W9-BNN-457

ENLIGHTENED BY DESIGN

ENLIGHTENED BY DESIGN

USING CONTEMPLATIVE WISDOM TO BRING PEACE, WEALTH, WARMTH, AND ENERGY INTO YOUR HOME

~

HELEN BERLINER

SHAMBHALA
BOSTON & LONDON · 1999

CONCLUSION: PUTTING IT ALL TOGETHER

PREFACE

ON A DARK AND STORMY NIGHT in Boston, circa 1970, I met an astrologer who told me two things. First, she said, "You are destined to be a healer, but you will heal with color"—which left me with more questions than answers about my destiny. Then she predicted, "You are about to meet someone the likes of whom you've never met, who will change your life forever." Two months later, I met Chögyam Trungpa Rinpoche—Tibetan Buddhist meditation master, artist, and poet—who was that someone.

Enlightenment means waking up!

Trungpa Rinpoche brought into the Western world the ancient Shambhala teachings on creating enlightened society. Based on the practice of meditation, this is a contemplative approach to living in the world. Accomplished in painting and calligraphy, and a master in the Japanese Sogetsu school of *ikebana* (flower arranging), he taught that realization was possible by working properly with perception and "wrote the book" on art in everyday life. In this spirit, he created furniture, banners, textiles, jewelry, and other applied and graphic designs as well as installations, theater pieces, and seasonal festivals.

Much of what Trungpa Rinpoche taught was communicated nonverbally through gesture, color, and environment. All of it was grounded in the ancient Tibetan tradition of mandala[1]—formulated in practice as "space awareness"[2]—and the five basic patterns, or styles, of energy in space. This, he taught, is the basic organization of our inner and outer worlds and the key to creating enlightened environments.

Basic mandala principle is very simple: It is that everything is related to everything else. It is quite simple and straightforward.

—CHÖGYAM TRUNGPA

He was especially interested in teaching the principles of enlightened home environment. Judith L. Lief, editor of *Dharma Art,* a collection of his teachings on creativity, writes: "He took an interest in all the details of his household, including architectural and interior design, landscape design, furniture arrangements, cooking, cleaning, forms of etiquette, dress, and service." Home meant "square one," "starting where you are"—and in his hands, home was "awake."[3]

Finally, he taught that art and life must not only be awake, they must also be in harmony with nature. Nature is a metaphor for enlightenment, which means "waking up." This view joins heaven and earth. Furthermore, life or art that is not aligned with heaven and earth "creates social chaos and natural disasters."[4] Working with the five styles of energy to join an awake mind with the natural world, we can create enlightened environments—and in this case, enlightenment begins at home!

This book—based on a contemplative approach to environmental design—could not have been written without him, and it is to him that it is dedicated.

~

To celebrate my move from the Wild West back to Philadelphia, the town where I was born and raised, my mother, daughter, and I filed off to lunch on the Main Line, a solid-gold outpost of East Coast domesticity. Lunch was followed by a "cultural seminar," How to Accessorize Your Home. Led by a local decorator with a wildly popular shop, it probed deep thoughts and gnarly questions such as how to arrange objects on your mantelpiece and whether figurines on occasional tables have to match. This was scary. Without a doubt, every woman in that well-appointed room—mostly young, some middle-aged—had a college education, if not a graduate degree. What was wrong with this picture? Scarier still, I became truly inspired—inspired to write a book reclaiming the home.

In the course of my life, I've lived in suburban developments (with and without sidewalks), a Catholic convent, dormitories, hotels, hospitals, a Mafia estate, and an urban commune housed in a New York brownstone that later became a historic landmark house. There were high-rises and high walk-ups—one with a vast kitchen window just inches from the darkly glowing stained-glass windows of a Russian Orthodox church—and lofts in SoHo and Chinatown and off-season houses by the sea. Living in Europe, I took shelter in a garden shed, a castle, a lopsided timber-and-beam house with flood marks that predated the plague, and yet another apartment just an arm's length away from sublime stained-glass windows of an ancient church. And then there were zendos, contemplative centers, retreat cabins, tents, yurts, rural communes, and hunting cabins. I had lived in mountains and deserts and on lakes in Nova Scotia and California (in a once-grand, trompe l'oeil treasure chest). Now I was living in a French provincial–style house northwest of Philadelphia, built in fields where I had learned to ride horses as a child. These were the homes of my spiritual journey and my bridge to the natural world. I determined to unearth their common ground.

Contemplating the underlying simplicity of earth-oriented traditions and agreeing with author Thomas Moore that "we have lived too long and too dangerously with a dysfunctional cosmology," I began to write.

This book will show you how to use your home to reclaim your connection with the universe. Step-by-step instructions show how to align your home with basic forces of nature: (1) heaven and earth, (2) the four directions, and (2) the five styles of energy that arise from them. You will learn theoretical and practical guidelines that apply to the outer and inner "homes" in which we live—body and mind, interior and exterior environments. You will learn how the same natural energies are at work in a studio apartment or an acre of architecture; in high-density urban housing, an isolated hogan, or the middle ground of suburbia.

If we do not belong in Nature we belong nowhere, and so must face final eviction and perpetual homelessness.
—Michael Dames

Enlightened homes are built on the common ground of wisdom traditions that preserve whole ways of living in the world. We will contemplate their universality and timelessness—necessary qualities of wisdom—and the skills they have to teach us. (In this book, I've presented those traditions with which I'm familiar. I encourage you to explore those to which you feel personally drawn or have an ancestral connection.)

Most traditional cultures orient themselves to "above and below" and the four cardinal directions (with multiple directions in between) and practice some form of geomancy[5] based on this orientation. You may be familiar with Chinese feng shui[6] or Native American, Celtic, Vedic, or African perspectives. Although the colors, symbols, elements, and other directional associations vary from culture to culture, from tribe to tribe, they reflect different perspectives on the world—like looking through yellow or blue glasses—and not fundamentally different worlds.

The practice of geomancy, which may roughly be defined as the science of putting human habitats and activities into harmony with the visible and invisible world around us, was at one time universal and vestiges of it remain in the landscape, architecture, ritual and folklore of almost all countries in the world.
—Nigel Pennick

The basic view of traditional cosmologies is similar: as holistic systems, they join mind and body (heaven and earth) with the vital energy of life, conceived variously as spirit, *ch'i*, or *lungta*.[7] This union is subtly embodied in spirits, gods or deities, subtle energies, or *drala*;[8] it manifests in the material world as wisdom, health, wealth, harmony, and power. Subsequent *interpretations* of the basic view, however, may be culturally specific or culturally biased. (Colors, shapes, and expressive styles, for instance, may have positive meanings in one culture, negative meanings in another.) This book will show you how to work spontaneously within your own context while holding fast to the view.

The *I Ching* talks about the sameness of diversity and the diversity of sameness. The common ground of diversity is wakefulness. Wakefulness is the ground of contemplative living and enlightened design. We experience it in practice as "space awareness," with five basic styles of energy defining that space.

Part I of this book, "Preparing the Ground," explains the principles of space

The aim of life is to live, and to live means to be aware, joyously, drunkenly, serenely, divinely aware.

—Henry Miller

awareness and describes how the five energies—in and out of balance—shape your space for better or for worse.

If you feel this is more ground than you want to cover, skip ahead to the practical applications in Parts II through VI. These chapters show you how to work with each energy style—its qualities, sensory associations, promises, and pitfalls—in your home. They explain how the five energies work in concert to realign your life by realigning your home with the forces of nature. Contemplative exercises will provide you with hands-on experience. To deepen your understanding, go back to "Preparing the Ground." Grounded in awareness, enlightened design always comes full circle!

ACKNOWLEDGMENTS

I owe a debt of gratitude to those teachers whose generosity can only be repaid by taking to heart their wisdom and guidance. These include teachers of Eastern and Western traditions, some of whom I first studied with in the 1970s, when I wrote my master's thesis on Tibetan-style space awareness—the study of energy in space.

Professor Cheng Man-ch'ing, T'ai Chi master and physician, initially bridged for me the disciplines of medicine and the arts. Tibetan physicians Drs. Yeshe Dhonden, Lobsang Dolma, and Trogawa Rinpoche planted seeds of understanding whose fruition is beyond the scope of this lifetime. Chandrashekhar G. Thakkur, Ayurvedic physician and astrologer, furthered my understanding of medical versus mathematical models of the world—sparking an ongoing interest in *Vastu Shastra*, the Vedic tradition of architecture.

Since the 1980s, I have been especially influenced by feng shui master Mr. J. S. Shiah; also by the written teachings of Professor Lin Yun along with Sarah Rossbach and the lineage of feng shui practitioners following in their footsteps; and more recently, by the work of Eva Wong, whose book *Feng Shui: The Ancient Wisdom of Harmonious Living for Modern Times* (Boston: Shambhala Publications, 1996) I had the pleasure of indexing. Because of my earlier studies with Michio Kushi—an ongoing source of spiritual and physical well-being—I am especially appreciative of the feng shui work of William Spear.

Howard Badhand, holder of Lakota Sioux wisdom tradition and teacher of the Chinese *Book of Changes (I Ching)*, has been and continues to be an invaluable teacher and guide.

Lady Elizabeth Pybus was a rare and treasured source of artistic inspiration and example. I am deeply saddened that she died shortly before publication of this book and before receiving this small token of my gratitude.

The writings of Nigel Pennick and Michael Dames many years ago stirred ancestral memories and launched an odyssey to Ireland. Experience of a Celtic wisdom tradition lost to our everyday lives begs commitment to its renewal.

For their keen interest, inspection, and support of *Enlightened by Design*, I thank the Venerable Khandro Rinpoche and her sister, Jetsun Dechen Paldron.

I am indebted and grateful to Judith L. Lief who generously read through several stages of the book with helpful suggestions; Christie Cashman for her role in shaping the section "How to Choose Your Site" and for permission to photograph her house; William Gordon and Margaret Jewell Gordon for their rigorous and artistic contributions; and to the insights and encouragement of Jeanne Ellgar, Dan Hessey, Douglas J. Penick, Katrina Pressman, and Richard Rice. For their contributions to the visual form of this book, heartfelt thanks to Leah Boyer, Barbara Craig for great logos and computer assistance, photographer Mitch Berger, and William Scheffel; to photographer John McQuade, instigator of my connection with Miksang photographers Carell Doerrbecker, Kathryn Munro, Michael Wood, and Alice Yang; along with photographers Alan Rabold and Liza Matthews, all of whom generously contributed their work—and to Liza, too, for her personal support and perfect cover design; to landscape architect Kim Turos for her photos, and to the wonderful students, clients, and friends I've worked with over the years, for their inspiration.

This book was written with the generous and unflagging support of my family: Stephen Boyer, an impassioned chanpion of the arts; my mother, Kathleen Boyer, who gave birth to the idea; and most especially my daughter, Lisa Haan Conrads, who not only made the book possible, but also made it better. It became a reality through the union of wisdom and skill offered by Shambhala editor Emily Hilburn Sell, to whom I am so grateful.

I

PREPARING THE GROUND

From a contemplative point of view, home design and ecology are one and the same. . . . Contemplate the seamlessness of your world when you find yourself asking, "What does this have to do with home design?"

1

HOME TRUTHS

In traveling to sacred places of the world, I keep realizing that it is the home which holds the greatest promise for transforming the world.
—SHAUN MCNIFF

THIS IS A BOOK ABOUT *home* in the most ordinary and extraordinary senses of the word. There was a time when "home," like the magic mountain, was an analogue for joining heaven and earth. There was a time when the "dwelling" was akin to the shaman's "central place," where spirit and human realms meet. And everyone knew that if you wanted to play with the planes of reality, with the spirit folk, angels, and other energies of the phenomenal world, you had to be "centered."

With magical thresholds joining the inner and outer worlds, magical gates symbolizing the gates of perception, and magical ladders, stairways, and chimneys—preserved in our Santa Claus stories—joining above and below worlds, homes were sacred space. They brought us into harmony with a world larger than ourselves. These are not the homes to which we retreat. They are the universal homes we left a long time ago and to which we will return in the future. Here is how to find your way back.

Entering the Gates of Perception

The cosmos isn't something that's far away, it's something that we're a part of. It touches our skin. As a matter of fact it goes through our bodies.
—LOUIE BERNSTEIN

A continuum of energy joins heaven/earth, mind/body, awareness and the world in which we live. Cycling through the gateways of our sense perceptions with its cargo of sights, sounds, smells, tastes, touch, and thoughts, it creates in us feelings of ease or dis-ease. Our personal and planetary health and well-being hang in the balance of this energy; in its sensory messages hangs our quality of life.

WAKEFULNESS

The cocreator of this sensory universe is an awake mind. Wakefulness is the product of mindfulness and awareness. Mindfulness attends to the details of everyday experience—the good, bad, and ugly—and makes them workable. Awareness is 360-degree mindfulness. It changes your way of seeing and "being" in your world. As architect Greg Van Mechelen suggests, "Becoming intimately aware of what already exists is the first step to shaping your environment."

ORDINARY MAGIC

Moment-by-moment mindfulness/awareness is a window of opportunity opening onto ordinary magic, which is the place where you—in your office, your kitchen, your car—and powers of the universe come together.

Magic begins with the choiceless "clear seeing" of ourselves and the world in which we live. The raw materials of our experience—sights, sounds, touch, tastes, thoughts, and feelings—house the magic we need in our lives. The mixing of an awake mind with the body of experience is the meaning of *contemplation*—and the path of enlightened design.

"Within a Space, to See Clearly"

> CONTEMPLATION: from the Latin *contemplari,* to observe carefully; from *com* (intensive) and *templum* (open space for observation, within a space to see clearly); space marked out by augurs for observation; temple, shrine.

Contemplation brings into the space of an open, or meditative, state of mind some object of mind—a candle, a passage of a book, a visualization of a deity, or an everyday activity—to "see clearly" the truth of things as they are. This truth is described in the Buddhist Heart Sutra like this: Form is emptiness, emptiness itself is form; form is no other than emptiness, emptiness is no other than form.

EMPTINESS

Empty means our minds are empty of preconceptions. They are open like the sky, like open space. In *Speaking of Silence,* psychotherapist Jack Engler describes contemplation as a "self-emptying process which happens over and over throughout the day." It is, he writes, an "opening to the invitation to go beyond whatever limiting assumptions we've made about ourselves at any given time. . . It is allowing ourselves to be challenged, to be blown open and catapulted into open space, that is contemplation."[1]

FORM

Form is our sensory experience of the world. It is made up of perceptions. Openness invites perceptions to speak for themselves. So the sensory messages we receive—no matter how familiar—are always fresh, uninhibited, and somewhat surprising.

The sight of your unmade bed with its flowery summer sheets, the sound of the newspaper landing on your step before dawn, the feel of straw rugs, the taste of hot tea, the mysterious songs of nocturnal birds—anything can spark the magic of awareness.

AWARENESS

Awareness is like oxygen: we don't *own* it, we tap into it—which is what is meant by "waking up." Awareness is the key to harmonious homes. It tunes us in to the energy dance of:

space/contents	warmth/coolness	movement/rest
order/chaos	richness/simplicity	above/below

Awareness enables us to diagnose deficient and excess energies, to restore balance, and to channel the energies we need and want in our lives. Living in balance is an intuitive process—and a form of prayer. "The Greek word *prosevkomai*, which is translated as 'prayer,'" writes Jeremy Hayward, "simply means to be in a mindful state of awareness."[2]

Home is a very personal topic. It reflects the harmony of your life on earth. From kibbles on the floor to stars in the sky, personal and cosmic truths are one in awareness. Now we will see how awareness translates into home design.

2

ENLIGHTENED HOME DESIGN

The Practice

ENLIGHTENED DESIGN BEGINS with an assessment of natural patterns of energy—rather than with individual needs and desires. *If we align our homes and lives with the five basic energies, our needs and desires will be met.* Those that are not met are those that we have historically abused or neglected—and so need some extra attention. In that sense, heaven and earth (which we will look at in Chapter 3) and the five basic energies are antidotes for a home/life out of balance. Here are some correspondences of natural energies and human concerns.

NATURAL ENERGIES AND HUMAN CONCERNS

All of the styles, remedies, and design ideas described in this book pertain to your state of mind, your body, and your relationship with the world as well as your home. In using them, it will be helpful to see them in relationship to your own particular concerns:

Space: You need more relaxation, gentleness, sanity in your life; you feel a lack of sacredness or spirituality.

Clarity: You need more focus. You are disorganized, and your goals are not clear. You want to address issues of schooling, personal development, or health. You want to simplify your life, find more meaning, get down to essentials.

Richness: Money and resources are a concern. You're not grounded; your life is not satisfying. You need to expand or enrich your horizons—and your confidence needs a boost. You want greater presence/influence in the world.

Warmth: Relationships are an issue. You feel isolated, unhappy, lonely. Your home is not comfortable. Pleasure and passion aren't part of your life. You are *not* having fun yet!

Energy: Work is out of control (even your space doesn't work for you). You want less speed and competitiveness in your life; more efficiency, productivity—more success! You are ready to be part of the action.

Above: Your "guiding lights" have grown dim. There is little presence of ancestors (guardian angels, higher powers) in your life. Home no longer brings out the best in you: familiarity has bred contempt.

Below: Practicalities (cooking, recycling, car maintenance, banking) overwhelm you. You have no time to deal with details. The physical world is a bother instead of a blessing.

Before Going Any Further . . .

It's not the pots we are forming, it's ourselves.
—M. C. Richards

I strongly suggest using workbooks to keep track of your progress. Begin gathering the five energies in them—as well as your insights and inspiration. Blank books and sketchbooks are fine, but ring binders are best for works in progress. You can add, delete, or change the sequence of pages.

Create separate workbooks for Parts II–VI and color-code them for each of the five styles. (Some binders have clear cover pockets where you can insert colored sheets of paper.) Use plastic page protectors to organize inspiration from those piles of magazines and catalogues (then recycle the rest). Add plastic pages with pockets to hold photos, postcards, and other treasures; and plenty of blank paper on which to write.

Draw, photograph, paste, and ponder the exercises indicated by » throughout this book. Research examples of the five styles in other times or places. Record your impressions as you explore each energy. As you fill your white, blue, yellow, red, and green workbooks, the energies will begin to speak for themselves—and to resonate in your home.

THE IDEAL HOME

DESIGN: from the Latin *designare*; to make or execute plans; to have a goal or purpose in mind; to point out.

Before going any further, visualize your ideal home on paper. What do you need and want in a domestic space? Let yourself dream! Think about location, about interior/exterior space. How would you divide up your domestic space and why? (Would you like a home with no separate rooms or interior walls—or many intimate spaces?) Think about color, building materials, (manufactured and natural,) and natural elements (earth, water, fire, and wind.) Note spontaneous details that flash into your mind.

The results of this exercise indicate what you require in a living space. Whatever ideas you have written down are variations of the five energies. Read on to see how—with or without money, with or without the option to move or to build—you can create an ideal space that is also in tune with the universe.

» If you can, set aside a space where you can work on this project over a period of time—a big basket or bookcase shelf will do to anchor your inspiration as you launch into space!

3

HEAVEN, EARTH, AND MAN

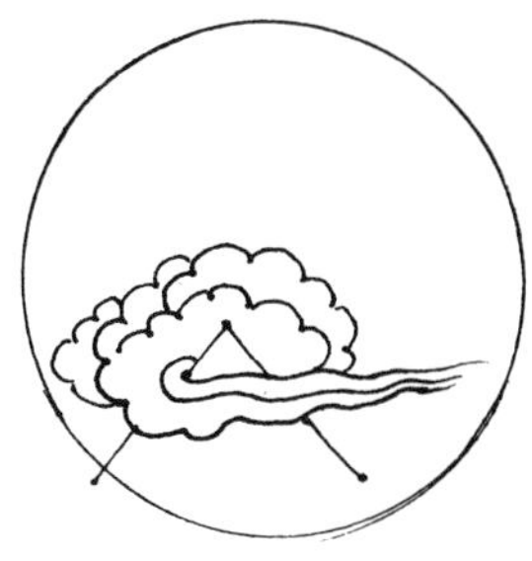

HEAVEN IS THE SKY ABOVE, earth is the ground beneath your feet, your heart beats in between. This is the principle of heaven, earth and man. This simple truth rules the world in which we live: our mental and physical health hangs in the balance of heaven and earth. When heaven and earth are in harmony, the vastness of heaven and the receptivity of earth manifest as abundance and well-being.

LHA, NYEN, AND LU

In Tibetan tradition, the principle of *lha*, *nyen*, and *lu* describes the "hierarchy" of heaven, earth, and man in the natural world (where the joining, or man, principle is nyen). "Lha, Nyen and Lu describe the protocol and the decorum of the earth itself," teaches Trungpa Rinpoche, "and they show how human beings can weave themselves into that texture of basic reality."[1]

For Navajos and Tibetans, the dialogue between earth and sky recognizes not the separate nature of the two aspects of the natural order but their inseparable, abiding union. Indeed, both cultures have very specific names and teachings concerning the inherent unity of opposite energies and qualities.

—PETER GOLD

Heaven

Heaven is space, vastness, the realm of gods and of energy beyond form. Inwardly, it's your mind, your loftiest ideals, your "vision." In the natural world, *lha* is high places and rarefied environments. It is a snow-capped mountain peak catching the first rays of sun. It's the sun, moon, stars, clouds, and the sky itself.

In the personal arrangement of body, speech, and mind, heaven is "mind" and especially your awareness. Physically, it's your head (especially your forehead and eyes)—as well as your hat and eyeglasses. At home, heaven is the roof and attic of your house. Heaven is upliftedness. It's connected with cherished or sacred objects—books, texts, relics, ancestral pictures or heirlooms—that you "raise up" in special places in your home. Uplift the environments in which you live and work and you can bring a bit of "heaven" to earth.

Earth

Earth is groundedness, solidity, and the energy of form. In the natural world, *lu*—connected with richness and fecundity—is fertile low-lying lands fed by streams and teeming with life. It's oceans, marshes, and jungles. It's the richness of earth symbolized by solid gold and the color yellow.

In everyday life, earth is the richness of relative truth. Earth is details, the nuts-and-bolts energy that supports life; it's the "ways and means" of demanding budgets, upkeep, age, health, and natural elements.

In the personal arrangement of body, speech, and mind, earth is "body." In the body itself, it's the lower areas (below the waist) that generate and support life—as well as your socks and shoes. At home, earth is the basement, plumbing, floors, and foundation of your house—as well as the cleaning supplies under the sink. A solid foundation provides heaven with a landing pad; attending to practical details (earth) makes it possible for heaven to land there.

Man Joins Heaven and Earth

> Heaven and Earth make love,
> and a sweet dew-rain falls.
> The people do not know why,
> But they are gathered together like music.
> —Tao-te Ching

Heaven and earth are joined in the simple relationships of everyday objects (the rug joining floor/furniture, the plant stand joining planter/floor). The sympathetic connection between heaven and earth is traditionally called "man," which refers not to gender but to a joining principle, like speech. Man is a bridge; a traditional metaphor is the saddle that joins horse and rider.

In the natural world, *nyen* refers to the foothills and middling plains—not too hot, not too cold—hospitable to man and beast. Physically, the man principle refers to your shoulders, torso, rib cage, and chest; and to your dress or suit—and the pin on your lapel that pulls the whole thing together. In the home, it's the furnishings and accessories that join the structure and space.

Ultimately, heaven and earth are inseparable. Their union doesn't need to be manufactured by us. When we speak of their "joining," we are simply going along with the way the world works. Enlightened design joins heaven and earth to realign our homes and lives with the natural order of things. Here are some practical guidelines:

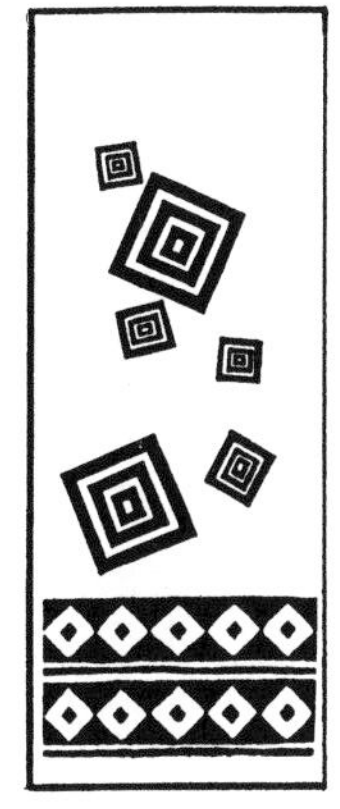

Borders above create a grounded feeling. Borders below create a sense of "heaven," or space. Borders above and below draw attention to "man," or center space.

- Before setting your heart on that ideal room design (heaven), consider the location of electrical outlets, phone jacks, and heating vents (earth). Consider how "traffic" flows through the room. See how light will hit your computer screen before moving your desk next to that window with the wonderful view.
- Don't lose sight of details (earth) in the grand scheme of things (heaven). Pay attention to hardware, trim, and moldings. Be mindful of lighting—natural and artificial. Look at surfaces (painted, natural, manufactured). Are they faded, harsh, bright and clean? What do fabrics contribute to your space? Don't worry about making changes right now; just record your impressions.
- Do you have half-dead flowers or plants (earth) in a beautifully decorated room (heaven)? The living things in your environment—flowers, plants, fish, birds—need to thrive to contribute uplifting energy to the space.

A QUESTION OF BALANCE

When the dance of "this and that" begins, the world becomes relational and balance is king. Life is an ongoing process of balance/imbalance—and "losing it" is part of the process. *Imbalance* can wake you up! It is the "practice" of contemplative practice (along with breaking the rules—but more about that later).

- Balance space (heaven) and sensory input (earth): for visual harmony, don't overdecorate or overstate colors, patterns, or forms; for tactile harmony, avoid extremes of hot/cold temperatures, hard/soft surfaces, furniture and accessories that are too casual/cozy or too severe. Balance sound with silence. Don't let televisions, radios, human, animal, or mechanical sounds chronically dominate the environment. Balance the need for openness with the need for privacy and protection. Work with the energies of opposites, which are ongoing and constantly in flux:

order/chaos	wet/dry	vertical/horizontal	rigid/flexible
body/mind	light/dark	hollow/solid	moving/still

Next, we will see how heaven and earth come together in the structure of your home.

CEILINGS ABOVE

Ceilings and floors are the heaven and earth of a house. Together with the height of walls, lighting, and contents of a room, they create the physical and visual balance necessary to enjoy a space.

The word for *ceiling* in many languages means "heaven." Ceilings that are too high (too much heaven) draw your awareness away from earth. They can make a room feel awe-inspiring or intimidating. (Cathedrals were designed for such an effect.) At home, steeply pitched or vaulted ceilings make it difficult to think, work, or focus on the here and now. Moreover, they make a room difficult to heat and light properly. Here are some ways to work with unsettling imbalances.

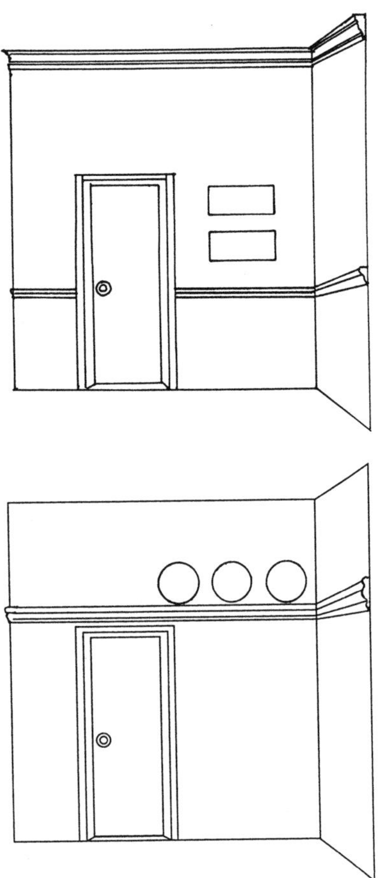

High ceilings *can* feel gracious and grand. In Victorian homes, their vast reaches were offset by richly colored or gilded ornamentation and elaborate crown moldings; by ceiling borders some two to three feet deep; and by equally rich and weighty draperies and furniture. You can adapt some of these same techniques:

- » Ground high ceilings with good lighting and visual interest at eye level—a mural or artwork, for instance (in a horizontal format) and dramatic window treatments. Highlight chair rails and wainscoting. Add a shelf above crown molding for more visual interest and balance. Use bold wall colors with heavy, rich furniture to lower the center of gravity.
- » Lower very high ceilings by filling the upper reaches of the room with decorative panels or banners (à la medieval castles).
- » Paint a too-high ceiling to create a canopy effect—overlapping the walls like a tent roof.
- » Create a real canopy using one or more parallel widths of muslin or canvas (also good for hiding unsightly ceiling fixtures).

Ceilings that are too low (including steeply inclined or sloping ceilings) can make a room feel oppressive. Pushing energy downward, they make it difficult to feel physically or mentally uplifted. (Some cultures, of course, *prefer* low-ceilinged rooms—which are easier to light and heat—and have developed their design sense around them.)

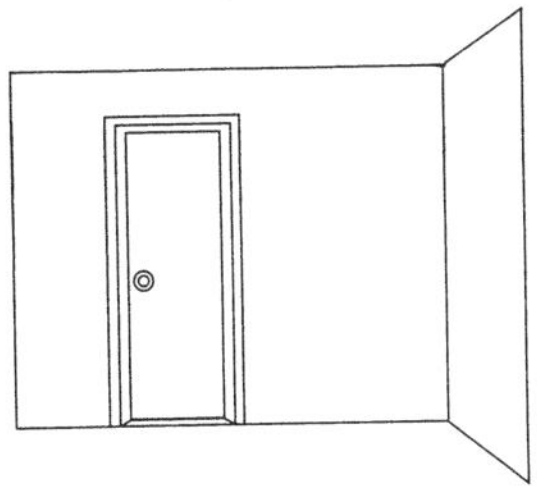

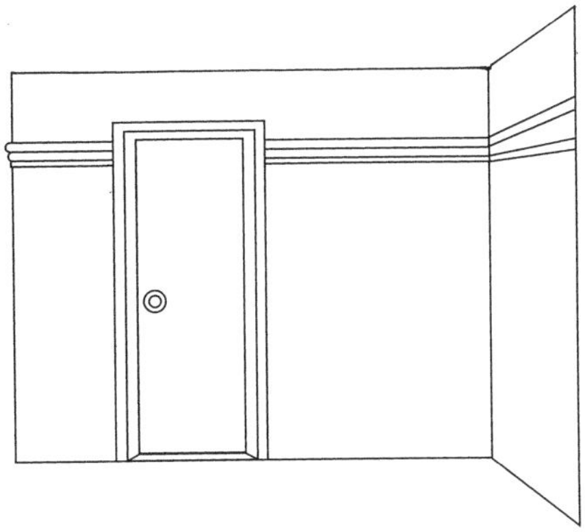

» To raise a low ceiling, hang a wallpaper border or crown molding below the wall/ceiling juncture. This brings your eye into the room itself and creates an illusion of space above the border. For best results, treat the space above/below the border differently using wallpaper or paint. Use vertical lines—plants, vertical art, or up-lights—to send the eye and energy up.

FLOORS BELOW

Floors can bring visual weight to a room that makes it feel just right. On the other hand, demanding or unimpressive floors can upset the balance of a room. To balance the energy of floor/ceiling, intensify floors when ceilings are too high or too low.

» Anchor a high-ceilinged room with a "riveting" floor (think of magnificent carpets in French castles or dramatic tiled floors in Persian mosques).
» Uplift a low-ceilinged room with highly interesting floors (like colorful hooked and rag rugs in early American log cabins or textured tatami mats in Japanese houses). Use dramatic or colorful accents below eye level.

Heaven and Earth in Action

In *The Poetics of Space*, Gaston Bachelard speaks of the house as a metaphor for humanness. *Humanness* is the intersection of heaven and earth, which are joined in our everyday activities. Align your home with heaven and earth, then relate to your home as a practice.

TEA AND TRAY CEREMONIES

In Japanese culture, many contemplative art forms—designed to train practitioners in the joining of heaven and earth—carry over into daily life. The elaborate and highly ritualized tea ceremony, for example—with its teahouse, flower arrangement, and artful accessories—was condensed into a simple but elegant "tray ceremony" adapted for everyday use. Every small gesture you make to join heaven and earth produces blessings in your environment.

- » Use a tray to join your coffee cup or tea snack (heaven) with your desk (earth) at work. (Carrying these items to your desk without one is somewhat unfocused and risky.) A tray puts you and your tea "on the spot." Use a cloth or paper napkin to join teacup (heaven) to tray (earth).
- » Use a tray for your pet's bowls as well (with a cloth or paper towel in between). Trays are a wonderful daily reminder of above and below, and a way to bring them together.

FLOWER AND OBJECT ARRANGING

If you have a fondness for flowers, consider taking a course or workshop on *ikebana*, which is based on the principles of heaven and earth. Using seasonal flowers and foliage, it also joins time (heaven) and place (earth). Ikebana is an accessible and inexpensive art form that can be practiced anywhere and mastered by anyone with a passion for flowers and a desire to bring harmony into the world.

Once you have mastered the principles, you can create "object arrangements" using whatever inspires you—found objects, theme objects, and so on—instead of flowers. Flower and object arrangements can be minuscule or monumental. They can stand alone or be used as centerpieces on tables.

HATS AND SHOES

To create a harmonious environment, join heaven and earth by mindful living as well as by design. Some of the suggestions below may seem simplistic—but they work! These are natural principles upon which traditional societies and governments—as well as personal health and well-being—are built.

- » Align your life with heaven and earth by not displacing their functions. Eating while working confuses physical and intellectual functions. Eating or reading in the bathroom confuses higher/lower functions.
- » Honor heaven and earth by not elevating things "below" above their station and vice versa. Socks and stockings are best housed "below" and should not migrate to the top drawer of your dresser. Hats are connected with your head and therefore heaven; they are best housed "above." Underwear is not "top-

drawer" but lives somewhere in the middle of the dresser, with socks below, scarves and jewelry above. Suits and dresses (man) hang in your closet between ceiling and floor. Shoes live on the floor and not on overhead shelves in your closet. Feet are not casually placed on tables or chairs—or on books (which represent ideas and therefore heaven).

HONORING SACRED THINGS

» Elevate, or "raise up," things that you respect and revere—sacred objects or texts, relics, ancestral pictures, heirlooms, even ordinary books that represent knowledge (heaven)—to special places. Such things should never be placed on the floor, under the bed, on the floor of your closet, or in bottom drawers; nor should they have anything placed, piled, or stored upon them—including coffee cups, ashtrays, or dust. (At certain times and places, sacred objects are placed on the earth, but the floor of your house is probably not one of them.)

SYNCHRONIZING MIND AND BODY

» Balance strenuous mental activity with physical work, exercise, or by walking (instead of driving) around your world. If you work at home, know that by making time to garden, wash vegetables, cook, and play with children or pets, you are joining heaven and earth and synchronizing body and mind.

RAKES, BROOMS, AND RAGS

We feel the forces of heaven and earth most keenly when they are out of balance (and imbalance of one affects all three). When heaven, earth, and man are not supporting one another, mental and physical dis-ease sets in.

You envision your home as a haven of peace and simplicity (heaven), but you exhaust yourself overmanaging your house and the forces of nature (too much man principle). The subsequent exertion—not to mention noise and expense—spent on snow- and leafblowers, lawn mowers, power pruning shears, vacuum cleaners, hairdryers, dishwashers, and Dustbusters (too much earth) is at odds with your dream.

If you bring your vision of peace (heaven) into harmony with falling leaves and snow and dirty dishes (earth), you might decide that a rake, a broom, and a rag would work best. Aspiration dances with practicality, and the balance of heaven and earth is restored.

Joining Heaven and Earth on the Spot

A Zen story tells of a man pursued by a ravenous tiger to the edge of a precipitous mountain cliff. There, between a rock and a hard place, in the moment of inescapable truth, he spies a berry bush, reaches out for a berry, puts it in his mouth, and exclaims—"*Delicious!*"

Delicious! is the taste of being on the spot with heightened awareness. Your spot may not be pleasant or comfortable, but it's true, which is preferable. A contemporary Buddhist saying—"Life is painful, suffering is optional"—celebrates the truth of here and now. From this point of view, "true" is a definition of *sacred*, and "nowness" is a personal experience of heaven and earth on the spot. From here, the world unfolds.

When heaven and earth are joined on the spot, that spot has a front, a back, and two sides. These are the four cardinal directions. In the next chapter, you will learn to align your home with their blessings.

4

THE FOUR DIRECTIONS

TRADITIONAL CULTURES—Indo-European, African, Asian, Native American—aligned themselves with heaven, earth, and the four cardinal directions through art and architecture, myths, rituals, and domestic customs. Some still do.

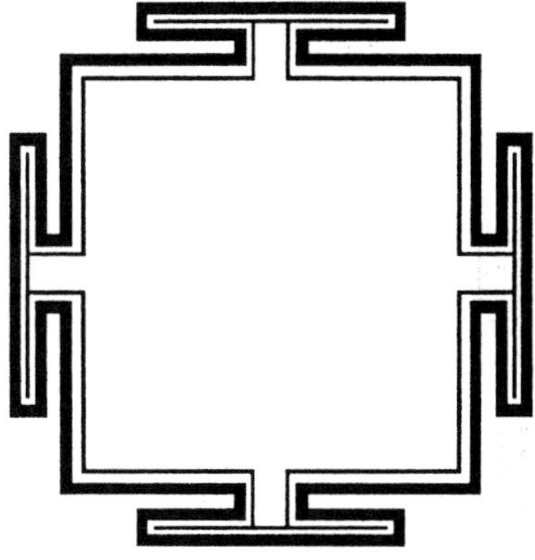

The four directions are represented by the four sides of the square which are symbolic of the stability of the center from which they originate.
—NIGEL PENNICK

Four Directions from Different Points of View

The four directions are universally connected with natural elements—earth, water, fire, and wind; with colors, deities, totem birds and animals, and specific human activities. In *Mythic Ireland*, Michael Dames explains how their names in Gaelic evoke mythic qualities rather than abstract geometry and how—in large and small ways—these *qualities* shape cosmic, individual, and community life.[1] Contemplate these profiles of the four directions to understand their influence on your home.

EAST

East is connected with vision, clarity, and the emergence of form. Its color is blue.[2] The sun rising in the east banishes darkness. By association, east represents "enlightenment" in the form of insight, intellectual learning, and spiritual vision. We face east to "wake up" and see things clearly. The element of east is clear water. Its energy is still and reflective. It is connected with purification, healing, and the taming of obstacles. We face east to restore mental and physical health. East brings clarity to your home, tames confusion and anxiety, and creates peace.

» Reflect the energy of the east in ponds, pools, bowls of water and artistic representations of the sun, bodies of water, and nautical themes.

The Gaelic word for east (*oithear*) is filled with "sunrise meanings," writes Dames, such as "beginning, forepart, future, and day to come." It also means "facade," or "front of a house," and by extension "supremacy," "perceiving intelligence," or "front part of the head."[3]

Most earth-based cultures and wisdom traditions orient their homes, villages, temples, churches, and healing mandalas to the east, the direction of the rising sun. They align the entrances of houses, hogans, and tepees—and their inhabitants—with the energy of "waking up" and making a fresh start. East is always awake, always "now."

The sun is the most consequential of the celestial influences because it is the earth's major source of energy. It supports life on earth and determines the growth, the strength, and the daily energy cycles of all life.
—Hua-Ching Ni

» Invite the light of the rising sun through windows, skylights, and doors.
» Situate rooms connected with your aspirations and ambition (offices, studios, dayrooms) in the "up-and-coming," sunrise side of the house. And from this point of view, situate your entrance/foyer to the east if you can.
» Reflect the seasons of the sun—winter, spring, summer, fall—in your environment. Make celebrations of solstices and equinoxes as significant as personal, social, and historical observances. (See "Conclusion: Putting It All Together" for more suggestions.)

The moon also rises in the east. The moon is for "viewing." It mirrors the truth of things as they *change*—birth, old age, sickness, death, and rebirth. The moon inspires reflection on change and impermanence. Both sacred and secular activities are universally coordinated with cycles and phases of the moon.

» Create a balcony, porch, or window for "moon viewing" and quiet contemplation. Find moon viewing reflected in the art, architecture, prose, and poetry of many cultures. Collect examples in your blue workbook.
» Use gold and silver to celebrate the energies of the sun and moon in your home.

WEST

The west is very seductive and colorful. Its color is red, and its element, fire. It is connected with warmth, passion, and the promise of pleasure—but also with endings and death. The sun and moon set in the west. West is connected with color and warmth in your home—and with relationships and the human dramas of life and death.

» Take advantage of warm afternoon sun for sunrooms, sitting rooms, and cozy spots for taking tea. Locate bedrooms and other private, "retiring" areas in the western side of the house.

- Celebrate the energy of the west with candles, wood fires, scarlet accessories, inviting fragrances, and the warmth of human companionship.

The Gaelic word for west, *iar*, refers to endings, extremities, "conclusion of a period," and "unhappy consequences"—with implications of wisdom gleaned from trial by fire.[†] Most Native American traditions associate west with thunder, lightning, and the spirit world—the land of the dead. West is painful as well as pleasurable. In the home, light from the setting sun can be too intense, creating glare and overwhelming the energy of a space. (We may suffer this irritation each afternoon, thinking it's "temporary.") Work won't go well under such influences, and eventually, physical and mental health will suffer as well.

- Protect rooms, especially workrooms, from the demanding energy of western windows and the setting sun with awnings, curtains, shades—or relocation.

The energy of the moon, which follows a very distinguishable cycle of waxing and waning, plays a significant role in our intellectual and emotional life, and influences sexual desire and women's menstruation as well as the ocean tides. The full moon may cause restlessness and impulsiveness, but can also make people very energetic. It is a good time for cultivation and creative expression.

—Hua-Ching Ni

NORTH

The energy of the north is a no-nonsense force to be reckoned with. The magnetic pole channels energy from north to south. (For this reason, dowsers align themselves north-south to begin their work; and there are various schools of thought about aligning the head of your bed with the north.) Wind is the element of north. Its color is green—the color of renewal/recovery, invincible growth, and long life. North brings vitality and the energy of success to your home.

- Celebrate the energy of the north in design with fans, kites, and real or representational moving objects (mobiles, wind chimes, birds/feathers, prints of sailing ships)—and with living plants and creatures and dynamic surface designs.

North light is the "coolest" light, especially in winter. Artists prefer this even light because it doesn't call attention to itself or interfere with the perception of color. Cool northern exposure, however, can also be gloomy and gray.

- Brighten northern rooms with fresh-cut flowers and songbirds.
- Use mirrors to increase natural and artificial light.

Northern exposure is vulnerable, in our hemisphere, to arctic wind and cold. Many old houses have *no* windows on the northern side, where they are further protected by barriers of trees.

» How are you using your rooms with northern exposure? Large windows and glass doors may be best installed elsewhere. Consider light, temperature, and energy in general before creating a home office with northern exposure.

North—associated with invincibility and warriorship—also represents danger. The Gaelic word for north (*tuaisceart*) means "left-hand side." It conveys a sense of danger as well as "arrogance, vanity, pride," "hammering, beating, smiting," and "anguished hearts."[5] North implies threats and the need for protection. (We will talk more about protection in Part VI, "Energy.")

» Some traditions post wrathful "roof guardians" to the north. Do you have a tradition of protectors or a vision of how to protect your home mandala from negative influences?

North is the energy that overcomes obstacles and ensures the success of any endeavor. Northern quarters were traditionally used for provisionary and protective energies—for the planning of campaigns and for the learning/teaching of skills.

» Locate sports and children's activities, working with tools, and stockpiling provisions (literally or figuratively) in the cool north.

SOUTH

South is associated with heat, strength, and fecundity. Its element is earth; its color is golden yellow. South is the energy of natural abundance and easy living ("mellow yellow"). In Gaelic, south (*dess*) means "being to the right of a person facing east"—a propitious condition giving rise to many positive qualities. By extension, it means "lucky," "favorable," "beauty," and "ears of corn."[6] Physical energy thrives in the south. The strongest source of solar heat and light (in the Northern Hemisphere) is southern exposure. The south's warm weather and long growing season put an abundance of food on our tables. South overcomes poverty and brings abundance and well-being to your home.

» Place banks of luxurious green and flowering plants in southern windows. They will flourish there.

» To invoke the energy of the south, bring earth (stone, sand, clay in the form of pottery or tiles) and things of the earth (rich natural fibers, plants, wood, straw baskets—preferably full—and plenty of good, nourishing food) into your home.

» Too much strong southern light and heat can be debilitating. Large windows, glass doors, decks, and porches are well placed in the south (especially in colder climates) if they're equipped with adequate protection from heat and glare.

Basic Orientation to the Four Directions

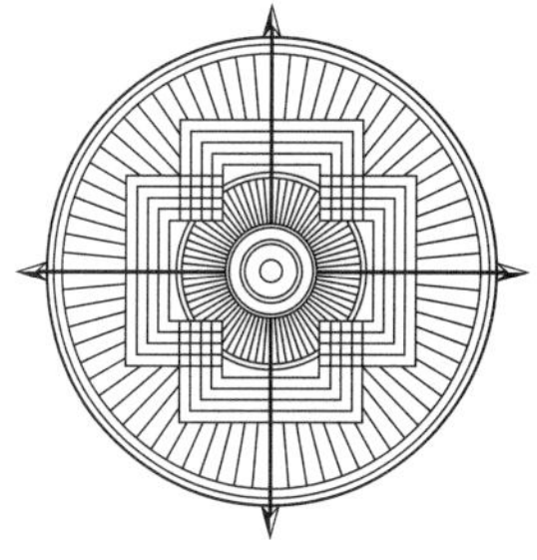

You can tune in to the energies of the four directions in two different ways, which are complementary and work together. First, to orient yourself physically to the east-west energies of sun and moon and the north-south polar axes, try the following exercise.

» Stand with your feet planted on the earth, your head rising up toward heaven. Feel the firmness of the earth supporting you and the space all around you. Feel your body joining heaven and earth. Imagine you are facing east—the direction of sunrise, of vision and new beginnings. New York is in front of you, San Francisco is behind you. Florida is the tip of your right hand, and Canada, the left. These very different directions express diverse colors, textures, passions, aggressions, lifestyles, and psychological states. Like magic, the world unfolds in this way.

It's great in practice, but it'll never work in theory!

This is the truth of the relative world and a simple, empirical approach to the four directions.

The second approach establishes your basic wakefulness as the center of any mandala. From this point of view, *wherever* you face is east, or awake. In practice, when you sit in a room, you sit facing the door—which represents the rising sun, wakefulness, and rising *ch'i*. The door wall is the "eastern gate" in the mandala of that room, with the western gate (the energy that "backs you up"—warmth, relations, ancestors/family) behind you, the northern gate (the energy of skillful means and helpful allies) to your left, and the southern gate (your wealth/resources) to your right. This is your interior mandala, regardless of exterior reference points.

The challenge is to integrate "within" and "without." Your house is literally charged with physical energies from four directions, which weave themselves—like brightly colored threads—into the one big picture you call home. It's up to you to create a happy, healthy pattern.

To do this, you must know how the directional energies—individually and collectively—work in the world and affect our lives.

The Powers of the Four Directions

The directional energies are traditionally connected with four actions, or powers (Sanskrit, *karmas*): pacifying, enriching, magnetizing, and destroying.[7] Clarity is connected with pacifying, richness with expansion or enriching, warmth with magnetizing, and energy with destroying obstacles. Activating the four quadrants of space, they show us how to *act* in the world. For this reason, Trungpa Rinpoche taught:

> When we begin to realize pacifying, enriching, magnetizing, and destroying as the natural expression of our desire to work with the whole universe, we are free from accepting too eagerly or rejecting too violently; we are free from push and pull. . . . [T]hat freedom is known as the mandala principle, in which everything is moderated by those four activities. In the mandala, east represents awake; south represents expansion; west represents passion or magnetizing; north represents action. That seems to be the basic mandala principle that has developed.[8]

The power of space, the fifth energy, is not traditionally called an "action" because space doesn't *do* anything—but it may be the most powerful of all. Space is basic sanity and openness—and we can talk about how to communicate that power through design.

The directional energies manifest as five basic patterns or styles in the world, which is our next discussion.

5

FIVE STYLES OF ENERGY

THE FOUR DIRECTIONS PLUS CENTER SPACE generate five basic energy patterns, or "styles." I have called these styles *space, clarity, richness, warmth,* and *energy.*[1] With the exception of space, each style is associated with a color, natural element, shape, and season. The five styles of energy are the "primary colors" of our sensory world. Depending on our makeup, we all respond differently to different styles. One individual might resonate with clarity (and its order, sharpness, and simplicity), another with richness (expansive, lush, weighty, and grand). We're excited by some energies and less comfortable with others.

» Ideally, our personal style is a "signature"—rather than a caricature—in harmony with the others. Cultivate appreciation of diverse styles for harmony at home and in the world.

Each style has a specific action, or power, which can be channeled in "enlightened" or "neurotic" ways. You can invoke the powers of the five styles into your life for specific purposes and incorporate them into your home.

> By trying to understand the five styles of energy, we are trying to get at some basic understanding of seeing things in their absolute essence, their own innate nature. We can use this knowledge with regard to painting or poetry or arranging flowers or making films or composing music. It is also connected with the relationships between people. These [five styles] seem to cover a whole area of new dimensions of perception. They are very important at all levels, and in all creative situations. —CHÖGYAM TRUNGPA

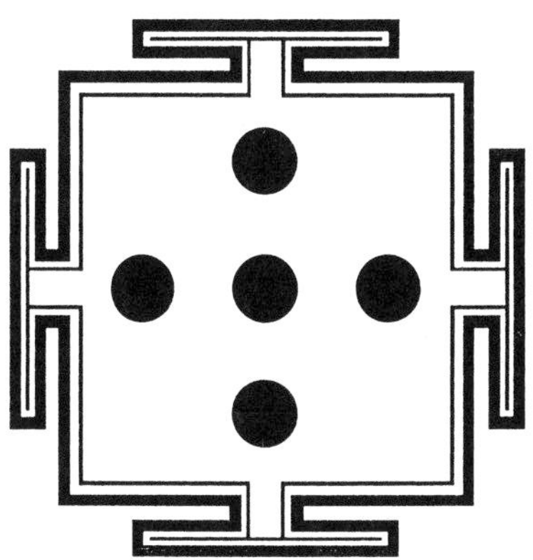

In Parts II through VI, we will see how the five styles function in the composition and design of domestic space. First, however, we will see how to initiate our connection.

6

THE ABCs OF ENLIGHTENED DESIGN

When we enter a space, we have an intuitive, if unspoken, sense of it. The space might feel uplifted, wholesome, inviting, energized—or anxious, depressing, cold, or chaotic. No decorator can make a house feel like a home or a cold space feel like a warm one. The combined "vibrations" of people, places, and things author the sensory messages available in the environment. And the receptivity, or spaciousness, of our sense organs enables us to read them.

Without mental and physical space, we cannot even experience our senses. Sound waves, for example, must undulate in space to be heard; light waves must travel through space to be experienced as color and sight. Sensory overstimulation (lack of space) causes sensory numbness and contributes to attention deficit disorder (ADD) in children and adults.

An Aesthetic Approach to Design

> AESTHETICS: from the Greek *aisthetikos*; of sensory perception; an ability to see, therefore to know, through the senses.

Sense perceptions—a function of space—are the ABCs of enlightened design, which is an *aesthetic* approach to design. Wakefulness restores us to our senses by restoring communication between body and mind. Enlightened design brings sense perceptions into harmony with space. The first space with which we work is mind. Mindfulness/awareness is 50 percent of "enlightened" interior, architectural, and environmental design.

In balance, all six sense organs work together to establish our world. Most of us these days are out of balance: relying heavily on conceptual mind, we often talk or read about things instead of putting them into practice. By flexing all of our sensory "muscles," we can balance overactive mind and join heaven and earth.

Architecture is illuminated not only by light but by sound, in fact it is brought into relief for us through all our senses.
—WILLIAM LETHABY

CREATING A SENSORY ENVIRONMENT

Mastering the ABCs of perception enables you to send and receive coherent sensory messages. Perceptual literacy creates conscious environments that are powerful and meaningful. Here's one example.

To create a rich and splendid space, you might start with one piece of furniture that says, "Look at me, I'm *rich*." From one seed of richness, you can "grow" a room—a fashion statement, performance piece, or public space. Richness—connected with abundance, dignity, generous scale and ornamentation, splendor, gold, and the color yellow—contains a world of associations. Express them through fabrics, rugs, accessories, artwork, and so on. Express richness through one or more of the sense perceptions. Needless to say, if you engage all the sense perceptions—sight, sound, touch, taste, and so on—you will create a very rich and powerful environment indeed.

The six tools of enlightened design are: eyes, ears, nose, tactile receptors, tongue—and in this tradition, mind (consciousness), which orchestrates the other five. Now we will look at the magic of the sense perceptions individually.

Sight

If a picture is worth a thousand words, our visual environment speaks volumes. Sight relies on light, and our eyes can literally enlighten us. Visual experiences have physical, emotional, and spiritual equivalents—and vice versa. They can be uplifting—or violent, depressing, and degrading. Interior design speaks mainly through the sense of sight.

Visual overstimulation is numbing. Visual chaos scrambles visual information, creating visual static and illiteracy. Both are forms of sensory pollution—and both contribute to attention deficit and other disorders in children and adults. These pressing challenges can be addressed on a daily basis by visual artists and designers. "The purpose of art," as Trungpa Rinpoche wrote, "is to wake people up; anything can wake you up!"

» Walk through your space with visual awareness and record what "strikes your eye." Stand in doorways and record your first impressions of the house, of a room. Are the organization and focus of each room clear? Then look at the objects around you. What are *they* contributing to your environment? Look at walls, doors, floors, and ceilings. Study the colors in and outside of your home. Are they warm, cold, pleasing, bright, or dingy? Notice the quality and color of your lighting. Don't plan any changes at this point; just record how your visual impressions make you *feel*.

Sound

Sound is not frontal like sight. We are immersed in sound that registers continually in our nervous and skeletal systems. Ambient sound can be irritating, soothing, or neutral (white noise). Sound can be used to promote growth—or to disorient, even kill, human beings, plants, and animals. Sound pollution, or noise, doesn't have to be loud to be toxic to our bodies, minds, health, and behavior. It is a leading cause of hearing loss, and it's as much a problem in the suburbs as in the city.

Sound is connected with body (sight is more connected with mind). Natural sounds—flowing water, wind, and birdsongs—are more soothing and pleasurable than mechanical sounds because, like our bodies, they're alive. Mechanical sounds—no matter how gentle—become irritating or debilitating. Sounds of children and animals connect us with the energy of life. The absence of seemingly insignificant sounds (birdcalls, rustling leaves) is the most often journalized loss after earthquakes, fires, and other natural disasters.

Because children are naturally raucous, parents may think they're insensitive to sound. In fact, children's hearing and attention spans can be seriously damaged by "noise pollution"—not the least of which are television and noisemaking toys. Children should not be relegated—contrary to the designs of many contemporary homes—to bedrooms or playrooms polluted with sounds of heat pumps, refrigerator motors, or other sounds objectionable to adults.

» Walk quietly through your home, relax your gaze, and pay attention to the sounds all around you. Listen for natural sounds (birds and animals, children, flowing water, wind) and mechanical sounds (refrigerators, heat pumps, plumbing, traffic, power tools and appliances, noisy toys). Listen for stressors such as squeaking doors, telephones (including call-interrupt and answering machines), sirens, and low-flying aircraft. Note how the "noise level" of your home makes you feel. Working with sound is important to home design.

Taste

The sense of taste may not seem relevant to environmental or interior design. We associate taste primarily with food, beverages, and other things we put in our mouths. In many traditional cultures, however, different kinds of tastes correspond with other sensory energies with similar kinds of effects. In Chinese and Ayurvedic medicine, for example, five flavors—sweet, sour, salty, bitter (astringent), hot (pungent)—correspond with the aromas, colors, elements, and so on, of the five basic energies. Balancing the energies of food helps to balance your environment. (See Appendix B, "References and Further Readings," for more information on this topic.)

Beyond that, we have a "taste" for certain kinds of experience. Taste implies discrimination (hence, "in good taste"). It is intimately connected with sensual pleasure (as in "What is your pleasure?") and, in James Hillman's words, "opening the soul's body to delight which anyway is implied by that sensate word 'taste.'"[1]

A spoon does not know the taste of soup, nor a learned fool the taste of wisdom.

—WELSH PROVERB

Taste is intimately connected with the sense of smell. Both convey worlds of information, and both contribute to feelings of well-being or distress. Taste and smell help us to understand, or "digest," situations. We literally and figuratively "taste" what we smell in our environment and vice versa; psychologically, we "taste" our experience. In old age, we lose the sense of taste, and interest in food—and other sensory experience—declines.

» Taste is not a question of good or bad, but of balance. Are the sweet, sour, salty, astringent, hot *energies* of your home in balance—or is your home too "sweet," too "bland," too "spicy"? Is it filled with things that "whet the appetite" and satisfy your soul? Or is your home the equivalent of a TV dinner? Are your cupboards literally filled with a discriminating selection of foods and beverages? Record your findings.

Everywhere I go I smell fresh paint.

—DIANA, PRINCESS OF WALES

Smell

The sense of smell conveys worlds of information that affect us for better or worse. Smells can pollute our world or have therapeutic effects. Many newer hospitals, for instance, have cozy, eat-in kitchens on floors caring for seriously ill patients: the cookies and breads baked fresh every day fill the space with wonderful and comforting aromas. "Good aromas can create refreshing and rejuvenating feeling," writes Greg Van Mechelen, "but too often our buildings smell of toxic materials and sick air systems."[2]

Smell is a warning system: it lets us know what's wholesome and what's not. In both Eastern and Western medicine, categories of smells—sweet, sour, astringent, and so on—are used in diagnosis. Every home has a unique smell that can be diagnosed as healthy or unhealthy. Smell is the sense perception most closely connected with memory.

Smells are used commercially to create "atmosphere" and positive associations and to seduce us to shop. When they are chemical, contrived, and used to manipulate, smells literally can be sickening. I was recently in a local gift boutique redolent of sugar and spice when a toddler accurately broadcast, "It stinks in here." On the other hand, the art and science of aromatherapy has brought relaxation, clarity, peace, healing, richness, harmony, love, energy, and delight to human beings all over the globe for thousands of years.

» Are the smells in your home fresh, reassuring, and "good" or stale and "bad"? (Do you know what to do about unwanted odors?) Record your findings. Don't forget bathrooms, closets, and basement.

Touch

The hands of those I meet are dumbly eloquent to me. The touch of some hands is an impertinence. I have met people so empty of joy, that when I clasped their frosty fingertips, it seemed as if I were shaking hands with a northeast storm. Others there are whose hands have sunbeams in them, so that their grasp warms my heart.

—Helen Keller

Touch connects us to the world through *contact*. We are constantly "in touch" with hard/soft, rough/smooth, pleasing/displeasing messages that inform us about our animate and inanimate world. The energies of soft (like the sky) and hard (like the earth) need to be in balance. Hardness can feel supportive and reassuring, or rejecting; softness can be comforting and friendly, or debilitating. If our world seems like too harsh a place, we may overcompensate with too much softness (and vice versa).

Temperature brings us into contact with the natural world. When we're deprived of that connection in temperature-controlled environments, we lose our ability to adapt to natural energies. Greg Van Mechelen notes that

> buildings used to be designed around variations in temperature, and people used them accordingly: fireplaces gave warmth in winter, courts provided coolness in summer. Today climate control makes the same house possible in Minneapolis or Miami. Many cultures associate important rituals with warmth: the Finnish sauna, the Japanese bath, or the sweat lodge of the native American. Passive heat transmitted through materials like stone flooring is known to be the healthiest. Other climate modifiers include soft surfaces, warm colors and yellow light for warmth.[3]

Beyond that, being touched means "to be moved," touched by the spirit—or slightly insane. Touch is a very significant sensory antenna and transmitter of sensory messages. It's also an important warning system. Contact with natural and synthetic fibers and building materials, for instance, provides us with a sense of well-being or dis-ease.

» How does *your* home "feel" to you? Are you in daily contact with wood, straw, cotton, and other "living, breathing" materials? Are you in touch with earth, fire, water, and the other elements in your daily life? What kind of contact do you make with your furniture? Are you constantly in touch with delightful surfaces or with sharp corners and tight squeezes? Can you easily control the temperature of your home? Do you use energy-intensive (fossil fuels, electricity) or energy-efficient (solar energy, a sweater) means to do that? Do you have a favorite cup to wrap your hands around for warmth? Notice the comfort level of your furniture (your kitchen cabinets, your office chair, your bed).

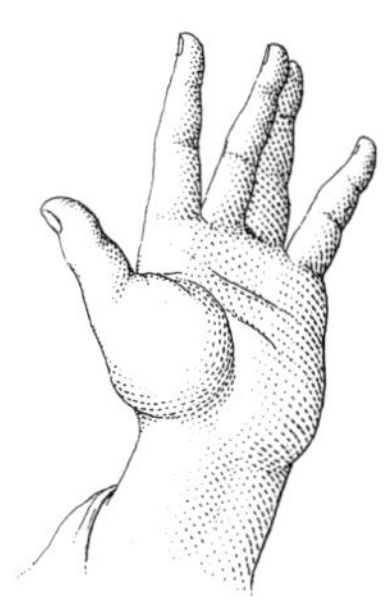

Mind

An awake mind is our ultimate home. In the Buddhist tradition, "taking refuge" means taking on the practice of wakefulness. Wandering from that, the thoughts, emotions, actions, and houses in which we seek shelter become like sandcastles or prisons.

Bringing wakefulness to every aspect of your home environment is as simple as cleaning your teapot. Colors, textures, shapes, and spatial organization can enlighten your world.

Awake means that when you clean your tea pot, then the tea pot wakes you up.

—Chögyam Trungpa

» Take time to sit quietly in each room of your home. Take a deep breath. Keeping your eyes open, count five relaxed out-breaths. Then, for the next five out-breaths, be aware not only of sights but also of sounds, smells, tactile sensations, tastes, and thoughts. Let each of them arise in your awareness, then let it go; come back to being in the room. You may notice that your home evokes feelings of satisfaction (sanity, well-being, renewal, peace) or distress (time pressures, feelings of isolation or intrusion). Notice those feelings and let them go. Ask yourself whether home is a spiritual power spot for you; whether you find personal and universal wisdom there; whether your home feels blessed.

BLESSING: honoring and invoking sacredness; something promoting or contributing to happiness, well-being, or prosperity; a boon; approbation; approval.

How to Use This Book

The next five parts of the book present each of the five styles from two basic perspectives: the power of the style and practical design applications.

THE POWER OF EACH STYLE

First, we'll take a look at the primary power of each energy and its effect on our lives. From a contemplative point of view, the ultimate power, or gift, of each energy is wisdom—its "awake" manifestation in space. The first chapter of each part also describes an energy's *imbalance* (in "Too Much of a Good Thing"), which you will learn to diagnose and correct; and sensory examples of each energy (in "Bringing It Home"), which will speak for themselves.

THE ROLE OF EACH STYLE IN HOME DESIGN

Then we'll translate each energy into practical applications. You will learn how to identify the energies in a room, to increase deficient energies, reduce excesses, and restore balance through design. Refer to the chart in Appendix A for an overview of the five styles.

» Use your workbook to record impressions of your space, to identify where you need or want certain qualities of energy, and to plan changes.

Important examples and exercises are repeated throughout the book. Please think of these repetitions as the heartbeats of living energies and your creative design process:

- The qualities of the five styles will be reviewed in Parts II through VI.
- Some design solutions pertain to several styles: boxes, baskets, and closed storage, for example, can eliminate clutter (creating space); organize space (clarity); decorate space (warmth); enrich space with their physical presence (richness); and make space work more efficiently (energy).

The discussion of each style ends with a summary design example and instructions for creating an "installation" in each style.

CREATING AN INSTALLATION

An installation focuses a particular energy—using its qualities, colors, natural element, and symbols—to channel it into your home. Large or small, it's a well defined statement that heightens your awareness of an energy, channels it into the space, and projects it into your world.

You can channel the energy of space, clarity, richness, warmth, or energy into any bounded space (including your body, your car, the top of your desk). You can create an installation in the foyer of your house or along the sight line of a particular room to set the tone, to empower a particular room of the house, or to celebrate a particular season. Here is one format that I've used throughout the book by way of demonstration, but you can do variations of your own:

Heaven: a panel of colored fabric or paper on the wall. I use 36-inch- to 48-inch-wide cotton duck or colored paper (bought by the roll)—and hang it from ceiling to floor. You can use smaller or larger panels and dye, paint, or sponge on color and augment the panel with artwork, a mirror, or a hanging scroll. This panel defines your installation space and its specific energy.

Earth: a table or base—in the appropriate style—in front of your backdrop.

Man: a statue or flower / object arrangement to evoke a specific energy—to bring heaven and earth into harmony (which can be enlivened with plants, a spotlight, or a fountain of running water).

Please Remember This!

A masterpiece can be created with a stone or the burned end of a stick! You don't need a lot of money, space, or professional help to apply these principles. You can realign your home with the forces of nature by rearranging your furniture and working with the contents of your house. You can train in these principles using cut/torn colored paper, fabric remnants, flowers, or the contents of your pocketbook (and join heaven and earth with an "installation" of Post-its and paper clips). You can, in fact, evoke a particular energy with just one object—a chair, a flower arrangement, or a rug.

» Start small. Use household objects and everyday situations to realign the energy of your home. One friend uses a tray of rocks, rearranging and relocating the tray in her home. The simplest, conscious gestures can change your life:

  Space: Eliminate clutter (everywhere—walls, floors, ceiling); open space up.
  Clarity: Make space spotless, restore order, and install good lights.
  Richness: Put a pumpkin (or a basket of ripe peaches) on the table.
  Warmth: Bring warm colors, flowers, and candles into the space.
  Energy: Ventilate the space—with fresh air and with furniture arrangements that encourage energy flow—and bring in live plants.

» Now take each of these suggestions and find it reflected in a painting or print (or do one of your own).

Whether you're working simply or on a grand scale, it's time to begin working with space.

II

SPACE

7

THE POWER OF SPACE

SPACE—WHICH CAN'T BE GRASPED and has no signature sites—brings sanity and relaxation to every area of the house. It is an antidote to pressure and stress. Its openness and gentleness are reassuring. Introduce the qualities of space when you want or need:

More relaxation / less ambition . . .	to let go of preoccupations
More gentleness . . .	to open up your mind/heart
More sanity . . .	to open up your physical space
More sacredness / spirituality in your life . . .	to center yourself

The ultimate power, or gift, of space is openness and relaxation. Spiritually, openness is called "all-accommodating wisdom"; in practice, it's the mind of meditation. In home design, openness is unadorned, spacious environments. Spacious environments—like spacious human beings—are a relief to be with. They're gentle (not stimulating or demanding) and accommodating (not uptight).

» Think of metaphors for gentleness—for example:

animal—kitten	landscape—sea / sand / sky
plant—soft grass	weather—mist, fog
flower—baby's breath	food—white rice, milk

Write down their qualities (soft, subtle, soothing, open, delicate, humble). How can you emulate these qualities in colors, fabrics, furniture, and lighting to create a gentle space?

Whereas *clarity* defines and organizes space; *richness* expands and dignifies it; *warmth* uplifts space, making it elegant and inviting; and *energy* makes space work—space itself is an all-pervasive port in the storm. Its animals—if it bothered to have any—might be the accommodating buffalo, sacred cow, wise owl, or ordinary sparrow.

Too Much of a Good Thing

Too much or too little personal space can be problematic and cause us to panic or feel confused. Too much space is isolating and can make us feel desolate. It can take the form of wasted or inflated space. The size of many homes is far greater than the needs of their occupants; the size of individual rooms is not "human-scale." And many homes stand empty for much of the year.

Imagine yourself living in a vast, empty palace (or world). Eventually, you will draw your awareness into yourself, creating a more comfortable "cocoon," and (à la couch potato) mentally go to sleep.

Too little space, on the other hand, feels claustrophobic and overcrowded. Overcrowding has been proved to cause madness in animals and human beings. The overcrowding of our sense perceptions has the same effect! Imagine living in an overcrowded apartment with too many roommates and too few rooms. You will soon start ignoring the energies bombarding you—demands, noise, clutter, things falling apart. To create more space, you might ignore answering machines, mail, and relationships. You find yourself procrastinating, in denial, "spacing out."

When you experience too much or too little space in your home, see it as a reminder to wake up and restore balance.

Bringing Space Home

Space isn't flashy. It has no highlights and doesn't call attention to itself. If space were a kind of fabric, it might be plain muslin, canvas, or mosquito netting (spacious materials open things up.) As a flower, baby's breath or the lowly daisy; as a piece of furniture, a shapeless beanbag, bed, or hammock. As a style of home design, space would be *no* style—neutral, artless, and nondescript—furnished with found objects, thrift-store bargains, or no furniture at all.

Pierced stucco window, 14th century. Museo Arquelogico, Granada.

» In your workbook, collect examples of *space* in architecture and design—in your own and other cultures. Include "spacious" fabric swatches.
» Collect visual and literary examples of this energy's natural element, physical space. How is it represented in art, architecture, and design?
» Include color samples. Color is the "realm," or atmosphere, of each energy. Space—which doesn't have a signature color—is "spacious" colors, neutrals,

and pastel colors mixed with white. Look for them in art and design, in everyday life, and especially in nature. Don't overlook clouds, fog, sand, and sky. (Think about *camouflage* colors in nature.)

We experience space as *spaciousness*, and through all of our senses, we can bring space into our homes.

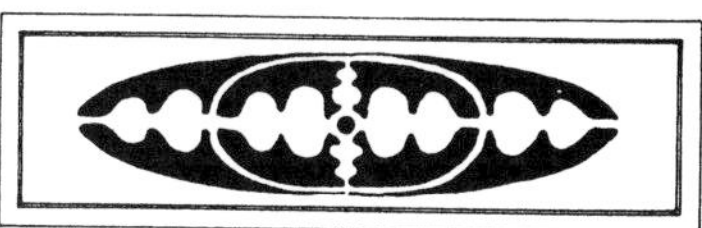

Openwork designs, Japanese transoms

SIGHT

Spaciousness is the absence or lessening of visual stimulation. It's a softening of focus and a sense of oneness with things. Colors are more gentle and subtle; materials, more natural and ordinary; edges are less sharp, less defined. Visually, space is the "isness" of things, the look of things when we just let them be.

» Study the sky each day while you're working with the space of your home. Once in the morning, afternoon, and at night—let your gaze and mind dissolve into the sky. Notice the changes; notice what, if anything, stays the same. Bring your observations and feelings of "sky" into your home.

SOUND

Spacious sound is wraparound (ambient) sound—chirping birds and giggling children, rustling trees, surging surf, and traffic. Spacious sound is gentle, unfocused, and full of "gaps"—the sounds of running water, wind chimes, a relaxed conversation. The most spacious sound is silence.

» Choose a quality of space—gentleness, for instance—and imagine it as a kind of music. Now vocalize that sound. Choose another quality of space—openness, accommodation, letting be—and translate it into music. Imagine these musical sounds cocreating a space in your home.

TASTE

If space were a taste, it might be "no taste" (institutional foods or fast-food sameness); comfort foods (mashed potatoes, rice pudding, hot milk); or bland, milky sweets. Sweet (*yin*) foods relax cell walls, creating a sense of comfort and well-being (irresistible when we're stressed or upset). Space in the home works the same way.

» The most "spacious" taste is no taste, or fasting. For one day, try fasting or eating only white or brown rice; translate fasting into home design. Create a space that's the equivalent of comfort food.

TOUCH

Spacious contact with the world is soft and gentle (a down comforter, a velvet pillow, the soft underbelly of a pet), ordinary and unassuming (a cotton sheet, terry cloth towel, meditation cushion). Space is a comfortable temperature (not too cold, not too hot) and being able to walk through a room without bumping your shins or squeezing past furniture.

» Pick a quality of space that you would like to *feel* in your home (gentleness, for instance) and visualize it as a piece of furniture. What material(s) would it be made of and why? How would it accommodate your body? Now create a room around that piece of furniture.

SMELL

If space were an aroma, it would, for starters, be free of olfactory pollution. Pollution is any sensory experience that is "solid," not ventilated with physical and mental space. This includes the stagnant or strong smells of stale air, molds, chemical cleaners, building or gardening materials, and artificial fragrances. *Toxic* smells—because of their extreme potency—need to be "ventilated" 100 percent. When the everyday smells of cooking, pets, people, and places are well ventilated, they are spacious and good. The *most* spacious smell is a lack of pollution—in other words, clean, fresh air.

» Identify olfactory pollution in your home—unpleasant or stagnant smells of smoke, chemicals, cooking, molds. What steps can you take to ensure proper ventilation throughout your house?

MIND

A spacious mind is open and unbiased: appreciating whatever arises, you remain unattached. Awareness ventilates your sense perceptions like fresh air. Spaciousness keeps mental energy from generating sensory pollution. For the sake of a sane environment, investigate ways to cultivate space in your mind.

- » Go outside and wander through space. Look upon everything you see as space: the sidewalk is space; the trees are space; all sounds are space; the temperature is space; your thoughts are space. *Whatever* you encounter is space. Like cool moonlight after the heat of a summer day, let your all your perceptions dissolve into space.
- » Investigate ways to bring more space to your mind. Notice what obliterates this space and how you return to it. Do a weekend workshop on meditation practice; learn a mind/body discipline like yoga or T'ai Chi. Trust the relationship of a spacious mind to a spacious world.

Although space has no signature sites, the qualities of space are a must in your bedroom for proper rest and relaxation. (Clarity will reflect them in a peaceful bedroom design.)

In the following chapters, you will learn seven basic ways to translate the experience of space into home design.

8

LETTING BE

A WARRIOR PROVERB COUNSELS THAT "sharpening a good sword blade makes it dull." Space is by nature self-existing and all-pervasive. The best way to "create" space is to acknowledge space in the world around you—and let it be. Your mental and physical health depends, in fact, on giving the spaciousness of life its due.

Contemplating the Empty Container

Don't just do something, stand there!

Let architectural and interior space speak for itself. Before designing or decorating interior space, contemplate the empty container; before filling space with contents, consider its form.

» Study the space of your home room by room. Take the time to walk, sit, or lie down in each space. Notice how structural shapes make you feel. Before "creating" space, let space speak for itself. To amplify its message, highlight surfaces (walls, floors, ceilings) and architectural details.

» In your effort to create space, refrain from filling space up. Take paintings *off* the wall; use less furniture, color, and surface decoration and fewer accessories to reduce or eliminate sensory stimulation. Arrange objects carefully—with an eye to the spaces in between.

Letting Be Brings Relief

Psychologically, letting be means letting go of mental demands and preoccupations. Our need to do this is expressed in idioms such as "go with the flow," "give it up," "let it all hang out." Psychological space is basic sanity. At home, a little more chaos and a messier desk might be just what the doctor orders.

» If you have a camera, walk through your house and shoot some pictures without worrying about subject matter or composition. Suspend any sense of "accepting or rejecting." Don't look for highlights. Appreciate things as they are—ordinary, familiar things—and let them be.

Letting be is an expression of trust. An attitude of no-struggle brings feelings of relaxation and gives overmanaging minds a break. (The world doesn't fall when we loosen our grip.) Trust is essential to sanity and sane space.

» Tap into the space of your perceptions. Sit quietly and—one by one—put your attention on each sense perception: sight, sound, touch, and so on, including your mind. For several seconds—longer, if you have the time—touch each sensory experience and then let it go. Just "touch" and let go. Notice how you feel as a result.
» Train in letting go through meditation, deep breathing, mental relaxation, or other contemplative disciplines. The more intense, or solid, your environment is, the more you need to learn ways to access space—especially the space of your mind.
» When you feel pressured by your environment, letting be might take the form of a deep breath or simply walking out of the space and closing the door. Shifting gears changes the experience of intense space.

Letting be brings relief. Relief ultimately means being able to trust the basic goodness and workability of your world—the good, the bad, the ugly. Trust is a basic human need, and you need to find it at home.

9

OPENNESS

HERE ARE SIX WAYS TO OPEN UP SPACE IN YOUR HOME: eliminate stuff and clutter; eliminate bulk; and open up space with doors, windows, spacious materials, and spacious arrangement of furniture. Let's look at them one by one.

Open Up Space by Eliminating Stuff and Clutter

A friend just back from vacation in Hawaii was shocked by the "high walls of clutter" in her home. Returning home from "wide-open spaces" can be an eye-opening experience. Sadly, we adapt to clutter—a form of pollution—and take it for granted. To open up space is to eliminate clutter.

» Eliminate anything not in regular use—outgrown clothes, toys, books and papers, old furniture and accessories. Find good homes for surplus cookware and appliances. Unclutter your cabinets and help someone else out at the same time.

» Eliminate sensory clutter: visual clutter (including busy prints, plaids, and loud colors), lingering smells, noise, and irritating tactile sensations (rough upholstery, user-unfriendly synthetics, temperature extremes).

OPEN SHELVING

Open shelving—full of books, magazines, files, papers, tools, CDs/tapes, and electronic equipment—creates visual clutter. If you don't have storage areas with doors and drawers, find creative ways to clean up the visual field—and keep closet doors closed for more visual space.

» Organize the contents of shelves into baskets or attractive boxes—and recycle the rest.

Mask open shelving to create visual space. The easiest solution is to hang *unpatterned* panels of fabric or paper over the shelves (with Velcro, tacks, or tape covered with a ribbon border).

» Try this experiment: tack newspaper or pillowcases over chaotic shelves and see what a difference it makes!
» Buy simple hinged doors or make them (from wood strips and fabric or paper).
» From the ceiling, hang cloth, rice paper, or reed shades (with or without valences) in front of open shelves—and create the impression of a window wall at the same time.

Open Up Space by Eliminating Bulk

Space is eaten up by bulky furniture and architectural structures (such as overhead beams, exposed heating systems, and irregular walls). Rooms feel more spacious when environmental energy flows easily.

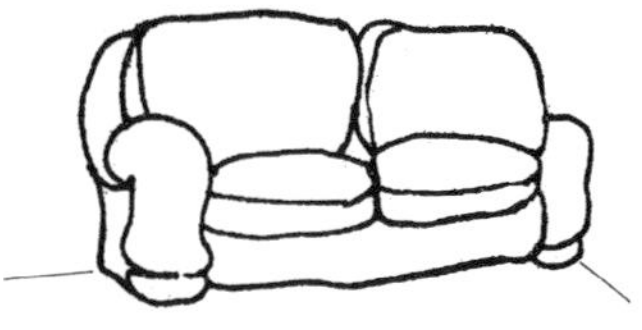

» Eliminate overstuffed furniture. It blocks the flow of energy and visually fills up space. Choose lighter, more versatile, furniture—old or new—with clean lines and unupholstered frames for more space.

» Mask or soften bulky duct systems (with a false ceiling or paint), low ceilings (with up-lights and a vertical plant or sculpture), and irregular walls (with plants or a mirror). Treat the downward-pressing (oppressive) energy of overhead beams as virtual walls and arrange furniture out of harm's way.

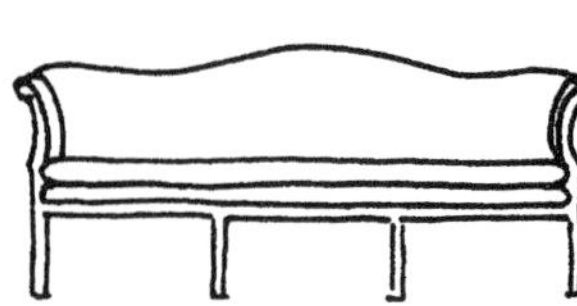

Next we will see how walls with doors, windows, or decorative openings create actual and visual space.

Open Up Space with Doors

Doors open up the space between rooms and between the inside and outside of your house. All doorways should be clear, unobstructed, and not too large or too small so that energy can flow easily—not excessively—in and out. (In a later chapter, we will talk about the flow of energy itself.)

» Open up interior/exterior space with sliding glass or French doors or with sliding shoji doors made out of translucent materials (paper or fabric). On a more modest scale, storm/screen doors let in winter light and summer breezes.

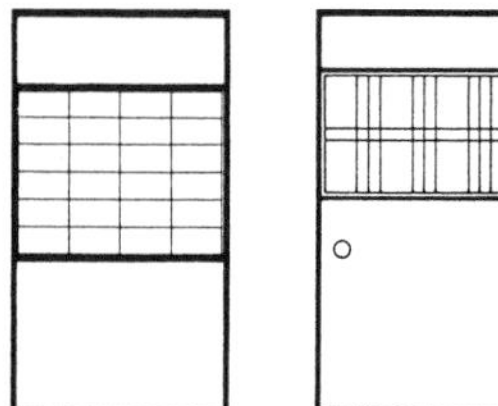

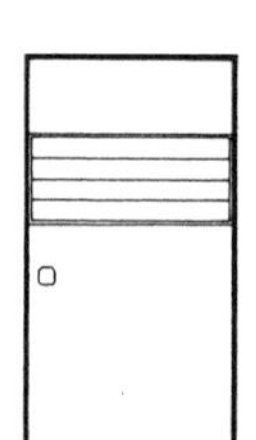

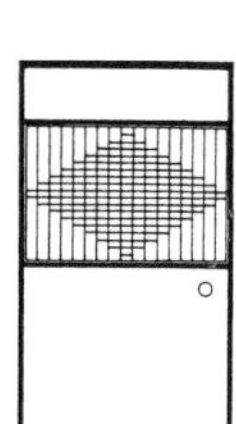

Doors that look too flat or solid—as hollow-core doors often do—visually take up space. Lighten them up or simply remove them.

» Replace solid doors with etched glass, slatted, latticed, or Dutch doors. (Salvage companies are a good source of used doors and ideas.) Lighten up flat doors with surface designs. For a low-budget solution, tack or glue moldings onto existing doors and paint to match; or create a simple "molded" effect with paint in subtly shaded colors. (Dark or contrasting colors will read as a graphic design—interesting, perhaps, but not as spacious.)

» Replace a solid door with a curtain that moves easily back and forth (on rings on a rod) or with a curtain of glass or wooden beads.

JAPANESE DOOR CURTAINS

A short or medium-length *noren* (Japanese door curtain) provides a light-handed but effective visual screen. Noren—in many colors, with and without designs—can be purchased in Japanese import stores. I've also used "panels" of starched vintage dishtowels, large linen napkins, mattress ticking, and handmade paper with great success. To create a sense of space, choose unpatterned, not decorative, fabrics.

Door curtains like this traditional-style noren (and the one below), create space by eliminating visual clutter.

» If you sew, stitch up your own door-curtains. They should fill approximately one third of the doorway, hang flat, and be split into two or three panels and hemmed. Hang them from springrods or from curtain clips stuck to the door frame.

Open Up Space with Windows and Half-Walls

Windows are the "eyes" of your house. When they are open, they suggest that the house is awake. When we're depressed, we draw our shades, shut out the light, and say "no" to the world. Windows provide light and spaciousness essential to mental and physical health. Keep this in mind when you "treat" your windows and don't get caught up in trends.

» Open up windowless areas, including bathrooms and halls, with skylights if you can. Use mirrors to reflect light and space into dark areas.

CURTAINS AND SHADES

Window treatments should be administered like medicinal poisons—in very small doses as needed. Their job is to provide privacy and to protect you from glare, darkness, and extreme temperatures; their decorative function is secondary. Don't smother openings with fabrics, plastic, or metal. Hang window treatments—especially, elaborate ones—in ways that maximize openness. This might require some thought on installation, but the rewards are more light, space, and the illusion of much larger windows.

» To maximize space vertically, keep valences and shades out of window openings. Hang valences *above*—not inside of—windows; they should stop at the frames and not cover the glass. Hang shades high enough so they can be drawn up to lie on the wall *above*—not inside of—the windows. If your window sills are low and the valences are hung at the ceiling you can create the impression of floor-to-ceiling windows or French doors.

» To maximize space horizontally, extend curtain rods beyond the windows so that curtains lie on the walls next to—not on—them when open. With two (or more) parallel windows, you can create the impression of a window wall. Hang extra panels in all sets of curtains and extend the rods across the wall. Curtain panels should lie between and beyond the windows when open.

» Mask "blind" windows. Hide unspacious "views" of air shafts and walls with decorative panels, screens, or interior shutters. Cover the window with translucent materials—sheer fabrics, rice paper, or several layers of moiré scrim—if it is a source of light. On large windows, hang etched or pebble-glass shower doors as "curtain panels" to create an illusion of light and space.

» Try not to block *any* window, even partially, with furniture. It creates a sense of obstruction (and exposes the unfortunate furniture to debilitating extremes of light, temperature, and humidity).

HALF-WALLS

Half-walls are "virtual" windows—but they don't always create a sense of space. For example, they are often used between kitchen and family rooms—affording a busy view of pots, pans, hanging knives, cabinets, and appliances (in the kitchen) from the family room, where you relax, socialize, and receive guests.

» Eliminate visual chaos by hanging a lightweight, translucent shade—try bamboo or rice paper—from the ceiling above the half-wall. Choose hardware that lets you pull the shade up and down without pulling it loose. You now have the option of screening off two rooms (creating more visual space in both) or rolling up the shade and joining them.

Open Up Space with Spacious Materials

Open-weave materials—mosquito netting, lace, gauze, latticework—are spacious; heavy and heavily patterned fabrics "fill" the space. Translucent materials—glass, plastic, and sheer fabrics—communicate the ever-changing energies of light and shade, seasons and weather that create a sense of space. In Japan, translucent paper walls in traditional homes create illusions of vast vistas in limited space.

» Nontraditional use of common building and design materials—glass bricks, corrugated plastic roofing, glass shower doors, theatrical scrims—can open up space in creative and affordable ways.

GAPS

A gap is an interval between two things—words, thoughts, pieces of furniture. A gap is space. Don't rush in to fill it up. Many cultures intentionally program "gaps" into architecture, art, and design to invite spirits, or subtle energies, to enter there. (Nothing can enter a space that's already full!)

Pueblo pottery is encircled by a line in which there is always a small gap called a "lifeline"—a design element that leaves small openings for the spirits to enter and

bless the pot. The lifeline is a symbol of blessings and of the way the spirits move in and out of everything in the house.

Like sleep and dreams, a gap is a brief interlude in "waking life." It can represent a moment of truth that—like space—is beyond mere definition. A flaw, or gap, is woven into the otherwise perfect design of all Persian carpets, for instance, as a nod to ultimate truth.

» Create space with a gap in your day. A tea or coffee break signals "relaxation" and brings a sense of space to the workplace. Make it a real gap: go outside, take a walk, or sit down with your tea and really relax. Inwardly, use breathing, mental relaxation, or mindfulness techniques to create gaps in physical stress and busy thoughts. A flower on your desk is a gap in visual business-as-usual.

Gaps are allies in design. They invite magic into interior space. Avoid making interiors too solid—objects on every surface, matching patterns on curtains/upholstery/walls—to enjoy the magic of space.

Open Up Space with Spacious Arrangement of Furniture

Realtors know that furnished homes appear much larger than unfurnished homes, which is why model homes are never shown empty. Spacious rooms are not necessarily empty rooms; they are rooms where the contents are arranged to open up space. What's important is not the size of home/room/contents but their relationships.

COMPOSITION

Composition—in art, architecture, and home design—is the conscious arrangement of objects in space. To create a spacious room, you must consciously arrange the contents of a room to create space. (The same objects could be used to create clutter!) Your intention to create space will guide you to a spacious arrangement.

Before rearranging your home, experiment with rocks in a sand tray, with objects on a shelf. Practice making space a priority.

» Now choose a room and do this exercise with furniture and accessories. Be aware of *opening up* rather than filling up space. In the following chapters, you will find more visual and energetic guidelines—but no fixed rules—for how this is done.

10

CREATING ILLUSIONS

ILLUSIONS ARE MADE OF "SMOKE AND MIRRORS" and skillful handling of objects (sleight of hand). Five simple ways to create illusions of space are mirrors, artwork, decorative screens, and the spatial illusions of contrast and sameness.

Creating Space with Mirrors

Mirrors can double the size of a room, multiply the light and loveliness of windows, and energize dark, dead areas. Like windows, they provide a room with a view and reflect patterns of natural light and life on interior walls.

On the other hand, mirrors can multiply glare, darkness, and interior/exterior chaos. Their "cool" reflective surfaces can bring a wintry chill to a room. Reflections from dirty, dark, broken, or odd-shaped mirrors are undesirable. Mirrors must be hung with care to create the illusion of space.

» *Do* use a mirror to create the illusion of more windows and open space; to enliven a dead area of a room; and to multiply desirable energies (greenery, art treasures, candles, chandeliers, and so on). In Chinese *feng shui*, mirrors are mounted behind the stove to multiply the blessings of fire and good food.

» *Do* hang a mirror at the back of your walk-in closet if the closet happens to face a window; it will brighten up the space.

» *Don't* "bounce" light/energy directly from window to mirror, especially if it "cuts" through seating or sleeping areas or interior traffic patterns. (In traditional feng shui, mirrors are used defensively to reflect troublesome energy back to its source. We will talk more about protective energy in Part VI.) To create an illusion of space, hang mirrors so they reflect gentle light and energy.

» *Don't* hang mirrors opposite cluttered shelves, messy work areas, or open doors (with constant comings and goings). You will eventually become overwhelmed by the chaos.

Creating Space with Artwork

Choosing artwork is a matter of personal preference; only you can determine how a piece makes you feel. If, however, you are choosing artwork *specifically* to create an illusion of space, there are some considerations (if no hard-and-fast rules).

REPRESENTATIONAL SPACE

Depictions of "real" space (land-, sky-, and seascapes) are generally most successful at conveying a sense of space because they spell out, or describe, space. Abstractions, no matter how "spacious," tend to read as objects on the wall—but there are always exceptions. Pattern painting—with no beginning or end—creates space through a sense of "ongoingness."

SPACIOUS STYLES

» Artwork done in a spacious, open style always evokes space. Choose spacious line drawings—large or small—as well as open styles of calligraphy, soft watercolors, pastels, and paintings done in soft colors.

LARGE-SCALE ARTWORK

» A large painting makes a generous statement and can make a small room seem less cramped. By the same token, "blowups" of familiar objects—a yard-high lipstick, a poster-sized teacup and saucer, a baseball as big as the mantle—can bring "bigness" to a small space.

» Create your own blowup (on paper or directly on the wall) with a good image, an overhead projector, and paint. (Subtle or bright colors will determine whether your image has a spacious or assertive effect on the space.)

Creating Space with Decorative Screens

Decorative screens, movable walls, and other room dividers create space in two ways: by virtue of surface design (spacious colors; depictions of sky, clouds, or wide vistas) and by concealing busy areas, traffic patterns, and clutter. Screens can be works of art or purely and simply (and beautifully) functional.

- Look at old and new screens (imported and domestic). Study their design and content. (Many European screens represent the four seasons; Asian screens often use symbolic natural motifs.)
- Make a simple screen using a wood, metal, or plastic frame covered with fabric or paper. Be creative: the rolling garment racks used in hotels and clothing stores make great frames for portable screens. Stretch them with fabric (as you would stretch a painting canvas); lash on fabric with rope and grommets (like a sail), or tie it on with ribbons. Hinge together panels of any lightweight, rigid material (plastic, wood, metal, cork) to make a freestanding screen. Decorate your screen with gentle colors and surface designs—try stenciling or sponging—to create an illusion of space.
- Create the visual effect of a floor-standing room divider with one or more panels hung from the ceiling. Use fabric panels—canvas, "grass" cloth, scrims, or satin for formal settings. Sheets of colored 1/8-inch acrylic or pebble-glass shower doors also can be used for this purpose.
- Use large green, leafy plants on multilevel plant stands as an ad hoc screen.

TABLE SCREENS

- Create an illusion of space with an inexpensive table screen (half the height of the average six-foot screen). Use it to hide clutter on the floor—including the busyness of chair/table legs, electrical plugs, cords, and computer cables. Place it on top of a large worktable to conceal a cluttered surface while creating an ad hoc wall. Stand one on top of your half-wall for the same effect. In summer, use a cool and spacious "half" screen to conceal your dormant hearth.

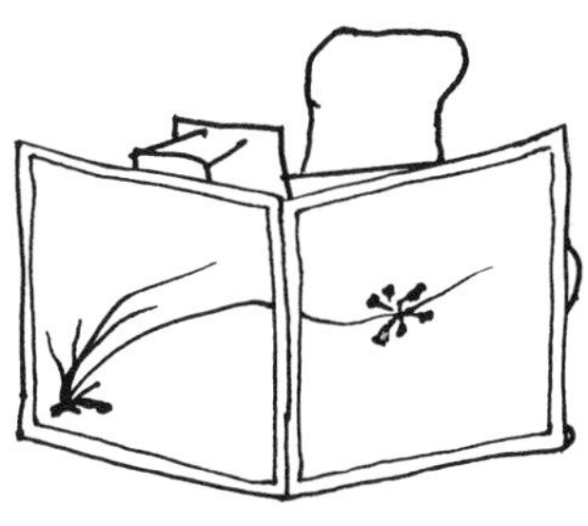

Creating Space with Contrast

If you put your hand in 98.6-degree water, you won't feel a thing. Change the temperature of hand or water, and the contrast creates feeling. Sensory experience relies on contrast.

In design, contrast exaggerates the difference between space and an object, heightening our experience of both the object and space. It's a dramatic way to enhance space. Here are three examples and some practical suggestions.

CONTRASTING LARGE AND SMALL

Contrast size, or scale, to create space: a tiny calligraphy, for example, can make an ordinary sheet of paper seem vast. By the same token, a visual focal point—a small photograph or painting, a focused arrangement of flowers or furniture—creates space. *Cluster* a group of paintings or photographs—or arrange them in focused rows, vertical or horizontal—for the same effect.

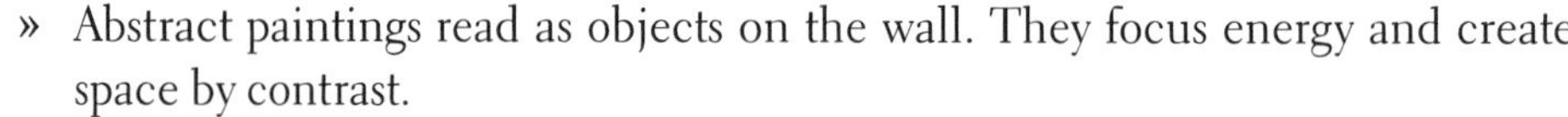

- » Abstract paintings read as objects on the wall. They focus energy and create space by contrast.
- » Framing a very small photograph or print (focal point) with a very generous mat/frame brings visual space into a room. (Framers who are set in their ways often balk at requests for outsized mats, urging standard proportions for your pictures. Take examples of wide-mat framing from magazines or museum catalogues to show them what you want.)
- » In a small, windowless room, a well-lit focal point (computer station, shrine, tool bench) can create usable space. Any concentrated, or focused, energy heightens a sense of space around it by contrast.
- » To balance a large space, a small object or group of objects must be very focused, intense, or highly defined. Without the contrast of boundaries and space, small things just become clutter.

CONTRASTING ABOVE AND BELOW

Floor-seated cultures—with their heightened sense of above/below—have their own ways of creating space through contrast. The concentration of floor mats, cushions, low tables, and other accessories (below) makes the room above seem very spacious.

Wainscoting in Western design has the same effect: less space below and more space *above* the chair rail creates an illusion of space by contrast.

- » Achieve the look of wainscoting by painting different colors on walls above and below an imaginary chair-rail line.

» To emulate a chair rail if you don't have one, mount one or more moldings on the wall. For a more decorative look, combine moldings with wallpaper borders.

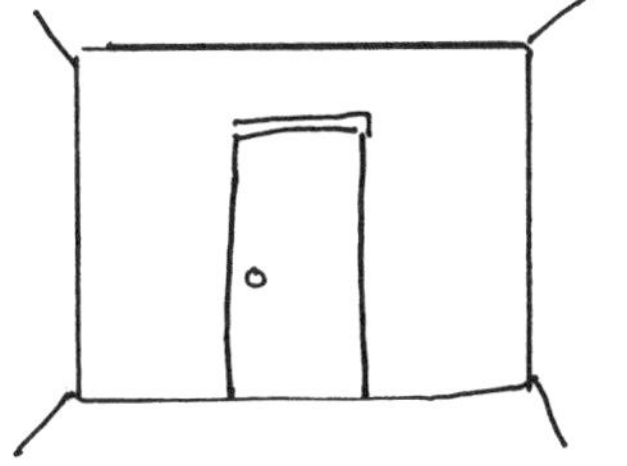

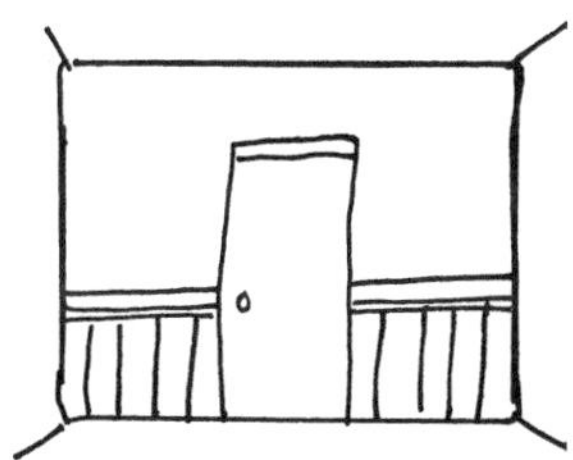

CONTRASTING COLORS

Contrasting colors create space: a black fly heightens our awareness of a bright, white wall.

» Consider this before choosing spacious white, pastel, and neutral colors (heaven) for carpets or floors (earth). They show every mark, by contrast. In bathrooms and kitchens wet areas attract foot- and pawprints that require constant cleaning up.

CONTRASTING FORM AND EMPTINESS

Contrast between form and emptiness creates space. When your senses are overloaded, for example, space seems "solid" and any *gap* is experienced as bliss. (Think of the silence that rolls over you when you turn the television off; think what an oasis a moment in the bathroom can be when you're surrounded by small children!) To restore balance to a stressful or intense environment, introduce the gentle qualities of space. They are antidotes to sensory overload. (Go back and read about letting be [Chapter 8].)

» Relieve sensory overload by turning off appliances, computers, and telephone ringers. Play soothing music when energy is running wild. Take a walk when you're overworked. Change your sheets to shift energy that's stuck. Shifting gears creates a gap—a breath of fresh air—and creates space by contrast.
» The flow of environmental energy—foot traffic, light, wind, and subtle energies—is balanced with the "emptiness" of space. Skillful arrangement of furniture (form) creates good boundaries and—by contrast—space.

Another way to create space through composition is "sameness."

Creating Space with Sameness

Sameness implies eternity, unendingness—and therefore space. With no highlights or reference points, it relieves the pressure of sensory stimulation and creates

a sense of space. This is the basic premise of flotation-tank therapy: in body-temperature water, the contrast between body and water dissolves, expanding the experience of personal "space." Psychologically, social conformity and the idea of "safety in numbers" works—for better or worse—the same way.

Sameness can be mindless: consider the unrelieved uniformity of some housing developments and institutional settings. The sameness of trekking through the desert or flying in the sky can make us very "spaced out"—if not terrified—due to lack of sensory signposts. To create an illusion of space, use sameness skillfully.

Sameness can refer to objects of uniform size (a collection of small statues); it can also mean energy "in kind" (a very large painting can bring visual "largeness" to a space; intense color can make a "big" statement).

» Group together real or representational objects of the same size (a collection of figurines or plates on a wall, a series of decorative motifs) to create an even, spacious effect.

» In a small room, balance a massive piece of furniture or large painting with strong colors on walls, floors, and upholstery; with rich textures; or with bright white room trim. (Otherwise, largeness will have just the opposite effect, drawing attention to itself and overwhelming the space.)

SAMENESS AS AN ANTIDOTE TO SENSORY OVERLOAD

The "Silver Garden" at Longwood Gardens, outside of Philadelphia, is a monochromatic realm of silvery plants, grasses, herbs, and ground covers, filled with the scents of lamb's ears and sage. The overall effect of this silver sensory world is immediate relaxation and peace.

» Use same-shade colors—pastels or neutral hues; shades of silver or gold; natural materials such as sisal, straw, wood—to create a soothing environment.

Sameness, like sand dunes, is undemanding and undramatic—but not without its own beauty. Used skillfully, uniformity—of color, texture, form, pattern, scale, and repetition—can provide a soothing antidote to sensory overload.

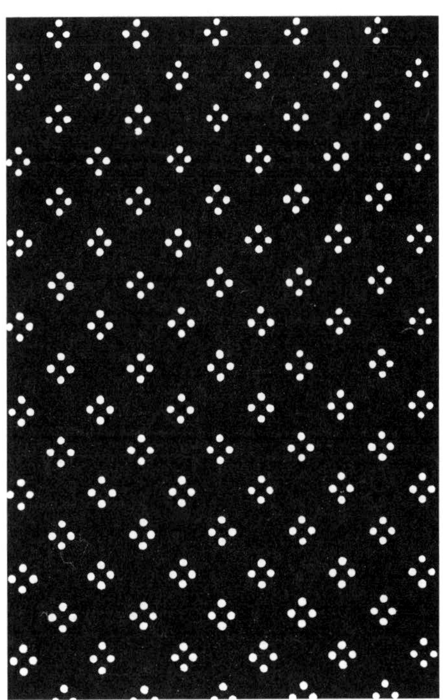

REPETITION

Repetition can be predictable and relaxing—as in our daily "routines." Mechanical or mindless repetition can also be used to torture human beings. Use repetition skillfully to create space.

» Choose wallpaper and textile patterns with regular (not random or dynamic) repeats that are unobtrusive in size and design. Find repetition in music, in the chiming of a clock, in visual "refrains."

SAMENESS INSIDE AND OUT

No matter where you live, you and your world are comprised of heaven and earth, water, fire, wind, and space. Congruence means your personal space is aligned with the natural environment; they're in harmony, "in touch." (If you don't want to be in touch with your environment, consider moving.)

» Unify indoor/outdoor space with natural materials (wood, paper, hemp, lacquer, stone, natural fabrics); surface design (sky, water, animals, leaves, flowers); and colors/textures that reflect nature and natural elements.

The congruence of home and nature creates space. Natural design, however, does not have to be rustic. Earth, water, fire, and wind are the building blocks—literally and symbolically—of all styles of design.

» If you're an urban dweller, think of ten ways (two for each element) to invoke earth, water, fire, wind, and space in your home. Your home will support life and living things if you do.

» Find pictures of traditional and contemporary, rustic and urban, home environments that are highly congruent with nature. Put them in your workbook and put them to work in your home. Look at examples of indigenous shelters in various climates and the work of Frank Lloyd Wright. (See Appendix B, References, and Further Readings, for more suggestions.)

11

SPACE IS A POSITIVE CONTEXT

We should find that all of our contexts for living—the workplace, home and family, places of learning, places of worship—are challenged to become more creatively dynamic and personally responsive. Whole people need creatively whole environments.

—CHARLES M. JOHNSTON, M.D.

SPACE PROVIDES THE CONTEXT FOR YOUR HOME—including the placement of your house on the lot and influences of the lot itself. From the point of view of enlightened design, the goodness of the universe is the basic context of your home. Work with the existing *positive* energy when you establish your home, and you will know how to overcome harmful influences.

Choosing Your Site

Your home should ideally be placed in a "lotuslike" location: cupped in the center of a site with protective walls of "petals" around it—*but elevated* in relation to the surrounding land mass. Another analogy for this ideal placement is a mother's lap.[1] In general, look for a moderate location—not too high, not too low—with mountains or hills (or higher buildings) to the rear for protection and a lower, preferably chalky, elevation to the front enclosing a gentle, open space. The environment should be alive with helpful energies and free of harmful influences (discussed later in the chapter).

When you find a suitable site, stand in the center and locate the four cardinal directions. Your new home should face east (next best choice is south). With east to the front and west to the back of the property, south is to your right as you face east, and north is to your left. The unique powers, or *drala*, of each direction should ideally be present in the natural landscape and subsequently invoked to protect the site from obstacles unique to those directions.

Helpful Influences

Since the most basic helpful influences are the five energies in balance, the rest of this book is about helpful influences! Working with them in the forms of colors, objects, elements, subtle energies, and spatial composition will fortify and sustain the positive context of your home.

Then there are helpful energies associated specifically with the four directions of your site. In this tradition, east—the front of the site—is symbolically represented by a white striped tiger, alert and powerful but meekly padding through space. The energy of the east overcomes anger/aggression. It appears in the landscape as described above. The drala of the east can be invoked by placing something white in the landscape (a white path, boulder, white flowers, a white fence) and by the gentleness and openness of the front of your site. If possible, include a peaceful body of water to the east (a birdbath or goldfish pond can serve this purpose). We will talk more about the relationship between mountain and water in Part IV, "Richness."

West—the rear of the site—is represented by the red garuda, a mythological Tibetan bird said to hatch full-grown from its egg. Outrageous and daring, the garuda is called "king of birds" and overcomes desire. The energy of the west appears in the landscape as a rocky mountain or hill, ideally covered with red lichen, which is called *lhari*, or Mountain of God. To invoke the drala of the west, Thrangu Rinpoche explains, "there should be a red rock or some red earth, which would be a sign of the red bird, and protection from obstacles in the West."

South—on your right as you face east—is represented by a glorious turquoise dragon connected with spontaneous fulfillment. The dragon is said to join heaven and earth and overcome pride: sleeping within the earth in the winter and rising up in the spring, the energy of the south brings blessings equally from above and below. It is ideally represented in the landscape by a river flowing through a valley in the shape of a dragon or by the presence of a forest or a tree.

The energy of the north is represented by a snow lion with a turquoise mane, connected with uplifted, youthful energy that overcomes laziness and envy. It appears in the landscape as a "network" of mountains resembling a tortoise's shell. (This direction is sometimes represented by the tortoise instead of the snow lion.) It is invoked by arranging small trees, shrubs, and grasses in patterns resembling the hard shell of a turtle—which stands, in part, for protection. (We will talk more about protection in Part VI, "Energy.")[2]

Harmful Influences

Harmful influences create a negative instead of a positive context and undermine the positive energy of your home. Here are some examples:

If the mountains and ridges (or buildings) to the north of your site are jagged and resemble "teeth," they represent danger or death.

If your site is at the head of a street funneling traffic energy into your home, you will feel invaded.

If your house is on an "island" surrounded by traffic, it's like a boat surrounded by sharks.

If some natural or manufactured formation—a boulder, sculpture, historic cannon, or billboard graphic—is "threatening" your home, your energy will suffer.

If your house is in a trough or valley, your energy might sink.

» See "References and Further Readings" for books on feng shui. Various schools of thinking on these topics offer remedies and compass-based relocation strategies.

Harmful influences can be remedied in some cases—but most should just be avoided.

Avoid houses with steep vertical inclines in front or back—including steep steps. They will present you with a constant sense of challenge.

Avoid houses built in risky places—on cliffs, eroding beaches, earthquake faults, and near high-power lines. They are like birds' nests built on water, like castles built on sand—not properly supported by nature and able to support life.

Avoid houses that overlook or are overlooked by a cemetery, crematorium, prison, or other facility harboring negative energy; negativity will loom large in your life.

Avoid houses or building sites with a history of events that are tragic (death, destruction) or negative (disputes, divorce, bankruptcy, loss.)

Avoid sites with significant decay or dead trees. Remove any such material on your site, after making offerings to whatever natural energies may be living there.

For Long-Term Commitments

Decide how deeply to investigate the context of your living situation. For short-term situations, only the most powerful, direct influences warrant your attention. For long-term commitments, the more you know, the better: your location may need to be remedied or changed.

» Get topographical maps (from city/county agencies or the library) showing the lay of the land and water tables. Check for geopathic stressors (the intersections of subterranean streams of energy). Hire a dowser to help you locate and work with them. (Karen Kingston's book *Creating Sacred Space with Feng Shui* is very good on this topic.)

» Get information about natural influences such as radon and termites.

» Check levels and sources of manufactured pollution—noise and air quality, chemical toxins, radioactive materials, and other waste. Look for high-power wires and transformers that generate electromagnetic pollution. Use a gauss-meter to measure electromagnetic fields (EMFs) in and around your home.[3]

» Get historical information about your home's location and its former inhabitants. (If bad or sad things have happened there, it's not a good place to be.)

Planetary Context

The planets revolving around earth create a heavenly context for your home. Their light and energy vibrations have a powerful influence on plants, animals, and human beings.

» Find out where the sun, moon, and stars rise and set—and which windows they shine in and when. Find a vantage point from which to follow their movements. Design your home within the context of their "rising" and "setting" energies.

A spacious environment is relaxing—and undaunted by our next topic, time!

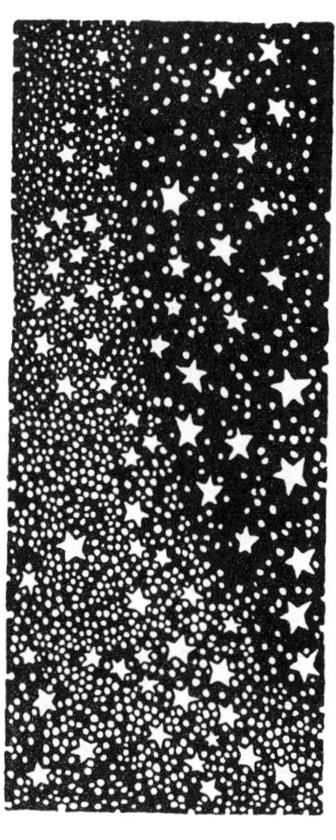

12

SPACE AND TIME

IN SPACIOUS SURROUNDINGS, we feel we have all the time in the world. When our lives are pressured and hectic, we feel we "need some space." Our experience of space and time is "simultaneous"—a fact often ignored in the West—and affects everything we design and build.

Many of us are happiest working into the night, when space is less demanding and we feel we have more time. From a contemplative point of view, however, the key to more space and time is wakefulness!

By creating space, or gaps, in our experience, wakefulness profoundly affects the perceptions that shape our sense of space/time. By creating more spacious sensory experiences—including our experience of conceptual mind and the clock—wakefulness creates a more spacious environment.

Flexibility and Change

Flexibility is spacious, bending this way and that like rushes in the wind. Flexibility is a spacious approach to everyday affairs and brings "space" into your life. In home design, flexibility is environments and materials that respond to change—changing seasons, weather, light, temperature, and times of day.

» Express flexibility through responsive materials that move, bend, sway, and give way to the touch. Flexible materials create gentle curves in space—in harmony with nature, where there are no straight lines. Flexibility in design implies "life."

» Find ways in your daily life to let go, go with, and give in. Flexibility will be rewarded with more space—mentally and environmentally.

CHANGING SEASONS

When I was a child, my grandmother cleaned her house from top to bottom every spring. Woolen rugs were taken up, sisal rugs were put down, and dark horsehair furniture was covered in bright cotton chintz. This simple ritual made the world open up like a flower—fresh and new, full of lovely possibilities. Change renews space and creates a sense of space in your home.

- » Change paintings, scrolls, and other artworks periodically—seasonally if you have pieces specific to a season. Change renews not only the space but also your ability to see your paintings. (We take for granted things we see on a regular basis and eventually don't see them at all.)
- » Change slipcovers, rugs, and accessories seasonally if you can. If you can't, use cotton or canvas throws as ad hoc slipcovers; put sisal rugs with summery decorative borders on top of permanent broadlooms.
- » Use seasonal flowers and plants to align your home with natural energy cycles. Keep wreaths, banners, and other accessories in tune with the times.

In the transitional seasons of spring and fall, put away unseasonable things and prepare for change.

- » In spring, remove andirons and decorative candles; clean out fireplaces and put summery fire screens in place. Replace decorative gourds and dried flowers with fresh flowers. In fall, pack up the chintz and put away fans, fire screens, and wildflower wreaths. Celebrate earth's bounty with signs of harvest and heavier, richer materials in deep seasonal colors.

Celebrate changing seasons with appropriate materials, colors, and natural elements. Work with earth, water, fire, and wind to balance and bless the environment.

- » In winter, use the warmth of fire (and all of its associations) to balance cold ice and snow (water). Maximize the importance of your fireplace if you have one: rearrange furniture; bring out warm woolly throws. Use wood and heavy, earthy objects to balance the north wind.
- » Balance summer heat (fire) with real and illusory experiences of water (fountains, glass vases, paintings of water) and with wind ("breezy" materials, wind

In Japan, concepts of space and time are simultaneously expressed by the word Ma. Ma . . . gives rise to both spatial and temporal formulations. The word Ma does not describe the West's recognition of time and space as different serializations. Rather, in Japan, both time and space have been measured in terms of intervals. Today's usage of the word Ma extends to almost all aspects of Japanese life—for Ma is recognized as their foundation; . . . architecture, fine arts, music, and drama are all known as "the art of Ma."

—Arata Isozaki

Firescreens balance the energy of fire/heat with cool vistas—snowcapped mountains, scenes of water—or seasonal flowers.

chimes, real and decorative fans). Cool off a hot environment with refreshing plants and flowers, and lightweight materials—mosquito netting, muslin, sisal, straw, and wicker.

CHANGING BY DESIGN

Nature is constantly changing—and human beings are part of nature. We are physiologically *designed* for impermanence and change. We thrive in adaptable environments and become physically and mentally ill in those that are not. (Extreme or out-of-control change, of course, is also an imbalance, causing unrest or loss of heart.)

Artificial environments that cut us off from change cut us off from life. Artificial lighting undermines your health and well-being by creating an illusion of permanence and unending daylight. Artificial temperature control has the same effect.

» Fill your home with natural light that changes with times of day and year. Use mirrors and skylights if you can. Relocate work or reading areas to sunny rooms; relegate TV and bedrooms to those with less daylight. Rearrange furniture and other accessories to take advantage of seasonal light and seasonal uses of space. Don't ignore your brain's need for natural, changing light. Consider aligning your sleep/wake cycles with natural cycles of light/dark and using less electricity. (I have considered this and cannot do it, but maybe you can.) Getting up with the sun enhances physical and spiritual well-being and is ritualized in many traditions.

» Balance natural and artificial temperature control. Wear sweaters and woolen socks when it's cold. Keep your heat low and turn it off at night. *Do* get a good feather bed. *Don't* use electric blankets. They are a source of electromagnetic pollution and undermine your body's health and energy. In summer, use floor-standing and overhead fans for a gentler form of air conditioning. Don't rob your body of its ability to adapt to the elements. (If you can't adapt to cold or hot climates, consider relocating or taking winter/summer vacations.)

STRESSORS IN ARTIFICIAL ENVIRONMENTS

Artificial environments subject your mind/body to a great deal of stress because they oppose impermanence and the need for renewal. To eliminate stress, use your home as a bridge between you and the natural world. Design your home around your physiological sensitivities to light, sound, temperature, time, and so on; and become less dependent on manufactured sources of energy. You will be healthier, happier—and save money as well.

» Use all of your senses—sight, sound, touch, smell, taste, and mind—to create living environments aligned with seasonal energies. Study your natural surroundings for ways to amplify the poetry of change in your home.

Finally and most important, we come to the significance of sacred space in our homes.

13

CENTER WITHOUT FRINGE

Labyrinths, the Western equivalent of mandala, lead us to our "center" and integrate outer/ inner realities.

When children make angels in the snow, they wave their arms in a circle around their central space. From that center, energy unfolds its wings and angels appear.

Center space is the heart and soul of any mandala. Psychologically, it's your source of inspiration, your spiritual core. "Center without fringe" means that—anytime, anywhere—you are *centered* in that inspiration. *Centrality* refers to its place in your life and in your home.

» In your workbook, put into words your central inspiration. How and where do you acknowledge that core truth in the home?

Creating a Place to Center Yourself

Centering is a way to come back to your core. When you are in touch with your "center," everything you touch is centered as well. "By the act of centering," M. C. Richards writes, "we resolve the oppositions in a single experience. The surrealists in France call it *le pointe supreme* and found it also at the center: *le foyer central*."[1]

In your home, center space honors your spirit and your spiritual lineage. Like the motionless hub of a wheel, it transcends the speed and frustrations of daily life. Center space—whether it takes the form of a wall shrine, a special room, or a corner of a room—is central to your spiritual well-being.

» The centerpiece on your table represents "center space." The next time you entertain, let an inspired centerpiece set the tone of the space.
» Create a central place for sacred objects, books, and pictures of special people (teachers, ancestors, guides).

IDENTIFYING YOUR PERSONAL LINEAGE

Each of us has a personal legacy of inspiration, teachings, and love—some heart connection to persons (living or dead) that we look up to and emulate. Because inspiration comes through your sense perceptions, you may have a visual lineage (favorite painters, designers, craftspeople), a sound lineage (musicians, singers, poets, and communicators), and so on—up to and including mind. Identifying your personal lineage helps to center you and your home.

» Identify your personal lineage. Consider all of the sense perceptions to fully appreciate your personal inspiration and ancestors. To center your lineage at home, provide them with a "seat," honor them, and invoke their blessings.

A TOKONOMA

Center space is not necessarily compass-center. The Japanese *tokonoma*—a recessed alcove in traditional homes and teahouses—is generally found near the door. Housing a seasonally appropriate flower arrangement, painting, or calligraphy, it provides a spiritual reminder as you enter/exit the house.

A MAGICAL GARDEN

Two friends of mine are devoted to the growing of gardens and two children. This is their life and contemplative practice. Instead of a shrine, they created a magical garden under the skylight in their living room—with plants, fountain, fish, figures of deities, and rock platforms for offerings—to celebrate their inspiration and center their home.

A SECRET PLACE

Architect Anthony Antoniades writes that one can't shape architecture without knowing what religious rituals it might contain. He tells of his experience with Greek Orthodox clients who, "though [they] will not state their deep devotion to their beliefs, feel much happier if the architect provides for an iconostatsis and a nook for the candle in a secret place that only they themselves will know exists."[2]

This simple wall shrine, hand-crafted by Takayuki Kida, could be used in kitchen or office.

SHRINES

In some cultures, spiritual "centers" are made in many rooms—with food offerings on the kitchen shrine, a scholar's shrine in the study (for deities and mentors of knowledge), and a guardian or good luck shrine in the baby's room. Here are some suggestions for creating a shrine:

» Honor the heaven principle by elevating sacred objects—a photograph, statue, or calligraphy—off the floor (earth). Use a table covered with a special piece of fabric or decorative paper; protect the top with a piece of glass cut to size; adorn it with candles, water bowls, seasonal flowers.
» Put incense, matches, and candle snuffer on the floor (earth) in front of this area. Place them on a tray or small rug (man). Burning incense at floor level allows the smoke to rise above and the ashes to fall below the shrine.
» Out of respect (heaven), don't point your feet (earth) toward this area (so don't place shrines or sacred objects and pictures at the foot of your bed). Don't rest your coffee mug or hairbrush on a shrine's surface (even temporarily). And if flowers or plants are arranged there, keep them fresh and well cared for.
» In the same spirit, keep your shrine space/room one-pointed—free of distractions. Don't let stacks of folded laundry migrate into that space or use it for storage (unless things are stored in closets with the doors closed).

Design your center space according to the principles of heaven, earth, and man. Then go there for meditation and prayer. "If you take care of that place," writes Jeremy Hayward in *Sacred World*, "simply going there can create a feeling of [space] . . . and bring freshness into your daily life."[3]

CHILDREN'S SHRINES

Children enjoy creating a special space in their rooms. A simple, meaningful shrine can help shape your child's inspiration and individual journey. If the room is small, use a shelf over the desk or bookcase for a shrine. In the Shambhala tradition, "children's day" is a celebrated at winter solstice with public and private children's shrines.

A MEMORIAL SHRINE

The elderly also benefit from a special space (many grew up with similar traditions). One seventy-eight-year-old woman lost several friends and family members within twelve months—a serious blow to her life on many levels. Creating a "memorial" shrine in her bedroom was a positive way to deal with her loss. It started with a simple white table runner on her late husband's dresser and became an ancestors shrine.

To create a memorial shrine, hang a colorful backdrop and a spiritually significant picture or symbol (heaven) over a table or shelf (earth). Include photos, mementos, and remembrances from memorial services (man). Over time, pack away or burn these tributes and keep only the main pictures on the shrine. Votive candles and incense may not be an option for many reasons; instead, focus the energy with a crystal, a small crystal ball on a stand, a cut-glass bowl of water, or a container of holy water.

RETREAT SPACE

A retreat cabin in a remote location surrounded by nature could be the core of your home mandala. Let it set the spiritual "tone" of your home. Build/buy/rent a place for contemplation and letting go. Let your retreat space center your home.

No matter what form your spiritual wellspring takes, it feeds everything that happens in your home. Tap into it on a regular basis. Without it, your home loses significance and power.

A Shambhala children's shrine embodies the principles heaven (king and queen dolls on the top level, pictured below); earth (rocks/minerals, plants, shells, representations of animals on the bottom level); and man (small figurines of musicians, dancers, and others on the middle level).

14

PUTTING SPACE IN PLACE

SPACE CREATES A GENTLE, RELAXED WORLD. It isn't localized and has no signature sites (an "installation" of space would be hard to find), but its impact on our lives is immeasurable. Working skillfully with space and spacious sensory experience is the foundation of enlightened design.

Space generates four other patterns of energy—all of them interdependent and ideally in balance. This energy dance creates our world. Our different personal styles are part of the dance: some of us are very spacious; the rest of us tend to be precise, expansive, passionate, or purposeful. We, too, are interdependent and ideally in balance.

Remedies for Excess

Clarity heightens our awareness of space by putting boundaries around it. By "framing" it, clarity draws our attention to a spacious experience (a painting, a piece of music, an aroma). With precision and order, clarity enhances space and prevents sloppiness or neglect.

Richness expands space and our sense of relaxation (more space/more time) and prevents anxiety.

Warmth increases our enjoyment of space and keeps it from being boring.

Energy brings a breath of fresh air into space and prevents lethargy (and lethargic environments).

The dance of form and emptiness begins with clarity, the energy of the east, and so will we.

Summing Up Space

Direction	*Color*	*Element*	*Season*	*Symbolic shape*
Center	White	Space	Timeless	Formless

Wisdom All-encompassing awareness.

In design Letting be, openness, illusion, accommodation, flexibility, change, sacred spaces.

Imbalance Ignorance (lack of awareness) results in dullness, lack of definition or boundaries, confusion/chaos, neglect/squalor.

Signature sites None. Space is all-pervasive. It is represented by the center of any mandala and associated with "spirit" and sacred sites.

Animals Buffalo, sacred cow, wise owl, ordinary sparrow.

III

CLARITY

15

THE POWER OF CLARITY

Clarity enlightens your home through precision and peace. Its energy—like the rising sun—is revealing and bright; its round shape, serene and still. Cool and unbiased, it encourages "clear-seeing." Clarity is an antidote to confusion and chaos. Channel it into your life when you want or need:

A slightly flawed cosmic mirror allows the universe to exist.

—HEADLINE, *Scientific American*, February 1988

More focus . . .	to clarify goals/intentions
More order/less chaos . . .	to simplify life
More insight . . .	to find more inspiration/meaning
More healing energy . . .	to refine an environment

The ultimate power of clarity—mirrorlike wisdom—is like the reflective surface of a lake. In design, it is clean lines and pure forms. Like water, clarity magnifies detail—drawing your attention to combed carpet fringe, the weave of linen, the texture of stone. Its traditional animal is the watchful tiger; its qualities are also embodied in the sleek otter, intelligent dolphin, peaceful crane, and visionary eagle.

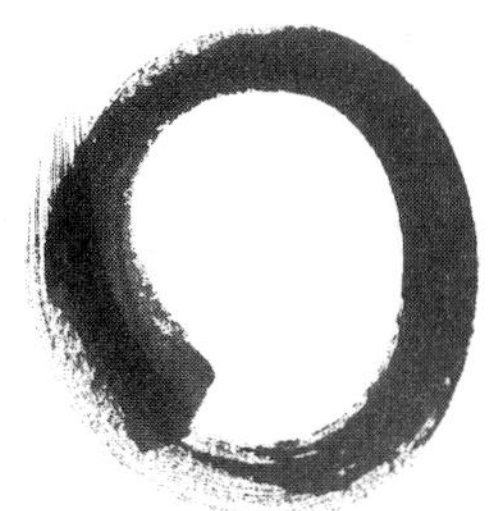

Too Much of a Good Thing

In excess, clarity's energy is like turbulent water (fragmenting reflections) or brittle and sharp like ice. Psychologically, it is too controlling, too conceptual, too "right." (Consider the overuse, especially in law and politics, of the word *clearly*.)

In design, excess clarity can be alienating, cold, and stark. Too intellectual with too many digitized systems (heating/cooling/lighting/coffee-making/security), it undermines any sense of well-being. Trying too hard to "get a grip," clarity creates anxious spaces that are overmanaged, overorganized, and claustrophobic. Warmth and spontaneity are squeezed out, as are softness and any sense of invitation. Like

ice, space becomes unresponsive and solid. Clarity of form becomes "pro forma"—hard-edged and humorless. Now let's look at the power of clarity in balance.

Bringing Clarity Home

If clarity were a kind of fabric, it would be starched white cotton, sharp pleats, or regimental stripes. As a style of design, it would be Art Deco or Japanese. Clarity is focused lighting (reading lights, up-lights, and spots) and clear white light in general. As a flower, it would be an orchid or bird-of-paradise. Clarity's cool color and style are ideal for hot climates.

We experience clarity through all our senses, and through them, we can clarify our environment.

SIGHT

Clarity is especially connected with sight. Vision—a function of objectivity and distance—is linear. It creates definition, form, and "lines of sight."

In design, clarity is clean lines, crisp patterns, and cool, wintry colors (especially blues). Clarity cools off the seduction of color, which takes a back seat to clear light. It's the sharp focus and high definition of photography, etching, and other print media (not colorful painting) and the drama of black/white calligraphy and black/white tiles. Clarity is spare and to the point (a Japanese flower arrangement, not a big bouquet of flowers; the precision of crystal and cut glass). Clarity's forms are still; its movements are restrained and precise (like the rising and setting of the sun)—even at high speeds (like flamenco dancing or Riverdance). More than 90 percent of design decisions are based on sight.

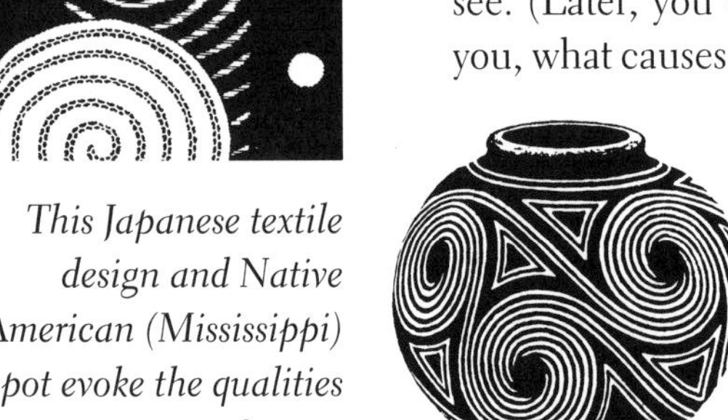

This Japanese textile design and Native American (Mississippi) pot evoke the qualities of water.

» Become a camera. Walk through your home and objectively record what you see. (Later, you can record how you *feel* about what you see—what pleases you, what causes you pain.)

» Collect visual representations of clarity's natural element, water. How is water represented in art, architecture, and design? What significance does it have?

» Research the *look* of clarity in other times and places, in architecture and design. Gather photos, fabric swatches, and natural materials. Include color samples. Look for the blues (and sharp black/white) of clarity everywhere—in art and design, in everyday life, and especially in nature. Don't overlook the clarity—and clear colors—of high-altitude lakes and exotic birds and animals.

Visual perception can be creative and open, the most powerful perception of all. It can be realistic and powerful and clear. And when extreme clarity takes place, that also brings a sense of humor.
—Chögyam Trungpa

SOUND

Clarity is the rustling of leaves and the clatter of dishes in the sink, the whisper of wind and the insistence of timers and clocks. The world speaks to us clearly through *all* the sounds we hear; all sound—even mumbling and confusion—is very precise. Clarity conveys clear messages of space, richness, warmth, and energy through qualities of sound.

» Close your eyes, listen, and let each sound "speak" to you—the telephone, television/radio, refrigerator, hair dryer, and other appliances; squeaking doors and floors; children and their toys, other people and pets; power tools in and around the house, sirens, rushing traffic, rushing streams. How do these sounds affect you? Write down an adjective for each significant sound. Write a poem using your adjectives as the first word of each line.

» Identify times or places of sound pollution—not the normal alternation of chaotic sound/silence but chronic sounds that fill the space. To clarify your environment, weed out noise.

SMELL

Clarity is clean, pure, and pungent aromas that wake up your sense of smell. In winter (clarity's season), aromatic energies and vapors contract. The smells we *do* experience are penetrating and sharp (wood smoke, pine, and wintergreen). They are cutting (like ice) and promote deep breathing (like camphor, eucalyptus, lavender). They are as refreshing as the wind after rain.

» Use clear aromas (lemon, frankincense, bergamot) to purify energy, restore health, and generally wake yourself up! And be clear, or precise, about the aromas you use for special effects. We will talk about the aromas connected with each energy in the following chapters. (See "References and Further Readings" for more on this topic.)

» More than 90 percent of our perception of taste is influenced by smell—so pay attention to the quality of air where you eat. Is it smoky, perfumed? Does your outdoor café serve traffic fumes with its food? Good smells enhance our eating experience, bad smells detract.

TASTE

Clarity is clean, distinct flavors (lemon and mint). It is palette cleansers (fresh herbs and grapefruit) and sharp, astringent tastes (wasabi and green tea). It's being clear about your taste experience (mindful of artificial, rancid, and impure tastes or tastes that are too extreme). It respects the tastes of others. Clarity of taste might take the form of a dietary regimen.

» What foods and beverages embody purity or healing? (A herbal tincture or medicine might come to mind.) Identify "meaningful" foods (think of health/dietary proscriptions). How clear—focused, simple, well-defined—is your diet?

» Consider the other meaning of *taste*. What does a *clear* sensibility or a sharp sense of style look like in design? Find examples for your workbook. Compare them to light, to purity, to mint tea.

TOUCH

Clarity is the feel of smooth satin, cool cotton, and crisp patent leather. It is smooth surfaces (plastic, marble, metal) and the wintry sharpness of hard edges, pleats, and points. It's a crisp, cold day and the crunchy textures of snow—or raw silk or sisal.

» Find the "touch" of clarity in your home. How and where do you make clear (precise, intelligent, simple, well-organized) contact with your interior world? Note how and where it's missing.

» If clarity were a chair, what would it look and feel like? Design a room around this chair. How does it feel to be in this room, and what would you do there?

MIND

Mental clarity wakes you up and overcomes depression and dullness. Like a crisp winter morning, it sharpens any sensory experience—even the experience of confusion: seeing confusion *clearly* is clarity of mind. Mental clarity is schematic, didactic, and precise. It takes the form of blueprints, design plans, and manufactured materials (products of mind). Computer programs are mental clarity at work; games—with their rules, roles, and diagrammatic terrains—are mental clarity at play.

» For one day, notice when you drift off and lose interest in your environment—it happens all the time. What brings you back? Record the perceptions that *wake you up*, stop your mind, and bring you into the present. Notice which of your senses is most awake.

» Walk outside with a mind open to sensory messages. See patterns of clouds in the sky, smell spring flowers, hear a haunting birdcall, feel your body moving through space. Record your impressions. Imagine they spell out an important message from a very wise person who has personally taken you under his or her wing. Now read that message and take it to heart!

Clarity brings peace to your whole home. Its signature sites are thoughtful, quiet rooms where learning takes place (libraries and studies); rooms for cleansing and purification (bathrooms, laundries, or spas—and healing places). Outside the home, they are hospitals, libraries, and universities.

There are seven basic ways to bring the power of clarity into your life. In the following chapters, we will translate each of them into home design.

16

LIGHT

LIKE THE SUN IN A CLOUDLESS SKY, clarity dispels darkness and illuminates the world. In the home, it's the luminosity of crystal chandeliers, glass-top tables, polished brass, shiny silver, and good lighting in general. Light rays—universally perceived as blessings—bless your home in many ways.

NATURAL LIGHT

Natural light is a powerful source of energy. Don't put obstacles in its way. Light is obstructed by fussy window coverings—as we saw in Chapter 9—and absorbed by oppressive colors or objects. Dark-colored interiors absorb light; white and light colors, on the other hand, reflect light—as do bright, shiny objects. Lightness of feeling is quashed by heavy, dark furniture—especially when placed on a window wall.

» Avoid placing very large pieces of furniture on window walls. Instead, put lighter-weight pieces (chairs, benches, occasional tables) and artwork on window walls.

» Use mirrors to reflect light, as well as crystal, glass, silver, and gold. (For personal viewing, choose mirrors that are clean and clear and don't darken or distort your reflection.)

» Illuminate your home with candles and gas lamps for special occasions. Use mirrors to enhance the glow; if you're shopping for sconces, look for those with mirrored backs.

[In Tibetan Buddhism] every particle is, in its true quality, light. Even in Western physics, a particle is made up of energy or dense light. So the world is not this gross, cold, rigid phenomenon; it is pure, clear, and transparent."
—TULKU THONDUP

ARTIFICIAL LIGHT

Good lighting is essential to good home design. Artificial light that's too cool (fluorescent and other "blue" light) is depressing and alienating. Lighting that's too "hot," or intense (glare, floodlights, exposed bulbs), is enervating. Lighting that's too dull has the same effect.

A young couple wanting a warm, earthy feeling in their home chose southwestern decor. And wanting to economize, they put fluorescent bulbs in all their lamps—with disastrous results. Cool blue light "killed" the warm colors of their adobe-colored walls, wooden floors, handwoven rugs, and Santa Fe–style furniture. Warm incandescent bulbs restored them to a more natural light environment.

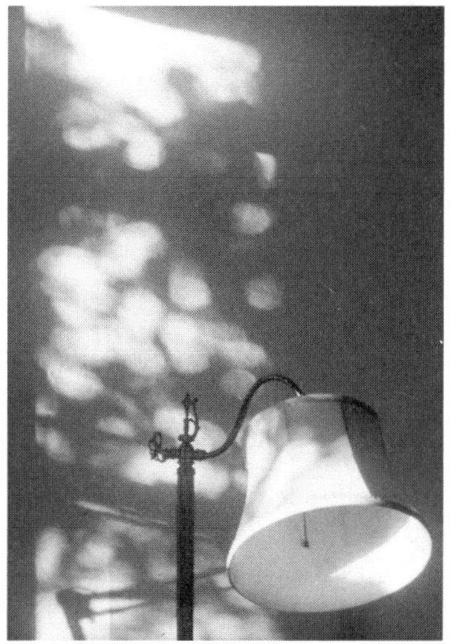

» Use incandescent lights or daylight—not fluorescent lights—to create a positive environment and sense of well-being. Look into the newest full-spectrum lighting fixtures.
» Install bulbs that are bright enough for reading, working, or lighting up dark passages. Use battery-operated utility lights in your closets (and stop fumbling around in the dark). Put bright, positive lights in stairwells and garage (especially if you enter the house there). But avoid the intense heat, glare, and electromagnetic distortion of halogen lamps.
» Avoid exposed bulbs. Choose overhead and floor lamps with shades or globes that mask their bulbs. Lamp shades are useless if they're *above* the bulb and you're below!

SPOTLIGHTS

Spotlights—from pencil-sized up-lights to track lighting—create focus and a sense of drama. They heighten the impact of art objects, flower arrangements, and seating areas.

» Use up- and down-lights to brighten up "dark corners." Put them behind furniture and plants and above paintings. Some nightlights (and the newer Christmas lights) are photosensitive and go on automatically.
» Always use the light over your stove or sink when you work there. It focuses your mind and brightens your activities.

THE EDGE OF DARKNESS

The *edge* of light/dark areas makes human beings uneasy. Light is connected with daylight and being in the world; darkness is a metaphor for the unexplored and unknown. Transiting light/dark areas affects our state of mind.

Waterford chandelier
(Courtesy of Waterford Wedgwood USA)

» Use focused lighting with care. Be mindful of light and dark areas of a room or house and create transitions that are comfortable, not scary.

The brightness of light describes "intelligence" as well as sensory experience.

Light as Intellect

Light is connected with intellect, learning—and ultimately enlightenment; seeing things as they really are, we're no longer "in the dark."

» Libraries, studies, and other reading areas need to be well lit. Choose lighting that lets you sit comfortably near it for a long time (reading with an exposed bulb by your head is irritating and unhealthy). Balance "cool" mental energy with warm light. Studying or doing mental work under fluorescent lights is very taxing.

INFORMATION

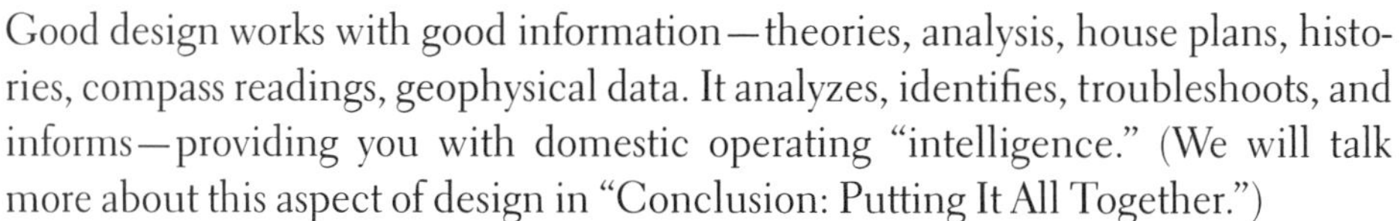

Good design works with good information—theories, analysis, house plans, histories, compass readings, geophysical data. It analyzes, identifies, troubleshoots, and informs—providing you with domestic operating "intelligence." (We will talk more about this aspect of design in "Conclusion: Putting It All Together.")

yes

» Good lighting lets you know how high the steps are, how long the hall. Changes in flooring materials/patterns tell you how a space is being used and warn you about the edges of steps. Operating manuals and technical resource books inform you about your house and surroundings. All of the design suggestions in this book provide you with sensory information of some kind.

WITTY SLOGANS AND STRUCTURES

Intellect takes the form of conceptual art (sculptures that demonstrate dazzling laws of physics) and intellectual surface design (witty slogans on pillows and cups). It is visible structures (the unupholstered frames of formal furniture) and structural supports (metal frames/joints/mechanical elements)—exposed and analytic. It is the heady aesthetics of manufactured materials and environments.

- Create designs that appeal to the mind: do a "flower" arrangement using plastic mesh, pipes, and computer cables; decorate with blowups of maps, structural diagrams, or architectural drawings (mount them under Plexiglas).
- Paint the interior trim (moldings and wainscoting) bright white or a contrasting color to "outline" a room, creating a diagrammatic (and intellectual) look.

Another form of intellect is organization. "Organizing power," writes Deepak Chopra, "is inherent in knowledge. Knowledge of any kind gets metabolized spontaneously and brings about a change in awareness from where it is possible to create new realities." Intellect is expressed through organization and order.

Organization and Order

Order "illuminates" your home, is revealing, and brings insight. Order and organization get a bad rap from those of us who appreciate spontaneity. We may feel overorganized and overmanaged at work and become defensive about chaos at home—or we may shift into supercontrol in self-defense. In either case, order is an "issue" rather than a way to light up our world.

ORDER AND CHAOS

In balanced environments (and people), order and chaos alternate like in- and out-breaths—with an emphasis on one or the other. Styles of clarity and energy tend toward order and conservation of energy; richness and warmth favor chaos and creativity. In the end, they're as inseparable as breathing in and out. (In biology, the most conservative form of organization, *habit*, begins innocently enough as a way to conserve energy for further creativity and change.)

Family members create order and chaos according to their particular styles of energy. Clarity and energy types prefer order, structure, and elimination of confusion; richness and warmth types tend to generate creative chaos along with their other gifts; and space "rangers" are wise enough to leave well enough alone.

One family member delighted in cleaning and organizing the environment. She had a real gift for "clarifying" space, which shone like a diamond when she was done. Nothing was out of place. There was no speck of dust. Her plants, however, were all dead in their pots! Focusing on form, she overlooked "function." Nature is messy; creative energy is chaotic. Indoor plants are a life-and-death process, with the occasional dribbles of water on furniture and floor.

Many artists find themselves cleaning and reorganizing their studios when they

When we see things as they are, they make sense to us: the way leaves move when they are blown by the wind, the way rocks get wet when there are snowflakes sitting on them. We see how things display their harmony and their chaos at the same time. So we are never limited by beauty alone, but we appreciate all sides of reality properly.

—Chögyam Trungpa

The attitude that nature is chaotic and that the artist puts order into it is a very absurd point of view, I think. All that we can hope for is to put some order into ourselves.

—Willem de Kooning

are about to dive into the chaos of a new project. Some have adopted this as a conscious ritual; others just accept it as part of their creative process.

- » Organize piles of chaos into useful, meaningful, or valuable collections of artifacts, memorabilia, magazines, and books. Turn material liabilities into assets and discard the rest. Anything worth saving is worth organizing in a way that enlightens your life and home.

THE COHERENCE OF WATER

Order reflects the coherence of water—gathering and channeling energy into orderly patterns for the good of the whole. The process of organizing domestic disaster areas will clarify your mind and your life.

- » Install a pool, pond, birdbath, or bowl of clear water to bring the energy of clarity into a space.
- » Thematic collections (nautical, sports, travel, theater, and so on) bring a sense of coherence to a space—if they're not mindless or slick. Gather thematic treasures together with care (and give the rejects away).

EASY ORGANIZATION AND STORAGE

The key to successful organization is ease. Make it easy to organize office supplies, papers, toys, kitchen tools, and closets on an ongoing basis. Good organization is a process that is in service of energy, not an energy prison. Like the banks of a river, it "goes with the flow."

- » Use baskets, boxes, and trays for instant organization. Commercial canvas laundry hampers on portable frames (available from restaurant supply houses) are great for large toys or patio cushions.
- » Color-code your file drawers/boxes for quick and easy visual organization: blue for ideas, intellectual pursuits, and health information; yellow for money and property files; red for love letters and other personal correspondence, and arts and entertainment files; green for active projects and work files.
- » Store bags of dry pet food in small plastic or metal trash cans with lids. More convenient than bags, they keep kibbles fresh and the floor clean.
- » Install a closet organizer, shelf dividers, and clear plastic drawers, boxes, and sweater/blanket bags (so you can see what's in there). Look through catalogues

and specialty stores for the latest selection of home organizers and storage units—if only for ideas.

» Storage units don't have to be built-in or permanent. Handsome canvas closets with removable wheels for portability are available. Commercial garment racks are also portable, if not pretty. Hide one behind a screen or bamboo shade (hung from the ceiling) or cover it with decorative fabric.

Organization creates focus and form, which is our next topic.

17

FOCUS AND FORM

CLARITY FOCUSES ENERGY and gives birth to form: to formulate a letter, you sit down at a desk, pen in hand, and focus your thoughts on paper. Interior spaces are shaped by their focus—entertaining, cooking and eating, sleeping, bathing—and give birth to their own forms of expression.

Energy enters a space, gathers/focuses for some purpose, and moves on. This process is much like eating a meal: nourishing energy enters our bodies through one "door"; gathers in a larger, stable midsection (focus area); and when its work is done, exits through another door. Like your stomach, the focus of any room must enjoy good energy circulation but not be disrupted by it.

» Arrange focus areas of furniture so they are not disrupted by traffic patterns or energy flowing through windows and doors.

Focus Creates Lines of Sight

Lines of sight—a theater term—are visual pathways into a home, a room, down a hall. They transmit visual information that determines what we think and feel about a space and creates our first impressions.

In a large front room, a client wanted to create a study with the look and feel of a library. Banks of bookcases, including two very tall ones, had been placed along side walls. From the doorway, however, the bookcases couldn't be seen, and the room didn't say "library." When the tall bookcases were moved to the wall opposite the door—flanking a velvet sofa with wall-mounted reading lamps—they created a library wall. Now you know at a glance how the energy is focused there.

» Stand in the entrance of your home. What is the first thing you see? Is this the first impression you would like to create? (We will talk more about entrances and spatial invitations in Chapter 34, "Hospitality.")

» Stand in the doorways of the rooms in your house. Is the intention/focus of each room immediately apparent? Would you enter the room for that reason?

Sight lines can support or sabotage any intentions you have for a space. Views that are clear, focused, and uplifting—or depressing, confusing, or threatening—create similar feelings in the viewer.

An underfunded social services facility used every available room for therapy groups. Upon entering one room, the first thing everyone saw was a bathroom—the door of which was always open. Group therapy began with a view of the toilet. (This problem was corrected with a spring hinge and an inexpensive decorative screen.)

The tone of this bedroom is set by the sight of a peaceful screen.

SIGHTS OUTSIDE

Entrances directly lined up with exits "funnel" energy in the front door and out the back. In the same way, a glass door or picture window opposite the entrance funnels your mind out of the house. Where the eye and mind go, physical energy soon follows (which means you may not reside there for long). Sight lines that send your eye/mind/energy too quickly through space have the effect of "cutting," or dividing, space.

» Check the alignment of front and back doors. If you can't relocate a door (or window) that's part of an energy funnel, create a visual diversion in your entrance hall. Use a decorative screen, freestanding wall, or hanging banner to tame incoming energy before it moves on.

From inside the house, sight lines lead your eye into the surrounding space outside. What you see there affects the quality of your life. Houses overlooking mortuaries, cemeteries, power plants, or disposal areas, for instance, do not promote health and well-being.

Sight lines operate on the principle of "What you see is what you get." By the end of this book, you will know how to focus visual energy in specific ways.

Manners are the happy way of doing things; each once a stroke of genius or of love—now repeated and hardened into usage. They form at last a rich varnish, with which the routine of life is washed, and its details adorned. If they are superficial, so are the dewdrops which give such depth to the morning meadows.

—RALPH WALDO EMERSON

Form

Focused energy expresses itself in simple forms—and in clean, spare lines, crisp surfaces, and pure environments.

» Focus on one ordinary object in your home—a plate, a chair, a roll of paper towels. Study it as an artifact. If you have time, draw it. If you have a camera, photograph it at various times of the day.

The external form, or shape, of anything is a clear picture of the way energy is focused within.

» Study the shape of your house from outside. Is the right or left side, front or back, significantly higher or lower? Study your house plans to see the shape of your house inside. Since this topic is too big to be fully addressed here, see "References and Further Readings" for recommended books.

Form and Formality

Form shapes the containers through which other energies flow. To do this, form must contain and conserve energy. Formality—like form—is "conservative" because it contains energy.

Formality communicates a sense of tradition, authority, and official sanction. Because it preserves proper procedure—and any preservation of procedure is "formal," from the most primordial and wild to the most urbane—formality is important to ritual, ceremony, and celebrations. Governments and corporations aspire to conserve and structure energy. The design of their official facilities and functions is formal. Formality is decorum, manners, and proper procedure.

Formality is rigorous. It focuses energy and prevents it from dissipating. Wisdom

Federal carved chairs, New York, circa 1790–1810.

traditions are preserved through form and therefore emphasize "proper," or "correct," ways of doing things. (Anglo-American cultural bias against form and formality is due largely to the loss of rituals and customs that channeled natural and spiritual energies into our lives.)

Excessive formality lacks heart. All form and no content is stiff and empty at the core. (James Thurber once called the ritual of formal banquets "a kind of dignified confusion that gradually unhinges the mind.") Ideally, formality and feeling support each other. Form and energy work as one.

The formal Washington dinner party has all the spontaneity of a Japanese imperial funeral.

—Simon Hoggart

FORMAL DESIGN

Formal design is seen in highly structured furniture, window treatments, and clothing ("formalwear") and "classical" accessories with historical (conservative) precedent. The *virtue* of form is conservation of energy (without which, energy dissipates). Its downfall is resistance to the process of change (without which, energy stagnates).

» To appreciate formal design—of places, people, and things—study the role of form in nature. Collect real and photographic examples of natural energy structures (leaves, shells, anatomical drawings, crystals, molecules, patterns of chaos in space). Notice their elegance, simplicity, and similarity to formal design.

FORMAL AND CASUAL STYLES

The style spectrum from "formal" (highly structured) to "casual" (unstructured) measures the importance of form. Design trends swing from one to the other; people, places, and things do, too. Form and function (the process of change)—seemingly conflicting energies—are two sides of one coin, with unique contributions to make to your home.

» In your workbook, collect examples of formal and casual styles from diverse times and places. What impact do they each have on you, on the environment? How do they work together?
» Identify formal and casual elements of your home. Look at furnishings, accessories, and surface designs. Are you using each style to best advantage?

Focus and form bring the energy of clarity into your home with the help of spatial definition and boundaries.

18

DEFINING SPACE

In the animal kingdom, the rule is, eat or be eaten; in the human kingdom, define or be defined.
—Thomas Szasz

Definition is the key to successful space planning. To define your space, you first need a vision. A vision of health and healing, for example, will generate a good medical center; a desire for warm human relations will give birth to social or intimate spaces; a nurturing vision will produce good kitchens and restaurants. When you visualize your space with a clear intention, you can define its boundaries, gather the energy you need to realize your dreams, and invite the world in.

» Decide where you need more/less definition in your home and why. This will determine how you will define your boundaries.

Boundaries

Boundaries shape energy and work like a magnifying glass to focus its intensity. Boundaries can be physical (walls/doors, office cubicles, screens, focused arrangements of furniture, large plants) or visual (changes in colors, patterns, materials, or textures of walls or floors). Boundaries prevent dissipation of energy from within and disruption from without, to balance your space.

» Choose a room (a bedroom, for instance) and visualize your intention for that space (restful sleep). Create good boundaries to define your intention and your space: in this case, window coverings that keep out unwanted light and a door that closes and locks for privacy. Psychological boundaries might mean no telephone or TV. (Psychological boundaries in the dining room might mean no answering of phones during meals.)

» Create boundaries around an entrance area with a focused arrangement of furniture.

- » Define a multipurpose space with visual boundaries—large areas of color painted on walls or floor; changes in floor covering (wood to tile, for instance, or an area rug); a hanging banner.

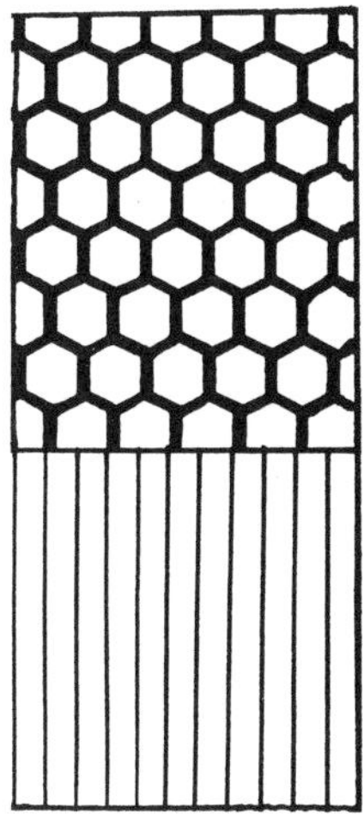

The best spatial—and psychological—boundaries are responsive, not permanent, rigid, or solid. Addressing the need for form and space joins heaven and earth—in a well-defined way.

WALLS . . .

Walls—for better or worse—define space. If you're stuck with your walls, visualize the purpose of your space, then use the walls to bring your intention into focus.

- » Ask yourself—from the perspective of the five styles—what does this wall need to do: open space up? pacify the space? enrich or beautify the space? make the space more functional? Choose paint colors, textures, and accessories appropriate to that energy. Heighten the energy with an appropriate style of artwork or installation. Create a wall that supports your intention for the space.

. . . OR NO WALLS

Open spaces such as lofts or studio apartments need good boundaries to meet all, not just some, of your needs. (A foldout couch is not enough to convert a work space into a restful sleeping area.)

- » Use furniture to create ad hoc boundaries: a rolltop desk can be closed up at night; closed cabinets can hide televisions, computers, and other equipment from view when you want to switch gears. (See Part II, "Space.")
- » Hang a curtain or rice paper shade in front of work/study/dressing/cooking areas. Some designer shower curtains are ideal for defining an all-purpose space.
- » Create luminous boundaries with glass bricks or colorful corrugated plastic panels—two building materials great for use indoors. For an intriguing effect, stretch layers of translucent material—scrim, organza, mosquito netting—on frames (as you would stretch a canvas) to make a simple freestanding screen or hanging panels. Use them (carefully) to hide overhead lights.

REMEDIES FOR BAD BOUNDARIES

When space feels chaotic, confusing, or threatening, we feel the need for better boundaries. (All of our boundaries—call screening, peepholes in doors, electronic surveillance systems—indicate the way we feel about our space.) When space is too "bound up," we feel claustrophobic and need more space. In this case, boundaries should be simplified, softened, or eliminated.

» Soften oppressive boundaries with mirrors, artwork, interesting textiles, textures, lighting, plants and flowers—and "soft" doors.
» Physically remove boundaries by taking out a wall or creating a half-wall or window. Light up narrow, dark hallways with skylights or half-walls, if possible, so no space feels boxed in. (One New York architect renovated his apartment so that no passage or room is without natural light.)

Details!

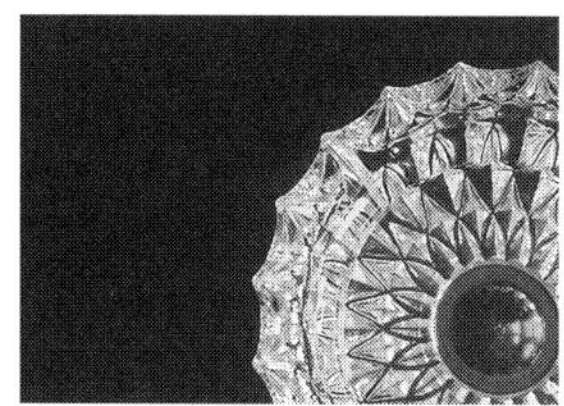

Details are a form of definition that says, "The picture's complete." Environmental clarity is like detailing your car—the perfect spit-and-polish job. It is shiny brass, fresh flowers, and clean overhead light fixtures (no dead flies). Design details (upholstery piping in contrasting colors, heating vents and returns in the style of your decor) say, "Nothing was overlooked."

Details are a celebration of mindfulness. We neglect them when we're preoccupied or stressed—which subtly undermines our sense of well-being and always undermines the power of the space. In *The Poetics of Space*, Gaston Bachelard tells of a distinguished psychologist, Mme. Minkowska, who interpreted the drawings of houses by children: "Often a simple detail suffices . . . to recognize the way the house functions. In one house, drawn by an eight-year-old child, she notes that there is 'a knob on the door; people go in the house, they live there.' It is not merely a constructed house, it is also a house that is 'lived-in.' Quite obviously the doorknob has a functional significance. This is the kinesthetic sign, so frequently forgotten in the drawing of 'tense' children."[1]

Men who wish to know about the world must learn about it in its particular details.
—Heraclitus

Details bring us down to earth. With too much heaven and not enough earth, we don't see the trees for the forest.

» Rely on details to make your design vision a reality. (For their role in the bigger picture, re-read "Earth" in Chapter 3: Heaven, Earth, and Man.)

» Go through your house with an eye to lighting and plumbing fixtures, doorknobs, hinges, and light-switch plates. (If they're brass, are they polished?) Look at baseboards, moldings, chair rails, and wainscoting. (Could they be enhanced, installed, removed?) Notice paint surfaces—matte or glossy? Do your paintings need viewing lights? Could their frames be more beautiful, more stark, more dramatic, less dull? In the kitchen and bathroom, check the toothbrush holder and soap dish you use every day—and what about the soaps? Do you need night-lights in dark corners? Check your office and desk: are they ready for a change of accessories? Being mindful of details clarifies your mind and environment.

Dying is the most embarrassing thing that can ever happen to you, because someone's got to take care of all your details.

—Andy Warhol

Flowers, Forks, and Other Numerical Considerations

When all's said and done, details are the signifiers, or messengers, of the phenomenal world. Odd and even numbers of things have different effects on composition and design—and different cultural meanings. In general, even (yin) numbers are passive, symmetrical, and connected with stillness and death. Odd (yang) numbers are "active," asymmetrical, and represent ongoing creative process and life.

Your dinner fork is a good example of the impact of odd and even numbers. Since forks are already an assertive shape and material (metal), a fork with four tines (an even, *nonassertive* number) is more balanced and pleasant to use than a fork with three tines (an odd and assertive number—and an unfortunately common contemporary style).

In Western civilization, even numbers stand for perfection in architecture and design. Balanced and unmoving, their stillness is a "container" for movement within. In Japan, even numbers (and symmetry) are considered "death" in design. The arts, architecture, and design are based on asymmetry, movement, and odd numbers of elements. Dynamic structures balance inner stillness.

» Use asymmetrical arrangements (of furniture, artwork, or objects) and odd numbers (three, not four, flowers in an arrangement) to invite viewer participation. Because symmetrical arrangements are "perfect," they create closure and distance between themselves and the viewer (and are often used to reinforce a sense of separateness and awe).

Details such as these define our material world. The next example is texture.

Texture as a Form of Definition

Textures are footprints in space—impressions of earth, water, fire, and wind; of urban and rustic virtues. They speak to your mind and heart as well as to your sense of touch and help create the "texture" of your life.

» Add your own to this list of interior textures:

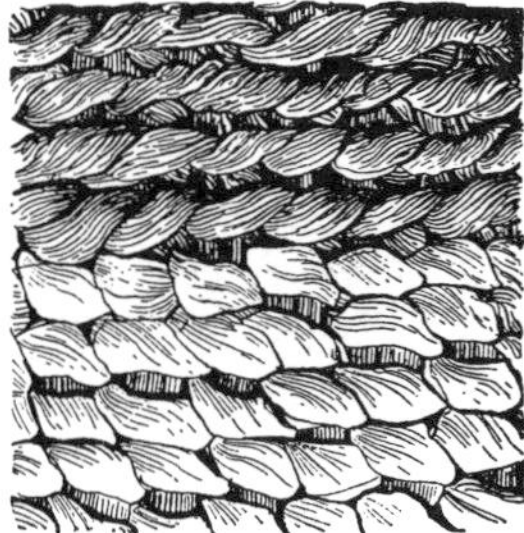

straw	handmade paper
sisal	glass
tiles	wood
fur	cast iron
velvet	rough/smooth stone
linen	brushed aluminum
feathers	leather
plastic	Brillo pads

Some textures can make you feel tense: ceramic-tile kitchen floors promise that whatever you drop will break; synthetic upholstery can be physically irritating; sharp corners on furniture are a subliminal threat, as is wicker furniture that snags stockings and clothes. The cumulative effect of "tense" textures—like the "Preponderance of the Small" in the *I Ching*—is a tense environment. And fake textures—wood veneers, synthetic rocks, artificial flowers—don't bring genuine energy messages into your environment like the "real" things.

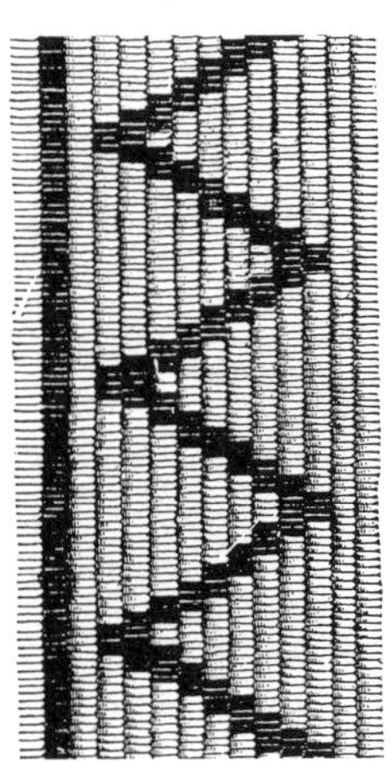

» What is the overall texture of your home? Take time to identify areas that are too hard, soft, rough, flat, unforgiving—or "unreal." Identify textures that feel right.

» Country styles (with handwoven textiles, carved woods, rough stone, hooked and braided rugs) tend to be more textured than urban styles (with more metals, plastic, smooth stone, and industrial carpets).

Texture, detail, boundaries, form, and focus are all design messengers, which bring us to the next topic, *meaning*.

One should not search for anything behind the phenomena. They themselves are the message.
—GOETHE

Meaning

Meaning is what we know of the world. Without this knowledge, we feel lonely and confused. It illuminates experience like the rising sun: when things "dawn" on us, we call it insight and say, "I see." A meaningless environment is benighted. Meaning makes living in the world worthwhile.

» Identify things in your home that are deeply meaningful to you—a photograph, a religious symbol, a mask, a diploma, as well as meaningful scents and sounds. To acknowledge their significance, frame, cluster, display, or enshrine meaningful things. Gather their energy and invoke their power into your life.

Meaning communicates itself through the senses. Sensory messages (like any language) are sympathetic vibrations that confirm—for better or worse—that we're one with our world. This is the *law of correspondence*: when a horse neighs out in the pasture, another horse—not a cow or a dog—responds. This is the way we cocreate our world.

» Take a walk through your house and read the "messages" all around you: carved into furniture, molded into silver, woven into textiles, inscribed or painted on clay. Know the real meanings of seasonal messages—wreaths, decorated trees, painted eggs. What messages are missing or meaningless? Is it time to replace old messages with new ones?

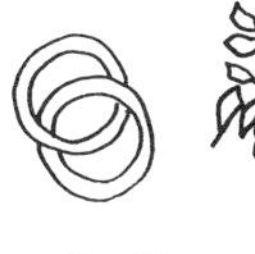

European style motifs symbolizing transformation (butterfly), spiritual quest (shells), connubial bliss, fidelity (interlocked rings), plenty (cornucopia), divine music, union of heaven/earth (lyre), longevity, wisdom (oak leaf/acorns).

MEANING IN MYTH AND HOME DESIGN

Mythical homes—inhabited by gods and spirits as well as humans—were meaningful. Coming and going, waking and sleeping, birthing and dying, bathing, dressing, and eating were poetic parallels of spiritual experience. Their meanings—preserved in language, myth, ritual, and symbol—join heaven and earth. (See "References and Further Readings" for more on this topic.) Understanding the spiritual and psychological significance of mirrors, stairs, thresholds, hallways, windows, and doors deepens our appreciation of structure. Here are some examples.

Mirrors	Reflect the soul, physical existence (mirrors are often covered at the time of death to prevent the soul from returning to its former body); timelessness; they are used for divination.
Stairs	Can symbolize ascending and descending energy connected with spiritual soul journeys.
Thresholds	Represent transitions/challenges; in Africa pregnant women know not to hesitate in thresholds.
Hallways	Signify narrow passages, journeys through the unknown, transitions; they are sometimes used as baffles/protection.
Windows	Are the eyes of the house, connected with vision, inspiration, blessings and children.
Front door	Is the mouth of the house and is connected with fortune, good or bad, and your relationship with the world.

» Remember how placement communicates meaning: the placement of religious or sacred symbols above doors, beds, or on thresholds and roofs, for instance; and the placement of meaningful pictures, such as ancestral portraits, above eye level.

» Take the symbolic associations of clarity—round shape, blue/white color, water element—and embody them in design. (On the wall, for example, hang a collection of round china plates with nautical themes.) Try this exercise for richness, warmth, and energy.

Meaning relies on the purity of our perception. In the next chapter, we will see how clarity purifies the environment.

Meaningful *symbols* bring us into harmony with heaven, with earth, and with each other. And beyond symbolic allusions, things are symbols of themselves: colors, shapes, and styles express themselves meaningfully. Ultimately, they communicate wakefulness (or not) and have the power to wake us up. This is the creative challenge of enlightened design.

BEAR TRACKS

FOOTPRINT

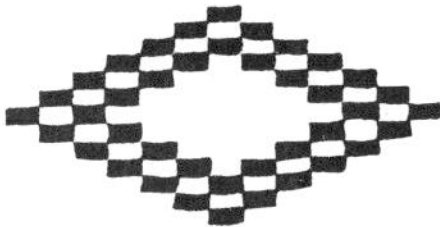

GOOSE TRACK

TADPOLE

BACKBONE

WAVE

RAVEN TAIL

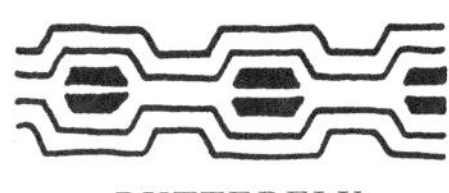

BUTTERFLY

SAND HILLS

Design units used in basketry, Tlingit (after Emmons)

19

PURITY

PURITY IS THE ESSENTIAL SHAPE OF THINGS—sights, sounds, ideas—seen clearly. Things "just as they are" are not perfect but pure! Purity in practice is compassion. In the home, it's a sense of basic goodness.

Perfection is finally attained not when there is no longer anything to add but when there is no longer anything to take away, when a body has been stripped down to its nakedness.

—ANTOINE DE SAINT-EXUPÉRY

Purifying the Environment

Purity gets to the goodness of things by getting rid of dirt, stagnation, and negative energy. It gets rid of the "dust on the mirror"—harmful habits and things that are stale, dead, or unproductive.

Native American wisdom advises us to walk away from places that "no longer grow corn." Get rid of things that no longer grow corn for you. Then the energy of goodness can shine through. (We will talk more about this in Part VI, "Energy.") Purifying the environment is essential to good energy and good design!

» Break old habits (subscriptions to papers or magazines you don't read, using coupons for undesirable things). Change ecologically unsound products (unrecyclable plastics or soaps, carcinogenic chemical cleansers) and practices (use of toxic bug or lawn spray). Restore the health of your home.

Clean everything and keep it completely clean. The spirit of the sky, the mountains, the valleys and the rivers are the perceptions themselves. When everything sparkles, all the world will resound here.

—DOUGLAS PENICK

CLEANING

Actually *cleaning* your home can be seen as a chore or an opportunity to purify the environment. Make it a ritual of renewal using the forces of nature as your elbow grease:

Earth is used by desert nomads, in the form of sand (or seeds), to scrub pots, to sweep clean the floor.

Water—sprinkled, washed, or poured—is universally used to purify people, places, and things. Used in house blessings, it often means purification and conception.

Fire purifies through destruction and is connected with transformation. By extension, smoke from cleansing herbs is used to purify homes in the form of incense and smudge sticks. Sunlight is used to purify people, places, and things. (Desert people put their shoes and clothes in the sun.) Salt, a form of fire, is used to clear confused energy and fortify earth.

Wind purifies the environment inside and out. It's connected with ventilation, the removal of obstacles, and renewal of energy.

There are very few cleaning jobs that can't be done with "clear" energy instead of chemicals. Reread "Bringing Clarity Home" (in Chapter 15), then put your sense perceptions to work. (See "References and Further Readings" for more information.)

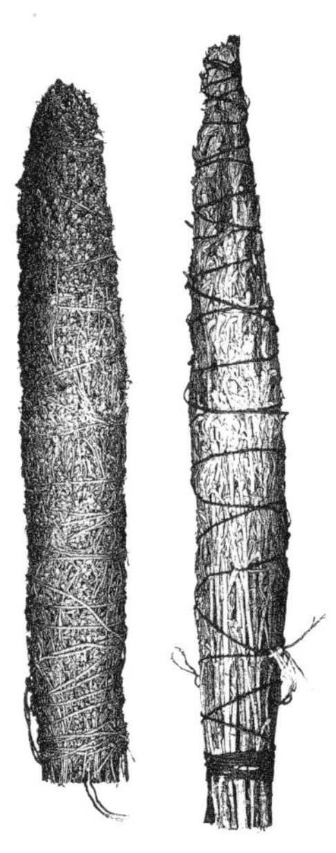

» Clean your house with pure water, lemon, and vinegar and with clear scents—eucalyptus, sage, lavender, pine, lemon. Smudge your home with sage, juniper, or cedar. Scrub it with water and baking soda. Use an open box of baking soda to deodorize your refrigerator (just leave it on a shelf). Combat unwanted guests naturally (lemon water for ants, borax for cockroaches, citronella candles for mosquitoes).

» Clean up the visual field. Cleaning the "dust off the mirror" has a powerful effect on the mind. Empty out cabinets under sinks; store only what you use and try to use as few products as possible.

» Purify the auditory environment of irritating sounds—noisy fans, motors, squeaking doors. Clean the coils of a noisy refrigerator. Get rid of noisy appliances if a task can be done by hand.

» Recycling is a powerful way to purify the environment inside and out. Recycle paper, metal, plastics, and usable goods—furniture, clothing, toys, and appliances. Call a local charity or church to take away domestic "time capsules." They will be timely and helpful to someone else.

» If you have interior or exterior walls that are porous (stone, plaster, brick) and unsealed, consider liming, or whitewashing, them. Liming your walls—an old way of protecting them from bacteria and molds while brightening them up—is coming back into fashion because of its luminous, soft look. You can tint limewash for chalky, pastel colors that resemble the icings on *petits fours*.

It may be necessary to clear the house of subtler unwanted energies.

EXAMPLES OF SPACE-CLEARING TECHNIQUES

Native Americans use smudge sticks of sage and other herbs to purify people, places, and things—and invoke blessings. Early Europeans used water, fire, and smoke in purification rituals—traditions continued in the Christian church. Tibetans also purify with water, fire, smoke, and other natural materials. In particular, the *lhasang* purification ceremony using juniper or cedar smoke is done to clear space and invoke the blessings of dralas.

» Do a purification ceremony when you move into a new home—or to dispel negativity from your current space. Ideally, invite a knowledgeable person to conduct this ceremony in the tradition of your choice so you can be a "benefactor."

» To rid a house of ghosts or negative energy, sprinkle salt in the four corners of the house and ask the presence to go away. Say why this is necessary and tell the energy to leave.

» Investigate space-clearing techniques. They are used throughout the world. Note that clearing and empowering are closely connected. Karen Kingston's book *Creating Sacred Space with Feng Shui* is especially good. (See "References and Further Readings.")

ELEMENTAL ETIQUETTE

To avoid *creating* negative energy, purify your contact (touch) with the world.

» Treat natural elements with respect: pour—don't "toss out"—water, to avoid offending spirits of water and earth. Observe "elemental etiquette" such as snuffing out—not blowing out—candles, to avoid setting wind against fire (or dousing fire with water).

» Here's a mindfulness exercise: For one day, pay attention to how you reach for, use, and discard things. Ask yourself whether you would like to be treated this way.

» Finally, investigate mindfulness/awareness disciplines to work with emotional and mental pollution. They can clarify our sense gates and our relationship with the phenomenal world.

Purity as Healing

Purifying a person or place of "sick" energy restores health. Healing into health—and particularly the purification of impurities and obstacles—is connected with the energy of the east, with light, the element water, and clarity's signature colors, blue and white. (Renewal of health—the healing of wounds and bones, healthy pregnancies, mental/physical growth—and the flourishing of wellness are more connected with energy, as we will see in Part VI.)

HEALING ENVIRONMENTS

An intentional healing environment is the work of clarity and its qualities:

Purity—of air, physical surroundings, medicinal supplies, food, and water—is essential.

Focus/form makes your vision of healing/health a reality and shapes clear-cut ways to reach your goal.

Order and simplicity help compromised energy and the energy of caregivers to move easily in the space. (Chaos and complexity are too demanding.)

Sight lines are especially important for bedridden patients. If a room doesn't have an uplifted view, bring in artwork, create a wall installation with backdrop and flowers.

Meaning can be introduced by placing meaningful pictures and objects where they can be easily seen or reached.

Peace—in the form of a peaceful, cool space that is undemanding—supports recovery.

» Medicine cabinets and first-aid kits are miniature healing environments. If you use medicinal herbs, give them a special place in your pantry or kitchen and label them with name, date, and directions for use. (If they're pushed to the back of a drawer or stored in an anonymous brown bag, they will never get used.)

For home health care, balance clarity with the energies of space, richness, warmth, and energy, so the space is not *too* cool or sterile. Home care is more well rounded than highly specialized hospital environments (especially surgeries and other technical areas, which are usually blue).

» Use colors, fabrics, and accessories with *spacious* (gentle, relaxing) qualities when energy is vulnerable. (See Part II, "Space.") If the patient's energy is agitated or heated (emotionally or physically), balance it with the cool colors and energies of space and clarity.

» To lift loneliness and depression, introduce shades of warm colors—reds and yellows rather than cool blues and greens. They are inviting, friendly, and warm up the space. Colorful flowers and throw rugs can be drawn on for emotional warmth.

» Shades of green (cool) express renewal of energy and growth. They may be helpful during recuperation, pregnancy, or the mending of bones—and may be irritating to people whose energy is profoundly weak.

» During recuperation or chronic illness, personal preference is very important. Work *with* the patient to create his or her home-care environment. Helping to choose colors, artwork, lighting, and furniture arrangements to balance the energy of the space can be very healing.

You don't have to repaint the sickroom to work with the healing potential of color. A blanket, throw rug, decorative screen, or simple fabric panels can set the tone of the room. Colored canvas or cotton duck panels (which can be sponged with similar colors for a softer, textured effect) can be easily moved, changed, and used as backdrops for pictures and paintings. Neutral canvas has a sturdy, reassuring presence. Or create several yards of hand-dyed gauzy muslin. It's an inexpensive way to brighten a sickroom—or any room of the house.

» Use your imagination working with colorful lengths of fabric—drape it over a curtain rod or chair, tack it to the wall, hang it from the ceiling.

Remember that cultural associations with colors and healing traditions vary. (Some traditions, for example, align compromised energy with very *strong* rather than gentle colors, drawing on them for strength.) Learning one set of guidelines makes us mindful of other possibilities.

» Be sensitive to personal preferences and cultural differences. Find out what the patient's requirements are.

WHEN SOMEONE IS VERY SICK OR DYING

When someone is sick or dying at home, energy is very focused. A truly healing environment—for everyone concerned—is balanced with the energies of space, richness, warmth, and energy. If you contemplate their qualities (letting go, centeredness, dignity, love, comfort, passion, playfulness, overcoming of obstacles), you will see how essential they are to healing.

» The patient's room provides, to a large extent, for the needs of caregivers and loved ones. Consult with them about their needs—a good chair, light for reading, throw rug, side table for a cup of tea—and make sure the room is kept clean and comfortable.

The outcome of healing is sometimes death. The environmental needs of a dying (or very elderly) person depend on his or her faculties and state of mind.

As sense fields fade, interest in the environment fades as well and, at some point, ceases. Prior to that, however, what focus there is is significant.

» Meaningful people and things—religious articles, family pictures, a prayer book—should be easily visible or reachable. Place them with care—not hidden behind a water jug or in a drawer with the Kleenex. Provide what sensory support you can for this significant and sometimes difficult life passage—but remember that the most significant sense faculty is the dying person's state of mind.
» Be prepared for the external environment to become less and less important; be ready to shift your focus. Disinterest is an all-important stage of letting go.

For the dying patient, the five styles of energy take an increasingly "inner" form: the space of letting go, the warmth of a hand held, the richness of the dying time, the energy of change. In the end, the five energies are like beautiful flowers in a garden: when their season is over, cover the beds and prepare the ground for rest and renewal.

Therapeutic Settings

Psychotherapists and other health professionals often create private offices that fall into one of two camps—his and hers. There are stylized versions of a heady, "masculine" approach and a more feeling, "feminine" style of therapeutic interiors. No style is right or wrong—but style needn't be formulaic. Designing your office is an excellent opportunity to determine the kind of therapeutic influence you would like to communicate—and the ways you could do this environmentally.

» Remember that anyone who walks into your office is there to feel *better*. The therapeutic setting can be a powerful part of the healing process. Its "message" should echo your own.

The secret to leading a positive life is to refine and harmonize one's energy so as to live in consonance with the order of the universe. . . .

—HUA-CHING NI

Purity as Refinement

Refinement—based on the word *fin*, or "end"—takes things to the nth degree. Burning away impurities, it's associated with reduction (and pain): something has to be given up for something to be gained. *Refining* means "of the essence"—subtle, well-processed, polished, precise. It is transformative, and transformation takes time; so refinement is about patience and cultivation. The aesthetic of refinement is renunciation and restraint. Its attitude is humble, its vision high.

In Japan, an aesthetic of "refined poverty," or *wabi*, evolved from the tea tradition. Influenced by Zen Buddhism, wabi is characterized by simplicity and humility. Because it celebrates the inner beauty of outwardly simple things, wabi is the aesthetic of impermanence, age, and imperfection.

» What area of your home life would you like to "refine," or cultivate, over time? It might be your collection of books, art, or music; your storage areas; your home office. In your workbook, make two columns—(1) dross, (2) gold—and go at it.

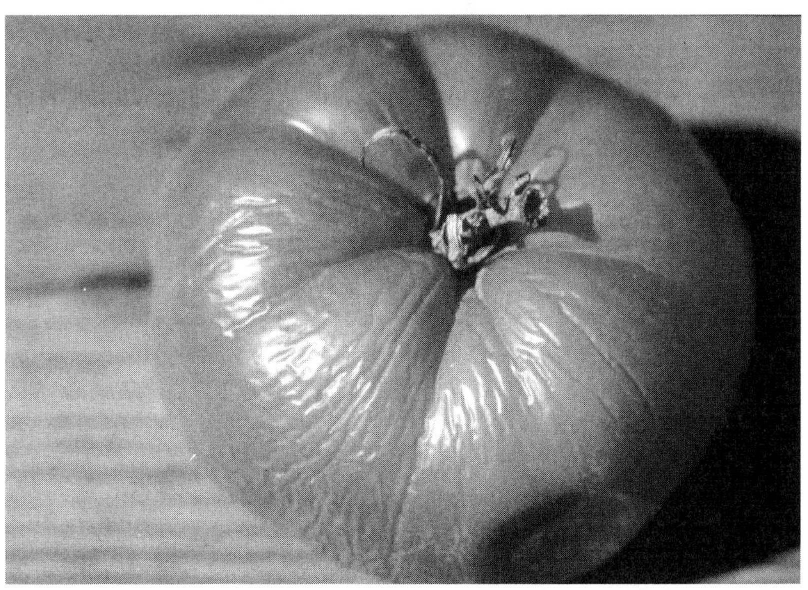

20

SIMPLICITY

Simplicity Is a State of Mind

IN THE RUGGED FRONTIER PAST, simplicity was despised as lowly and lacking in sophistication. In the overly complex present, we're nostalgic for a simplicity that has little to do with our lives. Genuine simplicity is a state of mind—whatever your style may be.

» Simplify your home by simplifying your thinking. On a page, make two columns: (1) What *must* my shelter provide? and (2) How do I envision my ideal home? Then bring those two lists together.
» Decorate simply and spontaneously: create one object arrangement, installation—or new look for your home—using only what you find in the house.
» Use what's at hand to simplify your life and home. If "simplifying" turns into a flurry of shopping, ordering, and styling, come back to the here and now.

Balance Simplicity and Complexity

Simplicity means "of the essence"—a good measure for quality of life. Paring down to essentials isn't "taking to the cloth" or simpleminded asceticism. It's having a simple relationship with life in all its complexity. What's essential is in everything; ultimately, simplicity means paring down to the best quality of life, which is awake.

The more you know, the less you need.
—AUSTRALIAN ABORIGINAL SAYING

SIMPLICITY JOINS HEAVEN AND EARTH

Homes that evolve from basic human needs bring simplicity and complexity into balance. Animals and birds burrow, nest, and hunker down to take shelter: home and homemaker fit hand in glove. When it comes to our homes, some "gloves" defy a human fit. (Consider the coxcombry of most contemporary "model" interiors.) Basic human needs are physical (earth), spiritual (heaven), and psychological (man). A simple home—large or small—joins heaven and earth.

Historically, Quakers, Shakers, and monastic traditions provide models of simplicity in Western design; more recently, modernism, Scandinavian, and Italian contemporary design. The lives and style of indigenous people and natural ecosystems were the best examples of simplicity and serve as models for the future.

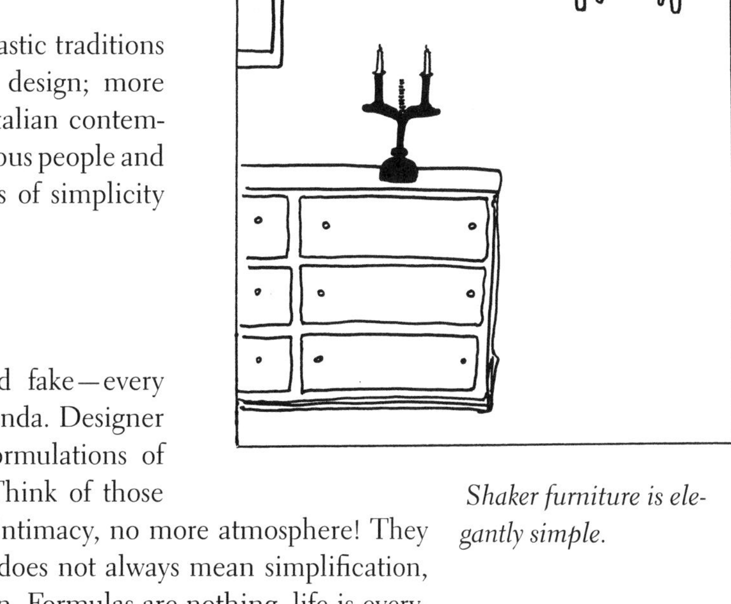

Shaker furniture is elegantly simple.

STYLIZED SIMPLICITY

Stylized simplicity can be formulaic and fake—every home a Japanese teahouse, an adobe hacienda. Designer Eileen Grey trounced the mechanical formulations of some modernist architects, exclaiming: "Think of those exaggerations [of simplicity] . . . no more intimacy, no more atmosphere! They simplified everything to death. Simplicity does not always mean simplification, and especially not such crude simplification. Formulas are nothing, life is everything. And life is simultaneously mind and heart."[1]

» Simplicity and complexity are two sides of one coin. Space is their common ground. Contemplate how simplicity and complexity can support each other in your home.

Finally, we will look at clarity's most powerful contribution to the environment, which is peace.

21

PEACE

A PEACEFUL ENVIRONMENT (and a peaceful mind) is like still water or a clean mirror: it lets us see things clearly. We may not always like what we see—but we see it for what it is! Turbulent water (or a dirty mirror) generates deception and disturbance. Peacefulness is the practice of truth. It is patient, unbiased, and deals with whatever comes up. Like a mirror, it shows things clearly; like a mirror, it doesn't become what it sees.

In home design, peace is an ongoing discipline, not a one-shot deal. The guidelines are similar to those in Part II, "Space"; space and clarity work hand in glove to pacify the environment. Work with the following exercises to bring peace to your home.

- » Walk through the house and identify areas of sensory distress—areas that are like "dust on the mirror" or patches of "rough water." Check open shelving (all visible storage tugs at your mind). Check walls, refrigerators, and bulletin boards for irrelevant printed matter and forgettable artifacts. Check corners where confusion masquerades as ad hoc storage—and miscellaneous stacks/piles on furniture and floors.
- » Pacify irritating energy in the environment, including untamed (too much/too little) light. Pacify sensory demands—sights, sounds, smells, tastes, tactile sensations—including jarring contact with furniture or anxious contact with slippery floors.

Peaceful Bedrooms

Bedrooms serve mainly two purposes—sleep and sex. Sleep is associated with space. A good night's sleep depends on the *spaciousness* of the environment. Contemplate the qualities of space when you set up your bedroom. Clarity can then reflect stillness in form and create a peaceful space. (In Part V, "Warmth," we will look at bedrooms from the other point of view!)

» Eliminate sensory pollution in the bedroom—including telephones and TVs. This is difficult if you are habituated to them, but you will notice the difference right away. Don't use electric outlets near your bed (especially near your head); plug reading lamps into another wall. Make sure window coverings keep out unwanted light. Replace the dry cold and noise of air conditioning with an overhead fan . Get a humidifier if your heat is dry, and turn off the heat at night And above all, don't work in bed.
» Choose "spacious" colors (neutrals, pastels, and natural materials). Gentle—not cold—shades of blue are especially conducive to restful sleep. Spacious colors can reflect different moods (rest, passion, recovery), which can be evoked with colorful accessories.
» For peace of mind, your bed should face the door. Never allow your bed/body to be broadsided by energy coming in through a door, or caught in crosscurrents between door and windows. Make sure your bed is not under an overhead beam (which oppresses the energy beneath it).
» Shut bedroom, closet, and bathroom doors to eliminate disruptive flow of traffic or ch'i through the bedroom. Maintain good bedroom boundaries with a door that you can lock if you so choose.

Restoring Peace

It's important to have quick and easy ways to restore peace after times of emotional or creative turmoil. Chaos comes with the creative territory. It inevitably accompanies artistic achievements (and cooking, sewing, or building projects); shifts in human relations; and just thinking (stewing, fermenting) or playing.

» Honor these messy times and the chaos they create. If you don't, you may find yourself boycotting the creativity of yourself and others—and just about anything that's fun.
» Use "quick and dirty" methods to get through rough patches of confusion. Don't think of temporary organization and storage as stopgap measures. They can have a powerful pacifying effect on your inner/outer environment.
» For art supplies, invest in carpenters' buckets hung with canvas pockets for brushes and tools. Fishing tackle boxes are great for drawing tools.

» Most important, design your home for "time out." Turn off the lights on occasion and use candles or gas lamps; unplug the telephone; close up your entertainment center and your office (or hide them behind a screen). Define a space where you can meditate or do yoga to pacify your mind

All of us need peace in our homes. If you follow these guidelines, you will pacify your environment and bring the energy of clarity into your life.

22

PACIFYING SPACE

CLARITY BRINGS PRECISION AND PEACE to the whole house. It especially rules libraries and studies (connected with intellect)—as well as the peace in your bedroom and the spotlessness of the bath and other areas of "purification." Here's an example of how clarity creates a library/study with the help of the other four energies.

Creating a Library/Study

Clarity is the intellectual focus of the library/study—a well-organized, peaceful space conducive to thought.

Richness is the wealth of wisdom and tradition gathered there: the books, ideas, and pictures—and your ongoing acquisition of them. It's the dignity, the stability, and the weight of the space.

Warmth is the attraction you feel to the room—the interesting titles, the leather-bound volumes, the comfortable chair that invites you to come in and spend time. It's a fire on the hearth and a glass of port by your elbow.

Energy is the efficient cataloguing of books that facilitates their use. It's the good shelving, reading stands, and lights that make the space work.

Space provides a quiet environment free from distractions and stress.

Creating an Installation to Pacify Space

To intensify the energy of clarity or pacify a specific space, create an installation. Put it along the sight line of a particular room to set the tone; in your study (or corner of a room where you want to focus your mind); in your bedroom to create peace; or in the foyer of your home at winter solstice. Bring the clarity of heaven, earth, and man together in one spot:

Heaven: a backdrop of clear blue or wintry white fabric/paper to define the space (enhanced perhaps with a seasonal painting, calligraphed poem, or mirror).

Earth: a table or pedestal that communicates the energy of the east.

Man: a statue or sculpture, flower or object arrangement (something crisp, penetrating, thoughtful, or intellectual) to bring heaven and earth into harmony.

Heighten the energy of your installation with a focus light. Depending on the season, include a bowl of water or mirror to symbolize ice; in summer, warmer blues/greens; in winter, purples, silver, black/white. And remember, these are only suggestions. Use your imagination and materials at hand to explore the possibilities—after all, the whole world is created this way!

Remedies for Excess

When clarity goes overboard in the environment, remedy it with the other four energies:

Space softens clarity and makes it "user-friendly," preventing anxious or alienating environments. It's the relaxed feel of mattress ticking instead of regimental stripes, a soft watercolor painting in a formal room.

Richness broadens clarity's horizons and prevents starkness or sterility. It replaces overhead light cans with a brilliant chandelier and expands your collection of good books. It fills your well-organized closet with good clothes (on heavy, aromatic cedar hangers) and transforms your dietary regimens (clarity) into gourmet meals.

Warmth brings out clarity's beauty, charm, and heart and keeps it from becoming humorless or uptight. It provides candlelight, beautiful frames for your architectural renderings and interplanetary maps, and decor that appeals to the mind (a display of antique game boards, a framed set of divination cards, or a lunar calendar showing phases of the moon).

Energy perks up clarity (with dynamic color, objects, and imagery) and keeps it from feeling unresponsive or cold. Energy makes sure all design concepts and organizational strategies actually *work*—and aren't just intellectually satisfying.

Summing Up Clarity

Power	*Direction*	*Color*	*Element*	*Season*	*Symbolic shape*
Pacifying:	East	Blue	Water	Winter	Circle

Wisdom Mirrorlike wisdom—which we experience as "clear-seeing"

In design Light, form, and focus; meaning; purity; healing; refinement; simplicity; peace

Imbalance Cold, stark, overmanaged, overorganized, conceptual, hard-edged, rigid, pro forma, precious, humorless

Signature sites Libraries/studies, bathrooms, laundries, home spas

Animals Otter, dolphin, crane, eagle—and traditionally, the tiger

IV

RICHNESS

Impeccable conduct is the key to richness. It aligns us with the ways richness works in the world. From a contemplative point of view, personal and environmental wealth have as much to do with conduct as with design.

23

THE POWER OF RICHNESS

RICHNESS BRINGS SATISFACTION AND WEALTH into your home. Its basic action— expanding/enriching—is an antidote to poverty mentality and anemic environments. Channel the energy of richness into your life when you want or need:

More wealth/resources . . .	to nurture your home/world
More stability . . .	to expand/upgrade your home
More generosity/less meanness in your life . . .	to proclaim yourself ("take your seat")
More splendor . . .	to foster confidence/self-esteem
More satisfaction . . .	to make great gestures
More of everything . . .	to ripen situations
	to overcome small-mindedness

The ultimate gift of richness, the wisdom of equanimity, is like a mountain, imposing and unmoving. It is not "going anywhere" because it is already fulfilled. It supports all manner of life because richness is its natural condition.

Psychologically, richness is confident and takes everything in its stride. It is dignified—with a positive sense of pride and display. It is symbolized by the stable square, which represents both equanimity (all sides are equal) and diversity (each side faces a different direction and has a different perspective)—and means "manifesting fully in the world." Richness is connected with fruition and things coming full circle; it is about becoming an elder and "taking your seat."

In design, richness is the *fullness* of things: a full color palette, full-bodied shapes, generous patterns and scale, and a house full of people and pets. It's not afraid of excess. It proclaims itself proudly (in upgrades, expansion, and acquisitions) and elaborately (through lavish texture and ornamentation). Its signature color is golden yellow. Its traditional animal is the dragon; but richness is also embodied in the majestic elephant, the steady ox, and the satisfied pig. Richness is both earthy and urbane and can express itself in opulent or rugged materials.

Too Much of a Good Thing

In excess, richness is too "full of itself." Filling space with stuff and clutter—all of which is too weighty, too expensive, too demanding—it squeezes other energies out. It is too big, too loud, too colorful, too perfumed, and generally overdone. Excess richness is greedy; instead of radiating splendor and well-being, it overwhelms space. Its attitude is "What's mine is mine, and what's yours is mine." Its motto is not "Less is more" but "More is more." In excess, it is ostentatious and suffocating. Now let's see how richness expresses itself sanely.

Bringing Richness Home

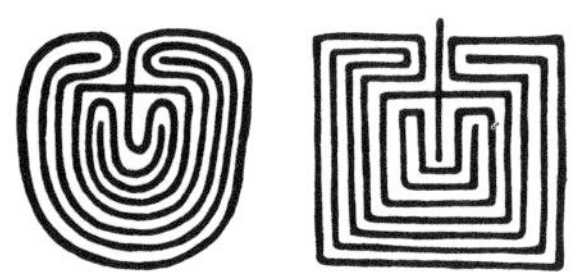

Native American (Hopi) mother-earth symbols

If richness were fabric, it would be heavy gold damask or an Italian brocade. As a style of furniture, rococo or Victorian. As a kind of illumination, richness would be banks of candles in elaborate candelabras; as a flower, protea blossoms. Richness is connected with earth and earthy materials; it's solid wooden furniture, stone sculptures, big plants, natural fibers, and ceramics and china (made of clay).

Richness fills *any* area of the house with a sense of satisfaction. Signature sites—dining rooms and kitchens—are connected with our first and most basic source of satisfaction, food. Outside the home, richness is opulent restaurants, bountiful vegetable gardens, and steamy jungles teeming with abundance.

Richness satisfies all the senses. Each of them can channel the energy of richness into your home.

SIGHT

Visual richness is deeply satisfying—like an ocean of melted butter or honey, like golden fields of grain. It is lustrous Russian icons and luxurious velvet drapes. It radiates presence like ormolu furniture and ornate gilt frames. It is an overflowing cornucopia (like Victorian parlors) that fills every inch of space (like baroque castles and Spanish mission–style homes). Richness is the generous surface designs of African textiles, Hawaiian and Balinese sarongs, Persian carpets, and Fortuny velvets stenciled in silver and gold. It is Indian architectural ornamentation, the Chinese imperial court, The Plaza on Fifth Avenue, and the five native colors of corn.

- » Identify visual richness in your home, including rich surfaces, colors, patterns, generous scale, and anything that enriches your visual field—your piano, family photos, your garden.
- » In your yellow workbook, collect rich photos, fabric swatches, and natural materials—include a sheet of gold leaf. Research expressions of richness in other times and places; collect examples from art, architecture, and design. Include color samples. Don't overlook the richness—and rich colors—of soil and rocks, vegetables, tropical birds, and flowers.
- » Collect visual and literary representations of earth, the natural element of richness. How is it represented in art, architecture, and design? What are its symbolic meanings?

SOUND

Rich sounds are deep and resonant (a didgeridoo, a cello, an organ), slow (time is as generous as space), and round (Big Ben striking the hour). Richness is Beethoven's Fifth Symphony, Russian choral music, *Aida* performed with live elephants. It's a wealth of sounds filling space—the cacophony of flocking geese, of children playing, of a family feast.

- » Enrich your environment through sound. Make music (play your CDs, tapes, or a good radio station); buy or rent a grand piano, a harpsichord, a Celtic harp.
- » Eat one meal with earplugs and listen to the sound of feasting.

TOUCH

Richness is weighty, reassuring, and rewarding to the touch—heavy brass fixtures softened by wear, weighty old textiles and silver. It is the feel of plush velvets, furs, buttery silks, luxurious satins, and lavish brocades. It is sheets with the highest thread count (300) and carpets with the greatest number of knots (about 320 knots per square inch). Richness is the patina of age (long life)—and the feel of weathered wood, old leather, and handwoven textiles. It is any physical *contact* with your world that's enriching and deeply satisfying. Ask yourself whether you're in touch with richness in your home—opulent and earthy—on a daily basis.

- » Provide richness through physical contact with people, pets, and things. Put a substantial paperweight on your desk (better yet, ask for one as a gift from someone who means a great deal to you—it adds weight to the object).

TASTE

Rich tastes satisfy body and mind and make them feel full. Rich foods—roast duck, chocolate cheesecake, and crème liqueur—are full of calories, full of fat, full of flavor. They satisfy all the senses with their wonderful colors, smells, and textures—a Hawaiian luau, buttered golden-jewel yams, stewed saffron and apricots come to mind. In design, "rich taste" affects your home the same way—aesthetically and energetically. Richness implies bigger, better, best—space, furniture, accessories—and no end of satisfaction!

» Enrich your home with delicious flavors—foods, beverages, smoking materials (if you indulge), and the real satisfaction of homegrown tomatoes, corn, and wild strawberries tasting of pine trees. Translate rich taste into design.

SMELL

Rich smells are full, complex, and satisfying—warm, moist earth in summer and steamy, wet hay in fall. (Water expands rich smells into the environment through stream and vapors.) Richness is the smell of coffee brewing, cookies baking, turkeys roasting. It's intimately connected to memory and our sense of taste—and food.

» Notice the richness of aromas in and around your home and what they mean to you. Expand your olfactory horizons; indulge in an aromatherapy session and learn more about scents that would be beneficial for you.

MIND

Wealth is an inborn attitude of mind, like poverty. The pauper who has made his pile may flaunt his spoils, but cannot wear them plausibly.
—JEAN COCTEAU

Richness is fundamentally a state of mind that delights in the richness of experience. It broadens our horizons and fills our hearts. We describe anything full of meaning, implication, or humor as "rich." Words like *prolific*, *comprehensive*, *exhaustive*, *encyclopedic*, and *acquisitive* describe a rich mind—as does "presence of mind," which indicates resourcefulness and confidence. Rich home design satisfies your mind. It works with self-existing wealth—the wealth you already possess—and is mindful of any negativity that undermines it.

» Go outside. Clear your mind, then connect with the richness around you. It is there. Take it in with a sense of living in a rich world. Then walk through your home and do the same thing. Treasures will come out of the woodwork.

There are six basic ways to channel the energy of richness into the environment. In the following chapters, we will translate each of them into home design.

24

WEALTH

WE ALL WANT WEALTH IN OUR LIVES. Wealth is desirable because *it's our natural condition*—and we all know that one form of wealth is money. But if money is our *only* wealth, we are as impoverished as if we had none. Money is a symbol, an indicator of wealth—a finger pointing to the moon. Real wealth is the richness of experience (which money cannot always buy). This chapter shows you how to bring real wealth into your home.

You may have only twenty dollars in your bank account, but you can still manifest richness in your world.
—CHÖGYAM TRUNGPA

If wealth feels beyond your grasp, you have yet to connect with self-existing richness. From a contemplative point of view, working with the energy of the south has as much to do with conduct as design. Two basic rules of wealth work with conduct; they are the key to wealth through design.

Rule 1. Be Mindful of the Richness of Everyday Life

To develop prosperity consciousness, you must first "weed your garden" and then "cultivate your flowers." To put this metaphor into practice:

1. Stop negativity in its tracks. Use attacks of poverty mentality, fear, envy, resentment, or fixation as red flags, or signals, to take a deep breath, raise your gaze, clear your mind.
2. Then, pay attention to richness: acknowledge your spiritual and emotional wealth; connect with richness in your environment; pay attention to your material wealth.

As we saw in Chapter 18, the law of correspondence teaches that when a cow moos, another cow answers (not a horse or a dog). Tuning forks work the same way. We attract to ourselves whatever we put out to the world.

Here are three exercises to cultivate your relationship with self-existing wealth:

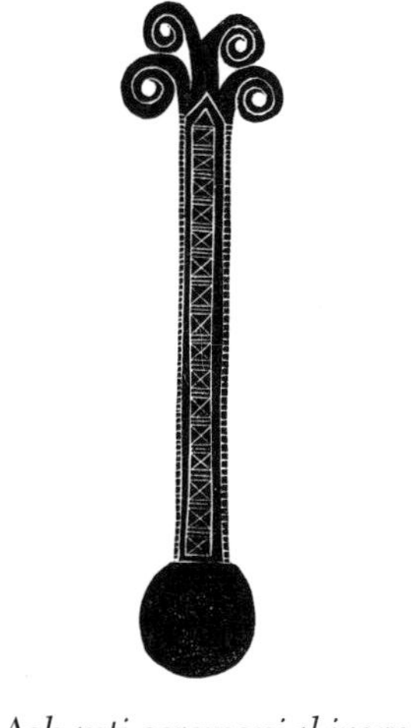
Ashanti ceremonial ivory spoon, Ghana

» Write down the qualities of richness—wealth, abundance, stability, weight, presence, dignity, increase, resources, diversity, and splendor.

  Next, make a corresponding list of the people, places, material objects, and ideas that bring these qualities into your life. (If your grandmother left you a cultural legacy, put her on the list.) Contemplate real "value" (an object made by someone you love is valuable). The veneration of your ancestral lineage, taught Trungpa Rinpoche, "can be a sign of respect for the accumulated wisdom of your culture."

» Now, incorporate this richness into your home—an heirloom chandelier, the handwork of people whose lives you admire, rugs from a favorite part of the world, framed photographs or posters of powerful places, an ancestor shrine. (You don't have to go out and buy these things; just unearth the treasures you already have.)

» To cultivate wealth, express gratitude for life's riches on a regular basis. Expressing gratitude—to yourself and others—shifts your focus from complaint or resentment to wealth. Focus brings fruition.

On a daily basis, find the richness in your experience and share the wealth. Take the rest of your life to do these exercises. Prosperity consciousness will bring infinite forms of real wealth into your world.

LUXURY

Consider the definition of *luxury* ("inessential but conducive to pleasure or comfort; expensive or hard to obtain")—and its opposite, *necessity*, which is connected with survival mentality. Luxury celebrates life: it can be as simple as a flower in your buttonhole. With or without money, make luxury part of your life.

Wealth is in applications of mind to nature; and the art of getting rich consists not in industry, much less in saving, but in a better order, in timeliness, in being at the right spot.
—Ralph Waldo Emerson

Rule 2. Cultivate Impeccable Conduct to Align Yourself with Richness in the World

The most basic way to increase richness—at home or in the world—is through "impeccable" conduct. The word *impeccable* means "not to be in sin," "without flaws or wrongdoing." The most impeccable conduct, from a contemplative point of view, is awareness. Awareness is the key to genuine richness because it aligns us with the ways richness works in the world.

» To align yourself—mentally and physically—with richness in the world, cultivate mindfulness; respect the natural laws of lha, nyen, and lu; and join heaven and earth (body/mind) in your conduct. (Go back to Part I and reread Chapter 3, "Heaven, Earth, and Man.")

If you put these suggestions into practice, you'll enjoy the energy of wealth. Now we will see how you can set up your home this way.

Wealth Is Abundance

Abundance literally means "overflowing." It's having enough of everything—time, space, and resources—and is the opposite of anxiety. From the point of view of enlightened design, abundance is the inherent goodness in every situation. Available anywhere, at any time, it is connected with "greatness"—and expresses itself through large scale, broad strokes, bold patterns, and a sense of not holding back.

» Abundance is dozens of flowers in a huge painted container (not a bud vase with one bloom). It's a jungle of giant houseplants (not a collection of African violets).

A genuinely rich environment is "top-drawer" (not "bottom-line"). Self-existing well-being has no need for workaholism, unnecessary efforting, or stress. It's beyond "survival mentality"; it's a sense of celebration.

» Deepen your relationship with abundance. In your workbook, make two columns: (1) scarcity and (2) abundance. In each room, be mindful of where and when feelings of scarcity occur. What do you feel you need more of? Under "abundance," record what's good about your world—include furniture, lighting, rugs, art, and appliances. Mindfulness brings further appreciation and change.

HIDDEN TREASURES

Richness says "treasure chest." Unearth the treasures in your basement and attic and put them on display—put photos of ancestors in antique gold frames; take that fabulous museum poster out of its mailing tube and put it on the wall; dust off the painting by your grandmother (conserve and frame it if it's good), the antique sword and helmet, the souvenirs from turn-of-the-last-century Paris. The key to richness is recognizing what you have. If you feel the need for more, you are connecting with neediness, not richness.

» Don't store all your wealth away. Put good dishes, silver, and linens into regular use; don't be shy about displaying grand wedding gifts. Let them enrich your environment.

African Kongo soapstone stele relief, Angola.

Abundance Is Food and Feasting

Food is the most basic form of abundance. Our first food is mother's milk. It's naturally produced, well packaged, readily available when needed, and completely satisfying—all qualities of abundance necessary to nurture your home.

» Select or grow good, wholesome foods that are not poisoned, irradiated, or denatured; prepare them mindfully; understand their properties (the powers they contribute to your life).

MINDFUL EATING

» To appreciate the richness of food, practice mindful eating. Choose one meal, one piece of fruit, or one cup of coffee and consume it mindfully, without reading, talking, or watching television. Appreciate its colors, textures, and tastes. Read meditation teacher Thich Nhat Hanh on mindful eating (see "References and Further Readings").

» Now enrich your relationship with food by taking each step of that relationship—cooking, serving, eating—further. Wealth is an accumulation of small measures. For maximum culinary satisfaction, enrich all the senses.

RITUAL MEALS

» Savor the importance of ritual meals—Thanksgiving, Passover, Christmas—and their seasonal associations. To enhance their power, align them with heaven (have a vision) and earth (provide the ground and attend to practicalities); align them with the four directions (include the energies of earth, water, fire, and wind). Make them highlights of your calendar to enrich your year.

» Make everyday meals a celebration of abundance (even if you live alone) with seasonal foods, flowers, and settings. Light candles at breakfast, lunch, and dinner in winter; choose seasonal colors for linens and dishes; create a centerpiece that enriches your day.

Dining Rooms

Formal dining rooms are like stage sets—not always in use but very powerful places when they are. Use the colors of richness (yellows and gold), the elemental energies (earth and water), and feeling (abundance, stability, dignity, splendor) to establish the tone. These qualities can enrich a dining room that is blue, green, or some other cool color.

» Enrich your table with beautiful dishes and silver. (If you rarely use your good sets, ask yourself what you're waiting for.) Excellent, heavyweight stainless flatware in rich patterns is very affordable; "picnic," or camp, cutlery with colorful plastic handles is inexpensive and attractive.

» If your taste is eclectic, collect serving and dining utensils from your favorite thrift shops, artists, or restaurant supply stores. Put together an exquisite collection of mismatched china, sterling silver, or vintage plastic piece by piece from consignment shops. The care and energy—not the money—you expend will enrich your table.

» A mirror in your dining room will reflect and multiply the glow of chandeliers, silver, colorful china, and good food. Buffet mirrors were traditionally hung over sideboards.

» If your dining room doubles as an office, make it easily—but completely—convertible. For work, focus the space and heighten the qualities of clarity and energy. For dining, rely on mobile workstations (to roll away equipment) and built-in storage (to hide work-related clutter)—then amplify the qualities of richness and warmth.

TRAY SERVICE

Some cultures traditionally gather to get their food from a central location, then go off a ways to eat separately. This practice is reflected in the style of their dishes and utensils. If yours is a movable feast—from kitchen to living room to porch—your accessories and setup for meals are especially important. To enrich your life, they should embody the qualities of richness—and a good dining room.

Trays are a simple and inexpensive way to enrich any serving situation. In our speedy society, trays are not a high priority, so they are easy to come by in consignment shops. They can be formal (black and red lacquer with gold trim) or informal (straw trays for summer). A nicely prepared tray can turn a fast-food meal into a rich and dignified dining experience.

- Start a collection of trays for all occasions. Japanese import stores carry elegant imitation lacquer and gold-leafed trays. Old faded wooden trays are beautiful when gold- or silver-leafed. Sterling silver trays are always available in consignment stores (but need polishing); stainless reproductions can be elegant for everyday use. Clear plastic trays come in rich, jewel-like colors, and theme trays are great for children.
- Get in the habit of preparing a tray to dignify meals, snacks, tea, or the water on your bedside table. Enrich it with a linen napkin, beautiful utensils, a flower.
- Keep a tray setup in your office. Enrich your workday with coffee or tea in a good china cup (bring your own). Serve it with a serviette and silver spoon.
- Teach children to use trays instead of casually carrying snacks through the house. They dignify a child's life and are a great way to teach them the principles of heaven, earth, and man. Children usually love to make up trays, especially if they're bright or amusing.

Kitchens

Kitchens are warm, nurturing places that satisfy all of our senses. User-friendly materials in warm, expansive colors—yellows, oranges, and reds, copper pots—reflect this energy. One very rich style of kitchen looks more like a sitting room, with wooden table and cushioned chairs, sofa, lamps, rugs, and framed art on the walls. At the other end of the spectrum is the crisp blue-and-white decor of French-style kitchens. Coolness is traditionally balanced, however, with warmly painted crockery, colorful displays of fruits and vegetables, venerable dark wooden floors and overhead beams—and more likely than not a richly framed print or painting.

- If your kitchen decor is "cool" (blue, white, green, black/white tiles), invoke richness with colorful dishes, glassware, copper pots/pans, and richly colored towels, napkins, and flowers.
- Use large, clear glass jars to display your abundance of grains, beans, and pastas—which are colorful as well as satisfying to see—and glass doors on kitchen cabinets to display dishes and food.
- Antique tins gilded with silver and gold are a "rich" way to store teas, coffee, cookies, and sugar. Look for them in consignment and thrift shops.
- Use excellent pots, pans, and knives to enrich your kitchen. Discard aluminum (read up on aluminum and Alzheimer's disease); pans with scratched nonstick surfaces that crumble into your food; and cooking utensils that don't work for you (no matter how expensive they were).

RUGS IN THE KITCHEN

Bring Oriental rugs into your kitchen to make it more opulent than utilitarian. They don't have to be your finest; older rugs or reproductions will serve the purpose. In Holland, Oriental rugs with white linen toppers cover traditional tables. In front of the sink, use (very inexpensive) Persian-style rugs with rubberized backing. Rugs redeem unattractive linoleum floors and enrich the space. Make sure they have nonskid pads underneath. (We will talk more about enriching your floors in the next chapter.)

EAT-IN KITCHENS

The site and setup of daily meals are more important than the occasional formal feast. Use your dining room more often if it's playing second fiddle to the kitchen; if your eat-in kitchen serves as your dining area, treat it as such and follow the dining room suggestions presented earlier in the chapter.

Larders and Pantries

Stockpiles of food and supplies express richness (as do banks, museums, and other sites of amassed wealth). Note that the emphasis of their design, however, is on the *organization* of wealth (clarity), not its energy in the world.

» Stock your home by buying in bulk (and paying less per item). If you have a rich shopping style (and you may not), you'll be willing to pay more up front for cases of wine, juice, toilet paper, toothpaste, and anything else you use on a regular basis.

Now we will look at how wealth manifests through stability in design.

25

STABILITY

RICHNESS IS CONNECTED WITH the stability of earth, which is symbolized by the square—solid, well built, and dependable.

The Stability of Earth

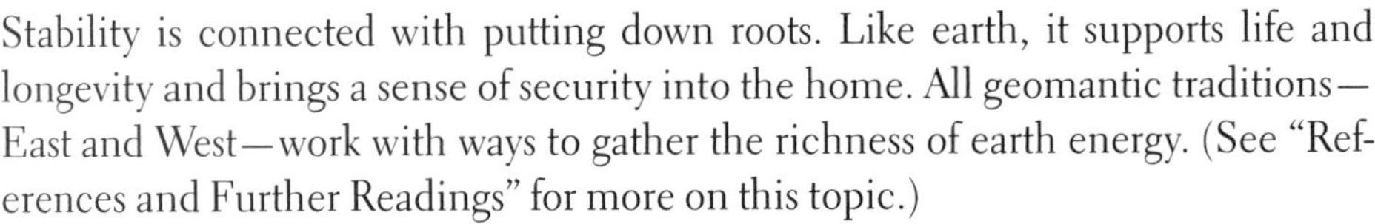

Stability is connected with putting down roots. Like earth, it supports life and longevity and brings a sense of security into the home. All geomantic traditions—East and West—work with ways to gather the richness of earth energy. (See "References and Further Readings" for more on this topic.)

» To gather the energy of richness into the yard, porch, or balcony outside your house, first look for natural manifestations of richness—a tree, boulder, or patch of land with the "presence," or qualities, of wealth. Amplify these pockets of richness. Landscape to enhance their settings.

» If you have very little earth around your house, cultivate (simply or elaborately); if you have none, consider installing planters or window boxes on the concrete or hanging some images of earth energy on your walls.

Stability, indoors, is the earth under your feet—and knowing that the rug's not going to be pulled out from under you. Rickety tables, chairs, and bookcases also undermine a sense of security.

» Secure throw rugs and runners with rubber pads. Put a nonskid mat on the floor of your shower.

» Put pads under the tablecloth on your dining room table for a thick, rich (and quieter) surface. If you don't have felt pads, use a folded sheet.

» Make sure furniture that gets heavy use is stable enough to serve its function with ease.

The Stability of Materials

There are no ideal building materials. All materials, natural or manufactured, embody the five energies and have unique practical, emotional, and poetic qualities.

NATURAL MATERIALS

Hopi coiled basket tray with figure of bird.

Natural materials are connected with "body" and living systems. They bring real vitality into your home and your home into harmony with nature. They are balanced with presence of mind to work well.

» Choose natural materials wisely. Woods, cottons, and other natural fibers that have been chemically treated might as well be plastic.
» Learn more about their production. Has an ecosystem been obliterated to provide your home with natural materials? Are natural artifacts and other products created by child or exploited labor? There are no easy answers to these questions; but if you design your world with such questions in mind, "natural" solutions will begin to shape what you do.

MANUFACTURED MATERIALS

Manufactured materials—products of mind—embody ingenuity, intelligence, and sometimes wit. They are best balanced with warm, physical energy. Since the nature of all materials—natural and manufactured—is empty, your mindfulness determines whether or not they will serve you well.

» Weigh the consequences of production, usage, and disposal when choosing your materials.

Tune in to the expressive qualities of your materials and choose those that communicate your vision. If you bring mindfulness and vision to home design, you can use whatever is at hand to express it.

THE WEIGHT OF MATERIALS

Richness is "worth its weight in gold." Weight implies substance. One symbol of richness is the elephant: it's heavy and takes up space. (In most traditional societies,

bodily weight was a sign of wealth and well-being.) Richness is people, places, and things that are heavy with blessings—heirlooms, ancestors, your spiritual lineage—and the accumulation of material wealth. At times, richness may feel like a burden. It's too weighty, too demanding; you need time to deal with it, to take it all in. Stability means staying the course.

Contemporary homes have become bigger and bigger—but less and less weighty and stable. Walls are drywall (not plaster); doors and doorknobs are hollow (not solid); floors/stairs are usually particleboard or unfinished pine concealed with carpet (not real wood). Flimsy materials create fluttery, ungrounded feelings in our bodies/minds. Although it is good and convenient for life's moving parts to be lightweight and not burdensome, some things in our lives need to convey a sense of stability and weight.

» If you own your home, replace flimsy with substantial materials over time—solid doors; doorknobs of china, cut glass, or solid brass; more substantial light fixtures and ventilation fans. Upgrade flooring or put rich carpets on the floors for weight.
» Use your heavy silver on a regular basis or buy stainless flatware with some heft. Use heavy linen napkins instead of paper—store them in hefty napkin rings for reuse. (For everyday use, don't worry whether they're ironed or not.)
» Heavy-duty containers make light work of their contents: weighty books that bend flimsy shelving out of shape are no problem for solid oak bookcases.
» Choose heavier fabrics (homespun, velvet, brocades, and leather) and heavily saturated, warm colors (deep reds, oranges, yellows, browns) to ground your home.
» Bringing warmth and weight indoors in winter balances the spare cold outside. (Summer's heavy heat is balanced with light, cool interiors.)
» Give life's necessities—food, clothing, and shelter—the "weight" they deserve and they will enrich your life.

Fewer and fewer Americans possess objects that have a patina, old furniture, grandparents' pots and pans—the used things, warm with generations of human touch, . . . essential to a human landscape. Instead, we have our paper phantoms, transistorized landscapes. A featherweight portable museum.
—Susan Sontag

The Stability of Foundations and Floors

Stability is the overall structure of a house, particularly the grounds, floors, and foundations. Solid foundations—physically and spiritually—create stability and a sense of well-being. Shaky foundations are poorly connected with richness and earth. Houses built on stilts, cliffs, and pilings have no depth and little connection to richness. They feel vulnerable and cannot afford to expand.

- The stability of your house rests on its foundation. Keep it in good repair. Check the foundation of any home you're thinking of buying.
- If you live in an apartment above the ground floor, the floor is your foundation. Make sure carpeting provides adequate soundproofing. You shouldn't have to tiptoe around your apartment or hear sounds from below.

Floors are not just a platform for furniture. They bring an added dimension of richness to your home. If you don't have much furniture to work with, floors can be the focus of your decor. Natural flooring materials are *grounding*: wood, wool, hemp and straw, cotton and silk—in some areas, stone and clay—keep the earth under your feet.

- Look for wooden floors under your wall-to-wall carpeting. Restore old floors to a deep, rich glow and adorn them with carpets.
- Consider a wooden floor for your kitchen. It's warmer and softer than tiles or stone, which can be slippery and unforgiving to dropped dishes. The price of real wood floorboards (prepacked, precut) is not prohibitive; and imitation wood panels don't have the same effect. Double the price to include installation or do it yourself. Wood with the right finish easily accommodates spills and washing. Cork is another natural alternative.

RUGS

Rugs are the easiest way to enrich floors with color, texture, and pattern. Make rugs the crowning glory of gleaming wooden floors or wall-to-wall carpeting. Your floors will be handsome and well padded and your rooms more soundproof.

- Take your time collecting rugs. Choose them with an eye to the future. Don't buy rugs to match your current decor; that will change.
- Rugs passed down from your family bring the richness of history to your home. Acquire several rugs that you will have forever.
- If you love a particular part of the world and its people, purchase their rugs. Take a rug-buying trip (if possible); see how your rug is made; learn about its symbols and colors. Buy rugs from the lands of your ancestors. Support those artisans who make handcrafted rugs.

If richness were merely stable, it would be stagnant—but it's not. Richness is the energy of increase, which is our next topic.

26

THE ENERGY OF INCREASE

INCREASE IS THE OPPOSITE OF SCARCITY: your cup is not only full, it runneth over. Increase leaves no dark corners, black holes, or empty pockets. It represents unconditional wealth and well-being, which is always available and never runs out because it doesn't depend on anything outside of itself. The energy of increase enriches your home.

Water Is an Agent of Increase

Richness (earth) is "married" to water. Water—earth's crown jewel—incubates life and is an agent of increase. Richness expands through watery mediums, including steam and vapors. Use them to expand richness into your home.

» Install an aquarium, fishbowl, fountain, or live plants to enrich the sense and increase the richness of a room.
» Enjoy the rich smells of cooking and baking that travel on steam and moist
» Make sure you have adequate humidity in your house. Central heating and air-conditioning create dry air. Excess dryness is as problematic as excess moisture

in the home. Excess dryness is as problematic as excess moisture in the home. Lack of humidity can cause physical complaints and mood disorders. Humidity is essential to physical and mental health.

Traditional "buffet mirror" enriches dining room.

Mirrors Increase Richness

Mirrors, like lakes, reflect and multiply abundance and increase the wealth in your home. Tibetan teacher Tai Situ Rinpoche described richness as a mountain with a beautiful lake in front: the lake reflects the mountain as well as the sun, moon, stars, and world around it. Mirrors multiply natural light and landscapes, candles and chandeliers, interior space and the richness in it.

The main rooms of the Bavarian nineteenth-century castle Neueschwanstein—a baroque fantasy in white and gold—were mirrored on all four walls to create an illusion of infinite space and opulence. On a smaller scale, traditional wall sconces are backed with mirrors to increase the candlelight.

» Place a mirror in your wealth corner or behind any rich object to increase its energy.
» Mirror the wall behind your stove (especially if you cook with gas) to "increase" the abundance of food and fire.

Richness can be reflected, multiplied, enhanced, amplified, spread out, given away, shared, expanded—and never exhausted! It's expansive and doesn't hold back. It's a never-ending feast for the senses.

Increase by Design

In design, richness goes the extra mile to increase sensory power and satisfaction. For example, an antique vase sits on your shelf looking lovely but visually lost. To increase the richness of the display:

Place the vase (heaven) on the shelf (earth) upon a richly carved rosewood stand (man).

Tack a beautiful strip of fabric (or ornamental paper) behind the vase as a backdrop—or run it behind and *under* the vase and over the edge of the shelf.

Spotlight your presentation to intensify the energy. Now your vase proclaims "richness"—and no museum display could do it better!

» Put a *basketful* of beautiful soaps in the bathroom (not just one bar of Ivory); cultivate large, lavish plants in your home (not just a few philodendrons). Provide guests with many pillows, quilts, towels, and reading materials; light banks of candles in winter; bring in armfuls of flowers in spring and summer.
» Be exuberant, bold, outrageous! Indulge your secret passion for polka dots or zebra stripes; for lava lamps, Christmas lights, life-size folk figurines. Make "mistakes." You can always tone things down (if you must) to restore balance.

Ndaka (*n.dah.!kuh*) people in Africa wrap a bride in so much cloth that no one knows how big she is. They circle her head with yards and yards of colorful material and make her a veil of sparkling clinking beads. Nadaka men lift her to their shoulders on a platform of young trees covered with flowers. A cloth stretched above her seat protects her from the hot sun. Flute players and singers dance gaily beside her as she rides to the groom's village.[1]

UPGRADES INCREASE RICHNESS

If something is worth having in your life, it's worth being wonderful. Increase richness by upgrading things you take for granted—paint, lighting, artwork, carpets, kitchen and office supplies.

» Refinish or cover tired furniture. (Have it done if you can't do it yourself.) Replace old drawer/door pulls with wonderful brass, glass, or ceramic fixtures.
» Create a clean, reflective surface on a table, shelf, or chest of drawers with a piece of glass cut to size. Place a fabulous piece of fabric, gold foil, or hand-printed paper under the glass.
» Go through your house with an eye for large and small ways to upgrade your environment. Replace coat hooks with an antique clothes tree—or an old clothes tree with high-tech metal hooks, if that's more your style. Replace all of your wire coat hangers with padded satin and cedar. (Your dry cleaner will be happy to take the wire ones back.) Add a lavish pillow or complementary ottoman to your one velvet chair; place an elegant table runner under the flower arrangement in the entrance hall; adorn draperies and tapestries with gold braided cords and tassels for festive occasions and dress straight-back chairs in extravagant satin tiebacks.

Resourcefulness Is the Energy of Increase

Resourcefulness "saves the day," "pulls rabbits out of hats," and turns velvet curtains into ball gowns à la Scarlett O'Hara. Necessity is the mother of invention; invention is the discovery of wealth—wealth of ideas, possibilities, workability. The greater the challenge, the richer the response. Resourcefulness is an attitude and expression of unconditional wealth: it depends on nothing but itself. Enrich your home and life by being resourceful.

There are ways of compensating for the absence of resources.

—Noam Chomsky

» If you only have one beautiful pillow sham or antique linen napkin, frame it handsomely and hang it in your bed- or dining room.

» Resourcefulness is versatility in design—from the most exalted modular furniture to the most humble innovations. Bedsheets become tablecloths, pillowcases become seat covers, shower curtains become room dividers, chipped teapots become flower containers, and garden furniture becomes an eclectic interior.

» Sheets and tablecloths make wonderful ad hoc curtains that don't have to look like your college dorm. Hang them with pushpins or staples or with clips on curtain rods. If you have bare windows with metal frames, get magnetic clips from an office supply store and hang large, flat sheets of luxurious handmade paper.

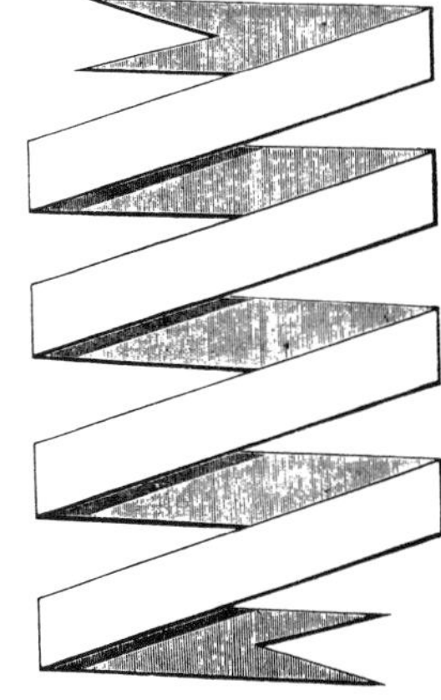

PAPER

» Decorate with especially beautiful gift wrap or hand-printed papers. Colorful designs can be mounted on the wall under Plexiglas (held with mirror clamps). Use them as backdrops for flower arrangements; change them seasonally. Put paper under the glass tops of tables or chests. Mount a favorite photograph on top of a special sheet of paper for a rich, custom border. (If the paper is not conservation grade, sandwich a piece of acid-free paper between the two.)

» Make a list of your most pressing visual design problems. Now see whether you can solve each of them using paper. Go to an art store and familiarize yourself with unusual papers. Go to a printing company or local newspaper—they're usually happy to sell "roll ends" (wide rolls of butcher paper or newsprint) for pennies per pound.

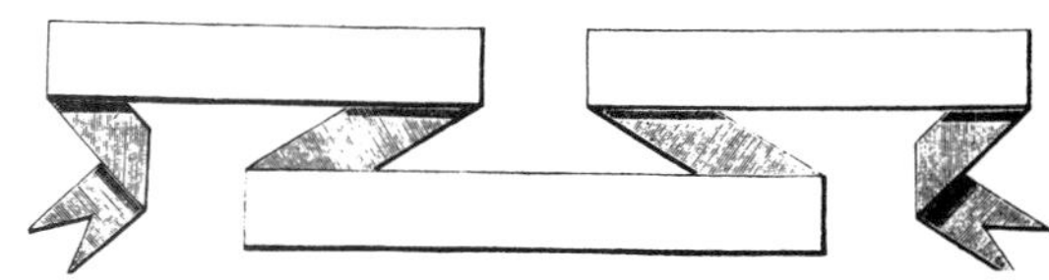

Diversity Is the Energy of Increase

We are never trapped in life, because there are constant opportunities for creativity, challenges for improvisation.
—Chögyam Trungpa

Richness is so full, so ongoing, it never runs out of ways to be. Infinite permutations of the five basic energies and their qualities are an expression of richness. It's no coincidence that *quality*—which means "unique or personal characteristic"—also means "excellence."

» Visit a large fish aquarium—with its neon colors, unfathomable shapes, styles, and outrageous surface designs—for a lesson in diversity in design.
» Be eclectic—"selective from many sources." Celebrate the diversity of your world—your travels, heritage, family, work, cultural interests, and natural surroundings—in home design.

You can do all of these exercises to cultivate richness without spending much money. Our next topic, however, is acquisitions.

Acquisitions Increase Richness

Acquisition of material things—gems, money, and other valuables—increases the energy of richness as much as the accumulation of spiritual virtue and immaterial blessings. From a contemplative point of view, the *point* of increasing wealth is to spread it around.

» Increase the power of collections—of art objects, books, heirlooms—by housing and displaying them properly. Consider their influence on your home. Who benefits from their energy and how? Think about your own collections of wealth. How do they enrich you and your world—intellectually, materially, spiritually—and how can they be expanded?
» Acquiring sacred objects connected with your personal heritage, lineage, or spiritual tradition or path can be a rescue operation if they're ransomed from the marketplace.
» Ordinary treasures can also be unearthed in unlikely places to enrich the world.

Ultimately, richness is the result of letting go. Letting go takes the form of generosity, our next topic. In home design, generosity challenges you to think big.

27

GENEROSITY

> Generosity is the ornament of the world;
> Through generosity one turns back from the lower realms;
> Generosity is the stairway to the higher realms;
> Generosity is the virtue that produces peace. . . .
> —FROM A BUDDHIST MEAL CHANT

GENEROSITY IS THE ATTITUDE and activity of wealth. In design, it expresses itself through abundance and generous gestures. Generous energy is willing to let go.

Generosity Is Letting Go

All wealth in nature is the result of letting go. If the heavily laden trees of autumn refused to let go, there would be no harvest; if mothers refused to let go, there would be no birth.

» Here is a personal exercise to practice letting go:

Hold both of your arms out in front of you, relaxed, bent at the elbow, yo hands open and palms up. Clench your fists tight. Gently open your finge until your hands are completely open again, as if you were offering a sma gift to someone or letting a butterfly fly away.

Now clench your fists again. This time, clench them as tightly as you can. Feel the muscles in your arms and shoulders getting tight. Quickly relax your grip and open your hands completely

Do this again, and clench even tighter. Think, "Tighter, tighter, tighter," for thirty seconds. Now suddenly open your hands; think, "Let go." As you let go, you might let out a little sigh or a soft "ahh."

The earth is a sacred vessel—and it cannot be owned or improved. If you try to possess it you will destroy it; if you try to hold on to it—you will lose it.

—Tao-te Ching

Do this again. This time, notice your state of mind as you clench tighter and let go. If negative or habitual emotion arises—anger, jealousy, resentment—imagine clenching that emotion in your fist. Hold, tighten—then let go.

Finally, imagine that you are holding in your hand your most precious possession. Hold, tighten, and let go. Now hold on to your most dearly held belief—hold, hold tighter, let go.[1]

Generous Styles of Design

Understanding that richness is too expansive to be held back, held onto, or denied overcomes misconceptions about generous lifestyles—and about generous styles of design. Make way for the generous energy of richness in your home.

Tis a sort of duty to be rich, that it may be in one's power to do good, riches being another word for power.

—Lady Mary Wortley Montagu

» Translate generosity into color. Immerse yourself in a full color palette, especially the rich, warm colors of fall. Buy a set of drinking glasses (or plastic tumblers) in deep, jewel-like colors. Replace a white tablecloth with orange, red, or black; top it with place mats in complementary colors or rustic straw.

» Translate generosity into pattern, shape, and scale. Enlarge decorative motifs by 200 percent. Buy a *huge* basket, flower container, painting, or ceramic platter (you could hang it on the wall) for a change. If you collect stamps, have several of your favorites blown up into posters.

» Take a generous attitude toward new possibilities and let go of stylistic habits and hang-ups. (If your style is habitually flamboyant, find richness in restraint.)

» Take a generous attitude toward others: let go of territoriality. Open your doors to friends, family, children, and pets. Welcome their friends and relatives. Host celebrations, meetings, study and social groups in your home. Keep your refrigerator, cookie jar, and wine cellar full. Nourish your guests mentally, physically, and spiritually. Through all the sense gates, share your treasures.

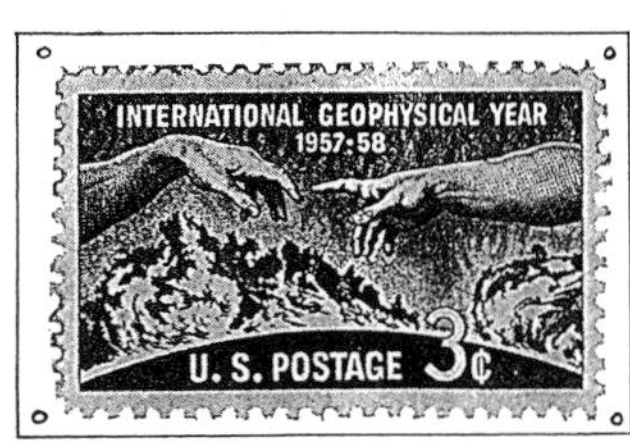
INTERNATIONAL GEOPHYSICAL YEAR
1957-58
U.S. POSTAGE 3¢

The *power* of richness radiates through your home and into the world as leadership and influence (presence), which is our next topic.

28

PRESENCE

In Middle English, "real" was a variant of "royal."
—Jeremy Hayward

Presence is the energy of "real" (not virtual) people, places, and things: it is real (not costume) jewelry, live (not silk) flowers, and real (not distressed) antique furniture. The overall effect of a room can have presence. Presence is commanding: like a king or queen, it conveys a sense of power and can empower the environment.[1] Presence is a form of richness. (The Tibetan word for "richness," *yang*, also means "presence.")

"(In Africa,) Ashanti weavers make a beautiful cloth called *kente*. They weave it in bright silk threads and give each different design a name. One, which is mostly yellow, is called "Gold Dust." Another, called "When the Queen Comes to Accra," is a favorite of many Ashanti women. "One Man Cannot Rule a Country" was designed especially for Ghana's first president. The Ashanti king drapes himself in a special kente that only he may wear."[2]

» Walk through your home with an open heart/mind. Genuine presence will command your attention with its energy—not just with visual appeal. Record any experience of *felt* presence. Try this exercise in a large museum. What objects are "holding court"? (If you don't feel anything, it may not be there!) Take notes.

» If you give them a proper seat (not lost among ordinary things), objects with real presence will enrich your environment. The trick is to tease it out. A gentle, receptive environment (space) that's clean and well defined (clarity) sets the stage for a powerful presence.

The next topic is dignity. Any dignified person or object has presence; any person or object with real presence is dignified.

Dignity

The root of the word *dignity* means "worthy," or noble. Real richness—not measured by your bank account—is anything worthy of respect. Because dignity doesn't need anything outside of itself, at heart it is simple and still. Real dignity can be found in the practice of sitting meditation, Trungpa Rinpoche taught: "Meditation practice begins by sitting down and assuming your seat on the ground. You begin to feel that by simply being on the spot, your life can become workable and even wonderful. You realize that you are capable of sitting like a king or queen on a throne. The regalness of that situation shows you the dignity that comes from being still and simple."[3]

Dignity's movements are stately and grand (even crowds, chaos, and the cosmos move in grand designs). To attract richness, translate an attitude of inherent nobility into dignified conduct and design.

» Cultivate dignity and pride in each room. In the kitchen, for instance, don't mix up human and pet dishes. In the family room, create time/space boundaries that honor everyone in the house. Close the doors to bathrooms (occupied or not). In any room, have visual reminders—photos, portraits, a piece of furniture, a flower in a vase—of a dignified life. Dignity invokes wealth; lack of dignity decreases richness.

Children's Rooms That Foster Dignity and Self-Esteem

To foster dignity and self-esteem in your child, follow the two rules of wealth: mindfulness of real richness and impeccable conduct. Align your child's room with heaven, earth, and man: shoes below, hats above, clothes in between. For a deeper understanding of dignity through design, reread Chapter 3, "Heaven, Earth, and Man," and Chapter 13, "Center without Fringe."

Create a child's room with the help of the other four energies for balance (knowing that "balance" is an ongoing process):

Clarity organizes the space. It's the physical definition of focus areas (a bureau, a mirror, perhaps a desk or an art corner).

Warmth makes a child's room attractive and enjoyable.

Energy is all the moving parts that make the room work for you and your child. It's child-height hanging bars, shelves, and mirrors, and child-size accessories.

Space provides a restful retreat. It's the gentleness (not overly stimulating) and restfulness of the room.

- » Honor children with symbols of inspiration and protection (pictures, statues, dolls). Place them "on high" in the room literally and figuratively. Hang a guardian angel figure, for instance, over the head of the bed and out of harm's way (not thrown in with the toys). In a special place, hang a richly framed picture of ancestors, of your child with a special family member or on a special occasion.
- » Help children cultivate respect for their everyday things—a clothes tree, a closet organizer for shoes, a bookcase with deep shelves; and for special things—a table for a vase of flowers or collection of shells, a corner shelf for a statue or personal awards. If the family dog sleeps with the children, provide a nice basket or pillow in a designated corner of the room (regardless of where Fido actually beds down).
- » To foster a child's sense of dignity and presence, avoid bunk beds. Placing one child above another violates the principles of heaven and earth, creating disharmonious feelings in both children.
- » Enlist the help of your children. Ask they what they want in their rooms and let them co-create space.

The power of richness manifests in very splendid—and very simple— ways.

29

SIMPLICITY AND SPLENDOR

THE WORD SPLENDOR—from the Latin verb "to shine"—means "great light or luster," "brilliance," "a magnificent appearance or display." Splendor is the radiation of richness. It's naturally occurring and can be found in a rock or patch of earth—and in people, places, and things. In design, splendor can express itself in simple things (a splendid porcelain bowl)—or in ways that are magnificent and grand (a black ebony grand piano).

Grandness doesn't fit easily in our speedy world. We are sometimes embarrassed by splendor; magnificence can make us feel small. (Simplicity, on the other hand, makes us feel noble.) In a *whole* world, however, splendor and simplicity are two sides of the coin of awareness—and both are cause for celebration. You could live splendidly in one room and simply in a palace.

"Lion Hunting": a magnificent brocade preserved at the famous Horyuji Temple in Nara, Japan. (Illustration courtesy of Kawade Shobo Shinsha, Publishers, Japan)

» Place a square of golden yellow acrylic (large or small) in a window with lots of light to stir your imagination.
» Take one piece of furniture and enrich it as much as you can—the surface, the fabrics, the trim. Choose one accessory for its splendid panache: a richly decorative pillow, a fur lap rug, a hand-painted or cloisonné lamp.
» Go to a high-end fabric store and find the richest fabric there by looking for rich colors, textures, and weight (not necessarily heavy, just "weighted" with richness). You can see and feel rich "vibrations" when they're there. Buy a yard or two and use it to create a power spot in a special place in your home.
» Enrich the tops of tables and bureaus with rich surfaces under glass. (See Chapter 26.) Use lavish papers—hand-print, marbleized, and gold or silver foil—or a Mexican wedding shawl. Glass tops make the whole surface lustrous.
» Emphasize colors associated with richness. In addition to yellow and gold,

black is often a color for earth, green for increase, and red for attraction. Use gold-colored objects—in addition to foils, gilding, and shiny brass, look for "gold-washed" accessories, tortoiseshell, and amber.

Gilding

Gilding the lily is an expression of richness and splendid display. On festive occasions throughout Indonesia, aristocrats wore sarongs coated with gold dust. In Western Renaissance pageantry, small children were often completely gilded (sometimes with deadly results).

Gilding can transform a simple space, contrasting dramatically with both white and colored walls.

» Use gold and silver leaf to transform odd pieces of furniture, dull wooden picture frames, or old serving trays. Gold- or silver-leaf the "wrong" side of glass for gilded tabletops. Gild moldings, cornices, cabinet trim, tiles, the odd wall (or your refrigerator). It's easy to do yourself (look for instruction books in your library or home improvement store) and produces very dramatic results.

Don't be shy about using gold leaf out of doors. Gilding was originally designed to enrich architectural structures and is still used mainly (on signs) outdoors. For exterior gilding (pediments, front door trim, address plaques), a good sign painter can do the job for a reasonable price, so that it's tarnish- and weatherproof.

Whether your palace is very small or very vast, you are at the center of it. If you pay attention to the many forms of wealth around you and draw them into your space, and cultivate wealth through conduct and design, richness will reign there.

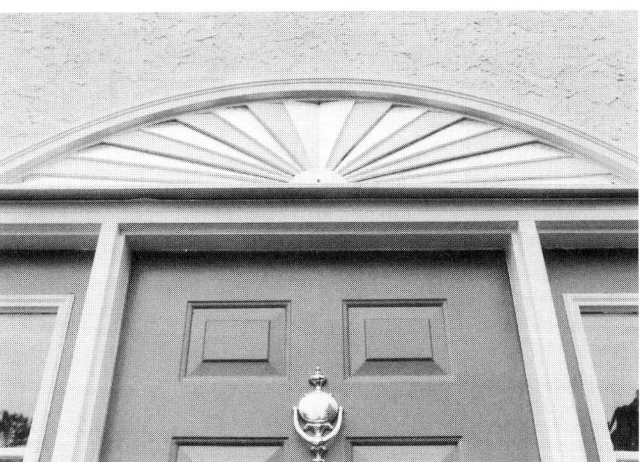

30

ENRICHING SPACE

RICHNESS BRINGS ABUNDANCE, POWER, and a sense of well-being to the whole house. It especially rules dining rooms and kitchens (connected with satisfaction), the material wealth of your home, and the dignity and generosity of your lifestyle. Here's an example of how richness creates a kitchen with the help of the other four energies.

Creating a Kitchen

Richness fills the kitchen with nurturing energy and lots of good food.

Clarity provides good lighting—and a cookbook, accurate recipes. Its element, water, purifies the space and everything in it. Clarity is the precision needed to tame the vagaries of fire, water, steam, and rising yeast.

Warmth pulls you into the kitchen with appetizing smells and the promise of pleasure. It's the seduction of cheerful colors, a pretty tablecloth—and brownies on the counter. It's the passion and artistry of food and the fire that makes things "cook."

Energy is the efficient ovens, clocks, Cuisinarts, and sharp knives that get the job done. It's helping hands and the skillful handling, cooking, and serving of food—concluding in a successful meal!

Space is an "open-door" policy (the more, the merrier). It accommodates the richness of the kitchen with physical space and emotional equilibrium.

Creating an Installation to Enrich Space

To intensify the energy of richness or enrich a specific space, create an installation. Put it along the sight line of a particular room to set the tone, in the "wealth corner" (southern quadrant) of your house or office to increase wealth from work, or in the foyer at harvest time. Bring the richness of heaven, earth, and man together on one spot. Here are some suggestions:

Heaven: a backdrop of rich yellow or gold fabric/paper to define the space (enriched further with an antique textile hanging, a gold china plate, an image of a figure making a gesture of generosity, a scroll painting of a calabash).

Earth: an opulent table or earthy platform (or boulder) that communicates richness.

Man: a generous statue, a big basket of flowers, or a power object to bring heaven and earth into harmony.

Amplify the richness of your installation with a mirror behind it; include live plants, fish, or a fountain of running water to increase the energy. Here are further suggestions:

» Challenge the limitations of scale and do a *miniature* richness installation: float a dandelion in the lid of a jar; in the kitchen, create a small but rich kitchen shrine to offer thanks and invoke abundance.

Remedies for Excess

Space allows room for richness to expand. It opens up new vistas and keeps richness from getting congested. Space and richness work "hand in glove."

Clarity organizes richness and prevents it from taking over the house. It's the *form* wealth takes—paintings, books, furniture, and their organization into collections. Clarity is also diets and dietary regimens, seasonal feasts, and other ways of organizing the consumption of food that keep richness from being greedy.

Warmth is the enjoyment of wealth that keeps richness from becoming proud and oppressive. It celebrates abundance and invites others to share the wealth. Warmth beautifies the dining room (lavishly) and the presentation of food.

Energy circulates richness internally and externally and keeps it from stagnating or getting stuck (think of earning/spending, eating/eliminating). Energy distributes wealth and prevents decadence.

Summing Up Richness

Direction	*Color*	*Element*	*Season*	*Action*
South	Golden yellow	Earth	Fall	Enriching

Wisdom Equanimity

In design Wealth, stability, increase, dignity, presence, generosity, splendor

Imbalance Overwhelming, ostentatious, indulgent, greedy, weighty, too demanding

Signature sites Dining room, kitchen, larder/pantry—and an overall sense of well-being in *any* room of the house

Animals Elephant, ox, pig—and traditionally, the dragon

V

WARMTH

31

THE POWER OF WARMTH

WARMTH COLORS AND BEAUTIFIES the environment and makes us smile. It is heartfelt. Hearts thrive in loving, warm environments. Much of our time, however, is spent in traffic, at work, and in a world filled with mental and physical stress. Warmth—and the spring season—are connected with softening, meeting, coming together; they're an antidote to coldness, desolation, humorlessness, and insensitivity. Channel the energy of warmth into your home when you want or need:

It is only with the heart that one can see rightly; what is essential is invisible to the eye.

—ANTOINE DE SAINT-EXUPÉRY

More love and understanding . . .	to work with relationships
More pleasure . . .	to improve your social life
More comfort . . .	to make life more beautiful
More intimacy . . .	to have more fun

The ultimate gift of warmth—discriminating awareness wisdom— discriminates "awake" from asleep and brings out the best in your world. Unconditionally loving, warmth is passion that doesn't get stuck. Psychologically, it manifests as compassion and communication.

In design, warmth is a sensory invitation. It's the *allure* of a space and everything in it. It creates beautiful rooms full of lovely things and hospitable homes full of heart. Warmth is deeply personal and, at the same time, vastly appreciative of others. With passion comes pleasure and playfulness. Its traditional animal in Tibet is the red garuda bird; its qualities are also embodied in loyal dogs, playful monkeys, elegant gazelles, and lovebirds—and in China, phoenixes, connected with fire. (Include them in your designs.)

Signature sites are the front door/foyer that invites us into the space as well as family rooms, inglenooks, and other intimate corners. Outside the home, they are *gemütlich* cafés, community/social centers, and theaters for the arts and entertainment.

Too Much of a Good Thing

Excess warmth is cloying and grasping. Out-of-control passion stems from neediness and poverty mentality. Taken to extremes, it's addiction—mesmerizing instead of truly magnetizing. Warmth becomes feverish; playfulness becomes frivolous and indulgent; seduction becomes a facade. The lovely, undulating movement of fire becomes a roller-coaster ride of highs and lows. In home design, the environment becomes "too-too"—overwrought, overdecorated—and fake.

> Painted cakes don't feed hunger.
> —SPANISH PROVERB

Too much warmth in design is too cute, treacly, garish, or tawdry. Like the "painted cakes" in the Spanish proverb, it doesn't really "feed hunger." Too much warmth sucks you in, intoxicates your senses, and puts you to sleep. Next we will see how warmth expresses itself sanely in home design.

Bringing Warmth Home

If warmth were a fabric, it might be pink chiffon, flowery chintz, or a soft red blanket. As a style of design, it might be *homey* (a rose-covered cottage), intimate (a boudoir), or fun (fifties furniture). It's a room filled with musical instruments, a jug of wine, and friends around the fire—or one candle and your lover. Warmth is a function of fire—as is candlelight, electricity, and the magic of color. To create warmth, choose red peonies over white orchids, provocative paintings over architectural renderings, sinuous bentwood rockers over practical folding chairs—and replace your electric stove with gas so you can cook with fire!

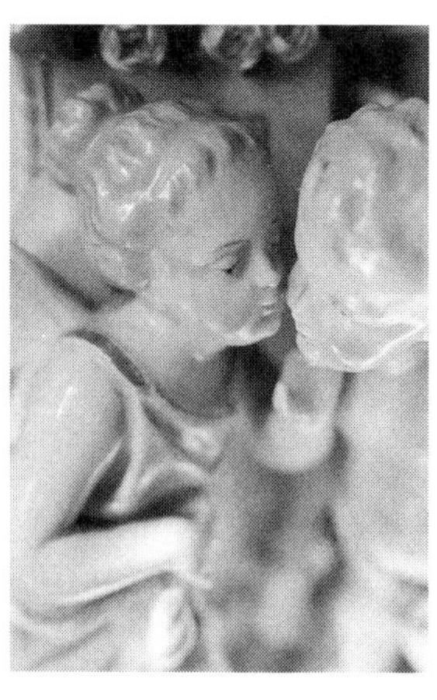

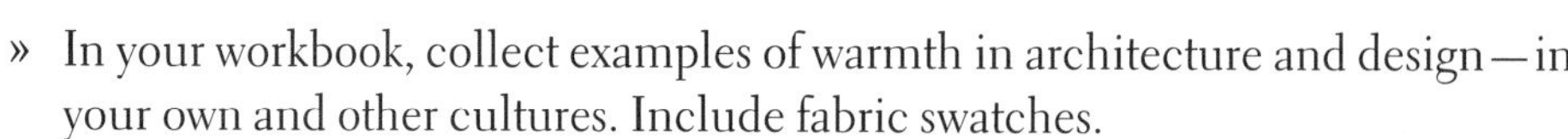

- In your workbook, collect examples of warmth in architecture and design—in your own and other cultures. Include fabric swatches.
- Collect visual and literary examples of warmth's natural element—fire. How is it represented in art, architecture, and design?
- Include color samples. Color is the "realm," or atmosphere, of each energy. Red—and all of its "warm" manifestations—is the signature color of warmth. Look for it everywhere—in art and design, in everyday life, and especially in nature. Look at insects, birds, animals, plant life, soil—and the reds in natural light.

We experience warmth through all of our senses, and through them, we can warm up our world.

SIGHT

Warmth is anything that catches your eye (like bright colors, especially red). It warms your heart (like pictures of people and places you love). It's anything delightful to look at or visually dramatic (like fields of wildflowers, sunsets, and rainbows). It magnetizes like fire (and the sight of a red velvet wing chair) and makes us smile (like a child's painting, a frog-shaped teapot, a *Star Wars* rug). It's provocative—now you see it, now you don't—as the sight of a lace slip showing. Like perfume, it's the essence of elegance. Warmth is channeled through color, arts, crafts, and attractive decor. Flowers—colorful, beautiful, fragrant—epitomize the energy of warmth!

» Look for visual warmth in your home—in colors, objects, and specific areas. What associations do they have for you? Do you need or want more (or less) warmth in your world?

SOUND

Warmth is especially connected with hearing—and the half-empty/half-full waves of undulating energy we perceive as sound. *All* sound, in fact, is a form of communication, or "speech." (Music is the universal "language.") Warm sounds captivate our bodies, minds, and souls. Like a lonely flute, they enthrall us. They entertain us—telling us stories, creating recognition, making us laugh. Warmth is melody, poetry, comedy, and communication in general. It's the sounds of children playing, people laughing, popcorn popping.

» If hospitality were a sound, what would it be? What sounds in your home invite your heart to open? What do they mean to you? What music would that be?

SMELL

Warm smells delight, invite, and sometimes intoxicate us (like the fragrance of a beautiful person walking by, the smell of attars and incense). Warm aromas create atmosphere and kindle memory (like the sweetness of spring flowers or sachets in your drawer, the inviting aromas of wood smoke and freshly brewed coffee).

» Write down pleasurable, enticing aromas in your home. Follow the thread to your heart. Write a poem, beginning each line with a fragrance. Follow that with an association and its meaning in your life.

TASTE

Warmth is the taste of desire—not so much nourishing as pleasurable, seductive, and diabolically delicious. It's chocolate mousse, excellent wine, desserts, and sweets in general (not medicines or things that are good for you). A taste for warmth in design is a taste for styles that are pleasurable, comfortable, elegant, or fun. (Don't make the mistake of trivializing warmth as too "feminine," cute, or frivolous; its energy is powerful and essential to life.)

» What furniture and accessories would you choose to create warmth? How did warmth look in other times and places? Collect design samples.

TOUCH

Warmth is pleasing to the touch. It's soft mohair throws, down comforters, and the delightful simplicity of cotton and linen. It's a luxurious leather chair and ottoman, and comfortable temperatures (the gentleness of an electric fan instead of chill air-conditioning, a toasty fire instead of dry artificial heat). Warmth is daily contact with human beings and pets and the feel of physical love.

» Note things in your home that are pleasing to the touch. How good does it feel to come into contact with your office, kitchen, and living room furniture, your lighting and accessories?

MIND

The aim of life is appreciation; there is no sense in not appreciating things; and there is no sense in having more of them if you have less appreciation of them.
—G. K. Chesterton

A warm mind is loving and genuinely interested in others. It warms to gossip and blow-by-blow accounts of romantic escapades. It's open (like a flower), kind (like warm weather), playful and willing to be amused. A warm mind is inquisitive and appreciative (not rejecting) of its world. It longs to communicate and loves to express itself in poetry, music, song, dance, fashion, and beautiful gestures.

» Record your feelings of longing, love, and appreciation. Choose one of these three feelings and send it out to the world through one of the senses you don't ordinarily use as a "gate." (If you are a writer, communicate it visually; if you usually express yourself through style and fashion (sight), communicate this particular feeling through sound, taste, or touch.

There are six basic ways to channel warmth into your home.In the following chapters, we will see how they translate into home design.

32

COLOR

ONE OF THE MOST POWERFUL EXPRESSIONS of warmth is color! Color arises from clear light, to which it ultimately returns. In many cultures, colors are connected with specific deities, or subtle energies, radiating qualities of wisdom just as light rays radiate from the sun. In any case, color—connected with luminosity, fire, and passion—is intimately connected with our physical and emotional life.

Color and the Emotions

Emotional *associations* with color come in large part from our experiences of nature: sun is yellow (and warm); moon and clouds are white (cool); fire and roses are red, as is blood (warm); water and sky are blue (cool); and so on. These realities are reflected in design.

Ceilings, for instance—universally connected with the heavens—are often painted blue with white (clouds) and gold (sun). Blue uniforms (the "boys in blue") designate authority and "higher-ups." Cool blue lacks the warmth and passion of red; we have the "blues" when we're lovelorn and lonely. (Icy blue walls in the bedroom can adversely affect your love life!)

Green is the color of new shoots fighting for their place in the sun; green lights tell us to start moving; we are "green" starting out in life and sometimes "green with envy" along the way.

Yellow is the color of the sun and the source of abundance. It is often used to designate food, fertility, royalty, and potency.

Red, like yellow, is connected with potential and potency.

Red—The Color of Warmth

Red—the color of our heart's blood—is the color of love, fire, and warmth. Like fire, red is magnetizing, hot, and provocative. It's connected with our appetite and digestion (a "cooking" process) and is helpful in eating areas—unlike neutral colors (grays, beiges), which are death to restaurants. Like the Golden Gate Bridge (which is red), it conveys a powerful sense of invitation. Teenagers and young adults are in the "red," or flowering, time of life. Red stops our minds; red lights tell us to "stop." Red says "wake up," "pay attention"—and is used to signal danger. (Imagine if warning flags were yellow or violet!) Red out of balance is manipulative: it says, "I want, I need," and speaks of grasping and clinging.

Color and the Five Styles of Energy

Colors vibrate with the powers and blessings of the four directions and center space. Each color is uniquely expressive. All colors speak to our emotions, intellect, nervous and endocrine systems, internal organs, and external energies—as well as our memories and projections. (If you knew only the favorite colors of your long-lost ancestors, you would know a great deal about your family heritage.)

I have a collection of colored glasses for workshops in which we spend time looking at the world through blue, yellow, red, green, or white lenses, being mindful of how that energy affects us. (Colored lightbulbs and slides of solid color fields create similar effects.) Taking the glasses off, we spend fifteen to twenty minutes "aim-

Blue (White)	*Yellow*	*Red*	*Green*	*White (Blue)*
Cool	Warm	Warm	Cool	All colors (in light)
Clarity	Richness	Warmth	Energy	Space
East	South	West	North	Center
Water	Earth	Fire	Wind	Emptiness
Winter	Fall	Summer	Spring	No-time
Circle	Square	Half-circle	Triangle	Formlessness
Pacifying	Enriching	Magnetizing	Destroying	(Openness)

lessly wandering," noticing how a particular energy affects our perception of the world.

- » With or without glasses, try to devote an hour (or a day) to each color: focus on it, feel it, see how it manifests in your world—when you're focused on a color, you will see it everywhere! Wear white, blue, yellow, red, or green clothes and see how they make you feel. Record your insights; write a poem. Explore this quality of energy in your home—and in other times and places.

Nature's Palette

The most magical and satisfying color schemes are based on nature. Nature's palette radiates the five energies and all their permutations. Each displays its own seasonal "theme" and vibrates on a specific physical, emotional, and spiritual plane. You can channel these energies into your home through color.

- » Study the colors of the natural world around you—sky, earth, near and distant vistas, qualities of light. (No exceptions for city dwellers! The city is a wonderful place to study the colors of nature.) Notice which natural energies dominate the landscape—those of heaven or earth. Notice naturally occurring color combinations in plants, animals, and birds (include their background colors, not just the highlights). Translate this color palette into home design.

Here's just one example of an urban color portrait. Do your own variations.

Earth: putty, charcoal gray, black (for the path in the park).
Water: silver (for the rain).
Fire: hot or fluorescent colors in small doses (for the sunset—and the sizzle of neon lights, a form of fire).
Wind: patterns of directional stripes—either multicolored or monochrome (for the life-forms speeding by).

- » Design a room based on the colors of a bird (landscape or plant) you find most visually interesting.
- » Invoke the energies of the sun and moon with silver and gold. Silvertone metal accessories are luminous and not too expensive; the same is true of silver and gold leaf. Brass accessories (plant holders, door knockers, and candlesticks) shine like the sun. Use silvers and golds to celebrate the sun and moon in your

home. (Read about "Warm and Cool Colors" in the next section for seasonal considerations.)

» Notice the commonsense colors in nature and emulate them in design. Use earth colors for floors, which are made to be walked on; beige and white floors are a constant hassle. (White is rarely the color of earth except for stone, and white stone floors work well in the right locations.) Stone, clay, and tile floors of any color are "cool" and good in hot climates.

PAINT COLORS

The colors and qualities of natural light change constantly with the seasons and times of day. Strong paint colors on our walls—dark reds, blues, greens, purples—on the other hand, make very "permanent" statements. For this reason, we tire of them quickly: because they're so dramatic, they soon beg relief. Deep wall colors can be great—they can balance massive furniture and high ceilings and make a small room seem bold—if you're prepared to redecorate when the thrill is gone.

Warm and Cool Colors

Any and *all* colors are warmer than black and white. Having said that, here is an overview of warm, cool, and neutral colors.

Color imbalances (too hot/too cold) in your home are generally reflected in your life. Notice which colors are dominant and which are missing in your home; think about their elements, energies, and associations.

» Do the colors of key areas (kitchen, living room, bedroom, office/study) enhance the activities performed there? Are they balanced with other energies? Is your office, for instance—a "cool," mental environment—balanced with warm accents (reds, golds, natural materials)? Record your feelings about the colors in your home.

Warm Colors	*Cool Colors*	*Neutral Colors*
Red (west, spring, fire)	Blue (east, winter, water)	White/light (center)
Yellow (south, fall, earth)	Green (north, summer, wind)	

» Is the color of your indoor lighting warm (pink/yellow), cold (blue/violet), or neutral (simulated daylight or full-spectrum lighting)?
» Work with color in your wardrobe as well. Adapt the exercise above to the colors you wear (and when and why). When you're feeling down or the weather's grim, a red blazer or scarf can lift your spirits and the spirits of those around you.

SEASONAL COLORS

Warm and cool colors are directly related to the seasons and environmental "heat." The colors of natural cycles alternate from cool to warm: cool in the beginning of a cycle (pale green in spring, pink/pale blue for baby) to the hot colors of summer and fall (bright reds, yellows, gold) to cool at the end (cool blues/whites/black of winter). Secondary shades arise from these palettes.

» To balance the cycles of life, nurture small children and the very old with warm (not hot or fluorescent) colors. Balance the heat of teenagers with cooler, more mental colors (blues, greens, violets), especially in rooms where they study/learn. (See "References and Further Readings" for more on this topic.)

Cool colors associated with water (blue, white) and wind (green) are especially refreshing in hot weather. Balance cold temperatures with warm colors associated with earth (yellows, golds, brown/black) and fire (reds, orange).

» Honor the stark colors of winter—black/white, silver, cool blues, and regal purples—but as in nature, balance them with warm, rich reds, deep oranges, and yellows. Use gold and natural materials (clay, wood, pine branches) for warmth. Display these in artworks, flower arrangements, and other accessories.
» Celebrate summer with hot, happy colors—balanced with icy white and stark black (or navy blue). Cool off with blues, greens, and gentle neutrals or pastels.

Extremes of hot/cold colors can be balanced with lots of space (and vice versa): a "hot" painting, for example, is happy on a large white wall; a neutral room, on the other hand, comes alive with a few persimmon pillows; as does a tawny woolen lap rug, with a bright red binding. One student instinctively balanced a very hot and chaotic summer in Los Angeles by painting her apartment various shades of blue and white.

The so-called L.A. style is a good example of visual balance. Los Angeles (hot, diverse) generated a style characterized by very hot and whimsical colors—combined, however, with very cool, hard-edged lines and shapes.

MIXING COLORS

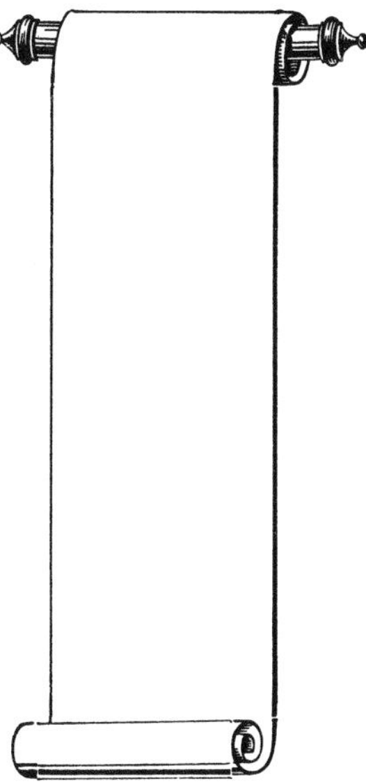

Complementary colors are exactly opposite each other on the color wheel. Mixed together in paint, they "gray" each other out. Side by side, they intensify each other; if they're the *same* intensity, they "sizzle," or vibrate, where they meet.

Mixing warm and cool colors can tip the temperature balance: red (warm) with a little blue in it (cool) is cooler than red with yellow. (Choose it for more formal or "elevated" situations or in later years of life.) Cool blues and greens are warmed up with reds or yellows (creating purple or turquoise). Red with deep yellow is a warm/warm, or "hot," combination.

» Mix white with any color to create a more spacious, less intense hue.

COLOR INSTALLATIONS

You don't have to repaint your apartment or house to work with the color of a space. Hanging panels of colored fabric or paper (which are easily moved or changed) is a simple, inexpensive way to channel a particular color energy. Intensify the color field with an energetically compatible flower arrangement, art object, or painting to change the "tone" of a space.

COLORED LIGHT

All translucent colored materials—glass, plastic, sheer fabrics—are magical because they radiate color as light. Stained glass is especially luminous and colorful. It doesn't have to be expensive or custom-made (and if stained glass isn't an option, simulate it using other materials). Remember to use colored light carefully and sparingly to avoid creating a "mood" in the room.

» Hang or stand a stained-glass panel in a window with good light—or use it to hide an unsightly lamp. Use squares of colored acrylic for a similar effect or buy colored cellophane and cut to size. Put a panel of each color in a window for one day and see how it affects the space. Acrylic panels can be installed into window panes (over the existing glass panes) with the small metal wedges from the backs of picture frames.

» Look for translucent colored clipboards, trays, glass dishes, bathroom soaps, and shower curtains. They're inexpensive enough to experiment and have fun with.
» Use colored lights, shades, and lanterns for special effects. (Lamp shades in everyday use, however, should convey clear, not colored, light.) Soften light with ivory or soft shell pink shades; sharpen it with bright white.

Interpreting Color

Color is a powerful and meaningful form of communication throughout the world. Cultural interpretations of color reflect both the universality and the differences of human experience. Designations such as "male/female" or "yin/yang" colors also differ. The importance of balancing their complementary energies, however, is universally the same. There are no fixed ways to interpret color, which is charged with cultural, spiritual, and personal associations—as well as shared meanings.

Europeans connect color with fire and life, and its absence (black) with darkness and death. In Japanese Zen tradition, black represents the richness of all color and stands for egolessness and liberation. In Chinese and Tibetan contexts, black represents water or earth and richness. In other contexts, black is thought to absorb light and attract negativity. It is a symbol of mourning in the West.

White, the color of purity in the West, is worn at weddings, where decorations, candles, and flowers are often snow-white. In China, white is the color of death and mourning (red is the color of happiness, used for weddings and celebrations). In African Yoruba tradition, white stands for purity and royalty (whose headpieces and robes are encrusted with shining white shells); and blue/indigo or green for "coolness" of character, which is considered godly.[1] In Chinese art and architecture, green stands for longevity; blue, for the heavens and blessings; and yellow, purple, and gold (which were used symbolically in robes, rugs, and ornamentation), for royalty.

» To use the language of color skillfully, take into consideration cultural interpretations (when in Rome, try to speak Italian).

Color is the language of passion, pleasure, and playfulness. Next we will see how to "flesh out" their energy in design.

33

PASSION, PLEASURE, AND PLAY

PASSION IS THE ENERGY OF LOVE—which is in large part longing. The pain and pleasure of love tenderize our hearts and make us human; they open us to the energies of heaven, earth, and other human beings. Don't underestimate the many ways you can manifest love in your life and your home.

» Express love in small gestures throughout the house. Don't leave any room out (hang a sachet in your closet).

Passion

Passion is seductive. The difference between "invitation" and "seduction" lies in their roots: the Latin root of *seduction* means "to lead astray." Seduction detours into desire and leads us on by intoxicating our senses. Its color is red, connected with "heat" and the provocative movement of fire. Seduction itself fulfills desire.

MYSTERY

Mystery is the Pied Piper of seduction. Seduction lies largely in the unknown—which tantalizes us, keeps us guessing and going on. It's a peek, not a full view; something suggested, not spelled out. (Romantic Japanese kimonos for women are "cool" on the outside, with scarlet linings that peek out suggestively at neck and wrists.) Mystery uses distance and restraint to advantage; it's the opposite of familiarity and "full disclosure." Mystery is in the service of passion.

SEDUCTIVE BEDROOMS

Bedrooms serve two basic purposes—sleep and sex. Because we rest, sleep, and renew ourselves for more hours than we play and make love, bedrooms need to be flexible. (It's not a good idea to make your primary bedroom into a passionate playground with red walls.)

One basic ground rule for seductive space: seduction is *special*, out of the ordinary! Dramatic colors and accessories in everyday use lose their effect. So first create a gentle, relaxing bedroom (see Part III, "Clarity"); then adorn it with "special effects."

- » Rely on romantic accessories for special occasions—gorgeous bedspreads and linens, a piano shawl thrown over a chair. Hang a length of dramatic fabric on the wall or draped over the bed. Investigate romantic surface designs—from your own and other cultures. Collect examples in your workbook.
- » Store special accessories in a special place—a cedar chest, trunk, or shelf in your closet.
- » Rely on *all* of the senses to send seductive messages. Use rich, warm velvet (touch) on the bed for special occasions. Hem or line it with a sensuous color.

- » Fragrant essential oils (smell) can be diffused, sprayed, rubbed on your body, dropped onto lightbulbs or into your tub. Fill a vase with fragrant flowers; use scented candles and incense. (In Japan, the art and science of incense was developed into a ritual similar to the tea ceremony.)
- » Choose warm colors—especially, red—and stimulating accent colors (remembering that, in tropical climates, cool colors might be more seductive).
- » Pay attention to lighting. Soft pink bulbs in the bedroom are flattering to any skin color—unlike stronger colored lights. Put an exotic scarf over your lamp (if it won't burn). Burn candles (in containers you don't have to worry about). Use a paper parasol or large scarf to disguise an overhead light.

» Don't wrap yourself in plastic in order to be seductive. Satin sheets are exotic but synthetic and not that pleasant to sleep on (the same goes for sexy lingerie). Fine cotton or silk is far more sensuous, as is the feel of fine cotton sheets. Red flannel sheets, while homey, are soft and visually stimulating.

» Avoid using mirrors as a "passion" device. They objectify your experience and are undesirable on ceilings or walls opposite your bed.

» Keep all doors in the bedroom—including closets and bathrooms—closed, so seductive energy isn't distracted or dissipated.

I live in my house as I live inside my skin: I know more beautiful, more ample, more sturdy and more picturesque skins; but it would seem to me unnatural to exchange them for mine.
—PRIMO LEVI

Pleasure

Warmth is the pleasure factor in your home. Pleasure is icing on the cake. It goes beyond comfort—it's possible to be comfortable without feeling your heart sing!—and it goes beyond mere function. It's humor, surprise, delight—and above all, beauty.

Pleasure is huge candles in glass globes, hand-painted tiles, extra-large bath towels, a good collection of music, your pets. Functional handcrafts—lamps/shades, textiles, ceramics, handblown and stained glass—are daily pleasures as well as works of art.

» Treat your home to something special on a regular basis. It doesn't have to be a purchase: garden flowers, a change of decor, trading artwork with a friend, a spring cleaning will do. Work the five energies and all of the senses. You don't need a lot of money to go beyond shelter to celebration.

PLEASURE IS A PERSONAL STYLE

Personal pleasures are the things that never fail to delight you—including styles of art, design, and decoration. They are the seeds of your personal style. A list of personal pleasures might look like this: early morning sun, crescent moon, wildlife, wild strawberries, mystery novels, crossword puzzles. If you begin to incorporate your favorite things into your home, your results might look like this:

- A breakfast nook with an east-facing window.
- A headboard painted or carved with a crescent moon.
- A tea set painted with wild strawberries; a framboise-colored slipcover on your easy chair.
- A large framed poster of an Agatha Christie movie.

- A blowup of a successful crossword puzzle (mount it under glass in your office or on top of your telephone table).

» In your workbook, make a list of personal pleasures. Becoming more conscious of them will help you see them in your world and in design.

» Identify your favorite painting (photograph, poem, or myth). Study it carefully. Imagine your painting—its colors, textures, and style of energy—as a room. Don't be afraid to bring drama or some serious design departures into your decor.

» Identify your favorite fragrances. Learn about "flower power"—the physical, emotional, and mythological associations of flowers/plants. Make sachets of your scent for your drawers.

Identifying your personal style is like choosing a medium in which to paint. Now translate the environmental energies into the medium of your choice.

Playfulness

Play is a lighthearted form of passion. It's seductive and basically gentle—as are people who are willing to play. It brings surprise, spontaneity, and creativity into our lives. Play has the power to inform, heal, expand our horizons, increase our energy, bring us joy, and wake us up.

Playfulness is a way of being in the world: it says, "I'm here, you're here, let's enjoy being here together." It doesn't mean everything's "funny," but it does make things fun.

Architecture can be playful and romantic as well: Victorian houses, for instance, were called "ladies" and adorned with "necklaces" of "carpenter's lace." The lacy openwork trim—made possible by the invention of the jigsaw—sprang from the sheer joy of invention. Play is the "open sesame" of creativity.

» Don't be afraid to let the whimsical, wild, and strange into your home. There are no rules: fun things fall into your life when you lighten up! In an artist's apartment, we used the Sunday comics (sealed with matte acrylic medium) to make a border to lower the very high ceilings in a playful way.

34

HOSPITALITY

Hospitality MEANS "TAKING CARE OF A GUEST" (from the same word root as *hospital* and *hospice*). In most traditional cultures, guests are seen and treated as deities. Coming from and going to worlds beyond our home, they are honored and put before oneself. Putting others before ourselves is a traditional practice of selflessness (called *tonglen* in Tibetan) that restores us to our natural state. Hospitality is an opportunity to exchange ourselves for others. All cultural customs surrounding hospitality—whether they arose from fear and loathing or love and compassion—strive to restore the wholeness of self and "other." The ground of good hospitality is empathy.

Hospitality is an antidote to dejection and disregard. You, too, are a guest in your home. If you provide yourself with proper hospitality, you will be able to extend it to others. If your home cheers you up, it will cheer up others as well; if it doesn't, it won't fool anyone.

» Treat yourself and those you live with as honored guests. Extend the same gracious concern for their comfort and accomodation.

Hospitality Is Inviting

Last year, a young friend of mine died of breast cancer. Her Buddhist funeral service was held in the Quaker school where she taught, drawing hundreds of people from the two communities. Among them was her daughter's teenage boyfriend, who—after the long and powerful outpouring of eulogies—timidly stood up and stopped our minds by saying very simply: "She always invited me in." In spite of his shyness, he explained, my friend had always made him feel welcome, and this had affected him deeply. There wasn't much more to say after that.

» Invite others into your home—family, neighbors, friends, and their children—for an impromptu tea, brunch, or dinner. What foods and beverages will you choose to delight, seduce, or pleasure your guests? (How is hospitality, passion, or harmony expressed in the culinary arts of other cultures?)
» Invite a family member to join you by the fire (make tea, bring lap rugs).
» Notice how powerfully all of your senses respond to inviting tastes, sounds, and aromas. (This is the magnetizing power of warmth!)
» Visualize hospitality—seasonal celebrations, dinners, housewarmings, and overnights—as home design. Learn how hospitality is extended in other cultures and times. What forms does it take? In your workbook, collect ideas and inspiration.

Hospitality begins with the good feeling established by your front door and foyer.

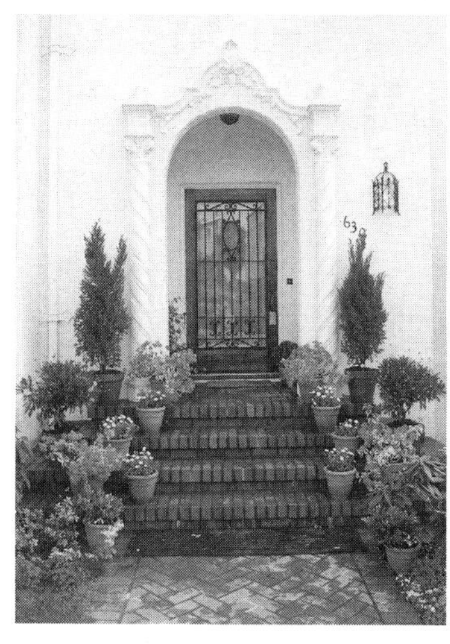

INVITING FRONT DOORS

The face of your house has windows for eyes and nose, and the front door as the "mouth." If you want life to beat a path to your door, make it very attractive!

» Sweep the front path and make sure it's well lit. Landscaping should be inviting—not neglected, sinister, or sad-looking. Trim any shrubbery that obstructs the path and cut away dead growth. Plant fragrant flowering bushes around the house (but not just outside the front door or you will have bees as guests). If you live in an apartment, make sure the lights are bright outside your door.
» If your entrance is recessed or tucked in a corner, brighten it up with bold color, attractive fixtures, and lots of light. Use artwork or a mirror to create an illusion of space and light (and to attract rather than repel your guests).
» Paint the "mouth" of your house. Red paint, like red lipstick, sends an intensely inviting message, as do red plants and bushes around the front door. Red is the most inviting color—but any color that's fresh and vibrant is attractive. (We will talk more about color later in the chapter.)
» If your door is natural wood or a more rustic style, make sure it shines with good health.
» Keep the door well oiled so it doesn't creak. (A creaking door is like creaking joints—depressing.) Keep hardware and locks working

smoothly; it shouldn't be a struggle to get in or out. Make your welcome mat as attractive as your new door (and just as wide). Get a new one if yours is faded (it's a daily message from you to your world).

» From the most commonsense to the most elaborate, door and entry customs are rich in tradition and meaning. Research them in your own and other cultures.

This wooden door panel from Ghana bears auspicious fish designs.

BRASS HARDWARE AND GOLD LEAF

Give your house a facelift with shiny brass hardware—a large French-style door handle, knocker, and kick plate; perhaps glass-and-brass carriage lamps with bright lights—and gold leaf. At our house, we gilded every other "ray" of a rising-sun pediment over the door. (For more on gilding, see Part IV.)

DOOR DEITIES

Front doors are often adorned with auspicious symbols to invite positive energies in and flanked with protectors to keep negative energies out. In Bali, spirits are invited to gather in their own little spirit house by the front door (where daily offerings are made). In China, main doors were often flanked by protective statuary in the form of stone lions or drums. Power objects are often hidden or built into lintels. (We'll talk more about protection in Part VI.)

SOFT DOORS

All doors invite us into another space. Soft doors—bead or reed curtains or drapes—make that space easily accessible and lend a veiled air of mystery, as do shoji screens. Hinged doors are necessary for privacy and protection.

» Replace an interior hinged door with a short or full-length door curtain for an attractive soft door.

A traditional Japanese style New Year's arrangement of pine and paper decorations is installed in the foyer.

INVITING FOYERS

The foyer inside the front door bridges outer/inner space and creates the first impression of your home. It's a very good place for guests to pause and regroup (and not the best place to store bikes and shopping carts). It's a good place to celebrate seasonal energy, as foyers are about transition and change. (We will talk more about *transitional* spaces in Part VI, "Energy.") Here are some ways to create an impressive foyer and uplift the spirits of your guests:

- » Use color, artwork, and personal style to create a representative foyer. Speak through your own medium if space permits—a piece of sculpture, a calligraphy, a painting, or an arrangement of flowers. Make your foyer as magical as it is functional.
- » Provide guests with a moment of mindfulness and delight before they move on. Do an installation using seasonal flowers on a pedestal or in a hanging basket; hang a colorful backdrop behind them. Do an object arrangement of local gourds, shells, or stones on the floor.
- » If you have no foyer—or you enter a hallway—use the ceiling (a hanging panel/banner or overhead lights) and floor (a well-chosen carpet, tile, change of flooring materials) to define an entry space. Add a piece of furniture, plants, or a screen to separate the entry from your living space. Hang an attractive mirror or painting to create a sense of invitation there.
- » If the entry hall is long and forbidding, light it well and use the ceiling and floor to create inviting "increments" of space. Hang a *series* of short banners, prayer flags, or door curtains from the ceiling; place several carpet runners (with space in between) on the floor rather than continuous flooring; and use one or more mirrors to reflect light in the hall.

INVITING GARAGE ENTRANCES

Finally, if you enter your home through an interior garage door—as more and more people do—bite the bullet and treat it as an entrance. Garage entrances can be quite grim (especially if you're coming and going in the dark). Garages don't need to be "prettified," but they can be uplifted.

- » Design a garage entrance as inviting as your front door. Clean and paint the interior of the garage, including the ceiling and floor if you can. (Some car buffs lay snappy linoleum on the floor.) Clear the entrance wall of tools and equipment (hang them on the other three walls out of sight). Paint the door from the garage to the house a bright color and light it well.

One woman painted the inside of her garage bright white, with a red door going into the house—around which she tacked a wide band of mirrored Indian fabric.

Another couple chose white and yellow for the garage, adding a wooden latticework screen door in the style of their garden patio.

» Make the garage entrance practical—with coat hooks and hat and shoe racks—and unobstructed. Remove clutter, trash cans, and garbage bags from the path to the door. Place an area rug or welcome mat out for yourself, and a nice table by the door for packages.
» Apartment dwellers who can't change garage or elevator entrances can compensate by creating an especially welcoming foyer.

Hospitality Is Comfortable

Real comfort is like wearing good shoes: when your body and mind are truly comfortable, you don't notice them. Comfort is at your service; it doesn't call attention to itself. Demanding, overdecorated homes are not comfortable because they put themselves—not you—first.

» For your comfort, choose natural fabrics and accessories that are pleasing but not intense. (A hot-pink room has its virtues, but comfort is not one of them.)

Comfort takes care of our fundamental needs: in hot weather, it's cold drinks, a ceiling fan, and cotton slipcovers (over heavier, hotter upholstery).

» It's not only comfortable but healthful to put your feet up. Provide ottomans and footstools (earth)—not tables (man)—for your feet. Gather lap rugs for cold weather, tray tables for comfortable dining by the fire or TV, and a book caddie for your favorite chair. Put cushions on the seats of wooden or metal chairs; or pad them with car seat cushions—the kind with both seat and back—and cover with simple slipcovers.

COMFORTABLE FURNITURE

Human beings are erect creatures. We lie down to sleep. We are not really mentally/physically comfortable in semiprone postures or in furniture that forces us to sprawl or lounge. Inevitably, a sense of self-doubt sets in. Comfortable furniture should encourage wakefulness at the same time.

» Check your sofas and chairs: Are the seats too soft or too deep (forcing an undignified sprawl)? Do your feet reach the floor (or stick out like a child's)?

COMFORTABLE SURROUNDINGS

Real comfort softens life's hard edges and celebrates the compatibility of things. Find the goodness wherever you are and enjoy it just as it is. If the exterior world is harsh, find its "soft spots," or heart. Reflect them in your living space. The world is more comfortable when inner/outer energies are in harmony.

» If you bring industrial chic to the country or a jungle paradise to Manhattan, bring them into harmony—or you will begin to feel disjointed. Create an interior retreat in harmony with your surroundings.

INTIMATE NOOKS AND CRANNIES

When I was a child, my family dined once a week in a quaint old restaurant called The Inglenook (which literally means "chimney corner," from the Gaelic for *fire*, *fireplace*, and *hearth*). Housed in a rambling old Victorian with beehive rooms, blazing fires, and family-style service, it was a memorably warm and intimate interior.

Intimacy—from the Latin root for "innermost"—means "being familiar," "being made known." Intimacy bonds parents and children, friends and lovers, you and your innermost self. In home design, intimacy is a cozy nook or cranny, a secluded spot for musing and secrets. It can be as simple as a table with two chairs, or a candle, rug, pillow, and screen.

Boundaries are essential to intimate space. The satisfaction of small needs and desires within those boundaries creates the feeling of being self-contained.

» Find a spot that you're drawn to—a spot of light, a woodstove, a window with a view—and create an intimate space there. Minimize outside influences; maximize pleasure and peace.

» Your bathroom—primarily connected with purification—is also an intimate space. Create a private spa experience with candles, hanging plants, and warm decor; relax and restore your energy there.

Next, we will see how warmth brings harmony into your home.

35

HARMONY

A HARMONIOUS ENVIRONMENT IS NOT "Pollyanna" or lukewarm—it's *workable*. Harmony is a sympathetic place that joins the richness of life with the spaciousness that keeps things going.

In Harmony with Children

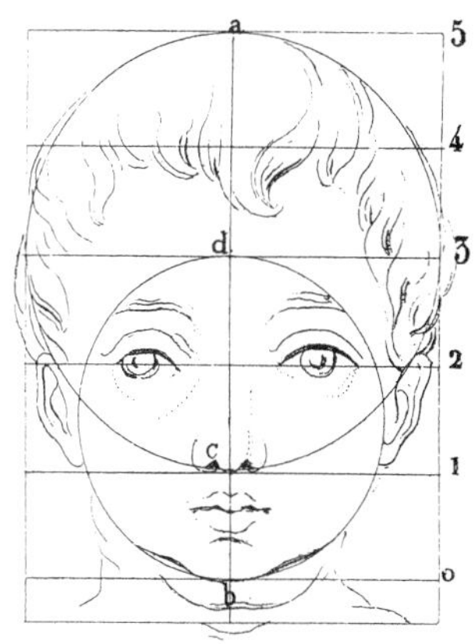
a
b
c
d
5
4
3
2
1
o

Children are like waxing moons: their energy is expansive but not fully developed. They need more space than babies but less than teenagers, who take up a lot of space. For harmony in a home with children, balance the five energies in design and within their limited orbit. Here's a checklist:

Space provides children with an accepting environment that offers gentleness and relaxation.
Clarity provides the good boundaries, physical and intellectual "enlightenment," and dependable havens of peace that children need.
Richness creates a stable, nurturing environment and fosters self-esteem. The richer their world in all ways, the wealthier children will be.
Warmth balances spaciousness and good boundaries with warm colors in the home. Children need physical and emotional warmth. (The hot and fluorescent colors of many of their toys and much of their clothing are exciting for children but overstimulating in large doses.)
Energy provides upliftedness and a sense of accomplishment—and good work areas for mastery and success.

OVERSTIMULATING CHILDREN'S ROOMS

Small children experience the bigness of their "container" very powerfully because of their size. Their experience of space (heaven) can be balanced by the limitations of practical tasks and physical exertion (earth)—as well as *focused* sensory input and periods of concentration. Children, like the elderly, derive a reassuring sense of self from dependable surroundings.

The rooms we create for children—if well intentioned—are often cluttered and overstimulating. In addition to intellectual stimulation, love, and rich surroundings, children need to experience space—a sense of "nothing happening," of silence. In spacious environments, they become mindful and relaxed. Ultimately, children are most at home in awareness, which is ageless.

In Harmony with Adults and the Elderly

For most of us, the world extends far beyond the walls of our home. The very old—like the very young—have limited range due to failing sensory and physical abilities. What space they do have must meet their specific needs and desires. (The balancing of energies for children, described in the preceding section, pertains to the very old as well.)

Adults arrive at environmental well-being differently than the very young and the very old. Young adults—who generally feel indestructible—thrive on environmental stimulus and change. With time, we feel more mortal but still crave sensory input and innovation.

SPACE FOR THE VERY OLD

The very old—who generally feel more vulnerable and overwhelmed by the world—do not thrive on wholesale stimulus and change. They are also less tied to the clock, which—with its many advantages—can also be somewhat disorienting. With personal loss and impermanence a daily challenge, a sense of well-being comes from the conservation of energy and dependable surroundings. In the home, workability is familiar things that stay put—in increasingly limited space. Use these parameters to create a space that is uplifted and dignified—a space that generates wakefulness and supports the process of letting go. (Ultimately, our "homes" drop away altogether. In many cultures, after the age of sixty, you become a wanderer or enter a monastery in preparation for this stage of your journey.)

Now let's look at how to create harmony in communal areas of your home.

Harmony in Communal Rooms

Most of us have our first go at domestic relations playing house. In play, we learn to be in our world. Common rooms are opportunities to be together. They invite communication, creativity, celebration—as well as time out. Before TV, "living rooms" were usually focused on the hearth and equipped with card/gaming tables, reading/sewing areas, and musical instruments.

» Balance the energies of age and gender in common rooms. Don't let toys, creative projects, sports broadcasts, or excessive formality dominate the space.

» Set boundaries on the use of electronic media, computer games, and work-related equipment in common rooms. Create a space in which you and your family can just be together.

Share your presence of mind as well as physical space to create a harmonious home. When you're awake, you are in harmony with the world around you; when you're in harmony with the world around you, you are awake!

» Foster wakefulness in the family room through attention to detail and decor. The beauty of a flower arrangement, the poetry of color, and the skillful arrangement of furniture will affect the minds and behavior of everyone using the space. (Fresh flowers on the coffee table delight the eye and mind and discourage people from putting their feet there. Sofas and chairs that face each other encourage conversation; lined up in front of the TV, they do not.)

» Diagnose the energy of communal rooms and choose energy "antidotes" to balance chaos, confusion, neglect, or stress.

Genuine warmth and wakefulness are a contemplative definition of elegance, which is our next topic.

36

ELEGANCE

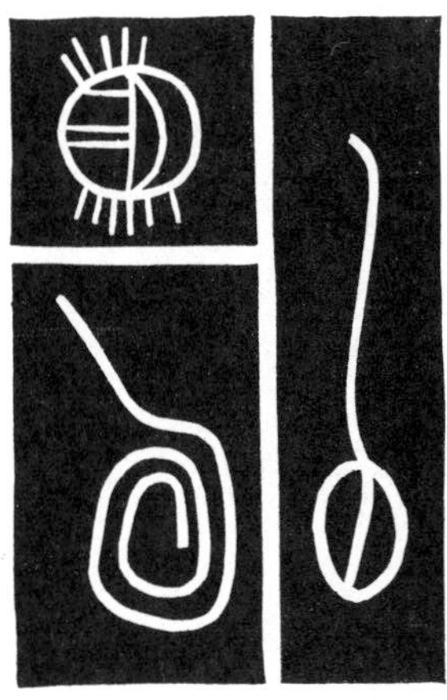

African Bushman drawings

THE WORD *elegance*—from the Latin *eligere*, "to select"—means "tasteful beauty of manner, form, or style." An expression of discriminating wisdom, elegance is based on a state of mind that is warm (inquisitive, willing, workable) and awake to possibilities.

» Find an example of something in your home that you find truly elegant. Study it carefully to discover why this is so.

Elegance is not a "me-first" style; it's the perfect blend of graciousness and glamour. It radiates without knocking you off of your pins. From a contemplative point of view, elegance is synonymous with "nonaggression," and nonaggression is synonymous with "art." Elegance is the art of living in harmony with your world.

"Function in Disaster, Finish in Style"

Elegance—like beauty—is easy to spot but hard to pin down. It's "flair," simplicity (even richness can be simply elegant), gentleness (as in "gentleman" or "gentlewoman"). But above all, elegance is brave. It communicates a pervasive sense of inspiration and workability; it allows no dark corners and is not afraid to relate with pain, sickness, old age, or death. Elegant homes are not havens *from* but havens *for* life's challenges. Elegance is summed up in the motto of the Madeira Girls School: "Function in disaster, finish in style."

Art is the mother of religion.
—ONISABURO DEGUCHI

Art

Art has the power to invoke the gods. It's a bridge (man principle) between your awake mind (heaven) and the world (earth). Whether it's a depiction of a blade of grass, a leaping steed, or a colorful abstraction, art—in the best sense—is a form of invocation.

Art has to move you; design does not, unless it's a good design for a bus.
—David Hockney

» Choose artistic expressions of space, clarity, richness, warmth, and energy to bridge you and the energies of the universe. Channel these energies into your home through art.
» Cultivate your passion for elegance and art. Look for art that wakes you up, touches your heart, makes you feel "real." See which pieces haunt you when you go home. Bring art into your home (if your favorite museum piece isn't affordable, get a reproduction).
» Circulate the art energy in your life: change the art on your walls, trade it, lend it to deserving venues, give it away.
» Bring your own creativity to the fore. Explore one or more artistic disciplines; incorporate at least one formal discipline into your life. In another time, we would put as much exertion into creative pursuits as we now put into physical culture.

Chinese vessels

Design and Decoration

Expressive arts appeal to our hearts; information appeals to our minds; applied arts—including design and decoration—fall somewhere in between. Their ordinary magic can bring wisdom, compassion, and power to the world. The opposite of ordinary magic is pro forma design moving along procedural or habitual tracks. Wakefulness is open-ended and spontaneous; without it, "design"—from the Latin root meaning "to signify" or "point out"—is meaningless.

> Design always has to be based on what the other person needs.
> —Khandro Rinpoche

» Bring sensory data together with wakefulness to get your message across. Decide which of the five energies you want to communicate and "send" it over one or more sensory "channels" by design.

Pueblo Indian pottery

SURFACE DESIGN

Artists have painted, carved, dyed, hammered, and imprinted their messages onto everyday objects since the beginning of time. Surface design is a powerful way to telegraph the five energies into your home.

Border from Roman painted wall decoration

We have to admit that the arts stimulate and satisfy a part of our nature that would otherwise be left untouched and that the emotions art arouses in us are of a different order to those aroused by experience of any other kind.

—JEANNETTE WINTERSON

» In your workbook, collect examples of clarity, richness, warmth, and energy in surface design—on fabrics, ceramics, and domestic objects. Invoke a specific energy (warmth, for example) into a designated area of your home through surface design.

Applied arts embody—for better or worse—the spirituality (heaven), morality (man principle), and practicality of life on earth. There is no separation between art, religion, and the living of life—only differences in degrees of elegance and quality of life. These can be determined by design.

DESIGNING FROM NATURE

Human beings are part of nature. We are physiologically *designed* according to natural laws—which are the guidelines for enlightened design.

The principles of natural design—heaven, earth, and man; the four directions; and the five styles of energy—transcend any conflict between nature, art, science, and technology and open up worlds of design possibilities. If you base your designs on the *principles* of nature, you may be surprised by the colors, shapes, and styles you come up with. Nature is not necessarily green and woodsy! (For more on this topic, go back and reread "Sameness Inside and Out" in Chapter 10.)

» Do a futuristic room design based on nature.

Pairs of birds, animals, or people in design bode well for relationships; solitary figures reinforce loneliness and isolation.

Decorative Arts

DECORATE: from the Latin root *dek*, meaning to take or accept, receptivity; connected with decency, appropriateness; suffixed forms meaning to teach (to cause to accept), as in docent, doctor, doctrine, etc.; and grace, seemliness, elegance, beauty, and dignity

Historically, what we call "decorative arts" were ways of educating, civilizing, inspiring, and empowering human beings. After World War I, Linda Lichter writes, "such discussions of the . . . influences of architecture and domestic decor had vanished. Form famously began to follow function, not philosophy. And this decline of the spiritualized home paralleled the appropriation of family functions by outside specialists like physicians, psychiatrists, and social workers."[1]

Decorative arts are what we live with on a daily basis. Philadelphia designer Bob Ingram summed up, "they define the texture of the culture."

» Choose the natural element most compelling for you (fire, for instance). Find evocative examples of fire in decorative arts from around the world. Do this exercise for *anything* that's important to you at the moment—love, healing, money. If you do it for all the five energies and their qualities, you will create a world.

DECORATING UNDER DURESS

The urge to decorate an unfinished home can become irresistible. Building or renovating usually takes longer than expected—and it's *very* difficult to pull a space together until it's done. There are some steps you can take:

» Target areas that are structurally ready and do the next level of improvement (electrical installation, finish carpentry, painting). While that's going on, begin decorating by identifying your needs and desires. (Go back and reread "Pleasure Is a Personal Style" in Chapter 33.) Your personal style in art, rugs, and objects isn't going to change as a result of renovating.

» The magic of design is a journey without goal; it places you firmly on the path of freshness and spontaneity. Putting one piece in place—even if it's a vase of your favorite flowers—is the first step of an ongoing journey.

If you want a golden rule that will fit everything, this is it: Have nothing in your houses that you do not know to be useful or believe to be beautiful.
—William Morris

Beauty

Beauty reflects the unconditional goodness and brightness of life—which is why we are drawn to it. Diana, Princess of Wales, was an example of such a beacon. Because it expresses the best of who and what we are, real beauty doesn't conform with conventional expectations or submit to comparisons. Because the best of who and what we are is unconditional, beauty has infinite manifestations, including—as in the Japanese tradition of wabi (and the French tradition of *belle laid*—the inner beauty of ugliness, old age, and imperfection.

» Take pictures, draw, paint, or just appreciate the beauty of ordinary things around you—a chair, a window, a toy, a head of garlic.

» Collect beautiful things around you. Don't be blinded by beauty, but don't underestimate its power.

> Beauty is an ecstasy; it is as simple as hunger. There is really nothing to be said about it. It is like the perfume of a rose: you can smell it and that is all.
> —W. Somerset Maugham

In the old-time Pueblo world, beauty was manifested in behavior and in one's relationships with other living beings. Beauty was as much a feeling of harmony as it was a visual, aural, or sensual effect.
—Leslie Marmon Silko

37

MAGNETIZING SPACE

WARMTH MAKES THE WHOLE HOUSE appealing and pleasurable. It especially rules communal rooms (connected with communication)—as well as the allure of your bedroom and other intimate areas. Here's an example of how warmth creates a social space with the help of the other four energies:

Creating a Social Space

Warmth makes us want to be in the room. It's beautiful colors and fabrics and interesting conversation. It's the "little pleasures"—a fire, flowers, a footstool—that invite you to come in and spend time.

Space is the gentleness conducive to relaxation and play.

Clarity organizes the space so that everyone can enjoy it. It arranges furniture for conversation and provides good lighting—in this case, soft and flattering. It's your streamlined entertainment center and games that challenge the mind.

Richness satisfies everyone's desires. On a large scale, it provides lots of comfortable chairs and elegant accessories, and a wealth of social possibilities and pleasurable pursuits. On a small scale, richness is the splendor of simple things (one perfect orange on a plate). In either case, it dignifies our social areas and creates a sense of well-being.

Energy brings vitality into the space through good traffic patterns and efficient technology—TV/video, CD player/radio—for entertainment and information. It's the lively competition of card games and debates.

Creating an Installation to Magnetize Space

To intensify the energy of warmth or bring magnetizing energy to a specific space, create an installation. Put it along the sight line of a particular room to set the tone; in your sitting room or sun porch where you enjoy getting together with people; in your bedroom to inspire passion; or in the foyer of your home for the summer equinox. Bring the warmth of heaven, earth, and man together in one spot. Here are some suggestions:

Heaven: A warm red backdrop that defines your installation space (adorned perhaps with a decorative pattern, colorful painting, or symbolic sun/fire).
Earth: An elegant (or playful) table or pedestal.
Man: An inviting, passionate, or playful statue, flower, or object arrangement that brings heaven and earth into harmony.

To intensify the energy of warmth, use real or representational fire (candles, a symbol of the sun); warm colors (red, yellow, orange); warm materials (wood, velvet, gold, straw); and a representation of a "fiery" bird or animal.

» To tap the energy of warmth, create an installation that takes the form of a celebration, a party, or an open house.

Remedies for Excess

Clarity focuses warmth's passion (into relationships, art, sculpture, music)—and prevents it from becoming too casual or chaotic. It's the formal aspect of warmth—a red rose in your lapel, good manners (and written invitations), courting customs, and decorous hospitality (with coasters on the table).
Space relaxes passion so it doesn't get feverish or carried away. It's humor, receptivity to change, a gap in conversation.
Richness prevents warmth from becoming superficial, needy, or burned out. It's grounding (heirlooms and family portraits) and expansive (the fruition of lovemaking is expansion of families). Richness is *generous* hospitality, with lots of good food, good company, and plenty of warm blankets.

Energy prevents warmth from being too dreamy or moody. It's decorative sconces that actually work, an attractive foyer *with* a place for your boots and umbrella. Energy keeps conversations moving, art forms uplifting, and cultural life dynamic. It doesn't invite you to "flop"; at the same time, energy provides a sense of protection.

Summing Up Warmth

Direction	*Color*	*Element*	*Season*	*Symbolic shape*
West	Red	Fire	Spring:	Half-circle

Wisdom Discriminating awareness wisdom

In design Color, passion, pleasure, playfulness, hospitality, harmony, elegance

Imbalance Cloying, mesmerizing, addictive, frivolous/fickle/superficial (lack of depth), overdecorated (too cute, treacly, garish, tawdry)

Signature sites Front door/entrance/foyer, living/family rooms and social areas, bedrooms, inglenooks, and other intimate spaces

Animals Loyal dog, playful monkey, elegant gazelle; lovebirds, Chinese phoenix—and traditionally, the red garuda

VI

ENERGY

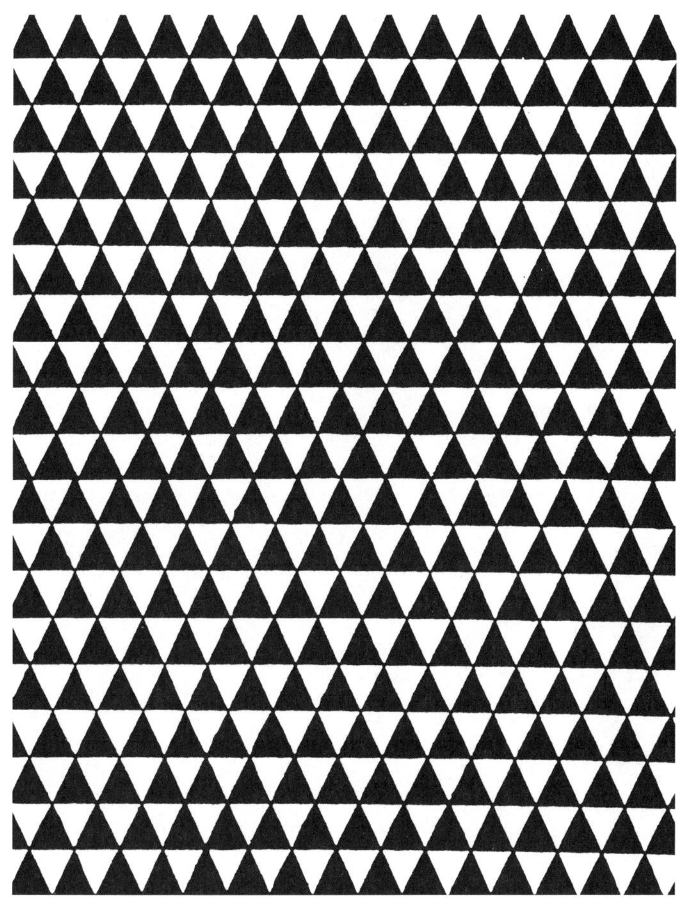

38

THE POWER OF ENERGY

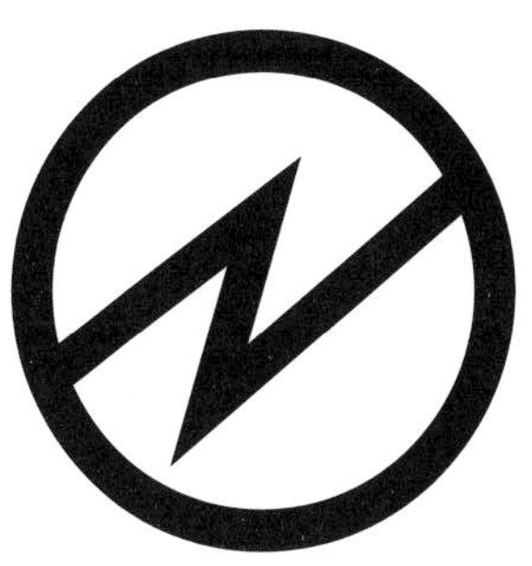

> It was the wind that gave them life. It is the wind that comes out of our mouths now that gives us life. When this ceases to blow we die. In the skin of our fingers we can see the trail of the wind; it shows us where the wind blew when our ancestors were created.
>
> —Washington Matthews, Navaho Legends

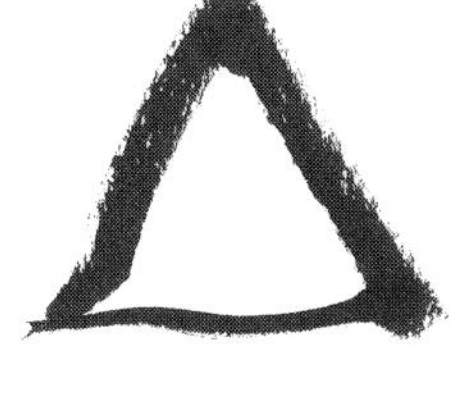

ENERGY—ASSOCIATED WITH THE NORTH, wind, the color green, and the shape of the triangle—is vitality in design. It's the life force of the other styles, circulating them through our homes and lives. It is "ascending" energy, and it is characteristically forceful and abrupt.

Channel energy into your world when you need or want:

More upliftedness/vitality . . .	to move your work out into the world
More growth/renewal . . .	to make a transition
More motivation . . .	to be more efficient/productive
More ease/less effort in action . . .	to overcome obstacles and negativity
More success in what you do . . .	to achieve your goals

The ultimate power of energy is all-accomplishing wisdom. From a contemplative point of view, the goal is already won. Energy takes a "can-do" approach and moves effortlessly about its business. Spiritually, it is enlightenment that needn't be designed. Psychologically, it is an antidote to depression, fear, and sloth. Like the wind—directional and undistracted—energy always gets the job done (and is therefore connected with work). It motivates us to work in the world.

Energy's traditional animal is the perky snow lion; energy is also embodied in busy beavers and bees, in swift-footed animals and soaring birds.

In design, energy is the vitality and overall success of your space. Moving quickly (like the wind), it's connected with tools, tasks, and utilitarian design; with fast foods, assembly lines, and a belief in progress. Signature sites are workplaces (office, basement, garage), exercise and sports areas, and transitional areas such as pathways, hallways, and stairs. Outside the home, energy is the marketplace, businesses, factories, and sports arenas—as well as airports, real (and virtual) highways, and other energy corridors.

Too Much of a Good Thing

Excess energy is frenetic and not effective (an imbalance of doing versus nondoing, moving versus staying still). Psychologically, it's "green with envy" and busy keeping up with the Joneses. It causes "hurry sickness" and time anxiety and manifests as ambition, workaholism, competitiveness, and war. Extreme excess becomes jealousy and paranoia (and overly concerned with security systems and weapons). Excess creates "type A" environments—speedy and insensitive, with an overemphasis on business, sports, and defense—and type A homes that make you feel as if you're running in place. In the next chapter, we will see how balanced energy restores the health of your home.

> [W]ithout basic sanity, there is no journey, no movement, there is no creative energy.
> —Chögyam Trungpa

Bringing Energy Home

If energy were a fabric, it would be *functional*—ripstop parachute silk, sturdy canvas and denim, spandex, waterproof nylon, and plastic—with dynamic surface designs. As a style of furniture, it's anything serviceable, portable, movable, and multipurpose—at best, "industrial chic." As lighting, it is energy-efficient fluorescent or zippy neon, adjustable lamps, an efficient flashlight—or a bolt of lightning. As a plant, it would probably be too busy to flower!

We experience energy through all of our senses—sight, sound, taste, smell, touch, and mind. Use them to energize your environment.

SIGHT

Energy—like wind—is invisible, but we can see its "footprints" (flags waving in the wind, the sweep of windswept pines), and the sight of them energizes space. Visual

energy is real or representational moving images: computer, TV, and video images; antique prints of windmills and mechanical devices; a colorful poster of mechanical toys—and an army of action figures. It's the sight of clocks and calendars that mark the passage of time; fire escapes and ladders that move us through space; and plumbing, pipes, cables, and wires that do the work of our homes. (Use all of them in your designs to create a dynamic space.)

Visual energy is communicated through dynamic color, angles, triangular shapes (the basis of energetic design)—and straight lines. Finally, energy is channeled through the sight of living/growing things—active children and pets (energy often lacking in the lives of the elderly), live plants, botanical pictures—and green, the color of growth.

- » In your workbook, collect examples of energy in architecture and design—in your own and other cultures. (Look at commercial, military, and sports design.)
- » Energy's signature color is green. Look for it in art and design, in everyday life, and especially in nature. Collect samples of color and color combinations of flying insects and birds, the oxidation of metals, moss—and especially plant life. Include fabric swatches.
- » Collect visual and literary examples of energy's natural element, wind. How is wind represented in art, architecture, and design (and what does it stand for)?
- » Use visual energy to intensify the other four styles. (Energize your earthy, nurturing kitchen with efficient equipment.)

SOUND

Energy is the *impact* of sound—rousing marching bands, clock alarms, car horns, three cheers! It's the clamor of people and machines doing their jobs—and the ongoing bells and whistles of refrigerators, furnaces, intercoms, beepers, and telephones at home. Energetic sound is intense (thunder, explosions, and the too-loud sound tracks of action movies). It's powerful (soaring jets, rushing traffic, wind, and water) and has the power to move us. The power of sound energy can energize (or overwhelm) your home.

- » Energize a space with wind chimes or a splashing fountain. Modify the sounds of your telephone, alarm clock, and doorbell so they are effective but not rude. Balance sound with silence.

TASTE

Energy is flavors that "pack a punch"—chilies, watercress, arugula, wasabi—and the herbs and spices that energize your cooking. It's the *impact* of a taste experience—sweet, salty, sour, bitter, astringent. Fast foods—symptomatic of a speedy environment—rely on instant taste sensation and are therefore too sweet, too salty, too spicy. Subtle flavors are lost when foods are nuked, frozen, and preserved for packaging. Metaphorically, energetic "taste" is the preference for an energetic, uplifted style—which, in excess, is fanatically functional.

» Be mindful of the flavors of your food. Potent tastes affect your health; they can be used medicinally or make you sick. The tastes of foods need to be in balance. Eliminate the taste of excess (especially in processed and fast foods). In design, balance function with feeling.

SMELL

Energy is the potency of smells—good, bad, or ugly—and the impact of smells on your mind. It's characterized by invigorating aromas—juniper, lemon grass, peppermint, carnation, bergamot, and fresh green growth—that uplift your mind and home. It's the smells of activity, exertion, and growth (and not the smells of stagnation and decay). Certain strong smells are warnings of environmental dangers, disease, death—and serve to protect us.

» Explore "flower power." Identify the energizing aromas best for you and your family. Use essential oils and incense as pick-me-ups. Work skillfully with the power of aromas in your home—and eliminate olfactory pollution.

TOUCH

Energy is the *impact* of touch. No matter what style—very sharp, very rich, very soft, very smooth—it is energetic contact with your environment. At best, it is bracing (a cool breeze, a hot cup of tea), stimulating (a new loofah), uplifting (a well-designed office chair). It is ease of handling (portable furniture, functional accessories), and it might be "charged" or intense. Above all, energy is the feel of ch'i flowing through space—and yourself flowing with it, purposeful and productive.

» Eliminate struggle from your environment. Rearrange furniture to encourage energy flow; replace furniture and accessories that are unwieldy, heavy, or hard to use.

MIND

Mental energy cuts through our preoccupations and uplifts our minds when we get stuck or carried away. It's the energy of wakefulness that connects us properly with environmental energy. (When our mental energy is boxed in, we are cut off and without real power.)

» Try this exercise outside: Close your eyes, relax your mind, and connect with the energy of sounds around you. Let your awareness dissolve into the sound of wind, rustling leaves, rush-hour traffic, or children squealing. (What are these sounds saying to you?) Now open your eyes. Let your visual focus dissolve into the energies of color, line, and forms around you. Extend your awareness further—without staring—to scurrying squirrels, soaring birds, waving grasses, racing clouds. (What is their message?)

Energy expresses itself sanely through five basic qualities that translate into uplifted, successful space. Use them when things are stuck or out of control; when you lack a sense of direction; when work isn't working for you; when your space doesn't work for you; when you (and your home) need more get-up-and-go.

(Illustration courtesy of Kawade Shobo Shinsha, Publishers, Japan)

39

DIRECTION

Realities are meaningless; practicalities are penetrating.
—CHÖGYAM TRUNGPA

WIND ALWAYS BLOWS IN ONE DIRECTION. Like the wind, energy travels one-pointedly through space to accomplish its goals. In design, it's efficient and to the point.

EFFICIENCY: effect, making things happen, creating change.

Making Things Happen

Efficient people, places, and things are concerned with the doing—not the philosophy, aesthetics, enjoyment, or importance—of a job. In design, efficiency is straight lines and easy-to-clean surfaces—utilitarian and unadorned. No elaboration slows it down or gets in the way of getting things done. Form follows function to the simplest "fit" between an object, its user, and use. It's the precision styling of a keyboard molded to the shape of your hand and the effectiveness of things that are good at what they do.

» Take a "bottom-line" approach to the design of any work space—but not to the exclusion of other energies or your work will be perfunctory and heartless.

Because efficiency is the shortest distance between two points, it saves time, money, and energy. In home design, efficiency means low-maintenance, easy-to-care-for environments that free up your energy for other things. And from the point of view of enlightened design, it does not sacrifice the other energies of the mandala.

» Write down your most compelling design inspiration. Divide it into practical steps. Now take the first step toward making it happen (get paint/paper samples, call the carpet store to measure your floors).
» Research and incorporate into your home as many energy-efficient measures as you can.

Efficient homes facilitate doing—loving, parenting, working, learning, socializing—and growing. When your home no longer "grows corn for you," it's time to move on. Energy is *about* moving on.

Goals

From a contemplative point of view, the ultimate goal of energy is an awake state of mind. Energy and mind move together; like the wind, where energy goes, the mind follows. In design, wakefulness translates into the upliftedness of your space. Upliftedness *releases* energy that is stuck or spinning its wheels. In Tibetan tradition, upliftedness is called a "breeze of delight."

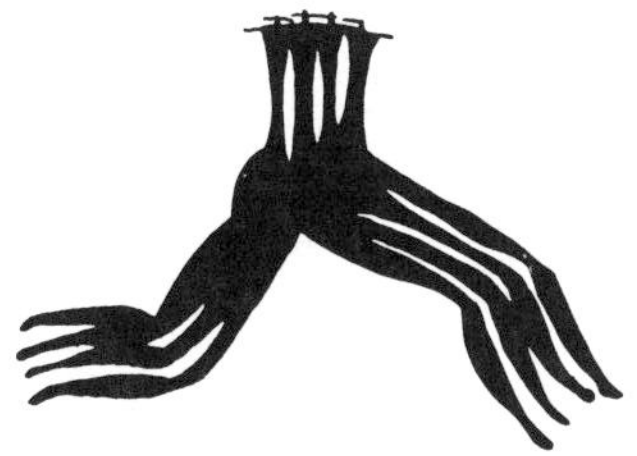

African Bushman rock figure.

BREEZE OF DELIGHT

You can uplift the energy of any space (or let it slide). Uplifting the environment begins with uplifting your mind. In the Tibetan tradition, this is called "raising windhorse."[1] There are formal and informal practices for doing this, which are beyond the scope of this book. If you are interested in pursuing them, please see "References and Further Readings" for recommended books. Here are two preliminary exercises to rouse energy in yourself and your space.

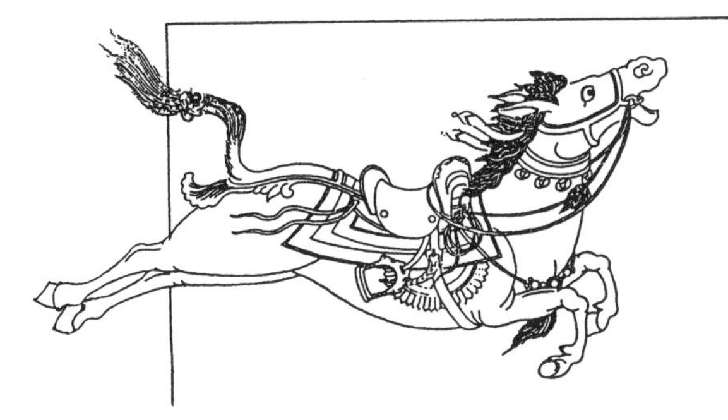

ROUSING YOURSELF

To rouse yourself, first take a good posture—erect, alert, eyes open. Then come to a full stop! Stop the discursiveness of your mind, emotions, sense perceptions. Hold that moment. Then feel the living, vibrating, energy of your world—the energy of heaven, of earth, and of everything in between. Hold . . . and *abruptly* let go. Take a deep breath, raise your gaze, and take a fresh start. Energy is *always* available to you. Rousing your mind tunes you in to that.

ROUSING THE ENVIRONMENT

To rouse the energy of the environment, start by noticing (not analyzing) how and where energy feels stuck—in depression, in speed, in confusion. Feel it in your body/mind and senses. Then—as above—come to a full stop. Straighten your posture. Connect with the dynamic energy flowing in- and outside of yourself, above and below. Hold that feeling . . . and abruptly let go. Project a breeze of delight into the space to clear the air; see the space in that light. (This brings energy, not obstacles, back into focus.) And again, let go! Take the first practical step that suggests itself to you after that.

» You may have to literally/physically "clear" a space in order to be able to rouse energy there. Go back and reread "Purifying the Environment" in Chapter 19 for more on this topic.
» Replace dead flowers with live ones. Arrange flowers so their greenery and main stems point upward toward the sun. They will bring ascending energy into the space. Leaves (and other elements of visual design) that point down take your energy in the same direction.
» Arrange furniture to promote the *flow* of energy and choose energetic colors, shapes, and surface design. Remove tarnish, rust, dust, and dirt from surfaces to rouse energy.
» Circulate a breeze of delight through your home with flags, fountains, dynamic colors and surface designs, and representations of wildlife, swimming fish, and sailing ships. Sports equipment and mechanical things—clocks, computers, the electric teakettle, and TV—also perk things up. (Fluttering banners and crossed swords on the wall would have done the job in your medieval castle.)

Energy can be channeled for specific purposes. If, however, it's too forceful, blocked, or misdirected (by oddly shaped rooms or poor placement of furniture, doors, and windows), those goals aren't reached. Treat interior energy like a good irrigation system: channel it into your space, promote good circulation throughout, and regulate it properly to avoid floods and drought.

40

FLOW

THE FLOW OF ENVIRONMENTAL ENERGY mirrors our internal circulation of ch'i. It distributes the vitality of earth, water, fire, and wind throughout the "body," dispels waste, and creates continuous change and activity along the way.

- Walk through your house visualizing your movement as a gently flowing river. Is your journey smooth—or obstructed and gnarly? How many times do you trip on unruly carpets, hit your shins on furniture, step over wastebaskets or wires? Do some interior landscaping to make the "river" flow smoothly.
- Now visualize your everyday tools and utensils "flowing" through your hands. Is the passage smooth—or awkward, uncomfortable, unwieldy? Notice how your furniture affects your energy (does it breathe? is it gentle or bruising?) and your posture (is it conducive to wakefulness or sloth?). Good design is essential for good energy flow.

Do not enjoy idleness; learn from flowing water which never decays. Therefore during both day and night always be gently in motion. Let your movement come from your creative nature, like the sun, moon and stars. Be a spontaneous expression of life without asking anything in return.
—HUA-CHING NI

Healthy Energy Flow

Healthy energy flow is *dynamic*, from Greek roots meaning "powerful" and "able." It's connected with renewal of physical health—especially the healing of wounds and bones, healthy pregnancies, mental/physical growth—and vitality.

- Use the qualities of energy—the element wind, the color green, and all of their sensory associations—to renew health. Rely on all of your sense perceptions when you need to channel energy into recovery.
- Uplift yourself and the environment with real and representational movement in design (mobiles, fountains, mechanical devices, equestrian pictures, a kite)

as well as *implied* movement (an eagle perched on a rock ledge, an archer with drawn bow, symbolic wings, or the feather of a high-flying bird—all imply flight).

THE PATH OF ENERGY

When you think of energy flowing through your house, think of meandering footpaths in nature (nature abhors straight lines). When you arrange your furniture in space, think of it as landscape design. Within the framework of your four walls, you can create a dynamic mandala. Here are some basic suggestions.

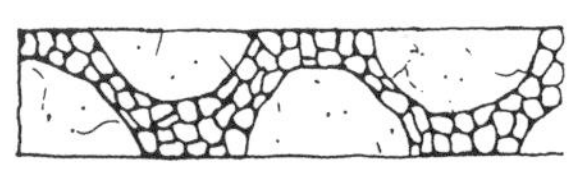

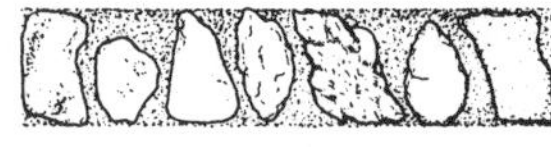

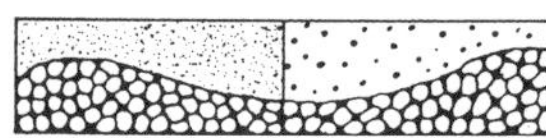

Japanese pathway designs

- » Arrange furniture to channel energy easily through rooms. In large rooms, islands of furniture surrounded by space allow energy to circulate easily. Use rugs to map out focus areas and pathways.
- » Avoid lining furniture up along the walls; it creates a boxed-in center space and too many (speedy) right angles.
- » Create asymmetrical arrangements of furniture and pictures to keep energy moving through space. Symmetrical or parallel arrangements create closure, which literally closes space up.
- » Choose furniture that allows energy to circulate and avoid pieces upholstered down to the floor. Don't stuff the space under beds with storage. (There are various feng shui remedies to activate blocked energy, but it's better to choose open furniture and to open up space.)

Energy flows along the course of least resistance, creating energy "paths." Most of us instinctively avoid the path of energy when we sit down to do something, when we choose a table in a restaurant, when we go to sleep. But sometimes we overlook the obvious. Avoid placing people or furniture in the path of flowing energy or both will be disrupted.

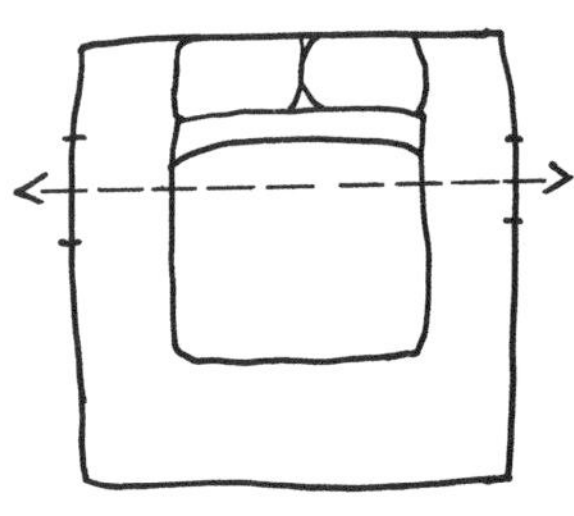

- » Don't put your bed, sofa, dining table and chairs, or office desk in the path of energy—which means directly in front of a door, between two facing doors or windows, or between a window and door. It will disrupt your physical and mental focus.
- » Divert traffic patterns and flowing energy (by rearranging furniture or creating boundaries) from conversation, work, or dining areas or they will sabotage the success of your gatherings.

Unhealthy Energy Flow

Healthy energy flow is gentle and continuous. Unhealthy energy is either deficient (stagnant or blocked) or excessive (too speedy or forceful).

STAGNANT ENERGY

Stagnant energy isn't the same as *stillness*, which is a healthy, restorative energy vibration. Stagnant or obstructed energy isn't serving its purpose and leads to dysfunction and disease. It needs to be unblocked or uplifted.

» To get stagnant energy moving, identify bottlenecks. Remove large objects blocking hallways, windows, or doors and rearrange furniture to promote energy flow. Remove dust, dirt, and clutter so energy can shine through. (See "Purifying the Environment," in Chapter 19.)

» Uplift the environment using the sense perceptions—dynamic colors, fresh air, a picture of cantering horses, a wind harp (for more examples, reread "Bringing Energy Home," in Chapter 38). Introduce the qualities of clarity, warmth, and richness to restore the environment.

EXCESS ENERGY

Excess energy is too speedy or forceful. It disrupts space, causing unsettled, angry, or upset feelings. Energy that rushes through a home is like a meal eaten on the run—it washes away virtue and deposits nothing of value.

» To remedy excessive energy, *slow it down*. Set up a barrier (a floor screen, statuary, or plants), redirect energy (by realigning furniture), or send it back (using a mirror remedy).

A standard arrangement, in traditional homes with large center halls, was to place a massive round table in the hall (on a suitable rug) to slow incoming energy. Topped with a dramatic plant or container of flowers, it created a beautiful visual focus (slowing mental energy) while physically redirecting traffic and incoming ch'i.

» A staircase ending at an outside door is an energy "chute." To redirect the energy, rehang the door or hang a mobile or crystal between the staircase and the door to act as a foil and prevent energy from rushing through the space.

CUTTING ENERGY

Metal, literally and figuratively, cuts materials such as paper and wood. The slats of metal blinds/Levelors send "cutting" energy into space. Metal furniture, accessories, or sculptures can cut you off from gentler natural energies. (See "References and Further Readings" for more on this topic.)

» Replace metal blinds with the softer energy of paper or fabric shades—which also bring the curvaceous shadow shapes of nature into your home—or with interior wooden shutters.

Cutting energy from sharp angles may come from outside: from the corner of a neighbor's home, a rock formation, a billboard, or speeding cars coming your way.

» Use a small mirror to send speedy or cutting energy back out of the space (place it on the outside of your home, reflecting the problematic ch'i). If street traffic is pointed toward your front door, hang a small mirror there to prevent it from speeding into your home.

STRAIGHT LINES AND SHARP ANGLES

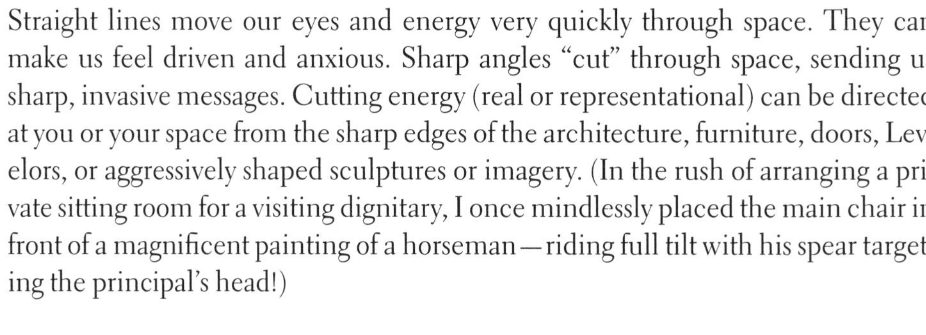

Straight lines move our eyes and energy very quickly through space. They can make us feel driven and anxious. Sharp angles "cut" through space, sending us sharp, invasive messages. Cutting energy (real or representational) can be directed at you or your space from the sharp edges of the architecture, furniture, doors, Levelors, or aggressively shaped sculptures or imagery. (In the rush of arranging a private sitting room for a visiting dignitary, I once mindlessly placed the main chair in front of a magnificent painting of a horseman—riding full tilt with his spear targeting the principal's head!)

» Walk through your house and identify areas with too many straight lines and sharp angles. Rearrange furniture to open angles up and redirect their energy; soften straight structural lines with fabrics or plants. Use furniture, artwork, and accessories to bring curves and physical weight into the space to slow energy down (include the vibrational weight of deep, rich color). You will find you have integrated space, warmth, and richness into the room.

OBJECT REMEDIES

The best way to regulate energy is to restore harmony among the five energies before relying on object remedies (crystals, mirrors, flutes, and so on). In some cases, a space should just be avoided, not remedied. Sometimes, however, object remedies are helpful and effective in correcting environmental influences and—more important—your awareness of them. Awareness will protect you from negativity (and in some cases, remind you to move on). Many excellent feng shui books are available if you would like to know more about object remedies (see "References and Further Readings" for suggestions), and I have suggested several simple ones above. But keep in mind, there is more to object remedies than meets the eye and much to learn.

Transitional times and places are particularly vulnerable to energy imbalances. Here are some suggestions for preventing and correcting them.

Regulating Energy in Transitional Times and Places

Transitional times and places are considered "dangerous" primarily because we don't pay attention to them. When we're in transition, with a foot in both worlds, we're off-center (imbalanced), easily distracted, and often unaware. This makes us vulnerable to attacks of negativity and accidents, and there are many traditional customs to correct that.

Changing seasons and changing times of day (sunrise, sunset) are times of transition. Traditionally, medical rituals are observed when the seasons change (herbal fortification in fall, cod liver oil and liver flush in spring). Prayers, chants, or rituals are done at the transitional times of dawn and dusk. Thresholds, doorways, foyers, halls, and stairs (transitional places) require the same vigilance.

THRESHOLDS

Thresholds are places of coming and going and represent, in Martin Heidegger's words, the "dependability of the middle which must never yield either way." Embodying the impermanence and discontinuity of our lives, they are good places for reminders of wakefulness.

» Thresholds are variously marked with mezuzahs, holy water fonts, protector deities, mirrors, prayers, and protective customs (removing shoes, taking off

outer garments, leaving your "sword" by the door. Have you ever noticed how dogs place their toys and bones in thresholds?) Wake up important thresholds in your home and in your life.

DOORS

The front door of your home—like your biological mouth—regulates energy flowing in and out. Maintain a balanced flow—no bingeing—to attract blessings and protect from excess.

» If your front door is one end of an energy "funnel," (vis-à-vis a back door or window), it will disrupt the wholeness of your house. If you can't move the back door, provide an energy "windbreak"—standing screen, hanging banner, or bank of plants—to keep energy from flying out the back.
» Erect a barrier (such as a freestanding wall) if your front door opens onto a powerful energy source (an ocean, a wind tunnel, street traffic coming toward your home) or if it's simply too big. If incoming energy is too invasive, you or your door may need to be moved.
» Doors tucked into or leading into small, dark, or complicated entryways need to be well lit, adorned with reflective objects (a mirror, shiny brass fixtures), and/or brightly painted so that energy flowing through them does not become confused, stuck, or "depressed."

FOYERS

Your foyer is a place to collect yourself before entering a new space. A moment of mindfulness can renew your energy. Many decorative customs throughout the world honor this tradition. (Go back and reread "Inviting Foyers," in Chapter 34, for more suggestions.) It's also an invitation to move on. Facilitate wakefulness and the flow of energy in your foyer.

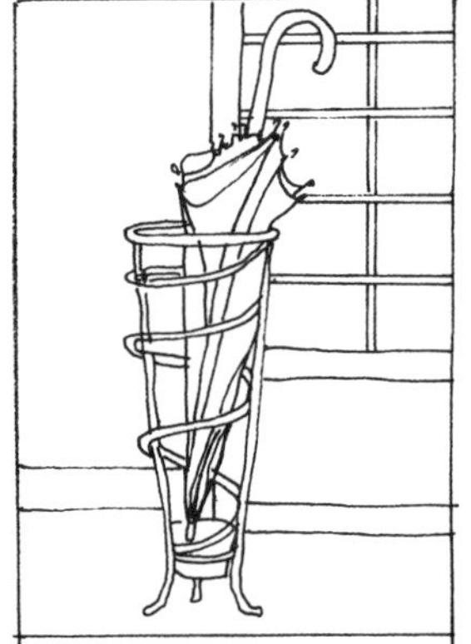

» For design ideas, study public foyers that are designed to manage energy flow beautifully and effectively. (Look at the lobbies of good hotels.)
» A warmly welcoming foyer must also be aware of guests' practical needs (umbrella stands, coat/hat hooks, shoe/boot racks).
» Don't use your foyer for unorganized storage or energy will get stuck there.
» If your house or apartment doesn't have a foyer, create an entry area. If you can, arrange furniture to set the boundaries, with an area rug, screen, sculpture,

plants, or floor-standing baskets to demarcate the space (or simply use an area rug with an umbrella stand). Then see what a difference it makes not to walk directly into the house.

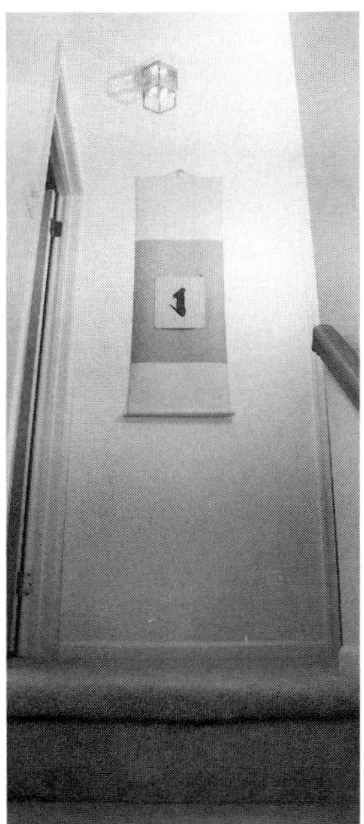

STAIRS

Many cultures have prayers and contemplations on the power of ascending and descending energy. Going up and down stairs joins heaven and earth. Use stairs to remind you of your aspirations (going up) and your mission in life (coming down the stairs).

» Hang an inspiring picture or image at the top of your stairs (not a good place for pictures of sunsets or demise). The opposite wall (over the descending stairs) is usually ignored—and usually very dead space—because it's difficult to reach. Adorn that wall with an image representing "blessings from above" or the energy you would like to bring down to earth. Make it simple and direct (a calligraphy, banner, or scroll), as you can't really study it coming down the stairs.

NOMADIC LIFESTYLES

Trungpa Rinpoche once remarked that it's very difficult for the drala (subtle energies) of richness to gather in our households because North Americans tend to live out of suitcases and move around too much.[1] For some cultures however, dwellings, like life, are designed to be impermanent.

» If your lifestyle is nomadic, learn how traditional nomads balance their lives by living in harmony with nature and natural cycles of time. Stabilize your life with the sun, moon, and seasons. Create stability at the center of your life and move around that. Keep significant reminders of your center (pictures, texts, objects—contemplative disciplines) with you on your travels.
» Consciously create seasonal homes and live on a seasonal "circuit." Make creative arrangements to rent, share, and exchange space.
» Find stillness within movement. Cultivate mindfulness practices and things that are timeless. Bring stillness to your mind and the moment.

Regulating the flow of energy creates a healthy home with a sense of purpose, or direction, which we will talk about next.

41

WORK

WORK IS SOMETHING WE DO OURSELVES. Unless you are ill or elderly, a certain amount of personal work is needed to create a personal life and home. (All family members can learn to pick up after themselves, wash their dishes, and maintain their space.) Depending on others or depending on machines to do all our work creates an energy imbalance in the mandala.

Working at Home

The workplace is energy's signature site. In the home, its location is especially important if you are creating a home-based business. A business office needs to draw energy *in* from and project energy *out* to the world. Work areas benefit from "rising" energy (to the east) and are brought down by setting-sun energy in the west. A successful home office needs to command a good space and circulate ch'i from outside windows. To maximize the potential of working at home, balance the five energies in your workspace.

CLARITY AT WORK

Clarity provides boundaries for your work space, plus good light and intellectual inspiration. It organizes your office (with filing cabinets, bookshelves, desk organizers) and your time. It creates a peaceful space where you can focus on your projects and goals.

» To maintain home/work boundaries, use a second desk for personal and household paperwork, preferably in another room. (Some homes have kitchen offices or a built-in desk for preparing menus and paying bills.) If that's not possible, keep the two domains separate in your office.

RICHNESS AT WORK

Richness is the wealth of excellent reference books, journals, equipment, and supplies. It radiates dignity (your desk commands the room and door), stability (your workspace is not makeshift or vulnerable), and the "weight" of your work (even if you're a stand-up comedian, your livelihood is in earnest). Richness is the *abundance* of work coming your way.

» Bring earthy materials (wood, stone, clay pots) and opulence (a power object, an heirloom, a very good pen) into your work space. Create a wealth corner there: if you can, place it in the southwest corner, where magnetizing and enriching energies meet. (Stand in the center of the room and face the door, which is east; west is behind you, south is to your right, southwest is their junction.) Use gold colors and good energy. Frame a meaningful picture (connected with your inspiration) in a goldleafed (not metal) frame to support creative energy.

If we use our work life as a tool for healing, we can transform our lives into an emotional and spiritual gold mine. We can do this by cultivating a peaceful center in ourselves in every situation our work presents. Whatever we do—office work, gardening, carpentry, painting, or writing—we can use the work as an expression of our peaceful inner nature. Try to find work that is naturally interesting to you, but also try to be interested in any work that you do.

—TULKU THONDUP

WARMTH AT WORK

Warmth creates an attractive workspace. You want to be there and feel good when you are. Creative energy blossoms, with an amusing screen saver, a found object, a child's painting—and beauty (defined by you). The allure of the elements (a clear bowl of water, a candle, a sand tray) and the senses (music, a vase of lavender) go to work with you. Warmth provides comfortable chairs and a tea table for consults with clients. It puts heart in the space where you work (and pictures of loved ones on your desk).

» Bring interesting furniture and accessories into your office. Put your office in a room with a fireplace or wood stove if you can. Put flowers on your desk often.

ENERGY AT WORK

Energy is channeled through efficient office systems and time-/space-saving devices that make light of your work. It's flexible lighting, cordless phones, and portable/mobile equipment—and troubleshooting devices (surge protectors, screen savers) to keep things from going wrong. It's efficient traffic patterns throughout the space and all five energies working as an unbeatable team. Energy is the overall success of the space and the work that you do there.

» Choose accessories that keep energy moving (a rug protector under your chair, for instance, for easy rolling around). Energize the space with live plants (keep a mister scented with bergamot in your desk drawer).

» Don't put your desk directly in front of a door; you will feel overwhelmed by your work—especially if there's a window behind you. Place the desk facing the door but off to one side.

» Protect the floors of an in-house studio or workroom from the throes of creative work by tacking/stapling wall-to-wall canvas over the carpets or floor. (Use padding on bare floors for a more cushioned feeling. Canvas floors—found in stately traditional American homes—are soothing and impervious surfaces (a good balance for energy), easy to remove and made to get painted on!

Left to its own devices, energy can become too one-pointed. Spaciousness lightens things up.

SPACE AT WORK

Space is the openness you feel when you enter your office or studio. It ventilates energy's ambition and workaholic tendencies. It's a window for daydreaming and deep breathing to relieve stress. It helps you meet deadlines by letting you take breaks.

Spaciousness brings peripheral vision to energy's one-pointed goals. In *Speaking of Silence*, Mother Tessa Bielecki writes: "I think one of the greatest obstacles to contemplative living in this culture is the neurotic compulsion to work. We overwork. Now, work in itself is good, and it is an important element in contemplative life: it is not only humanizing and energizing, but it is also a good preparation for contemplation. But if we are neurotically compelled to work then that is an obstacle. Our work has to be balanced by play, which is an equally crucial dimension of contemplative life."[1]

» Hang out in your work space without a task or goal. Make yourself comfortable. Remember to breathe. Put your work in perspective. Put your inspiration in front of you, your problems behind you, and then begin to work!

Your office is a success if you enjoy working there and get things done. If you work in cooperation with all-accomplishing energy, your work will succeed.

Success

> When campaigning, be swift as the wind; in leisurely march, majestic as the forest; in raiding and plundering, like fire; in standing firm, firm as the mountains; as unfathomable as the clouds, move like a thunderbolt.
> —Sun Tzu

Things "work" when they succeed easily without efforting. The key to effortless success is *cooperation*—you and your house working together with the basic forces of nature. Earth is augmented by water, water is warmed by fire, fire needs wind, wind enlivens the whole mandala, which is accommodated by space. This kind of cooperation is the modus operandi of enlightened design.

» How cooperative is your environment? (Your bedroom works if it restores your body and mind; your kitchen and dining room work if they're a source of satisfaction.) Make a list of rooms that work for you and a list of those that don't. Diagnose the rooms that don't work by identifying their deficient/excess energies.

EXAMPLES OF NATURAL ENERGY OPPOSITIONS

The opposite of cooperation is conflict. Natural energy oppositions can be seen as conflicts of interest among the natural elements. They manifest as hot/cold, wet/dry, moving/still, heavy/light, wholeness/disintegration. Avoid natural energy oppositions for a successful space:

Placing a refrigerator next to an oven is to be avoided; it's an opposition of hot and cold, fire and water/ice. (Move the oven or place an insulating panel in between.)

Placing a bathroom near a kitchen creates a natural opposition of offering and eliminating, feeding and flushing. (Move the powder room, or at the very least, keep the seat down and the door closed.)

Blowing out candles is frowned upon in some traditions; it creates an opposition of wind and fire. (Snuff candles out instead.)

Having created a successful space, you will want to sustain your environment and protect it from harm—which is our next topic.

42

PROTECTION

> Attainments always arise with hindrances.
> —Tibetan Buddhist teaching

THE POWERFUL ENERGY OF THE NORTH is connected with protection. When its force is misdirected, agitated, or blocked, however, energy actually causes accidents, illness, and other misfortunes—creating *need* of protection. (In Chapters 7, 15, 23, 31, and 38, reread the section "Too Much of a Good Thing" for each of the five styles; their imbalances are all fueled by basic energy.) Energy's northern direction is often represented by the tortoise, with its heavy, hard shell. Throughout Asia, hexagonal patterns are woven into textiles and patterned into ceilings and floors for long life and protection from harm.

There are three basic kinds of protection—physical, energetic, and spiritual. Good home design provides protection through physical means; through alignment with subtler energies (including spirits, deities, *kami*, drala, and so on, depending on your tradition); and through spiritual alignment with cosmic principles and basic wakefulness.

Physical Protection

Physical problems are the ultimate outcome of energy imbalances—for which, prevention is the best cure. Reread Chapter 11, "Space is a Positive Context" to prevent problems before they happen.

SAFETY

Protect your personal safety with rug pads, handrails, night-lights, outdoor lights, smoke and carbon monoxide detectors (if necessary).

- Childproofing and elder care require special measures. Ask your pediatrician or library for guidelines. Get a pamphlet on special safety features for the elderly from your local senior center. It should list local suppliers and installers of safety devices.

LIGHT AND DARK

- Protect your home from exposure to intense summer sun with old-fashioned canvas awnings or cloth roller shades. They create mellow light and peaceful interiors—and eliminate the cutting energy of venetian blinds and Levolors. But keep an open mind: Levolors and slatted windows work well on the ground floor, where shades can't afford privacy, and on windows where strong sun beats in. They are favored in the tropics, where the sharp contrasts of strong sun and shadows balance each other—and disintegrate fabrics. In such situations, interior shutters also work well.
- If you live in the glow of street lights, install curtains or window shades that provide maximum light protection, especially in the bedroom.
- Protect interior space from the energy of darkness outside, which can be enervating or threatening. Gather energy inside after dark and create a greater sense of well-being by drawing your curtains—unless you're gazing at the moon!

NOISE

- Protect your home from outside noise with double-pane windows, weather stripping, and soundproofing. Locate sleeping areas away from busy streets. Subdue interior noise with soundproofing and well-padded carpeting. Install rubber stripping around doors to stop their slamming. Control a very noisy space with heavy drapes on windows and between rooms with no doors (popular in Victorian homes). Keep a pair of earphones or earplugs in your office at home for unavoidable loud noise; they prevent hearing loss and let you keep working in peace.
- Eliminate electronic devices that disrupt the environment in the name of "protection"—too-sensitive car alarms or complex home-protection systems. Boycott noisy, battery-driven toys for your children.

THE SIX EVILS

Environmental dangers in the form of "aberrant" energies are traditionally described in Chinese medicine as *natural* dangers called the "six evils" (including excessive heat, cold, damp, dryness, and so forth). "In present times," writes Daniel Reid, "these have been eclipsed in magnitude and danger by man-made energies such as the 'dry-heat' of central heating; the 'dry-cold' of air conditioning; the 'evil winds' of microwave radiation and artificial electromagnetic fields; the internal 'damp-heat' of white sugar, alcohol, and chemical drugs; and other artificial industrial sources of abnormal energies that wreak havoc with the natural balance and patterns of human energies."[1]

» Protect against exposure to extremes of heat and cold—including drafts or stuffiness due to lack of fresh air. Overheating is a major problem in most of our living and work spaces. Avoid extremes of heat/cold in visual—and other sensory—environments.
» To protect yourself from manufactured pollution, reread Chapter 12, "Space and Time."
» Learn more about how other traditions work with aberrant energy and what they recommend to restore balance. (See "References and Further Readings" for suggestions.)

FEAR

We should take sensible measures to protect our homes from obvious dangers. An overemphasis on problems, protection, and remedies, however, may indicate a fearful state of mind or poor quality of life in your present location. At some point, you may need to shift from remedy to relocation—and to cultivate your sense of unconditional well-being. Energy is especially connected with fear and the development of fearlessness. The best and only fail-safe protection is an awake mind and a loving heart.

Examples of Tibetan "armor" pattern, based on the tortoise shell, can be found on textiles, thankas (scroll paintings), walls, and floors.

Subtle Energy Protection

Energy take many forms—seen and unseen. From the gross physical plane (earth) to the heavenly realms, subtle energies—as deities, spirits, drala, angels, or "helpful energies," depending on your tradition—join heaven and earth. They can be embodied in trees, rocks, animals, the elements, and human conduct and can empower people, places, and things. When imbalances are tamed, helpful energies can be invoked into your home mandala.

MYTHIC HOME

Home is a natural "landing pad" for subtle energies, which are traditionally invited *into* a space. World mythologies describe their fancy for caves, granaries, ritual enclosures, wells, magical circles—and the mythology of home is enlivened by spirit. Michael Dames describes a house without gods as a "mythless shell." Helpful subtle energies restore the connection.

INVOKING HELPFUL ENERGIES

Customs abound for propitiating subtle energies and invoking blessings when laying a foundation and building a house (placing the first beam, pouring the first slab, putting the roof on). These include offerings of food, wine, smoke, and precious objects, as well as honorific behaviors (circumambulating, bowing, clapping, prostrating). "To some," writes Mary Low, "this might seem like 'magic' or naked superstition, to others it is the body-language of prayer."[2]

» To expand your understanding of protection in a broader sense, contemplate the continuum of energy between visible and invisible realms. Learn one ritual, one custom, one daily practice to invoke that energy; look for examples in art and architecture.

Invocations of the four directions, above and below, as well as the powers of local animals, birds, trees, rocks, and water are traditionally made with offerings of food, drink, incense, and prayers for the benefit of beings on earth. Local customs and warnings abound ("Don't kill the house snake," "Don't cut the birch tree"). The subtle energies of natural elements are called on for specific blessings and protection (water protects from fire, fire from cold, earth from famine, wind from obstacles). Please go back to "Choosing Your Site," in Chapter 11, to review the protectors of the four directions.

DRALA

The Tibetan word for the subtle energies that empower the physical world is *drala*. Trangu Rinpoche, a close friend and colleague of Trungpa Rinpoche, was struck by Trungpa Rinpoche's remarks on drala in North America—and because this relates directly to our discussion here, I will quote him:

> Although America is a highly developed country . . . the people suffer inwardly from diminished or depressed life energy, or *yang*, and diminished or damaged drala. That was a problem that he found existing. . . . Because of this, because there was no [connection to] native tradition, there was much damage. There was damage to the customs of respect and kindness. So for one thing, people weren't happy, and for another, since it was a democracy, there was no situation where there could be mutual respect or love and kindness for people. Generally in other societies, the people respect those higher than they, and are kind to those lower (benevolent hierarchy), but this kind of custom has been lost here. . . . Another symptom of damaged drala is being homeless, and he noticed that people in America were always moving around and always thinking about moving: "I'm going to go to New York, and I think now I'll move to California . . ." Thinking in that way comes about from damaged drala. When drala is restored then a person starts to feel connected to one place and decide, "I'm going to stay here, this is my home," and gains more confidence in himself or herself.[3]

External drala (Tibetan, *dralha*) is completely connected with your internal drala (Tibetan, *drabla*): you can't have one without the other, as you will see below.

Spiritual Protection

In the West, we rely on mechanical means—alarms and electronic devices—for protection. Traditional cultures—East and West—teach that negative energies are symptomatic of the breakdown of internal virtue. The ultimate virtue is basic wakefulness. The best protection is to reconnect with the goodness of the environment. The best remedy is mindfulness/awareness; with it, you can prevent problems—and their causes.

» Consider working with a mindfulness discipline—meditation, T'ai Chi, yoga—to protect your physical and mental well-being.

» Work with the principles of heaven and earth and the four directions to prevent imbalances.

» Now ask yourself what are you protecting. Write down the things you most cherish. How can you best protect them? Create a sense of protection based on blessings.

43

OVERCOMING OBSTACLES TO SUCCESS

ENERGY CIRCULATES THROUGHOUT the whole house, overcoming any obstacles to space's working well. It especially rules work areas—and other functional areas of the house. We have just seen an example (Chapter 41) of how energy creates a work space.

Now we will see how to channel energy into specific areas.

Installation to Destroy Obstacles in Space

Energy's power, or action, is destroying: it destroys obstacles to vitality and success. The main obstacle is *laziness*—lazy energy and lazy, or unawake, states of mind. That's what energy destroys (not people, places, or things!). Trimming back an overgrown pathway, rearranging furniture that blocks energy flow, or rousing a lazy state of mind—all destroy obstacles to energy. Destroying action is administered in small doses—its purpose, after all, is to free up the full spectrum of energy, not to call attention to itself. To intensify energy, remove obstacles.

Then "rouse" energy—with a flourishing plant, wind chimes, a faceted crystal, a spotlight—in strategic places. These are your energy "installations"; use them as acupuncture points along meridians of flowing energy—in *small* doses. (What's important is the energy *flow* and not the point.) Put them along the sight line of a particular room, in your work space—anyplace that needs a lift. Use them in "pointed" ways to channel energy into specific locations.

Installations will mushroom as projects, a flourishing business, a dynamic household. At summer equinox, energy is a busy garden (arrange a sampling in your foyer to celebrate the season). Indoors energy is fresh green color, a bank of plants, a large decorative fan. It is images of birds in flight, busy bees, galloping horses. It might take the form of a dynamic sculpture, a flower, or an object arrangement (try tubes, pipes, and functional objects), a fountain of running water, mechanical toys, or a spotlight.

Remedies for Excess

Clarity provides the intention of the space so energy has a place to go—and boundaries to keep it from going haywire. It's plumbing and wiring systems, and intellectual understanding of tasks and equipment (owner's manuals, diagrams, technical instructions).

Richness stabilizes energy and rounds it out—preventing stressful, unsettling environments. It's the weight of furniture, objects, and building materials that keeps energy from spinning out of control.

Warmth brings joy to hard work (flowers on your desk) and prevents insensitive environments and interpersonal negativity. (For meals on the run, it's an English picnic basket with hand-painted china.)

Space provides room to move. Without spaciousness, energy is confined and too intense. Space, in the end, is how the whole thing hangs together.

Summing Up Energy

Direction	*Color*	*Element*	*Season*	*Symbolic shape*
North	Green	Wind	Summer	Triangle

Wisdom All-accomplishing wisdom

In design Energy flow/movement, direction, efficiency, upliftedness, protection, success

Imbalance Speedy, restless, insensitive, impatient, driven

Signature sites Work space, office, basement, garage; sport/exercise areas; transitional areas (pathways, doorways, halls, and stairs)

Animals Swift-footed (like the wind)—horse, antelope, greyhound, big cats (traditionally, the snow lion), and birds in flight

CONCLUSION

PUTTING IT ALL TOGETHER

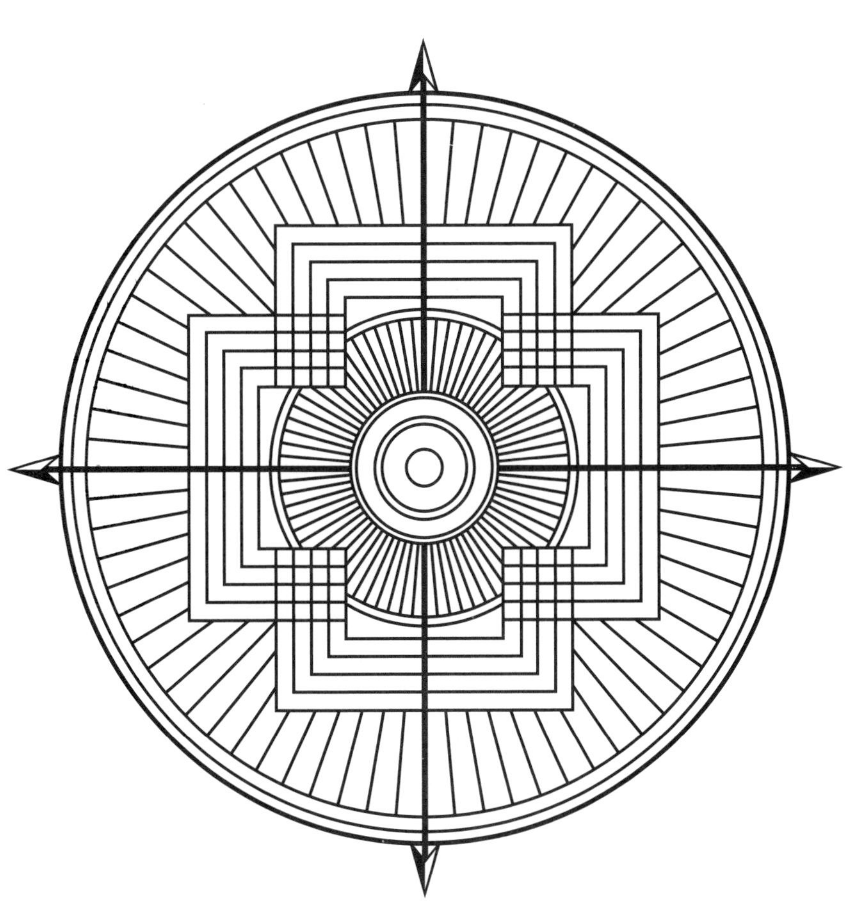

44

HOW TO DIAGNOSE YOUR HOME

THE WORLD DOESN'T NEED HEALING or saving, teaches Lakota Sioux elder Howard Badhand, "she's invincible. You just have to learn how the world works." If we align our homes and lives with heaven, earth, and the four directions, we are reconnecting with the way the world works. Healing begins at home.

Healing begins with a vision of health: imagine the sun in a cloudless sky and a peaceful, rich, inviting, vital world around you. *Diagnosis* identifies any obstacles to that (they stick out like sore thumbs). Combine intellect and intuition to learn more. Intellect will take you through the systematic process described in this chapter; intuition is more spontaneous.

INTUITION AND INTELLECT

Intuition is heart—feelings, associations, insight, and inspiration. Your personal relationship with the five styles of energy is living and real. You are making real observations and connections. You are the key that unlocks their magic and power in your home.

Intellect supplies your objective tools—theory and analysis, house plans, compass readings, the history of the house and its inhabitants. Go through the house once for first impressions and again for in-depth analysis.

Now Is the Time, This Is the Place

STEP 1. APPROACHING THE HOUSE

Begin with your approach to the house. What are the surroundings like? What do you notice about the landscaping, lot, pathway, and porch? How do you feel approaching the front door? Notice colors, stairs, lighting.

STEP 2. ENTERING THE SPACE

Entering the space engages all of your senses, including your mind (thoughts/emotions). Again, rouse a sense of health and well-being. Then, let go. Enter the space with an open mind (and no distractions).

STEP 3. HEAVEN AND EARTH

Be aware of the balance/imbalance of heaven and earth as you continue through the space. It will provide all the clues you need as to causes of unsettling energy and will help determine your "treatment plan."

HEAVEN AND EARTH

Heaven	*Earth*
The grand scheme of things	Details (hardware, trim, and moldings)
Ideal room design (include dreams, fantasies)	The reality of electrical outlets, phone jacks, heating vents, traffic patterns—and money
A panoramic view	Glare/reflections dealt with
Vision of a cheerful space	Dead flowers removed, plants watered, fish/birds and people cared for
Roof and ceilings	Basement and floors
Spiritual energy	The material world
Uplifted	Down-to-earth

STEP 4. THE FOUR DIRECTIONS

Take a compass reading to determine the four cardinal directions. Where do planetary energies rise and set? How do they affect your home? Please go back to "Choosing Your Site," in Chapter 11, to review the dralas of the four directions.

STEP 5. THE FIVE STYLES OF ENERGY

Then, walk through the house. What is going on in each room (work, study, dining, socializing, sleeping, bathing)? Identify the energy connected with that room (richness, clarity, and so on), its quadrant of the mandala (south, east, and so on), its qualities and practical associations. What qualities are missing?

Remember that all five energies must circulate *throughout* the house, but each of them rules specific areas/activities. Go through a mental checklist:

Space opens things up; experienced as letting be, accommodation, flexibility and change, sacredness; pervades the whole house; is connected with centering, sleep, and relaxation.

Clarity pacifies space; experienced as light energy (intellect), focus, form, organization, meaning, purity, healing, simplicity, peace; connected with water and with peace, a peaceful bedroom, and library/study (focused thought).

Richness expands/enriches space; experienced as wealth/abundance, stability, weight, good quality, generosity, presence/power, dignity, splendor; connected with earth, overall abundance, and especially kitchens and dining rooms.

Warmth magnetizes energy in space; experienced as color, passion, pleasure, playfulness, hospitality, harmony, and beauty; connected with fire and with intimate spaces, social areas—and elegant art and design.

Energy destroys obstacles in space; experienced as flow/circulation, direction, efficiency, production, upliftedness, success, protection; connected with wind and overall vitality, especially work areas—and keeping everything in working order.

» Design a table setting for each of the five styles. What kind of cuisine would you choose for clarity, richness, warmth, energy? How would you set the table (colors, centerpiece) and serve the guests (formal service, home-style)?

Through the apertures of human anatomy, the architecture of the cosmos enters its sentient home.

—MICHAEL DAMES

THE FIVE STYLES AND YOUR PHYSICAL HEALTH

The mandala of five energies pertains to any bounded space, including your body. (The teachings of Tibetan medicine are rooted in it.) Many cultures (including Indian, African, and Irish) model the construction of their homes after the structure of the human body and, by extension, the physical universe. The spine is most commonly the central pillar, with a center, or "heart" space, in the middle of the house. Michael Dames writes of the "Cosmos-House-Human amalgam" and refers to the description in hatha yoga texts of the "house with one column [the spine] and nine doors."

Personal and universal alignment take place in your home. Working with your physical environment will directly affect your physical health. Here is a simple checklist:

Space: rest/sleep, relaxation, peace of mind; yoga, T'ai Chi, or basic body work (to open up the physical space).

Clarity: purity—of all of your physical systems, including your food and water; connected with self-discipline (dietary/physical regimens).

Richness: nourishment—good food, good digestion, and physical strength.

Warmth: bodily pleasure—a happy heart, good circulation, and strong liver.

Energy: tonification of the body—easy breathing, physical exercise, and overall flow of ch'i.

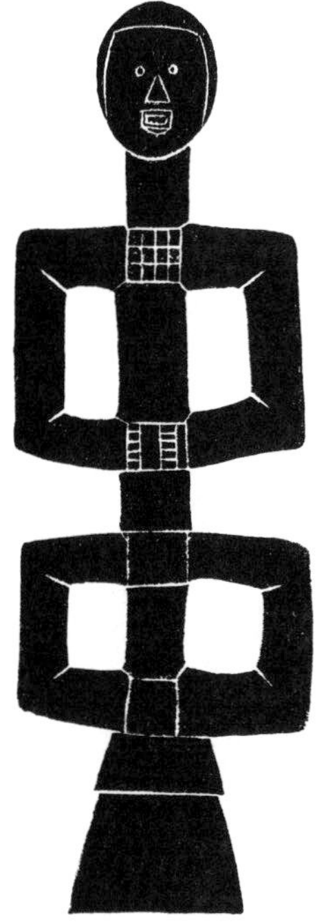

Zulu carved wooden figure, Republic of South Africa.

45

AMBIENT HOME

THE WORD *ambient* means "surrounding" or "encircling" (like ambient sound or ambient air). Ambient home is the *world* in which we live. Use nature's design—and all of the senses—to realign your world with space, clarity, richness, warmth, and energy.

I had three chairs in my house: one for solitude, two for friendship, three for society.

—HENRY DAVID THOREAU

THE MAGIC OF THE SENSE PERCEPTIONS

The purity of a snow-white napkin next to your plate is all the purity in the world. The fire on your hearth or the end of a match is cosmic fire. The water in your shower is the rain that joins heaven and earth. The air that you breathe is the breath of life.

Use the sense perceptions to awaken the ordinary magic of public space. And use them to work with the environment in times of tragedy, sickness, or death. They can communicate caring, if not relief, to very dark times and places. Sensory remedies for difficult situations—from the simplest flower or food offering to state-of-the-art hospital design—occur on a daily basis all over the world, with powerful, if unsung, effects on our quality of life.

CASE HISTORY

One summer evening, I was serving as chaplain in a local hospital where a toddler died, the result of a tragic home accident. Because the parents were in no way ready to relinquish their child's body, we appealed to a kindly ER staff to find us a room for the night. The best they could do, however, was a stainless-steel room with fluorescent lights, plastic chairs, and drastically lowered temperature. Here the distressed parents were able to hold their child and come to grips with death.

To comfort them in their agony, we created a more comforting space. From the maternity ward came wooden rocking chairs, and from the laundry, warm blankets; from the corner market, flowers, and from the church, tall votive candles (whose comforting glow was mercifully overlooked by the staff). Over the next twelve hours, as relatives and friends arrived from all over the country, soup and bread arrived from the all-night supermarket. During that long night, a great deal of support and compassion were extended to a grieving family—not only in words but in space.

Heaven and Earth in the World

> Traditionally it is said that, when human beings live in harmony with the principles of heaven and earth, then the four seasons and the elements of the world will also work together harmoniously. . . . But if human beings violate their connection, or lose their trust in Heaven and Earth, then there will be social chaos and natural disasters.
>
> —Chögyam Trungpa

When heaven and earth are out of balance, the world is like the Wizard of Oz—a head without a body. We can begin healing our cultural relationship with the natural world by design, following the same principles we applied at home. There are countless examples throughout the world from which to learn.

EXAMPLES IN NATURE

Nature shows us how to restore balance with simple examples such as the rain (heaven) that softens the soil (earth), which promotes growth (man), and the rainbows bridging heaven and earth like the magical bridges in shamanic traditions made of smoke, clouds, ladders, or rope.

EXAMPLES IN HUMAN AFFAIRS

In Western civilization, a man's necktie is a vestige of the magical rope (and shamanic power) that once joined the worlds of above and below.[1]

In earlier European cultures, dowsing (earth) and astronomy (heaven) were combined to create agricultural boundaries in accord with natural order.[2]

Spiritual traditions that practice in nature—and not in manufactured structures—relate to heaven and earth as sacred space.

Ritual bowing joins heaven and earth; and all martial arts are based on these principles. If you're a writer, your computer joins your inspiration (heaven) and your literary production (earth).

Sacred architecture around the world—cathedrals, temples, mosques, stupas, pagodas, tori gates—is designed to join heaven and earth. The great Asian sites of Borobadur in Indonesia and the once magnificent Nalanda University in India are three-dimensional mandalas of the four directions and monumental examples of joining heaven and earth by design.

Domestic architecture did the same. Traditional Swiss farmhouses were built on three levels: a lower level housing livestock, a middle living area, and a top level for sleeping quarters and storage. (The animals provided valuable heat and humidity, which rose up through the living levels.) Traditional Japanese houses were also built with above and below "zones": an earthen entry level, higher areas with wooden floors, and areas of highest regard covered in tatami—topped with massive symbolic straw roofs.[3]

The symbolism of a Tibetan style stupa is based on the five basic shapes/energies and their wisdoms.

JOINING HEAVEN AND EARTH THROUGH RITUAL

We have public and private rituals for love and marriage, fertility, birth, sickness, death—and rites of passage for everything in between; as well as seasonal rituals, rituals for natural elements, the rituals of birds and animals; and private rituals for eating, sleeping, and purifying ourselves. Domestic architecture is imbued with rituals for construction, pathways, gates, and thresholds. Home—once the seat of sacred rituals and spirit guests—is still the site of the Sabbath and of prayers and rituals of everyday life.

» Learn more about the rituals in wisdom traditions. Think of them as ways to organize human affairs. Think of small daily rituals as ways to organize life in public spaces—restaurants, offices, parks. (Your ritual afternoon tea could create an intimate tea shop in your town.)

The Four Directions in the World

Ed McGaa explains the sacred meaning that the number four has for Native American people:

> There are four faces, or ages: the face of the child, the face of the adolescent, the face of the adult, the face of the aged. There are Four Directions or four winds, four seasons, four quarters of the universe, four races of man and

woman—red, yellow, black, and white. There are four things that breathe: those that crawl, those that fly, those that are two-legged, those that are four-legged. There are four parts to the green things: roots, stem, leaves, fruit. There are four divisions of time: day, night, moon, year. There are four elements: fire, water, air, earth. Even the human heart is divided into four compartments.[4]

Plaited prayer mat from Zanzibar, Tanzania.

The mandala of the four directions has universally been—with various interpretations—the foundation of kingdoms, cities, villages, temples, and homes. Nigel Pennick describes the four provinces of ancient Ireland, "with Tara—seat of the high kings—at its geomantic center, where "centre stood for kingship, the North was reserved for the warrior caste, the east for craftspeople, the South for musicians, and the West for the learned."[5] Some early cultures aligned "sacred and profane" affairs with the four directions. Eleanor Lynn Nesmit describes the first Roman forum, with "political facilities to the West, while religious structures were clustered to the East."[6] Use the directional axes to design malls, social centers, cities.

» Consider the east-west energies of the sun and moon when you plan special events. Do you want rising- or setting-sun energy for your wedding? Do you want to launch your new business on the waxing or waning moon?

The Five Styles in the World

You can set up your world the same way you set up your home.

SPACE IN THE WORLD

Space is connected with our sacred ground—and the sacredness of ordinary life in the world. No matter how large or small the physical space, it is open and receptive. Space allows you to relax and feel good in public places, accommodating the details of daily life so you can appreciate them.

» Choose a public place—school, hospital, mall—and consider how you would introduce the qualities of space.

To enhance the experience of space in public places, create boundaries (clarity); energy dissipates in undefined space. The millions of empty houses in this country are an example of spatial excess and adversely affect the environment.

CLARITY IN THE WORLD

Clarity is connected with libraries, schools, health/healing centers, hospitals—and all manner of organizations. In public spaces, clarity pacifies energy and gives it focus and form. It eliminates confusion and aggression. It is an antidote to violence.

» Choose a public place—a mall or community center—and consider how you would introduce clarity's light, boundaries, focus, form, meaning, simplicity, purity, and peace.

Clarity is channeled through cleansing and healing rituals, rituals of light, and sunrise ceremonies. Here is a simple sunrise prayer:

> When you get up in the morning, go outside and greet the sun, saying, "Good morning sun, good morning world, good morning middle world." Repeat this three times—once for spiritual power, or luminosity; once for the physical sun, earth, and everything in between; and once for the sun of basic goodness in your body, mind, and life.

» Celebrate winter solstice and the energy of the east with others. Include all of the senses and qualities of clarity. Use deep winter colors (blues, black/white, blue-purples, and silver) but balance them with warm colors; balance cold darkness with warm light (fire, candles, and the "light" of inspiration); balance nature's dormancy with abundant food and drink. Reflect clarity's clear seeing in round shapes (a crystal ball, a round mirror, a bowl of water).

RICHNESS IN THEWORLD

Richness is a world of well-being and abundance. It is connected with restaurants, malls, museums, and banks; jungles and teeming gardens and markets. It fosters a sense of dignity and community pride.

MENU

» Design a housing complex that radiates the qualities of richness: abundance (perhaps food), stability, diversity, dignity, generosity, splendor—and a sense of well-being.

Richness is channeled through ritual feasts, harvest festivals, and empowerment ceremonies.

» Celebrate richness at the fall equinox (September 21). It's time to harvest rewards and share the wealth. Include all of the senses. Create a golden decor with deep, rich music, earthy abundance, and rich fare. Include all the qualities of richness. Remember that the real power of richness is letting go: do a "giveaway." (The cross-quarter day, or halfway point, between the fall equinox and the winter solstice is Halloween, a remembrance of the dead.) Plant a community garden, share the work and rewards.

Colored and white rice paper banners create a festive entrance to a public space.

WARMTH IN THE WORLD

Warmth creates places for getting together for conversation and friendship (cafés, pubs, and community centers) and places for entertainment and pleasure (theaters, art galleries, dance halls, and parks). Warmth is the *heart* of our cultural life. Warmth is community. In some African tribes, there is no word for an individual house; the word *house* refers to community, the collective circle of dwellings, or village.

» Design a social services center to include the energy of warmth: color, hospitality, passion, pleasure, play, harmony, and elegance—and a sense of caring and joy.
» Research creative forms of community and housing for all stages of life. What human needs and desires aren't currently met in housing—within your own family, within your community?

Warmth is channeled through rituals of intimacy, hospitality, friendship, and communication.

» Celebrate the spring equinox with friends and lovers—and delightful fragrances, foods, intoxicating beverages, harmonious music, and so on. Include all the qualities of warmth, remembering that the real power of warmth is love.

ENERGY IN THE WORLD

Energy takes the form of work spaces (offices, retail stores, factories, and other commercial sites), all corridors of transportation/movement (airports, train/bus stations, and highways)—as well as sports arenas and gymnasiums. Energy brings vitality, efficiency, and workability to any public place.

» Consider how you would bring energy—movement, direction, workability, efficiency, upliftedness, and security—into a public place so the space really "works."

Energy is ritualized through rites of passage for successful journeying through all stages of life. They are an antidote for age-specific suffering of young and old. From a contemplative point of view, energy celebrates your chosen path.

» Celebrate the summer solstice with great fanfare. Include all of the senses (banners, flags, rousing music, and activities) and qualities of energy (vigor, efficiency—and a first-aid kit for protection). Remember, the real power of energy is moving on.

Bringing Enlightenment Home

> One never reaches home, but wherever friendly paths intersect, the whole world looks like home for a time.
> —Hermann Hesse

The five styles are like Halloween costumes—colorful displays in convincing shapes and forms. Taken too seriously, they become caricatures of themselves. Awareness lets us see the five styles as they really are—celebrations of space. Their conventions and rules are containers for wisdom that can't be contained; how we obey, break, or play with them is a question of balance.

The only way to implement our vision for society is to bring it down to the situation of a single household.
—Chögyam Trungpa

To work with the five energies properly, avoid the temptation to solidify them. When you find yourself saying "her house is so *this* style" or "he is so *that* style," say it knowing that it's not entirely so. The cultures, cuisines, landscapes, seasons, and psychological characteristics used to exemplify styles are just that—examples. Descriptions are gateways into the space we call our homes, our bodies, ourselves.

ARTISTS CHANGE THE WORLD

Enlightened design is about creating your home as a work of art, where *art* is defined as "enlightenment" and *decorating* is defined—in the true sense of the word *decorum*—as "how you live your life." From this point of view, you have the power to enlighten your life and your world by aligning your home with heaven and earth, the four directions, and the five basic energies that make us up.

NOTES

Preface

1. *Mandala* (Tibetan, *kyil kor*) means "center without fringe" and refers to the interdependence of things within the nature of emptiness. It is represented as a circle, sometimes within a square, and describes the basic workability of domestic, social, economic, and spiritual realities and the way they all work together. In the *I Ching*, mandala principle is described as the "diversity of sameness and the sameness of diversity."
2. Space awareness is a contemplative approach to working with energy in space, based on ancient Tibetan Buddhist Tantric teachings and the sitting practice of meditation. It studies both the enlightened and confused energies—physical, psychological, and spiritual—that make up our world and the specific forms they take. There are specific practices and postures related to each style of energy, which are done in specially shaped, monochromatic rooms of the appropriate color.

   Space awareness practices (and their environments) were originally designed by Chögyam Trungpa Rinpoche as a way of working with people too disturbed for formal practice, and they remain—as "maitri space awareness"—the heart of the contemplative psychology program at The Naropa Institute. They are also the foundation of contemplative arts and environmental design in this tradition and are taught in seminars and workshops at Shambhala and Buddhist centers listed in Appendix C.
3. Awake refers to a state of mind free from self-deception and habitual patterns of perception.
4. Chögyam Trungpa, Shambhala: *The Sacred Path of the Warrior*, p. 130.
5. *Geomancy* literally means "divination by means of lines and figures or by geographic features" (Middle English *geomancie*, from the Latin *geomantia* and the Greek *geomanteia*, "divination by signs from the earth"). It refers to land-based systems of interpretation used throughout the world to determine auspicious sites for building and burials and skillful ways of working with various levels of energetic influences.

Traditional symbols of the five wisdoms of each energy "family": buddha, vajra, ratna, padma, karma.

6. *Feng shui*—literally, "wind and water"—refers to the Chinese art and science of geomancy. Developed as a way to chart wind and waterways for irrigation, it was used to determine energetically appropriate burial sites for powerful ancestors (and ensure their continued influence). Domestic *feng shui* works, first, with the movement of energy and, second, with qualities of energy. Two main traditions—form and compass schools—utilize temporal/spatial tools such as astrology, compass and bagua (or metaphysical "map"), geographical formations, and energy pathways of all kinds to align energy with desirable influences, channel its movement, and focus its impact by shaping its "container."
7. *Lungta*, or "windhorse," in Tibetan tradition refers to the energy of basic goodness and is used to describe both the experience and formal practice of rousing that energy.
8. *Drala*, which literally means "beyond enemy or conflict," is the wisdom and power of nonduality that reverberate within us and in the world of our sense perceptions. It is invoked through proper conduct of body, speech, and mind.

Chapter 1: Home Truths

1. Susan Walker, ed. *Speaking of Silence: Christians and Buddhists on the Contemplative Way*, p. 293.
2. Jeremy Hayward quotes Greek Orthodox priest Father George Timko, *Sacred World*, p. 67.

Chapter 3: Heaven, Earth, and Man

1. Chögyam Trungpa, *Shambhala: The Sacred Path of the Warrior*, p. 134.

Chapter 4: The Four Directions

1. Michael Dames, *Mythic Ireland*, p. 17.
2. Sometimes the colors of east and center are reversed, in which case east is associated with white and center with blue. The reasons for this reversal are beyond the scope of this book.
3. Michael Dames, *Mythic Ireland*, p. 120.
4. Ibid., p. 152.
5. Ibid., p. 46.
6. Ibid., p. 63.
7. *Four actions*, or *four karmas*, are the dynamic principle of mandala and an expression of "authentic presence" (*Tibetan, wangthang*), which literally means "field of power." They are directly connected with how we experience and perceive the world.
8. Chögyam Trungpa, *Dharma Art*, p. 102.

Chapter 5: Five Styles of Energy

1. As originally taught by Trungpa Rinpoche, the five styles, or "Buddha families," were called by their Sanskrit names: *Buddha* (space), *vajra* (clarity), *ratna* (richness), *padma* (warmth), *karma* (action).
2. *Windhorse* was described by Trungpa Rinpoche as:

   > raising a wind of delight and power and riding on, or conquering, that energy. Such wind can come with great force, like a typhoon that can blow down trees and buildings and create huge waves in the water. The personal experience of this wind comes as a feeling of being completely and powerfully in the present. The horse aspect is that, in spite of the power of this great wind, you also feel stability. You are never swayed by the confusion of life, never swayed by excitement or depression. You can ride on the energy of your life. So windhorse is not purely movement and speed, but it includes practicality and discrimination, a natural sense of skill. (*Shambhala: The Sacred Path of the Warrior*, p. 114)

3. Energy is sometimes connected with spring (and the greening of nature) and warmth, with summer (and its seductiveness). Generally, however, warmth describes spring and the thaw that makes possible the high production of summer and the style called "energy."
4. Rudolf Arnheim, *The Dynamics of Architectural Form*, p. 242.

Chapter 6: The ABCs of Enlightened Design

1. James Hillman, from a transcript of "Beauty," a conference held by Pacifica Graduate Institute in San Francisco, CA, 1991.
2. Greg Van Mechelen, "A Home for the Whole Person," *Shambhala Sun*, March 1996.
3. Ibid.

Chapter 7: The Power of Space

1. This exercise was adapted with the kind permission of Jeremy Hayward.

Chapter 10: Creating Illusions

1. Marc Treib, *Tokyo: Form and Spirit*, (Walker Art Center/Harry Abrams, N.Y., 1986) p. 113.

Chapter 11: Space Is a Positive Context

1. The first of these analogies is from Mr. J.S. Shiah; the second is from Chögyam Trungpa, "The Pön Way of Life,"in *The Heart of the Buddha*, p. 226.

2. See Chögyam Trungpa's "The Pön Way of Life" for more on this topic. The tradition of tiger, lion, garuda, dragon, and windhorse was taught by Chögyam Trungpa Rinpoche in the context of the Shambhala teachings. (See his book *Shambhala: The Sacred Path of the Warrior* for further information.) Teachings on the symbolic animals specifically connected with geomancy were explained by him in "The Pön Way of Life," p. 226–27, and by the Venerable Thrangu Rinpoche in a talk at the Shambhala Center, Halifax, Nova Scotia, July 14, 1995, and printed in the Shambhala Center *Banner* 9, no. 6, November 1995. The tradition he describes is based on the teachings of Rolpe Dorje, "related to the Chinese system which goes back to Manjushri [who] resides in Mount Wu-t'ai Shan. . . . He manifested as the Emperor K'ang-hsi who was an emanated king and taught this method of prognostication." In this tradition, the animal of the north is the turtle, which in Tibet and India is represented by the snow lion.
3. Many full-service hardware and building supply stores sell/rent gaussmeters. To obtain an accurate reading, however, they must be able to measure both electric and magnetic components. If you are not knowledgeable about this technology, hire someone who is (and not from the electric company).

Chapter 13: Center without Fringe

1. M. C. Richards, *Centering in Pottery, Poetry, and the Person*, p. 24.
2. Anthony Antoniades, *Poetics of Architecture: Theory of Design*, New York: Van Nostrand Reinhold, 1990, p. 97.
3. Jeremy Hayward, *Sacred World*, p. 177.

Chapter 18: Defining Space

1. Gaston Bachelard, *The Poetics of Space*, p. 73.

Chapter 20: Simplicity

1. Peter Adam, *Eileen Gray: Architect/Designer*, p. 234.

Chapter 26: The Energy of Increase

1. Margaret Musgrove, *Ashanti to Zulu*.

Chapter 27: Generosity

1. Adapted with permission from Jeremy Hayward.

Chapter 28: Presence

1. In human beings, presence is called *wangthang* in Tibetan, which means "field of power."

2. Margaret Musgrove, *Ashanti to Zulu.*
3. Chögyam Trungpa, *Shambhala: The Sacred Path of the Warrior,* p. 37.

Chapter 32: Color

1. Robert Farris Thompson, *Flash of the Spirit,* p. 13.

Chapter 36: Elegance

1. Linda Lichter, "Home Truths," *Commentary,* June 1994.

Chapter 39: Direction

1. See Chögyam Trungpa, *Shambhala: The Sacred Path of the Warrior,* and Jeremy Hayward, *Sacred World,* for discussions of "raising lungta" (windhorse).

Chapter 40: Flow

1. Chögyam Trungpa, quoted by Trangu Rinpoche in *Shambhala Sun* "Remembering the Vidyadhara," p. 21 (12/90–1/91).

Chapter 41: Work

1. Susan Walker, ed, *Speaking of Silence,* p. 295.

Chapter 42: Protection

1. Daniel Reid, *Shambhala Guide to Chinese Medicine,* p. 48.
2. Mary Low, *Celtic Christianity and Nature: Early Irish and Hebridean Tradition* (Belfast: Blackstaff Press, 1996).
3. Trangu Rinpoche, *Shambhala Sun.*

Chapter 45: Ambient Home

1. Mircae Eliade, *Shamanism* (New York: Bollingen Foundation, 1964).
2. Nigel Pennick, *The Ancient Science of Geomancy,* p. 53.
3. Mark Treib, *Tokyo: Form and Spirit,* p. 109.
4. Ed McGaa, *Mother Earth Spirituality,* p. 33. New York: Harper Collins, 1990.
5. Nigel Pennick, *The Ancient Science of Geomancy,* p. 97.
6. Eleanor Lynn Nesmit, *Instant Architecture,* p. 51. New York: Fawcett Columbine, 1995.

APPENDIX A

The Five Styles of Energy

	Space	*Clarity*	*Richness*	*Warmth*	*Energy*
Direction	Center	East	South	West	North
Color	White*	Blue	Yellow	Red	Green
Element	Space	Water	Earth	Fire	Wind
Shape	none	circle	square	half-circle	triangle
Season	timeless	winter	fall	spring	summer
Qualities	open relaxing	simple organized	satisfying abundant	beautiful comfortable	successful efficient
Power	accommodates	pacifies	enriches/ expands	magnetizes	overcomes obstacles
Wisdom	all-encompassing	mirrorlike	equanimity	discriminating	accomplishing
Psychological Imbalance	ignorance lack of awareness	aggression anger	pride greed	passion clinging	jealousy paranoia
Design Imbalance	structural oversights neglect	cold conceptual	oppressive pretentious	frivolous moody	speedy driven

*The colors of center and east are sometimes reversed—in which case, space is associated with blue and clarity with white.

APPENDIX B

References and Further Readings

These are good books for readers interested in topics related to enlightened design—contemplative disciplines, feng shui, art, and design in general—and I wish to extend deepest appreciation to their creators. The best way to pursue this path is with the personal guidance of qualified teachers and with the discipline of personal practice.

Art, Architecture, and Design

Adam, Peter. *Eileen Gray: Architect/Designer*. New York: Abrams, 1987.

Alexander, Christopher, Sara Ishikawa, Murray Silverstein with Max Jacobson, Ingrid Fikdahl King, and Scholomo Angel. *A Pattern Language*. New York: Oxford University Press, 1977.

Architects for Social Responsibility: *A Source Book for Sustainable Design: A Guide to Environmentally Responsible Building Materials and Processes*. 248 Franklin St., Cambridge, MA

Arnheim, Rudolf. *The Dynamics of Architectural Form*. Berkeley: University of California Press, 1977.

Ashihara, Yoshinobu. *The Hidden Order: Tokyo through the Twentieth Century*. New York: Kodansha, 1989.

Bachelard, Gaston. *The Poetics of Space*. Translated by Maria Jolas. Boston: Beacon Press, 1994.

Bakker, Rosemary. *Elder Design*. New York: Penguin Books, 1997.

Bang, Molly. *Picture This*. New York: Little, Brown, 1991.

Morris, William. *Hopes and Fears for Art: Five Lectures*. London: Longmans, Green, and Company, 1910.

Day, Christopher. *Places for the Soul: Architecure as a Healing Art*. Glasgow: Collins, 1990.

Hale, Jonathan. *The Old Way of Seeing: How Architecture Lost Its Magic (And How to Get It Back)*. New York: Houghton Mifflin Company, 1994.

Wilde, Judith, and Richard Wilde. *Visual Literacy*. New York: Watson-Guptill, 1991.
Winterson, Jeannette. *Art (Objects)*. New York: Knopf, 1995.
Wright, Frank Lloyd. The Natural House. New York: Bramhall House, 1954.
Zeither, Laura C. *The Ecology of Architecture*. New York: Whitney Library of Design, Watson-Guptill Publications, 1996.

Contemplative Arts and Disciplines

Hayward, Jeremy. *Sacred World: A Guide to Shambhala Warriorship in Daily Life*. New York: Bantam, 1995.
McNiff, Shaun. *Earth Angels: Engaging the Sacred in Everyday Things*. Boston: Shambhala Publications Publications, 1997.
Ni, Hua-Ching. *Entering the Tao*. Boston: Shambhala Publications, 1997.
Richards, M. C. *Centering in Pottery, Poetry and the Person*. Middletown, CT: Wesleyan University Press, 1989.
Trungpa Rinpoche, Chögyam. *Dharma Art*. Boston: Shambhala Publications, 1996.
———. *Shambhala: The Sacred Path of the Warrior*. Boston: Shambhala Publications, 1988.
Walker, Susan, ed. *Speaking of Silence: Christians and Buddhists on the Contemplative Way*. New York: Paulist Press, 1987.

Feng Shui, Geomancy, and Wisdom Traditions

Beck, Peggy, Nia Francisco, and Anna Lee Walters. *The Sacred: Ways of Knowledge, Sources of Life*. Flagstaff, AZ: Northland Publishers, 1991.
Dames, Michael. *Mythic Ireland*. London: Thames & Hudson, 1992.
Gold, Peter. *Navajo and Tibetan Sacred Wisdom: The Circle of the Spirit*. Rochester, VT: Inner Traditions, 1994.
Govinda, Lama Anagarika. *The Inner Structure of the I Ching*. New York: Weatherhill, 1981.
Friedman, Mildred, ed. *Tokyo: Form and Spirit*. New York: Abrams, 1986.
Kingston, Karen. *Creating Sacred Space with Feng Shui*. New York: Broadway Books, 1997.
Levine, Norma. *Blessing Power of the Buddhas: Sacred Objects, Sacred Lands*. Rockport, MA: Element Books, 1993.
Lin, Jamie. *Contemporary Earth Design: A Feng Shui Anthology*. Miami: Earth Design, 1997.
Low, Mary. *Celtic Christianity and Nature: Early Irish and Hebridean Tradition*. Belfast: Blackstaff Press, 1996.
Matsuoka, Seigow, ed. *Ma: Space-Time in Japan*. New York: Cooper-Hewitt Museum.
Matthews, Washington. *Navaho Legends*. American Folklore Society, 1897.
Musgrove, Margaret. *Ashanti to Zulu*. New York: Dial Books, 1976.

Nesmit, Eleanor Lynn. *Instant Architecture*. New York: Fawcett Columbine, 1995.
Neutra, Richard. *Survival through Design*. New York: Oxford University Press, 1954.
Pennick, Nigel. *The Ancient Science of Geomancy*. London: Thames and Hudson, 1979.
Rossbach, Sarah. *Interior Design with Feng Shui*. New York: Dutton, 1987.
Silko, Leslie Marmon. *Yellow Woman and a Beauty of the Spirit*. New York: Simon & Schuster, 1996.
Spear, William. *Feng Shui Made Easy*. New York: HarperCollins, 1995.
Steer, Diana. *Native American Women*. Barnes and Noble Books, 1996.
Thompson, Robert Farris. *Flash of the Spirit: African and Afro-American Art and Philosophy*. New York: Vintage Books, 1984.
Tiao Chang, Amos. *Intangible Content in Architectonic Form*. Princeton, NJ: Princeton University Press, 1956.
Wong, Eva. *Feng Shui*. Boston: Shambhala Publications, 1997.

The Five Styles of Energy

Trungpa Rinpoche, Chögyam. Cutting through Spiritual Materialism. Boston: Shambhala Publications, 1987.
———. *Dharma Art*. Boston: Shambhala Publications, 1996.
———. *The Heart of the Buddha*. Boston: Shambhala Publications, 1991.
———. *Journey without Goal: The Tantric Wisdom of the Buddha*. Boulder: Prajna Press, 1981.
———. *Lion's Roar*. Boston: Shambhala Publications, 1992.
———. *Myth of Freedom*. Boston: Shambhala Publications, 1976
———. *Orderly Chaos*. Boston: Shambhala Publications, 1991.
———. *Transcending Madness*. Boston: Shambhala Publications, 1992.

Food and Mindful Eating

Kushi, Michio. *The Book of Macrobiotics*. Tokyo: Japan Publications, 1987.
Spear, William. *Feng Shui Made Easy*. New York: HarperCollins, 1995.
Thich Nhat Hanh. *Living Buddha, Living Christ*. New York: Berkeley Publishing Group, 1995.
———. *Peace Is Every Step*. New York: Bantam, 1992.

Health and Healing

Greenpeace: For information about nontoxic living, contact Greenpeace, 1436 U Street NW, Washington, DC 20009.
Harwood, Barbara. *The Healing House*. Carlsbad, CA: Hay House, 1997.
Hay, Louise L., et al. *Gratitude: A Way of Life*. Carlsbad, CA: Hay House, 1996.

Kingston, Karen. *Creating Sacred Space with Feng Shui*. New York: Broadway Books, 1997.
Microwave News. Reports on nonionizing radiation; publishes resource directory: P.O. Box 1299, Grand Central Station, New York, NY 10163; (212) 517-2800.
Mojay, Gabriel. *Aromatherapy for Healing the Spirit*. New York: Henry Holt and Company, 1996.
Ni, Hua-Ching. *Entering the Tao*. Boston: Shambhala Publications Publications, 1997.
Pearson, David. *The Natural House Book*. London: Conran Octopus, 1991.
Reid, Daniel. *Shambhala Guide to Chinese Medicine*. Boston: Shambhala Publications, 1996.
Thondup, Tulku. *The Healing Power of Mind: Simple Exercises for Health, Well-Being, and Enlightenment*. Boston: Shambhala Publications, 1996.

Wealth

Chopra, Deepak. *Creating Affluence: Wealth Consciousness in the Field of All Possibilities*. San Rafael, CA: Amber-Allen/New World Library, 1995.

APPENDIX C

Contemplative Training

Contemplative training begins with the sitting practice of meditation. Shambhala centers offer basic instruction in Buddhist meditation as well as classes, discussion groups, and opportunities to study/practice contemplative arts.

Shambhala International
1084 Tower Road
Halifax, Nova Scotia
Canada B3H 2Y5

Introductory and advanced programs are offered at two residential contemplative centers, Karmê Chöling and Rocky Mountain Shambhala Center:

Karmê Chöling
4921 County Road 68C, Barnet, VT 05821.
(802) 633-2384, <KarmeCholing@shambhala.org>

Rocky Mountain Shambhala Center
Red Feather Lakes, CO 80545
(970) 881-2184,
www.rmsc. shambhala.org, <rmsc@shambhala.org>

If you would like to pursue the secular path of Shambhala warriorship, Shambhala Training offers weekend programs on mindfulness/awareness meditation with talks, discussion groups, and opportunities for private and group interviews. Advanced residential programs offer further training and practices, including the practice of raising windhorse (lungta) discussed in this book.

Shambhala Training International
1084 Tower Road
Halifax, Nova Scotia
Canada B3H 2Y5
(902) 423-3266

Space Awareness

Training programs—called Maitri Space Awareness—are periodically available through Shambhala centers, Karmê Chöling, and Rocky Mountain Shambhala Center. Maitri Space Awareness is also offered as an integral part of the contemplative psychology degree program at The Naropa Institute.

The Naropa Institute
2130 Arapahoe Avenue
Boulder, CO 80302
(303) 444-0202

The Naropa Institute is a private, nonsectarian liberal arts college offering undergraduate/graduate degrees in the arts, humanities, and social sciences. It is characterized by its unique Buddhist educational heritage and is accredited by the North Central Association of Colleges and Schools.

For information on training programs outside of the United States, call either Shambhala Training International or Shambhala International at the numbers above.

Miksang Society

Programs in contemplative photography are offered by the Miksang Society. For information, contact the Toronto Shambhala Centre at (416)588-5465.

Helen Berliner can be reached for workshops and consultation at

107 Brook Lane
Lansdale, PA 19446
(215) 362-0758
www.enlightenedbydesign.com, <sambhok@aol.com>

Credits for Illustrations and Photographs

These images and those from Dover's Pictorial Archives collections are used with kind permission of the following individuals, publishers, and businesses. Several images from secondary and tertiary sources have evaded dogged attempts to determine author/ownership; the author will gladly amend if they are not in public domain. All illustrations not credited below are by the author.

Mandala (p. ii); and tiger, garuda, dragon, and lion (p.57) with permission from Shambhala International, with thanks to the artist, Sherab Palden Beru; also thanks to Sherab Palden for the windhorse (p. 185).

Mosaics (pp. 13 and 36), textile (p.55), labyrinth (p. 64), and Hopi earth symbols (p. 114) from *Pattern Design*, Archibald Christie, New York, Dover Publications, 1969.

The drawing on p. 14 is after an ikebana design by Shusui Komoda (*Ikebana Spirit and Technique*, Shusui Komoda/Horst Pointner. Poole, Dorset: Blandford Press, 1976.)

The water, fire, wind, and earth logos on pp. 18–20,the sun logo on p. 207, and the heaven/earth symbol on p. 212 are © 1981, Rubber Poet Rubber Stamps, Box 218, Rockville, Utah 84763-0218; (435) 772-3441; toll free FAX (800) 906-Poet.

The mandala/compass on pp. 21 and 205 was designed by Pam Kerr/Kerr Designs, 333 S. 21st St., Philadelphia, PA 19103.

The logos for clarity (p.73), richness (p. 113), warmth (p. 145), and energy (p. 179) by Barbara Craig, Philadelphia.

The textile design (p. 33), the kitchen shrine (p. 66, hand-crafted by Takayuki Kida), and the windchimes (p. 181) are from Ziji Book & Gift Catalogue, 9148 Kerry Road, Boulder, CO 80303, <Ziji@csd.net>, tel. (303) 661-0034.

The openwork transoms (p. 37), the doors (p. 44), the transom (p. 37), and the pathway designs (p. 188) are from *The Japanese Home Style Book*, ed. Peter Goodman, Stone Bridge Press, Berkeley, CA.

The shoji screen (p. 51) is from Miya Shoji & Interiors, 109 W. 17th St., New York, NY, (212) 243-6774; FAX (212) 243-6780.

The lotus (p.56) and the armor patterns (p. 200) are courtesy of Robert Beer, London, England.

The water/reeds (p. 60), textile designs (pp. 71, 111, 143), water design (p. 74), and birds (p. 172), are from *Japanese Design Through Textile Patterns*, Frances Blakemore. New York: Weatherhill, 1978.

Stripes (p. 74), energy (p. 177), and horses (p. 183) are from *Designer's Guide to Japanese Patterns*, Jeanne Allen, courtesy of Kawade Shobo Shinsha Publishers, Japan.

The decorated pot (p. 74) and Tlingit basketry designs (p. 94) are from *American Indian Design and Decoration*, Leroy H. Appleton, Dover Publications, 1971.

The "Yes" calligraphy (p. 80) was done by Paul Higley shortly before his death, 1991. Collection of author.

The portable closets (p. 82) are after a photograph in "Hold Everything" catalogue from Williams Sonoma.

The Federal style chairs (p. 86) are courtesy of C. L. Prickett, Fine Authenticated American Antiques, 930 Stony Hill Road, Yardley, PA, (215) 493-4284.

The snowflake (p. 87) is from *The Power of Limits* by György Doczi,© 1981. Reprinted by arrangement with Shambhala Publications, Inc., Boston.

The textures (p. 92), the Hopi basket tray (p. 125), and the scrolls/frets (p. 171) are from *Indian Basketry*, George W. James, Dover Publications, 1972.

Ashanti spoon (p. 118), some textures (p. 92), the Kongo soapstone stele relief, Angola (p. 120), the door panel, Ghana (p. 163), the rock engravings, S. Africa (p. 170), the rock painting, S. Africa (p. 185), and the prayer mat, Zanzibar, Tanzania (p. 214) from *African Design from Traditional Sources*, Geoffrey Williams, Dover Publications, 1971.

Scan of sage smudge sticks (p. 96) by John Kyrk.

Shaker furniture (p. 103) after photograph of Shaker furniture from Metropolitan Museum of Art.

Heating vents (p. 130) after photograph in Front Gate, Spring Catalogue, 1998.

Balinese protector statue (p. 191), Balinese protector statue (p. 198) after designs from Thunder Lake Garden Sculpture, 2919 Shady Hollow East, Boulder, CO, 80304, (303) 245-0910.

Umbrella stand (p. 192) after a design by Wireworks, 131A Broadley Street, London, England, NW8 8BA; tel. 44-171-724-8856; FAX: 44-171-258-1528.

Great Stupa design (p. 213) from Rocky Mountain Shambhala Center, Red Feather Lakes, CO.

Photographs

All photographs not credited were taken by the author.

Gerald Ackerman: Kissing statues (p. 146). Collection of the author.

Mitch Berger: Sightline into bedroom (p. 85), teapot hand painted by the author (p. 159).

Carell Doerrbecker: Dancing statues, (p. 160).

Gordon Kidd: Chinese Round Doorway (p. 43).

John McQuade: Bed/flower (p. 166), gauze curtain (p. 39), doorknob (p. 90), mystery (p. 149).

Liza Matthews: Christie's herb shelves (p. 99), teacup (p. 41).

Kathryn Munro: Chair radiator cap (p. 184).

Ethan Neville: Children's shrine (p. 67).

Emily Sell: Home office (p. 194).

Kim Turos: Landscaping of front path/door (p. 162).

Chögyam Trungpa: Hand and bowl (p. 5). Photograph used by permission of Diana J. Mukpo, courtesy of the Shambhala Archives.

Waterford Wedgwood USA: Waterford chandelier (p. 80).

Michael Wood: Chair/light (p. 16), radiator (p. 54), chair/space (p. 103), lamp (p. 79), elegant bowl (p. 106), water glass (p. 83).

Index

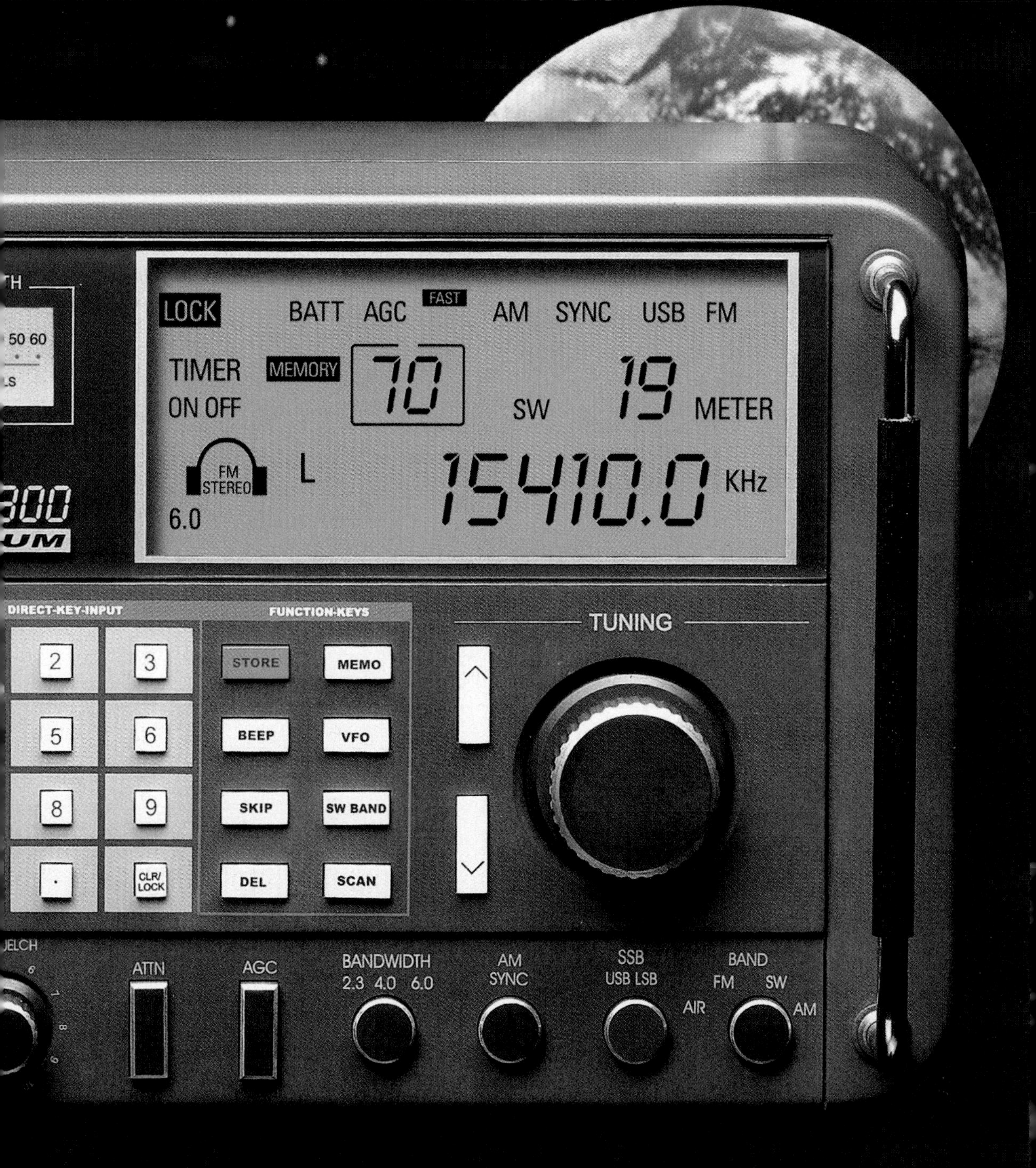

2002 Passport® to

TABLE OF CONTENTS

Radio's World

Compleat Idiot's Guide to Getting Started

985

What to Listen With: PASSPORT REPORTS—2002

World Band Radio

TABLE OF CONTENTS

ISSN 0987-0157

OUR READER IS THE MOST IMPORTANT PERSON IN THE WORLD!

Library of Congress Cataloging-in-Publication Data

Passport to World Band Radio.
1. Radio Stations, Shortwave—Directories. I. Magne, Lawrence
TK9956.P27 2001 384.54'5 01-22739
ISBN 0-914941-82-8

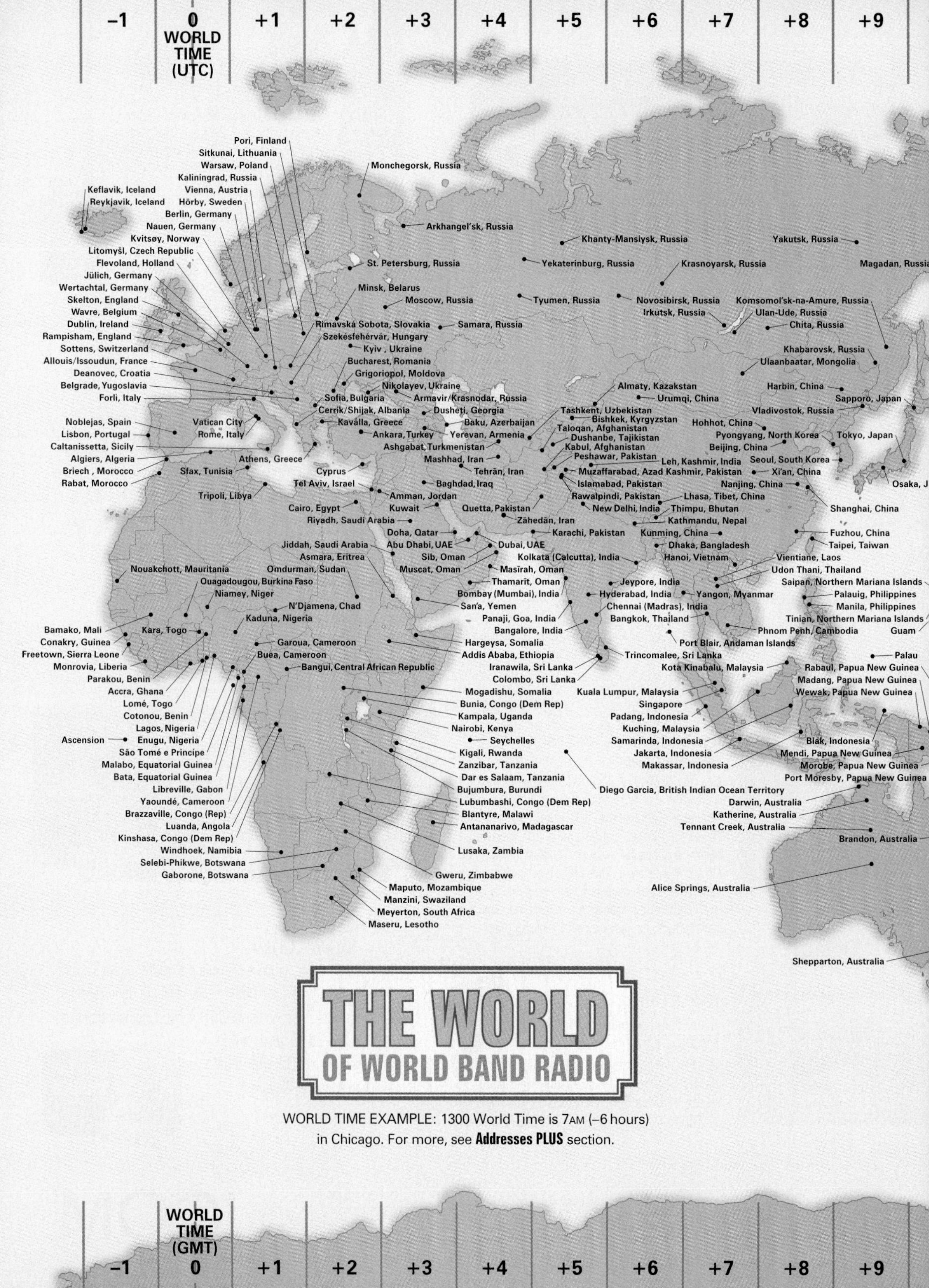

–1
0
WORLD TIME (UTC)
+1
+2
+3
+4
+5
+6
+7
+8
+9
Pori, Finland
Sitkunai, Lithuania
Warsaw, Poland
Kaliningrad, Russia
Vienna, Austria
Hörby, Sweden
Berlin, Germany
Nauen, Germany
Kvitsøy, Norway
Litomyšl, Czech Republic
Flevoland, Holland
Jülich, Germany
Wertachtal, Germany
Skelton, England
Wavre, Belgium
Dublin, Ireland
Rampisham, England
Sottens, Switzerland
Allouis/Issoudun, France
Deanovec, Croatia
Belgrade, Yugoslavia
Forlì, Italy
Keflavik, Iceland
Reykjavik, Iceland
Monchegorsk, Russia
Arkhangel'sk, Russia
St. Petersburg, Russia
Minsk, Belarus
Moscow, Russia
Rimavská Sobota, Slovakia
Samara, Russia
Székesfehérvár, Hungary
Kyiv , Ukraine
Bucharest, Romania
Grigoriopol, Moldova
Nikolayev, Ukraine
Sofia, Bulgaria
Armavir/Krasnodar, Russia
Cerrik/Shijak, Albania
Dusheti, Georgia
Kavalla, Greece
Baku, Azerbaijan
Ankara, Turkey
Yerevan, Armenia
Ashgabat, Turkmenistan
Mashhad, Iran
Tehrān, Iran
Khanty-Mansiysk, Russia
Yekaterinburg, Russia
Krasnoyarsk, Russia
Yakutsk, Russia
Magadan, Russia
Tyumen, Russia
Novosibirsk, Russia
Komsomol'sk-na-Amure, Russia
Irkutsk, Russia
Ulan-Ude, Russia
Chita, Russia
Khabarovsk, Russia
Ulaanbaatar, Mongolia
Almaty, Kazakstan
Harbin, China
Urumqi, China
Sapporo, Japan
Tashkent, Uzbekistan
Vladivostok, Russia
Bishkek, Kyrgyzstan
Hohhot, China
Taloqan, Afghanistan
Dushanbe, Tajikistan
Pyongyang, North Korea
Tokyo, Japan
Kabul, Afghanistan
Beijing, China
Peshawar, Pakistan
Leh, Kashmir, India
Seoul, South Korea
Muzaffarabad, Azad Kashmir, Pakistan
Xi'an, China
Islamabad, Pakistan
Nanjing, China
Osaka, J
Rawalpindi, Pakistan
Lhasa, Tibet, China
New Delhi, India
Thimpu, Bhutan
Shanghai, China
Quetta, Pakistan
Zahedān, Iran
Kathmandu, Nepal
Noblejas, Spain
Lisbon, Portugal
Vatican City
Rome, Italy
Caltanissetta, Sicily
Algiers, Algeria
Athens, Greece
Briech , Morocco
Sfax, Tunisia
Cyprus
Rabat, Morocco
Tel Aviv, Israel
Baghdad, Iraq
Tripoli, Libya
Amman, Jordan
Cairo, Egypt
Kuwait
Riyadh, Saudi Arabia
Doha, Qatar
Karachi, Pakistan
Kunming, China
Fuzhou, China
Jiddah, Saudi Arabia
Abu Dhabi, UAE
Dubai, UAE
Dhaka, Bangladesh
Taipei, Taiwan
Asmara, Eritrea
Sib, Oman
Kolkata (Calcutta), India
Hanoi, Vietnam
Vientiane, Laos
Nouakchott, Mauritania
Omdurman, Sudan
Muscat, Oman
Masirah, Oman
Udon Thani, Thailand
Ouagadougou, Burkina Faso
Thamarit, Oman
Jeypore, India
Saipan, Northern Mariana Islands
Niamey, Niger
Bombay (Mumbai), India
Hyderabad, India
Yangon, Myanmar
Palauig, Philippines
N'Djamena, Chad
San'a, Yemen
Chennai (Madras), India
Manila, Philippines
Kaduna, Nigeria
Panaji, Goa, India
Bangkok, Thailand
Tinian, Northern Mariana Islands
Bamako, Mali
Kara, Togo
Bangalore, India
Phnom Penh, Cambodia
Guam
Conakry, Guinea
Garoua, Cameroon
Hargeysa, Somalia
Port Blair, Andaman Islands
Freetown, Sierra Leone
Buea, Cameroon
Addis Ababa, Ethiopia
Trincomalee, Sri Lanka
Palau
Monrovia, Liberia
Bangui, Central African Republic
Iranawila, Sri Lanka
Kota Kinabalu, Malaysia
Rabaul, Papua New Guinea
Parakou, Benin
Colombo, Sri Lanka
Madang, Papua New Guinea
Accra, Ghana
Mogadishu, Somalia
Kuala Lumpur, Malaysia
Wewak, Papua New Guinea
Lomé, Togo
Bunia, Congo (Dem Rep)
Singapore
Cotonou, Benin
Kampala, Uganda
Padang, Indonesia
Lagos, Nigeria
Nairobi, Kenya
Kuching, Malaysia
Ascension
Enugu, Nigeria
Seychelles
Samarinda, Indonesia
Biak, Indonesia
São Tomé e Príncipe
Kigali, Rwanda
Jakarta, Indonesia
Mendi, Papua New Guinea
Malabo, Equatorial Guinea
Zanzibar, Tanzania
Makassar, Indonesia
Morobe, Papua New Guinea
Bata, Equatorial Guinea
Dar es Salaam, Tanzania
Port Moresby, Papua New Guinea
Libreville, Gabon
Bujumbura, Burundi
Diego Garcia, British Indian Ocean Territory
Yaoundé, Cameroon
Lubumbashi, Congo (Dem Rep)
Darwin, Australia
Brazzaville, Congo (Rep)
Blantyre, Malawi
Katherine, Australia
Luanda, Angola
Antananarivo, Madagascar
Tennant Creek, Australia
Kinshasa, Congo (Dem Rep)
Brandon, Australia
Windhoek, Namibia
Lusaka, Zambia
Selebi-Phikwe, Botswana
Gaborone, Botswana
Gweru, Zimbabwe
Maputo, Mozambique
Alice Springs, Australia
Manzini, Swaziland
Meyerton, South Africa
Maseru, Lesotho
Shepparton, Australia
THE WORLD
OF WORLD BAND RADIO
WORLD TIME EXAMPLE: 1300 World Time is 7AM (–6 hours)
in Chicago. For more, see Addresses PLUS section.
WORLD TIME (GMT)
–1
0
+1
+2
+3
+4
+5
+6
+7
+8
+9

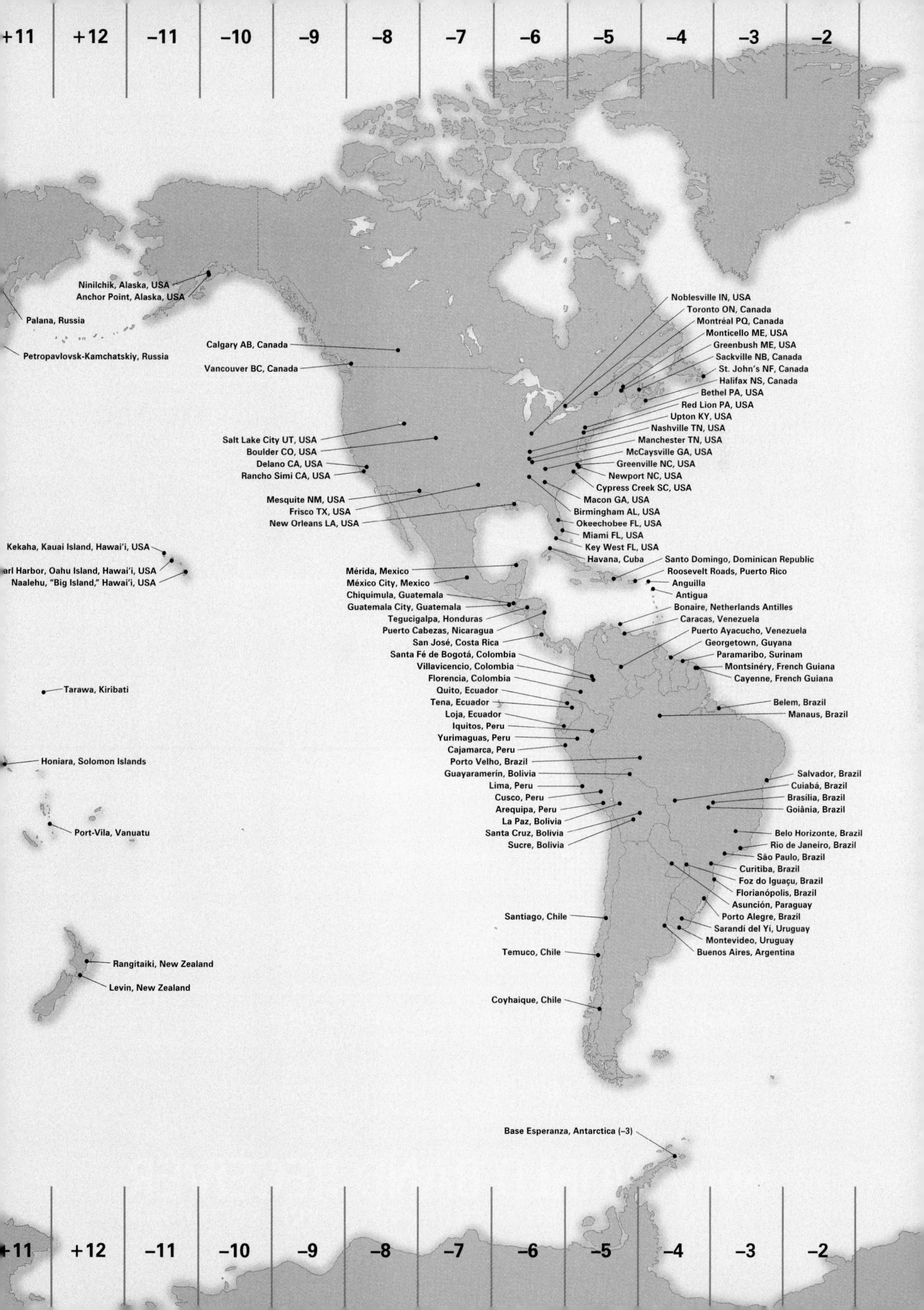

+11 +12 –11 –10 –9 –8 –7 –6 –5 –4 –3 –2

Ninilchik, Alaska, USA
Anchor Point, Alaska, USA
Palana, Russia
Petropavlovsk-Kamchatskiy, Russia
Calgary AB, Canada
Vancouver BC, Canada
Salt Lake City UT, USA
Boulder CO, USA
Delano CA, USA
Rancho Simi CA, USA
Mesquite NM, USA
Frisco TX, USA
New Orleans LA, USA
Noblesville IN, USA
Toronto ON, Canada
Montréal PQ, Canada
Monticello ME, USA
Greenbush ME, USA
Sackville NB, Canada
St. John's NF, Canada
Halifax NS, Canada
Bethel PA, USA
Red Lion PA, USA
Upton KY, USA
Nashville TN, USA
Manchester TN, USA
McCaysville GA, USA
Greenville NC, USA
Newport NC, USA
Cypress Creek SC, USA
Macon GA, USA
Birmingham AL, USA
Okeechobee FL, USA
Miami FL, USA
Key West FL, USA
Havana, Cuba
Santo Domingo, Dominican Republic
Roosevelt Roads, Puerto Rico
Anguilla
Antigua
Kekaha, Kauai Island, Hawai'i, USA
arl Harbor, Oahu Island, Hawai'i, USA
Naalehu, "Big Island," Hawai'i, USA
Mérida, Mexico
México City, Mexico
Chiquimula, Guatemala
Guatemala City, Guatemala
Tegucigalpa, Honduras
Puerto Cabezas, Nicaragua
San José, Costa Rica
Santa Fé de Bogotá, Colombia
Villavicencio, Colombia
Florencia, Colombia
Quito, Ecuador
Tena, Ecuador
Loja, Ecuador
Iquitos, Peru
Yurimaguas, Peru
Cajamarca, Peru
Porto Velho, Brazil
Guayaramerín, Bolivia
Lima, Peru
Cusco, Peru
Arequipa, Peru
La Paz, Bolivia
Santa Cruz, Bolivia
Sucre, Bolivia
Bonaire, Netherlands Antilles
Caracas, Venezuela
Puerto Ayacucho, Venezuela
Georgetown, Guyana
Paramaribo, Surinam
Montsinéry, French Guiana
Cayenne, French Guiana
Belem, Brazil
Manaus, Brazil
Salvador, Brazil
Cuiabá, Brazil
Brasília, Brazil
Goiânia, Brazil
Belo Horizonte, Brazil
Rio de Janeiro, Brazil
São Paulo, Brazil
Curitiba, Brazil
Foz do Iguaçu, Brazil
Florianópolis, Brazil
Asunción, Paraguay
Porto Alegre, Brazil
Sarandí del Yí, Uruguay
Montevideo, Uruguay
Buenos Aires, Argentina
Santiago, Chile
Temuco, Chile
Coyhaique, Chile
Tarawa, Kiribati
Honiara, Solomon Islands
Port-Vila, Vanuatu
Rangitaiki, New Zealand
Levin, New Zealand
Base Esperanza, Antarctica (–3)

+11 +12 –11 –10 –9 –8 –7 –6 –5 –4 –3 –2

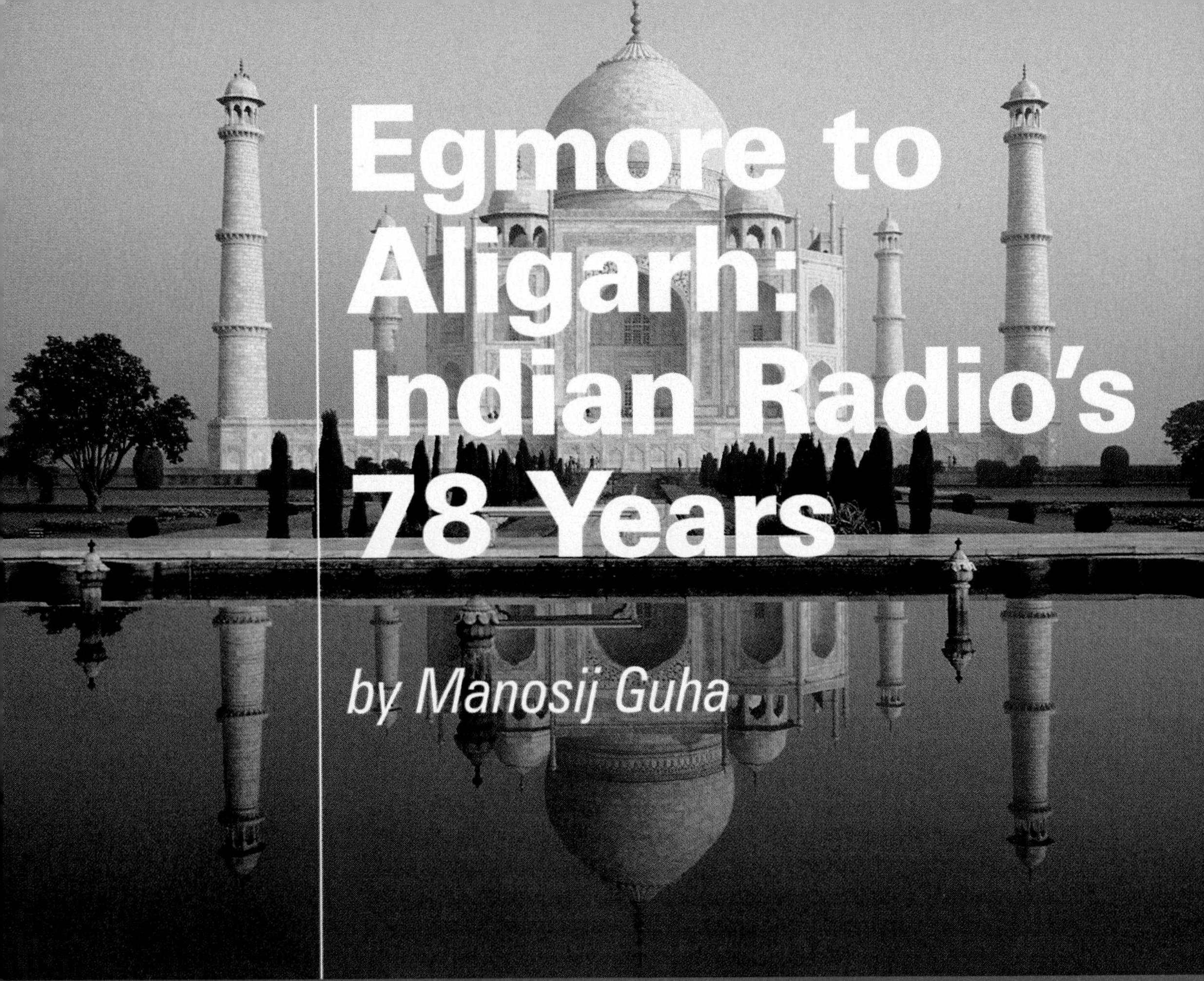

Egmore to Aligarh: Indian Radio's 78 Years

by Manosij Guha

Often touted as the underbelly of Asia, India is a behemoth of nearly a billion people. It is home to 25 major cultures speaking in over a thousand different tongues, including some that are among the oldest in the world. Yet, even with one-sixth of the world's population, it is packed into an area only a third the size of the continental United States.

Rarely has there been a country whose first steps into world band radio have been as unsteady as India's. Broadcasting there began largely as a private initiative—ironic, given the decades-long stranglehold that the government's All India Radio has had on broadcasting. The first moves began in 1923, when amateur radio clubs in Bombay and Calcutta began experimenting with shortwave hardware lent by the Marconi Company. Later, when enthusiast C. V. Krishnaswamy Chetty returned from England with a suitcase full of electronic components, he unknowingly kick-started shortwave radio in India.

Rudyard Kipling gives his first talk over the BBC Empire Service on July 12, 1933. BBC

Chetty formed the Madras Presidency Radio Club on May 16, 1924 at Holloways Garden in Egmore. Located in present-day Chennai in southern India, the site is now a ballfield at the local school. He assembled the components into a 40 Watt shortwave transmitter with the nondescript callsign of 2GR, which was used for India's first world band broadcast. This took place on the last day of July 1924, and consisted of two hours of music, along with talks in the evening.

The homebrew transmitter had a range of only five miles or eight kilometers, so it was replaced by one of 200 Watts. But this pioneering service ran into financial shoals, so the government came to the rescue with funds from radio license fees. Despite this and other efforts, the station was forced to close down in 1927. India's world band airwaves remained silent for three years.

Shortwave Revived in 1930

Goaded by the success of this impromptu broadcasting effort, the station was revived by the municipality of Madras after the defunct club donated its dormant transmitter. On the first day of April 1930, the station began airing regular stories and music lessons for schoolchildren at 4:00-4:30 PM weekdays, local time, followed an hour later by two hours of music. Sixty minutes of soothing gramophone music was featured on Sundays and holidays at 10:00 AM.

Because so few people owned radios, the government installed loudspeakers on beaches, within schools and in city parks. This continued until June 16, 1938, when the station was swallowed by the Madras outlet of All India Radio, then fleshed out with a relatively muscular 10 kW shortwave transmitter.

OPPORTUNITY LOST

"A great opportunity has been lost in India. In 1924, I had tried to get the India Office to take the potentialities of broadcasting seriously . . . but without official support or interest it was not surprising that little progress was made. Later on Lord Willingdon did his utmost to put things on a proper basis as will be told in due course; it was too late. If broadcasting had been taken seriously in 1924, subsequent events in India might have been very different."

—*Sir J. C. W. Reith, first Director General of the BBC*

BBC Empire Broadcasting Station at Daventry, 1933. BBC

The holy festival of Mahakumbhmela, where in February, 2001 over 75 million marched to the Ganges to wash away their sins. M. Guha

Station Refuses to Die

There's more to the saga of free enterprise. In 1927 a private company, the Indian Broadcasting Company, was licensed to operate with the blessing of the British Empire. Its first station was set up amid a fanfare on July 23, 1927 in Bombay—present-day Mumbai—in western India, with proceedings led by the British Viceroy, Lord Irwin. Programs emanated from a rudimentary studio in Radio House at Apollo Bunder, which was connected by phone line to a 1.5 kW shortwave transmitter at Worli. It had a callsign of 7BY, which later became VUB to conform to international convention.

Makeshift studio acoustics were augmented by colorful, eye-popping draperies. These were simpler times, so the studio's bold visual statement caused a stir. Soon the drapes became the talk of the town, earning columns of ink in local newspapers.

Flush with enthusiasm, the station quickly expanded. A mere five weeks later a 1.5 kW shortwave transmitter calling itself 7CA and later VUC was installed in Calcutta, inaugurated by no less than the Governor of Bengal, Sir Stanley Jackson. Alas, the initial euphoria was short lived—mounting losses compelled the company to liquidate on March 1, 1930. But the station didn't stay down for long. Exactly one month later the government decided to take it over as a public service, christening it the Indian Broadcasting Service.

But it was now the government's turn to go broke, so on October 10, 1931 the station's two transmitters once again fell silent. This caused widespread resentment so, bowing to public pressure, the government reincarnated the stubborn little station on November 23. Later, in 1935, a tiny 250 Watt transmitter called VUB began being heard on 9565 kHz.

Pigmy Transmitters for Princely States

Indian broadcasting wasn't limited to British India. About the same time, broadcasts were taking place in the adjacent princely states, which were technically not part of British India. Here, maharajas and nizams governed their minions in a laid-back existence.

Leading the pack, Mysore set up its own radio station in 1935. Not to be outdone, the princedoms of Baroda, Hyderabad, Aurangabad and Travancore followed suit—all had low-powered shortwave stations up and running by 1939. With their newfangled toys, these exalted highnesses could now launch "a thousand voices" and transport their durbar to the remotest corners of their fiefdoms.

BBC Success Boosts Indian Broadcasting

Meanwhile, the British masters of this prized colony had been toying with stronger broadcasting links. Indian listeners thus got a boost in December of 1932, when the British Broadcasting Corporation began its Empire Service. This was beamed to India for two hours a day from a shortwave transmitter in England, but within months this daily "Zone 2" service to India, Ceylon, Burma and Malaya had been expanded to four hours from two transmitters.

The BBC's growing presence on the dials greatly boosted sales of radios among the many European colonists in India. The increase in license fees resulting from the jump in radio ownership went to the fledgling Indian broadcasting apparatus, finally giving it the money to perform the task it had initially set out to do.

All India Radio Formed

By 1934 the government of India was convinced of the importance of broadcasting, so it decided to add a station in Delhi, the new viceregal capital. Collaborative efforts between the BBC and the Indian Broadcasting Service ensued, and in August of 1935 the venerated Lionel Fielden took over as Controller of Broadcasting. The same year saw the setting up of an experimental low-powered shortwave transmitter in Calcutta, under the generic callsign VUC, to relay AIR's mediumwave AM channel to the rural audience.

Fielden had the entire administrative bulwark overhauled, then on June 8, 1936 had it renamed "All India Radio" (AIR). AIR's radio empire then grew rapidly, expanding to nine stations as far-flung as Peshawar,

THE NAME GAME

Lionel Fielden describes how he tricked the then-Viceroy of India, Lord Linlithgow, into accepting the name "All India Radio" despite severe opposition from the cabinet.

"I cornered Lord Linlithgow after a Viceregal banquet, and said plaintively that I was in great difficulty and needed his advice. (He usually responded well to such an opening.) I said that I was sure that he agreed with me that ISBS was a clumsy title. After a slight pause, he nodded his long head wisely. Yes, it was rather a mouthful.

"I said that perhaps it was a pity to use the word broadcasting at all, since all Indians had to say 'broadcasting'—broad was for them an unpronounceable word. But I could not, I said, think of another title; could he help me? 'Indian State,' I said, was a term which, as he well knew, hardly fitted into the 1935 Act. It should be something general.

"He rose beautifully to the bait. 'All India'? I expressed my astonishment and admiration. The very thing. But surely not 'Broadcasting'? After some thought he suggested 'Radio'? Splendid, I said – and what beautiful initials. The Viceroy concluded that he had invented it, and there was no more trouble. His pet name must be adopted.

Thus, All India Radio was born."

New Delhi's broadcasting mast was to house a revolving restaurant, but terrorist attacks killed the plan. M. Guha

Stations Shuffled at Independence

"Long years ago we made a tryst with destiny, and now the time comes when we shall redeem our pledge, not wholly or in full measure, but very substantially. At the stroke of the midnight hour, when the world sleeps, India will awake to life and freedom. A moment comes, which comes but rarely in history, when we step out from the old to the new, when an age ends, and when the soul of a nation, long suppressed, finds utterance. It is fitting that at this solemn moment, we take the pledge of dedication to the service of India and her people and to the still larger cause of humanity."

This landmark speech on the midnight of August 14, 1947 was made by Jawaharlal Nehru in the Constituent Assembly, which later became the Indian Parliament. Nehru, who was to become India's first prime minister, ushered in a new era both for the country and its broadcasting organ, All India Radio.

When Indian independence finally came a day later, it was not exactly a win-win situation for All India Radio. The partition of India into three geographical entities—India, West Pakistan and East Pakistan—caused AIR to lose its outlets in Peshawar, Lahore and Dacca. Yet, this was more than offset by India's annexation the neighboring princely states, which resulted in AIR's gaining five more stations.

Part of the Punjab state in the northwestern frontier was partitioned over to Pakistan, so on the first day of November 1947, India set up a new station in nearby Jallandhar. Later that year a crisis arose in the northern state of Kashmir when it was attacked by a Pakistani-backed tribal army. This prompted the creation of a new station in Jammu exactly one month later.

Classical Indian music is AIR's chief offering. This has nurtured native musicians who lost the patronage of maharajas and nawabs after their courts folded. M. Guha

PRINCELY STATES' GLORY YEARS

In the Princely State of Mysore, Dr. M. V. Gopalaswamy, Professor of Psychology at the University of Mysore, started experimental broadcasts using a mere 30 Watt transmitter housed in his residence. It was formally inaugurated on September 10, 1935, airing classical Carnatic music and various talks from 6:00 to 8:30 PM daily except Sundays.

Subsequently, a 250 Watt transmitter was imported to improve coverage. Private support and grants from the Mysore Municipality enabled the station to provide regular nightly transmissions until 1942, when it was taken over by the Mysore State at the behest of His Highness Nalvadi Krishnaraja Wodeyar. The station was absorbed into the AIR network on April 1, 1950 after the princely states were integrated into India proper. Its on-air identification of "Akashvani" is still used to this day.

H.H. Nalvadi Krishnaraja Wodeyar, radio king of Mysore.

Travancore Follows Mysore

Early in 1936 the Trade Agent for the Travancore State at Bombay (now Mumbai) consulted the Controller of Broadcasting to set up a radio network. His Highness the Maharaja of Travancore showed great interest, and formed a committee of top officials to evaluate the possibility of installing a transmitter at the capital Trivandrum (now Thiruananthapuram).

All India Radio provided advice, and an engineer from Travancore was subsequently trained to carry out the onerous task. A 5 kW mediumwave transmitter was finally installed on March 12, 1943 and continued broadcasting until April 1, 1950, when like its Mysore cousin it joined the fraternity of AIR stations.

"External Service" Quickly Crushed

His Exalted Highness the Nizam commissioned a 4-to-5 kW mediumwave AM station on 411 meters at the capital of Hyderabad, and a small 250 Watt station in Aurangabad to the south on 319 meters. Technical knowhow was provided by All India Radio. The Hyderabad station came on air on February 3, 1935 with the callsign VUV, and the one at Aurangabad a bit later.

When the princedom refused to join the Indian Union and instead maintained direct ties with Britain, the station began identifying itself as the "external service of the Indian State of Hyderabad," airing what India felt was "propaganda." This defiance was quickly put down by Indian security forces in September 1948.

Gwalior Proposes, AIR Disposes

The Durbar in the princedom of Gwalior in central India also sought advice from AIR to set up a station. The foundation stone to the Baroda (now Vadodara) Broadcasting Station was laid by His Highness the Gaekwad on May 1, 1939.

After independence, on December 16, 1948, the BBS became the first princely station to merge with AIR.

आकाशवाणी
ALL INDIA RADIO
कार्यालय अधीक्षण अभियन्ता
OFFICE OF THE SUPERINTENDING ENGINEER
उच्च शक्ति प्रेषित्र
HIGH POWER TRANSMITTERS
KINGSWAY DELHI - 110009

It is illegal to photograph this sign, but okay to take pictures of people and equipment inside. M. Guha

On July 1, 1948, a shortwave transmitter of 2.5 kW went on the air from Srinagar, ostensibly to serve the divided Kashmiri peoples on both sides of the border. Shortly thereafter a 100 kW world band transmitter, as powerful as existed at the time, was installed in Delhi to add heft and range India's international radio voice.

The next few years saw a spate of new stations, mostly on mediumwave AM. The 5 kW shortwave transmitter was shut down in the erstwhile princely state of Mysore in 1955, while the following year a 2.5 kW transmitter was added at Simla. Shimla, as it is known in the local tongue, is the capital of the then-new state of Himachal Pradesh in the Himalayan foothills.

Also in 1948, the Portuguese authorities set up a radio station, Emissora de Goa, at Panjim (now Panaji) in their Subcontinental colony of Goa. On December 18, 1961, shortly after attacking Indian forces entered Goa, Emissora de Goa fell silent. On January 9, 1962, with Goa now incorporated into India, it was revived as AIR Panaji.

Armed Conflicts Prompt Changes

Though India's foreign policy was one of nonalignment, its overtly cordial relationship with the Soviet Union made its northern

EMISSORA DE GOA

The first radio broadcast from the old Portuguese colony of Goa took place on May 28, 1946 from a 0.5 kW American transmitter operated by the Post and Telegraph Department. Three years later a temporary 1 kW transmitter was installed in Panjim (now Panaji), the small capital city, and was active a few hours each day on 9610 kHz.

In 1950 Adventist World Radio began a weekly broadcast from Emissora de Goa, which was then still just a 1 kW station on the 49 meter band. Later that same year a new radio site was constructed some nine miles or 14 km from the city, with its first transmitter, 7.5 kW, commencing experimental broadcasts in March 1951 on 6023 kHz. With this facility operational, the Panjim shortwave transmitter was dropped.

In 1956 plans were laid to install several additional 10 kW shortwave transmitters. Only one was actually ever installed, three years later. However, in 1961 test broadcasts began from a relatively powerful new 50 kW transmitter. It was widely heard on 15410 kHz to Africa, 15385 kHz to the Persian Gulf and 17835 kHz to the Far East.

After Indian armed forces drove the Portuguese from Goa, an era came to an end. Emissora de Goa closed down forever at 8:00 AM on December 18, 1961.

—Adrian Peterson, AWR

Last of a breed, this technician and his veteran colleagues have been all but replaced by cadres of young techno-geeks.

M. Guha

neighbor nervous. China, flexing new-found military muscle, made a downward push into India on October 20, 1962, catching Indian forces off guard. This lead to an indecisive war in which Chinese forces seized two sizable chunks of territory, leading to discord and minor border incidents which are still commonplace. India's sanctuary of thousands of Tibetans and their venerated leader, the Dalai Lama, has reduced Sino-Indian relations to much like a game of catch-me-if-you-can.

After the Chinese attack, shortwave stations were hurriedly fired up in the far northeastern corner of the country. On January 4, 1963, an independent AIR station was set up in Kohima, the capital of Nagaland, with a 10 kW shortwave transmitter to serve the surrounding hilly terrain. Similarly, another was inaugurated on August 15 at Imphal in the neighboring tribal state of Mizoram. About the same time a 20 kW shortwave station was installed at Kurseong in northern West Bengal.

In 1974 India fought yet another war, with Pakistan. AIR was fearful of centralizing its broadcasting operations in Delhi, which were well within the reach of enemy air attack. So its first external service relay station was created on April 4, 1971 in the sleepy town of Aligarh, about 60 miles or 97 km east of Delhi along the main railway line to Calcutta. The site covers an area of over 823 acres or 333 hectares, and started with two 250 kW shortwave transmitters pumping signals into 39 arrays over 15 miles (25 km) of feeder lines, but there was a rub: Its 50-foot (15-meter) antenna masts were dead giveaways to enemy planes. These remain a source of worry to security conscious officials in Broadcasting House, even now.

Two similar transmitters were added in 1983. Since then, things have gone downhill. Nilgais—large grey Indian antelope—have been electrocuted while grazing in the antenna fields. There continues to be a lack of adequate electrical power, and aging transmitters suffer from a shortage of spare parts.

But the future is looking up. Soon, two of the old transmitters are to be replaced by energy-efficient 250 kW units that call for less electricity. Hopefully, the nilgais will fare equally well.

Manosij Guha, on assignment for PASSPORT *in India, is a media developer and reporter currently based in the United States.*

GRUNDIG The Ultimate ir

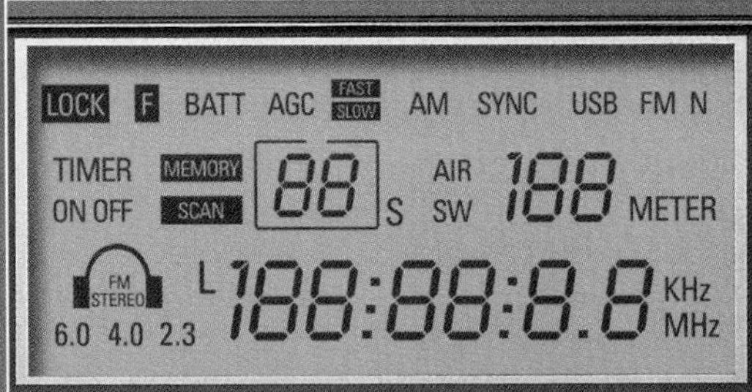
LOCK F BATT AGC FAST SLOW AM SYNC USB FM N
TIMER MEMORY 88 AIR 188
ON OFF SCAN S SW METER
FM STEREO L 188:88:8.8 KHz MHz
6.0 4.0 2.3

The LCD

Big! Bold! Brightly Illuminated 6" by 3½".
Liquid Crystal Display shows all important data: Frequency, Meter band, Memory position, Time, LSB/USB, Synchronous Detector and more.

The Signal Strength Meter

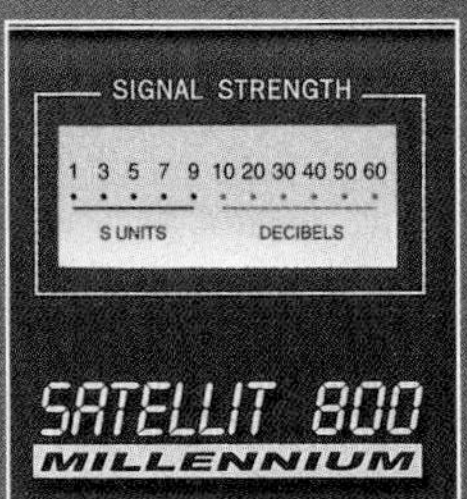
SIGNAL STRENGTH
1 3 5 7 9 10 20 30 40 50 60
S UNITS DECIBELS
SATELLIT 800
MILLENNIUM

Elegant in its traditional Analog design, like the gauges in the world's finest sports cars. Large. Well Lit. Easy to read.

The Frequency Coverage

Longwave, AM and shortwave: continuous 100-30,000 KHz. FM: 87-108 MHz VHF Aircraft Band: 118-137 MHz.

The Tuning Controls

• For the traditionalist: a smooth, precise tuning knob, produces no audio muting during use. Ultra fine-tuning of 50Hz on LSB/USB, 100Hz in

TUNING
MEMO
VFO
SCAN
BANDWIDTH
2.3 4.0 6.0
AM SYNC
SSB USB LSB
BAND
AIR FM SW AM

SW, AM and Aircraft Band and 20 KHz in FM.

• For Fixed-step Tuning: Big, responsive Up/Down tuning buttons.

• For direct frequency entry: a responsive, intuitive numeric keypad.

CLOCK
TIMER
LAMP
GRUNDIG
POWER
VOLUME
BASS
TREBLE

THESE ARE THE SATELLIT 800 MILLENNIUM'S MAJOR FEATURES.
FOR A DETAILED SPECIFICATION SHEET, CONTACT GRUNDIG.

Digital Technology

DIRECT-KEY-INPUT
1 2 3
4 5 6
7 8 9
0 · CLR/LOCK

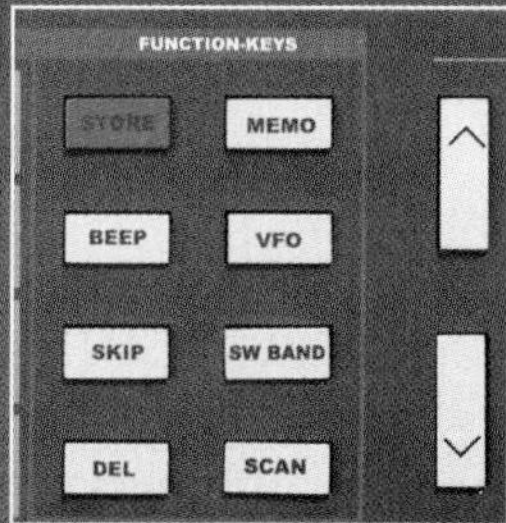
FUNCTION-KEYS
STORE MEMO
BEEP VFO
SKIP SW BAND
DEL SCAN

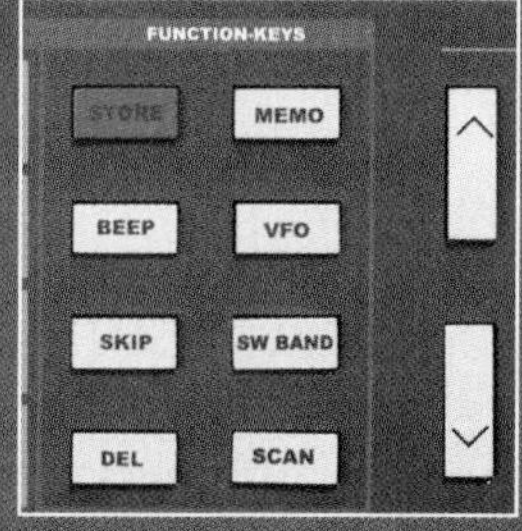

The Operational Controls

Knobs where you want them; Buttons where they make sense. The best combination of traditional and high-tech controls.

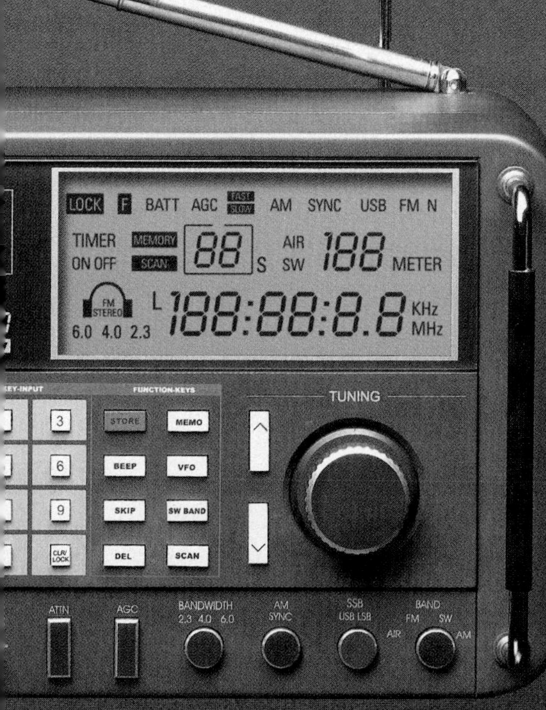
LOCK F BATT AGC FAST SLOW AM SYNC USB FM N
TIMER ON OFF MEMORY SCAN 88 S AIR SW 188 METER
FM STEREO 6.0 4.0 2.3 L 188:88:8.8 KHz MHz
FUNCTION-KEYS
STORE MEMO
BEEP VFO
SKIP SW BAND
DEL SCAN
TUNING
ATTN AGC BANDWIDTH 2.3 4.0 6.0 AM SYNC SSB USB LSB BAND FM SW AIR AM

The Sound

Legendary Grundig Audio Fidelity with separate bass and treble controls, big sound from its powerful speaker and FM-stereo with the included high quality headphones.

The Technology

Today's latest engineering:

- Dual conversion superheterodyne circuitry.
- PLL synthesized tuner.

The Many Features

- 70 user-programmable memories.
- Two, 24 hour format clocks.
- Two ON/OFF sleep timers.
- Massive, built-in telescopic antenna.
- Connectors for external antennas – SW, AM, FM and VHF Aircraft Band.
- Line-out, headphone and external speaker jacks.

The Power Supply

A 110V AC adapter is included for North America (a 220V AC adapter is available upon request). Also operates on 6 size D batteries. (not included)

Dimensions: 20.5″ L × 9″ H × 8″ W

Weight: 14.50 lbs.

by GRUNDIG

Lextronix / Grundig, P.O. Box 2307, Menlo Park, CA 94026 • Tel: 650-361-1611 • Fax: 650-361-1724
Shortwave Hotlines: (US) 1-800-872-2228 (CN) 1-800-637-1648 • Web: www.grundigradio.com • Email: grundig@ix.netcom.com

"This Is All India Radio"

by Manosij Guha

All India Radio is the heart of India's broadcasting, and its crown jewel is the quaint Broadcasting House. Located in the capital of New Delhi, this is AIR's headquarters and broadcasting hub where most nationwide radio programs are created and distributed.

Broadcasting House boasts 30 studios, including two for news. Fifteen are dedicated to live programs, while others are for recording and dubbing. There are two master control rooms which can carry a dozen channels of programming at a time. Although one is ancient, the other is state of the art—technicians are still in the process of learning how to operate it. Work is being moved in phases from the old to the new until it becomes a totally automated operation—a slow process, as the engineers' and technicians' unions, fearing job cuts, have traditionally resisted automation.

The entire complex is a high security area, with X-ray scanners and gun-toting guards that give it the feel of a military zone. The adjacent Akashvani Bhavan is more of an administrative annex, while a new broadcasting house is being built behind the existing complex.

News is in English over AIR's General Overseas Service. M. Guha

Large Network, Larger Bureaucracy

AIR's technical infrastructure and facilities are among the largest in the broadcasting world. When India attained independence in 1947, AIR had only six stations and 18 transmitters—just 2.5 percent of the country and 11 percent of the population were covered.

Starting in 1951, rapid expansion took place through a series of ambitious five-year plans. This increased the reach of AIR's broadcasts and helped improve literacy among the largely illiterate populace. Equally important, these nationwide broadcasts helped unify the country.

Now, over 9,000 engineers and technicians are responsible for planning, designing, installing, operating and maintaining 237 installations. These include 303 transmitters, 48 for shortwave; eight External Service centers; 32 Vividh Bharati commercial stations; 106 studio-to-transmitter links; 345 satellite radio terminals; and 189 studios.

For every employee turning out programs there are two bureaucrats.

The Home Services employ over 6,500 staffers churning out programs in 24 languages and 146 dialects. These broadcasts reach 90 percent of India and 97 percent of the population. The External Services air 26 languages—16 from India, plus ten foreign tongues.

For every employee involved in turning out programs, there are nearly two functionaries. Fully 11,000 administrative and support personnel bloat the payroll, making the organization exceptionally unwieldy.

The External Services' new control room uses leading-edge technology. AIR's engineers are still trying to get the hang of it.

M. Guha

Numerous Regional World Band Stations

AIR makes extensive use of world band radio to supplement FM and mediumwave AM. This creative mix of transmission media allows the network to reach even the most remote parts of India's vast countryside.

Twenty-five regional shortwave transmitters, ranging from 10 kW to 50 kW, ensure seamless coverage. Stations are as far-flung as Aizawl, Bhopal, Kolkata (formerly Calcutta), Chennai (formerly Madras), Delhi-Kingsway, Gangtok, Guwahati, Hyderabad, Imphal, Itanagar, Jaipur, Jeypore, Jammu, Kohima, Kurseong, Leh, Lucknow, Mumbai (formerly Bombay), Port Blair, Ranchi, Shillong, Shimla, Srinagar and Thiruananthapuram (formerly Trivandrum).

Station Originates in Victorian Building

On New Year's Day, 1936, AIR's Delhi station started broadcasting on medium-wave AM from a cramped bungalow on 18 Alipore Road, located within the Civil Lines which formed the European quarter in the old part of the city. It was an old-fashioned building in the style of the colonial period, with verandas out front and back. There were also four hexagonal tower-type rooms at each corner—one for the station's director, another for his assistant. A third served as the duty room, where an outdoor loudspeaker blared away for the benefit of passersby.

Honking Forbidden at Al Fresco Sessions

There were three studios in the back veranda—one for talks, one for European music and dramas, and a multi-purpose Indian music studio. Still, space was limited, so when military bands were booked it was sometimes difficult to squeeze in all the players. Performances wound up being recorded outside, with staff placed on vigilant duty to keep cars and horse-driven "tonga" carriages from honking.

When a shortwave transmitter was finally installed in December 1937, additional studio space was rented at nearby 4 Underhill Road. This continued to function until May 1943, when the operation was moved to Broadcasting House on Parliament Street in New Delhi, where it continues to this day. The Alipore Road premises are now a charitable hospital for eye diseases.

VOA-AIR DEAL SQUASHED

"This program has come to you from the Voice of America relay in Calcutta."

Strange as it may seem, that was almost a possibility in 1963. This proposed transmission facility would have been run by AIR personnel in cooperation with a VOA liaison officer. Both broadcasters' programs would have been aired, but at different times.

Alas, when the draft agreement became public it was emphatically denounced by the prime minister and others in a frenzy of nationalist indignation. Thus was the end of any consideration of a VOA relay station in India, and the beginning of an anti-relay mindset which continues to this day.

Rumors suggested the proposed VOA facility would be shared with a covert CIA listening post, presumably for the agency's Foreign Broadcast Information Service (FBIS). When the deal fell through, the CIA station shifted base to the port city of Chittagong, now in Bangladesh, while the VOA scouted for a less controversial relay base. They finally zeroed in on Udorn Thani in northern Thailand and Ekala in Sri Lanka.

Kingsway Camp, AIR's first external service shortwave facility. It is more like Kingsway Swamp now, thanks to its low-lying location.

M. Guha

Kingsway Becomes Swamp

On May Day, 1944, after AIR had outgrown its original facility, a new and spacious 256 acre (104 hectare) shortwave transmitter site was set up a few miles down the road. It was located at Kingsway Camp, a military base established to celebrate the coronation of King George V.

The same year saw the installation of India's first set of high-powered shortwave transmitters—two 100 kW General Electric behemoths the size of small rooms. These American-made units carried the external service war effort for the remainder of World War II.

Also installed were two 7.5 kW shortwave transmitters to carry national programs originating from the Delhi studios. These were joined a year later by a pair of 20 kW AWA units, which served primarily to feed national programs to outlying transmitters throughout the country.

In 1978 the nearby Yamuna river overflowed, damaging Kingsway's transmitters. The flood water never fully receded, so the antenna fields became mired in swamps inhospitable to maintenance crews.

Site Cleaned Up, Revived

Nevertheless, the site was refurbished in three stages. The first began in 1983, when a new hall was built for two compact, energy-efficient 100 kW Brown Boveri transmitters. These carried the bulk of the national hookup, as well as the northern beam of the external service to neighboring countries.

Second, the antediluvian General Electric and AWA transmitters were originally kept on standby, but were finally retired and dismantled. In 1986 four 50 kW Brown Boveri units were installed in their place to carry more national programs, the Vividh Bharati service and some external services.

The final stage of development for this site was completed in 1996, when a third hall was built to house three more 50 kW BEL transmitters to carry the Delhi A regional service, certain national programs, and a southern beam of the external service to neighboring countries.

The transmitter plant guzzles more electricity than all of Delhi, while two hundred staff, including ten engineers, beaver away in three rotating shifts. They operate the bevy of transmitters in a factory-like atmosphere,

RadioShack Canada has the best selection of high-quality shortwave radios

Shortwave radio enthusiasts take pleasure in listening to programming from all over the world–on the best equipment they can find. At RadioShack Canada, you'll find high-quality Grundig shortwave radios. Grundig is famous for the craftsmanship of their radios. Many hours of planning and crafting goes into each Grundig radio. Crisp, clear sound makes you forget that you're listening to a news program broadcast from Europe or Asia–you'll start to think you're listening to the local FM radio station. Grundig shortwave radios have the features and styles you want–from the Satellit 800 Millennium down to the popular travel sizes with dual alarm functions and more. Come to RadioShack Canada for the best choice in shortwave radios–Grundig.

Grundig Satellit 800 Millennium.
A perfect balance of form and function. Band coverage is complete: shortwave from 100KHz to 30MHz, plus AM/FM and VHF aircraft band (118 to 137 MHz). Synchronous detector for superior reception and more. Includes AC adapter and headphones. 2018104

YB300PE shortwave radio.
Features PLL tuning and 24 station presets, titanium-look finish, dynamic micro speaker and external antenna connector. Includes travel cover, AC adapter, earphones and supplementary antenna. 2018103

KASHMIR: TIT *VS.* TAT

Once touted as the Switzerland of India, the vale of Kashmir is a bone of contention between two siblings of the former British Indian empire. India has been fighting with Pakistan over Kashmir since the Hindu king of a predominantly Muslim region decided to join a predominantly Hindu India.

Some days battles are fought on the cricket playing field, while at other times the struggle takes place over the airwaves. Despite the divisive efforts of governments on both sides, radio broadcasting across the border has played a unifying role, as demonstrated by the many letters AIR has received from listeners outside Indian territory.

Maharaja Inaugurates Early Affiliate

Uzbekistan
Kyrgyzstan
Tajikistan
China
Afghanistan
Kashmir
Pakistan
India
Nepal

Kashmir, like Berlin of old, is divided into three zones—Indian (tan), Pakistani (yellow) and Chinese (purple).

One of the first stations to be opened anywhere in the AIR network was on December 1, 1947 in the city of Jammu, located in Jammu and Kashmir. Although that name makes it sound like two separate entities, "Jammu and Kashmir" is actually just a single Indian state.

Radio Kashmir, Jammu, was inaugurated at a local high school by Maharaja Hari Singh, the erstwhile King of Kashmir who had joined the Indian Union despite intense opposition. The station, along with its counterpart in Srinagar, was operated by the state government with technical assistance from AIR, in keeping with the special status given to Jammu and Kashmir. But it was not until 1961 that it radiated on world band, using a 1 kW shortwave transmitter. This was later upgraded to 2 kW, then finally shut down in 1994. Patient efforts are underway to resume shortwave using a 50 kW BEL transmitter.

Heroic Rescue Saves Station

Another Radio Kashmir station, using only 250 Watts, was opened in the maharaja's pavilion at the Polo Ground in the state's capital, Srinagar, on July 1, 1948. Unlike the outlet in Jammu, the one serving Kashmir used shortwave to improve coverage throughout the region's mountainous terrain.

About three years later an electrical short caused the studios to be gutted. The whole building was ablaze in minutes, fueled by a storeroom packed with presto-discs. But thanks to swift aid from local citizens, almost all the equipment was saved. Most daring was the rescue of the transmitter, which was wrenched out by breaking a concrete beam just before the roof caved in.

AIR erected a tent, allowing broadcasts to resume in only two hours. They then continued for three days until space was found in the government's arts emporium. In 1957 the gutted building at the Polo Ground was eventually rebuilt and the transmitter upgraded to 7.5 kW. Later, it was further boosted to 10 kW, ostensibly to cater to the divided peoples on both sides of the border, then that transmitter was replaced by an indigenous BEL 50 kW unit.

By then, the station had finally moved to a spacious building on Sherwani Road in 1964, where it still exists in fortified surroundings. It has been the target of several terrorist and rocket attacks, and personnel have even been assassinated.

With an Indian army patrol only minutes away, Pakistani-supported rebels attack bus passengers in the Indian sector of Kashmir. M. Guha

Azad Kashmir Faces Indian Clandestines

The Pakistanis also had their bag of tricks. Their nonofficial station, started on April 16, 1948, was called Azad Kashmir Radio, or Radio Free Kashmir—Azad Kashmir is the name for the Kashmir's Pakistani-held area. For 12 years it operated in Trarkhel from mobile units in two army trucks. To counter this, the Indian Army, in cooperation with intelligence agencies and AIR, aired "black" clandestine radio transmissions from mobile military transmitters.

Pakistan fired back with additional clandestine operations from Sada-e Hurriyat-e Kashmir (Voice of Kashmiri Freedom), purportedly run by Kashmiri freedom fighters. But direction finding showed that these originated from Azad Kashmir Radio in Muzzaffarabad. On October 15, 1971, Azad Kashmir Radio moved to its permanent residence in Muzzaffarabad. The tiny mobile unit was replaced by a nominally 10 kW shortwave transmitter that is much harder for faraway DXers to receive than the official power would suggest.

Stations Provide Surrogate Propaganda

The special status of these shadowy stations came in handy when the prime ministers of India and Pakistan agreed not to broadcast propaganda against each other. This prompted a charade where both sides refrained from hostile remarks over official outlets, but aired volleys of vituperation against each other through their nonofficial stations.

As Miss Piggy would say, "Who, moi"?

Curious onlookers gather in the remote Kashmiri village of Tanmarg, where only journalists now dare to tread. M. Guha

A decaying fan and rusting racks are all that remain of once-majestic STC transmitters. They await their grim fate at AIR's Khampur facility in Delhi. M. Guha

switching between 36 curtain arrays strung on 15 antenna masts with nine miles or 15 kilometers of feeder lines. Ten program channels come in by microwave and satellite from a repeater in the nearby village of Nangloi.

With all this going on, the Kingsway site was getting overcrowded. Adding to the congestion were such extraneous factors as land grabbing and construction activity by influential mobsters. This left little room for growth, so on January 1, 1958 yet another site was established on 500 acres, about 200 hectares, of sparsely populated farmland near the village of Khampur outside Delhi. The first transmitter to be installed was a 100 kW Marconi, which subsequently was sold for scrap.

The war with China meant more horsepower, so two 20 kW AWA units were installed in 1962 under what was known as the Colombo Plan. These were powered by diesel generators, which came in quite handy during the numerous extended power failures throughout the war years. At one time these two transmitters carried the entire program load of the national services in a cacophony of regional languages.

Khampur Facility Still Growing

With the fear of Chinese intrusion in mind, new transmitters were installed three years later at Khampur. Two were of 50 kW, another two of 100 kW, all made by the State Trading Corporation (STC) of Australia. Only one of these transmitters' halls stands today, but it has been converted into a dingy storeroom. It serves as a dispirited graveyard for the once-majestic STC units entombed within, waiting for the next auctioneer's hammer or the torch of a scrap dealer.

A three-stage modernization plan was undertaken to rapidly transform Khampur into an external service transmission facility. In 1989 the first of two 250 kW Brown Boveri transmitters was commissioned exclusively for the External Services. An oblong but spacious antenna switching hall was built next to where the job was formerly done by men pulling long levers.

Second, in June 2000 a pair of 250 kW Continental Electronics units was delivered to the new hall. Alas, their operation was interrupted the following January because of overmodulation and careless operation.

Finally, rounding out the Khampur modernization scheme will be three new 250 kW Thomson-CSF transmitters. These should fire up sometime in 2002.

Rusty Rifle Protects "Secret" Site

The powers that be would like to keep the beefy Khampur site something of a secret, which is like trying to hide an airplane in a school parking lot. The site has 49 curtain arrays dangling from 15 towering antenna masts, all linked by nine miles or 15 kilometers of thick feeder lines—a dead giveaway to all but the truly blind, despite noble intentions to keep everything under wraps.

The veil of secrecy can be dumbfounding, as is the rusty vintage rifle carried by Khampur's lone guard. But AIR could be in worse company—a number of world band organizations from other major democracies also treat transmitter site information as hush-hush.

Muscular Transmitters Reach Worldwide

One of AIR's grandest projects has been the superpower shortwave transmitting facility at Dodhballapur, near the southern city of Bangalore. This station now carries the bulk of the external service load to far-flung regions.

Commissioned on March 10, 1990, Dodhballapur is spread across 632 acres (256 hectares) of sparsely populated countryside. This prestigious complex consists of six 500 kW Brown Boveri transmitters, which like Intel microprocessors have been named after regional rivers. Like Khampur, it is anything but secret, what with 36 antennas, 21 masts and a spaghetti bowl of feeder lines visible for miles around.

That same year, AIR consolidated its service to neighboring Nepal with a new shortwave transmitting station at Gorakhpur, not far from the Indo-Nepalese border. It has a lone 50 kW BEL indigenous transmitter for AIR's Nepali service, plus national programs at other times.

In order to strengthen its presence in the Persian Gulf, where there is a sizable Indian migrant population, another external service transmission site was set up on November 6, 1994. This was at Bambolim, not far from Panaji, capital of the former Portuguese colony of Goa. Spread over 53 acres or 21 hectares, this facility has two 250 kW Brown Boveri transmitters fed by nine curtain antenna arrays.

Global Relays Rejected by Ministers

For listeners in the Americas, in particular, it seems puzzling that AIR's External Services have never provided them with world class signals.

AIR-Khampur's new 250 kW transmitters operate at reduced power, thanks to bureaucratic wrangling.

M. Guha

Yet, it is not for lack of trying. AIR executives have repeatedly pushed their ministerial chiefs to extend the External services' reach via relays and exchanges of transmitter time. This would allow the station to reach larger numbers of the Indian diaspora and others in the Americas and beyond.

Thus far the shadow of the abortive fiasco with VOA seems to have set an unhappy precedent among those in high office. However, as cautious veterans retire and fresh blood steps in, AIR may yet take these steps, allowing it a place of distinction among international news and cultural sources.

Manosij Guha, on assignment for PASSPORT *in India, is a media developer and reporter currently based in the United States.*

Ten of the Best: 2002's Top Shows

World band radio offers an exceptional lineup of news, sports, music, theater, comedy and other entertainment—much of it difficult or impossible to find elsewhere. So that you won't miss the finest of these listening opportunities, PASSPORT's monitors have winnowed through hundreds of today's shows to select ten of the very best.

Times and days are in World Time, while "winter" and "summer" refer to seasons in the Northern Hemisphere, where summer is in the middle of the year.

"Play of the Week"
BBC World Service

Gone are the days when BBC World Service listeners thrilled to serialized adaptations of books by Dick

Francis, John Le Carré and others in "Thirty-Minute Theatre." Today, Sid Halley and George Smiley have been replaced by "Westway," a politically correct soap with as much snap as a dead alligator.

Yes, PC has come to the BBC World Service, along with other measures that are dumbing down this onetime pearl of the airwaves. But even while programming is being made lite, management says it is targeting today's World Service to "elites." Eviscerating substance to appeal to educated elites has it backwards, so smart money is betting that there is another agenda, perhaps to have the World Service evolve into a commercial broadcaster.

Is the BBC World Service going commercial?

In the meantime, not all is lost. Even the BBC's hip new planners could not do away with a long-running *tour de force* like "Play of the Week." Whether it's a centuries-old classic, a newly commissioned work from an established playwright, or a show written by a listener in India—it is theater at its very best. And the actors are world class. Each play lasts between 60 and 90 minutes, and there are usually no interludes.

Following the BBC's cutbacks in its transmissions to the Americas, listeners in eastern *North America* have just one opportunity, at 2301 Saturday (may be one hour later in winter) on 5975 kHz. 12095 kHz (beamed to South America) may also be usable, though it tends to suffer from teletype interference unless your radio has synchronous selectable sideband. Listeners on the West Coast should tune to the BBC's Asian stream on 9740 kHz at 1131 Sunday.

Europe has a Sunday slot at 1701; choose from 6195, 9410 and (summer) 12095 kHz.

In the *Middle East*, it's the same time summer as for Europe; winter timing may be one hour later. Best bet is 15575 kHz, although 12095 kHz should also provide adequate reception.

Chilean playwright and author Ariel Dorfman (scarf) visits with the "Play of the Week" cast for his *Konfidenz*: (clockwise, from lower left) Anton Lesser, Andrew Wincott, Gavin Muir, producer Rosalynd Ward, Jonathan Broadbent and Luisa Bradshaw-Wright.

BBC World Service Press Office

Svetlana Yekimenko prepares "Music and Musicians," 47 outstanding minutes of classical Russian offerings.

VoR

For *Southern Africa*, the performance starts at 1501 Sunday on 6190, 11940 and 21470 kHz.

In *East* and *Southeast Asia*, tune in at 1131 Sunday on 6195, 9740, 9815 and 15280 kHz. Of these, 6195 and 9740 kHz are best for *Southeast Asia*.

Australasia, like North America, is no longer an official target for the BBC World Service. However, reception at 1131 Sunday on 9740 kHz should be more than adequate.

"Music and Musicians" Voice of Russia

Shortwave is hardly the ideal medium for music, yet some of the finest classical offerings are found on the world band airwaves.

One of the most consistently enjoyable is "Music and Musicians," a 47-minute jewel from the Voice of Russia. Whether it is Rachmaninoff at his most romantic, or the latest from a festival for young composers, the flavor is unequivocally Russian. Short interviews, historical anecdotes and other informative tidbits complete the program, but never at the expense of the music.

There is no specific airing for *North America*, but listeners on the East Coast should try the frequencies for Europe.

Winter slots for *Europe* are at 1711 Saturday on 7170 kHz; 1811 Sunday on 5940, 6045, 7340, 9775 and 9890 kHz; and 2111 Sunday on 5940, 5950, 6045, 7300, 7340 and 9890 kHz. In summer, tune in at 1711 Sunday on 9480, 9685, 9775, 9890 and 11675 kHz; and 2011 Sunday on 9480, 9775, 9890, 11675, 12070 and 15455 kHz.

Winter in the *Middle East*, try 1711 Saturday on 9470 and 9830 kHz, and 1811 Sunday on 9830 kHz. In summer, check 11985 and 15540 kHz at 1611 Saturday, and 11985 kHz at 1711 Sunday.

For *Southeast Asia* the only winter opportunity is at 0811 Monday on 17655 kHz. Summer, there's a choice between 0811 Sunday and 0711 Monday on 15490 kHz.

In *Australasia* the winter schedule is 0911 Sunday on 9905, 15460, 15470, 17495 and 17525 kHz; and 0811 Monday on 9905, 15460, 15470, 17495, 17525 and 17570 kHz. Midyear, it's 0811 Sunday on 17495, 17525, 17635 and 17685 kHz; and 0711 Monday on 17495, 17525, 17635 and 17685 kHz.

"EuroQuest" Radio Netherlands

"EuroQuest" is news from and about Europe—no surprise there. What is unusual is that politics is kept to a minimum, with most airtime being given over to environmental and social issues, the arts, and topics of general interest.

Muslims in secular Turkey, Belgium's relations with its former colonies, young people in post-war Bosnia, or opera performances on a Bavarian farm—no matter how varied the topics, the show is seamlessly put together by host Jonathan Groubert.

All editions are broadcast on local Mondays within target areas.

"Reporting Religion" BBC World Service

The title says it all: straight news, focusing on religious topics.

Yet, it is anything but another folded-hands offering for the pious. Some items are interesting but non-controversial, while others can set off sparks. A report on stopping dam construction to avoid flooding the Buddha's birthplace might not stir the juices, but an interview at a Hamas school for "martyrs" is another matter.

Faith guides much in the way of politics, so understanding religion can help us make sense of events in faraway cultures. "Reporting Religion" lasts only 15 minutes, but is worth soaking up even if you are militantly secular.

All editions are broadcast on Sunday.

North America gets a raw deal, being the only area without a fixed time year round. The summer slot of 2145 Sunday clashes with the BBC's flagship news program, "Newshour," in winter, so it gets shifted back many hours to 0130, which corresponds to Saturday evening local American date. The 0130 and 2145 transmissions are both on 5975 and 12095 kHz; the latter is audible even though it is beamed to South America, but it tends to suffer from teletype interference unless your radio has synchronous selectable sideband. For western North America, the best option is to try the Asian stream on 15360 kHz at 0530 and 0915.

Europe is well taken care of at 0530 on 6195, 9410 and 12095 kHz; and 0915 on 12095, 15565 and 17640 kHz.

For the *Middle East* it's 0915 on 11760 and 15575 kHz ; and in *Southern Africa* the same edition airs on 6190, 11940 and 21470 kHz.

East Asia choices are 0530 and 0915, both on 15360, 17760 and 21660 kHz. For *Southeast Asia* at the same times, there's 9740 and 15360 kHz, with the latter also audible in *Australasia*.

Prepared by Don Swampo and the staff of PASSPORT TO WORLD BAND RADIO.

www.passband.com

The Many Voices of Vietnam

by Hans Johnson

Vietnam: Its very mention evokes images of a sanguinary past, but today it's a new ball game. One quarter of the population wasn't even born until after the war ended in 1975, and many others are too young to remember.

Vietnam is barely larger than New Mexico, with a population of about 80 million. More than ninety percent are ethnic Vietnamese who live mainly along the coast near the Gulf of Tonkin and South China Sea. The remaining ten percent is a mosaic of no fewer than fifty-odd ethnic groups. These intriguing subcultures are concentrated in Vietnam's highlands and mountainous regions, well away from the majority coastal population.

World Band Thrives

Outside Indochina, world band listeners keep in touch through the external service of the Voice of Vietnam. It offers extensive programming in English and other languages, and is easily heard thanks in part to relay transmitters in faraway lands (see sidebar).

Those with talent, location, superior receiving equipment—and luck—can also eavesdrop on Vietnam's numerous domestic services on shortwave. National networks from Hanoi are relatively easy to hear, but provincial stations are faint and challenging.

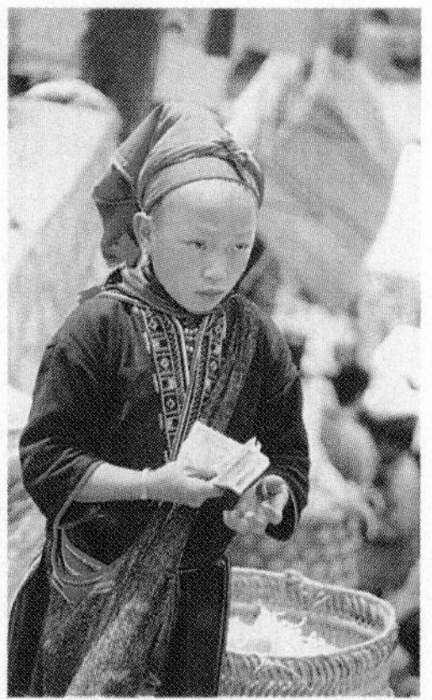

Red Dao girl heads to the village market.

Global Spectrum

Domestic Services Heard Worldwide

Two of Vietnam's three national domestic networks use world band frequencies to blanket the country in Vietnamese. These are regularly heard around sunrise in North America, as well as at various times elsewhere around the world.

Voice of Vietnam-One, the primary network, focuses on news and current affairs. Using a 50 kW transmitter nominally in Hanoi but possibly around Dak Lak province in the south, its channel of 5975 kHz is aired from 2200 to 1600 (1700 Fridays) World Time, along with another 50 kW unit in Hanoi on 9530 kHz. Another frequency, 7210 kHz, is used at 2300-2330, 0000-0330, 0500-0930 and 1100-1600, with minority-language programming during the three gaps, but is easier to receive. It uses a 20 kW transmitter, same location.

Hanoi is easy to hear, but provincial stations are tougher.

Voice of Vietnam-Two helps unify the country by presenting cultural and educational programs. Its main frequency of 5925 kHz is on from 2200 to 1600 World Time from a 50 kW transmitter at Xuân Mai, southwest of Hanoi. Its other frequency, 6020 kHz, is much harder to pick up. It is aired at 2300-0400, 0500-0930 and 1030-1600 World Time from a 20 kW transmitter in Hanoi shared with the Voice of Vietnam's minority-language service.

Hà Van Sicong weaves baskets in the tradition of Vietnam's Thai ethnic minority. M. Richer

VIETNAM'S GLOBAL VOICE WIDELY HEARD

The Viet Minh inaugurated the Voice of Vietnam's external service broadcasts in September 1945. Initially these emanated from Hanoi with programs in English, French and Chinese from a 50 kW shortwave utility, or point-to-point, transmitter.

A few years earlier the French had agreed to Vietnam's independence, provided the Viet Minh would join with the Allies in their fight against the Japanese occupation army. Although the Viet Minh upheld their end of the bargain, the French changed their minds after the war.

During the resulting struggle, the Viet Minh had to flee Hanoi as the French colonial army reestablished its presence in Vietnam. A similar situation occurred in the south of the country, where the Viet Minh had to abandon a world band transmitter site in Saigon (now Ho Chi Minh City) before they could even transmit from it.

For the next several years, Vietnamese forces operated on the run from the French, changing the location of their station over a dozen times. The Voice of Vietnam also survived French psychological warfare efforts, as well as at least one raid by French paratroops.

World Band Expands after French Defeat

After the Viet Minh reoccupied Hanoi in 1953, they pressed the former French regional station into service. A 10 kW shortwave utility station, call sign "HVA," was also used for broadcasts.

With Chinese assistance in the 1960s and early 1970s, the North Vietnamese built up their fleet of shortwave transmitters, but the Voice of Vietnam's domestic and external services were still difficult to hear abroad. This worsened in 1972 when the Christmas B-52 bombing campaign knocked much of the station off the air.

Relays Improve Reception

Today, the Voice of Vietnam includes three domestic networks and the external service. The external service uses eleven 100 kW transmitters at Son Tây, northwest of Hanoi.

In the last decade these have been supplemented by overseas transmitter sites, a practice similar to that which began when Radio Habana Cuba aired the "Voice of Vietnam" over world band during the Vietnam War. That was not a relay as such, but rather a separate program jointly prepared in Havana by both stations. Still, it brought North Vietnamese newscasts to millions who otherwise would not have had a chance to hear it.

Genuine relay broadcasts began from Krasnodar, Russia on New Year's Day of 1995, improving reception of the Voice of Vietnam in Europe and North America. The station further strengthened its reception in North America by concluding an agreement with Britain's Merlin Communications in mid-2000. It provides for relaying VoV programs in English and Vietnamese from the powerful Radio Canada International facility at Sackville NB, Canada.

The relay via Russia is heard in English on 12070 kHz at 1700-1730 World Time summer, 7440 kHz at 1800-1830 winter. From Canada, English for eastern North America is at 0100-0130 and 0230-0300 on 9525 kHz; for western North America, tune in at 0330-0400 on 9795 kHz.

Industry scuttlebutt is that the Voice of Vietnam's external service may make greater use of overseas relays before long. Among options reportedly being considered is the Sentech shortwave facility at Meyerton, South Africa. If so, Vietnam's global voice may begin to rival those of the world's major international broadcasters.

COMPAQ
Rinnai
AGFA

You can buy everything from eels to baguettes at the Ben Thanh Market. This is the former Saigon's largest market, dating back to French colonial times. S. Bailey

Minority Languages from Hanoi

What about those colorful ethnic groups that live inland?

Vietnam has a national network exclusively for them, with programs in various minority languages. At least three separate program streams have been monitored so far: 7210 kHz with the first stream, which shares a transmitter with VoV-One; and 6020 kHz with the second stream, which shares a transmitter with VoV-Two. Both transmitters are active 2200-1600 World Time, carrying national and minority programs.

The third stream is entirely in the Hmong ("Meo") language. Numbering just over half a million, the Hmong are the seventh-largest minority group in Vietnam, and suffered exceptionally after having allied themselves with the Americans during the war. Nearly all are concentrated in the mountain provinces northwest of Hanoi. The Hmong have no written language and are eighty percent illiterate—many, especially women, can't even speak Vietnamese, so Hmong-language radio is a "must." Broadcasting from Xuân Mai on 6165 kHz and the variable frequency of 5034 kHz, these broadcasts air at 2200-2300, 0500-0600 and 1200-1330 World Time; all are 15 kW except 6165 kHz at 0400-0500, when it is 50 kW. In North America, the best hope for reception is after 1200 on 6165 kHz.

Provincial Broadcasts Added

In 1948 the French established Vietnam's first regional shortwave stations in four towns of southern Vietnam. Serving close-by regions, these 1 kW stations filled the exact role that provincial stations were to play a few decades later.

However, by the time South Vietnamese authorities took over the stations in 1954,

With each boat adorned in blue, the fishing fleet at Nha Trang pulls in some of Vietnam's best seafood.

S. Bailey

only Hue and Dalat remained on the air. The authorities added a small 0.2 kW facility at Nha Trang in 1960, but all this and all others were moved over to mediumwave AM by 1970.

In North Vietnam, shortwave broadcasting was confined to Hanoi until the 1960s, when the first provincial stations went on the air from two northern autonomous regions. The government rapidly expanded the number of stations in the late 1970s, using sites of former regional broadcasters as well as provincial capitals in the north. At their peak in 1980 fully eighteen provincial stations were active, but deteriorating equipment and skimpy budgets have driven several off the air.

Vietnam now focuses on FM and mediumwave AM for provincial and district broadcasting, so most provincial shortwave transmitters are more than 20 years old. Given their age, the country's humid climate and a scarcity of spare parts, it has become impossible to keep some of these transmitters going.

Today, the stronghold of local shortwave broadcasting lies in the extreme north, where hills and mountains create a rugged landscape largely inhabited by ethnic minorities. Here, shortwave outperforms FM and mediumwave AM, so world band signals continue to emit from no less than six provincial capitals.

Vietnam's far north is also one of the least developed parts of Vietnam, with few roads and rough terrain that inhibits travel. Northern minority peoples suffer from poverty and illiteracy, but with their traditional way of living and colorful dress and crafts, they are among the biggest attractions in Vietnam's growing tourist industry.

Yet, even a seven-dollar Chinese radio is too costly, so a program tailored for the northern region subsidizes radio purchases. The government has also given away two million radios nationwide.

Provinces Offer Challenging Reception

Provincial stations offer DX aficionados an exceptional challenge. For starters, broadcasts are in Vietnamese and other languages that few understand outside Vietnam.

Another hurdle is that transmitters have only modest power—around one kilowatt—and sometimes drift in frequency or have poor modulation.

Fortunately, they often operate on out-of-band frequencies, making use of a special provision of the ITU regulations. These small stations might be overwhelmed within crowded world band segments, but transmitting in the "wide open spaces" allows a weak signal a better chance of squeaking through.

Some provincial stations relay large chunks of national programming from Hanoi, but most create the bulk of their own programming. The draw for foreign listeners is indigenous music, which ranks as some of the most enjoyable on the planet. Through songs and ballads, provincial stations offer a delightful window on the culture of Vietnam's minority peoples.

Six Provinces Audible on World Band

Six Vietnamese provinces have stations on world band frequencies, although they are anything but easy to receive.

Son La is the name of both the province and its capital. Best known for having a famous horse market, the town is flanked by mountains and enjoys a climate that is temperate year round.

World band broadcasts began here about 1967 in what was then known as the Tay Bac autonomous region. Son La originally had two transmitters, one in the 6 MHz range and one around 4.7 MHz. The 6 MHz unit gave up the ghost in 1995, but the latter is still soldiering away. For several years it regularly alternated between 4740 and 4795 kHz, but now has settled on 4795-6v kHz. Son La airs local programming at 2300-0030 and 1200-1400 World Time, but it is the final transmission, during local evening hours, that's by far the most widely heard outside Indochina.

Lai Chau province is where the 1954 battle of Dien Bien Phu was fought between French and Viet Minh forces. Here, Vietnam won its independence from France, paving the way for the ill-fated Geneva accords and military intervention by the United States.

Lai Chau is inhabited by the Tai (Thai) people, an ethnic group not to be confused with the Thais of Thailand. They live in traditional stilt houses set among rolling hills, where men farm rice and woman weave cloth so elaborate that it looks like embroidery.

Like Son La, Lai Chau once had transmitters operating on both 4 and 6 MHz. Both were

During a break, farmers search for crayfish in their rice paddy. M. Richer

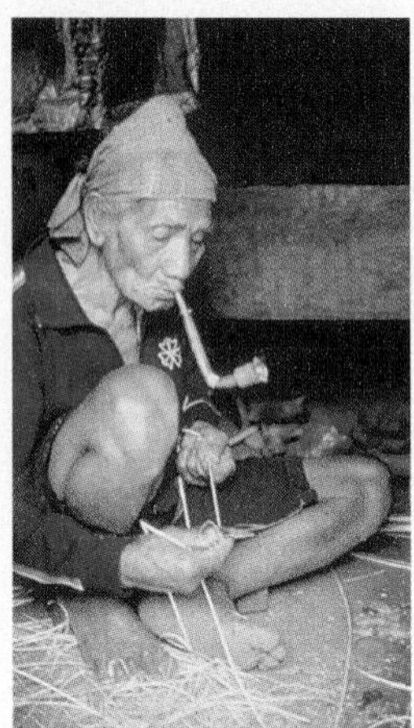

An elder of a Central Highlands' hill tribe smokes his pipe while starting to weave a basket. S. Bailey

commissioned in 1978, but the 4 MHz unit lasted only a few years. Luckily for world band listeners, the 6 MHz unit still provides good service on 6381 kHz at 2200-2400, 0300-0500 and 1100-1400, with programs in Vietnamese, Hmong and Tai.

The provincial capital of **Lao Cai** uses the same name as its province. It completely defies the stereotypical image of Vietnam as a land of rice paddies and jungle—from here, visitors look out over snow-capped peaks during the winter.

The town of Lao Cai is on the Red River, along the Sino-Vietnamese border and just opposite the Chinese town of Hekou. Lao Cai province is just northeast of Lai Chau, so ethnic Tai also live here.

Lao Cai fired up world band transmissions in 1978. As Vietnam's relations with China were tense, the station began airing programs in Chinese. When a border war erupted the following year, the Chinese briefly occupied the town.

In 1993 a new world band transmitter began operating in the 6 MHz range. Today, two birdcage-type shortwave antennas stretch over the station's compound on the west end of town. These transmit the same programs on 5597 and 6724 kHz, although both transmitters drift—the latter by dozens of kilohertz. They are on from 0300 to 0430, 0945 to 1100 and 1145 to 1400 World Time, but only the last two are ever heard outside Asia. Programming is in Vietnamese, as well as the languages of the Miao-yao and Tai peoples.

Ha Giang is Vietnam's northernmost province. Its station operated in the 4 MHz range when transmissions began in 1979, but it now operates on 7156 kHz.

Many girls have already started to wear the distinctive headdress for which the Red Hmong people of northern Vietnam are famous. FEBC

Hmong women sit down to lunch in the village of Sapa. They excel at embroidery, while their crafts and colorful dress draw in tourists.

Global Spectrum

Ha Giang is one of the most difficult provincial stations to hear. Yet, it is easy to identify because, unlike most other regional outlets, it relays the Voice of Vietnam-One from Hanoi at 0858-1300 World Time.

From 1300 until sign-off at 1400, Ha Giang airs local programming. This consists mostly of spoken programs, as unlike other provincial stations Ha Giang carries little indigenous music. Ha Giang is also on the air at 2300-0130 and 0300-0600, although hours vary—it may or may not relay Hanoi at these times. Modulation (volume) is invariably low and the signal is weak, making reception an aural strain. Indeed, Ha Giang's transmitter is probably the weakest of the provincials, with a power of well under 1kW.

Cao Bang is also on the Sino-Vietnamese border. The most famous attraction here is the Pac Bo cave, where in 1941 Ho Chi Minh made his headquarters after returning to Vietnam from exile abroad. The station's single world band transmitter has been active since 1977.

Cao Bang's frequency of 6493 kHz drifts slightly, but the station puts out a nice signal and has decent modulation. It operates at 0300-0500 and 1200-1400 World Time, signing on each time with a brief offering of instrumental music, followed by a man and a woman giving the station's identification in Vietnamese.

Lang Son is Vietnam's hardest-to-hear regional broadcaster. First noted in 1979, this station now drifts between 4660 and 4740 kHz. It is so weak that it is difficult to hear even within Vietnam.

Lang Son may be confused with the Laotian regional station at Houa Phan, also on 4660 kHz. The easiest way to tell the two apart is that Lang Son relays the "One" Network from Hanoi for much of the day.

Distinctive Regional Music

Vietnam's national minorities have created music as distinctive as their dress. Commonly heard on provincial stations are a capella songs—no instruments, just the standalone eloquence of the human voice.

The reasons for this are simple and practical. "A capella is a prominent fact of [their] music," explains Dr. Pho Nguyen, ethnomusicologist at Kent State University in Ohio. He adds that many among Vietnam's minorities still work as farmers and peasants. Like Africans, they sing while they work, where it is impractical to play instruments. The popularity of this style has spilled over into radio, where it is shared with fortunate world band enthusiasts.

In the Hmong tradition, a capella is also used during courtship by young women, according to Jason Gibbs, an American researcher of Vietnamese music. "The Hmong have strong imitation of their tonal language in both their vocal and instrumental music," adds Gibbs.

Hill tribe children at home outside Dalat. S. Bailey

Nonetheless, instruments are used for certain pieces. In Hmong music a type of mouth organ, called the geng or khenh, is used, with the player often dancing to his own music. In the Central Highlands, gongs are preferred—so much so, according to Nguyen, that it is said, "gong music is in your blood."

Minorities aren't alone in producing exceptional music. The majority Vietnamese use instruments such as lutes, including the single-stringed variety, to create haunting and beautiful tunes.

Vietnam is an aural paradise for radio aficionados. Listeners in much of the world can kick back and enjoy the Voice of Vietnam's English and other programs from powerful transmitters. Meanwhile, DXers can go beyond this by eavesdropping on Vietnam's bouillabaisse of elusive provincial stations.

Hans Johnson is the founder of Cumbre DX *(www.cumbredx.org), the world's largest weekly shortwave newsletter. This article was made possible in part by valuable input from Alan Davies in Malaysia and* Cumbre *contributors.*

985

Hanoi's Army Museum is a national showplace. This tank smashed through the Presidential Palace gate in Saigon when North Vietnamese troops entered in April 1975. S. Bailey

GRUNDIG Gift Collection

GRUNDIG
DESIGN BY F·A·PORSCHE
6:05

A gift for the auto enthusiast

Maneuver the Porsche Design G2000A Digital Radio Alarm Clock

... to all points around the globe. Wake up to sports and talk radio on AM, soothing stereo (with earphones) on FM or fascinating shortwave from around the world... select from 13 International bands from 2.3 - 7.4 and 9.4 - 26.1 MHz. Punch in any station or lock your favorites into 20 memories... other features include digital clock and alarm with Quartz accuracy... earphones... butter-soft handcrafted leather case. Designed by F. A. Porsche, the G2000A is a pleasure to own and operate. Requires 3 AA batteries (not included).

Dimensions: 5.5″ L × 3.5″ H × 1.375″ W
Weight: 11.52 oz.

HI-FI Sound
960
GRUNDIG Classic

A gift for the collector

50th Anniversary Edition Classic 960

AM/FM Stereo Shortwave Radio Nostalgia... remember when a radio was a center piece... handcrafted wooden cabinet ...unforgettable European styling... legendary sound. Those days are back! With the solid-state 960, Grundig's Famous 1950s Classic is updated and improved... two 3″ side speakers, left and right, and the 4″ front speaker will fill your room with exquisite sound... and let you travel the globe without leaving home... receives shortwave continuously from 2.3-22.3 MHz... additional features include: stereo inputs for CD, tape, VCR, or TV sound.

Dimensions: 15.5″ L × 11.25″ H × 7″ W
Weight: 9 lbs. 9.6 oz.

PASSPO

raveller II PE (TR2PE)

he world's best-selling travel radio. A compact adio with outstanding performance! This practical and stylish travel companion features AM, FM and five shortwave bands, plus a world clock for 24-time zones and simultaneous display of home and world time in a digital display. Titanium-look inish. Comes with 3 AA batteries, earphones, carrying pouch.

uner Frequency Ranges:

FM	88-108 MHz
AM	530-1600KHz
SW Bands	49, 41, 31, 25 and 19 meters
)utput:	Micro Speaker or earphones
3atteries:	3 AA (included)
)imensions:	5.5" L × 3.5" H × 1.25" W
Veight:	9.92 oz.

MINI WORLD 100 PE
GRUNDIG
PASSPORT

Aini World 100 PE (Mini). Grundig's smallest ocket World Band Radio....Travel with the world in our pocket. Another exciting breakthrough in world and technology. A well built radio that fits in the alm of your hand. AM/FM-Stereo/SW radio with ED indicator, six shortwave broadcast bands, elescopic antenna, earphones and belt clip make stening easy. Comes with soft carrying case.

uner Frequency Ranges

M	88-108MHz
M	525-1625MHz
W1	5.80-6.40MHz
W2	6.90-7.50MHz
W3	9.40-7.50MHz
W4	11.65-12.15MHz
W5	15.00-15.65MHz
W6	17.50-18.14MHz
)utput:	Micro Speaker or Earphones
atteries:	2 AA (included)
imensions:	2.75" L × 4" H × .75" W
Veight:	4.48 oz.

by **GRUNDIG**

Lextronix / Grundig, P.O. Box 2307, Menlo Park, CA 94026 • Tel: 650-361-1611 • Fax: 650-361-1724
Shortwave Hotlines: (US) 1-800-872-2228 (CN) 1-800-637-1648 • Web: *www.grundigradio.com* • Email: *grundig@ix.netcom.com*

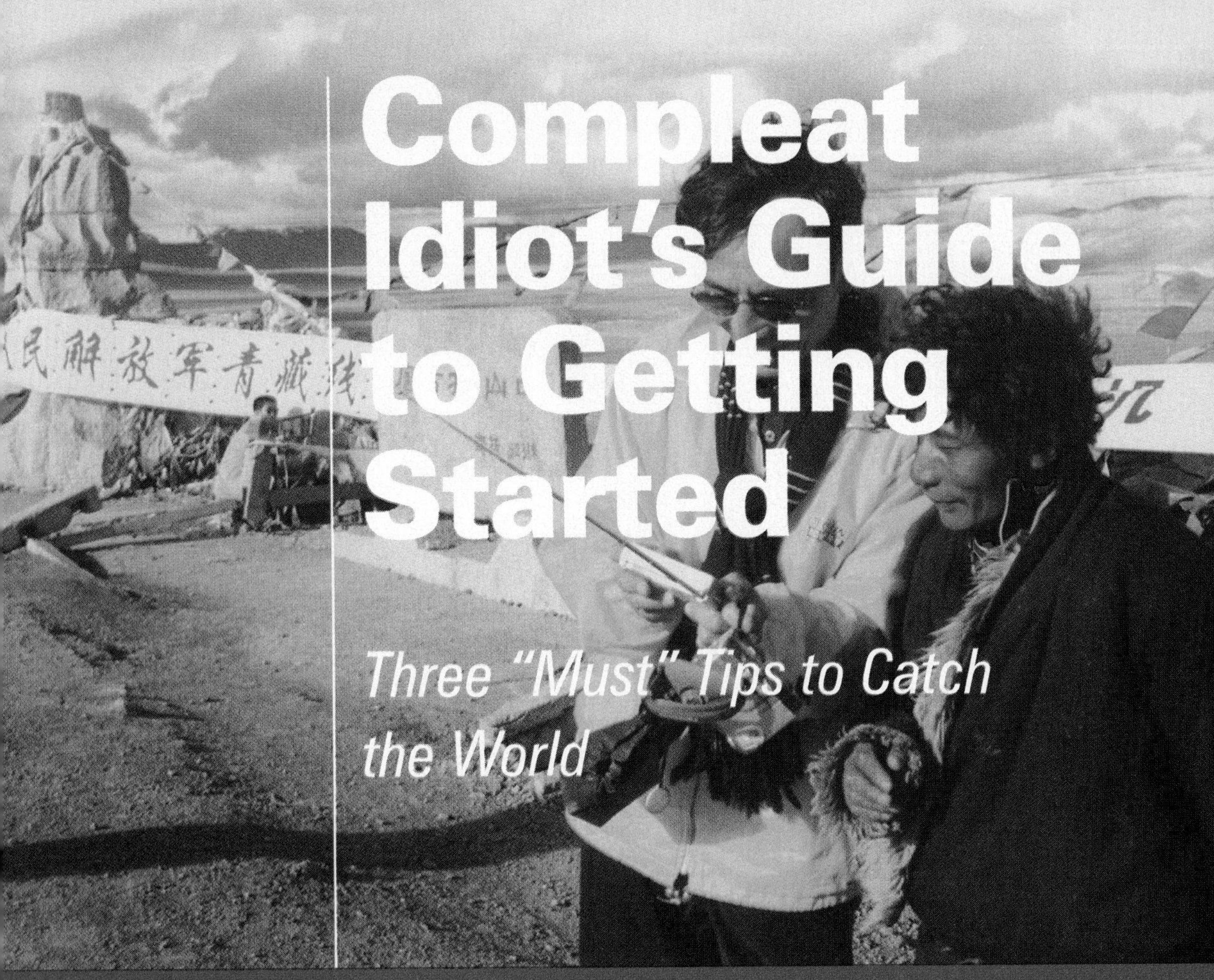
民解放军青藏线

Compleat Idiot's Guide to Getting Started

Three "Must" Tips to Catch the World

World band radio is your unfiltered connection to what's going on, but it differs from conventional radio. Here are three "must" tips to get started.

"Must" #1: World Time and Day

World band schedules use a single time, *World Time*. After all, world band radio is global, with stations broadcasting around-the-clock from virtually every time zone.

Imagine the chaos if each station used its own local time for scheduling. In England, 9:00 PM is different from nine in the evening in Japan or Canada. How would anybody know when to tune in?

World Time, or Coordinated Universal Time (UTC), is also known as Greenwich Mean Time (GMT) or, in the military, "Zulu." It is announced in 24-hour format, so 2 PM is 1400 ("fourteen hundred") hours.

There are four easy ways to know World Time. First, around North America tune to one of the standard time stations, such as WWV in Colorado and WWVH in Hawaii or CHU in Ottawa. WWV and WWVH are on 5000, 10000 and 15000 kHz, with WWV also on 2500 and 20000 kHz; CHU is on 3330, 7335 and 14670 kHz.

Second, tune to a major international broadcaster, such as the BBC World Service or Voice of America. Most announce World Time at the hour.

Third, on the Internet you can access World Time at various sites, including tycho.usno.navy.mil/what.html and www.nrc.ca/inms/time/cesium.shtml.

Fourth, see the sidebar to set your 24-hour clock. For example, if you live on the East Coast of the United States, *add* five hours winter (four hours summer) to your local time to get World Time. So, if it is 8 PM EST (the 20th hour of the day) in New York, it is 0100 hours World Time.

Once you know the correct World Time, adjust your radio's 24-hour clock. No clock? Get one now unless you enjoy doing weird computations in your head (it's 6:00 PM here, so add five hours to make it 11:00 PM, which on a 24-hour clock converts to 23:00 World Time—but, whoops, it's summer so I should have added four hours instead of five . . .). It will be the best money you've ever spent.

Remember that at midnight a new *World Day* arrives. This can trip up even experienced listeners—sometimes radio stations, too. So if it is 9 PM EST Wednesday in New York, it is 0200 hours World Time *Thursday*. Don't forget to "wind your calendar"!

Known in radio circles as RAFARS 4323, Mikiko uses a Packard Bell PC with an Icom IC-PCR1000 to listen from Surrey, England.

PASSPORT'S THREE-MINUTE START

No time? Try this:

1. Night time is the right time, so wait until evening when signals are strongest. In a concrete-and-steel building put your radio by a window or balcony.
2. Make sure your radio is plugged in or has fresh batteries. Extend the telescopic antenna fully and vertically. Set the DX/local switch (if there is one) to "DX," but otherwise leave the controls the way they came from the factory.
3. Turn on your radio. Set it to 5900 kHz and begin tuning slowly toward 6200 kHz; you can also try 9400-9900 kHz. You should hear stations from around the world.

Other times? Read "Best Times and Frequencies for 2002."

What happens at midnight, World Time? A new *World Day* arrives, as well.

SETTING YOUR WORLD TIME CLOCK

PASSPORT's "Addresses PLUS" lets you arrive at the local time in another country by adding or subtracting from World Time. Use that section to determine the time within a country you are listening to.

This box, however, gives it from the other direction—that is, what to add or subtract from your local time so you can determine World Time. Use this to set your World Time clock.

Wherever in the world you live, you can also use Addresses PLUS, instead of this sidebar, to determine World Time simply by reversing the time difference. For example, Addresses PLUS states that Burundi's local time is "World Time +2." So if you're in Burundi, to set your World Time clock you would take Burundi time *minus* two hours.

WHERE YOU ARE — *TO DETERMINE WORLD TIME* 

North America

Newfoundland St. John's NF, St. Anthony NF	Add 3½ hours winter, 2½ hours summer
Atlantic St. John NB, Battle Harbour NF	Add 4 hours winter, 3 hours summer
Eastern New York, Atlanta, Toronto	Add 5 hours winter, 4 hours summer
Central Chicago, Mexico City, Nashville, Winnipeg	Add 6 hours winter, 5 hours summer
Mountain Denver, Salt Lake City, Calgary	Add 7 hours winter, 6 hours summer
Pacific San Francisco, Vancouver	Add 8 hours winter, 7 hours summer
Alaska	Add 9 hours winter, 8 hours summer
Hawaii	Add 10 hours

Central America & Caribbean

Bermuda	Add 3 hours
Bahamas, Barbados, Puerto Rico, Virgin Islands	Add 4 hours
Cuba	Add 5 hours winter, 4 hours summer
Jamaica	Add 5 hours
Costa Rica	Add 6 hours

Europe

United Kingdom, Ireland, Portugal	Same time as World Time winter, subtract 1 hour summer

Continental Western Europe; parts of Central and Eastern Continental Europe	Subtract 1 hour winter, 2 hours summer
Estonia, Lithuania	Subtract 2 hours year round
Elsewhere in Continental Europe: Belarus, Bulgaria, Cyprus, Finland, Greece, Latvia, Moldova, Romania, Russia (Kaliningradskaya Oblast), Turkey, Ukraine	Subtract 2 hours winter, 3 hours summer
Moscow	Subtract 3 hours winter, 4 hours summer

Mideast & Africa

Côte d'Ivoire, Ghana, Guinea, Liberia, Mali, Morocco, Senegal, Sierra Leone	World Time exactly
Angola, Benin, Chad, Congo, Nigeria, Tunisia	Subtract 1 hour
Egypt, Israel, Jordan, Lebanon, Syria	Subtract 2 hours winter, 3 hours summer
South Africa, Zambia, Zimbabwe	Subtract 2 hours
Ethiopia, Kenya, Kuwait, Saudi Arabia, Tanzania, Uganda	Subtract 3 hours
Iran	Subtract 3½ hours winter, 4½ hours summer

Asia & Australasia

Pakistan	Subtract 5 hours
India	Subtract 5½ hours
Bangladesh, Sri Lanka	Subtract 6 hours
Laos, Thailand, Vietnam	Subtract 7 hours
China (including Taiwan), Malaysia, Philippines, Singapore	Subtract 8 hours
Japan, Korea	Subtract 9 hours
Australia: ***Victoria, New South Wales, Tasmania***	Subtract 11 hours local summer, 10 local winter (midyear)
Australia: ***South Australia***	Subtract 10½ hours local summer, 9½ hours local winter (midyear)
Australia: ***Queensland***	Subtract 10 hours
Australia: ***Northern Territory***	Subtract 9½ hours
Australia: ***Western Australia***	Subtract 8 hours
New Zealand	Subtract 13 hours local summer, 12 hours local winter (midyear)

Digital Technology

GRUNDIG
YB 400PE
40 STATION MEMORIES
SSB
LW/MW/SW/FM STEREO PLL SYNTHESIZED DUAL CONVERSION

GRUNDIG
YB 300PE
24 STATION MEMORIES

Yacht Boy 400PE

Powerful performance and sleek titanium look design combined with sophisticated features make the YB 400PE a value! Covers shortwave, AM, FM-stereo and longwave: SW 1.6-30 MHz, AM 530-1710 KHz, FM 88-108 MHz, LW 150-353 KHz. SSB circuitry for reception of shortwave single sideband two-way communications, e.g. ham radio, aeronautical and marine. 2 clocks. 40 memories. Built-in antennas. External SW antenna socket. Includes AC adapter, case, earphones, supplementary SW antenna. Uses 6 AA batteries (not included). Dimensions: 7.75″ L x 4.5″ H x 1.5″ W.
Weight: 1 lb. 5 oz.

Yacht Boy 300PE

Listen to broadcasts from countries around the globe on all 13 shortwave international broadcast bands. Local AM and FM-stereo too. Fully digital PLL. Direct frequency entry. Auto scan. Push-button tuning. Clock, alarm and 10 to 90 minute sleep timer. 24 memories. Titanium color. Easy-read LCD. Display light. External SW antenna socket. Carrying strap. Includes AC adapter, case, earphones, batteries, supplementary SW antenna. Compact. Dimensions: 5.75″ L x 3.5″ H x 1.25″ W.
Weight: 12 oz.

GRUNDIG
GRUNDIG
DESIGN BY F·A·PORSCHE

Porsche Design
G200A AM/FM/SW Radio

Wake up to sports and talk radio on AM, soothing stereo (with earphones) on FM or fascinating shortwave from around the world... select from 13 International bands from 2.3 - 7.4 and 9.4 - 26.1 MHz. Punch in any station or lock your favorites into 20 memories... other features include digital clock and alarm with Quartz accuracy... earphones... buttersoft handcrafted leather case. Designed by F.A. Porsche, the G2000A is a pleasure to own and operate. Uses 3 AA batteries (not included). Dimensions: 5.5″ L x 3.5″ H x 1.375″ W
Weight: 11.52 oz.

Lextronix / Grundig, P.O. Box 2307, Menlo Park, CA 94026 • Tel: 650-361-1611 • Fax: 650-361-1724
Shortwave Hotlines: (US) 1-800-872-2228 (CN) 1-800-637-1648 • Web: www.grundigradio.com • Email: grundig@ix.netcom.com

BEST TIMES AND FREQUENCIES FOR 2002

With world band, if you dial randomly you're just as likely to get dead air as a program. That's because some world band segments are alive and kicking only by day, while others spring to life at night. Others fare better at certain times of the year.

This guide is most accurate if you're listening from north of Africa or South America. Even then, what you'll actually hear will vary—depending upon your location, where the station transmits from, the time of year and your radio (*see* Propagation in the glossary). Although world band is active around the clock, signals are usually best from an hour or two before sunset until sometime after midnight. Too, try a couple of hours on either side of dawn. **Nighttime** refers to your local hours of darkness, plus dawn and dusk.

Possible Reception Nighttime

2 MHz (120 meters) **2300-2495 kHz**—overwhelmingly domestic stations, with 2496-2504 kHz for time stations only.

Limited Reception Nighttime

3 MHz (90 meters) **3200-3400 kHz**—overwhelmingly domestic stations.

Good-to-Fair in Europe and Asia except Summer Nights; Elsewhere, Limited Reception Nighttime

4 MHz (75 meters) **3900-4050 kHz**—international and domestic stations, primarily not in or beamed to the Americas; 3900-3950 kHz mainly Asian and Pacific transmitters; 3950-4000 kHz also includes European and African transmitters; 4001-4050 kHz currently out-of-band.

Some Reception Nighttime; Regional Reception Daytime

5 MHz (60 meters) **4750-4995 kHz** and **5005-5100 kHz**—mostly domestic stations, with 4996-5004 kHz for time stations only and 5061-5100 kHz currently out-of-band.

Excellent Nighttime; Regional Reception Daytime

6 MHz (49 meters) **5730-6300 kHz**—5730-5899 kHz and 6201-6300 kHz currently out-of-band.

Good Nighttime; Regional Reception Daytime

7 MHz (41 meters) **6890-6990 kHz** and **7100-7600 kHz**—6890-6990 kHz and 7351-7600 kHz currently out-of-band; 7100-7300 kHz no American-based transmitters and few transmissions targeted to the Americas.

9 MHz (31 meters) **9250-9995 kHz**—9250-9399 kHz and 9901-9995 kHz currently out-of-band; 9996-10004 kHz for time stations only.

Good Nighttime except Mid-Winter; Some Reception Daytime and Winter Nights; Good Asian and Pacific Reception Mornings in America

11 MHz (25 meters) **11500-12200 kHz**—11500-11599 kHz and 12101-12200 kHz currently out-of-band.

#2: How to Find Stations

tation schedules three ways: by country, time of day and frequency. By-country is best to hear a given station. "What's On Tonight," the time-of-day section, is like *TV Guide* and includes program descriptions from our listening panel. The by-frequency Blue Pages are ideal for when you're dialing around the bands.

World band frequencies are usually given in kilohertz (kHz), but a few stations use Megahertz (MHz). Forget all the technobabble—the main difference is three decimal places, so 6170 kHz is the same as 6.17 MHz, 6175 kHz identical to 6.175 MHz, and so on. All you need to know is that, either way, it refers to a certain spot on your radio's dial.

You're already used to hearing FM and mediumwave AM stations at the same spot on the dial, day and night, or Webcasts at the same URLs. But things are a lot different when you roam the international airwaves.

World band radio is like a global bazaar where a variety of merchants come and go at different times. Similarly, stations routinely enter and leave a given spot—frequency—on the dial throughout the day and night. Where you once tuned in, say, a French station, hours later you might find a Russian or Chinese broadcaster roosting on that same spot.

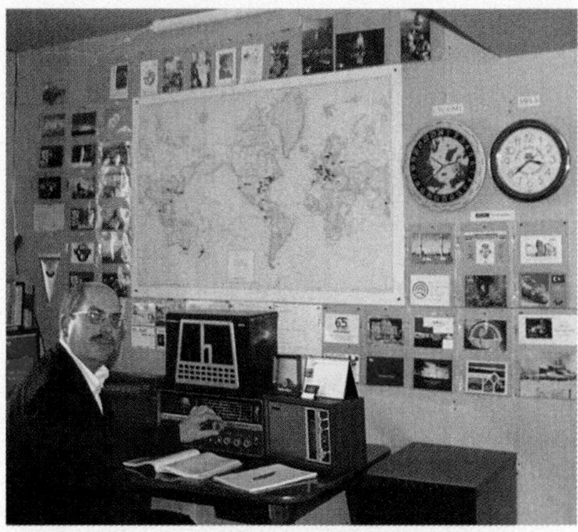

Leo Jacobson of Minneapolis enjoys his vintage Hallicrafters. "Hollow state" receivers, once consigned to molder in basements, are undergoing a revival.

Or on a nearby perch. If you suddenly hear interference from a station on an adjacent channel, it doesn't mean something is wrong with your radio; it probably means another station has begun broadcasting on

Good Daytime; Good Summer Nighttime

13 MHz (22 meters) **13570-13870 kHz**

15 MHz (19 meters) **15005-15800 kHz**—14996-15004 kHz for time stations only; 15005-15099 kHz currently out-of-band.

Good Daytime; Variable, Limited Reception Summer Nighttime

17 MHz (16 meters) **17480-17900 kHz**

19 MHz (15 meters) **18900-19020 kHz**

21 MHz (13 meters) **21450-21850 kHz**

Some Reception Daytime

25 MHz (11 meters) **25670-26100 kHz**

World band radio is free from regulation, free from fees—and largely free from ads, as well.

a nearby frequency. There are more stations on the air than there is space for them, so sometimes they try to outshout each other.

Technology to the rescue! To cope with this, purchase a radio with superior adjacent-channel rejection, also known as selectivity, and give preference to radios with synchronous selectable sideband. PASSPORT REPORTS, a major section of this book, tells you which stand out.

One of the most pleasant things about world band radio is cruising up and down the airwaves. Daytime, you'll find most stations above 11500 kHz; night, below 16000 kHz. Tune slowly, savor the sound of foreign tongues alongside English offerings. Enjoy the music, weigh the opinions of other peoples, hear the events that shape their lives and yours.

If a station can't be found or fades out, there is probably nothing wrong with your radio. The atmosphere's sky-high ionosphere deflects world band signals earthward, whereupon they bounce back up to the ionosphere, and so on like a dribbled basketball until they get to your radio. This is why world band radio is so unencumbered—its signals don't rely on cables or satellites or the Internet, just layers of ionized gases which have enveloped our planet for millions of years. World band is free from regulation, free from taxes, free from fees—and largely free from ads, as well.

WORLD TIME CLOCKS

Because World Time uses 24-hour format, digital clocks are easier to read than analog timepieces with hands. Some radios include a World Time clock that is displayed fulltime—these are best. Many other radios have World Time clocks, but you have to press a button to have time replace frequency in the display.

Some radios include a World Time clock that is displayed fulltime—these are best.

Basic Models

If your radio has no clock, a separate 24-hour digital clock or watch is a virtual "must." Here are two affordable choices, listed in order of cost.

MFJ-107B, $9.95. Bare-bones, but this battery-powered LCD "Volksclock" is good enough for many. Seconds not displayed numerically.

MFJ-118, $24.95, is similar to the '107B, but with large (1¼" or 32 mm) LCD numerals. Additionally, has an adjustable flip stand and a multilingual 100-year calendar. Seconds not displayed numerically.

Sophisticated Timepieces

For those who want only the very best, there are any number of high-tech 24-hour clocks ranging from under $100 to over $2,000. Nearly all display seconds numerically, and some synchronize the displayed time with one or another of the official atomic clock standards.

12:52
26

Moneray and MFJ solar-powered "atomic" clocks are synchronized with U.S. time station WWVB. Moneray

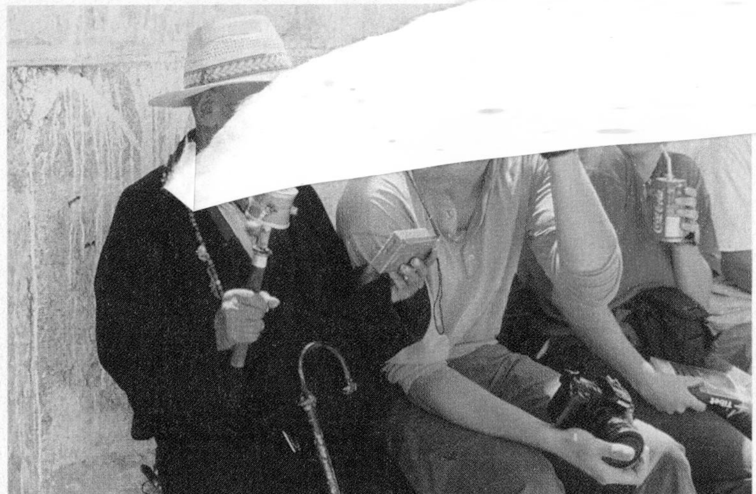

A. Hozour

But nature's ionosphere, like the weather, changes constantly, so world band stations have to adjust as best they can. The result is that broadcasters operate in different parts of the world band spectrum, depending upon the time of day and season of the year.

That same changeability can also work in your favor, especially if you like to eavesdrop on signals not intended for your part of the world. Sometimes stations from exotic locales—places you would not ordinarily hear—become surprise arrivals at your radio, thanks to the shifting characteristics of the ionosphere.

"Must" #3: The Right Radio

Choose carefully, but you shouldn't need a costly set. Avoid cheap radios, as they suffer from one or more major defects. With one of the better-rated portables you'll be able to hear much more of what world band has to offer.

Two basics: First, purchase a radio with digital frequency display—all radios tested for Passport Reports have digital readouts, but some vendors still carry analog models. Its accuracy and related digital features will make tuning far easier than with outmoded slide-rule tuning. Second, ensure the radio covers at least 4750-21850 kHz with no significant tuning gaps. Otherwise, you may not be able to tune in some stations you'd otherwise be able to hear.

You won't need an exotic outside antenna unless you're using a tabletop model. All portables, and to some extent portatops, are designed to work well off the built-in telescopic antenna—or, if you want it to perform a bit better, with several yards or meters of insulated wire clipped on.

If you just want to hear the major stations, you'll do fine with a moderately priced portable. Beyond that, portatop models have a better chance of bringing in faint and difficult signals, and they usually sound better, too. Tabletop receivers are aimed at experienced DX enthusiasts, so they tend to be unnecessarily costly and complex for most program listeners to operate.

Radio in hand, read or at least glance over your owner's manual—yes, it's worth it. You'll find that, despite a few unfamiliar controls, your new world band receiver isn't all that much different from radios you have used all your life, and you'll never get a blue-screen crash.

Prepared by Jock Elliott, Tony Jones and Lawrence Magne.

First Tries: Ten Easy Catches

Here are ten mighty stations in English that you should be able to hear well even on a simple radio. Many offer top-notch programs, too.

Times and days are in World Time, while "winter" and "summer" refer to seasons in the Northern Hemisphere, where summer is in the middle of the year.

EUROPE

France

Radio France Internationale has some of the most popular English-language news programs on the international airwaves, but declines to beam it to either Europe or North America—"We don't want to be seen as catering to the Anglo-Saxons," sniffed one RFI official in 1991.

RFI concentrates its efforts on reaching audiences in Africa, the Middle East and southern Asia. Listeners outside these areas have to make do with eavesdropping on signals beamed elsewhere.

☞ RECOMMENDED PROGRAM: All are first-rate.

North America: Nothing direct, but try 11710 kHz winter and 21620 kHz summer at 0600-0630; 15605 kHz at 0700-0800; 15540 kHz at 1200-1230; and 11995 kHz winter at 1600-1700. These transmissions to West Africa are from RFI's Gabon relay, but are heard well beyond.

Middle East: 1400-1500 on 17620 kHz; also 1600-1730 winter on 11615 kHz and summer on 15605 kHz, though this slot is intended mainly for East Africa.

South Asia: 1400-1500 on 11610kHz. This channel can also be heard in western parts of *Southeast Asia* and *Australia*.

Africa: RFI's broadcasts to Africa have a large audience, and deservedly so. Audible at 0400-0430 on any two frequencies from 11910, 11995, 13610 and 15155 kHz; 0500-0530 on 13610 (winter), 15155 and (summer) 17800 kHz; 0600-0630 on two or more frequencies from 11710, 15155, 17800 and 21620 kHz; 0700-0800 on 15605 kHz; 1200-1230 on 15540 kHz; 1600-1700 on 11615, 11995, 12015, 15605, 17605 and 17850 kHz; and at 1700-1730 on any two channels from 11615, 15605 and 17605 kHz.

Jean-Paul Cluzel, Président Directeur Général de RFI.

RFI

Germany

Deutsche Welle, the Voice of Germany, is renowned for its superb coverage of European affairs, but is no slouch in reporting events from other parts of the world, as well. Unsurprisingly, their 45-minute English broadcasts also contain features on German life and culture.

☞ RECOMMENDED PROGRAM: "NewsLink."

North and Central America: 0100-0145 winter on 6040, 6145, 9640, 9700 and 9765 kHz; summer on 6040, 9640, 11810 and 13720 kHz. The second edition goes out at 0300-0345: winter on 6020, 6045, 9535, 9640, 9700 and 11985 kHz; summer on 9535, 9640, 13780 and 15105 kHz. The third and final broadcast is at 0500-0545, winter on 5960, 6120, 9670 and 11795 kHz; and summer on 9670, 9785 and 11985 kHz. This last offering is best for western North America.

Europe: 0600-1900 year-round on 6140 kHz; and 2000-2045 winter on 6180 kHz, replaced summer by 7130 kHz.

East & Southern Africa: 0400-0445 winter—summer in the Southern Hemisphere—on 6015, 7195, 9565 and 9710 kHz; summer on 7225, 9565, 9765 and 13690 kHz. The second slot is available 0900-0945 winter on 11785, 15410, 17860 and 21560 kHz; and summer on 12035, 15410, 17800 and 21790 kHz. A third broadcast goes out at

Helen Seeney of Deutsche Welle's English Service.

DW

DEUTSCHE WELLE
DW

Deutsche Welle offers commanding coverage of European affairs. Its Cologne headquarters exemplify the "look forward, not back" architecture favored in Germany. DW

1100-1145 on 15410 and (summer) 11785 kHz; and the fourth and final airing is at 1600-1645 on 9735 and 21840 kHz.

East Asia: 0900-0945 winter on 7300 kHz, and summer on 15470 kHz.

Southeast Asia and Australasia: 0900-0945 winter on 6160, 17820 and 17845 kHz; summer on 6160, 17715, 17770, 17820 and 21680 kHz. A second broadcast—nominally to Australasia but also well heard in Southeast Asia—airs at 2100-2145 winter on 9765, 15275 and 17560 kHz; summer on 9670, 9765 and 11915 kHz. There's also an additional transmission for Southeast Asia at 2300-2345: winter on 9470, 9815 and 13690 kHz; summer on 9815, 12055, 13610 (or 13640) and 21790 kHz.

Holland

Radio Nederland—also called **Radio Netherlands**—is home to any number of thoughtful and entertaining programs. Many focus on controversial topics reflecting progressive views popular in Holland, yet relatively unknown in, say, the United States.

The station's newscasts are of relentlessly high quality, especially welcome in light of the BBC World Service's loss of gravitas in recent years. Among the most popular broadcasters on the world bands, and a rising star.

☞ RECOMMENDED PROGRAM: "EuroQuest."

Eastern North America: 1130-1325 (one hour earlier in summer) on 5965 kHz, and 2330-0125 on 6165 and 9845 kHz.

Western North America: 1430-1625 on 15220 kHz, and 0430-0530 on 6165 and 9590 kHz. The 2330-0125 broadcast on 6165 kHz is also worth trying.

Europe: 1130-1325 winter on 6045 and 9855 (or 9860) kHz, and 1030-1225 summer on 6045 and 9860 kHz.

Southern Africa: 1730-1925 on 6020 kHz.

East and Southeast Asia: 0930-1125 winters on 7260 and 12065 kHz, and summers on 12065 and 13710 kHz.

Australia and the Pacific: 0930-1125 on 9790 kHz. Frequencies for East and Southeast Asia are also widely heard within the region.

Russia

The **Voice of Russia** has a difficult path to tread. On the one hand, it has to present the official line of the Russian government—after all, they foot the bill. On the other hand, it tries to "tell it as it is." The station's

Globally Recognized
Monitoring Times

Olga Shapovalova co-produces "Music and Musicians" at the Voice of Russia, which excels at cultural presentations. VoR

superior staff and management manage to pull this off quite well, but where the Voice of Russia really shines is in its cultural offerings.

☞ RECOMMENDED PROGRAM: "Music and Musicians."

Eastern North America: 0200-0600 winter on 7125 (0400-0600), 7180 and (0200-0300) 9765 kHz; summer, one hour earlier, it's 9665 kHz at 0100-0500, 9725 kHz at 0100-0300, 11750 kHz at 0300-0500, and 11825 at 0100-0200. During winter afternoons, try frequencies beamed to Europe—some make it to eastern North America.

Western North America: Best bets for winter are: 0200-0400 on 12020, 13665 and 15470 kHz; and 0400-0600 on 12010, 13665 (till 0500), 12020, 15470, 15445, 15595 and 17595 kHz. For summer reception, one hour earlier, use 12000 and 17595 kHz at 0100-0300; and 12000, 17565, 17650, 17660 and 17690 kHz at 0300-0500.

Europe: Winter: At 1800-2000 use 5940 , 5950 (from 1900), 6045, 7340, 9775 and 9890 kHz; for 2000-2200, choose from 5940, 5950, 7300 (from 2100), 9775 (till 2100) and 9890 kHz. Summer: At 1700-1900 there's 9480, 9685, 9775, 9890, 11630 (from 1800) and 11675 kHz. For 1900-2100, look at 9480, 9685 (till 2000), 9775, 9890 11675, 12070 and (from 2000) 15455 kHz. Note that 5940 and 6045 kHz (winter) and 9480 and 11675 kHz (summer) are only available weekends during the first hour.

Middle East: 1600-1900 (1500-1800 in summer). Winter, there's 6005 kHz (1600-1700), 9470 kHz (1700-1800), and 9830 kHz (1600-1900). In summer, use 7325 kHz at 1500-1600, 15540 kHz at 1600-1700, and 11985 kHz at 1500-1800.

Southern Africa: Officially, there's virtually nothing beamed this way, but winter try 9875 kHz at 1500-1600, and 9875 and 11510 kHz at 1900-2000. Midyear, go for 9495 kHz at 1700-1900 and 11510 kHz at 1800-1900. These channels are targeted at East Africa, but should make it farther south.

Southeast Asia: 0600-0900 winter on 17655 kHz, and summer on 15490 kHz; 1400-1500 summer on 12055 kHz; and 1500-1600 (year round) on 11500 kHz. In addition, some of the channels for Australasia are also well heard in Southeast Asia.

Australasia: 0600-0800 winter on 15460 (from 0630), 15470, 15525, 17570 and 21790 kHz; and 0800-1000 on 9905 (from 0830), 15460, 15470, 17495, 17570 (till 0900) and 17525 kHz. Midyear, 0500-0900 on 17495 (from 0700), 17525 (from 0700), 17635 (from 0530), 17685 and (till 0700) 21790 kHz.

United Kingdom

That was the station that was. In recent years the **BBC World Service** has managed not only to reduce audibility in the Western Hemisphere and Australasia, but also to dumb down content. With many shows now being produced on the cheap—independently, rather than in-house—several long-running favorites have lost their sparkle.

It's not as though the money isn't there. The BBC as a whole has managed to toss over a hundred million pounds into Internet schemes that haven't gone anywhere, while broadcasting basics have fallen to pot. As Bush House insiders put it, the highest levels of BBC management see themselves as visionaries, rather than managers, emphasizing early adoption of emerging technologies. This may be a formula for latter-day Da Vinci status, but it has deprived the world of what has arguably been its most effective civilizing influence.

Nevertheless, there are still a number of excellent shows, and the BBC's overall news coverage—although questioned during 2001—is still superior to that of its competitors. Radio Netherlands, for example, doesn't have the budget to afford the foreign correspondents and bureaus that are essential to the World Service's level of international reporting.

Another advantage of the BBC? It is 24/7, with a wider choice of English programs than any of its counterparts.

☞ RECOMMENDED PROGRAM: "Play of the Week."

North America: There are no longer any broadcasts officially targeted at the United States and Canada. These former transmissions were dropped at the start of July 2001, and replaced by an English broadcast to Mexico—go figure. However, thanks to the long-haul properties of shortwave, the BBC is still heard well throughout most of the United States and Canada.

Best for North America is the service for the Caribbean: 1000-1100 on 6195 kHz, 1100-1400 on 6195 and 15220 kHz, 1400-1700 on 17840 kHz, and 2100-0400 on 5975 kHz. The transmission for South America at 2100-0300 on 12095 kHz is also heard in parts of eastern North America, but tends to suffer from teletype interference unless your radio has synchronous selectable sideband. Too, some daytime frequencies for Europe

Li Dan presides over today's China Radio International. The station has evolved into a serious professional organization with thoughtful programs. CRI

and the Mideast can be heard— particularly during summer—but times vary, depending on your location and the time of year.

For nighttime and early morning reception in western North America, tune to the BBC's East Asia stream on 15360 (0500-1030) and 9740 kHz (1000-1600). The latter channel, especially, is well heard on the West Coast.

Europe: A powerhouse 0300-2300 on 6195, 9410, 12095, 15485, 15565 and 17640 kHz, with times varying for each channel. Three frequencies—12095 (part of the time), 15565 and 17640 kHz— carry the program stream intended for the Mideast.

Middle East: 0200-2000. Key frequencies—times for each vary according to whether it is winter or summer—are 9410, 11760, 12095, 15575 and 17640 kHz. 12095 and 17640 kHz are mainly intended for Eastern Europe, but provide acceptable reception in northern parts of the Mideast.

Southern Africa: 0300-2200 on, among others, 3255, 6005, 6190, 11940, 15400 and 21470 kHz—times vary for each channel.

East and Southeast Asia: 0000-0300 on 6195 (till 0200), 15280 and 15360 kHz; 0300-0500 on 15280, 15360 (till 0330), 17760 and 21660 kHz; 0500-1030 on 6195 (from 0900), 9740, 11765 (from 0900), 11945 (from 0900), 15280 (till 0530), 15360, 17760 and 21660 kHz; 1030-1100 on 6195 and 9740 kHz; 1100-1300 on 6195, 9740, 9815 and 15280 kHz; 1300-1600 on 6195, 9740 and 9815 kHz; 1600-1700 on 3915, 6195 and 7160 kHz; and 1700-1800 (to Southeast Asia) on 3915 and 7160 kHz. Local mornings, it's 2100-2200 on 3915, 5965, 6195, and (summer) 11945 kHz; 2200-2300 on 5965, 6195, 7105, and 11955 kHz; and 2300-2400 on 3915, 5965, 6195, 7105, 11945, 11955 and 15280 kHz. If you would like different programs, try the stream for South Asia on 15310 kHz, easily audible in Southeast Asia at 1400-1700.

Australasia: Like North America, Australasia is no longer an official target for BBC broadcasts. Fortunately, some transmissions for Southeast Asia are easily heard in Australia and New Zealand. Best bets: 0500-1030 on 15360 kHz; 1100-1600 on 9740 kHz; and 2200-2400 on 11955 kHz. At 2200-2300, 12080 kHz is also available for the southwestern Pacific.

ASIA

China

China Radio International is now heard virtually everywhere. Powerful transmitters on home soil are supplemented by relay facilities in Europe, Africa and the Americas. The result is global coverage, like Sherwin-Williams paint.

New production facilities and a thoroughly professional staff ensure that CRI now ranks as a serious international broadcaster—a far cry from the old days of Radio Peking, with its paeans to Mao and mutterings about "running dogs."

☞ RECOMMENDED PROGRAM: "Music from China."

Eastern North America: 0100-0200 on 9570 kHz, 0300-0400 on 9690 kHz, 0400-0500

CRI

China Radio International has had its Long March. Programs are vastly improved, as are the building and studios. CRI

on 9730 kHz, 1300-1400 on 9570 kHz, and 2300-2400 on 5990 kHz. As we went to press, CRI was testing out two additional broadcasts: 0100-0200 on 9790 kHz, and 2300-2400 on 13680 kHz.

Western North America: 0300-0400 on 9690 kHz, 0400-0500 on 9730 kHz, 0500-0600 (0400-0500 in summer) on 9560 kHz, and 1400-1600 on 7405 kHz.

Europe: 2000-2200 winter on 5965 and 9840 kHz, and summer on 11790 and 15110 kHz. A relay via Moscow can be heard winters at 2200-2300 on 7170 (or 7175) kHz, and summers on 9880 kHz.

Middle East: There are no listed broadcasts for this area, but try the following: 1700-1800 on 9670 kHz; 1900-2000 winter on 6165 and 9585 kHz, and summer on 11610 and 13790 kHz; also 1900-2100 on 9440 kHz, intended for North Africa.

Southern Africa: 1400-1600 on 13685 and 15125 kHz; 1600-1700 winter on 13650 kHz, and summer on 9565 kHz ; 1700-1800 on 9570, 9695 and (summer) 15265 kHz; and 2000-2130 on 11735 and 13640 kHz.

Asia: (Southeast) 1200-1300 on 11980 kHz (9730 kHz may also be used in winter), and 1300-1400 on 11980 and 15180 kHz; *(South)* 1400-1500 winter on 7180, 9700, 11675 and 11765 kHz; summer on 9700, 11675, 11825 and 15110 kHz; and 1500-1600 on 7160 and 9785 kHz.

Australasia: 0900-1100 on 11730 and 15210 kHz; 1200-1300 on 9760, 11675 (or 11760) and 15415 kHz; and 1300-1400 on 11675 (or 11760) and 11900 kHz.

China (Taiwan)

Radio Taipei International has profited from a major reorganization of its broadcasting schedule during 2001, including new transmissions to East and South Asia. It is now easily heard in much of the world, thanks in part to shortwave relays in Florida and the United Kingdom.

While Radio Beijing has evolved to become a relatively serious broadcaster, Taipei's content tends to be lighter and more relaxing, with a strong focus on Taiwanese topics and issues. As a result, a number of people now listen to both stations.

☞ RECOMMENDED PROGRAM: "Jade Bells and Bamboo Pipes."

Eastern North America: 0200-0400 on 5950 kHz.

Western North America: 0200-0300 on 9680 kHz; 0300-0400 on 5950 and 9680 kHz; and 0700-0800 on 5950 kHz.

Central America: 0200-0300 on 11740 kHz; 0300-0400 and 0700-0800 on 5950 kHz.

Europe: 1800-1900 on 3955 kHz; and 2200-2300 on (winter) 5810 and 9355 kHz, and (summer) 11565 and 15600 kHz.

Middle East: There is nothing specifically targeted to the Mideast, but try the 2200-2300 broadcast to Europe via the Florida relay.

Southern Africa: Another area which is not officially targeted, but the 1600-1800 broadcast for South Asia on 11550 kHz is the best bet.

Asia: (East) 0200-0300 on 15345 kHz; 1100-1200 on 11985 kHz; and 1200-1300 on 7130 kHz; *(Southeast)* 0200-0300 on 15320 kHz; 0300-0400 on 11875 and 15320 kHz; 1100-1200 on 7445 kHz; and 1400-1500 on 15265 kHz; *(South)* 1600-1800 on 11550 kHz.

Australasia: 1200-1300 on 9610 kHz.

Radio Japan is audible nearly everywhere. Many programs are in English or Japanese. Digital Stock

Japan

Radio Japan is another Asian station with a worldwide relay network—it's heard almost everywhere. It carries with it a strong commitment to news and current events, but it also airs a wide range of Japanese music and other entertaining material.

☞ RECOMMENDED PROGRAM: "Hello from Tokyo."

Eastern North America: Best bets are 1100-1200 on 6120 kHz and 0000-0100 on 6145 kHz, both via the Canadian relay at Sackville, New Brunswick.

Western North America: 0500-0600 on 6110, 9835 (winter) and (summer) 13630 kHz; 0600-0700 winter on 9685 and 9835 kHz, and summer on 13630 and 17870 kHz; 1400-1500 and 1700-1800 on 9505 kHz; and 2100-2200 on 17825 and 21670 kHz.

Europe: 0500-0600 on 5975 kHz; 0500-0700 on 7230 kHz; 1700-1800 on 11970 kHz; 2100-2200 on 6115, 6180 and 11830 kHz.

Middle East: 0100-0200 on 9515 (winter), 11870 and (summer) 11880 kHz; and 1400-1500 on 11880 or 17755 kHz.

Southern Africa: 1700-1800 on 15355 kHz.

Asia: 0000-0015 on 13650 and 17810 kHz; 0100-0200 on 11860, 15325, 17810 and 17845 kHz; 0500-0600 on 11715, 11760, 15195 and 17810 kHz; 0600-0700 on 11740 and 15195 kHz; 1000-1200 on 9695 and 15590 kHz; 1400-1600 on 7200, 9845 (winter) and (summer) 11730 kHz; and 1500-1600 on 7200, 9750, 9845 (winter) and (summer) 11730 kHz. Transmissions to Asia are often heard in other parts of the world, as well.

Australasia: 0100-0200 on 17685 kHz; 0300-0400 on 21610 kHz; 0500-0700 and 1000-1100 on 21755 kHz; and 2100-2200 on 6035 (or 11920) and 11850 (or 17860) kHz.

NORTH AMERICA
Canada

When it finally appeared that **Radio Canada International** had secured solid funding for at least the next few years, 2001 saw the station facing yet another threat to its existence.

Some of RCI's best programs originate from the domestic networks of its parent organization, the Canadian Broadcasting Corporation, so it may not seem surprising that there is a move afoot to fully incorporate RCI into the CBC. This might seem to make sense, except that the underlying motive appears to be to take RCI's funding and transfer it to the CBC's domestic empire. If this were successful, Canada would lose its voice to the world.

While this is being sorted out, the number of broadcasts has been reduced, and even more content is being relayed from the CBC's home networks.

☞ RECOMMENDED PROGRAM: "Quirks and Quarks."

North America: Morning reception is much better in eastern North America than farther west, but evening broadcasts fare somewhat better. Winter, morning broadcasts air at 1300-1400 weekdays, 1400-1600 (daily) and 1600-1700 Sunday, all on 9515, 9640 and 17710 kHz (13650 kHz may be used part of the time). In summer, the transmissions are one hour earlier, on 9640, 15305 and 17800 kHz. During winter, evening broadcasts air at 2300-0100 on 5960, 6175, 9590 and 9755 kHz; and 0200-0300 on 6040, 9755 and 11990 kHz. The summer schedule is 2200-2400 on 6175, 9590, 9755, 13670 and 17695 kHz; and 0100-0200 on 5960, 9755, 13670, 15170 and 15305 kHz.

Europe: 2100-2200 winter on 5995, 7235, 9805 and 13650 kHz; and 2000-2100 summer on 5995, 11690, 15325, 17870 and 21570 kHz.

Middle East: 1900-2000 winter on 9805 kHz, and 1800-1900 summer on 13690 kHz.

Southern Africa: Try 1900-2000 winter (summer in Southern Hemisphere) on 13740 kHz, and 1800-1900 summer on 17820 kHz.

Asia: To East Asia at 1200-1300 winter on 6150 and 11730 kHz, and summer on 9660 and 15190 kHz; to Southeast Asia at 0000-0100 on 11895 kHz, and 1200-1300 on (winter) 11730 and (summer) 15190 kHz; to South Asia at 0200-0300 on 15150 (winter), 15260 (summer) and 17860 kHz; and 1500-1600 winter on 15360 and 17820 kHz, replaced summer by 15455 and 17720 kHz.

United States

Once upon a time, the **Voice of America** was a highly respected and much-enjoyed station. But that was a decade ago and beyond. Today, after some years of incompetent management by friends of leading political figures, the VOA is being guided by commercial broadcasting interests who are moving it away from its public-service mission. As at the "new" BBC World Service, the emphasis is now on emerging technologies, with content having to fit the technologies rather than the other way around.

Dissent is unwelcome. Meanwhile, staff morale is at an all-time low as the feeling sets in that political contributors are using the VOA as their pet plaything. Under fire from senators and criticized by listeners, it is now but a shadow of its former greatness.

Still, the VOA is heard well, and some programs are worthy.

☞ RECOMMENDED PROGRAM: "Music Time in Africa."

North America: There is a widespread misconception that because the VOA isn't beamed to an American audience, it can't be heard within the United States. In reality, it comes in quite well on world band, allowing American taxpayers to hear firsthand what their government is telling the world in their name. The two best times to listen are when the VOA broadcasts to South America and the Caribbean. These times are 0000-0200 Tuesday through Saturday—local weekday evenings in the Americas—on 5995, 6130, 7405, 9455, 9775, 11695 (till 0100) and 13740 (or 13790) kHz; and 1000-1100 daily on 5745

Vocal legend Miriam Makeba visits the Voice of America's "Music Time in Africa." Host Leo Sarkisian's musical archives go back 55 years and are being preserved by the University of Michigan. In 2002 Rita Rochelle (right) celebrates her 25th anniversary as co-host. VOA

(or 6165), 7370 and 9590 kHz. The African Service can also be heard in parts of North America; tune in the evening transmission at 1800-2200 on 15580 and, from 2000, 17580 or 17895 kHz.

There's not much for *Europe*, but try 0400-0700 on 7170 kHz, 0500-0700 winter on 11825 kHz, 1500-1700 (1800 in winter) on 15205 kHz, 1700-2100 on 9760 kHz, and 2100-2200 on 6040 and 9760 kHz.

Middle East: 0400-0700 winter on 11825 (from 0500) and 15205 kHz, and 0400-0700 summer on 11965 and 15205 kHz; 1400-1500 (winter) on 15205 kHz; 1500-1700 on 9575 (winter), 9700 (summer) and 15205 kHz; 1700-1800 winter on 6040, 9760 and 15205 kHz; and summer on 9700 and 9760 kHz; 1800-2100 on 9760 kHz (6040 also available winter till 1900); and 2100-2200 on 6040, 9595 (winter) and 9760 kHz.

Southern Africa: 0300-0500 on 6080, 7105, 7290, 7340 (to 0330), 7415 (winter), 9575, 9775 and (till 0430) 9885 kHz; 0500-0630 (to 0700 weekends) on 6035 and 12080 kHz; 1600-1800 on 11920 (winter), 12040 (winter), 13710 (till 1700), 15240 (or 15410) and 17895 kHz; and 1800-2200 on 7415 (from 1900 winter), 11920 (winter, to 2000), 15240 (or 15410), 15445 (midyear, from 1900), 15580 and (till 1900) 17895 kHz.

East and Southeast Asia: 0800-1000 winter on 11995, 13615 and 15150 kHz; summer on 11930, 13610 and 15150 kHz; 1100-1300 on 6110 (winter), 6160 (summer), 9760, 11705 (winter) and (summer) 15160 kHz; 1300-1500 on 9760, 11705 (winter) and (summer) 15160 kHz; 1900-2000 on 15180 kHz; 2100-2200 on 15185 and 17820 kHz; 2200-2400 on 7215, 9770, 9890 (winter), 15185, 15290, 15305 (summer) and 17820 kHz; and 0000-0100 on 7215, 9770 (summer), 15185, 15290 and 17820 kHz.

Australasia: 1000-1200 on 5985 (winter), 9645 (from 1100), 9770 (midyear) and 15425 kHz; 1200-1500 on 9645 (till 1400) and 15425 kHz; 1900-2000 on 9525 and 11805 (or 11870) kHz; 2100-2200 on 9705 (midyear), 11870 and 17735 (or 17740) kHz; 2200-2400 on 9705 (midyear), 9770 (winter), 11760 and 17735 (or 17740) kHz; and 0000-0100 on 11760 and 17740 kHz.

Prepared by Don Swampo and the staff of PASSPORT TO WORLD BAND RADIO.

How to Choose a World Band Radio

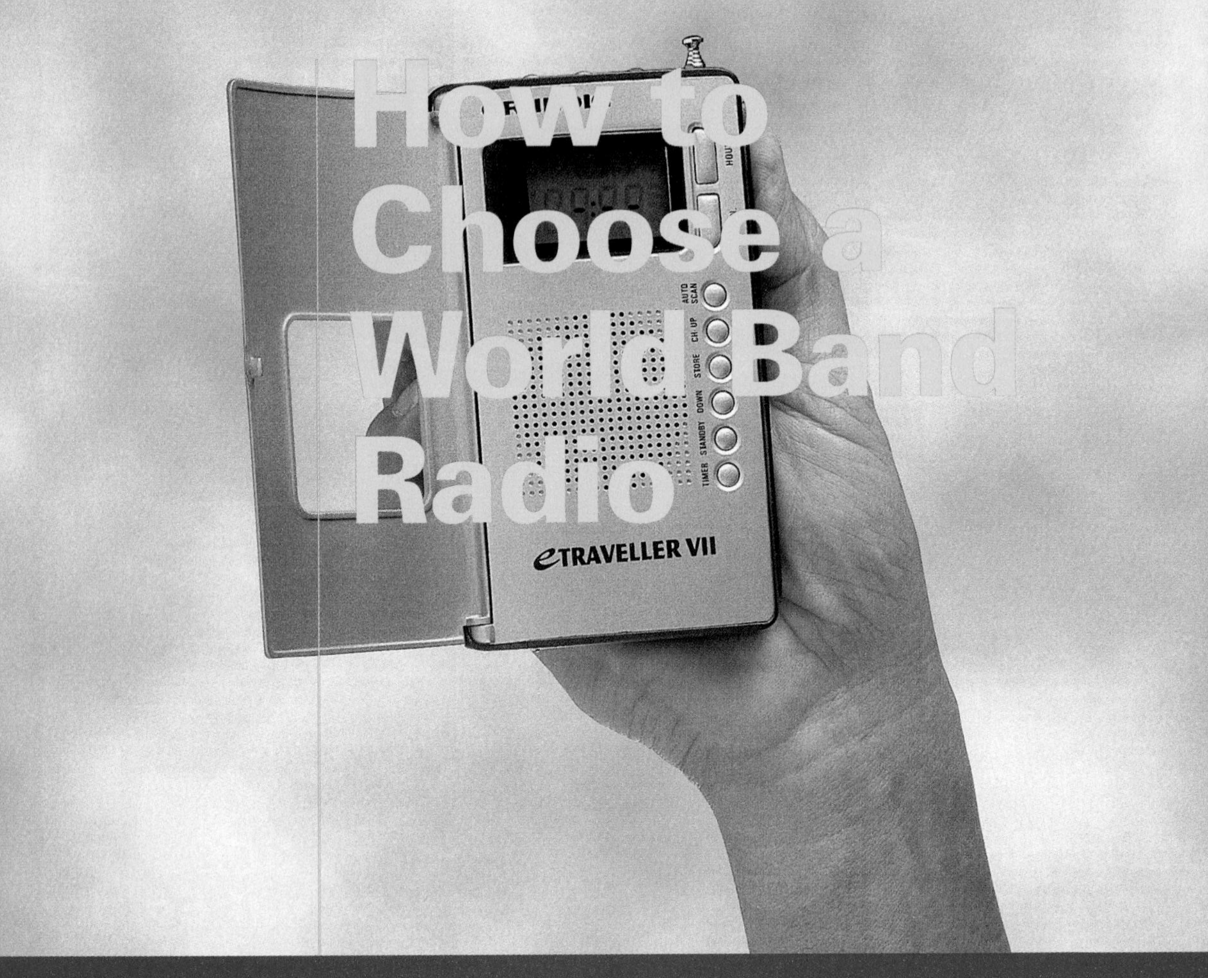
AUTO SCAN
CH UP
STORE
DOWN
STANDBY
TIMER
eTRAVELLER VII

Some electronic products are almost commodities. With a little common sense you can get what you want without fuss or bother.

Not so world band receivers, which vary greatly from model to model. As usual, money talks, but even that's a fickle barometer. Fortunately, many perform well and we rate them accordingly. Yet, even among models with comparable star ratings it helps to choose a radio that fits your requirements.

No Elbow Room

World band radio is a jungle: 1,100 channels, with stations scrunched cheek-by-jowl. It's much more crowded than FM or mediumwave AM, and to make matters worse a global voyage can make signals weak and quavery. To cope, a radio has to perform exceptional electronic gymnastics. Some succeed, others don't.

This is why PASSPORT REPORTS was created. At IBS we've tested hundreds of world band radios and accessories since 1977. These evaluations include rigorous hands-on use by listeners, plus specialized lab tests we've developed over the years. These form the basis of PASSPORT REPORTS, and for some popular premium receivers and antennas there are also the soup-to-nuts Radio Database International White Papers®.

Army buddies in Tibet listen up with a portable. For them, small size is paramount. E.A. Hozour

Four-Point Checklist

✔ **Price.** Do you want to hear big stations, or flush out soft voices from exotic lands? Powerful evening signals, or weaker signals by day? Decide, then choose a radio that surpasses your needs by a good notch or so—this helps ensure against disappointment without wasting money.

Once the novelty wears thin, most people give up on cheap radios—they're clumsy to tune, often receive poorly and can sound terrible. That's why we don't cover analog-tuned models, but even some digitally tuned models can disappoint.

Most find satisfaction with portables selling for $105-200 in the United States or £90-130 in the United Kingdom with a rating of ✪✪⅞ or more. If you're looking for elite performance, shoot for a portable or portatop rated ✪✪✪¾ or better—at least $350 or £300—or consider a five-star tabletop model.

PASSPORT'S STANDARDS

At International Broadcasting Services we have been analyzing shortwave equipment since 1977. Our reviewers, and no one else, write everything in PASSPORT REPORTS. These include our laboratory findings, all of which are done by an independent laboratory recognized as the world's leader. (For more on this, please see the Radio Database International White Paper, *How to Interpret Receiver Lab Tests and Measurements*.)

Our review process is completely separate from equipment advertising, which is not allowed within PASSPORT REPORTS. Our team members may not accept review fees from manufacturers, nor may they "permanently borrow" radios. International Broadcasting Services does not manufacture, sell or distribute world band radios or related hardware.

Choose a radio that slightly surpasses your needs.

PASSPORT recognizes superior products regardless of when they first appear on the market. We don't bestow annual awards, but instead designate each exceptional model, regardless of its year of introduction, as *Passport's Choice*.

FEATURES FOR SOLID PERFORMANCE

A signal should not just be audible, but actually sound pleasant. Radios can have several features help bring this about—some keep out unwanted sounds, others enhance audio quality. Of course, just because a feature exists doesn't mean it functions properly, but we check for this in PASSPORT REPORTS.

"Must" Features for Quality Reception

Full world band coverage from 2300-26100 kHz is best, although 3200-21850 kHz or even 4750-21850 kHz is usually adequate. If coverage is less, look at "Best Times and Frequencies for 2002" elsewhere in this book to ensure that important world band segments are completely covered.

Synchronous selectable sideband greatly enhances rejection of adjacent-channel interference while reducing fading distortion. It is found on some models selling for over $150 or £110.

Especially if a receiver doesn't have synchronous selectable sideband, it helps to have two or more *bandwidths* for superior adjacent-channel rejection. Some premium models incorporate this *and* synchronous selectable sideband—a killer combo. Multiple bandwidths are found on a number of models over $140 or £95.

Multiple conversion or *double conversion* helps reject spurious "image" signals—unwanted growls, whistles, dih-dah sounds and the like. Few models under $100 or £70 have it; nearly all over $150 or £100 do.

Other Helpful Attributes

High-quality speakers are an aural plus, as are *tone controls*—preferably continuously tunable with separate bass and treble adjustments. For world band reception, *single-sideband* (SSB) reception capability is only marginally relevant, but it is essential for utility or "ham" signals, as well as reception of low-powered signals from the U.S. Armed Forces Radio & Television Network. On costlier models you'll get it whether you want it or not.

Heavy-hitting tabletop models are designed to flush out virtually the most stubborn signal, but they usually require experience to operate and are overkill for casual listening. Among these look for a tunable *notch filter* to zap howls; *passband offset* (a/k/a *passband tuning* and *IF shift*) for superior adjacent-channel rejection and audio contouring, especially in conjunction with synchronous selectable sideband; and multiple *AGC* decay rates. At electrically noisy locations a *noise blanker* is essential; some work much better than others.

Digital signal processing (DSP) is the latest attempt to enhance mediocre signal quality. Until recently it has been much smoke, little fire, but the technology is improving. Watch for more DSP receivers in the years to come, but don't worship at their altar.

With portables and portatops an *AC adaptor* reduces operating costs and may improve weak-signal performance. Some of these are poorly made and cause hum, but most are quite good. With tabletop models an *inboard AC power supply* is preferable but not essential.

Looking ahead, *digital shortwave transmission* is being tested by Digital Radio Mondiale (www.drm.org). However these tests come out, it will be years before existing analog transmissions are phased out in favor of digital.

tables are more like laptop PCs. There are compact models with three or more stars that sell for around the equivalent of $150 to $200—you can't go wrong with these workhorses. But there are also compacts that sell for much less which are good enough for occasional use. These are excellent values for trips, although even travel warriors should think twice before going mini. A pocket model makes sense only if weight is paramount and you have a larger radio at home.

Not surprisingly, top-rated portables are also among the largest, but they're not huge. PASSPORT staffers routinely use Sony ICF-2010 lap portables while globetrotting, for example.

World Band Rebounds in North America

Since the Gulf War there has been a shift in the world band radio landscape in North America, and to a lesser degree Europe and Australasia. All but vanished are cheap analog radios with such dismal performance that they drove newcomers away from world band. At the same time demand has slackened for tabletop and portatop receivers, although this may be turning around.

Find major updates to the 2002 PASSPORT REPORTS at www.passband.com.

The lion's share of world band radios are now priced from $99.95 to $499.95, and it is that market segment which is growing. The manufacturer lineup has become more focused, as well. Grundig and Sony increasingly run the show, although Sangean and Radio Shack continue to be major players.

Most of the recent promotional efforts have been focused on the United States, a double-digit growth market where between a million and 1.5 million world band radios are sold annually. However, Canada and the United Kingdom are also in manufacturers' cross-hairs for 2002, and there is talk of eventual thrusts into continental Europe, East Asia and South Africa.

New for 2002 is the Sony ICF-SW7600GR (opposite) and Grundig eTraveller VII.

Longwave Useful for Some

The longwave band is still used for some domestic broadcasts in Europe, North Africa and Russia. If you live or travel there, longwave coverage may be a slight plus. Otherwise, forget it.

Who's the Toughie?

Thankfully, the days of poorly made world band portables appear to be largely behind us. At the same time, truly robust models are becoming harder to find as production and design economies take their toll. With any brand of world band radio, experience suggests that you should avoid models which have been recently introduced and are technologically sophisticated.

Most Sony world band radios are made in Japan, whereas all Grundig and all but one of Sangean's models are now made in China. "Made in China" was once enough to raise a caution flag on high. However, build quality from Chinese plants, although still rarely equal to Japanese or Taiwanese standards, is now much better and continues to improve.

Fix It?

Portables aren't meant to be friends for life, and are priced accordingly. Even the most robust model will probably be ready for the landfill after ten years of routine use, while some pedestrian models might give no more than a few years of regular service. At that point, they aren't worth fixing.

Of course, if you own a particularly robust model, listen infrequently, avoid static charges, live where it's pollution-free and dry, and cover the receiver when it's not in use, who knows but that your portable might last a quarter century before sheer age does it in.

If you wind up purchasing a genuinely defective new portable, insist upon an immediate exchange without a restocking fee—manufacturers' repair facilities tend to have a disappointing record. That having been said, Grundig in Europe and North America, and Sangean America in the United States and Canada appear to be providing better in-warranty service on portables than most, but even their post-warranty service can seriously disappoint. If quality of service is important to you, consider a portatop or tabletop model, instead.

Many vendors and virtually all world band specialty outlets will cooperate if a just-sold radio turns out to be defective or DOA. While most radios are warrantied for a year, some, such as Radio Shack in certain countries, come only with a 90-day warranty.

Also available are 15-day and other return policies The downside is that those returned units have to wind up somewhere. Whether a given outlet puts returns back in inventory, or resells them as used or for employee purchases, is usually anybody's guess.

Still, you can spot clues. For example, we purchased two house-brand units from a Radio Shack outlet in Pennsylvania—Radio Shack has a chain-wide 30-day return policy. One had the plastic bag taped close twice, while the other had batteries in it even though it wasn't supposed to. Perhaps these were opened to demonstrate the radio or for some other innocuous reason, and in fact both radios worked just fine. But in general it is better to get a radio that isn't somebody else's reject.

Some manufacturers sometimes go out of their way to avoid this problem. In North America, for example, Grundig checks out and repackages radios returned to stores for any reason—gift recipients who aren't interested in shortwave, for example. These are then sold openly as refurbished units, rather than stuck back into the normal distribution chain. Unfortunately, this fits into the "no good deed goes unpunished" category, as this has been widely misinterpreted as indicating Grundig radios have a high failure rate.

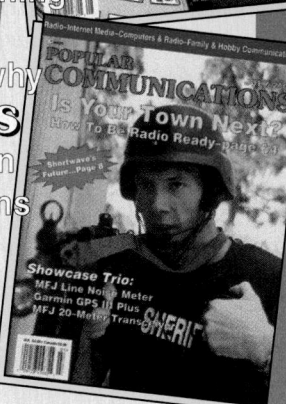

WHAT TO LOOK FOR

• **Tuning features.** Digitally tuned models are so superior to analog that these are now the only models tested by PASSPORT. Look for such handy tuning aids as direct-frequency access via keypad, station presets (programmable channel memories), up-down tuning via tuning knob and/or slewing keys, band/segment selection, and signal-seek or other scanning. These make the radio easier to tune—no small point, given that a hundred or more channels may be audible at any one time.

• **Audio quality.** Unlike many portatop and tabletop models, portables don't have rich, full audio. However, some are better than others.

• **Adjacent-channel rejection I: *selectivity, bandwidth*.** World band stations are packed together about twice as closely as ordinary mediumwave AM stations, so they tend to slop over and interfere with each other. Radios with superior selectivity are better at rejecting this. However, enhanced selectivity also means less high-end ("treble") audio response and muddier sound. So, having more than one bandwidth allows you to choose between superior selectivity ("narrow bandwidth") when it is warranted, and more realistic audio ("wide bandwidth") when it is not.

• **Adjacent-channel rejection II: *synchronous selectable sideband*.** This is the first major advance in world band listening quality in decades. With powerful stations "out in the clear," it has little audible impact. However, for tougher signals it improves audio quality by minimizing selective-fading distortion, while reducing adjacent-channel interference by selecting the "better half" of a signal.

• **Single-sideband demodulation.** If you are interested in hearing non-broadcast shortwave signals—"hams" and utility signals—single-sideband circuitry is *de rigeur*. Too, the popular low-powered U.S. Armed Forces Radio-Television Service (AFRTS/AFN) can only be heard intelligibly on receivers with single-sideband capability. No portable excels, but those that stand out are cited in PASSPORT REPORTS.

• **Weak-signal sensitivity.** This is important if you live in a weak-signal location or tune to DX or daytime stations. Since the BBC's cutbacks in 2001, this also become relevant for hearing the World Service within North America and Australasia. On the other hand, most portables have enough sensitivity to pull in major stations evenings if you're in such places as Europe or North Africa—even the east coast of North America.

☞ A simple outboard antenna enhances sensitivity, as well as the signal-to-noise ratio, on nearly any good portable.

• **Ergonomics.** Some radios are easy to use because they don't have complicated features. But even complex models can be designed to operate intuitively.

• **World Time clock.** A World Time clock—24-hour format—is a "must." You can obtain these separately, but many radios have them built in; the best display time whether the radio is on or off. Some radios have clocks that display more than one time zone. However, nearly all these additional zones read out in the 24-hour format familiar to Europeans, but not Americans.

• **AC adaptor.** An outboard AC adaptor is virtually a necessity except on trips. One provided by the manufacturer is usually best and should be free from hum and noise.

In general, stores that sell returned radios as new will provide a complete refund, while those that dispose of returned radios as used invariably charge a 10-20 percent restocking fee. The choice is yours.

Shelling Out

Street prices are given, including European and Australian VAT/GST where applicable. These vary plus or minus, so take them as the general guide they are meant to be. Shortwave specialty outlets and a growing number of other retailers have attractive prices, whereas duty-free shopping is not always a bargain you might expect.

We try to stick to plain English, but some specialized terms have to be used. If you come across something that's not clear, check with this edition's glossary.

All Current Models Included

PASSPORT REPORTS evaluates virtually every digitally tuned portable that meets reasonable minimum standards. Here, then, are the results of our hands-on and laboratory tests of current models.

What PASSPORT's Ratings Mean

Star ratings: ✪✪✪✪✪ is best. Stars reflect overall performance and meaningful features, plus to some extent ergonomics and build quality. Price, appearance, country of manufacture and the like are not taken into account. Nevertheless, to facilitate comparison, the portable rating standards are very similar to those used for the portatop, tabletop and professional models reviewed elsewhere in this PASSPORT.

A rating of at least ✪✪½ should please most who listen to major stations regularly during the evening. However, for casual use on trips virtually any small portable may suffice.

Passport's Choice. La crème de la crème. Our test team's personal picks of the litter—digitally tuned portables we would buy or have bought for our personal use.

¢: A relative bargain, with decidedly more performance than the price would suggest.

How Portables Are Listed

Models are listed by size; and, within size, in order of world band listening suitability. Street prices are cited, including VAT where applicable. Models designed for certain countries cannot receive single-sideband signals and may have reduced tuning ranges.

Unless otherwise indicated, each digital model has:

- Tuning by keypad, up/down slewing keys, station presets and signal-seek bandscanning.
- Digital frequency readout to the nearest kilohertz.
- Coverage of the world band shortwave spectrum from at least 3200-26100 kHz.
- Coverage of the usual 87.5-108 MHz FM band.
- Coverage of the AM (mediumwave) band in selectable 9 and 10 kHz channel increments from about 530-1700 kHz.
- Adequate spurious-signal ("image") rejection.
- No synchronous selectable sideband or single-sideband demodulation. However, when there is synchronous selectable sideband, the unwanted sideband is rejected approximately 25 dB via phasing, not IF filtering.

POCKET PORTABLES

Perfect for Travel, Inappropriate for Home

Pocket portables weigh under a pound, or half-kilogram, and are between the size of an audio cassette jewel box and a handheld calculator. They operate off two to four ordinary small "AA" (UM-3 penlite) batteries. These diminutive models do one job well:

SONY
LONDON
18:44

Sony's ICF-SW100 series has top overall performance among pocket portables, but speaker audio is tinny. With earpieces, it's a winner.

provide news and entertainment when you're traveling.

Don't expect much more. Listening to tiny speakers can be tiring, so pocket portables aren't great for everyday listening except through earpieces.

There is also a vast choice among compact models. Their bigger speakers sound better, and they're still small enough for carry-on bags.

✪✪✪

Sony ICF-SW100S

Price: $359.95 in the United States. CAN$599.00 as available in Canada. £199.95 in the United Kingdom.

Pro: Tiny. Superior overall world band performance for size category. High-tech synchronous selectable sideband generally

TIPS FOR GLOBETROTTING

Airline security and customs are rarely issues in most countries—with the preponderance of laptop computers, world band portables now rarely rate a suspicious glance. A number of PASSPORT editors have traveled unmolested throughout Western Europe, North America and the Caribbean for years, with Sony ICF-2010s in tow.

However, in some other parts of the world officials can be downright ornery. To avoid hassles with these folks:

- Bring a pocket or compact model. Terrorists like big radios.
- Stow your radio in a carry-on bag, not in checked luggage or on your person.
- Take along fresh batteries so you can demonstrate that the radio actually works.
- If asked what the radio is for, say for personal use.
- If traveling in zones of war or civil unrest, or off the beaten path in much of Africa or parts of South America, take along a radio you can afford to lose and which fits inconspicuously in a pocket.
- If traveling to Bahrain, avoid taking a radio which has the word "receiver" on its cabinet. Security personnel may think you're a spy.

Theft? Radios, cameras, binoculars, laptop computers and the like are almost always stolen to be resold. The more worn the item looks—affixing scuffed stickers helps—the less likely it is to be confiscated by corrupt inspectors or stolen by thieves.

performs well, reducing adjacent-channel interference and selective-fading distortion on world band, longwave and mediumwave AM signals, while adding slightly to weak-signal sensitivity and audio crispness (*see* Con). Single bandwidth, especially when synchronous selectable sideband is used, exceptionally effective at adjacent-channel rejection. Relatively good audio, provided supplied earbuds or outboard audio are used (*see* Con). FM stereo through earbuds. Numerous helpful tuning features, including keypad, two-speed slewing, signal-seek-then-resume scanning (*see* Con), five handy "pages" with ten presets each. Presets can display station name. Tunes in relatively precise 0.1 kHz increments. Good single-sideband performance (*see* Con). Good dynamic range. Worthy ergonomics for size and features. Illuminated display. Clock for many world cities, which can be made to work as a *de facto* World Time clock (*see* Con). Timer/snooze. Travel power lock. Longwave and Japanese FM bands. Amplified outboard antenna, supplied, in addition to usual built-in antenna, enhances weak-signal reception (*see* Con). Weak-battery indicator; about 16 hours from a set of batteries (*see* Con). High-quality travel case for radio. *Except for North America:* Self-regulating AC adaptor, with American and European plugs, adjusts automatically to all local voltages worldwide.

Con: Tiny speaker, although innovative, has mediocre sound, limited loudness and little tone shaping. Closing clamshell reduces speaker loudness and high-frequency response. Weak-signal sensitivity could be better, although supplied outboard active antenna helps. Expensive. No tuning knob. Clock not readable when station frequency displayed. As "London Time" is used by the clock for World Time, the summertime clock adjustment cannot be used if World Time is to be displayed accurately. Rejection of certain spurious signals ("images"), and 10 kHz "repeats" when synchronous selectable sideband off, could be better. In some urban locations, FM signals from 87.5 to 108 MHz can break through into world band segments with distorted sound, e.g. between 3200 and 3300 kHz. Synchronous selectable sideband tends to lose lock if batteries weak, or if NiCd cells are used. Synchronous selectable sideband alignment can vary with temperature, factory alignment and battery voltage, causing synchronous selectable sideband reception to be slightly more muffled in one sideband than the other. Some readers report BFO pulling causes audio quavering, not found in our test units. Batteries run down faster than usual when radio off. Tuning in 0.1 kHz increments means that non-synchronous single-sideband reception can be mis-tuned by up to 50 Hz, so audio quality varies. Signal-seek scanner sometimes stops 5 kHz before a strong "real" signal. No meaningful signal-strength indicator. Supplied accessory antenna performs less well than another Sony accessory antenna, the AN-LP1. Mediumwave AM reception only fair. Mediumwave AM channel spacing adjusts peculiarly. Flimsy battery cover. No batteries (two "AA" required). *North America:* AC adaptor only 120 Volts.

☞ In early production samples, the cable connecting the two halves of the "clamshell" case tended to lose continuity with extended use because of a very tight radius and an unfinished edge; this was successfully resolved with a design change in early 1996. Those with early units who encounter this problem should go to www.tesp.com/sw100faq.htm for repair information.

Verdict: The mighty midget. A shoehorning *tour de force*, complete with synchronous selectable sideband and an effective bandwidth filter that, taken together, make this tops in its size class for rejecting adjacent-channel interference. Speaker and, to a lesser extent, weak-signal sensitivity keep it from being all it could have been, and the accessory antenna isn't Sony's latest or best. Yet, this Japanese-made model still is the handiest pocket portable, and a nifty gift idea for your favorite soldier.

✪✪✪

Sony ICF-SW100E

Price: *ICF-SW100E:* £179.95 in the United Kingdom. *ACE-30 AC adaptor:* £24.95 in the United Kingdom.

Verdict: This version, not available in North America, nominally includes only a case, tape-reel-type passive antenna and earbuds. Otherwise, it is identical to the Sony ICF-SW100S, above.

✪✪✪ Ⓟ *Passport's Choice*

Sangean ATS 606AP, Roberts R617, Roberts R876

Price: *ATS 606AP:* $139.95 in the United States. CAN$219.00 in Canada. £104.95 in the United Kingdom. *R617:* £119.95 in the United Kingdom. *Sangean AC adaptor for ATS 606AP:* $14.95 in the United States. *R876:* £129.95 in the United Kingdom. *ATS 606AP:* $149.95 in the United States.

SANGEAN
TIMER
FM
LW
MW
SW
ENTER
FREQ
ATS 606A

The Sangean ATS 606 is not the smallest pocket portable and lacks synchronous selectable sideband. But it has reasonable audio quality and is affordable.

Pro: Speaker audio quality less bad than most pocket models—comparable to a mediocre-sounding compact model (*see* Con). Speaker audio unusually intelligible. Single bandwidth reasonably effective at adjacent-channel rejection, while providing reasonable audio bandwidth. Weak-signal sensitivity, although not optimum, a bit above average. Various helpful tuning features, including keypad, 54 presets, slewing, signal-seek tuning and meter band selection. Keypad has superior feel and tactile response. Longwave. Dual-zone 24-hour clock. Illuminated LCD. Alarm. 15/30/45/60-minute snooze. Travel power lock (*see* Con). Multi-level battery strength indicator; also, weak-battery warning. Stereo FM through earphones or earbuds. Above-average FM sensitivity, selectivity, dynamic range and capture ratio. Memory scan (*see* Con). Rubber feet reduce sliding while elevation panel in use. *R876 and ATS 606AP:* UL-approved 120/230V AC adaptor, with American and European plugs, adjusts to proper AC voltage automatically; also ANT-60 reel-in outboard wire antenna. *ATS 606AP:* In North America, service provided by Sangean America to models sold under its name.

Con: No tuning knob. Audio quality, although superior for size class, lacks low-frequency ("bass") response. Clock not readable while frequency displayed. No meaningful signal-strength indicator. Memory scan doesn't function on shortwave. Keypad not in telephone format. Power lock doesn't disable LCD illumination button. No carrying strap or handle. No batteries (three "AA" needed). On our unit, clock initially refused to be set. *All Sangean models:* Country of manufacture (China) not specified on radio or box.

Verdict: Easily the best buy in a pocket model—an excellent value. In the land of the deaf, the guy with a hearing aid is king. In that spirit, this model has the best sound among pocket models.

Money aside, choosing between the Sony ICF-SW100 series and this model is a no-brainer. If maximum freedom from adjacent-channel interference and/or smallness of size are paramount, the innovative little Sony wins. If audio quality and ease of use are primary, spring for the Sangean *et al.*

✪✪✪ Ⓔ *Passport's Choice*
Sangean ATS 606A

Identical to the Sangean ATS 606AP, preceding, but priced lower and with fewer accessories and no AC adaptor. Still available in some stores.

New for 2002
✪✪½ Ⓔ
Grundig eTraveller VII

Price: $129.95 in the United States. CAN$129.95 in Canada. Plans are to make this model widely available in the United Kingdom, continental Europe, South Africa and beyond.

Pro: Weak-signal sensitivity, although not optimum, is above average. Good rejection of spurious "image" signals, unusual at this price. Single bandwidth reasonably effective at adjacent-channel rejection, while providing adequate audio bandwidth. Audio quality above average for size class (*see* Con). Auto scan/slew-tuning works better than most—thankfully, as there are almost no other tuning features (*see* Con). Hinged protective travel cover, like on a Flip Phone, protects front of radio (*see* Con). World Time clock, with snooze and two-event timer that activates last-tuned frequency. Power/standby switch not easy to turn on accidentally while packed away in luggage (*see* Con). FM stereo through earbuds, included. Also comes with 117V AC adapter, desk stand, soft travel case and two "AA" alkaline batteries. *North America:* Excellent toll-free tech support.

Con: Paucity of helpful tuning facilities, including no keypad or tuning knob and only ten world band presets (plus 20 more for FM and mediumwave AM). Audio quality, although decent for size class, lacks low-frequency ("bass") response. Antenna does not rotate or swivel. Almost large and heavy enough to qualify as a compact model. Tunes world band only in 5 kHz steps. Even-numbered frequencies displayed with final zero omitted; e.g., 5.73 rather than conventional 5.730 or 5730. No signal-strength indicator. Hinged front cover can get in the way, although it may be removed. Clock not readable while frequency displayed, although time replaces frequency briefly if button is pushed. No travel power lock, although power/standby function provides considerable protection. Turning radio on for the first time is thoroughly counterintuitive. No LCD illumination. No carrying strap or handle.

☞ AC adaptors included during the initial production run, sold only in North America, generated considerable ripple and hum; better adaptors have since been provided. By the time you read this, none of these early samples should still be on sale new. Those with old adaptors should contact Grundig (US 800/872-2228, Canada 800/637-1648) for an exchange.

Verdict: A handsome, affordable package with pleasant performance. Yet, the eTraveller's hinged front cover and paucity of tuning features make it more appropriate for traveling than for routine daily use—hardly surprising, given its name. Like all Grundig radios of recent times, it is made in China at what Grundig's Lextronix spokesman says is a plant controlled by them.

Evaluation of New Model: Grundig has been bringing panache to portables on and off over the past few years, and they've done it again with the new eTraveller VII. It's designed to be seen, priced to move, and has more performance than its tag suggests.

GRUNDIG
HOUR
MIN
eTRAVELLER VII

Grundig's new eTraveller VII is another creative design from Grundig. The flip-open panel is useful for frequent travelers, but can be removed if it gets in the way.

What sets it apart is its physical configuration. Not since the days of beefy shortwave "portables" half a century ago has there been a portable with a protective hinged cover. Yet, today's eTraveller is anything but beefy—it fits right into a pocket, although at half a pound it tugs at shirts more than a pack of Marlboros.

It comes with just about everything you could possibly want: handy desk stand, soft travel case, stereo earbuds, AC adaptor and alkaline batteries. That adaptor initially produced considerable AC ripple and hum, but this has since been remedied.

The set's hinged cover is chic and practical, helping to protect the LCD and front-panel controls. But it also gets in the way. Should you wish to remove it, open the cover partway, then press outward on the inner cover near the hinge midpoint until bending "shortens" the cover so a hinge pin slips from its mounting hole. It's just as easy to reinstall.

Scanner Rescues Tuning

There is no keypad or tuning knob, only ten world band presets—no "meter band" selector for shortwave, either. This lays much of the tuning burden on the up/down slewing buttons, which serve two very different functions: slow channel-to-channel tuning, and lightning frequency movement to burn rubber from one part of the shortwave spectrum to another. The result is a mediocre compromise.

Hold the button down for under two seconds, then let up, slewing stops—this allows for fine tuning, and works reasonably well. However, when held down longer it takes off like a Batmobile on afterburner; to stop, the button is pushed again. Usually by that point the desired frequency has been sailed past, so the exercise has to be repeated in the other direction, and so on back and forth until the frequency landed on is close enough to poke-poke-poke the button to get there by fine tuning.

With enough practice you will acquire the reflexive skill needed to hit around the bull's eye, like throwing darts at a pub. But this seems like a high-tech throwback to the early days of radio, when tuning shortwave required the fingers of a safecracker and the patience of Job.

Thankfully, another of the eTraveller's tuning features comes to the rescue: the "signal-seek" scanner, which functions uncommonly well. A button-push turns on the scanner, then a mere tap on the up/down slew buttons get it going. It stops precisely on the next reasonably active signal, then with another tap it gets going again.

Read Manual to Turn Radio On

Those who insert the batteries and don't read the manual will be in for a rude surprise when they push the power button: The radio won't turn on!

Why? The clock needs to be set before the power button will work, which makes as much sense as having to open the glove box before starting your car. You can get around this by this by using the "sleep" function—another tip secreted in the owner's manual—but it's the first time in 24 years of testing that we've had to check the owner's manual to figure out how to turn on a radio.

The two timers and snooze control are both godsends for travelers and fit in with the overall orientation of this radio. Yet, with all the attention to detail there is no LCD illumination for the traveler stuck in a dimly lit hotel room or when the electricity fails.

Superior Weak-Signal Reception

Although the eTraveller has its share of operating idiosyncrasies, its performance is quite respectable. Weak-signal sensitivity is important anywhere, but especially in such modest-signal parts of the world as western North America, the Caribbean, sub-Saharan Africa, the Middle East, Pacific islands, East Asia and Australasia. In this regard, the eTraveller acquits itself well, especially considering its short antenna which neither rotates nor swivels, a disappointment at this price. Clip a short length of wire onto that antenna, and weak-signal reception springs to life even more—arguably too much more for Europe, North Africa, the Near East and other strong-signal regions. Even in North America a simple inverted-L outdoor antenna can cause the receiver to overload.

Audio Relatively Pleasant, Intelligible

Selectivity, or adjacent-channel rejection, is reasonably good, but not equal to that of a number of other models. This helps keep the audio from sounding muffled, and is what most listeners want for listening to major stations. But for chasing tough DX catches, this single bandwidth is too broad.

There is no such thing as good audio in a pocket portable, at least in today's market, and the eTraveller is no exception—even with earbuds and on FM, it lacks bass response. However, the eTraveller's crisp audio and bandwidth filtering make for audio that's more pleasant and intelligible than is expected from a small speaker.

Dual-conversion circuitry results in superior rejection of spurious "image" signals. This is done in a cost-effective manner, with only one niggling drawback: signals can't be received between 10.4-11.0 MHz. No world band stations are in that range.

Tuning is strictly in 5 kHz increments, but this rarely compromises reception quality. Frequencies are displayed in the offbeat XX.XXx MHz format for odd frequencies, XX.XX MHz for even frequencies, just as they are on some other low-cost Chinese-made portables. Some engineer on the mainland came up with this peculiar idea years ago, and like Leadbelly's old gray goose it just can't seem to get killed off. It's one of those things, like IBM relocating the shift key many years back, that you get used to even as you shake your head, wondering why people persist in doing such things.

Sensible Choice for Frequent Fliers

The Grundig eTraveller performs nicely, although its you-need-to-get-used-to-it characteristics make it more suitable to frequent flyers than occasional vacationers. Otherwise, it is eminently affordable and a delightful eyeful. With its superior weak-signal sensitivity and shirt-pocket convenience, the eTraveller VII is an obvious choice for travel within the Western Hemisphere, Pacific rim and beyond.

✪½

Grundig G4 Executive Traveller

Price: $99.95 in the United States.

Pro: Novel concept—comes with and fits into luxurious black leather wallet with room for passport, money, spare batteries,

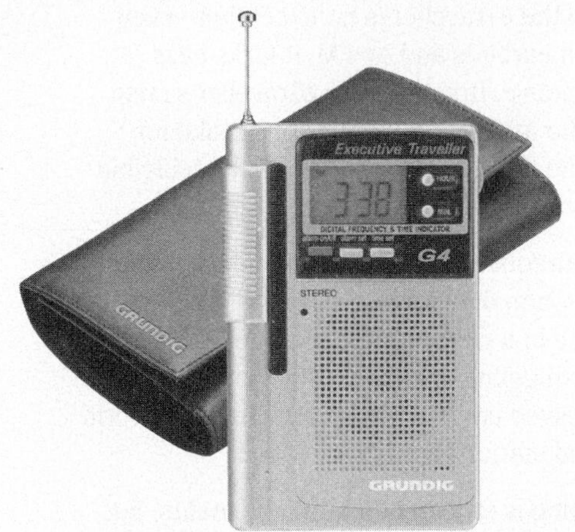
Executive Traveller
G4
STEREO
GRUNDIG
GRUNDIG

Some readers tell us they like the tiny Grundig G4 Executive Traveller more than we do. Sans accessories it is also available under the Kaiwa and Tecsun brand names.

earbuds and credit cards. Packaged with batteries and earbuds. Sensitivity to world band signals at least average for pocket model. Clock with alarm (*see* Con). Toll-free tech support.

Con: Analog radio with a digital frequency counter, so lacks tuning except by knob. Does not tune 90, 60, 22, 13 or 11 meter segments. Frequency counter completely omits last digit so, say, 9575 kHz appears as either 9.57 or 9.58 MHz. Clock in 12-hour format only. Poor image rejection. Mediocre audio quality. Telescopic antenna does not rotate or swivel. Mediumwave AM lacks weak-signal sensitivity. Pedestrian FM, with spurious signals. On one of our new units the telescopic antenna immediately fell apart.

Verdict: Innovative and stylish. A novel idea that includes a five-star wallet, but the Chinese-made radio is of a far lesser caliber.

✪½

Kaiwa KA-818, Tecsun R-818

Price: $29.95 in the United States; up to $40 elsewhere.

Verdict: Same as the Grundig G4 Executive Traveller, above, but with carrying pouch and belt clip instead of wallet, and no batteries supplied. *KS-818:* Warranty only 90 days in United States.

COMPACT PORTABLES

Nice for Travel, Okay for Home

Compact portables are the most popular because of their intersection of price, performance, size and speaker audio. They tip in at one to two pounds, under a kilogram, and are typically sized 8 × 5 × 1.5 inches, or 20 × 13 × 4 cm. Like pocket models, they feed off "AA" (UM-3 penlite) batteries—but, usually, more of them. They travel almost as well as pocket models, but sound better and usually receive better, too. They can also suffice as home sets.

✪✪✪¼ *Passport's Choice*

Sony ICF-SW07

Price: $419.95 in the United States. CAN$699.00 in Canada. £249.95 in the United Kingdom.

Pro: Best non-audio performance among travel portables. Eye popper. High-tech synchronous selectable sideband generally performs very well; reduces adjacent-channel interference and selective-fading distortion on world band, longwave and mediumwave AM signals while adding slightly to weak-signal sensitivity. Unusually small and light for a compact model. Numerous tuning aids, including pushbutton access of frequencies for four stations stored on a replaceable ROM, keypad, two-speed up/down slewing, 20 presets (ten for world band) and "signal-seek, then resume" bandscanning. Clamshell design aids in handiness of operation, and is further helped by illuminated LCD readable from a wide variety of angles. Hump on the rear panel places the keypad at a convenient operating angle. Comes with AN-LP2 outboard "tennis racquet" antenna, effective in enhancing weak-signal sensitivity on world band; this antenna, unlike the AN-LP1, has automatic preselector tuning. Good single sideband performance (*see* Con). Clock covers most international time zones, as well as World Time. Outstanding reception of weak and crowded FM stations, with limited urban FM overloading resolved by variable-level attenuator. FM stereo through earpieces, supplied. Longwave and Japanese FM bands. Above-average reception of mediumwave AM band. Travel power lock. Closing clamshell does not interfere with speaker. Low-battery indicator. Presets information is non-volatile, can't be erased when batteries changed. Two turn-on times for alarm/clock radio. Sixty-minute snooze. Hinged battery cover can't be misplaced. AC adaptor.

Con: Pedestrian audio quality, made worse by the lack of a second, wider, bandwidth and meaningful tone control. Lacks tuning knob. Display shows time and tuned frequency, but not both at the same time. Tuning resolution of 0.1 kHz above 1620 kHz means that non-synchronous single-sideband reception can be mis-tuned by up to 50 Hz, so audio quality varies. Synchronous selectable sideband tends to lose lock if batteries weak, or if NiCd cells are used. Synchronous selectable sideband alignment can vary with temperature, factory alignment and battery voltage, causing synchronous selectable sideband reception to be slightly more muffled in one sideband than the other. No meaningful signal-strength indicator. LCD frequency/time numbers relatively small for size of display, with only average contrast. AN-LP2 accessory antenna has to be physically disconnected for proper mediumwave AM reception. 1621-1700 kHz portion of American AM band is erroneously treated as shortwave, although this does not harm reception quality. Low battery indicator misreads immediately after batteries installed; clears up when radio is turned on. No batteries (two "AA" required). UTC, or World Time, displays as "London" time even during the summer, when London is an hour off from World Time. DST key can change UTC in error.

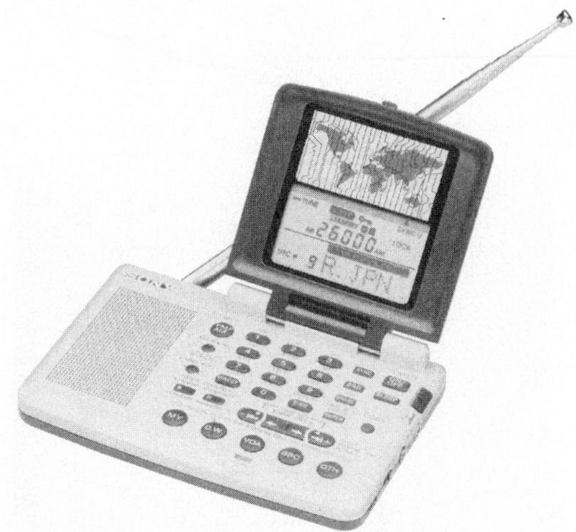
26000
9R. JPN

Where price is no object, the Sony ICF-SW07 is the best travel portable. It comes with an excellent little active antenna to enhance the built-in whip.

Verdict: Speaker audio aside, this Japanese-made model is the best available for travel—and a killer eyeful.

New for 2002

✪✪✪⅛ Ⓔ *Passport's Choice*
Sony ICF-SW7600GR

Price: $169.95 in the United States. CAN$299.00 in Canada. *When available:* Likely around £139.95 in the United Kingdom, AUS$459.00 in Australia. *AC-E60HG 120V AC adaptor:* $19.95 in the United States.

Pro: One of the great values in world band radio. Far and away the least-costly model available with high-tech synchronous selectable sideband; this generally performs well, reducing adjacent-channel interference and selective-fading distortion on world band, longwave and mediumwave AM

With solid performance, advanced technology and robust build quality, the new Sony ICF-SW7600GR is a bargain.

signals (*see* Con). Single bandwidth, especially when synchronous selectable sideband is used, exceptionally effective at adjacent-channel rejection. Seemingly robust—similar predecessor had superior quality of components and assembly for price class, and held up unusually well. Numerous helpful tuning features, including keypad, two-speed up/down slewing, 100 presets and "signal-seek, then resume" bandscanning. For those with limited hearing of high-frequency sounds, such as some men over the half-century mark, audio quality may be preferable to that of Grundig Yacht Boy 400PE (*see* Con). Single-sideband performance arguably the best of any portable; analog clarifier, combined with LSB/USB switch, allow single-sideband signals (e.g., AFRTS, utility, amateur) to be tuned with uncommon precision, and thus with superior carrier phasing and the resulting natural-sounding audio. Dual-zone 24-hour clock with single-zone readout, easy to set. Reel-in outboard passive antenna accessory aids slightly with weak-signal reception. Snooze/timer. Illuminated LCD has high contrast when read head-on or from below. Travel power lock. Superior reception of difficult mediumwave AM stations. Superior FM capture ratio helps separate co-channel stations. FM stereo through earpieces or headphones. Longwave and Japanese FM bands. Superior battery life. Weak-battery indicator. Stereo line output for taping. Hinged battery cover can't be mislaid.

Con: Audio lacks tonal quality for pleasant world band or mediumwave AM music reproduction, and speaker audio tiring for any type of FM program. Weak-signal sensitivity, although respectable, not equal to that of the top handful of top-rated portables; helped considerably by extra-cost Sony AN-LP1 active antenna reviewed elsewhere in this edition. Image rejection adequate, but not excellent. Three switches, including those for synchronous selectable sideband, located unhandily at the side of the cabinet. No tuning knob. When using up/down slewing buttons, muting slows down manual bandscanning. No meaningful signal-strength indicator. Synchronous selectable sideband holds lock decently, but less well on weak signals than in Sony's larger models; too, it tends to lose lock even more if batteries weak or if NiCd cells used. Synchronous selectable sideband alignment can vary with temperature, factory alignment and battery voltage, causing synchronous selectable sideband reception to be slightly more muffled in one sideband than the other. 1621-1700 kHz portion of American AM band is erroneously treated as shortwave, although this does not harm reception quality. Even though it has a relatively large LCD, same portion of display is used for clock and frequency digits; thus, clock not readable when radio is switched on. Factory AC adaptor a costly extra and not worth the premium; shop around for something better and/or cheaper. No earphones or earpieces. No batteries (four "AA" needed).

Verdict: The Sony ICF-SW7600GR provides excellent bang for the buck, even though it is manufactured in high-cost Japan. Its advanced-tech synchronous selectable sideband helps greatly in rejecting adjacent-channel interference and selective-fading distortion. Top drawer single-sideband reception for a portable, too, along with superior tough-signal FM and mediumwave reception. However, musical audio quality is only *ordinaire*.

Years of widespread use of its similar predecessor model suggests that it is built to last, and is outstandingly priced for all it does.

Evaluation of New Model: This is the latest in a series of models derived from the original 1983 Sony ICF-2002, also sold as the ICF-7600D. A slightly improved version, the ICF-2003, came out in 1987 and was also sold as the ICF-7600DS; this is what the original President Bush used while he was in the White House. That was replaced in 1990 by the ICF-SW7600, and again in 1994 by the substantially improved ICF-SW7600G.

The newly released ICF-SW7600GR is, like the earlier ICF-2003, an incremental improvement over its predecessor rather than a wholesale redesign. Cosmetics aside—the plastic front cabinet is now permeated with aluminum color—there are 100 programmable station presets (formerly 20), clustered in "pages" of ten. Accessing active frequencies among them is straightforward, so you can quickly find frequencies with receivable signals for a favorite major station whose various frequencies you've stored within a given page. Of course, the radio has no way of knowing whether it's your desired station on that frequency—different stations share the same frequency—but it's a definite tuning aid. Also new for 2002 is a dual-zone 24-hour clock, along with a handier travel lock and a fully variable attenuator.

The secret behind the ICF-SW7600GR's low price is its inclusion of just those features which are appropriate to obtaining reliable, racket-free world band reception. For example, it has numerous tuning aids: direct-frequency entry, up/down slewing and signal-seek scanning. Fully a hundred station presets, too—a major improvement over the prior version, which had only 20. But there's no free lunch; to save cost, there is no tuning knob, and several controls are unhandily located on the sides of the radio. There is only one bandwidth, too, although it is very selective.

Lowest Price for Synchronous Selectable Sideband

But what makes this radio really stand out is that it incorporates the most important high-tech feature available: synchronous selectable sideband. This not only can greatly diminish adjacent-channel interference, it also reduces fading distortion. These benefits are apparent not only on world band, but also mediumwave AM and longwave.

Sure, other world band radios have synchronous selectable sideband, but look at their price tags. And if anyone doubts the value of this feature, they should try listening to the BBC on 12095 kHz, now an important frequency for North Americans. With ordinary reception, particularly in the Western Hemisphere, it is clobbered by teletype. Turn the synchronous selectable sideband onto "LSB," and the BBC becomes fully usable, sometimes even pleasant.

That synchronous circuit also does wonders in defeating the extreme distortion sometimes encountered in mediumwave AM fringe zones, where the fulltime groundwave is sometimes phase-cancelled by the skywave which appears around dark. Add to that a selective bandwidth filter, solid dynamic range and superior antenna directionality, and the '7600GR turns out to be a truly excellent long-distance mediumwave AM receiver.

Audio for Voice, not Music

Long-distance FM reception is also commendable, but to listen for any time calls for good earpieces. FM audio through the speaker is unpleasant.

There is also a dual-zone 24-hour clock, although only one zone reads out at a time. However, time displays only when the radio is off—a pity, as the LCD is large enough to accommodate frequency and time digits simultaneously. There is also a basic timer/ sleep feature.

The '7600GR comes with a vinyl carrying case and a useful "tape measure" passive outboard wire antenna to complement the usual built-in telescopic. Yet, there is no AC adaptor or even free batteries. No earpieces, either.

The '7600GR's weak-signal sensitivity is respectable, although not outstanding. Ditto image rejection, as the occasional image signal appear 910 kHz below the "real" signal. Most other measures of performance are in line with competing models at the top end of the '7600GR's price and size class.

Audio quality is good for speech, and those with aging hearing will appreciate this enhanced intelligibility. Nevertheless, for music it is only fair at best.

GRUNDIG
40 STATION MEMORIES SSB

Grundig's Yacht Boy 400PE is a popular as crawfish in Acadia Parish. For its size, audio quality is pleasant, and there are two bandwidths instead of the usual one.

Appears Robust

The predecessor ICF-SW7600G had its share of manufacturing glitches when it first came out. However, with the shakedown cruise completed, it became one of the most reliable and rugged of compact portables we have tested. Overall, the '7600GR appears to be in that same league.

Sony does a superior job of engineering, manufacturing and pricing for its line of digital world band receivers. Yet, perhaps ironically, they are not as easy to find in stores as are some others. But the ICF-SW7600GR provides performance that normally costs much more, so it is well worth beating the bushes for.

Discontinued

✪✪✪⅛ © *Passport's Choice*

Sony ICF-SW7600G, Sony ICF-SW7600GS

Price: *ICF-SW7600G:* £139.95 in the United Kingdom. *ICF-SW7600GS (includes AN-71 active antenna):* AUS$509.00 in Australia.

Similar to the Sony ICF-SW7600GR, preceding, and at comparable prices—but with various minor differences and fewer presets. Still available in some stores outside North America.

✪✪✪ © *Passport's Choice*

Grundig Yacht Boy 400PE

Price: *YB-400PE:* $149.95 in the United States. CAN$199.99 in Canada. £99.95 in the United Kingdom. AUS$299.00 in Australia. *YB-400PE refurbished units, as available:* $99.95 in the United States. CAN$149.00 in Canada.

Pro: Audio quality tops in size category for those with sharp hearing. Two bandwidths, both well-chosen. Ergonomically superior, a pleasure to operate. A number of helpful tuning features, including keypad, up/down slewing, 40 station presets, "signal seek" frequency scanning and scanning of station presets. Signal-strength indicator. Dual-zone 24-hour clock, with one zone shown at all times; however, clock displays seconds only when radio is off. Illuminated display. Alarm/snooze. Tunable BFO allows for superior signal phasing during single-sideband reception. Reel-in outboard wire antenna supplements telescopic antenna. Generally superior FM performance. FM in stereo through headphones. Longwave. AC adaptor. *North America:* Toll-free tech support.

Con: Circuit noise ("hiss") can be slightly intrusive with weak signals. No tuning knob. At many locations there can be breakthrough of powerful AM or FM stations into the world band spectrum. Keypad not in telephone format. No LSB/USB switch. No batteries (four "AA" needed).

☞ Refurbished units reportedly include gift and similar returns from department stores and other outlets where customers tend to be unfamiliar with world band radio. Everything but the radio itself is supposed to be replaced. Limited availability.

Verdict: An exceptional value in a legendary and pleasant receiver for hearing world band programs. Superior audio quality, dual bandwidths and simplicity of operation set this Chinese-made compact receiver apart—even though circuit noise with weak signals could be lower.

✪✪✪

Sangean ATS 909, Sangean ATS 909 "Deluxe," Radio Shack DX-398, Roberts R861

Price: *ATS 909:* $259.95 in the United States. CAN$369.00 in Canada. £169.95 in the United Kingdom. AUS$399.00 in Australia. *ATS 909 "Deluxe":* $289.90 in the United States. *AC adaptor:* £16.95 in the United Kingdom. *DX-398:* $249.99 or less in the United States. *R861:* £179.95 in United Kingdom.

SANGEAN
MEMO
PLL

The Sangean ATS 909 features advanced tuning, but is wanting in weak-signal sensitivity and battery consumption.

Pro: Exceptionally wide range of tuning facilities and hundreds of world band presets, including one which works with a single touch. "Page" tuning system uses 29 pages and alphanumeric station descriptors for world band. Two voice bandwidths. Tunes single sideband in unusually precise 0.04 kHz increments, making this one of the best portables for listening to single-sideband signals (*see* Con). Dynamic range slightly above average for portable. Travel power lock. 24-hour clock shows at all times, and can display local time in various cities of the world (*see* Con). 1-10 digital signal-strength indicator. Low-battery indicator. Clock radio feature offers three "on" times for three discrete frequencies. Snooze feature. FM is sensitive to weak signals (see Con) and performs well overall, has RDS feature (*see* Con), and is in stereo through earpieces, supplied. Illuminated display. Superior ergonomics, including tuning knob with tactile detents. Longwave. *ATS 909 (North American units), ATS 909 "Deluxe" and Roberts:* Superb multivoltage AC adaptor with North American and European plugs. ANT-60 reel-in outboard wire antenna. Sangean service provided by Sangean America to models sold under its name. *ATS 909 "Deluxe," available only from*

C. Crane Company): Enhanced tuning knob operation and elimination of muting between stations. *DX-398:* 30-day money-back period in the United States.

Con: Weak-signal sensitivity not equal to that of comparable models. Tuning knob tends to mute stations during bandscanning (C. Crane Company offers a "Deluxe" modification to remedy this). Large and heavy for a compact. Signal-seek bandscanning, although flexible and relatively sophisticated, tends to stop on few active shortwave signals. Although scanner can operate out-of-band, reverts to default (in-band) parameters after one pass. Two-second wait between when preset is keyed and station becomes audible. Although synthesizer tunes in 0.04 kHz increments, frequency readout only in 1 kHz increments. Other software oddities; e.g., under certain conditions, alphanumeric station descriptor may stay on full time. Page tuning system cumbersome for some. Audio quality only so-so, not aided by three-level treble-cut tone control. No carrying handle or strap. 24-hour clock set up to display home time, not World Time, although this is easily overcome by not using world-cities-time feature. Clock does not compensate for daylight (summer) time in each displayed city. FM can overload in high-signal-strength environments, causing false "repeat" signals to appear; capture ratio average. RDS, which can automatically display FM-station IDs and update clock, is of limited use, as it requires a stronger signal than it should to activate. Heterodyne interference, possibly related to the digital display, sometimes interferes with reception of strong mediumwave AM signals. Battery consumption well above average; would profit from lower current draw or larger (e.g., "C") cell size. No batteries (four "AA" required). Elevation panel flimsy. *Sangean:* AC adaptor lacks UL approval. *Radio Shack:* Warranty only 90 days in the United States and some other countries.

Verdict: A wide range of operating features and relatively precise tuning of single-sideband signals, but weak-signal sensitivity not all it should be. This is the only Sangean model still made in Taiwan, rather than China.

26.100
SANGEAN

Want a bargain? Try Sangean's ATS-808A, also sold as the Roberts R809. Nice performance for under $120 or £85.

✪✪⅞ ©

Sangean ATS-808A, Roberts R809

Price: *Sangean:* $119.95 in the United States. CAN$199.00 in Canada. £84.95 in the United Kingdom. *ADP-808 120V AC adaptor:* $10.95 in the United States. *Roberts:* £99.95 in the United Kingdom.

Pro: The best value on the thrifty side of the Sony ICF-SW7600GR. Dual bandwidths, a major plus that's exceptional anywhere near this price class (*see* Con). Relatively simple to operate for technology class. Various helpful tuning features include two-speed tuning knob, although only 18 presets for world band. Weak-signal sensitivity a bit better than most. Keypad has exceptional feel and tactile response. Longwave. Dual-zone 24-hour clock, displayed separately from frequency. Alarm/snooze. Seven-level signal strength and battery indicator. Travel power lock. Stereo FM via earpieces, supplied. Superior FM reception.

Con: Fast tuning tends to mute receiver when tuning knob is turned quickly. Narrow bandwidth performance only fair. Spurious-signal ("image") rejection, although above average, not equal to that of top-rated portables. Pedestrian audio quality with two-level tone switch. Display not illuminated. Keypad not in telephone format. No carrying strap or handle. AC adaptor extra. No batteries (six "AA" needed). Country of manufacture (now China) not specified on radio or box.

Verdict: This Sangean offering is the best value in an under-$145 world band radio, with relative simplicity of operation and superior overall performance. If you don't need single-sideband capability, the ATS-808A is a better overall choice than the sibling ATS 505, below, for reception of weak or interfered world band signals.

SANGEAN
ATS 505
4745
POWER
DISPLAY
MODE
TUNING

The least costly route to decent single-sideband reception is the Sangean ATS 505.

Enhanced for 2002

✪✪¾

Sangean ATS 505, Sangean ATS 505P, Radio Shack DX-402, Roberts R9914

Price: *ATS 505:* $129.95 in the United States. CAN$179.00 in Canada. £99.95 in the United Kingdom. AUS$229.00 in Australia. *ATS 505P:* $139.95 in the United States. *ADP-808 120V AC Adaptor:* $10.95 in the United States. *DX-402:* $149.99 or less in the United States. *R9914:* £99.95 in the United Kingdom.

Pro: Numerous helpful tuning features, including two-speed tuning knob, keypad, presets (*see* Con), up/down slewing, meter-band carousel selection, signal-seek bandscan tuning and scanning of presets (*see* Con). Automatic-sorting feature arranges presets in frequency order. Analog clarifier with center detent and stable circuitry allows single-sideband signals to be tuned with uncommon precision and to stay properly tuned, thus allowing for superior audio phasing for a portable (*see* Con). Illuminated LCD. Dual-zone 24/12-hour clock. Alarm/snooze. Modest battery consumption. Nine-level battery-reserve indicator. Travel power lock (*see* Con). FM stereo through earbuds, supplied. Longwave. *ATS 505 and ATS 505P:* In North America, service provided by Sangean America to models sold under its name. *ATS 505P:* AC adaptor. Tape measure antenna. *DX-402:* 30-day money-back period in the United States and Canada; in Canada, product cannot have been opened. *R9914:* AC adaptor.

Con: Bandwidth slightly wider than appropriate for a single-bandwidth receiver (try detuning slightly to reduce 5 kHz world band heterodyne interference). Large for a compact. Only 18 world band presets (divided up between two "pages" with nine presets apiece). Tuning knob tends to mute stations during bandscanning by knob, especially when tuning rate is set to fine (1 kHz); muting with coarse (5 kHz) tuning is much less objectionable. Keys respond slowly, needing to be held down momentarily rather than simply tapped. Stop-listen-resume scanning of presets is slow.

Pedestrian overall single-sideband reception because of excessively wide bandwidth and occasional distortion caused by AGC timing. Clock does not display independent of frequency. No meaningful signal-strength indicator. No carrying handle or strap. Country of manufacture (China) not specified on radio or box. Travel power lock does not deactivate LCD illumination key. No batteries (four "AA" needed). *AST 505 and DX-402:* No AC adaptor. *DX-402:* Warranty only 90 days in the United States and some other countries.

☞ The Sangean ATS 505P, a new variation for 2002, includes an AC adaptor and tape-measure-type outboard antenna.

Verdict: The best bet in a low-cost portable that demodulates single-sideband signals, but you should also consider other models if this feature is not needed.

✪✪¾ ✐
Sony ICF-SW35

Price: $89.95 in the United States. CAN$179.95 as available in Canada. £79.95 in the United Kingdom. AUS$269.00 in Australia. *AC-E45HG 120V AC adaptor:* $19.95 in the United States.

SONY
POWER
ON/OFF
SLEEP
LIGHT
HOLD
STANDBY MEMORY
PAGE MEMORY PRESET
MEMORY SCAN
50 MEMORY PRESET

Superior reception and rock-bottom price are hallmarks of the Sony ICF-SW35. The catch: sparse tuning features.

Pro: Superior reception quality, with excellent and spurious-signal rejection. Fifty world band presets, which can be scanned within five "pages." Signal-seek-then-resume scanning works unusually well. Two-speed slewing. Illuminated display. Dual-zone 24-hour clock. Dual-time alarm. Snooze feature (60/45/30/15 minutes). Travel power lock. FM stereo through headphones, not supplied. Weak-battery indicator. Receives longwave and the Japanese FM band.

Con: No keypad or tuning knob. Synthesizer muting and poky slewing degrade bandscanning. Audio quality clear, but lacks low-frequency response ("bass"). Clock not displayed independent of frequency. LCD lacks contrast when viewed from above. AC adaptor, relatively needed, is extra and pricey. No batteries (three "AA" required).

Verdict: The new Sony ICF-SW35 is notable mainly for its superior rejection of spurious image signals that are the bane of nearly all other under-$100 models. This Chinese-made compact lacks a keypad, which is partially overcome by the large number of presets and effective scanning. Overall, a decent low-cost choice if you listen to a predictable roster of stations.

✪✪⅝ ✐
Radio Shack DX-396

Price: $99.99 or less in the United States.

Pro: Superior weak-signal sensitivity, particularly in higher bands used during the daytime. Several handy tuning features, including keypad, slewing, signal-seek scanning, memory scanning and meter-band selection. Also has 30 ergonomically excellent presets (10 for world band)—simply pushing one key brings in your station, a major convenience. Dual-zone 24/12-hour clock, one zone labeled "World Time" (*see* Con). Stereo FM through headphones, not supplied. Travel power lock.

Alarm. 15/30/45/60-minute snooze. Batteries (two "C" cells) power the radio for many, many hours. Weak battery indicator. 30-day money-back period.

Con: Spurious-signal ("image") rejection and dynamic range only fair. Lacks tuning knob. Tunes shortwave only in 5 kHz increments. Clocks don't display when frequency is shown, although pushbutton allows World Time to replace frequency. Signal-strength indicator merely a single LED. AC adaptor extra. Does not tune above 21850 kHz. FM capture ratio just fair. Warranty only 90 days.

☞ According to the manufacturer, the built-in ferrite rod antenna is used not only for mediumwave AM, but also for shortwave 2300-7095 kHz, and there is no external antenna jack. Nevertheless, if an outboard shortwave antenna is clipped to the built-in telescopic antenna it will impact signals below 7100 kHz.

Verdict: An excellent and surprisingly affordable travel radio with minimal need for battery changes. This Chinese-made model is a solid low-cost choice for daytime reception, as well as for nighttime listening where signal strengths are substandard. Especially during Radio Shack's periodic sales, the DX-396 is hard to resist.

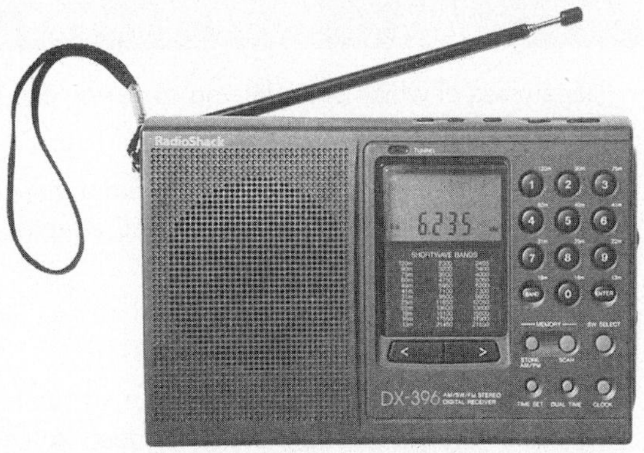
RadioShack
DX-396

Radio Shack's DX-396 performs well at capturing weak signals, and includes a keypad. During sale markdowns it is tempting, especially for traveling.

✪✪½
Sony ICF-SW40

Price: $119.95 in the United States. £84.95 in the United Kingdom. *AC-E45HG 120V AC adaptor:* $19.95.

Pro: Relatively affordable. Technologically unintimidating for older traditionalists, as its advanced digital tuning circuitry is disguised to look like slide-rule, or analog, tuning. 24-hour clock. Two "on" timers and snooze. Travel power lock. Illuminated LCD. Covers Japanese FM band.

Con: Single bandwidth is relatively wide, reducing adjacent-channel rejection. No keypad. Lacks coverage of 1625-1705 kHz portion of North American mediumwave AM band. AC adaptor, much-needed, is extra and overpriced. No batteries (three "AA" required).

Verdict: If you're turned off by things digital and complex, Sony's Japanese-made ICF-SW40 will feel like an old friend in your hands. Otherwise, forget it.

SONY
SW
LW/MW
FM

Sony's retro ICF-SW40 looks like a Nixon-era analog portable, but is really digital in drag.

MAKE YOUR PORTABLE "HEAR" BETTER

Regardless of which portable you own, you can boost weak-signal sensitivity on the cheap. How cheap? Nothing, for starters.

Look for "sweet spots" to place your radio: near windows, appliances, telephones, I-beams and the like. If your portable has an AC adaptor, try that, then batteries; sometimes the AC adaptor does better, sometimes not.

Outdoor Antenna Can Help

An outdoor antenna isn't necessary, but it can help. Good news: With compact and smaller portable receivers, simplest is often best. Run several meters or yards of insulated wire to a tree, then clip one end to your set's telescopic antenna with an alligator or claw clip available from Radio Shack and such. It's fast and cheap, yet effective.

Use it only when needed—disconnect during thunder, snow or sand storms and when the radio is off. And don't touch any antenna during dry weather, as you may discharge static electricity into your radio's vulnerable innards.

Sophisticated outdoor wire antennas? With most portables these can cause "overloading," usually at certain times of the night or day on frequency segments with powerful signals. You'll know this when you tune around and most of what you hear sounds like murmuring in a TV courtroom scene. Remedy: Disconnect the wire, then use the radio's telescopic antenna until you're ready to tune to another frequency segment.

If you are in a weak-signal location, such as central or western North America or Australia, and want stronger signals from a travel-sized portable, best is to erect an inverted-L (so-called "longwire") antenna. These are available at Radio Shack (278-758, $9.99) and other radio specialty outlets, or may be constructed from detailed instructions found in the RDI White Paper, PASSPORT *Evaluation of Popular Outdoor Antennas*. Antenna length is not critical, but keep the lead-in wire reasonably short.

However, portables are more susceptible to static damage than are tabletop and portatop models. Disconnect any outdoor antenna when storms are nearby or the radio isn't in use.

Creative Indoor Solutions

All antennas work best out of doors, away from the multitude of electrical noises found inside your home. If your supplementary antenna has to be indoors, run it along the middle of a window with Velcro, tape or suction cups. Another solution, in a reinforced-concrete building which absorbs radio signals: Affix a long whip or telescopic car antenna outdoors, almost horizontally, onto a windowsill or balcony rail. Antennas like these are all but invisible.

Active Antennas Now Practical

Amplified ("active") antennas are small and handy. However, in the past they usually did more harm than good with portables.

The aim of any antenna is a good signal-to-noise ratio, not just raw gain which can overwhelm circuitry. Inexpensive electronic signal-booster devices also tend to fare poorly, although anecdotal evidence suggests that some help in given listening situations. Purchase these on a money-back basis so you can experiment with little risk.

Sony has come up with a surprisingly good active antenna for portables, the eighty dollar AN-LP1. ("LP" stands for "loop.") It connects to almost any world band portable through its external-antenna socket or by being clipped onto the telescopic antenna. The 'LP1 comes with a variety of adapters for this purpose.

As detailed elsewhere in PASSPORT REPORTS, the AN-LP1 can be used with nearly any portable tested. We have found that it is a superior performer with portatop and tabletop models, as well. A variation, the AN-LP2, is identical except for automatic instead of manual preselection. For now, the 'LP2 only comes bundled with the ICF-SW07 portable and cannot be used with any other radio. However, as sophisticated new Sony models appear, presumably they will be designed to work with it.

Both versions use a small amplifier module powered by two "AA" cells, along with a separate loop antenna that looks like the Jolly Green Giant's tennis racket. The two lightweight parts are joined together by over a dozen feet—four meters—of cable which can be reeled into the amplifier module, like a tape measure. The amplifier, in turn, connects to the radio. For traveling, the "tennis racquet" part of the antenna folds so it can fit into a briefcase, handbag or small carry-on.

With a few radios the antenna's circuitry picks up traces of digital hash being emitted by the receiver itself—fundamentally the result of imperfect receiver shielding. Perhaps for this reason, the AN-LP1 is not supposed be used with the Sony ICF-SW77, although in practice the combination appears to work satisfactorily. With the Sony ICF-2010 only a bit of digital hash comes through.

Our tests show that the AN-LP1 provides varying degrees of improvement, depending upon the receiver. As a rough rule of thumb, smaller models benefit more than larger ones, but all show at least some audible improvement. As the ICF-SW07 portable was designed to work specifically with the AN-LP2, it really helps with weak signals.

In all, Sony's AN-LP1 and AN-LP2 antennas do yeoman's service with world band radios in need of a modest improvement in weak-signal performance. For many receivers, there's nothing better.

☞ Sony makes other models of active antennas (e.g., AN-1, AN-102). These are passable performers, but for world band the AN-LP1 and AN-LP2 are much better and are priced about the same.

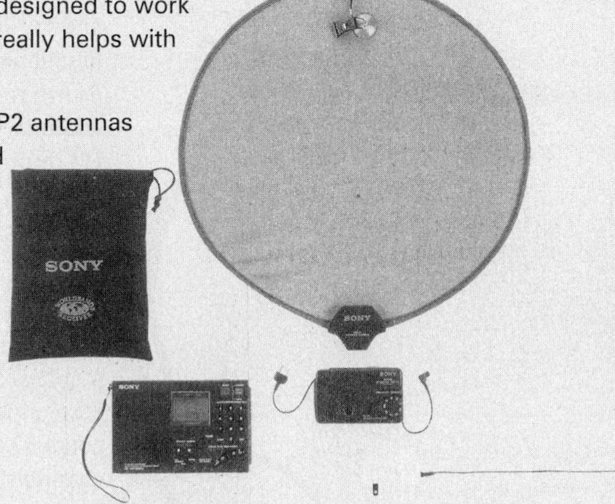
SONY
SONY

Sony's AN-LP1 active antenna is great for hearing weak stations. Swats flies, too.

SANGEAN
ATS 404
POWER
DISPLAY
ALARM
BAND
SW SELECT
MEMO SCAN
TUNING
ENTER
AUTO PRESET
FM/MW/14 SW METER BAND
SYNTHESIZED RECEIVER

Sangean's ATS 404 snares weak signals and is priced to move, but for similar money there are better choices.

✪✪½

Sangean ATS 404, Roberts R881

Price: *Sangean:* $99.95 in the United States. CAN$129.00 in Canada. £59.95 in the United Kingdom. AUS$162.00 in Australia. *ADP-808 120V AC adaptor:* $10.95 in the United States. *Roberts:* £79.95 in the United Kingdom.

Pro: Superior weak-signal sensitivity. Several handy tuning features. Stereo FM through earpieces, supplied. Dual-zone 24/12-hour clock displays seconds numerically. Alarm/snooze. Travel power lock. Illuminated LCD. Battery indicator.

Con: Poor spurious-signal ("image") rejection. No tuning knob. Overloading, controllable by shortening telescopic antenna on world band and collapsing it on mediumwave AM band. Picks up some internal digital hash. Tunes only in 5 kHz increments. No signal-strength indicator. Frequency and time cannot be displayed simultaneously. Power lock does not disable LCD illumination. No handle or carrying strap. AC adaptor extra. Country of manufacture (China) not specified on radio or box. No batteries (four "AA" needed).

Verdict: Value priced.

GRUNDIG
YB 300PE
ON/OFF
SLEEP
LIGHT
MODE
METER
MEMORY
TIME SET
24 STATION MEMORIES

The Grundig Yacht Boy 300PE is basic but affordable for traveling or the beach.

✪✪½

Grundig Yacht Boy 300PE, Tecsun PL757

Price: *YB-300PE:* $79.95 in the United States. CAN$99.99 in Canada. *YB-300PE refurbished units, as available:* $59.95 in the United States.

Pro: Sensitive to weak world band and FM signals. Various helpful tuning features. World Time clock with alarm, clock radio and 10-90 minute snooze (*see* Con). Illuminated LCD (*see* Con). 120V AC adaptor (North America) and supplementary antenna. Travel power lock (*see* Con). Stereo FM through earbuds, supplied. *North America:* Toll-free tech support.

Con: Mediocre spurious-signal ("image") rejection. No tuning knob. Few presets; e.g., only six for 2300-7800 kHz range. Tunes world band only in 5 kHz steps. Even-numbered frequencies displayed with final zero omitted; e.g., 5.73 MHz rather than usual 5730 kHz. Keypad entry of even channels with all digits (e.g., 6 - 1 - 9 - 0, Enter) tunes radio 5 kHz higher (e.g., 6195); remedied by not entering trailing zero (e.g., 6 - 1 - 9, Enter). Unhandy carouseling "MW/SW1/SW2/FM" control required for tuning within 2300-7800 kHz *vs.* 9100-26100 kHz range or *vice versa*. Clock not displayed independent of frequency; button alters which one is visible. Nigh-useless signal-strength indicator. LCD illumination not disabled by travel power lock.

Verdict: Except for LCD illumination being permanently enabled, the Chinese-made Grundig Yacht Boy 300PE is priced and sized to be an unusually sensible choice for traveling, as well as for where signals tend to be weak.

REALISTIC
SW BROADCAST BAND
15.425
PRESET/DIRECT ACCESS
DX-375
VOICE OF THE WORLD

Radio Shack's DX-375 is only found in Canada. A proven performer, it is similar to the DX-396 found in other countries.

✪✪½

Radio Shack DX-375

Price: CAN$199.99.

Pro: Several handy tuning features. Weak-signal sensitivity a bit above average. Stereo FM through headphones, not supplied. Travel power lock. Timer. 30-day money-back period in Canada; product cannot have been opened.

Con: Mediocre spurious-signal ("image") rejection. Unusually long pauses when tuning from channel to channel. Lacks tuning knob. Doesn't tune 6251-7099 kHz. Tunes only in 5 kHz increments. Antenna swivel sometimes needs tightening. Static discharges may disable microprocessor (usually remediable if batteries removed for a time, then replaced). No World Time clock. Signal-strength indicator only a single LED. AC adaptor extra.

Verdict: Made in China, this is similar to the DX-396.

✪✪

Grundig G2000A "Porsche Design," Grundig Porsche P2000

Price: *G2000A:* $99.95 in the United States. CAN$149.95 in Canada. *P2000:* £69.95 in the United Kingdom. AUS$249.00 in Australia. *G2ACA 120V AC adaptor:* $12.95 in the United States.

Pro: One of the most functionally attractive world band radios on the market, with generally superior ergonomics that include an effective and handy lambskin protective case. Superior adjacent-channel rejection—selectivity—for price and size class. Keypad (in proper telephone format), handy meter-band carousel control, signal-seek bandscanning and up/down slew tuning. Twenty station presets, of which ten are for world band and the rest for FM and mediumwave AM stations. FM stereo through earpieces, supplied. World Time clock. Timer/snooze/alarm. Illuminated

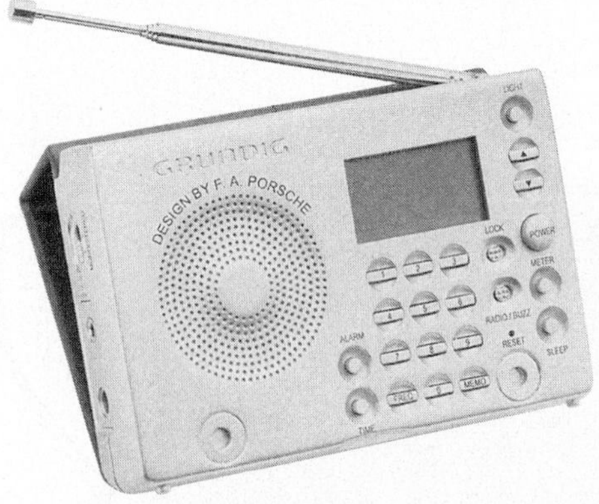
GRUNDIG
DESIGN BY F. A. PORSCHE

Porsche's protective lambskin cover folds back to become an elevation panel. Yes, *that* Porsche.

display. Travel power lock. Microprocessor reset control. *North America:* Toll-free tech support.

Con: Pedestrian audio. Sensitivity mediocre between 9400-26100 kHz, improving slightly between 2300-7400 kHz. Poor spurious-signal ("image") rejection. Does not tune such important world band ranges as 7405-7550 and 9350-9395 kHz. Tunes world band only in 5 kHz steps and displays in nonstandard XX.XX MHz/XX.XX5 MHz format. No tuning knob. Annoying one-second pause when tuning from one channel to the next. Old-technology SW1/SW2 switch complicates tuning. Protruding power button can get in the way of nearby slew-tuning and meter-carousel keys. Leather case makes it difficult to retrieve folded telescopic antenna. Magnetic catches weak on leather case. No carrying strap. Signal-strength indicator nigh useless. Clock not displayed separately from frequency. No batteries (three "AA" required).

Verdict: This German-styled, Chinese-manufactured portable is the ultimate in tasteful design for men and women alike, although performance is of a lesser caliber.

✪½
Bolong HS-490

Price: ¥360 in China.

BOLONG
HS-490

Bolong HS-490—hard to tune, so-so performance, but a hit in China because it's cheap and easily found.

Pro: Inexpensive for a model with digital frequency display, ten world band station presets, and ten station presets for mediumwave AM and FM. World Time clock (*see* Con). Reel-type outboard passive antenna accessory. AC adaptor. Illuminated display. Alarm/snooze. FM stereo (*see* Con) via earbuds, included.

Con: Seemingly nearly impossible to find outside China. Requires patience to get a station, as it tunes world band only via 10 station presets and multi-speed up/down slewing/scanning. Tunes world band only in 5 kHz steps. Even-numbered frequencies displayed with final zero omitted; e.g., 5.75 rather than conventional 5.750 or 5750. Poor spurious-signal ("image") rejection. So-so adjacent-channel rejection (selectivity). World Time clock not displayed independent of frequency. Does not receive relatively unimportant 6200-7100 kHz portion of world band spectrum. Does not receive 1615-1705 kHz portion of expanded AM band in the Americas. No signal-strength indicator. No travel power lock. Mediumwave AM 9/10 kHz tuning increments not selectable, which may make for inexact tuning in some parts of the world other than where the radio was purchased. FM selectivity and capture ratio mediocre. FM stereo did not trigger on our unit.

Verdict: Made by a joint venture between Xin Hui Electronics and Shanghai Huaxin Electronic Instruments. No prize, but as good you'll find among the truly cheap, which probably accounts for this model's being the #1 seller among digital world band radios in China.

LAP PORTABLES

Pleasant for Home, Acceptable for Travel

A lap portable is probably your best bet for use primarily around the home and yard, plus on occasional trips. They are large enough to perform well, sound better than

Portables don't get any better than this, the Sony ICF-2010. Tough and proven, with unsurpassed performance.

compact models, yet they are not too big to fit into a carry-on or briefcase. Most take 3-4 "D" (UM-1) or "C" (UM-2) cells, plus they may also use a couple of "AA" (UM-3) cells for memory backup.

These are typically just under a foot wide—that's 30 cm—and weighing in around 3-4 pounds, or 1.3-1.8 kg. For air travel, that's okay if you are a dedicated listener, but a bit much otherwise. Too, larger sets with snazzy controls occasionally attract unwanted attention from suspicious customs and airport-security personnel in some parts of the world (see sidebar).

Two models stand out for most listeners: the Sony ICF-2010 and Sony ICF-SW77, which unfortunately are hard to find outside the United States. They have the same overall rating, but many who favor one don't much care for the other. The Sangean ATS-818 is hardly in the same league, but at its current American pricing it is an attractive option.

Retested for 2002

✪✪✪¾ 🗉 *Passport's Choice*

Sony ICF-2010

Price: *ICF-2010:* $349.95 in the United States. CAN$599.00 in Canada. Not distributed by Sony elsewhere, but widely available worldwide by mail order or email from major American world band specialty firms. *Padded carrying case #0395:* $29.95 from Universal Radio in the United States. *Franzus F11 240-to-120 VAC,50 Watt, travel transformer:* about $10 at airports, travel shops and online merchants.

Pro: High-tech synchronous selectable sideband, thanks to Sony's proprietary chip with sideband phase canceling; this well-executed feature performs, overall, better for program listening than on any other portable in reducing adjacent-channel interference and selective-fading distortion on world band, longwave and mediumwave AM signals; it can also add slightly to weak-signal sensitivity (*see* Con). This is further aided by two bandwidths (10.4 kHz and 4.3 kHz) which offer a listener-oriented tradeoff between wideband audio fidelity and relatively tighter adjacent-channel rejection (selectivity), especially when used in concert with synchronous selectable sideband. Use of 32 separate one-touch station preset keys in rows and columns is ergonomically the best to be found on any model, portable or tabletop, at any price—simply pushing one key brings in your station, a major convenience (*see* Con). Numerous other helpful tuning features. Excellent weak-signal sensitivity above 4 MHz (noise floor typically –131 dBm, sensitivity typically 0.15 microvolts) (*see*

FAST FIX FOR SONY ICF-2010

The Sony ICF-2010 is a tireless workhorse—units routinely soldier on for 15 years or more without acting up.

Yet, sometimes an intermittent tab contact causes it to quit operating from batteries and an "Error 3" message to appear. This happens with older receivers because of oxidation and wear, but it has also shown up in recent production because tabs were not always bent sufficiently at the factory.

Too, sometimes jiggling the radio will cause the presets and clock setting to erase. This is inherent in the radio's design, but can be minimized with a little tweaking.

No Parts, Simple Tools

We checked with Universal Radio to see how they handle these issues, as they are the world's largest seller and exporter of '2010s. The remedy is simple—virtually anybody can do it.

- *Time:* 10-20 minutes.
- *Parts:* none.
- *Tools:* needle-nose pliers, #2 Phillips screwdriver. Optional: ethyl alcohol, Q-Tip and white eraser (reddish erasers, often on wooden pencils, corrode metal).

1. Remove all batteries and AC adaptor.
2. Remove seven Phillips screws from the back panel, where they are marked by arrows—one in the battery cavity, one in each lower corner and four at the top (including three under the antenna shaft, which needs to be angled up).
3. Lift off the back—it should come loose easily—placing the speaker to the right. Blow out cobwebs and dust.
4. Optional: Near the DC jack, where the AC adaptor plugs in, is a small circuit board is marked BATT+. Using a clean white eraser (rub on paper as needed), burnish the half-inch, or 10 mm, solder blob just above "BATT+." Blow away eraser dust, then wipe the blob with a clean cloth.
5. Stretch the "AA" battery spring slightly with needle-nose pliers, but don't break the plastic base .
6. Hold the back panel, inside facing you, with the antenna mount in the upper-left corner. Near the lower-left corner is a stainless-steel "D" cell battery tab; it has a pointed tip with a small hole and points up slightly. Use pliers to bend that tip to the right about 1/8 inch, or 3 mm.
7. Hold the lowest coil of the "D" battery spring firmly in place with a finger, then use pliers to stretch the spring slightly.
8. Optional: Dip one end of Q-Tip into straight alcohol, rub off excess, then wipe positive and negative battery-holder contacts (two springs and two tabs) for "AA" and "D" cells. Immediately burnish those same contacts with dry end of Q-Tip.
9. Replace the back panel, placing the short screw in "D" battery cavity.
10. The radio should now work off batteries. If not, repeat this procedure, but at step 6 tweak the pointed tip only an additional 1/16 inch or so—a millimeter or two.

Con). Superior dynamic range (DR-20 = 80 dB, DR-5 = 68 dB) and third-order intercept point (IP3-20 = –9 dBm, IP3-5 = –21 dBm). Good overall distortion (under 3.5 percent). Tunes and displays in relatively precise 0.1 kHz increments (*see* Con). Generally superior performance with single-sideband signals (*see* Con). Separate World Time clock, easily set, displays continuously and keeps exact time for months on end. Exceptionally robust, with superior quality of construction underscored by the huge numbers in use worldwide over the past many years; only exception, battery-spring contact, easily remediable by user (*see* Con). First IF rejection excellent, 85 dB. Excellent AGC threshold, 0.6 microvolts. Alarm/snooze, with four-event timer. Illuminated LCD. Travel power lock. Excellent ten-LED digital signal-strength indicator much better than those on most other portables; also seconds as a useful indication of battery strength. Overall reception of fringe and distant mediumwave AM signals is as good as it gets in a portable, thanks to the combination of synchronous selectable sideband, dual bandwidths and splendid field sensitivity (with its built-in ferrite-rod antenna; an external AM antenna may disappoint). Longwave and Japanese FM bands. FM very sensitive to weak signals, making it well suited for fringe reception (*see* Con). Passable reception of air band signals. Hum-free 120 VAC adaptor (center-pin negative, unlike other Sony models; *see* Con). Comes with length of outboard wire antenna that attaches to a separate antenna connector, also supplied.

Con: Distributed by Sony only in North America; however, routinely exported worldwide from American world band specialty firms. Audio quality only average for size class, with simple three-level treble-cut tone control. Station presets and clock/timer features immediately erase whenever microprocessor/memory batteries are replaced, and also sometimes when set is jostled (changing to a different brand of "AA" batteries may help). Similarly, when the "D" cells lose contact an "Error 3" message appears; stretching the battery springs helps. On some new and aging samples, positive battery spring sometimes does not make contact with jack PC board, preventing operation on batteries ("Error 3"); easily remediable, see sidebar. Wide bandwidth unusually broad, although this is typically a problem only when the synchronous selectable sideband is not in use; traveling DXers sometimes prefer the tighter bandwidths of the ICF-SW77, or '2010 replacement bandwidth filters offered by such aftermarket firms as Kiwa, with the tradeoff for less interference being relatively muffled audio. Signal-seek bandscanning works poorly. Telescopic antenna swivel gets slack with heavy use, requiring periodic adjustment of tension screw. Synchronous selectable sideband tends to lose lock if batteries weak, or if NiCd cells are used (NiCd cells put out relatively low voltage). Synchronous selectable sideband alignment can vary with temperature, factory alignment and battery voltage, causing synchronous selectable sideband reception to be slightly more muffled in one sideband than the other—notably with the narrow bandwidth. Synchronous selectable sideband adds minor digital hash to weak signals. On some, especially older, samples, or with depleted batteries, frequency readout can be off by up to 0.6 kHz in "lower" sync mode. Lacks up/down slewing controls. Keypad not in telephone format. LCD not clearly visible when radio viewed from above. Tuning resolution in 0.1 kHz increments means that non-synchronous single-sideband reception can be out of phase by up to 50 Hz, so audio quality varies. Image rejection, although 62 dB (good), is 18 dB less than on ICF-SW77. Blocking (109 dB) only fair. Weak-signal sensitivity (noise floor –118 dBm, sensitivity 0.75 microvolts) only fair within 120 meter tropical segment. Superior dynamic range invites use of external antennas, which if left connected when storms nearby can cause a transistor to blow; fortunately, it is not difficult for a technician to replace. Only 32 presets offered. Shoulder strap instead of handle, but this can be user-replaced. In high-signal-strength environments, FM band can overload, causing false "repeat" signals to appear. FM capture ratio only fair, limiting ability to separate co-channel stations. Air band insensitive to weak signals. No 240V AC adaptor known to be offered by Sony; best bet is to plug the Sony 120V AC adaptor into a Franzus F11 travel transformer or other 2:1 transformer. No batteries (three "D" required).

Verdict: With consumer electronic products and PCs, the best is often the newest or the most costly. Not so with world band radios, where the last wave of technological advances occurred between 1976 and 1984. Except for everyday audio quality and urban FM, the '2010 is the favorite portable of most PASSPORT panelists, as well as myriad radio monitors and DXers. It is among the best for rejection of one of world band's major bugaboos, adjacent-channel interference. This is thanks in large part to its synchronous selectable sideband feature, which allows for unusually broadband audio even if only one sideband is free from adjacent-channel interference. Alone among sophisticated receivers, it allows dozens of stations to be brought up at the single touch of a key. Although it is costlier to manufacture than newer models—it is made in Japan, and has discrete controls that are too costly for newly designed models—it sells at a surprisingly affordable price because its development costs have been written off. Sony of America emphasizes that they plan to keep this model in their line indefinitely.

Evaluation of Latest Units: This year we purchased two ICF-2010s for travel monitoring. Like another unit tested last year, these are both slightly more sensitive to weak signals than earlier production units. Alignment for the changeover point from LSB to USB with synchronous selectable sideband is also spot on: a perfect x.9/x.0 kHz for 2002, x.8/x.9 kHz for 2001, x.6/x.7 kHz for our mid-1980s units. However, changeover points can differ slightly from sample-to-sample, as batteries weaken and radios age. (Similarly, if the AC adaptor is in use the changeover point can shift slightly with wide swings in local AC mains voltage.)

The '2010 uses a long, well-made shoulder strap. For air travelers with their hands full, a shoulder strap can be mighty welcome. Otherwise, a carrying handle is much more convenient.

Originally, this strap was a continuous length of half-inch (13 mm) nylon webbing, whereas now beefy 1³⁄₁₆ inch (30 mm) material is used. The original strap could be cut down to make into a short handle, but not so the new version. However, you can obtain narrower webbing at a dry goods, luggage repair or sewing store, then use the '2010's strap hardware to affix your homebrew handle to the radio. If after this you want to have your cake and eat it, too, you can get a special radio carrying case made by Universal Radio. It's padded with a large shoulder strap, making it ideal for air trips.

The volume slider control has a touch more slack than it did in early production. More significant is that over the past year or so we have encountered complaints about new units failing to operate off batteries, with the display reading "Error 3." Fortunately, should this arise you can fix it yourself in a few minutes (see sidebar).

An *RDI WHITE PAPER* is available for this model.

✪✪✪¾

Sony ICF-SW77, Sony ICF-SW77E

Price: $469.95 in the United States. £329.95 as available in the United Kingdom. ¥8,000 in China. *Padded carrying case*

#0395: $29.95 from Universal Radio in the United States.

Pro: A rich variety of tuning and other features, including sophisticated "page" tuning that some enjoy but others dislike; includes 162 presets, two-speed tuning knob, signal-seek bandscanning (*see* Con), keypad tuning and meter-band access. Synchronous selectable sideband is exceptionally handy to operate; it significantly reduces selective-fading distortion and adjacent-channel interference on world band, longwave and mediumwave AM signals; although the sync chip part number was changed recently, its performance is virtually unchanged (*see* Con). Two well-chosen bandwidths (6.0 kHz and 3.3 kHz) provide superior adjacent-channel rejection. Excellent image rejection and first-IF rejection, both 80 dB. Excellent-to-superb weak-signal sensitivity (noise floor –133 dBm, sensitivity 0.16 microvolts) in and around lower-middle portion of shortwave spectrum where most listening is done (*see* Con). Superb overall distortion, almost always under one percent. Dynamic range (82 dB) and third-order intercept point (–10 dBm) fairly good and only slightly less than those of the ICF-2010 at 20 kHz separation (*see* Con). Tunes in very precise 0.05 kHz increments; displays in 0.1 kHz increments; these and other factors make this model superior to any other portable for single-sideband reception, although portatop and tabletop models usually fare better yet. Continuous bass and treble tone controls, a rarity. Two illuminated multi-function liquid crystal displays. Dual-zone clock, displays separately from frequency. Station name appears on LCD when station presets used. 10-level signal-strength indicator (*see* Con). Excellent stability, less than 20 Hz drift after ten-second warmup. Excellent weak-signal sensitivity (noise floor –130 dBm, sensitivity 0.21 microvolts) within little-used 120 meter segment (*see* Con). Flip-up chart for calculating time differences. VCR-type five-event timer controls radio and optional outboard recorder alike. Superior FM audio quality. Stereo FM through earpieces, supplied. Longwave and Japanese FM bands. AC adaptor, hum-free, and reel-in outboard antenna. No batteries (four "C" required). Rubber strip helps prevent sliding.

SONY

The only real competition to the Sony ICF-2010 is another Sony, the ICF-SW77.

Con: "Page" tuning system relatively complex to operate; many find that station presets can't be accessed simply. World band and mediumwave AM audio slightly muffled even when wide bandwidth in use. Synthesizer chugging degrades reception quality during bandscanning by knob. Dynamic range (64 dB) and third-order intercept point (–37 dBm) only fair at 5 kHz separation. Weak-signal sensitivity varies from fair to superb, depending on where between 2 and 30 MHz receiver is being tuned. Synchronous selectable sideband holds lock less well than ICF-2010 model. Synchronous selectable sideband tends to lose lock if batteries weak, or if NiCd cells are used. Synchronous selectable sideband alignment can vary with temperature, factory alignment and battery voltage, causing synchronous selectable sideband reception to be slightly more muffled in one sideband than the other. Signal-seek bandscanning skips over weaker signals. Flimsy 11-element telescopic antenna (the older version of the 'SW77 had nine elements). LCD characters small for size of receiver. Display illumination does not stay on with AC power. Unusual tuning knob design disliked by some. On mediumwave AM band, relatively insensitive, sometimes with spurious sounds during single-sideband reception; this doesn't apply to world band reception, however. Mundane reception of difficult FM signals. Signal-strength indicator grossly overreads, covering only a 20 dB range with maximum reading at only 3 microvolts. AGC threshold, 2 microvolts (good), inferior to that of ICF-2010. Painted surfaces can wear off with heavy use. Getting harder to find outside the United States.

☞ For those seeking to have their ICF-SW77 repaired, a helpful source at Sony of America suggests: Sony Service Center, 1504 Grundy's Lane, MD #12, Bristol PA 19007 USA.

Verdict: The Japanese-made '77 has been a strong contender among portables since it was improved some time back, and for single-sideband reception it is the best portable by a skosh. It's also one of the very few models with continuously tuned bass and treble controls. Ergonomics, however, are a mixed bag, so if you're interested consider trying it out first.

✪✪½

Sangean ATS-818, Roberts R827

Price: *Sangean:* $174.95 in the United States. CAN$239.00 in Canada. £139.95 in

NUMBERS: TOP TWO PORTABLES

	Sony ICF-2010	**Sony ICF-SW77**
Max. Sensitivity/Noise Floor	0.15 µV, Ⓢ/–131 dBm, Ⓔ[1]	0.16 µV, Ⓢ/–133 dBm, Ⓔ[2]
Blocking	109 dB, Ⓕ	121 dB, Ⓖ
Bandwidths *(Shape Factors)*	10.4 *(1:1.8,* Ⓔ*)*, 4.3 *(1:2.0,* Ⓖ*)* kHz	6.0 *(1:1.9,* Ⓔ*)*, 3.3 *(1:2.0,* Ⓖ*)* kHz
Ultimate Rejection	70 dB, Ⓖ	70 dB, Ⓖ
Front-End Selectivity	Ⓕ	—[3]
Image Rejection	62 dB, Ⓖ	80 dB, Ⓔ
First IF Rejection	85 dB, Ⓔ	80 dB, Ⓔ
Dynamic Range/IP3 (5 kHz)	68 dB, Ⓕ/–21 dBm, Ⓖ	64 dB, Ⓕ/–37 dBm, Ⓕ
Dynamic Range/IP3 (20 kHz)	80 dB, Ⓕ/–9 dBm, Ⓖ	82 dB, Ⓕ/–10 dBm, Ⓖ
Phase Noise	114 dBc, Ⓖ	122 dBc, Ⓔ
AGC Threshold	0.6 µV, Ⓔ	2.0 µV, Ⓖ
Overall Distortion, sync	2.9%, Ⓖ/3.5%, Ⓖ[4]	2.3%, Ⓔ/3.3%, Ⓖ[4]

IBS Lab Ratings: Ⓢ Superb Ⓔ Excellent Ⓖ Good Ⓕ Fair Ⓟ Poor

(1) Measurements flat from 5-29 MHz, but drop to 0.75 µV, Ⓕ/-118 dBm, Ⓕ at 2 MHz.

(2) Sensitivity varies considerably by frequency at 2 MHz and between 10-29.9 MHz; *viz.*, from 0.16 µV to1.40 µV, Ⓢ - Ⓕ. Noise floor varies by frequency from –133 dBm to –117 dBm, Ⓔ - Ⓕ. Neither measurement could be made at 5 MHz because of spurious responses, noise and leakage.

(3) Cannot be determined.

(4) Wide/narrow bandwidths.

The bad news we already reported on as we went to press last year, which is that Drake has finally dropped its robust SW8 portatop. It used to be that in 1932 you could buy any Ford so long as it was black, and now in 2002 you can obtain any portatop so long as it is a Grundig Satellit 800.

The good news is that the Satellit's manufacturing quality has continued to improve. It is now noticeably more consistent from sample-to-sample that it was at the time of its introduction. Additionally, the tuning knob mechanism and AC adaptor that formerly brought complaints have been successfully re-engineered, and pre-improvement units have long since disappeared from dealers' shelves.

In 2002 you can obtain any portatop so long as it is a Grundig Satellit 800.

What PASSPORT's Rating Symbols Mean

Star ratings: ✪✪✪✪✪ is best. Stars reflect overall performance and meaningful features, plus to some extent ergonomics and build quality. Price, appearance, country of manufacture and the like are not taken into account. With portatop models there is a balanced emphasis on listening quality, on one hand, and the ability to flush out tough, hard-to-hear signals on the other. Nevertheless, to facilitate comparison the portatop rating standards are very similar to those used for the professional, tabletop and portable models reviewed elsewhere in this PASSPORT.

Passport's Choice. *La crème de la crème.* Our test team's personal picks of the litter—models we would buy or have bought for our personal use.

¢: A relative bargain, with decidedly more performance than the price would suggest.

Revised for 2002

✪✪✪✪⅜ ¢ *Passport's Choice*

Grundig Satellit 800, Grundig Satellit 800 EU

Price: *S-800:* $499.95 including 120 VAC adaptor and headphones in the United States. CAN$599.99 including 120 VAC adaptor and headphones in Canada. *S-800 refurbished units, as available:* $399.95 in the United States. *S-800 EU:* £549.00 including 240V AC adaptor and headphones in the United Kingdom.

Pro: Outstanding price, especially in North America, for level of performance. Superior, room-filling tonal quality by world band, even if not audiophile, standards—whether with the internal speaker, outboard speakers or headphones; only receiver tested that comes with full-size audiophile-style padded headphones. Tonal shaping aided by continuous separate bass and treble tone controls, a rarity among world band receivers at any price. Excellent-performing synchronous selectable sideband, with 27 dB of unwanted-sideband rejection; this reduces adjacent-channel interference and selective-fading distortion with world band, longwave and mediumwave AM signals. Synchronous selectable sideband also boosts recoverable audio from some of the weakest of signals, and halves overall distortion from 5.3% in the ordinary AM mode to 2.4% on audio frequencies from 100-3,000 Hz. Three voice/music bandwidths; wide measures around 7 kHz, while medium and narrow measure in the vicinity of 5.8 kHz and 2.6 kHz (*see* Con). Bandwidths generally have excellent shape factors (*see* Con) and excellent ultimate rejection; all bandwidths are selectable independent of mode (or dependent, if the user prefers), and work in concert with the synchronous selectable sideband feature to provide superior adjacent-channel rejection. Slow/fast AGC decay (*see* Con). Numerous helpful tuning aids, including 70 tunable station presets that store many variables (*see* Con); also, presets may be scanned (*see* Con). Excellent ergonomics, including many dedicated, widely spaced controls; exceptionally smooth knob tuning aided by ball bearings (*see* Con); and foolproof frequency entry. Superb LCD with huge, bold characters has high contrast and can be viewed clearly from virtually any angle; it is even readable by many with faltering eyesight (*see* Con). Analog signal-strength indicator, a rarity at this price, has gradations in useful S1-9/+60 dB standard (*see* Con). Single-sideband reception above the portable norm (*see* Con), with rock-solid frequency stability and 50 Hz tuning increments. High- and low-impedance inputs for 0.1-30 MHz external antennas. Weak-signal shortwave sensitivity with built-in telescopic antenna comparable to that of best-rated portables; weak-signal shortwave and mediumwave AM performance is even better with appropriate

NUMBERS: GRUNDIG SATELLIT 800	
Max. Sensitivity/Noise Floor	0.43 µV, G/–124 dBm, G (1)
Blocking	132 dB, E
Bandwidths *(Shape Factors)*	7.1 *(1:1.6,* E*)*, 5.8 *(1:1.6,* E*)*, 2.6 *(1:2.2,* G*)* kHz
Ultimate Rejection	75 dB, E
Front-End Selectivity	F
Image Rejection	65 dB, G
First IF Rejection	83 dB, E
Dynamic Range/IP3 (5 kHz)	67 dB, F/–26 dBm, G (2)
Dynamic Range/IP3 (20 kHz)	92 dB, E/+11 dBm, S (2)
Phase Noise	111 dBc, G
AGC Threshold	0.8 µV, S
Overall Distortion, sync	2.4%, E

IBS Lab Ratings: S Superb E Excellent G Good F Fair P Poor

(1) Sample-to-sample variation from 0.23 to 0.43 µV, –129 to –124 dBm.

(2) Estimated, as ability to measure limited by birdies, phase noise and other mixing products.

SATELLIT 800
MILLENNIUM
GRUNDIG
15410.0

Even when power fails and all is dark, the Grundig Satellit 800 provides no-compromise performance. Engineered by the legendary R.L. Drake Company of Franklin, Ohio, which also provides service in and out of warranty.

external antennas (*see* Con). Weak-signal shortwave sensitivity with an external antenna can be boosted by setting antenna switch to "whip," thus adding preamplification (and, in such locations as Europe evenings, sometimes generating overloading as well). Superior blocking performance aids consistency of weak-signal sensitivity. Generally superior dynamic range and third-order intercept point to the extent they can be divined amidst receiver phase noise and such. Two-event on/off timer and two 24-hour clocks (*see* Con). Large, tough telescopic antenna includes spring-loaded detents for vertical, 45-degree and 90-degree swiveling; also rotates freely 360 degrees (*see* Con). Clever display and signal strength meter illumination—with batteries in use, light automatically comes on for 15 seconds either at the touch of any button or when receiver is knob or slew tuned; 15-second illumination cycle can be aborted by pushing the light button a second time. FM—mono through built-in speaker, stereo through outboard speakers, headphones and line output—performs well, although capture ratio only average and nearby FM transmitters may cause some overloading. Covers longwave down to 100 kHz. Built-in ferrite rod antenna may be used for 0.1-1.8 MHz. Covers the 118-137 MHz aeronautical band, but only in the AM mode without synchronous selectable sideband; performs about as well as a simple handheld scanner. Excellent, long carrying handle. Comes with AC adaptor—120 VAC or 220 VAC, depending upon where radio is sold; otherwise, alkaline batteries need changing every 35 hours or so, about 25 cents per hour. Battery-strength indicator (*see* Con). Rack-type handles protect front panel should radio fall over. Repairs in and out of one-year warranty is performed by the R.L. Drake Company, long known for superior service (*see* Con). *North America:* Excellent toll-free tech support.

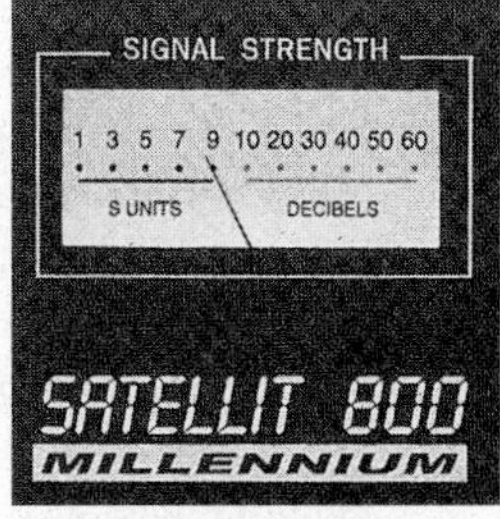
SIGNAL STRENGTH
1 3 5 7 9 10 20 30 40 50 60
S UNITS
DECIBELS
SATELLIT 800
MILLENNIUM

Bean counters have practically driven the analog signal-strength indicator into extinction, but not on this receiver.

Con: Huge (20⅜ inches—517 mm—wide) and weighty (15 pounds or 6.8 kg with batteries). Plastic cabinet and other components are not in the same radiophile-hardware league as tabletop models. Synthesizer phase noise, only fair, slightly impacts reception of weak-signals adjacent to powerful signals and in other circumstances; also, limits ability to make certain laboratory measurements accurately. Lacks notch filter, noise blanker, passband tuning and digital signal processing (DSP) found on some tabletop models. When ungrounded (e.g., AC adaptor is not connected) and powered by batteries, there is vigorous "hash" while the tuning knob is being handled within some portions of the mediumwave AM band; this ceases when the tuning knob is released, and reception quality of the received station is not affected. Each key push must each be done within three seconds, lest receiver wind up being mis-tuned or placed into an unwanted operating mode. No signal-seek frequency scanning. Signal-strength indicator greatly underreads, although arguably this is preferable to the overreading often found with other models. Outboard AC adaptor in lieu of inboard power supply. Single sideband's 50 Hz synthesizer increments allow tuning to be out of phase by up to 25 Hz, diminishing audio fidelity. Fast AGC decay setting is handy for bandscanning, but sometimes causes distortion with powerful signals; remedied by going to slow AGC when no longer actively bandscanning. Numerous modest birdies on longwave, mediumwave AM, shortwave and FM bands; these rarely cause heterodyne interference to world band signals, approximately one time in 250 they might heterodyne utility, ham and Eastern Hemisphere mediumwave signals. Spurious signal on 20,000 kHz obscures WWV reception. Ergonomics, although excellent, are not ideal; e.g., no rows and columns of dedicated buttons for station presets, as is found on the Sony ICF-2010. Sharp bevel on tuning knob. Neither clock displays when frequency is shown; however, pushbutton allows time to replace frequency on the display for three seconds. Both clocks in 24-hour format and neither displays seconds numerically; 12-hour format not selectable for local time. For faint-signal DXing, recoverable audio with an outboard antenna, although good, not fully equal to that of most tabletop and professional models. Using the built-in antenna, sensitivity to weak signals is not of DX caliber in the mediumwave AM band; remedied by using Terk AM Advantage or similar accessory antenna. Some frontal (only) radiation of digital noise from LCD, rarely causes problem in actual use. No adjustable feet or elevation rod to angle receiver upwards for handy operation. When receiver leaned backward, the telescopic antenna, if angled, spins to the rear. Battery-strength indicator doesn't come on until immediately before radio mutes from low battery voltage. Misleading location of battery spring clips makes it easy to insert half the batteries in the wrong direction, albeit to no permanent ill effect. Battery cover may come loose if receiver bumped in a specific and unusual manner. Antenna switches located unhandily on rear panel. "USB" on LCD displays as "LISB." No schematic or repair manual available, making service difficult except at authorized repair facilities. No batteries (6 "D" needed).

☞ Refurbished units reportedly include gift and similar types of returns from department stores and other outlets where customers tend to be unfamiliar with world band radio. Refurbishing is done at Drake's facility in Ohio.

Verdict: The improved Grundig Satellit 800 is a benchmark receiver, being the first ever to offer such a level of near-tabletop performance at portable prices. Its audio quality and ergonomics are among the best of any world band receiver on the market, regardless of price.

The Satellit 800 continues to provide exceptional performance at a surprisingly affordable price, especially now that it incorporates improved tuning and quality control.

Evaluation of Improved Version: Perhaps "version" is an overstatement, but clearly the Grundig Satellit 800 is better for 2002 than it was when it first appeared in mid-2000. For example, although the original tuning knob worked properly, on some samples it tended to wobble. No more—Matsushita ball bearings now make it rock stable.

Quality control used to be another and more serious problem. But with the "shakedown cruise" over, sample-to-sample manufacturing consistency appears to be approaching average for a portable-type receiver. Dealers report lower returns, and our lab tests no longer show unusual swings in measurement readings.

Still, it helps to know that if you buy one and it acts up at the outset, nearly all dealers will swap it out for a new replacement. And there's plenty of hand-holding: Grundig's North American toll-free customer support for the '800 is arguably the best in the business.

Canadians have special reason to cheer, as in late 2001 the manufacturer dropped the price by $100. The Satellit 800 continues to be relatively costly in the United Kingdom, but even there street price has dropped by £50 in recent months.

An *RDI WHITE PAPER* is available for this model.

The PASSPORT *portatop review team includes Lawrence Magne, Tony Jones, Craig Tyson and George Zeller, with Avery Comarow, George Heidelman and John Wagner. Laboratory measurements by Robert Sherwood.*

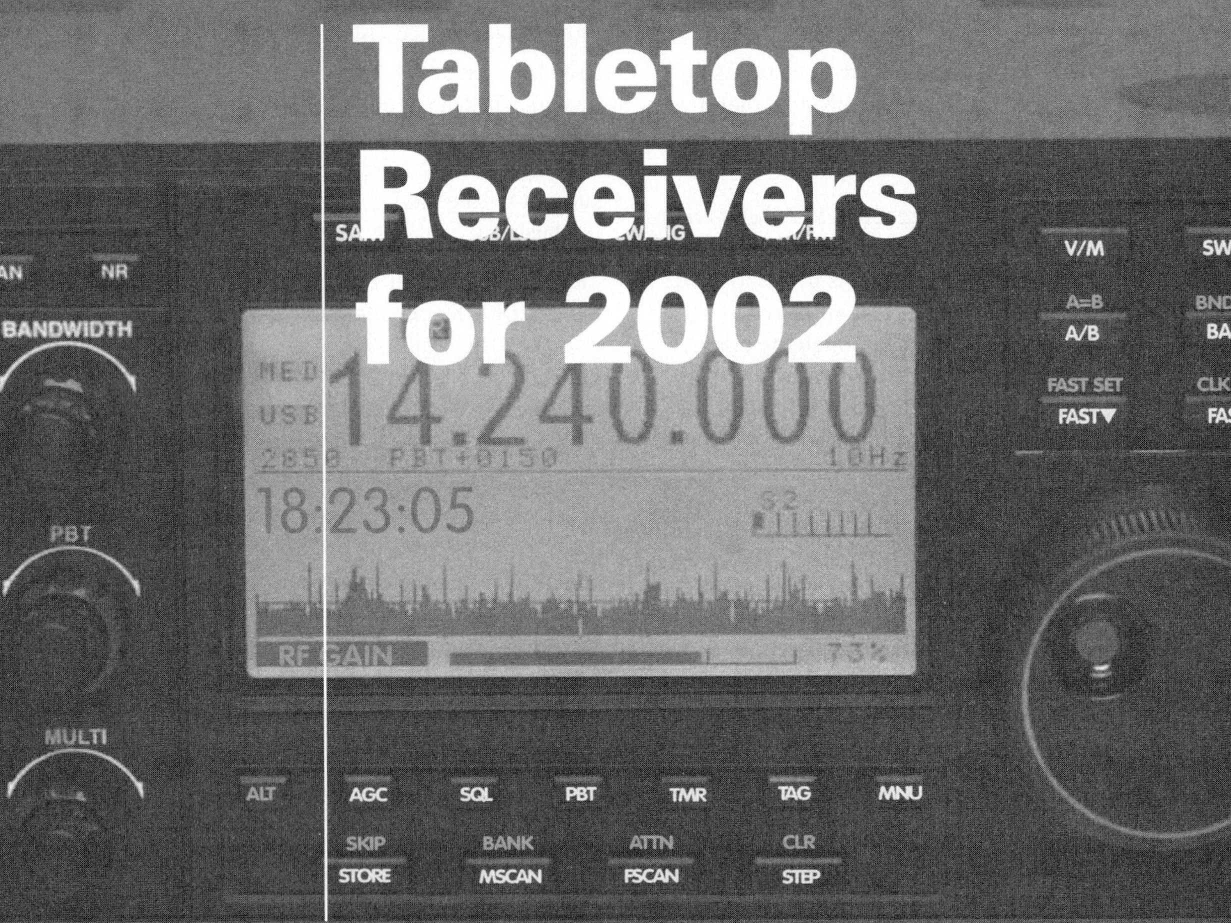
NR
BANDWIDTH
14.240.000
USB
PBT+0150
10Hz
18:23:05
RF GAIN
PBT
MULTI
V/M
A=B
A/B
FAST SET
FAST▼
ALT
AGC
SQL
PBT
TMR
TAG
MNU
SKIP
STORE
BANK
MSCAN
ATTN
PSCAN
CLR
STEP

Tabletop Receivers for 2002

Tabletop receivers flush out tough game—faint stations swamped by competing signals. That's why they are prized by radio aficionados known as "DXers," an old telegraph term meaning long distance.

But tabletop models aren't for everybody, and it shows. Even in prosperous North America and Europe, tabletop unit sales are minimal even while the roster of choices is as great as ever. Professional models are tempting alternatives to tabletop offerings, and are built to last. These are reviewed elsewhere in PASSPORT REPORTS, but steep prices keep most buyers away.

Most tabletop receivers are pricier than portables or portatops, yet less expensive than professional supersets. For that money you tend to get not only excellent performance, but also a fairly robust device. Tabletop models are not only manufactured to a higher standard than portables and portatops, but also are relatively easy to service and backed up by knowledgeable repair facilities. What you rarely find in a tabletop is reception of the everyday 87.5-108 MHz FM band—for this coverage in a premium receiver, look to a portatop.

Find major updates to the 2002 Passport Reports at www.passband.com.

Where in the World Is San Diego, Carmen?

Tabletop sets, like portatop and professional models, are heavy artillery for where signals are routinely weak—places like the North American Midwest and West, or Australia and New Zealand. Even elsewhere there can be a problem when world band signals have to follow paths over or near the geomagnetic North Pole. To check, place a string on a globe—a conventional map won't do—between you and from where the received station is transmitted (this is indicated in the Blue Pages). If the string passes near or above latitude 60° north, beware.

Tough-signal reception is especially relevant in North America and Australasia, now that the BBC World Service has throttled back on shortwave transmissions. Pleasant, reliable listening to the BBC now all but mandates superior weak-signal sensitivity and synchronous

NUMBERS: TOP TWO TABLETOPS

	Drake R8B	**AOR AR7030**
Max. Sensitivity/Noise Floor	0.2 µV, Ⓔ/–131 dBm, Ⓔ	0.2 µV, Ⓔ/–128 dBm, Ⓖ
Blocking	135 dB, Ⓢ	>130 dB, Ⓔ
Shape Factors, voice BWs	1:2.09–1:2.92, Ⓖ	1:1.52–1:1.96, Ⓔ
Ultimate Rejection	80 dB, Ⓔ	90 dB, Ⓢ
Front-End Selectivity	Half octave, Ⓔ	High/low pass, Ⓕ
Image Rejection	85 dB, Ⓔ	>100 dB, Ⓢ
First IF Rejection	>90 dB, Ⓢ	95 dB, Ⓢ
Dynamic Range/IP3 (5 kHz)	75 dB, Ⓖ/–20 dBm, Ⓔ	82 dB, Ⓔ/+1 dBm, Ⓢ
Dynamic Range/IP3 (20 kHz)	89 dB, Ⓖ/+2 dBm, Ⓔ	100 dB, Ⓢ/+28 dBm, Ⓢ
Phase Noise	114 dBc, Ⓖ	130 dBc, Ⓢ
AGC Threshold	0.9 µV, Ⓢ	2.25 µV, Ⓖ
Overall Distortion, sync	0.4%, Ⓢ	2.0%, Ⓔ
Notch filter depth	55 dB, Ⓢ	55 dB, Ⓢ

IBS Lab Ratings: ⓈSuperb ⒺExcellent ⒼGood ⒻFair ⓅPoor

selectable sideband. Tabletop and other high-performance receivers thus make more sense now than they did just a year ago.

Daytime Signals Weaker

Since the end of the Cold War a number of stations have compressed their schedules. Yet others, attempting to prognosticate the future, have shifted resources to satellites or the Internet. So some programs formerly heard at prime time are now audible only during your local daytime.

Daytime signals tend to be weaker, especially when not beamed to your part of the world. However, thanks to the scattering properties of shortwave, you can still eavesdrop on many of these "off-beam" signals. But it's harder, and that's where a superior receiver's longer reach comes in.

However, if you are already using a portable with an outdoor antenna and it is being disrupted by electrical noise from nearby motors, dimmers and such, you probably won't benefit from a tabletop model. Its superior circuitry boosts local noise as much as signals.

Antennas for High-Rises

In high-rise buildings—especially urban—portables can disappoint. Reinforced buildings soak up signals, while local broadcast and cellular transmitters can interfere.

Here, a good bet for tough stations is a well-rated tabletop or portatop model fed by a homebrew insulated-wire antenna along, or just outside, a window or balcony. Also, try an ordinary telescopic car antenna stuck perpendicularly out a window or balcony ledge. If your radio has a built-in preamplifier, all the better. With some portatop models, the built-in preamplifier can be accessed by connecting the external antenna to the receiver's telescopic-antenna input.

Another alternative is to amplify these homebrew antennas with an active preselector. You can also try amplified ("active") antennas that have reception elements and amplifiers in separate modules. Active preselectors and antennas are evaluated elsewhere in this PASSPORT REPORTS.

Antennas for the Backyard

Tabletop receiver performance is greatly determined by antenna quality and placement. If you don't live in an apartment, go with a first-rate passive (unamplified) outdoor wire antenna, like those from Antenna Supermarket and Alpha Delta—usually under $100. A good world band specialty antenna is a must if your tabletop model is to perform properly. For performance findings and specifics for best installation, check with the Radio Database International White Paper, *Popular Outdoor Antennas*, as well as the reports on antennas elsewhere in this book.

If yard space is minimal or there are legal restrictions, consider an active antenna. Passive wire antennas are still best, but in doing this year's PASSPORT REPORTS' tests we found one English manufacturer that turns out surprisingly good active models.

Complete Findings Now Available

Our unabridged laboratory and hands-on test results for each receiver are too exhaustive to reproduce here. However, they are available for selected models as PASSPORT's Radio Database International White Papers—details on availability are elsewhere in this book.

Tips for Using this Section

Receivers are listed in order of suitability for listening to difficult-to-hear world band stations. Important secondary consideration is given to audio fidelity and ergonomics. Street prices are given, including European and Australian VAT/GST where applicable. Prices vary, so take them as the general guide they are meant to be.

Unless otherwise stated, all tabletop models have:

- Digital frequency synthesis and display.
- Full coverage of at least the 155-29999 kHz longwave, mediumwave AM and shortwave spectra—including all world band frequencies—but no coverage of the FM broadcast band (87.5-108 MHz). Models designed for sale in certain countries have reduced shortwave tuning ranges.
- A wide variety of helpful tuning features.
- Synchronous selectable sideband via high-rejection IF filtering (not lower-rejection phasing), which greatly reduces adjacent-channel interference and selective-fading distortion.
  ☞ **ECSS:** Many tabletop models can tune to the nearest 10 Hz or even 1 Hz, allowing the user to use the receiver's single-

COMING UP: TEN-TEC TARGETS DRAKE'S MARKET

A new DSP receiver is in the wings: the American-made Ten-Tec RX-350, due out before early 2002. The price is $1,338—$1,199 is for the receiver, $139 for an encoder/keypad. This puts the RX-350 head to head against the top-rated Drake R8B and AOR AR7030+3.

Much is derived from the existing Ten-Tec Jupiter transceiver. Planned are 35 bandwidths, DSP automatic notch and noise reduction, synchronous selectable sideband, 1 Hz tuning and frequency readout, and an LCD spectrum display.

Tuning is by knob, multi-step up/down slewing, 128 presets storing alphanumeric tags and other variables, memory scanning and bandscanning. The receiver has no keypad; instead, there is an optional mouse-type keypad with a second tuning knob. It lays flat, so it is more comfortable than a built-in keypad.

The manufacturer promises a multi-event timer, like on a VCR, and a 24/12-hour clock which displays fulltime and shows seconds numerically. The inboard 115/230V AC power supply will be able to be automatically backed up by 13.8V DC. No continuous EQ or tone controls, just high-boost for aging ears.

The manufacturer's lab numbers are not terribly meaningful. However, should we test the '350 well in advance of Passport 2003, summary findings will be at www.passband.com.

Thus far consumer-grade DSP receivers have been better on paper than in execution. The culprit is a tradeoff between cost and power for microprocessors, which has kept DSP models from reaching their potential. Only time will tell whether Ten-Tec has overcome this with the forthcoming RX-350.

14.240.000
TEN-TEC
RX-350
Ten-Tec RX-350: Will it fly?

F1
F2
F3
7
8
9
4
5
6
1
2
3
0
E
Mouse keypad lays flat.

sideband circuitry to manually phase its BFO (internally generated carrier) with the station's transmitted carrier. Called "ECSS" (exalted-carrier, selectable-sideband) tuning, this can be used in lieu of synchronous selectable sideband. However, in addition to the relative inconvenience of this technique, unlike synchronous selectable sideband, which re-phases continually and perfectly, ECSS is always slightly out of phase. This causes at least some degree of harmonic distortion to music and speech, while tuning to the nearest Hertz can generate slow-sweep fading (for this reason, mis-phasing by two or three Hertz may provide better results).

- Proper demodulation of modes used by non-world-band shortwave signals, except for models designed to be sold in certain countries. These modes include single sideband (LSB/USB) and CW ("Morse code"); also, with suitable ancillary devices, radioteletype (RTTY), frequency shift key (FSK) and radiofax (FAX).
- Meaningful signal-strength indication.
- Illuminated display.

What PASSPORT's Rating Symbols Mean

Star ratings: ✪✪✪✪✪ is best. Stars reflect overall performance and meaningful features, plus to some extent ergonomics and build quality. Price, appearance, country of manufacture and the like are not taken into account. With tabletop models there is a slightly greater emphasis on the ability to flush out tough, hard-to-hear signals, as this is one of the main reasons these sets are chosen. Nevertheless, to facilitate comparison the tabletop rating standards are very similar to those used for the professional, portatop and portable models reviewed elsewhere in this PASSPORT.

Passport's Choice. *La crème de la crème.* Our test team's personal picks of the litter—models we would buy or have bought for our personal use.

⊘: A relative bargain, with decidedly more performance than the price would suggest. However, none of these receivers is cheap.

✪✪✪✪✪ *Passport's Choice*
Drake R8B

Price: *R8B:* $1,379.00 in the United States. CAN$2,095.00 in Canada. *MS8 Speaker:* US$49.00 in the United States. CAN$75.00 in Canada. *VHF Converter:* US$249.00 plus installation in the United States. CAN$379.00 plus installation in Canada.

Pro: Superior all-round performance for listening to world band programs and hunting DX catches, as well as utility, amateur and mediumwave AM signals. Mellow, above-average audio quality, especially with suitable outboard speaker or headphones. Synchronous selectable sideband excels at reducing distortion caused by selective fading, as well as at diminishing or eliminating adjacent-channel interference; also has synchronous double sideband. Five well-chosen bandwidths, four suitable for world band. Highly flexible operating controls, including a powerful tunable AF notch filter (tunes to 5,100 Hz AF, but *see* Con) and an excellent passband offset control. Best ergonomics of any five-star model (*see* Con), plus LCD unusually easy to read. Tunes and displays in precise 10 Hz increments. Slow/fast/off AGC with superior performance characteristics. Exceptionally effective noise blanker. Helpful tuning features include 1,000 presets and sophisticated scanning functions; presets can be quickly accessed via tuning knob and slew buttons. Built-in preamplifier. Accepts two antennas, selectable via front panel. Two 24-hour clocks, with seconds displayed numerically and two-event timer (*see* Con). Helpful operating manual. Superior factory service, although older models aren't supported for as long as they used to be.

Con: Virtually requires a good outboard speaker for non-headphone listening, although optional Drake MS8 outboard speaker not equal to the receiver's audio potential; try a good amplified computer speaker or high-efficiency passive speaker instead. Some "birdies." Neither clock shows when frequency displayed. Lightweight tuning knob lacks flywheel effect. No IF output. Otherwise-excellent tilt bail difficult to open. Notch filter does not tune below 500 Hz (AF). Fifteen-day money-back trial period if ordered from factory. Virtually impossible to find at dealers outside North America. When changing from 90-132V to 180-264V AC, a resistor must be removed from receiver, usually by a technician. Power cord detaches handily from receiver, making it easy to replace. Optional VHF converter difficult to install; best is to have this done when receiver is purchased, which adds another $20 or so.

Verdict: The American-made Drake R8B is the only non-professional receiver we have ever tested that gets *everything* right, where something important isn't missing or sputtering. This means there's little point spending money on such performance-enhancing accessories as the Sherwood SE-3, although a better—outboard—speaker allows the receiver to live up to its fidelity potential.

An *RDI WHITE PAPER* is available for this model.

✪✪✪✪✪ *Passport's Choice*

AOR AR7030, AOR AR7030+3

Price: *AR7030:* CAN$1,995.00 in Canada. £799.00 in the United Kingdom (£680.00 plus shipping for export). AUS$2,890.00 in Australia. *AR7030+3:* $1,399.95 in the United States. CAN$2,515.00 in Canada. £949.00 in the United Kingdom (£765.10 plus shipping for export). AUS$3,250.00 in Australia.

Pro: In terms of sheer performance for program listening, as good a radio as we've ever tested. Except for sensitivity to weak signals (*see* Con), easily overcome, the same comment applies to DX reception. Exceptionally quiet circuitry. Superior audio quality when used with a first-rate outboard speaker or audio system. Synchronous selectable sideband performs exceptionally well at reducing distortion caused by selective fading, as well as at diminishing or eliminating adjacent-channel interference; also has synchronous double sideband. Best dynamic range of any consumer-grade radio tested. Nearly all other lab measurements are top-drawer. Four voice bandwidths (2.3, 7.0, 8.2 and 10.3 kHz), with cascaded ceramic filters, come standard; up to six, either ceramic or mechanical, upon request (*see* Con). Advanced tuning and operating features aplenty, including passband tuning. Tunable audio (AF) notch and noise blanker now available, albeit as an option; notch filter extremely effective, with little loss of audio fidelity. Built-in preamplifier (*see* Con). Automatically self-aligns and centers all bandwidth filters for optimum performance, then displays the actual measured bandwidth of each. Remote keypad (*see* Con). Accepts two antennas. IF output. Optional improved processor unit now has 400 memories, including 14-character alphanumeric readout for station names. World Time clock, which displays seconds, calendar and timer/snooze features. Superior mediumwave AM performance. Superior factory service.

DRAKE
13760.0

PASSPORT's top-rated tabletop, the Drake R8B, is also the best seller—and rightly so.

Con: Unusually convoluted ergonomics, including tree-logic operating scheme, especially in +3 version; once the initial

by up to 30 Hz, especially at higher tuned frequencies, and gets worse as the months pass by. Presets don't store synchronous-AM settings. Audio amplifier lacks oomph with some poorly modulated signals. No IF output, nor can one be retrofitted. NRD Win software, at least the current v1.00, handles only uploads, not downloads, and works only on com port 1 that is usually already in use. World Time clock doesn't show when frequency displayed. No tilt bail or feet. Anti-reflective paint on buttons and knobs becomes shiny with wear.

Verdict: In many ways Japan Radio's NRD-545 is a remarkable performer, especially for utility and tropical-bands DXing. With its first-class ergonomics and the fine feel of superior construction quality, it is always a pleasure to operate. Yet, more is needed to make this the ultimate receiver it could be. By now Japan Radio should have issued a ROM upgrade to remedy at least some of these long-standing issues, but *nada* as yet.

Whether "monkey chatter" and other manifestations of DSP overload are an issue varies markedly from one listening situation to another. It depends on the type of signals being received, what part of the world you are in, and your own aural perceptions. Among our panelists, all noticed it eventually, but reaction varied from "no big deal" to howls of derision.

New for 2002

✪✪✪✪⅜

Japan Radio "NRD-545SE"

Price: *NRD-545SE:* $1,899.00 in the United States. *Retrofit to change an existing receiver to "SE":* $104.00 plus receiver shipping both ways.

Pro: Dynamic range, 5 kHz, improves from 66 dB to 73 dB.

Con: Not available outside North America. *With 8 kHz replacement filter:* Audio bandwidth reduced by 20 percent at the high end. *With 6 kHz replacement filter (not tested):* Audio bandwidth reduced by about 40 percent at the high end.

☞ For all except those who confine their listening to tough DX or utility catches, the 8 kHz filter is a preferable choice over the 6 kHz option.

Verdict: Sherwood Engineering, an American firm, replaces the stock DSP protection filter with one of two narrower filters of comparable quality. In principle, this should provide beaucoup decibels of audible improvement in the "monkey chatter" encountered on the '545 from adjacent-channel signals. Alas, our listening panel couldn't hear the difference, but did notice an unwelcome reduction in audio crispness with world band signals—as well as, of course, with mediumwave AM reception.

The "SE" modification yields a slight improvement in close-in dynamic range, but bottom line is nice try, no cigar. Adventurous DXers may wish to consider the 6 kHz filter-replacement option in lieu of the 8 kHz option tested.

For utility DXing, as well as intense world band DXing, the reduction in high-end audio response is not a real issue. For these applications, the "SE" may represent a marginal improvement over the stock '545.

✪✪✪✪¼

Icom IC-R75/Icom IC-R75E

Price: *Receiver only:* $774.95 or less in the United States. CAN$1,399.00 in Canada. £575.00 in the United Kingdom. AUS$1,640 in Australia. *Receiver, including UT-106 DSP unit:* £699.99 in the United Kingdom. AUS$1,820.00 in Australia. *UT-106 DSP unit:* $139.95 in the United States. £85.00 in the United Kingdom. AUS171.00 in Australia. *Icom Replacement Bandwidth Filters:* $160-200 or equivalent worldwide. *Sherwood SE-3 Mark III (aftermarket):* $490.00 ($590.00 for deluxe version) including down converter and installation, plus shipping, in the United States. $460.00 ($560.00 for deluxe version) including down converter but not installation, plus shipping, outside the United States.

Pro: Dual passband tuning acts as variable bandwidth and a form of IF shift (*see* Con). Reception of faint signals alongside powerful competing ones aided by excellent ultimate selectivity and good dynamic range. Outstanding rejection of spurious signals. Excellent reception of utility and ham signals, as well as world band signals painstakingly tuned via "ECSS" technique, explained earlier in this article. Tunes and displays in precise 0.001 kHz increments. Two-level preamp allows excellent sensitivity to weak signals. DSP unit with automatic variable notch filter helps improve intelligibility of some tough signals and reduce heterodyne ("whistle") interference. Fairly good ergonomics. Adjustable AGC—fast, slow, off. Pretty good audio with suitable outboard speaker. Effective noise blanker. Two antenna inputs, switchable. Signal-strength indicator unusually linear above S-9, and can be set to hold a peak reading briefly. Audio-out port for recording or feeding low-power FM transmitter to hear world band around the house. Tunes to 60 MHz, including 6 meter VHF ham band.

Con: No synchronous selectable sideband without aftermarket SE-3 installed. Dual passband tuning usually has little impact on received world band signals and is inoperative when synchronous detection is in use. Double-sideband synchronous detector works so poorly as to be virtually useless. DSP's automatic variable notch tends not to work with AM-mode signals not received via "ECSS" technique (tuning AM-mode signals as though they were single sideband). Mediocre audio through internal speaker and no tone controls. Keypad requires frequencies to be entered in MHz format with decimal or trailing zeroes, a pointless inconvenience. Some knobs small. Weird

ICOM
IC-R75
COMMUNICATIONS RECEIVER
TWIN PBT
PHONES

Icom's IC-R75 is not tops for world band, but it excels at receiving utility and amateur signals.

knob adjusts RF gain to 12 o'clock position, then becomes a squelch control. Some distortion in AM mode, but only below 400 Hz AF. Uses outboard AC adaptor in lieu of internal power supply. Can read clock or frequency, but not both at the same time.

☞ The above star rating rises to ✪✪✪✪½ when the receiver is equipped with the Sherwood SE-3 aftermarket accessory. However, because the 'R75 uses two intermediate frequencies (IFs) for bandwidth filtering, the SE-3's offset has to be tweaked when going from a bandwidth having one IF to another with a different IF.

Verdict: The Icom IC-R75 is a first-rate receiver for unearthing tough utility and ham signals, as well as world band signals received via manual "ECSS" tuning. Even though it is not all it could have been for top-notch world band reception, it is now fully equipped and priced to move—for utility DXing it is a bargain. Watch for occasional factory-sponsored sale prices.

✪✪✪✪

Icom IC-R8500A

Price: *IC-R8500A-02 (no cellular reception):* $1,699.95 or less in the United States. *IC-R8500A:* $1,799.95 for government use or export in the United States. CAN$2,849.00 in Canada. £1,349.00 in the United Kingdom. AUS$3,200.00 in Australia. *External*

The Icom IC-R8500 covers much of the radio spectrum, all in one box.

speakers: Up to three Icom speakers available worldwide, with prices ranging from under $65 to over $300 or equivalent.

Pro: Wide-spectrum multimode coverage from 0.1-2000 MHz includes longwave, mediumwave AM, shortwave and scanner frequencies. Physically very rugged, with professional-grade cast-aluminum chassis and impressive computer-type innards. Generally superior ergonomics, with generous-sized front panel having large and well-spaced controls, plus outstanding tuning knob with numerous tuning steps. 1,000 presets and 100 auto-write presets have handy naming function. Superb weak-signal sensitivity. Pleasant, low-distortion audio aided by audio peak filter. Passband tuning ("IF shift"). Unusually readable LCD. Tunes and displays in precise 10 Hz increments. Three antenna connections. Clock-timer, combined with record output and recorder-activation jack, make for superior hands-off recording of favorite programs, as well as for feeding a low-power FM transmitter to hear world band around the house.

Con: No synchronous selectable sideband. Bandwidth choices for world band and other AM-mode signals leap from a very narrow 2.7 kHz to a broad 7.1 kHz with nothing between, where something is most needed; third bandwidth is 13.7 kHz, too wide for world band, and no provision is made for a fourth bandwidth filter. Only one single-sideband bandwidth. Unhandy carousel-style bandwidth selection with no permanent indication of which bandwidth is in use. Poor dynamic range, surprising at this price point. Passband tuning ("IF shift") does not work in the AM mode, used by world band and mediumwave AM-band stations. No tunable notch filter. Built-in speaker mediocre. Uses outboard AC adaptor instead of inboard power supply.

☞ The Icom IC-R8500 is available in two similarly priced versions. That sold to the public in the United States is blocked so it cannot receive the 824-849 and 869-894 MHz cellular bands. In the U.S., the unblocked version is sold only to government-approved organizations, although Canadian mail-order firms will ship this version to customers in the United States

☞ Also tested with Sherwood SE-3 non-factory accessory, which proved to be outstanding at adding selectable synchronous sideband. It also provides passband tuning in the AM mode used by nearly all world band stations. Adding the SE-3 and replacing the widest bandwidth with a 4 to 5 kHz bandwidth filter dramatically improve performance on shortwave, mediumwave AM and longwave.

Verdict: The large Icom IC-R8500 is really a scanner that happens to cover world band, rather than *vice versa*. As a standalone world band radio, it makes little sense, but it is well worth considering if you want an all-in-one scanner/shortwave receiver.

✪✪✪✪

AOR AR5000+3

Price: *AR5000+3 receiver:* $2,099.95 in the United States. CAN$3,860.00 in Canada. £1,799.00 in the United Kingdom. AUS$4,360.00 in Australia. *Collins 6 kHz mechanical filter (recommended):* $109.95 in the United States. £76.00 in the United Kingdom.

Pro: Ultra-wide-spectrum multimode coverage from 0.1-2,600 MHz includes longwave, mediumwave AM, shortwave and scanner frequencies. Helpful tuning features include 2,000 presets. Narrow bandwidth filter and optional Collins wide filter both have superb skirt selectivity (standard wide filter's skirt selectivity unmeasurable because of limited ultimate rejection). Synchronous selectable and double sideband (*see* Con). Front-end selectivity, image rejection, IF rejection, weak-signal sensitivity, AGC threshold and frequency stability all superior. Exceptionally precise frequency readout to nearest Hertz. Most accurate displayed frequency measurement of any receiver tested to date. Superb circuit shielding results in virtually zero radiated digital "hash." IF output (*see* Con). Automatic Frequency Control (AFC) works on AM-mode, as well as FM, signals. Owner's manual, important because of operating system, unusually helpful.

Con: Synchronous detector loses lock easily, especially if selectable sideband feature in use, greatly detracting from the utility of this high-tech feature. Substandard rejection of unwanted sideband with selectable synchronous sideband. Overall distortion rises when synchronous detector used. Ultimate rejection of "narrow" 2.7 kHz bandwidth filter only 60 dB. Ultimate rejection mediocre (50 dB) with standard 7.6 kHz "wide" bandwidth filter, improves to an uninspiring 60 dB when replaced by optional 6 kHz "wide" Collins mechanical filter. Installation of optional Collins filter requires expertise, patience and special equipment. Poor dynamic range. Cumbersome ergonomics. No passband offset. No tunable notch filter. Needs good external speaker for good audio quality. World Time clock does not show when frequency displayed. IF output frequency 10.7 MHz instead of standard 455 kHz.

Verdict: Unbeatable in some respects, inferior in others—it comes down to what use you will be putting the radio. The optional 6 kHz Collins filter is strongly recommended, but it should be installed by your dealer at the time of purchase.

AOR AR5000
COMMUNICATIONS RECEIVER

The AOR AR5000+3 is unusual for a wide-spectrum receiver, as it focuses on world band performance.

✪✪✪✪

Palstar R30, Palstar R30C, Lowe HF-350

Price: *R30:* $495.00 in the United States. *R30C:* $550.00 in the United States. *HF-350:* £375.00 in the United Kingdom.

☞ We tested the R30. The R30C is identical, except that a Collins mechanical filter is used for the narrow bandwidth—puzzling, in that the standard version already has superb skirt selectivity and ultimate rejection. The HF-350, like the R30, uses two MuRata ceramic filters, but the wide bandwidth is narrower—nominally 4 kHz, but in practice it could be closer to 5 kHz. Regardless, adjacent-channel interference would be reduced, but at the cost of audio bandwidth.

Pro: Superb skirt selectivity (1:1.4) and ultimate rejection (90 dB); bandwidths measure 7.7 kHz (*see* Con) and 2.7 kHz, using MuRata ceramic filters (*see* Con). Generally good dynamic range. Pleasant audio quality with 7.7 kHz bandwidth (*see* Con). Overall distortion averages 0.5 percent, superb, in single-sideband mode (in AM mode, averages 2.9 percent, good, at 60% modulation and 4.4 percent, fair, at 95% modulation). Without exception, every other performance variable measures either good or excellent in PASSPORT's lab. Features include selectable slow/fast AGC decay; 20-100 Hz/100-500 Hz VRIT (slow/fast variable-rate incremental tuning) knob; 1 MHz slewing; and 100 non-volatile station presets that store frequency, bandwidth, mode, AGC setting and attenuator setting. Analog signal-strength indicator reads in useful S1-9/+60 dB standard and is reasonably accurate (*see* Con). Also operates from ten firmly secured "AA" internal batteries (*see* Con). Lightweight and small (*see* Con). Appears to be robust. Good longwave mediumwave AM weak-signal sensitivity. Switchable illumination of LCD and signal-strength indicator. Self-resetting circuit breaker. Optional AA30A and AM-30 active antennas, evaluated elsewhere in this Passport Reports.

Con: No keypad for direct frequency entry, not even as an outboard mouse-type option; virtually all other receivers over $130 come with or offer a keypad. No synchronous selectable sideband. Wide bandwidth slightly broad for a model lacking synchronous selectable sideband, often allowing adjacent-channel (5 kHz) heterodyne whistles to be heard; the HF-350 version's narrower wide bandwidth should resolve this, albeit by reducing audio bandwidth. Lacks features found in top-gun receivers, such as tunable notch filter, noise blanker, passband tuning and adjustable RF gain. No visual indication of which bandwidth is being used. No tone controls. Our unit's frequency readout off by 100 Hz. Signal-strength indicator drops about two "S" units when going from wide to narrow bandwidths. Several significant birdies, including one on 20,002 kHz; numerous other and faint birdies don't impact reception. Minor digital "hash" radiates about six inches or 15 centimeters from the front panel. Tiny identical front-panel buttons, including the MEM button which if accidentally pressed can erase a preset. Presets not as intuitive or easy to select as with various other models; lacks frequency information on existing presets during memory storage. Uses AC adaptor instead of built-in power supply. High battery consumption. Batteries uniquely difficult to install, requiring partial disassembly of the receiver and care not to damage speaker connections or confuse polarities. Receiver's lightness allows it to slide around, especially when tuning knob is pushed in to change VRIT increments; the added weight of batteries helps slightly.

☞ Works best when grounded.

PALSTAR, INC.™
SIGNAL
R30 HF RECEIVER
AM
LSB
USB
TUNE
PUSH
20/500 HZ
MEM MODE ATT BW AGC
AF GAIN
OFF
MHz

The Palstar R30 lacks important features found even on $150 portables. Yet, what it does, it does to a high standard, and it has battery backup for emergencies.

Verdict: Although the Ohio-made Palstar R30 family of receivers is woefully lacking in tuning and performance features, what it sets out to do, it does to a high standard. If you can abide the convoluted battery installation procedure, it can also be used as a quasi-portable.

Nevertheless, this receiver lacks a distinct identity. Although the audio is pleasant, it doesn't have synchronous selectable sideband, needed to make it a premium listener's radio; it even omits tuning features found on portables costing a fourth as much. At the same time, its commendable electronic performance serves a limited purpose because the receiver lacks important features which help snare DX the way sophisticated tabletop models can.

But not everybody fits neatly into these either-or categories. One size doesn't fit all, and to that end the R30's straightforward concept and quality performance adds diversity and choice to the roster of available models.

11.845.00
YAESU

The "Frog" 100 is the last Yaesu that tunes only below 30 MHz. Discontinued, but still found at some dealers.

Discontinued

✪✪✪¾

Yaesu FRG-100

Price (as available): $599.95 in the United States. CAN$999.00 in Canada. £399.00 in the United Kingdom. AUS$999.00 in Australia.

Pro: Excellent performance in many respects. Includes three bandwidths, a noise blanker, selectable AGC, two attenuators, the ability to select 16 pre-programmed world band segments, two clocks, on-off timers, 52 tunable station presets that store frequency and mode data, a variety of scanning schemes and an all-mode squelch.

Con: No keypad for direct frequency entry. No synchronous selectable sideband. Lacks features found in "top-gun" receivers: passband tuning, notch filter, adjustable RF gain. Simple controls and display, combined with complex functions, can make certain operations confusing. Dynamic range only fair. Uses AC adaptor instead of built-in power supply.

Verdict: While sparse on features, in many respects the Yaesu FRG-100 succeeds in delivering worthy performance within its price class. According to the manufacturer, this model was discontinued in mid-1999. Yet, well over a year later it was still available, so it's anybody's guess when the last units will finally fly off dealer shelves.

An *RDI WHITE PAPER* is available for this model.

New for 2002

✪✪✪

Yaesu VR-5000

Price: *VR-5000 Receiver, including single-voltage AC adaptor:* $889.95 or less in the United States. CAN$1,499.00 in Canada. £699.00 in the United Kingdom. *DSP-1 digital notch, bandpass and noise reduction unit:* $119.95 in the United States. *DVS-4 16-second digital audio recorder:* $47.00 in the United States. CAN$80.00 in Canada. *FVS-1A voice synthesizer:* $43.00 in the United States. CAN$75.00 in Canada. £38.00 in the United Kingdom.

Pro: Unusually wide frequency coverage, 100 kHz through 2.6 GHz (U.S. version omits cellular frequencies 869-894 MHz). Two thousand alphanumeric-displayed presets, which can be linked to any of up to 100 groupings of presets. Up to 50 programmable start/stop search ranges. Large and potentially useful "band scope" spectrum display (*see* Con). Bandwidths have superb skirt selectivity, with shape factors between 1:1.3 and 1:1.4. Wide AM bandwidth (17.2 kHz) allows local mediumwave AM stations to be received with superior fidelity (*see* Con). Flexible software settings provide a high degree of control over selected

1280.00000
WORLD TIME
UTC+ 9:00
TOKYO
12:00
DSP

The Yaesu VR-5000 has wideband frequency coverage and a spectrum display, but disappointing world band performance.

parameters. Sophisticated scanning choices, although of limited use because of false signals generated by receiver's inadequate dynamic range (*see* Con). Dual-receive function, with sub-receiver circuitry feeding "band scope" spectrum display; when spectrum display not in use, two signals may be monitored simultaneously, provided they are within 20 MHz of each other. Sensitivity to weak signals excellent-to-superb within shortwave spectrum, although combined with receiver's inadequate dynamic range this tends to cause overloading when a worthy antenna is used (*see* Con). Appears to be robustly constructed. External spectrum display, fed by receiver's 10.7 MHz IF output, can perform very well for narrow-parameter scans (*see* Con). Two 24-hour clocks, both of which are shown except when spectrum display mode not in use; one clock tied into an elementary map display and database of time in a wide choice of world cities. On-off timer allows for up to 48 automatic events. Snooze/alarm timers. Lightweight and compact. Multi-level display dimmer (*see* Con). Optional DSP unit includes adjustable notch filtering, a bandpass feature and noise reduction. Tone control. Built-in "CAT" computer control interface.

Con: Exceptionally poor dynamic range (49 dB at 5 kHz separation, 64 dB at 20 kHz) and IF/image rejection (as low as 30 dB) for a tabletop model; for listeners in such high-signal parts of the world as Europe, North Africa and eastern North America, this shortcoming all but cripples reception of shortwave signals; the degree to which VHF-UHF is degraded depends *inter alia* upon the extent of powerful transmissions in the vicinity of the receiver. No synchronous selectable sideband, a major drawback for world band and mediumwave AM listening, but not for shortwave utility/ham, VHF or UHF reception. Has only one single-sideband bandwidth, a relatively broad 4.0 kHz. Wide AM bandwidth (17.2 kHz) of no use for shortwave reception. For world band listening, the middle (8.7 kHz) AM bandwidth lets through adjacent-channel 5 kHz heterodyne, while narrow bandwidth (consistently 3.9 kHz, not the 4.0 kHz of the SSB bandwidth) produces muffled audio. Line output level low. Audio distorts at higher volume settings. Limited bass response. Audio hissy without DSP option, especially noticeable with a good outboard speaker; according to unconfirmed reports, this is to be improved in future production. Phase noise measures 94 dBc, poor. AGC threshold measures 11 microvolts, poor. No adjustment of AGC decay. Single-sideband AGC decay too slow. Signal-strength indicator has only five levels and overreads; an alternative software-selectable signal-strength indicator—not easy to get in and out of—has no markings other than a single reference level. Built-in spectrum display's dynamic range only 20 dB (–80 to –100 dBm), with a very slow scan rate. Long learning curve: Thirty buttons (often densely spaced, lilliputian and multifunction)—along with carouseling mode/tune-step selection and a menu-driven command scheme—combine to produce ergonomics that are not intuitive. Marginally informative owner's manual; an improved manual continues to be promised by the manufacturer. Mediocre tuning-knob "feel." Only one low-impedance antenna connector, inadequate for a wideband device that calls for multiple antennas. Longwave sensitivity mediocre. Clocks don't display seconds numerically. Marginal display contrast. Display bright even when dimmed. Although four LEDs used for backlighting, the result is unevenly distributed. Uses AC adaptor instead of built-in power supply. AC adaptor and receiver both tend to run warm. Tilt feet have inadequate rise.

Verdict: A basic VHF/UHF scanner with basic shortwave, the new Japanese-made Yaesu VR-5000 wideband receiver falls shy for world band reception in strong-signal parts of the world. Elsewhere, it fares better on shortwave, but VHF/UHF performance depends on the number and strength of local transmitters.

Evaluation of New Model: Yaesu is now part of Vertex-Standard, so it should not be surprising that the VR-5000 bears some resemblance to the Standard AX-700/CCR-708 scanner from nearly a decade ago. However, since then security and public-safety organizations have "gone digital" with their communications, so there has been less for scanners to receive and a resulting downturn in scanner sales. At the same time, world band listeners have gravitated en masse to portables, leaving the hobby-oriented shortwave tabletop market in a state of decline.

So, the reasoning goes, why not design a single wideband tabletop receiver to appeal to both markets? This reduces costs at several levels, and given today's technology it would seem to be feasible.

Bottom line, thus far it hasn't worked except with such models as the Icom IC-R9000. The rub is that these have been so expensive to produce that they wind up costing consumers more than separate scanners and world band receivers of comparable quality. Much as a single "do it all" receiver may be an accountant's dream, it hasn't been able to pass muster in the real world.

Alas, the new Yaesu VR-5000, although sensibly priced, is no exception. In much of the world, wholesale overloading makes this receiver an inferior choice to most world band portables, and for VHF/UHF scanning the results are often little better. Even the built-in spectrum display, a potentially exciting feature, falls flat. To round out a roster of disappointing findings, hardware and software ergonomics are mediocre.

Our unit has firmware version 1u.13—later versions should incorporate software improvements. But for now if you must have a single receiver with wide frequency coverage, look to better alternatives from Icom and AOR.

VOLUME
COMMUNICATIONS RECEIVER
TUNING
14.210
CLARIFY

Brits looking for a bargain can turn to the AKD Target HF3 series. Like the Palstar/Lowe offerings, these are woefully lacking in features but do the basics well.

✪✪✪

AKD Target HF3, AKD Target HF3M, AKD Target HF3S, AKD Target HF3E, NASA HF-4/HF-4E

Price: *HF-4/HF-4E (not tested):* £149.00 in the United Kingdom. *HF3:* £159.95 in the United Kingdom. *HF3M:* £209.95 in the United Kingdom. *HF3S (not tested):* £159.95 in the United Kingdom. *HF3E (not tested):* £299.00 in the United Kingdom.

Pro: *HF-4/HF-4E, HF3 and HF3M:* Superior rejection of spurious "image" signals. Third-order intercept point indicates superior strong-signal handling capability. Bandwidths have superb ultimate rejection. *HF-4/HF-4E, HF3M:* Equipped for weatherfax ("WEFAX") reception. *HF-4/HF-4E:* Two AM-mode bandwidths. Illuminated LCD.

Con: No keypad, and variable-rate tuning knob is difficult to control. Broad skirt selectivity. Single-sideband bandwidth relatively wide. Volume control fussy to adjust. Synthesizer tunes in relatively coarse 1 kHz increments, supplemented by an analog fine-tuning "clarifier" control. Single sideband requires both tuning controls to be adjusted. No synchronous selectable sideband, notch filter or passband tuning. Frequency readout off by 2 kHz in single-sideband mode. Uses AC adaptor instead of built-in power supply. No clock, timer or snooze feature. Apparently not available outside United Kingdom. *HF3 and HF3M:* Bandwidths not selectable independent of mode. Only AM-mode bandwidth functions for world band reception. LCD not illuminated. *HF3:* Only one preset. No elevation feet or tilt bail. When switched on, goes not to the last-tuned frequency and mode, but rather to the frequency and mode in the lone preset. *HF3S and HF-4/HF-4E, HF3M:* Only ten presets.

☞ These U.K.-made receivers sometimes undergo minor enhancements and designations over time. According to Target, the HF3S is identical to the HF3 but with ten presets, whereas the HF3E is comparable to the HF3M, but with a "quasi-synchronous" detector and illuminated LCD.

Verdict: Surprisingly pleasant world band performance for the price, but seriously lacking in features and frustrating to operate.

Radio Shack
DX-394

Radio Shack's DX-394 is still available at some stores. Unlike Palstar, Lowe and AKD models, the '394 is relatively long on features but short on performance.

Discontinued

✪✪½

Radio Shack DX-394

Price (as available): CAN$299.99 in Canada. £149.95 in the United Kingdom.

Pro: Low price in those parts of the world where dealers still have units in stock. Advanced tuning features include 160 tunable presets (*see* Con). Tunes in precise 10 Hz increments. Modest size, light weight and built-in telescopic antenna provide some portable capability. Bandwidths have superior shape factors and ultimate rejection. Two 24-hour clocks, one of which shows independent of frequency display. Five programmable timers. 30/60 minute snooze feature. Noise blanker. In Canada, 30-day money-back period; conditions may apply.

Con: What appear to be four bandwidths turn out to be virtually one bandwidth, and it is too wide for optimum reception of many signals. Bandwidths, such as they are, not selectable independent of mode. No synchronous selectable sideband. Presets cumbersome to use. Poor dynamic range for a tabletop, a potential problem in Europe and other strong-signal parts of the world if an external antenna is used. Overall distortion, although acceptable, higher than desirable.

Verdict: Modest dimensions and equally modest performance, but cheap for a tabletop model.

The Passport *tabletop-model review team consists of Tony Jones, Lawrence Magne, Chuck Rippel, David Walcutt, David Zantow and George Zeller; also, George Heidelman, with Craig Tyson. Laboratory measurements by J. Robert Sherwood.*

ROLL YOUR OWN

During the golden era of kits—the fifties and early sixties—most came from the Heath Company of Benton Harbor, Michigan. These all but vanished after Heath dropped out, but American and British firms have revived radio kit building in recent years.

Weekend Exercise

Most shortwave kits are novelties, but there is one exception: Ten-Tec's 1254 world band radio. This tabletop receiver is actually smaller than some portables, and tunes 100 kilohertz through 30 Megahertz. Including shipping it sells for $204 to the continental United States, and US$210 to Hawaii, Alaska and Canada. In the United Kingdom, dealers offer it for £189.95. Parts quality appears to be excellent, and assembly runs at least 24 hours.

The straightforward 1254 has precious few features: no keypad, for example, and no signal-strength indicator. No synchronous selectable sideband or tilt bail, either, or LSB/USB settings for single-sideband—much less adjustable AGC or any of the other goodies found on tabletop supersets. It uses an AC adaptor and won't accept inboard batteries.

Digitally synthesized tuning is in increments as small as 500 Hz for single sideband and 5 kHz for AM-mode reception, such as world band. Bright red LEDs read out to the nearest 2.5 kHz in the single-sideband mode, the nearest 5 kHz in the AM mode. There is also a fast-tuning rate for the knob, much needed for going from one part of the radio spectrum to another. For tweaking between synthesizer tuning increments, there is an analog clarifier. Rounding out the minimalist roster of features are 15 presets.

Prosaic Performance

The internal speaker is mediocre and phase noise is poor. Front-end selectivity is little better, as is evidenced by false signals within the longwave spectrum. Sensitivity on longwave and mediumwave AM is poor, and the set's digital circuitry radiates hash. AGC decay is somewhat fast for world band.

The lone bandwidth is 5.6 kHz, a good choice for AM-mode reception, and has worthy ultimate rejection—70 dB. Also showing up well in PASSPORT's lab are image rejection, sensitivity to weak world band signals, blocking (related to sensitivity), AGC threshold and frequency stability. Dynamic range is fair, yet superior for its price class; first IF rejection is fair, too. Overall distortion averages out as good, and with an external speaker the audio is surprisingly pleasant.

Robust

Ten-Tec's Model 1254 kit is no DX wonder and is painfully slim on features. The assembled Sony ICF-SW7600G, for example, has numerous useful features, is a better overall performer and costs less. But the 1254 has something else: It's a fun weekend project, and the manufacturer's track record for hand-holding means that even if you put "X" where "Y" belongs, in the end the radio will really work.

The spirit of Heathkit lives on in the Ten-Tec 1254 kit. Assembly runs 24 hours or more.

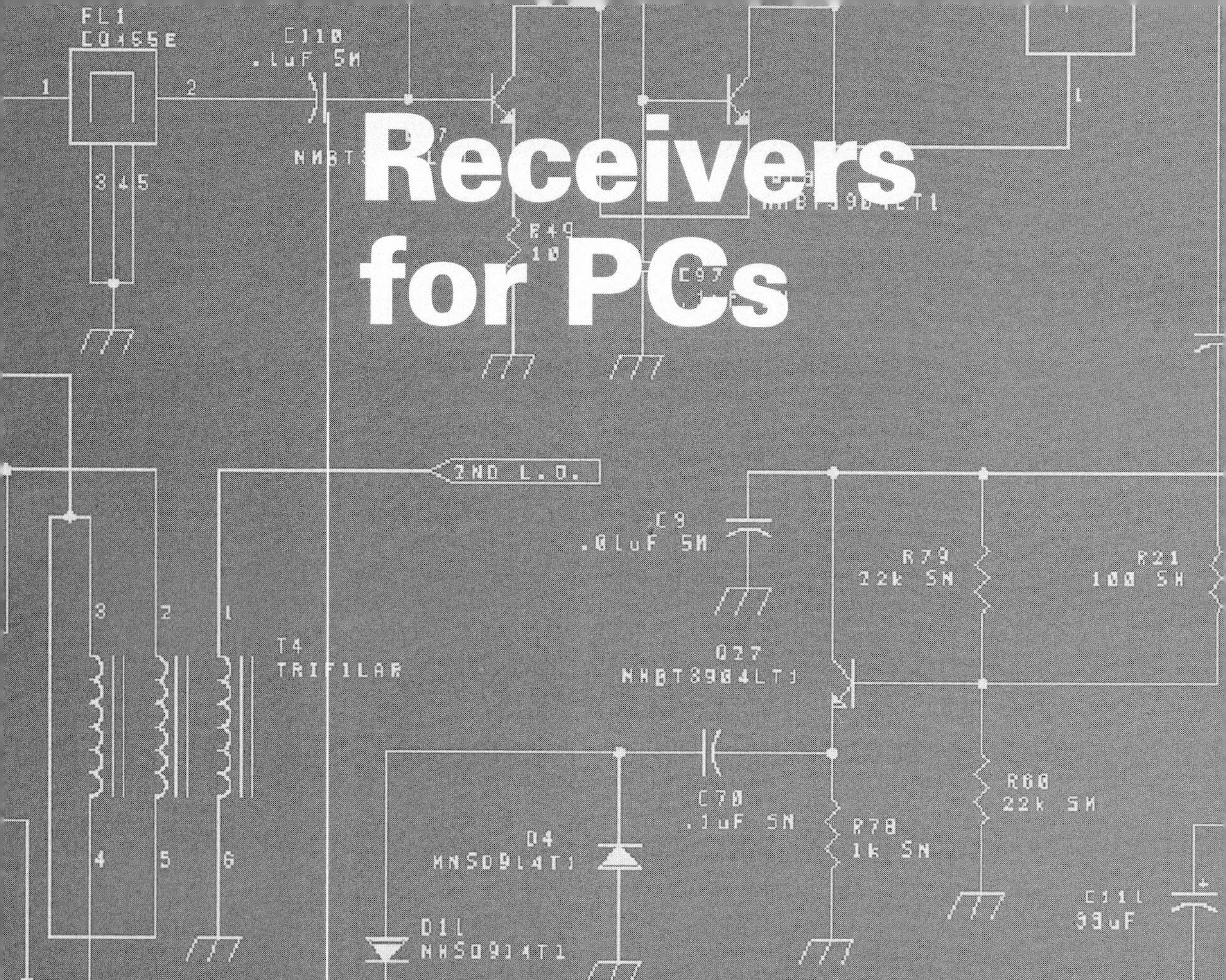
FL1
CQ455E
C110
.1uF 5M
2ND L.O.
C9
.01uF 5M
R79
22k 5M
R21
100 5M
T4
TRIFILAR
Q27
C70
.1uF 5M
R78
1k 5M
R80
22k 5M
D4
D11
C111
33uF

Receivers for PCs

Much of the enjoyment of world band comes from using a variety of knobs and buttons to unearth stations and enhance their reception quality. But one size doesn't fit all. A small but visible group prefers to have their receivers controlled by a PC.

These receivers have no controls, so only computers can operate them. Marrying shortwave receivers to PCs allows the performance of each to enhance the capabilities of the other. Yet, benefits are offset by drawbacks, such as convoluted hardware configurations and radio interference from PC hardware. Professional operations are set up to avoid these, but for a person at home it's a lot tougher.

Sales reflect this. Although proponents of PC-controlled receivers are enthusiastic and voluble, especially on the Internet, it turns out there's far more smoke than fire. Reliable industry sources report that actual sales levels have been consistently negligible following the initial months after product introduction.

PASSPORT's tests show that only one offering really cuts the mustard for world band: the $295 Ten-Tec RX-320, which earns four stars and is scheduled to remain in Ten-Tec's lineup indefinitely. Runner-up is the three-star Icom IC-PCR1000, which works equally well as a VHF+ scanner; its IC-PCR100 sibling is more rudimentary. The two-star WiNRADiO 1500e has been replaced by the 1550e that reportedly incorporates some degree of improvement; the 1500e has served much better as a scanner than as a world band receiver.

✪✪✪✪ Ⓟ *Passport's Choice*

Ten-Tec RX-320

Price: *RX-320:* $295.00 plus shipping worldwide. *Third-party control software:* Free-$99 worldwide.

Pro: Superior dynamic range. Apparently superb bandwidth shape factors (*see* Con). In addition to the supplied factory control software, third-party software is available, often for free, and may improve operation. Up to 34 bandwidths with third-party software. Tunes in extremely precise 1 Hz increments (10 Hz with tested factory software); displays to the nearest Hertz, and frequency readout is easily user-aligned. Large, easy-to-read digital frequency display and faux-analog frequency bar. For PCs with sound cards, outstanding freedom from distortion aids in providing good audio quality with most but not all cards and speakers. Fairly good audio, but with limited treble, also available through radio for PCs without sound cards. Superb blocking performance helps maintain consistently good world band sensitivity. Passband offset (*see* Con). Spectrum display with wide variety of useful sweep widths (*see* Con). World time on-screen clock (*see* Con). Adjustable AGC decay. Thousands of memories (presets), with first-rate memory configuration, access and sorting—including by station name and frequency. Only PC-controlled model tested which returns to last tuned frequency when PC turned off. Superior owner's manual. Outstanding factory help and repair support.

Con: No synchronous selectable sideband, although George Privalov's Control Panel Program now automates retuning of drifty AM-mode signals received as "ECSS." Some characteristic "DSP roughness" in the audio under certain reception conditions. Synthesizer phase noise measures only fair; among the consequences are that bandwidth shape factors cannot be measured exactly. Some tuning ergonomics only fair as compared with certain standalone receivers. No tunable notch filter. Passband offset doesn't function in AM mode. Signal-strength indicator, calibrated 0-80, too sensitive, reading 20 with no antenna connected and 30 with only band noise being received. Mediocre front-end selectivity can allow powerful mediumwave AM stations to

For world band, the best "black box" is the Ten-Tec RX-320. Missing: synchronous selectable sideband.

"ghost" into the shortwave spectrum, thus degrading reception of world band stations. Uses AC adaptor instead of built-in power supply. Spectrum display does not function with some third-party software and is only a so-so performer. Mediumwave AM reception below 1 MHz suffers from reduced sensitivity, and longwave sensitivity is atrocious. No internal speaker on receiver module. World Time clock tied into computer's clock, which may not be accurate without periodic adjustment. Almost no retail sources outside the United States.

☞ PASSPORT's four-star rating is for the RX-320 with third-party control software. With factory software the rating is slightly lower.

Verdict: No contest, the American-made Ten-Tec RX-320 is the star of the PC show when it is coupled to solid control software. Unless you live near a mediumwave AM station, this receiver runs circles around most receivers of any sort near its price class.

✪✪✪

Icom IC-PCR1000

Price: *IC-PCR1000:* $399.95 in the United States. CAN$799.00 in Canada. £319.95 in the United Kingdom. AUS$899.00 in Australia. *UT-106 DSP Unit:* $139.95 in the United States. £82.00 in the United Kingdom. US$171 in Australia.

Pro: Wideband frequency coverage. Spectrum display with many useful sweep widths for shortwave, as well as good real-time performance. Tunes and displays in extremely precise 1 Hz increments. Comes with reasonably performing control software (*see* Con). Excellent sensitivity to weak signals. AGC, adjustable, performs well in AM and single-sideband modes. Nineteen banks of 50 memories each, with potential for virtually unlimited number of memories. Passband offset (*see* Con). Powerful audio with good weak-signal readability and little distortion (*see* Con).

Con: Poor dynamic range. Audio quality, not pleasant, made worse by presence of circuit hiss. No line output to feed PC sound card and speakers, so no alternative to using receiver's audio. No synchronous selectable sideband. Only two AM-mode bandwidths—8.7 kHz (nominal 6 kHz) and 2.4 kHz (nominal 3 kHz)—both with uninspiring shape factors. Synthesizer phase noise, although not measurable, appears to be only fair; among the effects of this are that bandwidth shape factors cannot be exactly measured. Mediocre blocking slightly limits weak-signal sensitivity when frequency segment contains powerful signals. Tuning ergonomics only fair as compared with some standalone receivers. Automatic tunable notch filter with DSP audio processing (UT-106, not tested) an extra-cost option. Lacks passband offset in AM mode. Uses AC adaptor instead of built-in power supply. Spectrum display mutes audio when single-sideband or CW signal being received. No clock. Mediocre inboard speaker, remediable by using outboard speaker. Sparse owner's manual.

☞ A similar but more rudimentary model, the IC-PCR100, is available worldwide at roughly two-thirds the price of the IC-PCR1000. It has only one (broad) bandwidth.

ICOM

If you need a broadband PC receiver, the Icom IC-PCR is the way to go. Overall, a passable performer.

Verdict: Among tested PC-controlled receivers, the Japanese-made Icom IC-PCR1000 is the most appropriate for wideband frequency coverage and first-rate shortwave spectrum display.

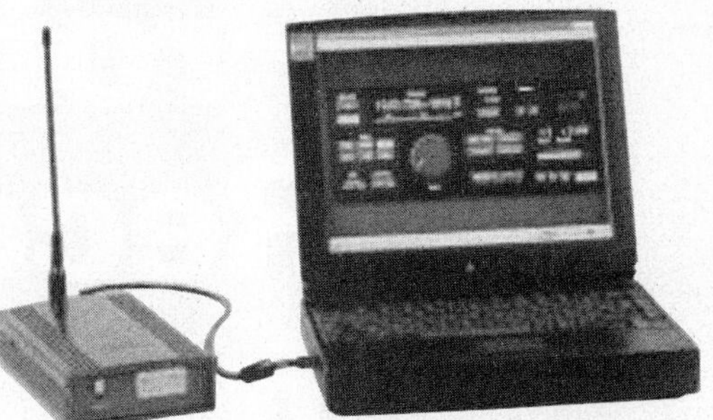

Tested WiNRADiO models have been cleverly marketed, but bring up the rear in performance. Manufacturer claims ongoing improvements.

✪✪

WiNRADiO 1500e

Price: $549.95 in the United States. CAN$899.00 in Canada. £369.00 in the United Kingdom. AUS$951.23 in Australia.

Pro: Wideband frequency coverage. AM-mode bandwidth has superb shape factor and good ultimate rejection. Spectrum display with good real-time performance (*see* Con). Tunes in precise 10 Hz increments; display has 1 Hz resolution, but of course can show only tuned 10 Hz increments. Comes with reasonably performing control software (*see* Con). Excellent sensitivity to weak signals, generally best among PC-controlled receivers tested (*see* Con). Passband offset (*see* Con). World time on-screen clock (*see* Con). High quality of assembly and construction.

Con: Dreadful dynamic range, a crucial shortcoming for world band (*see* ☞, below). Only one AM-mode bandwidth (6.5 kHz). Audio lacks power quality. No decent line output to feed PC sound card and speakers, so receiver's audio has to be used. Microphonics from internal speaker, making outboard speaker *de rigeur*. No synchronous selectable sideband. AGC not adjustable. No tunable notch filter. Poor blocking limits weak-signal sensitivity when band contains powerful signals. Long learning curve due to complexity. Tuning ergonomics only fair as compared with some standalone receivers. Lacks passband offset in AM mode. Uses AC adaptor instead of built-in power supply. Spectrum display of limited utility because of numerous spurious signals (*see* ☞, below). World Time clock tied into computer's clock, which may not be accurate. Comes with 9/25-pin cable and 25/9 adaptor, which doesn't fit onto some laptops, rather than usual 9/9 cable. Sparse owner's manual.

Verdict: As tested, this model is ill suited to world band applications.

☞ The 1500e has been replaced by the similar WR-1550e, which the manufacturer claims has improved dynamic range and spurious-signal rejection. Their official emailed product-release announcement also claims better sensitivity, although the WiNRADiO Website says improved selectivity with no mention of sensitivity.

☞ The pricey WiNRADiO 3100e we tested is very similar to the 1500e, above, but with improved dynamic range and reduced sensitivity to weak shortwave signals. $1,849.95 in the United States, CAN$3,199.00 in Canada, £1,169.00 in the United Kingdom and AUS$2,629.44 in Australia. It has been replaced by the WR-3150e with what the manufacturer calls "similar improvements."

Chuck Rippel, Robert Sherwood and David Zantow, with Lawrence Magne; also, Craig Tyson.

Professional Receivers for 2002

POWER
REMOTE
DWELL
STEP SIZE
CHANNEL VIEW
CHANNEL EXECUTE
SIGNAL LEVEL
WATKINS-JOHNSON
WJ-8711 HF RECEIVER
SCAN SETUP
CHANNEL STORE
CHANNEL INCLUDE
SCAN
SCAN TYPE
CHANNEL
FREQUENCY LOCKOUT
CLEAR
CHANNEL SKIP
PAUSE
F1 → F2
F1 → F2 w/LOCK
PHONES
SPEAKER
RF INPUT
USB
BOTH
LSB
PREAMP
NORM
ATTN

F. Scott Fitzgerald famously wrote about the rich, "They are different from you and me." And so it is that professional-grade receivers are manufactured not for most folks, but for an elite audience—and priced to match.

Like Hummers, the root market for professional receivers is not the public, even the rich public. No, they are primarily for prosperous commercial, maritime, surveillance and military outfits. Their requirements have much in common with the needs of world band listening, but like the wealthy they are . . . different.

Some of these variants make for better results, others worse. But when it all comes together like planets in alignment, this is the hardware that will scale the toughest, most extreme heights of DX reception.

Receivers in Three Flavors

There are numerous categories of professional receivers—indeed, some are made with only one narrow application in mind. But, *au fond*, these boil down to three groups: straightforward for human operation, complex for human operation and no human operation.

The first are designed so laymen can tune "utility" signals with minimal training. After all, if a B-52 takes shrapnel and the radioman is out, the more straightforward a radio is to operate, the more likely it is that other crew members will be able to carry on. Trouble is, simplicity of operation can also result in performance compromises, making these potentially inferior choices for world band cognoscenti.

Find major updates to the 2002 PASSPORT REPORTS at www.passband.com.

The second category goes to the other extreme, with features and performance that are "no holds barred." These assume a high degree of operator skill, and are the type of professional receiver we analyze in PASSPORT REPORTS. They are well worth considering if you aren't put off by their complexity of operation and sticker shock.

Simplest are "black box" professional receivers, which have virtually no controls. These are operated only by computers, often at hush-hush surveillance centers. We don't cover this here, as some of the best models are available only to U.S. Federal agencies or NATO organizations. However, consumer-grade versions are evaluated elsewhere within PASSPORT REPORTS.

Major Shared Characteristics

All professional receivers should be physically and electrically robust, with resistance to hostile environments and rough handling, as well as a high mean time between failures (MTBF). Additionally, their components need to be unusually consistent so board swapping and other field repair can be accomplished without disturbing alignment and the like.

The two best models PASSPORT REPORTS has tested were developed to replace the nonprofessional Icom IC-R71A. This was being used by the U.S. National Security Agency in offshore surveillance, but it had limitations. The reclusive folks at Fort Meade choose carefully, so their implied endorsement amounts to something of a "Good Housekeeping Seal of Approval."

Good Antenna Essential

Top-rated, properly erected antennas are an absolute "must" if these receivers are to reach their full potential. For test results and installation information, see the Radio Database International White Paper, *Popular Outdoor Antennas*, as well as reviews of antennas found elsewhere in PASSPORT REPORTS.

If reception at your location is already disrupted by electrical noises even when a suitable antenna is in use, a better receiver would be a waste of money. Before buying, try eliminating the source of noise or reorienting your antenna.

Volts with Jolts

Professional receivers tend to be unusually rugged, and in fact tend to include MOV surge protection before the power supply. Nevertheless, it helps to plug your pricey receiver into a non-MOV surge arrestor, such as Zero-Surge (www.zerosurge.com) or Brick Wall (www.brickwall.com).

Any receiver's outdoor antenna always should be fed through a suitable static arrestor, but this is especially important with the Watkins-Johnson WJ-8711A if it isn't equipped with the 8711/PRE option.

Audio with DSP Receivers

In principle, there is no reason DSP (digital signal processing) receivers can't produce audio quality equal to, and in some ways better than, conventional models. Witness the audio quality of digital CDs, for example.

But a multi-stage receiver is much more complex than a CD, so it requires a great deal of processing horsepower. Today's DSP receivers still fall short in this regard, one result being that audio quality is not all it could be. In particular, static crashes tend to sound much harsher.

Helping offset this is that hard-core DXers find recoverable audio to be slightly greater with DSP receivers. Of course, this same benefit would continue to accrue should overall audio quality be improved through greater microprocessor power.

The consensus of our panelists who own the two top-rated professional DSP receivers is that the Sherwood SE-3 fidelity-enhancing accessory is virtually *de rigueur*. Indeed, unlike with top-rated tabletop receivers, which don't need the SE-3, it is nearly a "must" for all professional receivers—DSP or not—being used to tune world band stations. While it doesn't fundamentally resolve the DSP audio issue, it tames it considerably while also providing high-quality synchronous selectable sideband. These are enormous pluses, but there are downsides, too: extra cost, operating complexity and a BFO that is not fully as stable as those on the top two professional receivers.

Ready for Digital Broadcasts?

Today's DSP receivers process analog radio signals digitally. However, analog broadcasts will eventually be superceded by digital, although it should be years before digital supplants analog for world band transmissions.

With conventional portable, portatop and tabletop receivers this hardly matters, as these are not intended to be friends for life. However, professional models are designed to keep humming for decades, not just years. What happens if digital transmissions begin to appear while your second-mortgage receiver is still in its prime?

Manufacturers are not yet position to promise future upgrades to receive digital. Nevertheless, among professional models tested by PASSPORT, those that look most encouraging for eventual digital reception are the Watkins-Johnson WJ-8711A and Ten-Tec RX-340. Indeed, a digital signal output board is already being offered for the '8711A.

Tips for Using this Section

Professional receivers are listed in order of suitability for listening to difficult-to-hear world band stations. Important secondary consideration is given to audio fidelity, ergonomics and reception of utility signals. We cite actual selling prices as of when we go to press, including European and Australian VAT/GST where applicable.

Unless otherwise stated, all professional models have:

- Digital frequency synthesis and display.
- Full coverage of at least the 155-29999 kHz longwave, mediumwave AM and shortwave spectra—including all world band frequencies—but no coverage of the FM broadcast band (87.5-108 MHz).
- A wide variety of helpful tuning features.
- Synchronous selectable sideband via high-rejection IF filtering (not lower-rejection phasing), which greatly reduces adjacent-channel interference and fading distortion. On some units this is referred to as "SAM" (synchronous AM).
  ☞ **ECSS:** Professional models can tune to the nearest 10 Hz or even 1 Hz, allowing the user to use the receiver's single-sideband circuitry to manually phase its BFO (internally generated carrier) with the station's transmitted carrier. Called "ECSS" (exalted-carrier, selectable-sideband) tuning, this can be used with AM-mode signals in lieu of synchronous selectable sideband. However, in addition to the relative inconvenience of this technique, unlike synchronous detection, which re-phases continually and essentially perfectly, ECSS is always slightly out of phase. This causes at least some degree of harmonic distortion to music and speech, while tuning to the nearest Hertz can generate slow-sweep fading (for this reason, high-pass audio filtering or mis-phasing by two or three Hertz may provide better results).
- Proper demodulation of modes used by non-world-band shortwave signals. These modes include single sideband (LSB/USB and sometimes ISB) and CW ("Morse code"); also, with suitable ancillary devices, radioteletype (RTTY), frequency shift key (FSK) and radiofax (FAX).
- Meaningful signal-strength indication.
- Illuminated display.
- Superior build quality, robustness and sample-to-sample consistency as compared to consumer-grade tabletop receivers.
- Audio output for recording or low-power FM transmission to hear world band around your domicile.

What Passport's Rating Symbols Mean

Star ratings: ✪✪✪✪✪ is best. Stars reflect overall performance and meaningful features, plus to some extent ergonomics and build quality. Price, appearance, country of manufacture and the like are not taken into account. With professional models there is a strong emphasis on the ability to flush out tough, hard-to-hear signals, as this is usually the main reason these sets are chosen by world band enthusiasts. Nevertheless, to facilitate comparison professional receiver rating standards are very similar to those used for the tabletop, portatop and portable models reviewed elsewhere in this Passport.

Passport's Choice. La crème de la crème. Our test team's personal picks of the litter—models we would buy or have bought for our personal use.

Retested for 2002

✪✪✪✪✪ *Passport's Choice*

Watkins-Johnson WJ-8711A

Price (receiver, factory options): *WJ-8711A:* $5,295.00 plus shipping worldwide. *871Y/SEU DSP Speech Enhancement Unit:* $1,130.00. *8711/PRE Sub-Octave Preselector:* $1,030.00. *871Y/DSO1 Digital Signal Output Unit:* $1,070.00.

Price (aftermarket options): *Ten-Tec #19-0525 cabinet:* $217.24 in the United States.

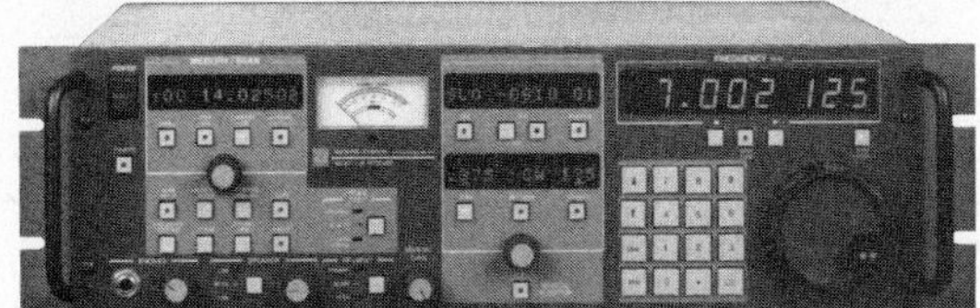

Running neck-and-neck for top DX receiver is the Watkins-Johnson WJ-8711A. For best world band performance, it needs to be equipped with specific accessories.

Sherwood SE-3 MK III accessory: $549.00 plus shipping worldwide.

Pro: Proven robust. BITE diagnostics and physical layout allows technically qualified users to make most repairs on-site. Users can upgrade receiver performance over time by EPROM replacement. Exceptional overall performance. Unsurpassed reception of feeble world band DX signals, especially when mated to the Sherwood SE-3 synchronous selectable sideband device and the WJ-871Y/SEU noise-reduction unit (*see* Con). Unusually effective "ECSS" reception, tuning AM-mode signals as though they were single sideband. Superb reception of non-AM mode "utility" stations. Generally superior audio quality when coupled to the Sherwood SE-3 fidelity-enhancing accessory, the W-J speech enhancement unit and a worthy external speaker (*see* Con). Unparalleled bandwidth flexibility, with no less than 66 outstandingly high-quality bandwidths. Tunes and displays in ultra-precise 1 Hz increments; trimmer inside radio allows frequency readout to be user-aligned against a known frequency standard, such as WWV/WWVH or a laboratory device. Extraordinary operational flexibility—virtually every receiver parameter is adjustable. One hundred station presets. Synchronous detection, called "SAM" (synchronous AM), reduces selective-fading distortion with world band, mediumwave AM and longwave signals, and works even on very narrow voice bandwidths (*see* Con). Rock stable. Built-in preamplifier. Tunable notch filter. Effective noise blanking. Highly adjustable scanning of both frequency ranges and channel presets. Easy-to-read displays. Large tuning knob. Can be fully and effectively computer and remotely controlled. Passband shift (*see* Con). Numerous outputs for data collection and ancillary hardware, including 455 kHz IF-out which makes for instant installation of Sherwood SE-3 accessory and balanced line outputs (connect to balanced hookup to minimize "hash" radiation). Remote control and dial-up data collection; Windows control software available from manufacturer. Among the most likely of all world band receivers tested to be able to be retrofitted for eventual reception of digital world band broadcasts. Inboard AC power supply, which runs unusually cool, senses incoming current and automatically adjusts to anything from 90-264 VAC, 47-440 Hz—a plus during brownouts or with line voltage or frequency swings. Superior-quality factory service (*see* Con). Comprehensive and well-written operating manual, packed with technical information and schematic diagrams.

Con: Static crashes and modulation-splash interference sound noticeably harsher than on analog receivers, although this has been improved in latest operating software. Synchronous detection not sideband-selectable, so it can't reduce adjacent-channel interference (remediable by Sherwood SE-3). Basic receiver has mediocre audio in AM mode; "ECSS" tuning or synchronous detection, along with the speech enhancement unit (W1 noise-reduction setting), required to alleviate this. Some clipping distortion in the single-sideband mode. Complex to operate to full advantage. Circuitry puts out a high degree of digital noise ("hash"), relying for the most part on the panels for electrical shielding; one consequence is that various versions emanate hash through the nonstandard rear-panel audio terminals, as well as through the signal-strength meter and front-panel headphone jack—this problem is lessened when the Sherwood SE-3 is used. Antennas with shielded (e.g., coaxial) feedlines are less likely to pick up receiver-generated hash. Passband shift operates only in CW mode. Jekyll-and-Hyde ergonomics: sometimes wonderful, sometimes awful. Front-panel rack "ears" protrude, with the right "ear" getting in the way of the tuning knob; fortunately, these are easily removed. Mediocre front-end selectivity, remediable by 8711/PRE option (with minor 2.5 dB insertion loss); e.g. for those living near mediumwave AM transmitters. 871Y/SEU option reduces audio gain and is extremely difficult to install; best to have all options factory-installed. Most recent sample's tuning knob has rotational play that causes a very slight pause when reversing direction. Signal-strength indicator's gradations in dBm only. No DC power input. Factory service can take as much as two months. Cabinet extra, available from Ten-Tec. Plastic feet have no front elevation and allow receiver to slide around. Available only through U.S. manufacturer (+1-301/948-7550); receiver and factory options have been subjected to a number of price increases since British Aerospace takeover.

☞ In 1999 Watkins-Johnson was taken over by Marconi, the British electronics goliath, which only months later was swallowed up by British Aerospace. As a result, Watkins-Johnson is now "BAE Systems."

Verdict: The American-made WJ-8711A is, by a hair, the ultimate machine for down-and-dirty world band DXing when money is no object; after all, fully tricked out this receiver costs as much as some cars. Had there not been digital hash, inexcusable at this price—and had there been better audio quality, a tone control, passband shift and synchronous selectable sideband—the '8711A would have been even better, especially for program listening. Fortunately, the Sherwood SE-3 accessory remedies virtually all these problems and improves DX reception, to boot; W-J's 871Y/SEU complements, rather than competes with, the SE-3 for improving recovered audio.

Overall, the WJ-8711A DSP receiver is exceptionally well-suited to demanding aficionados with suitable financial wherewithal—provided they want an exceptional degree of manual receiver control.

Evaluation of Latest Unit: The latest iteration of this majestic performer is all but identical to the unit dissected in last year's Passport—the only difference we could find was that the new tuning knob has the very slightest of pauses when changing directions. The WJ-8711A, when mated to the 871Y speech enhancement unit and Sherwood SE-3, continues to be most of our panelists' top choice in a world band DX superset. No slouch for program listening, either.

Revised for 2002

✪✪✪✪✪ *Passport's Choice*

Ten-Tec RX-340

Price: $3,950.00 in the United States. Actively seeking dealers for other parts of the world. *Ten-Tec #19-0525 cabinet:* $217.24 in the United States. *Sherwood SE-3 MK III accessory:* $549.00 plus shipping worldwide.

Pro: Appears to be robust (*see* Con). BITE diagnostics and physical layout allows

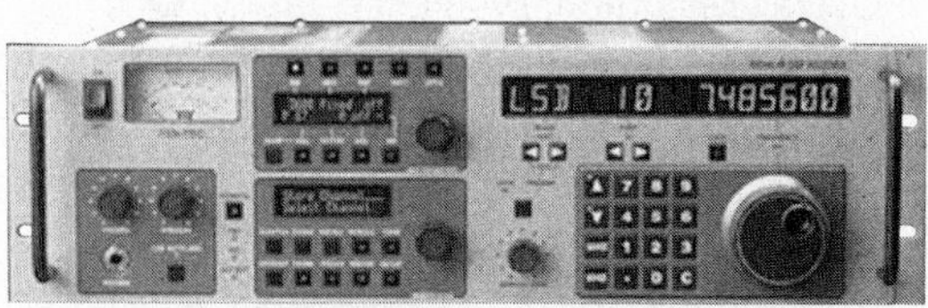
LSB 10 7485600

Ten-Tec's RX-340 is superb. Costs less than Watkins-Johnson's offering, too.

technically qualified users to make most repairs on-site. Users can upgrade receiver performance over time by replacing one or another of three socketed EPROM chips. Superb overall performance, including for reception of feeble world band DX signals, especially when mated to the Sherwood SE-3 device; in particular, superlative image and IF rejection, both >100 dB. Few birdies. Audio quality usually worthy when receiver coupled to the Sherwood SE-3 accessory and a good external speaker (*see* ☞). Average overall distortion in single-sideband mode a breathtakingly low 0.2 percent; in other modes, under 2.7 percent. Exceptional bandwidth flexibility, with no less than 57 outstandingly high-quality bandwidths having shape factors of 1:1.33 or better; bandwidth distribution exceptionally good for world band listening and DXing, along with other activities (*see* Con). Tunes and displays accurately in ultra-precise 1 Hz increments. Extraordinary operational flexibility—virtually every receiver parameter is adjustable; for example, the AGC's various time constants have 118 million possible combinations, plus pushbutton AGC "DUMP" to temporarily deactivate AGC (*see* Con). Worthy front-panel ergonomics, valuable given the exceptional degree of manual operation; includes easy-to-read displays (*see* Con). Also, large, properly weighted rubber-track tuning knob with fixed dimple and Oak Grigsby optical encoder provide superior tuning "feel" and reliability. Attractive front

NUMBERS: TOP TWO PROFESSIONAL RECEIVERS

	Watkins-Johnson WJ-8711A	**Ten-Tec RX-340**
Max. Sensitivity/Noise Floor	0.13 µV, (S)/–136 dBm, (E)	0.17 µV, (S)/–132 dBm, (E)[1]
Blocking	123 dB, (G)	109 dB, (F)
Shape Factors, voice BWs	1:1.21-1:1.26, (S)	1:1.15-1:1.33, (S)
Ultimate Rejection	>80 dB, (E)	70 dB, (G)
Front-End Selectivity	Wideband, (F)/Half octave, (E)[2]	Half octave, (E)
Image Rejection	80 dB, (E)	>100 dB, (S)
First IF Rejection	—[3]	>100 dB, (S)
Dynamic Range/IP3 (5 kHz)	74 dB, (G)/–18 dBm, (E)	46 dB, (P)/–53 dBm, (P)
Dynamic Range/IP3 (20 kHz)	99 dB, (S)/+20 dBm, (S)	84 dB, (G)/+4 dBm, (E)
Phase Noise	115 dBc, (G)	113 dBc, (G)
AGC Threshold	0.1 µV, (P)	0.3 µV, (G)[4]
Overall Distortion, sync	8.2%, (P)	2.6%, (G)
Notch filter depth	58 dB, (S)	58 dB, (S)

IBS Lab Ratings: (S) Superb (E) Excellent (G) Good (F) Fair (P) Poor

(1) Preamp on. With preamp off, 0.55 µV, (G)/–122 dBm, (G).

(2) (F) standard/(E) with optional preselector.

(3) Adequate, but could not measure precisely.

(4) Preamp on. With preamp off, 1.3 µV, (E).

panel. Two hundred station presets, 201 including the scratchpad. Synchronous selectable sideband, called "SAM" (synchronous AM), reduces selective-fading distortion, as well as at diminishing or eliminating adjacent-channel interference, with world band, mediumwave AM and longwave signals (*see* Con). Built-in half-octave preselector comes standard. Built-in preamplifier (*see* Con). Adjustable noise blanker, works well in most situations (*see* Con). Stable as Gibraltar, as good as it gets. Tunable DSP notch filter with exceptional depth of 58 dB (*see* Con). Passband shift (passband tuning) works unusually well (*see* Con). Unusually effective "ECSS" reception by tuning AM-mode signals as though they were single sideband. Superb reception of "utility" (non-AM mode) stations using a wide variety of modes and including fast filters for delay-critical digital modes. Highly adjustable scanning of both frequency ranges and channel presets. Can be fully and effectively computer and remotely controlled. Numerous outputs for data collection and ancillary hardware, including 455 kHz IF-out for instant hookup of Sherwood SE-3 accessory. Remote control and dial-up data collection. Superb analog signal-strength indicator (*see* Con). Among the most likely of all world band receivers tested to be able to be retrofitted for eventual reception of digital world band broadcasts. Inboard AC power supply senses incoming current and automatically adjusts to anything from 90-264 VAC, 48-440 Hz—a plus during brownouts or with line voltage or frequency swings. Superior control of fluorescent display dimming (*see* Con). Superior-quality factory service, reasonably priced by professional standards, with helpful online/phone tech support. Comprehensive and well-written operating manual, packed with technical information and schematic diagrams.

Con: Synchronous selectable sideband loses lock relatively easily; e.g., if listening to one sideband and there is a strong signal impacting the other sideband, lock can be momentarily lost; resolved by Sherwood SE-3 fidelity device. DSP microprocessor limitations result in poor dynamic range/IP3 at 5 kHz signal spacing. Blocking, phase noise and ultimate rejection all pretty good, but not of professional caliber. Complex to operate to full advantage. Audio profits from Sherwood SE-3 accessory and good outboard speaker. Static crashes sound harsher than on analog receivers. Not all bandwidths available in all modes. Spurious signals noted around 6 MHz segment (49 meters) at night at one test location having superb antennas. When 9-10 dB preamplifier turned on, AGC acts on noise unless IF gain reduced by 10 dB. Notch filter does not work in AM, synchronous selectable sideband or ISB modes. Passband shift tunes only plus or minus 2 kHz and does not work in the ISB or synchronous selectable sideband modes; remediable with Sherwood SE-3. Occasional "popping" sound, notably when synchronous selectable sideband or ISB in use—DSP overload? No AGC off except by holding down DUMP button. Noise blanker not effective at all test locations; for example, other receivers work better in reducing noise from electric fences. Audio power, especially through headphones, could be greater. On our unit, right-channel headphone audio cuts out at full volume. On our unit, occasional minor buzz from internal speaker. Keypad not in telephone format. Some ergonomic clumsiness when going back and forth between the presets and VFO tuning; too, "Aux Parameter" and "Memory Scan" knobs touchy to adjust. Signal-strength indicator illuminated less than display. Digital hash from fluorescent display emits from front of receiver, although not elsewhere. On our latest unit, stick-on decal with front-panel markings has peeled loose above the main display, and pushing it back into place hasn't helped; this has not been a problem on other units. No DC power input. Cabinet extra. Cabinet excessively deep, requiring operator to reach in far to get to rear panel.

Verdict: With an extreme degree of manual control, the Ten-Tec RX-340, when coupled to fidelity-enhancing hardware, is a superb DSP receiver for those who want no-compromise performance for years to come. It's a sensible value, too—with bells and whistles, it costs considerably less than a fully equipped WJ-8711A.

Evaluation of Revised Model: Version 1.10A of Ten-Tec's outstanding RX-340 receiver is free of most of the former software oddities and bugs. Additionally, presets have been doubled, an adjustable noise blanker incorporated, and a 9 kHz tuning step added for mediumwave AM outside the Americas.

These improvements are welcome, but a number of issues persist: Synchronous selectable sideband doesn't hold lock as well as it should, and various features are limited by mode choice.

Nevertheless, there is nothing else on the Scotch side of a kilofin that quite equals the performance or build quality of the Ten-Tec RX-340. It is a great receiver, indeed, and keeps getting fine-tuned over time.

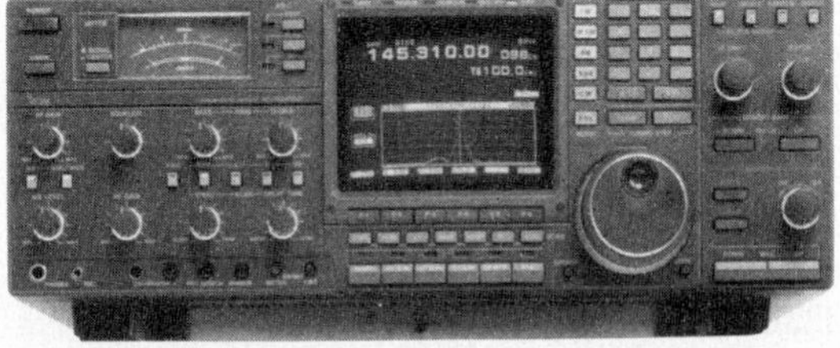

With the right options, the Icom IC-R9000L is a superb receiver with better audio than most other professional models. The rub: It's illegal for the public to purchase within the United States. In the aftermath of the World Trade Center attack, it has become more difficult for Americans to import via Canadian dealers, as well.

✪✪✪✪✪ *Passport's Choice*

Icom IC-R9000L

Price (receiver): $8,499.95 by special order to Federal government purchasers, or for export, in the United States. CAN$15,999.00 in Canada or for export. AUS$21,824.00 by special order in Australia.

Price (aftermarket options): *Three new filter bandwidths, installed by Sherwood:* $499.00. *Synchronous selectable sideband (Sherwood SE-3 with 9 MHz-to-455 kHz IF down converter):* $720.00, installed.

Pro: Exceptional tough-signal performance, especially with faint DX signals that may be unreadable on other top-rated receivers. Flexible, above-average audio for a tabletop model when used with suitable outboard speaker; outstanding audio quality when used with Sherwood SE-3. Tunes and displays frequency in precise 10 Hz increments. Video display of radio spectrum occupancy, a rarely found feature. Sophisticated scanner/timer. Extraordinarily broad and high-quality coverage of radio spectrum, including portions forbidden to be listened to by the general public in the United States. Exceptional assortment of flexible operating controls and sockets. Good ergonomics. Superb reception of utility and ham signals. Superb reception of longwave DX, mediumwave DX, VHF/UHF scanner frequencies and FM broadcasts (monaural). Noise blanker is the best we have tested. Arguably the best available receiver for TV DX, using the built-in monochrome display. Reliability, originally questionable, found to be above average in recent years. Two 24-hour clocks.

Con: In the United States, available only to Federal agencies, as it receives cellular frequencies; this ban is routinely circumvented by purchasing from Canadian Icom dealers (service is available to any owner within the United States). Not physically robust; one tested sample failed when subjected to ordinary shipment; nonetheless, it has a high MTBF during fixed use, so it appears to be electronically dependable. Power supply runs hot, although over the years this has not caused premature component failure. No synchronous selectable sideband; remediable with Sherwood SE-3. Two AM-mode bandwidths too broad for most world band applications; remediable with Sherwood aftermarket filter option. Both single-sideband bandwidths almost identical. Dynamic range merely adequate. Front-panel controls of only average quality, although robust. Keypad frequency entry only in MHz, decimal and all.

☞ The five-star rating, above, applies for world band applications only when it is equipped with aftermarket accessory filters and synchronous selectable sideband.

☞ Rack mounted, but an optional cabinet is available for desktop use.

Verdict: The Icom IC-R9000L is virtually identical to the IC-R9000 and IC-R9000A except that the "L" version's spectrum display uses an LCD instead of a CRT. Our experience confirms what the eye suggests, which is that this is not a receiver designed to take vibration and other physical punishment. Indeed, its high heat would hint at a low MTBF even in fixed applications, but over the years the receiver has proven to be electrically reliable.

With changed AM-mode bandwidth filters—available from at least one world band specialty firm—this receiver is about as good as it gets for DX reception of faint, tough signals throughout the radio spectrum. With the Sherwood SE-3 it is also top drawer for fastidious listening to world band programs. And it shines if you want a visual indication of spectrum occupancy and certain other characteristics of stations within a designated segment of the radio spectrum.

An *RDI WHITE PAPER* is available for the IC-R9000/R9000A.

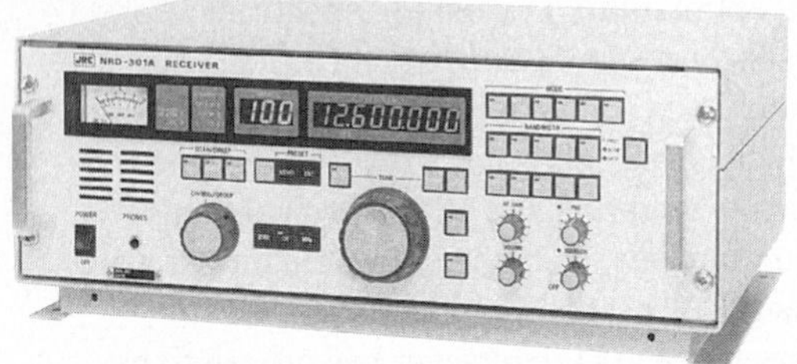

Each professional receiver stands out in a certain way. The Japan Radio NRD-301 is designed to weather the high seas, so its high card is build quality and ease of repair. Not bombproof, but close.

⭘⭘⭘⭘½

Japan Radio NRD-301A

Price: Under $8,000 in the United States—actual price varies considerably. *Cabinet #MPBX10832:* $449.95 if ordered with receiver, $749.95 if ordered separately, in the United States. *Aftermarket voice bandwidth filters:* approximately $150 each, installed ($139.95 uninstalled), in the United States. *Sherwood SE-3:* $549 plus shipping worldwide.

Pro: Uncommonly easy to repair on the spot—aided by built-in test equipment (BITE), plug-in circuit boards and a spare-parts kit. Superior overall performance in nearly all respects. Superior ergonomics. Passband shift, operates in AM mode. Tunes in ultra-precise 1 Hz increments. Three hundred presets, and VFO operates from presets' channels. Effective noise blanker. Adjustable AGC decay. Sophisticated scanning system. AF (audio) filter narrows high- and low-frequency audio response. Comes with spare parts for on-site repair. Operates from a wide range of AC voltages, using an easily adjusted inboard power supply and 24 VDC ship's power. Can be computer controlled. Room for additional bandwidths. Unlike other professional models, the actual selling price varies enormously—attractive pricing can be found in some quarters.

Con: Usually available only on special order. Lacks the operating flexibility of such professional supersets as the Watkins-Johnson WJ-8711A. Only two voice bandwidths (*see* Pro), although both perform nicely and are well chosen. No keypad tuning, a major omission. No synchronous selectable sideband; remediable by adding Sherwood SE-3 outboard accessory, which uses off-tuning to select sidebands. No tunable notch filter. Unusual audio, antenna and AC cord jacks. Signal-strength indicator not illuminated. Slight whine from LED display at high brightness after receiver has been on for over an hour. Slight AC "tingle" when touching cabinet, remediable by grounding the receiver or, for receive-only applications, by removing marine-oriented C1 and C2 capacitors from across the back of the AC socket. AC power transformer runs very hot and sometimes buzzes. Distribution limited to Japan Radio dealers, offices, and a few specialty organizations such as shipyards. Rack mounted, so cabinet is extra and pricey.

☞ The above star rating is for the receiver "as is" from the factory. With the addition of at least one more AM-mode voice filter and the Sherwood SE-3, the rating improves by a quarter star.

Verdict: Japan Radio's NRD-301A receiver is exceptional. It is probably fit to be handed down from one generation to the next, what with its seemingly bulletproof construction, ease of repair and superior overall performance. Yet, as it comes from the factory it lacks certain features of use for everyday world band listening and DXing.

The Passport *professional-model review team consists of Tony Jones, Lawrence Magne, Chuck Rippel, David Walcutt, David Zantow and George Zeller. Laboratory measurements by J. Robert Sherwood.*

Choosing a Premium Receiver?

Get premium advice before you buy!

If you could, you'd spend weeks with each receiver, learning its charms and foibles. Seeing for yourself how it handles—*before* you spend.

Now, you can do the next best thing—better, some folks insist. Radio Database International White Papers®, from the PASSPORT® TO WORLD BAND RADIO library of in-depth test reports, put the facts right into your hands. We test run each receiver for you. Put it through comprehensive laboratory and bench tests to find out where it shines. And where it doesn't.

Then our panel takes over: DXers, professional monitors, program listeners. They're mean, grumpy, hypercritical . . . and take lots of notes. They spend weeks with each receiver, checking ergonomics and long-run listening quality with all kinds of stations. Living with it day and night.

With PASSPORT's RDI White Papers®, these findings—the good, the bad and the ugly—are yours, along with valuable tips on how to operate your radio to best advantage. Each receiver report covers one model in depth, and is US$6.95 postpaid in the United States and Canada; $9.95 airmail elsewhere:

- Drake R8B
- Drake SW8
- Grundig Satellit 800
- Icom IC-R9000/'R9000A
- Lowe HF-150
- Sony ICF-2010/ICF-2001D
- Yaesu FRG-100
- How to Interpret Receiver Specifications and Lab Tests
- Popular Outdoor Antennas, including installation

PASSPORT RDI White Papers for vintage receivers:

- AOR AR3030
- Drake R8/R8E
- Drake R8A
- Grundig Satellit 500
- Grundig Satellit 650 (and Satellit 600)
- Icom IC-R71
- Kenwood R-5000
- Japan Radio NRD-93
- Japan Radio NRD-525 (includes summary evaluation of Japan Radio NRD-515)
- Japan Radio NRD-535D/NRD-535
- Lowe HF-125
- Lowe HF-225 and Lowe HF-235
- Sony CRF-V21
- Ten-Tec RX325
- Yaesu FRG-8800

Available direct or from dealers. For VISA/Master Card orders, click on www.passband.com or call our 24-hour autovoice order line: +1 (215) 598-9018; also, fax +1 (215) 598 3794. Or send your check or money order, specifying which reports you want, to:

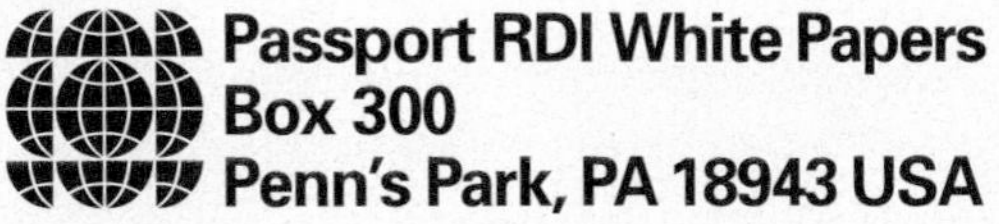
Passport RDI White Papers
Box 300
Penn's Park, PA 18943 USA

"We strongly recommend the PASSPORT RDI White Papers before purchasing any receiver over $100. The *Consumer Reports* of shortwave radio."

—What's New, *Monitoring Times*

Passive Antennas: Wires That Work

Part of the allure of world band as opposed to Webcasts is no wires. Yet, for those seeking the best in world band performance, an outdoor antenna can be surprisingly effective—and most are made from wire.

If you decide to spring for a serious outdoor wire antenna, there are three "musts" for optimum results:

- Mate the type of antenna to the type of receiver.
- Purchase the best antenna of the type you want which fits outdoors.
- Erect the antenna safely and for best performance.

Signal-to-Noise

An outdoor antenna will almost always help with weaker signals by providing more signal and overcoming local electrical noises and receiver circuit noise. The result—more signal, less noise—is an improvement in the *signal-to-noise ratio*. It's like getting rid of crackling and hiss on a noisy telephone line.

The signal-to-noise ratio is important because increasing signal strength means little if you also increase background noise by a similar amount. These noises can be from local sources—appliances, fluorescent lights, computers, dimmers and the like—as well as from "hiss" and other circuit noises generated within your receiver.

When an Antenna Won't Help

Nevertheless, muscular stations already coming in well probably won't sound better. Your receiver's signal-strength indicator may read higher, but its automatic-gain control (AGC) ensures that what you hear probably won't sound much different than it does with your existing antenna.

If you are using a simple portable, forget sophisticated antennas—outdoor or indoor, passive or active. Rather, either make do with the built-in telescopic antenna, or for more oomph stick to a simple inverted-L wire outdoor antenna or the Sony AN-LP1 active loop. Among the best inverted-L antennas in the United States is Radio Shack's ten-buck "SW Antenna Kit" with wire, insulators and other goodies, plus $2 for a claw/alligator clip or other connector. In Australia Dick Smith Electronics offers the comparable K 3490 Short Wave Antenna.

These inverted-L antennas may be too long for your radio, causing "overload" from too much incoming signal; yet, you can always shorten it. Experiment, but as a rough rule of thumb the less costly the portable, the shorter the antenna.

At the other extreme, tabletop world band receivers usually don't even come with built-in antennas, as these can't begin to do justice to their exceptional potential. A good antenna is as essential to these elite receivers as high-octane gasoline is to a Ferrari.

Location, Location

Antenna location is as important as the type of antenna chosen. An antenna placed out in the fresh air—high up, and away from electrical lines, communications cables and other sources of noise—will excel in improving the "noise" portion of the signal-to-noise ratio.

Unamplified *vs*. Amplified Antennas

There are two basic types of outboard antennas: "unamplified" (typically outdoor) and "amplified" or "active" (indoor, outdoor or both).

An unamplified antenna consists of a healthy length of wire or other metal receiving element to provide a radio signal directly to the receiver. It has no electrical amplification. An amplified or active antenna, on the other hand, typically uses a much shorter rod or wire receiving element, plus one or more stages of electrical amplification to make up for the relatively modest signal input of the diminutive receiving element.

Amplified antennas are popular because they are compact—for apartments, ideal. Even some homeowners prefer them because they can be easy to erect and relatively inconspicuous.

But amplified antennas have four drawbacks. First, their short receiving elements don't provide the signal-to-noise enhancement that comes when longer elements are used. Second, the antenna's amplifier can generate noise of its own. Third, the antenna's amplifier can itself overload, with results comparable to those found when a receiver overloads . . . a mishmash of jumbled-sounding stations up and down the dial; indeed, if amplifier gain is excessive it can also overload the receiver. Fourth, most amplified antennas have mediocre front-end selectivity, and thus are prone to commingling signals from local mediumwave AM stations with those from world band radio stations. This makes them potentially bad news for the very urban areas in which apartment dwellers and powerful radio/TV signals coexist in close proximity.

So, while there are a few good amplified antennas on the market today, these are not the antennas of choice except when installation of a first-rate unamplified antenna is simply not feasible.

Of course, if you're an apartment dweller with high-quality receiving gear, there is really precious little choice—it's dictated by where you live and the whims of your landlord or tenants' association. Unless you have access to a long roof or parcel of ground and the blessing of your landlord or tenants' association, you'll usually have to make do with an amplified antenna simply because there's no legit way to erect a long outdoor antenna.

Still, determined apartment dwellers have put their creative juices to full use with a wide variety of hidden or camouflaged outdoor wire antennas, such as phoney "clotheslines." Or they have simply capitalized on urban apathy by erecting a good outdoor wire antenna, then seeing whether any adverse reaction materializes. For these circumstances, the alternative least likely to attract attention is an inverted-L of moderate length, using wire that's not too thick or brightly colored.

Static Protection

An effective static protector is essential during thunderstorms, windy snowfalls and sandstorms. These storms tend to generate static charges, "sparks" strong enough to send your radio to the repair shop. Among the best protectors are those made by Alpha Delta Communications.

Installation

Most antennas are robustly constructed to withstand ice buildup during storms. However, those which require guying need hardware comparable in strength to that of the antenna. Also give consideration to the use of bungee cords to provide elasticity in the event of heavy ice buildup.

Safety is paramount during installation, especially to avoid falls or making contact with potentially lethal electrical utility and

Alpha Delta's DX-Ultra presents some erection challenges, but is a top performer.

other lines. There's much more to this than we can cover here, but you can find specifics in the RADIO DATABASE INTERNATIONAL report, *Evaluation of Popular Outdoor Antennas*, as well as at www.universal-radio.com/catalog/sw_ant/safeswl.html.

Which Are Best?

For our RADIO DATABASE INTERNATIONAL report, *Evaluation of Popular Outdoor Antennas*, we tested a number of popular outdoor wire antennas for shortwave listening. The best of those are reported on here. All are dipoles, most of which rely on traps for frequency resonance. Three layouts are used: end-fed sloper, with the antenna pitched about 30 degrees from horizontal; center-fed tapered wing, with a tall (about 20 feet or 6 meters) center mounting and two end mountings which are lower; and center-fed horizontal, hung between two points of comparable height.

Passive antennas are among the most difficult devices to evaluate properly. First, the quality of reception is frequency-dependent, so any overall rating is only a generalization. Second, performance depends to a noticeable extent on how well the antenna is erected, and even the type of soil, moisture and bedrock immediately underneath.

Star Ratings for 2002

In PASSPORT 2001 we evaluated active antennas on their own, and in our current RDI WHITE PAPER we evaluate passive antennas on their own. Star ratings for these reports have been based on each type of antenna in isolation, but for this year's PASSPORT we are awarding star ratings based on any and all types of antennas—three stars, for example, means the same thing regardless of whether an antenna is active or passive. This facilitates comparison of a given passive antenna with an active antenna that might otherwise seem equally suitable.

Inverted-L Alternatives

What about inverted-L antennas, sometimes referred to as "longwires"? They are simple and inexpensive, and for most radios they provide excellent results, even doing reasonably well on mediumwave AM.

Simple inverted-L antennas of moderate length are available at radio stores—these usually rate three stars, sometimes four, and are much too short to be called "longwires." Huge homemade versions, detailed in the RDI White Paper on outdoor antennas, can run over 200 feet, or 60 meters—Universal Radio and others sell the necessary specialized parts.

These long inverted-L antennas can perform fully as well as the Alpha Delta DX-Ultra, sometimes better because their enormous capture wavelength tends to improve the signal-to-noise ratio. But they are a night-mare to keep erect during ice storms and other extremes of weather, which can also cause sagging because of stretched wire.

✪✪✪✪¾ *Passport's Choice*

Alpha Delta DX-Ultra

Price: $119.95 in the United States.

Pro: Best overall performer of any antenna tested, passive or active. Little variation in performance from one world band segment to another. Rugged construction. Comes with built-in static protection. Wing design appropriate for certain yard layouts. Covers mediumwave AM band.

Con: Assembly a major undertaking, with stiff wire having to be bent and fed through spacer holes, then affixed. Unusually lengthy, 80 feet or 25 meters. Does not include needed coaxial cable lead-in. Relatively heavy, adding to erection effort. Warranty only six months.

For many backyards the Alpha Delta DX-SWL Sloper and Eavesdropper Sloper fit in nicely.

Verdict: The Alpha Delta DX-Ultra rewards sweat equity—it is really more of a kit than a finished product. First, you have to purchase the needed lead-in cable and other hardware bits, then assemble, bend and stretch the many stiff wires, section-by-section.

Because the wire used should outlast the Pyramids, assembly is a trying and unforgiving exercise. Each wire needs to be rigorously and properly affixed, lest it slip loose and the erected antenna comes tumbling down, as it did at one of our test sites.

While all outdoor antennas require yard space, the Ultra is the longest manufactured antenna tested. It is also relatively heavy, making installation an even more tiresome chore than it already is. In ice-prone climates, be sure any trees or poles attached to the antenna are sturdy.

But if you have the yard space and don't object to leaping assembly and erection hurdles, you are rewarded with a robust antenna that is outperformed only by hugely long inverted-L antennas and professional-grade antennas beyond the financial reach of even the most enthusiastic listener.

✪✪✪✪½ *Passport's Choice*

Alpha Delta DX-SWL Sloper

Price: $79.95 in the United States.

Pro: Rugged construction. Sloper design, using traps to save space, unusually practical for some yard layouts. Covers mediumwave AM band.

Con: Requires assembly, a significant exercise. Does not include static protection. Does not include needed coaxial cable lead-in. Warranty only six months.

☞ A shortened version, the 40-foot (12 meter) DX-SWL-S, not tested by us, is available for $69.95. Its nominal coverage is 3.2-22 MHz, omitting the 2 MHz (120 meter) world band segment. Although both Sloper versions nominally don't cover the 25 MHz (11 meter) world band segment, our measurements of the full-length Sloper show excellent results at 25650-26100 kHz.

Verdict: An excellent choice if you find that a 60-foot (18 meter) sloper will fit better into your yard than the Ultra or a very long inverted-L wire. However, it is a chore to assemble.

⭘⭘⭘⭘⅛ *Passport's Choice*
Eavesdropper Model T, Eavesdropper Model C

Price: *Models T and C:* $89.95 in the United States.

Pro: Exceptionally compact, only 43 feet or 13 meters, making it relatively likely to fit into a yard. Comes with built-in static protection. One-year warranty, after which repairs made "at nominal cost." *Model T:* Easiest to install of any Passport's Choice antenna—just unpack it and it's ready to hang. Comes with ribbon lead-in wire, which tends to have less signal loss than coaxial cable. *Model C:* Easier than most to install, with virtually everything included and assembled but the coaxial cable lead-in.

Con: Some performance drop in 2 MHz (120 meter) and 3 MHz (90 meter) tropical segments. *Model C:* Coaxial cable not included.

☞ Eavesdropper also makes a fully assembled $89.95 sloper antenna, not tested by us, similar to the Alpha Delta DX-SWL Sloper. It comes with lead-in wire and a static arrestor.

Verdict: There's no getting around the rule that the longer the antenna, the more likely it is to do well at low frequencies. The Eavesdropper's designer told PASSPORT some years back that their research showed little tuning taking place below 4.7 MHz, while on the other hand many folks had problems with yard space, or just wanted a shorter antenna less likely to come down in an ice storm. So he designed the Eavesdropper to be relatively compact, yet perform optimally above 4.7 MHz while still doing decent service lower down.

Our tests confirm this. The Eavesdropper horizontal trap dipoles perform quite nicely above 4.7 MHz, with a notch less gain in the 2 MHz and 3 MHz tropical segments.

The Eavesdropper T comes "ready to go" and is straightforward to erect. In practice the ribbon lead-in wire used by the T works very well, using phasing to cancel out much electrical noise. Too, it stands up to weather and usually has less signal loss than the coaxial cable used by its C sibling. The C version is helpful when there is significant electrical noise in the immediate vicinity of the feedline.

Prepared by Stephen Bohac, Jock Elliott, Tony Jones, Lawrence Magne and David Walcutt.

Eavesdropper's Model T comes ready to erect, with built-in static protection. Mounting is easy with two high points.

Active Antennas: Where Space Is Limited

Do you listen during the day, when signals are harder to hear? Do you like to flush out weaker, more unusual stations?

If so, a good outboard antenna can be your radio's best friend. Problem is, the most effective world band antennas are passive—unamplified—and require yard space. If you have little room outdoors, or are in an apartment or hotel, something else is needed.

That "something else" is an active antenna. These include a relatively small rod ("whip"), loop or wire—the receiving element—to snare signals from the airwaves. But because these elements are not lengthy, signals they pass on to the receiver tend to be weak. If something weren't done to overcome this, it would be like powering a car with a golf cart engine.

Active antennas resolve this by electrically amplifying signals before they get to the receiver. Although a passive wire antenna has inherent advantages, compact active antennas can do a surprisingly good job. The challenge is to sort out winners from losers.

Tempus Fugit

Active antennas used to be considered strictly as also-rans. Early models were noisy, overloaded easily, generated harmonic "false" signals and suffered from the ravages of outdoor use. Actives quickly earned a reputation for failing to perform even close to what serious listeners demanded.

There are well-engineered active antennas from Wellbrook and Dressler—even Sony.

In recent years, all this has changed for the better. The introduction of robust, well-engineered models from Wellbrook and Dressler—even Sony—has changed the game considerably. While none yet equals the performance of a proper outdoor wire antenna, the gap has closed considerably.

The two new Wellbrook antennas top our ratings. At least as important is that the company has been making continuing improvements, and as we go to press is researching another upgrade to its newest model, the ARA 330. Our laboratory made an approximate replication of that potential upgrade, and test results have been encouraging.

Price Not the Key

Price bears little relation to performance. One of the best-rated antennas is among the least costly, while the most expensive ranks near the bottom—at least for users in much of the world.

We limited our testing to designs likely to perform satisfactorily under a wide range of circumstances. However, various other amplified antennas are available at low cost for portables. In general, the weaker the overall signal strengths at your location, the greater the chances these budget offerings will suffice.

For mediumwave AM DXers and emergency listeners wanting only the very best, the Yaesu G-5550 twin-axis rotor allows the Wellbrook ALA 1530 to reduce co-channel interference by tilting, as well as rotating.

Proximate *vs.* Remote

Active antennas can be either proximate or remote. A proximate model requires that the receiving element be located near the receiver, as it is mounted on a control box which must be close to the radio. Remote models allow the receiving element to be placed a considerable distance away—either indoors or, with some models, out in the open weather where reception is superior.

Remote units are almost always the better bet, as they allow the receiving element to be placed where electrical noise is low and incoming signals are strong. Proximate models give you no choice unless you are willing to move the entire receiver to where reception happens to be optimum, which may not be a satisfactory place to listen.

If you do choose a proximate model, keep in mind that many radios put out some degree of electrical noise. Typically, this radiates forward from the receiver's digital display, so it is best to locate a proximate antenna behind or to either side of the radio.

WHERE TO INSTALL A REMOTE ANTENNA

The good news is that if an excellent active antenna is installed optimally, it can perform very well. The bad news is that if you have room outdoors to mount it optimally, you may also have room for a passive wire antenna that will perform better, yet. Probably cheaper, too.

Still, here are a few practical tips on placement of weather-resistant remote models. As always with antennas, creativity rules—don't be afraid to experiment.

• If you can mount your antenna's receiving element outdoors, try to do it in the clear. Use a nonconductive mast or capped PVC pipe, as metal masts or pipes are likely to degrade performance. Optimum height from ground is around 10-25 feet or 3-8 meters, but keep in mind that "ground" refers to electrical ground, which includes non-wooden roofs and the like.

If this is not feasible, try a nearby tree. This works less well because tree sap is electrically conductive, but is a reasonable fallback, especially with hardwood varieties. Ensure that leaves and branches can't brush against the element under most weather conditions.

• If outdoor mounting is impractical, then have the receiving element protrude out into the fresh air as much as possible. Even if you are in a high-rise building, this can work so long as a window opens or there is a balcony. For example, if your antenna's receiving element is a whip you can stick it away from the building 45 degrees or so, like a wall flagpole. If that is too visible, then try using a string or rope to pull it up, out of view, by day.

If you are in a house with an attic, especially one with no foil-lined insulation along the pitched roof, and the roof is not metal, this can often work in lieu of an outdoor placement. Indeed, with the large Wellbrook models this is a tempting alternative to placement within a room, especially if a rotor is used.

• If all these choices are impractical, then at least place the receiving element up against a large window. Glass blocks signals much less than masonry or metal, including to a limited extent insulation foil and aluminum siding.

Preselection *vs.* Broadband

Broadband electronic amplifiers have the potential for all sorts of mischief. Some add noise and spurious signals, especially from the mediumwave AM band; others may overload a receiver with too much gain.

A partial solution is to have effective tunable or switchable preselection. Preselection limits the band of frequencies which get full amplification, and in so doing reduces the odds of spurious signals being created by the antenna or the receiver.

Problem is, preselection adds to manufacturing cost. And because it requires manual tuning, it also increases operating complexity—although it doesn't have to. As indicated in our review of the Sony ICF-SW07 elsewhere in PASSPORT REPORTS, preselection can be automated if the antenna and receiver are designed to work together. So far only the 'SW07 can do this.

A simplified variant of preselection is to substantially reduce gain at frequencies below around two Megahertz. The top-rated Wellbrook ALA 330 takes this approach, which is a great help in keeping powerful local mediumwave AM stations from disrupting world band reception.

Amplified Wire Beats Whip

The MFJ-1020B, about to be replaced by the similar '1020C, performs only modestly with its little built-in antenna. However, it does nicely as an active preselector when used with a short inverted-L wire antenna, especially if the wire is placed outdoors. If this is feasible at your location, the combo can provide superior performance at an affordable price.

How Much Is Too Much?

With a first-rate receiver and passive outdoor wire antenna, there is rarely any need for electrical gain between the antenna and receiver. In principle, a good active antenna should replicate that "natural" level of gain—or, better, the signal-to-noise ratio. Too little gain, then overall circuit noise appears, if only from the receiver. Too much gain and the receiver's dynamic range is strained unnecessarily.

AC Can Cause Hum, Buzz

Active antennas work best when powered by battery. This eliminates all possibility of hum and buzzing caused by an AC-to-DC power supply. Problem is, using batteries tends to be impractical.

Switching over to an AC adaptor isn't a flawless solution, either. Hum and buzzing persisted to a greater or lesser degree throughout our tests of several active antennas powered by AC adaptors. The best practical solution: Keep all AC adaptors as far as possible from the antenna's receiving element.

Steps You Can Take

Antenna performance is roughly one part technology, one part geography and geology, and one part installation. This report covers the first, with tips on the third, but in the end all it can accomplish is to boost your odds of success. After all, much of the outcome depends on where you live and what you do once the antenna arrives.

Antenna location and installation details can make all the difference. Consider experimenting with different locations before doing a permanent installation, and if your receiver has multiple antenna inputs don't be afraid to see which works best.

What PASSPORT's Ratings Mean

Star ratings: ✪✪✪✪✪ is best for any type of antenna, but in reality even the best of active antennas don't yet merit more than four stars when compared against passive antennas. To help with in making a purchase decision, starting with this edition star ratings for active antennas may be compared directly against those for passive antennas, which almost always outperform active models. Stars reflect overall performance on shortwave and meaningful features, plus to some extent ergonomics and build quality. Price, appearance, country of manufacture and the like are not taken into account.

Passport's Choice. *La crème de la crème.* Our test team's personal picks of the litter—models we would buy or have bought for our personal use.

¢: A relative bargain, with decidedly more performance than the price would suggest.

Active antennas are listed in descending order of merit. Unless otherwise indicated each has a one-year warranty.

New for 2002

★★★½ *Passport's Choice* as tested

★★★¾ with ~10 dB greater amplifier gain, *see* ☞

Wellbrook ALA 330

Remote, broadband, outdoor-indoor, 2.3-30 MHz

Tops are the Wellbrook ALA 330 and ALA 1530, especially with rotor (shown). Chuck Rippel

Price: Existing versions (same gain as ALA 1530): *ALA 330:* £119.95 plus £10.00 shipping in the United Kingdom. £129.95 plus £25.00 shipping to North America. *ALA 330P:* £109.95 plus £10.00 shipping in the United Kingdom. £109.95 plus £25.00 shipping elsewhere. **Replacement versions with higher gain, if introduced:** add £25.00.

Pro: Best signal-to-noise ratio, on all shortwave frequencies, of any active model tested that has reasonable gain; against the runner-up Dressler antennas its raw gain tended to be greater above 18 MHz; below that, relative gain varied from one test site to another (*see* ☞). Its aluminum loop receiving element allows it to be affixed to a low-cost TV rotor to improve reception by directionally nulling local electrical noise and static. Sometimes, rotatability also can slightly reduce co-channel shortwave interference; as is to be expected, this modest nulling of co-channel skywave interference is best at frequencies below 5 MHz. Superior build quality, including rigorous weatherproofing (*see* Con). Supplied AC adaptor, even though unregulated, is among the best tested for not causing hum or buzzing. Although any large loop is inherently susceptible to inductive pickup of local thunderstorm static, during our tests the antenna's amplifier never suffered static damage during storms; indeed, even nearby 1 kW shortwave transmissions did no damage to the antenna amplifier (since our tests the manufacturer has changed the static protection to improve overall reception performance, but in principle static protection should still be first-rate). Protected circuitry, using an easily-replaced 315 mA slow-blow fuse.

Con: Modest gain for reception within the Western Hemisphere, Asia and Australasia; can be significantly improved by adding 9-12 dB of high-quality electrical preamplification; or, depending to some extent on the receiver's antenna impedance, a passive antenna tuner (*see* ☞). No mediumwave AM coverage. Balanced loop receiving element, about one meter across, not easy to mount and large for shipment. Mounting mast and optional rotor add to cost. BNC connector at the receiving element's base is open to the weather and thus needs to be user-sealed with Coax Seal, electrical putty or similar. Encapsulated amplifier makes repair unusually difficult. Adaptor supplied for 117V AC runs hot after being plugged in for a few hours, while amplifier tends to run slightly warm. No coaxial cable supplied. Available for purchase or export only two ways: via cheque through the English manufacturer (www.wellbrook.uk.com), or with credit card via a dealer's unsecured email address in England, although a secure order page is being considered.

☞ The manufacturer advises that it is considering boosting the '330's amplifier gain around 9-12 dB. In order to replicate this, we tested the current version with a high-quality 10 dB preamp. The result was enough of an improvement in weak-signal performance to raise PASSPORT's overall rating. Should the manufacturer boost the gain of the amplifier by a like amount—they are researching this as we go to press—the antenna should be a more suitable choice for weak-signal shortwave reception in the Western Hemisphere, Middle East, central and southern Africa, Asia and Australasia.

☞ If your receiver has antenna inputs with varying impedances, experiment to see which provides the greatest signal strength.

☞ The "P" version uses a semi-rigid plastic loop rather than aluminum. It is intended for indoor use only.

Verdict: If its dimensions and purchase hurdles don't deter you, you will not find a better active antenna for shortwave reception than the U.K.-made Wellbrook ALA 330. While the tough ALA 330 does not equal the performance of a high-performance wire antenna, it is the best-performing active antenna we have tested.

Wellbrook's antennas mount easily in attics or not-so-easily on high poles—with or without rotor. Chuck Rippel

Should the manufacturer boost the antenna amplifier's gain, the ALA 330 should perform similarly to a simple inverted-L outdoor wire antenna of modest length. Otherwise, the '330's gain can be improved almost to the same degree if your receiver includes a built-in switchable preamplifier.

Optimally, mounting should be outdoors with a rotor. However, worthy results can be expected indoors sans rotor, provided the usual caveats are followed for placement of the reception element.

New for 2002

✪✪✪ (North America)

✪✪✪½ *Passport's Choice*
(most locations outside North America)

Wellbrook ALA 1530, Wellbrook ALA 1530P

Remote, broadband, outdoor-indoor, 0.05-30 MHz

Price: *ALA 1530:* £119.95 plus £10.00 shipping in the United Kingdom. £129.95 plus £25.00 shipping to North America. *ALA 1530P:* £109.95 plus £10.00 shipping in the United Kingdom. £109.95 plus £25.00 shipping elsewhere. *Yaesu G-5550 twin-axis*

rotor: $599.95 in the United States. CAN$1060.00 in Canada.

☞ To avoid problems with circuit stress from powerful mediumwave AM signals, the manufacturer advises that amplifier gain will not be increased on the '1530, regardless of whether it is boosted on the ALA 330. For that same reason, irrespective of location the ALA 1530 should not be used with an accessory preamplifier.

☞ Mediumwave AM and longwave performance directionality may suffer if the '1530 is not mounted well away from other antennas.

☞ The "P" version, not tested by us, uses a semi-rigid plastic loop rather than aluminum. It is intended for indoor use only.

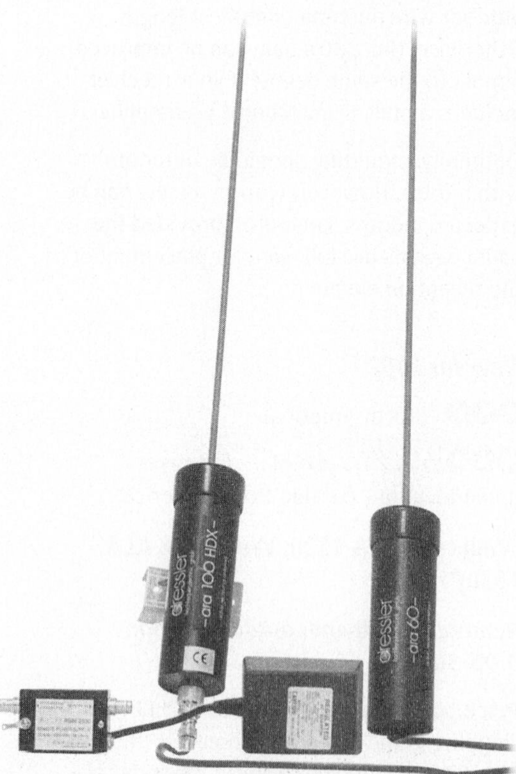
dressler
ara 100 HDX
dressler
ara 60

The Dressler ARA 100 HDX and ARA 60 do yeoman's service while remaining inconspicious. Robert Sherwood

Verdict: Virtually identical to the Wellbrook ALA 330, reviewed above, but also covers mediumwave AM and longwave bands—and does so brilliantly. This is thanks in no small part to the effectiveness of directional reception on frequencies below the shortwave spectrum. Mediumwave AM reception is particularly aided by the Yaesu G-5500 rotor, used in our tests, which has twin-axis capability. Although costly, it allows the receiving element to be both rotated and tilted to enhance nulling of co-channel interference below 1.7 MHz.

However, the '1530's extended frequency range also can result in mediumwave AM signals surfacing within the shortwave spectrum, degrading reception—this is usually a more significant issue in urban and suburban North America than elsewhere. Yet, for this, too, a rotor can be of help, as it allows the problem to be minimized by turning the antenna perpendicular to an offending mediumwave AM signal's axis.

✪✪✪¼ *Passport's Choice*
Dressler ARA 100 HDX

Remote, broadband, outdoor-indoor, 0.04-40 MHz

Price: $529.95 in the United States. £325.00 on special order in the United Kingdom.

Pro: Superior build quality, with fiberglass whip and foam-encapsulated head amplifier to resist the weather (*see* Con). Very good gain below 20 MHz (*see* Con). Outstanding dynamic range. Superior signal-to-noise ratio. Handy detachable "N" connector on bottom. AC adaptor with regulated DC output is better than most.

Con: Encapsulated design makes most repairs impossible. Above 20 MHz gain begins to fall off slightly. Body of antenna runs slightly warm. "N" connector at the head amplifier/receiving element exposed to weather, needs to be sealed with Coax Seal, electrical putty or similar by user. Gain

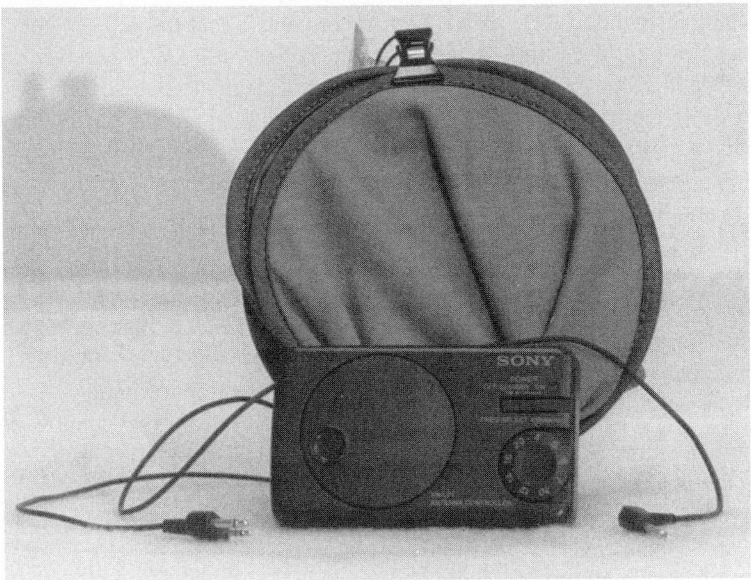
SONY

For most portables nothing beats the Sony AN-LP1. It folds neatly into handbags, briefcases and carry-ons. Jane Brinker

control cumbersome to adjust; fortunately, in practice it is rarely needed. Reader reports suggest that ordering direct from the factory can be a frustrating experience.

Verdict: The robust Dressler ARA 100 HDX, made in Germany, is an excellent but costly low-noise antenna.

✪✪✪ *Passport's Choice*
Dressler ARA 60

Remote, broadband, outdoor-indoor, 0.04-60/100 MHz

Price: $289.95 in the United States. £169.00 in the United Kingdom.

Pro: Superior build quality, with fiberglass whip and foam-encapsulated head amplifier to resist weather (*see* Con). Very good and consistent gain, even above 20 MHz. Outstanding dynamic range. AC adaptor with regulated DC output is better than most.

Con: Encapsulated design makes most repairs impossible. RG-58 coaxial cable permanently attached on antenna end, making user replacement impossible (*see* ☞, below). Gain control cumbersome to adjust; fortunately, in practice it is rarely needed. Reader reports suggest that ordering direct from the factory can be a frustrating experience.

Verdict: Very similar to the ARA 100 HDX—even its dynamic range and overloading performance are virtually identical. This makes the German-made ARA 60 an excellent lower-cost alternative to the ARA 100 HDX.

✪✪✪ *Passport's Choice*
MFJ-1020B

This rating only for when used with short outdoor inverted-L antenna.

See review of the MFJ-1020B towards the end of this article.

✪✪¾ *Passport's Choice*
Sony AN-LP1

Remote, manual preselection, indoor/portable, 3.9-4.3 + 4.7-25 MHz

Price: $79.95 in the United States. CAN$185.00 in Canada. £69.95 in the United Kingdom.

Pro: Very good overall performance, including generally superior gain (*see* Con), especially within world band segments—yet surprisingly free from side effects. Compact folding design for airline and other travel; also handy for hospital, prison or other institutional use where an antenna must be stashed away periodically. Can be used even with portables that have no antenna input jack (*see* Con). Plug-in filter to reduce local electrical noise (*see* Con). Low battery consumption (*see* Con). Powered by the radio when used with Sony ICF-SW7600G or ICF-SW1000T portables.

Con: Battery operation only—no AC power supply, not even a socket for an AC adaptor. Only remote model tested which can't be mounted outdoors during inclement weather. Functions acceptably on shortwave only between 3.9-4.3 MHz and 4.7-25 MHz, with no mediumwave AM coverage. Gain varies markedly throughout the shortwave spectrum, in large part because the preselector's step-tuned resonances lack variable peaking. Preselector bandswitching complicates operation slightly. Consumer-grade plastic construction with no shielding. When clipped onto a telescopic antenna instead of fed through an antenna jack, the lack of a ground connection reduces performance. Plug-in noise filter unit reduces signal strength by several decibels.

TUNABLE PREAMP - ANTENNA
AMECO
OUT
IN
PREAMP.
TUNE
BAND (MHz)
GAIN
ON
OFF
POWER
MODEL TPA

Every greybeard ham remembers the name "Ameco." The same family still turns out the Ameco TPA active antenna. Robert Sherwood

☞ Sony recommends that the AN-LP1 not be used with the Sony ICF-SW77 receiver. However, our tests indicate that so long as the control box and loop receiving element are kept reasonably away from the radio, the antenna performs well.

☞ The Sony ICF-SW07 compact portable comes with an AN-LP2 antenna. This is virtually identical in concept and performance to the AN-LP1, except that because it is designed solely for use with the 'SW07 it has automatic preselection to simplify operation. At present the AN-LP2 cannot be used with other radios, even those from Sony.

Verdict: A real winner if the shoe fits. Hands down, this is the best model for world band reception on portables—it is often a worthy choice for portatop and tabletop models, as well, provided you don't mind battery-only operation. This Japanese-made model has generally excellent gain, low noise and few side effects. The price is right, too.

Yet, there is limited frequency coverage—90/120 meter DXers should look elsewhere—and the loop receiving element cannot be mounted permanently outdoors. Too, the lack of variable preselector peaking causes gain to vary greatly by frequency; this especially limits utility DX performance. Otherwise, the Sony AN-LP1 is nothing short of a bargain.

✪✪½ ⊘

Ameco TPA

Proximate, manual preselection, indoor, 0.22-30 MHz

Price: $69.95 in the United States.

Pro: Highest recovered signal with the longest supplied whip of the four proximate models tested. Most pleasant unit to tune to proper frequency. Superior ergonomics, including easy-to-read front panel with good-sized metal knobs (*see* Con). Superior gain below 10 MHz.

Con: Proximate model, so receiving element has to be placed near receiver. Above 15 MHz gain slips to slightly below average. Overloads with external antenna; because gain potentiometer is in the first stage, decreasing gain may increase overloading as current drops through the FET. Preselector complicates operation, compromising otherwise-superior ergonomics. No rubber feet, slides around in use; user-remediable. No AC adaptor. Consumer-grade plastic construction with no shielding. Comes with no printed information on warranty; however, manufacturer states by telephone that it is the customary one year.

Verdict: The Ameco TPA, made in the United States, is the best proximate model tested for bringing in usable signals with the factory-supplied whip—signal recovery was excellent. However, when connected to an external antenna it overloads badly, and reducing gain doesn't help.

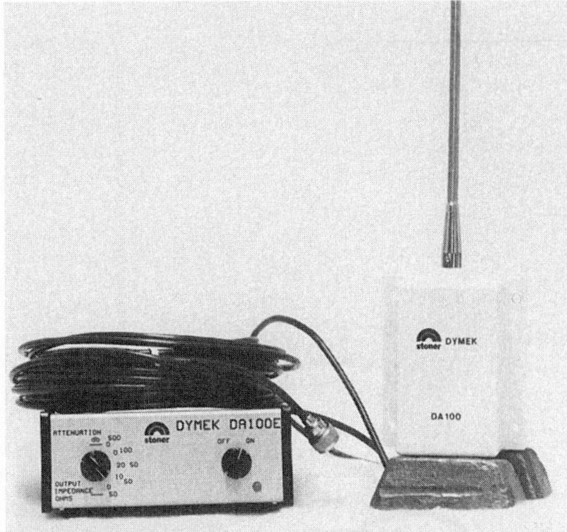
DYMEK DA100E
stoner
DYMEK
DA100

One of the first good active antennas was the McKay Dymek DA100. It has been improved over the years, and now is in its "E" incarnation. Robert Sherwood

✪✪½

McKay Dymek DA100E, McKay Dymek DA100EM, Stoner Dymek DA100E, Stoner Dymek DA100EM

Remote, broadband, indoor-outdoor-marine, 0.05-30 MHz

Price: *DA100E:* $179.95 in the United States. *DA100EM (marine version, not tested):* $199.95 in the United States.

Pro: Respectable gain and noise. Generally good build quality, with worthy coaxial cable and an effectively sealed receiving element; marine version (not tested) appears to be even better yet for resisting weather. Jack for second antenna when turned off. Minor gain rolloff at higher shortwave frequencies. *DA100EM (not tested):* Weather-resistant fiberglass whip and brass fittings help ensure continued optimum performance.

Con: Slightly higher noise floor compared to other models. Some controls may confuse initially. Dynamic range among the lowest of any model tested; for many applications in the Americas this is adequate, but for use near local transmitters, or in Europe and other strong-signal parts of the world, the antenna is best purchased on a returnable basis. *DA100E:* Telescopic antenna allows moisture and avian waste penetration between segments, and thus potential resistance and/or spurious signals; user should seal these gaps with Coax Seal, electrical putty or similar. Telescopic antenna could, in principle, be de-telescoped by birds, ice and the like, although we did not actually encounter this. Warranty only 30 days.

Verdict: The DA100E is a proven "out of the box" choice, with generally excellent weatherproofing and coaxial cable. Because its dynamic range is relatively modest, it is more prone than some other models to overload, especially in an urban environment or other high-signal-strength location. In principle the extra twenty bucks for the marine version should be a good investment, provided its fiberglass whip is not too visible for your location.

MFJ REMOTE ACTIVE
ANTENNA

The MFJ 1024 is widely available, making it a popular choice. Robert Sherwood

✪✪¼

MFJ 1024

Remote, broadband, indoor-outdoor, 0.05-30 MHz

Price: $139.95 in the United States. CAN$220.00 in Canada.

Pro: Overall good gain and low noise. A/B selector for quick connection to another receiver. "Aux" input for passive antenna. 30-day money-back guarantee if purchased from manufacturer.

Con: Significant hum with supplied AC adaptor; remedied when we substituted a suitable aftermarket adaptor. Non-standard power socket complicates substitution of AC adaptor; also, adaptor's sub-mini plug can spark when inserted while the adaptor is plugged in; adaptor should be unplugged beforehand. Dynamic range among the lowest of any model tested; for many applications in the Americas it is adequate, but for use near local transmitters, or in Europe and other strong-signal parts of the world, antenna is best purchased on a returnable basis. Slightly increased noise floor compared to other models. Telescopic antenna allows moisture and avian waste penetration between segments, and thus potential resistance and/or spurious signals; user should seal these gaps with Coax Seal, electrical putty or similar. Telescopic antenna could, in principle, be de-telescoped by birds, ice and the like after installation, although we did not actually encounter this. Control box/amplifier has no external weather sealing to protect from moisture, although the printed circuit board nominally comes with a water-resistant coating. Coaxial cable to receiver not provided. Mediocre coaxial cable provided between control box and receiving element. On our unit, a coaxial connector came poorly soldered from the factory.

Verdict: The MFJ 1024, made in America, performs almost identically to the Stoner Dymek DA100E, but sells for $40 less. However, that gap lessens if you factor in the cost of a worthy AC adaptor—assuming you can find or alter one to fit the unusual power jack—and the quality of the 1024's coaxial cable is not in the same league.

✪✪

Vectronics AT-100

Proximate, manual preselection, indoor, 0.3-30 MHz

Price: $79.95 in the United States. CAN$109.00 in Canada.

Pro: Good—sometimes excellent—gain (*see* Con), especially in the mediumwave AM band. Good dynamic range. Most knobs are commendably large.

Con: Proximate model, so receiving element has to be placed near receiver. No

AC power; although it accepts an AC adaptor, the lack of polarity markings complicates adaptor choice (it is center-pin positive). Preselector complicates operation, especially as it is stiff to tune and thus awkward to peak. Our unit oscillated badly with some receivers, limiting usable gain—although it was more stable with other receivers, and thus appears to be a function of the load presented by a given receiver.

Verdict: If ever there were a product that needs to be purchased on a returnable basis, this is it. With one receiver, this American-made model gives welcome gain and worthy performance; with another, it goes into oscillation nearly at the drop of a hat.

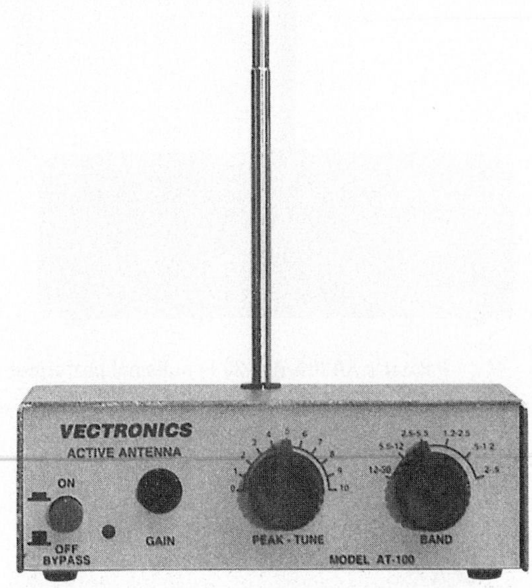
VECTRONICS
ACTIVE ANTENNA
ON
OFF
BYPASS
GAIN
PEAK - TUNE
BAND
MODEL AT-100

Vectronics' AT-100 is low-priced, but performance is hard to predict. Robert Sherwood

✪¾ Sony AN-1

Remote, broadband, indoor-outdoor, 0.15-30 MHz

Price: $89.95 in the United States. CAN$160.00 in Canada. £64.95 in the United Kingdom.

Pro: Connects easily to any portable or other receiver, using supplied cables and inductive coupler. Unusually appropriate for low-cost portables lacking an outboard antenna input. Only portable-oriented model tested with weather resistant remote receiving element. Unlike Sony AN-LP1, it covers entire shortwave spectrum, plus mediumwave AM and longwave. AC adaptor jack, although antenna designed to run on six "AA" batteries. Good quality coaxial cable. Coaxial cable user-replaceable once head unit is disassembled. Switchable high-pass filter helps reduce intrusion of mediumwave AM signals into shortwave spectrum; rolloff begins at 3 MHz. Receiving element's bracket allows for nearly any mounting configuration (*see* Con).

Con: Poor gain, with pronounced reduction as frequency increases. Mediocre mediumwave AM performance. Clumsy but versatile mounting bracket makes installation tedious. No AC adaptor.

☞ Sony offers a number of active antennas in various world markets. All appear to be similar to the AN-1, except for the very different AN-LP1.

Verdict: The Japanese-made Sony AN-1 has feeble gain, rendering it practically useless on higher frequencies and little better below. However, for outdoor mounting and use on lower frequencies it provides passable performance.

SONY
SONY
SONY

Sony AN-1's size and broadband performance make it a favorite for portable surveillance of utility and mediumwave stations. Robert Sherwood

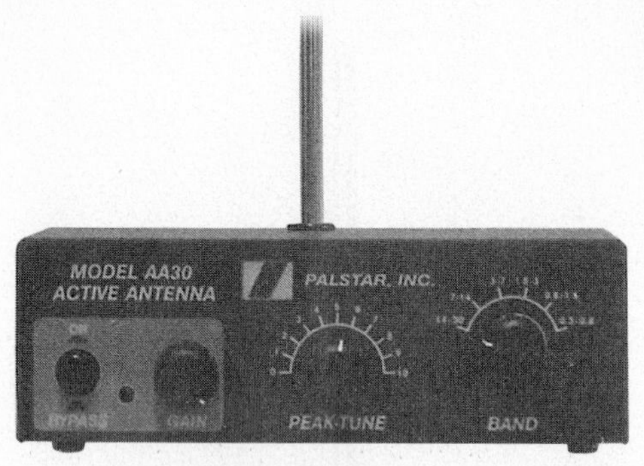
MODEL AA30
ACTIVE ANTENNA
PALSTAR, INC.
BYPASS
GAIN
PEAK TUNE
BAND

Palstar's AA30A/AM-30 is a dismal performer, especially above 14 MHz. Robert Sherwood

✪¾
Palstar AA30A "Active Antenna Matcher", Palstar AM-30 "Active Antenna Matcher"

Proximate, manual preselection, indoor, 0.3-30 MHz

Price: *AA30A:* $65.95 in the United States. *AM-30 (not tested):* £69.95 in the United Kingdom.

Pro: Moderate-to-good gain. Tuning control easily peaked. Can be powered directly by the Palstar R30/R30C and Lowe HF-350 tabletop receivers (reviewed elsewhere in PASSPORT REPORTS), an internal battery or an AC adaptor.

Con: Spurious oscillation throughout 14-30 MHz range. Overloads with external antenna. Proximate model, so receiving element has to be placed near receiver. Preselector complicates operation. No AC adaptor.

☞ At present, the AA30A's cabinets are silk screened simply as "AA30," although the accompanying owner's manual refers to the "AA30A."

☞ The Palstar AM-30, not tested, is sold in Europe. It appears to be comparable to the AA30A.

Verdict: Oscillation makes this a dubious choice except for reception below 14 MHz. Manufactured in the United States.

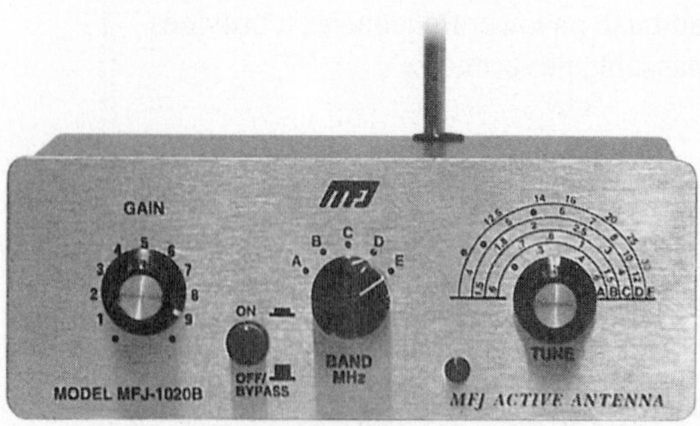
GAIN
ON
OFF/BYPASS
BAND MHz
TUNE
MODEL MFJ-1020B
MFJ ACTIVE ANTENNA

The MFJ-1020B is no prize on its own. Yet, when used as a preselector with a small wire antenna, it becomes an excellent and thrifty choice. Robert Sherwood

✪¾
MFJ-1020B

Proximate, manual preselection, indoor, 0.3-30 MHz

Price: $79.95 in the United States. CAN$125.00 in Canada.

Pro: Superior dynamic range. Rating rises to three stars if converted from a proximate to a remote model by removing the built-in antenna and connecting the active preselector module to a user-purchased inverted-L antenna. Choice of PL-259 or RCA connections. 30-day money-back guarantee if purchased from manufacturer.

Con: Proximate model, so receiving element has to be placed near receiver (*see* Pro). Low gain, excessive noise. Preselector complicates operation and tuning capacitor hard to peak. Knobs small and not easy to adjust. Confusing markings on front panel. Two manufacturing flaws found on our unit: a defective lowest frequency inductor or switch, as the unit would not tune below 530 kHz; also, crooked front panel. No AC adaptor.

☞ The '2010B is about to be replaced by the '1020C, which reportedly is to be similar but cover 0.3-40 MHz.

Verdict: The MFJ-1020B, made in the United States, is uninspiring with its own telescopic antenna. However, the '1020B works very well when coupled to a short wire in lieu of the built-in telescopic antenna.

✪½

RF Systems DX-One Professional

Remote, broadband, outdoor-indoor, 0.02-54 MHz

Price: $599.95 in the United States. £295.00 in the United Kingdom. AUS$1,170.00 in Australia.

Pro: Outstanding dynamic range. Very low noise. Outputs for two receivers. Comes standard with switchable high-pass filter to reduce the chances of most mediumwave AM signals ghosting into the shortwave spectrum; it is effective below 1.4 MHz (*see* Con); manufacturer offers an optional brick wall filter to cut off the entire mediumwave AM band. Receiving element has outstanding build quality (*see* Con). Coaxial connector at head amplifier is completely shielded from the weather by a clever mechanical design. Superior low noise, high gain performance on mediumwave AM. Operates from either 120 or 230 VAC (*see* Con).

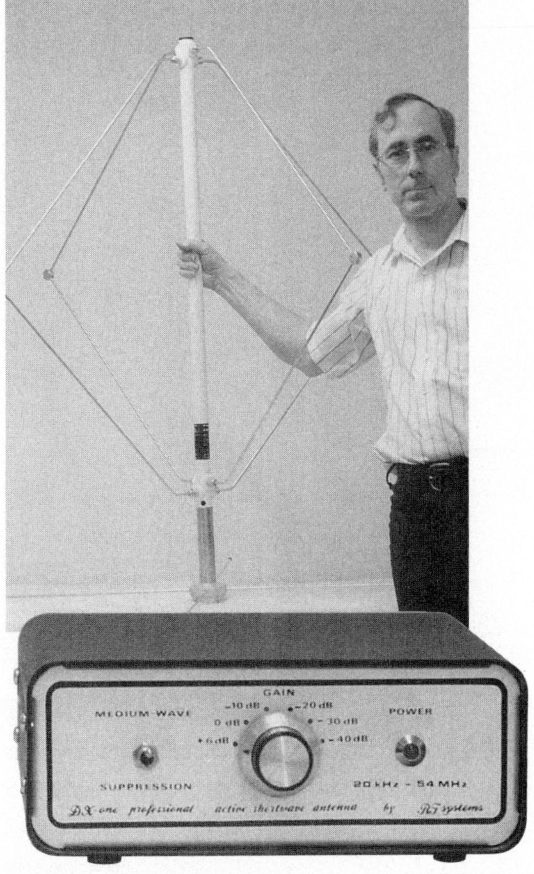
GAIN
MEDIUM-WAVE
-10 dB
-20 dB
0 dB
-30 dB
+6 dB
-40 dB
POWER
SUPPRESSION
20 kHz - 54 MHz
DX-one professional active shortwave antenna by RF systems

The RF Systems DX-One Professional sells well to certain professional surveillance organizations. However, try as we might we could not share their enthusiasm. Robert Sherwood (shown)

Con: Low gain. Control box build quality appears to be lacking. Amplifier appears to be susceptible to static damage, as on the first of our two units it failed; the manufacturer says it was not grounded properly, allowing static to blow the amp, but none of the other tested models suffered such a fate. Modest hum due to AC adaptor's not being thoroughly bypassed (*see* ☞). Supplied high-pass filter provides only limited rejection of 1.4-1.7 MHz mediumwave AM signals. No coaxial cable supplied. Control unit has a European-style plug on the 117 VAC American version; user-remediable by purchasing a travel adaptor plug (*see* ☞). AC voltage change requires disassembly of AC adaptor, followed by cutting and soldering; no instructions are supplied to explain how this should be done (*see* ☞). Warranty only six months.

☞ According to industry reports, this has been replaced by the $699.95 DX-One Professional Mk II.

☞ Star rating is for the Americas and Australasia only. In high-signal parts of the world, such as Europe, the Near East and North Africa, the DX-One Professional could

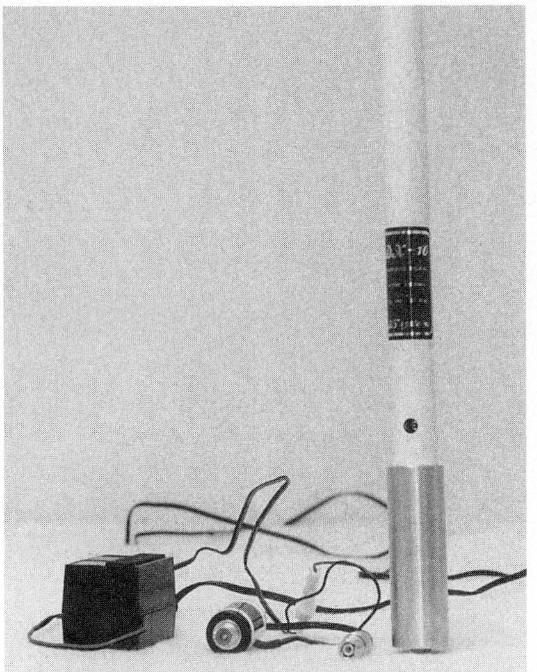

RF System's DX-10 falls flat with the supplied AC adaptor for North America and Japan. Assuming this will have been remedied by the time you read this, it should perform similarly to its costlier sibling.

Robert Sherwood

be a sensible choice, provided the receiving element is optimally erected, and the receiver possesses a superior noise floor, AGC threshold and recovered audio. This antenna should be especially attractive in an urban environment, where its high dynamic range reduces the chances of overloading caused by a potpourri of local signals.

Verdict: Clearly not in the running as a high-gain device for shortwave, although it does very nicely below that. If the receiving element can be mounted high, in the clear and outdoors, within suitable environments it should function acceptably as a very low-noise, low-gain shortwave antenna. Made in The Netherlands.

RF Systems DX-10

Remote, broadband, outdoor-indoor, 0.1-30 MHz

Price: $289.95 in the United States. £125.00 in the United Kingdom. AUS$490.00 in Australia.

Pro: Outstanding dynamic range. Very low noise. Very small, unobtrusive design. Well-constructed receiving element.

Con (all versions): Low gain within shortwave spectrum. Weather sealing mediocre on our unit. User must supply coaxial feed line. Warranty only six months.

Con (unique to North American version—see ☞): *Because of the supplied AC power supply, which lacks rectifier bypass capacitors, there are exceptional problems that would be avoided with a proper power supply:* Buzzes and spurious signals appear throughout the mediumwave AM spectrum, as well as on shortwave to about 4 MHz; lesser hum and buzzing appear throughout the remainder of the tuning range. AC adaptor provided for North America rated as 100 VAC input, rather than conventional 120 Volts. No substitute AC adaptor can be put into use without cutting the power cord.

☞ According to industry reports, this model has been replaced by the $239.95 DX-10 Pro.

Verdict: The noisy and permanently attached 100 VAC power supply for North America is awful, but the manufacturer may have taken steps to alleviate this in the recently introduced DX-10 Pro.

Prepared by Robert Sherwood, with George Heidelman, Chuck Rippel and David Zantow; also, Lawrence Magne.

WHERE TO FIND IT: INDEX TO RADIOS & ANTENNAS

PASSPORT REPORTS evaluates nearly every digitally tuned receiver and many antennas on the market. Here's where they are found, with those that are new, forthcoming, revised or retested in **bold**.

Comprehensive PASSPORT® Radio Database International White Papers® are available for the many popular premium receivers and outdoor antennas. Each RDI White Paper®—$6.95 in North America, $9.95 airmail elsewhere—contains virtually all our panel's findings and comments during hands-on testing, as well as laboratory measurements and what these mean to you. These unabridged reports are available from key world band dealers, or you can contact our 24-hour VISA/MC order channels (www.passband.com, autovoice +1 215/598-9018, fax +1 215/598 3794), or write us at PASSPORT RDI White Papers, Box 300, Penn's Park, PA 18943 USA.

📄 *Radio Database International White Paper®* available.

What's On Tonight?

PASSPORT's Hour-by-Hour Guide to World Band Shows

World band is the Gibraltar of news. It reaches out across borders without wires or gatekeepers, raw and unfiltered. Nothing else comes close, especially when the chips are down.

However, not everybody wants an earful of news. Some are interested in a few pleasant stations—entertainment from a favorite country, or inspiration from a religious ministry. That's where PASSPORT's "Worldwide Broadcasts in English" and "Voices from Home" fit in.

Others like to surf the airwaves, scouring the buzz. With the Blue Pages, they can figure out what they're hearing or what's causing interference.

PASSPORT's Picks

Yet, most of us simply want to know what's on, and when—that's what this section is about. So here are PASSPORT's Picks from all over, hour by hour. Most are enjoyable, but icons mark the best:

- ■ Station superior, most shows excellent
- ● Show worth hearing

Some stations provide schedules, others don't. Yet, even among those that do, data isn't always credible or complete. To resolve this, PASSPORT monitors stations around the world, firsthand, to detail schedule activity throughout the year.

PASSPORT's Picks. What's on, when—hour by hour.

Additionally, to be as useful as possible PASSPORT's schedules consist not just of observed activity, but also that which we have creatively opined will appear well into the year ahead. This predictive material is based on decades of experience, and is original from us. Although it is inherently less exact than real-time data, over the years it has been of solid value.

Primary frequencies are given for North America, Western Europe, East Asia and Australasia, plus the Middle East, Southern Africa and Southeast Asia. "Worldwide Broadcasts in English" and the Blue Pages also include secondary and seasonal channels, as well as frequencies for other parts of the world.

World Time and World Day are used—both covered in the "Compleat Idiot's Guide to Getting Started" and glossary. "Summer" and "winter" refer to seasons in the Northern Hemisphere.

Bathers converge on Prayag—the confluence of the Ganga, Yamuna and the mythical Saraswati—during the Mahakumbhmela. This happened on the most auspicious day of the millennium in the Hindu calendar. M. Guha

0000-0559
North America—Evening Prime Time
Europe & Mideast—Early Morning
Australasia & East Asia—Midday and Afternoon

00:00

■BBC World Service for the Americas. Tuesday through Saturday winter (weekday evenings in the Americas), opens with five minutes of *news*. Next comes the long-running *Outlook*, and the hour is rounded off with a 15-minute feature (very much a mixed bag). Sunday brings ●*Play of the Week* (world theater at its best), replaced Monday by *World Briefing*, ●*Sports Roundup* and *The World Today*. Summer, starts with five minutes of *news*, then Tuesday through Saturday there's *Meridian* (the arts). The second half hour is mostly popular music, except for 15 minutes of *Westway* (a soap) on Thursday and Saturday. Weekends, there's the final part of Sunday's ●*Play of the Week* (or *World Briefing* and ●*Sports Roundup*) followed by *Arts in Action*; replaced Monday by the same lineup as in winter. Continuous programming to North America and the Caribbean on 5975 kHz. Listeners in eastern North America can also try 12095 kHz, targeted at South America; a radio with synchronous selectable sideband helps reduce teletype interference.

■BBC World Service for East and Southeast Asia. Starts with 20 minutes of *World Briefing*, followed by ●*Sports Roundup*. Except for Sunday, ●*World Business Report/Review* can then be heard on the half-hour. The final 15-minute slot is taken by ●*Analysis* (Tuesday, Wednesday, Friday and Saturday), ●*From Our Own Correspondent* (Thursday) and ●*Letter from America* on Monday. The only 30-minute show is *Agenda* at 0030 Sunday. Audible in East Asia on 15280, 15360 and (till 0030) 17615 kHz; and in Southeast Asia on 3915 (to 0030), 6195, 7105 (to 0030) and 15360 kHz.

Radio Bulgaria. Winter only at this time. *News*, music and features. Tuesday through Saturday (weekday evenings in North America), the news is followed by *Events and Developments*, replaced Sunday by *Views Behind the News* and Monday by the delightfully exotic ●*Folk Studio*. The next slot consists of weekly features. Take your pick from *Plaza/Walks and Talks* (Monday), *Magazine Economy* (Tuesday), *Arts and Artists* (Wednesday), *History Club* (Thursday), *The Way We Live* (Friday), *DX Programed* (Saturday) and *Answering Your Letters*, a listener-response show, on Sunday. Tuesday through Sunday, the broadcast ends with *Keyword Bulgaria*. Sixty minutes to eastern North America and Central America on 7375 and 9400 kHz. One hour earlier in summer.

Radio Canada International. Winter only at this time. Tuesday through Saturday (weekday evenings in North America), it's the final hour of the CBC domestic service news program ●*As It Happens*, which features international stories, Canadian news and general human interest features. Weekends, you can hear two of Canada's best radio shows—Sunday's ●*Quirks and Quarks* (science) and Monday's ●*Global Village* (world music), both from the CBC's domestic output. To North America on 5960, 6175, 9590 and 9755 kHz. One hour earlier in summer. For a separate year-round broadcast to Asia, see the next item.

Radio Canada International. Tuesday through Saturday, it's ●*The World At Six*; and a shortened version of ●*As It Happens*, both news-oriented programs. These are replaced Sunday by ●*Quirks and Quarks* (a science show) and Monday by *Tapestry*. One hour to Southeast Asia on 11895 kHz, and also heard in much of East Asia, especially during summer.

Radio Japan. *News*, then Tuesday through Saturday (weekday evenings local American date) it's *Japan and World 44 Minutes* (an in-depth look at current trends and events in Japan and elsewhere). This is replaced Sunday by *Hello from Tokyo*, and Monday by *Weekend*

Square. One hour to eastern North America on 6145 kHz via the powerful relay facilities of Radio Canada International in Sackville, New Brunswick. A separate 15-minute news bulletin for Southeast Asia is aired on any two frequencies from 11815, 13650 and 17810 kHz.

Radio Exterior de España ("Spanish National Radio"). *News*, then Tuesday through Saturday (local weekday evenings in the Americas) it's *Panorama*, which features a recording of popular Spanish music, a commentary or a report, a review of the Spanish press, and weather. The remainder of the program is a mixture of literature, science, music and general programming. Tuesday (Monday evening in North America), there's *Sports Spotlight* and *Cultural Encounters*, replaced Wednesday by *People of Today* and *Entertainment in Spain*; Thursday brings *As Others See Us* and, biweekly, *The Natural World* or *Science Desk*; Friday has *Economic Report* and *Cultural Clippings*; and Saturday offers *Window on Spain* and *Review of the Arts*. The broadcast ends with a language course, *Spanish by Radio*, considered by many to be the best on the air. The Sunday lineup is *Hall of Fame* and *Gallery of Spanish Voices*, replaced Monday by *Window on Spain*, then a feature on Spanish music (well worth hearing) and *Radio Club*, a listener-response program. Sixty minutes to eastern North America winter on 6055 kHz, and summer on 6055 or 15385 kHz. Popular with many listeners.

Radio for Peace International, Costa Rica. Continues with a six-hour cyclical block of social-conscience and counterculture programming audible in Europe and the Americas on 15050 and (upper sideband) 21815 kHz.

Voice of Korea, North Korea. Strictly of curiosity value only, this broadcasting dinosaur is almost totally removed from reality. Terms like "Great Leader" and "Beloved Comrade" abound, as do reports on visits to iron factories and other state enterprises. An hour of old-style communist programming to North America on 11710, 13760 and 15180 kHz.

Radio Ukraine International. Summer only at this time. An hour's ample coverage of just about everything Ukrainian, including news, sports, politics and culture. Well worth a listen is ●*Music from Ukraine*, which fills most of the Monday (Sunday evening in the Americas) broadcast. Sixty minutes to Europe on 5905 kHz, to eastern North America on 13590 kHz, and to West Asia on 9640 kHz. One hour later in winter. Budget and technical limitations have reduced audibility of Radio Ukraine International to only a fraction of what it used to be.

Radio Australia. *World News*, then a feature. Monday's offering—unusual, to say the least—is *Awaye*, a program dealing with indigenous affairs. This is replaced Tuesday by *Science Show* and Wednesday by *The National Interest* (topical events). Thursday's *Background Briefing* (investigative journalism) and Friday's historical *Hindsight* complete the weekday lineup. *Feedback* (a listener-response show) and *Country Breakfast* fill the Saturday slots, and Sunday's feature is *The Europeans*. Targeted at Asia and the Pacific on 9660, 12080, 15240, 15415, 17580, 17750 (from 0030), 17775, 17795 and 21740 kHz. In North America (best during summer) try 17580, 17795 and 21740 kHz; and in East Asia go for 15240 kHz. For Southeast Asia there's 15415, 17750 and 17775 kHz.

Radio Prague, Czech Republic. Summer only at this time; see 0100 for specifics. Thirty minutes to eastern North America and the Caribbean on 7345 and 11615 kHz. One hour later in winter.

HCJB—Voice of the Andes, Ecuador. Tuesday through Saturday (weekday evenings in North America), you can hear *Insight for Living* and other religious features. This is replaced weekends by Sunday's *Nite Brite Kid's Club* and *Saludos Amigos,* and Monday's *Hour of Decision* and *Mountain Meditations*. To North America on 9745 and (winter) 11840 or (summer) 15115 kHz.

Voice of America. The first 60 minutes of a two-hour broadcast to the Caribbean and Latin America which is aired Tuesday through Saturday (weekday evenings in the Americas). *News Now*, a rolling news format covering political, business and other developments.

00:00–00:30

Radio Prague staff (from left): Bill Bathurst, Dita Asiedu, Pavla Navratilova, Daniela Lazarova, Vladimir Tax, Peter Smith, Olga Szantova, Rob Cameron, Nick Carey, Ita Dungan, and Alena Skodova.

J. Moravec

On 5995, 6130, 7405, 9455, 9775, 11695 and 13740 kHz. The final hour of a separate service to East and Southeast Asia and Australasia (see 2200) can be heard on 7215, 9770, 11760, 15185, 15290, 17735 and 17820 kHz.

Radio Thailand. *Newshour*. Thirty minutes to eastern and southern parts of Africa (who listens at this hour?), winter on 9680 kHz and summer on 9690 kHz. A full hour is available for Asia on 9655 and 11905 kHz, though these channels tend to operate intermittently.

All India Radio. The final 45 minutes of a much larger block of programming targeted at East and Southeast Asia, and heard well beyond. To East Asia on 9950 and 13605 kHz, and to Southeast Asia on 9705, 11620 and 13605 kHz.

Radio Cairo, Egypt. The final half hour of a 90-minute broadcast to eastern North America. *Arabic by Radio* can be heard on the hour, and there's a daily *news* bulletin at 0015. See 2300 for more specifics. Easy reception on 9900 kHz.

Radio New Zealand International. A friendly package of *news* and features sometimes replaced by live sports commentary. Part of a much longer broadcast for the South Pacific, but also heard in parts of North America (especially during summer) on 17675 kHz.

WJCR, Upton, Kentucky. Twenty-four hours of gospel music targeted at North America on 7490 and (at this hour) 13595 kHz. Also heard elsewhere, mainly during darkness hours. For more religious broadcasting at this hour, try **WYFR-Family Radio** on 6085 and 9505 kHz, and **KTBN** on (winter) 7510 or (summer) 15590 kHz. For something a little more controversial, tune to Dr. Gene Scott's University Network, via **WWCR** on 13845 kHz or **KAIJ** on 13815 kHz. Traditionalist Catholic programming can be heard via **WEWN** on 5825 and 9355 (or 13615) kHz.

AFRTS Shortwave, USA. Network news, live sports, music and features in the upper-sideband mode from the Armed Forces Radio & Television Service. Transmitted from modestly powered U.S. Navy stations around the globe. Try 4278.5, 4319, 4995, 5765, 6350, 6458.5, 10320, 10940.5, 12579, 12689.5 and 13362 kHz.

00:30

■**Radio Netherlands.** Opens with a feature, then Tuesday through Saturday (weekday evenings in North America) there's ●*Newsline* (current events). Take your pick from ●*EuroQuest* (Tuesday), ●*A Good Life* (Wednesday), *Dutch Horizons* (Thursday), ●*Research File* (Friday), and Saturday's award-winning ●*Documentary*. Sunday fare consists of ●*Roughly Speaking*, a news bulletin and *Europe Unzipped*; Monday, it's *Sound Fountain* followed by news and *Wide Angle*. The second of two hours to North America on 6165 and 9845 kHz.

Radio Vilnius, Lithuania. A half hour that's heavily geared to news and background reports about events in Lithuania. Of broader appeal is *Mailbag*, aired every other Sunday (Saturday evenings local American date). For a little Lithuanian music, try the next evening, towards the end of the broadcast. To eastern North America winter on 6120 (or 6155) kHz, and summer on 9855 kHz.

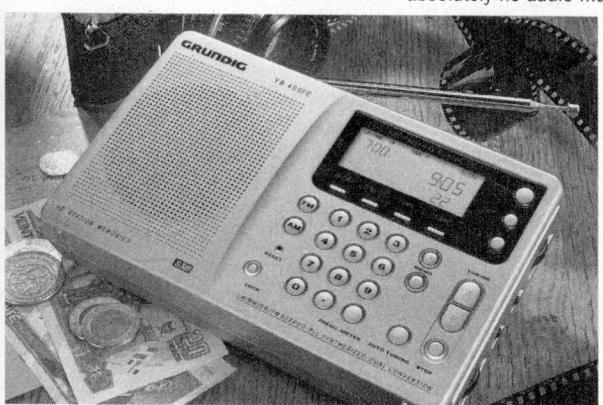

00:30–01:00

Voice of the Islamic Republic of Iran. A one-hour package of news, commentary and features with the accent strongly on Islam and Islamic culture. Reflects a way of life not found in western countries. One hour to eastern North America and Central America winter on 6065, 6135 and 9022 kHz, and summer on 9022, 9835 and 11970 kHz.

Radio Thailand. *Newshour*. Thirty minutes to central and eastern North America, winter on 13695 kHz and summer on 15395 kHz.

Radio Yugoslavia. Monday through Saturday (Sunday through Friday evenings local American date) and summer only at this time. Thirty minutes of news and short features to eastern North America on 11870 kHz. One hour later in winter.

01:00

■**BBC World Service for the Americas.** Tuesday through Saturday winter (weekday evenings in the Americas), five minutes of *news* are followed by *Meridian* (the arts). The second half hour is mostly popular music, except for 15 minutes of *Westway* (a soap) on Thursday and Saturday. The Sunday lineup is split between *The World Today*; ●*Reporting Religion* and ●*Letter from America*, replaced Monday by a full hour of *The World Today*. In summer, opens with five minutes of *news*, then it's some of the best of the BBC's output. The best double bill is undoubtedly Tuesday (Monday evening local American date), when ●*Health Matters* shares the stage with ●*Everywoman*. Also recommended are ● *Focus on Faith* (0130 Wednesday), *Sports International* and *Pick of the World* (Thursday), ●*One Planet* and *People and Places* (Friday), and *Discovery* (0105 Saturday). On Sunday, 30 minutes of *The World Today* are followed by ●*Reporting Religion* and the long-running ●*Letter from America*; Monday, there's five minutes of *news* and 55 minutes of *Wright Round the World*. Continuous programming to North America and the Caribbean on 5975 kHz, and to western North America and Central America on 9525 (winter) or (summer) 11835 kHz. In parts of eastern North America, 12095 kHz (nominally to South America) is also audible; a radio with synchronous selectable sideband helps reduce teletype interference.

■**BBC World Service for East and Southeast Asia.** Monday through Saturday, there's five minutes of *World News*, replaced Sunday by a half hour of *The World Today*. Tuesday through Saturday at 0105, look for *Outlook*, one of the BBC's longest running shows (though not as good as it used to be). Monday, this gives way to *Talking Point* (a call-in show). On weekdays, the final 15 minutes carry ●*Off the Shelf*, serialized readings from the best of world literature. At the same time Saturday you can hear *Write On* (a listener-response program), and the religious *In Praise of God* can be heard at 0130 Sunday. Continuous to East Asia on 15280 and 15360 kHz, and to Southeast Asia on 6195 and 15360 kHz.

Radio Canada International. Summer only at this time. *News*, followed Tuesday through Saturday (weekday evenings local American date) by *Canada Today*. The Sunday opener is *Canada Newsweek*, replaced Monday by a listener-response show, *The Mailbag*. On the half-hour, it's *Canada Review* both days. Sixty minutes to North, Central and South America on 5960, 9755, 13670, 13770, 15170 and 15305 kHz. One hour later in winter.

■**Deutsche Welle,** Germany. *News*, followed Tuesday through Saturday (weekday evenings in the Americas) by the comprehensive ●*NewsLink*—commentary, interviews, background reports and analysis. This is followed by ●*Insight* (analysis, Tuesday); ●*Man and Environment* (ecology, Wednesday); *Living in Germany* (Thursday), *Spotlight on Sport* (Friday), or Saturday's *German by Radio*. Sunday fare is *Talking Point* and ●*Inside Europe*, replaced Monday by *Religion and Society* and *Arts on the Air*. Forty-five minutes of very good reception in North America and the Caribbean, winter on 6040, 6145, 9640, 9700 and 9765 kHz; and summer on 6040, 9640, 11810 and 13720 kHz.

Radio Slovakia International. *Slovakia Today*, a 30-minute window on Slovakia and its culture. Tuesday (Monday evening in the

Americas) there's a variety of short features; the Wednesday focus is on tourism and Slovak personalities; Thursday's spotlight is on business and economy; and Friday there's a mix of politics, education and science. Saturday fare includes cultural features, *Slovak Kitchen* and the off-beat *Back Page News*; while Sunday brings the *"Best of"* series. Monday's menu is very much a mixed bag, and includes *Listeners' Tribune* and some enjoyable Slovak music. A friendly half hour to eastern North America and the Caribbean on 5930 and 6190 (or 7230) kHz, and to South America on 9440 kHz.

Radio Budapest, Hungary. Summer only at this time. *News* and features, most of which are broadcast on a non-regular basis. Thirty minutes to North America on 9560 kHz. One hour later in winter.

Radio Prague, Czech Republic. *News*, then Tuesday through Saturday (weekday evenings in the Americas), there's *Current Affairs* and a feature. Tuesday, it's either *Spotlight* (a look at Czech regional affairs) or *One on One* (an informal interview show); Wednesday, there's *Talking Point* (issues shaping the lives of people in the Czech Republic); and the Thursday show is either *Czechs in History* or *Central Europe Today*. *Economic Report* fills the Friday slot, and Saturday's feature is *Magazine* ("the show that starts where the news ends"). Weekends, following the news, the Sunday lineup consists of *Readings from Czech Literature* and an excellent musical feature (strongly recommended), and is replaced Monday by *A Letter from Prague*, *The Arts* and *Mailbag*. Thirty minutes to eastern and central North America and the Caribbean on 5915 (summer), 6200 (winter) and 7345 kHz.

Radio Exterior de España ("Spanish National Radio"). Repeat of the 0000 transmission. Sixty minutes to eastern North America winter on 6055 kHz, and summer on 6055 or 15385 kHz. One of the better broadcasts aired at this hour.

RAI International—Radio Roma, Italy. Actually starts at 0055. *News* and Italian music make up this 20-minute broadcast to North America on 6010 (winter), 9675 and 11800 kHz.

Radio Japan. *News*, then Tuesday through Saturday there's *Japan and World 44 Minutes* (an in-depth look at trends and events in Japan and beyond). This is replaced Sunday by *Pop Goes Asia*, and Monday by *Hello from Tokyo*. One hour to East Asia on 17845 kHz; to South Asia on 15325 kHz; to Southeast Asia on 11860 and 17810 kHz; to Australasia on 17685 kHz; to South America on 17835 kHz; and to the Mideast on 11870 (or 9700) and 11880 kHz. The broadcast on 17685 kHz may differ somewhat from the other transmissions, and may include alternative features.

Radio for Peace International, Costa Rica. Continues with a six-hour cyclical block of social-conscience and counterculture programming audible in Europe and the Americas on 15050 and (upper sideband) 21815 kHz.

China Radio International. Starts with *News*, and Tuesday through Saturday (Monday through Friday evenings in the Americas) is followed by special reports. The rest of the broadcast is devoted to features. Regulars include *People in the Know* (Tuesday), *Sportsworld* (Wednesday), *China Horizons* (Thursday), *Voices from Other Lands* (Friday), and *Life in China* on Saturday. Sunday's lineup includes *Global Review* and *Listeners' Garden* (has some interesting Chinese music) and the Monday menu offers *Report from Developing Countries* and *In the Spotlight*. One hour to North America on 9570 kHz, via CRI's Cuban relay.

Voice of Vietnam. A relay via the facilities of Radio Canada International. Begins with *news*, then there's *Commentary* or *Weekly Review*, followed by short features and some pleasant Vietnamese music (especially at weekends). Thirty minutes to eastern North America, with reception better to the south. Winter on 6175 kHz and summer on 9525 kHz. Repeated at 0230 on the same channels.

Voice of Russia World Service. Summer only at this hour, and the start of a four-hour block of programming for North America. *News*, then Tuesday through Saturday (weekday evenings in North America), there's *Commonwealth Update*, replaced Sunday by *News and Views*,

01:00–01:30

Huge curtain antennas at Biblis, Germany focus RFE-RL's signals for best reception in target countries.

A. Blechschmidt

and Monday by *Sunday Panorama* and *Russia: People and Events*. The second half-hour contains some interesting fare, with just about everyone's favorite being Tuesday's ●*Folk Box*. Other popular shows include Friday's ●*Music at Your Request* (may alternate with *Yours for the Asking* or ●*Music Around Us*), ●*Moscow Yesterday and Today* (Sunday), Wednesday's ●*Jazz Show*, and Friday's evocative ●*Christian Message from Moscow*. Where to tune? In eastern North America there's 9665, 9725 and 11825 kHz; farther west, use 12000 and 17595 kHz.

Radio Habana Cuba. The start of a two-hour cyclical broadcast to North America. Tuesday through Sunday (Monday through Saturday evenings in North America), the first half hour consists of international and Cuban *news* followed by *RHC's Viewpoint*. The next 30 minutes consist of a *news* bulletin and the sports-oriented *Time Out* (five minutes each) plus a feature: *Caribbean Outlook* (Tuesday and Friday), *DXers Unlimited* (Wednesday and Sunday), the *Mailbag Show* (Thursday) and *Weekly Review* (Saturday). Monday, the hour is split between *Weekly Review* and *Mailbag Show*. To eastern and central North America on 6000 and 9820 kHz. Also available to Europe on 11705 kHz upper sideband, though not all radios, unfortunately, can process such signals.

Voice of Korea, North Korea. Repeat of the 0000 broadcast; see there for specifics. An hour of old-style communist programming (albeit a little mellower than in the past). To North America and South East Asia on 11735, 15230 and 17735 kHz.

Radio Australia. Part of a 24-hour service to Asia and the Pacific, but which can also be heard at this time in parts of North America (better to the west). Begins with world *news*, then Tuesday through Saturday there's *Asia Pacific* (regional current events), replaced Sunday by *Correspondents' Report*. Weekdays on the half-hour, there's yet more reporting: *Health Report* (Monday), *Law Report* (Tuesday), *Religion Report* (Wednesday) and *Media Report* (Thursday). Friday brings some relief, with *Sports Factor*. Weekend fare consists of Saturday's *Arts Talk* and Sunday's musical *Oz Sounds*. Targeted at Asia and the Pacific on 9660, 12080, 15240, 15415, 17580, 17775 (till 0130), 17795 and 21725 kHz. In North America (best during summer) try 17580 and 17795 kHz; in East Asia go for 15240 and 21725 kHz; and best for Southeast Asia are 15415, 17750 and 17775 kHz. Some channels may carry a separate sports service on winter Saturdays.

Voice of Croatia. Summer only at this time, and actually starts three minutes into a predominantly Croatian broadcast. Approximately 15 minutes of news from and about Croatia. To eastern North America on 9925 kHz. One hour later in winter.

HCJB—Voice of the Andes, Ecuador. Tuesday through Saturday (weekday evenings in North America) it's *Studio 9*, featuring nine minutes of world and Latin American *news*, followed by 20 minutes of in-depth reporting on Latin America. The second half hour is given over to one of a variety of 30-minute features—including *Inside HCJB* (Tuesday), *Ham Radio Today* (Thursday), *Woman to Woman* (Friday), and the delightful ●*Música del Ecuador* on Saturday. On Sunday (Saturday evening in the Americas), the news is followed by *DX Partyline*, and Monday by *Musical Mailbag*. Continuous programming to North America on 9745 and (winter) 11840 or (summer) 15115 kHz.

Voice of America. The second and final hour of a two-hour broadcast to the Caribbean and Latin America which is aired Tuesday through Saturday (weekday evenings in the Americas). *News Now*, a rolling news format covering political, business and other developments. On the half-hour, a program in "Special" (slow-speed) English is carried on 7405, 9775 and 13740 kHz; with mainstream programming continuing on 5995, 6130 and 9455 kHz.

Radio Ukraine International. Winter only at this time; see 0000 for program details. Sixty minutes of informative programming targeted at Europe, eastern North America and West Asia. Poor reception in most areas due to limited transmitter availability. Try 6020, 9560 and 9610 kHz. One hour earlier in summer.

Radio New Zealand International. A package of *news* and features sometimes replaced by live sports commentary. Part of a much longer broadcast for the South Pacific, but also heard in parts of North America (especially during summer) on 17675 kHz.

Radio Tashkent, Uzbekistan. *News* and features with a strong Uzbek flavor; some exotic music, too. A half hour to West and South Asia and the Mideast, occasionally heard in North America; winter on 5040, 5955, 5975, 7205 and 9540 kHz; and summer on 7190, 9375, 9530 and 9715 kHz.

WJCR, Upton, Kentucky. Continues with country gospel music for North American listeners on 7490 and 13595 kHz. Also with religious programs to North America at this hour are **WYFR-Family Radio** on 6065 and 9505 kHz, **WWCR** on 13845 kHz and **KTBN** on 7510 kHz. For traditionalist Catholic programming, tune to **WEWN** on 5825 and 9355 (or 13615) kHz.

AFRTS Shortwave, USA. Network news, live sports, music and features in the upper-sideband mode from the Armed Forces Radio & Television Service. Transmitted from modestly powered U.S. Navy stations around the globe. Try 4278.5, 4319, 4995, 5765, 6350, 6458.5, 10320, 10940.5, 12579, 12689.5 and 13362 kHz.

01:30

Radio Austria International. Summer only at this time. ●*Report from Austria*, which includes a brief bulletin of *news* followed by a series of current events and human interest stories. Tends to spotlight national and regional issues, and is an excellent source of news about Central Europe. Thirty minutes to eastern North America on 9870 kHz. One hour later in winter.

Radio Sweden. Tuesday through Saturday, it's *news* and features in *Sixty Degrees North*, concentrating heavily on Scandinavian topics. Several of the features rotate from week to week, but a few are fixtures. Tuesday's *SportScan* is replaced Wednesday by *Close Up* or an alternative feature, and Thursday by *Money Matters*. Friday's carousel is *Nordic Report*, *GreenScan* (the environment), *Heart Beat* (health), and *S-Files*, with *Weekly Review* filling the Saturday slot. The Sunday rotation is *Weekend*, *Spectrum*, *Sweden Today* and *Studio 49*, while Monday's offering is *In Touch with Stockholm* (a listener-response program) or the musical *Sounds Nordic*. Thirty minutes to South Asia and beyond, winter on 9495 kHz and summer on 13625 kHz.

Radio Yugoslavia. Monday through Saturday (Sunday through Friday evenings local American date) and winter only at this time. Thirty minutes of news and short features to eastern North America on 7115 kHz. One hour earlier in summer.

01:45

Radio Tirana, Albania. Summer only at this time. Approximately 15 minutes of *news* and commentary from this small Balkan country. To North America on 6115 and 7160 kHz. One hour later in winter.

02:00

■BBC World Service for the Americas. Tuesday through Saturday winter (weekday evenings in the Americas), starts with five minutes of *news*, then it's some of the best of the BBC's output. Pick of an excellent litter are ●*Health Matters* and ●*Everywoman* (Tuesday), ● *Focus on Faith* (0130 Wednesday), *Sports International* and *Pick of the World* (Thursday), ●*One Planet* and *People and Places* (Friday), and *Discovery* (science, 0105 Saturday). On Sunday, 30 minutes of *The World Today* are followed by ●*Reporting Religion* and the long-running ●*Letter from America*; Monday, there's five minutes of *news*, with *Wright Round the World* occupying the remainder of the hour. Summer, it's 30 minutes of ●*The World Today*, then Tuesday through Saturday there's a quarter hour of ●*World Business Report* followed most days by ●*Analysis* (current events). The exception is Thursday's ●*From Our Own Correspondent* (another edition airs at 0230 Sunday). The second Monday slot goes to an extra half hour of *The World Today*. Continuous programming to North America and the Caribbean on 5975 kHz, and to western North America and Central America on 9525 (winter) or (summer) 11835 kHz. In parts of eastern North America, 12095 kHz (nominally to South America) is also audible; a radio with synchronous selectable sideband helps reduce teletype interference.

■BBC World Service for the Mideast. Summer only at this time. News and current events in *The World Today*. One hour weekdays but reduced to 30 minutes at weekends, when Saturday's *Global Business* and Sunday's ●*From Our Own Correspondent* complete the hour. On 9410 and 11760 kHz.

■BBC World Service for East Asia. Weekdays, the first half hour consists of *News* and an arts show, *Meridian*. In a brutal switch from highbrow to lowbrow, the next 30 minutes are a mixed bag of popular music and *Westway*, a soap. Weekends there's 30 minutes of *The World Today*, with Saturday's *Global Business* or Sunday's ●*From Our Own Correspondent* completing the hour. Continuous to East Asia on 15280 and 15360 kHz, and to Southeast Asia on 15360 kHz.

Radio Cairo, Egypt. Repeat of the 2300 broadcast, and the first hour of a 90-minute potpourri of *news* and features about Egypt and the Arab world. Fair reception, but often mediocre audio quality. To North America on 9475 kHz.

Radio Argentina al Exterior—R.A.E. Tuesday through Saturday only. *News* and short features spotlighting Argentina and its people. One of only a handful of stations which still give prominence to music from the provinces, and well worth a listen. Tangos, too, for listeners who like nostalgia. Fifty-five minutes to North America on 11710 kHz. Sometimes pre-empted by live soccer commentary in Spanish.

Radio Budapest, Hungary. Winter only at this time. *News* and features, most of which are broadcast on a non-regular basis. Thirty minutes to North America on 9835 kHz. One hour earlier in summer.

Wales Radio International. This time summer Saturdays (Friday evenings American date) only. News, views and music from the land of "Sospan Fach." Thirty minutes to North America on 9795 kHz, and one hour later in winter.

Radio Canada International. *News*, followed Tuesday through Saturday (weekday evenings local American date) by *Canada Today*. On the remaining days, opens Sunday with *Canada Newsweek*, and Monday with *The Mailbag* (a listener-response show). On the half-hour, it's *Canada Review* both days. One hour winter to North America on 6040, 9755 and 11990 kHz; and year round to South Asia on 15150 (winter), 15260 (summer) and 17860 kHz.

■Deutsche Welle, Germany. *News*, then Tuesday through Saturday there's the excel-

lent ●*NewsLink*—commentary, interviews, background reports and analysis. The final part of the broadcast consists of a feature. Choose from ●*Insight* (analysis, Tuesday); ●*Man and Environment* (ecology, Wednesday); *Living in Germany* (Thursday); *Spotlight on Sport* (Friday); and Saturday's *German by Radio*. The Sunday offerings are *Weekend Review* and *Mailbag*, replaced Monday by *Weekend Review* (second part) and ●*Marks and Markets*. Forty-five minutes nominally targeted at South Asia, but widely heard elsewhere. Winter on 7285, 9615, 9765 and 11965 kHz; and summer on 11965, 13720 and 15370 kHz.

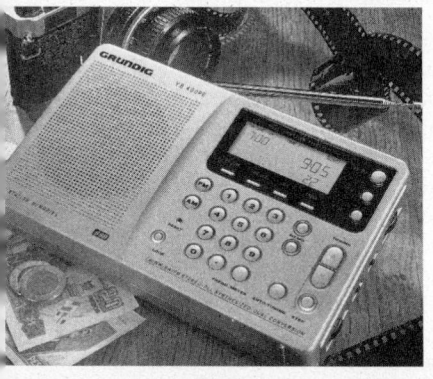

KNLS' inspirational programming emanates from the backwoods of Anchor Point, Alaska. KNLS

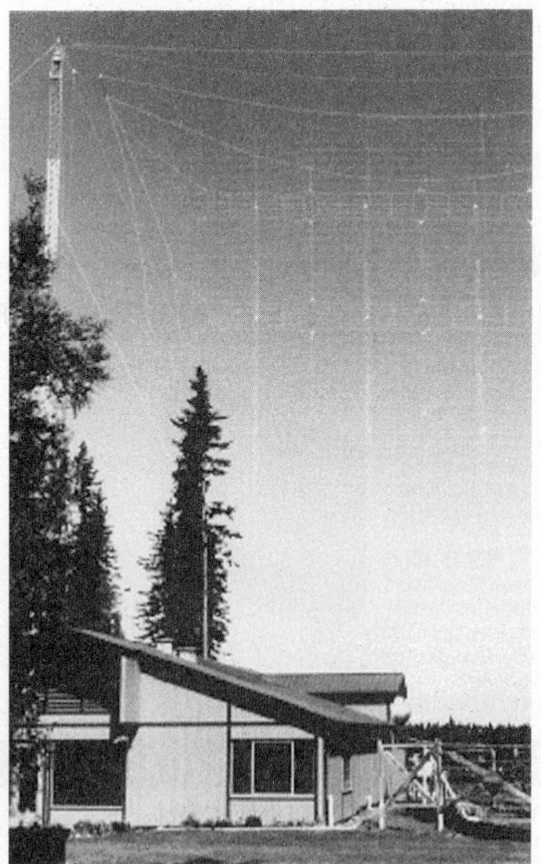

Radio Bulgaria. Summer only at this time. Starts with *news*, then Tuesday through Saturday (weekday evenings in North America) there's *Events and Developments*, replaced Sunday by *Views Behind the News* and Monday by 15 minutes of Bulgarian exotica in ●*Folk Studio*. Additional features include *Answering Your Letters* (a listener-response show, Monday), *Plaza/Walks and Talks* (Tuesday), *Magazine Economy* (Wednesday). *Arts and Artists* (Thursday), *History Club* (Friday), *The Way We Live* (Saturday) and *DX Programed*, a Sunday show for radio enthusiasts. Wednesday through Monday, the broadcast ends with *Keyword Bulgaria*. Sixty minutes to eastern North America and Central America on 9400 and 11700 kHz. One hour later in winter.

Radio Prague, Czech Republic. Winter only at this time. Repeat of the 0100 broadcast; see there for specifics. A half hour to North America on 6200 and 7345 kHz.

HCJB—Voice of the Andes, Ecuador. A mixed bag of religious programming, depending on the day of the week. Continuous to North America on 9745 and (winter) 11840 or (summer) 15115 kHz.

Voice of Croatia. Winter only at this time, and actually starts around 0203. Approximately six minutes of news from and about Croatia. To eastern North America on 7280 (or 9925) kHz. One hour earlier in summer.

Radio Taipei International, Taiwan. Opens with 15 minutes of *News*, and with the exception of Sunday, closes with *Let's Learn Chinese*, which has a series of segments for beginning, intermediate and advanced learners. In between, there are either one or two features, depending on which day it is. Monday (Sunday evening in North America) there's the pleasurable and exotic ●*Jade Bells and Bamboo Pipes* (Taiwanese music); Tuesday's combo is *Culture Express* and *Trends*; Wednesday's slots are *Taiwan Today* and the esoterically titled *Confucius and Inspiration Beyond*; Thursday's double bill is *Journey into Chinese Culture* and *Instant Noodles*; and Friday's coupling brings together *Taipei Magazine* and *East Meets West*. These are replaced Saturday by *Kaleidoscope* and *Naluwan*, and Sunday by *Great Wall Forum* and *Mailbag Time*. One hour to North and Central America on 5950, 9680 and 11740 kHz; East Asia on 15345 kHz; and Southeast Asia on 15320 kHz.

Voice of Russia World Service. Winter, the start of a four-hour block of programming to North America; summer, it's the beginning of the second hour. *News*, features and music to suit all tastes. Winter fare includes *Commonwealth Update* (0211 Tuesday through Saturday), replaced Sunday by *News and Views* and Monday by *Sunday Panorama*. The second half hour includes ●*Folk Box* (Tuesday), ●*Jazz Show* (Wednesday),●*Music at Your Request* or ●*Music Around Us* (Friday), ●*Christian Message from Moscow* (Saturday), ●*Moscow Yesterday and Today* (Sunday) and *Timelines* (Monday). In summer, take your pick from *Moscow Mailbag* (0211 Sunday, Monday and Thursday), *Newmarket* (business, same time Wednesday and Saturday), and *Science and Engineering* (0211 Tuesday and Friday). There's a news summary on the half-hour, then ●*Audio Book Club* (Saturday), *Songs from Russia* (Sunday), *This is Russia* (Monday), *Kaleidoscope* (Tuesday), *Musical Portraits from the Twentieth Century* and *Russia: People and Events* (Wednesday), ●*Moscow Yesterday and Today* (Thursday) or Friday's *Russian by Radio*. Note that these days are World Time; locally in North America it will be the previous evening. For eastern North America winter, tune to 7180 and 9765 kHz; summer, it's 9665 and 9725 kHz. Listeners in western states should go for 12020, 13665 and 15470 kHz in winter; and 12000 and 17595 kHz in summer.

Radio Habana Cuba. The second half of a two-hour broadcast to eastern and central North America. Tuesday through Sunday (Monday through Saturday evenings in North America), opens with 10 minutes of international *news*. Next comes *Spotlight on the Americas* (Tuesday through Saturday) or Sunday's *The World of Stamps*. The final 30 minutes consists of news-oriented programming. The Monday slots are *From Havana* and ●*The Jazz Place* or *Breakthrough* (science). On 6000 and 9820 kHz. Also available to Europe on 11705 kHz upper sideband.

Radio Australia. Continuous programming to Asia and the Pacific, but well heard in parts of North America (especially to the west). Begins with *World News*, then Monday through Friday it's *The World Today* (comprehensive coverage of world events). Weekends, there's Saturday's *Background Briefing* and *Earthbeat, replaced* Sunday by *Margaret Throsby* (interviews and music). Targeted at Asia and the Pacific on 9660, 12080, 15240, 15415, 15515, 17580, 17750 and 21725 kHz. Best heard in North America (especially during summer) on 15515 and 17580 kHz; in East Asia on 15240 and 21715 kHz; and in Southeast Asia on 15415 and 17750 kHz. Some of these channels carry a separate sports service on summer (midyear) weekends and winter Saturdays.

Radio for Peace International, Costa Rica. Continues with a six-hour cyclical block of social-conscience and counterculture programming audible in Europe and the Americas on 7445 (upper sideband) and 15050 kHz.

Radio Korea International, South Korea. Opens with *news* and commentary, followed Tuesday through Thursday (Monday through Wednesday evenings in the Americas) by *Seoul Calling*. Weekly features include *Echoes of Korean Music* and *Shortwave Feedback* (Monday), *Tales from Korea's Past* (Tuesday), *Korean Cultural Trails* (Wednesday), *Pulse of Korea* (Thursday), *From Us to You* (a listener-response program) and *Let's Learn Korean* (Friday), *Let's Sing Together* and *Korea Through Foreigners' Eyes* (Saturday), and Sunday's *Discovering Korea*, *Korean Literary Corner* and *Weekly News*. Sixty minutes to the Americas on 11725, 11810 and 15575 kHz; and to East Asia on 7275 kHz.

Voice of Korea, North Korea. Repeat of the 0000 broadcast; see there for specifics. Abominably bad programs, but improvement may be on the way now that the country is beginning to accept outside help. In the meantime, it's one hour of old-fashioned communist programming to North America and South East Asia on 11845 and 13650 kHz.

Radio Romania International. *News*, commentary, press review and features on

02:00–03:00

Taliban military commander battles against rebel forces. Afghanistan's opposition, reported on firsthand in PASSPORT 2000, received no backing from the West until after the World Trade Center attack. M. Guha

Romania. Regular spots include Wednesday's *Youth Club* (Tuesday evening, local American date), Thursday's *Romanian Musicians*, and Friday's *Listeners Letterbox* and ●*Skylark* (Romanian folk music). Fifty-five minutes to North America on 9570, 11830 (winter) and (summer) 11940 kHz; to East Asia winter on 9690 and 11740 kHz, and summer on 11885 and 15105 kHz; and to Australasia winter on 9510 and 11940 kHz, and summer on 15380 and 17790 kHz.

Voice of Greece. Actually starts around 0202 Approximately seven minutes of English *news* in a predominantly Greek broadcast. To North America winter on 7450, 9375 and 9420 kHz; and summer on 9420, 12110 and 15630 kHz.

WJCR, Upton, Kentucky. Continues with country gospel music for North American listeners on 7490 kHz. Also with religious broadcasts to North America at this hour are **WYFR-Family Radio** on 6065 and 9505 kHz, **WWCR** on 5935 kHz, **KAIJ** on 5755 kHz, and **KTBN** on 7510 kHz. Traditionalist Catholic programming can be heard via **WEWN** on 5825 kHz.

AFRTS Shortwave, USA. Network news, live sports, music and features in the upper-sideband mode from the Armed Forces Radio & Television Service. Transmitted from modestly powered U.S. Navy stations around the globe. Try 4278.5, 4319, 4995, 5765, 6350, 6458.5, 10320, 10940.5, 12579, 12689.5 and 13362 kHz.

02:30

Kol Israel. Summer only at this time. A thirty-minute "temporary" relay from Israel Radio's domestic network, aired over WRMI-Radio Miami International. Commenced in September 2001 for a "limited," but indefinite, period. To North America and Caribbean basin on 7385 kHz. One hour later in winter.

Radio Austria International. Winter only at this time. ●*Report from Austria*, a popular compilation of news, current events and human interest stories. Good coverage of national and regional issues. Thirty minutes to eastern North America on 7325 kHz. One hour earlier in summer.

Radio Sweden. Tuesday through Saturday (weekday evenings in North America), it's *news* and features in *Sixty Degrees North*, with the accent heavily on Scandinavian topics. See 0330 for full program specifics. Sunday, there's *Spectrum* (the arts), *Weekend*, *Sweden Today* or *Studio 49*. A listener-response program, *In Touch with Stockholm*, is aired on the first Monday of each month, and replaced by *Sounds Nordic* on the remaining weeks. Thirty minutes to North America on 9495 kHz.

Radio Tirana, Albania. Summer only at this time. Thirty minutes of Balkan news and music to North America on 6115 and 7160 kHz. One hour later during winter.

Radio Budapest, Hungary. Summer only at this time. *News* and features, not many of which are broadcast on a regular basis. Thirty minutes to North America on 9570 kHz. One hour later in winter.

Radio Yugoslavia. Winter only at this time. Thirty minutes of news and short features to western North America on 7115 kHz. Two hours later in summer.

Voice of Vietnam. Repeat of the 0100 broadcast; see there for specifics. A relay to eastern North America via the facilities of

Radio Canada International, winter on 6175 kHz and summer on 9525 kHz. Reception is better to the south.

02:45

Radio Tirana, Albania. Winter only at this time. Approximately 15 minutes of *news* and commentary from one of Europe's least known countries. To North America on 6115 and 7160 kHz. One hour earlier in summer.

Vatican Radio. Actually starts at 0250. Concentrates heavily, but not exclusively, on issues affecting Catholics around the world. Twenty minutes to eastern North America on 7305 and 9605 kHz.

03:00

■BBC World Service for the Americas. Winter, there's some newsy but interesting fare, with *World Briefing* and ●*Sports Roundup* filling the first half hour. These are followed Tuesday through Saturday (weekday evenings local American date) by 15 minutes of ●*World Business Report* and (most days) ●*Analysis* (current events). The exception is Thursday's ●*From Our Own Correspondent*. On the remaining days, it's either Sunday's *Science in Action* or a Monday documentary. Tuesday through Saturday summer, there's five minutes of *news*, then a 25-minute feature. Best is Tuesday's light entertainment show, with a variety of music programs on the remaining days. There's another feature at 0330, and ●*Off the Shelf* (readings from the best of world literature) completes the hour. *World Briefing* and ●*Sports Roundup* fill the first 30 minutes on Sunday and Monday, and are followed by *Science in Action* and *Westway* (a soap), respectively. Continuous programming to North America and the Caribbean on 5975 kHz, and to western North America and Central America on 9525 (winter) or (summer) 11835 kHz.

■BBC World Service for Eastern Europe and the Mideast. Starts with *World Briefing* and ●*Sports Roundup*, then Monday through Saturday there's top-notch financial reporting in ●*World Business Report/Review*. The final 15-minute slot goes to ●*Analysis* (Tuesday, Wednesday, Friday and Saturday), *Write On* or *Waveguide* (Monday), and ●*From Our Own Correspondent* on Thursday. A full half hour of ●*Science in Action* airs at 0330 Sunday. To Eastern Europe on 6195 and (summer) 9410 kHz, and to the Mideast on 9410, 11760 and 11955 kHz.

■BBC World Service for Southern Africa. Same as the service for the Mideast until 0330, then Monday through Friday it's *Network Africa*, a fast-moving breakfast show. This is replaced Saturday by *African Quiz* or *This Week and Africa*, and Sunday by *Postmark Africa*. The first 60 minutes of a 19-hour block of programming. On 3255, 6005, 6190 and 7125 kHz.

■BBC World Service for East and Southeast Asia. Monday through Saturday, starts with five minutes of *news*. Best of the weekday features which follow are ●*One Planet* and *People and Places* (Monday), *Discovery* and *Essential Guide* (Tuesday), Wednesday's excellent combo of ●*Health Matters* and ●*Everywoman*, Thursday's ●*Focus on Faith* (0330) and Friday's *Sports International* and *Pick of the World*. On Saturday, the news is followed by 55 minutes of *Wright Round the World*. The Sunday lineup consists of *World Briefing*, ●*Sports Roundup* and *Science in Action*. Audible in East Asia on 15280, 15360 (to 0330), 17760 and 21660 kHz. For Southeast Asia there's only 15360 kHz until 0330.

Voice of Croatia. Summer only at this time, and actually starts several minutes into a predominantly Croatian broadcast. Approximately six minutes of news from and about Croatia. To western North America on 9925 kHz. One hour later in winter.

Wales Radio International. This time winter Saturdays (Friday evenings American date) only. News, interviews and music from the land of the druids. Worth a listen for the occasional song from renowned Welsh choirs. Thirty minutes to North America on 9735 kHz, and one hour earlier in summer.

Radio Taipei International, Taiwan. Opens with 15 minutes of *News*, and closes Monday through Wednesday with *Let's Learn Chinese*. The remaining airtime is taken up by features. Monday (Sunday evening in North America) there's *Taiwan Economic Journal* followed by *People*; Tuesday's pairing is *Culture Express* and *Trends*; Wednesday's single feature is *New Music Lounge*; Thursday's offerings are the delightfully named *Instant Noodles*, *Life Unusual* and *Naluwan*; and Friday's lineup consists of *Weekend Zoo* and *Business Chinese*. The Saturday slots are filled by *Kaleidoscope* and *Mailbag Time*, with *Great Wall Forum* and *Asia Pacific* making up the Sunday menu. One hour to North and Central America on 5950 and 9680 kHz, and to Southeast Asia on 11875 and 15320 kHz.

China Radio International. Starts with *News*, then Tuesday through Saturday (weekday evenings in the Americas) there's in-depth reporting. The rest of the broadcast is devoted to features. Regular shows include *People in the Know* (Tuesday), *Sportsworld* (Wednesday), *China Horizons* (Thursday), *Voices from Other Lands* (Friday), and *Life in China* on Saturday. Sunday's lineup includes *Global Review* and *Listeners' Garden* (reports, music and Chinese language lessons), while Monday's broadcast has *Report from Developing Countries* and *In the Spotlight*. One hour to North America on 9690 kHz.

■**Deutsche Welle,** Germany. *News*, then Tuesday through Saturday (weekday evenings in North America) it's ●*NewsLink*—an impressive package of commentary, interviews, background reports and analysis. The final slot is a feature:●*Insight* (Tuesday), ●*Man and Environment* (Wednesday), *Living in Germany* (Thursday), *Spotlight on Sport* (Friday) and *German by Radio* on Saturday. The Sunday offerings are *Weekend Review* and ●*Spectrum* (science); while Monday brings *Weekend Review* (second part) and *Arts on the Air*. Forty-five minutes to North America and the Caribbean, winter on 6020, 6045, 9640, 9700 and 11985 kHz; and summer on 9535, 9640, 13780 and 15105 kHz.

Radio Ukraine International. Summer only at this time, and a repeat of the 0000 broadcast See there for specifics). Sixty minutes to Europe and the Mideast on 6020 kHz, to North America on 13590 kHz, and to West Asia on 9640 kHz. One hour later in winter. Generally poor reception due to budget and technical limitations.

Voice of America. Three and a half hours (four at weekends) of continuous programming aimed at an African audience. Monday through Friday, there's the informative and entertaining ●*Daybreak Africa*, with the remaining airtime taken up by *News Now*—a mixed bag of sports, science, business and other news and features. Although beamed to Africa, this service is widely heard elsewhere, including parts of the United States. Try 6035 (winter), 6080, 6115 (summer), 7105, 7275 (summer), 7290, 7415 (winter), 9575 (winter) and 9885 kHz.

Voice of Russia World Service. Continuous programming to North America at this hour. *News*, then winter it's a listener-response program, *Moscow Mailbag* (Monday, Thursday and Sunday), the business-oriented *Newmarket* (Wednesday and Saturday), or *Science and Engineering* (Tuesday and Friday). At 0331, there's ●*Audio Book Club* (Saturday), *This is Russia* (Monday), *Kaleidoscope* (Tuesday), *Musical Portraits from the Twentieth Century* and *Russia: People and Events* (Wednesday), ●*Moscow Yesterday and Today* (Thursday), *Russian by Radio* (Friday) and *Songs from Russia* on Sunday. Note that these days are World Time, so locally in North America it will be the previous evening. In summer, look for *News and Views* at 0311 Tuesday through Sunday, replaced Monday by *Sunday Panorama* and *Russia: People and Events*. After a brief news summary on the half-hour, there's Sunday's *Kaleidoscope*, Monday's ●*Audio Book Club*, and a changing roster of features on the remaining days. In eastern North America, use 7180 kHz in winter, and 9665 and 11750 kHz in summer. In western North America, the situation is a little better—for winter, try 12020, 13665 and 15470 kHz; in summer, take your pick from 12000, 17565, 17650, 17660 and 17690 kHz.

XERMX—Radio México Internacional. Summer only at this time. Tuesday through Saturday (weekday evenings in North America) there's an English summary of the

Spanish-language *Antena Radio*, replaced Sunday by *Mailbox*, a listener-response show. Monday's programming is in Spanish. Thirty minutes to North America on 9705 and 11770 kHz. One hour later in winter.

Radio Australia. *World News*, then Monday through Friday there's *Regional Sports*, *Pacific Focus* and a 20-minute music feature—*Oz Music Show* (Monday), *Music Deli* (music from different cultures, Tuesday), *Blacktracker* (indigenous music and stories, Wednesday), *Australian Country Style* (Thursday), and *Jazz Notes* (Friday). Saturday, the out-of-town *Rural Reporter* is paired with *In the Pipeline*, and Sunday's *Feedback* (a listener-response show) is followed by some cutting scientific commentary in ●*Ockham's Razor*. Continuous to Asia and the Pacific on 9660, 12080, 15240, 15415, 15515, 17580, 17750 and 21725 kHz. Also heard in North America (best in summer) on 15515 and 17580 kHz. In East Asia, tune to 15240 or 21725 kHz; for Southeast Asia, there's 15415 and 17750 kHz. Some of these channels carry a separate sports service at weekends.

Radio Habana Cuba. Repeat of the 0100 broadcast. To eastern and central North America on 6000 and 9820 kHz, and also available to Europe on 11705 kHz upper sideband.

Radio Thailand. *News Magazine*. Thirty minutes to western North America winter on 15460 kHz, and summer on 15395 kHz. Also available to Asia on 9655 and 11905 kHz, although operation on these channels tends to be somewhat irregular.

HCJB—Voice of the Andes, Ecuador. Predominantly religious programming at this hour. Try *Radio Reading Room* at 0330 Monday (local Sunday evening in North America). Continuous to the United States and Canada on 9745 and (winter) 11840 or (summer) 15115 kHz.

Radio Prague, Czech Republic. Summer only at this time. Repeat of the 0000 and 0100 broadcasts; see 0100 for specifics. A half hour to North America on 7345 and 9870 kHz. This is by far the best opportunity for listeners in western states. One hour later in winter.

Radio Cairo, Egypt. The final half-hour of a 90-minute broadcast to North America on 9475 kHz.

Radio Bulgaria. Winter only at this time; see 0200 for specifics. A distinctly Bulgarian potpourri of news, commentary, interviews and features, plus a fair amount of music. Not to be missed is the musical ●*Folk Studio* at 0310 Monday (Sunday evening local American date). Sixty minutes to eastern North America and Central America on 7375 and 9400 kHz. One hour earlier in summer.

Radio Japan. *News*, then weekdays there's *Asian Top News*. This is followed by a 35-minute feature. Choose between Monday's *Unforgettable Musical Masterpieces* (postwar popular songs with brief historical items of the period), Japanese language lessons (Tuesday and Thursday), *Japan Music Log* (Wednesday), and *Music Beat* (Japanese popular music, Friday). *Weekend Square* fills the Saturday slot, and *Hello from Tokyo* is aired Sunday. Sixty minutes to Australasia on 21610 kHz, and to Central America on 17825 kHz.

Radio New Zealand International. A friendly broadcasting package targeted at a regional audience. Part of a much longer transmission for the South Pacific, but also heard in parts of North America (especially during summer) on 17675 kHz. Often carries commentaries of local sporting events.

Voice of Turkey. Summer only at this time. *News*, followed by *Review of the Turkish Press* and features (some of them unusual) with a strong local flavor. Selections of Turkish popular and classical music complete the program. Fifty minutes to eastern North America on 11655 kHz, to the Mideast on 6155 kHz, and to Southeast Asia and Australasia on 21715 kHz. One hour later during winter.

WJCR, Upton, Kentucky. Continues with country gospel music for North American listeners on 7490 kHz. Also with religious programs to North America at this hour are **WYFR-Family Radio** on 6065 and 9505 kHz, **WWCR** on 5935 kHz, **KAIJ** on 5755 kHz and **KTBN** on 7510 kHz. For traditionalist Catholic fare, try **WEWN** on 5825 kHz.

03:00–04:00

Radio for Peace International, Costa Rica. Continues with a variety of counterculture and social-conscience features. Audible in Europe and the Americas on 7445 (upper sideband) and 15050 kHz.

AFRTS Shortwave, USA. Network news, live sports, music and features in the upper-sideband mode from the Armed Forces Radio & Television Service. Transmitted from modestly powered U.S. Navy stations around the globe. Try 4278.5, 4319, 4995, 5765, 6350, 6458.5, 10320, 10940.5, 12579, 12689.5 and 13362 kHz.

03:30

Kol Israel. Winter only at this time. A thirty-minute "temporary" relay from Israel Radio's domestic network, aired over WRMI-Radio Miami International. Commenced in September 2001 for a "limited," but indefinite, period. To North America and Caribbean basin on 7385 kHz. One hour earlier in summer.

United Arab Emirates Radio, Dubai. *News*, then a feature devoted to Arab and Islamic history or culture. Twenty minutes to North America on 12005, 13675 and 15400 kHz; heard best during the warm-weather months.

Radio Sweden. Tuesday through Saturday (weekday evenings local American date), it's *news* and features in *Sixty Degrees North*, concentrating heavily on Scandinavian topics. Several of the features rotate from week to week, but a few are fixtures. Tuesday's *SportScan* is replaced Wednesday by *Close Up* or an alternative feature, and Thursday by *Money Matters*. Friday's roundabout is *Nordic Report*, *GreenScan* (the environment), *Heart Beat* (health), and *S-Files*, and *Weekly Review* fills the Saturday slot. The Sunday rotation is *Weekend*, *Spectrum*, *Sweden Today* and *Studio 49*, while Monday's offering is *In Touch with Stockholm* (a listener-response program) or the musical *Sounds Nordic*. Thirty minutes to North America, winter on 9495 (or 9755) kHz and summer on 9495 or 15240 kHz.

Radio Prague, Czech Republic. Summer only at this time. *News*, then Tuesday through Saturday, there's *Current Affairs* and a feature. Tuesday, *Spotlight* (a look at Czech regional affairs) alternates with *One on One* (an informal interview show); Wednesday, there's *Talking Point* (issues shaping the lives of people in the Czech Republic); and the Thursday show is either *Czechs in History* or *Central Europe Today*. Friday's business-oriented *Economic Report* is substituted Saturday by *Magazine* ("the show that starts where the news ends"). On the remaining days, the news is followed by Sunday's *Readings from Czech Literature* and an enjoyable musical feature, and Monday's *A Letter from Prague*, *The Arts* and *Mailbag*. A friendly half hour to the Mideast and South Asia on 11600 and 15470 kHz. One hour later in winter.

Radio Budapest, Hungary. This time winter only. *News* and features, most of which are broadcast on a non-regular basis. Thirty minutes to North America on 9835 kHz. One hour earlier in summer.

Voice of Vietnam. A relay via the facilities of Radio Canada International. Begins with *news*, then there's *Commentary* or *Weekly Review*, followed by short features and some pleasant Vietnamese music (particularly at weekends). A half hour to western North America, winter on 6175 kHz and summer on 9795 kHz.

Radio Tirana, Albania. Winter only at this time. *News*, features and lively Albanian music. Thirty minutes to North America on 6115 and 7160 kHz. One hour earlier in summer.

04:00

■BBC World Service for the Americas. Tuesday through Saturday winter (weekday evenings in North America), there's five minutes of *news*, then a 25-minute feature (a very mixed bag). This is followed by another feature at 0330, and ●*Off the Shelf* (readings from the best of world literature) rounds off the hour. *The World Today* fills the first half hour on Sunday and Monday, and is followed by *Global Business* and *Westway* (a soap), respectively. Monday through Friday summer

CRI

China Radio International's vast schedule has programs in many languages, including Russian. During the cold war, these were sometimes transmitted to the Soviet Union with the tape being played backwards. CRI

(Sunday through Thursday evenings in North America), it's 50 minutes of news and current events in *The World Today*, with ●*Sports Roundup* closing the hour. On the remaining days, *The World Today* is cut to 30 minutes, and is followed by Saturday's ●*Assignment* (or another documentary), and Sunday's *Global Business*. Continuous programming to western North America and Central America on 5975, 6135 (winter) and (summer) 11835 kHz.

■**BBC World Service for Europe.** Identical to the service for the Americas, except for 0430 summer Saturdays, when ●*Weekend* replaces ●*Assignment*. Continuous to Europe and North Africa on 6195, 9410 and (summer) 12035 kHz.

■**BBC World Service for the Mideast.** Similar to the service for the Americas, but *In Praise of God* replaces *Global Business* at 0430 Sunday. Continuous programming on 11760 and 15575 kHz.

■**BBC World Service for Southern Africa.** Thirty minutes of ●*The World Today*, followed Monday through Friday by *Network Africa*. Weekends at 0430, look for Saturday's *Talkabout Africa* or Sunday's *African Perspective*. Continues on 3255, 6190, 7125 and (winter) 11765 kHz.

■**BBC World Service for East Asia.** Monday through Friday, it's 50 minutes of news and current events in *The World Today*, then ●*Sports Roundup* closes the hour. On the remaining days, *The World Today* is cut to 30 minutes, and is followed by Saturday's ●*Assignment* (or another documentary), and Sunday's ●*Omnibus* or light entertainment (including the unique ●*Brain of Britain* for part of the year). Continuous to East Asia on 15280, 17760 and 21660 kHz.

Voice of Croatia. Winter only at this time, and actually starts several minutes into a predominantly Croatian broadcast. Approximately six minutes of news from and about Croatia. To western North America on 6130 (or 7285) kHz. One hour earlier in summer.

Radio Habana Cuba. Repeat of the 0200 broadcast. To east and central North America on 6000 and 9820 kHz. Also available to Europe on 11705 kHz upper sideband.

Radio Vlaanderen Internationaal, Belgium. Tuesday through Saturday (weekdays evenings in North America), starts with *News*, then *Belgium Today*, *Press Review* and features. Take your pick from *Focus on Europe* and *Sports* (Tuesday), *Green Society* (Wednesday), *The Arts* (Thursday and Saturday), *Around Town* (Thursday), *Economics* and *International Report* (Friday) and Saturday's *Tourism*. Closes with *Soundbox*. These are replaced Sunday by *Music from Flanders*, and Monday by *Radio World*, *Tourism*, *Brussels 1043* (a listener-response program) and *Soundbox*. A half hour to western North America winter on 11985 kHz, and summer on 15565 kHz.

Radio Prague, Czech Republic. Winter only at this time. A repeat of the 0100 and 0200 broadcasts; see 0100 for specifics. Thirty minutes to North America on 7345 and 9435 kHz. By far the best opportunity for western parts. One hour earlier in summer.

■Radio France Internationale. Starts with a bulletin of African *news* and an international newsflash. Next, there's a review of the French dailies, an in-depth look at events in Africa , the main news event of the day in France, and sports. Thirty information-packed minutes to East Africa on any two channels from 11910, 11995, 13610 and 15155 kHz. Heard well beyond the intended target area.

Radio Ukraine International. Winter only at this time, and a repeat of the 0100 broadcast. See 0000 for program details. Sixty minutes of informative programming targeted at Europe, North America and West Asia. Generally poor reception due to budget and technical limitations. Try 6020, 9600 and 9610 kHz. One hour earlier in summer.

XERMX—Radio México Internacional. Tuesday through Saturday winter (weekday evenings in North America) there's an English summary of the Spanish-language *Antena Radio*, replaced Sunday by a listener-response program, *Mailbag*. Monday's programming is in Spanish. The summer lineup consists of *Regional Roots and Rhythms* (Tuesday), *Mosaic of Mexico* (Wednesday), *Mailbox* (Thursday), *Magical Trip* (Friday), *Mirror of Mexico* (Saturday) and *DXperience* (a show for radio enthusiasts, Sunday). There are no programs on Monday. Thirty minutes to North America on 9705 and 11770 kHz.

HCJB—Voice of the Andes, Ecuador. Tuesday through Saturday (weekday evenings in North America) it's *Studio 9*, featuring nine minutes of world and Latin American *news*, followed by 20 minutes of in-depth reporting on Latin America. The second half hour is given over to one of a variety of 30-minute features—including *Inside HCJB* (Tuesday), *Ham Radio Today* (Thursday), *Woman to Woman* (Friday), and the unique and enjoyable ●*Música del Ecuador* on Saturday. On Sunday (Saturday evening in the Americas), the news is followed by *DX Partyline*, and Monday by *Musical Mailbag*. Continuous programming to North America on 9745 and (winter) 11840 or (summer) 15115 kHz.

Radio Australia. *World News*, then Monday through Friday it's music and interviews with *Margaret Throsby*. Weekend fare consists of *Pacific Focus* followed by Saturday's *The Buzz* or Sunday's *Arts Talk*. Continuous to Asia and the Pacific on 9660, 12080, 15240, 15415, 15515, 17580, 17750 (from 0530) and 21725 kHz. Should also be audible in parts of North America (best during summer) on 15515 and 17580 kHz. In East Asia, choose between 15240 and 21725 kHz; for Southeast Asia, there's 15415 and 17750 kHz. Some channels carry separate sports programming at weekends.

■Deutsche Welle, Germany. *News*, followed Tuesday through Saturday by ●*NewsLink* and *Hallo Africa* (except Saturday, when there's *German by Radio*). The Sunday lineup is *Weekend Review* and ●*Inside Europe*, and the Monday menu features *Weekend Review* (second edition) and ●*Marks and Markets*. A 45-minute broadcast aimed primarily at eastern and southern Africa, but also heard in parts of the Mideast. Winter on 6015, 7195, 9565 and 9710 kHz; and summer on 7225, 9565, 9765 and 13690 kHz.

Voice of America. Directed to Africa and the Mideast, but widely heard elsewhere. *News Now*—a mixed bag of sports, science, business and other news and features. Weekdays on the half-hour, the African service leaves the mainstream programming and carries its own ●*Daybreak Africa*. To North Africa year round on 7170 kHz, and to the Mideast summer on 11965 kHz. The African service is available on 6035 (winter), 6080, 7265 and 7275 (summer), 7415 (winter), 9575, 9775 (winter) and 9885 kHz. Some of these are only available until 0430. Reception of some of these channels is also possible in North America.

Radio Romania International. Similar to the 0200 transmission (see there for specifics).

04:00–05:00

Fifty-five minutes to North America winter on 9570 and 11830 kHz, and summer on 11940 and 15105 kHz.

Voice of Turkey. Winter only at this time. See 0300 for specifics. Fifty minutes to Europe and eastern North America on 6010 and 9655 kHz, to the Mideast on 7240 kHz, and to Southeast Asia and Australasia on 21715 kHz. One hour earlier in summer.

WJCR, Upton, Kentucky. Continues with country gospel music for North American listeners on 7490 kHz. Also with religious programs to North America at this hour are **WYFR-Family Radio** on 6065 and 9505 kHz, **WWCR** on 5935 kHz, **KAIJ** on 5755 kHz and **KTBN** on 7510 kHz. Traditionalist Catholic programming is available via **WEWN** on 5825 kHz

Kol Israel. Summer only at this time. *News* for 15 minutes from Israel Radio's domestic network. To Europe and eastern North America on 9435 and 15640 kHz, and to Australasia on 17545 kHz. One hour later in winter.

China Radio International. Repeat of the 0300 broadcast; one hour to North America on 9730 and (summer only) 9560 kHz.

Radio New Zealand International. Continues with regional programming for the South Pacific. Part of a much longer broadcast, which is also heard in parts of North America (especially during summer) on 17675 kHz. Sometimes carries commentaries of local sporting events.

Radio for Peace International, Costa Rica. Part of a six-hour cyclical block of predominantly social-conscience and counterculture programming. Audible in Europe and the Americas on 7445 (upper sideband) and 15050 kHz.

Voice of Russia World Service. Continues to North America at this hour. Tuesday through Sunday winter, it's *News and Views*, replaced Monday by *Sunday Panorama* and *Russia: People and Events*. During the second half hour, the Sunday slot goes to *Kaleidoscope*, replaced Monday by ●*Audio Book Club*. The rest of the lineup is variable, and often chosen at short notice. The summer schedule has plenty of variety, and includes ●*Jazz Show* (0431 Monday), ●*Music at Your Request* or ●*Music Around Us* (same time Tuesday), the business-oriented *Newmarket* (0411 Thursday), *Science and Engineering* (same time Wednesday and Saturday), ●*Folk Box* (0431 Thursday), ●*Audio Book Club* (0431 Thursday), *Moscow Mailbag* (0411 Tuesday and Friday) and the retrospective ●*Moscow Yesterday and Today* (0431 Sunday). In eastern North America, tune to 7125 and 7180 kHz in winter, and 9665 and 11750 kHz in summer. Best winter bets for the west coast are 12010, 12020, 13665, 15445, 15470, 15595 and 17595 kHz; in summer, choose from 12000, 17565, 17650, 17660 and 17690 kHz.

AFRTS Shortwave, USA. Network news, live sports, music and features in the upper-sideband mode from the Armed Forces Radio & Television Service. Transmitted from modestly powered U.S. Navy stations around the globe. Try 4278.5, 4319, 4995, 5765, 6350, 6458.5, 10320, 10940.5, 12579, 12689.5 and 13362 kHz.

04:30

■**Radio Netherlands.** Tuesday through Saturday (weekday evenings in North America), starts with ●*Newsline*, then a feature program. The lineup includes ●*Research File* (science, Tuesday); *Music 52-15* (eclectic, Wednesday); the excellent award-winning ●*Documentary* (Thursday); ●*Encore* (Friday); and ●*A Good Life* (Saturday). The Sunday fare is *Europe Unzipped*, *Insight* and *Sound Fountain*, replaced Monday by *Sincerely Yours*, a program preview and *Dutch Horizons*. One hour to western North America on 6165 and 9590 kHz.

Radio Prague, Czech Republic. Winter only at this time; see 0330 for specifics. Thirty minutes to the Mideast and South Asia on 9865 and 11600 kHz. One hour earlier in summer.

Radio Yugoslavia. Summer only at this time. Thirty minutes of news and short features to western North America on 11870 kHz. Two hours earlier in winter.

05:00

■**BBC World Service for the Americas.** Winter only at this time. With the exception of Sunday (Saturday night local American date), when five minutes of *news* are followed by *Wright Round the World*, it's a full hour of news and current events in *The World Today*. The final hour to western North America and Central America on 6135 kHz.

■**BBC World Service for Europe.** Monday through Friday, a full hour of news in ●*The World Today*. Weekends, the second half hour is replaced Saturday by ●*Weekend* (winter) or *Arts in Action* (summer), and Sunday by ●*Reporting Religion* and ●*Letter from America*. Continuous to Europe and North Africa on 6195, 9410 and (summer) 12095 kHz.

■**BBC World Service for the Mideast.** Same as for Europe, except that the 0530 Sunday slot is occupied by *Global Business*.

■**BBC World Service for Africa.** ●*The World Today*, then weekdays on the half-hour there's a continuation of *Network Africa*. Weekends, the final 30 minutes are filled by Saturday's *African Quiz* or *This Week and Africa*, and Sunday's *Artbeat*. Continuous programming on 3255 (midyear), 6190, 11765 and (winter) 11940 kHz.

■**BBC World Service for East and Southeast Asia and the Pacific.** Starts with 30 minutes of ●*The World Today*. Thereafter, it's a mixed bag of features. Favorites are ●*Off the Shelf* (serialized readings from world literature, 0545 weekdays) and ●*Reporting Religion* and ●*Letter from America* (0130 and 0145 Sunday). Continuous to East Asia on 15280 (till 0530), 15360, 17760 and 21660 kHz; and to Southeast Asia on 9740 and 15360 kHz. Heard in Australasia on 15360 kHz.

■**Deutsche Welle,** Germany. Repeat of the 45-minute 0100 transmission to North America, except that Sunday's *Inside Europe* is replaced by ●*Marks and Markets*; and Monday's *Arts on the Air* gives way to *Cool*. Winter on 5960, 6120, 9670 and 11795 kHz; and summer on 9670, 9785, and 11985 kHz. This slot is by far the best for western North America.

All India Radio's curtain antennas at Khampur are switched manually to serve diverse audiences. M. Guha

Radio Exterior de España ("Spanish National Radio"). *News*, then Tuesday through Saturday (local weekday evenings in the Americas) it's *Panorama*, which features a recording of popular Spanish music, a commentary or a report, a review of the Spanish press, and weather. The remainder of the program is a mixture of literature, science, music and general programming. Tuesday (Monday evening in North America), there's *Sports Spotlight* and *Cultural Encounters*; Wednesday features *People of Today* and *Entertainment in Spain*; Thursday brings *As Others See Us* and, biweekly, *The Natural World* or *Science Desk*; Friday has *Economic Report* and *Cultural Clippings*; and Saturday offers *Window on Spain* and *Review of the Arts*. A language course, *Spanish by Radio*, closes the hour. On the remaining days, you can listen to Sunday's *Hall of Fame* and *Gallery of Spanish Voices*; and Monday's *Visitors' Book*, a feature on Spanish music and *Radio Club*. Sixty minutes to the eastern and southern United States on 6055 kHz.

■**Radio France Internationale.** Similar to the 0400 broadcast, but without the international newsflash. A half hour to East Africa (and heard well beyond) on 13610 (winter), 15155 and (summer) 17800 kHz.

Vatican Radio. Summer only at this time. Twenty minutes of programming oriented to Catholics. To Europe on 4005, 5880 (variable) and 7250 kHz. One hour later in winter.

05:00–05:30

Radio Denmark's office staff: Marie Villumsen (standing), Dorte Skott and Marianne Lillelund. Erik Koie, R. Denmark

Voice of Croatia. Summer only at this time, and actually starts about three minutes into a predominantly Croatian broadcast. Approximately six minutes of news from and about Croatia. To Australasia on 9470 kHz. One hour later in winter.

XERMX—Radio México Internacional. Tuesday through Saturday (weekday evenings local American date) and winter only at this time. Take your pick from *Regional Roots and Rhythms* (Tuesday), *Mosaic of Mexico* (Wednesday), *Mailbox* (Thursday), *Magical Trip* (Friday), *Mirror of Mexico* (Saturday) and Sunday's *DXperience*, a program for radio enthusiasts. The station is off the air on Monday. Thirty minutes to North America on 9705 and 11770 kHz. One hour earlier in summer.

Radio Japan. *News*, then Monday through Friday there's *Japan and World 44 Minutes* (an in-depth look at current trends and events). This is replaced Saturday by *Hello from Tokyo* and Sunday by *Pop Goes Asia*. One hour to Europe on 5975 and 7230 kHz; to East Asia on 11715, 11760 and 15195 kHz; to Southeast Asia on 17810 kHz; to Australasia on 21755 kHz; and to western North America on 6110 and 13630 (or 9835) kHz.

China Radio International. This time winter only. Repeat of the 0300 broadcast; one hour to North America on 9560 kHz via a Canadian relay.

HCJB—Voice of the Andes, Ecuador. Predominantly religious programming at this hour. For a general audience, try Friday's *Inspirational Classics* (Thursday night in North America) or *Saludos Amigos* (same time Sunday). Continuous programming to North America on 9745 and (winter) 11840 or (summer) 15115 kHz.

Voice of America. Continues with the morning broadcast to Africa and the Mideast. *News Now*—a mixed bag of sports, science, business and other news and features. To North Africa on 7170 and (winter only) 5995 and 11805 kHz; to the Mideast on 11825 (winter) or (summer) 11965 kHz; and to the rest of Africa on 5970, 6035, 6080, 7195 (summer), 7295 (winter), 9630 (summer) and 12080 kHz. Some of these channels are audible in parts of North America.

Radio Habana Cuba. The start of a two-hour broadcast for the East Coast and western North America. Tuesday through Sunday (Monday through Saturday evenings in North America), the first half hour consists of international and Cuban news followed by *RHC's Viewpoint*. The next 30 minutes consist of a news bulletin and the sports-oriented *Time Out* (five minutes each) plus a feature: *Caribbean Outlook* (Tuesday and Friday), *DXers Unlimited* (Wednesday and Sunday), the *Mailbag Show* (Thursday) and *Weekly Review* (Saturday). Monday, the hour is split between *Weekly Review* and *Mailbag Show*. In the east, use 9550 kHz; in the west, 9820 kHz (also audible in parts of Australasia). Additionally available to Europe on 9830 kHz upper sideband.

Voice of Nigeria. Targeted mainly at West Africa, but also audible in parts of Europe and North America, especially during winter. Monday through Friday, opens with the lively *Wave Train* followed by *VON Scope*, a half hour of *news* and press comment. Pick of the weekend programs is ●*African Safari*, a musical journey around the African continent, which can be heard Saturdays at 0500. This is replaced Sunday by five minutes of *Reflections* and 25 minutes of music in *VON Link-Up*, with the second half-hour taken up by *News*. The first 60 minutes of a daily two-hour broadcast on 7255 and (when the transmitter is repaired) 15120 kHz.

Radio New Zealand International. Continues with regional programming for the South Pacific. Part of a much longer broadcast, which is also heard in parts of North America (especially during summer) on 11725 or 15340 kHz.

Radio Australia. *World News*, then Monday through Friday there's *Pacific Beat* (background reporting on events in the Pacific)—look for a sports bulletin at 0530. Weekends, the news is followed by *Pacific Focus* and Saturday's *Lingua Franca* and *Business Weekend* or Sunday's *Fine Music Australia*. Continuous to Asia and the Pacific on 9660, 12080, 15240, 15415, 15515, 17580, 17750 (from 0530) and 21725 kHz. In North America (best during summer) try 15515 and 17580 kHz. Best for East Asia are 15240 and 21725 kHz; in Southeast Asia use 15415 or 17750 kHz. Some channels carry alternative sports programming at weekends.

Voice of Russia World Service. Winter, the *news* is followed by a wide variety of programs. These include *Jazz Show* (0531 Monday), ●*Music at Your Request* or ●*Music Around Us* (same time Tuesday), the business-oriented *Newmarket* (0511 Thursday), *Science and Engineering* (same time Wednesday and Saturday), ●*Folk Box* (0531 Thursday), ●*Audio Book Club* (0531 Friday), *Moscow Mailbag* (0511 Tuesday and Friday), and the retrospective ●*Moscow Yesterday and Today* (0531 Sunday). Tuesday through Saturday summer, there's *Focus on Asia and the Pacific*, replaced Sunday by *Science and Engineering* and Monday by *Moscow Mailbag*. On the half-hour, look for *This is Russia* (Monday and Friday), ●*Audio Book Club* (Sunday), ●*Moscow Yesterday and Today* (Thursday), ●*Christian Message from Moscow* (Saturday) and *Russian by Radio* on Wednesday. Winter only to eastern North America on 7125 and 7180 kHz, and to western parts on 12010, 12020, 15445, 15470, 15595 and 17595 kHz. Available summer to Australasia on 17635 (from 0530), 17685 and 21790 kHz.

Radio for Peace International, Costa Rica. Continues with a six-hour cyclical block of social-conscience and counterculture programming. Audible in Europe and the Americas on 7445 (upper sideband) and 15050 kHz.

Kol Israel. Winter only at this time. *News* for 15 minutes from Israel Radio's domestic network. To Europe and eastern North America on any two channels from 6280, 7520, 9435 and 11605 kHz, and to Australasia on 17545 kHz. One hour earlier in summer.

WJCR, Upton, Kentucky. Continues with country gospel music for North American listeners on 7490 kHz. Also with religious programs to North America at this hour are **WYFR-Family Radio** on 5985 kHz, **WWCR** on 5935 kHz, **KAIJ** on 5755 kHz and **KTBN** on 7510 kHz. For traditionalist Catholic programming, tune to **WEWN** on 5825 kHz.

AFRTS Shortwave, USA. Network news, live sports, music and features in the upper-sideband mode from the Armed Forces Radio & Television Service. Transmitted from modestly powered U.S. Navy stations around the globe. Try 4278.5, 4319, 4995, 5765, 6350, 6458.5, 10320, 10940.5, 12579, 12689.5 and 13362 kHz.

05:30

Radio Austria International. Summer only at this time and actually starts at 0532. ●*Report from Austria*, which includes a brief bulletin of *news*, followed by a series of current events and human interest stories. A popular source of news about Central Europe. Thirty minutes to Europe on 6155 and 13730 kHz, and to the Mideast on 17870 kHz.

United Arab Emirates Radio, Dubai. See 0330 for program details. Twenty minutes to East Asia and Australasia on 15435, 17830 and 21700 kHz.

Radio Thailand. Thirty minutes of *news* and short features relayed from one of the station's domestic services. To Europe winter on 13780 kHz, and summer on 21795 kHz. Also available to Asia on 9655 and 11905 kHz, although operation on these channels tends to be somewhat irregular.

0600-1159
Australasia & East Asia—Evening Prime Time
Western North America—Late Evening
Europe & Mideast—Morning and Midday

06:00

■**BBC World Service for Europe.** Monday through Friday winter, a full hour of *The World Today* (news and current events). Weekends, it's reduced to 30 minutes and followed by Saturday's ●*People and Politics* or Sunday's ●*Agenda*. Summer weekdays, you can hear 20 minutes of *World Briefing* followed by ●*Sports Roundup*, ●*World Business Report* and ●*Analysis* (replaced Monday by ●*Letter from America* and Thursday by ●*From Our Own Correspondent*). Saturday and Sunday, the first half hour is the same as during the week, with the final 30 minutes being filled with the same features as winter. Continuous to Europe and North Africa on 6195, 9410, 12095 and (summer) 15485 kHz.

■**BBC World Service for Eastern Europe and the Mideast.** Tuesday through Saturday, starts with *News*, then the popular ●*Outlook* (except Monday, when there's *Talking Point*, a call-in show). Weekdays, the final 15 minutes are filled by ●*Off the Shelf* (readings from the best of world literature). The Saturday slot goes to *Write On* or *Waveguide*, and Sunday's lineup is *World Briefing*, ●*Sports Roundup* and ●*Agenda* (current events). Continues on 11760, 15565 and 15575 kHz.

■**BBC World Service for Southern Africa.** Identical to the service for the Mideast at this hour. Continuous programming on 6190, 11765 and 11940 kHz.

■**BBC World Service for East and Southeast Asia and the Pacific.** Five minutes of *news*, then Monday through Friday there's an arts show, *Meridian*. The next half hour consists mostly of a mixed bag of music and light entertainment. Exceptions are winter Thursdays (●*Omnibus*) and summer Mondays (●*Omnibus* and *Composer of the Month*). Weekends, starts with *World Briefing* and ●*Sports Roundup*, then it's either Saturday's ●*People and Politics* or Sunday's *Westway* (a soap). Continuous to East Asia on 15360, 17760 and 21660 kHz; to Southeast Asia on 9740 and 15360 kHz; and to Australasia on 15360 kHz.

■**Deutsche Welle, Germany.** Repeat of the 0400 broadcast. Forty-five minutes to West Africa (and often heard in Europe), winter on 7225, 9565 and 11785 kHz; and summer on 11925, 13790 and 17860 kHz. The same programs also form part of a separate one hour broadcast to Europe on 6140 kHz. The bonus for Europeans is an extra 15-minute feature: *Business German* (Monday), *People in Europe* (Tuesday), *German by Radio* (Wednesday), ●*Insight* (Thursday), ●*Man and Environment* (Friday), *Women on the Move* or *Development Forum* (Saturday) and Sunday's *Around Germany*.

Radio Habana Cuba. The second half of a two-hour broadcast for the East Coast and western North America. Tuesday through Sunday (Monday through Saturday evenings in North America), opens with 10 minutes of international news. Next comes *Spotlight on the Americas* (Tuesday through Saturday) or Sunday's *The World of Stamps*. The final 30 minutes consists of news-oriented programming. The Monday slots are *From Havana* and ●*The Jazz Place* or *Breakthrough* (science). Tune to 9550 kHz in the east, and 9820 kHz out west. Also available to Europe on 9830 kHz upper sideband. Listeners in Australasia can try 9820 kHz, as it's also beamed their way.

Radio Japan. *News*, then weekdays there's *Asian Top News*. This is followed by a 35-minute feature: *Unforgettable Musical Masterpieces* (Monday), Japanese language lessons (Tuesday and Thursday), *Japan Music Log* (Wednesday), and *Music Beat* (Japanese popular music, Friday). On the remaining days, *Pop Goes Asia* fills the Saturday slot and

Weekend Square is aired on Sunday. One hour to Europe on 7230 kHz; to East Asia on 15195 kHz; to Southeast Asia on 11740 kHz; to Australasia on 21755 kHz; to western North America on 13630 (or 9835) kHz; and to Hawaii and Central America on 17870 (or 9685) kHz. This last broadcast may differ somewhat from the other transmissions, and may include alternative features.

Voice of Croatia. Winter only at this time, and actually starts around 0603. Approximately six minutes of news from and about Croatia. To Australasia on 9470 (or 11970) kHz. One hour earlier in summer.

■**Radio France Internationale.** Similar to the 0400 broadcast (see there for specifics), but includes a report on the day's main international story. A half hour to East Africa on two or more channels from 11710, 15155, 17800 and 21620 kHz.

Voice of America. Final segment of the transmission to Africa and the Mideast. Monday through Friday, the mainstream African service carries just 30 minutes of ●*Daybreak Africa*, with other channels carrying a full hour of *News Now*—a mixed bag of sports, science, business and other news and features. Weekend programming is the same to all areas—60 minutes of *News Now*. To North Africa on 5995 (winter), 7170, 9680 (summer) and 11805 kHz; to the Mideast on 11825 (winter) or (summer) 11965 kHz; and to mainstream Africa on 5970, 6035, 6080, 7195 (summer), 7285 (winter), 9630 (summer), 11950 (winter), 11995 (summer), 12080 and (winter) 15600 kHz. Some of these channels are audible in North America.

Radio Australia. Opens with *News*, then the weekday lineup is *Regional Sports*, *Pacific Focus* and a 20-minute feature—*Oz Music Show* (Monday), *Music Deli* (music from different cultures, Tuesday), *Blacktracker* (indigenous music and stories, Wednesday), *Australian Country Style* (Thursday), and *Jazz Notes* (Friday). Saturday's pairing is *Feedback* (a listener-response program) and *Oz Sounds*, replaced Sunday by *The Europeans*. Continuous to Asia and the Pacific on 9660, 12080, 15240, 15415, 15515, 17580, 17750 and 21725 kHz. Listeners in western North America should try 15515 and 17580 kHz. In East Asia, tune to 15240 or 21725 kHz; for Southeast Asia, use 15415 or 17750 kHz. Some channels carry an alternative sports program until 0700 on weekends (0800 midyear).

Voice of Nigeria. The second (and final) hour of a daily broadcast intended mainly for listeners in West Africa, but also heard in parts of Europe and North America (especially during winter). Features vary from day to day, but are predominantly concerned with Nigerian and West African affairs. There is a listener-response program at 0600 Friday and 0615 Sunday, and other slots include *Across the Ages* and *Nigeria and Politics* (Monday), *Southern Connection* and *Nigerian Scene* (Tuesday), *West African Scene* (0600 Thursday) and *Images of Nigeria* (0615 Friday). There is a weekday 25-minute program of *news* and commentary on the half-hour, replaced weekends by the more in-depth *Weekly Analysis*. To 0657 on 7255 and (when operating) 15120 kHz.

Radio New Zealand International. Continues with regional programming for the South Pacific. Part of a much longer broadcast, which is also heard in parts of North America (especially during summer) on 11725 or 15340 kHz.

Voice of Russia World Service. *News*, then winter it's *Focus on Asia and the Pacific* (Tuesday through Saturday), *Science and Engineering* (Sunday), and *Moscow Mailbag* (Monday). On the half-hour, look for *This is Russia* (Monday and Friday), ●*Audio Book Club* (Sunday), ●*Moscow Yesterday and Today* (Thursday), ●*Christian Message from Moscow* (Saturday) and *Russian by Radio* on Wednesday. In summer, the news is followed by *Science and Engineering* (Monday and Friday), the business-oriented *Newmarket* (Wednesday and Saturday), and a listener-response program, *Moscow Mailbag*, on the remaining days. The lineup for the second half hour includes ●*Moscow Yesterday and Today* (Wednesday), ●*Audio Book Club* (Thursday), *Timelines* (Sunday), *Russian by Radio* (Mon-

06:00–07:00

day); the eclectic *Kaleidoscope* (Tuesday and Friday) and *This is Russia* on Saturday. Continuous programming to Australasia and Southeast Asia. Winter in Australasia (local summer in the Southern Hemisphere), tune to 15460 (from 0630), 15470, 15525, 17570 and 21790 kHz; midyear, go for 17635, 17685 and 21790 kHz. For Southeast Asia, there's 17655 kHz in winter, and 15490 kHz in summer.

Radio for Peace International, Costa Rica. Continues with counterculture and social-conscience programs. Audible in Europe and the Americas on 7445 (upper sideband) and 15050 kHz.

Vatican Radio. Winter only at this time. Twenty minutes with a heavy Catholic slant. To Europe on 4005, 5880 (variable) and 7250 kHz. One hour earlier in summer.

WJCR, Upton, Kentucky. Continues with country gospel music to North America on 7490 kHz. Also with religious programs for North American listeners at this hour are **WYFR-Family Radio** on 5985 kHz, **WWCR** on 5935 kHz, **KAIJ** on 5755 kHz, **KTBN** on 7510 kHz, and **WHRI-World Harvest Radio** on 5760 and 7315 kHz. Traditionalist Catholic fare is available on 5825 kHz.

Voice of Malaysia. Actually starts at 0555 with opening announcements and program summary, followed by *News*. Then comes *This is the Voice of Malaysia*, a potpourri of news, interviews, reports and music. The hour is rounded off with *Personality Column*. Part of a 150-minute broadcast to Southeast Asia and Australia on 6175, 9750 and 15295 kHz.

HCJB—Voice of the Andes, Ecuador. Predominantly religious programming at this hour. A favorite with HCJB listeners is Monday's *Mountain Meditations* (Sunday night in North America). To North America on 9745 and (winter) 11840 or (summer) 15115 kHz. For a separate service to Europe, see the next item.

HCJB—Voice of the Andes, Ecuador. Summer only at this time. Monday through Friday it's *Studio 9*, featuring nine minutes of world and Latin American *news*, followed by 20 minutes of in-depth reporting on Latin America. The second half hour is devoted to one of a variety of 30-minute features—including *Inside HCJB* (Monday), *Ham Radio Today* (Wednesday), *Woman to Woman* (Thursday), and the thoroughly enjoyable ●*Música del Ecuador* on Friday. On Saturday, the news is followed by *DX Partyline*, and Monday by *Musical Mailbag*. The first of two hours to Europe on 11680 kHz. One hour later in winter.

AFRTS Shortwave, USA. Network news, live sports, music and features in the upper-sideband mode from the Armed Forces Radio & Television Service. Transmitted from modestly powered U.S. Navy stations around the globe. Try 4278.5, 4319, 4995, 5765, 6350, 6458.5, 10320, 10940.5, 12579, 12689.5 and 13362 kHz.

06:40

Radio Romania International. Actually starts at 0641. A 15-minute broadcast to Europe winter on 7105, 9510, 11755 and 15105 kHz; and summer on 9570, 9665, 11885 and 15250 kHz.

07:00

■**BBC World Service for Europe.** Winter, you can hear 20 minutes of *World Briefing* followed by ●*Sports Roundup*, then weekdays there's ●*World Business Report* and ●*Analysis* (replaced Monday by ●*Letter from America* and Thursday by ●*From Our Own Correspondent*). Weekends, these give way to Saturday's *Arts in Action* and Sunday's ●*Assignment* (or substitute documentary). Monday through Saturday summer, starts with *News*, then the long-running *Outlook* (except Monday, when there's *Talking Point*, a call-in show). Weekdays, the final 15 minutes go to ●*Off the Shelf* (readings from the best of world literature); Saturday, the slot is filled by *Write On*. Sunday's lineup is *World Briefing*, ●*Sports Roundup* and ●*Assignment* (or an alternative documentary). Continuous to Europe and North Africa on 6195, 9410, 12095, 15485 and 15565 kHz.

■**BBC World Service for Eastern Europe and the Mideast.** Five minutes of *News*, then it's either the weekday *Meridian* (an arts

08:00–09:00

Sixty minutes to Europe on 13670 kHz, and to Australasia on 9570 kHz.

AFRTS Shortwave, USA. Network news, live sports, music and features in the upper-sideband mode from the Armed Forces Radio & Television Service. Transmitted from modestly powered U.S. Navy stations around the globe. Try 4278.5, 4319, 4995, 5765, 6350, 6458.5, 10320, 10940.5, 12579, 12689.5 and 13362 kHz.

08:10

Voice of Armenia. Summer Sundays only. Twenty minutes of Armenian *news* and culture, mainly of interest to Armenians abroad. To Europe on 15270 kHz, and to the Mideast on 4810 kHz. One hour later in winter.

08:30

Swiss Radio International. *Newsnet*—news and background reports on world and Swiss events. Look for some lighter fare on Saturdays, when *Capital Letters* (a biweekly listener-response program) alternates with *Name Game* (first Saturday) and *Sounds Good* (third Saturday). To southern Africa on 21770 kHz.

09:00

■**BBC World Service for Europe.** Monday through Saturday winter, opens with five minutes of *News*, then weekdays it's *Meridian* (an arts show). The second half hour is a mixed bag of popular music or *Westway* (a soap). Saturday has youth-oriented programming, replaced Sunday by *World Briefing*, ●*Reporting Religion* and *In Praise of God*. Summer (except Sunday), starts with *News*, then weekdays there's an interesting collection of features: ●*One Planet* and *People and Places* (Monday), *Discovery* and *Essential Guide* (Tuesday), ●*Health Matters* and ●*Everywoman* (Wednesday),●*Focus on Faith* (0930 Thursday) and *Sports International* and *Pick of the World* on Friday. Saturday brings *World Briefing*, ●*Letter from America* and *Global Business*, and Sunday's programming is the same as winter. Continuous to Europe and North Africa on 12095, 15485 and 15565 kHz.

■**BBC World Service for Eastern Europe and the Mideast.** Weekdays, identical to the service for Asia and the Pacific. On the weekends, *World Briefing* is followed by Saturday's ●*Letter from America* and *Global Business*, or Sunday's *Reporting Religion* and ●*People and Politics*. Continuous programming on 11760, 15565, 15575 and 17640 kHz.

■**BBC World Service for East and Southeast Asia and the Pacific.** Winter, starts with *World Briefing*, then weekdays it's ●*Sports Roundup*. The lineup for the 0945 feature is ●*Analysis* (Tuesday, Wednesday and Friday), ●*From Our Own Correspondent* (Thursday) and *Write On* (a listener-response program, Monday). Saturday features are ●*Analysis* and *Global Business*, and Sunday there's ●*Reporting Religion* and *In Praise of God*. Monday through Friday summer, there's one hour of *World Update*; Saturday, it's *World Briefing* followed by ●*Letter from America* and *Global Business*; and Sunday's programs are the same as winter. To East Asia on 9740, 11945, 15360, 17760 and 21660 kHz; to Southeast Asia on 6195, 9740 and 15360 kHz; and to Australasia on 15360 kHz.

■**Deutsche Welle,** Germany. *News*, followed Monday through Friday by ●*NewsLink*, and then a feature. Monday, it's *Development Forum* or *Women on the Move*; Tuesday brings ●*Insight*; Wednesday has the interesting ●*Man and Environment*; Thursday, there's *Living in Germany*; and Friday's slot is *Spotlight on Sport*. Weekend fare consists of Saturday's *Talking Point* and ●*Marks and Markets*; and Sunday's *Religion and Society* and *Cool*. Forty-five minutes to East Asia winter on 7300 kHz, replaced summer by 15470 kHz; and to Southeast Asia and Australasia, winter on 6160, 17820 and 17845 kHz; and summer on 6160, 17715, 17770, 17820 and 21680 kHz. For a separate service to Africa, see the next item.

■**Deutsche Welle,** Germany. Similar to the service for Asia and the Pacific, except that Saturday's *Marks and Markets* is replaced by *African Kaleidoscope*. Forty-five minutes to eastern and southern Africa, winter on 11785, 15410, 17860 and 21560 kHz; and midyear on 12035, 15410, 17800 and 21790 kHz. This service is also available to West Africa on 17800 (winter) or (summer) 21560 kHz. For yet another service, to Europe, see the next entry.

■**Deutsche Welle,** Germany. Same as for Asia and the Pacific, but with an extra 15-minute feature: *Business German* (Monday), *German History* (Tuesday), *German by Radio* (Wednesday), ●*Insight* (Thursday), ●*Man and Environment* (Friday), *Women on the Move* or *Development Forum* (Saturday) and Sunday's *Living in Germany*. One hour to Europe on 6140 kHz.

HCJB—Voice of the Andes, Ecuador. Monday through Friday it's *Studio 9*, featuring nine minutes of world and Latin American *news*, followed by 20 minutes of in-depth reporting on Latin America. The second half hour is devoted to a 30-minute feature—including *Inside HCJB* (Monday), *Ham Radio Today* (Wednesday), *Woman to Woman* (Thursday), and the unique ●*Música del Ecuador* on Friday. Saturday, the news is followed by *DX Partyline*, and Sunday by *Musical Mailbag*. Continuous to Australasia on 11755 kHz.

China Radio International. Starts with *News*, then weekdays there are background reports. The rest of the broadcast is devoted to features. Regular shows include *People in the Know* (Monday), *Sportsworld* (Tuesday), *China Horizons* (Wednesday), *Voices from Other Lands* (Thursday), and *Life in China* on Friday. The Saturday lineup includes *Global Review* and *Listeners' Garden* (reports, music and Chinese language lessons), and Sunday's broadcast has *Report from Developing Countries* and *In the Spotlight*. One hour to Australasia on 11730 and 15210 kHz.

Radio New Zealand International. Continuous programming for the islands of the South Pacific, where the broadcasts are targeted. On 9885 or 11675 kHz. Audible in much of North America.

Voice of Russia World Service. Winter only at this time. *News*, followed by ●*Update* on Wednesday and Friday. This is replaced Monday by *Science and Engineering*, Tuesday by *Focus on Asia*, Thursday by *Newmarket* and Saturday by *Moscow Mailbag*. Sunday's offering is the 45-minute ●*Music and Musicians*—not to be missed if you are an aficionado of classical music. Choice pickings from the second half hour include ●*Moscow Yesterday and Today* (Monday), ●*Folk Box* (Thursday) ●*Jazz Show* (Friday) and Saturday's ●*Christian Message from Moscow*. The Tuesday and Wednesday slots are also worth a listen. To Australasia on 9905, 15460, 15470, 17495 and 17525 kHz.

Radio Prague, Czech Republic. Summer only at this time. *News*, then Monday through Friday there's *Current Affairs* and a feature. Monday, it's either *Spotlight* (a look at Czech regional affairs) or *One on One* (an informal interview show); Tuesday, there's *Talking Point* (issues shaping the lives of people in the Czech Republic); and the Wednesday show is either *Czechs in History* or *Central Europe Today*. *Economic Report* fills the Thursday slot, and the Friday feature is *Magazine*. Weekends, following the news, the Saturday lineup consists of *Readings from Czech Literature* and an enjoyable musical feature (strongly recommended), replaced Sunday by *A Letter from Prague*, *The Arts* and *Mailbag*. Thirty minutes to South Asia and West Africa on 21745 kHz, and heard well beyond. One hour later in winter.

RFE-RL's control room at Biblis, Germany directs programs to the correct transmitters. A. Blechschmidt

09:00–10:00

Radio Australia. *World News*, then weekdays it's a call-in show, *Australia Talks Back*. This is replaced Saturday by *Science Show* and *Business Weekend*, and Sunday by *The National Interest* (topical events). Continuous to Asia and the Pacific on 11880, 13605 and 21820 kHz; and heard in North America on 13605 kHz. Best for East and Southeast Asia is 11880 kHz, and listeners in Europe should try 21820 kHz.

KTWR-Trans World Radio, Guam. Final 30 minutes of evangelical programming to Australasia on 15330 kHz.

Radio for Peace International, Costa Rica. Continues with counterculture and social-conscience programs. To the Americas on 7445 (upper sideband) and 15050 kHz.

WJCR, Upton, Kentucky. Continues with country gospel music to North America on 7490 kHz. Other U.S. religious broadcasters operating at this hour include **WWCR** on 5935, **KAIJ** on 5755, **KTBN** on 7510 kHz, and **WHRI-World Harvest Radio** on 5745 and 9495 kHz. Traditionalist Catholic programming is aired via **WEWN** on 5825 kHz.

AFRTS Shortwave, USA. Network news, live sports, music and features in the upper-sideband mode from the Armed Forces Radio & Television Service. Transmitted from modestly powered U.S. Navy stations around the globe. Try 4278.5, 4319, 4995, 5765, 6350, 6458.5, 10320, 10940.5, 12579, 12689.5 and 13362 kHz.

09:10

Voice of Armenia. Winter Sundays only, and mainly of interest to Armenians abroad. Twenty minutes of Armenian *news* and culture. To Europe on 15270 kHz, and to the Mideast on 4910 kHz. One hour earlier in summer.

09:30

■**Radio Netherlands.** Monday through Friday it's ●*Newsline*, then a feature. Top picks are ●*Research File* (science, Monday), Thursday's ●*Encore*, ●*A Good Life* (Friday), and Wednesday's well produced ●*Documentary*. Tuesday, you can hear the eclectic *Music 52-15*. Weekends, there's a bulletin of *news* followed by Saturday's *Europe Unzipped*, *Insight* and *Sound Fountain*; and Sunday's *Sincerely Yours* (a listener-response program) and *Dutch Horizons*. The first of two hours to East and Southeast Asia and Australasia on 7260 (winter), 9790, 12065 and (summer) 13710 kHz. Recommended listening.

Radio Vilnius, Lithuania. Summer only at this time; see 1030 for program specifics. Thirty minutes to western Europe on 9710 kHz. One hour later in winter.

10:00

■**BBC World Service for the Americas.** Monday through Friday winter, opens with a half hour of *World Update* (news and current events) and closes with 15 minutes of ●*Sports Roundup*. In between , you can hear ●*Letter from America* (Monday), ●*Analysis* (Tuesday, Wednesday and Friday) and ●*From Our Own Correspondent* on Thursday. Weekends, the first 30 minutes are divided between *World Briefing* and ●*Sports Roundup*, with the second half hour consisting of Saturday's *Science in Action* or Sunday's ●*Agenda*. In summer, the weekday lineup is *World Briefing*, ●*World Business Report* and ●*Sports Roundup*, with weekend programs the same as in winter. To the Caribbean on 6195 kHz, and audible in much of the southern and eastern United States. Listeners farther west can tune to the Asian stream on 9740 kHz.

■**BBC World Service for Europe.** Winter weekdays, opens with *News*, then there's an interesting collection of features: ●*One Planet* and *People and Places* (Monday), *Discovery* and *Essential Guide* (Tuesday), ●*Health Matters* and ●*Everywoman* (Wednesday),●*Focus on Faith* (0930 Thursday) and *Sports International* and *Pick of the World* on Friday. Saturday brings *World Briefing*, ●*Letter from America* and *Global Business*; and Sunday there's *World Briefing*, ●*Sports Roundup* and ●*Agenda*. In summer, starts with *World Briefing*, then Monday through Friday there's ●*World Business Report* and ●*Sports Roundup*. Weekends, ●*Sports Roundup* moves to 1020 and is followed by Saturday's ●*Science in Action* or Sunday's ●*Weekend*. Continuous to Europe and North Africa on 12095, 15485 and 15565 kHz.

■BBC World Service for Eastern Europe and the Mideast. Starts with a half hour of *World Briefing* (shorter at weekends, when the final ten minutes are taken by ●*Sports Roundup*). The 1030 weekday slot goes to *The Learning Zone*, an educational program. Saturday and Sunday, it's the same as for the Americas. Continues on 11760, 15565, 15575 and 17640 kHz.

■BBC World Service for East and Southeast Asia and the Pacific. Monday through Friday, the format is *World Update* (*World Briefing* in summer), ●*World Business Report* and ●*Sports Roundup*. Saturday's *news* bulletin is followed by *Jazzmatazz* and *The Greenfield Collection* (a classical music request show), and Sunday's feature is a first-rate concert of classical music—not to be missed if you appreciate top-notch performances. Continuous to East Asia on 9740 and (till 1030) 15360, 17760 and 21660 kHz; to Southeast Asia on 6195, 9740 and (till 1030) 15360 kHz. For Australasia there's 15360 kHz. Well heard in western North America on 9740 kHz.

■Deutsche Welle, Germany. A partial relay of the station's satellite service, consisting of just features. Monday's pairing is ●*Spectrum* (science) and *Around Germany*; Tuesday has an international joint production, *Women on the Move* (or *Development Forum*) and ●*Insight*; Wednesday there's ●*Marks and Markets*, *Business Germany* and *German by Radio*; Thursday features *Arts on the Air* and ●*Great Performers*; and Friday's lineup is *Cool* and *Hits* (or *Melody Time*). Weekends, the Saturday airing is ●*Inside Europe*, replaced Sunday by *Concert Hour*. Sixty minutes to Europe on 6140 kHz.

Radio Australia. *World News*, then weekdays there's *Asia Pacific* and a feature on the half-hour. Monday, it's health; Tuesday, law; Wednesday, religion; Thursday, media; and Friday, sport. Saturday's lineup consists of *Pacific Review* and *In Conversation*, replaced Sunday by *The Buzz* and *Rural Reporter*. Continuous to Asia and the Pacific on 11880, 13605 and 21820 kHz; and heard in North America on 13605 kHz. Listeners in East and Southeast Asia should tune to 11880 kHz, and 21820 kHz is often heard in Europe.

Radio Jordan. Summer only at this time. A 60-minute partial relay of the station's domestic broadcasts, beamed to western Europe and eastern North America on 11690 or 17580 kHz. One hour later in winter.

Radio Prague, Czech Republic. This time winter only. See 0900 for specifics. Thirty minutes to South Asia and West Africa on 21745 kHz, but audible well beyond. One hour earlier in summer.

Radio Japan. *News*, then Monday through Friday there's *Japan and World 44 Minutes* (an in-depth look at current trends and events). This is replaced Saturday by *Hello from Tokyo*, and Sunday by *Weekend Square*. One hour to East Asia on 15590 kHz, to Southeast Asia on 9695 kHz, and to Australasia on 21755 kHz.

Voice of Vietnam. Begins with *news*, then there's *Commentary* or *Weekly Review* followed by short features and pleasantly exotic Vietnamese music (especially at weekends). Thirty minutes to Southeast Asia on 9840 and 12020 kHz.

Voice of America. The start of the VOA's daily broadcasts to the Caribbean. *News Now*—a mixed bag of sports, science, business and other news and features. On 6165, 7405 and 9590 kHz. For a separate service to Australasia, see the next item.

Voice of America. The ubiquitous *News Now*, but unlike the service to the Caribbean, this is part of a much longer broadcast. To Australasia on 5985, 11720, and 15425 kHz.

China Radio International. Repeat of the 0900 broadcast, but with news updates. One hour to Australasia on 11730 and 15210 kHz.

All India Radio. *News*, then a composite program of commentary, press review and features, interspersed with exotic Indian music. One hour to East Asia on 11585, 15020 and 17840 kHz; and to Australasia on 13700, 15020, 17510 and 17895 kHz.

10:00–10:30

WJCR, Upton, Kentucky. Continues with country gospel music to North America on 7490 kHz. Other U.S. religious broadcasters operating at this hour include **WWCR** on 5935 kHz, **KTBN** on 7510 kHz, **WYFR-Family Radio** on 5950 kHz, and **WHRI-World Harvest Radio** on 6040 and 9495 kHz. For traditionalist Catholic programming, try **WEWN** on 5825 (or 7425) kHz.

HCJB—Voice of the Andes, Ecuador. Sixty minutes of religious programming to Australasia on 11755 kHz.

AFRTS Shortwave, USA. Network news, live sports, music and features in the upper-sideband mode from the Armed Forces Radio & Television Service. Transmitted from modestly powered U.S. Navy stations around the globe. Try 4278.5, 4319, 4995, 5765, 6350, 6458.5, 10320, 10940.5, 12579, 12689.5 and 13362 kHz.

10:30

Radio Korea International, South Korea. Summer only at this time. Starts off with *News*, followed Monday through Wednesday by *Economic News Briefs*. The remainder of the 30-minute broadcast is taken up by a feature: *Shortwave Feedback* (Sunday), *Seoul Calling* (Monday and Tuesday), *Pulse of Korea* (Wednesday), *From Us to You* (Thursday), *Let's Sing Together* (Friday) and *Weekly News Focus* (Saturday). On 11715 kHz via their Canadian relay, so this is the best chance for North Americans to hear the station. One hour later in winter.

Radio Prague, Czech Republic. This time summer only. Repeat of the 0700 broadcast; see 1130 for program specifics. A half hour to Europe on 9880 and 11615 kHz. One hour later during winter.

■Radio Netherlands. The second of two hours targeted at East and Southeast Asia and Australasia. Opens with a feature. Quality shows include ●*EuroQuest* (Monday), ●*A Good Life* (Tuesday), ●*Research File* (science, Thursday), ●*Roughly Speaking* (Saturday) and Friday's excellent ●*Documentary*. Other offerings include *Dutch Horizons* (Wednesday) and *Sound Fountain* (Sunday). Monday through Friday, the final 25 minutes are given to ●*Newsline*, replaced weekends by a simple *news* bulletin and Saturday's *Europe Unzipped* or Sunday's *Wide Angle*. On 7260 (winter), 9790, 12065 and (summer) 13710 kHz. For a separate summer broadcast to western Europe and eastern North America, see the next item.

■Radio Netherlands. Summer only at this time, and the first 60 minutes of an approximately two-hour broadcast. Weekdays, opens with ●*Newsline* (current events), which is replaced weekends by a *news* bulletin. The second half hour (more at weekends) is devoted to features. Choice pickings include ●*EuroQuest* (Monday), ●*A Good Life* (Tuesday), ●*Research File* (science, Thursday), ●*Roughly Speaking* (Saturday) and Friday's excellent ●*Documentary*. Other offerings include *Dutch Horizons* (Wednesday), *Europe Unzipped* and *Insight* (Saturday), and *Wide Angle* and *Sound Fountain* (Sunday). To western Europe on 6045 and 9860 kHz, and to eastern North America on 5965 kHz.

Radio Vilnius, Lithuania. Winter only at this time. A half hour that's mostly *news* and background reports about events in Lithuania. Of broader appeal is *Mailbag*, aired every other Sunday. For a little Lithuanian music, try the second half of Monday's broadcast. To western Europe on 9710 kHz. One hour earlier in summer.

Voice of Mongolia. Most days, it's *news*, reports and short features, all with a local flavor. The programs provide an interesting insight into the life and culture of a nation largely unknown to the rest of the world. The entire Sunday broadcast is devoted to exotic Mongolian music. Thirty minutes to Australasia on 12015 or 12085 kHz. Tends to be well heard in parts of the United States during March and September.

United Arab Emirates Radio, Dubai. *News*, then a feature dealing with one or more aspects of Arab life and culture. Weekends, there are replies to listeners' letters. To Europe and North Africa on 13675, 15370, 15395 and 21605 kHz.

OF
OUR LORD
CHURCH

This Russian Orthodox church is still going strong in Ninilchik, Alaska. The village is also home to America's newest shortwave station, owned by Aurora Communications. It expects to start broadcasting in 2002.

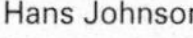
Hans Johnson

11:00

■**BBC World Service for the Americas.** Monday through Saturday winter, the lineup is *World Briefing*, *British News*, ●*World Business Report* (replaced by ●*World Business Review* on Saturday) and ●*Sports Roundup*. Sunday fare is the same for the first 30 minutes, but then it's *Arts in Action*. In summer, the first weekday half hour consists of special programming for the Caribbean, then a feature: ●*Letter from America* (Monday), ●*From Our Own Correspondent* (Thursday) and ●*Analysis* on the remaining days. The final 15-minute slot is filled by ●*Sports Roundup*, except for Friday's *Football Extra* (soccer). Weekend programs are the same as those for winter. Continuous programming to eastern North America and the Caribbean on 6195 and 15190 (or 15220) kHz. Listeners farther west should tune to the Asian stream on 9740 kHz.

■**BBC World Service for Europe.** Winter, identical to the service for the Americas, except that *Arts in Action* replaces ●*Agenda* at 1130 Sunday. Monday through Saturday summer, there's *World Briefing*, *British News*, ●*Analysis* (replaced Monday be ●*Letter from America* and Thursday by ●*From Our Own Correspondent*) and ●*Sports Roundup* (preempted Friday by *Football Extra*). Sunday, there's more of the same during the first 30 minutes, with *Arts in Action* completing the hour. Continuous to Europe and North Africa on 12095, 15485 and 15565 kHz.

■**BBC World Service for Eastern Europe and the Mideast.** *News*, then Monday through Friday there's an arts show, *Meridian*. The next half hour consists of a mixed bag of music and light entertainment, except for Thursday's ●*Omnibus*. On Saturday, the news if followed by *Wright Round the World*, and Sunday fare consists of *World Briefing*, *British News* and *Arts in Action*. Continues on 11760, 15565, 15575 and 17640 kHz.

■**BBC World Service for East and Southeast Asia and the Pacific.** Weekdays there's five minutes of *news*, then a pair of features: ●*Health Matters* and ●*Everywoman* (Monday), *Science View* and ●*Focus on Faith* (Tuesday), *Sports International* and *Pick of the World* (Wednesday), ●*One Planet* and *People and Places* (Thursday), and *Discovery* and *Essential Guide* on Friday. Some of the BBC's better offerings. Weekends, opens with *World Briefing* and *British News*, then it's Saturday's ●*Science in Action* or Sunday's first half hour of ●*Play of the Week* (the best in world theater). Continuous to East Asia on 9740, 9815 and 15280 kHz; to Southeast Asia on 6195 and 9740 kHz;

and to Australasia on 9740 kHz (also heard in western North America).

Radio Taipei International, Taiwan. Opens with 15 minutes of *News*, and Monday through Wednesday closes with *Let's Learn Chinese*. The remaining airtime is devoted to features. Monday's *Taiwan Economic Journal* is followed by *People*; Tuesday's shows are *Culture Express* and *Trends*; Wednesday's single offering is *New Music Lounge*; Thursday's triple bill brings *Instant Noodles*, *Life Unusual* and *Naluwan*; while Friday's slots are *Weekend Zoo* and *Business Chinese*. Weekend fare consists of Saturday's *Kaleidoscope* and *Mailbag Time*, and Sunday's *Great Wall Forum* and *Asia Pacific*. Sixty minutes to Southeast Asia on 7445 kHz, also audible in western parts of Australasia. Replaces the former Voice of Asia broadcast. For a separate transmission to East Asia, see the next item.

Radio Taipei International, Taiwan. Opens with 15 minutes of *News*, and with the exception of Sunday, closes with *Let's Learn Chinese*, which has a series of segments for beginning, intermediate and advanced learners. In between, there are either one or two features, depending on the day of the week. Monday, there's the pleasurable and exotic ●*Jade Bells and Bamboo Pipes* (Taiwanese music); Tuesday's lineup is *Culture Express* and *Trends*; Wednesday's slots are *Taiwan Today* and *Confucius and Inspiration Beyond*; Thursday's offerings are *Journey into Chinese Culture* and *Instant Noodles*; and Friday's coupling is *Taipei Magazine* and *East Meets West*. These are replaced Saturday by *Kaleidoscope* and *Naluwan*, and Sunday by *Great Wall Forum* and *Mailbag Time*. One hour to East Asia on 11985 kHz.

■**Deutsche Welle,** Germany. *News*, then weekdays it's ●*NewsLink* and *Hallo Africa* (not Monday). These are replaced Saturday by *Talking Point* and *African Kaleidoscope*, and Sunday by *Religion and Society* and *Cool*. Forty-five minutes to Africa on 11785 (summer), 15410, 17800 (winter), 17860 (summer) and 21780 kHz. Best for southern Africa is 15410 kHz. For a separate service to Europe, see the next item.

■**Deutsche Welle,** Germany. Similar to the service for Africa, but with an additional 15-minute feature: *Business German* (Monday), *People in Europe* (Tuesday), *German by Radio* (Wednesday), ●*Insight* (Thursday), ●*Man and Environment* (Friday), *Women on the Move* or *Development Forum* (Saturday) and Sunday's *Around Germany*. One hour to Europe on 6140 kHz.

Radio Australia. *World News*, with the remainder of the first half hour going to *Asia Pacific* (replaced Sunday by *Correspondents' Report*). Monday through Friday, the next 30 minutes consist of a sports bulletin and *Life Matters* (personal and social issues). Weekends, there's *Fine Music Australia* (classical music) at 1130 Saturday, and *Business Report* at the same time Sunday. Continuous to East Asia and the Pacific on 5995, 6020, 9580, 11880, 12080, 13605 and 21820 kHz; and heard in much of North America on 6020, 9580 and 13605 kHz. Listeners in Europe should try 21820 kHz.

Radio Bulgaria. Summer only at this time. Starts with *news*, then Tuesday through Saturday there's *Events and Developments* (preceded Saturday by *In Focus*). The remaining lineup includes *Answering Your Letters* (a listener-response show, Sunday), the enjoyable and exotic ●*Folk Studio* (Monday), *Magazine Economy* (Tuesday). *Arts and Artists* (Wednesday), *History Club* (Thursday), *The Way We Live* (Friday) and *DX Programed*, a Saturday show for radio enthusiasts. Tuesday through Sunday, the broadcast ends with *Keyword Bulgaria*. Sixty minutes to Europe on 15700 and 17500 kHz. One hour later during winter.

Radio Ukraine International. Summer only at this time. An hour's ample coverage of just about all things Ukrainian, including news, sports, politics and culture. Well worth a listen is ●*Music from Ukraine*, which fills most of the Sunday broadcast. Sixty minutes to Australasia on 21520 kHz, and one hour later in winter. Tends to be irregular due to financial limitations.

HCJB—Voice of the Andes, Ecuador. First 60 minutes of more than three hours of religious programming to the Americas on 12005 and 15115 kHz.

11:00–11:30

Voice of America. A mixed bag of sports, science, business and other news and features. To East Asia on 6110 (or 6160), 9760, 11705 (winter) and 15160 kHz, and to Australasia on 5985 (or 9770), 9645, 11720 and 15425 kHz.

Radio Jordan. A 60-minute partial relay of the station's domestic broadcasts, beamed to western Europe and eastern North America on 11690 or 17580 kHz.

Radio Japan. *News*, then weekdays there's *Asian Top News*. This is followed by a 35-minute feature: *Unforgettable Musical Masterpieces* (Monday), Japanese language lessons (Tuesday and Thursday), *Japanese Musical Log* (Wednesday), and Friday's *Music Beat* (Japanese popular music—old and new). *Pop Goes Asia* fills the Saturday slot, and is replaced Sunday by *Hello from Tokyo*. One hour to eastern North America on 6120 kHz; to East Asia on 15590 kHz; and to Southeast Asia on 9695 kHz.

Radio Singapore International. A three-hour package for Southeast Asia, and widely heard beyond. Starts with nine minutes of *news* (five at weekends), then Monday through Friday there's *Business and Market Report*, replaced Saturday by *Asia Below the Headlines*, and Sunday by *The Film Programed*. These are followed on the quarter-hour by *Arts Arena* (Monday), *Profile* (Tuesday), and *Star Trax* (Wednesday). A self-denominated lifestyle magazine—*Living*—pairs up with *Afterthought* on Thursday, and the eclectic and informative *Frontiers* fills the Friday slot. Weekends, look for *Regional Press Review* (1120 Saturday) and *Business World* (1115 Sunday). There's a daily 5-minute news bulletin on the half-hour, then one or more short features. Weekdays, take your pick from *Wired Up* (Internet, Monday), *Vox Box* (a radio soapbox, Tuesday), *Reflections* (musings, Wednesday), *The Film Programed* (Thursday), and *The Written Word* (Friday). The hour is rounded off with the 15-minute *Newsline*. Saturday fare consists of *Eco-Watch*, *Comment* and *Business World*; Sunday, there's *Frontiers* and *Regional Press Review*. On 6015 and 6150 kHz.

CBC North-Québec, Canada. Summer only at this time; see 1200 for specifics. Intended for a domestic audience, but also heard in the northeastern United States on 9625 kHz.

Voice of the Islamic Republic of Iran. The first hour of a 90-minute block of news, commentary and features, plus a little Iranian music. Strongly reflects an Islamic point of view. To West, South and Southeast Asia, but widely heard elsewhere. On 15185 (winter), 15385, 15430 (summer), 15585, 21470 and 21730 kHz.

WJCR, Upton, Kentucky. Continues with country gospel music to North America on 7490 kHz. Other U.S. religious broadcasters operating at this hour include **WWCR** on 5935 (or 15685) kHz, **KTBN** on 7510 kHz, **WYFR-Family Radio** on 5950 and 7355 (or 5850) kHz, and **WHRI-World Harvest Radio** on 6040 and 9495 kHz. Traditionalist Catholic programming can be found on **WEWN** on 5825 (or 7425) kHz.

AFRTS Shortwave, USA. Network news, live sports, music and features in the upper-sideband mode from the Armed Forces Radio & Television Service. Transmitted from modestly powered U.S. Navy stations around the globe. Try 4278.5, 4319, 4995, 5765, 6350, 6458.5, 10320, 10940.5, 12579, 12689.5 and 13362 kHz.

11:30

Radio Austria International. Summer only at this time. ●*Report from Austria*, which includes a brief bulletin of *news* followed by a series of current events and human interest stories. Tends to spotlight national and regional issues, and is an excellent source of news about Central Europe. Thirty minutes to Europe on 6155 and 13730 kHz. One hour later in winter.

Radio Korea International, South Korea. Winter only at this time. See 1030 for program details. A half hour on 9650 kHz via their Canadian relay, so a good chance for North Americans to hear the station. One hour earlier in summer.

■**Radio Netherlands.** Winter weekdays, opens with ●*Newsline* (current events), which

11:00–11:30

The Caribbean is an ideal location for world band relay stations. Propagation is so good that North Americans receive BBC World Service signals from there clearly, even though they are beamed elsewhere.

J.M. Brinker

is replaced weekends by a *news* bulletin. The second half hour (more at weekends) is given over to features. The lineup includes ●*EuroQuest* (Monday), ●*A Good Life* (Tuesday), ●*Research File* (science, Thursday), ●*Roughly Speaking* (Saturday) and Friday's excellent ●*Documentary*. Other offerings include *Dutch Horizons* (Wednesday), *Europe Unzipped* and *Insight* (Saturday), and *Wide Angle* and *Sound Fountain* (Sunday). Summer, starts with a feature and ends with ●*Newsline* (Monday through Friday) or a *news* bulletin (Saturday and Sunday). Pick of the litter are ●*Research File* (science, Monday), ●*Encore* (Thursday) ●*A Good Life* (Friday) and Wednesday's award-winning ●*Documentary*. On the remaining days, you can hear *Music 52-15* (Tuesday), *Sound Fountain* and *Europe Unzipped* (Saturday) and *Dutch Horizons* and *Sincerely Yours* on Sunday. To western Europe on 6045 and 9860 kHz, and to eastern North America on 5965 kHz.

Radio Vlaanderen Internationaal, Belgium. Weekdays, starts with *News*, then *Belgium Today*, *Press Review* and features. The lineup includes *The Arts* (Monday and Thursday), *Tourism* (Monday), *Focus on Europe* and *Sports* (Tuesday), *Green Society* (Wednesday), *Around Town* (Thursday), and *Economics* and *International Report* (Friday). Closes with *Soundbox*. These are replaced Saturday by *Music from Flanders*, and Sunday by *Radio World*, *Tourism*, *Brussels 1043* (a listener-response program) and *Soundbox*. Thirty minutes to southern Europe summer on 9925 kHz (one hour later in winter); and year round to East Asia and Australasia on 9865 kHz.

Radio Prague, Czech Republic. Winter only at this time. *News*, then Monday through Friday it's *Current Affairs* plus a feature. *Spotlight* (a jaunt around the Czech Republic) alternates with *One on One* (a series of informal interviews) on Mondays; *Talking Point* occupies the Tuesday slot; and the Wednesday show is either *Czechs in History* or *Central Europe Today*. Thursday's feature is the business-oriented *Economic Report*, and *Magazine* is heard on Friday. Weekends, the news is followed by Saturday's *Readings from Czech Literature* and an excellent musical feature (strongly recommended), and Sunday by *A Letter from Prague*, *The Arts* and *Mailbag*. Thirty minutes to Europe on 11640 kHz, and to East Africa on 21745 kHz. The latter channel is also audible in parts of the Mideast.

Wales Radio International. Winter Saturdays only at this time. Thirty minutes of news, interviews and music for Australasia on 17625 (or 17650) kHz. One hour later in summer (Oz winter).

Radio Sweden. Summer only at this time; see 1230 for program details. To North America on 18960 kHz.

1200-1759
Western Australia & East Asia—Evening Prime Time
North America—Morning and Lunchtime
Europe & Mideast—Afternoon and Early Evening

12:00

■**BBC World Service for the Americas.** A full hour of news and current events in ●*Newshour* (may be one hour later in winter), except for the first 20 minutes summer weekdays, when there's alternative programming for the Caribbean. Continuous to North America and the Caribbean on 6195 and 15190 (or 15220) kHz. Listeners in western states may get a better signal from the Asian stream on 9740 kHz.

■**BBC World Service for Europe.** Winter, you can hear the daily ●*Newshour*—60 minutes of news and current events. Monday through Friday summer, starts with a *news* bulletin and is followed by *Outlook* and a 15-minute feature. Weekends, the news is followed by Saturday's *Wright Round the World* or Sunday's *The Alternative* (popular music) and *Global Business*. Continuous to Europe and North Africa on 12095, 15485 and 15565 kHz.

■**BBC World Service for Eastern Europe and the Mideast.** ●*Newshour*—the best in news and analysis. Some general interest items, too. Continuous programming on 11760, 15565, 15575 and 17640 kHz.

■**BBC World Service for East and Southeast Asia and the Pacific.** Monday through Friday, five minutes of *news* are followed by *Outlook* (news and human interest stories). The hour ends with a 15-minute feature. Saturday fare consists of a *news* bulletin, some light entertainment (●*Brain of Britain* part of the year) and the excellent ●*Assignment* (or alternative documentary). Sunday, it's the final part of ●*Play of the Week*, which runs till 1230 or 1300. If the former, ●*Agenda* takes over the second half hour. Continuous to East Asia on 6195, 9740, 9815 (summer) and 15280 kHz; to Southeast Asia on 6195 and 9740 kHz; and to Australasia on 9740 kHz. Also audible in western North America on 9740 kHz.

Radio Canada International. Summer weekdays only at this time. The first 60 minutes of a three-hour block of the Canadian Broadcasting Corporation's *This Morning*. To eastern North America and the Caribbean on 9640, 15305 and 17820 kHz. For a separate year-round service to Asia, see the next item.

Radio Canada International. *News*, then Monday through Friday it's *World Report* and *Canada Today*. These are replaced Saturday by *The House* (Canadian politics), and Sunday by the informative and entertaining *Quirks and Quarks* (a science show). One hour to East and Southeast Asia winter on 9660 and 11730 kHz, and summer on 9660 and 15190 kHz.

Radio Tashkent, Uzbekistan. *News* and commentary, followed by features such as *Life in the Village* (Wednesday), a listeners' request program (Monday), and local music (Thursday). Heard better in Asia, Australasia and Europe than in North America. Thirty minutes winter on 5060, 5975, 6025 and 9715 kHz; and summer on 7285, 9715, 15295 and 17775 kHz.

■**Radio France Internationale.** Opens with a *news* bulletin, then there's a 25-minute feature— *French Lesson*, *Crossroads*, *Voices*, *Rendez-Vous*, *World Tracks*, *Weekend* or *Club 9516* (a listener-response program). A half hour to West Africa (and audible in parts of eastern North America) on 15540 kHz, and to East Africa on 25820 kHz.

Radio Bulgaria. This time winter only; see 1100 for specifics. Unlike most other stations, Radio Bulgaria continues to feature folk music in its program lineup. Particularly worthy of note is the 15-minute ●*Folk Studio* aired at 1210 Monday. Sixty minutes to Europe on 15700 and 17500 kHz. One hour earlier in summer.

Radio Polonia, Poland. This time summer only. Sixty minutes of news, commentary, features and music—all with a Polish accent. Monday through Friday, it's *News from*

Poland—a potpourri of news, reports and interviews. This is followed by an arts program, *Focus*, and *Chart Show* (a cultural clash, Monday); *Day in the Life* and *Request Concert* (Tuesday); *Cookery Corner* and *The Best of Polish Radio* (Wednesday); *Letter from Poland* and *Multimedia Show* (Thursday); and Friday's *Business Week* and *Discovering Chopin* (or an alternative classical music feature). The Saturday broadcast begins with a bulletin of *news*, then there's *Panorama* (investigative reporting) and *Soundcheck*. Sundays, you can hear *The Weeklies*, *Europe East* and *Postbag*, a listener-response program. To Europe on 6095, 7145, 7270, 9525 and 11820 kHz. One hour later in winter.

Radio Australia. *World News*, then Monday through Thursday it's *Late Night Live* (round-table discussion). On the remaining days, there's Friday's *Sound Quality* (music), Saturday's *The Spirit of Things*, and Sunday's *Country Club* (not all country music comes from Nashville!). Continuous to Asia and the Pacific on 5995, 6020, 9580, 11650, 11880 and 21820 kHz; and well heard in much of North America on 6020, 9580 and 11650 kHz. Listeners in Europe should try 21820 kHz.

Radio Jordan. A 60-minute partial relay of the station's domestic broadcasts, beamed to western Europe and eastern North America on 11690 or 17580 kHz.

Radio Ukraine International. Winter only at this time. See 1100 for specifics. Sixty minutes to Australasia on 21510 kHz, and one hour earlier in summer. Tends to be irregular due to financial limitations.

Radio Korea International, South Korea. Opens with *news* and commentary, followed Monday through Wednesday by *Seoul Calling*. Weekly features include *Echoes of Korean Music* and *Shortwave Feedback* (Sunday), *Tales from Korea's Past* (Monday), *Korean Cultural Trails* (Tuesday), *Pulse of Korea* (Wednesday), *From Us to You* (a listener-response program) and *Let's Learn Korean* (Thursday), *Let's Sing Together* and *Korea Through Foreigners' Eyes* (Friday), and Saturday's *Discovering Korea*, *Korean Literary Corner* and *Weekly News Focus*. Sixty minutes to East Asia on 7285 kHz.

CBC North-Québec, Canada. Part of an 18-hour multilingual broadcast for a domestic audience, but which is also heard in the northeastern United States. Weekend programming at this hour is in English, and features *news* followed by the enjoyably eclectic ●*Good Morning Québec* (Saturday) or *Fresh Air* (Sunday). Starts at this time winter, but summer it is already into the second hour. On 9625 kHz.

HCJB—Voice of the Andes, Ecuador. Continuous religious programming to the Americas on 12005 and 15115 kHz.

Radio Singapore International. Continuous programming to Southeast Asia and beyond. Starts with five minutes of *news*, a weather report, and either the weekday *Front Page* (headlines from local and regional dailies) or instrumental music (Saturday and Sunday). Weekdays, the next 20 minutes are devoted to music. Take your pick from *E-Z Beat* (Monday and Tuesday), *Classic Gold* (Wednesday and Friday) and *Love Songs* on Thursday. There are two Saturday slots, *Star Trax* and *Currencies*, replaced Sunday by *Comment* and *Profile*. On the half-hour, it's either the weekday *Business and Market Report* or a five-minute news bulletin. The next 25 minutes are given over to features. Monday, it's *The Written Word* and *Business World*; Tuesday, there's *Living* and *Asia Below the Headlines*; and Wednesday's pairing is *Wired Up* and *Frontiers*. Thursday's offerings are *Vox Box* and *Arts Arena*; and Friday brings *Reflections* and *Profile*. Weekends are devoted to repeats of shows aired earlier in the week—Saturday's features are *Arts Arena* and *Wired Up*; and Sunday's lineup is *Living*, *Snapshots*, *Afterthought* and *Currencies*. On 6015 and 6150 kHz.

Radio Taipei International, Taiwan. Opens with 15 minutes of *News*, and with the exception of Sunday, closes with *Let's Learn Chinese*. The remaining airtime is filled with either one or two features, depending on which day it is. Monday, there's the thoroughly enjoyable ●*Jade Bells and Bamboo Pipes* (Taiwanese music), replaced Tuesday by *Culture Express* and *Trends*; Wednesday's slots are *Taiwan Today* and *Confucius and Inspiration*

12:00–12:30

Beyond; Thursday's lineup is *Journey into Chinese Culture* and *Instant Noodles*; and Friday's combo is *Taipei Magazine* and *East Meets West*. These are replaced Saturday by *Kaleidoscope* and *Naluwan*, and Sunday by *Great Wall Forum* and *Mailbag Time*. One hour to East Asia on 7130 kHz, and to Australasia on 9610kHz.

Voice of the Islamic Republic of Iran. Final half hour of a 90-minute broadcast with the accent firmly on Islam and Islamic culture. To West, South and Southeast Asia, but widely heard beyond. On 15185 (winter),15385, 15430 (summer), 15585, 21470 and 21730 kHz.

Voice of Korea, North Korea. Just about the last of the old-time communist stations, with quaint terms like "Great Leader" and "Unrivaled Great Man" seemingly destined for immortality. Starts with *"news,"* with much of the remainder of the broadcast devoted to revering the late Kim Il Sung. Abominably bad programs, but worth the occasional listen just to hear how awful they are. One hour to Africa and the Mideast on 9660 and 9975 kHz, and to Southeast Asia and the Americas on 9850, 11335 and 13650 kHz.

Voice of America. A mixed bag of current events, sports, science, business and other news and features. To East Asia on 6110 (or 6160), 9760, 11715, 11705 (winter) and 15160 kHz; and to Australasia on 9645, 11715 and 15425 kHz.

China Radio International. *News*, followed weekdays by in-depth reports. Next come features, including regular shows like *People in the Know* (Monday), *Sportsworld* (Tuesday), *China Horizons* (Wednesday), *Voices from Other Lands* (Thursday) and Friday's *Life in China*. The weekend lineup includes Saturday's *Global Review* and *Listeners' Garden*, and Sunday's *Report from Developing Countries* and *In the Spotlight*. One hour to Southeast Asia on 11980 kHz, and to Australasia on 9760, 11675 (or 11760) and 15415 kHz.

WJCR, Upton, Kentucky. Continues with country gospel music to North America on 7490 kHz. Other U.S. religious broadcasters operating at this hour include **WWCR** on 5935 (or 13845) and 15685 kHz, **KTBN** on 7510 kHz, **WYFR-Family Radio** on 5950, 7355 (or 5850), 11830 (winter) and 11970 (or 17750) kHz, and **WHRI-World Harvest Radio** on 6040 and 9495 kHz. For traditionalist Catholic programming, tune **WEWN** on 5825 (or 7425) kHz.

AFRTS Shortwave, USA. Network news, live sports, music and features in the upper-sideband mode from the Armed Forces Radio & Television Service. Transmitted from modestly powered U.S. Navy stations around the globe. Try 4278.5, 4319, 4995, 5765, 6350, 6458.5, 10320, 10940.5, 12579, 12689.5 and 13362 kHz.

12:15

Radio Cairo, Egypt. The start of a 75-minute package of news, religion, culture and entertainment, much of it devoted to Arab and Islamic themes. The initial quarter hour consists of virtually anything, from quizzes to Islamic religious talks, then there's *news* and commentary, which in turn give way to political and cultural items. To Asia on 17595 kHz.

12:30

Radio Austria International. Monday through Saturday, winter only, at this time (the Sunday broadcast is at 1310 on the same frequencies). ●*Report from Austria*, a compilation of national and regional news, current

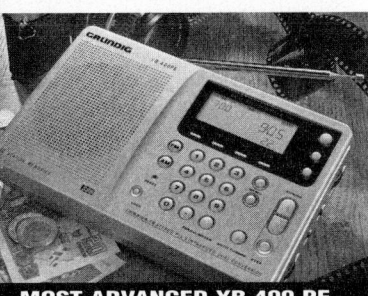

events and human interest stories. Thirty minutes to Europe on 6155 and 13730 kHz. One hour earlier in summer.

Radio Bangladesh. *News*, followed by Islamic and general interest features and pleasant Bengali music. Thirty minutes to Southeast Asia, also heard in Europe, on 7185 and 9550 kHz. Frequencies may vary slightly.

■Radio Netherlands. Winter only at this time. The second of two hours for listeners in western Europe and eastern North America. Starts with a feature and ends with ●*Newsline* (Monday through Friday) or a *news* bulletin (weekends). Quality shows include ●*Research File* (science, Monday), ●*Encore* (Thursday) ●*A Good Life* (Friday) and Wednesday's award-winning ●*Documentary*. On the remaining days, you can hear *Music 52-15* (Tuesday), *Sound Fountain* and *Europe Unzipped* (Saturday) and *Dutch Horizons* and *Sincerely Yours* on Sunday. To western Europe on 6045 and 9860 kHz, and to eastern North America on 5965 kHz.

Radio Vlaanderen Internationaal, Belgium. Winter only at this time; see 1130 for specifics. A half hour to southern Europe on 9925 kHz. One hour earlier in summer.

Voice of Vietnam. Repeat of the 1000 transmission. A half hour to Southeast Asia on 9840 and 12020 kHz. Frequencies may vary slightly.

Radio Thailand. Thirty minutes of *news* and short features. To Southeast Asia and Australasia, winter on 9810 kHz and summer on 9885 kHz. Also available to Asia on 9655 and 11905 kHz, although operation on these channels tends to be somewhat irregular.

Voice of Turkey. This time summer only. Fifty-five minutes of *news*, features and Turkish music beamed to Europe on 17830 kHz, and to Southeast Asia and Australasia on 21540 kHz. One hour later in winter.

Radio Sweden. Monday through Friday, it's *news* and features in *Sixty Degrees North*, concentrating heavily on Scandinavian topics. The Monday slot goes to *SportScan*, replaced Tuesday by *Close Up* or an alternative feature, and Wednesday by *Money Matters*. Thursday features a different show each week of the month—*Nordic Report*, *GreenScan*, *Heart Beat* or *S-Files*, while Friday offers a review of the week's news. Saturday's slot is filled by *Weekend*, *Spectrum* (the arts), *Sweden Today* or *Studio 49*, and Sunday fare consists of *In Touch with Stockholm* (a listener-response program) or the musical *Sounds Nordic*. A year-round half hour to North America on 18960 kHz; and summer to Asia and Australasia on 17505 and 21530 kHz.

Radio Korea International, South Korea. Starts off with *news*, followed Monday through Wednesday by *Economic News Briefs*. The remainder of the broadcast is taken up by a feature: *Shortwave Feedback* (Sunday), *Seoul Calling* (Monday and Tuesday), *Pulse of Korea* (Wednesday), *From Us to You* (Thursday), *Let's Sing Together* (Friday) and *Weekly News Focus* (Saturday). Thirty minutes to East and Southeast Asia on 6055, 9570, 9640 and 13670 kHz.

Wales Radio International. Summer Saturdays only at this time. News, interviews and local music from Britain's westernmost region. Thirty minutes to Australasia on 17650 kHz, and one hour earlier in winter.

13:00

■BBC World Service for the Americas. A five-minute *news* bulletin is followed by the long-running *Outlook* (unfortunately not as good as it used to be) and the enjoyable ●*Off the Shelf* (readings from world literature). There's a possibility ●*Newshour* may be switched to this slot for winter, in which case the other programs would be aired one hour earlier. Continuous programming to North America and the Caribbean on 6195 and 15190 (or 15220) kHz. The Asian stream on 9740 kHz is likely to provide better reception in western North America.

■BBC World Service for Europe. Monday through Friday winter, starts with a *news* bulletin, then it's *Outlook* (news and human interest stories) and a 15-minute feature. Weekends, the news is followed by Saturday's

Wright Round the World or Sunday's *The Alternative* (popular music) and *Global Business*. Summer weekdays, five minutes of *news* are followed by an arts show, *Meridian* (except Monday, when ●*Omnibus* is aired in its place). The next half hour consists of a mixed bag of music and light entertainment. Saturday, there's 60 minutes of news and current events in ●*Newshour*, reduced Sunday to a half hour, and complemented by *Sportsworld*. Continuous to Europe and North Africa on 12095, 15485 and 15565 kHz.

■**BBC World Service for Eastern Europe and the Mideast.** Starts with *News*, then it's all features. Pick of the weekday litter are *Discovery* (science, 0705 Monday), Tuesday's pairing of ●*Health Matters* and ●*Everywoman*, Wednesday's ●*Focus on Faith* (0730) and Friday's ●*One Planet* (0705). Weekend fare consists of Saturday's *Jazzmatazz* and ●*People and Politics*, and Sunday's quiz or panel game followed by *Global Business*. Continuous programming on 11760, 15565, 15575 and 17640 kHz.

■**BBC World Service for East and Southeast Asia and the Pacific.** Fifty minutes of ●*Newshour* (a full hour on weekends), with ●*World Business Report* occupying the remaining 10-minute weekday slot. To East and Southeast Asia on 6195 and 9740 kHz, and to Australasia on 9740 kHz (also audible in western North America).

Radio Canada International. Monday through Friday winter, and daily in summer. Winter, it's the first 60 minutes of a three-hour block of the Canadian Broadcasting Corporation's *This Morning*; summer weekdays, the second hour thereof. Summer Saturdays, there's a look at Canadian politics in *The House*, and Sunday it's the start of yet another three-hour show, *The Sunday Edition*. To eastern North America and the Caribbean winter weekdays on 9515, 9640 and 17710 kHz. The summer schedule is a little more complicated: Monday through Friday on 9640, 15305 and 17820 kHz; and weekends on 9640, 15305 and 17800 kHz.

China Radio International. Repeat of the 1200 broadcast; see there for specifics. One hour to Southeast Asia on 11980 and 15180 kHz; and to Australasia on 11675 (or 11760) and 11900 kHz. Also available to eastern North America on 9570 kHz; and summer only to western North America on 7405 kHz.

Radio Polonia, Poland. This time winter only. *News*, commentary, music and a variety of features. See 1200 for specifics. Sixty minutes to Europe on 6095, 7270, 9525 and 11820 kHz. Listeners in southeastern Canada and the northeastern United States should also try 11820 kHz. One hour earlier during summer.

Radio Prague, Czech Republic. Summer only at this time. *News*, then Monday through Friday there's *Current Affairs* and a feature. Monday, it's either *Spotlight* (a look at Czech regional affairs) or *One on One* (an informal interview show); Tuesday, there's *Talking Point* (issues shaping people's lives in the Czech Republic); and the Wednesday show is either *Czechs in History* or *Central Europe Today*. *Economic Report* fills the Thursday slot, and the Friday feature is *Magazine*. Weekends, following the news, the Saturday lineup consists of *Readings from Czech Literature* plus an excellent musical feature (strongly recommended), replaced Sunday by *A Letter from Prague*, *The Arts* and *Mailbag*. Thirty minutes to Europe on 13580 kHz, and to South Asia (audible in parts of the Mideast) on 21745 kHz.

Radio Jordan. A partial relay of the station's domestic broadcasts, beamed to Europe on 11690 kHz. Continuous till 1630 (1730 in winter).Also audible in parts of eastern North America, especially during winter.

Radio Cairo, Egypt. The final half-hour of the 1215 broadcast, consisting of listener participation programs, Arabic language lessons and a summary of the latest news. To Asia on 17595 kHz.

CBC North-Québec, Canada. Continues with multilingual programming for a domestic audience. *News*, then winter Saturdays it's the second hour of ●*Good Morning Québec*, replaced Sunday by *Fresh Air*. In summer, the news is followed by *The House* (Canadian politics, Saturday) or the highly professional

13:00–14:00

●*Sunday Morning*. Weekday programs are mainly in languages other than English. Audible in the northeastern United States on 9625 kHz.

Radio Romania International. First afternoon broadcast for European listeners. *News*, commentary, press review, and features about Romanian life and culture, interspersed with lively Romanian folk music. Fifty-five minutes winter on 11940 and 15390 kHz, and summer on 15390 and 17770 kHz. Also targeted at Canada: winter on 15335 and 17735 kHz, and summer on 15250 and 17790 kHz.

Radio Australia. Monday through Friday, there's a quarter-hour of *news* followed by 45 minutes of World Music in ●*The Planet*. Weekends, after five minutes of *news*, it's either Saturday's *Science Show* or the second part of Sunday's *Country Club*. Continuous programming to Asia and the Pacific on 5995, 6020, 9580, 11650, 11660 (from 1330), 11880 (till 1330) and 21820 kHz; and easily audible in much of North America on 6020, 9580 and 11650 kHz. In Europe, try 21820 kHz.

Radio Singapore International. The third and final hour of a daily broadcasting package to Southeast Asia and beyond. Starts with a five-minute bulletin of the latest *news*, then most days it's music: *Singapop* (local talent, Monday and Thursday); *Music and Memories* (nostalgia, Tuesday); *Spin the Globe* (world music, Wednesday and Saturday); and *Hot Trax* (new releases, Saturday). *Friends of the Airwaves*, a listener-participation show, occupies the Sunday slot. There's more news on the half-hour, then a short feature. Monday's offering is *Snapshots*, replaced Tuesday by *Afterthought*. Wednesday and Thursday feature *Eco-Watch*, with the Thursday edition repeated the following Wednesday. The rest of the lineup consists of *Comment* (Friday), *The Written Word* (Saturday) and Sunday's *Reflections*. Weekdays, these are followed by *Newsline*, replaced Saturday by *Regional Press Review*, and Sunday by *Vox Box*. The broadcast ends with yet another five-minute news update. On 6015 and 6150 kHz.

WJCR, Upton, Kentucky. Continues with country gospel music to North America on 7490 kHz. Other U.S. religious broadcasters operating at this hour include **WWCR** on 5935 (or 13845) and 15685 kHz, **KTBN** 7510 kHz, **WYFR-Family Radio** on 11740, 11830, 11970, 13695 and 17750 kHz, and **WHRI-World Harvest Radio** on 6040 and 15105 kHz. Traditionalist Catholic programming is available via **WEWN** on 11875 kHz.

HCJB—Voice of the Andes, Ecuador. A further 60 minutes of religious broadcasting to the Americas on 12005 and 15115 kHz.

Voice of America. A mix of current events and sports, science, business and other news and features. To East Asia on 6110 (or 6160), 9760, 11705 (winter) and 15160 kHz; and to Australasia on 9645 and 15425 kHz. Both areas are also served by 11715 kHz until 1330.

AFRTS Shortwave, USA. Network news, live sports, music and features in the upper-sideband mode from the Armed Forces Radio & Television Service. Transmitted from modestly powered U.S. Navy stations around the globe. Try 4278.5, 4319, 4995, 5765, 6350, 6458.5, 10320, 10940.5, 12579, 12689.5 and 13362 kHz.

13:30

United Arab Emirates Radio, Dubai. *News*, then a feature on an Arab or Islamic theme. Twenty minutes to Europe and North Africa (also audible in eastern North America) on 13630, 13675, 15395 and 21605 kHz.

Radio Austria International. ●*Report from Austria*, which consists of a short bulletin of *news* followed by a series of current events and human interest stories. Good coverage of national and regional issues. To Asia and Australasia winter on 17855 kHz, and summer on 21780 kHz. Also to Europe, summer only, on 6165 and 13730 kHz (one hour later in winter).

Radio Yugoslavia. Winter only at this time. Thirty minutes of news and short features to Australasia on 11835 kHz. Moves to 2200 in summer.

Voice of Turkey. This time winter only. *News*, followed by *Review of the Turkish Press* and features (some of them unusual) with a strong local flavor. Selections of Turkish popular and classical music complete the program. Fifty-five minutes to Europe on 17815 kHz, and to Southeast Asia and Australasia on 17685 kHz. One hour earlier in summer.

Radio Sweden. See 1230 for program details. Thirty minutes to North America summer on 18960 kHz. Also to Asia and Australasia winter on 9430 and year round on 17505 kHz.

Voice of Vietnam. Begins with *news*, then there's *Commentary* or *Weekly Review*, followed by short features and pleasant Vietnamese music (particularly at weekends). A half hour to Europe on 7145 (winter), 9730 and (summer) 13740 kHz.

All India Radio. The first half hour of a 90-minute package of exotic Indian music, regional and international *news*, commentary, and a variety of talks and features of general interest. To Southeast Asia and beyond on 9690, 11620 and 13710 kHz.

Radio Tashkent, Uzbekistan. *News* and commentary, then features. Look for an information and music program on Tuesdays, with more music on Sundays. Apart from Wednesday's *Business Club*, most other features are broadcast on a non-weekly basis. Heard in Asia, Australasia, Europe and occasionally in North America; winter on 5060, 5975, 6025 and 9715 kHz; and summer on 7285, 9715, 15295 and 17775 kHz.

14:00

■BBC World Service for the Americas. *News*, then weekdays there's 25 minutes of *Meridian* (the arts). The second half hour is much more lowbrow—popular music and (Wednesday and Friday) a soap. Weekend programming consists of a five-minute *news* bulletin followed by Saturday's *Sportsworld* or a Sunday call-in show, *Talking Point*. Continuous to North America and the Caribbean on 15190 (or 17840) kHz. Listeners in the western United States may get better reception from the Asian stream on 9740 kHz.

■BBC World Service for Europe. Winter weekdays, five minutes of *news* are followed

Lifelong veteran of RFE-RL and frequency manager for Family Radio, Stanley Leinwoll comes as close as anybody to being "Mister Shortwave." M. Leinwoll

by an arts show, *Meridian*. The next half hour consists of a mixed bag of music and light entertainment. Same time summer, the *news* is followed by two features, including some of the BBC's better offerings—*Discovery* and *Essential Guide* (Monday), ●*Health Matters* and ●*Everywoman* (Tuesday), ●*Focus on Faith* (1430 Wednesday), *Sports International* and *Pick of the World* (Thursday) and Friday's ●*One Planet* and *People and Places*. Weekend programs are the same all year: five minutes of *news* followed by Saturday's *Sportsworld* or Sunday's *Talking Point*, a call-in show. Continuous to Europe and North Africa on 12095, 15485 and 15565 kHz.

■BBC World Service for Eastern Europe and the Mideast. Similar to the service for Asia and the Pacific, except for the first half hour weekdays, when *World Briefing* and ●*World Business Report* take the place of *East Asia Today*. Continuous programming on 15565, 15575 and 17740 kHz.

■BBC World Service for East and Southeast Asia and the Pacific. The weekday lineup is *East Asia Today*, *British News* and ●*Sports Roundup*. Weekends, starts with *news*, then it's either Saturday's live *Sportsworld* or Sunday's call-in show, *Talking Point*. Continuous to East and Southeast Asia on 6195 and 9740 kHz, and to Australasia on 9740 kHz (also audible in western North America).

14:00–14:00

Radio Japan. *News*, then Monday through Friday there's *Japan and World 44 Minutes* (an in-depth look at current trends and events). This is replaced Saturday by *Weekend Square*, and Sunday by *Pop Goes Asia*. One hour to the Mideast winter on 11880 kHz, and summer on 17755 kHz; to western North America on 9505 kHz; to South Asia on 9845 (winter) or (summer) 11730 kHz; and to Southeast Asia on 7200 kHz.

■**Radio France Internationale.** Weekdays, opens with international and Asian *news*; then come in-depth reports, a look at the main news event of the day in France, and sports. *Asia-Pacific*, replaces the international report on Saturday, and Sunday fare includes a weekly report on cultural events in France and a phone-in feature. These are followed on the half-hour by a 25-minute feature— *French Lesson*, *Crossroads*, *Voices*, *Rendez-Vous*, *World Tracks*, *Weekend* or *Club 9516* (a listener-response program). An hour of interesting and well-produced programming to the Mideast and beyond on 17620 kHz; and to South Asia on 11610 kHz.

The Voice of Turkey not only provides timely news, but also details Turkish culture and history, including this from Anatolia. VoT

Voice of Russia World Service. Summer only at this time. Eleven minutes of *News*, followed Monday through Saturday by much of the same in *News and Views*. Completing the lineup is *Sunday Panorama* and *Russia: People and Events*. On the half-hour, the lineup includes some of the station's better entertainment features. Try ●*Folk Box* (Monday), ●*Music at Your Request* or ●*Music Around Us* (Tuesday and Thursday), ●*Jazz Club* (Wednesday) and Friday's retrospective ●*Moscow Yesterday and Today*, all of which should please. Making up the roster are Saturday's *Timelines* and Sunday's *Kaleidoscope*. Targeted at South and Southeast Asia at this hour. Best for Southeast Asia is 12055 kHz, although 15510 kHz should also provide reasonable reception.

Radio Australia. *World News* is followed Monday through Friday by a continuation of ●*The Planet* (world music) , Saturday's *New Dimensions* or Sunday's *Books and Writing*. Continuous to Asia and the Pacific on 5995, 6080, 9580, 11650 and 11660 kHz (5995, 9580 and 11650 kHz are audible in North America, especially to the west). In Southeast Asia, use 6080 or 11660 kHz.

Radio Prague, Czech Republic. Winter only at this time. *News*, then weekdays there's *Current Affairs* and a feature. On Monday, *Spotlight* (a look at Czech regional affairs) alternates with *One on One* (an informal interview show); Tuesday's regular spot is *Talking Point* (issues shaping the lives of people in the Czech Republic); and the Wednesday show is either *Czechs in History* or *Central Europe Today*. Thursday's business-oriented *Economic Report* is substituted Friday by *Magazine* ("the show that starts where the news ends"). Weekends, the news is followed Saturday by *Readings from Czech Literature* plus an excellent musical feature, and Sunday by *A Letter from Prague*, *The Arts* and *Mailbag*. A friendly half hour to eastern North America and East Africa on 21745 kHz.

Voice of America. This time winter only. The first of several hours of continuous programming to the Mideast. *News*, current events and short features covering sports, science, business, entertainment and other topics. On 15205 kHz.

14:00–14:30

Chinese tourists explain a Grundig world band portable to their Tibetan guide. E.A. Hozour

XERMX—Radio México Internacional. Summer only at this time. Monday through Friday, there's an English summary of the Spanish-language *Antena Radio*, replaced Saturday by *Mirror of Mexico*, and Sunday by *Regional Roots and Rhythms*. Thirty minutes, best heard in western and southern parts of the United States on 9705 and 11770 kHz. One hour later in winter.

Radio Taipei International, Taiwan. Opens with 15 minutes of *News*, and closes Monday through Wednesday with *Let's Learn Chinese*. The remaining airtime is taken up by features. Monday, there's *Taiwan Economic Journal* followed by *People*; Tuesday's pairing is *Culture Express* and *Trends*; Wednesday's single show is *New Music Lounge*; Thursday's offerings are the delightfully named *Instant Noodles*, *Life Unusual* and *Naluwan*; and Friday's combination is *Weekend Zoo* and *Business Chinese*. The Saturday slots are filled by *Kaleidoscope* and *Mailbag Time*, with *Great Wall Forum* and *Asia Pacific* making up the Sunday menu. One hour to Southeast Asia on 15265 kHz.

China Radio International. Starts with *News*, then weekdays there are background reports. The rest of the broadcast is devoted to features. Regular shows include *People in the Know* (Monday), *Sportsworld* (Tuesday), *China Horizons* (Wednesday), *Voices from Other Lands* (Thursday), and *Life in China* on Friday. The Saturday lineup includes *Global Review* and *Listeners' Garden* (reports, music and Chinese language lessons), and Sunday's broadcast has *Report from Developing Countries* and *In the Spotlight*. One hour to western North America on 7405 and 17720 kHz; to South Asia on 7180 (winter), 9700, 11675, 11765 (winter), and (summer) 11825 and 15110 kHz; and to East Africa on 13685 and 15125 kHz.

All India Radio. The final hour of a 90-minute package of regional and international *news*, commentary, features and exotic Subcontinental music. To Southeast Asia and beyond on 9690, 11620 and 13710 kHz.

Radio Canada International. Winter weekdays, it's the second of three hours of *This Morning*; summer, the final 60 minutes of the same. Winter Saturdays, there's a look at Canadian politics in *The House*; summer, it's the entertaining ●*Vinyl Café*. On the remaining day, there's 60 minutes of another three-hour show, *The Sunday Edition*. To eastern North America and the Caribbean winter on 9515, 9640 and 17710 kHz; and summer on 9640,

15305 and (Monday through Friday) 17820 kHz. Weekends, 17820 kHz is replaced by 17800 kHz.

HCJB—Voice of the Andes, Ecuador. The final 30 minutes of religious fare to the Americas on 12005 and 15115 kHz.

CBC North-Québec, Canada. Continues with multilingual programming for a domestic audience. *News*, followed winter Saturdays by *The House* (Canadian politics). In summer, it's *The Great Eastern*, a magazine for Newfoundlanders. Sundays, there's the excellent ●*Sunday Morning*. Weekday programs are in languages other than English. Audible in the northeastern United States on 9625 kHz.

Radio Jordan. A partial relay of the station's domestic broadcasts, beamed to Europe on 11690 kHz. Continuous till 1630 (1730 in winter). Also audible in parts of eastern North America, especially during winter.

Voice of America. *News* and reports on a variety of topics. To East Asia on 6110 (or 6160), 9760, 11705 (winter) and 15160 kHz; and to Australasia on 15425 kHz.

Radio Thailand. Thirty minutes of tourist features for Southeast Asia and Australasia; winter on 9530 kHz, and summer on 9830 kHz. Also available to Asia on 9655 and 11905 kHz, although operation on these channels tends to be somewhat irregular.

WJCR, Upton, Kentucky. Continues with country gospel music to North America on 7490 kHz. Other U.S. religious broadcasters operating at this hour include **WWCR** on 13845 and 15685 kHz, **KTBN** on 7510 kHz, **WYFR-Family Radio** on 11740, 11830, 11970 (or 17760) and 17750 kHz, and **WHRI-World Harvest Radio** on 6040 and 15105 kHz. For traditionalist Catholic fare, try **WEWN** on 11875 kHz.

CFRX-CFRB, Toronto, Canada. Audible throughout much of the northeastern United States and southeastern Canada during the hours of daylight with a modest, but clear, signal on 6070 kHz. This pleasant, friendly station carries news, sports, weather and traffic reports—most of it intended for a local audience. Call in if you'd like at +1 (514) 790-0600—comments from outside Ontario are welcomed. Weekdays at this hour, you can hear *The Charles Adler Show*.

AFRTS Shortwave, USA. Network news, live sports, music and features in the upper-sideband mode from the Armed Forces Radio & Television Service. Transmitted from modestly powered U.S. Navy stations around the globe. Try 4278.5, 4319, 4995, 5765, 6350, 6458.5, 10320, 10940.5, 12579, 12689.5 and 13362 kHz.

14:30

■**Radio Netherlands.** The first 60 minutes of a two-hour block of programming. Monday through Friday it's ●*Newsline* (current events) and a feature. Pick of an excellent pack are ●*Research File* (science, Monday), ●*Encore* (Thursday), ●*A Good Life* (Friday) and Wednesday's award-winning ●*Documentary*. Making up the roster is Tuesday's *Music 52-15*, good at its best but a little uneven from week to week. Weekend programming opens with *News*, then it's either Saturday's *Europe Unzipped*, *Insight* and *Sound Fountain*; or Sunday's *Sincerely Yours*, a program preview and *Dutch Horizons*. To South Asia winter on 12070, 12080 and 15595 kHz; and summer on 9890, 11835 and 12075 kHz. Also year round to western North America on 15220 kHz.

Radio Austria International. Winter only at this time. ●*Report from Austria* (see 1330 for more details). Thirty minutes to Europe on 6155 and 13730 kHz. One hour earlier in summer.

Radio Sweden. Winter only at this time. Monday through Friday, it's *news* and features in *Sixty Degrees North*, concentrating heavily on Scandinavian topics. Several of the features rotate from week to week, but a few are fixtures. Monday's *SportScan* is replaced Tuesday by *Close Up* or an alternative feature, and Wednesday by *Money Matters*. Thursday's carousel is *Nordic Report*, *GreenScan* (the environment), *Heart Beat* (health), and *S-Files*, with *Weekly Review* filling the Saturday slot. The Sunday rotation is *Weekend*, *Spectrum*,

14:30–15:00

Sweden Today and *Studio 49*, while Monday's offering is *In Touch with Stockholm* (a listener-response program) or the musical *Sounds Nordic*. Thirty minutes to North America on 18960 kHz, and to Asia and Australasia on 17505 kHz.

15:00

■**BBC World Service for the Americas.** Starts with five minutes of *news*, then come several of the BBC's better offerings—●*One Planet* and *People and Places* (Monday), *Discovery* (science) and *Essential Guide* (Tuesday), ●*Health Matters* and ●*Everywoman* (Wednesday), *Science View* and ●*Focus on Faith* (Thursday), *Sports International* and *Pick of the World* (Friday), and *Sportsworld* on Saturday. Winter Sundays, there's ●*From Our Own Correspondent* and ●*People and Politics*, replaced summer by an hour of the finest in classical music (features vary). Continuous programming to the Caribbean and North America on 15190 (or 17840) kHz. In western states, try the Asian stream on 9740 kHz—you may well get better reception.

■**BBC World Service for Europe.** Winter, identical to the service for the Americas. In summer, the format is *World Briefing*, *British News* and ●*Analysis* (except Wednesday, when you can hear ●*From Our Own Correspondent*). Saturday, it's a continuation of *Sportsworld*, and Sunday there's some fine classical music (features vary). Continuous to Europe and North Africa on 9410 (winter), 12095, 15485 and 15565 kHz.

■**BBC World Service for Eastern Europe and the Mideast.** The weekday lineup is *News*, ●*Outlook* and a 15-minute feature (very much a mixed bag). The Saturday news is followed by a continuation of *Sportsworld*, and Sunday it's time for the BBC's weekly concert of classical music (definitely worth hearing). On 15575 kHz (additional frequencies may be available winter).

■**BBC World Service for East and Southeast Asia and the Pacific.** *News*, then Monday through Friday, *Meridian* (the arts). The second half hour is totally different—either a soap or popular music. These are replaced Saturday by the live *Sportsworld*, and Sunday by *The Alternative* (popular music) and ●*Omnibus* (winter) or *Composer of the Month* (summer). Continuous to East and Southeast Asia on 6195 and 9740 kHz, and to Australasia on 9740 kHz (also heard in western North America).

China Radio International. See 1400 for program details. Sixty minutes to western North America on 7405 (winter) and 17720 kHz. Also available year round to South Asia on 7160 and 9785 kHz; and to East Africa on 13685 and 15125 kHz.

Radio Australia. *World News*, then weekdays there's *Asia Pacific* and a feature on the half-hour. Monday, it's health; Tuesday, law; Wednesday, religion; Thursday, media; and Friday, sport. These are replaced Saturday by *Melisma* (classical music), and Sunday by *Encounter* and *Business Weekend*. Continuous programming to the Pacific on 5995, 9580 and 11650 kHz (also well heard in western North America). Additionally available to Southeast Asia on 6080 and 11660 kHz.

Voice of America. Continues with programming to the Mideast. A mixed bag of current events and sports, science, business and other news and features. Winter on 9575 and 15205 kHz, and summer on 9700 and 15205 kHz. Also heard in much of Europe.

Radio Canada International. Daily in winter, but weekends only in summer. Winter weekdays, it's the final 60 minutes of *This Morning*; replaced Saturday by the unique ●*Vinyl Café* (readings and music). Summer, the Saturday slot goes to ●*Quirks and Quarks* (a science show with a difference). On the remaining day (winter and summer) it's *The Sunday Edition*. To North America and the Caribbean, winter on 9515, 9640 and 17710 kHz; and summer on 9640, 15305 and 17800 kHz. For a separate broadcast to South Asia, see the next item.

Radio Canada International. *News*, then weekdays there's *Canada Today*. On the remaining days, opens Saturday with *Canada Newsweek*, and Sunday with *The Mailbag* (a listener-response show). On the half-hour, it's

Canada Review both days. Sixty minutes to South Asia winter on 15360 and 17820 kHz, and summer on 15455 and 17720 kHz. Heard well beyond the intended target area, especially to the west.

XERMX—Radio México Internacional. Winter weekdays, there's an English summary of the Spanish-language *Antena Radio*, replaced Saturday by *Mirror of Mexico*, and Sunday by *Regional Roots and Rhythms*. The summer lineup consists of *Mirror of Mexico* (Monday), *Mailbox* (Tuesday and Sunday), *Magical Trip* (Wednesday), *DXperience* (for radio enthusiasts, Thursday), *Regional Roots and Rhythms* (Friday) and *Mosaic of Mexico* (Saturday). Thirty minutes to North America, best heard in western and southern parts of the United States on 9705 and 11770 kHz.

Radio Japan. *News*, then Monday through Friday there's *Asian Top News* and a 35-minute feature. Take your pick from *Unforgettable Musical Masterpieces* (Monday), Japanese language lessons (Tuesday and Thursday), *Japan Music Log* (Wednesday), and *Music Beat* (Japanese popular music, Friday). *Pop Goes Asia* fills the Saturday slot, and Sunday's offering is *Hello from Tokyo*. One hour to East Asia on 9750 kHz; to South Asia on 9845 (winter) or (summer) 11730 kHz; and to Southeast Asia on 7200 kHz.

Voice of Russia World Service. Predominantly news-related fare for the first half-hour, then a mixed bag, depending on the day and season. At 1531 winter, look for ●*Folk Box* (Monday), ●*Jazz Show* (Wednesday), ●*Music at Your Request* or ●*Music Around Us* (Tuesday and Thursday), *Kaleidoscope* (Sunday) and Friday's retrospective ●*Moscow Yesterday and Today*. Summer at this time, look for some listener favorites. The lineup includes *This is Russia* (Monday), ●*Moscow Yesterday and Today* (Tuesday), ●*Audio Book Club* (dramatized reading, Wednesday), the incomparable ●*Folk Box* (Thursday), and *Songs from Russia* on Friday. Weekend fare is split between Saturday's *Kaleidoscope* and Sunday's *Russian by Radio*. To the Mideast summer on 7325 and 11985 kHz, and year round to Southeast Asia on 11500 kHz.

Voice of Mongolia. *News*, reports and short features, with Sunday featuring lots of exotic Mongolian music. Thirty minutes to South and Southeast Asia on 9720 (or 12015) and 12085 kHz. Frequencies may vary slightly.

WJCR, Upton, Kentucky. Continues with country gospel music to North America on 7490 and 13595 kHz. Other U.S. religious broadcasters operating at this hour include **WWCR** on 13845 and 15685 kHz, **KTBN** on 7510 (or 15590) kHz, and **WYFR-Family Radio** on 11830 and 17750 (or 17760) kHz. Traditionalist Catholic programming is available from **WEWN** on 11875 kHz.

Radio Jordan. A partial relay of the station's domestic broadcasts, beamed to Europe on 11690 kHz. Continuous till 1630 (1730 in winter). Audible in parts of eastern North America, especially during winter.

15:00–16:00

CFRX-CFRB, Toronto, Canada. See 1400. Monday through Friday, it's a continuation of *The Charles Adler Show*. Look for *News and Commentary* summer at 1550. Weekend fare consists of *The CFRB Gardening Show* (Saturday) replaced the following day by *CFRB Sunday*. On 6070 kHz.

AFRTS Shortwave, USA. Network news, live sports, music and features in the upper-sideband mode from the Armed Forces Radio & Television Service. Transmitted from modestly powered U.S. Navy stations around the globe. Try 4278.5, 4319, 4995, 5765, 6350, 6458.5, 10320, 10940.5, 12579, 12689.5 and 13362 kHz.

15:30

■**Radio Netherlands.** The second of two hours targeted at western North America and South Asia. Monday through Friday, starts with a feature and ends with ●*Newsline* (current events). Choice pickings include ●*EuroQuest* (Monday), ●*A Good Life* (Tuesday), ●*Research File* (science, Thursday) and Friday's ●*Documentary* (winner of several prestigious awards). The weekend format is feature-news-feature. Saturday, you can hear ●*Roughly Speaking* (an award-winning youth program) and *Europe Unzipped*; Sunday, there's *Sound Fountain* and *Wide Angle*. To South Asia winter on 12070, 12080 and 15595 kHz; and summer on 9890, 11835 and 12075 kHz. Also year round to western North America on 15220 kHz.

Radio Austria International. Summer only at this time, and may start around 1533. See 1630 for program specifics. Twenty-five minutes to western North America on 17865 kHz, via the facilities of Radio Canada International. One hour later in winter.

Voice of the Islamic Republic of Iran. A one-hour broadcast of news, commentary and features, heavily reflecting the Islamic point of view. To South and Southeast Asia and Australasia on 7115 (winter), 7245 (summer), 9635, 11775 and (winter) 11870 kHz. Frequency usage tends to be a little erratic, though not as much as in the past.

16:00

■**BBC World Service for the Americas.** Monday through Friday winter, it's *World Briefing*, ●*Analysis* (except Wednesday's ●*From Our Own Correspondent*) and ●*Sports Roundup*; summer, there's ●*Europe Today*, ●*World Business Report* and ●*Sports Roundup*. Weekends, year round, there's a short *news* bulletin followed by live sports. The final hour to the Caribbean and North America on 15190 (or 17840) kHz.

■**BBC World Service for Europe.** Monday through Saturday, is identical to the service for East and Southeast Asia. Sunday, the winter offering is a concert of classical music (well worth hearing); summer, there's live sports. Continuous to Europe and North Africa on 9410, 12095 and 15565 kHz.

■**BBC World Service for Eastern Europe and the Mideast.** *News*, then Monday through Friday, *Meridian* (the arts) and a soap or popular music. Weekends, there's live sports. Continuous programming on 15565 and 15575 kHz.

■**BBC World Service for East and Southeast Asia.** Winter weekdays, there's *World Briefing*, *British News*, ●*Analysis* (except for Thursday's ●*From Our Own Correspondent*), and ●*Sports Roundup*. These are replaced in summer by ●*Europe Today*, ●*World Business Report* and ●*Sports Roundup*. Saturdays and summer Sundays, a five-minute *news* bulletin is followed by live sports. In winter, the Sunday lineup is *World Briefing*, *British News*, ●*Reporting Religion* and ●*Sports Roundup*. The final hour to East Asia on 6195 kHz; and continuous to Southeast Asia on 3915 and 7160 kHz.

■**Radio France Internationale.** The first half hour includes *news* and reports from across Africa, international newsflashes and news about France. Next is a 25-minute feature—*French Lesson*, *Crossroads*, *Voices*, *Rendez-Vous*, *World Tracks*, *Weekend* or *Club 9516* (a listener-response program). A fast-moving hour to Africa and the Mideast on 11615, 11995, 12015, 15605, 17605 and 17850 kHz. Best for the Mideast is 11615 kHz in winter, and 15605 kHz in summer. For southern Africa, 12015 and 17850 kHz should be more than enough.

United Arab Emirates Radio, Dubai. A 15-minute feature on Arab history or culture, and preceded and followed by programming in Arabic. A little later, around 1630, there's a short bulletin of *news*. To Europe and North Africa (also heard in eastern North America) on 13630, 13675, 15395 and 21605 kHz.

■Deutsche Welle, Germany. *News*, then Monday through Friday it's ●*NewsLink* followed by *Africa Report*. Weekends, the Saturday news is followed by *Talking Point* and ●*Spectrum*, with *Religion and Society* and *Arts on the Air* filling the Sunday slots. Forty-five minutes aimed primarily at eastern, central and southern parts of Africa, but also audible outside the continent. Winter on 9735, 15455 and 21840 kHz; and summer on 9735, 11665, 17595 and 21840 kHz. For a separate service to South Asia and beyond, see the next entry.

■Deutsche Welle, Germany. Similar to the broadcast for Africa (see previous entry), except that *Asia-Pacific Report* replaces *Africa Report*, and *Cool* is aired in place of Sunday's *Arts on the Air*. Nominally to South Asia, but heard well beyond. Winter on 6170, 7225, 11695 and 13605 kHz; and summer on 6170, 7225 and 17595 kHz.

Kol Israel. Summer only at this time. Thirty minutes from Israel Radio's domestic network. To Europe and eastern North America on 15640 kHz. One hour later in winter.

Radio Korea International, South Korea. Opens with *news* and commentary, followed Monday through Wednesday by *Seoul Calling*. Weekly features include *Echoes of Korean Music* and *Shortwave Feedback* (Sunday), *Tales from Korea's Past* (Monday), *Korean Cultural Trails* (Tuesday), *Pulse of Korea* (Wednesday), *From Us to You* (a listener-response program) and *Let's Learn Korean* (Thursday), *Let's Sing Together* and *Korea Through Foreigners' Eyes* (Friday), and Saturday's *Discovering Korea*, *Korean Literary Corner* and *Weekly News Focus*. One hour to East Asia on 5975 kHz, and to the Mideast and much of Africa on 9515 and 9870 kHz.

Radio Taipei International, Taiwan. Opens with 15 minutes of *News*, and with the exception of Sunday, closes with *Let's Learn Chinese*, which has a series of segments for beginning, intermediate and advanced learners. In between, there are either one or two features, depending on the day of the week. Monday, there's the pleasurable and exotic ●*Jade Bells and Bamboo Pipes* (Taiwanese music), replaced Tuesday by *Culture Express* and *Trends*; Wednesday's slots are *Taiwan Today* and *Confucius and Inspiration Beyond*; Thursday brings *Journey into Chinese Culture* and *Instant Noodles*; and Friday's coupling is *Taipei Magazine* and *East Meets West*. These are replaced Saturday by *Kaleidoscope* and *Naluwan*, and Sunday by *Great Wall Forum* and *Mailbag Time*. The first of two hours to South Asia on 11550 kHz.

Radio Pakistan. Fifteen minutes of *news* from the Pakistan Broadcasting Corporation's domestic service. Intended for the Mideast and Africa, but heard well beyond. Try 11570, 15100 and 15725 kHz.

Radio Prague, Czech Republic. Summer only at this time. *News*, then weekdays it's *Current Affairs* plus a feature. *Spotlight* (a jaunt around the Czech Republic) alternates with *One on One* (a series of informal interviews) on Mondays; *Talking Point* occupies the Tuesday slot; and the Wednesday show is either *Czechs in History* or *Central Europe Today*. Thursday's feature is the business-oriented *Economic Report*, and *Magazine* is heard on Friday. Weekends, the news is followed by Saturday's *Readings from Czech Literature* plus an excellent musical feature, and Sunday by *A Letter from Prague*, *The Arts* and *Mailbag*. A half hour to Europe on 5930 kHz, and to East Africa on 21745 kHz. One hour later in winter.

Radio Algiers, Algeria. *News*, then western and Arab popular music, with an occasional feature thrown in. One hour of so-so reception in Europe, and sometimes heard in eastern North America. On 11715 and 15160 kHz. Operation was irregular during 2001.

Radio Australia. Continuous programming to Asia and the Pacific. At this hour *World News* is followed by *Margaret Throsby* (interviews and

16:00–17:00

Large earphones permit world band listening even within a noisy Indian throng. M. Guha

music, Monday), *The Comfort Zone* (Tuesday), *Verbatim* (personal experiences) and *Earshot* (Wednesday), *Hindsight* (a look back into history, Thursday), and Friday's show of Australian indigenous music and stories, *Awaye* Saturday brings a continuation of *Melisma*, replaced Sunday by *The National Interest* (topical events). Beamed to the Pacific on 5995, 9580 and 11650 kHz (and well heard in western North America). Additionally available to East and Southeast Asia on 6080, 9475 and 11660 kHz.

Radio Ethiopia. An hour-long broadcast divided into two parts by the 1630 *news* bulletin. Regular weekday features include *Kaleidoscope* and *Women's Forum* (Monday), *Press Review* and *Africa in Focus* (Tuesday), *Guest of the Week* and *Ethiopia Today* (Wednesday), *Ethiopian Music* and *Spotlight* (Thursday) and *Press Review* and *Introducing Ethiopia* on Friday. For weekend listening, there's *Contact* and *Ethiopia This Week* (Saturday), or Sunday's *Listeners' Choice* and *Commentary*. Best heard in parts of Africa and the Mideast, but sometimes audible in Europe. On 7165 and 9560 kHz.

Radio Jordan. A partial relay of the station's domestic broadcasts, beamed to Europe on 11690 kHz. The final half hour in summer, but a full 60 minutes in winter. Audible in parts of eastern North America, especially during winter.

Voice of Russia World Service. Continuous programming to the Mideast and West Asia at this hour. *News*, then very much a mixed bag, depending on the day and season. Winter weekdays, there's *Focus on Asia and the Pacific*, with Saturday's *Newmarket* and Sunday's *Moscow Mailbag* making up the week. On the half-hour, choose from *This is Russia* (Monday), ●*Moscow Yesterday and Today* (Tuesday), ●*Audio Book Club* (dramatized reading, Wednesday), the exotic and eclectic ●*Folk Box* (Thursday), and Friday's *Songs from Russia*. Weekend fare is split between Saturday's *Kaleidoscope* and Sunday's *Russian by Radio*. Summer, the news is followed by the business-oriented *Newmarket* (Monday and Thursday), *Science and Engineering* (Tuesday and Sunday), *Moscow Mailbag* (Wednesday and Friday), and Saturday's showpiece, ●*Music and Musicians*. The features after the half-hour tend to be variable. Audible in the Mideast winter on 6005 and 9830 kHz, and summer on 11985 and 15540 kHz.

Radio Canada International. Winter weekends only at this hour. Saturday, there's ●*Quirks and Quarks* (science), and Sunday it's the final hour of *The Sunday Edition*. To North America and the Caribbean on 9515, 9640 and 17710 kHz.

XERMX—Radio México Internacional. Winter only at this time. Take your pick from *Mirror of Mexico* (Monday), *Mailbox* (Tuesday and Sunday), *Magical Trip* (Wednesday), *DXperience* (a show for radio enthusiasts, Thursday), *Regional Roots and Rhythms* (Friday) and *Mosaic of Mexico* (Saturday). Thirty minutes to western and southern parts of the United States on 9705 and 11770 kHz. One hour earlier in summer.

China Radio International. Starts with *News*, then weekdays continues with in-depth reports. The remainder of the broadcast is made up of features. Regular shows include *People in the Know* (Monday), *Sportsworld* (Tuesday), *China Horizons* (Wednesday), *Voices* *from Other Lands* (Thursday) and Friday's *Life in China*. Saturday, there's *Global Review* and *Listeners' Garden* (reports, music and a Chinese language lesson), replaced Sunday by *Report from Developing Countries* and *In the Spotlight*. One hour to eastern and southern Africa winter on 7190 and 13650 kHz, and midyear on 9565 and 9870 kHz.

Voice of America. Several hours of continuous programming aimed at an African audience. At this hour, there's a split between mainstream programming and news and features in "Special" (slow-speed) English. The former can be heard on 6035, 13710, 15225 and 15410 kHz, and the "Special" programs on 13600, 15445 and (summer) 17895 kHz. For a separate service to the Mideast, see the next item.

Radio for Peace International, Costa Rica. The first 60 minutes of a six-hour cyclical block of social-conscience and counterculture programming audible in Europe and the Americas on 15050 and (upper sideband) 21815 kHz.

Voice of America. *News Now*—a mixed bag of news and reports on current events, sports, science, business and more. To the Mideast winter on 9575 and 15205 kHz, and summer on 9700 and 15205 kHz. Also heard in much of Europe.

WJCR, Upton, Kentucky. Continues with country gospel music to North America on 7490 and 13595 kHz. Other U.S. religious broadcasters operating at this hour include **WWCR** on 13845 and 15685 kHz, **KTBN** on 15590 kHz, and **WYFR-Family Radio** on 11830, 15215 (or 15600) and 17750 (or 17760) kHz. Traditionalist Catholic programming can be heard via **WEWN** on 11875 and 13615 kHz.

CFRX-CFRB, Toronto, Canada. See 1400. Winter weekdays, it's the final part of *The Charles Adler Show*, with *The CFRB Gardening Show* and *CFRB Sunday* the weekend offerings. Summer, look for *The Motts* Monday through Friday, and ●*The World at Noon* on weekends.

AFRTS Shortwave, USA. Network news, live sports, music and features in the upper-sideband mode from the Armed Forces Radio & Television Service. Transmitted from modestly powered U.S. Navy stations around the globe. Try 4278.5, 4319, 4995, 5765, 6350, 6458.5, 10320, 10940.5, 12579, 12689.5 and 13362 kHz.

16:30

Radio Slovakia International. Summer only at this time; see 1730 for specifics. Thirty minutes of friendly programming to western Europe on 5920, 6055 and 7345 kHz. One hour later in winter.

Radio Austria International. Winter only at this time. Twenty-five minutes of ●*Report from Austria*, which tends to spotlight national and regional issues, and is an excellent source of news about Central Europe. To western North America on 17865 kHz, via the facilities of Radio Canada International. One hour earlier in summer.

Voice of Vietnam. *News*, then *Commentary* or *Weekly Review* followed by short features and pleasant Vietnamese music (especially at weekends). A half hour to Europe on 7145 (winter), 9730 and (summer) 13740 kHz.

Radio Cairo, Egypt. The first 30 minutes of a two-hour package of Arab music and features reflecting Egyptian life and culture, with *news*, commentary, quizzes, mailbag shows, and answers to listeners' questions. To southern Africa on 15255 kHz.

17:00

■BBC World Service for Europe. Identical to the service for Southeast Asia. Continuous to Europe and North Africa on 6195 and 9410 kHz

■BBC World Service for Eastern Europe and the Mideast. Starts weekdays with five minutes of *news*, then there's a pair of features: ●*Health Matters* and ●*Everywoman* (Monday), *Science View* and ●*Focus on Faith* (Tuesday), *Sports International* and *Pick of the World* (Wednesday), ●*One Planet* and *People and Places* (Thursday), and *Discovery* and *Essential Guide* on Friday. Some of the BBC's best. Saturday's lineup consists of *World*

17:00–17:00

Briefing, *British News* and *Westway* (a soap); Sunday, it's the first hour of ●*Play of the Week*. On 11980 (winter), 12095 and 15575 kHz.

■BBC World Service for Southern Africa. *News*, *Focus on Africa*, and ●*Sports Roundup*. Part of a 19-hour daily service on a variety of channels. At this hour, on 3255, 6190 and 15400 kHz.

■BBC World Service for Southeast Asia. Monday through Friday winter, there's ●*Europe Today*, ●*World Business Report* and ●*Sports Roundup*. Summer replacements are a five-minute *news* bulletin, *Outlook* (news and human interest stories) and a 15-minute feature (very much a mixed bag). Winter Saturdays, it's *World Briefing*, *British News* and ●*Sportsworld*, replaced summer by ●*From Our Own Correspondent* and ●*Agenda*. Sunday's winter offerings are *Global Business* and ●*Agenda*, with ●*Play of the Week* filling the summer slot. The final hour to Southeast Asia, on 3915 and 7160 kHz.

Radio Prague, Czech Republic. See 1600 for program specifics. A half hour of *news* and features year round to Europe on 5930 kHz; also winter to West and Central Africa on 17485 kHz, and summer to central and southern Africa on 21745 kHz.

Radio Romania International. *News*, commentary, a press review, and several short features. Music, too. Thirty minutes to Europe winter on 9625 11740, 11940 and 15365 kHz; and summer on 15250, 15390, 17735 and 17805 kHz.

Radio Australia. Continuous programming to Asia and the Pacific. Starts with *World News*, then Monday through Friday there's *Bush Telegraph*, a light-hearted look at rural and regional issues in Australia. Replaced Saturday by *The Spirit of Things*, and Sunday by *New Dimensions*. Beamed to the Pacific on 5995, 9580, 9815 and 11880 kHz; and to East and Southeast Asia on 6080 and 9475 kHz. Listeners in Japan should tune to 9815 kHz. Also audible in parts of western North America on 5995, 9580 and 11880 kHz.

Radio Polonia, Poland. This time summer only. Monday through Friday, it's *News from Poland*—a compendium of news, reports and interviews. This is followed by *Cookery Corner* and *The Best of Polish Radio* (Monday), *Letter from Poland* and *Multimedia Show* (Tuesday), *Day in the Life* and *Discovering Chopin* (Wednesday), *Focus* (the arts in Poland) and *Soundcheck* (Thursday), and Friday's *Business Week* followed by *Postbag*, a listener-response show. The Saturday broadcast begins with a bulletin of *news*, then there's *Europe East, The Weeklies* and *Chart Show*. Sundays, it's five minutes of *news* followed by *Panorama* and *Request Concert*. Sixty minutes to Europe on 6000 and 7285 kHz. One hour later during winter.

Radio Jordan. Winter only at this time. The last 30 minutes of a partial relay of the station's domestic broadcasts, beamed to Europe on 11690 kHz.

Voice of Russia World Service. *News*, then it's a mixed bag, depending on the day and season. Winter, the news is followed by the business-oriented *Newmarket* (Monday and Thursday), *Science and Engineering* (Tuesday and Sunday), *Moscow Mailbag* (Wednesday and Friday) and Saturday's 45-minute ●*Music and Musicians*. The choice of features for the second half hour tends to be variable. In summer, the news is followed by a series of features: *Moscow Mailbag* (Monday, Thursday and Saturday), *Newmarket* (Tuesday and Friday), *Science and Engineering* (Wednesday), and one of Moscow's musical jewels, ●*Music and Musicians*, on Sunday. On the half-hour, the lineup includes *Kaleidoscope* (Monday), ●*Music at Your Request* or ●*Music Around Us* (Tuesday), ●*Moscow Yesterday and Today* (Wednesday), Friday's ●*Folk Box* and Saturday's *Songs from Russia*. Summer only to Europe on 9685, 9775 and 9890 kHz, plus weekends on 9480 and 11675 kHz. For the Mideast, tune to 9470 and 9830 kHz in winter, and 11985 kHz in summer.

Radio for Peace International, Costa Rica. Continues with social-conscience and counterculture programming. Audible in Europe and the Americas on 15050 and (upper sideband) 21815 kHz.

Kol Israel. Winter only at this time. Thirty minutes from Israel Radio's domestic network.

To Europe and eastern North America on 17545 kHz. One hour earlier in summer.

Radio Japan. *News*, then weekdays look for some in-depth reporting in *Japan and World 44 Minutes*. Saturday's feature is *Hello From Tokyo*, replaced Sunday by *Pop Goes Asia*. One hour to Europe on 11970 kHz; to southern Africa on 15355 kHz; to South Asia winter on 9845 kHz; and to western North America on 9505 kHz.

Radio Taipei International, Taiwan. The final 60 minutes of a two-hour block of programs to South Asia. Opens with 15 minutes of *News*, and Monday through Wednesday closes with *Let's Learn Chinese*. The remaining airtime is devoted to features. Monday, there's *Taiwan Economic Journal* and *People*; Tuesday's shows are *Culture Express* and *Trends*; Wednesday's single offering is *New Music Lounge*; Thursday's triple bill consists of *Instant Noodles*, *Life Unusual* and *Naluwan*; while Friday's slots are *Weekend Zoo* and *Business Chinese*. Weekend fare consists of Saturday's *Kaleidoscope* and *Mailbag Time*, and Sunday's *Great Wall Forum* and *Asia Pacific*. On 11550 kHz.

China Radio International. Repeat of the 1600 transmission; see there for specifics. One hour to eastern and southern parts of Africa winter on 7150, 9570 and 9695 kHz; and summer on 9570, 9695, 11920 and 15265 kHz. Also available year round to the Mideast on 9670 kHz.

RAI

RAI branch office in Italy. Arto Mujunen

Voice of America. Continuous programming to the Mideast and North Africa. *News*, then Monday through Friday it's the interactive *Talk to America*. Weekends, there's the ubiquitous *News Now*. Winter on 6040, 9760 and 15205 kHz; and summer on 9760, 15135 and 15255 kHz. Also heard in much of Europe. For a separate service to Africa, see the next item.

Voice of America. Programs for Africa. Monday through Saturday, identical to the service for Europe and the Mideast (see previous item). Sunday on the half-hour, look for the entertaining ●*Music Time in Africa*. Audible well beyond where it is targeted. On 6035, 7415, 11920, 11975, 12040, 13710, 15410, 15445 and 17895 kHz, some of which are seasonal. For yet another service (to East Asia and the Pacific), see the next item.

Voice of America. Monday through Friday only. *News*, followed by the interactive *Talk to America*. Sixty minutes to Asia on 5990, 6045, 6110/6160, 7125, 7215, 9525, 9645, 9670, 9770, 11945, 12005 and 15255 kHz, some of which are seasonal. For Australasia, try 9525 and 15255 kHz in winter, and 7150 and 7170 kHz in summer.

■**Radio France Internationale.** An additional half-hour (see 1600) of predominantly African fare. Monday through Friday, focuses on *news* from the eastern part of Africa. Weekends, there's *Spotlight on Africa*, health issues, features on French culture, sports, media in Africa, and a phone-in feature, *On-Line*. To East Africa and the Mideast on any two channels from 11615, 15605 and 17605 kHz. Occasionally heard in North America.

17:00–18:00

Radio Cairo, Egypt. See 1630 for specifics. Continues with a broadcast to southern Africa on 15255 kHz.

WJCR, Upton, Kentucky. Continues with country gospel music to North America on 7490 and 13595 kHz. Other U.S. religious broadcasters operating at this hour include **WWCR** on 13845 and 15685 kHz, **KTBN** on 15590 kHz, and **WHRI-World Harvest Radio** on 13760 and 15105 kHz.

CFRX-CFRB, Toronto, Canada. See 1400. Winter weekends at this time, there's ●*The World at Noon*; summer, it's *The Mike Stafford Show*. Monday through Friday, look for *The Motts*. On 6070 kHz.

AFRTS Shortwave, USA. Network news, live sports, music and features in the upper-sideband mode from the Armed Forces Radio & Television Service. Transmitted from modestly powered U.S. Navy stations around the globe. Try 4278.5, 4319, 4995, 5765, 6350, 6458.5, 10320, 10940.5, 12579, 12689.5 and 13362 kHz.

17:30

■**Radio Netherlands.** The first of three hours targeted at Africa, and heard well beyond. Monday through Friday, the initial 30 minutes are taken up by ●*Newsline* (current events), with a feature filling the second half hour. Best of a good bunch are ●*Research File* (Monday), ●*Documentary* (Wednesday), ●*Encore* (Thursday) and ●*A Good Life* on Friday. For a change of pace, try the eclectic *Music 52-15* aired each Tuesday. Weekend fare consists of *news* followed by Saturday's *Europe Unzipped*, *Insight* and *Sound Fountain*; and Sunday's *Sincerely Yours* (a listener-response show) and *Dutch Horizons*. Sixty minutes on 6020 (best for southern Africa), 7120 (summer) and 11655 kHz.

Radio Slovakia International. Winter only at this time. *Slovakia Today*, a 30-minute look at Slovakia and its people. Monday, there's a bag of short features; Tuesday spotlights tourism and Slovak personalities; Wednesday's slot goes to business and economy; and Thursday brings a mix of politics, education and science. Friday offerings include cultural items, *Slovak Kitchen* and the off-beat *Back Page News*; and Saturday brings the *"Best of"* series. Sunday's show is more relaxed, and includes *Listeners' Tribune* and some enjoyable Slovak music. A friendly half hour to western Europe on 5915, 6055 and 7345 kHz. One hour earlier in summer.

Radio Sweden. Summer only at this hour; see 1830 for program specifics. Thirty minutes of Scandinavian fare for Europe, Monday through Saturday on 6065 kHz, and Sunday on 13580 kHz. One hour later during winter.

Swiss Radio International. *Newsnet*—news and background reports on world and Swiss events. Some lighter fare on Saturdays, when the biweekly *Capital Letters* (a listener-response program) alternates with *Name Game* (first Saturday) and *Sounds Good* (third Saturday). Thirty minutes to the Mideast and East Africa winter on 9605, 13790 and 15555 kHz; and summer on 15220, 17735 and 21720 kHz.

Radio Vlaanderen Internationaal, Belgium. Summer only at this time. Weekdays, starts with *News*, then *Belgium Today*, *Press Review* and features. The lineup includes *Focus on Europe* and *Sports* (Monday), *Green Society* (Tuesday), *The Arts* (Wednesday and Friday), *Around Town* (Wednesday), *Economics* and *International Report* (Thursday), and Friday's *Tourism*. Closes with *Soundbox*. These are replaced Saturday by *Music from Flanders*, and Sunday by *Radio World*, *Tourism*, *Brussels 1043* (a listener-response program) and *Soundbox*. Thirty minutes to Europe on 5910 and 9925 kHz; and to the Mideast on 13710 kHz. One hour later in winter.

17:45

All India Radio. The first 15 minutes of a two-hour broadcast to Europe, Africa and the Mideast, consisting of regional and international *news*, commentary, a variety of talks and features, press review and exotic Indian music. Continuous till 1945. To Europe on 7410 and 9950 kHz; to the Mideast on 13620 kHz; and to Africa on 11935, 13795 (or 15155), 15075 (or 15120) and 17670 kHz.

1800-2359
Europe & Mideast—Evening Prime Time
East Asia—Early Morning
Australasia—Morning
Eastern North America—Afternoon and Suppertime
Western North America—Midday

18:00

BBC World Service for Europe. Monday through Friday winter, *News* is followed by *Outlook* (news and human interest stories) and a mixed bag of 15-minute features. Weekend fare is *World Briefing*, *British News* and either Saturday's ●*Agenda* or Sunday's ●*Assignment*. Summer weekdays, there's *news*, *Meridian* (the arts) and a soap or popular music. These are replaced Saturday by *World Briefing*, *British News*, *World Business Review* and *Letter from America*. Sunday, it's the final part of ●*Play of the Week*. If it ends at 1820, you also get *British News* and *Assignment* (or an alternative documentary); if it makes it to 1830, you get just the documentary; and if it goes the full hour, just sit back and enjoy it! Continuous to Europe and North Africa on 6195 and 9410 kHz.

BBC World Service for Eastern Europe and the Mideast. Except Sunday, starts with 20 minutes of *World Briefing*, with *British News* making up the half hour. Weekdays, the next 30 minutes bring ●*World Business Report* and ●*Analysis* (except 1845 Wednesday, when it's ●*From Our Own Correspondent*). At the same time Saturday, there's ●*World Business Review* and ●*Letter from America*. Sunday, it's a continuation of ●*Play of the Week*. Continuous programming on 11980 (winter), 12095 and (summer) 15575 kHz.

■**BBC World Service for Southern Africa.** Starts weekdays with five minutes of *News*, then it's a couple of features: ●*Health Matters* and ●*Everywoman* (Monday), *Science View* and ●*Focus on Faith* (Tuesday), *Sports International* and *Pick of the World* (Wednesday), ●*One Planet* and *People and Places* (Thursday), and *Discovery* and *Essential Guide* on Friday. Not a bad one among them. Weekends, the first 30 minutes are taken by *World Briefing* and *British News*. After the half-hour, it's Saturday's ●*World Business Review* and ●*Letter from America* or Sunday's ●*Assignment* (sometimes replaced by an alternative documentary). Continuous programming on 3255, 6190 and 15400 kHz.

Radio Kuwait. The start of a three-hour package of *news*, Islamic-oriented features and western popular music. Some interesting features, even if you don't particularly like the music. There is a full program summary at the beginning of each transmission, to enable you to pick and choose. To Europe and eastern North America on 11990 kHz.

Voice of Vietnam. Begins with *news*, which is followed by *Commentary* or *Weekly Review*, short features and some pleasant Vietnamese music (especially at weekends). A half hour to Europe on 7145 (winter), 7440 (winter), 9730 and (summer) 12070 and 13740 kHz. The 7440 and 12070 kHz channels are via relays in western Russia, and should provide good reception.

Radio for Peace International, Costa Rica. Continues with social-conscience and counterculture programming. Audible in Europe and the Americas on 15050 and (upper sideband) 21815 kHz.

All India Radio. Continuation of the transmission to Europe, Africa and the Mideast (see 1745). *News* and commentary, followed by programming of a more general nature. To Europe on 7410 and 9950 kHz; to the Mideast on 13620 kHz; and to Africa on 11935, 13795 (or 15155), 15075 (or 15120) and 17670 kHz.

Radio Prague, Czech Republic. Winter only at this time. *News*, then Monday through Friday there's *Current Affairs* and a feature. Monday, it's either *Spotlight* (a look at Czech regional affairs) or *One on One* (an informal interview

18:00–18:30

show); Tuesday, there's *Talking Point* (issues shaping people's lives in the Czech Republic); and the Wednesday show is either *Czechs in History* or *Central Europe Today*. *Economic Report* fills the Thursday slot, and the Friday feature is *Magazine*. Weekends, following the news, the Saturday lineup consists of *Readings from Czech Literature* plus an excellent musical feature, replaced Sunday by *A Letter from Prague*, *The Arts* and *Mailbag*. A half hour to Europe on 5930 kHz, and to Australasia on 7315 kHz.

Radio Australia. Sunday through Friday, *World News* is followed by *Pacific Beat* (a news magazine), replaced Saturday by *Lifelong Learning*. As we went to press, the future content of the second half hour was yet to be decided. Part of a continuous 24-hour service, and at this hour beamed to the Pacific on 6080, 7240, 9580, 9815 and 11880 kHz. Additionally available to East Asia on 9475 and 9815 kHz. In western North America, try 9580 and 11880 kHz.

Radio Polonia, Poland. This time winter only. See 1700 for program specifics. *News*, features and music reflecting Polish life and culture. Sixty minutes to Europe on 6000 and 7285 kHz. One hour earlier in summer.

Voice of Russia World Service. Continuous programming to Europe at this time. Predominantly news-related fare during the initial half hour in summer, but the winter schedule offers a more varied diet. Winter, the news is followed by a series of features: *Moscow Mailbag* (Monday, Thursday and Saturday), *Newmarket* (Tuesday and Friday), *Science and Engineering* (Wednesday) and the outstanding ●*Music and Musicians* on Sunday. On the half-hour, the lineup includes *Kaleidoscope* (Monday), ●*Music at Your Request* or ●*Music Around Us* (Tuesday), ●*Moscow Yesterday and Today* (Wednesday), *Folk Box* (Friday) and Saturday's *Songs from Russia*. Summer weekdays, the first half hour consists of news followed by *Commonwealth Update*, while the features that follow tend to be variable. The Saturday slots are filled by *Science and Engineering* and *This is Russia*, replaced Sunday by *Musical Portraits of the Twentieth Century* and ●*Christian Message from Moscow* (an insight into Russian Orthodoxy). Best winter bets are 5940, 6045, 7340, 9775 and 9890 kHz; likely summer channels include 9480, 9685, 9775, 9890, 11630 and 11675 kHz. Also available winter only to the Mideast on 9830 kHz.

Radio Argentina al Exterior—R.A.E. Monday through Friday only. A freewheeling presentation of news, press review, short features and local Argentinian music. The press review is possibly unique, since the items are often translated on-air as the announcer reads the newspaper in the studio. From the ubiquitous tango to lesser known styles like the milongo and zamba, there's plenty to enjoy. Fifty-five minutes to Europe on 15345 kHz.

Voice of America. Continuous programming to the Mideast and North Africa. *News Now*—reports and features on a variety of topics. On 6040 (winter) and 9760 kHz. For a separate service to Africa, see the next item.

Voice of America. Monday through Friday, it's *News Now* and *Africa World Tonight*. Weekends, there's a full hour of the former. To Africa—but heard well beyond—on 7275, 11920, 11975, 12040, 13710, 15410, 15580 and 17895 kHz, some of which are seasonal.

Radio Cairo, Egypt. See 1630 for specifics. The final 30 minutes of a two-hour broadcast to southern Africa on 15255 kHz.

Radio Taipei International, Taiwan. Opens with 15 minutes of *News*, and closes Monday through Wednesday with *Let's Learn Chinese*. The remaining airtime is devoted to features. Monday's pairing is *Taiwan Economic Journal* and *People*, replaced Tuesday by *Culture Express* and *Trends*; Wednesday's show is *New Music Lounge*; Thursday brings *Instant Noodles*, *Life Unusual* and *Naluwan*; and Friday's combo is *Weekend Zoo* and *Business Chinese*. The Saturday slots are filled by *Kaleidoscope* and *Mailbag Time*, with *Great Wall Forum* and *Asia Pacific* making up the Sunday menu. One hour to western Europe on 3955 kHz.

WJCR, Upton, Kentucky. Continues with country gospel music to North America on 7490 and 13595 kHz. Other U.S. religious broadcasters operating at this time include **WWCR** on 13845 and 15685 kHz, **KTBN** on 15590 kHz, and **WHRI-World Harvest Radio** on 13760 and 15105 kHz. For traditionalist Catholic programming, tune **WEWN** on 11875 and 13615 kHz.

CFRX-CFRB, Toronto, Canada. Audible throughout much of the northeastern United States and southeastern Canada during the hours of daylight with a modest, but clear, signal on 6070 kHz. This pleasant, friendly station carries news, sports, weather and traffic reports—most of it intended for a local audience. Winter weekdays at this hour, it's *The Motts*; summer, look for *The John Oakley Show*. Weekends feature *The Mike Stafford Show*.

AFRTS Shortwave, USA. Network news, live sports, music and features in the upper-sideband mode from the Armed Forces Radio & Television Service. Transmitted from modestly powered U.S. Navy stations around the globe. Try 4278.5, 4319, 4995, 5765, 6350, 6458.5, 10320, 10940.5, 12579, 12689.5 and 13362 kHz.

18:15

Radio Bangladesh. *News*, followed by Islamic and general interest features; some nice Bengali music, too. Thirty minutes to Europe on 7190 and 9550 kHz, and irregularly on 15520 kHz. Frequencies may be slightly variable.

18:30

■**Radio Netherlands.** The second part of a three-hour block of programming for Africa, but also well heard in parts of North America at this hour. Monday through Friday, the first half hour is occupied by ●*Newsline*, then comes a 30-minute feature. Some excellent shows, including ●*EuroQuest* (Monday), ●*A*

18:30–19:00

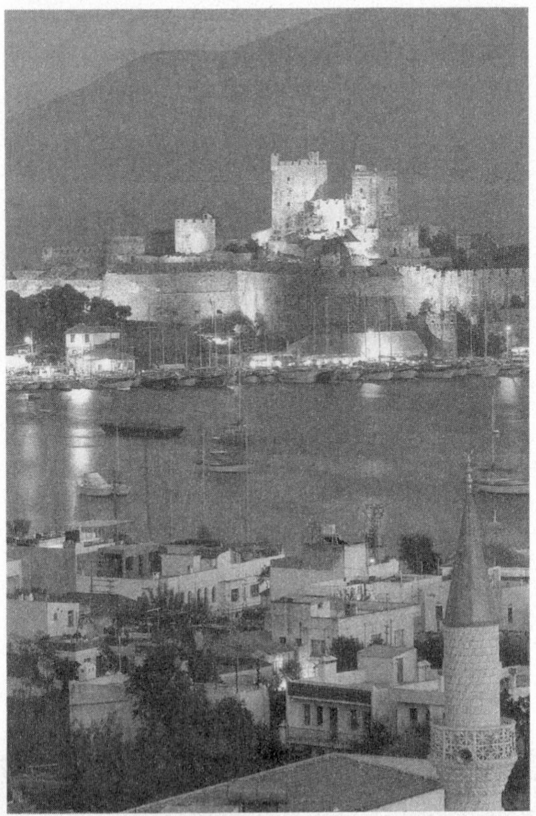

Ancient castle overlooks Bodrum, Turkey.

Good Life (Tuesday), ●*Research File* (science, Thursday) and Friday's excellent ●*Documentary*. The weekend menu consists of a bulletin of *news* followed by two or more features. Saturday's lineup is *Europe Unzipped*, *Insight* and ●*Roughly Speaking* (an award-winning youth program), while *Wide Angle* and *Sound Fountain* are the Sunday offerings. On 6020, 7120 (summer), 9895, 11655, 13700, 17605 and (summer) 21590 kHz. The last two frequencies, via a relay in the Netherlands Antilles, are widely heard in the United States. In southern Africa, tune to 6020 kHz.

Radio Austria International. Summer only at this time. ●*Report from Austria*; see 1930 for more details. Thirty minutes to Europe on 5945 and 6155 kHz. One hour later in winter.

Radio Slovakia International. Summer only at this time; see 1930 for specifics. Thirty minutes of *news* and features with a strong Slovak flavor. To western Europe on 5920, 6055 and 7345 kHz. One hour later in winter.

Radio Vlaanderen Internationaal, Belgium. Winter only at this time. See 1730 for specifics. Thirty minutes to Europe on 5910 and 9925 kHz; and to the Mideast on 13770 kHz. One hour earlier in summer.

Radio Yugoslavia. Summer only at this time. Thirty minutes of news and short features to Europe on 6100 kHz. One hour later in winter.

Voice of Turkey. This time summer only. *News*, followed by *Review of the Turkish Press*, then features on Turkish history, culture and international relations, interspersed with enjoyable selections of the country's popular and classical music. Fifty minutes to Western Europe on 9785 and 11765 kHz. One hour later in winter.

Radio Sweden. Monday through Friday, it's *news* and features in *Sixty Degrees North*, concentrating heavily on Scandinavian topics. The Monday slot goes to *SportScan*, replaced Tuesday by *Close Up* or an alternative feature, and Wednesday by *Money Matters*. Thursday features a different show each week of the month—*Nordic Report*, *GreenScan*, *Heart Beat* or *S-Files*, while Friday offers a review of the week's news. Saturday's slot is filled by *Weekend*, *Spectrum* (the arts), *Sweden Today* or *Studio 49*, and Sunday fare consists of *In Touch with Stockholm* (a listener-response program) or the musical *Sounds Nordic*. Thirty minutes to Europe, Monday through Saturday on 6065 kHz, and Sunday on 5840 kHz. One hour earlier in summer.

19:00

■**BBC World Service for Europe.** Monday through Friday winter, there's *news*, *Meridian* (the arts) and a soap or popular music. Weekends, the first half hour consists of *World Briefing* and ●*Sports Roundup*, with the final

30 minutes going to Saturday's ●*World Business Review* and ●*Letter from America* or Sunday's *Science in Action*. Summer weekdays, opens with five minutes of *news*, and then it's features: ●*Health Matters* and ●*Everywoman* (Monday), ●*Focus on Faith* (1930 Tuesday), *Sports International* and *Pick of the World* (Wednesday), ●*One Planet* and *People and Places* (Thursday), and *Discovery* and *Essential Guide* on Friday. Some of the BBC's better offerings. Weekend fare is similar to that in winter, except for 1930 Saturday, when there's a 30-minute soap. Continuous to Europe and North Africa on 6195 and 9410 kHz.

■**BBC World Service for Eastern Europe and the Mideast.** Weekdays, starts with *World Briefing* and ●*Sports Roundup*, and ends with ●*Off the Shelf* (readings from world literature). In between, there's a 15-minute feature. On the weekend, a five-minute *news* bulletin is followed by Saturday's *Classical Request* and ●*Omnibus*, or Sunday's *Jazzmatazz* and ●*From Our Own Correspondent*.

■**BBC World Service for Southern Africa.** Monday through Friday, *News* is followed by 25 minutes of *Focus on Africa*. The second half hour consists of popular music or *Westway*, a soap. Weekend programming opens with *World Briefing*, Saturday's ●*Sports Roundup* ●*Science in Action* or Sunday's news bulletin followed by *Wright Round the World*. Continuous on 3255, 6190 and 15400 kHz. The last frequency can often be heard in eastern North America during summer.

Radio Australia. Begins with *World News*, then Sunday through Thursday it's *Pacific Beat* (in-depth reporting on the region). Friday's slots go to *Pacific Focus* and *In Conversation*, replaced Saturday by *Earthbeat* (the environment) and *Lingua Franca*. Continuous to Asia and the Pacific on 6080, 7240, 9500, 9580, 9815 and 11880 kHz. Listeners in western North America should try 9580 and 11880 kHz, and best for East Asia are 6080 and 9500 kHz.

Radio Kuwait. See 1800; continuous to Europe and eastern North America on 11990 kHz.

Kol Israel. Summer only at this time. ●*Israel News Magazine*. Twenty-five minutes of even-handed and comprehensive news reporting from and about Israel. To Europe and North America on 9435, 11605, 15650 and 17545 kHz; and to Africa and South America on 15640 kHz. One hour later in winter.

All India Radio. The final 45 minutes of a two-hour broadcast to Europe, Africa and the Mideast (see 1745). Starts off with *news*, then continues with a mixed bag of features and Indian music. To Europe on 7410 and 9950 kHz; to the Mideast on 13620 kHz; and to Africa on 11935, 13795 (or 15155), 15075 (or 15120) and 17670 kHz.

Radio Bulgaria. Summer only at this time. Starts with *news*, then Monday through Friday there's *Events and Developments*, replaced Saturday by *Views Behind the News* and Sunday by 15 minutes of Bulgarian exotica in ●*Folk Studio*. Additional features include *Magazine Economy* (Monday), *Arts and Artists* (Tuesday), *History Club* (Wednesday), *The Way We Live* (Thursday) and *DX Programed*, a Friday slot for radio enthusiasts. Saturday is interactive day, with *Answering Your Letters*, a listener-response show, and *Walks and Talks* fills the Sunday slot. Monday through Friday, the broadcast ends with *Keyword Bulgaria*. Sixty minutes to Europe on 9400 and 11700 kHz. One hour later during winter.

HCJB—Voice of the Andes, Ecuador. Summer only at this time. The first of three hours of religious and secular programming targeted at Europe. Monday through Friday it's *Studio 9*, featuring nine minutes of world and Latin American *news*, followed by 20 minutes of in-depth reporting on Latin America. The final portion is given over to one of a variety of 30-minute features—including *Inside HCJB* (Monday), *Ham Radio Today* (Wednesday), *Woman to Woman* (Thursday) and Friday's exotic and enjoyable ●*Música del Ecuador*. Saturday, the news is followed by *DX Partyline*, and Sunday by *Musical Mailbag*. On 17660 kHz. One hour later in winter.

Radio Exterior de España ("Spanish National Radio"). Summer weekdays only at this time. See 2000 for program specifics. Sixty minutes to Europe on 15285 kHz. One hour later in winter.

19:00–19:30

Old contrasts with new in Milan, Italy. The RAI Lombardia radio tower peeks out in the background to ensure no passersby go into a time warp. Arto Mujunen

Radio Budapest, Hungary. Summer only at this time. *News* and features, few of which are broadcast on a regular basis. Thirty minutes to Europe on 6025 and 7130 kHz. One hour later in winter.

■**Deutsche Welle,** Germany. *News*, then Monday through Friday it's ●*NewsLink* followed by *Africa Report*. Weekends, the Saturday news is followed by *Talking Point* and ●*Spectrum* (science); Sunday, by *Religion and Society* and *Arts on the Air*. Forty-five minutes to Africa, but also well heard in parts of eastern North America. Winter, choose from 11765, 11810, 13780, 15275, 15390 and 17810 kHz; in summer, go for 11805, 11965, 13720, 15390 and 17810 kHz. Best winter options for North America are 11810 and 15275 kHz; and summer, 15390 kHz.

Voice of Russia World Service. Continuous programming to Europe at this hour. *News*, then winter weekdays there's *Commonwealth Update* (news and reports from and about the CIS), replaced Saturday by *Science and Engineering*, and Sunday by *Musical Portraits of the Twentieth Century*. Monday through Saturday summer, it's *News and Views*, with *Sunday Panorama* and *Russia: People and Events* filling the Sunday slots. Winter weekends at 1931, there's Saturday's *This is Russia*, and Sunday's emotive ●*Christian Message from Moscow*. During the week, the feature lineup is somewhat variable. Summer offerings at this time include ●*Moscow Yesterday and Today* (Monday), *This is Russia* (Tuesday and Sunday), *Kaleidoscope* (Wednesday), ●*Audio Book Club* (Thursday), *Russian by Radio* (Friday) and Saturday's ●*Christian Message from Moscow*. Winter, choose from 5940, 5950, 6045, 7340, 9775 and 9890 kHz; in summer, try 9480, 9685, 9775, 9890, 11675 and 12070 kHz.

China Radio International. Repeat of the 1600 transmission. One hour to North Africa and the Mideast on 6165 (winter), 9440, 9585 (winter), and (summer) 11610 and 13790 kHz.

Radio Thailand. A 60-minute package of *news*, features and (if you're lucky) enjoyable Thai music. To Northern Europe winter on 9535 kHz, and summer on 7155 kHz. Also available to Asia on 9655 and 11905 kHz, although operation on these channels tends to be somewhat irregular.

Voice of Korea, North Korea. Strictly of curiosity value only. An hour of old-style communist programming to Europe on 6575 and 9335 kHz, and to North America on 11710 and 13760 kHz.

Radio for Peace International, Costa Rica. Continues with a variety of counterculture and social-conscience features. Audible in Europe and North America on 15050 and (upper sideband) 21815 kHz.

Voice of Vietnam. Repeat of the 1800 transmission (see there for specifics). A half hour to Europe on 7145 (winter), 9730 and (summer) 13740 kHz.

Voice of America. Continuous programming to the Mideast and North Africa. *News Now*—news and reports on a wide variety of topics. On 9760 and (summer) 9770 kHz. Also heard in Europe. For a separate service to Africa, see the next item.

Voice of America. *News Now*, then Monday through Friday it's *World of Music*. Best of the weekend programs is ●*Music Time in Africa* at 1930 Sunday. Continuous to most of Africa on 6035, 7375, 7415, 11920, 11975, 12040, 15410, 15445 and 15580 kHz, some of which are seasonal. For yet another service, to Australasia, see the following item.

Voice of America. Sixty minutes of news and reports covering a variety of topics. One hour to Australasia on 9525, 11870 and 15180 kHz.

Radyo Pilipinas, Philippines. Part of a much longer two-hour broadcast mainly in Tagalog. The amount of programming in English varies widely, sometimes starting at 1830 or earlier, but at other times does not appear until around 1915, or not at all! To the Mideast winter on 11730, 11890 and 15190 kHz; and summer on 11720, 15190 and 17720 kHz. Occasionally heard in North America, mainly during summer.

Radio Korea International, South Korea. Opens with *news* and commentary, followed Monday through Wednesday by *Seoul Calling*. Weekly features include *Echoes of Korean Music* and *Shortwave Feedback* (Sunday), *Tales from Korea's Past* (Monday), *Korean Cultural Trails* (Tuesday), *Pulse of Korea* (Wednesday), *From Us to You* (a listener-response program) and *Let's Learn Korean* (Thursday), *Let's Sing Together* and *Korea Through Foreigners' Eyes* (Friday), and Saturday's *Discovering Korea*, *Korean Literary Corner* and *Weekly News Focus*. Sixty minutes to East Asia on 5975 and 7275 kHz.

WJCR, Upton, Kentucky. Continues with country gospel music to North America on 7490 and 13595 kHz. Other U.S. religious broadcasters operating at this time include **WWCR** on 13845 and 15685 kHz, **KTBN** on 15590 kHz, and **WHRI-World Harvest Radio** on 13760 kHz. For traditionalist Catholic programming, try **WEWN** on 11875 and 13615 kHz.

CFRX-CFRB, Toronto, Canada. See 1800. Weekdays at this time, you can hear *The John Oakley Show*; weekends, it's replaced by *The Mike Stafford Show*. On 6070 kHz.

AFRTS Shortwave, USA. Network news, live sports, music and features in the upper-sideband mode from the Armed Forces Radio & Television Service. Transmitted from modestly powered U.S. Navy stations around the globe. Try 4278.5, 4319, 4995, 5765, 6350, 6458.5, 10320, 10940.5, 12579, 12689.5 and 13362 kHz.

19:30

Radio Polonia, Poland. Summer only at this time. Monday through Friday, it's *News from Poland*—news, reports and interviews on the latest events in the country. This is followed by *Cookery Corner* and *The Best of Polish Radio* (Monday), *Letter from Poland* and *Multimedia Show* (Tuesday), *Day in the Life* and *Discovering Chopin* (Wednesday), *Focus* (the arts in Poland) and *Soundcheck* (Thursday), and Friday's *Business Week* followed by *Postbag*, a listener-response show. The Saturday broadcast begins with a bulletin of *news*, then there's *Europe East, The Weeklies* and *Chart Show*. Sundays, look for five minutes of *news* followed by *Panorama* and *Request Concert*. Sixty minutes to Europe on 6035, 7185, 7265 and 9525 kHz. One hour later during winter.

Radio Austria International. Winter only at this time. ●*Report from Austria*, a half hour of news and human interest stories. Ample coverage of national and regional issues. To Europe on 5945 and 6155 kHz. One hour earlier in summer.

Radio Slovakia International. Winter only at this time. *Slovakia Today*, a 30-minute review of Slovak life and culture. Monday has a potpourri of short features; Tuesday's focus is on tourism and Slovak personalities; Wednesday features business and economy; and Thursday brings a mix of politics, education and science. Friday offerings include cultural items, cooking recipes and the off-beat *Back Page News*; and Saturday has the *"Best of"* series. Sunday's show is a melange of this and that, and includes *Listeners' Tribune* and some enjoyable Slovak music. A friendly 30 minutes to Western Europe on 5915, 6055 and 7345 kHz. One hour earlier in summer.

Swiss Radio International. *Newsnet*—news and background reports on world and Swiss events. Some lighter fare on Saturdays, when the biweekly *Capital Letters* (a listener-response program) alternates with *Name Game* (first Saturday) and *Sounds Good* (third Saturday). Thirty minutes to Africa, winter on 9605, 11910, 13660 and 17735 kHz; summer on 13770, 15220 and 17580 and 17735 kHz. Easy reception in southern Africa on 17735 kHz.

Radio Yugoslavia. Winter only at this time. Thirty minutes of news and short features to Europe on 6100 kHz. One hour earlier in summer.

Voice of Turkey. Winter only at this time. See 1830 for program details. Some unusual programming and friendly presentation make this station worth a listen. Fifty minutes to Europe on 6175 and 6180 kHz. One hour earlier in summer.

Voice of the Islamic Republic of Iran. A one-hour broadcast of news, commentary and features with a strong Islamic influence. Reflects a way of life not found in western countries. To Europe winter on 6110, 9022 and 9625 kHz; and summer on 9022, 11670 and 13730 kHz. Apart from 9022 kHz, frequency usage tends to be a little erratic. As of winter 2001, also available to southern Africa on 11685 and 15105 kHz (summer channels not known).

Radio Vlaanderen Internationaal, Belgium. Summer only at this time. Weekdays, starts with *News*, then *Belgium Today*, *Press Review* and features. The lineup includes *Focus on Europe* and *Sports* (Monday), *Green Society* (Tuesday), *The Arts* (Wednesday and Friday), *Around Town* (Wednesday), *Economics* and *International Report* (Thursday), and Friday's *Tourism*. Closes with *Soundbox*. These are replaced Saturday by *Music from Flanders*, and Sunday by *Radio World*, *Tourism*, *Brussels 1043* (a listener-response program) and *Soundbox*. Thirty minutes to western Europe on 9925 kHz. There is no corresponding winter broadcast on shortwave, only on Medium Wave AM.

Radio Sweden. Summer only at this time, and a repeat of the 1730 broadcast. See 1830 for program details. Thirty minutes to Europe on 6065 kHz.

■Radio Netherlands. Monday through Friday, starts with a feature and ends with ●*Newsline*, replaced weekends by a *news* bulletin and a second feature. Quality fare, including ●*Research File* (science, Monday), ●*Encore* (Thursday) ●*A Good Life* (Friday) and Wednesday's award-winning ●*Documentary*. On the remaining days, you can hear *Music 52-15* (Tuesday), *Sound Fountain* and *Europe Unzipped* (Saturday) and *Dutch Horizons* and *Sincerely Yours* (a listener- response show) on Sunday. The end of a three-hour broadcast to Africa on 6020 (best for southern parts), 7120 (summer), 9895, 11655, 13700, 17605 and (summer) 21590 kHz. The last two frequencies are audible in much of the United States.

RAI International—Radio Roma, Italy. Actually starts at 1935. Approximately 12 minutes of *news*, then some Italian music. Twenty minutes to western Europe winter on 5970, 7285 and 9760 kHz, and summer on 5970 and 9750 kHz.

19:40

Voice of Armenia. Monday through Saturday, summer only at this time. Twenty minutes of Armenian *news* and culture, mainly of interest to Armenians abroad. To Europe on 9960 or 9965 kHz, and to the Mideast on 4810 kHz. One hour later in winter.

19:50

Vatican Radio. Summer only at this time. Twenty minutes of programming oriented to Catholics. To Europe on 4005, 5880 (variable) and 7250 kHz. One hour later in winter.

kHz. Other U.S. religious broadcasters operating at this hour include **WWCR** on 13845 and 15685 and kHz, **KTBN** on 15590 kHz, and **WHRI-World Harvest Radio** on 13760 kHz. Traditionalist Catholic programming is available from **WEWN** on 11875 and 13615 kHz.

AFRTS Shortwave, USA. Network news, live sports, music and features in the upper-sideband mode from the Armed Forces Radio & Television Service. Transmitted from modestly powered U.S. Navy stations around the globe. Try 4278.5, 4319, 4995, 5765, 6350, 6458.5, 10320, 10940.5, 12579, 12689.5 and 13362 kHz.

21:30

BBC World Service for the Falkland Islands. *Calling the Falklands* has been running for so long that it has almost ceased to be the broadcasting curiosity it used to be. This twice-weekly transmission for a small community in the South Atlantic consists of news and short features, often on unusual topics. Decidedly different from the usual world band fare. Audible for 15 minutes Tuesday and Friday on 11680 kHz, and easily heard in parts of eastern North America.

Radio Austria International. Summer weekdays only at this time. Thirty minutes of news and human-interest stories in ●*Report from Austria*. A good source of national and regional news. To Europe on 5945 and 6155 kHz. One hour later during winter.

Radio Prague, Czech Republic. Summer only at this time. See 2230 for program details. *News* and features dealing with Czech life and culture. A half hour to Southeast Asia and Australasia on 11600 kHz, and to West Africa on 15545 kHz.

Radio Budapest, Hungary. This time summer only. *News* and features, few of which are broadcast on a regular basis. Thirty minutes to Europe on 3975 kHz. One hour later in winter.

21:30–22:00

Usu, Bidang Siaran Musik, in overalls, and Toto Harmanto, Tehnik Rekaman, coordinate programs at RRI Jakarta, Indonesia. Juichi Yamada

Wales Radio International. Winter Fridays only at this time. News, interviews and music from the Land of the Red Dragon. Thirty minutes to Europe on 6010 kHz, and one hour earlier in summer.

Radio Tashkent, Uzbekistan. Thirty minutes of news, commentary and features, plus some exotic Uzbek music. To Europe winter on 7105 and 9540 (or 9430) kHz, and summer on 9540 (or 9530) and 11905 kHz.

Radio Tirana, Albania. Summer only at this time. *News*, short features and some lively Albanian music. Thirty minutes to Europe on 7130 and 9540 kHz. One hour later in winter.

Voice of Turkey. This time winter only. *News*, followed by *Review of the Turkish Press* and features (some of them unusual) with a strong local flavor. Selections of Turkish popular and classical music complete the program. Fifty minutes to Southeast Asia and Australasia on 9525 kHz. One hour earlier in summer.

Radio Sweden. Summer only at this time. Thirty minutes of predominantly Scandinavian fare (see 2230 for specifics). To Europe on 6065 kHz, and to Southeast Asia and Australasia on 15255 kHz.

Voice of the Islamic Republic of Iran. A one-hour package of news, commentary and features with a distinctly Islamic slant. Definitely not for listeners who seek lighter fare. To Australasia winter on 9780 and 11740 kHz, and summer on 9570 and 13745 kHz.

22:00

■BBC World Service for the Americas. Monday through Friday winter, five minutes of *news* are followed by ●*World Business Report*, *British News*, ●*Sports Roundup* and ●*Analysis* (replaced Wednesday by ●*From Our Own Correspondent*). Summer, it's a full hour of *The World Today*, with the exception of Friday, when the final 30 minutes are taken up by ●*People and Politics*. Weekend programs are year round, with *The World Today* filling the first half hour, followed by Saturday's ●*From Our Own Correspondent* or Sunday's ●*Agenda*. Continuous programming to the Caribbean and eastern North America on 5975 kHz. Also audible in some areas on 12095 kHz, beamed to South America; a radio with synchronous selectable sideband helps reduce teletype interference.

BBC World Service for Europe. Winter weekdays, there's *News*, ●*World Business Report*, *British News*, ●*Sports Roundup* and ●*Off the Shelf* (readings from world literature). Weekends, *News* is followed by *Jazzmatazz* and ●*Omnibus* (Saturday), and *Meridian* (the arts) and ●*Weekend* on Sunday. Summer, it's news and current events in *The World Today*, reduced to 30 minutes Friday and Saturday, when it is followed by ●*People and Politics* and ●*From Our Own Correspondent*, respectively. The final 60 minutes of a 19-hour block of programming to Europe and North Africa. On 6195 kHz.

■BBC World Service for East and Southeast Asia and the Pacific. Sunday through Thursday (local Asian weekdays), it's a full hour of news and current events in ●*The World Today*. Friday and Saturday, there's 30 minutes of the same, followed by ●*People and Politics* and ●*From Our Own Correspondent*, respectively. Continuous to East Asia on 5965 and 6195 kHz; to Southeast Asia on 6195, 7110, 9660 and 11955 kHz; and to Australasia on 9660, 11955 and 12080 kHz.

Radio Bulgaria. This time winter only. See 2100 for specifics. News and culture from the Balkans—don't miss ●*Folk Studio* (Bulgarian music) at 2210 Sunday. Sixty minutes to Europe, also heard in parts of eastern North

America, on 7535 and 7545 kHz. One hour earlier in summer.

Radio Cairo, Egypt. The second half of a 90-minute broadcast to Europe on 9990 kHz; see 2115 for program details.

Radio Exterior de España ("Spanish National Radio"). Winter weekends only at this time. A popular package of *news* and features. Sunday's series on Spanish music is highly recommended. One hour to Europe on 9680 kHz, and to North and West Africa on 9595 kHz. One hour earlier in summer.

China Radio International. Repeat of the 2000 transmission; see there for specifics. One hour to Europe, winter on 7170 (or 7175) kHz and summer on 9880 kHz.

Voice of America. The beginning of a three-hour block of programs to East and Southeast Asia and the Pacific. The ubiquitous *News Now*—news and reports on current events, sports, science, business, entertainment and more. To East and Southeast Asia on 7215, 9705, 9770, 11760, 15185, 15290, 15305, 17735 (or 17740) and 17820 kHz; and to Australasia on 15185, 15305 and 17735 kHz. The first half hour is also available weekday evenings to Africa on 7340, 7375 and 7415 kHz.

Radio Australia. *News*, followed Sunday through Thursday by *AM* (current events) and, on the half-hour, a feature. The lineup starts with Sunday's *Australian Music Show* (contemporary music) and ends with Thursday's *Jazz Notes*. In between, there's *Music Deli* (samplings from different cultures, Monday); *Blacktracker* (contemporary aboriginal music, Tuesday); and *Australian Country Style* (Nashville Down Under, Wednesday). Friday's features are *Asia Pacific* and a later-than-usual edition of *AM*; and Saturday's pairing is *Correspondents' Report* and *Business Report*. Continuous programming to the Pacific on 17715, 17795 and 21740 kHz (audible in parts of North America, especially during summer), and to Southeast Asia on 13620 or 13780 kHz.

Radio Taipei International, Taiwan. Opens with 15 minutes of *News*, and with the exception of Sunday, closes with *Let's Learn Chinese*. In between, there are either one or two features, depending on the day of the week. Monday, there's the pleasurable and exotic ●*Jade Bells and Bamboo Pipes* (Taiwanese music); Tuesday has *Culture Express* and *Trends*; Wednesday's slots are *Taiwan Today* and *Confucius and Inspiration Beyond*; Thursday's offerings are *Journey into Chinese Culture* and *Instant Noodles*; and Friday's pairing is *Taipei Magazine* and *East Meets West*. These are replaced Saturday by *Kaleidoscope* and *Naluwan*, and Sunday by *Great Wall Forum* and *Mailbag Time*. Sixty minutes to western Europe, winter on 5810 and 9355 kHz, and summer on 11565 and 15600 kHz.

Radio Tirana, Albania. Winter only at this time. Thirty minutes of news, short features and Albanian music. To Europe on 7130 and 9540 kHz. One hour earlier in summer.

Radio Habana Cuba. Monday through Saturday, the first half hour consists of international and Cuban news followed by commentary in *RHC's Viewpoint*. The next 30 minutes consist of a news bulletin and the sports-oriented *Time Out* (five minutes each) followed by a feature: *Caribbean Outlook* (Monday and Thursday), *DXers Unlimited* (Tuesday and Saturday), the *Mailbag Show* (Wednesday) and *Weekly Review* (Friday). Sunday, the hour is split between *Weekly Review* and *Mailbag Show*. Sixty minutes to the Caribbean and southern United States on 9550 kHz.

Radio Budapest, Hungary. Winter only at this time. *News* and features, most of which are broadcast on a non-regular basis. Thirty minutes to Europe on 6025 kHz. One hour earlier in summer.

Radio Yugoslavia. Thirty minutes of news and short features. Winter only to Europe on 6100 or 6185 kHz, and one hour earlier in summer. Sunday through Friday summer only to Australasia on 7230 kHz, and moves to 1330 for winter.

Voice of Turkey. Summer only at this time. *News*, followed by *Review of the Turkish Press* and features with a strong local flavor. Selections of Turkish popular and classical music complete the program. Fifty minutes to Europe on 7190 and 13640 kHz, and to

22:00–23:00

eastern North America on 13640 kHz. One hour later during winter.

Radio Canada International. Summer only at this hour, and a relay of CBC domestic programming. Monday through Friday, opens with ●*The World at Six*; Saturday and Sunday, *The World This Weekend*. On the half-hour there's the weekday ●*As It Happens*, Saturday's *Madly Off in All Directions* (sometimes replaced by another comedy show), and Sunday's *The Inside Track*. Sixty minutes to North America on 6175, 9590, 9755, 13670 and 17695 kHz. One hour later in winter.

RAI International—Radio Roma, Italy. Actually starts at 2205. Approximately ten minutes of *news* followed by a quarter-hour feature (usually music). Twenty-five minutes to East Asia on 9675, 11900 and (summer) 15265 kHz.

Radio Korea International, South Korea. Winter only at this hour. Starts with *news*, followed Monday through Wednesday by *Economic News Briefs*. The remainder of the broadcast is taken up by a feature: *Shortwave Feedback* (Sunday), *Seoul Calling* (Monday and Tuesday), *Pulse of Korea* (Wednesday), *From Us to You* (Thursday), *Let's Sing Together* (Friday) and *Weekly News Focus* (Saturday). Thirty minutes to Europe on 3980 kHz, and one hour earlier in summer.

HCJB—Voice of the Andes, Ecuador. Winter only at this time. The final 60 minutes of a three-hour block of predominantly religious programming to Europe on 11890 kHz. One hour earlier in summer.

Radio Ukraine International. Winter only at this time. A potpourri of things Ukrainian, with the Sunday broadcast often featuring some excellent music. Sixty minutes to Europe and beyond on 5905, 6020, 6080 and 9560 kHz. Often mediocre reception due to financial and technical limitations. One hour earlier in summer.

Radio for Peace International, Costa Rica. Continues with counterculture and social-conscience programs. Audible in Europe and North America on 15050 and (upper sideband) 21815 kHz.

XERMX—Radio México Internacional. Monday through Friday summer, there's an English summary of the Spanish-language *Antena Radio* (weekend programs are in Spanish). Winter, there's a daily feature: *Mosaic of Mexico* (Monday and Friday), *DXperience* (a show for radio enthusiasts, Tuesday and Sunday), *Regional Roots and Rhythms* (Wednesday), *Mirror of Mexico* (Thursday) and Saturday's *Magical Trip*. Best heard in western and southern parts of the United States on 9705 and 11770 kHz.

All India Radio. The final half-hour of a transmission to Western Europe and Australasia, consisting mainly of news-related fare. To Europe on 7410, 9650 and 9950 kHz; and to Australasia on 7150, 9910, 11620 and 11715 kHz. Frequencies for Europe are audible in parts of eastern North America, while those for Australasia are also heard in Southeast Asia.

WJCR, Upton, Kentucky. Continues with country gospel music to North America on 7490 and 13595 kHz. Other U.S. religious broadcasters heard at this hour include **WWCR** on 13845 kHz, **KAIJ** on 13815 kHz, **KTBN** on 15590 kHz, and **WHRI-World Harvest Radio** on 5745 kHz. For traditionalist Catholic programming, try **WEWN** on 9355 and 13615 kHz.

CFRX-CFRB, Toronto, Canada. See 2100.

AFRTS Shortwave, USA. Network news, live sports, music and features in the upper-sideband mode from the Armed Forces Radio & Television Service. Transmitted from modestly powered U.S. Navy stations around the globe. Try 4278.5, 4319, 4995, 5765, 6350, 6458.5, 10320, 10940.5, 12579, 12689.5 and 13362 kHz.

22:30

Radio Sweden. Monday through Friday, it's *news* and features in *Sixty Degrees North*, concentrating heavily on Scandinavian topics. The Monday slot goes to *SportScan*, replaced Tuesday by *Close Up* or an alternative feature, and Wednesday by *Money Matters*. Thursday features a different show each week of the month—*Nordic Report*, *GreenScan*, *Heart Beat* or *S-Files*, while Friday offers a review of the week's news. Saturday's slot is filled by *Weekend*, *Spectrum* (the arts), *Sweden Today* or *Studio 49*, and Sunday fare consists of *In Touch with Stockholm* (a listener-response program) or the musical *Sounds Nordic*. Thirty minutes to Europe on 6065 and 7325 kHz, with the latter frequency also audible in Africa and the Mideast. One hour earlier in summer.

Radio Austria International. Winter weekdays only at this time. The informative and well-presented ●*Report from Austria*. Ample coverage of national and regional issues. Thirty minutes to Europe on 5945 and 6155 kHz. One hour earlier in summer.

Radio Budapest, Hungary. Winter only at this time. *News* and features, few of which are broadcast on a regular basis. Thirty minutes to Europe on 3975 kHz. One hour earlier in summer.

Radio Vlaanderen Internationaal, Belgium. Summer only at this time. Weekdays, starts with *News*, then *Belgium Today*, *Press Review* and features. The lineup includes *Focus on Europe* and *Sports* (Monday), *Green Society* (Tuesday), *The Arts* (Wednesday and Friday), *Around Town* (Wednesday), *Economics* and *International Report* (Thursday), and Friday's *Tourism*. Closes with *Soundbox*. These are replaced Saturday by *Music from Flanders*, and Sunday by *Radio World*, *Tourism*, *Brussels 1043* (a listener-response program) and *Soundbox*. Thirty minutes to North America winter on 13660 kHz, and summer on 15565 kHz.

Radio Prague, Czech Republic. *News*, then Monday through Friday there's *Current Affairs* and a feature. Monday, *Spotlight* (a look at Czech regional affairs) alternates with *One on One* (an informal interview show); Tuesday, there's the regular *Talking Point* (issues in the Czech Republic); and the Wednesday spot is either *Czechs in History* or *Central Europe Today*. Thursday, it's business and related topics in *Economic Report*, replaced Friday by *Magazine*. Weekend fare after the news consists of Saturday's *Readings from Czech Literature* plus an excellent musical feature, and Sunday's *A Letter from Prague*, *The Arts* and *Mailbag*. A half hour to eastern North America winter on 7345 kHz, and summer on 11600 and 15545 kHz; also to West Africa winter on 9435 kHz.

22:45

All India Radio. The first 15 minutes of a much longer broadcast, consisting of Indian music, regional and international *news*, commentary, and a variety of talks and features of general interest. Continuous till 0045. To East Asia on 9950 and 13605 kHz, and to Southeast Asia on 9705, 11620 and 13605 kHz.

23:00

■BBC World Service for the Americas. Monday through Thursday winter, a full hour of *The World Today*. On the remaining days, it's reduced to 30 minutes and followed by *Global Business* (Friday), *Arts in Action* (Saturday) or Sunday's *The Greenfield Collection* (classical music). Summer weekdays, opens with five minutes of *news*. Next comes the long-running *Outlook*, and the hour is rounded off with a 15-minute feature (very much a mixed bag). Saturday brings ●*Play of the Week* (world theater at its best), replaced Sunday by the same programs as in winter. Continuous to the Caribbean and eastern North America on 5975 kHz. Also audible in some areas on 12095 kHz, targeted at South America; a radio with synchronous selectable sideband helps reduce teletype interference.

■BBC World Service for East and Southeast Asia and the Pacific. Sunday through Thursday (weekday mornings in Asia), it's the second hour of *The World Today*, a breakfast news show for the region. On the remaining days there's 30 minutes of the same, followed by Friday's *Global Business* or Saturday's *Arts in Action*. Continuous to East Asia on 5965, 6035, 6195, 11945, 11955 and 15280 kHz; to Southeast Asia on 3915, 6195, 7105 and 11955 kHz; and to Australasia on 11955 kHz.

Voice of Turkey. Winter only at this hour. See 2200 for program details. Fifty minutes to

23:00–23:30

Europe on 6135 and 9655 kHz, and to eastern North America on 9655 kHz. One hour earlier in summer.

■**Deutsche Welle,** Germany. Repeat of the 2100 broadcast to Southeast Asia and Australasia (see there for specifics). Forty-five minutes to South and Southeast Asia, winter on 9470, 9815 and 13690 kHz; and summer on 9815, 12055, 13610 (or 13640) and 21790 kHz.

Radio Australia. *World News*, followed Sunday through Thursday by *Asia Pacific* (replaced Friday by *Lingua Franca*, and Saturday by some sharp scientific commentary in ●*Ockham's Razor*). On the half-hour, look for a feature. *Earthbeat* (the environment) occupies the Sunday slot, and is replaced Monday by *The Buzz*. Then come Tuesday's *Arts Talk*, Wednesday's *Rural Reporter*, Thursday's *Media Report*, Friday's *Sports Factor*, and Saturday's *Innovations*. Continuous to the Pacific on 9660, 12080, 17715, 17795 and 21740 kHz; and to Southeast Asia on 13620 or 13780 kHz. Listeners in North America should try 17715, 17795 and 21740 kHz, especially in summer.

Radio Canada International. Summer weekdays, the final hour of ●*As It Happens*; winter, the first 30 minutes of the same, preceded by the up-to-the-minute news program ●*World at Six*. Summer weekends, look for ●*Quirks and Quarks* (science, Saturday) and ●*Global Village* (world music, Sunday). These are replaced winter by *The World This Weekend* (both days), a comedy show (Saturday) and *The Inside Track* (Sunday). To North America on 5960 (winter), 6175, 9590, 9755 and (summer) 13670 and 17695 kHz.

China Radio International. Starts with *News*, and weekdays continues with in-depth reports. The remainder of the broadcast is made up of features. Regular shows include *People in the Know* (Monday), *Sportsworld* (Tuesday), *China Horizons* (Wednesday), *Voices from Other Lands* (Thursday) and Friday's *Life in China*. Saturday, there's *Global Review* and *Listeners' Garden* (reports, music and a Chinese language lesson), replaced Sunday by *Report from Developing Countries* and *In the Spotlight*. Sixty minutes to the Caribbean and southern United States on 5990 kHz, via CRI's Cuban relay. May also be available to the United States on 13680 kHz.

Radio for Peace International, Costa Rica. Continues with a six-hour cyclical block of social-conscience and counterculture programming audible in Europe and the Americas on 15050 and (upper sideband) 21815 kHz.

Radio Cairo, Egypt. The first hour of a 90-minute broadcast to eastern North America. A 10-minute *news* bulletin is aired at 2315, with the remaining time taken up by short features on Egypt, the Middle East and Islam. For the intellectual listener there's *Literary Readings* at 2345 Monday, and *Modern Arabic Poetry* at the same time Friday. More general fare is available in *Listener's Mail* at 2325 Thursday and Saturday. Easy reception on 9900 kHz.

Radio Romania International. *News*, commentary and features, plus some enjoyable Romanian music. Fifty-five minutes to Europe on 7195 (winter), 9690 and (summer) 11830 kHz; also to eastern North America winter on 9570 and 11940 kHz, and summer on 11775 and 15105 kHz.

Radio Bulgaria. Summer only at this time. *News*, music and features. Monday through Friday (weekday evenings in North America), the news is followed by *Events and Developments*, replaced Saturday by *Views Behind the News* and Sunday by the enjoyable and exotic ●*Folk Studio*. The next slot consists of weekly features. Take your pick from *Plaza/Walks and Talks* (Sunday), *Magazine Economy* (Monday), *Arts and Artists* (Tuesday), *History Club* (Wednesday), *The Way We Live* (Thursday), *DX Programed* (Friday) and *Answering Your Letters*, a listener- response show, on Saturday. Monday through Saturday, the broadcast ends with *Keyword Bulgaria*. Sixty minutes to eastern North America on 9400 and 11700 kHz. One hour later during winter.

XERMX—Radio México Internacional. Winter weekdays only. An English summary of the Spanish-language *Antena Radio*. Weekend programs are in Spanish. One hour earlier in summer. Thirty minutes to North America on 9705 and 11770 kHz, and best heard in western and southern parts of the United States.

Voice of America. Continues with programs aimed at East Asia and the Pacific on the same frequencies as at 2200.

WJCR, Upton, Kentucky. Continuous country gospel music to North America on 7490 and 13595 kHz. Other U.S. religious broadcasters heard at this time include **WWCR** on 13845 kHz, **KAIJ** on 13815 kHz, **KTBN** on 15590 kHz, and **WHRI-World Harvest Radio** on 5745 kHz. For traditionalist Catholic programming, tune **WEWN** on 9355 and 13615 kHz.

AFRTS Shortwave, USA. Network news, live sports, music and features in the upper-sideband mode from the Armed Forces Radio & Television Service. Transmitted from modestly powered U.S. Navy stations around the globe. Try 4278.5, 4319, 4995, 5765, 6350, 6458.5, 10320, 10940.5, 12579, 12689.5 and 13362 kHz.

23:30

■**Radio Netherlands.** Opens Monday through Friday with ●*Newsline*, replaced weekends by a *news* bulletin. The next 30 minutes are devoted to features: the well produced ●*Research File* (science, Monday); *Music 52-15* (eclectic, Tuesday); the outstanding ●*Documentary* (Wednesday); ●*Encore* (Thursday); and ●*A Good Life* (Friday). The Saturday offerings are *Europe Unzipped*, *Insight* and *Sound Fountain*, replaced Sunday by *Sincerely Yours*, a program preview and *Dutch Horizons*. The first of two hours to North America on 6165 and 9845 kHz.

Radio Prague, Czech Republic. Winter only at this time; see 2230 for program specifics. A half hour to eastern North America on 7345 and 9435 kHz.

Swiss Radio International. *Newsnet*—news and background reports on world and Swiss events. Some lighter fare on Saturdays, when the biweekly *Capital Letters* (a listener-response program) alternates with *Name Game* (first Saturday) and *Sounds Good* (third Saturday). Thirty minutes to South America on 9885, 11660 (winter) and (summer) 11905 kHz. As a result of SRI's decision to discontinue shortwave broadcasts to all parts of the world except the Middle East, Africa and South America (and these are also to be phased out eventually), this slot is far and away the best opportunity for listeners in North America.

Radio Canada International's studios are located in the heart of cosmopolitan Montréal, Quebec. This exceptional station has had more near-death experiences than John Wayne, but since the World Trade Center attack it has once again been receiving urgent financial infusions. RCI

All India Radio. Continuous programming to East and Southeast Asia. A potpourri of *news*, commentary, features and exotic Indian music. To East Asia on 9950 and 13605 kHz, and to Southeast Asia on 9705, 11620 and 13605 kHz.

Voice of Vietnam. *News*, then *Commentary* or *Weekly Review*. These are followed by short features and some pleasant Vietnamese music. A half hour to Southeast Asia (often heard in Europe) on 9840 and 12020 kHz. Frequencies may vary slightly.

Prepared by Don Swampo and the staff of PASSPORT TO WORLD BAND RADIO.

www.passband.com

Addresses PLUS—2002

Station Email and Postal Addresses . . . PLUS *Websites, Webcasts, Who's Who, Phones, Faxes, Bureaus, Future Plans, Items for Sale, Giveaways . . .* PLUS *Summer and Winter Times in Each Country!*

Other parts of PASSPORT show how stations reach out to you, but Addresses PLUS flips things around—it shows how you can reach out to stations. It also reveals ways besides world band that stations can inform and entertain.

"Applause" Replies

When radio broadcasting was in its infancy, listeners sent in "applause" cards to inform stations about reception and program quality. To say "thanks," stations would reply with a letter or illustrated card verifying ("QSLing") that the station the listener heard was, in fact, theirs. While they were at it, some would also throw in a free souvenir—a station calendar, perhaps, or a pennant or sticker.

This is still being done today to

some extent. You can learn how to provide technical feedback by looking under Verification in PASSPORT's glossary, then making use of Addresses PLUS for contact specifics.

Some stations sell goods, as well—things like radios, CDs, publications, clothing, tote bags, caps, watches, clocks, pens, knives, letter openers, lighters, refrigerator magnets and keyrings.

Paying Postfolk

Most stations reply to listener correspondence—even email—through the postal system. That way, they can send out printed schedules, verification cards and other "hands-on" souvenirs. Big stations usually do so for free, but smaller ones often seek reimbursement for postage.

Some stations offer unusual CDs, publications and souvenirs.

Most effective, especially for Latin American and Indonesian stations, is to enclose some unused (mint) stamps from the station's country. These are available from Plum's Airmail Postage, 12 Glenn Road, Flemington NJ 08822 USA, phone +1 (908) 788-1020, fax +1 (908) 782 2612. One way to help ensure your return-postage stamps will be put to the intended use is to affix them onto a pre-addressed return airmail envelope. The result is a self-addressed stamped envelope, or SASE as it is referred to in Addresses PLUS.

You can also prompt reluctant stations by donating one or more U.S. dollars, preferably hidden from prying eyes by a piece of foil-covered carbon paper or the like. Registration helps, too, as cash tends to get stolen. Additionally, International Reply Coupons (IRCs), which recipients may exchange locally for air or surface stamps, are available at a number of post offices worldwide. Thing is, they're increasingly hard to find, relatively costly, not fully effective, and aren't accepted by postal authorities in some countries.

U.S.
MAIL

A dip in the muddy Ganga washes away all sins. It also reaffirms faith according to the Hindu tradition. M. Guha

Stamp Out Crime

Yes, even in 2002 mail theft is a problem in several countries. We identify these, and for each one offer proven ways to help avoid theft. Remember that a few postal employees are stamp collectors, and in certain countries they freely steal mail with unusual stamps. When in doubt, use everyday stamps or, even better, a postal meter or PC-generated postage. Another option is to use an aerogram.

¿Que Hora Es?

World Time, explained elsewhere in this book, is essential if you want to find out when your favorite station is on. But if you want to know what time it is in any given country, World Time and Addresses PLUS work together to give you local times within each country.

So that you don't have to wrestle with seasonal changes in your own time, we give local times for each country in terms of hours' difference from World Time, which stays the same year-round. For example, if you look below under "Algeria," you'll see that country is World Time +1; that is, one hour ahead of World Time. So, if World Time is 1200, the local time in Algeria is 1300 (1:00 PM). On the other hand, México City is World Time –6; that is, six hours behind World Time. If World Time is 1200, in México City it's 6:00 AM.

Times shown in parentheses are for the middle of the year—roughly April-October; specific dates of seasonal-time changeovers for individual countries can be obtained (U.S. callers only) by dialing the OAG toll-free 1-800-342-5624 during working hours, or (worldwide) fax +1 (630) 574 6565.

Spotted Something New?

Has something changed since we went to press? A missing detail? Please let us know! Your update information, especially photocopies of material received from stations, is highly valued. Contact the IBS Editorial Office, Box 300, Penn's Park, PA 18943 USA, fax +1 (215) 598 3794, email addresses@passband.com.

Muchas gracias to the kindly folks and helpful organizations mentioned at the end of this chapter for their tireless cooperation in the preparation of this section. Without you, none of this would have been possible.

Using PASSPORT's Addresses PLUS Section

Stations included: All stations are listed if known to reply, however erratically. Also, new stations which possibly may reply to correspondence from listeners.

Leased-time programs: Private organizations/NGOs that lease air time, but which possess no world band transmitters of their own, are usually not listed. However, they may be reached via the stations over which they are heard.

Postal addresses. Communications addresses are given. These sometimes differ from the physical transmitter locations given in the Blue Pages.

Email addresses and Websites. Given in Internet format. Periods, commas and semicolons at the end of an address listing are normal sentence punctuation, not part of the address, and "http://" is used only when there is no "www."

Phone and fax numbers. To help avoid confusion, telephone numbers are given with hyphens, fax numbers without. All are configured for international dialing once you add your country's International access code (011 in the United States and Canada, 010 in the United Kingdom, and so on). For domestic dialing within countries outside the United States, Canada and the Caribbean, replace the country code (1-3 digits preceded by a "+") by a zero.

Giveaways. If you want freebies, say so politely in your correspondence. These are usually available until supplies run out.

Webcasting. World band stations which simulcast and/or provide archived programming over the Internet are indicated by 🖥.

Unless otherwise indicated, stations:

- Reply regularly within six months to most listeners' correspondence in English.
- Provide, upon request, free station schedules and verification ("QSL") postcards or letters (see "Verification" in the glossary for further information). We specify when other items are available for free or for purchase.
- Do not require compensation for postage costs incurred in replying to you. Where compensation is required, details are provided.

Local times. These are given in difference from World Time. For example, "World Time –5" means that if you subtract five hours from World Time, you'll get the local time in that country. Thus, if it were 1100 World Time, it would be 0600 local time in that country. Times in (parentheses) are for the middle of the year—roughly April-October. For exact changeover dates, see above explanatory paragraph.

Allan Weiner, general manager of WBCQ and founder of Radio Newyork International. WBCQ

In Afghanistan this butcher shop quickly sells beef as food. Other unfortunate cattle roam freely on Afghan fields as live mine detectors. Bakhtar Agence

AFGHANISTAN World Time +4:30

NOTE: Postal service to this country is sometimes suspended.

ISLAMIC EMIRATE OF AFGHANISTAN (under Taliban control)

Radio Voice of Shari'ah, Afghan Radio TV, P.O. Box 544, Ansari Wat, Kabul, Afghanistan, via Pakistan (while direct postal service is unavailable)—under normal conditions, replace "Afghanistan, via Pakistan" with "Islamic Emirate of Afghanistan." Phone: +92 (91) 287-454. Fax: +92 (81) 447 300. Email: (English Service) english.program@usa.net. Web: (RealAudio only) www.taleban.com. External telephone links are currently suspended, except for a limited service provided by Pakistan Telecom. Contact: Abdul Rahman Nasseri, Department of Planning and Foreign Relations; Ahmad Shoaib Sharafi, English Program Producer; or Mir Ahmad Niazmand, Director of Foreign Relations. Correspondence in Dari, Farsi, Pashto or Urdu preferred, but reception reports in English are sometimes verified, especially when directed to Mr. Nasseri. Given the erratic postal system that operates via Pakistan, replies may take several months.

NEW YORK OFFICE: Representative of the Islamic Emirate of Afghanistan to the United Nations, 55/16 Main Street, Flushing NY, USA. Phone: +1 (718) 359-0457; (Newsline) +1 (718) 762-8095. Fax: +1 (718) 661 2721. Email: AMujahid@aol.com. Web: www.taleban.com. Contact: Mulawi Abdul Hakeem Mujahid; or Noorullah Zadran.

ISLAMIC STATE OF AFGHANISTAN (Northern Afghanistan, pro-Rabbani)

Takhar Radio, Operations Complex, Taloqan, Takhar Province, Islamic State of Afghanistan, via Dushanbe, Tajikistan. Contact: (administration) Sayd Habib, Director; Habib Inayatullah, Deputy Director; (technical) Mohammed Taher Ramin, Engineer. Although there is no official verification policy, reception reports are welcomed. Correspondence in English, Dari or Farsi is best directed to Mr. Arayanfar at the embassy in Dushanbe (*see*, below), though listeners in North America may prefer sending their correspondence c/o the Afghan Mission to the United Nations.

TAJIKISTAN ADDRESS: Embassy of the Islamic State of Afghanistan, ul. Pushkina, House 34, Dushanbe, Tajikistan. Phone: +7 (3772) 062-057. Fax: +7 (3772) 276 061. Contact: Shamsul Haq Arayanfar, Cultural Attaché.

USA ADDRESS: Permanent Mission of the Islamic State of Afghanistan to the United Nations, 360 Lexington Avenue, 11th Floor, New York NY 10017 USA. Phone: +1 (212) 972-1212/3. Fax: +1 (212) 972 1216. Email: Afgwatan@aol.com, or afghangovernment@afghangovernment.org. Web: www.afghangovernment.org.

ALBANIA World Time +1 (+2 midyear)

Radio Tirana, External Service, Rruga Ismail Qemali Nr. 11, Tirana, Albania. Phone: (general) +355 (42) 23-239; (Phone/fax, Technical Directorate) +355 (42) 26203. Fax: (External Service) +355 (42) 23650; (Technical Directorate) +355 (42) 27 745. Email: (general) radiotirana@radiotirana.net; radiotirana@interalb.net; (Technical Directorate) 113566.3011@compuserve.com; or dcico@artv.tirana.al. Web: (general) www.radiotirana.net; http://rtsh.sil.at; (RealAudio from Radio Tirana 1, domestic service) http://rtsh.sil.at/online.htm. Contact: Bardhyl Pollo, Director of External Services; Adriana Bislea, English Department; Marjeta Thoma; Pandi Skaka, Producer; or Diana Koci; (Technical Directorate) Irfan Mandija, Chief of Radio Broadcasting, Technical Directorate; Hector Karanxha; or Rifat Kryeziu, Director of Technical Directorate; (Frequency Management) Mrs. Drita Cico, Head of RTV Monitoring Center. May send free stickers and postcards. Replies from the station are again forthcoming, but it is advisable to include return postage ($1 should be enough).

Trans World Radio—*see* Monaco.

ALGERIA World Time +1 (+2 midyear)

Radio Algiers International—same details as "Radio Algérienne," below.

Radio Algérienne (ENRS)

NONTECHNICAL AND GENERAL TECHNICAL: 21 Boulevard des Martyrs, Algiers 16000, Algeria. Phone: (Direction Générale) +213 (21) 230-821; (Direction Commerciale) +213 (21) 590-700; (head of international relations) +213 (21) 594-266; (head of technical direction) +213 (21) 692-867. Fax: +213 (21) 230 823. Email: (information) information@algerian-radio.dz; (Direction Générale) dg@algerian-radio.dz; (Direction Technique, including reception reports) technique@algerian-radio.dz. Web: (includes Windows Media) www.algerian-radio.dz. Contact: (nontechnical) L. Zaghlami; Chaabane Lounakil, Head of International Arabic Section; Mrs. Zehira Yahi, Head of International Relations; or Relations Extérieures; (technical) M. Lakhdar Mahdi, Head of Technical Direction. Replies irregularly. French or Arabic preferred, but English accepted.

FREQUENCY MANAGEMENT OFFICE: Télédiffusion d'Algérie, Centre Nsdal, Bouzareah 1850, Algeria. Phone: +213 (21) 904-512; or +213 (21) 901-717. Fax: +213 (21) 901 499 or +213 (21) 901 522. Email: tda@ist.cerist.dz. Contact: Slimane Djematene; or Karim Zitouni.

ANGOLA World Time +1

Rádio Ecclésia (when operating), Rua Comandante Bula 118, São Paulo, Luanda, Angola; or C.P. 3579, Luanda, Angola. Phone: (general) +244 (2) 443-041; (studios) +244 (2) 445-484. Fax: +244 (2) 443 093. Email: ecclesia@snet.co.ao. Web: http://

ecclesia.snet.co.ao/noticias.htm. Contact: Fr. Antônio Jaca, General Manager. A Catholic station founded in 1954 and which broadcast continuously from March 1955 until closed by presidential decree in 1978. Reestablished in March 1997, when it was granted a permit to operate on FM. Experimented with shortwave transmissions via Radio Nederland facilities during July 2000, but these were terminated for technical reasons. Restarted transmissions in April 2001 via facilities of Germany's Deutsche Telekom (*see*). Eventually hopes to resume shortwave broadcasts via its own transmitter, if and when the current tight regulations in Angola are relaxed.

Rádio Nacional de Angola, C.P. 1329, Luanda, Angola. Fax: +244 (2) 391 234. Email: (technical) rochapinto@rna.so Web: (includes RealAudio) www.rna.ao; if the audio link doesn't work, try www.netangola.com/p/default.htm. Contact: Júlio Mendonça, Diretor dos Serviços de Programas; Lourdes de Almeida, Chefe de Secção; or Manuel Rabelais, Diretor Geral; (technical) Cândido Rocha Pinto, Diretor dos Serviços Técnicos. Formerly replied occasionally to correspondence, preferably in Portuguese, but replies have been more difficult recently. $1, return postage or 2 IRCs most helpful.

ANTARCTICA World Time -3 Base Antárctica Esperanza

Radio Nacional Arcángel San Gabriel—LRA36, Base Esperanza, 9411 Antártida Argentina, Argentina. Phone/Fax: +54 (2964) 421 519. Email: lra36@infovia.com.ar. Web: www.fcapital.com.ar/esperanza/pagina_otras.htm. Return postage required. Replies to correspondence in Spanish, and sometimes to correspondence in English and French, depending on who is at the station. If no reply, try sending your correspondence (but don't write the station's name on the envelope) and 2 IRCs via the helpful Gabriel Iván Barrera, Casilla 2868, C1000WBC Buenos Aires, Argentina.

ANGUILLA World Time -4

Caribbean Beacon, Box 690, Anguilla, British West Indies. Phone: +1 (264) 497- 4340. Fax: +1 (264) 497 4311. Contact: Monsell Hazell, Chief Engineer. $2 or return postage helpful. Relays Dr. Gene Scott's University Network—*see* USA.

ANTIGUA World Time -4

BBC World Service—Caribbean Relay Station, P.O. Box 1203, St. John's, Antigua. Phone: +1 (268) 462-0994. Fax: +1 (268) 462 0436. Contact: (technical) David George. Nontechnical correspondence should be sent to the BBC World Service in London (*see*).

Deutsche Welle—Relay Station Antigua—same address and contact as BBC World Service, above. Nontechnical correspondence should be sent to Deutsche Welle in Germany (*see*).

ARGENTINA World Time -3

Radiodifusión al Exterior—RAE, Casilla de Correos 555, Correo Central, C1000WBC Buenos Aires, Argentina. Phone/fax: +54 (11) 4325-6368. Fax: +54 (11) 4325 9433. Email: (Marcela Campos) camposrae@fibertel.com.ar, or camposrae@skytel.com.ar. Contact: (general) John Anthony Middleton, Head of English Team; María Dolores López; (administration) Señora Marcela G. R. Campos, Directora; (technical) Gabriel Iván Barrera, DX Editor. Free paper pennant and tourist literature. Return postage or $1 appreciated.

Radio Nacional Buenos Aires, Maipú 555, C1006ACE Buenos Aires, Argentina. Phone: +54 (11) 4325-9100. Fax: (management—Gerencia General) +54 (11) 4325 9433; (technical—Gerencia Operativa) +54 (11) 4327 4149. Email: (general) dnsor@sion.com; (Director) mmanuele@sion.com. Contact: (general) Marcelo Manuele, Gerente General; (technical) Miguel Angel Amaya, Gerente Operativo. $1 helpful. Prefers correspondence in Spanish, and usually replies via RAE (*see* above). If no reply, try sending your correspondence (but don't write the station's name on your envelope) and 1 IRC via the helpful Gabriel Iván Barrera, Casilla 2868, C1000WBC Buenos Aires, Argentina.

ARMENIA World Time +3 (+4 midyear)

Armenian National Radio/Voice of Armenia, Radio Agency, Alek Manoukyan Street 5, 375025 Yerevan, Armenia. Phone: +374 (2) 570-970, +374 (2) 554-761 or +374 (2) 552-650. Fax: +374 (2) 151 600. Contact: V. Voskanian, Deputy Editor-in-Chief; R. Abalian, Editor-in-Chief; Armenag Sansaryan, International Relations Bureau; Laura Baghdassarian, Deputy Manager, Radioagency; or Dr. Levon V. Ananikian, Director. Free postcards and stamps. Replies slowly.

ASCENSION World Time exactly

BBC World Service—Atlantic Relay Station, English Bay, Ascension (South Atlantic Ocean). Fax: +247 6117. Contact: (technical) Jeff Cant, Staff Manager; M.R. Watkins, A/Assistant Resident Engineer; or Mrs. Nicola Nicholls, Transmitter Engineer. Nontechnical correspondence should be sent to the BBC World Service in London (*see*).

Radio Japan, Radio Roma and Voice of America via BBC Ascension Relay Station—All correspondence should be directed to the regular addresses in Japan, Italy and USA (*see*).

AUSTRALIA World Time +11 (+10 midyear) Victoria (VIC), New South Wales (NSW), Australian Capital Territory (ACT) and Tasmania (TAS); +10:30 (+9:30 midyear) South Australia (SA); +10 Queensland (QLD); +9:30 Northern Territory (NT); +8 Western Australia (WA)

Australian Broadcasting Corporation Northern Territory HF Service—ABC Radio 8DDD Darwin, Administrative Center for the Northern Territory Shortwave Service, ABC Box 9994, GPO Darwin NT 0820, Australia. Phone: +61 (8) 8943-3222; (engineering) +61 (8) 8943-3209. Fax: +61 (8) 8943 3235 or +61 (8) 8943 3208. Contact: (general) Tony Bowden, Branch Manager; (administration) Carole Askham, Administrative Officer; (technical) Peter Camilleri or Yvonne Corby. Free stickers and postcards. "Traveller's Guide to ABC Radio" for $1. T-shirts US$20. Three IRCs or return postage helpful.

Australian Defence Forces Radio, Department of Defence, EMU (Electronic Media Unit) ANZAC Park West, APW 1-B-07, Reid, Canberra, ACT 2601, Australia. Phone: +61 (2) 6266-6669. Fax: +61 (2) 6266 6565. Contact: (general) Adam Iffland, Presenter; (technical) Hugh Mackenzie, Managing Presenter; or Brian Langshaw. SAE and 2 IRCs needed for a reply. Formerly broadcast irregularly using its own transmitters, but currently airs via the facilities of Radio Australia. Replies to verification inquiries only.

BBC World Service via Radio Australia—For verification direct from the Australian transmitters, contact John Westland, Director of English Programs at Radio Australia (*see*). Nontechnical correspondence should be sent to the BBC World Service in London (*see*).

Radio Australia—ABC
STUDIOS AND MAIN OFFICES: GPO Box 428G, Melbourne VIC 3001, Australia. Phone: ("Openline" voice mail for listeners' messages and requests) +61 (3) 9626-1825; (switchboard) +61 (3) 9626-1800; (English programs) +61 (3) 9626-1922; (marketing manager) +61 (3) 9626 1723. Fax and Faxpoll: (general) +61 (3) 9626 1899; (engineering) +61 (3) 9626 1917. Email: (general) english@ra.abc.net.au; (marketing manager) mccaig.anne@abc.net.au; (Radio Australia transmissions and programs) raelp@radioaus.abc.net.au; (Pacific Services) rapac@radioaus.abc.net.au; (Internet and Web Coordinator) naughton.russell@a2.abc.net.au. Web: (includes RealAudio) www.abc.net.au/ra/. Contact: (general) John Westland, Head, English Language Programming; Roger Broadbent, Producer "Feedback"; Tony Hastings, Director of Programs; Caroline Bilney, Information Officer; Anne McCaig, Marketing Manager; or Jean-Gabriel Manguy, General Manager; (technical) Nigel Holmes, Transmission Manager, Transmission Management Unit. Free stickers and sometimes pennants and souvenirs available. On-air language courses available in Chinese, Indonesian, Khmer and Vietnamese. Course notes available at cost price. Radio Australia will attempt to answer listener's letters even though this will largely depend on the availability of resources and a reply may no longer be possible in all cases. All reception reports received by Radio Australia will now be forwarded to the Australian Radio DX Club for assessment and checking. ARDXC will forward completed QSLs to Radio Australia for mailing. For further information, contact John Westland, Director of English Programs at Radio Australia (Email: westland.john@a2.abc.net.au); or John Wright, Secretary/Editor, ARDXC (Email: dxer@fl.net.au). Plans to add new aerials and re-locate 250 kW transmitters.
NEW YORK BUREAU, NONTECHNICAL: Room 2260, 630 Fifth Avenue, New York NY 10020 USA. Phone: (representative) +1 (212) 332-2540; or (correspondent) +1 (212) 332-2545. Fax: +1 (212) 332 2546. Contact: Maggie Jones, North American Representative.
LONDON BUREAU, NONTECHNICAL: 54 Portland Place, London W1N 4DY, United Kingdom. Phone: +44 (20) 7631-4456. Fax: (administration) +44 (20) 7323 0059, (news) +44 (20) 7323 1125. Contact: Robert Bolton, Manager.
BANGKOK BUREAU, NONTECHNICAL: 209 Soi Hutayana off Soi Suanplu, South Sathorn Road, Bangkok 10120, Thailand. Fax: +66 (2) 287 2040. Contact: Nicholas Stuart.
SAN FRANCISCO OFFICE, SCHEDULES: 2654 17th Avenue, San Francisco CA 94116 USA. Phone: +1 (415) 564-9968. Email: GPoppin@aol.com. Contact: George Poppin. This address, a volunteer office, only provides Radio Australia schedules to

TIPS FOR EFFECTIVE CORRESPONDENCE

Write to be read. Be interesting and helpful from the recipient's point of view, yet friendly without being chummy. Comments on specific programs are almost always appreciated, even if you are sending in what is basically a technical report.

Incorporate language courtesies. Using the broadcaster's tongue is always a plus—Addresses PLUS indicates when it is a requirement—but English is usually the next-best bet. When writing in any language to Spanish-speaking countries, remember that what gringos think of as the "last name" is actually written as the penultimate name. Thus, Juan Antonio Vargas García, which can also be written as Juan Antonio Vargas G., refers to Sr. Vargas; so your salutation should read, *Estimado Sr. Vargas*.

What's that "García" doing there, then? That's *mamita's* father's family name. Latinos more or less solved the problem of gender fairness in names long before Anglos.

But, wait—what about Portuguese, used by all those stations in Brazil? Same concept, but in reverse. *Mamá's* father's family name is penultimate, and the "real" last name is where English-speakers are used to it, at the end.

In Chinese, the "last" name comes first. However, when writing in English, Chinese names are sometimes reversed for the benefit of *weiguoren*—foreigners. Use your judgement. For example, "Li" is a common Chinese last name, so if you see "Li Dan," it's "Mr. Li." But if it's "Dan Li"—and certainly if it's been Westernized into "Dan Lee"—he's already one step ahead of you, and it's still "Mr. Li" (or Lee). Less widely known is that the same can also occur in Hungarian. For example, "Bartók Béla" for Béla Bartók.

If in doubt, fall back on the ever-safe "Dear Sir" or "Dear Madam," or use email, where salutations are not expected. And be patient—replies by post usually take weeks, sometimes months. Slow responders, those that tend to take many months to reply, are cited in Addresses PLUS, as are erratic repliers.

listeners. All other correspondence should be sent directly to the main office in Melbourne.

Radio Christian Voice, PMB 5777, Darwin NT 0801, Australia. Phone: +61 (8) 8981-6591; (station manager) +61 (7) 5477-1555. Fax: +61 (8) 8981 2846; (Station Manager) +61 (7) 5477 1727. Email: (Edmiston) mike.edmiston@christianvoice.com.au; (Moti) moti@christianvoice.com.au. Web: www.christianvoice.com.au. Contact: (general) Mike Edmiston, Director; Raymond Moti, Station Manager; or Mrs. Lorna Manning, Site Administrator; (technical) Andrew Flynn, Acting Chief Engineer (replacement expected shortly). Also, *see* entry under Chile for Radio Voz Cristiana and further contact details.

Radio VNG (official time station)

PRIMARY ADDRESS: National Standards Commission, P.O. Box 282, North Ryde, NSW 1670, Australia. Toll-free telephone (Australia only) (1800) 251-942. Phone: +61 (2) 9856-0300. Fax: +61 (2) 9856 0399. Email: rbrittain@nsc.gov.au. Contact: Dr. Richard Brittain, Secretary, National Time Committee. Station offers a free 16-page booklet about VNG and free promotional material. Free stickers and postcards. One IRC or $1 helpful. Likely to close June 30th 2002.

ALTERNATIVE ADDRESS: VNG Users Consortium, GPO Box 1090, Canberra, ACT 2601, Australia. Fax: +61 (2) 6249 9355. Contact: Dr. Marion Leiba, Honorary Secretary. Three IRCs appreciated.

AUSTRIA World Time +1 (+2 midyear)

Radio Austria International

MAIN OFFICE: ierstrasse 31, A-1040 Vienna, Austria. Phone: (management) +43 (1) 87878-12130; (answering machine/listener's service) +43 (1) 87878-13636; (technical) +43 (1) 87878-12629. Fax: (management) +43 (1) 87878 14404; (technical) +43 (1) 87878 12773; (listener's service) +43 (1) 87878 14404. Email: (frequency schedules, comments, reception reports) roi.service@orf.at; (intermedia programme) intermedia@orf.at; (Internet programming service) roi@orf.at; (frequency management) hfbc@orf.at. Web: (general, including RealAudio) http://roi.orf.at; (RealAudio news in German) www.wrn.org/ondemand/austria.html. Contact: (general) Vera Bock, Listener's Service; "Postbox"/"Hörerbriefkasten/Flash des Ondes" listeners' letters shows; Wolf Harranth, Editor, "Intermedia"; (management) Roland Machatschke, Managing Director; or Michael Kerbler, Deputy Director, Head of German Department & Director of Programs; (English Department) David Ward; (French Department) Lucien Giordani; (Spanish Department) Jacobo Naar-Carbonell; (Internet Programming Service) Marianne Veit or Oswald Klotz; (technical) Ing. Ernst Vranka, Frequency Manager; Ing. Klaus Hollndonner, Chief Engineer; Martin Cargnelli, Monitoring Department; or Listener's Service. Program schedule twice a year, as well as quiz prizes. Mr. Harranth seeks collections of old verification cards and letters for the highly organized historical archives he is maintaining. Radio Austria International is facing an uncertain future due to increasing funding cuts. Major programming cuts or even complete closure of the station is possibe.

WASHINGTON NEWS BUREAU: 1206 Eaton Ct. NW, Washington DC 20007 USA. Phone: +1 (202) 822-9570. Contact: Eugen Freund.

AZERBAIJAN World Time +3 (+4 midyear)

Radio Dada Gorgud (Voice of Azerbaijan), Medhi Hüseyin küçäsi 1, 370011 Baku, Azerbaijan. Phone: +994 (12) 398-585. Fax: +994 (12) 395 452. Contact: Mrs. Tamam Bayatli-Öner, Director; or Kamil Mamedov, Director of Division of International Relations. May run station contests at various times during the year. Free postcards, and occasionally, books. $1 or return postage helpful. Replies irregularly to correspondence in English.

BANGLADESH World Time +6

Bangladesh Betar

NONTECHNICAL CORRESPONDENCE: External Services, Bangladesh Betar, Shahbagh Post Box No. 2204, Dhaka 1000, Bangladesh; (physical address) Betar Bhaban Sher-e-Bangla Nagar, Agargaon Road, Dhaka 1207, Bangladesh. Phone: (director general) +880 (2) 8615-294; (Rahman Khan) +880 (2) 8613-949; (external services) +880 (2) 8618-119. Fax:(director general) +880 (2) 8612 021. Email: (Office of Director General) dgbetar@bd.drik.net; (external services) tsbetar@bdonline.com. Contact: Mrs. Dilruba Begum, Director, External Services; Ashfaque-ur Rahman Khan, Director - Programmes; or (technical) Muhammed Nazrul Islam, Station Engineer. $1 helpful. For further technical contacts, *see* below.

TECHNICAL CORRESPONDENCE: National Broadcasting Authority, NBA Bhaban, 121 Kazi Nazrul Islam Avenue, Shahabagh, Dhaka 1000, Bangladesh. Phone: +880 (2) 500-143/7, +880 (2) 500-490, +880 (2) 500-810, +880 (2) 505-113 or +880 (2) 507-269; (Shakir) +880 (2) 818-734; (Das) +880 (2) 500-810. Fax: +880 (2) 817 850; (Shakir) +880 (2) 817 850. Email: dgradio@drik.bgd.toolnet.org, or rrc@aitlbd.net. Contact: Syed Abdus Shakir, Chief Engineer; (reception reports) Manoranjan Das, Station Engineer, Dhaka; or Muhammed Romizuddin Bhuiya, Senior Engineer (Research Wing). Verifications not common from this office.

BELARUS World Time +2 (+3 midyear)

Belarusian Radio—*see* Radio Belarus, below, for details.

Radio Grodno (Hrodna)—contact via Radio Belarus, below.

Radio Mogilev (Mahiliou)—contact via Radio Belarus, below.

Radio Belarus/Radio Minsk, ul. Krasnaja 4, 220807 Minsk, Belarus. Phone: (domestic Belarusian Radio) +375 (17) 239-5810; (external services, general) +375 (17) 239-5830; (English Service) +375 (17) 239-5831; (German Service) +375 (17) 239-5875. Fax: (all services) +375 (17) 236 6643. Email: radio-minsk@tvr.by. Web: (includes several music files in MP3) www.tvr.by. Contact: Natalia Khlebus, Director; Grigori Mityushnikov, Editor, English Service; Jürgen Eberhardt, Editor, German Service. Free Belarus stamps.

BELGIUM World Time +1 (+2 midyear)

RTBF-International, B-1044 Brussels, Belgium. Phone: +32 (2) 737-4024. Fax: +32 (2) 737 3032. Email: relint.r@rtbf.be, or rtbfi@rtbf.be. Web: (RTBF-International) www.rtbf.be/ri/; ("La Première") www.rtbf.be/premiere/; (RealAudio) www.rtbf.be/jp/. Contact: Jean-Pol Hecq, Directeur des Relations Internationales (or "Head, International Service" if writing in English). Broadcasts are essentially a relay of news and information programs from the domestic channel "La Première" of RTBF (Radio-Télévision Belge de la Communauté Française) via facilities of Deutsche Telekom (*see*) in Jülich, Germany. Return postage not required. Accepts email reports.

Paro Airport is the transit point for foreign mail to and from Bhutan. M. Guha

Radio Vlaanderen Internationaal (RVI)

NONTECHNICAL AND GENERAL TECHNICAL: B-1043 Brussels, Belgium; (English Section) RVI Brussels Calling, B-1043 Brussels, Belgium. Phone: +32 (2) 741-5611, +32 (2) 741-3806/7 or +32 (2) 741-3802. Fax: (administration and Dutch Service) +32 (2) 732 6295; (other language services) +32 (2) 732 8336. BBS: +32 (3) 825-3613. Email: info@rvi.be. Web: (text and RealAudio) www.rvi.be; (RealAudio in English, French, German and Dutch) www.wrn.org/ondemand/belgium.html. Contact (general) Deanne Lehman, Producer, "Brussels 1043" letterbox program; Liz Sanderson, Head, English Service; Maryse Jacob, Head, French Service; Martina Luxen, Head, German Service; or Wim Jansen, Station Manager; (general technical) Frans Vossen, Producer, "Radio World." Sells RVI T-shirts (large/extra large) for 400 Belgian francs. May send free music CD. Remarks and reception reports can also be sent c/o the following diplomatic addresses:

NIGERIA EMBASSY: Embassy of Belgium, 1A, Bak Road, Ikoyi-Island, Lagos, Nigeria.

ARGENTINA EMBASSY: Embajada de Bélgica, Defensa 113 - 8° Piso, 1065 Buenos Aires, Argentina.

FREQUENCY MANAGEMENT OFFICE: BRTN, August Reyerslaan 52, B-1043 Brussels, Belgium. Phone: +32 (2) 741-5020. Fax: +32 (2) 741 5567. Email: (De Cuyper) hector.decuyper@vrt.be. Contact: Hector De Cuyper, Frequency Manager.

BENIN World Time +1

Office de Radiodiffusion et Télévision du Benin, Boite Postale 366, Cotonou, Bénin. Phone: +229 300-481, +229 301-096 or +229 301-347. Fax: +229 302 184. Web: http://elodia.intnet.bj/bol/ortb.htm. Contact: (Cotonou) Damien Zinsou Ala Hassa; Emile Desire Ologoudou, Directeur Generale; or Leonce Goohouede; (technical) Anastase Adjoko, Chef de Service Technique. Return postage, $1 or IRC required. Replies irregularly and slowly to correspondence in French.

PARAKOU REGIONAL STATION: ORTB-Parakou, Boite Postale 128, Parakou, Benin. Phone: +229 610-773. Fax: +229 610-881. Contact: (general) J. de Matha, Le Chef de la Station; (technical) Léon Donou, Chef des Services Techniques. Return postage required. Replies tend to be extremely irregular, and a safer option is to send correspondence to the Cotonou address.

BHUTAN World Time +6

Bhutan Broadcasting Service

STATION: Department of Information and Broadcasting, Ministry of Communications, P.O. Box 101, Thimphu, Bhutan. Phone: +975 (2) 323-071/72. Fax: +975 (2) 323 073. Email: (News and Current Affairs) news@bbs.com.bt; (Kinga Singye) ks@bbs.com.bt; (Thinley Tobgay Dorji) thinley@bbs.com.bt; (Sonam Tobgay) toby@bbs.com.bt. Web: (includes news and songs in MP3) www.bbs.com.bt. Contact: (general) Thinley Tobgay Dorji, News Coordinator; or Kinga Singye, Executive Director; (technical) Sonam Tobgay, Station Engineer. Two IRCs, return postage or $1 required. Replies irregularly; correspondence to the U.N. Mission (*see* following) may be more fruitful.

UNITED NATIONS MISSION: Permanent Mission of the Kingdom of Bhutan to the United Nations, Two United Nations Plaza, 27th Floor, New York NY 10017 USA. Fax: +1 (212) 826 2998. Contact: Mrs. Kunzang C. Namgyel, Third Secretary; Mrs. Sonam Yangchen, Attaché; Ms. Leki Wangmo, Second Secretary; or Hari K. Chhetri, Second Secretary. Free newspapers and booklet on the history of Bhutan.

BOLIVIA World Time –4

NOTE ON STATION IDENTIFICATIONS: Many Bolivian stations listed as "Radio . . ." may also announce as "Radio Emisora . . ." or "Radiodifusora . . ."

Galaxia Radiodifusión—*see* Radio Galaxia, below.

Hitachi Radiodifusión—*see* Radio Hitachi, below.

Paitití Radiodifusión—*see* Radio Paitití, below.

Radio Abaroa, Calle Nicanor Gonzalo Salvatierra 249, Riberalta, Beni, Bolivia. Contact: René Arias Pacheco, Director. Return postage or $1 required. Replies occasionally to correspondence in Spanish.

Radio Animas, Chocaya, Animas, Potosí, Bolivia. Contact: Julio Acosta Campos, Director. Return postage or $1 required. Replies irregularly to correspondence in Spanish.

Radio Camargo—*see* Radio Emisoras Camargo, below.

Radio Centenario "La Nueva"

MAIN OFFICE: Casilla 818, Santa Cruz de la Sierra, Bolivia. Phone: +591 (3) 529-265. Fax: +591 (3) 524 747. Email: mision.eplabol@scbbs-bo.com. Contact: Napoleón Ardaya B., Director. May send a calendar. Free stickers. Return postage or $1 required. Audio cassettes of contemporary Christian music and Bolivian folk music $10, including postage; CDs of Christian folk music $15, including postage. Replies to correspondence in English and Spanish.

U.S. BRANCH OFFICE: LATCOM, 1218 Croton Avenue, New Castle PA 16101 USA. Phone: +1 (412) 652-0101. Fax: +1 (412) 652 4654. Contact: Hope Cummins.

Radio Eco

MAIN ADDRESS: Correo Central, Reyes, Ballivián, Beni, Bolivia. Contact: Gonzalo Espinoza Cortés, Director. Free station literature. $1 or return postage required. Replies to correspondence in Spanish.

ALTERNATIVE ADDRESS: Rolmán Medina Méndez, Correo Central, Reyes, Ballivián, Bolivia.

Radio Eco San Borja (San Borja la Radio), Correo Central, San Borja, Ballivián, Beni, Bolivia. Contact: Gonzalo Espinoza Cortés, Director. Free station poster promised to correspondents. Return postage appreciated. Replies slowly to correspondence in Spanish.

Radio El Mundo (when operating), Casilla 1984, Santa Cruz de la Sierra, Bolivia. Phone: +591 (3) 464-646. Fax: +591 (3) 465 057. Contact: Freddy Banegas Carrasco, Gerente; Lic. José

Luis Vélez Ocampo C., Director; or Lic. Juan Pablo Sainz, Gerente General. Free stickers and pennants. $1 or return postage required. Replies irregularly to correspondence in Spanish.

Radio Emisoras Ballivián (when operating), Correo Central, San Borja, Beni, Bolivia. Replies to correspondence in Spanish, and sometimes sends pennant.

Radio Emisora Dos de Febrero (if reactivated), Calle Vaca Diez 400, Rurrenabaque, Beni, Bolivia. Contact: John Arze von Boeck. Free pennant, which is especially attractive. Replies occasionally to correspondence in Spanish.

Radio Emisora Galaxia—*see* Radio Galaxia, below.

Radio Emisora Padilla—*see* Radio Padilla, below.

Radio Emisora Villamontes—*see* Radio Villamontes, below.

Radio Emisoras Camargo, Casilla 09, Camargo, Provincia Nor-Cinti, Bolivia. Contact: Pablo García B., Gerente Propietario. Return postage or $1 required. Replies slowly to correspondence in Spanish.

Radio Emisoras Minería—*see* Radiodifusoras Minería.

Radio Fides, Casilla 9143, La Paz, Bolivia. Fax: +591 (2) 379 030. Email: rafides@caoba.entelnet.bo (rafides@wara.bolnet.bo may also work). Replies occasionally to correspondence in Spanish.

Radio Galaxia (if reactivated), Calle Beni s/n casi esquina Udarico Rosales, Guayaramerín, Beni, Bolivia. Contact: Dorián Arias, Gerente; Héber Hitachi Banegas, Director; or Carlos Arteaga Tacaná, Director-Dueño. Return postage or $1 required. Replies to correspondence in Spanish.

Radio Grigotá (when operating), Casilla 203, Santa Cruz de la Sierra, Bolivia. Phone/fax: +591 (3) 326-443. Fax: +591 (3) 362 795. Contact: (general) Víctor Hugo Arteaga B., Director General; (technical) Tania Martins de Arteaga, Gerente Administrativo. Free stickers, pins, pennants, key rings and posters. $1 or return postage required. Replies occasionally to correspondence in English, French, Portuguese and Spanish. May replace old Philips transmitter.

Radio Illimani, Casilla 1042, La Paz, Bolivia. Phone: +591 (2) 376-364. Fax: +591 (2) 359 275. Email: illimani@communica.gov.bo. Contact: Gabriel Astorga Guachala. $1 required, and your letter should be registered and include a tourist brochure or postcard from where you live. Replies irregularly to friendly correspondence in Spanish.

Radio Integración, Casilla 1722, La Paz, Bolivia. Contact: Lic. Manuel Liendo Rázuri, Gerente General; Benjamín Juan Carlos Blanco Q., Director Ejecutivo; or Carmelo de la Cruz Huanca, Comunicador Social. Free pennants. Return postage required.

Radio Juan XXIII [Veintitrés], Avenida Santa Cruz al frente de la plaza principal, San Ignacio de Velasco, Santa Cruz, Bolivia. Phone: +591 (962) 2087. Phone/Fax: +591 (962) 2188. Contact: Pbro. Elías Cortezón, Director; or María Elffy Gutiérrez Méndez, Encargada de la Discoteca. Return postage or $1 required. Replies occasionally to correspondence in Spanish.

Radio La Cruz del Sur, Casilla 1408, La Paz, Bolivia. Email: cruzdel-sur@zuper.net. Contact: Presbítero Reyes Baltazar Quispe, Director. Pennant $1 or return postage. Replies slowly to correspondence in Spanish.

Radio La Palabra, Parroquia de Santa Ana de Yacuma, Beni, Bolivia. Phone: +591 (848) 2117. Contact: Padre Yosu Arketa, Director. Return postage necessary. Replies to correspondence in Spanish.

Radio La Plata, Casilla 276, Sucre, Bolivia. Phone: +591 (64) 31-616. Fax: +591 (64) 41 400. Contact: Freddy Donoso Bleichner, Director Ejecutivo.

Radio Mallku (formerly Radio A.N.D.E.S.), Casilla No. 16, Uyuni, Provincia Antonio Quijarro, Departamento de Potosí, Bolivia. Phone: +591 (693) 2145. Email: (FRUTCAS parent organization) frutcas@yahoo.es. Contact: Freddy Juárez Huarachi, Director; Erwin Freddy Mamani Machaca, Jefe de Prensa y Programación. Spanish preferred. Return postage in the form of two U.S. dollars appreciated, as the station depends on donations for its existence. Station owned by La Federación Unica de Trabajadores Campesinos del Altiplano Sud (FRUTCAS).

Radio Mauro Núñez (when operating), Centro de Estudios para el Desarrollo de Chuquisaca (CEDEC), Casilla 196, Sucre, Bolivia. Phone: +591 (64) 25-008. Fax: +591 (64) 32 628. Contact: Jorge A. Peñaranda Llanos; Ing. Raúl Ledezma, Director Residente "CEDEC"; José Peneranda; or Jesús Urioste. Replies to correspondence in Spanish.

Radio Minería—*see* Radiodifusoras Minería.

Radio Mosoj Chaski, Casilla 4493, Cochabamba, Bolivia. Phone: +591 (42) 220-641 or +591 (42) 220-644. Fax: +591 (42) 251 041. Email: chaski@bo.net. Web: http://tunari.socs.utsedu.au/rmc/.

Radio Movima, Calle Baptista No. 24, Santa Ana de Yacuma, Beni, Bolivia. Contact: Rubén Serrano López, Director; Javier Roca Díaz, Director Gerente; or Mavis Serrano, Directora. Return postage or $1 required. Replies irregularly to correspondence in Spanish.

Radio Nacional de Huanuni, Casilla 681, Oruro, Bolivia. Contact: Rafael Linneo Morales, Director General; or Alfredo Murillo, Director. Return postage or $1 required. Replies irregularly to correspondence in Spanish.

Radio Norte, Calle Warnes 195, 2do piso del Cine Escorpio, Montero, Santa Cruz, Bolivia. Phone: +591 (92) 20-970. Fax: +591 (92) 21 062. Contact: Leonardo Arteaga Ríos, Director.

Radio Padilla, Padilla, Chuquisaca, Bolivia. Contact: Moisés Palma Salazar, Director. Return postage or $1 required. Replies to correspondence in Spanish.

Radio Paititi, Casilla 172, Guayaramerín, Beni, Bolivia. Contact: Armando Mollinedo Bacarreza, Director; Luis Carlos Santa Cruz Cuéllar, Director Gerente; or Ancir Vaca Cuéllar, Gerente-Propietario. Free pennants. Return postage or $3 required. Replies irregularly to correspondence in Spanish.

Radio Panamericana, Casilla 5263, La Paz, Bolivia; (physical address) Av. 16 de Julio, Edif. 16 de Julio, Of. 902, El Prado, La Paz, Bolivia. Phone: +591 (2) 324-606, +591 (2) 325-239 or +591 (2) 358-945. Fax: +591 (2) 392 353. Email: pana@panamericana-bolivia.com (may no longer work). Web: (includes RealAudio) www.panamericana-bolivia.com. Contact: Daniel Sánchez Rocha, Director. Replies irregularly, with correspondence in Spanish preferred. $1 or 2 IRCs helpful.

Radio Perla del Acre (if reactivated), Casilla 7, Cobija, Departamento de Pando, Bolivia. Return postage or $1 required. Replies irregularly to correspondence in Spanish.

Radio Pío XII [Doce], Siglo Veinte, Potosí, Bolivia. Phone: +591 (58) 20-250. Fax: +591 (58) 20 544. Email: radiopio@nogal.oru.entelnet.bo. Contact: Pbro. Roberto Durette, OMI, Director General; or José Blanco. Return postage necessary. As mail delivery to Siglo Veinte is erratic, latters may be sent instead to: Casilla 434, Oruro, Bolivia; to the attention of Abenor Alfaro Castillo, periodista de Radio Pío XX (Phone: +591 (52) 76-163).

Radio San Gabriel, Casilla 4792, La Paz, Bolivia. Phone: +591 (2) 414-371. Phone/fax: +591 (2) 411 174. Email: rsg@fundayni.rds.org.bo. Contact: Hno. José Canut Saurat, Director General; or Sra. Martha Portugal, Dpto. de Publicidad. $1 or return postage helpful. Free book on station, Aymara calendars and *La Voz del Pueblo Aymara* magazine. Replies fairly regularly to correspondence in Spanish. Station of the Hermanos de la Salle Catholic religious order.

Radio San Miguel, Casilla 102, Riberalta, Beni, Bolivia. Phone: +591 (852) 8268 or +591 (852) 8363. Fax: +591 (852) 8268. Contact: Félix Alberto Rada Q., Director; or Gerin Pardo Molina, Director. Free stickers and pennants; has a different pennant each year. Return postage or $1 required. Replies irregularly to correspondence in Spanish. Feedback on program "Bolivia al Mundo" (aired 0200-0300 World Time) especially appreciated.

Radio Santa Ana, Calle Sucre No. 250, Santa Ana de Yacuma, Beni, Bolivia. Contact: Mario Roberto Suárez, Director; or Mariano Verdugo. Return postage or $1 required. Replies irregularly to correspondence in Spanish.

Radio Santa Cruz, Emisora del Instituto Radiofónico Fé y Alegría (IRFA), Casilla 672 (or 3213), Santa Cruz, Bolivia. Phone: +591 (3) 521-814. Fax: +591 (3) 532 257. Email: irfacruz@roble.scz.entelnet.bo. Contact: Padre Francisco Flores, S.J., Director General; Srta. María Yolanda Marco Escobar, Secretaria de Dirección; Señora Mirian Suárez, Productor, "Protagonista Ud."; or Lic. Silvia Nava S. Free pamphlets, stickers and pennants. Welcomes correspondence in English, French and Spanish, but return postage required for a reply.

Radio Villamontes, Avenida Méndez Arcos No. 156, Villamontes, Departamento de Tarija, Bolivia. Contact: Gerardo Rocabado Galarza, Director. $1 or return postage required.

Radio Yura (La Voz de los Ayllus), Casilla 326, Yura, Provincia Quijarro, Departamento de Potosí, Bolivia. Phone: +591 (81) 36-216. Email: canal18@cedro.pts.entelnet.bo. Contact: Rolando Cueto F., Director.

Radiodifusoras Integración—*see* Radio Integración.

Radiodifusoras Minería, Casilla de Correo 247, Oruro, Bolivia. Phone: +591 (52) 77-736. Contact: Dr. José Carlos Gómez Espinoza, Gerente Propietario; or Srta. Costa Colque Flores, Responsable del programa "Minería Cultural." Free pennants. Replies to correspondence in Spanish.

Radiodifusoras Trópico, Casilla 60, Trinidad, Beni, Bolivia. Contact: Eduardo Avila Alberdi, Director. Replies slowly to correspondence in Spanish. Return postage required for reply.

BOTSWANA World Time +2

Radio Botswana, Private Bag 0060, Gaborone, Botswana. Phone: +267 352-541 or +267 352-861. Fax: +267 357 138. Contact: (general) Ted Makgekgenene, Director; or Monica Mphusu, Producer, "Maokaneng/Pleasure Mix"; (technical) Kingsley Reetsang, Principal Broadcasting Engineer. Free stickers, pennants and pins. Return postage, $1 or 2 IRCs required. Replies slowly and irregularly.

Voice of America/IBB—Botswana Relay Station

TRANSMITTER SITE: Voice of America, Botswana Relay Station, Moepeng Hill, Selebi-Phikwe, Botswana; or VOA-Botswana Transmitting Station, Private Bag 38, Selebi-Phikwe, Botswana. Phone: +267 810-932. Contact: Station Manager. This address for specialized technical correspondence only, although some reception reports may be verified, depending on who is at the site. During 2001, a number of verifications were received from Gabriel Tjitjo, Supervisor, Transmission Plant. All other correspondence should be directed to the regular VOA or IBB addresses (*see* USA).

BRAZIL World Time -1 (-2 midyear) Atlantic Islands; -2 (-3 midyear) Eastern, including Brasília and Rio de Janeiro, plus the town of Barra do Garças; -3 (-4 midyear) Western; -5 Acre. Most, if not all, northern states keep midyear time year round.

NOTE: Postal authorities recommend that, because of the level of theft in the Brazilian postal system, correspondence to Brazil be sent only via registered mail.

Emissora Rural A Voz do São Francisco, C.P. 8, 56300-000 Petrolina PE, Brazil. Contact: Maria Letecia de Andrade Nunes. Return postage necessary. Replies to correspondence in Portuguese.

Rádio Alvorada (Londrina), Rua Senador Souza Naves 9, 9 Andar, 86010-921 Londrina PR, Brazil. Web: www.miliciadaimaculda.org.br. Contact: Padre José Guidoreni, Diretor; Padre Manuel Joaquim; or Sonia López. Pennants $1 or return postage. Replies to correspondence in Portuguese.

Rádio Alvorada (Parintins), Rua Governador Leopoldo Neves 516, 69151-440 Parintins AM, Brazil. Contact: Raimunda Ribeira da Motta, Diretora; or M. Braga. Return postage required. Replies occasionally to correspondence in Portuguese.

Rádio Alvorada (Rio Branco), Avenida Ceará 2150—Altos de Gráfica Globo, 69900-470 Rio Branco AC, Brazil. E-mail: severian@mdnet.com.br. Contact: José SeverianoOccasionally replies to correspondence in Portuguese.

Rádio Araguaia—FM sister-station to Rádio Anhanguera (*see* next entry) and sometimes relayed via the latter's shortwave outlet. Web: (general) www.opopular.com.br/araguaia/; (RealAudio) www2.opopular.com.br/radio.htm. Usually identifies as "Araguaia FM."

Rádio Anhanguera, BR-157 Km. 1103, Zona Rural, 77804-970 Araguaína TO, Brazil. Return postage required. Occasionally replies to correspondence in Portuguese. Often airs programming from sister-station Rádio Araguaia, 97.1 FM (*see* previous item) or from the Rede Somzoomsat satellite network.

Rádio Anhanguera, C.P. 13, 74823-000 Goiânia GO, Brazil. Web: (RealAudio only) www2.opopular.com.br/radio.htm. Contact: Rossana F. da Silva; or Eng. Domingo Vicente Tinoco. Return postage required. Replies to correspondence in Portuguese. Although—like its namesake in Araguaína (*see*, above)—a member of the Sistema de Rádio da Organização Jaime Câmara, this station is also an affiliate of the CBN network and often identifies as "CBN Anhanguera," especially when airing news programming.

Rádio Aparecida, Avenida Getulio Vargas 185, 12570-000 Aparecida SP, Brazil; or C.P. 14547, 03698-970 Aparecida SP, Brazil. Phone: +55 (12) 565-1133. Fax: +55 (12) 565 1138. Email: (nontechnical) radioaparecida@redemptor.com.br. Web: www.radioaparecida.com.br. Contact: Padre C. Cabral; Savio Trevisan, Departamento Técnico; Cassiano Alves Macedo, Producer, "Encontro DX"; Ana Cristina Carvalho, Secretária da Direção; Padre Cesar Moreira; or João Climaco, Diretor Geral. Return postage or $1 required. Replies occasionally to correspondence in Portuguese.

Rádio Bandeirantes, C.P. 372, Rua Radiantes 13, Morumbi, 01059-970 São Paulo SP, Brazil. Fax: +55 (11) 3743 5391. Email: rbradio@band.com.br. Web: (includes Windows Media) www.radiobandeirantes.com.br. Contact: Marcelo Parada, Diretor Geral; or Carlos Newton. Free stickers, pennants and canceled Brazilian stamps. $1 or return postage required.

Rádio Baré, Avenida Santa Cruz Machado 170 A, 69010-070 Manaus AM, Brazil. Contact: Fernando A.B. Andrade, Diretor Programação e Produção. The Diretor is looking for radio catalogs.

Rádio Brasil, C.P. 625, 13000-000 Campinas, São Paulo SP, Brazil. Contact: Wilson Roberto Correa Viana, Gerente. Return postage required. Replies to correspondence in Portuguese.

Rádio Brasil Central, C.P. 330, 74001-970 Goiânia GO, Brazil. Contact: Ney Raymundo Fernández, Diretor Administrativo; Sergio Rubens da Silva; or Arizio Pedro Soárez, Diretor Gerente. Free stickers. $1 or return postage required. Replies to correspondence in Portuguese.

Rádio Brasil Tropical, C.P. 405, 78005-970 Cuiabá MT, Brazil (street address: Rua Joaquim Murtinho 1456, 78020-830 Cuiabá MT, Brazil). Phone: +55 (65) 321-6882 or +55 (65) 321-6226. Fax: +55 (65) 624 3455. Email: rcultura@nutecnet.com.br. Contact: Klécius Antonio dos Santos, Diretor Comercial; or Roberto Ferreira, Gerente Comercial. Free stickers. $1 required. Replies to correspondence in Portuguese. Shortwave sister-station to Rádio Cultura de Cuiabá (*see*).

Rádio Caiari, Av. Carlos Gomes 932, 78900-030 Porto Velho RO, Brazil. Contact: Carlos Alberto Diniz Martins, Diretor Geral; or Ronaldo Rocha, Diretor Executivo. Free stickers. Return postage helpful. Replies irregularly to correspondence in Portuguese.

Rádio Canção Nova, C.P. 57, 12630-000 Cachoeira Paulista SP, Brazil; (physical address) Rua João Paulo II s/n, Alto da Bela Vista, 12630-000 Cachoeira Paulista SP, Brazil. Phone: +55 (12) 560-2022. Fax: +55 (12) 561 2074. Email: (general) radio@cancaonova.org.br; (Director) adriana@cancaonova.org.br. Web: (includes RealAudio) www.cancaonova.org.br/cnova/radio/. Contact: (general) Benedita Luiza Rodrigues; Ana Claudia de Santana; or Valera Guimarães Massafera, Secretária; (administration) Adriana Pereira, Diretora da Rádio. Free stickers, pennants and station brochure sometimes given upon request. May send magazines. $1 helpful.

Rádio Capixaba, C.P. 509, 29000-000 Vitória ES, Brazil; or (street address) Av. Santo Antônio 366, 29025-000 Vitória ES, Brazil. Email: radiocap@terra.com.br. Contact: Jairo Gouvea Maia, Diretor; or Sr. Sardinha, Técnico. Replies occasionally to correspondence in Portuguese.

Rádio Clube de Ribeirao Preto (if reactivated), Ribeirao Preto SP, Brazil. Phone/fax: +55 (16) 610-3511. Email: scc@clube.com.br; clubeam@clube.com.br. Web: (includes RealAudio) www.clube.com.br.

Rádio Clube de Rondonópolis (when active), C.P. 190, 78700-000 Rondonópolis MT, Brazil. Contact: Canário Silva, Departamento Comercial; or Saúl Feliz, Gerente-Geral. Return postage helpful. Replies to correspondence in Portuguese.

Rádio Clube do Pará, C.P. 533, 66000-000 Belém PA, Brazil. Email: online form. Web: (includes Windows Media) www.radioclubedopara.com.br. Contact: Edyr Paiva Proença, Diretor Geral; or José Almeida Lima de Sousa. Return postage required. Replies irregularly to correspondence in Portuguese.

Radio Clube Paranaense, Rua Rockefeller 1311, Prado Velho, 80230-130 Curitiba PR, Brazil. Phone: +55 (41) 332-4255 or +55 (41) 332-6644. Contact: Vicente Mickosz, Superintendente.

Rádio Clube Varginha, C.P. 102, 37000-000 Varginha MG, Brazil. Contact: Juraci Viana. Return postage necessary. Replies slowly to correspondence in Portuguese.

Rádio Coari—*see* Rádio Educação Rural-Coari.

Rádio Copacabana, Rua Visconde Inhauma 37, 12 Andar, Rio de Janeiro. Phone: +55 (21) 233-9269 or +55 (21) 263-8567. Replies slowly to correspondence in Portuguese.

Rádio Cultura Araraquara, Avenida Feijó 583 (Centro), 14801-140 Araraquara SP, Brazil. Phone: +55 (16) 232-3790. Fax: +55 (16) 232 3475. Email: cultura@techs.com.br. Web: www.techs.com.br/cultura/. Contact: Antonio Carlos Rodrigues dos Santos, Diretor Artistico e Comercial. Return postage required. Replies slowly to correspondence in Portuguese.

Rádio Cultura de Campos, C.P. 79, 28100-970 Campos RJ, Brazil. $1 or return postage necessary. Replies to correspondence in Portuguese.

Rádio Cultura de Cuiabá—AM sister-station of Rádio Brasil Tropical (*see*) and whose programming is partly relayed by RBT. Email: rcultura@nutecnet.com.br. Web: www.solunet.com.br/rcultura/.

Rádio Cultura do Pará, Avenida Almirante Barroso 735, 66090-000 Belém PA, Brazil. Phone: +55 (91) 228-1000. Fax: +55 (91) 226 3989. Contact: Ronald Pastor; or Augusto Proença. Return postage required. Replies irregularly to correspondence in Portuguese.

Rádio Cultura Filadelfia, Rua Antonio Barbosa 1353, C.P. 89, 85851-090 Foz do Iguaçu PR, Brazil. Phone: +55 (45) 523-2930. A Finnish listener reports receiving a reply from Andre Antero (andreantero@hotmail.com); however, this person's connection with the station is unknown.

Rádio Cultura Ondas Tropicais, Rua Barcelos s/n Praça 14, 69020-060 Manaus AM, Brazil. Phone: +55 (92) 633-3857/2030. Fax: +55 (92) 633 3332. Contact: Luíz Fernando de Souza Ferreira; or Maria Jerusalem dos Santos, Chefe da Divisão de Rádio. Replies to correspondence in Portuguese. Return postage appreciated. Station is part of the FUNTEC, Fundação Televisão e Rádio Cultura do Amazonas network.

Rádio Cultura São Paulo, Rua Cenno Sbrighi 378, Agua Branca, 05036-900 São Paulo, Brazil; or Caixa Postal 11544, 05049-970 São Paulo, Brazil. Phone: (general) +55 (11) 3874-3122; (Cultura AM) +55 (11) 3874-3081; (Cultura FM) +55 (11) 3874-3082. Fax: +55 (11) 3611 2014. Email: (Cultura AM, relayed on 9615 and 17815 kHz) falecom@radiocultura.am.br; (Cultura FM, relayed on 6170 kHz) falecom@radioculturasp.fm.br. Web: (includes Windows Media) www.tvcultura.com.br. Contact: Thais de Almeida Dias, Chefe de Produção e Programação; Eduardo Weber; Sra. Maria Luíza Amaral Kfouri, Chefe de Produção; or Valvenio Martins de Almeida, Coordenador de Produção. $1 or return postage required. Replies slowly to postal correspondence in Portuguese.

Rádio Difusora Acreana, Rua Benjamin Constant 161, 69908-520 Rio Branco AC, Brazil. Contact: Washington Aquino, Diretor Geral. Replies irregularly to correspondence in Portuguese.

Rádio Difusora Cáceres, C.P. 297, 78200-000 Cáceres MT, Brazil. Contact: Sra. Maridalva Amaral Vignardi. $1 or return postage required. Replies occasionally to correspondence in Portuguese.

Rádio Difusora de Aquidauana, C.P. 18, 79200-000 Aquidauana MS, Brazil. Phone: +55 (67) 241-3956 or +55 (67) 241-3957. Contact: Primaz Aldo Bertoni, Diretor; or João Stacey. Free tourist literature and used Brazilian stamps. $1 or return postage required. This station sometimes identifies during the program day as "Nova Difusora," but its sign-off announcement gives the official name as "Rádio Difusora, Aquidauana."

Rádio Difusora de Londrina, C.P. 1870, 86000-000 Londrina PR, Brazil. Contact: Walter Roberto Manganoti, Gerente. Free tourist brochure, which sometimes seconds as a verification. $1 or return postage helpful. Replies irregularly to correspondence in Portuguese.

Rádio Difusora de Roraima, Avenida Capitão Ene Garcez 830, 69304-000 Boa Vista RR, Brazil. Phone: +55 (95) 623-1871, +55 (95) 623-2085 or +55 (95) 623-2131. Contact: Francisco G. França, Diretor Gerente; Galvão Soares, Diretor Geral; Benjamin Monteiro, Locutor; or Francisco Alves Vieira. Return postage required. Replies occasionally to correspondence in Portuguese.

Rádio Difusora do Amazonas (if reactivated), C.P. 311, 69000-000 Manaus AM, Brazil. Contact: J. Joaquim Marinho, Diretor. Joaquim Marinho is a keen collector and especially interested in Duck Hunting Permit Stamps, stamp booklets and stamp sheets. Will reply to correspondence in Portuguese or English. $1 or return postage helpful.

Rádio Difusora Jataí, C.P. 33 (or Rua de José Carvalhos Bastos 542), 75800-000 Jataí GO, Brazil. Contact: Zacarías Faleiros, Diretor Gerente.

Rádio Difusora Macapá, C.P. 2929, 68900-000 Macapá AP, Brazil. Contact: Paulo Roberto Rodrigues, Gerente; Francisco de Paulo Silva Santos; Rui Lobato; or Eng. Arquit. Benedito Rostan Costa Martins, Diretor. $1 or return postage required. Replies irregularly to correspondence in Portuguese. Sometimes provides stickers, key rings and—on rare occasions—T-shirts.

Rádio Difusora Poços de Caldas, C.P. 937, 37701-970 Poços de Caldas MG, Brazil; or (street address) Rua Rio Branco 681 primeiro andar, 37701-001 Poços de Caldas MG, Brazil. Phone/fax: +55 (35) 722-1530. Email: difusora@pocos-net.com.br. Web: www.pocos-net.com.br/difusora/. Contact: Marco Aurelio C. Mendoça, Diretor; or Dr. Wanderley de Mello, Gerente. $1 or return postage required. Replies to correspondence in Portuguese.

Rádio Difusora "6 de Agosto," Rua Pio Nazário 31, 69930-000 Xapuri AC, Brazil. Contact: Francisco Evangelista de Abreu. Replies to correspondence in Portuguese.

Rádio Difusora Taubaté (when operating), Rua Dr. Sousa Alves 960, 12020-030 Taubaté SP, Brazil. Contact: Emilio Amadei Beringhs Neto, Diretor Superintendente. May send free stickers, pens, keychains and T-shirts. Return postage or $1 helpful.

Rádio Educação Rural—Campo Grande, C.P. 261, 79002-233 Campo Grande MS, Brazil. Phone: +55 (67) 384-3164, +55 (67) 382-2238 or +55 (67) 384-3345. Contact: Ailton Guerra, Gerente-Geral; Angelo Venturelli, Diretor; or Diácono Tomás Schwamborn. $1 or return postage required. Replies to correspondence in Portuguese.

Rádio Educação Rural—Coari, Praça São Sebastião 228, 69460-000 Coari AM, Brazil. Contact: Lino Rodrigues Pessoa, Diretor Comercial; Joaquim Florencio Coelho, Diretor Administrador da Comunidade Salgueiro; or Elijane Martins Correa. $1 or return postage helpful. Replies irregularly to correspondence in Portuguese.

Rádio Educadora da Bahia, Centro de Rádio, Rua Pedro Gama 413/E, Alto Sobradinho Federação, 40230-291 Salvador BA, Brazil. Phone: +55 (71) 339-1180. Fax: +55 (71) 339 1170. Web: (includes RealAudio) www.educadora.com.br. Contact: Elza Correa Ramos; or Walter Sequieros R. Tanure. $1 or return postage required. May send local music CD. Replies to correspondence in Portuguese.

Rádio Educadora de Bragança, Rua Barão do Rio Branco 1151, 68600-000 Bragança PA, Brazil. Contact: José Rosendo de S. Neto; Zelina Cardoso Gonçalves; or Adelino Borges, Aux. Escritório. $1 or return postage required. Replies to correspondence in Portuguese.

Rádio Educadora de Guajará Mirim, Praça Mario Correa No.90, 78957-000 Guajará Mirim RO, Brazil. Contact: Padre Isidoro José Moro. Return postage helpful. Replies to correspondence in Portuguese.

Rádio Educadora de Limeira, C.P. 105, 13480-970 Limeira SP, Brazil. Email: (Bortolan) bab@zaz.com.br. Contact: Bruno Arcaro Bortolan, Gerente.

Rádio Gaúcha, Avenida Ipiranga 1075 2do andar, Azenha, 90169-900 Porto Alegre RS, Brazil. Phone: +55 (51) 223-6600. Email: (general) gaucha@rdgaucha.com.br; (technical) gilberto.kussler@rdgaucha.com.br. Web: (includes RealAudio) http://radiogaucha.clicrbs.com.br. Contact: Marco Antônio Baggio, Gerente de Jornalismo/Programação; Armindo Antônio Ranzolin, Diretor Gerente; Gilberto Kussler, Gerente Técnico; Geraldo Canali. Replies occasionally to correspondence, preferably in Portuguese.

Rádio Gazeta, Avenida Paulista 900, 01310-940 São Paulo SP, Brazil. Fax: +55 (11) 285 4895. Contact: Shakespeare Ettinger, Supervisor Geral de Operação; Bernardo Leite da Costa; José Roberto Mignone Cheibub, Gerente Geral; or Ing. Aníbal Horta Figueiredo. Free stickers. $1 or return postage necessary. Replies to correspondence in Portuguese. Currently leasing all its airtime to the "Deus é Amor" Pentecostal church, but has been observed in the past to sometimes carry its own programming on at least one of its three shortwave channels.

Rádio Globo, Rua do Russel 434-Glória, 22210-210 Rio de Janeiro RJ, Brazil. Phone: +55 (21) 555-8375. Fax: +55 (21) 558 6385. Email: (administration) gerenciaamrio@radioglobo.com.br. Web: (includes RealAudio) www.radioglobo.com.br/globorio/. Contact: Marcos Libretti, Diretor Geral. Replies irregularly to correspondence in Portuguese. Return postage helpful.

Rádio Globo, Rua das Palmeiras 315, Santa Cecilia, 01226-901 São Paulo SP, Brazil. Phone: +55 (11) 3824-3217. Fax: +55 (11) 3824 3210. Email: (Rapussi) margarete@radioglobo.com.br. Web: (includes RealAudio) www.radioglobo.com.br/globosp/. Contact: Ademar Dutra, Locutor, "Programa Ademar Dutra"; Margarete Rapussi; Guilherme Viterbo; or José Marques. Replies to correspondence, preferably in Portuguese.

Rádio Guaíba, Rua Caldas Júnior 219, 90019-900 Porto

Alegre RS, Brazil. Phone: +55 (51) 215-6222. Email: guaiba@cpovo.net. Web: (includes RealAudio) www.guaiba.com.br. Return postage helpful.

Rádio Guarani, Avenida Assis Chateaubriand 499, Floresta, 30150-101 Belo Horizonte MG, Brazil. Web: (includes RealAudio) www.guarani.com.br/index.html. Contact: Junara Belo, Setor de Comunicações. Replies slowly to correspondence in Portuguese. Return postage helpful.

Rádio Guarujá

STATION: C.P. 45, 88000-000 Florianópolis SC, Brazil. Contact: Mario Silva, Diretor; Joana Sempre Bom Braz, Assessora de Marketing e Comunicação; or Rosa Michels de Souza. Return postage required. Replies irregularly to correspondence in Portuguese.

NEW YORK OFFICE: 45 West 46 Street, 5th Floor, Manhattan, NY 10036 USA.

Rádio Inconfidência, C.P. 1027, 30650-540 Belo Horizonte MG, Brazil. Fax: +55 (31) 296 3070. Email: inconfidencia@plugway.com.br. Web: (includes RealAudio) www.plugway.com.br/inconfidencia/. Contact: Isaias Lansky, Diretor; Manuel Emilio de Lima Torres, Diretor Superintendente; Jairo Antolio Lima, Diretor Artístico; or Eugenio Silva. Free stickers and postcards. May send CD of Brazilian music. $1 or return postage helpful.

Rádio Integração (when active), Rua Alagoas 270, 69980-000 Cruzeiro do Sul AC, Brazil. Contact: Oscar Alves Bandeira, Gerente. Return postage helpful.

Rádio IPB AM, Rua Itajaí 473, Bairro Antonio Vendas, 79041-270 Campo Grande MS, Brazil. Contact: Iván Páez Barboza, Diretor Geral (hence, the station's name, "IPB"); Pastor Laercio Paula das Neves, Dirigente Estadual; Agenor Patrocinio S., Locutor; Pastor José Adão Hames; or Kelly Cristina Rodrigues da Silva, Secretária. Return postage required. Replies to correspondence in Portuguese. Most of the airtime is leased to the "Deus é Amor" Pentecostal church.

Rádio Itatiaia, Rua Itatiaia 117, 31210-170 Belo Horizonte MG, Brazil. Fax: +55 (31) 446 2900. Email: itatiaia@itatiaia.com.br. Web: (includes RealAudio) www.itatiaia.com.br. Contact: Lúcia Araújo Bessa, Assistente da Diretória; or Claudio Carneiro.

Rádio Jornal "A Crítica" (when active), C.P. 2250, 69061-970 Manaus AM, Brazil; or Av. Andre Araujo s/n, Aleixo, 69060-001 Manaus AM, Brazil. Contact: Sr. Cotrere, Gerente.

Rádio Liberal, C.P 498, 66017-970 Belém PA, Brazil; (street address) Av. Nazaré 350, 66035-170 Belém PA, Brazil. Phone: +55 (91) 213-1500. Fax: +55 (91) 224 5240. Email: radio@radioliberal.com.br. Web: (includes RealAudio) www.radioliberal.com.br. Contact: Flavia Vasconcellos; Advaldo Castro, Diretor de Programação AM; João Carlos Silva Ribeiro, Coordenador de Programação AM.

Rádio Marumby, C.P. 296, 88010-970 Florianópolis SC, Brazil; Rua Angelo Laporta 841, C. P. 62, 88020-600 Florianópolis SC, Brazil; or (missionary parent organization) Gideões Missionários da Última Hora—GMUH, Ministério Evangélico Mundial, Rua Joaquim Nunes 244, C.P. 4, 88340-000 Camboriú SC, Brazil. Email: (GMUH parent organization) gmuh@gmuh.com.br. Web: www.gmuh.com.br/aradio.htm. Contact: Davi Campos, Diretor Artístico; Dr. Cesario Bernardino, Presidente, GMUH; Pb. Claudiney Nunes, Coordenador Rádio e Jornalismo; or Jair Albano, Diretor. $1 or return postage required. Free diploma and stickers. Replies to correspondence in Portuguese.

Rádio Marumby, Curitiba—*see* Rádio Novas de Paz, Curitiba, below.

Rádio Meteorologia Paulista, C.P. 91, 14940-970 Ibitinga, São Paulo SP, Brazil. Contact: Roque de Rosa, Diretora. Replies to correspondence in Portuguese. $1 or return postage required.

Rádio Missões da Amazônia, Travessa Ruy Barbosa 142, 68250-000 Obidos PA, Brazil. Contact: Max Hamoy; Edérgio de Moras Pinto; or Maristela Hamoy. Return postage required. Replies occasionally to correspondence in Portuguese.

Rádio Mundial, Av. Paulista 2198-Térreo, Cerqueira Cesar, 01310-300 São Paulo, Brazil. Phone: +55 (11) 253-0082. Phone/Fax: +55 (11) 283 5833. Email: radiomundial@radiomundial.com. Web: (includes Windows Media) www.radiomundial.com.br. Contact: (nontechnical) Luci Rothschild de Abreu, Diretora Presidente.

Rádio Nacional da Amazônia, SCRN 702/3 Bloco-B, Ed. Radiobrás, 70710-750 Brasília DF, Brazil. Fax: +55 (61) 321 7602. Web: (includes Windows Media) www.radiobras.gov.br/primeira.htm (click on "Amazônia"). Contact: (general) Luíz Otavio de Castro Souza, Diretor; Fernando Gómez da Câmara, Gerente de Escritório; or Januario Procopio Toledo, Diretor. Free stickers, but no verifications.

Rádio Nacional Brasília—same postal and Web addresses as Rádio Nacional da Amazônia, above.

Rádio Nacional São Gabriel da Cachoeira, Avenida Alvaro Maia 850, 69750-000 São Gabriel da Cachoeira AM, Brazil. Contact: Luíz dos Santos França, Gerente; or Valdir de Souza Marques. Return postage necessary. Replies to correspondence in Portuguese.

Rádio Novas de Paz, Avenida Paraná 1896, 82510-000 Curitiba PR, Brazil; or C.P. 22, 80000-000 Curitiba PR, Brazil. Phone: +55 (41) 257-4109. Contact: João Falavinha Ienzen, Gerente. $1 or return postage required. Replies irregularly to correspondence in Portuguese.

Rádio Nova Visão

STUDIOS: Rua do Manifesto 1373, 04209-001 São Paulo SP, Brazil. Contact: José Eduardo Dias, Diretor Executivo. Return postage required. Replies to correspondence in Portuguese. Free stickers. Relays Rádio Trans Mundial fulltime.

TRANSMITTER: C.P. 551, 97000-000 Santa Maria RS, Brazil; or C.P. 6084, 90000-000 Porto Alegre RS, Brazil. Reportedly issues full-data verifications for reports in Portuguese or German, upon request, from this location. If no luck, try contacting, in English or Dutch, Tom van Ewijck, via email at egiaroll@mail.iss.lcca.usp.br. For further information, see the entry for Rádio Trans Mundial.

Rádio Oito de Setembro, C.P. 8, 13690-000 Descalvado SP, Brazil. Contact: Adonias Gomes. Replies to corrrespondence in Portuguese.

Rádio Pioneira de Teresina, Rua 24 de Janeiro 150 sul/centro, 64001-230 Teresina PI, Brazil. Phone: +55 (86) 222-8121. Fax: +55 (86) 222 8122. Email: pioneira@ranet.com.br. Contact: Luíz Eduardo Bastos; or Padre Tony Batista, Diretor. $1 or return postage required. Replies slowly to correspondence in Portuguese.

Rádio Progresso (when operating), Estrada do Belmont s/n, B° Nacional, 78903-400 Porto Velho RO, Brazil. Return postage required. Replies occasionally to correspondence in Portuguese.

Rádio Record

STATION: C.P. 7920, 04084-002 São Paulo SP, Brazil. Email: radiorecord@rederecord.com.br. Web: www.rederecord.com.br (click on "Rádio"). Contact: Mário Luíz Catto, Diretor Geral. Free stickers. Return postage or $1 required. Replies occasionally to correspondence in Portuguese.

NEW YORK OFFICE: 630 Fifth Avenue, Room 2607, New York NY 10111 USA.

Rádio Relógio, Rua Paramopama 131, Ribeira, Ilha do Governador, 21930-110 Rio de Janeiro RJ, Brazil. Phone: +55 (21) 467-0201. Fax: +55 (21) 467 4656. Email: radiorelogio@ig.com.br. Contact: Olindo Coutinho, Diretor Geral; or Renato Castro. Replies occasionally to correspondence in Portuguese.

Rádio RGS—*see* Rádio Rio Grande do Sul, below.

Rádio Ribeirão Preto, C.P. 1252, 14025-000 Ribeirão Preto SP, Brazil (physical address: Av. 9 de Julho 600, 14025-000 Ribeirão Preto SP, Brazil). Phone/fax: +55 (16) 610-3511. Contact: Lucinda de Oliveira, Secretária; Luis Schiavone Junior; or Paulo Henríque Rocha da Silva. Replies to correspondence in Portuguese.

Rádio Rio Grande do Sul, Rede Pampa de Comunicação, Rua Orfanatrófio 711, 90840-440 Porto Alegre RS, Brazil. Phone: +55 (51) 233-8311. Fax: +55 (51) 233-4500. Email: pampa@pampa.com.br. All the station's shortwave outlets carry programming from Sistema LBV Mundial (*see*), to where all program and reception related correspondence should be sent.

Rádio Rio Mar, Rua José Clemente 500, 69010-070 Manaus AM, Brazil. Replies to correspondence in Portuguese. Contact: Jairo de Sousa Coelho, Diretor de Programação e Jornalismo. $1 or return postage helpful.

Rádio Rural Santarém, Rua São Sebastião 622, 68005-090 Santarém PA, Brazil. Contact: João Elias B. Bentes, Gerente Geral; or Edsergio de Moraes Pinto. Replies slowly to correspondence in Portuguese. Free stickers. Return postage or $1 required.

Rádio Trans Mundial, Caixa Postal 18300, 04626-970 São Paulo SP, Brazil. Phone: +55 (11) 533-3533. Fax: +55 (11) 533 5271. Email: (general) rtm@transmundial.com.br; (technical) tecnica@transmundial.com.br; ("Amigos do Rádio" DX-program) amigosdoradio@transmundial.com.br. Web: (includes RealAudio) www.transmundial.com.br. Contact: José Eduardo Dias, Diretor; or Rudolf Grimm, programa "Amigos do Rádio." Sells religious books and casettes and CDs of religious music (from choral to bossa nova). Prices, in local currency, can be found at the Website (click on "catálogo"). Program provider for Rádio Nova Visão—*see*, above.

Rádio Senado. Caixa Postal 070-747, 70359-970 Brasília DF, Brazil. E-mail: radio@senado.gov.br; (Maintenance Engineer) arenato@senado.gov.br. Web: (includes RealAudio) www.senado.gov.br/radio/. Contact: Aldo Renato B. de Assis, Engenheiro de Manutenção.

Rádio Tupi (when operating), Avenida Nadir Dias Figueiredo 1329, 02110-901 São Paulo SP, Brazil. Contact: Alfredo Raymundo Filho, Diretor Geral; Montival da Silva Santos; or Elia Soares. Free stickers. Return postage required. Replies occasionally to correspondence in Portuguese.

Rádio Universo/Rádio Tupi, C.P. 7133, 80000-000 Curitiba PR, Brazil. Contact: Luíz Andreu Rúbio, Diretor. Replies occasionally to correspondence in Portuguese. Rádio Universo's program time is rented by the "Deus é Amor" Pentecostal church, and is from the Rádio Tupi network. Identifies on the air as "Radio Tupi, Sistema Universo de Comunicação" or, more often, just as "Radio Tupi."

Rádio Verdes Florestas, C.P. 53, 69981-970 Cruzeiro do Sul AC, Brazil. Contact: Marlene Valente de Andrade. Return postage required. Replies occasionally to correspondence in Portuguese.

Rádio Voz do Coração Imaculado (when operating), C.P. 354, 75001-970 Anápolis GO, Brazil. Contact: P. Domingos M. Esposito A religious station which started shortwave operation in 1999 with the transmitter formerly used by Rádio Carajá. Operation tends to be irregular, as the station is funded entirely from donations.

Rede SomZoom Sat—a satellite network based in Fortaleza, Ceara, whose programming is sometimes carried by Brazilian world band stations (usually during night hours). Email: somzoomsat@somzoom.com.br. Web: (includes Windows Media) www.somzoom.com.br/Radio/radio.htm.

Sistema LBV Mundial, Legião da Boa Vontade, Av. Sérgio Tomás 740, Bom Retiro, 01131-010 São Paulo SP, Brazil; or Rua Doraci 90, Bom Retiro, 01134-020 São Paulo SP, Brazil. Phone: 3225-4500. Fax: +55 (11) 3225 4639. Web: (general) http://sistema.lbv.org; (LBV parent organization, includes RealAudio) www.lbv.org. Contact: André Tiago, Diretor; Sandra Albuquerque, Secretária; or Gizelle Almeida, Gerente do Dept. de Rádio. Replies slowly to correspondence in all main languages. Program provider for Radio Rio Grande do Sul (*see*).

NEW YORK OFFICE: 383 5th Avenue, 2nd Floor, New York NY 10016 USA. Phone: +1 (212) 481-1004. Fax: +1 (212) 481 1005. Email: lgw2000@aol.com.

Voz de Libertação. Ubiquitous programming originating from the "Deus é Amor" Pentecostal church's Rádio Universo (1300 kHz) in São Bernardo do Campo, São Paulo, and heard over several shortwave stations, including Rádio Universo, Curitiba (*see*) and Rádio Gazeta, São Paulo (*see*). A RealAudio feed is available at the "Deus é Amor" Website, www.ipda.org.br.

Voz do Coração Imaculado—*see* Rádio Voz do Coração Imaculado.

BULGARIA World Time +2 (+3 midyear)

Bulgarian National Radio, 4 Dragan Tsankov Blvd., 1040 Sofia, Bulgaria. Phone: +359 (2) 652-871. Fax: (weekdays) +359 (2) 657 230. Web: (includes RealAudio) www.nationalradio.bg. Contact: Borislav Djamdjiev, Director; Iassen Indjev, Executive Director; or Martin Minkov, Editor-in-Chief.

Radio Bulgaria

NONTECHNICAL AND TECHNICAL: P.O. Box 900, BG-1000, Sofia, Bulgaria. Phone: (general) +359 (2) 661-954 or +359 (2) 854-633; (Managing Director) +359 (2) 854-604. Fax: (general, usually weekdays only) +359 (2) 871 060, +359 (2) 871 061 or +359 (2) 650 560; (Managing Director) +359 (2) 946 1576; or +359 (2) 988 5103; (Frequency Manager) +359 (2) 963 4464. Email: rcoresp1@fon15.bnr.acad.bg; or rbul1@nationalradio.bg. Web: (RealAudio in English, French and Russian) www.nationalradio.bg/real.htm. Contact: (general) Mrs. Iva Delcheva, English Section; Kristina Mihailova, In Charge of Listeners' Letters, English Section; Christina Pechevska, Listeners' Letters, English Section; Svilen Stoicheff, Head of English Section; (administration and technical) Anguel H. Nedyalkov, Managing Director; (technical) Atanas Tzenov, Director. Replies regularly, but sometimes slowly. Return postage helpful, as the station is financially overstretched due to the economic situation in the country. For concerns about frequency usage, contact BTC, below, with copies to Messrs. Nedyalkov and Tzenov of Radio Bulgaria.

FREQUENCY MANAGEMENT AND TRANSMISSION OPERATIONS: Bulgarian Telecommunications Company (BTC), Ltd., 8 Totleben Blvd., 1606 Sofia, Bulgaria. Phone: +359 (2) 88-00-75. Fax: +359 (2) 87 58 85 or +359 (2) 80 25 80. Contact: Roumen Petkov, Frequency Manager; or Mrs. Margarita Krasteva, Radio Regulatory Department.

Radio Varna, 22 blv. Primorski, 9000 Varna, Bulgaria. Replies irregularly. Return postage required. If no reply is forthcoming, try sending an email to rcorresp1@bnr.acad.bg.

BURKINA FASO World Time exactly

Radiodiffusion-Télévision Burkina, B.P. 7029, Ouagadougou, Burkina Faso. Phone: +226 310-441. Contact: (general) Raphael L. Onadia or M. Pierre Tassembedo; (technical) Marcel Teho, Head of Transmitting Centre. Replies irregularly to correspondence in French. IRC or return postage helpful.

BURMA—*see* MYANMAR.

BURUNDI World Time +2

La Voix de la Révolution, B.P. 1900, Bujumbura, Burundi. Phone: +257 22-37-42. Fax: +257 22 65 47 or +257 22 66 13. Email: rtnb@cbinf.com. Contact: (general) Grégoire Barampumba, Head of News Section; or Frederic Havugiyaremye, Journaliste; (administration) Gérard Mfuranzima, Le Directeur de la Radio; or Didace Baranderetse, Directeur Général de la Radio; (technical) Abraham Makuza, Le Directeur Technique. $1 required.

CAMBODIA World Time +7

National Radio of Cambodia (when operating)
STATION ADDRESS: 106 Preah Kossamak Street, Monivong Boulevard, Phnom Penh, Cambodia. Phone: +855 (23) 423-369 or +855 (23) 422-869. Fax: + 855 (23) 427 319. Contact: (general) Miss Hem Bory, English Announcer; Kem Yan, Chief of External Relations; or Touch Chhatha, Producer, Art Department; (administration) In Chhay, Chief of Overseas Service; Som Sarun, Chief of Home Service; Van Sunheng, Deputy Director General, Cambodian National Radio and Television; or Ieng Muli, Minister of Information; (technical) Oum Phin, Chief of Technical Department. Free program schedule. Replies irregularly and slowly. Do not include stamps, currency, IRCs or dutiable items in envelope. Registered letters stand a much better chance of getting through. Has been increasingly off the air in recent years.

CAMEROON World Time +1

NOTE: Any CRTV outlet is likely to be verified by contacting via registered mail, in English or French with $2 enclosed, James Achanyi-Fontem, Cameroon Link, Shortwave Monitors, P.O. Box 1460, Douala, Cameroon.

Cameroon Radio Television Corporation (CRTV)—Bafoussam (if reactivated), B.P. 970, Bafoussam (Ouest), Cameroon. Contact: (general) Boten Celestin; (technical) Ndam Seidou, Chef Service Technique. IRC or return postage required. Replies irregularly in French to correspondence in English or French.

Cameroon Radio Television Corporation (CRTV)—Bertoua (if reactivated), B.P. 230, Bertoua (Eastern), Cameroon. Rarely replies to correspondence, preferably in French. $1 required.

Cameroon Radio Television Corporation (CRTV)—Buea, P.M.B., Buea (Sud-Ouest), Cameroon. Contact: Ononino Oli Isidore, Chef Service Technique. Three IRCs, $1 or return postage required.

Cameroon Radio Television Corporation (CRTV)—Douala (if reactivated), B.P. 986, Douala (Littoral), Cameroon. Contact: (technical) Emmanual Ekite, Technicien. Free pennants. Three IRCs or $1 required.

Cameroon Radio Television Corporation (CRTV)—Garoua, B.P. 103, Garoua (Nord/Adamawa), Cameroon. Contact: Kadeche Manguele. Free cloth pennants. Three IRCs or return postage required. Replies irregularly and slowly to correspondence in French.

Cameroon Radio Television Corporation (CRTV)—Yaoundé, B.P. 1634, Yaoundé (Centre-Sud), Cameroon. Phone: +237 214-035, +237 208-037. Fax: +237 204 340. Email: crtv@crtv.cm. Web: (includes RealAudio and MP3) www.crtv.cm. Contact: (technical or nontechnical) Prof. Gervais Mendo Ze, Directeur-Général; (technical) Eyébé Tanga, Directeur Technique. $1 required. Replies slowly (sometimes extremely slowly) to correspondence in French.

CANADA World Time –3:30 (–2:30 midyear)

Newfoundland; –4 (–3 midyear) Atlantic; –5 (–4 midyear) Eastern, including Quebec and Ontario; –6 (–5 midyear) Central; except Saskatchewan; –6 Saskatchewan; –7 (–6 midyear) Mountain; –8 (–7 midyear) Pacific, including Yukon

Canadian Broadcasting Corporation (CBC)—English Programs, P.O. Box 500, Station A, Toronto, Ontario, M5W 1E6, Canada. Phone: (Audience Relations) +1 (416) 205-3700. Email: cbcinput@toronto.cbc.ca. Web: (includes RealAudio) www.radio.cbc.ca. CBC prepares some of the programs heard over Radio Canada International (*see*).
LONDON NEWS BUREAU: CBC, 43-51 Great Titchfield Street, London W1P 8DD, England. Phone: +44 (20) 7412-9200. Fax: +44 (20) 7631 3095.
PARIS NEWS BUREAU: CBC, 17 avenue Matignon, F-75008 Paris, France. Phone: +33 (1) 4421-1515. Fax: +33 (1) 4421 1514.
WASHINGTON NEWS BUREAU: CBC, National Press Building, Suite 500, 529 14th Street NW, Washington DC 20045 USA. Phone: +1 (202) 383-2900. Contact: Jean-Louis Arcand, David Hall or Susan Murray.

Canadian Broadcasting Corporation (CBC)—French Programs, Société Radio-Canada, C.P. 6000, succ. centre-ville, Montréal, Québec, H3C 3A8, Canada. Phone: (Audience Relations) +1 (514) 597-6000. Email (comments on programs): auditoire@montreal.radio-canada.ca. Welcomes correspondence sent to this address but may not reply due to shortage of staff. Web: (includes RealAudio) www.radio-canada.ca. CBC prepares some of the programs heard over Radio Canada International (*see*).

CBC Northern Quebec Shortwave Service—*see* Radio Canada International, below.

CFRX-CFRB
MAIN ADDRESS: 2 St. Clair Avenue West, Toronto, Ontario, M4V 1L6, Canada. Phone:(main switchboard) +1 (416) 924-5711; (talk shows switchboard) +1 (416) 872-1010; (news centre) +1 (416) 924-6717; (CFRB information access line) +1 (416) 872-2372. Fax: (main fax line) +1 (416) 323 6830; (CFRB news fax line) +1 (416) 323 8616. Email: (comments on programs) cfrbcomments@cfrb.com; (News Director) news@cfrb.com; (general nontechnical) info@cfrb.com; or opsmngr@cfrb.com; (technical) ian.sharp@cfrb.com. Web: (includes Windows Media and MP3) www.cfrb.com. Contact: (nontechnical) Carlo Massaro, Information Officer; or Steve Kowch, Operations Manager; (technical) Ian Sharp. Reception reports should be sent to the verification address, below.
VERIFICATION ADDRESS: Ontario DX Association, P.O. Box 161,

Station 'A', Willowdale, Ontario, M2N 5S8, Canada, or by email: odxa@compuserve.com. General information about CFRB/CFRX can be seen at the ODXA Website: www.odxa.on.ca. General information about CFRB/CFRX reception may be directed to the QSL Manager, Steve Canney, VA3SC (email: scanney@home.com). A free CFRB/CFRX information sheet and an ODXA brochure is enclosed with your verification card. Reports are processed quickly if sent to this address.

CFVP-CKMX, AM 1060, Standard Broadcasting, P.O. Box 2750, Station 'M', Calgary, Alberta, T2P 4P8, Canada. Phone: (general) +1 (403) 240-5800; (news) +1 (403) 240-5844; (technical) +1 (403) 240-5867. Fax: (general and technical) +1 (403) 240 5801; (news) +1 (403) 246 7099. Contact: (general) Gary Russell, General Manager; or Beverley Van Tighem, Exec. Ass't.; (technical) Ken Pasolli, Technical Director.

CHNX-CHNS (if reactivated), P.O. Box 400, Halifax, Nova Scotia, B3J 2R2, Canada. Phone: +1 (902) 422-1651. Fax: +1 (902) 422 5330. Email: chnx@chnsradio.com; (Olson) molson@mbsradio.com. Contact: Garry Barker, General Manager; (programs) Troy Michaels, Operations Manager; (technical, & reception reports) Mark Olson, Station Engineer. Program schedules, stickers and small souvenirs sometimes available. Return postage or $1 helpful. Replies irregularly. According to the station engineer, the shortwave transmitter "died" in summer 2001 and the station has insufficient funds to purchase a replacement.

CHU, Time and Frequency Standards, Bldg. M-36, National Research Council, Ottawa, Ontario, K1A 0R6, Canada. Phone: (general) +1 (613) 993-5186; (administration) +1 (613) 993-1003 or +1 (613) 993-2704. Fax: +1 (613) 993 1394. Email: time@nrc.ca. Web: www.cisti.nrc.ca/inms/time/ctse.html. Contact: Dr. Rob Douglas; Dr. Jean-Simon Boulanger, Group Leader; or Ray Pelletier, Technical Officer. Official standard frequency and World Time station for Canada on 3330, 7335 and 14670 kHz. Brochure available upon request.Those with a personal computer, Bell 103 compatible modem and appropriate software can get the exact time, from CHU's cesium clock, via the telephone; details available upon request, or direct from the Website.

CKZN, CBC Newfoundland and Labrador, P.O. Box 12010, Station 'A', St. John's, Newfoundland, A1B 3T8, Canada. Phone: +1 (709) 576-5155. Fax: +1 (709) 576 5099. Email: (administration) radiomgt@stjohns.cbc.ca; (engineer) keith_durnford@cbc.ca. Web: (includes RealAudio) www.stjohns.cbc.ca. Contact: (general) Heather Elliott, Communications Officer; (technical) Shawn R. Williams, Manager, Transmission and Distribution; Keith Durnford, Station Engineer; Jerry Brett, Transmitter Department; or Janet Ferweda. Free CBC sticker and verification card with the history of Newfoundland included. Don't enclose money, stamps or IRCs with correspondence, as they will only have to be returned. Relays CBN (St. John's, 640 kHz) except at 1000-1330 World Time (one hour earlier in summer) when programming comes from CFGB Goose Bay.

CFGB ADDRESS: CBC Radio, Box 1029 Station 'C', Happy Valley, Goose Bay, Labrador, Newfoundland A0P 1C0, Canada.

CKZU-CBU, CBC, P.O. Box 4600, Vancouver, British Columbia, V6B 4A2, Canada—for verification of reception reports, mark the envelope, "Attention: Engineering." Toll-free telephone (U.S and Canada only) 1-800-961-6161. Phone: (general) +1 (604) 662-6000; (engineering) +1 (604) 662-6060. Fax: +1 (604) 662 6350. Email: (general) webmaster@vancouver.cbc.ca; (Newbury) newburyd@vancouver.cbc.ca. Web: (includes RealAudio) www.vancouver.cbc.ca. Contact: (general) Public Relations; (technical) Dave Newbury, Transmission Engineer.

Radio Canada International

NOTE: (CBC Northern Quebec Service) The following RCI address, fax and email information for the Main Office and Transmission Office is also valid for the CBC Northern Quebec Shortwave Service, provided you make your communication to the attention of the particular service you seek to contact.

MAIN OFFICE: P.O. Box 6000, Montréal, Quebec, H3C 3A8, Canada; or (street address) 1400 boulevard René Lévesque East, Montréal, Québec, H2L 2M2, Canada. Phone: (general) +1 (514) 597-7500; (Audience Relations, Ms. Maggy Akerblom) +1 (514) 597-7555; (Communications) +1 (514) 597-7551. Fax: (general) +1 (514) 597 7076; (Audience Relations) +1 (514) 597 7760. Email: rci@montreal.radio-canada.ca. Web: (includes RealAudio) www.rcinet.ca. Contact: (general) Maggy Akerblom, Audience Relations; Stéphane Parent, Producer/Host "Le courrier mondial"; or Mark Montgomery, Producer/Host "The Maple Leaf Mailbag"; (Communications) Ousseynou Diop, Manager; (administration) Denis Doucet, Executive Director; or Ms. Joy Sellers, Programming and Operations; (technical—verifications) Bill Westenhaver. Free stickers & lapel pins on request.

TRANMISSION OFFICE: 1400 boulevard René Lévesque East, Montréal, Québec, H2L 2M2, Canada. Phone: +1 (514) 597-769/20. Fax: +1 (514) 284 2052. Email: (Théorêt) gtheoret@montreal.radio-canada.ca; (Bouliane) jboulian@montreal.radio-canada.ca. Contact: (general) Gérald Théorêt, Manager, Frequency Management; or Ms. Nicole Vincent, Frequency Management; (administration) Jacques Bouliane, Coordinator, Plant Engineering. This office only for informing about transmitter-related problems (interference, modulation quality, etc.), especially by fax. Verifications not given out at this office; requests for verification should be sent to the main office, above.

TRANSMITTER SITE: CBC, P.O. Box 6131, Sackville New Brunswick, E4L 1G6, Canada. Phone: +1 (506) 536-2690/1. Fax: +1 (506) 536 2342. Contact: Raymond Bristol, Plant Manager Transmitting Stations. All correspondence not concerned with transmitting equipment should be directed to the appropriate address in Montréal, above. Free tours given during normal working hours.

RCI MONITORING STATION: P.O. Box 322, Station C, Ottawa, Ontario, K1Y 1E4, Canada. Phone: +1 (613) 831-2801. Fax: +1 (613) 831 0343. Contact: Derek Williams, Manager Monitoring Station.

Radio Monte-Carlo Middle East (via Radio Canada International)—*see* France.

Shortwave Classroom, R. Tait McKenzie Public School, 175 Paterson Street, Almonte, Ontario, K0A 1A0, Canada. Phone: +1 (613) 256-8248. Fax: +1 (613) 256 4791. Contact: Neil Carleton, VE3NCE, Editor & Publisher. *The Shortwave Classroom* newsletter was published three times per year as a nonprofit volunteer project for teachers around the world that use shortwave listening in the classroom, or as a club activity, to teach about global perspectives, media studies, world geography, languages, social studies and other subjects. Although no longer published, a set of back issues with articles and classroom tips from teachers around the globe is available for $10.

CENTRAL AFRICAN REPUBLIC World Time +1

Radio Centrafrique, Radiodiffusion-Télévision Centrafricaine, B.P. 940, Bangui, Central African Republic. Contact: (technical) Jacques Mbilo, Le Directeur des Services Techniques; or Michèl Bata, Services Techniques. Replies on rare occasions to correspondence in French; return postage required.

Radio Ndeke Luka, c/o PNUD, Av. de l'Indépendance, B.P. 872, Bangui, Central African Republic. Operated by the Hirondelle Foundation, and successor to the UN-run Radio MINURCA. Currently off shortwave, but eventually hopes to acquire a transmitter.

CHAD World Time +1

Radiodiffusion Nationale Tchadienne—N'djamena, B.P. 892, N'Djamena, Chad. Web: www.tit.td/rnt/. Contact: Djimadoum Ngoka Kilamian; or Ousmane Mahamat. Two IRCs or return postage required. Replies slowly to correspondence in French.

Radiodiffusion Nationale Tchadienne—Radio Moundou (when operating), B.P. 122, Moundou, Logone, Chad. Contact: Dingantoudji N'Gana Esaie.

CHILE World Time -3 (-4 midyear)

Radio Esperanza

OFFICE: Casilla 830, Temuco, Chile. Phone: +56 (45) 213-790. Phone/fax: +56 (45) 367 070. E-mail: ciacym@chilesat.net. Website: www.acym.cl/radio.htm. Contact: (general) Juanita Cárcamo, Departmento de Programación; Eleazar Jara, Dpto. de Programación; Ramón P. Woerner K., Publicidad; or Alberto Higueras Martínez, Locutor; (verifications) Rodolfo Campos, Director; Juanita Carmaco M., Dpto. de Programación; (technical) Juan Luis Puentes, Dpto. Técnico. Free pennants, stickers, bookmarks and tourist information. Two IRCs, $1 or 2 U.S. stamps appreciated. Replies, often slowly, to correspondence in Spanish or English.

STUDIO: Calle Luis Durand 03057, Temuco, Chile. Phone/fax: +56 (45) 240-161.

Radio Santa María, Apartado 1, Coyhaique, Chile. Phone: +56 (67) 23-23-98, +56 (67) 23-20-25 or +56 (67) 23-18-17. Fax: +56 (67) 23 13 06. Contact: Pedro Andrade Vera, Coordinador. $1 or return postage required. May send free tourist cards. Replies to correspondence in Spanish and Italian.

Radio Triunfal Evangélica (if reactivated), Calle Las Araucarias 2757, Villa Monseñor Larrain, Talagante, Chile. Phone: +56 (1) 815-4765. Contact: Fernando González Segura, Obispo de la Misión Pentecostal Fundamentalista. Two IRCs required. Replies to correspondence in Spanish.

Radio Voz Cristiana, Casilla 490-3, Santiago, Chile. Phone: (engineering) +56 (2) 855-7046. Fax: +56 (2) 855 7053. Email: (engineering) vozing@interaccess.cl, aflynn@interaccess.cl or AndrewFlynn@compuserve.com; (administration) vozcrist@interaccess.cl. Web: (includes Windows Media) www.vozcristiana.com. Contact: (technical) Andrew Flynn, Head of Engineering. Free program and frequency schedules. Sometimes sends small souvenirs. All QSL requests should be sent to the Miami Address.

INTERNATIONAL OFFICE: Christian Vision, Ryder Street, West Bromwich, West Midlands B70 0EJ, United Kingdom. Email: (Bennett) terryb@christianvision.com. Contact: Terry Bennett, Operations Director.

MIAMI ADDRESS: P.O. Box 2889, Miami FL 33144 USA. Phone: +1 (305) 231-7704. Fax: +1 (305) 231 7447. Email: cvusa@msn.com; (Gallardo) jmarkgallardo@msn.com. Contact: (nontechnical) Mark Gallardo.

CHINA World Time +8; still nominally +6 ("Urümqi Time") in the Xinjiang Uighur Autonomous Region, but in practice +8 is observed there, as well.

NOTE: China Radio International, the Central People's Broadcasting Station and certain regional outlets reply regularly to listeners' letters in a variety of languages. If a Chinese regional station does not respond to your correspondence within four months—and many will not, unless your letter is in Chinese or the regional dialect—try writing them c/o China Radio International.

Central People's Broadcasting Station (CPBS)—China National Radio (Zhongyang Renmin Guangbo Diantai), P.O. Box 4501, Beijing 100866, China. Phone: +86 (10) 6851-2435 or +86 (10) 6851-5522. Fax: +86 (10) 6851 6630. Email: zhangzr@mail.cnradio.com.cn, or wgblaze@mail.cnradio.com. Web: (includes RealAudio) www.cnradio.com.cn. Contact: Wang Changquan, Audience Department, China National Radio. Tape recordings of music and news $5 plus postage. CPBS T-shirts $10 plus postage; also sells ties and other items with CPBS logo. No credit cards. Free stickers, pennants and other small souvenirs. Return postage helpful. Responds regularly to correspondence in English and Standard Chinese (Mandarin). Although in recent years this station has officially been called "China National Radio" in English-language documents, all on-air identifications in Standard Chinese continue to be "Zhongyang Renmin Guangbo Dientai" (Central People's Broadcasting Station). To quote from the Website of China's State Administration of Radio, Film and TV: "The station moved to Beijing on March 25, 1949. It was renamed the Central People's Broadcasting Station (it [sic] English name was changed to China National Radio later on) . . ."

China Huayi Broadcasting Company, P.O. Box 251, Fuzhou, Fujian 350001, China. Contact: Lin Hai Chun, Announcer; or Wu Gehong. Replies to correspondence in English and Chinese. On-air, announces in English as "Corporation" but the correct translation from the Chinese name is "Company."

China National Radio—*see* Central People's Broadcasting Station (CPBS), above.

China Radio International

MAIN OFFICE, NON-CHINESE LANGUAGES SERVICE: 16A Shijingshan Street, Beijing 100040, China; or P.O. Box 4216, CRI-2 Beijing 100040 China. Phone: (Director's office) +86 (10) 6889-1676; (Audience Relations.) +86 (10) 6889-1617 or +86 (10) 6889-1652; (English newsroom) +86 (10) 6889-1619; (current affairs) +86 (10) 6889-1588; (Technical Director) +86 (10) 6609-2577. Fax: (Director's office) +86 (10) 6889 1582; (English Service) +86 (10) 6889 1378 or +86 (10) 6889 1379; (Audience Relations) +86 (10) 6851 3175; (administration) +86 (10) 6851 3174; (German Service) +86 (10) 6889 1941; (Spanish Service) +86 (10) 6889 1909. Email: (English) crieng@cri.com.cn; or msg@cri.com.cn; (Chinese) chn@cri.com.cn; (German) ger@box.cri.com.cn (*see* also the entry for the Berlin Bureau, below); (Japanese) jap@cri.com.cn; (Spanish) spa@cri.com.cn; ("Voices from Other Lands" program) voices@box.cri.com.cn. Web: (official, including RealAudio) www.cri.com.cn; (unofficial, but regularly updated) http://pw2.netcom.com/~jleq/cril.htm. Contact: Ms. Qi Guilin, Director of Audience Relations, English Service; Ying Lian, English Service; Shang Chunyan, "Listener's Letterbox"; Xu Ming, Editor; or Xia Jixuan, Director of English Service; (technical) Wang Guoqing, Technical

Director; (administration) Li Dan, President, China Radio International; Wang Guoqing, Cong Yingmin and Wong Rufeng, Deputy Directors, China Radio International; Xin Liancai, Director International Relations, China Radio International. Free bi-monthly *Messenger* newsletter for loyal listeners, pennants, stickers, desk calendars, pins and handmade papercuts. Sometimes, China Radio International holds contests and quizzes, with the overall winner getting a free trip to China. T-shirts for $8. Two-volume, 820-page set of *Day-to-Day Chinese* language-lesson books $15, including postage worldwide; a 155-page book, *Learn to Speak Chinese: Sentence by Sentence*, plus two cassettes for $15. Two chinese music tapes for $15. Various other books (on arts, medicine, Chinese idioms etc.) in English available from Audience Relations Department, English Service, China Radio International, 100040 Beijing, China. Payment by postal money order to Mr. Li Yi. Every year, the Audience Relations Department will renew the mailing list of the *Messenger* newsletter. CRI is also relayed via shortwave transmitters in Canada, Cuba, France, French Guiana, Mali, Russia and Spain.
FREQUENCY PLANNING DIVISION: Radio and Television of People's Republic of China, 2 Fuxingmenwai Street, Beijing 100866, China; or P.O. Box 2144, Beijing 100866, China. Phone: (Wang Xiulan) +86 (10) 6609-2080 or +86 (10) 6609-2627; (Yang Minmin) +86 (10) 6609-2070. Fax: +86 (10) 6801 6436 or +86 (10) 6609 2176. Email: (Wang Xiulan) plc2000@btamail.net.cn; (Yang Minmin & Li Guohua) pdc@abrs.chinasartft. Contact: Ms. Wang Xiulan; Ms. Li Guohua; Ms. Yang Minmin; or Zheng Shuguang.
MAIN OFFICE, CHINESE LANGUAGES SERVICE: China Radio International, Beijing 100040, China. Prefers correspondence in Chinese (Mandarin), Cantonese, Hakka, Chaozhou or Amoy.
ARLINGTON NEWS BUREAU: 2000 South Eads Street APT#712, Arlington VA 22202 USA. Phone: +1 (703) 521-8689. Contact: Mr. Zhenbang Dong.
BERLIN BUREAU: Berliner Büro, Gürtelstr. 32 B, D-10247 Berlin, Germany. Phone: +49 (30) 2966-8998. Fax: +49 (30) 2966 8997. Email: deyubu@hotmail.com. Correspondence to CRI's German Service can be sent to this office.
CHINA (HONG KONG) NEWS BUREAU: 387 Queen's Road East, Room 1503, Hong Kong, China. Phone: +852 2834-0384. Contact: Ms. Zhang Jiaping.
JERUSALEM NEWS BUREAU: Flat 16, Hagdud Ha'ivri 12, Jerusalem 92345, Israel. Phone: +972 (2) 566-6084. Contact: Mr. H. Yi.
LONDON NEWS BUREAU: 13B Clifton Gardens, Golders Green, London NW11 7ER, United Kingdom. Phone: +44 (20) 8458-6943. Contact: Ms. Xu Huazhen
NEW YORK NEWS BUREAU: 630 First Avenue #35K, New York NY 10016 USA. Fax: +1 (212) 889 2076. Contact: Mr Li.
SYDNEY NEWS BUREAU: Unit 53, Block A15 Herbert Street, St. Leonards NSW 2065, Australia. Phone: +61 (2) 9436-1493. Contact: Mr. Shi Chungyong.
SAN FRANCISCO OFFICE, SCHEDULES: 2654 17th Avenue, San Francisco CA 94116 USA. Phone: +1 (415) 564-9968. Email: GPoppin@aol.com. Contact: George Poppin. This address, a volunteer office, only provides CRI schedules to listeners. All other correspondence should be sent directly to the main office in Beijing.

Fujian People's Broadcasting Station, 2 Gutian Lu, Fuzhou, Fujian 350001, China. $1 or IRC helpful. Contact: Audience Relations. Replies occasionally and usually slowly. Prefers correspondence in Chinese.

Gannan People's Broadcasting Station, 49 Renmin Xije, Hezuo Zhen, Xiahe, Gian Su 747000, China. Verifies reception reports written in English. Return postage not required.

Gansu People's Broadcasting Station, 226 Donggang Xilu, Lanzhou 730000, China. Phone: +86 (931) 841-1054. Fax: +86 (931) 882 5834. Contact: Li Mei. IRC helpful.

Guangxi Foreign Broadcasting Station, 12 Min Zu Avenue, Nanning, Guangxi 530022, China. Phone: +86 (771) 585-4191, +86 (771) 585-4256 or +86 (771) 585-4403. Email: 101@gxfbs.com or 103@gxfbs.com; (Thanh Mai) thanhmai@gxfbs.com. Web: www.gxfbs.com. Contact: Thanh Mai, Vietnamese Section. Free stickers and handmade papercuts. IRC helpful. Replies irregularly. Broadcasts in Vietnamese and Cantonese to listeners in Vietnam.

Guangxi People's Broadcasting Station, 75 Min Zu Avenue, Nanning, Guangxi 530022, China. Email: gxbs@public.nn.gx.cn. Web: www.gxpbs.com. IRC helpful. Replies irregularly.

Guizhou People's Broadcasting Station, 259 Qingyun Lu, Guiyang, Guizhou 550002, China. Phone: +86 (851) 582-2495. Fax: +86 (851) 586 9983.

Heilongjiang People's Broadcasting Station, 181 Zhongshan Lu, Harbin, Heilongjiang 150001, China. Phone: +86 (451) 262-7454. Fax: +86 (451) 289 3539. Email: am621@sina.com. Web: www.am621.com.cn. $1 or return postage helpful.

Honghe People's Broadcasting Station, 32 Jianshe Donglu, Gejiu, Yunnan 661400, China. Contact: Shen De-chun, Head of Station; or Mrs. Cheng Lin, Editor-in-Chief. Free travel brochures.

Hubei People's Broadcasting Station, 563 Jiefang Dadao, Wuhan, Hubei 430022, China.

Hunan People's Broadcasting Station, 27 Yuhua Lu, Changsha, Hunan 410007, China. Phone: +86 (731) 554-7202. Fax: +86 (731) 554 7220.

Jiangxi People's Broadcasting Station, 111 Hongdu Zhong Dadao, Nanchang, Jiangxi 330046, China. Email: gfzq@public.nc.jx.cn. Contact: Tang Ji Sheng, Editor, Chief Editor's Office. Free gold/red pins. Replies irregularly. Mr. Tang enjoys music, literature and stamps, so enclosing a small memento along these lines should help assure a speedy reply.

Nei Menggu (Inner Mongolia) People's Broadcasting Station, 19 Xinhua Darjie, Hohhot, Nei Menggu 010058, China. Web: www.nmrb.com.ch. Contact: Zhang Xiang-Quen, Secretary; or Liang Yan. Replies irregularly.

Qinghai People's Broadcasting Station, 96 Kunlun Lu, Xining, Qinghai 810001, China. Contact: Liqing Fangfang; or Ghou Guo Liang, Director, Technical Department. $1 helpful.

Sichuan People's Broadcasting Station, 119-1 Hongxing Zhonglu, Chengdu, Sichuan 610017, China. Web: www.swww.com.cn/scsb/. Replies occasionally.

Voice of Jinling (Jinling zhi Sheng), P.O. Box 268, Nanjing, Jiangsu 210002, China. Fax: +86 (25) 413 235. Contact: Strong Lee, Producer/Host, "Window of Taiwan." Free stickers and calendars, plus Chinese-language color station brochure and information on the Nanjing Technology Import and Export Corporation. Replies to correspondence in Chinese and to simple correspondence in English. $1, IRC or 1 yuan Chinese stamp required for return postage.

Voice of Pujiang (Pujiang zhi Sheng), P.O. Box 3064, Shanghai 200002, China. Phone: +86 (21) 6208-2797. Fax: +86 (21) 6208 2850. Contact: Jiang Bimiao, Editor and Reporter.

Voice of the Strait (Haixia zhi Sheng), People's Liberation Army Broadcasting Centre, P.O. Box 187, Fuzhou, Fujian 350012, China. Email: hxzs@mail.radiohx.com. Web: (includes RealAudio) www.radiohx.com. Replies irregularly.

Wenzhou People's Broadcasting Station, 19 Xianxue Qianlu, Wenzhou, Zhejiang 325000, China.

Xilingol People's Broadcasting Station, Xilin Dajie, Xilinhot, Nei Menggu 026000, China.

Xinjiang People's Broadcasting Station, 84 Tuanjie Lu, Urümqi, Xinjiang 830044, China. Email: mw738@21cn.com. Web: www.xjbs.com.cn. Contact: Zhao Ji-shu. Free tourist booklet, postcards and used Chinese stamps. Replies to correspondence in Chinese and to simple correspondence in English.

Xizang People's Broadcasting Station, 180 Beijing Zhonglu, Lhasa, Xizang 850000, China. Contact: Lobsang Chonphel, Announcer; or Miss Wenxin, host of "Tonights Appointment" program. Free stickers and brochures. Enclosing an English-language magazine may help with a reply.

Yunnan People's Broadcasting Station, 73 Renmin Xilu, Central Building of Broadcasting and TV, Kunming, 650031 Yunnan, China. Phone: +86 (871) 531-0270. Fax: +86 (871) 531 0360. Contact: Sheng Hongpeng or F.K. Fan. Free Chinese-language brochure on Yunnan Province, but no QSL cards. $1 or return postage helpful. Replies occasionally.

Zhejiang People's Broadcasting Station, 111 Moganshan Lu, Hangzhou, Zhejiang 310005, China. Phone: +86 (571) 807-7050. Email: radiozjy@163.com. Contact: Yin Weiling, Editor.

CHINA (TAIWAN) World Time +8

Central Broadcasting System (CBS), 55 Pei'an Road, Tachih, Taipei 104, Taiwan, Republic of China. Phone: +886 (2) 2591-8161 or +886 (2) 2885-6168. Email: cbs@cbs.org.tw. Web (includes RealAudio): www.cbs.org.tw. Contact: Lee Ming, Deputy Director. Free stickers.

China Radio, 53 Min Chuan West Road 9th Floor, Taipei 10418, Taiwan. Phone: +886 (2) 2598-1009. Fax: +886 (2) 2598 8348. Email: (Adams) readams@usa.net. Contact: Richard E. Adams, Station Director. Verifies reception reports. A religious broadcaster, sometimes referred to as "True Light Station," transmitting via leased facilities in Petropavlovsk-Kamchatskiy, Russia.

Radio Taipei International, P.O. Box 24-38, Taipei 106, Taiwan, Republic of China. Phone: +886 (2) 2885-6168. Fax: +886 (2) 2885 2254. Email: (general) cbs@cbs.org.tw; (English) prog@cbs.org.tw; (German) deutsch@cbs.org.tw. Web: (includes RealAudio) www.cbs.org.tw; (online reception report form for Radio Taipei International and Voice of Asia broadcasts) www.cbs.org.tw/RadioReport/NewRadio.asp. Contact: (general) Daniel Dong, Chief, Listeners' Service Section; Paula Chao, Producer, "Mailbag Time";Yea-Wen Wang; Huan Wen-lin; Bonnie Cheng; or Carlson Wong; (administration) John C.T. Feng, Director; or Dong Yu-Ching, Deputy Director; (technical) Wen-Bin Tsai, Engineer, Engineering Department; Tai-Lau Ying, Engineering Department; Tien-Shen Kao; or Huang Shuh-shyun, Director, Engineering Department. Free stickers, caps, shopping bags, annual diary, "Let's Learn Chinese" language-learning course materials, booklets, newsletters and other publications, and Taiwanese stamps. T-shirts $5. Broadcasts to the Americas are relayed via WYFR-Family Radio transmitters in Okeechobee, Florida, USA (*see*).

BERLIN OFFICE: Postfach 08 05 36, D-10005 Berlin, Germany.

OSAKA NEWS BUREAU: C.P.O. Box 180, Osaka Central Post Office, Osaka 530-091, Japan.

TOKYO NEWS BUREAU: P.O Box 21, Azubu Post Office, Tokyo 106, Japan.

SAN FRANCISCO NEWS BUREAU: P.O. Box 192793, San Francisco CA 94119-2793 USA.

Voice of Asia, P.O. Box 24-777, Taipei, Taiwan, Republic of China. Phone: +886 (2) 2771-0151, X-2431. Fax: +886 (2) 2751 9277. Web: same as for Radio Taipei International, above. Free shopping bags, inflatable globes, coasters, calendars, stickers and booklets. T-shirts $5. As of June 2001, no longer broadcasts in English.

CLANDESTINE

Clandestine broadcasts are often subject to abrupt change or termination. Being operated by anti-establishment political and/or military organizations, these groups tend to be suspicious of outsiders' motives. Thus, they are more likely to reply to contacts from those who communicate in the station's native tongue, and who are perceived to be at least somewhat favorably disposed to their cause. Most will provide, upon request, printed matter on their cause, though not necessarily in English.

For more detailed information on clandestine stations, refer to the annual publication, *Clandestine Stations List*, about $10 or 10 IRCs postpaid by air, published by the Danish Shortwave Clubs International, Tavleager 31, DK-2670 Greve, Denmark; phone (Denmark) +45 4290-2900; fax (via Germany) +49 6371 71790; email 100413.2375@compuserve.com. For CIA media contact information, *see* USA. Available on the Internet, *The Clandestine Radio Intel Webpage* specializes in background information on these stations and is organized by region and target country. The page can be accessed at: www.ClandestineRadio.com. Another informative Web page specializing in clandestine radio information and containing a twice monthly report on the latest news and developments affecting the study of clandestine radio is *Clandestine Radio Watch*, found at www.listen.to/qip/.

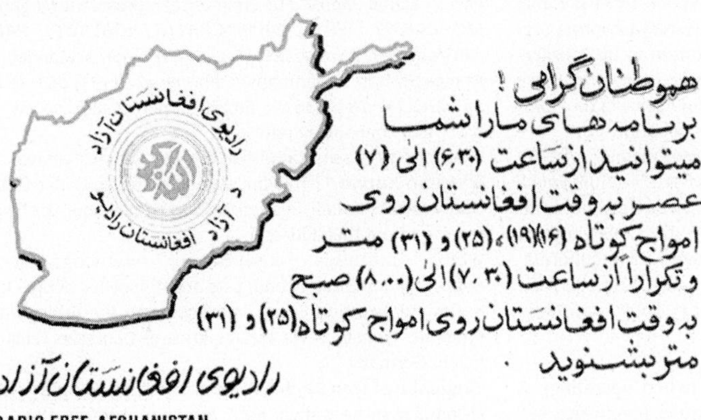
هموطنان گرامی !
برنامه های ما را شما
میتوانید از ساعت (۶.۳۰) الی (۷)
عصر بوقت افغانستان روی
امواج کوتاه (۱۶)(۱۹)، (۲۵) و (۳۱) متر
و تکرارا از ساعت (۷.۳۰) الی (۸.۰۰) صبح
بوقت افغانستان روی امواج کوتاه (۲۵) و (۳۱)
متر بشنوید .
رادیوی افغانستان آزاد
RADIO FREE AFGHANISTAN

Being unprepared: RFE-RL aired "Radio Free Afghanistan" from 1985-1993. Attempts to revive it after the September 11 attacks were hampered by a lack of transmitters, as American shortwave facilities were being closed down as recently as mid-2001. RFE-RL

"Democratic Voice of Burma" ("Democratic Myanmar a-Than")
STATION: DVB Radio, P.O. Box 6720, St. Olavs Plass, N-0130 Oslo, Norway. Phone: +47 (22) 20-0021. Phone/fax: +47 (22) 36-2525. Email: dvbburma@online.no. Web: (includes RealAudio) www.communique.no/dvb/. Contact: (general) Dr. Anng Kin, Listener Liaison; Aye Chan Naing, Daily Editor; or Thida, host for "Songs Request Program"; (administration) Harn Yawnghwe, Director; or Daw Khin Pyone, Manager; (technical) Saw Neslon Ku, Studio Technician; or Technical Dept. Free stickers and booklets to be offered in the near future. Norwegian kroner requested for a reply, but presumably Norwegian mint stamps would also suffice. Programs produced by Burmese democratic movements, as well as professional and independent radio journalists, to provide informational and educational services for the democracy movement inside and outside Burma. Opposes the current Myanmar government. Transmits via the facilities of Radio Norway International, among others.
AFFINITY GROUPS Web:
BURMA NET. Email: (BurmaNet News editor, Free Burma Coalition, USA) strider@igc.apc.org; (Web coordinator, Free Burma Coalition, USA) freeburma@pobox.com. Web: (BurmaNet News, USA) http://sunsite.unc.edu/freeburma/listservers.html.
FREE BURMA COALITION. Email: justfree@ix.netcom.com. Web: http://danenet.wicip.org/fbc/.

"National Radio of the Democratic Saharan Arab Republic"—*see* Radio Nacional de la República Arabe Saharaui Democrática, Western Sahara.

"Netsanet Le-Ethiopia Radio," Netsanet Le-Ethiopia, P.O. Box 5398, Takoma Park MD 20913 USA. Voicemail: +1 (301) 562-8597. Email: netsanet@netsanet.com. Web: (includes RealAudio) www.netsanet.com. Opposed to the Ethiopian government.

"Radio Anternacional," BM Box 1499, London WC1N 3XX, United Kingdom. Phone: +44 (20) 8962-2707. Fax: +44 (20) 8346 2203. Email: radio7520@yahoo.com. Web: (includes Windows Media) www.anternacional.org. Contact: Ms. Azar Majedi. A broadcast in Persian sponsored by the Committee for Humanitarian Assistance to Iranian Refugees (CHAIR)—*see* below— and aired via transmitting facilities in Moldova. Reportedly has ties to the Worker-Communist Party of Iran.
SPONSORING ORGANIZATION: Committee for Humanitarian Assistance to Iranian Refugees (CHAIR), GPO, P.O. Box 7051, New York NY 10116 USA. Phone: +1 (212) 747-1046. Fax: +1 (212) 425 7260. Email: info@chair.org. Web: www.chair.org.

"Radio Bopeshawa," P.O. Box 22266, London SE5, United Kingdom. Phone: (Arabic Section) +44 (789) 006-5933; (Kurdish Section) +44 (779) 625-7020. Email: bopeshawa@wpiraq.org. Web: www.wpiraq.org/kurdish/bop/. Station of the Worker-Communist Party of Iraq. If no reply is forthcoming from these sources, try the contact addresses listed for "Voice of the Communist-Worker Party of Iraq" later in this section.

"Radio Free Vietnam," P.O. Box 29245, New Orleans LA 70189 USA. Phone: +1 (504) 254-2304. Fax: +1 (504) 254-2305. Email: vkyson@bigfoot.com. Web: www.radiofreevietnam.com. Contact: Vuong Ky-Son, Director in Chief. Transmits via hired facilities in Central Asia. Not to be confused with a California-produced program of the same name, broadcast over KWHR.

"Radio Freedom, Voice of the Ogadeni People"—*see* Radio Xuriyo.

"Radio Free Iraq"—*see* USA.

"Radio Independence Bougainville" (when operating), 2 Griffith Avenue, Roseville NSW 2069, Australia. Phone/fax: +61 (2) 9417-1066. Contact: Sam Voron, Australian Director. $5, AUS$5 or 5 IRCs required. Station is operated from Panguna, Central Bougainville by the pro independence forces of the Meekamui Defence Force led by Fransis Ona. Opposed to the Papua New Guinea government.

"Radio International"—*see* "Radio Anternacional"

"Radio Iran of Tomorrow" ("Radio-ye Iran-e Farda"). Fax: +33 (1) 5301 0899. E-mail: riot_studio@hotmail.com. Web: (RealAudio only) www.ri-ot.com. Contact: A. Qat. Supports the struggle of clerics and religious forces who wish to see the separation of religion and government in Iran. Describes itself as "the voice of all of Iran's national and free thinking forces." Believed to hire airtime via facilities in Tajikistan.

"Radio Kurdistan"—*see* Iraq.

"Radio Liberté" (when operating). E-mail: mlcongo@compuserve.com. Web: www.mlc-congo.org. Contact: Olivier Kamitatu. Broadcasts in support of the rebel Congolese Liberation Movement. Broadcasts from Gbadolite in the northeast of the Democratic Republic of Congo, on the border with the Central African Republic.

"Radio Nacional de la República Arabe Saharaui Democrática"—*see* Western Sahara.

"Radio Rainbow" ("Kestedamena rediyo ye selamena yewendimamach dimtse"), c/o RAPEHGA, P.O. Box 140104, D-53056 Bonn, Germany. Contact: T. Assefa. Supposedly operated by an Ethiopian opposition group called Research and Action Group for Peace in Ethiopia and the Horn of Africa. Broadcasts via hired shortwave transmitters in Germany.

"Radio Sedaye Iran"—*see* KRSI, USA.

"Radio Voice of Hope"— *see* Holland.

"Radio Voice of Liberty and Renewal," ("Idha'at sawt al-hurriyah wa al-tajdid, sawt quwwat al-tahaluf al-sudaniyyah, sawt al-intifadah al-sha'biyyah al-musallahah"). E-mail: infosaf@eol.com.er. Web: (Sudan Alliance Forces) www.safsudan.com. Contact: Fathi Abdelaziz, Sudan Alliance Forces Secretary for Culture and Information. The Sudan Alliance Forces are an opposition guerrilla army of ex-government northern soldiers, affiliated to the Asmara, Eritrea-based National Democratic Alliance (NDA). Opposes the current Sudanese government. Also identifies as "Voice of the Sudan Alliance Forces" and "Voice of the Popular Armed Uprising." Claims to operate in liberated areas on the Sudanese side of the Sudan-Eritrea border.

"Radio Voice of the Mojahed"—*see* "Voice of the Mojahed," later in this section.

"Radio Voice of the People," P.O. Box CY 3093, Causeway, Harare, Zimbabwe. Airs via Radio Nederland facilities in Madagascar and is opposed to Zimbabwean president Mugabe.
MOVEMENT FOR DEMOCRATIC CHANGE PARENT ORGRANIZATION: Harvest House, 6th Floor, N.Mandela Ave/Angwa St, Harare, Zimbabwe. Phone: +263 (91) 367-151/2/3 or +263 (4) 781-138/9. Email: support@mdc.co.zw. Web: www.mdczimbabwe.com.

"Radio VOP"—*see* "Radio Voice of the People," above.

"Radio Xuriyo," ("Halkani wa Radio Xuriyo, Codkii Ummada Odageniya"). Email: ogaden@yahoo.com (some verifications received from this address).
Web: (includes RealAudio) www.ogaden.com/radio_Freedom.htm. Broadcasts are supportive of the Ogaden National Liberation Front, and hostile to the Ethiopian government. Transmits via the facilities of Deutsche Telekom in Jülich, Germany.

"Republic of Iraq Radio, Voice of the Iraqi People" ("Idha'at al-Jamahiriya al-Iraqiya, Saut al-Sha'b al-Iraqi"), Broadcasting Service of the Kingdom of Saudi Arabia, P.O. Box 61718, Riyadh 11575, Saudi Arabia. Phone: +966 (1) 442-5170. Fax: +966 (1) 402 8177. Contact: Suliman A. Al-Samnan, Director of Frequency Management. Anti-Saddam Hussein "black" clandestine supported by CIA, British intelligence, the Gulf Cooperation Council and Saudi Arabia. The name of this station has changed periodically since its inception during the Gulf crisis. Via transmitters in Saudi Arabia.

SPONSORING ORGANIZATION: Iraqi National Congress, 17 Cavendish Square, London W1M 9AA, United Kingdom. Phone: +44 (20) 7665-1812; (office in Arbil, Iraq) +873 (682) 346-239. Fax: +44 (20) 7665 1201; (office in Arbil, Iraq) +873 (682) 346 240. Email: pressoffice@inc.org.uk. Web: www.inc.org.uk.

"Voice of China" ("Zhongguo zhi Yin"), P.O. Box 273538, Concord CA 94527 USA; or (sponsoring organization) Foundation for China in the 21st Century, P.O. Box 11696, Berkeley CA 94701 USA. Contact: Bang Tai Xu, Director. Mainly "overseas Chinese students" interested in the democratization of China. Financial support from the Foundation for China in the 21st Century. Has "picked up the mission" of the earlier Voice of June 4th, but has no organizational relationship with it. Transmits via facilities of the Central Broadcasting System, Taiwan (*see*).

"Voice of Biafra International." Email: oguchi@pacbell.net. Web: (parent organization) www.biafraland.com. Contact: Oguchi Nkwocha, M.D.

"Voice of Democratic Eritrea" ("Sawt Eritrea al-Dimuqratiya-Sawtu Jabhat al-Tahrir al-Eritrea") (when active), ELF-RC, P.O. Box 200434, D-53134 Bonn, Germany. Phone: +49 (228) 356-181. Email: (Eritrean political opposition) meskerem@erols.com. Web: (includes RealAudio) http:users.erols.com/meskerem/. Contact: Seyoum O. Michael, Member of Executive Committee, ELF-RC. Station of the Eritrean Liberation Front-Revolutionary Council, hostile to the government of Eritrea. Transmits via facilities in Jülich, Germany.

"Voice of Ethiopian Medhin," EMDP, P.O. Box 13875, Silver Spring, MD 20911 USA; Medhin Dimts, Postfach 111423 D-60049 Frankfurt/Main, Germany. Web: (includes RealAudio) www.medhin.org. Broadcast produced by overseas members of the Ethiopian Medhin Democratic Party (EMDP) based in the USA, a broad-based coalition of Ethiopians aiming to democratize their country. Transmits via facilities in Jülich, Germany.

MEDHIN INFORMATION AND PUBLIC RELATIONS DEPARTMENT: Postfach 4432, D-90023 Nueremberg, Germany. Phone/fax: +49 (911) 209 433.

"Voice of Iranian Kurdistan"—Contact one of the PDKI (Democratic Party of Iranian Kurdistan parent organization) offices, below.

PDKI INTERNATIONAL BUREAU: AFK, Boite Postale 102, F-75623 Paris Cedex 13, France. Phone: +33 (1) 4585-6431. Fax: +33 (1) 4585 2093. Email: pdkiran@club-internet.fr; Web: www.pdk-iran.org.

PDKI CANADA BUREAU: P.O. Box 29010, London, Ontario N6G 2V3, Canada. Email: pdkiontario@pdki.org, or pdkivancouver@pdki.org. Web: www.pdki.org.

PDKI REPRESENTATIVE IN USA: Email: pdkiusa@pdki.org.

"Voice of Iraqi Kurdistan"—*see* Iraq.

"Voice of Jammu Kashmir Freedom" ("Sada-i Hurriyat-i Jammu Kashmir"), P.O. Box 102, Muzaffarabad, Azad Kashmir, via Pakistan. Contact: Islam-ud Din Butt. Favors Azad Kashmiri independence from India; pro-Moslem, sponsored by the Kashmiri Mojahedin organization. Believed to transmit via facilities in Pakistan. Return postage not required.

"Voice of Khmer Krom," P.O. Box 121, Pensauken NJ 08110 USA. Email: vokk@khmerkrom.org. Web: (includes RealAudio) http://radio.khmerkrom.org. Targeted at the inhabitants of what used to be South Vietnam, via hired transmission facilities in Central Asia.

"Voice of Liberty and Renewal"—*see* "Radio Voice of Liberty and Renewal," above.

"Voice of National Salvation" ("Gugugui Sori Pangsong"), Grenier Osawa 107, 40 Nando-cho, Shinjuku-ku, Tokyo, Japan. Phone: + 81 (3) 5261-0331. Fax: +81 (3) 5261 0332. Email: (National Salvation Front) kuguk@alles.or.jp. Web: (National Salvation Front parent organization) www.alles.or.jp/~kuguk/. Pro-North Korea, pro-Korean unification; supported by North Korean government. On the air since 1967, but not always under the same name. Via North Korean transmitters located in Pyongyang, Haeju and Wongsan.

"Voice of Oromo Liberation" ("Segalee Bilisummaa Oromoo"), Postfach 510610, D-13366 Berlin, Germany; or SBO, Prinzenallee 81, D-13357 Berlin, Germany. Phone: +49 (30) 494-1036. Fax: +49 (30) 494 3372. Email: sbo13366@aol.com. Web: (includes RealAudio) www.oromoliberationfront.org. Contact: Taye Teferah, European Coordinator. Occasionally replies to correspondence in English or German. Return postage required. Station of the Oromo Liberation Front of Ethiopia, an Oromo nationalist organization transmitting via facilities in Germany and, irregularly, elsewhere.

OROMO LIBERATION FRONT USA OFFICE: P.O. Box 73247, Washington DC 20056 USA. Phone: +1 (202) 462-5477. Fax: +1 (202) 332 7011.

"Voice of Palestine, Voice of the Palestinian Islamic Revolution" ("Saut al-Filistin, Saut al-Thowrah al-Islamiyah al-Filistiniyah")—for many years considered a clandestine station, but is now officially listed as part of the Arabic schedule of the Voice of the Islamic Republic of Iran, over whose transmitters the broadcasts are aired. *See* "Iran" for potential contact information. Supports the Islamic Resistance Movement, Hamas, which is anti-Arafat and anti-Israel.

"Voice of Peace and Brotherhood,"—*see* "Radio Rainbow," above.

"Voice of Rebellious Iraq" ("Sawt al-Iraq al-Tha'ir"), P.O. Box 11365/738, Tehran, Iran; P.O. Box 37155/146, Qom, Iran; or P.O. Box 36802, Damascus, Syria. Anti-Iraqi regime, supported by the Shi'ite-oriented Supreme Assembly of the Islamic Revolution of Iraq, led by Mohammed Baqir al-Hakim. Supported by the Iranian government and transmitted from Iranian soil. Hostile to the Iraqi government.

SPONSORING ORGANIZATION: Supreme Council for Islamic Revolution in Iraq (SCIRI), 27a Old Gloucester St, London WC1N 3XX, United Kingdom. Phone: +44 (20) 7371-6815. Fax: +44 (20) 7371 2886. Email: 101642.1150@compuserve.com. Web: http://ourworld.compuserve.com/homepages/sciri/.

"Voice of the Communist Party of Iran" ("Seda-ye Hezb-e Komunist-e Iran"), B.M. Box 2123, London WC1N 3XX, United Kingdom. Email: ib@cpiran.org. Web: www.cpiran.org. Sponsored by the Communist Party of Iran (KOMALA, formerly Tudeh).

"Voice of the Communist-Worker Party of Iraq" (Aira dangi kizb-e communist-e kargar-e iraqa") (if reactivated), WCPI Radio, Zargata, Sulaimania, Iraq. Email: radio@wpiraq.org. Web: (WCPI parent organization) www.wpiraq.org. Station of the Worker-Communist Party of Iraq, and may have been replaced by Radio Bopeshawa (*see*).

WCPI CANADIAN OFFICE: P.O. Box 491, Don Mills Postal Station, North York, Ontario M3C 2T4, Canada.

WCPI GERMAN OFFICE: A.K.P.I., Postfach 160244, D-10336 Berlin, Germany.
WCPI SWEDISH OFFICE: W.P.C.I., Box 1211, SE-17224, Sundbyberg, Sweden
"Voice of the Democratic Path of Ethiopian Unity," Finote Democracy, P.O. Box 88675, Los Angeles CA 90009 USA. Email: efdpu@finote.org. Web: (includes RealAudio) www.finote.org. Transmits via Jülich, Germany.
EUROPEAN ADDRESS: Finote Democracy, Postbus 10573, 1001 EN, Amsterdam, Netherlands.
"Voice of the Iranian Revolution" ("Aira Dangi Shurashi Irana")—*see* "Voice of the Communist Party of Iran," above, for details.
"Voice of the Islamic Revolution in Iraq"—*see* "Voice of Rebellious Iraq," above, for contact information. Affiliated with the Shi'ite-oriented Supreme Assembly for Islamic Revolution in Iraq, led by Mohammed Baqir al-Hakim. Transmits via the facilities of Islamic Republic of Iran Broadcasting.
"Voice of the Kurdistan People"—*see* Iraq.
"Voice of the Mojahed" ("Seda-ye Mojahed ast")
PARIS BUREAU: Mojahedines de Peuple d'Iran, 17 rue des Gords, F-95430 Auvers-sur-Oise, France; or Mojahed, c/o CCI, 147 rue St. Martin, F-75003 Paris, France. Fax: +33 (1) 4271-5627. Email: (People's Mojahedin Organization of Iran parent organization) mojahed@mojahedin.org. Web: (RealAudio) www.iran.mojahedin.org/Pages/seda/; (People's Mojahedin Organization of Iran parent organization) www.iran.mojahedin.org. Contact: Majid Taleghani. Station replies very irregularly and slowly. Pre-prepared verification cards and SASE helpful, with correspondence in French or Persian almost certainly preferable. Sponsored by the People's Mojahedin Organization of Iran (OMPI) and the National Liberation Army of Iran.
OTHER BUREAUS: Voice of the Mojahed, c/o Heibatollahi, Postfach 502107, 50981 Köln, Germany; or P.O. Box 3133, Baghdad, Iraq (Contact: B. Moradi, Public Relations).
"Voice of the Popular Armed Uprising,"—*see* "Radio Voice of Liberty and Renewal," above.
"Voice of the Sudan Alliance Forces,"—*see* "Radio Voice of Liberty and Renewal," above.
"Voice of the Worker"—station of the Worker-Communist Party of Iran. Web: (includes historical archives in Windows Media) www.kvwpiran.org.
WORKER-COMMUNIST PARTY OF IRAN PARENT ORGANIZATION: Email: wpi@wpiran.org. Web: www.wpiran.org.
"Voice of Tibet"
ADMINISTRATIVE OFFICE: Welhavensgate 1, N-0166 Oslo, Norway. Phone: (administration) +47 2211-2700; (studio) +47 2211-1209. Fax: +47 2211 5474. Email: voti@online.no; (Norbu) votibet@online.no. Web: (includes RealAudio) www.vot.org. Contact: Øystein Alme, Project Manager [sometimes referred to as "Director"]; or Chophel Norbu, Project Coordinator.
MAIN EDITORIAL OFFICE: Voice of Tibet, Editor-in-Chief, Narthang Building, Gangchen, Kyishong, Dharamsala-176 215 H.P., India. Phone: +91 (1892) 28179 or +91 (1892) 22384. Fax: +91 (1892) 24913. Email: vot@nde.vsnl.net.in. Contact: Sonam Dargyay.
A joint venture of the Norwegian Human Rights House, Norwegian Tibet Committee and World-View International. Programs focus on Tibetan culture, education, human rights and news from Tibet. Opposed to Chinese control of Tibet. Those seeking a verification for this program should enclose a prepared card or letter. Return postage helpful. Verifications have been received from both addresses. Broadcasts via transmitters in Central Asia.
"Voice of Tigers" (when operating). Web: (archived news in RealAudio) www.eelamweb.com/vot/. No direct contact information is known, but try the following: c/o Eelamweb, 170 Lees Avenue #902, Ottawa, Ontario K1S 5G5, Canada (email: webmaster@eelamweb.com, or feedback@eelamweb.com). Station operated by Liberation Tigers of Tamil-Eelam.
"Voz de la Resistencia"
Email: (FARC-EP parent organization) farc-ep@comision.internal.org; or elbarcino@laneta.apc.org (updated transmission schedules and QSLs available from this address, but correspond in Spanish). Web: www.resistencianacional.org/radio.htm; www.radioresistencia.com; (FARC-EP parent organization) http://burn.ucsd.edu/~farc-ep/. Contact: Olga Lucía Marín, Comisión Internacional de las FARC-EP. Station of the Fuerzas Armadas Revolucionarias de Colombia - Ejercito del Pueblo.

COLOMBIA World Time -5

NOTE: Colombia, the country, is always spelled with two o's. It should never be written as "Columbia."
Armonías del Caquetá, Apartado Aéreo 71, Florencia, Caquetá, Colombia. Phone: +57 (88) 352-080. Contact: Padre Alvaro Serna Alzate, Director. Replies occasionally and slowly to correspondence in Spanish. Return postage required.
Caracol Arauca—see La Voz del Cinaruco.
Caracol Colombia
MAIN OFFICE: Apartado Aéreo 9291, Santafé de Bogotá, D.C., Colombia. Phone: +57 (1) 337-8866. Fax: +57 (1) 337 7126. Web: (includes RealAudio) www.caracol.com.co/webasp2/homeneo.asp. Contact: Hernán Peláez Restrepo, Jefe Cadena Básica; Efraín Jiménez, Director de Operaciones; or Oscar López M., Director Musical. Free stickers. Replies to correspondence in Spanish and English.
MIAMI OFFICE: 2100 Coral Way, Miami FL 33145 USA. Phone: +1 (305) 285-2477 or +1 (305) 285-1260. Fax: +1 (305) 858 5907.
Caracol Florencia (when active), Apartado Aéreo 465, Florencia, Caquetá, Colombia. Phone: +57 (88) 352-199. Contact: Guillermo Rodríguez Herrera, Gerente; or Vicente Delgado, Operador. Replies occasionally to correspondence in Spanish.
Caracol Villavicencio—*see* La Voz de los Centauros.
Colmundo Bogotá, Diagonal 58 No. 26-29, Santafé de Bogotá, Colombia; or Apartado Aéreo 36750, Santafé de Bogotá, Colombia. Fax: +57 (1) 217 9358. Contact: María Teresa Gutiérrez, Directora Gerente; Marcela Aristizábal, Presidente; Jorge Eliecer Hernández, Gerente Nacional de Programación; Carlos Arturo Echeverry, Chief Engineer; or Néstor Chamorro, Presidente de la Red Colmundo. Email: colradio@latino.net.co.Actively seeks reception reports from abroad, preferably in Spanish. Free stickers and program schedule.
Ecos del Atrato, Apartado Aéreo 196, Quibdó, Chocó, Colombia. Phone: +57 (49) 711-450. Contact: Absalón Palacios Agualimpia, Administrador. Free pennants. Replies to correspondence in Spanish.
Ecos del Orinoco (if reactivated), Gobernación del Vichada, Puerto Carreño, Vichada, Colombia.
La Voz de la Selva—*see* Caracol Florencia.
La Voz de los Centauros (Caracol Villavicencio), Cra. 31 No. 37-71 Of. 1001, Villavicencio, Meta, Colombia. Phone: +57 (986) 214-995. Fax: +57 (986) 623 954. Contact: Carlos Torres Leyva, Gerencia; or Olga Arenas, Administradora. Replies to correspondence in Spanish.
La Voz del Cinaruco (if reactivated), Calle 19 No. 19-62,

Arauca, Colombia. Contact: Efrahim Valera, Director. Pennants for return postage. Replies rarely to correspondence in Spanish; return postage required.

La Voz del Guaviare, Carrera 22 con Calle 9, San José del Guaviare, Colombia. Phone: +57 (986) 840-153/4. Fax: +57 (986) 840 102. Contact: Luis Fernando Román Robayo, Director General. Replies slowly to correspondence in Spanish.

La Voz del Llano, Calle 41B No. 30-11, Barrio La Grama, Villavicencio, Meta, Colombia; or (postal address in Bogotá) Apartado Aéreo 67751, Santafé de Bogotá, Colombia. Phone: +57 (986) 624-102. Fax: +57 (986) 625 045. Contact: Manuel Buenaventura, Director; Rafael Rodríguez R., or Edgar Valenzuela Romero. Replies occasionally to correspondence in Spanish. $1 or return postage necessary.

La Voz del Río Arauca

STATION: Carrera 20 No. 19-09, Arauca, Colombia. Phone: +57 (818) 52-910. Contact: Jorge Flórez Rojas, Gerente; Luis Alfonso Riaño, Locutor; or Mario Falla, Periodista. $1 or return postage required. Replies occasionally to correspondence in Spanish; persist.

BOGOTÁ OFFICE: Cra. 10 No. 14-56, Of. 309/310, Santafé de Bogotá, D.C., Colombia.

La Voz del Yopal (when active), Calle 9 No. 22-63, Yopal, Casanare, Colombia. Phone: +57 (87) 558-382. Fax: +57 (87) 557 054. Contact: Pedro Antonio Socha Pérez, Gerente; or Marta Cecilia Socha Pérez, Subgerente. Return postage necessary. Replies to correspondence in Spanish.

Ondas del Meta (when active), Calle 41B No. 30-11, Barrio La Grama, Villavicencio, Meta, Colombia. Phone: +57 (986) 626-783. Fax: +57 (986) 625 045. Contact: Yolanda Plazas Agredo, Administradora. Free tourist literature. Return postage required. Replies irregularly and slowly to correspondence in Spanish. Plans to reactivate from a new antenna site.

Ondas del Orteguaza, Calle 16, No. 12-48, piso 2, Florencia, Caquetá, Colombia. Phone: +57 (88) 352-558. Contact: Sandra Liliana Vásquez, Secretaria; Señora Elisa Viuda de Santos; or Henry Valencia Vásquez. Free stickers. IRC, return postage or $1 required. Replies occasionally to correspondence in Spanish.

Radio Auténtica (when operating), Calle 38 No. 32-41, piso 7, Edif. Santander, Villavicencio, Meta, Colombia. Phone: +57 (986) 626-780. Phone/fax: +57 (986) 624 507. Web: (Cadena Radial Auténtica de Colombia parent organization) www.cmb.org.co/cra/. Contact: (general) Pedro Rojas Velásquez; or Carlos Alberto Pimienta, Gerente; (technical) Sra. Alba Nelly González de Rojas, Administradora. Sells religious audio cassettes for 3,000 pesos. Return postage required. Replies slowly to correspondence in Spanish.

Radiodifusora Nacional de Colombia

MAIN ADDRESS: Edificio Inravisión, CAN, Av. Eldorado, Santafé de Bogotá, D.C., Colombia. Phone: +57 (1) 222-0415. Fax: +57 (1) 222 0409 or +57 (1) 222 8000. Email: radio_oc@inravision.com.co; radiodifusora@hotmail.com. Web: (includes online reception report form) www.inravision.com.co/radiodifusora/onda/. Contact: Janeth Jiménez M., Coordinadora de Onda Corta; or Dra. Athala Morris, Directora. Free lapel badges, membership in Listeners' Club and monthly program booklet.

RCN (Radio Cadena Nacional)

MAIN OFFICE: Apartado Aéreo 4984, Santafé de Bogotá, D.C., Colombia. Phone: +57 (1) 314-7070. Fax: +57 (1) 285 0121 or +57 (1) 288 6130. Email: rcn@impsat.net.co. Web: (RealAudio, news and correspondence) www.rcn.com.co. Contact: Antonio Pardo García, Gerente de Producción y Programación. Will verify all correct reports for stations in the RCN network. Spanish preferred and return postage necessary.

Radio Melodía (Cadena Melodía) (when active), Apartado Aéreo 58721, Santafé de Bogotá, D.C., Colombia; or Apartado Aéreo 19823, Santafé de Bogotá, D.C., Colombia. Phone: +57 (1) 217-0423, +57 (1) 217-0720, +57 (1) 217-1334 or +57 (1) 217-1452. Fax: +57 (1) 248 8772. Contact: Gerardo Páez Mejía, Vicepresidente; Elvira Mejía de Pérez, Gerente General; or Gracilla Rodríguez, Asistente Gerencia. Stickers and pennants. $1 or return postage.

Radio Mira (when opeerating), Apartado Aéreo 165, Tumaco, Nariño, Colombia. Phone: +57 (27) 272-452. Contact: Padre Jairo Arturo Ochoa Zea. Return postage required.

Radio Super (Ibagué) (when active), Parque Murillo Toro 3-31, P. 3, Ibagué, Tolima, Colombia. Phone: +57 (982) 611-652 or +57 (982) 637-004. Fax: +57 (82) 611 471. Contact: Fidelina Caycedo Hernández; or Germán Acosta Ramos, Locutor Control. Free stickers. Return postage or $1 helpful. Replies irregularly to correspondence in Spanish.

CONGO (DEMOCRATIC REPUBLIC) (formerly Zaïre) World Time +1 Western, including Kinshasa; +2 Eastern

Radio Bukavu (when active), B.P. 475, Bukavu, Democratic Republic of the Congo. Contact: Jacques Nyembo-Kibeya; Kalume Kavue Katumbi; or Baruti Lusongela, Directeur. $1 or return postage required. Replies slowly. Correspondence in French preferred.

Radio CANDIP Bunia (formerly La Voix du Peuple, and prior to that, Radio CANDIP), B.P. 373, Bunia, Democratic Republic of Congo. Letters should preferably be sent via registered mail. $1 or return postage required. Correspondence in French preferred.

Radio Kisangani (when active), B.P. 1745, Kisangani, Democratic Republic of the Congo. Letters should be sent via registered mail. $1 or 2 IRCs required. Correspondence in French preferred.

Radio Lubumbashi (when active), B.P. 7296, Lubumbashi, Democratic Republic of the Congo. Contact: Senga Lokavu, Chef du Service de l'Audiovisuel; Bébé Beshelemu, Directeur; or Mulenga Kanso, Chef du Service Logistique. Letters should be sent via registered mail. $1 or 3 IRCs helpful. Correspondence in French preferred.

Radio-Télévision Nationale Congolaise, B.P. 3171, Kinshasa-Gombe, Democratic Republic of the Congo. Contact: Faustin Mbula, Ingenieur Technicien. Letters should be sent via registered mail. $1 or 3 IRCs helpful. Correspondence in French preferred.

CONGO (REPUBLIC) World Time +1

Radiodiffusion Nationale Congolaise (also announces as "Radio Liberté," "Radio Nationale" or "Radio Congo"), Radiodiffusion-Télévision Congolaise, B.P. 2241, Brazzaville, Congo. Contact: (general) Antoine Ngongo, Rédacteur en chef; (administration) Alphonse Bouya-Dimi, Directeur; or Zaou Mouanda. $1 required. Replies irregularly to letters in French sent via registered mail.

COSTA RICA World Time -6

Faro del Caribe—TIFC

MAIN OFFICE: Apartado 2710, 1000 San José, Costa Rica. Phone: +506 (226) 2573 or +506 (226) 2618. Fax: +506 (227)

1725. Email: al@casa-pres.go.cr. Web: www.cristo.net/faro/faro.html. Contact: Carlos A. Rozotto Piedrasanta, Director Administrativo; or Mauricio Ramires; (technical) Minor Enrique, Station Engineer.Free stickers, pennants, books and bibles. $1 or IRCs helpful.

U.S. OFFICE, NONTECHNICAL: Misión Latinoamericana, P.O. Box 620485, Orlando FL 32862 USA.

Radio Casino, Apartado 287, 7301 Puerto Limón, Costa Rica. Phone: +506 758-0029. Fax: +506 758 3029. Contact: Edwin Zamora, Departamento de Notícias; or Luis Grau Villalobos, Gerente; (technical) Ing. Jorge Pardo, Director Técnico; or Geraldo Moya, Técnico.

Radio Exterior de España—Cariari Relay Station, Cariari de Pococí, Costa Rica. Phone: +506 767-7308, +506 767-7311. Fax: +506 225 2938.

Radio For Peace International (RFPI)

MAIN OFFICE: Apartado 88, Santa Ana, Costa Rica. Phone: +506 249-1821. Fax: +506 249 1095. Email: info@rfpi.org; radiopaz@racsa.co.cr; rfpicr@sol.racsa.co.cr. Web: (includes RealAudio) www.rfpi.org. Contact: (general) Debra Latham, General Manager of RFPI, Editor of *VISTA* and co-host of "RFPI Mailbag"; (programming) Joe Bernard, English Program Coordinator; Willie Barrantes, Director, Spanish Department; or Ms. Sabine Kapuschinski, Host of German program; (nontechnical or technical) James Latham, Station Manager. Replies sometimes slow in coming because of the mail. Quarterly *VISTA* newsletter, which includes schedules and program information, $40 annual membership ($50 family/organization) in "Friends of Radio for Peace International"; station commemorative T-shirts and rainforest T-shirts $20; thermo mugs $10 (VISA/MC). Free bumper stickers. Actively solicits listener contributions. Free online verification of email reports, but $1 or 3 IRCs required for verification by QSL card. Limited number of places available for volunteer broadcasting and journalism interns; those interested should send résumé. RFPI was created by United Nations Resolution 35/55 on December 5, 1980.

U.S. OFFICE, NONTECHNICAL: P.O. Box 20728, Portland OR 97294 USA. Phone: +1 (503) 252-3639. Fax: +1 (503) 255 5216. Contact: Dr. Richard Schneider, Chancellor CEO, University of Global Education (formerly World Peace University). Newsletter, T-shirts and so forth, as above. University of the Air courses (such as "Earth Mother Speaks" and "History of the U.N.") $25 each, or on audio cassette $75 each (VISA/MC).

Radio Reloj (when operating), Sistema Radiofónico H.B., Apartado 341, 1000 San José, Costa Rica. Contact: Roger Barahona, Gerente; or Francisco Barahona Gómez. Can be very slow in replying. $1 required.

Radio Universidad de Costa Rica, Apartado 1-06, 2060 Universidad de Costa Rica, San Pedro de Montes de Oca, San José, Costa Rica. Phone: (general) +506 207-4727; (studio) +506 225-3936. Fax: +506 207 5459. Email: radioucr@cariari.ucr.ac.cr. Web: http://cariari.ucr.ac.cr/~radioucr/radioucr/. Contact: Marco González Muñoz; Henry Jones, Locutor de Planta; or Nora Garita B., Directora. Marco González is a radio amateur, call-sign TI3AGM. Free postcards, station brochure and stickers. Replies slowly to correspondence in Spanish or English. $1 or return postage required.

University Network—*see* entry under "USA," later in this section.

CROATIA World Time +1 (+2 midyear)

Croatian Radio-Television (Hrvatska Radio-Televizija, HRT)

MAIN OFFICE: Hrvatska Radio-Televizija (HRT), Prisavlje 3, HR-10000 Zagreb, Croatia. Phone: (operator) +385 (1) 634-3366; (Managing Director) +385 (1) 634-3308; (Technical Director) +385 (1) 634-3663. Fax: (Technical Director) +385 (1) 634 3636. Email: (Managing Director) i.lucev@hrt.hr; (Technical Director) nikola.percin@hrt.hr; (technical, including reception reports) z.klasan@hrt.hr. Web: (includes RealAudio) www.hrt.hr. Contact: (general) Ivanka Lucev, Managing Director; (Technical Director) Nikola Percin.

Voice of Croatia, External Radio Service (Glas Hrvatske)—same address as "Hrvatska Radio," above. Phone: (Editor-in-Chief) +385 (1) 634-2602; (Shortwave Technical Coordinator) +385 (1) 634-3428; (Shortwave Technical Coordinator, mobile) +385 9857-7565. Fax: (Editor-in-Chief) +385 (1) 634 3305; (Shortwave Technical Coordinator) +385 (1) 634 3347. E-mail: (Editor-in-Chief) ivana.jadresic@hrt.hr; (staff) kratki.val@hrt.hr; (Shortwave Technical Coordinator) z.klasan@hrt.hr. Contact: (Editor-in-Chief) Ivana Jadresic; (Shortwave Technical Coordinator, domestic & external) Zelimir Klasan.

Croatian Radio operates two services on world band: the domestic (first) national radio program, transmitted via HRT's Deanovec shortwave station for listeners in Europe and the Mediterranean; and a special service in Croatian, with news segments in English and Spanish for Croatian expatriates, which airs via facilities of Deutsche Telekom (*see*) in Jülich, Germany and is sponsored by the Croatian Heritage Organization. The previous Croatian external broadcasting service known as "Radio Hrvatska" and produced by the Croatian Information Center (Hrvatski Informativni Centar, HIC) was discontinued on October 1st 2000. The external service resumed its transmissions on April 18th 2001 as Glas Hrvatske (Voice of Croatia) under the authority of HRT.

WASHINGTON NEWS BUREAU: Croatian-American Association, 2020 Pennsylvania Avenue NW, Suite 287, Washington DC 20006 USA. Phone: +1 (202) 429-5543. Fax: +1 (202) 429 5545. Email: 73150.3552@compuserve.com. Web: www.hrnet.org/CAA/. Contact: Frank Brozovich, President.

CUBA World Time –5 (–4 midyear)

Radio Habana Cuba, P.O. Box 6240, Habana, Cuba 10600. Phone: (general) +53 (7) 784-954 or +53 (7) 334-272; (English Department) +53 (7) 794-943; (Coro) +53 (7) 814-243 or (home) +53 (7) 301-794. Fax: (general) +53 (7) 783 518; (English Department) +53 (7) 705 810. Email: (general) radiohc@ip.etecsa.cu; (English Service) english@radiohc.cu; (Arnie Coro) arnie@radiohc.org. Web: (includes online reception report form) www.radiohc.cu/home.asp; (includes archived scripts of "DXers Unlimited") www.radiohc.org. Contact: (general) Lourdes López, Head of Correspondence Dept.; Jorge Miyares, English Service; or Mike La Guardia, Senior Editor; (administration) Ms. Milagro Hernández Cuba, General Director; (technical) Arnaldo Coro Antich, ("Arnie Coro"), Producer, "DXers Unlimited"; or Luis Pruna Amer, Director Técnico. Free wallet and wall calendars, pennants, stickers, keychains and pins. DX Listeners' Club. Free sample *Granma International* newspaper. Contests with various prizes, including trips to Cuba.

Radio Rebelde, Departamento de Relaciones Públicas, Apartado 6277, Habana 10600, Cuba; or (street address) Calle 23 No. 258 entre L y M, El Vedado, Habana, Cuba 10600. For technical correspondence (including reception reports), substitute "Servicio de Onda Corta" in place of "Departamento de Relaciones Públicas." Reception reports can also be emailed

626-4562 or +972 (3) 626-4500. Fax: +972 (3) 626 4559. Email: (Oren) moshe_oren@bezeq.co.il; mosheor@bezeq.com. Web: www.bezeq.co.il. Contact: Moshe Oren, Frequency Manager. Bezeq is responsible for transmitting the programs of the Israel Broadcasting Authority (IBA), which *inter alia* parents Kol Israel. This address only for pointing out transmitter-related problems (interference, modulation quality, network mixups, etc.), especially by fax, of transmitters based in Israel. Verifications not given out at this office; requests for verification should be sent to the English Department of Kol Israel (*see* below).

Galei Zahal (Israel Defence Forces Radio), Zahal, Military Mail No. 01005, Israel. Phone: +972 (3) 512-6666. Fax: +972 (3) 512 6760. Email: ofer@glz.co.il. Web: (includes Windows Media) www.glz.co.il. Israeli law allows the Galei Zahal, as well as the Israel Broadcasting Authority, to air broadcasts beamed to outside Israel. Occasionally heard on Kol Israel frequencies when the latter is affected by industrial action; also more regularly on out-of-band channels via unknown transmitters.

Israel Radio International—*see* Kol Israel, below.

Kol Israel (Israel Radio, the Voice of Israel)

STUDIOS: Israel Broadcasting Authority, P.O. Box 1082, Jerusalem 91010, Israel. Phone: (general) +972 (2) 302-222; (Engineering Dept.) +972 (2) 535-051; (administration) +972 (2) 248-715; Hebrew voice mail for Reshet Bet expatriate program) +972 (3) 765-1929. Fax: (English Service) +972 (2) 530 2424; (Engineering Dept.) +972 (2) 388 821; (other) +972 (2) 248 392 or +972 (2) 302 327. Email: (general) ask@israel-info.gov.il; (English Service) englishradio@iba.org.il; (correspondence relating to reception problems, only) engineering@israelradio.org; (Reshet Bet program for Israelis abroad) radio1@iba.org.il. Web: (schedule, RealAudio) www.israelradio.org; (IBA parent organization, including RealAudio in Hebrew and Arabic) www.iba.org.il. Contact: Edmond Sehayeq, Head of Programming, Arabic, Persian and Yemenite broadcasts; Yishai Eldar, Reporter, English News Department; Steve Linde, Head of English News Department; or Sara Gabbai, Head of Western Broadcasting Department; (administration) Shmuel Ben-Zvi, Director; (technical, frequency management) Raphael Kochanowski, Director of Liaison and Coordination, Engineering Dept. Various political, religious, tourist, immigration and language publications. IRC required for reply. Announces in English as "Israel Radio International" but continues to refer to itself as "Kol Israel" in other languages, such as French and Spanish.

SAN FRANCISCO OFFICE, SCHEDULES: 2654 17th Avenue, San Francisco CA 94116 USA. Phone: +1 (415) 564-9968. Email: GPoppin@aol.com. Contact: George Poppin. This address, a volunteer office, only provides Kol Israel schedules. All other correspondence should be sent directly to the main office in Jerusalem.

ITALY World Time +1 (+2 midyear)

Adventist World Radio, AWR-Europe, Casella Postale 383, I-47100 Forlì, Italy. Phone: +39 (0543) 766-655. Fax: +39 (0543) 768 198. Email: english@awr.org. Web: www.awr.org. Contact: Erika Gysin, Listener Mail Services; (technical) Brook Powers, Chief Engineer. Listener mail in English should be sent to: Adventist World Radio, 39 Brendon Street, London W1H 5HD, United Kingdom; correspondence in continental European languages should go to the Forlì address, above. Free religious printed matter, stickers and program schedules. Return postage, IRCs or $1 appreciated. Airs "Radio Magazine," a DX program produced by Dario Villani. AWR has a license to operate the station at Forlì, as well as a new facility soon to be built near Argenta. Also, *see* AWR listings under Germany, Guam, Guatemala, Kenya, Madagascar, United Kingdom and USA.

EDXC officials Luigi Cobisi and Paolo Morandotti.

A. Mujunen

Italian Radio Relay Service, IRRS-Shortwave, Nexus-IBA, C.P. 10980, 20100 Milano, Italy; or alternatively, to expedite cassette deliveries only: NEXUS-IBA, Attn. Anna Boschetti, P.O. Box 11028, I-20110 Milano, Italy. Phone: +39 (02) 266-6971. Fax: +39 (02) 7063 8151. Email: (general) info@nexus.org; ("Hello There" program, broadcast on special occasions only) ht@nexus.org; (reception reports of test transmissions) reports@nexus.org; (International Public Access Radio, a joint venture of IRRS and WRMI, USA) IPAR@nexus.org; (Alfredo Cotroneo) aec@nexus.org; (Ron Norton) ron@nexus.org. Web: (general) www.nexus.org; (RealAudio) www.nexus.org/IRN/index.html; (schedules) www.nexus.org/NEXUS-IBA/Schedules; (International Public Access Radio) www.nexus.org/IPAR; (Internet Services) www.nexus.org/NEXUS-IBA/Services/index-english.html. Contact: (general) Ms. Anna S. Boschetti, Verification Manager; Alfredo E. Cotroneo, President and Producer of "Hello There"; (technical) Ron Norton. Due to recent funding cuts, this station cannot assure a reply to all listener's mail. Email correspondence and reception reports by email are answered promptly and at no charge. A number of booklets and sometimes stickers and small souvenirs are available for sale, but check their Website for further details. Two IRCs or $1 helpful.

Radio Europe, P.O. Box 12, 20090 Limito di Pioltello, Milan, Italy. Phone: +39 (02) 9210-0246. Fax: +39 (02) 8645 0149. Email: radioeurope@iol.it. Contact: Dario Monferini, Foreign Relations Director; or Alex Bertini, General Manager. Pennants $5 and T-shirts $25. $30 for a lifetime membership to Radio Europe's Listeners' Club. Membership includes T-shirt, poster, stickers, flags, gadgets, and so forth, with a monthly drawing for prizes. Application forms available from station. Sells airtime for $20 per hour. Two IRCs or $1 return postage appreciated.

Radio Maria Network Europe, Spoleto relay (when active), Via Turati 7, 22036 Erba, Italy. Fax: +39 (031) 611 288. Web: www.cta.it/aziende/r_maria/info.htm.

Radio Roma-RAI International (external services)

MAIN OFFICE: External/Foreign Service, Centro RAI, Saxa Rubra, 00188 Rome, Italy; or P.O. Box 320, Correspondence Sector, 00100 Rome, Italy. Phone: +39 (06) 33-17-2360. Fax: +39 (06) 33 17 18 95 or +39 (06) 322 6070. Email: raiinternational@rai.it. Web: (shortwave) www.raiinternational.rai.it/radio/indexoc.htm. Contact: (general) Rosaria Vassallo, Correspondence Sector; or Augusto Milana, Editor-in-Chief, Shortwave Programs in Foreign Languages; Esther Casas, Servicio Español; (administration) Angela Buttiglione, Managing Director; or Gabriella Tambroni, Assistant Director. Free stickers, banners, calendars and *RAI Calling from Rome* magazine. Can provide supplementary materials, including on VHS and CD-ROM, for Italian-language video course, "Viva l' italiano," with an audio equivalent soon to be offered, as well. Is constructing "a new, more powerful and sophisticated shortwave transmitting center" in Tuscany; when this is activated, RAI International plans to expand news, cultural items and music in Italian and various other language services—including Spanish & Portuguese, plus new services in Chinese and Japanese. Responses can be very slow. Pictures of RAI's Shortwave Center at Prato Smeraldo can be found at www.mediasuk.org/rai/.

SHORTWAVE FREQUENCY MONITORING OFFICE: RAI Monitoring Station, Centro di Controllo, Via Mirabellino 1, 20052 Monza (MI), Italy. Phone: +39 (039) 388-389. Phone/fax (ask for fax): +39 (039) 386-222. Email: cqmonza@rai.it. Contact: Signora Giuseppina Moretti, Frequency Management; Lucia Luisa La Franceschina; or Mario Ballabio.

ENGINEERING OFFICE, ROME: Via Teulada 66, 00195 Rome, Italy. Phone: +39 (06) 331-70721. Fax: +39 (06) 331 75142 or +39 (06) 372 3376. Email: isola@rai.it. Contact: Clara Isola.

ENGINEERING OFFICE, TURIN: Via Cernaia 33, 10121 Turin, Italy. Phone: +39 (011) 810-2293. Fax: +39 (011) 575 9610. Email: allamano@rai.it. Contact: Giuseppe Allamano.

NEW YORK OFFICE, NONTECHNICAL: 1350 Avenue of the Americas—21st floor, New York NY 10019 USA. Phone: +1 (212) 468-2500. Fax: +1 (212) 765 1956. Contact: Umberto Bonetti, Deputy Director of Radio Division. RAI caps, aprons and tote bags for sale at Boutique RAI, c/o the aforementioned New York address.

SAN FRANCISCO OFFICE, SCHEDULES: 2654 17th Avenue, San Francisco CA 94116 USA. Phone: +1 (415) 564-9968. Email: GPoppin@aol.com. Contact: George Poppin. This address, a volunteer office, only provides RAI schedules to listeners. All other correspondence should be sent directly to the main office in Rome.

Radio Speranza, Modena (when operating), Largo San Giorgio 91, 41100 Modena, Italy. Phone/fax: +39 (059) 230-373. Email: radiosperanza@radiosperanza.it. Web: www.radiosperanza.com. Contact: Padre Luigi Cordioli, Missionario Redentorista. Free Italian-language newsletter. Replies enthusiastically to correspondence in Italian. Return postage appreciated.

RTV Italiana-RAI (domestic services)

CALTANISSETTA: Radio Uno, Via Cerda 19, 90139 Palermo, Sicily, Italy. Contact: Gestione Risorse, Transmission Quality Control. $1 required.

ROME: Centro RAI, Saxa Rubra, 00188 Rome, Italy. Fax: +39 (06) 322 6070. Email: grr@rai.it. Web: www.rai.it.

Tele Radio Stereo, Roma, Via Bitossi 18, 00136 Roma, Italy. Fax: + 39 (06) 353 48300.

JAPAN World Time +9

NHK Fukuoka, 1-1-10 Ropponmatsu, Chuo-ku, Fukuoka-shi, Fukuoka 810-77, Japan.

NHK Osaka, 3-43 Bamba-cho, Chuo-ku, Osaka 540-01, Japan. Fax: +81 (6) 6941 0612. Contact: (technical) Technical Bureau. IRC or $1 helpful.

NHK Sapporo, 1-1-1 Ohdori Nishi, Chuo-ku, Sapporo 060-8703, Japan. Fax: +81 (11) 232 5951. Sometimes sends postcards, stickers or other small souvenirs.

NHK Tokyo/Shobu-Kuki, 3047-1 Oaza-Sanga, Shobu-cho, Minamisaitama-gun, Saitama 346-0104, Japan. Fax: +81 (3) 3481 4985 or +81 (480) 85 1508. IRC or $1 helpful. Replies occasionally. Letters should be sent via registered mail.

Radio Japan/NHK World (external service)

MAIN OFFICE: NHK World, Nippon Hoso Kyokai, Tokyo 150-8001, Japan. Phone: +81 (3) 3465-1111. Fax: (general) +81 (3) 3481 1350; ("Hello from Tokyo" and Production Center) +81 (3) 3465 0966. Email: (general) info@intl.nhk.or.jp; ("Hello from Tokyo" program) hello@intl.nhk.or.jp. Web: includes RealAudio) www.nhk.or.jp/rjnet/. Contact: (administration) Isao Kitamoto, Deputy Director General; Hisashi Okawa, Senior Director International Planning; (general) Yoshiki Fushimi; H. Kawamoto, English Service; Ms. Hirotani Kyoko, Programming Division; or K. Terasaka, Programming Division.

ENGINEERING ADMINISTRATION DEPARTMENT: Nippon Hoso Kyokai, Tokyo 150-8001, Japan. Phone: +81 (3) 5455-5395 or +81 (3) 5455-2288. Fax: +81 (3) 3485 0952. E-mail: yoshimi@eng.nhk.or.jp or kurasima@eng.nhk.or.jp. Contact: Tetsuya Itsuk or Toshiki Kurashima.

MONITORING SECTION: NHK World/Radio Japan. Fax: +81 (3) 3481 1877.

HONG KONG OFFICE: Phone: +852 2577-5999.

LONDON OFFICE: Phone: +44 (20) 7334-0909.

LOS ANGELES OFFICE: Phone: +1 (310) 816-0300.

NEW YORK OFFICE: Phone: +1 (212) 755-3907.

SINGAPORE OFFICE: Phone: + 65 225-0667.

Radio Tampa/NSB

MAIN OFFICE: Nihon Shortwave Broadcasting, 9-15 Akasaka 1-chome, Minato-ku, Tokyo 107-8373, Japan. Fax: +81 (3) 3583

9062. Email: web@tampa.co.jp. Web: (in Japanese only) www.tampa.co.jp. Contact: H. Nagao, Public Relations; M. Teshima; Ms. Terumi Onoda; or H. Ono. Sending a reception report may help with a reply. Free stickers and Japanese stamps. $1 or 2 IRCs helpful.

NEW YORK NEWS BUREAU: 1325 Avenue of the Americas #2403, New York NY 10019 USA. Fax: +1 (212) 261 6449. Contact: Noboru Fukui, reporter.

JORDAN World Time +2 (+3 midyear)

Radio Jordan, P.O. Box 909, Amman, Jordan; or P.O. Box 1041, Amman, Jordan. Phone: (general) +962 (6) 477-4111; (International Relations) +962 (6) 477-8578; (English Service) +962 (6) 475-7410 or +962 (6) 477-3111; (Arabic Service) +962 (6) 463-6454; (Saleh) +962 (6) 474-8048; (Al-Areeny) +962 (6) 420-7845 or +962 (6) 475-7404. Fax: (general) +962 (6) 478 8115; (English Service) +962 (6) 420 7862. Email: (general) general@jrtv.gov.jo; (programs) rj@jrtv.gov.jo; (schedule) feedback@jrtv.gov.jo; (technical) eng@jrtv.gov.jo. Web: www.jrtv.com/radio.htm. Contact: (general) Jawad Zada, Director of Foreign Service; Mrs. Firyal Zamakhshari, Director of Arabic Programs; or Qasral Mushatta; (administrative) Hashem Khresat, Director of Radio; Mrs. Fatima Massri, Director of International Relations; or Muwaffaq al-Rahayifah, Director of Shortwave Services; (technical) Fawzi Saleh, Director of Engineering; or Yousef Al-Areeny, Director of Radio Engineering. Free stickers. Replies irregularly and slowly. Enclosing $1 helps.

KENYA World Time +3

Adventist World Radio, AWR Africa, P.O. Box 42276, Nairobi, Kenya. Phone: +254 (2) 573-277. Fax: +254 (2) 568 433. Web: www.awr.org. Contact: (general) Samuel Misiani, Regional Director. Free home Bible study guides, program schedule and other small items. Return postage (IRCs or 1$) appreciated. This office will sometimes verify reception reports direct, but replies are slow. Also, *see* AWR listings under Germany, Guam, Guatemala, Italy, Madagascar, United Kingdom and USA.

Kenya Broadcasting Corporation, P.O. Box 30456, Harry Thuku Road, Nairobi, Kenya. Phone: +254 (2) 334-567. Fax: +254 (2) 220 675. Email: (general) kbc@swiftkenya.com; (management) mdkbc@swiftkenya.com; (technical services) kbctechnical@swiftkenya.com. Web: (general) www.kbc.co.ke; (RealAudio) www.africaonline.co.ke/AfricaOnline/netradio.html. Contact: (general) Henry Makokha, Liaison Office; (administration) Joe Matano Khamisi, Managing Director; (technical) Nathan Lamu, Senior Principal Technical Officer; Augustine Kenyanjier Gochui; Lawrence Holnati, Engineering Division; or Daniel Githua, Assistant Manager Technical Services (Radio). IRC required. Replies irregularly. If all you want is verfication of your reception report(s), you may have better luck sending your letter to: Engineer in Charge, Maralal Radio Station, P.O. Box 38, Maralal, Kenya.

KIRIBATI World Time +12

Radio Kiribati (if reactivated), P.O. Box 78, Bairiki, Tarawa, Republic of Kiribati. Phone: +686 21187. Fax: +686 21096. Email: bpa@tskl.net.ki. Contact: (general) Atiota Bauro, Programme Organiser; Mrs. Otiri Laboia; Batiri Bataua, News Editor; or Moia Tetoa, Radio Manager; (technical) Tooto Kabwebwenibeia, Broadcast Engineer; Martin Ouma Ojwach, Senior Superintendent of Electronics; or T. Fakaofo, Technical Staff. Cassettes of local songs available for purchase. $1 or return postage required for a reply (IRCs not accepted). Currently off air due to transmitter problems. Has no immediate plans to repair the transmitter as the Chief Engineer is on long term sick leave.

KOREA (DPR) World Time +9

Radio Pyongyang, External Service, Korean Central Broadcasting Station, Pyongyang, Democratic People's Republic of Korea (*not* "North Korea"). Phone and fax numbers valid only in those countries with direct telephone service to North Korea. Free book for German speakers to learn Korean, sundry other publications, pennants, calendars, newspapers, artistic prints and pins. Do not include dutiable items in your envelope. Replies are irregular, as mail from countries not having diplomatic relations with North Korea is sent via circuitous routes and apparently does not always arrive. Indeed, some PASSPORT readers continue to report that mail to Radio Pyongyang in North Korea results in their receiving anti-communist literature from *South* Korea, which indicates that mail interdiction has not ceased. One way around the problem is to add "VIA BEIJING, CHINA" to the address, but replies via this route tend to be slow in coming. Another gambit is to send your correspondence to an associate in a country—such as China, Ukraine or India—having reasonable relations with North Korea, and ask that it be forwarded. If you don't know anyone in these countries, try using the good offices of the following person: Willi Passman, Oberhausener Str. 100, D-45476, Mülheim, Germany. Send correspondence in a sealed envelope without any address on the back. That should be sent inside another envelope. Include 2 IRCs to cover the cost of forwarding.

Regional Korean Central Broadcasting Stations—Not known to reply, but a long-shot possibility is to try corresponding in Korean to: Korean Central Broadcasting Station, Ministry of Posts and Telecommunications, Chongsung-dong (Moranbong), Pyongyang, Democratic People's Republic of Korea. Fax: +850 (2) 812 301 (valid only in those countries with direct telephone service to North Korea). Contact: Chong Ha-chol, Chairman, Radio and Television Broadcasting Committee.

KOREA (REPUBLIC) World Time +9

Korean Broadcasting System (KBS), 18 Yoido-dong, Youngdeungpo-gu, Seoul, Republic of Korea 150-790. Phone: +82 (2) 781-1000. Fax: +82 (2) 781 1698, +82 (2) 781 2399. Email: pr@kbs.co.kr. Web: (includes Windows Media) www.kbs.co.kr.

Radio Korea International

MAIN OFFICE: Overseas Service, Korean Broadcasting System, 18 Yoido-dong, Youngdeungpo-gu, Seoul, Republic of Korea 150-790. Phone: (general) +82 (2) 781-3650/60/70; (English Service) +82 (2) 781-3674/5/6; (German Service) +82 (2) 781-3682/3/9; (Japanese Service) +82 (2) 781-3674/5/6 (Spanish Service) +82 (2) 781-3679/81/97. Fax: +82 (2) 781 3694/5/6. Email: (general) rki@kbs.co.kr; (English) english@kbs.co.kr; (German) german@kbs.co.kr; (Japanese) rkijp@kbs.co.kr; (Spanish) spanish@kbs.co.kr. Web: (includes Windows Media) www.rki.kbs.co.kr. Contact: Cho Won-Suk, Executive Director; Ms. Shin Joo-Ok, Director Division 1; or Ms. Han Hee-Joo, Director Division 2, and is also the Producer/Co-Host of "*Multiwave Feedback*" show. QSLs, time/frequency schedule, station stickers, calendars, *Let's Learn Korean* book and a wide

variety of other small souvenirs. *History of Korea* is available on CD-ROM (upon request) and via the station's Website.
"EDXP NEWS REPORTS": Web: www.members.tripod.com/-bpadula/edxp.html. Special news reports concentrating on shortwave broadcasts to and from Asia, the Far East, Australia, the Pacific and the Indian sub-continent, compiled by EDXP and aired once a week on a Sunday (UTC) during the Radio Korea International *"Multiwave Feedback"* program in English. Special EDXP QSLs will be offered for the shortwave releases (not for RealAudio). Reports of the EDXP feature should be sent to: Bob Padula, EDXP QSL Service, 404 Mont Albert Road, Surrey Hills, Victoria 3127, Australia. Return postage appreciated. Outside of Australia, 1 IRC or $1; within Australia, four 45c Australian stamps. Email reports welcome at edxp@bigpond.com, and verified with Web-delivered animated QSLs.

KUWAIT World Time +3

Ministry of Information, P.O. Box 193, 13002 Safat, Kuwait. Phone: +965 241-5301. Fax: +965 243 4511. Web: www.moinfo.gov.kw. Contact: Sheik Nasir Al-Sabah, Minister of Information.
FREQUENCY SECTION: Ministry of Information, P.O. Box 967 13010 Safat, Kuwait. Phone: +965 243-6193 or +965 241-7830. Fax: +965 241 5498. Contact: Ms. Wesam Najaf, Head of Frequency Section; or Ahmad Alawdhi, Communication Engineer.
Radio Kuwait, P.O. Box 397, 13004 Safat, Kuwait; (technical) Department of Frequency Management, P.O. Box 967, 13010 Safat, Kuwait. Phone: (general) +965 242-3774; (technical) +965 241-0301, +965 242-1422. Fax: (general) +965 245 6660; (technical) +965 241 5946. Email: (technical, including reception reports) kwtfreq@hotmail.com; (frequency matters) kwtfreq@ncc.moc.kw; (general) radiokuwait@radiokuwait.org or info@moinfo.gov.kw. Web: (technical) www.moinfo.gov.kw/ENG/FREQ/; (RealAudio) www.radiokuwait.org. Contact: (general) Manager, External Service; (technical) Nasser M. Al-Saffar, Frequency Manager; or Wessam Najaf. Sometimes gives away stickers, calendars, pens or key chains.

KYRGYZSTAN World Time +5 (+6 midyear)

Kyrgyz Radio, Kyrgyz TV and Radio Center, 59 Jash Gvardiya Boulevard, 720300 Bishkek, Kyrgyzstan. Phone: (general) +996 (312) 253-404 or +996 (312) 255-741; (Director) +996 (312) 255-700 or +996 (312) 255-709; (Assemov) +996 (312) 650-7341 or +996 (312) 255-703; (Atakanova) +996 (312) 251-927; (technical) +996 (312) 257-771. Fax: +996 (312) 257 952. Note that from a few countries, the dialing code is still the old +7 (3312). Email: trk@kyrnet.kg. Contact: (administration) Mrs. Baima J. Sutenova, Vice-Chairman - Kyrgyz Radio; or Eraly Ayilchiyev, Director; (general) Talant Assemov, Editor - Kyrgyz/Russian/German news; Gulnara Abdulaeva, Announcer - Kyrgyz/Russian/German news; Nargis Atakanova, Announcer - English news; (technical) Mirbek Uursabekov, Technical Director. Kyrgyz and Russian preferred, but correspondence in English and German can also be processed. For quick processing of reception reports, use email in German to Talant Assemov. Reports are regularly verified and verifications are usually signed by Mrs. Sutenova.
TRANSMISSION FACILITIES: Ministry of Transport and Communications, 42 Issanova Street, 720000 Bishkek, Kyrgyzstan. Phone: +996 (312) 216-672. Fax: +996 (312) 213 667. Contact: Jantoro Satybaldiyev, Minister. The shortwave transmitting station is located at Krasny-Retcha (Red River), a military encampment in the Issk-Ata region, about 40 km south of Bishkek.

LAOS World Time +7

Lao National Radio, Luang Prabang (when active), Luang Prabang, Laos; or B.P. 310, Vientiane, Laos. Return postage required (IRCs not accepted). Replies slowly and very rarely. Best bet is to write in Laotian or French directly to Luang Prabang, where the transmitter is located.
Lao National Radio, Vientiane, Laotian National Radio and Television, B.P. 310, Vientiane, Laos. Phone: +856 (21) 212-429. Fax: +856 (21) 212 430. Contact: Khoun Sounantha, Manager-in-Charge; Bounthan Inthasai, Director General; Mrs. Vinachine, English/French Sections; Ms. Mativarn Simanithone, Deputy Head, English Section; or Miss Chanthery Vichitsavanh, Announcer, English Section who says, "It would be good if you send your letter unregistered, because I find it difficult to get all letters by myself at the post. Please use my name, and 'Lao National Radio, P.O. Box 310, Vientiane, Laos P.D.R.' It will go directly to me." Sometimes includes a program schedule and Laotian stamps when replying. The external service of this station is currently off shortwave.

LEBANON World Time +2 (+3 midyear)

Voice of Charity, Rue Fouad Chéhab, B.P. 850, Jounieh, Lebanon. Phone: +961 (9) 914-901 or +961 (9) 918-090. Email: radiocharity@opuslibani.org.lb. Web: (includes RealAudio) www.radiocharity.org.lb/. Contact: Frère Elie Nakhoul, Managing Director. Program aired via facilities of Vatican Radio from a station founded by the Order of the Lebanese Missionaries. Basically, a Lebanese Christian educational radio program. Replies to correspondence in English, French and Arabic, and verifies reception reports.
Voice of Lebanon (if reactivated), P.O. Box 165271, Al-Ashrafiyah, Beirut, Lebanon; or (street address) Radio Voice of Lebanon Bldg., Bachir Gémayel Avenue, Beirut, Lebanon. Phone: +961 (1) 201-380 or +961 (1) 323-458. Fax: +961 (1) 219 290. Email: vdl@cyberia.net.lb. Web: (includes RealAudio) www.vdl.com.lb. Contact: Sheik Simon El-Khazen, General Manager. $1 required. Replies occasionally to correspondence in French or Arabic. Operated by the Phalangist organization.

LESOTHO World Time +2

Radio Lesotho, P.O. Box 552, Maseru 100, Lesotho. Phone: +266 323-371 or +266 323-561. Fax: +266 323 003. Web: www.lesotho.gov.ls/radio/Radiolesotho/. Contact: (general) Mamonyane Matsaba, Acting Programming Director; or Sekhonyana Motlohi, Producer, "What Do Listeners Say?"; (administration) Ms. Mpine Tente, Principal Secretary, Ministry of Information and Broadcasting; (technical) Lebohang Monnapula, Chief Engineer; Basia Maraisane, Transmitter Engineer; or Motlatsi Monyane, Studio Engineer. Return postage necessary.

LIBERIA World Time exactly

NOTE: Mail sent to Liberia may be returned as undeliverable.
ELBC (if reactivated), Liberian Broadcasting System, P.O. Box 10-594, 1000 Monrovia 10, Liberia. Phone: +231 224-984 or +231 222-758.

Radio ELWA, c/o SIM Liberia, 08 B.P. 886, Abidjan 08, Côte d'Ivoire. Contact: Moses T. Nyantee, Station Manager; or Chief Technician.

Radio Liberia International, Liberian Communications Network/KISS, P.O. Box 1103, 1000 Monrovia 10, Liberia. Phone: +231 226-963 or +231 227-593. Fax: (during working hours) +231 226 003. Contact: Issac P. Davis, Engineer-in-Charge/ QSL Coordinator. $5 required for QSL card.

Radio Veritas (if reactivated), P.O. Box 3569, Monrovia, Liberia. Phone: +231 226-979. Contact: Steve Kenneh, Manager.

LIBYA World Time +1 (+2 midyear)

Libyan Jamahiriyah Broadcasting (frequency management only), Box 333, Soug al Jama, Tripoli, Libya. Phone: +218 (21) 361-4508. Fax: +218 (21) 489 4240. Contact: Youssef Moujrab; Salah Zayani; or Abdessalem Zaglem.

Voice of Africa, P.O. Box 4677, Tripoli, Libya. Phone: +218 (21) 444-0112, +218 (21) 444-9106 or +218 (21) 444-9872. Fax: +218 (21) 444 9875. Email: africanvoice@hotmail.com. The external service of Libyan Jamahiriyah Broadcasting, it identifies as "Voice of Africa" in its English and French programs, while in Arabic it may use the same identification as for the domestic service or refer to itself as the "Voice of Libya." Replies slowly and irregularly.

MALTA OFFICE: P.O. Box 17, Hamrun, Malta. Replies tend to be more forthcoming from this address than direct from Libya.

LITHUANIA World Time +2

Lietuvos Radijo ir Televizijos Centras (LRTC), Sausio 13-osios 10, LT-2044 Vilnius, Lithuania. Phone: +370 (2) 459-397. Fax: +370 (2) 706 919. Email: info@lrtc.lt. Web: www.lrtc.net; www.lrtc.lt. Contact: A. Vydmontas, Director General. This organization operates the transmitters used by Lithuanian Radio.

Lithuanian Radio

STATION: Lietuvos Radijas, S. Konarskio 49, LT-2674 Vilnius MTP, Lithuania. Phone: +370 (2) 333-182. Fax: (general) +370 (2) 263 282; (Technical Director) +370 (2) 232 465. Email: format is initiallastname@rtv.lrtv.ot.lt, so to contact, say, Juozas Algirdas Vilciauskas, it would be jvilciauskas@rtv.lrtv.ot.lt; (reception reports) peles@lrtc.lt. Web: (includes RealAudio) www.lrtv.lt/lt_lr.htm. Contact: (general) Mrs. Kazimiera Mazgeliene, Programme Director; or Guoda Litvaitiene, International Relations; (technical) Mr. Petras Leskevicius; or Juozas Algirdas Vilciauskas, Technical Director.

ADMINISTRATION: Lietuvos Nacionalinis Radijas ir Televizija (LNRT), Konarskio 49, LT-2674 Vilnius MTP, Lithuania. Phone: (general) +370 (2) 263-383; (Director General) +370 (2) 263-292. Fax: +370 (2) 263 282. Web: www.lrtv.lt/lt_lrtv.htm. Contact: Juraté Lauciuté, Acting Director General.

STATE RADIO FREQUENCY SERVICE: Algirdo str. 27, LT-2006 Vilnius, Lithuania. Phone: +370 (2) 231-550; or +370 (2) 261-177. Fax: +370 (2) 261 564. Email: (Medeisis) medeisis@radio.lt; (Norkunas) enorkuna@radio.lt; (Cesna) acesna@radio.lt. Contact: Arturas Medeisis, Head of Division of Strategic Planning; Augutis Cesna, Deputy Head of EMC Division; or Eugenijus Norkunas, Director.

Radio Vilnius, Lietuvos Radijas, Konarskio 49, LT-2674 Vilnius, Lithuania. Phone: (voicemail) +370 (90) 71297. Fax: +370 (2) 233 526. Email: ravil@rtv.lrtv.ot.lt. Web: (includes RealAudio) *see* Lithuanian Radio, above. Contact: Ms. Rasa Lukaite, "Letterbox"; Audrius Braukyla, Editor-in-Chief; or Ilonia Rukiene, Head of English Department. Free stickers, pennants, Lithuanian stamps and other souvenirs.

MADAGASCAR World Time +3

Adventist World Radio

ADMINISTRATION: B.P. 700, Antananarivo, Madagascar. Phone: +261 (2022) 404-65.

STUDIO: B.P. 460, Antananarivo, Madagascar.

TECHNICAL AND NON-TECHNICAL (e.g. comments on programs)—see USA and Italy. AWR Broadcasts in Malagasy and French on leased airtime from Radio Nederland's Madagascar Relay. Reception reports concerning these broadcasts are best sent to the AWR Italian office. Also, *see* AWR listings under Germany, Guam, Guatemala, Italy, Kenya, United Kingdom and USA.

Radio Madagasikara, B.P. 442, Antananarivo 101, Madagascar. Email: radmad@dts.mg. Web: http://takelaka.dts.mg/radmad/. Contact: Mlle. Rakotonirina Soa Herimanitia, Secrétaire de Direction, a young lady who collects stamps; Mamy Rafenomanantsoa, Directeur; or J.J. Rakotonirina, who has been known to request hi-fi catalogs. $1 required, and enclosing used stamps from various countries may help. Tape recordings accepted. Replies slowly and somewhat irregularly, usually to correspondence in French.

Radio Nederland Wereldomroep—Madagascar Relay, B.P. 404, Antananarivo, Madagascar. Contact: (technical) Rahamefy Eddy, Technische Dienst; or J.A. Ratobimiarana, Chief Engineer. Nontechnical correspondence should be sent to Radio Nederland Wereldomreop in Holland (*see*).

MALAWI World Time +2

Malawi Broadcasting Corporation (when operating), P.O. Box 30133, Chichiri, Blantyre 3, Malawi. Phone: +265 671-222. Fax: +265 671 257 or +265 671 353. Email: dgmbc@malawi.net. Contact: (general) Wilson Bankuku, Director General; J.O. Mndeke; or T.J. Sineta; (technical) Edwin K. Lungu, Controller of Transmitters; Phillip Chinseu, Engineering Consultant; or Joseph Chikagwa, Director of Engineering. Currently off air due to lack of transmitter spares. Return postage or $1 helpful, as the station is underfunded.

MALAYSIA World Time +8

Asia-Pacific Broadcasting Union, P.O. Box 1164, 59700 Kuala Lumpur, Malaysia; or (street address) 2nd Floor, Bangunan IPTAR, Angkasapuri, 50614 Kuala Lumpur, Malaysia. Phone: (general) +60 (3) 2282-3592; (Programme Department)+60 (3) 2282-2480; (Technical Department) +60 (3) 2282-3108. Fax: +60 (3) 2282 5292. Email: (Office of Secretary-General) sg@abu.org.my; (Programme Department) prog@abu.org.my; (Technical Department) tech@abu.org.my. Web: www.abu.org.my. Contact: (administration) Hugh Leonard, Secretary-General; (technical) Sharad Sadhu and Rukmin Wijemanne, Senior Engineers, Technical Department.

Radio Malaysia Kota Kinabalu, RTM Sabah, Jalan Tuaran, 2.4 KM, 88614 Kota Kinabalu, Sabah, Malaysia. Phone: +60 (88) 212-086, +60 (88) 213-444. Fax: +60 (88) 223 493. Email: rtmkk@rtm.net.my. Web: www.p.sabah.gov.my/rtm/. Contact: Benedict Janil, Director of Broadcasting; Hasbullah Latiff; or Mrs. Angrick Saguman. Registering your letter may help. $1 or return postage required.

Radio Malaysia, Kuala Lumpur
MAIN OFFICE: RTM, Angkasapuri, Bukit Putra, 50614 Kuala Lumpur, Malaysia. Phone: +60 (3) 2282-5333 or +60 (3) 2282-4976. Fax: +60 (3) 2282 4735, +60 (3) 2282 5103 or +60 (3) 2282 5859. Email: sabariah@rtm.net.my. Web: (general) www.rtm.net.my; (Radio 1, includes Windows Media) www.radio1.com.my. Contact: (general) Madzhi Johari, Director of Radio; (technical) Ms. Aminah Din, Deputy Director Engineering (Radio); Abdullah Bin Shahadan, Engineer, Transmission and Monitoring; or Ong Poh, Chief Engineer. May sell T-shirts and key chains. Return postage required.
TRANSMISSION OFFICE: Controller of Engineering, Department of Broadcasting (RTM), 43000 Kajang, Selangor Darul Ehsan, Malaysia. Phone: +60 (3) 8736-1530, +60 (3) 8736-1863. Fax: +60 (3) 8736 1227. Email: rtmkjg@rtm.net.my. Contact: Jeffrey Looi.

Radio Malaysia Sarawak (Kuching), RTM Sarawak, Jalan Satok, 93614 Kuching, Sarawak, Malaysia. Phone: +60 (82) 248-422. Fax: +60 (82) 241 914. Email: rtmkuc@rtm.net.my. Contact: (general) Yusof Ally, Director of Broadcasting; Mohd. Hulman Abdollah; or Human Resources Development; (technical, but also nontechnical) Colin A. Minoi, Technical Correspondence; (technical) Kho Kwang Khoon, Deputy Director of Engineering. Return postage helpful.

Radio Malaysia Sarawak (Miri), RTM Miri, Bangunan Penyiaran, 98000 Miri, Sarawak, Malaysia. Phone: +60 (85) 423-645. Fax: +60 (85) 411 430. Contact: Clement Stia. $1 or return postage helpful.

Radio Malaysia Sarawak (Sibu), RTM Sibu, Bangunan Penyiaran, 96009 Sibu, Sarawak, Malaysia. Phone: +60 (84) 323-566. Fax: +60 (84) 321 717. Contact: Clement Stia, Divisional Controller, Broadcasting Department. $1 or return postage required. Replies irregularly and slowly.

Voice of Islam—Program of the Voice of Malaysia (*see*, below).

Voice of Malaysia, Suara Malaysia, Wisma Radio Angkasapuri, P.O. Box 11272, 50740 Kuala Lumpur, Malaysia. Phone: (general) +60 (3) 2288-7824; (English Service) +60 (3) 2282-7826. Fax: +60 (3) 2284 7594. Email: vom@rtm.net.my; (technical, Kajang transmitter site) rtmkjg@po.jaring.my. Web: www.rtm.net.my/radio/vom/. Contact: (general) Mrs. Mahani bte Ujang, Supervisor, English Service; Hajjah Wan Chuk Othman, English Service; (administration) Santokh Singh Gill, Director; or Mrs. Adilan bte Omar, Assistant Director; (technical) Lin Chew, Director of Engineering; (Kajang transmitter site) Kok Yoon Yeen, Technical Assistant. Free calendars and stickers. Two IRCs or return postage helpful. Replies slowly and irregularly.

MALDIVES World Time +5

Voice of Maldives (if and when reactivated), Ministry of Information, Arts and Culture, Moonlight Higun, Malé 20-06, Republic of Maldives. Phone: (administration and secretaries) +960 321-642; (Director General) +960 322-577; (Director of Programs) +960 322-746; (Duty Officer) +960 322-841; (programme section) +960 322-842; (studio 1) +960 325-151; (studio 2) +960 323-416; (newsroom) +960 322-253, +960 324-506 or + 960 324-507; (office assistant/budget secretary) +960 320-508; (FM Studio) +960 314-217; (technical, office) +960 322-444 or +960 320-941; (residence) +960 323-211. Fax: +960 328 357 or +960 325 371. Email: informat@dhivehinet.net.mv. Contact: Maizan Ahmed Manik, Director General of Engineering. Long inactive on the world bands, the station is hoping to resume shortwave broadcasts sometime in the future with a newly installed 10 kilowatt transmitter on the island of Mafushi.

MALI World Time exactly

Radiodiffusion Télévision Malienne, B.P. 171, Bamako, Mali. Phone: +223 21-20-19 or +223 21-24-74. Fax: +223 21 42 05. Email: (Traore) cotraore@sotelma.ml. Contact: Karamoko Issiaka Daman, Directeur des Programmes; (administration) Abdoulaye Sidibe, Directeur General; (Technical) Nouhoum Traore. $1 or IRC helpful. Replies slowly and irregularly to correspondence in French. English is accepted.

MALTA World Time +1 (+2 midyear)

Voice of the Mediterranean (Radio Melita), St Francis Ravelin, Floriana VLT 15, Malta; or P.O. Box 143, Valetta CMR 01, Malta. Phone: +356 240-421 or +356 248-080. Fax: +356 241 501. Email: vomradio@vom-malta.org.mt. Web: (includes RealAudio) www.vom-malta.org.mt. Contact: (administration) Dr. Richard Vella Laurenti, Managing Director; (German Service and listener contact) Ingrid Huettmann; Victoria Farrugia. Letters and reception reports welcomed. May send blank QSL cards, stickers and bookmarks.

MAURITANIA World Time exactly

Radio Mauritanie, B.P. 200, Nouakchott, Mauritania. Phone: +222 (2) 52287. Fax: +222 (2) 51264. Email: rm@mauritania.mr. Contact: Madame Amir Feu; Lemrabott Boukhary; Madame Fatimetou Fall Dite Ami, Secretaire de Direction; Mr. El Hadj Diagne; or Mr. Hane Abou. Return postage or $1 required. Rarely replies.

MEXICO World Time -6 (-5 midyear) Central, including D.F.; -7 (-6 midyear) Mountain; -8 (-7 midyear) Pacific

Candela FM—*see* RASA Onda Corta.

La Hora Exacta—XEQK (if reactivated), Real de Mayorazgo 83, Barrio de Xoco, 03330-México 13, D.F., Mexico. Phone: +52 (5) 628-1731, +52 (5) 628-1700 Ext. 1648 or 1659. Fax: +52 (5) 604-8292. Web: www.imer.gob.mx (click on the corresponding icon). Contact: Lic. Santiago Ibarra Ferrer, Gerente.

La Jarocha—XEFT (if reactivated), Apartado Postal 21, 91701-Veracruz, VER, Mexico. Phone: +52 (29) 322-250. Contact: C.P. Miguel Rodríguez Sáez, Sub-Director; or Lic. Juan de Dios Rodríguez Díaz, Director. Free tourist guide to Veracruz. Return postage, IRC or $1 probably helpful. Likely to reply to correspondence in Spanish.

Radio Educación Onda Corta—XEPPM, Apartado Postal 21-940, 04021-México 21, D.F., Mexico. Phone: (general) +52 (5) 559-6169. Phone/Fax: (Director's Office) +52 (5) 575 6566. Email: (general) radioe@conaculta.gob.mx; (Lidia Camacho) lidiac@conaculta.gob.mx. Web: www.cnca.gob.mx/cnca/buena/radio/temas.html; (includes Windows Media) www.radioeducacion.edu.mx. Contact: (general) Lic. María Del Carmen Limón Celorio, Directora de Producción y Planeación; (administration) Lic. Lidia Camacho Camacho, Directora General; (technical) Ing. Jesús Aguilera Jiménez, Subdirector de Desarrollo Técnico. Free stickers, calendars and station photo. Return postage or $1 required. Replies, sometimes slowly, to correspondence in English, Spanish, Italian or French.

Radio Huayacocotla—XEJN

STATION ADDRESS: "Radio Huaya," Dom. Gutiérrez Najera s/n, Apartado Postal 13, 92600-Huayacocotla, VER, Mexico. Phone: +52 (775) 80067. Fax: +52 (775) 80178. E-mail: radiohua@sjsocial.org, or framos@uibero.uia.mx. Web: www.sjsocial.org/Radio/huarad.html. Contact: Martha Silvia Ortiz López, Coordinadora. Return postage or $1 helpful. Replies irregularly to correspondence in Spanish.

Radio México Internacional—XERMX, Instituto Méxicano de la Radio, Apartado Postal 21-300, 04021-México 21, D.F., Mexico. Phone: +52 (5) 604-7846 or +52 (5) 628-1720. Fax: +52 (5) 628 1710. E-mail: rmi@eudoramail.com. Web: www.imer.gob.mx (click on the appropriate icon); http://hello.to/rmi. Contact: Lic. Ana Cristina del Razo Esqueda, Gerente; or Juan Josi Miroz, host "Mailbag Program." Free stickers, post cards and stamps. Sometimes free T-shirts and CDs. Welcomes correspondence, including inquiries about Mexico, in Spanish, English and French. $1 helpful. A bilingual reception report form can be downloaded and printed from the website.

Radio Mil Onda Corta—XEOI, NRM, Avda. Insurgentes Sur 1870, Col. Florida, 01030- México 20 D.F., Mexico; or Apartado Postal 21-1000, 04021-México 21, D.F., Mexico (this address for reception reports and listeners' correspondence on the station's shortwave broadcasts, and mark the envelope to the attention of Dr. Julián Santiago Díez de Bonilla). Phone: (station) +52 (5) 662-1000 or +52 (5) 662-1100; (Núcleo Radio Mil network) +52 (5) 662-6060, +52 (5) 663-0739 or +52 (5) 663 0590. Fax: (station) +52 (5) 662 0974; (Núcleo Radio Mil network) +52 (5) 662 0979. E-mail: info@nrm.com.mx. Web: www.nrm.com.mx/estaciones/radiomil/. Contact: (administration) Edilberto Huesca P., Vicepresidente Ejecutivo del Núcleo Radio Mil; or Lic. Gustavo Alvite Martínez, Director; (shortwave service) Dr. Julián Santiago Díez de Bonilla. Free stickers. $1 or return postage required.

Radio Transcontinental—XERTA (when operating), Plaza de San Juan 5, Primer piso, Despacho 2, Esquina con Ayuntamiento, Centro, 06070-México, D.F., Mexico. Phone: +52 (5) 518-4938. Contact: Roberto Najera Martínez, Presidente de Radio Transcontinental.

Radio Universidad Autónoma de México (UNAM)—XEYU (if reactivated), Adolfo Prieto 133, Colonia del Valle, 03100-México 12, D.F., Mexico. Phone: +52 (5) 523-2633. E-mail: radiounam@www.unam.mx. Web: (includes RealAudio) www.unam.mx/radiounam/. Contact: (general) Lic. Fernando Escalante Sobrino, Directora General de Radio UNAM; (technical) Ing. Gustavo Carreño, Departamento Técnico. Free tourist literature and stickers. $1 or return postage required. Replies irregularly to correspondence in Spanish.

RASA Onda Corta—XEQM (when operating), Apartado Postal 217, 97001-Mérida, YUC, Mexico. Phone: +52 (99) 236-155. Fax: +52 (99) 280 680. Contact: Lic. Bernardo Laris Rodríguez, Director General del Grupo RASA Mérida. Replies irregularly to correspondence in Spanish. Currently relays programs from FM sister station "Candela Tropicaliente," but hopes eventually to produce its own programming based on the best programs of each station in the network.

MOLDOVA World Time +2 (+3 midyear)

Radio Moldova International (if reactivated), Mioriţa str. 1, 277028 Chişinău, MD-2028 Moldova. Phone: +373 (2) 721-792, + (373) (2) 723-369, +373 (2) 723-379 or +373 (2) 723-385. Fax: +373 (2) 723 329 or +373 (2) 723 307. E-mail: rmi.engl@mail.md or rmi@mail.md. Web: (includes Windows Media) www.trm.md/radio/. Because of a severely reduced budget, the station suspended its world band broadcasts in September 2000, and thereafter has only been audible via its Website. Even there, the broadcasts are restricted to five days per week.

MONACO World Time +1 (+2 midyear)

Trans World Radio

STATION: B.P. 349, MC-98007 Monte-Carlo, Monaco-Cedex. Phone: +377 (92) 16-56-00. Fax: +377 (92) 16 56 01. Web: (transmission schedule) www.gospelcom.net/twr/broadcasts/europe.htm. Contact: (general) Mrs. Jeanne Olson; (administration) Richard Olson, Station Manager; (Technical) *see VIENNA OFFICE, TECHNICAL: see* Vienna address, below. Free paper pennant. IRC or $1 helpful. Also, *see* USA.

GERMAN OFFICE: Evangeliums-Rundfunk, Postfach 1444, D-35573 Wetzlar, Germany. Phone: +49 (6441) 957-0. Fax: +49 (6441) 957-120. Email: erf@erf.de; or siemens@arf.de. Web: (includes RealAudio) www.erf.de. Contact: Jürgen Werth, Direktor.

HOLLAND OFFICE, NONTECHNICAL: Postbus 176, NL-3780 BD Voorthuizen, Holland. Phone: +31 (0) 34-29-27-27. Fax: +31 (0) 34 29 67 27. Contact: Beate Kiebel, Manager Broadcast Department; or Felix Widmer.

VIENNA OFFICE, TECHNICAL: Postfach 141, A-1235 Vienna, Austria. Phone: +43 (1) 863-1233 or +43 (1) 863-1247. Fax: +43 (1) 863 1220. Email: (Menzel) 100615.1511@compuserve.com; (Schraut) eurofreq@twr.org; bschraut@twr.org; or 101513.2330@compuserve.com; (Dobos) kdobos@twr-europe.at. Contact: Helmut Menzel, Director of Engineering; Bernhard Schraut, Frequency Manager; Charles K. Roswell; or Kalman Dobos, Frequency Coordinator.

SWISS OFFICE: Evangelium in Radio und Fernsehen, Witzbergstrasse 23, CH-8330 Pfäffikon ZH, Switzerland. Phone: +41 (951) 0500. Fax: +41 (951) 0540. Email: erf@erf.ch. Web: www.erf.ch.

MONGOLIA World Time +8

NOTE: Due to telecommunication network expansion, it is possible that some of the numbers below will no longer work. If you encounter difficulty, try inserting an additional "1" after the country code.

Mongolian Radio (Postal and email addresses same as Voice of Mongolia, *see* below). Phone: (administration) +976 (1) 323-520 or +976 (1) 328-978; (editorial) +976 (1) 329-766; (MRTV parent organization) +976 (1) 326-663. Fax: +976 (1) 327 234. Email: radiomongolia@magicnet.mn. Contact: A. Buidakhmet, Director.

Voice of Mongolia, C.P.O. Box 365, Ulaanbaatar 13, Mongolia. Phone: +976 (1) 321-624 or (English Section) +976 (1) 327-900. Fax: +976 (1) 323 096 or (English Section) +976 (1) 327 234. Email: (general) radiomongolia@magicnet.mn, radio-internet@magicnet.mn, or (International Relations Office) mrtv@magicnet.mn. Web: (includes RealAudio) www.mongol.net/vom/. Contact: (general) Mrs. Narantuya, Chief of Foreign Service; D. Batbayar, Mail Editor, English Department; N. Tuya, Head of English Department; Dr. Mark Ostrowski, Consultant, MRTV International Relations Department; or Ms. Tsegmid Burmaa, Japanese Department; (administration) Ch. Surenjav, Director; (technical) Ing. Ganhuu, Chief of Technical Department. Correpondence should be directed to the relevant language section and 2 IRCs or 1$ appreciated. Sometimes very slow in replying. Accepts taped reception reports, preferably containing five-minute excerpts of the broadcast(s) reported, but cassettes cannot be returned. Free pennants, postcards, newspapers and Mongolian stamps.

MOROCCO World Time exactly

Radio Medi Un

MAIN OFFICE: B.P. 2055, Tanger, Morocco (physical location: 3, rue Emsallah, 90000 Tanger, Morocco). Phone/fax: +212 (9) 936-363 or +212 (9) 935-755. Email: (general) medi1@medi1.com; (technical) technique@medi1.com. Web: (includes RealAudio) www.medi1.com; www.medi1.co.ma. Contact: J. Dryk, Responsable Haute Fréquence. Two IRCs helpful. Free stickers. Correspondence in French preferred.

PARIS BUREAU, NONTECHNICAL: 78 Avenue Raymond Poincaré, F-75016 Paris, France. Phone: +33 (1) 45-01-53-30. Correspondence in French preferred.

Radio Mediterranée Internationale—*see* Radio Medi Un.

Radiodiffusion-Télévision Marocaine, 1 rue El Brihi, Rabat, Morocco. Phone: +212 (7) 766-881/83/85, +212 (7) 701-740; or +212 (7) 201-404. Fax: +212 (7) 722 047, or +212 (7) 703 208. Email: rtm@rtm.gov.ma; (technical) hammouda@rtm.gov.ma. Web: (general) www.rtm.gov.ma; (radio) www.rtm.gov.ma/Radiodiffusion/Radiodiffusion.htm; (RealAudio) www.maroc.net/rc/live.htm. Contact: (nontechnical and technical) Ms. Naaman Khadija, Ingénieur d'Etat en Télécommunication; Rahal Sabir; (technical) Tanone Mohammed Jamaledine, Technical Director; Hammouda Mohamed, Engineer; or N. Read. Correspondence welcomed in English, French, Arabic or Berber.

Voice of America/IBB—Morocco Relay Station, Briech. Phone: (office) +212 (9) 93-24-81. Fax: +212 (9) 93 55 71. Contact: Station Manager. These numbers for urgent technical matters only. Otherwise, does not welcome direct correspondence; *see* USA for acceptable VOA and IBB Washington addresses and related information.

MOZAMBIQUE World Time +2

Rádio Moçambique (when operating), Rua da Rádio no. 2, Caixa Postal 2000, Maputo, Mozambique. Phone: +258 (1) 431-679/80. Fax: +258 (1) 421 816. Web: www.teledata.mz/radiomocambique/. Contact: (general) João Baptista de Sousa, Administrador de Produção; Izidine Faquira, Diretor de Programas; Orlanda Mendes, Produtor, "Linha Direta"; (technical) Eng. Eduardo Rufino de Matos, Administrador Técnico; or Daniel Macabi, Diretor Técnico. Free medallions and pens. Cassettes featuring local music $15. Return postage, $1 or 2 IRCs required. Replies to correspondence in Portuguese or English.

MYANMAR (BURMA) World Time +6:30

Radio Myanmar

STATION: GPO Box 1432, Yangon-11181, Myanmar; or Pyay Road, Yangon-11041, Myanmar. Contact: Ko Ko Htway, Director of Radio.

NAGORNO-KARABAGH World Time +3 (+4 midyear)

Voice of Justice, Tigranmetz Street 23a, Stepanakert, Nagorno-Karabagh. Contact: Michael Hajiyan, Station Manager. Replies to correspondence in Armenian, Azeri, Russian and German.

NAMIBIA World Time +2 (+1 midyear)

Radio Namibia/Namibian Broadcasting Corporation, P.O. Box 321, Windhoek 9000, Namibia. Phone: (general) +264 (61) 291-3111; (studio, during "Chat Show" and "Openline") +264 (61) 236-381. Fax: (general) +264 (61) 217 760; (Duwe, technical) +264 (61) 231 881. Web: www.nbc.com.na. Contact: (technical) P. Schachtschneider, Manager, Transmitter Maintenance; Joe Duwe, Chief Technician. Free stickers.

NEPAL World Time +5:45

Radio Nepal, P.O. Box 634, Singha Durbar, Kathmandu, Nepal. Phone: (general) +977 (1) 223-910; (engineering) +977 (1) 225-467. Fax: +977 (1) 221 952. Email: radio@rne.wlink.com.np; (engineering) radio@engg.wlink.com.np. Web: (includes RealAudio in English and Nepali) www.radionepal.com. Contact: (general) S.R. Sharma, Executive Director; M.P. Adhikari, Deputy Executive Director; Jayanti Rajbhandari, Director - Programming; or S.K. Pant, Producer, "Listener's Mail"; (technical) Ram Sharan Kharki, Director - Engineering. 3 IRCs necessary, but station urges that neither mint stamps nor cash be enclosed, as this invites theft by Nepalese postal employees.

NETHERLANDS—*see* Holland

NETHERLANDS ANTILLES World Time –4

Radio Nederland Wereldomroep—Bonaire Relay, P.O. Box 45, Kralendijk, Netherlands Antilles. Contact: Leo Kool, Manager. Nontechnical correspondence should be sent to Radio Nederland Wereldomreop in Holland (*see*).

NEW ZEALAND World Time +13 (+12 midyear)

Radio New Zealand International (Te Reo Irirangi O Aotearoa, O Te Moana-nui-a-kiwa), P.O. Box 123, Wellington, New Zealand. Phone: +64 (4) 474-1437. Fax: +64 (4) 474 1433 or +64 (4) 474 1886. Email: info@rnzi.com. Web: (includes RealAudio and online reception report form) www.rnzi.com. Contact: Florence de Ruiter, Listener Mail; Myra Oh, Producer, "Mailbox"; or Walter Zweifel, News Editor; (administration) Ms. Linden Clark, Manager; (technical) Adrian Sainsbury, Technical Manager. Free stickers, schedule/flyer about station, map of New Zealand and tourist literature available. English/Maori T-shirts for US$20; sweatshirts $40; interesting variety of CDs, as well as music cassettes and spoken programs, in Domestic "Replay Radio" catalog (VISA/MC). Two

IRCs or $2 for QSL card, one IRC for schedule/catalog. Email reports verified by email only.

Radio Reading Service—ZLXA, P.O. Box 360, Levin 5500, New Zealand. Phone: (general) +64 (6) 368-2229; (engineering) +64 (25) 985-360. Fax: +64 (6) 368 7290. Email: (general) nzrpd@xtra.co.nz; (Bell) ABell@radioreading.org; (Little) Alittle@radioreading.org; (Stokoe) BStokoe@radioreading.org. Web: www.radioreading.org. Contact: (general) Ash Bell, Manager/Station Director; (administration) Allen J. Little, Executive President; (technical, including reception reports) Brian Stokoe. Operated by volunteers 24 hours a day, seven days a week. Station is owned by the "New Zealand Radio for the Print Disabled Inc." Free brochure, postcards and stickers. $1, return postage or 3 IRCs appreciated.

NICARAGUA World Time -6

Radio Miskut, Barrio Pancasan, Puerto Cabezas, R.A.A.N., Nicaragua. Phone: +505 (282) 2443. Fax: +505 (267) 3032. Contact: Evaristo Mercado Pérez, Director de Operación y de Programas; or Abigail Zúñiga Fagoth. T-shirts $10, and *Resumen Mensual del Gobierno y Consejo Regional* and *Revista Informativa Detallada de las Gestiones y Logros* $10 per copy. Station has upgraded to a new shortwave transmitter and is currently improving its shortwave antenna. Replies slowly and irregularly to correspondence in English and Spanish. $2 helpful, as is registering your letter.

NIGER World Time +1

La Voix du Sahel, O.R.T.N., B.P. 361, Niamey, Niger. Fax: +227 72 35 48. Contact: (general) Adamou Oumarou; Issaka Mamadou; Zakari Saley; Souley Boubacou; or Mounkaïla Inazadan, Producer, "Inter-Jeunes Variétés"; (administration) Oumar Tiello, Directeur; (technical) Afo Sourou Victor. $1 helpful. Correspondence in French preferred. Correspondence by males with this station may result in requests for certain unusual types of magazines and photographs.

NIGERIA World Time +1

WARNING—MAIL THEFT: For the time being, correspondence from abroad to Nigerian addresses has a relatively high probability of being stolen.

WARNING—CONFIDENCE ARTISTS: For years, now, correspondence with Nigerian stations has sometimes resulted in letters from highly skilled "pen pal" confidence artists. These typically offer to send you large sums of money, if you will provide details of your bank account or similar information (after which they clean out your account). Other scams are disguised as tempting business proposals; or requests for money, free electronic or other products, publications or immigration sponsorship. Persons thus approached should contact their country's diplomatic offices. For example, Americans should contact the Diplomatic Security Section of the Department of State [phone +1 (202) 647-4000], or an American embassy or consulate.

Radio Nigeria—Enugu, P.M.B. 1051, Enugu (Anambra), Phone: +234 (42) 254-137. Fax: +234 (42) 255354. Nigeria. Contact: Louis Nnamuchi, Assistant Director Technical Services. Two IRCs, return postage or $1 required. Replies slowly.

Radio Nigeria—Ibadan, Broadcasting House, P.M.B. 5003, Ibadan, Oyo State, Nigeria. Phone: +234 (22) 241-4093 or +234 (22) 241-4106. Fax: +234 (22) 241 3930. Contact: V.A. Kalejaiye, Technical Services Department; Rev. Olukunle Ajani, Executive Director; Nike Adegoke, Executive Director; or Dare Folarin, Principal Public Affairs Officer. $1 or return postage required. Replies slowly.

Radio Nigeria—Kaduna, P.O. Box 250, Kaduna (Kaduna), Nigeria. Contact: Yusuf Garba, Ahmed Abdullahi, R.B. Jimoh, Assistant Director Technical Service; or Johnson D. Allen. May send sticker celebrating 30 years of broadcasting. $1 or return postage required. Replies slowly.

Radio Nigeria—Lagos, P.M.B. 12504, Ikoyi, Lagos, Nigeria. Phone: +234 (1) 269-0301. Fax: +234 (1) 269 0073. Contact: Willie Egbe, Assistant Director for Programmes; Babatunde Olalekan Raji, Monitoring Unit. Two IRCs or return postage helpful. Replies slowly and irregularly.

Voice of Nigeria, P.M.B. 40003 Falomo Post Office, Ikoyi, Lagos, Nigeria. Phone: +234 (1) 269-3078/3245/3075/. Fax: +234 (1) 269 1944. Contact: (general) Alhaji Lawal Yusuf Saulawa, Director of Programming; Mrs. Stella Bassey, Deputy Director Programmes; Alhaji Mohammed Okorejior, Acting Director News; or Livy Iwok, Editor; (administration) Taiwo Alimi, Director General; Abubakar Jijiwa, Chairman; Frank Iloye, Station Manager; or Dr. Walter Ofonagoro, Minister of Information; (technical) T. Gyang, Director, Department of Transmission Engineering; J.O. Kurunmi, Deputy Director Engineering Services. Replies from station tend to be erratic, but continue to generate unsolicited correspondence from supposed "pen pals" (*see WARNING—CONFIDENCE ARTISTS*, above); faxes, which are much less likely to be intercepted, may be more fruitful. Two IRCs or return postage helpful.

NORTHERN MARIANA ISLANDS World Time +10

Far East Broadcasting Company—Radio Station KFBS Saipan

MAIN OFFICE: FEBC, P.O. Box 209, Saipan, Mariana Islands MP 96950 USA. Phone: (main office) +1 (670) 322-3841. Fax: +1 (670) 322 3060. Email: saipan@febc.org. Web: www.febc.org. Contact: Chris Slabaugh, Field Director; Irene Gabbie, QSL Secretary; Mike Adams; or Robert Springer, Director. Replies sometimes take months. Also, *see* FEBC Radio International, USA.

NORWAY World Time +1 (+2 midyear)

Radio Norway International (Utenlandssendingen)

MAIN OFFICE, NONTECHNICAL: Utenlandssendingen, NRK, N-0340 Oslo, Norway. Phone: (general) + 47 (23) 048-441 or +47 (23) 048-444; (Norwegian-language 24-hour recording of schedule information +47 (23) 048-008 (Americas, Europe, Africa), +47 (23) 048-009 (elsewhere). Fax: (general) +47 (23) 047 134 or +47 (22) 605 719. Email: radionorway@nrk.no. Web: (includes RealAudio) www.nrk.no/radionorway/ (if it doesn't work, try www5 in place of www). Contact: (general) Kirsten Ruud Salomonsen, Head of External Broadcasting; or Grethe Breie, Consultant; (technical) Gundel Krauss Dahl, Head of Radio Projects. Free stickers and flags.

WASHINGTON NEWS BUREAU: Norwegian Broadcasting, 2030 M Street NW, Suite 700, Washington DC 20036 USA. Phone: +1 (202) 785-1481 or +1 (202) 785-1460. Contact: Bjorn Hansen or Gunnar Myklebust.

SINGAPORE NEWS BUREAU: NRK, 325 River Valley Road #01-04, Singapore.

FREQUENCY MANAGEMENT OFFICE: Statens Teleforvaltning, Dept. TF/OMG, Revierstredet 2, P.O. Box 447 Sentrum, N-0104

Oslo, Norway. Phone: +47 (22) 824-889 or +47 (22) 824-878. Fax: +47 (22) 824 891 or +47 (22) 824 790. Email: (Johnsbråthen) erik.johnsbraten@npt.no; (Ohta) ayumu.ohta@npt.no. Contact: Erik Johnsbråthen, Frequency Manager; or Ayumu Ohta.

UKEsenderen, Elgesetergate 1, N-7030 Trondheim, Norway. Email: uka@uka.no. Web: www.uka.ntnu.no. A student station which operates on 7215 kHz for approximately three weeks (mid-October to early November) in odd-numbered years.

OMAN World Time +4

BBC World Service—Eastern Relay Station (BERS), P.O. Box 23, Wilayat Masirah, Post Code 414, Sultanate of Oman. Technical correspondence should be sent to "Senior Transmitter Engineer"; nontechnical goes to the BBC World Service in London (*see* United Kingdom). Construction of a new transmission complex is under way at al-Ashkhara and will eventually replace the current facilities at Masirah, built in 1966.

Radio Sultanate of Oman, Ministry of Information, P.O. Box 600, Muscat, Post Code 113, Sultanate of Oman. Phone: +968 602-494 or +968 603-222. Fax: (general) +968 602 055 or +968 602 831; (technical) +968 604 629; or +968 607 239. Email: (technical) sjnornani@omantel.net.om; or abulukman@hotmail.com. Web: (RealAudio only) www.oman-tv.gov.om/. Contact: (Directorate General of Technical Affairs) Abdallah Bin Saif Al-Nabhani, Acting Chief Engineer; Salim Al-Nomani, Director of Frequency Management; or Ahmed Mohamed Al-Balushi, Head of Studio's Engineering. Replies regularly, and responses are from one to two weeks. $1, return postage or 3 IRCs helpful.

PAKISTAN World Time +5

Azad Kashmir Radio, Muzaffarabad, Azad Kashmir, Pakistan. Contact: (technical) M. Sajjad Ali Siddiqui, Director of Engineering; or Liaquatullah Khan, Engineering Manager. Registered mail helpful. Rarely replies to correspondence.

Pakistan Broadcasting Corporation—same address, fax and contact as "Radio Pakistan," below. Email: cnoradio@isb.comsats.net.pk. Web: (includes RealAudio) www.radio.gov.pk.

Radio Pakistan, P.O. Box 1393, Islamabad 44000, Pakistan. Email: same as for Pakistan Broadcasting Corporation, above. Phone: +92 (51) 921-0689. Fax: +92 (51) 920-1861. Web: www.radio.gov.pk/exter.html. Contact: (technical) Ahmed Nawaz, Senior Broadcast Engineer, Room No. 324, Frequency Management Cell; Syed Abrar Hussain, Controller of Frequency Management; Syed Asmat Ali Shah, Senior Broadcasting Engineer; or Nasirahmad Bajwa, Frequency Management. Free stickers, pennants and *Pakistan Calling* magazine. May also send pocket calendar. Very poor replier. Plans to replace two 50 kW transmitters with 500 kW units if and when funding is forthcoming.

PALAU World Time +9

KHBN—Voice of Hope, P.O. Box 66, Koror, Palau 96940, Pacific Islands. Phone: +680 488-2162. Fax: (main office) +680 488 2163; or (engineering) +680 544 1008. Email: (general) hamadmin@palaunet.com; or (engineering) khbntx@ palaunet.com.Contact: (general) Regina Subris, Station Manager; (technical) Ernie Fontanilla, Engineer. Free stickers and publications. IRC requested. Also, *see* High Adventure Ministries, USA.

PAPUA NEW GUINEA World Time +10

NOTE: Stations are sometimes off the air due to financial or technical problems which can take weeks or months to resolve.

KBBN ("Krai Bilong Baibel Bradkesting Netwok"), P.O. Box 617, Mt. Hagen W.H.P., Papua New Guinea. Email: bwells@daltron.com.pg. Contact: Brad Wells. A bible radio ministry initially broadcasting on FM, but which eventually hopes to add a shortwave transmitter.

National Broadcasting Corporation of Papua New Guinea, P.O. Box 1359, Boroko 111 NCD, Papua New Guinea. Phone: +675 325-5233, + 675 325-5949 or +675 325-6779. Fax: +675 323 0404, +675 325 0796 or +675 325 6296. Email: pom@nbc.com.pg. Web: www.nbc.com.pg. Contact: (general) Renagi R. Lohia, CBE, Managing Director and C.E.O.; or Ephraim Tammy, Director, Radio Services; (technical) Bob Kabewa, Sr. Technical Officer; or F. Maredey, Chief Engineer. Two IRCs or return postage helpful. Replies irregularly.

Radio Bougainville, P.O. Box 35, Buka, North Solomons Province (NSP), Papua New Guinea. Contact: Aloysius Rumina, Provincial Programme Manager; Ms. Christine Talei, Assistant Provincial Manager; or Aloysius Laukai, Senior Programme Officer. Replies irregularly.

Radio Central (when operating), P.O. Box 1359, Boroko, NCD, Papua New Guinea. Contact: Steven Gamini, Station Manager; Lahui Lovai, Provincial Programme Manager; or Amos Langit, Technician. $1, 2 IRCs or return postage helpful. Replies irregularly.

Radio Eastern Highlands (when operating), P.O. Box 311, Goroka, EHP, Papua New Guinea. Contact: Tonko Nonao, Program Manager; Ignas Yanam, Technical Officer; or Kiri Nige, Engineering Division. $1 or return postage required. Replies irregularly.

Radio East New Britain (when operating), P.O. Box 393, Rabaul, ENBP, Papua New Guinea. Contact: Esekia Mael, Station Manager; or Oemas Kumaina, Provincial Program Manager. Return postage required. Replies slowly.

Radio East Sepik, P.O. Box 65, Wewak, E.S.P., Papua New Guinea. Contact: Elias Albert, Assistant Provincial Program Manager; or Luke Umbo, Station Manager.

Radio Enga, P.O. Box 300, Wabag, Enga Province, Papua New Guinea. Phone: +675 547-1213. Contact: (general) John Lyein Kur, Station Manager; or Robert Papuvo, (technical) Gabriel Paiao, Station Technician.

Radio Gulf (when operating), P.O. Box 36, Kerema, Gulf, Papua New Guinea. Contact: Robin Wainetta, Station Manager; or Timothy Akia, Provincial Program Manager.

Radio Madang, P.O. Box 2138, Madang, Papua New Guinea. Phone: +675 852-2415. Fax: +675 852 2360. Contact: (general) Damien Boaging, Senior Programme Officer; Geo Gedabing, Provincial Programme Manager; Peter Charlie Yannum, Assistant Provincial Programme Manager; or James Steve Valakvi, Senior Programme Officer; (technical) Lloyd Guvil, Technician.

Radio Manus, P.O. Box 505, Lorengau, Manus, Papua New Guinea. Phone: +675 470-9029. Fax: +675 470 9079. Contact: (technical and nontechnical) John P. Mandrakamu, Provincial Program Manager. Station is seeking the help of DXers and broadcasting professionals in obtaining a second hand, but still usable broadcasting quality CD player that could be donated to Radio Manus. Replies regularly. Return postage appreciated.

Radio Milne Bay(when operating), P.O. Box 111, Alotau, Milne

Bay, Papua New Guinea. Contact: (general) Trevor Webumo, Assistant Manager; Simon Muraga, Station Manager; or Raka Petuely, Program Officer; (technical) Philip Maik, Technician. Return postage in the form of mint stamps helpful.

Radio Morobe, P.O. Box 1262, Lae, Morobe, Papua New Guinea. Fax: +675 472 6423. Contact: Ken L. Tropu, Assistant Program Manager; Peter W. Manua, Program Manager; Kekalem M. Meruk, Assistant Provincial Program Manager; or Aloysius R. Nase, Station Manager.

Radio New Ireland, P.O. Box 140, Kavieng, New Ireland, Papua New Guinea. Contact: Otto A. Malatana, Station Manager; or Ruben Bale, Provincial Program Manager. Return postage or $1 helpful.

Radio Northern (when operating), Voice of Oro, P.O. Box 137, Popondetta, Oro, Papua New Guinea. Contact: Roma Tererembo, Assistant Provincial Programme Manager; or Misael Pendaia, Station Manager. Return postage required.

Radio Sandaun, P.O. Box 37, Vanimo, Sandaun Province, Papua New Guinea. Contact: (nontechnical) Gabriel Deckwalen, Station Manager; Zacharias Nauot, Acting Assistant Manager; Celina Korei, Station Journalist; Elias Rathley, Provincial Programme Manager; Mrs. Maria Nauot, Secretary; (technical) Paia Ottawa, Technician. $1 helpful.

Radio Simbu, P.O. Box 228, Kundiawa, Chimbu, Papua New Guinea. Phone: +675 735-1038 or +675 735-1082. Fax: +675 735 1012. Contact: (general) Jack Wera, Manager; Tony Mill Waine, Provincial Programme Manager; Felix Tsiki; or Thomas Ghiyandiule, Producer, "Pasikam Long ol Pipel." Cassette recordings $5. Free two-Kina banknotes.

Radio Southern Highlands (when operating), P.O. Box 104, Mendi, SHP, Papua New Guinea. Contact: (general) Andrew Meles, Provincial Programme Manager; Miriam Piapo, Programme Officer; Benard Kagaro, Programme Officer; Lucy Aluy, Programme Officer; Jacob Mambi, Shift Officer; or Nicholas Sambu, Producer, "Questions and Answers"; (technical) Ronald Helori, Station Technician. $1 or return postage helpful; or donate a wall poster of a rock band, singer or American landscape.

Radio Western, P.O. Box 23, Daru, Western Province, Papua New Guinea. Contact: Robin Wainetti, Manager; (technical) Samson Tobel, Technician. $1 or return postage required. Replies irregularly.

Radio Western Highlands (when operating), P.O. Box 311, Mount Hagen, WHP, Papua New Guinea. Contact: (general) William Kie, Acting Station Manager; (technical) Esau Okole, Technician. $1 or return postage helpful. Replies occasionally. Often off the air because of theft, armed robbery or inadequate security for the station's staff.

Radio West New Britain, P.O. Box 412, Kimbe, WNBP, Papua New Guinea. Fax: +675 983 5600. Contact: Valuka Lowa, Provincial Station Manager; Darius Gilime, Provincial Program Manager; Lemeck Kuam, Producer, "Questions and Answers"; or Esekial Mael. Return postage required.

PARAGUAY World Time -3 (-4 midyear)

La Voz del Chaco Paraguayo, Filadelfia, Dpto. de Boquerón, Chaco, Paraguay. Contact: Erwin Wiens, Director; or Arnold Boschmann, Director de Programación. This station, currently only on medium wave (AM), hopes to add a world band transmitter within the 60-meter (5 MHz) band. Although it is located above the Tropic of Capricorn, and therefore eligible to use the tropical bands, the telecommunications authorities in Asunción, south of the line, have never supported broadcasting on tropical band frequencies within Paraguay.

Radio Encarnación (if reactivated), Gral. Artigas casi Gral. B. Caballero, Encarnación, Paraguay. Phone: +595 (71) 4376 or +595 (71) 3345. Fax: +595 (71) 4099. Contact: Bienvenida Kriskovich Vda. de Madelaire, Propietaria. $1 or return postage helpful. On February 6, 2001—after 43 years and a lengthy legal battle which went all the way to the Paraguayan supreme court—the station was returned to its rightful owners. Unfortunately, both the medium wave and shortwave transmitting equipment had been dismantled before being handed over, and was totally unusable. It remains to be seen if and when the station will be reactivated.

Radio Guairá (if reactivated), Alejo García y Presidente Franco, Villarrica, Paraguay. Phone: +595 (541) 2385 or +595 (541) 3411. Fax: +595 (541) 2130. Contact: (general) Lídice Rodríguez, Propietaria; (technical) Enrique Traversi. Welcomes correspondence in Spanish. $1 or return postage helpful.

Radio Nacional del Paraguay, Blas Garay 241 entre Yegros e Iturbe, Asunción, Paraguay. Phone: +595 (21) 449-213. Fax: +595 (21) 332 750. Free tourist brochure. $1 or return postage required. Replies, sometimes slowly, to correspondence in Spanish.

PERU World Time-5

NOTE: Obtaining replies from Peruvian stations calls for creativity, tact, patience—and the proper use of Spanish, not form letters and the like.

Emisoras JSV—*see* Radio JSV.

Estación C, Casilla de Correo 210, Moyobamba, San Martín, Peru. Contact: Porfirio Centurión, Propietario.

Estación Tarapoto (if reactivated), Jirón Federico Sánchez 720, Tarapoto, Peru. Phone: +51 (94) 522-709. Contact: Luis Humberto Hidalgo Sánchez, Gerente General; or José Luna Paima, Announcer. Replies occasionally to correspondence in Spanish.

Estación Wari, Calle Nazareno 108, Ayacucho, Peru. Phone: +51 (64) 813-039. Contact: Walter Muñoz Ynga I., Gerente.

Estación X (Equis), Calle Argentina 198, Bagua, Departamento de Amazonas, Peru.

Frecuencia Líder (Radio Bambamarca), Jirón Jorge Chávez 416, Bambamarca, Hualgayoc, Cajamarca, Peru. Phone: (office) +51 (74) 713-260; (studio) +51 (74) 713-249. Contact: (general) Valentín Peralta Díaz, Gerente; Irma Peralta Rojas; or Carlos Antonio Peralta Rojas; (technical) Oscar Lino Peralta Rojas. Free station photos. *La Historia de Bambamarca* book for 5 Soles; cassettes of Peruvian and Latin American folk music for 4 Soles each; T-shirts for 10 Soles each (sending US$1 per Sol should suffice and cover foreign postage costs, as well). Replies occasionally to correspondence in Spanish. Considering replacing their transmitter to improve reception.

Frecuencia San Ignacio, Jirón Villanueva Pinillos 330, San Ignacio, Cajamarca, Peru. Contact: Franklin R. Hoyos Cóndor, Director Gerente; or Ignacio Gómez Torres, Técnico de Sonido. Replies to correspondence in Spanish. $1 or return postage necessary.

Frecuencia VH—*see* Radio Frecuencia VH.

La Super Radio San Ignacio (when operating), Avenida Víctor Larco 104, a un costado del campo deportivo, San Ignacio, Distrito de Sinsicap, Provincia de Otuzco, La Libertad, Peru.

La Voz de Anta, Distrito de Anta, Provincia de Acobamba, Departamento de Huancavelica. Phone: +51 (64) 750-201.

La Voz de la Selva—*see* Radio La Voz de la Selva.

La Voz de San Juan—*see* Radio La Voz de San Juan.

La Voz del Campesino—*see* Radio La Voz del Campesino.

La Voz del Marañon—*see* Radio La Voz del Marañon.

Ondas del Suroriente—*see* Radio Ondas del Suroriente, below.

Radio Adventista Mundial—La Voz de la Esperanza, Jirón Dos de Mayo No. 218, Celendín, Cajamarca, Peru. Contact: Francisco Goicochea Ortiz, Director; or Lucas Solano Oyarce, Director de Ventas.

Radio Altura (Cerro de Pasco), Casilla de Correo 140, Cerro de Pasco, Pasco, Peru. Phone: +51 (64) 721-875, +51 (64) 722-398. Contact: Oswaldo de la Cruz Vásquez, Gerente General. Replies to correspondence in Spanish.

Radio Altura (Huarmaca), Antonio Raymondi 3ra Cuadra, Distrito de Huarmaca, Provincia de Huancabamba, Piura, Peru.

Radio Amauta del Perú, (when operating), Jirón Manuel Iglesias s/n, a pocos pasos de la Plazuela San Juan, San Pablo, Cajamarca, Nor Oriental del Marañón, Peru.

Radio Amistad, Manzana I-11, Lote 6, Calle 22, Urbanización Mariscal Cáceres, San Juan de Lurigancho, Lima, Peru. Phone: +51 (1) 392-3640. Email: radioamistad@peru.com. Contact: Manuel Mejía Barboza. Accepts email reception reports.

Radio Ancash, Casilla de Correo 221, Huaraz, Peru. Phone: +51 (44) 721-381,+51 (44) 721-359, +51 (44) 721-487, +51 (44) 722-512. Fax: +51 (44) 722 992. Contact: Armando Moreno Romero, Gerente General. Replies to correspondence in Spanish.

Radio Andahuaylas, Jr. Ayacucho No. 248, Andahuaylas, Apurímac, Peru. Contact: Sr. Daniel Andréu C., Gerente. $1 required. Replies irregularly to correspondence in Spanish.

Radio Andina (Huancabamba), Huáscar 201, Huancabamba, Piura, Peru. According to an on-air announcement, the station is expected to move to Avenida Ramón Castilla 254. Phone: +51 (74) 473-104. Contact: Manuel Campos Ojeda, Director.

Radio Andina (Huancayo), Real 175, Huancayo, Junín, Peru. Phone: +51 (64) 231-123. Replies infrequently to correspondence in Spanish.

Radio Apurímac (when operating), Jirón Cusco 206 (or Ovalo El Olivo No. 23), Abancay, Apurímac, Peru. Contact: Antero Quispe Allca, Director General.

Radio Arcángel San Miguel—*see* Radio San Miguel Arcángel.

Radio Arequipa, Avenida Unión 215, 3er piso, Distrito Miraflores, Arequipa, Peru. May identify as "Radio Arequipa Bethel" when carrying religious programming from the "Movimiento Misionero Mundial" evengelistic organization.

Radio Atlántida

STATION: Jirón Arica 441, Iquitos, Loreto, Peru. Phone: +51 (94) 234-452, +51 (94) 234-962. Contact: Pablo Rojas Bardales. *LISTENER CORRESPONDENCE:* Sra. Carmela López Paredes, Directora del prgrama "Trocha Turística," Jirón Arica 1083, Iquitos, Loreto, Peru. Free pennants and tourist information. $1 or return postage required. Replies to most correspondence in Spanish, the preferred language, and some correspondence in English. "Trocha Turística" is a bilingual (Spanish and English) tourist program aired weekdays 2300-2330.

Radio Ayaviri (La Voz de Melgar) (when operating), Apartado Postal 8, Ayaviri, Puno, Peru. Fax: +51 (54) 320 207, specify on fax "Anexo 127." Contact: (general) Sra. Corina Llaiqui Ochoa, Administradora; (technical) José Aristo Solórzano Mendoza, Director. Free pennants. Sells audio cassettes of local folk music for $5 plus postage; also exchanges music cassettes. Correspondence accepted in English, but Spanish preferred.

Radio Bahía, Jirón Alfonso Ugarte 309, Chimbote, Ancash, Peru. Phone: +51 (44) 322-391. Contact: Margarita Rossel Soria, Administradora; or Miruna Cruz Rossel, Administradora.

Radio Bambamarca—*see* Frecuencia Líder, above.

Radio Bolívar, Correo Central, Bolívar, Provincia de Bolívar, Departamento de La Libertad, Peru. Contact: Julio Dávila Echevarría, Gerente. May send free pennant. Return postage helpful.

Radio Cajamarca, Jirón La Mar 675, Cajamarca, Peru. Phone: +51 (44) 921-014. Contact: Porfirio Cruz Potosí.

Radio Chanchamayo, Jirón Tarma 551, La Merced, Junín, Peru.

Radio Chaski, Baptist Mid-Missions, Apartado Postal 368, Cusco, Peru; or Alameda Pachacútec s/n B-5, Cusco, Peru. Phone: +51 (84) 225-052. Contact: Andrés Tuttle H., Gerente; or Felipe S. Velarde Hinojosa M., Representante Legal.

Radio Chincheros, Jirón Apurímac s/n, Chincheros, Departamento de Apurímac, Peru.

Radio Chota, Jirón Anaximandro Vega 690, Apartado Postal 3, Chota, Cajamarca, Peru. Phone: +51 (44) 771-240. Contact: Aladino Gavidia Huamán, Administrador. $1 or return postage required. Replies slowly to correspondence in Spanish.

Radio Comas, Avenida Estados Unidos 327, Urbanización Huaquillay, km 10 de la Avenida Túpac Amaru, Distrito de Comas, Lima, Peru. Phone: +51 (1) 525-0859. Fax: +51 (1) 525 0094. Email: rtcomas@protelsa.com.pe; rtcomas@terra.com.pe. Web: http://homepages.go.com/homepages/r/a/d/radio_cantogrande/. Contact: Edgar Saldaña R.; Juan Rafael Saldaña Reátegui (Relaciones Públicas) or Gamaniel Francisco Chahua, Productor-Programador General.

Radio Comercial Naranjos, Avenida Cajamarca 464, Distrito de Pardo Miguel Naranjos, Provincia de Rioja, San Martín, Peru. Contact: Mario Cusma Vasquez, Propietario; Esperanza Galo Gomez, Gerente Adminitrativo; or Pepe Vasquez, Jefe de Producciones.

Radio Concordia (if reactived), Av. La Paz 512-A, Arequipa, Peru. If a reply is not forthcoming, try: Miguel Grau s/n Mz.2 Lt. 1, Arequipa, Peru. Phone: +51 (54) 446-053. Contact: Pedro Pablo Acosta Fernández. Free stickers. Return postage required.

Radio Continental (if reactivated), Av. Independencia 56, Arequipa, Peru. Phone: +51 (54) 213-253. Contact: J. Antonio Umbert D., Director General; or Leonor Núñez Melgar. Free stickers. Replies slowly to correspondence in Spanish.

Radio CORA, Compañía Radiofónica Lima, S.A., Paseo de la República 144, Centro Cívico, Oficina 5, Lima 1, Peru. Phone: +51 (1) 433-5005, +51 (1) 433-1188, +51 (1) 433-0848. Fax: +51 (1) 433 6134. Email: cora@peru.itete.com.pe; cora@lima.business.com.pe. Contact: (general) Juan Ramírez Lazo, Propietario y Director Gerente; Dra. Lylian Ramírez M., Directora de Prensa y Programación; Juan Ramírez Lazo, Director Gerente; or Srta. Angelina María Abie; (technical) Srta. Sylvia Ramírez M., Directora Técnica. Free station sticky-label pads, bumper stickers and may send large certificate suitable for framing. Audio cassettes with extracts from their programs $20 plus $2 postage; women's hair bands $2 plus $1 postage. Two IRCs or $1 required. Replies slowly to correspondence in English, Spanish, French, Italian and Portuguese.

Radio Coremarca, Jirón Jaime de Martínez, Bambamarca,

Peru. Contact: Virgilio Carranza Tello, Director. A small educational station, so include return postage with your correspondence.

Radio Cristal (if reactivated), Jirón Ucayali s/n, a un costado de la Carretera Marginal de la Selva, San Hilarión, Provincia de Picota, Región San Martín, Peru. Contact: Señora Marina Gaona, Gerente; or Lucho García Gaona.

Radio Cultural Amauta, Cahuide 278, Apartado Postal 24, Huanta, Ayacucho, Peru. Phone: +51 (64) 832-153. Email: arca@terra.com.pe or montessd@terra.com.pe. Contact: Demetria Montes Sinforoso (Administradora); Vicente Saico Tinco.

Radio Cusco, Apartado Postal 251, Cusco, Peru. Phone: (general)+51 (84) 225-851; (management) +51 (84) 232-457. Fax: +51 (84) 223 308. Contact: Sra. Juana Huamán Yépez, Administradora; or Raúl Siú Almonte, Gerente General; (technical) Benjamín Yábar Alvarez. Free pennants, postcards and key rings. Audio cassettes of Peruvian music $10 plus postage. $1 or return postage required. Replies irregularly to correspondence in English or Spanish. Station is looking for folk music recordings from around the world to use in their programs.

Radio del Pacífico, Apartado Postal 4236, Lima 1, Peru. Phone: +51 (1) 433-3275. Fax: +51 (1) 433 3276. Email: postmast@pacifico.com.pe. Contact: J. Petronio Allauca, Secretario, Departamento de Relaciones Públicas; or P.G. Ferreyra. $1 or return postage required. Replies occasionally to correspondence in Spanish.

Radio El Sol (Lima) (when active), Avenida Uruguay 355, 7°, Lima Peru. Phone: +51 (1) 330-0713, +51 (1) 424-6107. Rarely replies, and only to correspondence in Spanish.

Radio El Sol (Pucará), Avenida Jaén s/n, Distrito de Pucará, Jaén, Cajamarca, Peru.

Radio El Sol de los Andes, Jirón 2 de Mayo 257, Juliaca, Peru. Phone: +51 (54) 321-115. Fax: +51 (54) 322-981. Contact: Armando Alarcón Velarde.

Radio Estación Uno, Barrio Altos, Distrito de Pucará, Provincia Jaén, Nor Oriental del Marañón, Peru.

Radio Estudio 2000, Distrito Miguel Pardo Naranjos, Provincia de Rioja, Departamento de San Martín, Peru.

Radio Frecuencia VH ("La Voz de Celendín"; "RVC"), Jirón José Gálvez 1030, Celendín, Cajamarca, Peru. Contact: Fernando Vásquez Castro, Propietario.

Radio Frecuencia San Ignacio—*see* Frecuencia San Ignacio.

Radio Horizonte (Chachapoyas), Apartado Postal 69 (or Jirón Amazonas 1177), Chachapoyas, Amazonas, Peru. Phone: +51 (74) 757-793. Fax: +51 (74) 757 004. Contact: Sra. Rocío García Rubio, Ing. Electrónico, Directora; Percy Chuquizuta Alvarado, Locutor; María Montaldo Echaiz, Locutora; Marcelo Mozambite Chavarry, Locutor; Ing. María Dolores Gutiérrez Atienza, Administradora; Juan Nancy Ruíz de Valdez, Secretaria; Yoel Toro Morales, Técnico de Transmisión; or María Soledad Sánchez Castro, Administradora. Replies to correspondence in English, French, German and Spanish. $1 required.

Radio Horizonte (Chiclayo), Jirón Incanato 387 Altos, Distrito José Leonardo Ortiz, Chiclayo, Lambayeque, Peru. Phone: +51 (74) 252-917. Contact: Enrique Becerra Rojas, Owner and General Manager. Return postage required.

Radio Hualgayoc, Jirón San Martín s/n, Hualgayoc, Cajamarca, Peru. Contact: Máximo Zamora Medina, Director Propietario.

Radio Huamachuco (if reactivated), Jirón Bolívar 937, Huamachuco, La Libertad, Peru. Contact: Manuel D. Gil Gil, Director Propietario.

Radio Huanta 2000, Jirón Gervacio Santillana 455, Huanta, Peru. Phone: +51 (64) 932-105. Fax: +51 (64) 832 105. Contact: Ronaldo Sapaico Maravi, Departmento Técnico; or Sra. Lucila Orellana de Paz, Administradora. Free photo of staff. Return postage or $1 appreciated. Replies to correspondence in Spanish.

Radio Huarmaca, Av. Grau 454 (detrás de Inversiones La Loretana), Distrito de Huarmaca, Provincia de Huancabamba, Región Grau, Peru. Contact: Simón Zavaleta Pérez. Return postage helpful.

Radio Ilucán, Jirón Lima 290, Cutervo, Región Nororiental del Marañón, Peru. Phone: +51 (44) 737-010, +51 (44) 737-231. Contact: José Gálvez Salazar, Gerente Administrativo. $1 required. Replies occasionally to correspondence in Spanish.

Radio Imagen, Casilla de Correo 42, Tarapoto, San Martín, Peru; Jirón San Martín 328, Tarapoto, San Martín, Peru; or Apartado Postal 254, Tarapoto, San Martín, Peru. Phone: +51 (94) 522-696. Contact: Adith Chumbe Vásquez, Secretaria; or Jaime Ríos Tapullima, Gerente General. Replies irregularly to correspondence in Spanish. $1 or return postage helpful.

Radio Integración, Av. Seoane 200, Apartado Postal 57, Abancay, Departamento de Apurímac, Peru. Contact: Zenón Hernán Farfán Cruzado, Propietario.

Radio Internacional del Perú (when operating), Jirón Bolognesi 532, San Pablo, Cajamarca, Peru.

Radio Jaén (La Voz de la Frontera), Calle Mariscal Castilla 439, Jaén, Cajamarca, Peru. Contact: Luis A. Vilchez Ochoa, Administrador.

Radio JSV, Jirón Aguilar 742-744, Huánuco, Peru. Phone: +51 (64) 512-930. Return postage required.

Radio Juliaca (La Decana), Jirón Ramón Castilla 949, Apartado Postal 67, Juliaca, San Román, Puno, Peru. Phone: +51 (54) 321-372. Fax: +51 (54) 332-386. Contact: Robert Theran Escobedo, Director.

Radio JVL, Jirón Túpac Amaru 105, Consuelo, Distrito de San Pablo, Provincia de Bellavista, Departamento de San Martín, Peru. Contact: John Wiley Villanueva Lara—a student of electronic engineering—who currently runs the station, and whose initials make up the station name. Replies to correspondence in Spanish. Return Postage required.

Radio La Hora, Av. Garcilaso 180, Cusco, Peru. Phone: +51 (84) 225-615, +51 (84) 231-371. Contact: (general) Edmundo Montesinos G., Gerente; (reception reports) Carlos Gamarra Moscoso, who is also a DXer. Free stickers, pins, pennants and postcards of Cusco. Return postage required. Replies to correspondence in Spanish. Reception reports are best sent direct to Carlos Gamarra's home address: Av. Garcilaso 411, Wanchaq, Cusco, Peru. The station hopes to increase transmitter power to 2 kw if and when the economic situation improves.

Radio La Inmaculada, Parroquia La Inmaculada Concepción, Frente de la Plaza de Armas, Santa Cruz, Provincia de Santa Cruz, Departamento de Cajamarca, Peru. Phone: +51 (74) 714-051. Contact: Reverendo Padre Angel Jorge Carrasco, Gerente; or Gabino González Vera, Locutor.

Radio Lajas, Jirón Rosendo Mendívil 589, Lajas, Chota, Cajamarca, Nor Oriental del Marañón, Peru. Contact: Alfonso Medina Burga, Gerente Propietario.

Radio La Merced, Junín 163, La Merced, Junín, Peru. Phone: +51 (64) 531-199. Occasionally replies to correspondence in Spanish.

Radio La Oroya, Calle Lima 190, Tercer Piso Of. 3, Apartado Postal 88, La Oroya, Provincia de Yauli, Departamento de Junín, Peru. Phone: +51 (64) 391-401. Fax: +51 (64) 391 440. Email: rlofigu@net.cosapidata.com.pe. Web: www.cosapidata.com.pe/

empresa/rlofigu/rlofigu.htm. Contact: Jacinto Manuel Figueroa Yauri, Gerente-Propietario. Free pennants. $1 or return postage necessary. Replies to correspondence in Spanish.

Radio La Voz, Andahuaylas, Apurímac, Peru. Contact: Lucio Fuentes, Director Gerente.

Radio La Voz de Abancay, Avenida Noviembre Lote 6, Urbanización Micaela Bastidas, Abancay, Departamento de Apurímac, Peru. Contact: Lucio Fuentes, Propietario.

Radio La Voz de Chiriaco, Jirón Ricardo Palma s/n, Chiriaco, Distrito de Imaza, Provincia de Bagua, Departamento de Amazonas, Peru. Contact: Hildebrando López Pintado, Director; Santos Castañeda Cubas, Director Gerente; or Fidel Huamuro Curinambe, Técnico de Mantenimiento. $1 or return postage helpful.

Radio La Voz de Cutervo (if reactivated), Jirón María Elena Medina 644-650, Cutervo, Cajamarca, Peru.

Radio La Voz de Huamanga (if reactivated), Calle El Nazareno, 2do Pasaje No. 161, Ayacucho, Peru. Phone: +51 (64) 812-366. Contact: Sra. Aguida A. Valverde Gonzales. Free pennants and postcards.

Radio La Voz de la Selva, Jirón Abtao 255, Casilla de Correo 207, Iquitos, Loreto, Peru. Phone: +51 (94) 265-245. Fax: +51 (94) 264 531. Email: lvsradio@tvs.com.pe. Contact: Julia Jáuregui Rengifo, Directora; Marcelino Esteban Benito, Director; Pedro Sandoval Guzmán, Announcer; or Mery Blas Rojas. Replies to correspondence in Spanish.

Radio La Voz de las Huarinjas, Barrio El Altillo s/n, Huancabamba, Piura, Peru. Phone: +51 (74) 473-126 or +51 (74) 473-259. Contact: Alfonso García Silva, Gerente Director (also the owner of the station); or Bill Yeltsin, Administrador. Replies to correspondence in Spanish.

Radio La Voz de Oxapampa, Av. Mullenbruck 469, Oxapampa, Pasco, Peru. Contact: Pascual Villafranca Guzmán, Director Propietario.

Radio La Voz de San Juan, 28 de Julio 420, Lonya Grande, Provincia de Utcubamba, Región Nororiental del Marañón, Peru. Contact: Prof. Víctor Hugo Hidrovo; or Edilberto Ortiz Chávez, Locutor. Formerly known as Radio San Juan.

Radio La Voz de Santa Cruz (if reactivated), Av. Zarumilla 190, Santa Cruz, Cajamarca, Peru.

Radio La Voz del Campesino, Av. Ramón Castilla s/n en la salida a Chiclayo, Huarmaca, Provincia de Huancabamba, Piura, Peru. Contact: Hernando Huancas Huancas.

Radio La Voz del Marañón (if reactivated), Jirón Bolognesi 130, Barrio La Alameda, Cajamarca, Nor Oriental del Marañón, Peru. Contact: Eduardo Díaz Coronado.

Radio Libertad de Junín, Cerro de Pasco 528, Apartado Postal 2, Junín, Peru. Phone: +51 (64) 344-026. Contact: Mauro Chaccha G., Director Gerente. Replies slowly to correspondence in Spanish. Return postage necessary.

Radio Líder, Portal Belén 115, 2do piso, Cusco, Peru. Contact: Mauro Calvo Acurio, Propietario.

Radio Lircay (when operating), Barrio Maravillas, Lircay, Provincia de Angaraes, Huancavelica, Peru.

Radio Los Andes (Huamachuco) (if reactivated), Pasaje Damián Nicolau 108-110, 2do piso, Huamachuco, La Libertad, Peru. Phone: +51 (44) 441-240 or +51 (44) 441-502. Fax: +51 (44) 441 214. Contact: Monseñor Sebastián Ramis Torerns.

Radio Los Andes (Huarmaca), Huarmaca, Provincia de Huancabamba, Región Grau, Peru. Contact: William Cerro Calderón.

Radio Luz y Sonido, Apartado Postal 280, Huánuco, Peru; (physical address) Jirón Dos de Mayo 1286, Oficina 205, Huánuco, Peru. Phone: +51 (64) 512-394 or +51 (64) 518-500. Fax: +51 (64) 511 985. Email: luz.sonido@hys.com.pe. Web: www.hys.com.pe/page/luzysonido/. Contact: (technical) Jorge Benavides Moreno; (nontechnical) Pedro Martínez Tineo, Director Ejecutivo; Lic. Orlando Bravo Jesús; or Seydel Saavedra Cabrera, Operador/Locutor. Return postage or $2 required. Replies to correspondence in Spanish, Italian and Portuguese. Sells video cassettes of local folk dances and religious and tourist themes.

Radio Madre de Dios, Daniel Alcides Carrión 385, Apartado Postal 37, Puerto Maldonado, Madre de Dios, Peru. Phone: +51 (84) 571-050. Fax: +51 (84) 571 018 or +51 (84) 573 542. Contact: (administration) Padre Rufino Lobo Alonso, Director; (general) Alcides Arguedas Márquez, Director del programa "Un Festival de Música Internacional," heard Mondays 0100 to 0200 World Time. Sr. Arguedas is interested in feedback for this letterbox program. Replies to correspondence in Spanish. $1 or return postage appreciated.

Radio Majestad, Calle Real 1033, Oficina 302, Huancayo, Junín, Peru.

Radio Marañón (if reactivated), Apartado Postal 50, Jaén, Cajamarca, Peru. Phone: +51 (44) 731-147, +51 (44) 732-580. Fax: +51 (44) 733 464. Email: (director) tavaral@telemail.telematic.edu.pe. Contact: Padre Luis Távara Martín, S.J., Director. Return postage necessary. May send free pennant. Replies slowly to correspondence in Spanish.

Radio Marginal, San Martín 257, Tocache, San Martín, Peru. Phone: +51 (94) 551-031. Rarely replies.

Radio Máster, Jirón 20 de Abril 308, Moyobamba, Departamento de San Martín, Peru. Contact: Américo Vásquez Hurtado, Director

Radio Melodía, San Camilo 501, Arequipa, Peru. Phone: +51 (54) 232-071, +51 (54) 232-327, +51 (54) 285-152. Fax: +51 (54) 237 312. Contact: Hermogenes Delgado Torres, Director; or Señora Elba Alvarez de Delgado. Replies to correspondence in Spanish.

Radio Mi Frontera, Calle San Ignacio 520, Distrito de Chirinos, Provincia de San Ignacio, Región Nor Oriental del Marañón, Peru.

Radio Moderna, Jirón Arequipa 323, 2do piso, Celendín, Cajamarca, Peru.

Radio Mundial Adventista, Colegio Adventista de Titicaca, Casilla 4, Juliaca, Peru. Currently on medium wave (AM) only, but is expected to add shortwave sometime in the future.

Radio Naylamp, Avenida Andrés Avelino Cáceres 800, Lambayeque, Peru. Phone: +51 (74) 283-353. Contact: Dr. Juan José Grández Vargas, Director Gerente; or Delicia Coronel Muñoz, who is interested in receiving postcards and the like. Free stickers, pennants and calendars. Return postage necessary.

Radio Nor Andina, Jirón José Gálvez 602, Celendín, Cajamarca, Peru. Contact: Misael Alcántara Guevara, Gerente; or Víctor B. Vargas C., Departamento de Prensa. Free calendar. $1 required. Donations (registered mail best) sought for the Committee for Good Health for Children, headed by Sr. Alcántara, which is active in saving the lives of hungry youngsters in poverty-stricken Cajamarca Province. Replies irregularly to casual or technical correspondence in Spanish, but regularly to Children's Committee donors and helpful correspondence in Spanish.

Radio Nor Peruana, Emisora Municipal, Jirón Ortiz Arrieta 588, 1er. piso del Concejo Provincial de Chachapoyas, Chachapoyas, Amazonas, Peru. Contact: Carlos Poema, Administrador; or Edgar Villegas, program host for "La Voz de Chachapoyas," (Sundays, 1100-1300).

Radio Onda Imperial, Calle Sacsayhuamán K-10, Urbanización Manuel Prado, Cusco, Peru. Phone: +51 (84) 232-521, +51 (84) 233-032.

Radio Ondas del Huallaga, Jirón Leoncio Prado 723, Apartado Postal 343, Huánuco, Peru. Phone: +51 (64) 511-525, +51 (64) 512-428. Contact: Flaviano Llanos Malpartida, Representante Legal. $1 or return postage required. Replies to correspondence in Spanish.

Radio Ondas del [Río] Marañón, Jirón Amazonas 315, Distrito de Aramango, Provincia de Bagua, Departamento de Amazonas, Región Nororiental del Marañón, Peru. Contact: Agustín Tongod, Director Propietario. "Rio"—river—is sometimes, but not always, used in on-air identification.

Radio Ondas del Río Mayo, Jirón Huallaga 348, Nueva Cajamarca, San Martín, Peru. Phone: +51 (94) 556-006. Contact: Edilberto Lucío Peralta Lozada, Gerente; or Víctor Huaras Rojas, Locutor. Free pennants. Return postage helpful. Replies slowly to correspondence in Spanish.

Radio Ondas del Suroriente, Jirón Ricardo Palma 510, Quillabamba, La Convención, Cusco, Peru.

Radio Oriente, Vicariato Apostólico, Avenida Progreso 114, Yurimaguas, Loreto, Peru. Phone: +51 (94) 352-156. Fax: +51 (94) 352 128. Contact: (general) Sra. Elisa Cancino Hidalgo; or Juan Antonio López-Manzanares M., Director; (technical) Pedro Capo Moragues, Gerente Técnico. $1 or return postage required. Replies occasionally to correspondence in English, French, Spanish and Catalan.

Radio Origen, Acobamba, Departamento de Huancavelica, Peru.

Radio Paccha (if reactivated), Calle Mariscal Castilla 52, Paccha, Provincia de Chota, Departamento de Cajamarca, Peru.

Radio Panorama (when operating)

STATION: Centro-poblado Recopampa, Distrito de Sorochuco, Provincia de Celendín, Departamento de Cajamarca, Región Autónoma del Marañón, Peru. Phone: +51 (44) 820-321. This is a public phone booth, so the person who answers may not necessarily work at the station! Contact: Segundo Ayala Brione, Propietario.

ADDRESS OF SISTER STATION, RADIO LA VOZ DE LOS ANDES: Plaza de Armas, Distrito de Sorochuco, Provincia de Celendín, Departamento de Cajamarca, Región Autónoma del Marañón, Peru.

Radio Paucartambo, Emisora Municipal

STATION ADDRESS: Paucartambo, Cusco, Peru.

STAFFER ADDRESS: Manuel H. Loaiza Canal, Correo Central, Paucartambo, Cusco, Peru. Return postage or $1 required.

Radio Perú ("Perú, la Radio")

STUDIO ADDRESS: Jirón Atahualpa 191, San Ignacio, Región Nororiental del Marañón, Peru.

ADMINISTRATION: Avenida San Ignacio 493, San Ignacio, Región Nororiental del Marañón, Peru. Contact: Oscar Vásquez Chacón, Director General; or Idelso Vásquez Chacón, Director Propietario. Sometimes relays the FM outlet, "Estudio 97."

Radio Quillabamba, Jirón Ricardo Palma 432, Apartado Postal 76, Quillabamba, La Convención, Cusco, Peru. Phone: +51 (84) 281-002. Fax: +51 (84) 281 771. Contact: Padre Francisco Javier Panera, Director. Replies very irregularly to correspondence in Spanish.

Radio Real, Av. Ramón Castilla casi Limón y Nieto, Parque Leoncio Prado, Huarmaca, Provincia de Huancabamba, Piura, Peru.

Radio Regional, Jirón Grau s/n frente al Colegio Nuestra Señora del Carmen, Celendín, Cajamarca, Peru.

Radio Reina de la Selva, Jirón Ayacucho 944, Plaza de Armas, Chachapoyas, Región Nor Oriental del Marañón, Peru. Phone: +51 (74) 757-203. Contact: José David Reina Noriega, Gerente General; or Jorge Oscar Reina Noriega, Director General. Replies irregularly to correspondence in Spanish. Return postage necessary.

Richard Leiderman of Boynton Beach, Florida shows off his stash of shortwave equipment. S. Kane

Radio San Antonio, Parroquia San Antonio de Padua, Plaza Principal s/n, Callalli, Departamento de Arequipa, Peru.

Radio San Francisco Solano, Parroquia de Sóndor, Calle San Miguel No. 207, Distrito de Sóndor, Huancabamba, Piura, Peru. Contact: Reverendo Padre Manuel José Rosas Castillo, Vicario Parroquial. Station operated by the Franciscan Fathers. Replies to correspondence in Spanish. $1 helpful.

Radio San Ignacio, Jirón Victoria 277, San Ignacio, Región Nororiental del Marañón, Peru. Contact: César Colunche Bustamante, Director Propietario; or his son, Fredy Colunche, Director de Programación.

Radio San Juan, Distrito de Aramango, Provincia de Bagua, Departamento de Amazonas, Región Nororiental del Marañón, Peru.

Radio San Juan, 28 de Julio 420, Lonya Grande, Provincia de Utcubamba, Región Nororiental del Marañón, Peru. Contact: Prof. Víctor Hugo Díaz Hidrovo; or Edilberto Ortiz Chávez, Locutor.

Radio San Miguel, Av. Huayna Cápac 146, Huánchac, Cusco, Peru. Contact: Sra. Catalina Pérez de Alencastre, Gerente General; or Margarita Mercado. Replies to correspondence in Spanish.

Radio San Miguel Arcángel, Jirón Bolívar 356, a media cuadra de la Plaza de Armas, Provincia de San Miguel, Cajamarca, Peru.

Radio San Miguel de El Faique, Distrito de El Faique, Provincia de Huancabamba, Departamento de Piura, Peru.

Radio San Nicolás, Jirón Amazonas 114, Rodríguez de Mendoza, Peru. Contact: Juan José Grández Santillán, Gerente; or Violeta Grández Vargas, Administradora. Return postage necessary.

Radio Santa Rosa, Jirón Camaná 170, Casilla 4451, Lima 01, Peru. Phone: +51 (1) 427-7488. Fax: +51 (1) 426 9219. Email: santarosa@viaexpresa.com.pe. Web: www.viaexpresa.com.pe/santarosa/santarosa.htm. Contact: Padre Juan Sokolich Alvarado, Director; or Lucy Palma Barreda. Free stickers and pennants. $1 or return postage necessary. 180-page book commemorating station's 35th anniversary $10. Replies to correspondence in Spanish.

Radio Santiago (if reactivated), Municipalidad Distrital de Río Santiago, Puerto Galilea, Provincia de Condorcanqui, Amazonas, Peru. Contact: Juan Tuchía Oscate, Alcalde Distrital; Sara Sánchez Cubas, Locutora Comercial; or Guillermo Gómez García, Director. Free pennants and postcards. Return postage necessary. Replies to correspondence in Spanish.

Radio Satélite, Jirón Cutervo No. 543, Provincia de Santa Cruz, Cajamarca, Peru. Phone: +51 (74) 714-074, +51 (74) 714-169. Contact: Sabino Llamo Chávez, Gerente. Free tourist brochure. $1 or return postage required. Replies to correspondence in Spanish.

Radio Selecciones, Chuquibamba, Provincia de Condesuyos, Arequipa, Peru.

Radio Sicuani, Jirón 2 de Mayo 212, Sicuani, Canchis, Cusco, Peru; or Apartado Postal 45, Sicuani, Peru. Phone: +51 (84) 351-136 or +51 (84) 351-698. Fax: +51 (84) 351 697. Email: cecosda@mail.cosapidata.com.pe. Contact: Mario Ochoa Vargas, Director.

Radio Soledad, Centro Minero de Retama, Distrito de Parcoy, Provincia de Pataz, La Libertad, Peru. Contact: Vicente Valdivieso, Locutor. Return postage necessary.

Radio Sudamérica, Jirón Ramón Castilla 491, tercer nivel, Plaza de Armas, Cutervo, Cajamarca, Peru. Phone: +51 (74) 736-090 or +51 (74) 737-443. Contact: Jorge Luis Paredes Guerra, Administrador; or Amadeo Mario Muñoz Guivar, Propietario.

Radio Superior (Bolívar), Jirón San Martín 229, Provincia de Bolívar, Departamento de La Libertad, Peru.

Radio Tacna, Aniceto Ibarra 436, Casilla de Correo 370, Tacna, Peru. Phone: +51 (54) 714-871. Fax: +51 (54) 723 745. Email: radiotac@principal.unjbg.edu.pe. Web: http://principal.unjbg.edu.pe/radio/radta.html. Contact: (nontechnical and technical) Ing. Alfonso Cáceres Contreras, Sub-Gerente/Jefe Técnico; (administration) Yolanda Vda. de Cáceres C., Directora Gerente. Free stickers and samples of *Correo* local newspaper. $1 or return postage helpful. Audio cassettes of Peruvian and other music $2 plus postage. Replies irregularly to correspondence in English and Spanish.

Radio Tawantinsuyo, Av. Sol 806, Cusco, Peru. Phone: +51 (84) 226-955, +51 (84) 228-411. Contact: Ing. Raul Montesinos Espejo, Director Gerente. Has a very attractive QSL card, but only replies occasionally to correspondence, which should be in Spanish.

Radio Tarma, Jirón Molino del Amo 167, Apartado Postal 167, Tarma, Peru. Phone/fax: +51 (64) 321 167 or +51 (64) 321 510. Contact: Mario Monteverde Pomareda, Gerente General. Sometimes sends 100 Inti banknote in return when $1 enclosed. Free stickers. $1 or return postage required. Replies irregularly to correspondence in Spanish.

Radio Tayacaja, Correo Central, Distrito de Pampas, Tayacaja, Huancavelica, Peru. Phone: +51 (64) 22-02-17, Anexo 238. Contact: (general) J. Jorge Flores Cárdenas; (technical) Ing. Larry Guido Flores Lezama. Free stickers and pennants. Replies to correspondence in Spanish. Hopes to replace transmitter.

Radio Tingo María (when operating), Jirón Callao 115 (or Av. Raimondi No. 592), Casilla de Correo 25, Tingo María, Leoncio Prado, Departamento de Huánuco, Peru. Contact: Gina A. de la Cruz Ricalde, Administradora; or Ricardo Abad Vásquez, Gerente. Free brochures. $1 required. Replies slowly to correspondence in Spanish.

Radio Tropical, Casilla de Correo 31, Tarapoto, Peru. Phone: +51 (94) 522-083, +51 (94) 524-689. Fax: +51 (94) 522 155. Contact: Mery A. Rengifo Tenazoa, Secretaria; or Luis F. Mori Reátegui, Gerente. Free stickers, occasionally free pennants, and station history booklet. $1 or return postage required. Replies occasionally to correspondence in Spanish.

Radio Unión, Apartado Postal 833, Lima 27, Peru; or (street address) Avenida Central 717 - Piso 12, San Isidro, Lima 27, Peru. Phone: +51 (1) 440-2093. Fax: +51 (1) 440 7594. Email: runion@amauta.rcp.net.pe. Contact: Raúl Rubbeck Jiménez, Director Gerente; Juan Zubiaga Santiváñez, Gerente; Natividad Albizuri Salinas, Secretaria; or Juan Carlos Sologuren, Dpto. de Administración, who collects stamps. Free satin pennants and stickers. IRC required, and enclosing used or new stamps from various countries is especially appreciated. Replies irregularly to correspondence and tape recordings, with Spanish preferred.

Radio Uno, Av. Balta 1480, 3er piso, frente al Mercado Modelo, Chiclayo, Peru. Phone: +51 (74) 224-967. Contact: Luz Angela Romero, Directora del noticiero "Encuentros"; Plutarco Chamba Febres, Director Propietario; Juan Vargas, Administrador; or Filomena Saldívar Alarcón, Pauta Comercial. Return postage required.

Radio Uripa, Avenida Túpac Amaru s/n, Uripa, Provincia de Chincheros, Departamento de Apurímac, Peru. Contact: Lorenzo Quispe Nauto, Propietario.

Radio Victoria, Jr.Reynel 320, Mirones Bajo, Lima 1, Peru. Phone: +51 (1) 336-5448. Fax: +51 (1) 427 1195. Email: soermi@mixmail.com. Contact: Marta Flores Ushinahua. This station is owned by the Brazilian-run Pentecostal Church "Dios Es Amor," with local headquarters at Av. Arica 248, Lima; phone: +51 (1) 330-8023. Their program "La Voz de la Liberación" is produced locally and aired over numerous Peruvian shortwave stations.

Radio Virgen del Carmen ("RVC"), Jirón Virrey Toledo 466, Huancavelica, Peru. Phone: +51 (64) 752-740. Contact: Rvdo. Samuel Morán Cárdenas, Gerente.

Radiodifusoras Huancabamba, Calle Unión 409, Huancabamba, Piura, Peru. Phone: +51 (74) 473-233. Contact: Federico Ibáñez Maticorena, Director.

Radiodifusoras Paratón, Jirón Alfonso Ugarte 1090, contiguo al Parque Leoncio Prado, Huarmaca, Provincia de Huancabamba, Piura, Peru. Contact: Prof. Hernando Huancas Huancas, Gerente General; or Prof. Rómulo Chincay Huamán, Gerente Administrativo.

PHILIPPINES World Time +8

NOTE: Philippine stations sometimes send publications with lists of Philippine young ladies seeking "pen pal" courtships.

DUR2—Philippine Broadcasting Service (when operating), Bureau of Broadcasting Services, Media Center, Bohol Avenue, Quezon City, Philippines. Relays DZRB Radio ng Bayan and DZRM Radio Manila.

Far East Broadcasting Company—FEBC Radio International (External Service)

MAIN OFFICE: P.O. Box 1, Valenzuela, Metro Manila, Philippines 0560. Phone: (general) +63 (2) 292-5603, +63 (2) 292-9403 or +63 (2) 292-5790; (frequency management) +63 (2) 292-0253. Fax: +63 (2) 292 9430; +63 (2) 291 4982, but lacks funds to provide faxed replies; (Frequency Management) +63 (2) 294 0859. Email: febcomphil@febc.org.ph; (Peter McIntyre) pm@febc.jfm.org.ph; (Larry Podmore) lpodmore@febc.jmf.org.ph; (Peter Hsu) phsu@febc.org. Web: www.febc.org; www.febc.ph. Contact: (general) Peter McIntyre, Manager, International Operations Division; (administration) Carlos Peña, Managing Director; (engineering) Ing. Renato Valentin, Frequency Manager; Larry Podmore, IBG Chief Engi-

neer; or Peter Hsu, International Frequency Manager. Free stickers and calendar cards. Three IRCs appreciated for airmail reply. Plans to add a new 100 kW shortwave transmitter.
NEW DELHI BUREAU, NONTECHNICAL: c/o FEBA, Box 6, New Delhi-110 001, India.
Far East Broadcasting Company (Domestic Service), Bgy. Bayanan Baco Radyo DZB2, c/o ONF Calapan, Orr. Mindoro, Philippines 5200. Contact: (general) Dangio Onday, Program Supervisor/OIC; (technical) Danilo Flores, Broadcast Technician.
Radyo Pilipinas, the Voice of Democracy, Philippine Broadcasting Service, 4th Floor, PIA Building, Visayas Avenue, Quezon City 1100, Metro Manila, Philippines. Phone: (general) +63 (2) 924-2620; +63 (2) 920-3963; or +63 (2) 924-2548; (engineering) +63 (2) 924-2268. Fax: +63 (2) 924 2745. E-mail: pbs.pao@pbs.gov.ph. Contact: (nontechnical) Evelyn Salvador Agato, Officer-in-Charge; Mercy Lumba; Leo Romano, Producer, "Listeners and Friends"; Tanny V. Rodriguez, Station Manager; or Richard G. Lorenzo, Production Coordinator; (technical) Danilo Alberto, Supervisor; or Mike Pangilinan, Engineer. Free postcards and stickers.
Radio Veritas Asia
STUDIOS AND ADMINISTRATIVE HEADQUARTERS: P.O. Box 2642, Quezon City, 1166 Philippines. Phone: +63 (2) 939-0011 to 14, +63 (2) 939-4465 or +63 (2) 939-7476. Fax: (general) +63 (2) 938 1940; (Frequency and Monitoring) +63 (2) 939 7556. Email: (Program Dept.) veritas@mnl.sequel.net; (technical) info@radio-veritas.org.ph; or (Frequency Management) fmrva@pworld.net.ph. Web: www.rveritas-asia.org. Contact: (administration) Ms. Erlinda G. So, Manager; (general) Ms. Cleofe R. Labindao, Audience Relations Supervisor; Mrs. Regie de Juan Galindez; or Msgr. Pietro Nguyen Van Tai, Program Director; (technical) Honorio L. Llavore, Technical Director; Alex M. Movilla, Assistant Technical Director; or Alfonso L. Macaranas, Frequency Planning. Free caps, T-shirts, stickers, pennants, rulers, pens, postcards and calendars. Free bimonthly newsletter *UPLINK*. Return postage appreciated.
TRANSMITTER SITE: Radio Veritas Asia, Palauig, Zambales, Philippines. Contact: Fr. Hugo Delbaere, CICM, Technical Consultant.
BRUSSELS BUREAUS AND MAIL DROPS: Catholic Radio and Television Network, 32-34 Rue de l' Association, B-1000 Brussels, Belgium; or UNDA, 12 Rue de l'Orme, B-1040 Brussels, Belgium.
Voice of Friendship—*see* FEBC Radio International.

PIRATE

Pirate radio stations are usually one-person operations airing home-brew entertainment and/or iconoclastic viewpoints. In order to avoid detection by the authorities, they tend to appear irregularly, with little concern for the niceties of conventional program scheduling. Most are found in Europe chiefly on weekends, and mainly during evenings in North America, often just above 6200 kHz, just below 7000 kHz and just above 7375 kHz. These *sub rosa* stations and their addresses are subject to unusually abrupt change or termination, sometimes as a result of forays by radio authorities.

A worthy source of current addresses and other information on American pirate radio activity is: A*C*E, P.O. Box 12112, Norfolk VA 23541 USA (email: pradio@erols.com; Web: www.frn.net/ace/), a club which publishes a periodical ($20/year U.S., US$21 Canada, $27 elsewhere) for serious pirate radio enthusiasts.

For Europirate DX news, try:
SRSNEWS, Swedish Report Service, Ostra Porten 29, SE-442 54 Ytterby, Sweden. Email: srs@ice.warp.slink.se. Web: www-pp.kdt.net/jonny/index.html.
Pirate Connection, P.O. Box 4580, SE-203 20 Malmoe, Sweden; or P.O. Box 7085, Kansas City, Missouri 64113 USA. Phone: (home, Sweden) +46 (40) 611-1775; (mobile, Sweden) +46 (70) 581-5047. Email: etoxspz@eto.ericsson.se, xtdspz@lmd.ericsson.se or spz@exallon.se. Web: www-pp.hogia.net/jonny/pc. Six issues annually for about $23. Related to SRSNEWS, above.
FRS Goes DX, P.O. Box 2727, NL-6049 ZG Herten, Holland. Email: FRSH@pi.net; or peter.verbruggen@tip.nl. Web: http://home.pi.net/~freak55/home.htm.
Free-DX, 3 Greenway, Harold Park, Romford, Essex, RM3 OHH, United Kingdom.
FRC-Finland, P.O. Box 82, FIN-40101 Jyvaskyla, Finland.
Pirate Express, Postfach 220342, Wuppertal, Germany.
For up-to-date listener discussions and other pirate-radio information on the Internet, the usenet URLs are: alt.radio.pirate and rec.radio.pirate.

POLAND World Time +1 (+2 midyear)

Radio Maryja, ul. Żwirki i Wigury 80, PL-87-100 Toru , Poland. Phone: (general) +48 (56) 655-2361; (studio) +48 (56) 655-2333, +48 (56) 655-2366. Fax: +48 (56) 655 2362. Email: radio@radiomaryja.pl; (Kabulska) anna.kabulska@ radiomaryja.pl. Web: (includes RealAudio) www.radiomaryja.pl; (Windows Media only) http://nyas.radiomaria.org/mediaserver/index.htm (click the Poland button on the world map). Contact: Father Tadeusz Rydzk, Dyrektor; Father Jacek Cydzik; or Anna Kabulska, Secretary. Polish preferred, but also replies to correspondence in English. Transmits via facilities in Samara, Russia.
Radio Polonia
STATION: External Service, P.O. Box 46, PL-00-977 Warsaw, Poland. Phone: (general) +48 (22) 645-9305 or +48 (22) 444-123; (English Section) +48 (22) 645-9262; (German Section) +48 (22) 645-9333; (placement liaison) +48 (2) 645-9002. Fax: (general and administration) +48 (22) 645 5917 or +48 (22) 645 5919; (placement liaison) +48 (2) 645 5906. Email (general): piatka@radio.com.pl; (Polish Section) polonia@radio.com.pl; (English Section) english.section@radio.com.pl; (German Section) deutsche.redaktion@radio.com.pl; (Esperanto Section) esperanto.redakcio@radio.com.pl. Web: www.radio.com.pl/polonia/; (RealAudio in English and Polish) www.wrn.org/ondemand/poland.html. Contact: (general) Rafał Kiepuszewski, Head, English Section and Producer, "Postbag"; Peter Gentle, Presenter, "Postbag"; or Ann Flapan, Corresponding Secretary; (administration) Jerzy M. Nowakowski, Managing Director; Wanda Samborska, Managing Director; Bogumiła Berdychowska, Deputy Managing Director; or Maciej Łętowski, Executive Manager. On-air Polish language course with free printed material. Free stickers, pens, key rings and possibly T-shirts depending on financial cutbacks. DX Listeners' Club.
TRANSMISSION AUTHORITY: PAR (National Radiocommunication Agency), ul. Kasprzaka 18/20, PL-01-211 Warsaw, Poland. Phone: +48 (22) 608-8139/40, +48 (22) 608-8174 or +48 (22) 608-8191. Fax: +48 (22) 608 8195. Email: the format is initial.last name@par.gov.pl, so to reach, say, Filomena Grodzicka, it would be f.grodzicka@par.gov.pl. Contact: Mrs. Filomena Grodzicka, Head of BC Section; Lukasz Trzos; Mrs. Katalin Jaros; Ms. Urszula Rzepa or Jan Kondej. Responsible for coordinating Radio Polonia's frequencies.

Radio Racja

SHORTWAVE: P.O. Box 144, 220102 Minsk, Belarus. Email: rac@user.unibel.by, or r101@user.unibel.by. Web: (includes RealAudio) www.racja.pl.

BIALYSTOK FM STATION: Osrodek Radiowy w Bialymstoku, ul. Ciapla 1/7. PL-15-472 Bialystok, Poland. Contact: Wiktor Stachwiuk, Director.

Broadcasts in Belarusian and is opposed to President Lukashenko. The shortwave broadcasts are a joint Minsk-Warsaw production, and transmitted from Warsaw. The Bialystok station is part of the same organization, but has different programs which are intended for the Belarusian community in eastern Poland.

PORTUGAL

World Time exactly (+1 midyear); Azores World Time –1 (World Time midyear)

RDP Internacional—Rádio Portugal, Apartado 1011, 1001 Lisbon, Portugal; (street address) Av. Eng. Duarte Pacheco 26, 1070-110 Lisbon, Portugal. Phone: (general) +351 (21) 382-0000; (engineering) +351 (21) 382-2000. Fax: (general) +351 (21) 382 0165; (engineering) +351 (21) 387 1381. Email: (general) rdpinternacional@rdp.pt; (reception reports and listener correspondence) isabelsaraiva@rdp.pt, or christianehaupt@rdp.pt; (Frequency Management) teresaabreu@rdp.pt, or paulacarvalho@rdp.pt. Web: (includes Windows Media) www.rdp.pt/internacional/. Contact: (administration) José Manuel Nunes, Chairman; or Jaime Marques de Almeida, Director; (general) Isabel Saraiva or Christiane Haupt, Listener's Service Department; (technical) Eng. Francisco Mascarenhas, Technical Director; (Frequency Management) Teresa Abreu, Frequency Manager; or Ms. Paula Carvalho. Free stickers. May also send literature from the Portuguese National Tourist Office.

Radio Trans Europe (transmission facilities), 6º esq., Rua Braamcamp 84, 1200 Lisbon, Portugal. Transmitter located at Sines.

QATAR

World Time +3

Qatar Radio & Television Corporation, P.O. Box 3939, Doha, Qatar. Phone: (director) +974 86-48-05; (under secretary) +974 864-823; (engineering) +974 864-518; (main Arabic service audio feed) +974 895-895. Fax: +974 822 888 or +974 831 447. Contact: Jassim Mohamed Al-Qattan, Head of Public Relations. May send booklet on Qatar Broadcasting Service. Occasionally replies, and return postage helpful.

TECHNICAL OFFICE: Qatar Radio and Television Corporation, P.O. Box 1836, Doha, Qatar. Phone: +974 831-443, +974 864-057 or +974 894-613. Fax: +974 831 447. Contact: Hassan Al-Mass or Issa Ahmed Al-Hamadi, Head of Frequency Management.

ROMANIA

World Time +2 (+3 midyear)

Radio România Actualitati, Societatea Româna de Radiodifuziune, 60-62 Berthelot St., RO-70747 Bucharest, Romania. Phone: +40 (1) 615-9350. Fax: +40 (1) 223 2612. Web: (RealAudio only) www.ituner.com.

Radio România International

STATION: 60-62 Berthelot St., RO-70747 Bucharest, Romania; P.O. Box 111, RO-70756 Bucharest, Romania; or Romanian embassies worldwide. Phone: (general) +40 (1) 222-2556, +40 (1) 303-1172, +40 (1) 303-1488 or +40 (1) 312-3645; (English Department) +40 (1) 303-1357; (engineering) +40 (1) 303-1193. Fax: (general) +40 (1) 223 2613 [if no connection, try via the office of the Director General of Radio România, but mark fax "Pentru RRI"; that fax is +40 (1) 222 5641]; (Engineering Services) +40 (1) 312 1056/7 or +40 (1) 615 6992. Email: (general) rri@rri.ro; (English Service) engl@rri.ro; (Nisipeanu) emisie@radio.ror.ro; (Ianculescu) rianculescu@rri.ro. Web: (includes RealAudio) www.rri.ro. Contact: (communications in English or Romanian) Dan Balamat, "Listeners' Letterbox"; or Ioana Masariu, Head of the English Service; (radio enthusiasts' issues, English only) "DX Mailbox," English Department; (communications in French or Romanian) Doru Vasile Ionescu, Deputy General Director; (listeners' letters) Giorgiana Zachia; or Dan Dumitrescu; (technical) Sorin Floricu; Radu Ianculescu, Frequency Monitoring Engineer; or Marius Nisipeanu, Engineering Services. Free stickers, pennants, posters, pins and assorted other items. Listeners' Club. Annual contests. Replies slowly but regularly. Concerns about frequency management should be directed to the PTT (*see* below), with copies to the Romanian Autonomous Company (*see* farther below) and to a suitable official at RRI.

TRANSMISSION AND FREQUENCY MANAGEMENT, PTT: General Directorate of Regulations, Ministry of Communications, 14a Al. Libertatii, R-70060 Bucharest, Romania. Phone: +40 (1) 400-1312 or +40 (1) 400-177. Fax: +40 (1) 400 1230. Email: sfloricu@radio.ror.ro. Contact: Mrs. Elena Danila, Head of Frequency Management Department.

TRANSMISSION AND FREQUENCY MANAGEMENT, AUTONOMOUS COMPANY: Romanian Autonomous Company for Radio Communications, 14a Al. Libertatii, R-70060 Bucharest, Romania. Phone: +40 (1) 400-1072. Fax: +40 (1) 400 1228 or +40 (1) 335 5965. Contact: Mr. Marian Ionitá.

RUSSIA

(Times given for republics, oblasts and krays):

- World Time +2 (+3 midyear) Kaliningradskaya;
- World Time +3 (+4 midyear) Adygeya, Arkhangelskaya, Astrakhanskaya, Belgorodskaya, Bryanskaya, Chechnya, Chuvashiya, Dagestan, Ingushetiya, Kabardino-Balkariya, Kalmykiya, Kaluzhskaya, Karachayevo-Cherkesiya, Ivanovskaya, Karelia, Kirovskaya, Komi, Kostromskaya, Krasnodarskiy, Kurskaya, Leningradskaya (including St. Petersburg), Lipetskaya, Mariy-El, Mordoviya, Moskovskaya (including the capital, Moscow), Murmanskaya, Nenetskiy, Nizhegorodskaya, Novgorodskaya, Severnaya Osetiya, Orlovskaya, Penzenskaya, Pskovskaya, Rostovskaya, Ryazanskaya, Saratovskaya, Smolenskaya, Stavropolskiy, Tambovskaya, Tatarstan, Tulskaya, Tverskaya, Ulyanovskaya, Vladimirskaya, Volgogradskaya, Vologodskaya, Voronezhskaya, Yaroslavskaya;
- World Time +4 (+5 midyear) Samarskaya, Udmurtiya;
- World Time +5 (+6 midyear) Bashkortostan, Chelyabinskaya, Khanty-Mansiyskiy, Komi-Permyatskiy, Kurganskaya, Orenburgskaya, Permskaya, Sverdlovskaya, Tyumenskaya, Yamalo-Nenetskiy;
- World Time +6 (+7 midyear) Altayskiy, Novosibirskaya, Omskaya, Altayskiy;
- World Time +7 (+8 midyear) Evenkiyskiy, Kemerovskaya, Khakasiya, Krasnoyarskiy, Taymyrskiy, Tomskaya, Tyva;
- World Time +8 (+9 midyear) Buryatiya, Irkutskaya, Ust-Ordynskiy;
- World Time +9 (+10 midyear) Aginskiy-Buryatskiy, Amurskaya, Chitinskaya, Sakha;
- World Time +10 (+11 midyear) Khabarovskiy, Primorskiy, Yevreyskaya;
- World Time +11 (+12 midyear) Magadanskaya, Sakhalinskaya;
- World Time +12 (+13 midyear) Chukotskiy, Kamchatskaya, Koryakskiy;

VERIFICATION OF STATIONS USING TRANSMITTERS IN ST. PETERSBURG AND KALININGRAD: Transmissions of certain world band stations—such as the Voice of Russia, Radio Rossii and China Radio International—when emanating from transmitters located in St. Petersburg and Kaliningrad, may be verified directly from: World Band Verification QSL Service, Centre for Broadcasting and Radio Communications No. 2 (CRR-2), ul. Akademika Pavlova 13A, 197376 St. Petersburg, Russia. Phone: +7 (812) 234-1002. Fax: +7 (812) 234 2971 during working hours. Contact: Mikhail V. Sergeyev, Chief Engineer; or Mikhail Timofeyev, verifier. Free stickers. Two IRCs required for a reply, which upon request includes a copy of "Broadcast Schedule," which gives transmission details (excluding powers) for all transmissions emanating from three distinct transmitter locations: Kaliningrad-Bolshakovo, St. Petersburg and St. Petersburg-Popovka. This organization—which has 26 shortwave, three longwave, 15 medium wave (AM) and nine FM transmitters—relays broadcasts for clients for the equivalent of about $0.70-1.00 per kW/hour.

Government Radio Agencies

C.I.S. FREQUENCY MANAGEMENT ENGINEERING OFFICE: The Main Centre for Control of Broadcasting Networks, 7 Nikolskaya Str., 103012 Moscow, Russia. Phone: +7 (095) 298-3302. Fax: +7 (095) 956 7546 or +7 (095) 921 1624. Email: (Titov) titov@mccbn.ru; or titov@nsl.ru. Web: www.mccbn.ru. Contact: (general) Mrs. Antonia Ostakhova, Interpreter, Mrs. Nina Bykova; or Ms. Margarita Ovetchkina; (administration) Anatoliy T. Titov, Chief Director. This office is responsible for the operation of radio broadcasting in the Russian Federation, as well as for frequency usage of transmitters throughout much of the C.I.S. Correspondence should be concerned only with significant technical observations or engineering suggestions concerning frequency management improvement—not regular requests for verifications. Correspondence in Russian preferred, but English accepted.

CENTRE FOR BROADCASTING AND RADIO COMMUNICATIONS NO. 2 (GPR-2)—see VERIFICATION OF STATIONS USING TRANSMITTERS IN ST. PETERSBURG AND KALININGRAD, above.

STATE RADIO COMPANY: AS Radioagency Co., Pyatnitskaya 25, 113326 Moscow, Russia. Phone: (Khlebnikov and Petrunicheva) +7 (095) 233-6474; (Komissarova) +7 (095) 233-6660; (Staviskaia) +7 (095) 233-7003. Fax: (Khlebnikov, Petrunicheva and Komissarova) +7 (095) 233 1342; (Staviskaia) +7 (095) 230 2828 or +7 (095) 233 7648. Contact: Valentin Khlebnikov, Mrs. Maris Petrunicheva, Mrs. Lyudmila Komissarova or Mrs. Rachel Staviskaia.

STATE TRANSMISSION AUTHORITY: Russian Ministry of Telecommunication, ul. Tverskaya 7, 103375 Moscow, Russia. Phone: +7 (095) 201-6568. Fax: +7 (095) 292 7086 or +7 (095) 292 7128. Contact: Anatoly C. Batiouchkine.

STATE TV AND RADIO COMPANY: Russian State TV and Radio Company, Yamskogo polya, 5-ya ul. 19/21, 125124 Moscow, Russia. Phone: +7 (095) 213-1054, +7 (095) 213-1054 or +7 (095) 250-0511. Fax: +7 (095) 250 0105. Contact: Ivan Sitilenlov.

Adygey Radio (Radio Maykop), ul. Zhukovskogo 24, 352700 Maykop, Republic of Adygeya, Russia. Contact: A.T. Kerashev, Chairman. English accepted but Russian preferred. Return postage helpful.

Amur Radio, GTRK Amur, per Svyatitelya Innokentiya 15, 675000 Blagoveschensk, Russia. Contact: V.I. Kal'chenko, Chief Engineer.

Arkhangel'sk Radio, GTRK "Pomorye," ul. Popova 2, 163000 Arkhangel'sk, Arkhangel'skaya Oblast, Russia; or U1PR, Valentin G. Kalasnikov, ul. Suvorov 2, kv. 16, Arkhangel'sk, Arkhangel'skaya Oblast, Russia. Replies irregularly to correspondence in Russian.

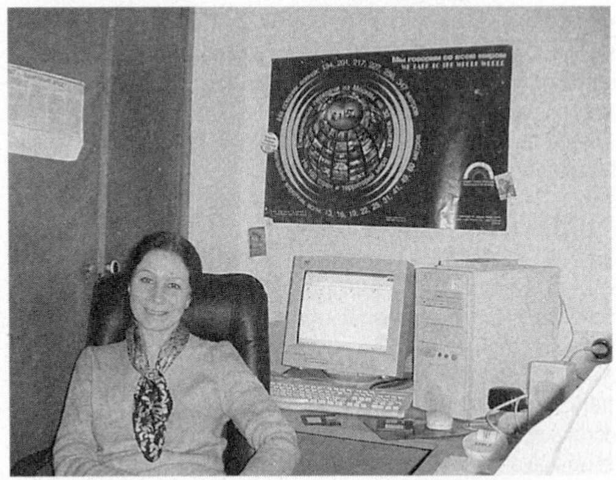

Irene Larina, host of the Voice of Russia's "Russian by Radio" course. VoR

Buryat Radio, Dom Radio, ul. Erbanova 7, 670013 Ulan-Ude, Republic of Buryatia, Russia. Contact: Z.A. Telin; Mrs. M.V. Urbaeva, 1st Vice-Chairman; or L.S. Shikhanova.

Kabardino-Balkar Radio (Radio Nalchik), ul. Nogmova 38, 360000 Nalchik, Republic of Kabardino-Balkariya, Russia. Contact: Kamal Makitov, Vice-Chairman. Replies to correspondence in Russian.

Kamchatka Radio, RTV Center, Dom Radio, ul. Sovietskaya 62-G, 683000 Petropavlovsk-Kamchatskiy, Kamchatskaya Oblast, Russia. Contact: A. Borodin, Chief OTK; or V.I. Aibabin. $1 required. Replies in Russian to correspondence in Russian or English. Currently inactive on shortwave, apart from a special program for fishermen—*see* next item.

Kamchatka Rybatskaya—a special service for fishermen off the coasts of China, Japan and western North America; *see* "Kamchatka Radio," above, for contact details.

Khabarovsk Radio (when operating), RTV Center, ul. Lenina 71, 680013 Khabarovsk, Khabarovskiy Kray, Russia; or Dom Radio, pl. Slavy, 682632 Khabarovsk, Khabarovskiy Kray, Russia. Web: (program schedule only) www.khb.ru/Afisha/Radio/kabar.htm. Contact: (technical) V.N. Kononov, Glavnyy Inzhener.

Khanty-Mansiysk Radio, Dom Radio, ul. Mira 7, 626200 Khanty-Mansiysk, Khanty-Mansyiskiy Avt. Okrug, Tyumenskaya Oblast, Russia. Contact: (technical) Vladimir Sokolov, Engineer.

Krasnoyarsk Radio, Krasnoyarskaya GTRK, "Tsentr Rossii," ul. Mechnikova 44A, 666001 Krasnoyarsk 28, Krasnoyarskiy Kray, Russia. E-mail: postmaster@telegid.krasnoyarsk.su. Contact: Valeriy Korotchenko; or Anatoliy A. Potehin, RAØAKE. Free local information booklets in English/Russian. Replies in Russian to correspondence in English or Russian. Return postage helpful.

Magadan Radio, RTV Center, ul. Kommuny 8/12, 685013 Magadan, Magadanskaya Oblast, Russia. Contact: Viktor Loktionov or V.G. Kuznetsov. Return postage helpful. Occasionally replies to correspondence in Russian.

Mariy Radio, Mari Yel, ul. Osipenko 50, 424014 Yoshkar-Ola, Russia. Contact: V. F. Melnikov, Director. Replies in Russian to correspondence in English or Russian. Return postage useful.

Mayak—*see* Radiostantsiya Mayak.

Murmansk Radio, Sopka Varnichnaya, 183042 Murmansk, Murmanskaya Oblast, Russia; or RTV Center, Sopka Varnichaya, 183042 Murmansk, Murmanskaya Oblast, Russia. Phone: +7 (8152) 561-527. Phone/fax: +7 (8152) 459-770. Fax: +7 (8152) 231 913. Email: tvmurman@sampo.ru; tvmurman@sampo.karelia.ru; murmantv@com.mels.ru. Web: www.sampo.ru/~tvmurman/radio/rmain.html. Contact: D. Perederi (chairman).

Perm Radio, Permskaya Gosudarstvennaya Telekinoradiokompaniya, ul. Technicheskaya 21, 614600 Perm, Permskaya Oblast, Russia; or ul. Krupskoy 26, 614060 Perm, Permskaya Oblast, Russia. Contact: M. Levin, Senior Editor; or A. Losev, Acting Chief Editor.

Radio Gardarika, Radio Studio Dom Radio, Ligovsky Prospekt 174, 197002 St. Petersburg, Russia. Email: studiosw@metroclub.ru. Contact: Dmitry Vasyliev, Shortwave Project Manager. Replies to correspondence in Russian and English. Return postage helpful.

Radio Maykop—*see* Adygey Radio, above.

Radio Mix-Master, Office 1, ul. Oktyabr'skaya 20/1, 677027 Yakutsk, Respublika Sakha, Russia. Phone: +7 (4112) 420-302. Web: http://mixmaster.ykt.ru.

Radio Nalchik—*see* Radio Kabardino-Balkar, above.

Radio Radonezh, Pyatnitskaya 25, 113326 Moscow, Russia. E-mail: radrad@mrezha.ru. Web: (includes RealAudio) www.radrad.ru. Replies to correspondence in English and Russian. A station independent of the Russian Orthodox Church, but which reflects its beliefs.

Radio Rossii (Russia's Radio), Yamskogo polya 5-ya ul. 19/21, 125124 Moscow, Russia. Phone: +7 (095) 213-1054, +7 (095) 250-0511 or +7 (095) 251-4050. Fax: +7 (095) 250 0105, +7 (095) 233 6449 or +7 (095) 214 4767. Web: (includes Windows Media) www.radiorus.ru. Contact: Sergei Yerofeyev, Director of International Operations [sic]; or Sergei Davidov, Director. Free English-language information sheet. For verification of reception from transmitters located in St. Petersburg and Kaliningrad, *see NOTE*, above, shortly after the country heading, "RUSSIA."

Radio Samorodinka, P.O. Box 898, Center, 101000 Moscow, Russia. Contact: Lev Stepanovich Shiskin, Editor. This station may be licensed as other than a regular broadcaster.

Radiostantsiya Mayak, ul. Pyatnitskaya 25, 113326 Moscow, Russia. Phone: +7 (095) 950-6767. Fax: +7 (095) 959 4204. Email: inform@radiomayak.ru. Web: (includes Windows Media) www.radiomayak.ru. Although no longer operating officially on shortwave from Russia, the station's programs can still be heard on the world bands via outlets such as Belarusian Radio's Program 2 and one or two regional stations in western Siberia. Unofficially, Mayak broadcasts are also aired over certain military transmitters in Belarus which operate in the 2, 3 and 5 MHz bands. Correspondence in Russian preferred, but English increasingly accepted.

Radiostantsiya Tikhiy Okean ("Radio Station Pacific Ocean"), RTV Center, ul. Uborevieha 20A, 690000 Vladivostok, Primorskiy Kray, Russia.

Sakha Radio, GTRK Respubliki Sakha, ul. Ordzhonikidze 48, 677007 Yakutsk, Respublika Sakha, Russia. Contact: (general) Alexandra Borisova; Lia Sharoborina, Advertising Editor; or Albina Danilova, Producer, "Your Letters"; (technical) Sergei Bobnev, Technical Director. Russian books $15; audio cassettes $10. Free station stickers and original Yakutian souvenirs. Replies to correspondence in English.

Sakhalin Radio, GTRK "Sakhalin," ul. Komsomolskaya 211, 693000 Yuzhno-Sakhalinsk, Sakhalinskaya Oblast, Russia. Phone: (Director of Radio) +7 (42422) 729-349. Phone/fax: (GTRK parent company) +7 (42422) 35286. Email: gtrk@sakhalin.ru; (Romanov) romanov@gtrk.sakhalin.su. Web: www.gtrk.ru/RV/radio.htm. Contact: S. Romanov, Director of Radio.

Tatarstan Awazy—*see* Voice of Tatarstan.

Tuva Radio, ul. Gornaya 31, 667003 Kyzyl, Tuva, Russia. Verifies reception reports written in Russian.

Tyumen' Radio, RTV Center, ul. Permyakova 6, 625013 Tyumen', Tyumenskaya Oblast, Russia. E-mail: regtumc@sbtx.tmn.ru. Contact: (general) Liliya Vycherova, Advertising Manager; (technical) V.D. Kizerov, Engineer, Technical Center. Sometimes replies to correspondence in Russian. Return postage helpful.

Voice of Russia, ul. Pyatnitskaya 25, Moscow 113326, Russia. Phone: (Chairman) +7 (095) 950-6331; (International Relations Department) +7 (095) 950-6440; (Technical Department) +7 (095) 950-6115. Fax: (Chairman & World Service in English) +7 (095) 230 2828; Email: letters@vor.ru. Web: (includes RealAudio) www.vor.ru. Contact: (Letters Department, World Service in English) Olga Troshina, Tanya Stukova, Elena Osipova or Elena Frolovskaya; (Chairman) Armen Oganesyan; (International Relations Department) Victor Kopytin, Director; (Technical Department) Ms. Rachel Staviskaya, Director; (World Service in English) Vladimir Zhamkin, Director. For language services other than English contact the International Relations Department.

Voice of Tatarstan, ul. Maksima Gor'kogo 15, 420015 Kazan, Tatarstan, Russia. Phone: (general) +7 (8432) 384-846; (editorial) +7 (8432) 367-493. Fax: +7 (8432) 361-283. Email: root@gtrkrt.kazan.su; postmaster@stvcrt.kazan.su. Contact: Hania Hazipovna Galinova.

ADDRESS FOR RECEPTION REPORTS: QSL Manager, P.O. Box 134, 420136 Kazan, Tatarstan, Russia. Contact: Ildus Ibatullin, QSL Manager. Offers an honorary diploma in return for 12 correct reports in a given year. The diploma costs 2 IRCs for Russia and 4 IRCs elsewhere. All reports to the QSL Manager address listed above. Accepts reports in English and Russian. Return postage helpful.

RWANDA World Time +2

Deutsche Welle—Relay Station Kigali—Correspondence should be directed to the main offices in Cologne, Germany *(see)*.

Radio Rwanda, B.P. 404, Kigali, Rwanda. Fax: +250 (7) 6185. Contact: Marcel Singirankabo. $1 required. Rarely replies, with correspondence in French preferred.

SAO TOME E PRINCIPE World Time exactly

Voice of America/IBB—São Tomé Relay Station, P.O. Box 522, São Tomé, São Tomé e Príncipe. Contact: Manuel Neves, Transmitter Plant Technician. Replies direct if $1 included with correspondence, otherwise all communications should be directed to the usual VOA or IBB addresses in Washington (*see* USA).

SAUDI ARABIA World Time +3

Broadcasting Service of the Kingdom of Saudi Arabia, P.O. Box 61718, Riyadh-11575, Saudi Arabia. Phone: (general)

+966 (1) 404-2795; (administration) +966 (1) 442-5493. Fax: (general) +966 (1) 402 8177. Web: (Holy Quran domestic service, RealAudio only) http://radio.kacst.edu.sa/ithaa.ram. Contact: (general) Mutlaq A. Albegami. Free travel information and book on Saudi history. For technical contacts including Engineering and Frequency Management, see the next entry.

Saudi Arabian Radio & Television, P.O. Box 8525, Riyadh-11492, Saudi Arabia. Phone: (technical & frequency managementl) +966 (1) 442-5170. Fax: (technical & frequency management) +966 (1) 404 1692. Email: alsamnan@yahoo.com. Contact: Suleiman Al-Samnan, Director of Engineering and Frequency Management; Suleiman Al-Kalifa, General Manager; Suleiman Al Haidari, Engineer; or Youssef Dhim.

SEYCHELLES World Time +4

BBC World Service—Indian Ocean Relay Station, P.O. Box 448, Victoria, Mahé, Seychelles; or Grand Anse, Mahé, Seychelles. Phone: +248 78-269. Fax: +248 78 500. Contact: (administration) Peter J. Loveday, Station Manager; (technical) Peter Lee, Resident Engineer; Nigel Bird, Resident Engineer; or Steve Welch, Assistant Resident Engineer. Nontechnical correspondence should be sent to the BBC World Service in London (*see*).

Far East Broadcasting Association—FEBA Radio

MAIN OFFICE: P.O. Box 234, Mahé, Seychelles, Indian Ocean. Phone: (main office) +248 282-2000 Fax: +248 242-146. Email: mmaillet@feba.org.sc. Web: www.feba.org.uk. Contact: (general) Hugh Barton, Seychelles Director; (technical) Richard Whittington, Schedule Engineer; or Andy Platts, Head of Engineering; (reception reports) N. Nugashe, QSL Secretary; Regina Duval; or Doreen Dugathe. Free stickers, pennants and station information sheet. $1 or one IRC helpful. Also, *see* FEBC Radio International—USA and United Kingdom.

CANADA OFFICE: 6850 Antrim Avenue, Burnaby BC, V5J 4M4 Canada. Phone: +1 (604) 430-8439. Fax: +1 (604) 430 5272. Email: dpatter@axionet.com.

INDIA OFFICE: FEBA India, P.O. Box 2526, 7 Commissariat Road, Bangalore-560 025, India. Phone: +91 (80) 558-5019. Fax: +91 (80) 558 5098. Email: febindia@giasbg01.vsn1.net.in. Contact: Peter Muthl Raj.

SIERRA LEONE World Time exactly

Sierra Leone Broadcasting Service, New England, Freetown, Sierra Leone. Phone: +232 (22) 240-123; +232 (22) 240-173; +232 (22) 240-497 or 232 (22) 241-919. Fax: +232 (22) 240 922. Contact: Cyril Juxon-Smith, Officer in Charge; or Henry Goodaig Hjax, Assistant Engineer.

SINGAPORE World Time +8

BBC World Service—Far Eastern Relay Station, Merlin Communications International Ltd., 51 Turut Track, Singapore 718930. Phone: + 65 260-1511. Fax: +65 253 8131. Contact: (technical) Far East Resident Engineer. Nontechnical correspondence should be sent to the BBC World Service in London (*see*).

Radio Corporation of Singapore, Farrer Road, P.O. Box 968, Singapore 912899; or (physical location) Caldecott Broadcast Centre, Caldecott Hill, Andrew Road, Singapore 299939. Phone: +65 251-8166, +65 251-8622 or +65 359-7340. Fax: +65 254 8062, +65 256 1995, +65 256 9533, +65 256 9556 or +65 256 9338. Email: (general) info@rcs.com.sg; (Engineering Dept.) engineering@rcs.com.sg. Web: (general) www.rcs.com.sg; (RealAudio) http://rcslive.singnet.com.sg. Contact: (general) Lillian Tan, Public Relations Division; Lim Heng Tow, Manager, International and Community Relations; Tan Eng Lai, Promotion Executive; Hui Wong, Producer/Presenter; or Lucy Leong; (administration) Anthony Chia, Director General; (technical) Asaad Sameer Bagharib, V.P. Engineering; or Lee Wai Meng. Free regular and Post-It stickers, pens, umbrellas, mugs, towels, wallets and lapel pins. Do not include currency in envelope.

Radio Nederland via Singapore—All correspondence should be directed to the regular address in Holland (*see*).

Radio Japan via Singapore—All correspondence should be directed to the regular address in Japan (*see*).

Radio Singapore International, Farrer Road, P.O. Box 5300, Singapore 912899, Singapore; or (physical address) Caldecott Broadcast Centre, Annex Building Level 1, Andrew Road, Singapore 299939. Phone: (general) + 65 251-8622. Fax: +65 259 1357 or +65 259 1380. Email: info@rsi.com.sg; or english@rsi.com.sg. Web: (includes RealAudio) www.rsi.com.sg. Contact: (general) Mrs. Sakuntala Gupta, Programme Manager, English Service; (technical) Mr Lim Wing Kee, RSI Engineering. Free souvenir T-shirts and key chains to selected listeners. Do not include currency in envelope.

SLOVAKIA World Time +1 (+2 midyear)

Radio Slovakia International, Mýtna 1, P.O. Box 55, 81755 Bratislava 15, Slovakia. Phone: (Editor-in-Chief) +421 (7) 5727-3730; (English Service) +421 (7) 5727-3736 or +421 (7) 5727-2737; (technical) +421 (7) 5727-3251. Fax: +421 (7) 5249 6282 or +421 (7) 5249 8247; (technical) +421 (7) 5249 7659. Email: (English Section) englishsection@slovakradio.sk; for other languages, the format is rsi_language@slovakradio.sk (e.g. rsi_german@slovakradio.sk); (Frequency Manager) chocolata@slovakradio.sk. Web: (general) www.slovakradio.sk; (RealAudio in English) www.wrn.org/ondemand/slovakia.html. Contact: Oxana Ferjenčíková, Director of English Broadcasting; (administration) PhDr. Karol Palkovič, Head of External Broadcasting; or Dr. Slavomira Kubickova, Head of International Relations; (technical) Ms. Edita Chocholatá, Frequency Manager; Jozef Krátky, Ing. May exchange stamps, recipes and coins. Free pennants, pocket calendars, T-shirts (occasionally) and other souvenirs and publications.

SOLOMON ISLANDS World Time +11

Solomon Islands Broadcasting Corporation, P.O. Box 654, Honiara, Solomon Islands. Phone: +677 20051. Fax: +677 23159 or +677 25652. email: sibcnews@solomon.com.sb. Web: (SIBC news in text format) www.commerce.gov.sb/Others/sibc_news_headlines.htm. Contact: (general) Julian Maka'a, Producer, "Listeners From Far Away"; Cornelius Teasi; or Silas Hule; (administration) Johnson Honimae, General Manager; (technical) John Babera, Chief Engineer. IRC or $1 helpful. Problems with the domestic mail system may cause delays.

SOMALIA World Time +3

Radio Galkayo (when operating), 2 Griffith Avenue, Roseville NSW 2069, Australia. Phone/fax: +61 (2) 9417-1066. Web: www. radiogalkayo.com. Contact: Sam Voron, Australian Director. $5, AUS$5 or 5 IRCs required. A community radio station in the Mudug region of northeastern Somalia, and operated by the Somali International Amateur Radio Club. Seeks volunteers and donations of radio equipment and airline tickets.

SOMALILAND World Time +3

NOTE: "Somaliland," claimed as an independent nation, is diplomatically recognized only as part of Somalia.

Radio Hargeysa, P.O. Box 14, Hargeysa, Somaliland, Somalia. E-mail: no known direct mail address, but try admin@radiohargeysa.com or radio@somaliland.com. Web: (includes RealAudio) www.radiohargeysa.com; (RealAudio archives only) www.radiosomaliland.com. Contact: Sulayman Abdel-Rahman, announcer. More likely to respond to correspondence in Somali or Arabic.

SOUTH AFRICA World Time +2

BBC World Service via South Africa—For verification direct from the South African transmitters, contact Sentech (*see* below). Nontechnical correspondence should be sent to the BBC World Service in London (*see*).

Channel Africa, P.O. Box 91313, Auckland Park 2006, South Africa. Phone: (executive editor) +27 (11) 714-2255; + 27 (11) 714-2551 or +27 (11) 714-3942; (technical) +27 (11) 714-3409. Fax: (executive editor) +27 (11) 482 3506; + 27 (11) 714 2546, +27 (11) 714 4956 or +27 (11) 714 6377; (technical) +27 (11) 714 5812. Email: (general) africancan@channelafrica.org; (news desk) news.africa@channelafrica.org. Web: (RealAudio in English, French and Portuguese, plus text) www.channelafrica.org; (RealAudio in English) www.wrn.org/ondemand/southafrica.html. Contact: (general) Tony Machilika, Head of English Service; Robert Michel, Head of Research and Strategic Planning; or Noeleen Vorster, Corporate Communications Manager; (technical) Mrs. H. Meyer, Supervisor Operations; or Lucienne Libotte, Technology Operations. T-shirts $11 and watches $25. Prices do not include shipping and handling. Free *Share* newsletter from the Department of Foreign Affairs, stickers and calendars. Reception reports are best directed to Sentech (*see* below), which operates the transmission facilities.

Radiosondergrense (Radio Without Boundaries), Posbus 91312, Auckland Park 2006, South Africa; or SABC, P.O. Box 2551, Cape Town 8000, South Africa. Phone: (general) +27 (89) 110-2525; (live studio on-air line) +27 (89) 110-4553; (station manager) +27 (11) 714-2702. Fax: (general) +27 (11) 714 6445; (station manager) +27 (11) 714 3472. Email: (general) info@rsg.co.za; (Myburgh) myburghs@sabc.co.za. Web: (includes RealAudio) www.rsg.co.za. Contact: Sarel Myburgh, Station Manager. Reception reports are best directed to Sentech (*see* below), which operates the shortwave transmission facilities. A domestic service of the South African Broadcasting Corporation (*see* below), and formerly known as Afrikaans Stereo. The shortwave operation is scheduled to be eventually replaced by a satellite and FM network.

Radio Lusofonia, P.O. Box 1586, Alberton 1450, South Africa. Phone: +27 (12) 361-8833. Fax: +27 (12) 348 3713. E-mail: dario.bettencourt@tollink.co.za.

Sentech (Pty) Ltd, Shortwave Services, Private Bag X06, Honeydew 2040, South Africa. Phone: (general) +27 (11) 475-5600; (shortwave) +27 (11) 475-1596; (Otto) +27 (11) 471-4658 or +27 (11) 471-4537. Fax: (general) +27 (11) 475 5112; (Otto) +27 (11) 471 4758 or +27 (11) 471 4754. Email: (general) comms@sentech.co.za; (Otto) ottok@sentech.co.za; (Smuts) smutsn@sentech.co.za. Web: (general) www.sentech.co.za; (schedules, unofficial) http://home.mweb.co.za/an/andre46/. Contact: Mr. Neël Smuts, Managing Director; Rodgers Gamuti, Client Manager; or Kathy Otto, HF Coverage Planner. Sentech issues its own verification cards, and is the best place to send reception reports for world band stations broadcasting via South African facilities.

South African Broadcasting Corporation

ADMINISTRATION AND GENERAL TECHNICAL MATTERS: Private Bag X1, Auckland Park 2006, South Africa. Phone: (Head Office) +27 (11) 714-9111; (information) +27 (11) 714-9797; (technical) +27 (11) 714-3409. Fax: (general) +27 (11) 714 4086 or +27 (11) 714 5055; (technical) +27 (11) 714 3106 or +27 (11) 714 5812. Web: (includes RealAudio) www.sabc.co.za. Contact: (administration) Mrs. Charlotte Mampane, Chief Executive, Radio. Reception reports are best directed to Sentech (*see*, above), which operates the transmission facilities.

RADIO PROGRAMME SALES: Private Bag X1, Auckland Park 2006, South Africa. Phone: (general enquiries) +27 (11) 714-5681, +27 (11) 714-6039 or +27 (11) 714-4044; (actuality programs) +27 (11) 714-4709; (music) +27 (11) 714-4315. Fax: +27 (11) 714 3671. Email: botham@sabc.co.za; snymane@sabc.co.za; or corbinm@sabc.co.za. Offers a wide range of music, book readings, radio drama, comedy and other types of programs.

Trans World Radio Africa

NONTECHNICAL CORRESPONDENCE: Trans World Radio—South Africa, Private Bag 987, Pretoria 0001, South Africa. Phone: +27 (12) 807-0053. Fax: +27 (12) 807 1266. Web: (includes online email form) www.twraro.org.za.

TECHNICAL CORRESPONDENCE: Reception reports and other technical correspondence are best directed to Sentech (*see*, above) or to TWR's Swaziland office (*see*). Also, *see* USA.

SPAIN World Time +1 (+2 midyear)

Radio Exterior de España (Spanish National Radio, World Service)

MAIN OFFICE: Apartado de Correos 156.202, E-28080 Madrid, Spain. Phone: (general) +34 (91) 346-1081/1083; (Audience Relations) +34 (91) 346-1149. Fax: +34 (91) 346 1815. Email: (Director) dir_ree.rne@rtve.es; (Spanish programming) audiencia.ree.rne@rtve.es; (foreign language programming, including English) lenguas_extranjeras.rne@rtve.es; (reception reports) dxree.rne@rtve.es. Web: (includes RealAudio and Windows Media) www.rtve.es/rne/ree/. Contact: (Audience Relations) Pilar Salvador M.; (Assistant Director) Pedro Fernández Céspedes; (Director) Javier Garrigós. Free stickers and tourist information. Reception reports can be sent to: Radio Exterior de España, Relaciones con la Audiencia, Sección DX, Apartado de Correos 156.202, E-28080 Madrid, Spain or to the email address listed above.

TRANSCRIPTION SERVICE: Radio Nacional de España, Servicio de Transcripciones, Apartado 156.200, Casa de la Radio (Prado del Rey), E-28223 Madrid, Spain.

HF FREQUENCY PLANNING OFFICE: Prado del Rey. Pozuelo de Alarcom, E-28223 Madrid, Spain. Phone: +34 (91) 346-1276 or +34 (91) 346-1978. Fax: +34 (91) 346 1401. Email: (Almarza) planif_red2.rne@rtve.es. Contact: Fernando Almarza, Frequency Planning.

NOBLEJAS TRANSMITTER SITE: Centro Emisor de RNE en Onda Corta, Ctra. Dos Barrios s/n, E-45350 Noblejas-Toledo, Spain.

COSTA RICA RELAY FACILITY—see Costa Rica.

MOSCOW OFFICE: P.O Box 88, 109044 Moscow, Russia.

WASHINGTON NEWS BUREAU: National Press Building, 529 14th Street NW, Suite 1288, Washington DC 20045 USA. Phone: +1 (202) 783-0768. Contact: Luz María Rodríguez.

SRI LANKA World Time +6:00

Deutsche Welle—Relay Station Sri Lanka, 92/2 D.S. Senanayake Mawatha, Colombo 08, Sri Lanka. Phone: +94 (1) 699-449. Fax: +94 (1) 699 450. Contact: R. Groschkus, Resident Engineer. Nontechnical correspondence should be sent to Deutsche Welle in Germany (*see*).

Radio Japan/NHK, c/o SLBC, P.O. Box 574, Torrington Square, Colombo 7, Sri Lanka. This address for technical correspondence only. General nontechnical listener correspondence should be sent to the usual Radio Japan address in Japan. News-oriented correspondence may also be sent to the NHK Bangkok Bureau (*see* Radio Japan, Japan).

Sri Lanka Broadcasting Corporation (also announces as "Radio Sri Lanka" in the external service), P.O. Box 574, Independence (Torrington) Square, Colombo 7, Sri Lanka. Phone: (general) +94 (1) 697-491 or +94 (1) 697-493; (Director General) +94 (1) 696-140. Fax: (general) +94 (1) 697 150 or +94 (1) 698 576; (Director General) +94 (1) 695 488; (Sooryia, Phone/fax) +94 (1) 696 1311. Email: slbc@sri.lanka.net; slbcweb@sri.lanka.net. Web: www.infolanka.com/people/sisira/slbc.html. Contact: Icumar Ratnayake, Controller, "Mailbag Program"; (SLBC administration) Eric Fernando, Director General; Newton Gunaratne, Deputy Director-General; (technical) H.M.N.R. Jayawardena, Engineer - Training and Frequency Management; Wimala Sooriya, Deputy Director - Engineering; or A.M.W. Gunaratne, Station Engineer, Ekala.

Voice of America/IBB—Iranawila Relay Station.
ADDRESS: International Broadcasting Bureau, Sri Lanka Transmission Station, c/o U.S. Embassy, 210 Galle Road, Colombo 3, Sri Lanka. Contact: Gary Wise, Station Manager. Nontechnical correspondence should be sent to the VOA address in Washington.

SUDAN World Time +3

Sudan National Radio Corporation, P.O. Box 572, Omdurman, Sudan. Phone: +249 (11) 553-151 or +249 (11) 552-100. Email: snrc@sudanmail.net. Web: (includes RealAudio) www.sudanradio.net. Contact: (general) Mohammed Elfatih El Sumoal; (technical) Abbas Sidig, Director General, Engineering and Technical Affairs; Mohammed Elmahdi Khalil, Administrator, Engineering and Technical Affairs; Saleh Al-Hay; or Adil Didahammed, Engineering Department. Replies irregularly. Return postage necessary.

SURINAME World Time -3

Radio Apintie, Postbus 595, Paramaribo, Suriname. Phone: +597 40-05-00. Fax: +597 40 06 84. Email: apintie@sr.net. Web: www.apintie.sr. Contact: Charles E. Vervuurt, Director. Free pennant. Return postage or $1 required. Email reception reports preferred, since local mail service is unreliable.

SWAZILAND World Time +2

Swaziland Commercial Radio (when operating)
NONTECHNICAL CORRESPONDENCE: P.O. Box 5569, Rivonia 2128, Transvaal, South Africa. Phone: +27 (11) 884-8400. Fax: +27 (11) 883 1982. Contact: Fernando Vaz-Osiori; Rob Vickers, Manager—Religion. IRC helpful. Replies irregularly.
TECHNICAL CORRESPONDENCE: P.O. Box 99, Amsterdam 2375, South Africa. Contact: Guy Doult, Chief Engineer.
SOUTH AFRICA BUREAU: P.O. Box 1586, Alberton 1450, Republic of South Africa. Phone: +27 (11) 434-4333. Fax: +27 (11) 434 4777.

Trans World Radio—Swaziland
MAIN OFFICE: P.O. Box 64, Manzini, Swaziland. Phone: +268 505-2781/2/3. Fax: +268 505 5333. Email: (James Burnett, Regional Engineer and Frequency Manager) jburnett@twr.org; (Chief Engineer) sstavrop@twr.org; (Mrs. L. Stavropoulos, DX Secretary) lstavrop@twr.org; (Greg Shaw, Follow-up Department) gshaw@twr.org. Web: (transmission schedule) www.gospelcom.net/twr/broadcasts/africa.htm. Contact: (general) Greg Shaw, Follow-up Department; G.J. Alary, Station Director; or Joseph Ndzinisa, Program Manager; (technical) Mrs. L. Stavropoulos, DX Secretary; Chief Engineer; or James Burnett, Regional Engineer. Free stickers, postcards and calendars. A free Bible Study course is available. May swap canceled stamps. $1, return postage or 3 IRCs required. Also, *see* USA.
AFRICA REGIONAL OFFICE: P.O. Box 4232, Kempton Park 1610, South Africa. Contact: Stephen Boakye-Yiadom, African Regional Director.
CÔTE D'IVOIRE OFFICE: B.P. 2131, Abidjan 06, Côte d'Ivoire.
KENYA OFFICE: P.O. Box 21514 Nairobi, Kenya.
MALAWI OFFICE: P. O. Box 52 Lilongwe, Malawi.
SOUTH AFRICA OFFICE: P.O. Box 36000, Menlo Park 0102, South Africa.
ZIMBABWE OFFICE: P.O. Box H-74, Hatfield, Harare, Zimbabwe.

SWEDEN World Time +1 (+2 midyear)

IBRA Radio (program producer)

MAIN OFFICE: International Broadcasting Association, Box 396, SE-105 36 Stockholm, Sweden; or Box 4033, SE-14104 Huddinge, Sweden. Phone: +46 (8) 619-2540. Fax: +46 (8) 619 2539. Email: hq@ibra.se; or ibra@ibra.se. Web: www.ibra.se/; www.ibra.org/. Contact: Mikael Stjernberg, Public Relations Manager; or Helene Hasslof. Free pennants and stickers. IBRA Radio's programs are aired over various world band stations, including Trans World Radio (Monaco); and also broadcast via transmitters in Germany and Russia. Accepts emailed reception reports.

CYPRUS OFFICE: P.O. Box 7420, 3315 Limassol, Cyprus. Contact: Rashad Saleem. Free schedules, calendars and stickers.

Radio La Voz del Pueblo, Box 122, SE-191 22 Solentuna, Sweden. Tested briefly during January 2001, and hopes eventually to broadcast regularly six days per week.

Radio Sweden

MAIN OFFICE: SE-105 10 Stockholm, Sweden. Phone: (general) +46 (8) 784-7200, +46 (8) 784-7207, +46 (8) 784-7288 or +46 (8) 784-5000; (listener voice mail) +46 (8) 784-7287; (technical department) +46 (8) 784-7286. Fax: (general) +46 (8) 667 6283; (polling to receive schedule) +46 8 660 2990. Email: (general) radiosweden@sr.se; (In Touch) intouch@p6.sr.se; (schedule on demand) english@rs.sr.se; (Roxström) sarah.roxstrom@rs.sr.se; (Hagström) nidia.hagstrom@rs.sr.se; (Wood) george.wood@p6.sr.se; (MediaScan) media@p6.sr.se; (Sounds Nordic) sono@p6.sr.se); (Beckman, technical manager) rolf-b@stab.sr.se. Web: (includes RealAudio) www.sr.se/rs/ .Contact: (general) Nidia Hagström, Host, "In Touch with Stockholm" [include your telephone number]; Sarah Roxström, Head, English Service; Greta Grandin, Program Assistant, English Service; Gabby Katz, Presenter of Heartbeat; Bill Schiller, Spectrum presenter; George Wood; Olimpia Seldon, Assistant to the Director; or Charlotte Adler, Public Relations and Information; (administration) Finn Norgren, Director General; (technical) Rolf Erik Beckman, Head, Technical Department; or Anders Baecklin, Editor, Technical Administration. T-shirts (three sizes) $10 or £8. Payment for T-shirts may be made by international money order, Swedish postal giro account No. 43 36 56-6 or internationally negotiable bank check.

NEW YORK NEWS BUREAU: Swedish Broadcasting, 747 Third Avenue, 8th floor, New York NY 10022 USA. Phone: +1 (212) 644-1224. Fax: +1 (212) 644 1227. Contact: Elizabeth Johansson.

WASHINGTON NEWS BUREAU: Swedish Broadcasting, 2030 M Street NW, Suite 700, Washington DC 20036 USA. Phone: +1 (202) 785-1727. Contact: Folke Rydén, Lisa Carlsson or Steffan Ekendahl.

TRANSMISSION AUTHORITY: TERACOM, Svensk Rundradio AB, P.O. Box 17666, SE-118 92 Stockholm, Sweden. Phone: (general) +46 (8) 555-420-00; (Nilsson) +46 (8) 555-420-66. Fax: (general) +46 (8) 555-420-01; (Nilsson) +46 (8) 555 420 60. Email: (general) info@teracom.se; (Nilsson) magnus.nilsson@teracom.se. Web: www.teracom.se. Contact: (Frequency Planning Dept.—Head Office): Magnus Nilsson; (Engineering) H. Widenstedt, Chief Engineer. Free stickers; sometimes free T-shirts to those monitoring during special test transmissions. Seeks monitoring feedback for new frequency usages.

SWITZERLAND World Time +1 (+2 midyear)

European Broadcasting Union, Case Postal 67, CH-1218 Grand-Saconnex, Geneva, Switzerland. Phone: +41 (22) 717-2111 or +41 (22) 717-2221. Fax: +41 (22) 798 5897 or +41 (22) 717 2481. Email: ebu@ebu.ch. Web: www.ebu.ch. Contact: Jean-Bernard Munch, Secretary-General; or Robin Levey, Strategic Information Service Database Manager. Umbrella organization for broadcasters in 49 European and Mediterranean countries.

International Telecommunication Union, Place des Nations, CH-1211 Geneva 20, Switzerland. Phone: (Fonteyne) +41 (22) 730-5983; or Pham) +41 (22) 730-6136. Fax: +41 (22) 730 5785. Contact: Jacques Fonteyne or Hai Pham. Email: (schedules and reference tables) Brmail@itu.int; (Fonteyne) jacques.fonteyne@itu.int; or (Pham) pham.hai@itu.int. Web: www.itu.ch. The ITU is the world's official regulatory body for all telecommunication activities, including world band radio. Offers a wide range of official multilingual telecommunication publications in print and/or digital formats.

Radio Réveil, Paroles, Les Chapons 4, CH-2022 Bevaix, Switzerland. Phone: +41 (32) 846-1655. Fax: +41 (32) 846 2547. Email: contact@paroles.ch. Web (includes RealAudio): www.paroles.ch. An evangelical radio ministry, part of the larger Radio Réveil Paroles de Vie organization, which apart from broadcasting to much of Europe on longwave, medium wave and FM, also targets an African audience via the shortwave facilities of Germany's Deutsche Telekom (*see*).

Swiss Radio International

MAIN OFFICE: Giacomettistrasse 1, CH-3000 Berne 15, Switzerland. Phone: (general) +41 (31) 350-9222; (English Department) +41 (31) 350-9790; (French Department) +41 (31) 350-9555; (German Department) +41 (31) 350-9535; (Italian Department) +41 (31) 350-9531); (Frequency Management) +41 (31) 350-9734. Fax: (general) +41 (31) 350 9569; (administration) +41 (31) 350 9744 or +41 (31) 350 9581; (Communication and Marketing) +41 (31) 350 9544; (Programme Department) +41 (31) 350 9569; (English Department) +41 (31) 350 9580; (French Department) +41 (31) 350 9664; (German Department) +41 (31) 350 9562; (Italian Department) +41 (31) 350 9678; (Frequency Management) +41 (31) 350 9745. Email: (general) format is language@sri.ch (e.g. english@sri.ch, german@sri.ch); (marketing) marketing@swissinfo.org; (technical) technical@swissinfo.org; (Frequency Management): ulrich.wegmueller@sri.ch. Web: (includes RealAudio and MP3) www.swissinfo.org. Contact: (general) Diana Zanotti, English Department; Marlies Schmutz, Listeners' Letters, German Programmes; Thérèse Schafter, Listeners' Letters, French Programmes; Esther Niedhammer, Listeners' Letters, Italian Programmes; Beatrice Lombard, Promotion; Giovanni D'Amico, Audience Officer; (administration) Ulrich Kündig, General Manager; Nicolas Lombard, Director; Walter Fankhauser, Head, Communication and Marketing Services; Rose-Marie Malinverni, Head, Editorial Co-ordination Unit; Ron Grünig, Head, English Programmes; James Jeanneret, Head, German Programmes; Philippe Zahne, Head, French Programmes; Fabio Mariani, Head, Italian Programmes; (technical) Paul Badertscher, Head, Engineering Services; Ulrich Wegmüller, Frequency Manager; or Bob Zanotti. Free station flyers, posters, stickers and pennants. Sells CDs of Swiss music, plus audio and video (PAL/NTSC) cassettes; also, Swiss watches and clocks, microphone lighters, briefcases, umbrellas, letter openers, books, T-shirts, sweatshirts and Swiss Army knives. VISA/EURO/AX or cash, but no personal checks. For catalog, write to SRI Enterprises, c/o the above address, fax +41 (31) 350 9581, or email shopping@sri.srg-ssr.ch. Swiss Radio International will gradually phase out its shortwave transmissions by the end of October 2004 in favor of alternative delivery sys-

tems such as the internet and to a lesser extent direct satellite broadcasting in English.
WASHINGTON NEWS BUREAU: 2030 M Street NW, Washington DC 20554 USA. Phone: (general) +1 (202) 775-0894 or +1 (202) 429-9668; (French-language radio) +1 (202) 296-0277; (German-language radio) +1 (202) 7477. Fax: +1 (202) 833 2777. Contact: Christophe Erbeck, reporter.

SYRIA World Time +2 (+3 midyear)

Radio Damascus, Syrian Radio and Television, P.O. Box 4702, Damascus, Syria. Phone: +963 (11) 221-7653. Fax: +963 (11) 222 2692. Contact: Mr. Afaf, Director General; Mr. Adnan Al-Massri; Adnan Salhab; Lisa Arslanian; or Mrs. Wafa Ghawi. Free stickers, paper pennants and *The Syria Times* newspaper. Replies can be highly erratic, but as of late have been more regular, if sometimes slow.

TAIWAN—*see* CHINA (TAIWAN)

TAJIKISTAN World Time +5

Radio Tajikistan, Chapaev Street 31, 734025 Dushanbe, Tajikistan; or English Service, International Service, Radio Tajikistan, P.O. Box 108, 734025 Dushanbe, Tajikistan. Phone: (Director) +7 (3772) 210-877 or +7 (3772) 277-417; (English Department) +7 (3772) 277-417; (Ramazonov) +7 (3772) 277-667 or +7 (3772) 277-347. Fax: +7 (3772) 211 198. Note that the country and city codes are scheduled to be changed in the near future, so the current +7 (3772) should then become +992 (372). Email: treng@td.silk.org. Contact: (administration) Mansur Sultanov, Director - Tajik Radio; Nasrullo Ramazonov, Foreign Relations Department. Correspondence in Russian or Tajik preferred. There is no official policy for verification of listeners' reports, so try sending reception reports and correspondence in English to the attention of Mr. Ramazonov, who is currently the sole English speaker at the station. Caution should be exercised when contacting him via email, as it is his personal account and he is charged for both incoming and outgoing mail. In addition, all email is routinely monitored and censored. Return postage of 5$ has been requested on at least one occasion, but enclosing currency notes is risky due to the high level of postal theft in the country. IRCs are not exchangeable, so including small souvenirs with your letter may help produce a reply.
TRANSMISSION FACILITIES: Television and Radiocommunications Ltd., ul. Internationalskaya 85, 734001 Dushanbe, Tajikistan. Phone: +7 (3772) 244-646. Fax: +7 (3772) 212 517. Email: nodir@uralnet.ru. Contact: Rakhmatillo Masharipovich Masharipov, Director General.
Tajik Radio, ul. Chapaeva 31, 734025 Dushanbe, Tajikistan. Contact information as for Radio Tajikistan, above.

TANZANIA World Time +3

Radio Tanzania, Nyerere Road, P.O. Box 9191, Dar es Salaam, Tanzania. Phone: +255 (51) 860-760. Fax: +255 (51) 865 577. Email: radiotanzania@raha.com. Contact: (general) Abdul Ngarawa, Director of Broadcasting; Mrs. Edda Sanga, Controller of Programs; Ms. Penzi Nyamungumi, Head of English Service and International Relations Unit; or Ahmed Jongo, Producer, "Your Answer"; (technical) Taha Usi, Chief Engineer; or Emmanuel Mangula, Deputy Chief Engineer. Replies to correspondence in English.
Voice of Tanzania Zanzibar, Department of Broadcasting, Radio Tanzania Zanzibar, P.O. Box 2503, Zanzibar, Tanzania—if this address brings no reply, try P.O. Box 1178; (Ali Bakari Muombwa, personal address) P.O. Box 2068, Zanzibar, Tanzania. Phone: +255 (54) 231-088. Fax: + 255 (54) 257 207. Contact: (general) Seti Suleiman, Director; Ndaro Nyamwolha; Ali Bakari Muombwa; Abdulrah'man M. Said; or Kassim S. Kassim; (technical) Khalid Hassan Rajab, Shortwave Transmitter Engineer; Nassor M. Suleiman, Maintenance Engineer. $1 return postage helpful.

THAILAND World Time +7

BBC World Service—Asia Relay Station, P.O. Box 20, Muang, Nakhon Sawan 60000, Thailand. Contact: Jaruwan Meesaurtong, Personal Assistant. Verifies reception reports.
Radio Thailand World Service, 236 Vibhavadi Rangsit Highway, Din Daeng, Huaykhwang, Bangkok 10400, Thailand. Phone: +66 (2) 277-1814, +66 (2) 274-9098. Phone/fax: +66 (2) 277-6139, +66 (2) 274-9099. Email: amporns@mozart.inet.co.th. Web: (includes RealAudio) www.prd.go.th/prdnew/eng/radio_e/index.html. Contact: Mrs. Amporn Samosorn, Chief of External Services; or Patra Lamjiack. Free pennants. Replies irregularly, especially to those who persist.

TOGO World Time exactly

Radio Lomé, B.P. 434, Lomé, Togo. Phone: + 228 212-492. Contact: (nontechnical) Batchoudi Malúlaba or Geraldo Isidine. Return postage, $1 or 2 IRCs helpful. French preferred but English accepted.

TUNISIA World Time +1

Radiodiffusion Télévision Tunisienne, 71 Avenue de la Liberté, TN-1070 Tunis, Tunisia. Phone: +216 (1) 801-177. Fax: +216 (1) 781 927. Email: info@radiotunis.com. Web: (includes RealAudio) www.radiotunis.com/news.html. Contact: Mongai Caffai, Director General; Mohamed Abdelkafi, Director; Kamel Cherif, Directeur; Masmoudi Mahmoud; Mr. Bechir Betteib; or Smaoui Sadok, Le Sous-Directeur Technique. Replies irregularly and slowly to correspondence in French or Arabic. $1 helpful. For reception reports try: Le Chef de Service du Controle de la Récepcion de l'Office National de la Télediffusion, O.N.T, Cité Ennassim I, Bourjel, B.P. 399, TN-1080 Tunis, Tunisia. Phone: +216 (1) 801-177. Fax: +216 (1) 781 927. Email: ont.@ati.tn. Contact: Abdesselem Slim.

TURKEY World Time +2 (+3 midyear)

Meteoroloji Sesi Radyosu (Voice of Meteorology), T.C. Tarim Bakanliği, Devlet Meteoroloji İşleri, Genel Müdürlüğü, P.K. 401, Ankara, Turkey. Phone: +90 (312) 359-7545, X-281. Fax: +90 (312) 314 1196. Contact: (nontechnical) Gühekin Takinalp; Recep Yilmaz, Head of Forecasting Department; or Abdullah Gölpinar; (technical) Mehmet Örmec , Director General. Free tourist literature. Return postage helpful.
Türkiye Polis Radyosu (Turkish Police Radio), T.C. Içişleri Bakanliği, Emniyet Genel Müdürlüğü, Ankara, Turkey. Contact: Fatih Umutlu. Tourist literature for return postage. Replies irregularly.
Voice of Turkey (Turkish Radio-Television Corporation External Service)
MAIN OFFICE, NONTECHNICAL: TRT External Services Depart-

Turkey's capital, Ankara, as viewed by Voice of Turkey's George Poppin and wife Dottie. This Muslim nation, with close ties to Europe, has been fighting terrorism for years. G. Poppin

ment, TRT Sitesi, Turan Güneş Blv., Or-An Çankaya, 06450 Ankara, Turkey; or P.K. 333, Yenişehir, 06443 Ankara, Turkey. Phone: (general) +90 (312) 490-9800/9801; (English Service) +90 (312) 490-9842. Fax: +90 (312) 490 9835/45/46. Email: (general) infotsr@tsr.gov.tr; (Turkish broadcasts) turkceyayin@tsr.gov.tr; (English Service) englishservice@tsr.gov.tr; same format applies for Arabic, French, German and Russian services, e.g. germanservice@tsr.gov.tr. Web: (includes RealAudio) www.trt.net.tr. Contact: (English and non-technical) Mr. Osman Erkan, Chief, English Service; Ms. Refside Morali, Host of "Letterbox" & "DX Corner"; (other languages) Mr. Rafet Esit, Director, Foreign Languages Section; (administration) Mr. Danyal Gurdal, Head, External Services Department. Technical correspondence, such as on reception quality should be directed to: Ms. Sedef Somaltin (*see* next entry below). On-air language courses offered in Arabic and German, but no printed course material. Free stickers, pennants, and tourist literature.
MAIN OFFICE, TECHNICAL (FOR EMIRLER AND ÇAKIRLAR TRANSMITTER SITES AND FOR FREQUENCY MANAGEMENT): TRT Teknik Yardimcilik, TRT Sitesi, Kat: 5/C, 06450 ORAN, Ankara, Turkey. Phone: +90 (312) 490-1730/2. Fax: +90 (312) 490 1733. Email: utis@turnet.net.tr or utis2@trt.net.tr; (Ms. Somaltin) sedef.somaltin@trt.net.tr. Contact: Mr. O. Haluk Buran, TRT Deputy Director General (Head of Engineering); or Ms. Sedef Somaltin, Engineer.
SAN FRANCISCO OFFICE, SCHEDULES: 2654 17th Avenue, San Francisco CA 94116 USA. Phone: +1 (415) 564-9968. Email: GPoppin@aol.com. Contact: George Poppin. This address, a volunteer office, only provides TRT schedules to listeners. All other correspondence should be sent directly to Ankara.

TURKMENISTAN World Time +5

Radio Turkmenistan, National TV and Radio Broadcasting Company, Mollanepes St. 3, 744000 Ashgabat, Turkmenistan. Phone: +993 (12) 251-515. Fax: +993 (12) 251 421. Contact: (administration) Yu M. Pashaev, Deputy Chairman of State Television and Radio Company; (technical) G. Khanmamedov; Kakali Karayev, Chief of Technical Department; or A.A Armanklichev, Deputy Chief, Technical Department. This country is currently under strict censorship and media people are closely watched. A lot of foreign mail addressed to a particular person may attract the attention of the security services. Best is not to address your mail to particular individuals but to the station itself.

UGANDA World Time +3

Radio Uganda
GENERAL OFFICE: P.O. Box 7142, Kampala, Uganda. Phone: +256 (41) 257-256. Fax: +256 (41) 256 888. Email: ugabro@infocom.co.ug. Contact: (general) Charles Byekwaso, Controller of Programmes; Machel Rachel Makibuuka; or Mrs. Florence Sewanyana, Head of Public Relations. $1 or return postage required. Replies infrequently and slowly. Correspondence to this address has sometimes been returned with the annotation "storage period overdue"—presumably because the mail is not collected on a regular basis.
ENGINEERING DIVISION: P.O. Box 2038, Kampala, Uganda. Phone: +256 (41) 256-647. Contact: Leopold B. Lubega, Principal Broadcasting Engineer; or Rachel Nakibuuka, Secretary. Four IRCs or $2 required. Enclosing a self addressed envelope may also help to get a reply.

UKRAINE World Time +2 (+3 midyear)

WARNING-MAIL THEFT: For the time being, letters to Ukrainian stations, especially containing funds or IRCs, are more likely to arrive safely if sent by registered mail.
Government Transmission Authority: RRT/Concern of Broadcasting, Radiocommunication and Television, 10 Dorogajtshaya St., 254112 Kyiv, Ukraine. Phone: +380 (44) 226-2262 or +380 (44) 444-6900. Fax: +380 (44) 440 8722; or +380 (44) 452 6784. Email: (Kurilov) ak@cbrt.freenet.kiev.ua. Contact: Mr. Mykola Kyryliuk, Technical Operations & Management; Alexej M. Kurilov; Alexey Karpenko; Alexander Serdiuk; Nikolai P. Kiriliuk, Head of Operative Management Service; or Mrs. Liudmila Deretskaya, Interpreter. This agency is responsible for choosing the frequencies used by Radio Ukraine International.
Radio Ukraine International, Kreshchatik str., 26, 252001 Kyiv, Ukraine. Phone: +380 (44) 228-2534, +380 (44) 229-1757, +380 (44) 229-1883 or (phone/fax) +380 (44) 228-7356. Fax: +380 (44) 229 4585 or +380 (44) 229 3477. Email: (QSL cards & complete schedules) vsru@nrcu.gov.ua; (reception reports) egorov@nrcu.gov.ua; mo@ukrradio.ru.kiev.ua. Web: www.nrcu.gov.ua/eng/program/vsru/vsru.html. Contact: (administration) Inna Chichinadze, Vice-Director of RUI; (technical) Anatolii Ivanov, Frequency Coordination, Engineering Services, Ukrainian Radio. Free stickers, calendars and Ukrainian stamps.

UNITED ARAB EMIRATES World Time +4

UAE Radio from Abu Dhabi (if reactivated), Ministry of Information and Culture, P.O. Box 63, Abu Dhabi, United Arab Emirates. Phone: +971 (2) 451-000. Fax: (Ministry of Information and Culture) +971 (2) 452 504. Contact: (technical) Ibrahim Rashid, Director General, Technical Department; or Fauzi Saleh, Chief Engineer. Free stickers, postcards and stamps. Do not enclose money with correspondence.

FREQUENCY MANAGEMENT: Abu Dhabi Radio, P.O. Box 63, Abu Dhabi, United Arab Emirates. Phone: +971 (2) 436-849. Fax: +971 (2) 451 155 or +971 (2) 450 205. Email: waleed_alzaabi@ebc.co.ae. Contact: Mr. Samir Iskander, Senior Engineer; or Mr. Waleed Al-Zaabi, Chief Engineer.

SHORTWAVE TRANSMITTER STATION: P.O. Box 3966, Abu Dhabi, United Arab Emirates. Phone: +971 (2) 406-2149 or +971 (2) 644-1936. Fax: +971 (2) 406 2149. Contact: Bahaaeldin Abdelrazek, Head of Transmitter Station.

Transmissions were discontinued in summer 2001and substituted with relays of other world band stations such as Radio Canada International and Adventist World Radio.

UAE Radio in Dubai, P.O. Box 1695, Dubai, United Arab Emirates. Phone: +971 (4) 370-255. Fax: +971 (4) 374 111, +971 (4) 370 283 or +971 (4) 371 079. Contact: Ms. Khulud Halaby; or Sameer Aga, Producer, "Cassette Club Cinarabic"; (technical) K.F. Fenner, Chief Engineer—Radio; or Ahmed Al Muhaideb, Assistant Controller, Engineering. Free pennants. Replies irregularly. Unconfirmed reports say the station may be operating under a new name, Emirates Radio.

UNITED KINGDOM World Time exactly (+1 midyear)

Adventist World Radio, 39 Brendon Street, London W1H 5HD, United Kingdom. Phone: +44 (1344) 401-401. Fax: +44 (1344) 401 419. Email: english@awr.org. Web: www.awr.org. Contact: Bert Smit, European Regional Director; or Victor Hulbert, Director English Listener Mail. All mail addressed to AWR and written in English is processed at this address. Also, *see* AWR listings under Germany, Guam, Guatemala, Italy, Kenya, Madagascar and USA.

BBC Monitoring, Caversham Park, Reading, Berkshire RG4 8TZ, United Kingdom. Phone: (switchboard) +44 (118) 948-6000; (Foreign Media Unit—Broadcast Schedules/monitoring) +44 (118) 948-6261; Marketing Department) +44 (118) 948-6289. Fax: (Foreign Media Unit) +44 (118) 946 1993; (Marketing Department) +44 (118) 946 3823. Email: (Marketing Department) marketing@mon.bbc.co.uk; (Foreign Media Unit/World Media) fmu@mon.bbc.co.uk; (Kenny) dave_kenny@mon.bbc.co.uk; (publications and real time services) marketing@mon.bbc.co.uk. Web: www.monitor.bbc.co.uk. Contact: (administration) Andrew Hills, Director of Monitoring; (Foreign Media Unit) Chris McWhinnie, Editor "World Media," Broadcast Schedules; Dave Kenny, Chief Sub Editor, "World Media," Broadcast Schedules; or Peter Feuilherade; (Publication Sales) Stephen Innes, Marketing. BBC Monitoring produces the weekly publication *World Media* which reports political, economic, legal, organisational, programming and technical developments in the world's electronic media. Its reports are based on material broadcast or published by radio and TV stations, news agencies, Websites and publications; other information issued but not necessarily broadcast by such sources and by other relevant bodies; and information obtained by BBC Monitoring's own observations of foreign media. Available on yearly subscription, costing £410.00. Price excludes postage overseas. *World Media* is also available online through the Internet or via a direct dial-in bulletin board at an annual cost of £425.00. Broadcasting Schedules, issued weekly by email at an annual cost of £99.00. VISA/MC/AX. The Technical Operations Unit provides detailed observations of broadcasts on the long, medium, short wave, satellite bands and Internet. This unit provides tailored channel occupancy observations, reception reports, and updates the *MediaNet* source information database (constantly updated on over 100 countries) and the *Broadcast Research Log* (a record of broadcasting developments compiled daily). BBC Monitoring works in conjunction with the Foreign Broadcast Information Service (*see* USA).

BBC World Service

MAIN OFFICE, NONTECHNICAL: Bush House, Strand, London WC2B 4PH, United Kingdom. Phone: (general) +44 (20) 7240-3456; (Press Office) +44 (20) 7557-2947/1; (International Marketing) +44 (20) 7557-1143. Fax: (Audience Relations) +44 (20) 7557 1258; ("Write On" listeners' letters program) +44 (20) 7436 2800; (Audience and Market Research) +44 (20) 7557 1254; (International Marketing) +44 (20) 7557 1254. Email: (general listener correspondence) worldservice.letters@bbc.co.uk; ("Write On") writeon@bbc.co.uk. Web: (general, including RealAudio and Windows Media) www.bbc.co.uk/worldservice/; (entertainment and information) www.beeb.com. Contact: Patrick Condren, Presenter, of "Write On"; Alan Booth, Controller, Marketing & Communications; Miles Palmer, Head of Business Development; or Mark Byford, Chief Executive. Offers *BBC On Air* magazine (*see* below). Also, *see* Antigua, Ascension, Oman, Seychelles, Singapore and Thailand. Does not verify reception reports due to budget limitations.

SAN FRANCISCO OFFICE, SCHEDULES: 2654 17th Avenue, San Francisco CA 94116 USA. Phone: +1 (415) 564-9968. Email: GPoppin@aol.com. Contact: George Poppin. This address, a volunteer office, only provides BBC World Service schedules to listeners. All other correspondence should be sent directly to the main office in London.

TECHNICAL: See Merlin Communications International, below.

BBC WORLD SERVICE—PUBLICATION AND PRODUCT SALES BBC World Service Shop, Bush House Arcade, Strand, London WC2B 4PH, United Kingdom. Phone: +44 (20) 7557-2576. Fax: +44 (20) 7240 4811. Sells numerous audio/video (video PAL/VHS only) cassettes, publications, portable world band radios, T-shirts, sweatshirts and other BBC souvenirs available by mail order to UK addresses only.

"BBC On Air" monthly program magazine, Room 310 NW, Bush House, Strand, London WC2B 4PH, United Kingdom. Phone: (editorial office) +44 (20) 7557-2211; (Circulation Manager) +44 (20) 7557-2855; (advertising) +44 (20) 7557-2873; (subscription voice mail) +44 (20) 7557-2211. Fax: +44 (20) 7240 4899. Email: on.air.magazine@bbc.co.uk. Contact: (editorial) Dionne St. Hill, Editor; (subscriptions) Rosemarie Reid, Circulation Manager; (advertising) Adam Ford. Subscription $32 or £20 per year. VISA/MC/AX/Barclay/EURO/Access, Postal Order, International Money Draft or cheque in pounds sterling.

Commonwealth Broadcasting Association, CBA Secretariat, 17 Fleet Street, London EC4Y 1AA, United Kingdom. Phone: +44 (20) 7583-5550. Fax: +44 (20) 7583 5549. Email: cba@cba.org.uk. Web: www.cba.org.uk. Publishes the annual *Commonwealth Broadcaster Directory* and the quarterly *Commonwealth Broadcaster* (online subscription form available).

Everest Radio, 226 Greenford Avenue, Hanwell, London W7

3QT, United Kingdom. Email: (general) everestradio@hotmail.com; (Bijaya Thapa) bijaya@everesttimeslondon.com. Web: (includes RealAudio) www.everestradio.co.uk. Contact: Bijaya Thapa, Director. A production of Everest Media Services for the Nepalese diaspora, transmitted from Moosbrunn, near the Austrian capital, Vienna.

Far East Broadcasting Association (FEBA), Ivy Arch Road, Worthing, West Sussex BN14 8BX, United Kingdom. Phone: +44 (1903) 237-281. Fax: +44 (1903) 205 294. Email: reception@febaradio.org.uk; or (Richard Whittington) dwhittington@febaradio.org.uk. Web: www.feba.org.uk. Contact: Tony Ford or Richard Whittington, Schedule Engineer. This office is the headquarters for FEBA worldwide.

High Adventure Ministries Global Broadcasting Network—"European Beacon", P.O. Box 2801, Eastbourne, East Sussex BN21 2EQ, United Kingdom. Phone: +44 (1323) 639-798. Fax: +44 (1323) 722 716. Email: hamukmartin@hotmail.com. Contact: Martin Thompson. Broadcasts via transmitters of Deutsche Telekom (*see*) in Jülich, Germany. Also, *see* High Adventure Radio, USA.

IBC-Tamil, P.O. Box 1505, London SW8 2ZH, United Kingdom. Phone: +44 (20) 7787-8000. Fax: +44 (20) 7787 8010. Contact: A.C. Tarcisius, Managing Director; S. Shivaranjith, Manager; K. Pillai; or Public Relations Officer.

London Radio Service (LRS), Medialink, 7 Fitzroy Square, London W1P 5AH, United Kingdom. Phone: +44 (20) 7554-3300. Fax: +44 (20) 7554 3326. Email: (Stoddart) hstoddart@lrs.co.uk; (Allen) callen@lrs.co.uk. Web: (includes RealAudio) www.lrs.co.uk. Contact: Helen Stoddart, Marketing/Production Coordinator; or Charlotte Allen, Media Relations Executive. LRS is an award-winning producer and syndicator of news and feature programs in English, Arabic, Russian, Spanish and Portuguese, on behalf of the Foreign and Commonwealth Office. On world band, heard in English and Spanish via WWCR, USA (*see*).

Merlin Communications International Limited, 20 Lincoln's Inn Fields, London WC2A 3ES, United Kingdom. Phone: +44 (171) 969-0000. Fax: +44 (171) 396 6223. Email: marketing@merlincommunications.com. Web: www.merlincommunications.com. Contact: Fiona Lowry, Chief Executive; Rory Maclachlan, Director of International Communications & Digital Services; Kevin Cawood, Director of Global Facilities; Ciaran Fitzgerald, Head of Engineering & Operations; Richard Hurd, Head of Transmission Sales; Ravi Maheswaran, Head of Facilities Management; or Laura Jelf, Marketing Manager.Merlin is a leading global communications facilities management company providing world class core communications , facilities management and technical services to prestigious customers including BBC World Service and the British Ministry of Defence (MoD). Operating the world's leading commercial short wave network, Merlin delivers over 1000 hours of short and medium wave broadcasts every day for internationnal and religious broadcasters in over 100 countries worldwide. International terrestrial transmission customers include Radio Canada International, Voice of America and NHK. Merlin are founder members of the Digital Radio Mondiale consortium, working to bring affordable digital AM radio to the marketplace. Does not verify reception reports.

Radio Ezra (when operating), Water Into Wine Ministry, P.O. Box 16, Stockton on Tees TS18 3GN, United Kingdom. Email: radio@water-into-wine.com. Web: http://radioezra.members.easyspace.com. Contact: John D. Hill. Broadcasts irregularly from different transmission sites. Verifies reception reports.

Salama Radio, P.O. Box 126, Chessington, Surrey KT9 2WJ, United Kingdom. Phone/fax: +44 (208) 395-7425. Email: admin@salamaradio.org. Web: www.salamaradio.org. Contact: Dr. Jacob Abdalla, President, Harvestime Ministries; Mrs. Margaret Perera, International Director, Harvestime Ministries. *NIGERIA ADDRESS:* P.O. Box 287, Jos, Plateau State, Nigeria. Commenced operation on July 6, 2001, via the U.K. facilities of Merlin Communications International (*see*, above). A radio project of Harvestime Ministries.

Tamil Broadcasting Corporation—London ("TBC-London"), P.O. Box 383, Harrow, HA1 3FW, United Kingdom. Phone: +44 (20) 8864-0909. Fax: +44 (20) 8864 0700. Email: tbcradio@hotmail.com. Broadcasts to Sri Lanka and southern India from the Jülich facilities of Germany's Deutsche Telekom (*see*).

Wales Radio International, Preseli Radio Productions, Pros Kairon, Crymych, Pembrokeshire, SA41 3QE, Wales, United Kingdom. Phone: +44 (1437) 563-361. Fax: +44 (1239) 831 390. Email: jenny@wri.cymru.net. Web: (includes RealAudio) http://wri.cymru.net. Contact: Jenny O'Brien. A weekly broadcast via the facilities of Merlin Communications International (*see*).

World Radio Network, P.O. Box 1212, London SW8 2ZF, United Kingdom. Phone: +44 (20) 7896-9000. Fax: + 44 (20) 7896 9007. Email: (general) email@wrn.org, or letters@wrn.org; (WRN Boutique) boutique@wrn.org To contact individuals, the format is firstname.lastname (Cohen) jeffc@wrn.org; (Ayris) tim.ayris@wrn.org. Web: www.wrn.org. Contact: Karl Miosga, Managing Director; Kimberly Rivers, Sales Manager; Jeffrey Cohen, Director of Development; Tim Ashburner, Director of Technical Operations; Tim Ayris, Marketing and Rebroadcasting Manager. Sells numerous items such as Polo and T-shirts, baseball caps, pen knives and dual-time wristwatches. More details at the website, or contact WRN Boutique at the address above. Webcasts using RealAudio and Windows Media, plus program placement via satellite in various countries for nearly two dozen international broadcasters.

UNITED NATIONS World Time –5 (–4 midyear)

United Nations Radio, Secretariat Building, Room S-850-M, United Nations, New York NY 10017 USA; or write to the station over which UN Radio was heard. Phone: +1 (212) 963-5201. Fax: +1 (212) 963 1307. Email: (general) unradio@un.org; (comments on programs) audio-visual@un.org; (reception reports) smithd@un.org. Web: (general) www.un.org/av/radio; (RealAudio) www.wrn.org/ondemand/unitednations.html; www.internetbroadcast.com/un/. Contact: (general) Sylvester E. Rowe, Chief, Radio and Video Service; or Ayman El-Amir, Chief, Radio Section, Department of Public Information; (reception reports) David Smith; (technical and nontechnical) Sandra Guy, Secretary. Free stamps and *UN Frequency* publication. Reception reports (including those sent by email) are verified with a QSL card.

GENEVA OFFICE: Room G209, Palais des Nations, CH-1211 Geneva 10, Switzerland. Phone: +41 (22) 917-4222. Fax: +41 (22) 917 0123.

PARIS OFFICE: UNESCO Radio, 7 Place de Fontenoy, F-75007 Paris, France. Fax: +33 (1) 45 67 30 72. Contact: Erin Faherty, Executive Radio Producer.

URUGUAY World Time –3

NOTE: If you are trying to make direct contact with stations in Montevideo for QSL purposes and are unsuccessful, you might try Uruguayan DXer Gabriel Gómez, Casilla de Correo 24.066,

11800 Montevideo, Uruguay. E-mail: gomezdx@yahoo.com or gomezdx@hotmail.com. Enclose return postage with all reports.

Emisora Ciudad de Montevideo, Canelones 2061, 11200 Montevideo, Uruguay. Phone: +598 (2) 402-0142. Fax: +598 (2) 402 0700. Contact: Aramazd Yizmeyian, Director General. Free stickers. Return postage helpful.

La Voz de Artigas (if reactivated), Av. Lecueder 483, 55000 Artigas, Uruguay. Phone: +598 (772) 2447 or +598 (772) 3445. Fax: +598 (772) 4744. Contact: (general) Sra. Solange Murillo Ricciardi, Co-Propietario; or Luis Murillo; (technical) Roberto Murillo Ricciardi. Free stickers and pennants. Replies to correspondence in English, Spanish, French, Italian and Portuguese.

Radiodifusion Nacional—*see* S.O.D.R.E., below.

Radio Monte Carlo, Av. 18 de Julio 1224 piso 1, 11100 Montevideo, Uruguay. Phone: +598 (2) 901-4433 or +598 (2) 908-3987. Fax: +598 (2) 901 7762. Email: cx20@netgate.com.uy. Web: (includes RealAudio) http://netgate.com.uy/cx20/. Contact: Ana Ferreira de Errázquin, Secretaria, Departmento de Prensa de la Cooperativa de Radioemisoras; Gustavo Cirino, Jefe Técnico; Déborah Ibarra, Secretaria; Emilia Sánchez Vega, Secretaria; or Ulises Graceras. Correspondence in Spanish preferred.

Radio Oriental—Same mailing address as Radio Monte Carlo, above. Phone: +598 (2) 901-4433 or +598 (2) 900-5612. Fax: +598 (2) 901 7762. Email: cx12@radiooriental.com.uy. Web: (includes RealAudio) www.radiooriental.com.uy/. Contact: (technical) José A. Porro, Technician. Correspondence in Spanish preferred.

Radio Sarandí del Yí, Sarandí 328, 97100 Sarandí del Yí, Uruguay. Phone/fax: +598 (367) 9155. Email: (owner) norasan@adinet.com.uy. Contact: Nora San Martín de Porro, Propietaria.

Radio Universo, Ferrer 1265, 27000 Castillos, Dpto. de Rocha, Uruguay. Email: am1480@adinet.com.uy. Contact: Juan Héber Brañas, Propietario. Currently on 1480 kHz medium wave AM only, but is expected to commence shortwave operation sometime in 2002.

S.O.D.R.E., Radiodifusión Nacional, Casilla 1412, 11000 Montevideo, Uruguay. Phone: +598 (2) 916-1933. Email: info@sodre.gub.uy. Web: www.sodre.gub.uy. Contact: (administration) Dr. Jorge Mascheroni, Director de Radiodifusión Nacional; (publicity) Daniel Ayala González, Publicidad; (technical) Francisco Escobar, Dpto. Técnico. Reception reports may also be sent to the "Radioactividades" program (*see*, below).

MEDIA PROGRAM: "Radioactividades," Casilla 7011, 11000 Montevideo, Uruguay. Fax: +598 (2) 575 4640. Email: radioact@chasque.apc.org. Web: www.chasque.apc.org/radioact/. Contact: Daniel Muñoz Faccioli.

USA

World Time –4 Atlantic, including Puerto Rico and Virgin Islands; –5 (–4 midyear) Eastern, excluding Indiana; –5 Indiana, except northwest and southwest portions; –6 (–5 midyear) Central, including northwest and southwest Indiana; –7 (–6 midyear) Mountain, except Arizona; –7 Arizona; –8 (–7 midyear) Pacific; –9 (–8 midyear) Alaska, except Aleutian Islands; –10 (–9 midyear) Aleutian Islands; –10 Hawaii; –11 Samoa

Adventist World Radio

HEADQUARTERS: 12501 Old Columbia Pike, Silver Spring MD 20904 USA. Email: english@awr.org. Web: www.awr.org; (Chinese service, English/Chinese text) www.vohc.com—worth a visit just for the graphics. Send all letters and reception reports to: AWR, 39 Brendon Street, London W1H 5HD, United Kingdom.

INTERNATIONAL RELATIONS: Box 29235, Indianapolis IN 46229 USA. Phone/fax: +1 (317) 891-8540. Contact: Dr. Adrian M. Peterson, International Relations Coordinator. Provides publications with regular news releases and technical information. Sometimes issues special verification cards. QSL stamps and certificates also available from this address in return for reception reports.

DX PROGRAM: "Wavescan," prepared by Adrian Peterson; aired on all AWR facilities and other stations. Also available in RealAudio at the AWR Website, www.awr.org. Also, *see* AWR listings under Germany, Guam, Guatemala, Italy, Kenya, Madagascar and United Kingdom.

AFNL-American Farsi NetLink, 7417 Van Nuys Blvd., Van Nuys CA 91405 USA. Phone: +1 (818) 988-4241; (toll-free within the United States) 1-800-547-9986. Fax: +1 (818) 781 3666. Email: afnl@pacbell.net. Web: (includes MP3) www.afnl.com. A satellite broadcaster which commenced shortwave broadcasts via Moldova during summer 2000.

AFRTS-Armed Forces Radio and Television Service (Shortwave), Naval Media Center, NDW Anacostia Annex, 2713 Mitscher Road SW, Washington DC 20373-5819 USA. For verification of reception, be sure to mark the envelope, "Attn: Short Wave Reception Reports." Email: (verifications) qsl@mediacen.navy.mil. Web: (AFRTS parent organization) www.afrts.osd.mil; (2-minute news clips in RealAudio): www.defenselink.mil/news/radio/; (Naval Media Center) www.mediacen.navy.mil. Contact: Michael Foutch, Chief Broadcast Operations Specialist; or Jennifer Grey, Broadcast Operations Specialist. The Naval Media Center is responsible for all AFRTS broadcasts aired on shortwave.

Aurora Communications, Mile 129, Sterling Highway, Ninilchik, Alaska, USA. Hopes to commence broadcasts to Russia during 2002.

BBC World Service via WYFR—Family Radio. For verification direct from WYFR's transmitters, contact WYFR—Family Radio (*see* below). Nontechnical correspondence should be sent to the BBC World Service in London (*see*).

Broadcasting Board of Governors (BBG), 330 Independence Avenue SW, Room 3360, Washington DC 20237 USA. Phone: +1 (202) 619-2538. Fax: +1 (202) 619 1241. Email: pubaff@ibb.gov. Web: www.ibb.gov/bbg/. Contact: (general) Kathleen Harrington, Public Relations; (administration) Mark Nathanson, Chairman. The BBG, created in 1994 and headed by nine members nominated by the President, is the overseeing agency for all official non-military United States international broadcasting operations, including the VOA, RFE-RL, Radio Martí and Radio Free Asia.

FEBC Radio International

INTERNATIONAL HEADQUARTERS: Far East Broadcasting Company, Inc., P.O. Box 1, La Mirada CA 90637 USA. Phone: +1 (310) 947-4651. Fax: +1 (310) 943 0160. Email: febc@febc.org. Web: www.febc.org. Operates world band stations in the Northern Mariana Islands, the Philippines and the Seychelles. Does not verify reception reports from this address.

RUSSIAN OFFICE: P.O. Box 2128, Khabarovsk 680020, Russia. Email: khabarovsk@febc.org.

UNITED KINGDOM OFFICE: FEBA Radio, Ivy Arch Road, Worthing, West Sussex BN14 8BX, United Kingdom. Phone: +44 (903) 237-281. Fax: +44 (903) 205 294. Email: reception@feba.org.uk or jbartlett@feba.org.uk. Web: www.feba.org.uk.

Federal Communications Commission, 445 12th Street SW, Washington DC 20554 USA. Phone: +1 (202) 418-0190; (toll-free within U.S.) 1-888-225-5322. Fax: +1 (202) 418 0232.

Email: (general information and inquiries) fccinfo@fcc.gov; (Freedom of Information Act requests) FOIA@fcc.gov; (Polzin) tpolzin@fcc.gov. Web: (general) www.fcc.gov; (high frequency operating schedules) www.fcc.gov/ib/pnd/neg/hf_web/seasons.html; (FTP) ftp://ftp.fcc.gov/pub/. Contact: (International Bureau, technical) Thomas E. Polzin.

Fundamental Broadcasting Network, Grace Missionary Baptist Church, 520 Roberts Road, Newport NC 28570 USA. Phone: +1 (252) 223-6088; (toll-free, within the United States) 1-800-245-9685; (Robinson) +1 (252) 223-4600. Web: (text) www.clis.com/fbn/; (RealAudio) www.worthwhile.com/fbn/. Email: fbn@bmd.clis.com. Alternative address: Morehead City NC 28557 USA. Phone: +1 (252) 240-1600. Fax: +1 (252) 726 2251. Contact: Pastor Clyde Eborn; (technical) David Robinson, Chief Engineer. Verifies reception reports if 1 IRC or (within USA) an SASE is included. Accepts email reports. Plans to eventually broadcast in Chinese, French, Russian and Spanish in addition to English.

George Jacobs and Associates, Inc., 8701 Georgia Avenue, Suite 711, Silver Spring MD 20910 USA. Phone: +1 (301) 587-8800. Fax: +1 (301) 587 8801. Email: gja@gjainc.com; or gjainc_20910@yahoo.com. Web: www.gjainc.com/. Contact: (technical) Bob German or Mrs. Anne Case; (administration) George Jacobs, P.E. This firm provides frequency management and other engineering services for a variety of private U.S. and other world band stations and brokers time on worldwide shortwave, AM, FM, satellite and cable systems for international broadcasters.

Herald Broadcasting Syndicate—Shortwave Broadcasts (all locations), Shortwave Broadcasts, P.O. Box 1524, Boston MA 02117-1524 USA. Phone: (toll-free, U.S. only) 1-800-288-7090; (elsewhere) +1 (617) 450-2929 [with either number, it's extension 2060 to hear recorded frequency information, and 2929 for Shortwave Helpline and to request printed schedules and information]. Fax: +1 (617) 450 2283. Web: (includes RealAudio) www.tfccs.com/GV/CSPS/HERALD/bdcst/bdcst.html. Contact: Catherine Aitken-Smith, Director of International Broadcasting, Herald Broadcasting Syndicate (representative for station activity in Boston). Free schedules and information about Christian Science. *The Christian Science Monitor* newspaper and a full line of Christian Science books are available from: 1 Norway Street, Boston MA 02115 USA. *Science and Health with Key to the Scriptures* by Mary Baker Eddy is available in English $14.95 paperback ($16.95 in French, German, Portuguese or Spanish paperback; $24.95 in Czech or Russian hardcover) from Science and Health, P.O. Box 1875, Boston MA 02117 USA.

Herald Broadcasting Syndicate—WSHB Cypress Creek, 1030 Shortwave Lane, Pineland SC 29934 USA. Phone: (general) +1 (803) 625-5551; (station manager) +1 (803) 625-5555; (engineer) +1 (803) 625-5554. Fax: +1 (803) 625 5559. Email: (Station Manager) evansc@wshb.com; (Chief Engineer) centgrafd@wshb.com; (QSL coordinator) riehmc@wshb.com. Web: www.tfccs.com/GV/shortwave/shortwave_schedule.html. Contact: (technical) Damian Centgraf, Chief Engineer; C. Ed Evans, Senior Station Manager; or Cindy Riehm, QSL Coordinator. Free station stickers when available. Visitors welcome from 9 to 4 Monday through Friday; for other times, contact transmitter site beforehand to make arrangements. This address is for technical feedback on South Carolina transmissions only; other inquiries should be directed to Shortwave Broadcasts, P.O. Box 1524, Boston MA 02117-1524 USA.

High Adventure Ministries Global Broadcasting Network

MAIN OFFICE: P.O. Box 100, Simi Valley CA 93062 USA. Phone: +1 (805) 520-9460; toll-free (within USA) 1-800-517-4673. Fax: +1 (805) 520 7823. Email: mail@highadventure.net. Web: www.highadventure.org. Contact: (listeners' correspondence) Pat Kowalick, "Listeners' Letterbox"; (nontechnical) Ralph McDevitt, Program Manager; (administration, High Adventure Ministries) George Otis, President and Chairman; (administration, KVOH) Paul Johnson, General Manager, KVOH; (technical) Paul Hunter, Director of Engineering. Free program schedules and *Voice of Hope* book. Sells books, audio and video cassettes, T-shirts and world band radios. Booklist available on request. VISA/MC. A new site is currently under construction in northern Nigeria which will eventually be home to FM, medium wave (AM) and shortwave transmitters. Also, *see* Palau and United Kingdom. Return postage (IRCs) required. Replies as time permits.

WESTERN AUSTRALIA OFFICE, NONTECHNICAL: P.O. Box 545, Balcatta WA 6194, Australia. Phone: +61 (8) 9345-1300. Fax: +61 (8) 9345 5407. Email: caron@hatikvahfilm.com. Contact: Caron Hedgeland.

CANADA OFFICE, NONTECHNICAL: Box 425, Station 'E', Toronto, M6H 4E3 Canada. Phone: +1 (905) 898-5447. Fax: +1 (905) 898 5447. Email: hiadvcan@home.com. Contact: Don McLaughlin, Director.

MIDDLE EAST OFFICE: P.O. Box 53379, Limassol, Cyprus. Phone: +972 (6) 690-3037. Fax: +972 (6) 695 9174. Email: gronberg@zahav.net.il. Contact: Isaac Gronberg.

PALAU OFFICE, NONTECHNICAL: P.O. Box 66, Koror, Palau 96940, Pacific Islands. Phone: +680 488-2162. Fax: +680 488 2163. Contact: Rolland Lau.

SINGAPORE OFFICE, NONTECHNICAL: 265B/C South Bridge Road - Eu Yan Sang Annexe, Singapore 058814, Singapore. Phone: + 65 221-2054. Fax: +65 221 2059. Email: csarch@singnet.com.sg. Contact: Cyril Seah.

U.K. OFFICE: P.O. Box 2801, Eastbourne, East Sussex BN21 2EQ, United Kingdom. Phone: +44 (1323) 639-798. Fax: +44 (1323) 722 716. Email: hamukmartin@hotmail.com. Contact: Martin Thompson.

International Broadcasting Bureau (IBB)—Reports to the Broadcasting Board of Governors (*see*), and includes, among others, the Voice of America, RFE-RL, Radio Martí and Radio Free Asia. IBB Engineering (Office of Engineering and Technical Operations) provides broadcast services for these stations. Contact: (administration) Brian Conniff, Director; or Joseph O'Connell, Director of External Affairs. Web: www.ibb.gov/ibbpage.html.

FREQUENCY AND MONITORING OFFICE, TECHNICAL:
IBB/EOF: Spectrum Management Division, International Broadcasting Bureau (IBB), Room 4611 Cohen Bldg., 330 Independence Avenue SW, Washington DC 20237 USA. Phone: +1 (202) 619-1669. Fax: +1 (202) 619 1680. Email: (scheduling) dferguson@ibb.gov; (monitoring) bw@his.com. Web: (general) http://monitor.ibb.gov; (email reception report form) http://monitor.ibb.gov/now_you_try_it.html. Contact: Dan Ferguson (dferguson@ibb.gov); or Bill Whitacre (bw@his.com).

KAIJ

ADMINISTRATION OFFICE: Two-if-by-Sea Broadcasting Co., 22720 SE 410th St., Enumclaw WA 89022 USA. Phone/fax: (Mike Parker, California) +1 (818) 606-1254; (Washington State office, if and when operating) +1 (206) 825 4517. Contact: Mike Parker (mark envelope, "please forward"). Relays programs of Dr. Gene Scott's University Network (*see*). Replies occasionally.

STUDIO: Faith Center, 1615 S. Glendale Avenue, Glendale CA 91025 USA. Phone: +1 (818) 246-8121. Contact: Dr. Gene Scott, President.

TRANSMITTER: RR#3 Box 120, Frisco TX 75034 USA; or Highway 380 West, Prosper TX 75078 USA (physical location: Highway 380, 3.6 miles west of State Rt. 289, near Denton TX; transmitters and antennas located on Belt Line Road along the lake in Coppell TX). Phone: +1 (972) 346-2758. Contact: Walt Green or Fred Bithell. Station encourages mail to be sent to the administration office, which seldom replies, or the studio (*see* above).

KJES—King Jesus Eternal Savior

STATION: The Lord's Ranch, 230 High Valley Road, Vado NM 88072 USA. Phone: +1 (505) 233-2090. Fax: +1 (505) 233 3019. Email: KJES@aol.com. Contact: Michael Reuter, Manager. $1 or return postage appreciated.

SPONSORING ORGANIZATION: Our Lady's Youth Center, P.O. Box 1422, El Paso TX 79948 USA. Phone: +1 (915) 533-9122.

KNLS—New Life Station

OPERATIONS CENTER: 605 Bradley Ct., Franklin TN 37067 USA (letters sent to the Alaska transmitter site are usually forwarded to Franklin). Phone: +1 (615) 371-8707 ext.140. Fax: +1 (615) 371 8791. Email: knls@aol.com. Web: www.knls.org. Contact: (general) Dale Ward, Executive Producer; L. Wesley Jones, Director of Follow-Up Teaching; or Mike Osborne, Senior Producer, English Language Service; (technical) F.M. Perry, Frequency Coordinator. Free *Alaska Calling!* newsletter and station pennants. Free spiritual literature and bibles in Russian, Mandarin and English. Free Alaska books, tapes, postcards and cloth patches. Two free DX books for beginners. Special, individually numbered, limited edition, verification cards issued for each new transmission period to the first 200 listeners providing confirmed reception reports. Stamp and postcard exchange. Return postage appreciated.

TRANSMITTER SITE: P.O. Box 473, Anchor Point AK 99556 USA. Phone: +1 (907) 235-8262. Fax: +1 (907) 235 2326. Contact: (technical) Kevin Chambers, Chief Engineer.

KRSI—Radio Sedaye Iran, Suite 207, 9744 Wilshire Blvd, Beverly Hills CA 90212 USA. Email: krsi@glancing.com. Web: (includes Windows Media) www.krsi.com. Normally operates via a closed broadcasting system and the Internet, but started shortwave broadcasts from Moldova during 2000.

KTBN—Trinity Broadcasting Network:

GENERAL CORRESPONDENCE: P.O. Box A, Santa Ana CA 92711 USA. Phone: +1 (714) 832-2950. Fax: +1 (714) 730 0661. Email: comments@tbn.org. Web: (Trinity Broadcasting Network, including RealAudio) www.tbn.org; (KTBN) www.tbn.org/watch/how2watch/sw_radio/index.htm. Contact: Dr. Paul F. Crouch, Managing Director. Monthly TBN newsletter. Free booklets, stickers and small souvenirs sometimes available.

TECHNICAL CORRESPONDENCE: Engineering/QSL Department, 2442 Michelle Drive, Tustin CA 92780-7015 USA. Phone: +1 (714) 665-2145. Fax: +1 (714) 730 0661. Email: lreyes@tbn.org. Contact: Laura Reyes, QSL Manager; or Ben Miller, Vice President, Engineering. Responds to reception reports. Write to: Trinity Broadcasting Network, Attention: Superpower KTBN Radio QSL Manager, Laura Reyes, 2442 Michelle Drive, Tustin CA 92780 USA. Return postage (IRC or SASE) helpful. Although a California operation, KTBN's shortwave transmitter is located at Salt Lake City, Utah.

KVOH—Voice of Hope. *See* High Adventure Ministries Global Broadcasting Network.

KWHR-World Harvest Radio:

ADMINISTRATION OFFICE: see WHRI, USA, below.

TRANSMITTER: Although located 6 miles southwest of Naalehu, 8 miles north of South Cape, and 2000 feet west of South Point (Ka La) Road (the antennas are easily visible from this road) on Big Island, Hawaii, the operators of this rural transmitter site maintain no post office box in or near Naalehu, and their telephone number is unlisted, Best bet is to contact them via their administration office (*see* WHRI, below), or to drive in unannounced (it's just off South Point Road) the next time you vacation on Big Island.

Leinwoll (Stanley)—Telecommunication Consultant, 305 E. 86th Street, Suite 21S-W, New York NY 10028 USA. Phone: +1 (212) 987-0456. Fax: +1 (212) 987 3532. Email: stanL00011@aol.com. Contact: Stanley Leinwoll, President. This firm provides frequency management and other engineering services for some private U.S. world band stations, but does not correspond with the general public.

National Association of Shortwave Broadcasters, 10400 NW 20th Street, Okeechobee, FL 34972 USA; P.O. Box 8700, Cary NC 27512 USA. Phone: +1 (863) 763-0281. Fax: +1 (863) 763 8867. Email: nasbmem@rocketmail.com. Web: www.shortwave.org. Contact: Dan Elyea, Secretary-Treasurer. Association of most private U.S. world band stations, as well as a group of other international broadcasters, equipment manufacturers and organizations related to shortwave broadcasting. Includes committees on various subjects, such as digital shortwave radio. Interfaces with the Federal Communications Commission's International Bureau and other broadcasting-related organizations to advance the interests of its members. Publishes *NASB Newsletter* for members and associate members; free sample upon request on letterhead of an appropriate organization. Annual one-day convention held near Washington DC's National Airport early each spring; non-members wishing to attend should contact the Secretary-Treasurer in advance; convention fee typically $50 per person.

Overcomer Ministry ("Voice of the Last Day Prophet of God"), P.O. Box 691, Walterboro SC 29488 USA. Phone: (0900-1700 local time, Sunday through Friday) +1 (803) 538-3892. Email: (general) brotherstair@overcomerministry.com; (reception reports) overcomer@overcomerministry.com. Web: (includes RealAudio) www.overcomerministry.com. Contact: Brother R.G. Stair. Sample "Overcomer" newsletter and various pamphlets free upon request. Sells a Sangean shortwave radio for $50, plus other items of equipment and various publications at appropriate prices. Via Deutsche Telekom, Germany; and WBCQ, WINB and WWCR, USA.

Que Huong Radio, 2670 S. White Rd. #165, San Jose CA 95148 USA. Phone: +1 (408) 223-3130; (toll-free within the United States) 1-888-313-1120. Fax: +1 (408) 223-3131. Email: quehuong@quehuongmedia.com or qhradio@aol.com. Web: www.quehuongmedia.com. Contact: Nguyen Khoi, Manager. A Californian Vietnamese station operating on medium wave AM and which airs some of its programs on shortwave via the facilities of World Harvest Radio (*see*).

Radio Africa International, General Board of Global Ministries, United Methodist Church, 475 Riverside Drive, New York NY 10115 USA. Phone: (toll-free within U.S.) 1-800-862-4246; (Media Contact) +1 (212) 870 3803. Fax: +1 (212) 870 3748. E-mail: radio@gbgm-umc.org. Web: (GBGM-UMC parent organization) www.gbgm-umc.org. Contact: Donna Niemann, Executive Producer; Raphael Mbadinga, Senior Producer. Sells calendars, magazines, books, videos and CDs of Christian music. Transmits via Jülich, Germany.

Radio Free Asia, Suite 300, 2025 M Street NW, Washington DC 20036 USA. Phone: (general) +1 (202) 530-4900; (programming) +1 (202) 530-4907; (president) +1 (202) 457-4901; (vice-president) +1 (202) 536 4902; (technical) +1 (202) 530-4958.

Fax: +1 (202) 530 7794 or +1 (202) 721 7468. Email: (individuals) the format is lastnameinitial@rfa.org; so to reach, say, David Baden, it would be badend@rfa.org; (language sections) the format is language@www.rfa.org; so to contact, say, the Cambodian section, address your message to khmer@www.rfa.org; (general) Webmaster@www.rfa.org. Web: (includes audio in Audio Active format) www.rfa.org. Contact: (administration) Richard Richter, President; Craig Perry, Vice President; Daniel Southerland, Executive Editor; (technical) David Baden, Director of Technical Operations; (reception reports) Ms. Tetiana Iwanciw, Executive Assistant for Technical Operations. RFA, originally created in 1996 as the Asia Pacific Network, is funded as a private nonprofit U.S. corporation by a grant from the Broadcasting Board of Governors (*see*), a politically bipartisan body appointed by the President. The purpose of RFA is to deliver accurate and timely news, information, and commentary, and to provide a forum for a variety of opinions and voices from within Asian countries. RFA focuses on events occurring in those countries. RFA seeks to promote the rights of freedom of opinion and expression—including the freedom to seek, receive and impart information and ideas through any medium regardless of frontiers.

CHINA OFFICE: P.O. Box 28840, Hong Kong, China.

JAPAN OFFICE: P.O. Box 49, Central Post Office, Tokyo 100-91, Japan.

Radio Free Europe-Radio Liberty/RFE-RL

PRAGUE HEADQUARTERS: Vinohradská 1, 110 00 Prague 1, Czech Republic. Phone: +420 (2) 2112-1111; (president) +420 (2) 2112-3000; (news desk) +420 (2) 2112-3629; (public relations) +420 (2) 2112-3012; (technical operations) +420 (2) 2112-3700; (broadcast operations) +420 (2) 2112-3550; (affiliate relations). +420 (2) 2112-2539. Fax: +420 (2) 2112 3013; (president) +420 (2) 2112 3002; (news desk) +420 (2) 2112 3613; (public relations) +420 (2) 2112 2995; (technical operations) +420 (2) 2112 3702; (broadcast operations) +420 (2) 2112 3540; (affiliate operations) +420 (2) 2112 4563. Email: the format is lastnameinitial@rferl.org; so to reach, say, David Walcutt, it would be walcuttd@rferl.org. Web: (general, including RealAudio) www.rferl.org; (broadcast services) www.rferl.org/bd. Contact: Thomas A. Dine, President; Kestutis Girnius, Managing Editor, News and Current Affairs; Luke Springer, Deputy Director, Technology; Jana Horakova, Public Relations Coordinator; Uldis Grava, Marketing Director; or Christopher Carzoli, Broadcast Operations Director.

WASHINGTON OFFICE: 1201 Connecticut Avenue NW, Washington DC 20036 USA. Phone: +1 (202) 457-6900; (newsdesk) +1 (202) 457-6950; (technical) +1 (202) 457-6963. Fax: +1 (202) 457 6992; (news desk) +1 (202) 457 6997; (technical) +1 (202) 457 6913. Email and Web: *see* above. Contact: Jane Lester, Secretary of the Corporation; Ken Morehouse, Director of Technology Systems; or Paul Goble, Director of Communications; (news) Oleh Zwadiuk, Washington Bureau Chief; (technical) David Walcutt, Broadcast Operations Liaison. A private nonprofit corporation funded by a grant from the Broadcasting Board of Governors, RFE/RL broadcasts in 21 languages (but not English) from transmission facilities now part of the International Broadcasting Bureau (IBB), *see*.

Radio Free Iraq—a service of Radio Free Europe-Radio Liberty (*see*, above). Web: (includes RealAudio) www.rferl.org.bd/iq/index.html.

Radio Martí, Office of Cuba Broadcasting, 4201 N.W. 77th Avenue, Miami FL 33166 USA. Phone: +1 (305) 437-7000; (Director) +1 (305) 437-7117; (Technical Operations) +1 (305) 437-7051. Fax: +1 (305) 437 7016. Email: (Spanish) rcotta@ocb.ibb.gov; (English) webmaster@ocb.ibb.gov. Web: (includes RealAudio) www.ibb.gov/marti/. Contact: Roberto Rodríguez-Tejera, Director, Radio Martí; Martha Yedra, Director of Programs; (technical) Michael Pallone, Director of Technical Operations; or Tom Warden, Chief of Radio Operations.

Trans World Radio, International Headquarters, P.O. Box 8700, Cary NC 27512-8700 USA. Phone: +1 (919) 460-3700; toll-free (U.S. only) 1-800-456-7897. Fax: +1 (919) 460 3702. Email: info2@twr.org. Web: (includes RealAudio) www.gospelcom.net/twr/. Contact: (general) Jon Vaught, Public Relations; Richard Greene, Director, Public Relations; Joe Fort, Director, Broadcaster Relations; or Bill Danick; (technical) Glenn W. Sink, Assistant Vice President, International Operations. Free "Towers to Eternity" publication for those living in the U.S. Technical correspondence should be sent to the office nearest the country where the transmitter is located—Guam, Monaco or Swaziland. For information on TWR offices in Asia and Australasia, refer to the entry under "Guam."

CANADIAN OFFICE: P.O. Box 444, Niagara Falls ON, L2E 6T8 Canada. Web: http://twrcan.ca.

University Network, P.O. Box 1, Los Angeles CA 90053 USA. Phone: (toll-free within U.S.) 1-800-338-3030; (elsewhere, call collect) +1 (818) 240-8151. Email: drgenescott@mail.drgenescott.com (doesn't always work). Web: (includes RealAudio and Windows Media) www.drgenescott.com. Contact: Dr. Gene Scott. Sells audio and video tapes and books relating to Dr. Scott's teaching. Free copies of *The Truth About* and *The University Cathedral Pulpit* publications. Transmits over KAIJ and WWCR (USA); Caribbean Beacon (Anguilla, West Indies); the former AWR facilities in Cahuita, Costa Rica; and facilities in Samara, Russia.

USA Radio Network, 2290 Springlake #107, Dallas TX 75234 USA. Toll-free phone (within the U.S.) 1-800-829-8111. Email: (complaints/suggestions) tim@usaradio.com; (technical) david@usaradio.com. Web: (includes RealAudio, Windows Media and MP3) www.usaradio.com. Contact: (general) Tim Maddoux. Does not broadcast direct on shortwave, but some of its news and other programs are heard via KWHR, WHRA, WHRI and WWCR, USA.

Voice of America—All Transmitter Locations

MAIN OFFICE: 330 Independence Avenue SW, Washington DC 20237 USA. If contacting the VOA directly is impractical, write c/o the American Embassy in your country. Phone: (to hear VOA-English live) +1 (202) 619-1979; (Office of External Affairs) +1 (202) 619-2358 or +1 (202) 619-2039; (Audience Mail Division) +1 (202) 619-2770; (Africa Division) +1 (202) 619-1666 or +1 (202) 619-2879; ("Communications World") +1 (202) 619-3047; (Office of Research) +1 (202) 619-4965; (administration) +1 (202) 619-1088. Fax: (general information for listeners outside the United States) +1 (202) 376 1066; (Public Liaison for listeners within the United States) +1 (202) 619 1241; (Office of External Affairs) +1 (202) 205 0634 or +1 (202) 205 2875; (Africa Division) +1 (202) 619 1664; ("Communications World," Audience Mail Division and Office of Research) +1 (202) 619 0211; (administration) +1 (202) 619 0085; ("Communications World") +1 (202) 619 2543. Email: (general business) pubaff@voa.gov; (reception reports and schedule requests) letters@voa.gov; ("Communications World") cw@voa.gov; ("VOA News Now") newsnow@voanews.com; (VOA Special English) special@voa.gov; (VOA English to Africa) africanews@voa.gov. Web: (includes RealAudio) www.voa.gov. Contact: Mrs. Betty Lacy Thompson, Chief, Audience Mail Division, B/K. G759A Cohen; Larry James, Director, English Programs Division; Leo Sarkisian; Rita Rochelle,

INTERNATIONAL BROADCASTING STATION
KNLS
VISITORS WELCOME

PASSPORT author Hans Johnson has to step high at the verdant transmitter site of KNLS, Anchor Point, Alaska. H. Johnson

Africa Division; Kim Andrew Elliott, Producer, "Communications World"; or George Mackenzie, Audience Research Officer; (reception reports) Mrs. Irene Greene, QSL Desk, Audience Mail Division, Room G-759-C. Free stickers and calendars. If you're an American and miffed because you can't receive these goodies from the VOA, don't blame the station—they're only following the law. The VOA occasionally hosts international broadcasting conventions, and as of 1996 has been accepting limited supplemental funding from the U.S. Agency for International Development (AID). Also, *see* Ascension, Botswana, Greece, Morocco, Philippines, São Tomé e Príncipe, Sri Lanka and Thailand.

Voice of America/IBB—Delano Relay Station, Rt. 1, Box 1350, Delano CA 93215 USA; (physical address) 11015 Melcher Road, Delano CA 93215 USA. Phone: +1 (805) 725-0150. Fax: +1 (805) 725 6511. Contact: (technical) Brent Boyd, Manager; or John Vodenik. Photos of this facility can be seen at the following Website: www.hawkins.pair.com/voadelano.shtml. Nontechnical correspondence should be sent to the VOA address in Washington.

Voice of America/IBB—Greenville Relay Station, P.O. Box 1826, Greenville NC 27834 USA. Phone: +1 (919) 752-7115. Fax: +1 (919) 752 5959. Contact: (technical) Bruce Hunter, Manager; or Glenn Ruckleson. Nontechnical correspondence should be sent to the VOA address in Washington.

WBCQ—"The Planet," 97 High Street, Kennebunk ME 04043 USA. Email: wbcq@gwi.net. Web: (includes MP3) http://theplanet.wbcq.net/. Contact: Allan H. Weiner, Owner; or Elayne Star, Assistant Manager. Verifies reception reports if 1 IRC or (within USA) an SASE is included.

WEWN—EWTN Global Catholic Radio

TRANSMISSION FACILITY AND STATION MAILING ADDRESS: 1500 High Road, P.O. Box 176, Vandiver AL 35176 USA.

ENGINEERING AND MARKETING OFFICES: 5817 Old Leeds Rd., Irondale AL 35210 USA.

Phone: (general) +1 (205) 271-2900; (Station Manager) +1 (205) 271-2943; (Chief Engineer) +1 (205) 271-2959; (Marketing Manager) +1 (205) 271-2982; (Program Director, English) +1 (205) 271-2944; (Program Director, Spanish) +1 (205) 271-2900 ext. 2073; (Frequency Manager) +1 (205) 271-2900 ext. 2017. Fax: (general) +1 (205) 271 2926; (Marketing) +1 (205) 271 2925; (Engineering) +1 (205) 271 2953. Email: (general) wewn@ewtn.com; (Spanish) rcm@ewtn.com. To contact individuals, the format is initiallastname@ewtn.com; so to reach, say, Thom Price, it would be tprice@ewtn.com. Web: (English, including RealAudio) www.ewtn.com/wewn/; (Spanish, including schedule) www.ewtn.com/spanish/radio.htm. Contact: (general) Thom Price, Director of English Programming; or Doug Archer, Director of Spanish Programming; (marketing) Bernard Lockhart, Radio Marketing Manager; (administration) William Steltemeier, President; or Frank Leurck, Station Manager; (technical) Terry Borders, Vice President Engineering; Joseph A. Dentici, Frequency Manager; or Dennis Dempsey, Chief Engineer. Listener correspondence welcomed; responds to correspondence on-air and by mail. Free bumper stickers, program schedules and (sometimes) other booklets or publications. Sells numerous religious books, CDs, audio and video cassettes, T-shirts, sweatshirts and various other religious articles; list available upon request (VISA/MC). IRC or return postage appreciated for correspondence. Although a Catholic entity, WEWN is not an official station of the Vatican, which operates its own Vatican Radio (*see*). Rather, WEWN reflects the activities of Mother M. Angelica and the Eternal Word Foundation, Inc. Donations and bequests accepted by the Eternal Word Foundation.

WHRA-World Harvest Radio:

ADMINISTRATION OFFICE: see WHRI, USA, below.

TRANSMITTER: Located in Greenbush, Maine, but all technical and other correspondence should be sent to WHRI (*see* next entry).

WHRI—World Harvest Radio, WHRI/WHRA/KWHR, LeSEA Broadcasting, P.O. Box 12, South Bend IN 46624 USA. Phone: +1 (219) 291-8200. Fax: (station) +1 (219) 291 9043. Email: whr@lesea.com; (Joe Brashier) jbrashier@lesea.com; (Joe Hill) jhill@lesea.com. Web: (including RealAudio): www.whr.org; (LeSEA Broadcasting parent organization) www.lesea.com.

Contact: (listener contact) Loren Holycross; (general) Pete Sumrall, Vice President; or Joe Hill, Operations Manager; (programming or sales) Joe Hill or Joe Brashier; (technical) Douglas Garlinger, Chief Engineer. World Harvest Radio T-shirts available from 61300 S. Ironwood Road, South Bend IN 46614 USA. Return postage appreciated.

"EDXP NEWS REPORTS": Web: www.members.tripod.com/-bpadula/.html. Special news reports concentrating on shortwave broadcasts to and from Asia, the Far East, Australia, the Pacific and the Indian sub-continent, compiled by EDXP and aired on the first Friday of each month, (UTC) and repeated on the following Saturday and Sunday within the *"Dxing with Cumbre"* program, over the World Harvest Radio shortwave and RealAudio Networks. Special EDXP QSLs will be offered for the shortwave releases (not for RealAudio). Reports of the EDXP feature should be sent to: Bob Padula, EDXP QSL Service, 404 Mont Albert Road, Surrey Hills, Victoria 3127, Australia. Return postage appreciated. Outside of Australia, 1 IRC or $1; within Australia, four 45c Australian stamps. Email reports welcome at: edxp@bigpond.com, and verified with Web-delivered animated QSLs.

WINB—World International Broadcasters, WINB, World International Broadcasters, 2900 Windsor Road, P.O. Box 88, Red Lion PA 17356 USA. Phone: (all departments) +1 (717) 244-5360. Fax: +1 (717) 246 0363. Email: info@winb.com. Web: www.winb.com. Contact: (general) Mrs. Sally Spyker, Manager; (sales) Hans Johnson; (technical) Fred W. Wise, Technical Director; or John H. Norris, Owner. Return postage helpful outside United States. No giveaways or items for sale.

WJCR—Jesus Christ Radio, P.O. Box 91, Upton KY 42784 USA. Phone: +1 (502) 369-8614. Email: (general) wjcrfm@earthlink.net. Web: www.wjcr.com. Free religious printed matter. Return postage or $1 appreciated. Actively solicits listener contributions. Reportedly sold to a new owner in summer 2001.

WMLK—Assemblies of Yahweh, 190 Frantz Road, P.O. Box C, Bethel PA 19507 USA. Toll-free telephone (U.S only) 1-800-523-3827; (elsewhere) +1 (717) 933-4518 or +1 (717) 933-4880. Email: aoy@allsportsstuff.com. Web: www.assembliesofyahweh.com/Log.htm. Contact: (general) Elder Jacob O. Meyer, Manager and Producer of "The Open Door to the Living World"; (technical) Gary McAvin, Station Manager. Free *The Sacred Name Broadcaster* magazine published monthly, stickers and religious material. Bibles, audio and video (VHS) tapes and religious paperback books offered. Enclosing return postage ($1 or IRCs) helps speed things up.

World Beacon, 8133 Baymeadows Way, Jacksonville FL 32256 USA. Phone: +1 (904) 642-8902. Fax: +1 (904) 642-8916. Email: (general) info@wordbeacon.net; (reception reports) reception@worldbeacon.net. Web: (includes MP3) www.worldbeacon.net; (AMG parent organization) www.affiliatedmedia.com. Contact: Scott Westerman, President; Jeff Johnson, Program Director. A mission service of Affiliated Media Group. Currently broadcasts via transmitters of Merlin Communications International (*see*) in the U.K. and Sentech (*see*) in South Africa.

AFRICA OFFICE: World Beacon-African Service, Box 651525, Benmore, Postal Code 2010, South Africa.

WRMI—Radio Miami International, 175 Fontainebleau Blvd., Suite 1N4, Miami FL 33172 USA; or P.O. Box 526852, Miami FL 33152 USA. Phone: (general) +1 (305) 559-9764; (Engineering) +1 (305) 827-2234. Fax: (general) +1 (305) 559 8186; (Engineering) +1 (305) 819 8756. Email: info@wrmi.net. Web: www.wrmi.net. Contact: (technical and nontechnical) Jeff White, General Manager/Sales Manager; (technical) Indalecio "Kiko" Espinosa, Chief Engineer. Free station stickers and tourist brochures. Sells "public access" airtime to nearly anyone to say virtually anything for $1 or more per minute. Radio Miami Internacional also acts as a broker for Cuban exile programs aired via U.S. station WHRI.

WSHB—*see* Herald Broadcasting Syndicate, above.

WTJC, Fundamental Broadcasting Network, Grace Missionary Baptist Church, 520 Roberts Road, Newport NC 28570 USA.Phone: +1 (252) 223-6088; (toll free, within the United States) 1-800-245-9685; (Robinson) +1 (252) 223-4600. Email: (general) fbn@clis.com; (technical, David Robinson) davidwr@clis.com. Web: (includes RealAudio) www.fbnradio.com. Contact: Pastor Clyde Eborn; (technical) David Robinson, Chief Engineer. Verifies reception reports if an IRC or (within the USA) an SASE is included. Accepts email reports. Plans to eventually broadcast in Chinese, French, Russian and Spanish in addition to English. Station is operated by FBN, a religious and educational non-commercial broadcasting network.

WWBS, P.O. Box 18174. Macon GA 31209 USA. Phone: +1 (912) 477-3433. Email: (general) wwbsradio@aol.com. Contact: Charles C. Josey; or Joanne Josey. Include return postage if you want your reception reports verified.

WWCR—World Wide Christian Radio, F.W. Robbert Broadcasting Co., 1300 WWCR Avenue, Nashville TN 37218 USA. Phone: (general) +1 (615) 255-1300. Fax: +1 (615) 255 1311. Email: (general) wwcr@wwcr.com; ("Ask WWCR" program) askwwcr@wwcr.com. Web: www.wwcr.com. Contact: (administration) George McClintock, K4BTY, General Manager; Adam W. Lock, Sr., WA2JAL, Head of Operations; or Dawn Keen, Program Director; (technical) William Hair, Chief Engineer. Free program guides, updated monthly. Return postage helpful. For items sold on the air and tapes of programs, contact the producers of the programs, and *not* WWCR. Replies as time permits. Carries programs from various political organizations, which may be contacted directly.

WWFV—World Wide Freedom Voice, Box 1131, Copperhill TN 37317-1131 USA. Phone/fax: +1 (706) 492-5944. Email: wwfv@ellijay.com. Web: www.wwfv.net. Contact: Peter Taggart, General Manager; (technical) Dave Frantz, Chief Engineer. WWFV verification policy is that reception reports should be sent to individual broadcasters (i.e. program producers) with a request to forward the report to the station, which in turn will then verify it.

WWV/WWVB (official time and frequency stations): NIST Radio Station WWV, 2000 East County Road #58, Ft. Collins CO 80524 USA. Phone: +1 (303) 497-3914. Fax: +1 (303) 497 4063. Email: nist.radio@boulder.nist.gov; (Deutch) deutch@boulder.nist.gov. Contact: Matt Deutch, Engineer-in-Charge. Web: www.boulder.nist.gov/timefreq/stations/wwv.html. Along with branch sister station WWVH in Hawaii (*see* below), WWV and WWVB are the official time and frequency stations of the United States, operating over longwave (WWVB) on 60 kHz, and over shortwave (WWV) on 2500, 5000, 10000, 15000 and 20000 kHz.

PARENT ORGANIZATION: National Institute of Standards and Technology, Time and Frequency Division, 325 Broadway, Boulder CO 80305-3328 USA. Phone: +1 (303) 497-5453. Email: (Lowe) lowe@boulder.nist.gov. Contact: John Lowe, Group Leader.

WWVH (official time and frequency station): NIST Radio Station WWVH, P.O. Box 417, Kekaha, Kauai HI 96752 USA. Phone: +1 (808) 335-4361; (live audio) +1 (808) 335-4363. Fax: +1

(808) 335 4747. Email: nistwwvh@gte.net. Contact: (technical) Dean T. Okayama, Engineer-in-Charge. Along with headquarters sister stations WWV and WWVB (*see* preceding), WWVH is the official time and frequency station of the United States, operating on 2500, 5000, 10000 and 15000 kHz.

WYFR—Family Radio

NONTECHNICAL: Family Stations, Inc., 290 Hegenberger Road, Oakland CA 94621 USA; or P.O. Box 2140 Oakland CA 94621-9985 USA. Phone: (toll-free, U.S. only) 1-800-543-1495; (elsewhere) +1 (510) 568-6200; (engineering) +1 (510) 568-6200 ext. 240. Fax: (main office) +1 (510) 568-6200; (engineering) +1 (510) 562 1023. Email: (general) famradio@familyradio.com; (shortwave department) shortwave@familyradio.com; (technical) fsiyfr@okeechobee.com. Web: (Family Radio Network, including RealAudio) www.familyradio.com; (WYFR) www.familyradio.com/shortwave/swlinks.html; (foreign-language broadcasts in RealAudio) www.familyradio.com/foreign.htm. Contact: (general) Harold Camping, General Manager; or Thomas Schaff, Shortwave Program Manager; (technical) Dan Elyea, Station Manager; or Shortwave Department. Free gospel tracts (33 languages), books, booklets, quarterly *Family Radio News* magazine and frequency schedule. 2 IRCs helpful.

BELARUS OFFICE: B.A International, Chapaeva Street #5, 220600 Minsk, Belarus.

INDIA OFFICE: Family Radio, c/o Rev. Alexander, Tekkali 532201 Andra Pradesh India.

TECHNICAL: WYFR—Family Radio, 10400 NW 240th Street, Okeechobee FL 34972 USA. Phone: +1 (941) 763-0281. Fax: +1 (941) 763 1034. Contact: Dan Elyea, Engineering Manager; or Edward F. Dearborn, Assistant Engineering Manager.

UZBEKISTAN World Time +5

WARNING—MAIL THEFT: Due to increasing local mail theft, Radio Tashkent suggests that those wishing to correspond should try using one of the drop-mailing addresses listed below.

Radio Tashkent, 49 Khorazm Street, 700047 Tashkent, Uzbekistan. Phone: (Head of International Service) +998 (71) 133-8920; (Correspondence Section) +998 (71) 139-9657; (Shekhar) +998 (71) 139-0752 or +998 (71) 139-9521. Fax: +998 (71) 144 0021. Email: (Shekhar) alex@kirsh.silk.org. Contact: Sherzat Gulyamov, Head of International Service; Mrs. Alfia Ruzmatova, Head of Correspondence Section; Babur Turdieav, Head of English Service; Alok Shekhar, Announcer - Hindi Service. Correspondence is welcomed in English, German, Russian, Uzbek and nine other languages broadcast by Radio Tashkent. Reception reports are verified with colorful QSL cards. Free pennants, badges, wallet calendars and postcards. Has quizzes from time to time with prizes and souvenirs. Books in English by Uzbek writers are apparently available for purchase. Station offers free membership to the "Salum Aleikum Listeners' Club" for regular listeners.

LONDON OFFICE: 72 Wigmore Street, London W18 9L, United Kingdom.

BANGKOK OFFICE: 848-850 Ramapur Road, Bangkok 10050, Thailand.

TRANSMISSION FACILITIES: Pochta va Telekommunikasiyalar Agentligi, Aleksey Tolstoy küçă 1, 700000 Tashkent, Uzbekistan. Phone: +998 (71) 133-6645. Fax: +998 (71) 144 2603. Contact: Fatrullah Fazullahyev, Director General.

Uzbek Radio, Khorazm küçă 49, 700047 Tashkent, Uzbekistan. Phone: (general) +998 (71) 144-1210; (Director) +998 (71) 133-8920 or 998 (71) 139-9636; (technical) +998 (71) 136-2290. Fax: (general) +998 (71) 144 0021; (Director) +998 (71) 133 8920. Email: uzradio@eanetways.com. Contact: (administration) Fakhriddin N. Nizom, Director; (technical) Komoljon Rajapov, Chief Engineer.

VANUATU World Time +12 (+11 midyear)

Radio Vanuatu, Information and Public Relations, Private Mail Bag 049, Port Vila, Vanuatu. Phone: +678 22999 or +678 23026. Fax: +678 22026. Contact: Maxwell E. Maltok, General Manager; Ambong Thompson, Head of Programmes; or Allan Kalfabun, Sales and Marketing Consultant, who is interested in exchanging letters and souvenirs from other countries; (technical) K.J. Page, Principal Engineer; Marianne Berukilkilu, Technical Manager; or Willie Daniel, Technician.

VATICAN CITY STATE World Time +1 (+2 midyear)

Radio Vaticana (Vatican Radio)

MAIN AND PROMOTION OFFICES: 00120 Città del Vaticano, Vatican City State. Phone: (general) +39 (06) 6988-3551; (Director General) +39 (06) 6988-3945; (Programme Director) +39 (06) 6988-3996; (Publicity and Promotion Department) +39 (06) 6988-3045; (technical, general) +39 (06) 6988-4897; (frequency management) +39 (06) 6988-5258. Fax: (general) +39 (06) 6988 4565; (frequency management) +39 (06) 6988 5062. Email: sedoc@vatiradio.va; sedoc@vaticanradio-us.org; (Director General) dirigen@vatiradio.va; (frequency management) mc6790@mclink.it; (technical direction, general) sectec@vatiradio.va; (Programme Director) dirpro@vatiradio.va; (Publicity and Promotion Department) promo@vatiradio.va; (English Section) englishpr@vatiradio.va,

Worldwide Broadcasts in English—2002

Country-by-Country Guide to Best-Heard Stations

Dozens of countries reach out to us in English, and this section gives the times and frequencies where you're likely to hear them. If you want to know which shows are on hour-by-hour, check out "What's On Tonight."

• **When and where:** "Best Times and Frequencies," earlier in this edition, pinpoints where each world band segment is found and gives tuning tips. Best is late afternoon and evening, when most programs are beamed your way. Tune world band segments within the 5730-10000 kHz range in winter, 5730-15800 kHz during summer. Around breakfast, you can also explore segments within the 5730-17900 kHz range for fewer but intriguing catches.

• **Strongest (and weakest) frequencies:** Frequencies shown in italics—say, *5965* kHz—tend to be best, as they are from transmitters that may be located near you. However, other frequencies beamed your way might do almost as well. Some signals not beamed to you can also be heard, especially when they are targeted to nearby parts of the world. Frequencies with no target zones are typically for domestic coverage, so they are unlikely to be heard unless you're in or near that country.

Program Times

Some stations shift broadcast times by one hour midyear, typically April through October. These are indicated by ⇦ (one hour earlier) and ⇨ (one hour later). Frequencies used seasonally are labeled **S** for summer (midyear, typically April through October), and **W** for winter. Stations may also extend their hours of transmission, or air special programs, for national holidays, emergencies or sports events.

Times and days of the week are in World Time, explained in "Setting Your World Time Clock" earlier in this edition, as well as in PASSPORT's glossary.

Frequencies not beamed your way might also be heard.

Indigenous Music

Broadcasts in other than English? Turn to the next section, "Voices from Home," or the Blue Pages. Keep in mind that stations for kinsfolk abroad sometimes carry delightful chunks of native music. They make for enjoyable listening, regardless of language.

Schedules for Entire Year

To be as useful as possible over the months to come, PASSPORT's schedules consist not just of observed activity, but also that which we have creatively opined will take place during the forthcoming year. This predictive material is based on decades of experience and is original from us. Although inherently not as exact as real-time data, over the years it's been of tangible value to PASSPORT readers.

NATION SHALL SPEAK PEACE UNTO NATION

The first logo of the British Broadcasting Corporation, ca. 1927.

BBC Hand Book, 1928

AFGHANISTAN

VOICE OF SHARI'AH—(W Asia & Mideast)

1530-1545 7085

ALBANIA

RADIO TIRANA

0245-0300 &
0330-0400 ⬅ 6115 & 7160 (E North Am)
1945-2000 ⬅ 7210 & 9510 (W Europe)
2230-2300 ⬅ 7130 & 9540 (W Europe)

ALGERIA

RADIO ALGERIENNE—(Europe)

1600-1700 &
2000-2100 11715 & 15160

ARGENTINA

RADIO ARGENTINA AL EXTERIOR-RAE

0200-0300 Tu-Sa 11710 (Americas)
1800-1900 M-F 15345 (Europe & N Africa)

ARMENIA

VOICE OF ARMENIA

0910-0930 ⬅ Su 4810 (E Europe, Mideast & W Asia), Su 15270 (Europe)
2040-2100 ⬅ M-Sa 4810 (E Europe, Mideast & W Asia), M-Sa 9960/9965 (Europe)

AUSTRALIA

RADIO AUSTRALIA

0000-0100 21740 (Pacific & N America)
0000-0130 17775 (SE Asia)
0000-0200 17795 (Pacific & W North Am)
0000-0700 15240 (Pacific & E Asia)
0000-0800 9660 (Pacific), 17580 (Pacific & W North Am)
0000-0900 12080 (S Pacific), 15415 (SE Asia)
0030-0400 17750 (SE Asia)
0100-0900 21725 (E Asia)
0200-0700 15515 (Pacific & N America)
0430-0500 &
0530-0800 17750 (SE Asia)
0700-0900 15240 (Pacific & W North Am)
0800-0900 5995 & 9710 (Pacific)
0800-1200 13605 (Pacific & W North Am)
0830-0900 17750 (SE Asia)
0900-1330 11880 (E Asia & SE Asia)
0900-1400 21820 (Asia & Europe)
1100-1200 12080 (S Pacific)
1100-1400 5995 (Pacific), 6020 (Pacific & W North Am), 9475 (E Asia & SE Asia)
1100-2130 9580 (Pacific & N America)
1200-1700 11650 (Pacific & W North Am)
1330-1700 11660 (SE Asia)
1400-1800 5995 (Pacific & W North Am), 6080 (SE Asia)
1530-1900 9475 (E Asia & SE Asia)
1700-2100 9815 (Pacific & E Asia)
1700-2200 11880 (Pacific & W North Am)
1800-2000 6080 (Pacific & E Asia), 7240 (Pacific)
1900-2130 9500 (E Asia & SE Asia)
2100-2200 7240 & 9660 (Pacific)
2100-2400 17715 (Pacific & W North Am), 21740 (Pacific & N America)
2200-2400 13620/13780 & 15240 (SE Asia), 17795 (Pacific & W North Am)
2300-2400 9660 (Pacific), 12080 (S Pacific)
2330-2400 11695 (SE Asia)

RADIO CHRISTIAN VOICE

0000-0100 17850 (E Asia)
0000-1200 17645 (E Asia)
0030-0400 21680 (SE Asia)
0130-0700 21550 (E Asia)
0130-1000 17600 (SE Asia)
0430-0500 &
0530-0900 21680 (SE Asia)
0700-0900 17820 (E Asia)
0900-1600 13775 (E Asia)
1000-1200 17825 (S Asia & SE Asia)
1000-1300 17725 (S Asia & SE Asia)
1200-1600 15370 (E Asia)
1300-1700 13660 (S Asia & SE Asia)
1600-2000 9540 (E Asia)
1700-2130 11700 (S Asia & SE Asia)
2030-2130 9865/11935 (SE Asia)
2200-2400 17850 (E Asia)
2330-2400 9865/11935 (SE Asia)

AUSTRIA

RADIO AUSTRIA INTERNATIONAL

0130-0200 [S] 9870 (E North Am)
0230-0300 [W] 7325 (E North Am)
0530-0600 [S] 17870 (Mideast)
0735-0800 [W] 6155 & [W] 13730 (Europe)
1130-1200 [S] 6155 & [S] 13730 (Europe)

1230-1300 [W] M-Sa 6155 & [W] M-Sa 13730 (Europe)
1330-1400 [S] 6155 & [S] 13730 (Europe), [W] 17855 & [S] 21780 (S Asia, SE Asia & Australasia)
1335-1400 [W] Su 6155 & [W] Su 13730 (Europe)
1430-1500 [W] 6155 & [W] 13730 (Europe)
1630-1700 ⇐ *17865* (W North Am)
1630-1700 [W] 6155 & [W] 13730 (Europe)
1830-1900 [S] 5945 & [S] 6155 (Europe)
1930-2000 [W] 5945 & [W] 6155 (Europe)
2130-2200 [S] M-F 5945 & [S] M-F 6155 (Europe)
2230-2300 [W] M-F 5945 & [W] M-F 6155 (Europe)

BANGLADESH

BANGLADESH BETAR

1230-1300 7185 & 9550 (SE Asia)
1530-1545 15519 (Mideast & Europe)
1745-1815 &
1815-1900 7185, 9550 & 15519 (Irr) (Europe)

BELARUS

RADIO BELARUS/RADIO MINSK

0200-0230 [S] M/W/F-Su 6070 (W Europe & Atlantic)
0300-0330 ⇐ M/W/F-Su 7210 (N Europe)
0300-0330 [W] M/W/F-Su 5970 (W Europe & Atlantic)
2030-2100 &
2130-2200 ⇐ Tu/Th 7105 (Europe), Tu/Th 7210 (N Europe)

BELGIUM

RADIO VLAANDEREN INTERNATIONAAL

0400-0430 [W] *11985* & [S] *15565* (W North Am)
0800-0830 ⇐ *5985* (W Europe)
1130-1200 *9865* (E Asia & Australasia)
1230-1300 ⇐ 9925 (S Europe)
1730-1800 [S] *13710* (S Europe & Mideast)
1830-1900 ⇐ 5910 (S Europe), 9925 (S Europe & W Africa)
1830-1900 [W] *13770* (S Europe & Mideast)
1930-2000 [S] *9925* (Europe)
2230-2300 [W] *13660* & [S] *15565* (N America)

BULGARIA

RADIO BULGARIA

0000-0100 ⇐ 9400 (E North Am)
0000-0100 [W] 7375 (E North Am)
0200-0300 [S] 11700 (E North Am)
0300-0400 ⇐ 9400 (E North Am)
0300-0400 [W] 7375 (E North Am)
1200-1300 ⇐ 15700 & 17500 (Europe)
1900-2000 [S] 9400 & [S] 11700 (Europe)
2000-2100 [W] 5845 & [W] 7535 (Europe)
2100-2200 [S] 9400 & [S] 11700 (Europe)
2200-2300 [W] 7535 & [W] 7545 (Europe)
2300-2400 [S] 11700 (E North Am)

CANADA

CANADIAN BROADCASTING CORP—(E North Am)

0000-0300 ⇐ Su 9625
0200-0300 ⇐ Tu-Sa 9625
0300-0310 &
0330-0609 ⇐ M 9625
0400-0609 ⇐ Su 9625
0500-0609 ⇐ Tu-Sa 9625
1200-1255 ⇐ M-F 9625
1200-1505 ⇐ Sa 9625
1200-1700 ⇐ Su 9625
1600-1615 &
1700-1805 ⇐ Sa 9625
1800-2400 ⇐ Su 9625
1945-2015,
2200-2225 &
2240-2330 ⇐ M-F 9625

CFRX-CFRB—(E North Am)

24 Hr 6070

CFVP-CKMX—(W North Am)

0600-0400 ⇐ 6030

CKZN—(E North Am)

24 Hr 6160

CKZU-CBU—(W North Am)

24 Hr 6160

RADIO CANADA INTERNATIONAL

0000-0100 ⇐ 6175 (N America), 9590 (N America & C America), 9755 (E North Am & C America)
0000-0100 [W] 5960 (E North Am & C America), [W] *9750* & *11895* (SE Asia)
0100-0200 [S] 13670 (N America), [S] 13770 (S America), [S] 15170 & [S] 15305 (C America & S America)

Radio Romania's English Service: Sitting (left), Alexandra Dragomirescu, Ana Maria Palcu, Eugenia Chira. Standing, Iulian Muresan, Christine Lescu, Daniel Bilt, Cristina Mateescu, Georgiana Zachia, Ioana Masariu, Mihaela Ignatescu, Lacramioara Simion, Diana Vijeu, and Mihai Babic.

0200-0300 ←	6175 (N America & C America), 9755 (E North Am & C America)
0200-0300	[W] 6040 (E North Am & C America), [W] 11725 (C America & S America), [W] 11990 (N America), [W] *15150*, [S] *15260* & *17860* (S Asia)
1200-1300	[S] M-F 9640 (E North Am & C America), *9660* (E Asia), [W] *11730* & [S] *15190* (E Asia & SE Asia), [S] M-F 15305 (E North Am)
1200-1500	[S] M-F 17820 (C America)
1300-1400	[W] M-F 9515 (N America & C America), [W] M-F 13655 (E North Am & C America), [W] M-F 17710 (C America)
1300-1500	[S] 9640 (E North Am & C America), [S] 15305 (E North Am)
1400-1600	[W] 9515 (N America & C America), [W] 13655 (E North Am & C America), [W] 17710 (C America)
1400-1700	[S] Sa/Su 17800 (C America)
1500-1600	[S] Sa/Su 9640 (E North Am & C America), [S] Sa/Su 15305 (E North Am), [W] *15360*, [W] *15360*, [S] *15455*, [S] *17720* & [W] *17820* (S Asia)
1600-1700	[W] Sa/Su 9515 (N America & C America), [W] Sa/Su 13655 (E North Am & C America), [W] Sa/Su 17710 (C America)
2000-2100	[S] *5995* (W Europe), [S] *11690*, [S] 15325, [S] 17870 & [S] 21570 (Europe)
2100-2200	[W] 5995 (Europe), [W] *7235* (N Africa), [W] *9805* (C Africa & E Africa), [W] *11600* (Mideast), [W] 13650 (W Europe)
2200-2230	[W] *9805* (N Africa & W Africa), [S] M-F 15305 (C America & S America), [S] M-F 17880 (S America)
2200-2400	[S] 13670 & [S] 17695 (E North Am & C America)
2300-2330	[W] M-F 11865 & [W] M-F 13730 (C America & S America)
2300-2400 ←	6175 (N America), 9590 (N America & C America), 9755 (E North Am & C America)
2300-2400	[W] 5960 (E North Am & C America)

CHINA

CHINA RADIO INTERNATIONAL

0100-0200	*9570* (E North Am), *9790* (W North Am)
0300-0400	*9690* (N America & C America)
0400-0500	*9730* (W North Am)

0500-0600 ←	*9560* (W North Am)
0900-1100	11730 & 15210 (Australasia)
1200-1300	9760 & 15415 (Australasia)
1200-1400	11675/11760 (Australasia), 11980 (SE Asia)
1300-1400	*9570* (E North Am), 11900 (Australasia), 15180 (SE Asia)
1400-1500	[W] 7180, 9700, 11675, [W] 11765, [S] 11825 & [S] 15110 (S Asia)
1400-1600 ←	7405 (W North Am)
1400-1600	*13685* (E Africa & S Africa), *15125* (C Africa & E Africa), *17720* (W North Am)
1500-1600	7160 & 9785 (S Asia)
1600-1700	[W] 7190 (E Africa), [S] 9565 (S Africa), [S] 9870 (E Africa), [W] 13650 (S Africa)
1700-1800	[W] 7150 (E Africa), 9570 (E Africa & S Africa), 9670 (Mideast & W Asia), 9695 (S Africa), [S] 11920 (E Africa), [S] 15265 (S Africa)
1900-2000	[W] 6165 & [W] 9585 (Mideast), [S] 11610 (Mideast & N Africa), [S] 13790 (Mideast)
1900-2100	9440 (N Africa)
2000-2130	*11735* (E Africa & S Africa), *13635/13640* (E Africa)
2000-2200	[W] 5965, [W] 9840, [S] 11790 & [S] 15110 (Europe)
2200-2300	[W] *7170/7175* & [S] *9880* (W Europe)
2300-2400	*5990* (C America), *13680* (N America & C America)

CHINA (TAIWAN)

RADIO TAIPEI INTERNATIONAL

0200-0300	*5950* (E North Am), *11740* (C America), 15345 (E Asia)
0200-0400	*9680* (W North Am), 15320 (SE Asia)
0300-0400	*5950* (N America & C America), 11875 (SE Asia)
0700-0800	*5950* (W North Am & C America)
1100-1200	7445 (SE Asia), 11985 (E Asia)
1200-1300	7130 (E Asia), 9610 (Australasia)
1400-1500	15265 (SE Asia)
1600-1800	11550 (S Asia)
1800-1900	*3955* (W Europe)
2200-2300	[W] *5810*, [W] *9355*, [S] *11565* & [S] *15600* (Europe)

COSTA RICA

RADIO FOR PEACE INTERNATIONAL—(N America)

24 Hr	15049
0200-1000	7445 USB
1200-0200	21815 USB

CUBA

RADIO HABANA CUBA

0100-0500	6000 (E North Am), 9820 (N America), 11705 USB (E North Am & Europe)
0500-0700	9550 (E North Am), 9820 (W North Am), 9830 USB (E North Am & Europe)
2030-2130	13660 USB & 13750 (Europe & E North Am)
2230-2330	9550 (C America)

CZECH REPUBLIC

RADIO PRAGUE

0000-0030	[S] 7345 (N America & C America), [S] 11615 (Americas)
0100-0130	[S] 5915 & [W] 6200 (N America & C America), 7345 (N America)
0200-0230	[W] 6200 (N America & C America), [W] 7345 (N America)
0300-0330	[S] 7345 (N America), [S] 9870 (W North Am & C America)
0330-0400	[S] 11600 (Mideast), [S] 15470 (Mideast & S Asia)
0400-0430	[W] 7345 (N America), [W] 9435 (W North Am & C America)
0430-0500	[W] 9865 (Mideast), [W] 11600 (Mideast & S Asia)
0700-0730	[S] 9880 (W Europe)
0800-0830 ←	11600 (W Europe)
0800-0830	[W] 15255 (W Europe)
0900-0930	[S] 21745 (S Asia & W Africa)
1000-1030	[W] 21745 (S Asia & W Africa)
1030-1100	[S] 9880 & [S] 11615 (N Europe)
1130-1200	[W] 11640 (N Europe), [W] 21745 (E Africa)
1300-1330	[S] 13580 (N Europe), [S] 21745 (S Asia)
1400-1430	[W] 21745 (N America & E Africa)

1600-1630	[S] 21745 (E Africa)
1700-1730 ⬅	5930 (W Europe)
1700-1730	[W] 17485 (W Africa & C Africa), [S] 21745 (C Africa)
1800-1830 ⬅	5930 (W Europe)
1800-1830	[W] 7315 (E Europe, Asia & Australasia)
2000-2030	[S] 11600 (SE Asia & Australasia)
2100-2130 ⬅	5930 (W Europe)
2100-2130	[W] 9430 (SE Asia & Australasia)
2130-2200	[S] 11600 (SE Asia & Australasia), [S] 15545 (W Africa)
2230-2300	[W] 7345 (N America), [W] 9435 (W Africa), [S] 11600 & [S] 15545 (N America)
2330-2400	[W] 7345 & [W] 9435 (N America)

ECUADOR

HCJB-VOICE OF THE ANDES

0000-0100	[W] 11785 & [S] 17660 (S Asia)
0000-0400	9745 (E North Am)
0000-0700	[W] 11840 (N America & C America), [S] 15115 (N America)
0000-1430	21455 USB (Europe & Australasia)
0400-0700	9745 (W North Am)
0600-0800	[S] 11680 (Europe)
0700-0900	[W] 9780 (Europe)
0700-1100	11755 (Australasia)
1100-1430	12005 (C America), 15115 (N America & S America)
1900-2200	[S] 17660 (Europe)
2000-2130	[W] 12005 (W Europe)
2000-2300	[W] 11890 (W Europe)
2030-2200	21455 USB (Europe & Australasia)
2130-2300	[W] 9725 (Europe)
2300-2400	[W] 11785 & [S] 17660 (S Asia)

EGYPT

RADIO CAIRO

0000-0030	9900 (E North Am)
0200-0330	9475 (N America)
1215-1330	17595 (S Asia)
1630-1830	15255 (S Africa)
2030-2200	15375 (W Africa)
2115-2245	9990 (Europe)
2300-2400	9900 (E North Am)

ETHIOPIA

RADIO ETHIOPIA

1030-1100	M-F 5990, M-F 7110, M-F 9704
1600-1700	7165/7175 & 9560 (E Africa)

FRANCE

RADIO FRANCE INTERNATIONALE

0400-0430	[W] *11910*, [W] 11995, 13610 (Irr) & [S] 15155 (E Africa)
0500-0530	[W] 13610 (E Africa), [W] *15155* (E Africa & S Africa), [S] 17800 (E Africa)
0600-0630	[W] *11710* (W Africa), [W] 15155, 17800 & [S] 21620 (E Africa)
0700-0800	*15605* (W Africa)
1200-1230	*15540* (W Africa), 25820 (E Africa)
1400-1500	*11610* (S Asia), 17620 (Mideast)
1600-1700	11615 (Irr) (N Africa), *11995* (W Africa), *12015* (S Africa), 17850 (C Africa & S Africa)
1600-1730	[W] 11615 & [S] 15605 (Mideast), [W] 15605 & [S] 17605 (E Africa)

GERMANY

DEUTSCHE WELLE

0100-0145	[S] *6040* (N America & C America), [W] *6040* (E North Am & C America), [W] 6145 (N America & C America), [S] 9640 (E North Am), [W] *9640* (E North Am & C America), [W] *9700* (E North Am), [W] *9765* (N America), [S] *11810* (E North Am), [S] *13720* (E North Am & C America)
0200-0245	[W] 7285, [W] *9615*, [W] 9765, *11965*, [S] 13720 & [S] *15370* (S Asia)
0300-0345	[W] *6020* (W North Am), [W] 6045 (N America), [S] *9535* (W North Am), [S] *9640* (E North Am), [W] *9640* (E North Am & C America), [W] *9700* (N America), [W] *11985* (W North Am), [S] *13780* (E North Am & C America), [S] *15105* (W North Am & C America)

In early March of each year radio aficionados flock to Kulpsville, Pennsylvania. Shown, John Wagner (stripes), PASSPORT's Marie Lamb and Jane Brinker, and John Figliozzi of Save the BBC World Service Coalition. Tom Sundstrom

0400-0445	[W] *6015* (E Africa), [W] *7195* (S Africa), [S] *7225* (E Africa & S Africa), *9565* (S Africa), [W] 9710 & [S] *9765* (E Africa & S Africa), [S] 13690 (E Africa)
0500-0545	[W] 5960 & [W] *6120* (W North Am), [S] *9670* (N America), [W] *9670*, [S] *9785*, [W] *11795* & [S] *11985* (W North Am)
0600-0645	[W] *7225* & [W] 9565 (W Africa), [W] 11785 (C Africa), [S] *11925* (W Africa), [S] *13790* (Africa), [S] 17860 (W Africa & C Africa)
0600-1900	6140 (Europe)
0900-0945	*6160* (Australasia), [W] *7300* (E Asia), [W] *11785* (E Africa & S Africa), [S] *12035* (E Africa), *15410* (S Africa), [S] *15470* (E Asia), [S] *17715* & [S] *17770* (SE Asia & Australasia), [S] *17800* (S Africa), [W] *17800* (W Africa), [S] *17820* (SE Asia), [W] *17820* (SE Asia & Australasia), [W] *17845* (SE Asia), [W] *17860* (S Africa), [W] 21560 (Mideast & E Africa), [S] *21560* (W Africa), [S] 21680 (SE Asia & Australasia), [S] 21790 (C Africa & S Africa)
1100-1145	[S] *11785* (E Africa), *15410* (S Africa), [W] *17800* (W Africa & C Africa), [S] *17860* & 21780 (W Africa)
1600-1645	*6170* & *7225* (S Asia), *9735* (E Africa & S Africa), [S] *11665* (S Africa), [W] 11695 & [W] 13605 (S Asia, SE Asia & Australasia), [W] *15455* (S Africa), [S] 17595 (S Asia), 21840 (E Africa & S Africa)
1900-1945	[W] 11765 (W Africa), [S] *11805* & [W] *11810* (C Africa & W Africa), [S] *11965* (S Africa), [S] 13720 (W Africa), [W] 13780 (Africa), [W] *15275* & [S] *15390* (W Africa & C Africa), [W] *15390* (S Africa), *17810* (E Africa)
2000-2045	[W] *6180* (Europe), [S] 7130 (W Europe)
2100-2145	[W] *9615* (W Africa), [S] *9670* (SE Asia & Australasia), [W] 9690 (C Africa & S Africa), 9765 (Australasia), [S] *9875* & [S] 11865 (W Africa), [S] *11915* (SE Asia & Australasia), [S] *15135* (W Africa & C America), [W] *15275* (SE Asia & Australasia), [W] *15410* (W Africa & C America), [W] *17560* (Australasia), [W] *17835* (W Africa & C America)
2300-2345	[W] *9470* (E Asia & SE Asia), 9815, [S] *12055* & [S] *13610/13640* (S Asia & SE Asia), [W] *13690* (SE Asia), [S] *21790* (E Asia & SE Asia)

GHANA

GHANA BROADCASTING CORPORATION

0530-0900 4915, 6130/3366
0900-1200 Sa/Su//Holidays 4915
0900-1700 6130
1200-1700 M-F 6130
1200-2400 4915
1700-2400 3366

GUAM

KTWR-TRANS WORLD RADIO

0730-0900 15510/15200 (SE Asia)
0815-0930 15330 (Australasia & S Pacific)
1430-1600 15330 (S Asia)

GUYANA

VOICE OF GUYANA

24 Hr 5950/3290

HOLLAND

RADIO NETHERLANDS

0000-0125 *6165* (N America), *9845* (E North Am)
0430-0530 *6165* & *9590* (W North Am)
0930-1125 [W] *12065* (SE Asia), [S] *13710* (E Asia & Australasia)
0930-1130 [W] *7260* (E Asia & Australasia), *9790* (Australasia), [S] *12065* (E Asia & Australasia)
1130-1325 ⇦ *5965* (E North Am), *6045* & *9860* (W Europe)
1430-1625 [S] *9890*, [S] *11835*, [W] *12070*, [S] *12075* & [W] *12080* (S Asia), *15220* (W North Am), [W] *15595* (S Asia)
1730-2025 *6020* (S Africa), [S] *7120* (E Africa), [S] 11655 (W Africa), [W] *11655* (E Africa)
1830-2025 9895 & 13700 (W Africa), *17605* & [S] *21590* (W Africa & C Africa)
2330-2400 *6165* (N America), *9845* (E North Am)

HUNGARY

RADIO BUDAPEST

0100-0130 [S] 9560 (N America)
0200-0230 [W] 9835 (N America)
0230-0300 [S] 9570 (N America)
0330-0400 [W] 9835 (N America)
1900-1930 [S] 7130 (W Europe)
2000-2030 ⇦ 6025 (Europe)
2000-2030 [W] 7135 (W Europe)
2200-2230 ⇦ 6025 (Europe)
2230-2300 ⇦ 3975 (Europe)

INDIA

ALL INDIA RADIO

0000-0045 7410 (E Asia), 9705 (SE Asia), 9950 & 11620 (E Asia), 13625 (SE Asia)
1000-1100 11585 (E Asia), 13700 (Australasia), 15020 (E Asia & Australasia), 17510 (Australasia), 17840 (E Asia), 17895 (Australasia)
1330-1500 9690, 11620 & 13710 (SE Asia)
1745-1945 7410, 9950 & 11620 (Europe), 11935 (E Africa), 13750 (N Africa & W Africa), 15200 (Mideast & W Asia), 17670 (E Africa)
2045-2230 7150 (Australasia), 7410 & 9650 (Europe), 9910 (Australasia), 9950 (Europe), 11620 & 11715 (Australasia)
2245-2400 7410 (E Asia), 9705 (SE Asia), 9950 & 11620 (E Asia), 13625 (SE Asia)

INDONESIA

VOICE OF INDONESIA

0100-0200 9525/11785 (E Asia, SE Asia & Pacific)
0800-0900 11785/9525 (Australasia)
2000-2100 11785/9525 & 15150 (Europe)

IRAN

VOICE OF THE ISLAMIC REPUBLIC

0030-0130 [W] 6065 (C America), [W] 6135 (E North Am & C America), 9022 (C America), [S] 9835 (E North Am & C America), [S] 11970 (C America)
1100-1230 [W] 15185, 15385, [S] 15430 & 15585 (W Asia & S Asia), 21470 & 21730 (S Asia & SE Asia)

1530-1630 W 7115, S 7245 & 9635 (S Asia, SE Asia & Australasia), 11775 (S Asia & SE Asia), W 11870 (S Asia, SE Asia & Australasia)
1900-1930 7175, W 7255 & S 9745 (Mideast)
1930-2030 W 6110, 9022, W 9625 & S 11670 (Europe), W 11685 (S Africa), S 13730 (Europe), W 15105 (S Africa)
2030-2100 W 7200 (W Europe)
2130-2230 S 9570 (S Asia, SE Asia & Australasia), W 9780 & W 11740 (Australasia), S 13745 (S Asia, SE Asia & Australasia)

IRELAND

RTE OVERSEAS

0130-0200 *6155* (C America)
1000-1030 *11685* (Australasia)
1800-1830 W *9895* & S *15315* (Mideast)
1830-1900 W *13640* & S *13725* (N America), *21630* (C Africa & S Africa)

ISRAEL

KOL ISRAEL

0400-0415 S 15640 (W Europe & E North Am)
0500-0515 ← 9435 (W Europe & E North Am) & 17545 (Australasia)
0500-0515 W 11605/6280 (W Europe & E North Am)
1600-1630 S 15640 (W Europe & E North Am)
1700-1730 ← 17545 (W Europe & E North Am)
1700-1730 W 15650 (W Europe & E North Am)
1900-1925 S 11605, S 15650 & S 17545 (W Europe & E North Am)
2000-2025 ← 15640 (S Africa)
2000-2025 W 9435, W 11605/6285 & W 13725 (W Europe & E North Am)

ITALY

RADIO ROMA-RAI INTERNATIONAL

0055-0115 9675 (N America), 11800 (N America & C America)
0445-0500 W 5965, W 5975 & 7235 (S Europe & N Africa)
1935-1955 5970, S 9750 & W 9760 (W Europe)
2025-2045 S 7125, W 7220, S 9635, W 9710, S 11800 & W 11885 (Mideast)
2205-2230 W 9675, 11900 & S 15265 (E Asia)

JAPAN

RADIO JAPAN/NHK

0000-0015 13650 & 17810 (SE Asia)
0000-0100 *6145* (E North Am)
0100-0200 *11860* (SE Asia), 11870/9700 & *11880* (Mideast), 15325 (S Asia), 17685 (Australasia), 17810 (SE Asia), 17835 (S America), 17845 (E Asia)
0300-0400 17825 (C America), 21610 (Australasia)
0500-0600 *5975* (W Europe), *6110* (W North Am), 11715 & 11760 (E Asia), 17810 (SE Asia)
0500-0700 *7230* (Europe), 13630/9835 (W North Am), 15195 (E Asia), 21755 (Australasia)
0600-0700 *11740* (SE Asia), 17870 (Pacific)
1000-1100 21755 (Australasia)
1000-1200 9695 (SE Asia), 15590 (Asia)
1100-1200 *6120* (E North Am)
1400-1500 9505 (W North Am), *17755* (Mideast)
1400-1600 7200/9860 (SE Asia), W 9845 & S 11730 (S Asia)
1500-1600 9750 (E Asia)
1700-1800 9505 (W North Am), 11970 (Europe), *15355* (S Africa)
2100-2200 S *6035* (Australasia), *6115* (W Europe), *6180* & 11830 (Europe), W 11850 (Australasia), *11855* (C Africa), W *11920* (Australasia), 17825 (W North Am), S 17860 (Australasia), 21670 (Pacific)

JORDAN

RADIO JORDAN

1100-1530 ← 11690 (W Europe)
1530-1730 ← 17680 (E North Am)

KOREA (DPR)

VOICE OF KOREA

0000-0100	11710 (N America & C America), 13760 & 15180 (Americas)
0100-0200	3560 (E Asia), 11735 (N America), 15230 & 17735 (SE Asia & Americas)
0200-0300	11845 (N America)
1100-1200	9850 (SE Asia & C America)
1200-1300	3560 (E Asia), 9640 (SE Asia & C America), 9975 (N America & C America), 11335 (SE Asia & C America), 13650 (N America & C America)
1500-1600	6575 & 9335 (Europe), 11710 & 13760 (N America & C America)
1600-1700	3560 (E Asia), 6520, 9660 & 9975 (Mideast & Africa)
1900-2000	6575 & 9335 (Europe), 11710 (N America & C America), 13760 (N America)

KOREA (REPUBLIC)

RADIO KOREA INTERNATIONAL

0200-0300	7275 (E Asia), 11725 & 11810 (S America), 15575 (N America)
0800-0900	9570 (Australasia), 13670 (Europe)
1130-1200	*9650* (E North Am)
1300-1400	9570 (SE Asia), 9640 (E Asia), 13670 (SE Asia)
1600-1700	5975 (E Asia), 9515 & 9870 (Mideast & Africa)
1900-2000	5975 (E Asia), 7275 (Europe)
2100-2130	S *3970* & 6480 (Europe)
2100-2200	15575 (Europe)
2200-2230	W *3975* (Europe)
2200-2300	W *3955* (W Europe)

KUWAIT

RADIO KUWAIT

0500-0800	15110 (S Asia & SE Asia)
1800-2100	11990 (Europe & E North Am)

LIBERIA

LIBERIAN COMMUNICATIONS NETWORK

0450-0800	6100/5100
0800-1800	6100
1800-2400	5100/5000

MALAYSIA

VOICE OF MALAYSIA

0500-0700 &	
0700-0830	6175 & 9750 (SE Asia), 15295 (Australasia)

MALTA

VOICE OF THE MEDITERRANEAN

0600-0630	S M-Sa *6110* (Europe & N Africa)
0700-0730	W M-Sa *6010* (Europe & N Africa)
0900-1000 ⇐	Su *11770* (Europe & N Africa)
1900-2000	S Sa-Th *12060* (Europe & N Africa)
2000-2100	W Sa-Th *7440* (Europe)

MEXICO

RADIO MEXICO INTERNACIONAL—(W North Am & C America)

0400-0430 &	
0500-0530 ⇐	Tu-Su 9705 & Tu-Su 11770
1500-1530,	
1600-1630 &	
2200-2230 ⇐	9705 & 11770
2300-2330 ⇐	M-F 9705 & M-F 11770

MONACO

TRANS WORLD RADIO

0645-0655	S Sa/Su *6045* (W Europe)
0655-0820	S *6045* (W Europe)
0745-0755 ⇐	Sa/Su 9870 (W Europe)
0745-0755	W Sa/Su *12070* (W Europe)
0755-0920 ⇐	9870 (W Europe)
0755-0920	W *12070* (W Europe)

MONGOLIA

VOICE OF MONGOLIA

1030-1100	12015/12085 (E Asia & SE Asia)
1500-1530	W 9720 & S 12015 (E Asia & SE Asia), 12085 (S Asia)
2000-2030	W 9720 & S 12015 (Europe), 12085 (S Asia)
2100-2130	12085 (E Asia)

NEPAL

RADIO NEPAL

0215-0225 &	
1415-1425	5005, 7165/3230

0100-0400	[W] *9525* (C America & W North Am)
0200-0300	[S] 6195 (E Europe), [S] *9410* (E Europe & Mideast), [W] *9410* (W Asia), *9770* (E Africa)
0200-0500	[W] *11760* (Mideast)
0300-0400	*6005* (S Africa), [W] *9410* (E Europe), *11730* & [S] *12035* (E Africa), [S] *21830* (W Asia & S Asia)
0300-0500	*3255* (S Africa), [S] *7120* & [W] *11765* (W Africa), [S] *11835* (W North Am & C America), [S] *12095* (Mideast), [W] *12095* (E Africa), [S] *15575* (Mideast), *17760* (E Asia)
0300-0530	*21660* (E Asia)
0300-0600	*17790* (S Asia)
0300-0700	6195 (Europe), *7160* (C Africa)
0300-0800	*15310* (S Asia)
0300-2200	*6190* (S Africa)
0330-0600	*15420* (E Africa)
0400-0500	*5975* (C America & W North Am), [S] *12035* (Europe), [S] *17640* (E Africa), *21830* (W Asia & S Asia)
0400-0600	[W] *6135* (W North Am & C America)
0400-0700 ←	9410 (Europe)
0400-0720	*6005* (W Africa)
0400-0730	[W] *15575* (Mideast)
0500-0530	*17885* (E Africa)
0500-0700	*11765* (W Africa), *17640* (E Africa)
0500-0730	[S] *15575* (Mideast & W Asia)
0500-0800	*11760* (Mideast)
0500-1030	*15360* (E Asia, SE Asia & Australasia), *17760* (E Asia & SE Asia)
0500-1100	*9740* (SE Asia)
0500-1700	*11940* (S Africa), 12095 (Europe)
0530-0600	M-F *17885* (E Africa)
0530-1030	*21660* (E Asia & SE Asia)
0600-0700	[W] *15420* (E Africa), [S] 15565 (E Europe)
0600-0800	Sa/Su *17885* (E Africa)
0600-0805	*17790* (S Asia)
0700-0800	*11765* & 17830 (W Africa)
0700-0900 ←	9410 (W Europe)
0700-1000	*15400* (W Africa)
0700-1500	17640 (E Europe & W Asia)
0700-1600	15485 (W Europe & N Africa)
0700-1700	15565 (E Europe)
0730-0900	Sa/Su *15575* (Mideast & W Asia)
0800-0900	[S] *21470* (S Africa), 21830 (W Asia & S Asia)
0800-1000	*17830* (W Africa & C Africa)
0800-1400	*15310* (S Asia), *17885* (E Africa)
0900-1000	*15190* (S America)
0900-1100	*9605*, [W] *11765* & *11945* (E Asia), *17790* (S Asia)
0900-1300	[W] *15310* (Mideast), *21470* (S Africa)
0900-1400	*11760* (Mideast)
0900-1500	*15575* (Mideast & W Asia)
0900-1700	*6195* (SE Asia)
1000-1100	Sa/Su *15400* (W Africa), Sa/Su *17830* (W Africa & C Africa)
1000-1130	Sa/Su *15190* (S America)
1000-1400	*6195* (C America & N America)
1100-1130	*15400* (W Africa), *17790* (S America)
1100-1300	*15280* (E Asia)
1100-1400	*15190/15220* (Americas)
1100-1600	*9740* (E Asia, SE Asia & Australasia), [S] *9815* (E Asia)
1100-1700	*17705* (S Asia)
1100-2100	*17830* (W Africa & C Africa)
1300-1400	*15420* (E Africa)
1300-1900	*21470* (S Africa)
1400-1700	*15190/17840* (Americas), *15310* (S Asia), *21660* (E Africa)
1430-1700	[W] 6195 (W Europe)
1500-1530	*11860*, *15420* & *21490* (E Africa)
1500-1600	[W] 9410 (Europe)
1500-1830	*5975* (S Asia)
1500-1900	*15400* (W Africa)
1600-1700	[S] *9410* (W Europe), [S] 15485 (W Europe & N Africa)
1600-1800	*3915* & *7160* (SE Asia), *9740* (S Asia)
1600-2100	[W] *9410* (N Europe)
1615-1700	Sa/Su *11860*, Sa/Su *15420* & Sa/Su *21490* (E Africa)
1700-1745	[S] *6005* & *9630* (E Africa)
1700-1800	[S] *15485* (W Europe)
1700-1830	*9510* (S Asia)

1700-1900	*15420* (E Africa)
1700-2000	6195 (W Europe), [S] *9410* (Europe), *15575* (Mideast & W Asia)
1700-2100	[S] 12095 (E Europe)
1700-2200	*3255* (S Africa)
1830-2100	*6005* & *9630* (E Africa)
1900-2000	[W] *15400* (S Africa)
2000-2100	[S] *9410* (W Europe), *15400* (W Africa & S Africa)
2000-2300	6195 (Europe), 11835 (W Africa)
2100-2200	*3915* (S Asia & SE Asia), *6005* (S Africa), *9410* (W Europe), [S] *11945* (E Asia)
2100-2300	*15400* (W Africa)
2100-2400	*5965* (E Asia), *5975* (C America & N America), *6195* (SE Asia), *12095* (S America)
2115-2130	M-F *11675* & M-F *15390* (C America)
2130-2145	Tu/F 11680 (Atlantic & S America)
2200-2300	*9660* (SE Asia), *12080* (S Pacific)
2200-2400	*7105* (SE Asia), *11955* (SE Asia & Australasia)
2300-2400	*3915* (SE Asia), [W] 6195 (W Europe), *11945* & *15280* (E Asia)
2330-2400	*6035* (E Asia)

WALES RADIO INTERNATIONAL

0200-0230	[S] Sa 9795 (N America)
0300-0330	[W] Sa 9735 (N America)
1130-1200	[W] Sa 17625 (Australasia)
1230-1300	[S] Sa 17650 (Australasia)
2030-2100	[S] F 7325 (Europe)
2130-2200	[W] F 6010 (Europe)

UNITED NATIONS

UNITED NATIONS RADIO

1730-1745	M-F *6125* (S Africa), [S] M- F *15265* (E Africa), [W] M-F *15495* (E Africa & Mideast), [W] M-F *17580* & [S] M-F *17710* (W Africa & C Africa)

USA

ADVENTIST WORLD RADIO

0100-0130	[W] *9730* (W Asia & S Asia)
0330-0400	[S] *17635* (W Asia & S Asia)
0400-0430	[W] *9630* (E Africa)
0430-0500	[S] *11975* & [W] *12080* (E Africa)
0500-0530	*5960* & *6015* (S Africa)
0530-0600	[S] *11970* & [W] *15345* (W Africa & C Africa)
0600-0630	[W] *15345* (C Africa & E Africa)
0830-0900	[S] *9610* & [W] *9660* (Europe), [W] *12000* (W Europe), [S] *17780* (W Africa)
1000-1030	[S] *11560* (E Asia), [S] *11705* & [W] *15330* (SE Asia)
1000-1100	[W] *11660* (E Asia)
1130-1200	[W] *15225* (W Europe)
1230-1300	[S] *9610* (Europe)
1300-1330	[W] *15225* (S Asia & SE Asia), [S] *15385* (S Asia)
1330-1400	[S] *11705*, [W] *11755* & [S] *11980* (E Asia), *15495* (W Asia & S Asia)
1430-1500	[S] *17720* (S Asia)
1530-1600	[S] *7165* (Europe), [S] *17660* (W Asia & S Asia)
1600-1700	[S] *11850* & [W] *11980* (S Asia)
1630-1700	[W] *5970* (Europe)
1730-1800	[W] *7455*, [W] *11560* & [S] *11965* (Mideast & W Asia), *12130* (E Africa), [S] *13840* (Mideast)
1800-1830	*5960* & *6100* (S Africa), [W] *11690* (E Africa)
2000-2030	*11640* (Europe), [W] *17695* (C Africa & E Africa)
2030-2100	*9745* (C Africa & E Africa)
2100-2130	[S] *15195* (W Africa)
2100-2200	[W] *9660* (W Africa)
2130-2200	[W] *11960*, *11980* & [S] *15240* (E Asia)

AFRTS-ARMED FORCES RADIO & TV SERVICE

24 Hr	4279 USB (N America & C America), *4319/12579* USB (S Asia), *4995/10943* USB (Europe & N Africa), *5765/13362* USB (Pacific), 6350/10320 (Irr) USB (Atlantic), 6459 USB (C America), 12690 USB (Americas)

FAMILY RADIO

0000-0100	6085 (E North Am)
0000-0445	9505 (W North Am)
0100-0200	*15060* (S Asia)
0100-0445	6065 (E North Am)
0400-0445	9985 (Europe)

0400-0500 [W] 11550 (Europe & Mideast)
0445-0600 [S] 9985 (Europe)
0500-0600 [S] 11580 (Europe)
0600-0700 [W] 11550 (Europe & Mideast)
0600-0745 7355 (Europe)
0700-0800 [W] 9985 (W Africa), [W] 11580 (C Africa & S Africa), [S] 13695 (W Africa), [S] 15170 (C Africa & S Africa)
1000-1245 5950 (E North Am)
1100-1300 [W] 11830 (W North Am)
1200-1300 13695 (E North Am)
1200-1345 [W] 11970 (C America)
1200-1700 [S] 17750 (W North Am & C America)
1300-1500 *11550* (S Asia), [W] 11740 & [S] 11970 (E North Am), 17510 & 17575 (S America)
1300-1700 11830 (W North Am)
1400-1700 [W] 17760 (W North Am & C America)
1500-1600 *6280* (S Asia)
1500-1700 [W] *15525* & [S] *17730* (S Asia)
1600-1700 [S] 15600 (W North Am), 21525 (C Africa & S Africa)
1600-1800 *13855* (C Africa & E Africa), 21455 (Europe)
1600-1945 18980 (Europe)
1900-1945 [W] 15565 (Europe)
1900-2100 [W] *13855* & [S] *15775* (C Africa & S Africa)
1945-2145 [S] 18980 (Europe)
2000-2200 [W] *11670* & [S] *13855* (W Africa), 17575 (S America)
2000-2245 [W] 7580 (Europe), [W] 15565 & [S] 17845 (W Africa)
2100-2200 [W] 21525 (C Africa & S Africa)
2100-2245 [S] 15120 (C Africa & S Africa)
2200-2345 11740 (W North Am)
2300-2400 [W] 15170 & [W] 15400 (S America)

HERALD BROADCASTING

0000-0057 W/F-M 9430 (E North Am), M/W/F 15285 (C America & S America)
0100-0157 9430 (N America), M 15285 (C America & S America)
0200-0257 M/Th 7535 (W North Am & C America), Su/M 9430 (N America)
0300-0357 [W] M 7535 & [S] M 11930 (E Europe)
0400-0457 [W] M/Tu/Th/Sa 12020 & [S] M/Tu/Th/Sa 15195 (E Africa & C Africa)
0500-0557 [W] M 7535 (E Europe), [S] 9840 (S Africa), [S] M 11930 (E Europe), [W] 12020 (S Africa)
0600-0657 [W] M/W/F/Sa 7535 & [S] M/W/F/Sa 13650 (W Africa & C Africa)
0700-0757 [W] Tu/Th 7535 & [S] Tu/Th 13650 (W Africa)
0800-0857 [W] Sa/Su 7535 (Europe), Sa-Th 9845 (Australasia), [S] Sa/Su 9860 (Europe)
0900-0957 [W] Tu/Th 7535 & [S] Tu/Th 9860 (Europe)
1000-1057 M/W/Th 6095 (E North Am), Su 9455 (S America)
1000-1100 Th-Tu *11780* (E Asia)
1100-1157 Tu/F-Su 6095 (E North Am), M 11660 (C America & S America)
1200-1257 M/W/Th 6095 (E North Am), Sa 11660 (C America & S America)
1200-1300 [W] *5915* & [S] *9875* (E Asia & SE Asia), [W] *9880* & [S] *12065* (SE Asia)
1300-1357 Sa-Th 9430 (N America), Tu/F 9455 (W North Am & C America)
1300-1400 [W] *7460* & [S] *9940* (S Asia)
1600-1657 Sa 18910 (E Africa)
1700-1800 Tu/Th/Sa 18910 (C Africa)
1800-1857 Su 15665 (E Europe), Su/W 18910 (S Africa)
1900-1957 Su/Tu/Th 15665 (E Europe), 18910 (S Africa)
2000-2057 [W] Su/M/W/F 15665 & [S] Su/M/W/F 18910 (Africa)
2100-2157 [W] W/Sa-M 11550 & [S] W/Sa-M 15665 (W Europe), [W] F 15665 & [S] F 18910 (W Africa & C Africa)
2200-2257 [W] Su/Th 7510 & [S] Su/Th 13770 (W Europe), W/Su 15285 (S America)
2300-2357 [W] Su/W 7510 & [S] Su/W 13770 (S Europe & W Africa), Su 15285 (S America)

HIGH ADVENTURE MINISTRIES

0500-0600 9975 (C America)

0700-0715 W/F-Su *5975* (W Europe)
0700-0900 *5975* (W Europe)
0900-1200 *21590* (Mideast)
1200-1300 *15715* (Mideast)
1330-1530 *17550* (S Asia)
1415-1500 *13820* (E Asia)
1700-1800 &
1800-1900 *9495* (E Europe)

KAIJ—(N America)
0000-0200 5755/13815
0200-1200 5755
1200-1400 5755/13815
1400-2400 13815

KJES
0100-0230 7555 (W North Am)
1300-1400 11715 (N America)
1400-1500 11715 (W North Am)
1800-1900 15385 (Australasia)

KNLS-NEW LIFE STATION—(E Asia)
0800-0900 [W] 9615 & [S] 11765
1300-1400 9615

KTBN—(E North Am)
0000-0100 [W] 7510 & [S] 15590
0100-1500 7510
1500-1600 [W] 7510 & [S] 15590
1600-2400 15590

KWHR-WORLD HARVEST RADIO
0000-0100 M-Sa 17510 (E Asia)
0100-0400 17510 (E Asia)
0400-1000 17780 (E Asia)
0500-0700 M-F 11565 (Australasia)
0700-1045 11565 (Australasia)
1000-1030 Su-F 9930 (E Asia & SE Asia)
1030-1400 9930 (E Asia & SE Asia)
1045-1600 Sa/Su 11565 (Australasia)
1600-1800 9930 (E Asia & SE Asia)
1800-2000 [W] 9930 (E Asia & SE Asia), [S] 17510 (E Asia)
2000-2100 M-F 17510 (E Asia)
2330-2400 M-Sa 17510 (E Asia)

RADIO AFRICA INTERNATIONAL—(Africa)
0400-0600 [W] *9535/13810* & [S] *13810*
1700-1900 *15485*

UNIVERSITY NETWORK
0000-0200 [S] *9825* (S Asia)
0000-0215 *13749* (C America)
0000-0300 [W] *9940* (S Asia)
24 Hr *5030* (C America), *6150* (C America & S America), *9725* (N America), *11870* (S America)
0300-1700 [S] *17645* (S Asia)
0400-1400 [W] *17765* (S Asia)
1400-2400 [W] *9940* (S Asia)
1700-2400 [S] *9825* (S Asia)
2100-2400 *13749* (C America)

VOA-VOICE OF AMERICA
0000-0100 *7215*, [S] *9770* & [W] *9890* (SE Asia), Tu-Sa 11695 (C America & S America), *11760* (SE Asia), *15185* (SE Asia & S Pacific), *15290* (E Asia), *17740* (E Asia & S Pacific), *17820* (E Asia)
0000-0130 [W] Tu-Sa 13740 & [S] Tu- Sa 13790 (C America & S America)
0000-0200 Tu-Sa 5995, Tu-Sa 6130, Tu-Sa 7405, Tu-Sa 9455 & Tu-Sa 9775 (C America & S America)
0100-0300 7115, [W] 7200, [S] 9635, [W] 9850, 11705, [S] 11725, 11820, [S] *13650*, *15250*, [W] *15300*, *17740* & *17820* (S Asia)
0130-0200 Tu-Sa 13740 (C America & S America)
0300-0330 [W] M-F *4960* (W Africa & C Africa), *7340* (C Africa & E Africa)
0300-0400 [W] *6035* (E Africa & S Africa), *7105* (S Africa)
0300-0430 *9885* (C Africa)
0300-0500 [S] *5855* (E Africa & S Africa), *6080* (S Africa), [S] *7275* (Africa), *7290* (C Africa & E Africa), [W] *7415* (C Africa & S Africa), 9575 (W Africa & S Africa), [S] *17685* (E Africa & S Africa)
0400-0500 [S] *4960* (W Africa & C Africa)
0400-0600 [W] *9775* (C Africa & E Africa)
0400-0700 [W] *7170* & [S] *9530* (N Africa), [S] *11965* (Mideast), *15205* (Mideast & S Asia)
0500-0600 [W] *9700* (N Africa)
0500-0630 *5970* (W Africa & C Africa), 6035 (W Africa & S Africa), *6080*, [S] *7195* & [W] *7295* (W Africa), [W] *11835* (W Africa & S Africa), *12080* (Africa), [S] *13670* (C Africa)
0500-0700 [W] *11825* (Mideast)
0600-0630 [S] *11995* (E Africa), [W] *11995* (C Africa), [W] *15600* (C Africa & E Africa)

Friends and family of Dr. Abelkader Abbadi gather for fellowship and refreshments. Abbadi is a lifelong world band listener and retired Moroccan official at the United Nations. A. Abbadi

0600-0700	[W] *5995*, [S] *9680*, [S] *11805* & [W] *11930* (N Africa)
0630-0700	Sa/Su *5970* (W Africa & C Africa), Sa/Su 6035 (W Africa & S Africa), Sa/Su *6080*, [S] Sa/Su *7195* & [W] Sa/Su *7295* (W Africa), [W] Sa/Su *11835* (W Africa & S Africa), [S] Sa/Su *11995* (E Africa), [W] Sa/Su *11995* (C Africa), Sa/Su *12080* (Africa), [S] Sa/Su *13670* (C Africa), [W] Sa/Su *15600* (C Africa & E Africa)
0700-0730	Sa 10869/6873 (Europe)
0800-1000	[S] *11930*, [W] *11995*, [S] *13610*, [W] *13615*, [W] *13650* & *15150* (E Asia)
1000-1100	5745, [W] 7370 & 9590 (C America)
1000-1200	[W] 5985 & [S] 9770 (Pacific & Australasia), [W] *11720* (E Asia & Australasia), [W] *15250* (E Asia)
1000-1300	[S] *15240* (E Asia)
1000-1500	*15425* (SE Asia & Pacific)
1100-1300	[W] *6110* & [S] *6160* (SE Asia)
1100-1400	*9645* (SE Asia & Australasia)
1100-1500	*9760* (E Asia, S Asia & SE Asia), [W] *11705* & [S] *15160* (E Asia)
1200-1330	[W] *11715* (E Asia & Australasia)
1300-1400	[W] *21550* (S Asia & SE Asia)
1300-1800	[W] *6110* & [S] *6160* (S Asia & SE Asia)
1400-1430	Su 18275 (Europe)
1400-1500	[W] *21555* & [W] *21840* (S Asia)
1400-1800	*7125* & *9645* (S Asia), [W] *15205* (Mideast & S Asia), [S] *15255* (Mideast)
1500-1600	[S] *9590* & [S] *9760* (S Asia & SE Asia), [W] *9760* (E Asia, S Asia & SE Asia), [W] *9795*, [S] *9845* & *12040* (E Asia), [S] *15235* (SE Asia & Australasia), [W] *15460* (SE Asia)
1500-1700	[W] *9575* (Mideast & S Asia), [S] *15205* (Europe, N Africa & Mideast)
1500-1800	[W] *15395* (S Asia)
1600-1700	*6035* (W Africa), *9760* (S Asia & SE Asia), *13600* (C Africa & E Africa), *13710* (Africa), *15225* (S Africa), [S] *15410* (Africa)

1600-1800	[W] *12040* & *15445* (E Africa), *17895* (Africa)
1600-2000	[W] *13710* (C Africa & E Africa)
1600-2200	[W] *15240* (Africa)
1700-1800	M-F *5990* (E Asia), [W] M-F *6045* (E Asia & Australasia), [S] M-F *7170* (Australasia), [S] M-F *7215* (SE Asia), [W] M-F *9525* (E Asia, SE Asia & S Pacific), [S] M-F *9550* (E Asia & SE Asia), [W] M-F *9670* (E Asia, SE Asia & Australasia), [S] M-F *9770* (E Asia), [W] M-F *9785*, [W] M-F *9795* & [W] M-F *11955* (S Asia & SE Asia), [W] M-F *12005* (SE Asia), [S] M-F *15255* (E Asia & Australasia)
1700-1900	[W] *6040* (N Africa & Mideast)
1700-2100	[S] *9760* (N Africa & Mideast), [W] *9760* (Mideast & S Asia)
1700-2200	[S] *15410* (Africa)
1730-1800	[W] *13680* (S Africa)
1800-1900	[S] *7415* (C Africa & S Africa), *9770* (Mideast), [S] *17895* (Africa)
1800-2200	*6035* (W Africa), *11975* (C Africa & E Africa), [W] *13710* (Africa), 15580 (W Africa)
1830-1900	[S] Sa/Su *11690*, [W] Sa/Su *13675*, [S] Sa/Su *13740*, [W] Sa/Su *15445* & [S] Sa/Su *15525* (E Africa)
1900-2000	[W] M-F *5965*, [S] *6160* & [S] *7260* (Mideast), *9525* (Australasia), [S] *9550*, [S] *9680* & [W] *9785* (Mideast), M-F *9840* & [W] *11720* (Mideast & S Asia), [S] M-F *11780* (Mideast), [S] *11805* (S Pacific), [W] *11870* (Australasia), [S] M-F *11970* (SE Asia), [W] M-F *11970* (E Asia), [S] M-F *12015* (S Asia), [W] *12015*, [W] *13640*, [S] *13690*, [S] *13725* & [W] *13725* (Mideast), *15180* (Pacific), [W] *15205* (Mideast), [S] M- F *15235* (SE Asia), [W] M-F *15410* (E Asia)
1900-2030	*4950* (W Africa & C Africa)
1900-2100	[W] *9690* (Mideast & S Asia), [S] *9770* (N Africa & Mideast)
1900-2200	[S] *7375* (C Africa & S Africa), *7415* (E Africa & S Africa), [S] *15445* (Africa)
2000-2030	*11855* (W Africa)
2000-2100	[S] *17745* & [W] *17885* (W Africa & C Africa)
2000-2200	*6095* (Mideast), 17725/17785 (Africa)
2030-2100	Sa/Su *4950* (W Africa & C Africa)
2100-2200	*6040* (Mideast), [S] *9535* (N Africa & Mideast), [W] *9595* (Mideast & S Asia), [W] *9670* (SE Asia & Australasia), *9760* (E Europe & Mideast), *11870* (Australasia)
2100-2400	[S] *9705* (SE Asia), *15185* (SE Asia & S Pacific), *17735/17740* (E Asia & S Pacific), *17820* (E Asia)
2200-2230	[S] M-F *5855* (C Africa & S Africa), M-F *6035* (W Africa), [S] M-F *7375* (C Africa & S Africa), M-F *7415* (E Africa & S Africa), [W] M-F *11655* (C Africa & S Africa), M-F 11975 (C Africa & E Africa), [W] M-F *13710* (Africa)
2200-2400	*7215* & [S] *9770* (SE Asia), [W] *9770* (SE Asia & Australasia), [W] *9890* & *11760* (SE Asia), *15290* (E Asia), *15305* (E Asia & SE Asia)
2300-2400	[W] *6045*, [W] *7140*, [S] *7190*, [S] *7200*, *9545*, *11925*, [S] *13775* & [W] *15395* (E Asia)
2330-2400	[W] *7130*, [S] *7225*, [S] *7260*, [W] *9620*, *11805*, [S] *13735*, [W] *13745* & *15205* (SE Asia)

WBCQ-"THE PLANET"—(N America)

0000-0500 ⇦	7415
0000-0700 ⇦	9330/9335 USB
0500-0545 ⇦	Tu-Su 7415
0545-0700 ⇦	F/Su 7415
1300-1400 ⇦	Su 17495 USB
1500-2200 ⇦	M-F 9330/9335 USB
1800-1900 ⇦	M-Sa 17495 USB
1900-2200 ⇦	M-F 17495 USB
2100-2400 ⇦	7415
2200-2400 ⇦	M-Sa 9330/9335 USB

WEWN

0000-0200	[S] 5825 (E North Am), [W] 5825 (N America & C America), [W] 9355 (Europe), [S] 13615 (W North Am & C America)
0200-1000	5825 (N America & C America)

1000-1100 [W] 7465 & [S] 15745 (Europe)
1000-1300 [W] 5825 & [S] 7425 (N America & C America)
1100-2100 15745 (Europe)
1300-1600 11875 (N America & C America)
1600-2200 11875 (E North Am)
1600-2400 13615 (W North Am & C America)
2100-2200 [W] 9975 & [S] 15745 (Europe)
2100-2400 17575 (Africa)
2200-2400 9385 (E North Am), 9975 (Europe)

WHRA-WORLD HARVEST RADIO

0000-0500 7580 (Europe & Mideast)
0500-1000 [W] 7435 & [S] 11565 (Africa)
1600-2300 ⇐ 17650 (Africa)
2200-2300 [S] 7580 (Europe & Mideast)
2300-2400 7580 (Europe & Mideast)

WHRI-WORLD HARVEST RADIO

0000-1000 5745 (E North Am)
0045-0300 M 7315 (C America)
0300-1000 7315 (C America)
1000-1045 M-Sa 9495 (N America & C America)
1000-1500 6040 (E North Am)
1045-1300 9495 (N America & C America)
1300-1700 15105 (C America)
1500-1600 [W] 6040 (E North Am), [S] 13760 (E North Am & W Europe)
1600-1715 13760 (E North Am & W Europe)
1700-1800 [S] 9495 (N America & C America), [W] 15105 (C America)
1715-1730 M-Sa 13760 (E North Am & W Europe)
1730-2000 13760 (E North Am & W Europe)
1800-2400 9495 (N America & C America)
2000-2400 5745 (E North Am)

WINB-WORLD INTERNATIONAL BROADCASTERS—(C America & W North Am)

0000-0400 12160
1000-1200 13845
1200-2300 13570
2300-2400 13570/12160

WJCR

24 Hr 7490 (E North Am), 13595 (W North Am)

WMLK—(Europe, Mideast & N America)

0400-0900 &
1700-2200 Su-F 9465

WORLD BEACON

1400-1800 [S] *17795* (E Europe)
1500-1700 [W] *15340* (E Europe)
1700-1900 [W] *9575* (E Europe)
1800-2200 *3230* (S Africa), [S] *9675* (C Africa & S Africa), [W] *9675* (W Africa)

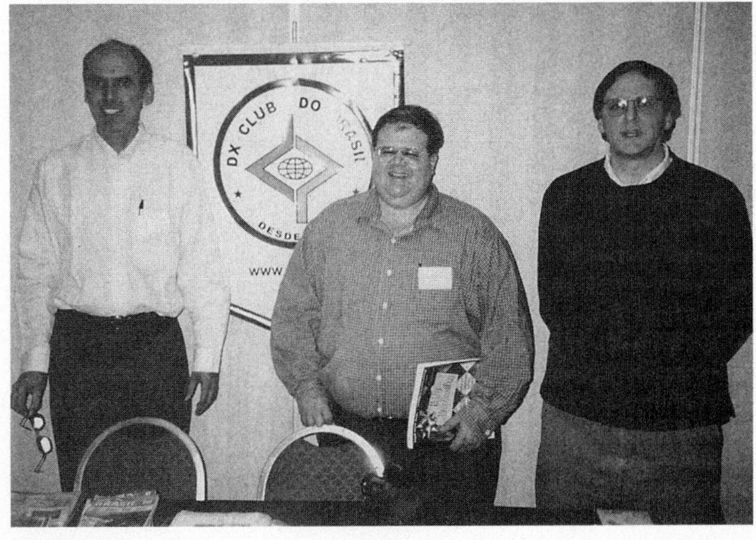
DX CLUB DO

Pedro de Castro, in white, of the DX Clube do Brasil, along with Jeff White of WRMI in Miami and the VOA's Kim Elliott. Elliott's weekly "Communications World" has an enthusiastic worldwide following.

L. Magne

WRMI-RADIO MIAMI INTERNATIONAL

Time	Frequency / Target
0100-0130 ⇦	M 9955 (C America & S America)
0130-0300 ⇦	Tu-Sa 7385 (N America)
0200-0230 ⇦	M 9955 (C America & S America)
0400-0545 ⇦	7385 (N America)
0545-0600 ⇦	M-Th/Sa 7385 (N America)
0600-0630 ⇦	Tu-Sa 7385 (N America)
0630-0700 ⇦	M-Sa 7385 (N America)
0700-0715 & 0715-1030 ⇦	Tu-Sa 7385 (N America)
1300-1500 ⇦	Su 9955 (C America)
1300-2400 ⇦	M-F 7385 (N America)
2100-2300 ⇦	Sa/Su 9955 (C America)
2300-2400 ⇦	Sa 9955 (C America)

WTJC—(N America)

Time	Frequency / Target
0000-0130 ⇦	9370
0130-0145 ⇦	Tu-Su 9370
0145-1105 ⇦	9370
1105-1120 ⇦	M-Sa 9370
1120-2400 ⇦	9370

WWBS—(E North Am)

Time	Frequency / Target
0000-0100	[S] Su/M 11910
0000-0200	[W] Su/M 11900
2300-2400	[S] Sa/Su 11910

WWCR

Time	Frequency / Target
0000-0100	3215/9475 (E North Am)
0000-0200	5935/13845 & 13845 (E North Am)
0000-0400	7435 (E North Am)
0000-1300	5070 (E North Am)
0100-0400	3215 (E North Am)
0200-1200	5935 (E North Am)
0400-0500	[W] 3215 (E North Am)
0400-0600	[W] 2390/7435 (E North Am)
0500-1000 ⇦	3210 (E North Am)
0600-1200 ⇦	2390 (E North Am)
1000-1100 ⇦	Su-F 7435 (E North Am)
1000-1100	[S] Su-F 9475 (E North Am)
1100-1200	[W] Su-F 12160 (E North Am & Europe)
1100-1300	[S] 15685 (E North Am & Europe)
1100-1400 ⇦	7435 (E North Am)
1200-1300	[W] 12160 (E North Am & Europe)
1200-1400	5935/13845 (E North Am)
1300-1400	[W] 5070 & [S] 9475 (Irr) (E North Am), [S] 12160 (E North Am & Europe)
1300-2100	15685 (E North Am & Europe)
1400-2100	9475 (E North Am)
1400-2200	12160 (E North Am & Europe)
1400-2400	13845 (E North Am)
2100-2145	[S] Sa/Su 15685 (E North Am & Europe)
2100-2200	[W] 15685/9475 (E North Am)
2145-2200	[S] 15685 (E North Am & Europe)
2200-2245	[S] 9475 & [W] Sa/Su 9475 (E North Am)
2200-2400	5070/12160 (E North Am & Europe), 7435 (E North Am)
2245-2300	9475 (E North Am)
2300-2400	3215/9475 (E North Am)

WWFV

Time	Frequency / Target
0000-0200 ⇦	6890 USB (W North Am)
0000-0600 ⇦	5085 USB (W North Am & C America)
0200-0600 ⇦	3270 USB (W North Am & C America)
1300-2400 ⇦	12172 (W North Am)
2300-2400 ⇦	6890 USB (W North Am)

UZBEKISTAN

RADIO TASHKENT

Time	Frequency / Target
0100-0130	[W] 5040 & 5060 (C Asia), [W] 5955 (S Asia), [W] 5975 (Mideast & W Asia), [W] 7105 (W Asia), [S] 7190 (Mideast & W Asia), [W] 7205 (Mideast), [S] 9375 (W Asia), [W] 9540 (Mideast & W Asia), [S] 9715 (Mideast & S Asia)
1200-1230 & 1330-1400	[W] 5060 & [W] 5975 (S Asia), [W] 6025 & [S] 7285 (W Asia & S Asia), 9715 & [S] 15295 (S Asia), [S] 17775 (S Asia & SE Asia)
2030-2100 & 2130-2200	[W] 7105 (W Asia), 9540 (Mideast & W Asia), [S] 9545 (W Asia)

VATICAN STATE

VATICAN RADIO

Time	Frequency / Target
0140-0200	[W] 7335, [S] 9650 & [S] 11935 (S Asia)
0250-0310	7305 (E North Am), 9605 (E North Am & C America)

"Information Central" at Radio Canada International is this highly automated control room. RCI

0600-0620 ⇦	4005 (Europe), 5880 (W Europe)
0620-0700 ⇦	5880 (W Europe)
0730-0745 ⇦	M-Sa 4005 (Europe), M-Sa 5880 (W Europe), M-Sa 7250 & M-Sa 9645 (Europe), M-Sa 11740 (W Europe & N Africa), M-Sa 15210/15215 (Mideast)
1120-1130 ⇦	M-Sa 7250 (Europe), M-Sa 11740 (W Europe), M-Sa 15210 (Mideast)
1615-1630	S 7250 (N Europe), S 11810 (Mideast)
1715-1730 ⇦	4005 (Europe), 5880 & 9645 (W Europe)
1715-1730	W 7250 (Mideast)
2050-2110 ⇦	4005 & 5880 (Europe)

VIETNAM

VOICE OF VIETNAM

0100-0130 & 0230-0300	*9525* (E North Am)
0330-0400	*9795* (W North Am)
1000-1030	9840 & 12020 (SE Asia)
1100-1130	7285 (SE Asia)
1230-1300	9840 & 12020 (SE Asia)
1330-1400	W 7145, 9730 & S 13740 (Europe)
1600-1630	W 7145 & 9730 (Europe)
1630-1700	S 13740 (Europe)
1700-1730	S *12070* (Europe)
1800-1830	W *5955* (W Europe), W 7145, 9730 & S 13740 (Europe)
1900-1930 & 2030-2100	W 7145, 9730 & S 13740 (Europe)
2330-2400	9840 & 12020 (SE Asia)

YEMEN

REPUBLIC OF YEMEN RADIO—(Mideast & E Africa)

0600-0700 & 1800-1900	9780

YUGOSLAVIA

RADIO YUGOSLAVIA

0000-0030	S M-Sa *11870* (E North Am)
0100-0130	W M-Sa *7115* (E North Am)
0200-0230	W *7130* (W North Am)
0430-0500	S *11870* (W North Am)
1330-1400	W *11835* (Australasia)
1930-2000 ⇦	*6100* (Europe)
2100-2130	S *6100* (Europe)
2200-2230	W *6100/6185* (Europe), S Su-F *7230* (Australasia)

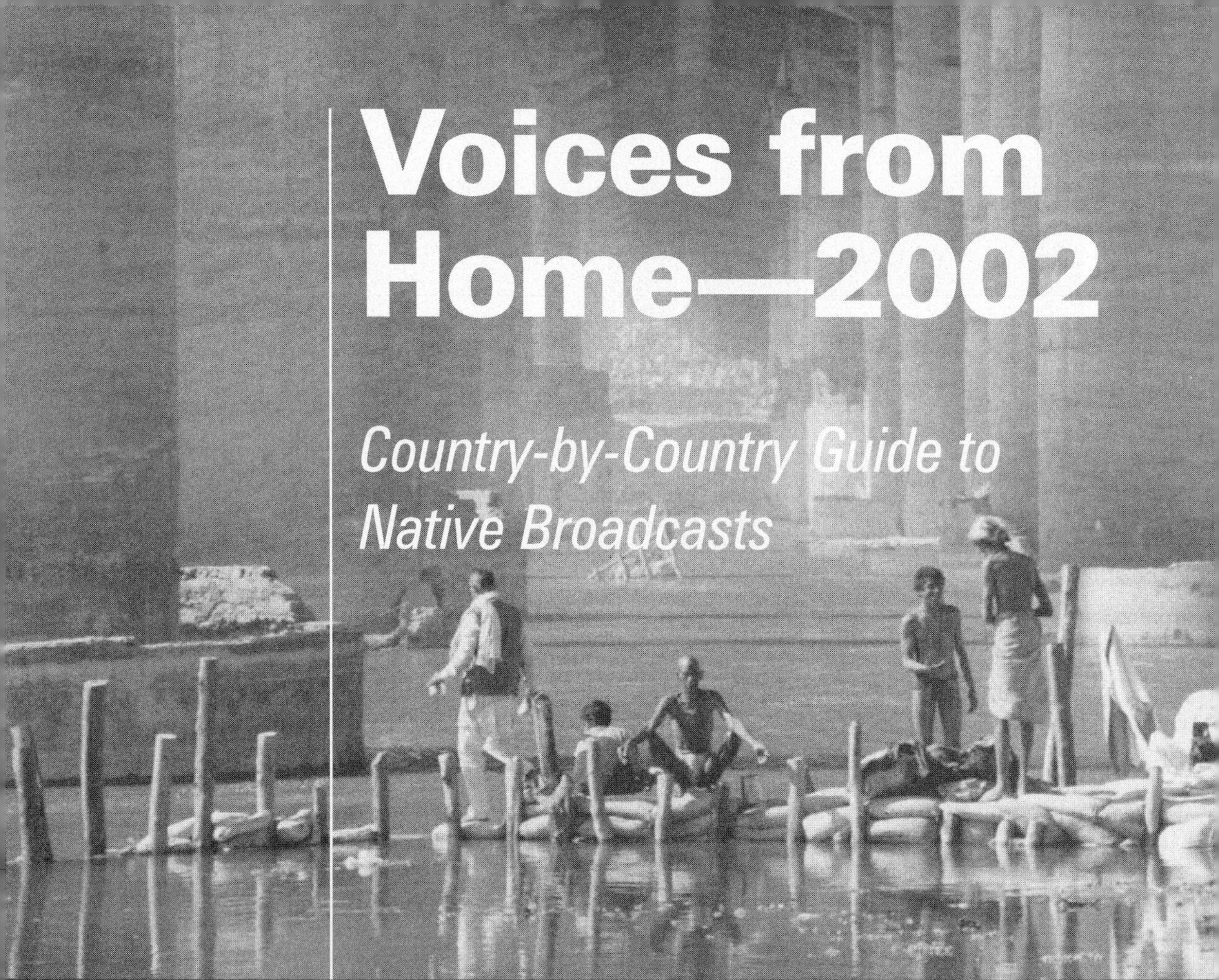

Voices from Home—2002

Country-by-Country Guide to Native Broadcasts

For some listeners, English offerings are merely icing on the cake. Their real interest is in eavesdropping on broadcasts for *nativos*—the home folks. These can be enjoyable regardless of language, especially when they offer traditional music.

Some you'll hear, many you won't, depending on your location and receiving equipment. Keep in mind that native-language broadcasts are sometimes weaker than those in English, so you may need more patience and better hardware. PASSPORT REPORTS shows which radios and antennas work best.

When to Tune

Some broadcasts come in better during the day within world band segments from 9300 to 21850 kHz. However, signals from Latin

America and Africa peak near or during darkness, especially from 4700 to 5100 kHz. See "Best Times and Frequencies" for specifics.

Times and days of the week are in World Time, explained in "Setting Your World Time Clock" and Passport's glossary; for local times in each country, see "Addresses PLUS." Midyear, some stations are an hour earlier (⇦) or later (⇨) because of daylight saving time, typically April through October. Those used only seasonally are labeled S for summer (midyear) and W for winter (January, etc.). Stations may also extend their hours for holidays, emergencies or sports events.

Frequencies in *italics* may be best, as they come from relay transmitters that might be near you, although other frequencies beamed your way might do almost as well. Some signals not beamed to you can also be heard, especially when they are targeted to nearby parts of the world. Frequencies with no target zones are usually for domestic coverage, so they are the least likely to be heard unless you're in or near that country.

Moroccan tower. World band is well heard in North Africa. A. Abbadi

Schedules for Entire Year

To be as useful as possible over the months to come, Passport's schedules consist not just of observed activity, but also that which we have creatively opined will take place during the forthcoming year. This predictive material is based on decades of experience and is original from us. Although inherently not as exact as real-time data, over the years it's been of tangible value to Passport readers.

ALBANIA—Albanian

RADIO TIRANA

0000-0430 ←	6090 & 7270 (E North Am)
0400-0900 ←	6100 (Europe)
0900-1000 ←	7110 (Europe)
1500-1800 ←	5985 (S Europe), 7270 (Europe)
2130-2300 ←	7295 & 9575 (Europe)

ARGENTINA—Spanish

RADIO ARGENTINA AL EXTERIOR-RAE

0800-1200	M-F 6060 (S America), M- F 15345 (Americas)
1200-1400	M-F 11710 (S America)
2200-2400	M-F 9690 (S America), M- F 15345 (Europe & N Africa)

RADIO NACIONAL

0000-0300	Su/M 6060 & 11710 (Irr) (S America), Su/M 15345 (Americas)
1700-2400	11710 (Irr) (S America)
1800-2400	Sa/Su 6060 (S America), Sa/ Su 15345 (Europe & N Africa)

ARMENIA—Armenian

VOICE OF ARMENIA

0300-0330 ←	9965 (S America)
0400-0430 ←	4810 (E Europe, Mideast & W Asia), 9965 (S America)
0800-0830 ←	Su 4810 (E Europe, Mideast & W Asia), Su 15270 (Europe)
1930-2000 ←	M-Sa 4810 (E Europe, Mideast & W Asia), M-Sa 9960/9965 (Europe)

Elayne Star, Assistant Manager of WBCQ, and Tim Smith at the station's Monticello office. WBCQ

AUSTRIA—German

RADIO AUSTRIA INTERNATIONAL

0000-0030	S 9870 (C America & S America), W 13730 (S America)
0100-0130	S 9870 (E North Am), W 9870 (C America & S America)
0200-0230	W 7325 (E North Am)
0400-0500	S 6155 & S 13730 (Europe)
0500-0530	S 17870 (Mideast)
0500-0630	6155 & 13730 (Europe)
0600-0630	S 17870 (Mideast)
0630-0700	W 6155 & W 13730 (Europe)
0700-0715	6155 & 13730 (Europe)
0715-0800	S 6155 & S 13730 (Europe)
0800-1100	6155 & 13730 (Europe)
1000-1200	W 21530/21630 (Africa)
1100-1200	W 6155 & W 13730 (Europe)
1100-1400	Su 9745 (W Europe)
1200-1300	S 6155, W Su 6155, S 13730 & W Su 13730 (Europe)
1300-1310	W Su 6155 & W Su 13730 (Europe)
1300-1330	S 6155 & S 13730 (Europe), W 17855 & S 21780 (S Asia, SE Asia & Australasia)
1300-1400	W M-Sa 6155 & W M-Sa 13730 (Europe)
1400-1430	6155 & 13730 (Europe)
1430-1500	S 6155 & S 13730 (Europe)
1500-1600	W 21560 (Africa)
1500-1630	6155 & 13730 (Europe)
1600-1630 ←	*17865* (W North Am)
1630-1700	S 6155 & S 13730 (Europe)
1700-1730	6155 & 13730 (Europe)
1730-1800	W 6155 & W 13730 (Europe)
1800-1830 & 1900-1930	5945 & 6155 (Europe)
2000-2030	W 5945 & W 6155 (Europe)
2000-2100	S M-Th/Sa 5945 & S M- Th/ Sa 6155 (Europe)
2100-2130	S 5945 & S 6155 (Europe)
2100-2200	W M-Th/Sa 5945 & W M- Th/ Sa 6155 (Europe)
2130-2200	S Sa/Su 5945 & S Sa/Su 6155 (Europe)
2200-2230	5945 & 6155 (Europe)
2230-2300	S 5945, W Sa/Su 5945, S 6155 & W Sa/Su 6155 (Europe)
2300-2330	5945 & 6155 (Europe), S 13730 (S America)
2330-2400	W 5945 & W 6155 (Europe)

BANGLADESH—Bangla

BANGLADESH BETAR

1200-1530 &
1545-1600 15519 (Mideast & Europe)
1600-1730 15519 (Mideast & Europe)
1630-1730 7185 & 9550 (Mideast)
1915-2000 7185, 9550 & 15519 (Irr) (Europe)

BELGIUM

RADIO VLAANDEREN INTERNATIONAAL

Dutch

0430-0500 [W] *11985* & [S] *15565* (W North Am)
0600-0700 ⇦ 5985 (S Europe)
0600-0700 [S] 13685 (S Europe & Mideast)
0600-0900 ⇦ 9925 (S Europe)
0700-0800 [W] 5985 (S Europe), [S] 13685 (Europe)
0800-0900 [W] 11700 (S Europe & W Africa), [S] 13685 (S Europe)
0900-1000 ⇦ 9925 (Europe)
0900-1000 [W] 13650 (S Europe)
1000-1100 [S] Su 17690 (C Africa)
1100-1130 [S] 13685 (S Europe & W Africa)
1100-1200 ⇦ Su 21630 (C Africa & S Africa)
1100-1200 [W] Su 17650 (C Africa)
1200-1230 ⇦ 9925 (S Europe)
1200-1230 *9865* (E Asia & Australasia), [W] *13650* (S Europe), [W] *17685* & [S] *17690* (SE Asia & Australasia), 21630 (C Africa & S Africa)
1400-1700 ⇦ Su 9925 (S Europe), Su 13710 (S Europe & W Africa)
1600-1630 [S] 13710 (S Europe & Mideast)
1700-1730 ⇦ 9925 (S Europe)
1700-1730 [W] 5910 (S Europe), [S] 13710 (S Europe & W Africa)
1800-1830 ⇦ 9925 (S Europe)
1800-1830 [W] 5910 (S Europe)
1800-1900 [S] *7195* (C Africa & S Africa), [S] *13710* (S Europe & Mideast), [S] *15515* (C Africa & S Africa)
1900-2000 ⇦ 5910 (S Europe), 9925 (S Europe & W Africa)
1900-2000 [W] *13645* (S Africa), [W] *13770* (S Europe & Mideast), [W] *15520* (C Africa & S Africa)
2000-2100 ⇦ Sa 5910 (S Europe), Sa 9925 (S Europe & W Africa)
2100-2200 ⇦ 5910 (S Europe), 9925 (S Europe & W Africa)
2300-2330 [W] *13660* & [S] *15565* (N America)

French

1630-1645 [S] 9925 (S Europe)
1730-1745 [W] 5910 (S Europe)
1900-1915 [S] 5960 (Europe)

RTBF INTERNATIONAL

French

0400-0530 ⇦ M-F *9490* (C Africa)
0400-0800 [S] 9970/9965 (S Europe)
0530-0600 ⇦ *9490* (C Africa)
0600-0812 ⇦ *17580* (C Africa)
0800-1700 9970/9965 (S Europe)
0812-0906 ⇦ Sa/Su *17580* (C Africa)
0906-1100 ⇦ Sa *17580* (C Africa)
1100-1200 ⇦ M-Sa *21565* (C Africa)
1200-1217 ⇦ *21565* (C Africa)
1217-1306 ⇦ M-F *21565* (C Africa)
1600-1700 ⇦ Su-F *17570* (C Africa)
1700-1715 [S] 9970/9965 (S Europe)
1700-1816 ⇦ *17570* (C Africa)

BRAZIL—Portuguese

RADIO BANDEIRANTES

24 Hr 6090, 9645, 11925

RADIO CULTURA SAO PAULO

0000-0200 ⇨ 6170, 9615, 17815
0700-2400 ⇨ 9615, 17815
0800-2400 ⇨ 6170

RADIO NACIONAL BRASILIA

0000-0230 ⇨ 6180/11780
0230-0700 ⇨ Su 6180/11780
2105-2300 ⇨ Sa/Su 6180/11780
2300-2400 ⇨ 6180/11780

RADIO NACIONAL DA AMAZONIA

0700-2105 ⇨ 6180/11780
2105-2300 ⇨ M-F 6180/11780

BULGARIA—Bulgarian

RADIO BULGARIA

0000-0100 [S] 9500 & [S] 11600 (S America), [S] 11700 (E North Am)
0100-0200 ⇦ 9400 (E North Am)
0100-0200 [W] 5900 (S America), [W] 7375 (E North Am), [W] 9415 (S America)
0300-0400 [S] 7500 (E Europe & W Asia)
0400-0500 ⇦ 5900 (E Europe & W Asia)
0400-0500 [W] 7400 (E Europe & W Asia)

1200-1500	[S] 7300 (Europe)
1300-1600 ⇦	13600 (Europe)
1300-1600	[W] 7500 (S Europe & Mideast)
1500-1600	[S] 13600 (Mideast)
1500-1800	[S] 9900 & [S] 11700 (E Europe & W Asia)
1600-1700 ⇦	17500 (S Africa)
1600-1700	[W] 9400 (Mideast)
1600-1900	[W] 5865 & [W] 7465 (E Europe & W Asia)
1800-1900	[S] 6000 (S Europe)
1800-2100	[S] 7400 (Mideast), [S] 7500 (Europe)
1900-2000	[W] 5855 (S Europe)
1900-2200	[W] 7500 (Mideast), [W] 7545 (Europe)

CANADA—French

CANADIAN BROADCASTING CORP—(E North Am)

0100-0300 ⇦	M 9625
0300-0400 ⇦	Su 9625 & Tu-Sa 9625
1300-1310 & 1500-1555 ⇦	M-F 9625
1700-1715 ⇦	Su 9625
1900-1945 ⇦	M-F 9625
1900-2310 ⇦	Sa 9625

RADIO CANADA INTERNATIONAL

0000-0100	[W] 6040 (E North Am & C America), [W] 11865 (C America & S America), [W] 13640 (E North Am & C America)
1100-1200	[S] 5990, [S] 9640 & [S] 11910 (E North Am & C America)
1200-1300	[S] Sa/Su 9640, [S] Sa/Su 11910, [W] 13655 & [W] 15425 (E North Am & C America)
1300-1400	[W] Sa/Su 13655 & [W] Sa/Su 15425 (E North Am & C America)
1700-1800 ⇦	21565 (C America)
1700-1800	[W] 17820 (C America)
1900-2000	[S] *5995* & [S] *7235* (S Europe & N Africa), [S] *13670* (N Africa & W Africa), [S] *15120* (C Africa & N Africa), [S] 15325 & [S] 21570 (Europe)
2000-2100	[W] 5995 (Europe), [W] *7235* (N Africa), [W] 9770 (W Europe), [W] *11725* (W Africa), [W] 13650 (W Europe), [W] *15325* (C Africa & N Africa)
2200-2300	[W] *9680* & [W] *11705* (E Asia & SE Asia), [S] *13710* (E Asia), [S] *17835* (E Asia & SE Asia)
2230-2300	[W] *9805* (N Africa & W Africa)
2300-2400	[S] 5960 (E North Am & C America)

CHINA

CENTRAL PEOPLE'S BROADCASTING STATION

Chinese

0000-0030	[W] 9775, [W] 9830, [W] 11990, [S] 17565, [S] 17605, [S] 17700
0000-0100	5880, 5915, 5955, [W] 6110, 6125, 6750, 7275, 7935, 9480, 9710, 9800/6125, [W] 9845, [W] 11710, [W] 11925, [S] 11960, [S] 17490, [S] 17550
0000-0103	[W] 6790, 9170, [S] 11000
0000-0130	7220
0000-0200	[W] 9900
0000-0500	7230, 11660
0000-0600	6030, 7200, 9625, 9645, 9675, 9700, 9810, 11610, 11670, 11800, 12030, 15480, 15500, 15540, 15550, 17625, 17890
0030-0600	17565, 17605, 17700
0055-0614	11100, 11935, 15710
0100-0400	11835
0100-0600	11960, 17490, 17550
0130-0500	17580
0200-0500	15390
0200-0600	15300
0200-1300	13700
0355-0603	11000, 15880
0500-0600	Sa-Th 7230, W-M 11660, 11835
0600-0800	W-M 11835
0600-0855	W-M 6030, Th-Tu 7200, W/Th/Sa-M 7230, Th-Tu 9625, W-M 9645, W-M 9675, Th-Tu 9700, Th-Tu 9810, Th-Tu 11610, Th-M 11660, Th-Tu 11670, Th- Tu 11800, W-M 11960, W- M 12030, W-M 15300, W- M 15480, Th-Tu 15500, Th-Tu 15540, W-M 15550, Th-Tu 17490, W-M 17550, W-M 17565, W-M 17605, Th-Tu 17625, Th-Tu 17700, W-M 17890

RCI
RADIO CANADA INTERNATIONAL
Monitoring Station
Station d'écoute

Radio Canada International's monitoring station. RCI

Time	Frequencies
0603-0955	Th-Tu 11000, Th-Tu 15880
0700-0855	W-M 11630, W-M 12055, W-M 15390, W-M 17580
0855-0930	11960
0855-1000	9700
0855-1030	9645, 15500
0855-1100	9675, 15550, 17490
0855-1130	17550, 17565, 17625
0855-1200	9810, 17700, 17890
0855-1230	15480
0855-1300	11610, 11660, [S] 11670
0855-1330	11800, 15540, 17605
0855-1400	12030
0855-1500	15300
0855-1602	7200, 9625
0855-1730	6030, 7230
0900-1130	11835
0900-1730	9480, 9710, 9800
0930-1300	[W] 6110, [S] 11960
0955-1230	11000, 15880
0955-2400	[W] 5090, [W] 7620, 9380, [S] 11100, [S] 11935
1000-1100	11630, 12055, 15390, 17580
1000-1300	[W] 4850
1000-1400	7935
1030-1300	[W] 4460, [W] 5010, [S] 9645
1030-1602	[S] 15500
1100-1200	[W] 5030, [S] 9675
1100-1230	[W] 7345, [S] 15550
1100-1300	[W] 11710, [S] 17490
1100-1730	5880, 5955, 6125, 6750, 13610
1130-1300	7275
1130-1330	[W] 9845, [S] 17550
1130-1602	9745
1130-1730	7335, 9830
1200-1230	15390
1200-1300	[W] 9775, [S] 17700
1200-1400	9820, 11630, [W] 11925, 12055/9455
1200-1602	[W] 5163, [S] 9810
1200-1730	5030, 7290
1230-1730	5320, 7345, 9655
1230-1804	[W] 6790, 9170, [S] 11000
1300-1400	[S] 13700
1300-1602	4850, 5010, [W] 6090, [W] 7140, 9775, [S] 11610, [S] 11660, 11710
1300-1730	4460, 6110
1330-1602	[W] 3290, 11730, [S] 11800
1330-1730	9845, 11990
1400-1600	11925
1400-1730	7250, 7275
2000-2200	4460, 6055, 7290
2000-2230	5320
2000-2300	6110, 7250, 7275, 7345, 9830, 9845, 11925
2000-2330	5030, 11990
2000-2400	5880, 5915, 5955, 6030, 6125, 6750, 7230, 7335, 7935, 9455, 9480, 9655, 9710, 9820, 9900, 11630
2055-2200	6790
2055-2400	9170

2100-2200	4850
2100-2230	W 3290, S 11800
2100-2300	5010, 6090, 7315, 9745, 9755, 9775, 11710, W 11730, S 15540
2100-2330	W 5163, W 7140, S 9810, S 11610
2100-2400	7200, 9625
2200-2300	W 4850, S 11670
2200-2400	W 4460, W 6790, 7220, W 7290, S 9645, S 11000, S 17890
2230-2400	9800/6125, 11800, 15480
2300-2400	W 5010, W 6110, W 7345, W 9745, W 9775, W 9830, W 9845, 11660, 11670, W 11710, 11720, W 11925, S 11960, 12030, S 15500, 15540, S 15550, S 17490, S 17550, S 17565, S 17625, S 17700
2330-2400	9675, 9810, 11610, W 11990, S 17605

CHINA RADIO INTERNATIONAL

Chinese

0200-0300	*9570* (E North Am), *9690* (N America & C America), 15435 (S America)
0300-0400	*9720* (W North Am)
0900-1000	W 6165 & S 9550 (E Asia), 11700 & 11875 (Australasia), S 11975 & W 15110 (E Asia), S 15250 (SE Asia), 15440 (Australasia)
0900-1100	7360, 15340/11685 & 17785 (SE Asia)
1200-1300	*9570* (E North Am)
1200-1400	11875 (Australasia), 15260, 15340/11685 & 17785 (SE Asia)
1300-1400	9440 (SE Asia)
1500-1600	W 7180, W 7265, S 11760 & S 11825 (S Asia)
1730-1830	W 6135 & W 7120 (Europe), W 7160 (W Africa & C Africa), W 7315 (N Africa), 9645 (W Africa & C Africa), S 9685 (Mideast & N Africa), W 9745 (Mideast), S 11660 (Europe), S 11760 (Mideast & N Africa), S 11835 (N Africa), S 13610 (Europe)
1830-2230	S 11660 (Europe)
2000-2100	W 6165 & W 7135 (Mideast), W 7225 (Europe), W 7245 (Mideast), W 7660 (E Europe), W 9585 & 9685 (Mideast), W 9720 & S 9765 (E Europe), S 11610 & S 11650 (Mideast & N Africa), S 11870 (E Europe), S 13775 (Europe), S 13790 (Mideast)
2230-2300	W 7150 & S 15110 (E Asia), *15500* (E Africa)
2230-2330	6140, 9460, W 9515/9550, 11945, 15100, 15260 & 15400 (SE Asia)
2230-2400	*11975* (N Africa)
2300-2400	*7170* (W Africa)

Cantonese

1000-1100	15440 (Australasia), 17755 (SE Asia)
1000-1200	11875 (Australasia)
1100-1200	9590, 15340/11685 & 17785 (SE Asia)
1700-1800	W 7220 (E Africa & S Africa), 9770 & S 15580 (E Africa)
1900-2000	W 7255 (Europe), W 9720 & S 9765 (E Europe), S 11895 (Europe)
2330-2400	6140, 9460, W 9515/9550, 11945, 15100, 15260 & 15400 (SE Asia)

CHINA (TAIWAN)

CENTRAL BROADCASTING SYSTEM- CBS

Chinese

0000-0100	9650 (E Asia)
0000-0200	9690, 11625 & 11985 (E Asia)
0100-0500	15460 (E Asia)
0100-1800	15355 (E Asia)
0200-0500	15290 (SE Asia)
0300-0500	9690 (E Asia)
0400-0500	6265 (E Asia)
0400-0600	11625, 11985, 15060 & 15430 (E Asia)
0600-0800	Sa/Su 15060 (E Asia)
0600-0900	Sa/Su 11625, Sa/Su 11985 & Sa/Su 15430 (E Asia)
0900-1400	11625 (E Asia)
0900-1500	6265 (E Asia)
0900-1700	6220 & 15060 (E Asia)
0900-1800	7365, 9650 & 9690 (E Asia)
1100-1200	9610 (Australasia)
1100-1700	11615 (E Asia)

जय भारत स्टेशनर्स
A.K.

The Pink City in Jaipur, India. Lars Rydén

1400-1800	3335 (E Asia)
1500-1700	15265 (SE Asia)
2200-2300	6265 (E Asia), 11875 (SE Asia)
2200-2400	*5950* (E North Am), 9650 & 11625 (E Asia), 11635 (SE Asia), 11985 & 15060 (E Asia), *15440* (W North Am & C America), 15460 (E Asia)
2300-2400	9690 (E Asia)

RADIO TAIPEI INTERNATIONAL

Amoy

0000-0100	*15440* (W North Am & C America)
0100-0300	11875 (SE Asia)
0500-0600	11550 (SE Asia)
0600-0800	15580 (SE Asia)
1000-1100	11605 (E Asia), 15465 (SE Asia)
1300-1400	11635 & 15465 (SE Asia)
2100-2200	11875 (Australasia)

Chinese

0100-0200	[W] *11825* & [S] *17845* (S America)
0400-0500	*5950* (N America & C America), *9680* (W North Am), 15320 & 15405 (SE Asia)
0900-1000	9610 (Australasia), 11605 (E Asia), 15320, 15405 & 15580 (SE Asia)
1200-1300	11605 (E Asia), 15405 & 15465 (SE Asia)
1900-2000	[W] *9355*, 9955, [S] *15600*, [S] *17750* & [W] *17760* (Europe)

Cantonese

0100-0200	*5950* (E North Am), *7520* (Europe), 15290 (SE Asia), *15440* (W North Am & C America)
0100-0300	6040 (E Asia)
0300-0400	*11740* (C America)
0500-0600	*5950* (N America & C America), *9680* (W North Am), 15320, 15405 & 15580 (SE Asia)
1000-1100	9610 (Australasia), 11635 & 15320 (SE Asia)
1000-1200	15405 (SE Asia)
1200-1400	6040 (E Asia), 11915 (SE Asia)

COLOMBIA—Spanish

RADIODIFUSORA NACIONAL DE COLOMBIA

1100-1700	Su 4955/9635
1700-0445	4955/9635

CROATIA—Croatian

CROATIAN RADIO—(Europe)

0500-1000 [←]	7365
0500-2400 [←]	6165
0600-1830 [←]	9830
0900-1000	[S] 13830
1000-2200	13830
2200-2300	[S] 13830

VOICE OF CROATIA

0000-0200 [←]	*9925* (S America)
0100-0300	[S] *9925* (E North Am)

0200-0400	[W] *7280/9925* (E North Am)
0300-0500	[S] *9925* (W North Am)
0400-0600	[W] *6130/7285* (W North Am)
0600-0800 ←	*9470/11970* (Australasia)
0800-1000 ←	*13820* (Australasia)

CUBA—Spanish

RADIO HABANA CUBA

0000-0100	6000 (E North Am), 9820 (N America)
0000-0500	5965 (C America & W North Am), 9505 (C America), 11760 (Americas), 11970 & 15230 (S America)
0200-0500	9550 (E North Am)
1100-1300	11705 (S America)
1100-1400	6000 (C America)
1100-1500	11760 (C America)
1200-1400	9550 (C America & W North Am), 15250 (S America)
1400-1830	Su 6140 & Su 9505 (C America), Su 9820 (N America), Su 11705 & Su 11875 (S America)
2100-2300	11705 USB (E North Am & Europe), 11760 & 13680 (Europe & N Africa)
2100-2400	15230 (S America)
2300-2400	6000 (E North Am)

RADIO REBELDE

24 Hr	5025
1000-1300	9600 (C America)
1100-1300	6140 (C America)

CZECH REPUBLIC—Czech

RADIO PRAGUE

0030-0100	[W] 7345 (N America), [W] 11615 (S America)
0130-0200	[S] 5915 (N America & C America), [S] 7345 (S America)
0230-0300	[W] 6200 (N America & C America), [S] 7345 (N America), [W] 7345 (S America), [S] 9870 (W North Am & C America)
0330-0400	[W] 7345 (N America), [W] 9435 (W North Am & C America)
0830-0900	[S] 11600 (W Europe), [S] 21745 (E Africa & Mideast)
0930-1000	[W] 15255 (W Europe), [S] 21745 (S Asia & W Africa), [W] 21745 (E Africa)
1030-1100	[W] 21745 (S Asia & W Africa)
1100-1130	[S] 11615 (N Europe), [S] 21745 (S Asia)
1200-1230	[W] 11640 (N Europe), [W] 21745 (S Asia, SE Asia & Australasia)
1330-1400 ←	6055 (Europe), 7345 (W Europe)
1330-1400	[S] 13580 (N Europe), [S] 21745 (S Asia)
1430-1500	[W] 21745 (N America & E Africa)
1530-1600	[S] 21745 (E Africa)
1630-1700 ←	5930 (W Europe)
1630-1700	[W] 17485 (W Africa & C Africa)
1730-1800	[S] 5930 (E Europe, SE Asia & Australasia), [S] 21745 (C Africa)
1830-1900	[W] 5930 (W Europe), [W] 7315 (E Europe, Asia & Australasia)
1930-2000	[S] 11600 (SE Asia & Australasia)
2030-2100 ←	5930 (W Europe)
2030-2100	[W] 9430 (SE Asia & Australasia)
2100-2130	[S] 11600 (SE Asia & Australasia), [S] 15545 (W Africa)
2200-2230	[W] 5930 (W Europe), [W] 9435 (W Europe & S America)
2330-2400	[S] 11615 (Americas), [S] 13580 (S America)

DENMARK—Danish

RADIO DANMARK

0030-0055	[W] *9935* (SE Asia), [W] *9945* (E North Am & C America), [S] *11635* (N America), [S] *13800* (E North Am & C America), [S] *13805* (SE Asia & Australasia)
0130-0155	[W] *7465* (E North Am & C America), [W] *7495* (S Asia), [W] *9945* & [S] *9985* (N America), [S] *11635* (E North Am & C America), [S] *13800* (S Asia)
0230-0255	[W] *7465* (E North Am & C America), [W] *7490* (S Asia), [W] *9590* (N America), [S] *13800* (S Asia)
0330-0355	[S] *7465* (Mideast), [W] *7465* (W North Am), [W] *7485* (Mideast), [W] *9945* (E Africa), [S] *11635* (W North Am), [S] *13800* (Mideast & E Africa)

0430-0455 S *7465* (Europe), W *7465* (W North Am), W *7485* (Mideast), S *9475* (E Europe & Mideast), W *9945* (E Europe & E Africa), S *11635* (W North Am), S *13800* (Mideast & E Africa)

0530-0555 W *5965* & S *7465* (Europe), W *7485* (E Europe & W Asia), S *11615* (Mideast), S *13800* (Africa)

0630-0655 W *5965* (W Europe), S *7180* (Europe), W *7180* & S *9590* (W Europe), W *9590* (W Africa), S *13800* (W Africa & Australasia), W *13800* (Africa), S *15705* (Africa & Australasia)

0730-0755 S *7180* (Europe), W *7180* (W Europe), S *9590* (Europe), W *9590* (W Europe), S *15705* (W Africa & Australasia)

0830-0855 W *15705* (Australasia), S *18910* (S America & Australasia), S *18950* (Mideast), W *18950* (E Asia & Australasia)

0930-0955 W *15705* (Australasia), S *18910* (S America & Australasia), W *18950* (E Asia & Australasia), W *21725* (Mideast), S *21755* (E Asia)

1030-1055 *13800* (Europe), W *21725* (S America), S *21755* (W Africa & S America)

1130-1155 S *13800* (Europe), W *13800* (W Europe), S *15735* (E North Am & C America), W *21760* (S America)

1230-1255 W *13800* (E Asia), S *15735* (N America), W *15735* (Europe), S *17535* (E Asia), W *18910* (SE Asia & Australasia), *18950* (E North Am & C America), S *21755* (SE Asia & Australasia)

1330-1355 *9590* (Europe), W *13800* (E Asia), S *15735* (N America), S *17535* (E Asia), W *18910* (SE Asia & Australasia), W *18950* (N America), S *21755* (SE Asia & Australasia)

1430-1455 W *15705* (Mideast & S Asia), S *17505* (W North Am), S *18950* (S Asia), W *18950* (N America)

1530-1555 *13800* (S Asia), W *15705* (Mideast), S *15735* (Mideast & S Asia), W *15735* & S *17505* (W North Am)

1630-1655 W *9590* (E Europe & W Asia), S *12080* (Europe), S *13800* (Mideast & S Asia), W *13800* (E Africa), W *18950* (W North Am), S *21730* (Mideast & E Africa)

1630-1700 S *21755* (E North Am & C America)

1730-1755 W *7485* (Europe), W *9985* (E Europe & W Asia), S *12080* (Europe), W *15705* (E Africa), S *15735* (Mideast), S *17505* (N America), W *18950* (E North Am & C America), S *21730* (Mideast & E Africa)

1830-1855 W *5960* & S *7485* (Europe), W *9985* & S *13800* (Australasia), W *13800* & S *13810* (Africa), W *18950* (E North Am & C America)

1930-1955 S *7485* (W Europe), W *7485* (Europe), *13800* (Africa), S *15705* (Australasia), W *15705* & S *17505* (W North Am)

2030-2055 W *7465* (Australasia), S *7485* (W Europe), W *7485* (Europe), S *9985* (Australasia)

2130-2155 W *7465* (Australasia), W *7485* (W Europe), S *11610* (Australasia)

2230-2255 W *9415* (S America), W *9480* (E Asia), S *11625* (S America), S *15735* (E Asia)

2330-2355 W *7465* (S America), W *9480* (E Asia), W *9580* & S *9935* (SE Asia & Australasia), W *9945* & S *13805* (E North Am & C America), S *15735* (E Asia)

2330-2400 S *11625* (S America)

EGYPT—Arabic

EGYPTIAN RADIO

0000-0030 ⬅ 9700 (N Africa), 11665 (C Africa & E Africa), 15285 (Mideast)

0150-2400 ⬅ 12050 (Europe & E North Am)

0200-2200 ⬅ 9755 (N Africa & Mideast)

0300-0600 ⬅ 9855 (N Africa & Mideast)

0300-2400 ⇦ 15285 (Mideast)
0350-0700 ⇦ 9620 & 9770 (N Africa)
0350-2400 ⇦ 9800 (Mideast)
0600-1400 ⇦ 11980 (N Africa & Mideast)
0700-1100 ⇦ 15115 (W Africa)
0700-1400 ⇦ 15475 (E Africa)
0700-1500 ⇦ 11785 (N Africa)
1100-2400 ⇦ 9850 (N Africa & Mideast)
1245-1900 ⇦ 17670 (N Africa)
1800-2400 ⇦ 9700 (N Africa)
1900-2400 ⇦ 11665 (C Africa & E Africa)

RADIO CAIRO

0000-0045 15590 (C America & S America), 17770 (S America)
0030-0430 9900 (E North Am)
1015-1215 17745 (Mideast & W Asia)
1100-1130 17800 (E Africa & S Africa)
1300-1600 15220 (C Africa)
2000-2200 11990 (Australasia)
2330-2400 17770 (S America)
2345-2400 15590 (C America & S America)

FRANCE—French

RADIO FRANCE INTERNATIONALE

0000-0030 [W] *15440* & [S] *17710* (SE Asia)
0000-0100 [W] 9805 & [S] 11660 (S Asia & SE Asia), [W] *12025* (SE Asia), *15200* (S America), [S] *15535* (SE Asia)
0100-0200 [W] *15440* & [S] *17710* (S Asia)
0130-0200 [W] 9790 (C America), [W] 9800 (S America), *9800* & *11665* (C America), [S] 11995 (S America)
0200-0230 *15200* (S America)
0300-0400 [W] 5915 (Mideast & E Africa), [S] *5925* (C Africa & E Africa), [W] *5925* (S Africa), [W] 5945 (E Europe & Mideast), 9550 (Mideast), [S] 9825, [S] 11700, 11995 & [S] 13610 (E Africa)
0300-0500 [W] 7315 (Mideast)
0300-0600 9790 (Africa), [W] 9845 (E Africa)
0300-0700 7135 (Africa)
0330-0500 [S] 9745 (E Europe)
0400-0430 [S] 11995 (E Africa)
0400-0445 [S] 7280 (E Europe)
0400-0500 [W] 3965 (N Africa), *4890* (C Africa), [S] 5925 (N Africa), [W] *9805* (C Africa), *11850* (Mideast)
0400-0600 ⇦ 11685 (Mideast)
0400-0600 [W] 9550 (Mideast), 11700 (C Africa & S Africa), [S] 15135 (E Africa), [S] 15605 (Mideast & W Asia)
0430-0445 [W] 5990 (E Europe)
0430-0500 ⇦ 7280 (E Europe)
0430-0500 [W] *11910*, 11995, 13610 (Irr) & [S] 15155 (E Africa)
0430-0600 ⇦ 6045 (E Europe)
0500-0600 *6175* (C Africa), [W] 11995 (E Africa), [S] 15300 (C Africa & S Africa), *15605* (N Africa & Mideast)
0500-0700 [W] 11700 (C Africa & S Africa), [S] 17620 (E Africa)
0530-0600 [W] 13610 (E Africa), [W] *15155* (E Africa & S Africa), [S] 17800 (E Africa)
0600-0700 [W] 5925 (N Africa), [W] 6175 (E Europe), 9790 (N Africa & W Africa), [S] *9790* (C Africa), [W] 15135 (Mideast), 15300 (C Africa & S Africa), *15315* (Irr) (W Africa), [S] 17650 (Mideast), [S] 17850 (C Africa & S Africa)
0600-0800 11700 (N Africa & W Africa)
0630-0700 [W] *11710* (W Africa), [W] 15155, 17800 & [S] 21620 (E Africa)
0700-0800 [W] 7135 (N Africa), [W] 9790 (N Africa & W Africa), *9790* (C Africa), 9805 (E Europe), [W] 11975 (N Europe), [S] 15300 (N Africa & W Africa), [W] 15300 (C Africa & S Africa), 15315 & [S] 17620 (W Africa), 17850 (C Africa & S Africa)
0700-1130 11670 (E Europe)
0800-0900 [S] 15315, 17620 & [W] 21685 (W Africa)
0800-1000 15300 (N Africa & W Africa), [W] 21580 (C Africa & S Africa)
0800-1600 11845 (N Africa)
0900-0930 [W] *9715* & [S] *11670* (S America)
0900-1000 [W] 17620 (W Africa)
0900-1200 21620 & 25820 (E Africa)
0900-1600 *21685* (W Africa)
1000-1100 15155 (E Europe), 15300 (W Africa), 17850 (C Africa & S Africa)
1000-1600 21580 (C Africa & S Africa)
1030-1100 *15435* (S America)

1030-1200	W *7140* & S *9830* (E Asia), W *9830*, S *11890* & S *15215* (SE Asia)
1100-1130	W 17610 (Irr) (E North Am & C America)
1100-1200	6175 (W Europe & Atlantic), *11600* (SE Asia), W *11670*, *13640* & *15515* (C America), S 17570 (E North Am & C America), *21755* (S Africa)
1100-1300	S 17620 (W Africa)
1100-1400	15300 (N Africa & W Africa)
1130-1200	W 17610 (E North Am & C America)
1200-1400	*9790* (C Africa)
1230-1300	*15515* (C America), *15540* (W Africa), *17860* (C America), 25820 (E Africa)
1300-1330	*17860* (C America)
1300-1400	17620 (W Africa), *21645* (C America)
1330-1400	M-Sa *17860* (C America)
1400-1500	17650 (Mideast)
1400-1600	15300 (W Africa)
1500-1600	W 15605 (Mideast & W Asia), 17605 & 17620 (E Africa), S 17650 (Mideast), 17850 (C Africa & S Africa), 21620 (E Africa)
1600-1700	*6090* (SE Asia), 11700 (N Africa), S 15300 (W Africa), W 17605 & S 21620 (E Africa)
1600-1800	W 15300 (Africa), S 21580 (C Africa & S Africa)
1700-1800	W 5960 (N Europe), S 11670 (E Europe), 11700 (Irr) (N Africa), S 15300 (N Africa & W Africa), S 17620 (W Africa & E Africa)
1700-2000	W 11965 (W Africa)
1730-1800	W 11615 & S 15605 (Mideast), W 15605 & S 17605 (E Africa)
1800-1900	W 5900 (E Europe), W 5970 (N Europe), W 11615 (N Africa), S 17620 (E Africa)
1800-2000	W 9790 (N Africa & W Africa), S 11615 (W Africa), 11705 (Africa), W 11995 (E Africa), 15300 (Africa), S 15460 (E Africa)
1800-2200	*7160* (C Africa), *11955* (W Africa)
1900-2000	W 3965 (Europe), W 6175 (N Europe), W 7315 (N Africa), W 9485 (E Africa), S 11670 (E Europe), S 17620 (W Africa)
2000-2100	W 6175 (N Africa), S 15300 (Africa)
2000-2200	W 5960 (S Europe), 7315 (N Africa), 9485 (E Africa), 9790 (N Africa & W Africa), W 9790 (C Africa & S Africa), 11995 (E Africa)
2100-2200	W 3965 (N Africa), S 5915 (E Europe), 6175 (N Africa), S 9805 (E Europe), S 15300 (C Africa & S Africa)
2200-2300	W 9790 (W Africa)
2230-2300	*17620* (S America)
2300-2400	W 9805 & S 11660 (S Asia & SE Asia), W *12025* (SE Asia), W *12075* (E Asia), W *15440*, S *15535*, S *15595* & S *17710* (SE Asia)
2330-2400	W 9790 (C America), W 9800 (S America), S 11670 (C America), S 11995, *15200* & *17620* (S America)

GABON—French

AFRIQUE NUMERO UN

0500-2300	9580 (C Africa)
0700-1600	17630 (W Africa)
1600-1900	15475 (W Africa & E North Am)

RTV GABONAISE

0500-0800	7270/4777
0800-1600	7270
1600-2100	4777

GERMANY—German

BAYERISCHER RUNDFUNK

24 Hr	6085

DEUTSCHE WELLE

0000-0200	6075 (Europe), **W** 6100 (E North Am), **S** 7130 (N Africa & S America), 9545 (S America), **W** *11795* (SE Asia), **W** *12000* (S America), **W** *12045* (E North Am), **W** *13750* (SE Asia), **S** 13780 (E North Am), **S** *13780* (S America), **W** *13780* (C America), **S** *15275* (C America & S America), **S** *15410* (E North Am & S America), **W** *15410* (S America), **S** *17860* & **S** *17875* (SE Asia)
0000-0355	**S** *11785* (C America)
0000-0400	**W** 7130 (S Europe & S America)
0000-0600	3995 (Europe)
0200-0300	**S** 9735 (N America)
0200-0400	**W** 6075 (Mideast & W Asia), **W** 6100 (C America), **W** 6145 (N America & C America), **W** *9870* (W Africa, C America & S America), **S** 11795 (E Africa), *15205* (S Asia)
0200-0600	6075 (Europe & N America), **S** 6100 (E North Am & C America)
0300-0600	**S** 9735 (N Europe & N America)
0400-0555	**S** 13780 (Africa)
0400-0600	**W** 6075 (E Europe & W Asia), **W** *6100* (W North Am), **W** 6145 (N America & C America), **W** *7225* (S Europe), **W** 9545 (Mideast & W Asia), **S** *9640* (N America & C America), **S** *9700* (S Africa), **W** 9735 (Mideast & Africa), **W** *11805* (S Africa), **S** 17810 (Africa)
0500-0600	**S** 9735 (Australasia)
0600-0800	**W** 3995 & 6075 (Europe), 9735 & *11985* (Australasia), **S** 21600 (C Africa & S Africa)
0600-1000	*9690* & 11795 (Australasia), 11865 (N Europe & E Europe), **S** 17845 (S Asia & SE Asia), *21640* (SE Asia & Australasia), **W** 21840 (Africa)
0600-1800	13780 (Mideast)
0600-2000	9545 (S Europe)
0800-1000	**S** 9735 (S Europe & N Africa), **W** 9735 (Australasia)
0800-1400	**W** 25740 (S Asia & SE Asia)
0800-1800	6075 (Europe)
0900-1200	*15135* (E Africa)
1000-1400	**W** *5905*, **W** *7400* & **S** *9900* (E Asia), **S** *13720* (S Asia & SE Asia), **W** *13810* (E Asia & SE Asia), **S** 17560 (Atlantic & W Africa), **W** 17845 (S Asia & SE Asia), **S** *17845* (SE Asia & Australasia), **S** *21640* (E Asia & SE Asia), **S** 21680 (E Europe & Asia), **S** 21790 (S Asia & SE Asia), **W** *21790* (E Asia & SE Asia), 21840 (Mideast)
1100-1300	**S** *17650* (W Europe)
1200-1400	*15135* (S Africa), **W** *17570* (W Europe), **W** 17650 (E Europe & W Asia), *17730* (E North Am), **S** *17730* & **W** *17765* (S America)
1200-1600	**W** *9480* & **S** *15480* (W Asia & C Asia)
1400-1600	15275 (S Asia & SE Asia), **S** 15275 (Atlantic & W Africa), **W** 15275 (S Europe & Mideast)
1400-1700	**W** *15515* (W North Am), *17730* (N America), *17765* (S America), **S** *17875* (N America & C America)
1400-1800	*9655* (S Asia), **W** *13720* (Mideast & W Asia), **W** 13780 (S Asia & SE Asia), **S** 17845 (Mideast), **S** 17845 (S Asia & SE Asia), **S** *21560* (Mideast)
1600-1800	**W** 11795 & **S** 15275 (S Asia)
1800-2000	**W** 3995 (Europe), **S** 13780 (Mideast)
1800-2155	**S** *11765* (SE Asia & Australasia)
1800-2200	6075 (Europe & E Africa), **S** 7185 & **W** 9735 (Africa), **S** *9735* (S Africa), **S** *11765* (Australasia), **S** 11795 (E Africa & S Africa), **W** *11795* (S Africa), **W** *12045* (Australasia), **S** 15275 (W Africa & S America), *17860* (W Africa & C America)

Radio New Zealand International's staff brings news and good cheer to the Pacific rim. It's even heard many nights in North America. RNZI

2000-2200	9545 (Atlantic & S America), *17810* (N America & S America)
2000-2400	3995 (Europe)
2200-2400	[W] *5925* (E Asia), 6075 (Europe), 9545 (S America), [W] *9610* (E Asia & SE Asia), [W] 9715 (S Asia & SE Asia), [S] *11785* (C America), [S] *11795* (E Asia), [W] *11795* & [S] 11895 (SE Asia), [W] *12000* (S America), [W] *12045* (E North Am), [S] *13690* (S Asia & SE Asia), [S] 13780 (E North Am), [S] *13780* (S America), [W] *13780* (C America), [S] *15250* (E Asia & SE Asia), [W] *15250* (E Asia), [S] *15275* (C America & S America), [S] *15410* (E North Am & S America), [W] *15410* (S America), *17860* (C America)

DEUTSCHLANDFUNK—(Europe)

24 Hr	6190

DEUTSCHLANDRADIO—(Europe)

24 Hr	6005

SUDWESTRUNDFUNK—(Europe)

24 Hr	7265
0455-2305 ←	6030

HOLLAND—Dutch

RADIO NEDERLAND

0000-0025	[S] *7280* (SE Asia), [W] *7280* & [S] *9590* (SE Asia & Australasia), [W] *9590*, [W] *15565*, [W] *17570* & [S] *17590* (SE Asia)
0130-0225	[S] *6010* (E North Am), [W] *6020* & [S] 11730 (E North Am & C America), *15315* (S America)
0330-0425	*6165* (N America), *9590* (W North Am), [S] *9845* & [W] *9860* (E Africa), *15560* (Mideast)
0600-0700 ←	7125 (Europe)
0600-0700	[W] 6020 (W Europe), [S] *13720* (N Europe)
0600-1800 ←	5955 (W Europe), 9895 (S Europe)
0700-0800	[W] *9715*, [S] *9820* & *11655* (Australasia)
0700-0900 ←	11935 (S Europe)
0800-1100	[S] 13700 (S Europe)
0930-1015	M-Sa *6020* (C America)
1030-1125	*9720* (Australasia), *13820* (E Asia), *17575* (Australasia), *21480* (SE Asia)
1100-1300	13700 (S Europe)
1300-1700	[S] 13700 (S Europe)
1330-1425	[W] *5930*, [W] *7375* & [S] *9890* (E Asia & SE Asia), [S] *12065* (SE Asia & Australasia), [S] *13695* (E Asia & SE Asia), [W] 13700 (Mideast & S Asia), [W] *13820* (SE Asia & Australasia), *17580* & *21480* (S Asia)
1600-1800	[W] 13700 (N Africa & W Africa)
1630-1725	*6020* (S Africa), *11655* (E Africa)
1730-1825	[S] 9895 & [S] 13700 (S Europe & Mideast), [S] 15560 (S Africa & E Africa), [S] *21590* (W Africa & C Africa)

1830-1925 [W] 11695 (Mideast & E Africa), [W] 15315 & [W] *21590* (W Africa)
2030-2125 *5835* (Europe), [W] 6015 (S Europe), [S] *6015* (S Africa), [S] 6020 (W Europe & N Africa), [W] *6020* (S Africa), [S] *7120* (C Africa & W Africa), 9895 (S Europe & N Africa), [S] 11655 (W Africa), [W] *11655* (W Africa & C Africa), *15315* & *17605* (W Africa), *21590* (W Africa & C Africa)
2130-2225 *6020* (C America), [S] 9895 (C America & S America), [W] 9895 (E North Am), [W] 11730 (C America & S America), [S] 13700 (S America), [W] *13700* & [S] *15155* (E North Am), *15315* (S America)
2330-2400 [S] *7280* (SE Asia), [W] *7280* & [S] *9590* (SE Asia & Australasia), [W] *9590*, [W] *15565*, [W] *17570* & [S] *17590* (SE Asia)

HUNGARY—Hungarian

RADIO BUDAPEST

0000-0100 [W] M 9580 (S America), [S] 9800 (N America), [W] M 11990 (S America)
0100-0200 [W] 9835 (N America)
0130-0230 [S] 9570 (N America)
0230-0330 [W] 9835 (N America)
0900-1300 ⇦ 6025 (Europe)
1100-1200 ⇦ 21560 (Australasia)
1200-1300 ⇦ Su 21560 (Australasia)
1300-1400 ⇦ M-Sa 6025 (Europe)
1400-1500 ⇦ Sa-Th 6025 (Europe)
1500-1530 ⇦ M-Sa 6025 (Europe)
1900-2000 ⇦ 3975 & 6025 (Europe)
1900-2000 [W] 9695 (Australasia)
2000-2100 [S] 17690 (N America)
2100-2200 ⇦ 3975 & 6025 (Europe)
2100-2200 [S] 11890 (Australasia)
2200-2300 [W] 9820 (N America), [S] 11870 & [S] 15455 (S America)
2300-2400 [W] 9580, [S] Su 11870, [W] 11990 & [S] Su 15455 (S America)

INDIA—Hindi

ALL INDIA RADIO

0315-0415 13695 (E Africa), 15075 (Mideast & W Asia), 15185 & 17715 (E Africa)
0430-0530 15075, 15185 & 17715 (E Africa)
1615-1730 7410 (Mideast & W Asia), 9950 (E Africa), 12025 (Mideast & W Asia), 13770 (W Asia & Mideast), 17670 (E Africa)
1945-2045 7410 & 9950 (Europe)
2300-2400 9910, 11740 & 13795 (SE Asia)

IRAN—Persian

VOICE OF THE ISLAMIC REPUBLIC

0000-0630 15084 (Europe & C America)
0130-0300 7275 (W Asia & S Asia)
0300-0400 [W] 7275 (W Asia & S Asia)
0730-1200 15084 (Europe & C America), [S] 15215 & [W] 15365 (W Asia & S Asia)
0930-1030 ⇦ 15115 (E Asia)
0930-1030 17785 (Europe)
0930-1100 13695 (W Asia)
1300-2400 15084 (Europe & C America)
1630-1730 9765 (Europe)
1930-2030 7105 (W Europe), 9775 (Australasia)

ISRAEL

KOL ISRAEL

Arabic

0400-2215 ⇦ 5915 (Mideast & N Africa), 9815 (Mideast), 12145 (Mideast & W Asia)

Hebrew

0000-0100 [S] 13635 (W Europe & E North Am)
0000-0245 11585 (W Europe & E North Am)
0000-0400 [S] 9345 (W Europe & E North Am)
0000-0500 [W] 7545 (W Europe & N America), [W] 9345/5790, [S] 9390 & [S] 15760 (W Europe & E North Am)
0245-0330 [W] 11585 & [S] 11590 (W Europe & E North Am)
0330-0355 11590 (W Europe & E North Am)
0355-0430 [W] 11590 (W Europe & E North Am)
0400-0500 [S] 17535 (W Europe & E North Am)

0500-1700	15760 & 17535 (W Europe & E North Am)
1600-1700	[S] 11590 (W Europe & E North Am)
1700-1755	11590 (W Europe & E North Am)
1700-1800	[S] 17535 (W Europe & E North Am)
1700-2000	[W] 9390 (W Europe & E North Am)
1700-2400	[W] 9345/5790 & [S] 15760 (W Europe & E North Am)
1755-1855	[W] 11590 (W Europe & E North Am)
1800-1900	[S] 11585 (W Europe & E North Am)
1900-2400	[S] 9345, 11585 & [S] 13635 (W Europe & E North Am)
2000-2400	9390 (W Europe & E North Am)
2100-2215 ◄	15640 (S America)

Yiddish

1600-1625	[S] 15650 (S Europe & N Africa)
1700-1725 ◄	9435 & 11605 (Europe)
1700-1725	[W] 15640 (S Europe & N Africa)
1800-1825 ◄	9435 & 11605 (Europe)

ITALY—Italian

RADIO ROMA-RAI INTERNATIONAL

0000-0055	9675 (N America), 9840 & 11755 (S America), 11800 (N America & C America)
0130-0230	*6110* (S America), *11765* (C America)
0130-0315	9675 (N America), 9840 & 11755 (S America), 11800 (E North Am & C America)
0435-0445	[W] 5965, [S] 5975 & 7235 (S Europe & N Africa)
0455-0530	15250 & 17780 (E Africa)
0630-1300	9670 (Europe & N Africa), 11800 (E Europe), 17710 & 21520 (E Africa)
1000-1100	*11920* (Australasia)
1345-1630	Su 9670 (N Europe)
1350-1730 ◄	Su//Holidays 17780 (N America), Su//Holidays 21520 (E Africa), Su//Holidays 21535 (S America), Su//Holidays 21710 (C Africa & S Africa)
1400-1430	M-Sa 17780 (N America), M-Sa 21520 (E North Am)
1500-1525	M-Sa 9670 (S Europe & N Africa), 11880 (Mideast)
1555-1625	M-Sa 9670 (Europe), 11880 (W Europe)
1630-1730	[W] Su 9670 (Irr) (N Europe)
1700-1800	9670 & 11910 (S Europe & N Africa), 15220/15230 (C Africa & S Africa), *15320* (S Africa), 17660 (C Africa & S Africa)
1830-1905	[W] 15250, 17780 & [S] 21520 (N America)
2240-2400	9675 (N America), 9840 & 11755 (S America), 11800 (N America & C America)

RAI-RADIOTELEVISIONE ITALIANA

0000-0003, 0012-0103, 0112-0203, 0212-0303, 0312-0403 & 0412-0500 ◄	6060 (Europe, Mideast & N Africa)
0500-2300 ◄	6060 & 9515 (Europe, N Africa & Mideast)
0500-2300	7175 (Europe, Mideast & N Africa)
2300-2400 ◄	6060 (Europe, Mideast & N Africa)

JAPAN—Japanese

RADIO JAPAN/NHK

0000-0100	11910 (E Asia), 17690 (SE Asia)
0100-0200	[W] 15195 (E Asia), 17855 (SE Asia)
0200-0300	*11860* (SE Asia), 17825 (C America), 17845 (E Asia), 21610 (Australasia)
0200-0400	*5960* (E North Am), 11870/9700 (Mideast), 15325 (S Asia), 17685 (Australasia), 17835 (S America), 17875 (W North Am)
0200-0500	15195 (E Asia), 17810 (SE Asia)
0300-0400	*9660* (S America), *11890* (S Asia), *11930* (Mideast & W Asia)
0500-0700	11910 (E Asia), 21600 (SE Asia)

0700-0800	6145, 6165 & 15195 (E Asia), 17870 (Pacific)
0700-0900	17860 (SE Asia)
0700-1000	*11740* (SE Asia), *11920* & 21755 (Australasia)
0800-1000	*9530* (S America), 9835 (W North Am), *11710* (Europe), 12030 (C America), 15230 (Pacific & S America), 15590 (S Asia), *17650* (W Africa), *21550* (Mideast)
0800-1500	9750 (E Asia)
0900-1500	11815 (SE Asia)
1300-1500	*11705* (E North Am)
1500-1600	11910 (E Asia), 17810 (SE Asia)
1500-1700	9505 (W North Am), W 9535 & S 11895 (C America), *12045* (S Asia)
1600-1700	9750 (E Asia), W 9845 & S 11730 (S Asia), W *21630* (E Africa)
1600-1800	7140 (Australasia)
1600-1900	6035 (E Asia), 7200/9860 (SE Asia)
1700-1800	W *9750* (Europe), *21600* (S America), *21630* (E Africa)
1700-1900	*6175* (W Europe), 9835 (Pacific & S America), *11880* (Mideast)
1800-1900	*15355* (S Africa)
1900-2000	W 11665 (SE Asia)
1900-2100	6165 (E Asia)
1900-2400	11910 (E Asia), S 13680 (SE Asia)
2000-2100	S *6035* (Australasia), 11830 (Europe), W 11850, W *11920* & S 17860 (Australasia)
2000-2200	W 7225 & 11665 (SE Asia)
2200-2300	*6110* (E North Am), *6115* (W Europe), *11895* (C America), *15220* (S America), 17825 (W North Am)
2200-2400	W 11665 (SE Asia)

RADIO TAMPA

0000-0800	3925, 9760
0000-1000	6115
0000-1300	3945
0000-1730	6055, 9595
0800-1500 & 2030-2300	3925
2030-2400	6055, 9595
2300-2400	3925, 3945, 6115, 9760

JORDAN—Arabic

RADIO JORDAN

0000-0205	6105 (Irr) (Mideast)
0000-0210	11930 (W Europe & E North Am), 15435 (S America)
0000-0600	11810 (Mideast & S Asia)
0400-0600	9630/13630 (Mideast & E Africa)
0400-0700	15435 (W Europe)
0600-0810	11960 (E Europe)
0830-1615	11810 (Mideast, S Asia & Australasia)
1100-1300	15290 (N Africa & C America)
1300-1625	13630 (Mideast & E Africa)
1600-2155	6105 (Mideast)
1630-2055	7155 (E Europe)
1800-2155	9830 (W Europe)
2155-2400	6105 (Irr) (Mideast)
2200-2400	11810 (Mideast & S Asia), 11930 (W Europe & E North Am), 15435 (S America)

KOREA (DPR)—Korean

KOREAN CENTRAL BROADCASTING STATION

0000-0630	6100
0000-0930	9665
0000-1800	2850, 11680
1010-1100	3560 & 7140 (E Asia), 9345 (Asia), 9850 (SE Asia & C America), 11335 & 13650 (SE Asia)
1400-1450	3560 (E Asia), 9640 (SE Asia & C America), 9975 (N America & C America), 11335 (SE Asia & C America), 13650 (N America & C America)
1500-1800	6100
1700-1750	6575 & 9335 (Europe), 11710 (N America & C America), 13760 (N America)
2000-2050	3560 (E Asia), 6520 (Mideast & Africa), 6575, 7505, 9325 & 9335 (Europe), 9660 & 9975 (Mideast & Africa), 11710 (N America & C America), 13760 (N America)
2000-2400	2850, 6100, 9665, 11680
2300-2350	3560 & 7140 (E Asia), 9345 (Asia), 9975 (E Asia), 11735 (SE Asia)

RADIO PYONGYANG

0000-0925	6250 (E Asia)
0700-0800	6195 & 7140 (E Asia), 9325 & 9345 (Asia)
0800-0900	3560, 6575 & 9975 (E Asia), 13760 & 15245 (E Europe & Asia)
0900-1000	6195 & 7140 (E Asia), 9325 & 9345 (Asia)
1100-1200 & 1300-1400	7140 (E Asia), 9325 & 9345 (Asia)
1500-1900	6250 (E Asia)
1700-1800	3560 (E Asia), 6520, 9660 & 9975 (Mideast & Africa)
2100-2400	6250 (E Asia)

KOREA (REPUBLIC)—Korean

RADIO KOREA INTERNATIONAL

0000-0100	5975 (E Asia), 15575 (N America)
0100-0200	7275 (E Asia), 11725 (S America)
0300-0400	7275 (E Asia), 11725 & 11810 (S America), 15575 (N America)
0700-0800	7550 & *9535* (Europe), 9570 (Australasia)
0900-1000	7550 (S America)
0900-1100	5975 & 7275 (E Asia), 9570 (Australasia), 13670 (Europe)
1100-1130	*6145* (E North Am), 9580 (S America), 9640 (E Asia), *9650* (E North Am)
1200-1300	7285 (E Asia)
1700-1900	5975 (E Asia), 7550 & 15575 (Europe)
2100-2200	5975 (E Asia), 9640 (SE Asia)
2300-2400	5975 (E Asia), 15575 (N America)

KUWAIT—Arabic

RADIO KUWAIT

0000-0530	11675 (W North Am)
0200-1305	6055 & 15495 (Mideast)
0400-0740	15505 (E Europe & W Asia)
0800-0925	15110 (S Asia & SE Asia)
0930-1605	13620 (Europe & E North Am)
1015-1740	15505 (W Africa & C Africa)
1200-1505	17885 (SE Asia)
1315-1600	15110 (S Asia & SE Asia)
1315-2130	9880 (Mideast)
1615-1800	11990 (Europe & E North Am)
1745-2130	15505 (Europe & E North Am)
1745-2400	15495 (W Africa & C Africa)
1815-2400	9855 (Europe & E North Am)
2145-2400	11675 (W North Am)

LIBYA—Arabic

RADIO JAMAHIRIYA—(Africa)

0000-0350 & 1000-2400	15415/17725 & 15435

MEXICO—Spanish

RADIO EDUCACION

0000-0830 ⇐	6185
0830-0900 ⇐	Th-Tu 6185
0900-1200 ⇐	6185

RADIO MEXICO INTERNACIONAL—(W North Am & C America)

0000-0400 ⇐	9705 & 11770
0400-0430 ⇐	M 9705 & M 11770
0430-0500 ⇐	9705 & 11770
0530-0600 ⇐	Tu/Th/Sa 9705 & Tu/Th/Sa 11770
1300-1500 & 1530-1600 ⇐	9705 & 11770
1630-1700 ⇐	Su/M/W/F 9705 & Su/M/W/F 11770
1700-2200 ⇐	9705 & 11770
2230-2300 ⇐	Su/M/W/F 9705 & Su/M/W/F 11770
2300-2330 ⇐	Sa/Su 9705 & Sa/Su 11770
2330-2400 ⇐	9705 & 11770

MOROCCO

RADIO MEDI UN—(Europe & N Africa)
French & Arabic

0500-0400	9575

RTV MAROCAINE
Arabic

0000-0500	[W] 7185 & [S] 11920 (N Africa & Mideast)
0900-2200	15345 (N Africa & Mideast)
1100-1500	15335 (Europe)
2200-2400	7160 (Europe)

NORWAY—Norwegian

RADIO NORWAY INTERNATIONAL

0000-0030	[W] 9935 (SE Asia), [W] 9945 (E North Am & C America), [S] 11635 (N America), [S] 13800 (E North Am & C America), [S] 13805 (SE Asia & Australasia)

0100-0130	W 7465 (E North Am & C America), W 7495 (S Asia), W 9945 (N America), S 11635 (E North Am & C America), S 13800 (S Asia)
0200-0230	W 7465 (E North Am & C America), W 7490 (S Asia), W 9590 (N America), S 13800 (S Asia)
0300-0330	S 7465 (Mideast), W 7465 (W North Am), W 7485 (Mideast), W 9945 (E Africa), S 11635 (W North Am), S 13800 (Mideast & E Africa)
0400-0430	S 7465 (Europe), W 7465 (W North Am), W 7485 & S 9475 (Mideast), W 9945 (E Europe & E Africa), S 11635 (W North Am), S 13800 (Mideast & E Africa)
0500-0530	W 5965 & S 7465 (Europe), W 7485 (E Europe & W Asia), S 11615 (Mideast), S 13800 (Africa)
0600-0630	W 5965 (W Europe), S 7180 (Europe), W 7180 & S 9590 (W Europe), W 9590 (W Africa), S 13800 (W Africa & Australasia), W 13800 (Africa), S 15705 (Africa & Australasia)
0700-0730	S 7180 (Europe), W 7180 (W Europe), S 9590 (Europe), W 9590 (W Europe), S 15705 (W Africa & Australasia)
0800-0830	W 15705 (Australasia), S 18910 (S America & Australasia), S 18950 (Mideast), W 18950 (E Asia & Australasia)
0900-0930	W 15705 (Australasia), S 18910 (S America & Australasia), W 18950 (E Asia & Australasia), W 21725 (Mideast), S 21755 (E Asia)
1000-1030	13800 (Europe), W 21725 (S America), S 21755 (W Africa & S America)
1100-1130	S 13800 (Europe), W 13800 (W Europe), S 15735 (E North Am & C America), W 21760 (S America)
1200-1230	W 13800 (E Asia), S 15735 (N America), W 15735 (Europe), S 17535 (E Asia), W 18910 (SE Asia & Australasia), 18950 (E North Am & C America), S 21755 (SE Asia & Australasia)
1300-1330	9590 (W Europe), W 13800 (E Asia), S 15735 (N America), S 17535 (E Asia), W 18910 (SE Asia & Australasia), W 18950 (N America), S 21755 (SE Asia & Australasia)
1400-1430	W 15705 (Mideast & S Asia), S 17505 (W North Am), W 18910 (N America), S 18950 (S Asia)
1500-1530	S 13800 (S Asia), W 15705 (Mideast), S 15735 (Mideast & S Asia), W 15735 & S 17505 (W North Am)
1600-1630	W 9590 (E Europe & W Asia), S 12080 (Europe), S 13800 (Mideast & S Asia), W 13800 (E Africa), W 18950 (W North Am), S 21730 (Mideast & E Africa), S 21755 (E North Am & C America)
1700-1730	W 7485 (Europe), W 9985 (E Europe & W Asia), S 12080 (Europe), W 15705 (E Africa), S 15735 (Mideast), S 17505 (N America), W 18950 (E North Am & C America), S 21730 (Mideast & E Africa)
1800-1830	W 5960 & S 7485 (Europe), W 9985 & S 13800 (Australasia), W 13800 & S 13810 (Africa), W 18950 (E North Am & C America)
1900-1930	S 7485 (W Europe), W 7485 (Europe), 13800 (Africa), S 15705 (Australasia), W 15705 & S 17505 (W North Am)
2000-2030	W 7465 (Australasia), S 7485 (W Europe), W 7485 (Europe), S 9985 (Australasia)
2100-2130	W 7465 (Australasia), W 7485 (W Europe), S 11610 (Australasia)
2200-2230	W 9415 (S America), W 9480 (E Asia), S 11625 (S America), S 15735 (E Asia)

2300-2330	[W] 7465 (S America), [W] 9480 (E Asia), [W] 9580 & [S] 9935 (SE Asia & Australasia), [W] 9945 (E North Am & C America), [S] 11625 (S America), [S] 13805 (E North Am & C America), [S] 15735 (E Asia)

OMAN—Arabic

RADIO SULTANATE OF OMAN

0000-0100	9760 (Europe & Mideast)
0100-0200	[W] 9760 (Europe & Mideast)
0100-0300	[S] 7235 (E Africa)
0200-0300	[W] 15355 (E Africa)
0200-0400	6085 (Mideast)
0400-0600	9515 (Mideast), [S] 15355 & [S] 17590 (E Africa)
0600-1000	17630 (Europe & Mideast)
0600-1400	13640 (Mideast)
1400-1800	15375 (Mideast & E Africa)
1500-1800	15140 (Europe & Mideast)
1800-2000	6190 (Mideast & E Africa), 15355 (E Africa)
2000-2200	6085 (Mideast & E Africa)
2000-2300	9735 (Europe & Mideast)
2300-2400	9760 (Europe & Mideast)

PARAGUAY—Spanish

RADIO NACIONAL DEL PARAGUAY

0800-0900 →	M-Sa 9737 (S America)
0900-1300 →	9737 (S America)
2000-0300 →	9737 (S America & E North Am)

POLAND—Polish

RADIO POLONIA

0700-0800	[S] 5995 (Europe)
1200-1225 ←	7270 (W Europe), 7285 (E Europe)
1630-1730 ←	6035 (W Europe), 7285 (E Europe)
2200-2255 ←	6035 (E Europe), 6095 (W Europe)
2200-2300 ←	7270 (E Europe)

PORTUGAL—Portuguese

RDP INTERNATIONAL-RADIO PORTUGAL

0000-0200	[S] Tu-Sa 13660 (S America)
0000-0300 ←	Tu-Sa 9715 (E North Am), Tu-Sa 11655 (W North Am), Tu-Sa 13700 (C America)
0000-0300	[W] Tu-Sa 12030/11980 & [W] Tu-Sa 13770 (S America)
0500-0700	[S] M-F 15555 (W Europe)
0500-0900	[S] M-F 11950 (W Europe)
0600-0800 ←	Tu-Sa 15585 (W North Am)
0600-0800	[W] M-F 11675 (Europe)
0600-1300 ←	M-F 9815 (W Europe), M-F 11960 (Europe)
0600-1300	[W] M-F 15140 (W Europe)
0645-0800	[S] M-F 11850 (Europe)
0700-1200	[S] 15555 (W Europe)
0700-1400	[S] Sa/Su 12020/9840 (Europe), [S] Sa/Su 13610 (W Europe)
0745-0900	[W] M-F 11660 (Europe)
0800-1100 ←	Sa/Su 21655 (W Africa & S America), Sa/Su 21830 (E Africa & S Africa)
0800-1500	[W] Sa/Su 11875 (Europe), [W] Sa/Su 12020 & [W] Sa/Su 15575 (W Europe)
0930-1100 ←	Sa/Su 11995 (Europe)
1100-1300 ←	21655 & M-F 21725 (W Africa & S America), 21830 (E Africa & S Africa)
1200-1600	[S] Sa/Su 15555 (W Europe)
1200-2000	[S] Sa/Su//Holidays 15180 (E North Am), [S] Sa/Su// Holidays 17615 (C America)
1300-1500	[S] M-F 17760 (Mideast & S Asia)
1300-1700 ←	Sa/Su 21655 (W Africa & S America), Sa/Su 21800 (S America)
1300-1800 ←	Sa/Su 21830 (E Africa & S Africa)
1300-2100	[W] Sa/Su//Holidays 15540 (N America), [W] Sa/Su//Holidays 17745 (C America)
1400-1600	[S] Sa/Su 13770 (S Europe), [W] M-F 15490 (Mideast & S Asia)
1500-2100	[W] Sa/Su 13660 (Europe), [W] Sa/Su 13790 (W Europe)
1600-1900	[S] 13770 (S Europe), [S] 15555 (W Europe), [S] M-F 17650 (S Europe)
1700-2000 ←	M-F 13625/13585 (S Europe), 17680 (E Africa & S Africa), 21655 (W Africa & S America), 21800 (S America)
1700-2000	[W] M-F 11800 (W Europe), [W] M-F 11860 (Europe)

PASSPORT's Craig "Tireless" Tyson enjoys a rare moment of leisure near his Western Australia office. C. Tyson

1900-2000	**S** Sa/Su 13770 (S Europe)
1900-2300	**S** 11945 (Irr) (S Africa), **S** 13720 (Irr) (W Europe), **S** 13770 (Irr) (C America), **S** 15555 (Irr) (W Europe)
2000-2300 ⇦	17680 (Irr) (E Africa & S Africa)
2000-2300	**S** 15180 (Irr) (E North Am)
2000-2400 ⇦	M-F 13625/13585 (Irr) (S Europe), Sa/Su 21655 (Irr) (W Africa & S America), 21800 (Irr) (S America)
2000-2400	**W** M-F 11675 (Irr) (S Europe), **W** M-F 11800 (Irr) (W Europe), **W** M-F 11860 (Irr) (Europe), **W** 13770 (Irr) (C America)
2100-2400	**W** 15540 (Irr) (N America)
2300-2400	**S** Tu-Sa 13660 (S America)

RUSSIA—Russian

VOICE OF RUSSIA

0100-0300	**S** *11750* (E North Am), **S** 12060 & **S** 12070 (S America), **S** 17565, **S** 17620, **S** 17660 & **S** 17690 (W North Am)
0200-0300	**S** 7330 (S America), **S** 17650 (W North Am)
0200-0400 ⇦	9480 (S America)
0200-0400	**W** *7125* (E North Am), **W** 7260 (Atlantic & C America), **W** 9810 (S America), **W** 12010, **W** 15445, **W** 15595, **W** 17565 & **W** 17595 (W North Am)
1200-1300	**S** 7315 (E Asia), **S** 15460 (W Asia & S Asia)
1200-1400	**S** 11640 (SE Asia), **S** 15510 (S Asia & SE Asia)
1200-1500	**S** 9920 (C Asia & S Asia)
1300-1400	**S** 7330 (E Asia), **S** 9495 (S Asia)
1300-1500	**W** 7155 (E Asia), **W** 7205 (E Asia & SE Asia), **W** 9490 (SE Asia), **W** 15460 (S Asia & SE Asia)
1330-2100	**S** 11695 (W Asia)
1400-1500	**W** 7315 (W Asia & S Asia)
1400-2000	**S** 9820 (W Asia)
1500-1600	**S** 12005 (Mideast), **S** 12055 (S Asia), **S** 15540 (Mideast), **S** 17580 (Mideast & E Africa)
1530-1800	**S** 7315 (W Asia & S Asia)
1600-1700	**W** 7170 (W Europe), **W** 7315 (W Asia & S Asia), **W** 9470 (Mideast), **W** 12030 (E Europe & Mideast)
1600-1800	**S** 7420 (Europe)
1700-1800	**S** 7300 & **S** 11630 (Europe), **S** 15540 (Mideast)
1800-1900	**W** 5950 (Europe), **W** 7170 (W Europe), **W** 7205 (Europe), **W** 9875 (E Europe)
1900-2000	**S** 11745 & **S** 15350 (Europe), **S** 17725 (S Europe)
1930-2000	**S** 11630 (Europe)
1930-2100	**S** 12020 (S Europe)
2000-2100	**W** 7170 (W Europe), **W** 7310, **W** 7330, **W** 7380, **S** 9450 & **S** 9685 (Europe), **S** 12000 (Europe & W Africa)
2000-2200	**W** 7205 & **W** 9905 (Europe)
2100-2200	**W** 7370 (S Europe & N Africa)

SAUDI ARABIA—Arabic

BROADCASTING SERVICE OF THE KINGDOM

0300-0600	9578 (Mideast & E Africa), 11818 (N Africa), 15170 (E Europe & W Asia), 15435 (W Asia), 21495 (C Asia)
0600-0800	17895 (C Asia)
0600-0900	15380 (Mideast), 17560 (W Asia), 17760 (N Africa)
0600-1500	21505 (N Africa), 21705 (W Europe)
0600-1700	11855 (Mideast & E Africa)
0900-1200	11935 (Mideast), 17880 (SE Asia), 21495 (E Asia & SE Asia)
1200-1400	15380 (Mideast), 21495 (SE Asia)
1200-1500	17560 (W Asia), 17895 (N Africa)
1200-1600	17760 (N Africa)
1500-1800	11948/11913 (W Asia), 13690/13610 & 15275 (N Africa), 15435 (W Europe)
1600-1800	11708 (N Africa), 15205/15345 (W Europe), 17560 (C Africa & W Africa)
1700-2200	9578 (Mideast & E Africa)
1800-2100	11948 (W Asia)
1800-2300	9555 (N Africa), 9870 & 11820 (W Europe), 11935 (N Africa), 15230/15275 (C Africa & W Africa)

SINGAPORE—Chinese

RADIO CORPORATION OF SINGAPORE

1400-1600 & 2300-1100	6000

RADIO SINGAPORE INTERNATIONAL—(SE Asia)

1100-1400	6000 & 9560

SLOVAKIA—Slovak

RADIO SLOVAKIA INTERNATIONAL

0130-0200	5930 & 6190/7230 (E North Am & C America), 9440 (S America)
0730-0800	[S] 9440, 15460, 17550/11990 & [W] 21705 (Australasia)
1530-1600	[S] 5920 (W Europe)
1630-1700 ▭	6055 & 7345 (W Europe)
1630-1700	[W] 5915 (W Europe)
1900-1930	[S] 5920 (W Europe)
2000-2030 ▭	6055 & 7345 (W Europe)
2000-2030	[W] 5915 (W Europe)

SPAIN

RADIO EXTERIOR DE ESPAÑA

Galician, Catalan & Basque

1240-1255	[S] M-F *9765* (C America), [S] M-F 15585 (Europe), [S] M-F 17595 (N America & C America), [S] M-F 21540 (C Africa & S Africa), [S] M-F 21570 (S America), [S] M-F 21610 (Mideast)
1340-1355	[W] M-F 15585 (Europe), [W] M-F 17595 (N America & C America), [W] M-F 21540 (C Africa & S Africa), [W] M-F 21570 (S America), [W] M-F 21610 (Mideast)

Spanish

0000-0100	[W] Su/M *9765* (C America), [W] Su/M *11880* (C America & S America), [W] Su/M *15170* (W North Am & C America)
0000-0200	[S] 11680 & [W] 11945 (S America)
0000-0400	[S] *6020* (C America)
0000-0500	[W] 6125 (S America), 9540 (N America & C America), 9620 & [S] 15160 (S America)
0100-0400	[W] Tu-Sa *3210* & [W] Tu-Sa *5970* (C America)
0100-0500	[W] Tu-Sa *9630* (C America)
0200-0500	6055 (N America & C America)
0200-0600	[S] *6125* (W North Am & C America), [S] *9765* (C America & S America)
0500-0700	[S] 9710 (Europe), [W] 11890 & [S] 17665 (Mideast)
0600-0800	[W] 9705 (Europe)
0600-0900 ▭	12035 (Europe)
0700-0900	17770 & 21610 (Australasia)
0800-0900	[S] 15585 (Europe)
0800-1000	M-F 21570 (S America)
0900-1240	15585 (Europe), 21540 (C Africa & S Africa), 21610 (Mideast)
1000-1200	*9660* (E Asia), [S] M-F 21700 (C America)
1000-1240	M-F 17595 (N America & C America), 21570 (S America)

Today's China Radio International is more than just radio. Like some other stations, they also prepare television programs. CRI

1100-1200	S M-F *9765* (C America)
1100-1400	W M-F *5970* & M-F *11815* (C America), W M-F *15170* (W North Am & C America)
1200-1240	S Su-F *9765* (C America)
1200-1400	*11910* (SE Asia)
1200-2000	Sa/Su 21700 (C America & S America)
1240-1255	S Su *9765* (C America), S Sa/Su 15585 & W 15585 (Europe), W M-F 17595 (N America & C America), S Sa/Su 21540 & W 21540 (C Africa & S Africa), S Sa/Su 21570 & W 21570 (S America), S Sa/Su 21610 & W 21610 (Mideast)
1255-1340	15585 (Europe), M-F 17595 (N America & C America), 21540 (C Africa & S Africa), 21570 (S America), 21610 (Mideast)
1255-1400	S Su *9765* (C America)
1340-1355	S 15585 & W Sa/Su 15585 (Europe), S M-F 17595 (N America & C America), S 21540 & W Sa/Su 21540 (C Africa & S Africa), S 21570 & W Sa/Su 21570 (S America), S 21610 & W Sa/Su 21610 (Mideast)
1355-1500	M-F 17595 (N America & C America), 21540 (C Africa & S Africa), 21610 (Mideast)
1355-1700	15585 (Europe), 21570 (S America)
1400-1700	W Sa/Su *15170* (W North Am & C America)
1400-1800	W Sa/Su *9765* (C America), W Sa/Su *15125* (C America & S America)
1400-2300	S Su *9765* (C America)
1500-1600	S Su *17850* (W North Am & C America)
1500-1700	S 21610 & W 21770 (Mideast)
1500-1900	17755 (C Africa & S Africa)
1600-1700	M-Sa 15375 (W Africa & C Africa)
1600-2300	S Sa/Su *17850* (W North Am & C America)
1700-1800	W Sa/Su *17850* (W North Am & C America)
1700-1900	17715 (S America)
1700-2000	Sa/Su 9665 (Europe)
1700-2300	7275 (Europe)
1800-2100	M-F 21700 (Irr) (C America & S America)
1800-2200	W *15125* (C America & S America), W *17850* (W North Am & C America)

1800-2400	W *9765* (C America)
1900-2100	Su 17755 (C Africa & S Africa)
1900-2300	15110 (N America & C America)
2000-2100	Sa 9665 (Europe), Sa 21700 (C America & S America)
2200-2300	7270 (N Africa & W Africa)
2200-2400	W *11880* (C America & S America), W *15170* (W North Am & C America)
2300-2400	W 6125 (S America), 9540 (N America & C America), 9620, S 11680, W 11945 & S 15160 (S America)

SWEDEN—Swedish

RADIO SWEDEN

0000-0030	W 9495 & S 13625 (S America)
0100-0130	W 9495/7290 (S Asia & S America), S 13625 (S America), S 13640 (E Asia & Australasia)
0200-0230	9495, W *9560* & S *9755* (N America)
0300-0330	S 9495/15245 & W 9495/9755 (N America)
0400-0430	S 9475 (N America)
0430-0700	S M-F 9495 (Europe)
0500-0700 ⇦	M-F 6065 (Europe), M-F 17505 (Mideast & E Africa)
0530-0600 ⇦	9495 (N America)
0600-0800	W M-F 9490 (Europe, N Africa & Mideast), S Sa 9495 (Europe)
0700-0900 ⇦	Sa 17505 (Africa)
0700-0900	W Sa 6065 (Europe), W Sa 9490 (Europe & N Africa), S Su 9495 (Europe)
0800-1000 ⇦	Su 17505 (Africa)
0800-1000	W Su 6065 (Europe), W Su 9490 (Europe & N Africa)
1000-1010	S 9490 (Europe), S 21530 (E Asia & Australasia)
1010-1030	S Sa/Su 9490 (Europe), S Sa/Su 21530 (E Asia & Australasia)
1030-1040	S 21530 (SE Asia & Australasia)
1040-1100	S Sa/Su 21530 (SE Asia & Australasia)
1100-1110 ⇦	6065 (Europe), 21810 (Africa)
1100-1110	W 17505 (E Asia & Australasia)
1110-1130 ⇦	Sa/Su 6065 (Europe), Sa/Su 21810 (Africa)
1110-1130	W Sa/Su 17505 (E Asia & Australasia)
1130-1140 ⇦	18960 (N America), 21810 (S America)
1130-1140	W 17505 (SE Asia & Australasia)
1140-1200 ⇦	Sa/Su 18960 (N America), Sa/Su 21810 (S America)
1140-1200	W Sa/Su 17505 (SE Asia & Australasia)
1200-1230	18960 (N America)
1300-1330 ⇦	17505 (E Asia & Australasia)
1300-1330	W 15240 (N America)
1400-1430 ⇦	17505 (E Asia & Australasia), 18960 (N America)
1500-1530 ⇦	15240 (N America), 17505 (Asia & Australasia), 18960 (N America)
1545-1600 ⇦	18960 (N America)
1545-1600	S 13580 (Mideast), W 15240 (N America)
1545-1610	S 17485 (W Europe & W Africa)
1545-1700 ⇦	6065 (Europe)
1600-1630	W 5840 (E Europe)
1645-1700	W 15495 (S Europe & W Africa)

Bergen's fishing fleet keeps in touch with home by tuning to Radio Norway International. Lars Rydén

1645-1710	[W] 13765 (Mideast)
1700-1710 ⇦	M-F 6065 (Europe)
1800-1830	[S] 15315 (Mideast), [S] 17505 (S Europe & Africa)
1800-1900 ⇦	Su 6065 (Europe & Mideast)
1900-1930 ⇦	6065 (Europe & Mideast)
1900-1930	[W] 9765 (Europe & N Africa)
2000-2030	[W] 9445 (Australasia)
2000-2100	[S] 13580 (Europe & Africa)
2100-2130	[S] 9435 (W Europe), [W] 11615 (Europe & N Africa), [S] 15255 (Australasia)
2100-2230 ⇦	6065 (Europe)
2200-2230 ⇦	7325 (Europe & Africa)

SWITZERLAND

SWISS RADIO INTERNATIONAL

French

0600-0630	[W] *9885* (W Africa), [W] *13635/12025* & [S] *15545* (N Africa), [W] 17665 (C Africa & S Africa), [S] *17685* (N Africa & W Africa), [S] 21750 (C Africa & S Africa)
1000-1030	21770 (C Africa & S Africa)
1800-1815	[W] *9605*, [W] *13790* & [S] *15220* (Mideast), [W] 15555 (Mideast & E Africa), [S] *17735* (Mideast), [S] 21720 (Mideast & E Africa)
2100-2130	[W] *9605* (N Africa & W Africa), [W] *11910* (E Africa), [W] 13660 (C Africa & S Africa), [S] 13770 (E Africa), [S] *15220* (C Africa & S Africa), [S] *17580* (N Africa & W Africa), *17735* (S Africa)
2200-2230	9885, [W] *11660* & [S] *11905* (S America)

German

0630-0700	[W] *9885* (W Africa), [W] *13635/12025* & [S] *15545* (N Africa), [W] 17665 (C Africa & S Africa), [S] *17685* (N Africa & W Africa), [S] 21750 (C Africa & S Africa)
0930-1000	21770 (C Africa & S Africa)
2030-2100	[W] *9605* (N Africa & W Africa), [W] *11910* (E Africa), [W] 13660 (C Africa & S Africa), [S] 13770 (E Africa), [S] *15220* (C Africa & S Africa), [S] *17580* (N Africa & W Africa), *17735* (S Africa)
2230-2300	9885, [W] *11660* & [S] *11905* (S America)

Italian

0700-0730	[W] *9885* (W Africa), [W] *13635/12025* & [S] *15545* (N Africa), [W] 17665 (C Africa & S Africa), [S] *17685* (N Africa & W Africa), [S] 21750 (C Africa & S Africa)
0900-0930	21770 (C Africa & S Africa)
1630-1700	[W] *9605*, [W] *13790* & [S] *15220* (Mideast), [W] 15555 (Mideast & E Africa), [S] *17735* (Mideast), [S] 21720 (Mideast & E Africa)
1830-1900	[W] *9605* (N Africa & W Africa), [W] *11910* (E Africa), [W] 13660 (C Africa & S Africa), [S] 13770 (E Africa), [S] *15220* (C Africa & S Africa), [S] *17580* (N Africa & W Africa), *17735* (S Africa)
2300-2330	9885, [W] *11660* & [S] *11905* (S America)

SYRIA—Arabic

RADIO DAMASCUS—(S America)

2215-2315	12085 & 13610

SYRIAN BROADCASTING SERVICE

0600-1600 ⇦	13610
0600-1700 ⇦	12085

THAILAND—Thai

RADIO THAILAND

0100-0200	[W] 13695 & [S] 15395 (E North Am)
0330-0430	[S] 15395 & [W] 15460 (W North Am)
1000-1100	[W] 7285 & [S] 11805 (SE Asia & Australasia)
1330-1400	[W] 7145 & [S] 11955 (E Asia)
1800-1900	[S] 9690 & [W] 11855 (Mideast)
2045-2115	[W] 9535 & [S] 9680 (Europe)

TUNISIA—Arabic

RTV TUNISIENNE

0200-0500	9720/12005 (N Africa & Mideast)
0400-0600	7275 (W Europe)
0400-0700	7110 (N Africa)
1200-1400	17735 (N Africa & Mideast)
1200-1700	[W] 15450 (N Africa & Mideast)
1400-1700	11730 (W Europe), [S] 17735 (N Africa & Mideast)
1400-1900	11655 (N Africa)

1700-2100	9720/12005 (N Africa & Mideast)
1700-2300	7225 (W Europe)
1900-2300	7110 (N Africa)

UNITED ARAB EMIRATES—Arabic

UAE RADIO IN DUBAI

0230-0330	12005, 13675 & 15400 (E North Am & C America)
0400-0530	15435 (Australasia), 17830 (E Asia), 21700 (Australasia)
0600-1030	13675, 15395 & 21605 (Europe)
1050-1200	15370 (N Africa)
1050-1330	13675, 15395 & 21605 (Europe)
1200-1330	13630 (N Africa)
1350-1600	13630 (N Africa), 13675, 15395 & 21605 (Europe)
1630-2050	11950 (Europe), 13630 (N Africa), 13675 & 15395 (Europe)

VENEZUELA—Spanish

ECOS DEL TORBES

0900-0400	4980
1200-2200	9640

RADIO NACIONAL—(C America)

0000-0100, 0300-0400, 1100-1200, 1400-1500, 1800-1900 & 2100-2200	9540 (Irr)

RADIO TACHIRA

1000-1400 & 2100-0400	4830

VIETNAM—Vietnamese

VOICE OF VIETNAM

0000-0100	[W] 7145, 9730 & [S] 13740 (C Africa)
0130-0230	*9525* (E North Am)
0400-0500	*9795* (W North Am)
1700-1800	[W] 7145, 9730 & [S] 13740 (Europe)
1730-1830	[S] *12070* (Europe)
1830-1930	[W] *5955* (W Europe)
1930-2030	[S] *12030* (Europe)
2030-2130	[W] *5970* (S Europe)

ORIENTAL CX-12
MONTE CARLO ORIENTAL
MONTECARLO
CX 20 MONTE CARLO
ADMINISTRACION ESTUDIOS
CX 12 ORIENTAL
Santander

Radio Monte Carlo and Radio Oriental are located together in downtown Montevideo, Uruguay. They also share a shortwave transmitter used to relay their mediumwave AM programs. Lars Rydén

YUGOSLAVIA—Serbian

RADIO YUGOSLAVIA

0000-0030	[S] Su *11870* (E North Am)
0030-0100	[W] *7115* & [S] *11870* (E North Am)
0100-0130	[W] Su *7115* (E North Am)
0130-0200	[W] *7115* (E North Am)
1400-1430	[W] *11835* (Australasia)
1400-1530 ←	*7200* (Europe)
2030-2100 ←	*6100* (Europe)
2030-2100 →	*7230* (Australasia)
2100-2130 ←	Sa *6100* (Europe)
2100-2130 →	Sa *7230* (Australasia)
2330-2400	[S] *11870* (E North Am)

Weird Words

PASSPORT's Ultimate Glossary of World Band Terms and Abbreviations

A rich variety of terms and abbreviations is used in world band radio. Some are specialized and benefit from explanation; several are foreign words that need translation; and yet others are simply adaptations of everyday usage.

Here, then, is PASSPORT's A-Z guide to what's what in world band buzzwords. For a thorough analysis of terms and norms used in evaluating world band radios, see the Radio Database International White Paper, *How to Interpret Receiver Specifications and Lab Tests*.

A. Summer schedule season. *See* S. *See* HFCC.
Active Antenna. An antenna that electronically amplifies signals. Active, or amplified, antennas are typically mounted indoors, but some models can also be mounted outdoors. Active antennas take up relatively little space, but their amplification circuits may introduce certain types of problems that can result in unwanted sounds being heard. *See* Passive Antenna.
Adjacent-Channel Rejection. *See* Selectivity.
AGC. *See* Automatic Gain Control.
AGC Threshold. The threshold at which the automatic gain control (AGC), *see*, chooses to act relates to both listening pleasure and audible sensitivity. If the threshold is too low, the AGC will tend to act on internal receiver noise and minor static, desensitizing the receiver. However, if the threshold is too high, variations in loudness will be uncomfortable to the ear, forcing the listener to manually twiddle with the volume control to do, in effect, what the AGC should be doing automatically. Measured in μV (microvolts).
Alt. Freq. Alternative frequency or channel. Frequency or channel that may be used in place of the regularly scheduled one.
Amateur Radio. *See* Hams.
AM Band. The local radio band, which currently runs from 520 to 1611 kHz (530–1705 kHz in the Western Hemisphere), within the Medium Frequency (MF) range of the radio spectrum. Outside North America, it is usually called the mediumwave (MW) band. However, in parts of Latin America it is sometimes called, by the general public and a few stations, *onda larga*—longwave—strictly speaking, a misnomer.
Amplified Antenna. *See* Active Antenna.
Analog Frequency Readout. Needle-and-dial or "slide-rule" tuning, greatly inferior to synthesized tuning for scanning world band airwaves. *See* Synthesizer.
Audio Quality. At PASSPORT, audio quality refers to what in computer testing is called "benchmark" quality. This means, primarily, the freedom from distortion of a signal fed through a receiver's entire circuitry—*not* just the audio stage—from the antenna input through to the speaker terminals. A lesser characteristic of audio quality is the audio bandwidth needed for pleasant world band reception of music. Also, *see* Enhanced Fidelity.
Automatic Gain Control (AGC). Smooths out fluctuations in signal strength brought about by fading, a regular occurrence with world band signals. *See* AGC Threshold.
AV. A Voz—Portuguese for "The Voice." In PASSPORT, this term is also used to represent "The Voice of."
B. Winter schedule season. *See* W. *See* HFCC.
Bandwidth. A key variable that determines selectivity (*see*), bandwidth is the amount of radio signal at -6 dB a radio's circuitry will let pass, and thus be heard. With world band channel spacing at 5 kHz, the best single bandwidths are usually in the vicinity of 3 to 6 kHz. Better radios offer two or more selectable bandwidths: at least one of 5 to 9 kHz or so for when a station is in the clear, and one or more others between 2 to 6 kHz for when a station is hemmed in by other signals next to it. Proper selectivity is a key determinant of the aural quality of what you hear, and some newer models of tabletop receivers have dozens of bandwidths. Synchronous selectable sideband *(see)* allows wider bandwidths to be used to provide improved fidelity.
Baud. Measurement of the speed by which radioteletype (*see*), radiofax (*see*) and other digital data are transmitted. Baud is properly written entirely in lower case, and thus is abbreviated as b (baud), kb (kilobaud) or Mb (Megabaud). Baud rate standards are usually set by the international CCITT regulatory body.
BC. Broadcasting, Broadcasting Company, Broadcasting Corporation.
Birdie. A silent spurious signal, similar to a station's open carrier, created by circuit interaction within a receiver. The fewer and weaker the birdies within a receiver's tuning range, the better, although in reality birdies rarely degrade reception.
Blocking. The ability of a receiver to avoid being desensitized by powerful adjacent signals or signals from other nearby frequencies. Measured in dB (decibels) at 100 kHz signal spacing.
Broadcast. A radio or television transmission meant for the general public. *Compare* Utility Stations, Hams.
BS. Broadcasting Station, Broadcasting Service.
Cd. Ciudad—Spanish for "City."
Channel. An everyday term to indicate where a station is supposed to be located on the dial. World band channels are spaced exactly 5 kHz apart. Stations operating outside this norm are "off-channel" (for these, PASSPORT provides resolution to better than 1 kHz to aid in station identification).
Chugging, Chuffing. The sound made by some synthesized tuning systems when the tuning knob is turned. Called "chugging" or "chuffing," as it is suggestive of the rhythmic "chuf, chuf" sound of steam locomotives or "chugalug" gulping of beverages.
Cl. Club, Clube.
Cult. Cultura, Cultural.
Default. The setting at which a control of a digitally operated electronic device, including many world band radios, normally operates, and to which it will eventually return (e.g., when the radio is next switched on).
Digital Frequency Display, Digital Tuning. *See* Synthesizer.
Digital Radio Mondiale (DRM). International organization (www.drm.org/indexeuz.htm) heavily involved in the effort to convert world band transmissions from traditional analog mode to digital mode. *See* Mode.
Digital Signal Processing (DSP). Where digital circuitry and software are used to perform radio circuit functions traditionally done using analog circuits. Used on certain world band receivers; also, available as an add-on accessory for audio processing only.
Dipole Antenna. *See* Passive Antenna.
Distortion. *See* Overall Distortion.
Domestic Service. *See* DS.
DS. Domestic Service—Broadcasting intended primarily for audiences in the broadcaster's home country. However, some domestic programs are beamed on world band to expatriates and other kinfolk abroad, as well as interested foreigners. *Compare* ES.
DSP. *See* Digital Signal Processing.
DX, DXers, DXing. From an old telegraph term "to DX"; that is, to communicate over a great distance. Thus, DXers are those who specialize in finding distant or exotic stations that are considered to be rare catches. Few world band listeners are considered to be regular DXers, but many others seek out DX stations every now and then—usually by bandscanning, which is greatly facilitated by PASSPORT's Blue Pages.
Dynamic Range. The ability of a receiver to handle weak signals in the presence of strong competing signals within or near the same world band segment (*see* World Band Spectrum). Sets with inferior dynamic range sometimes "overload," especially with external antennas, causing a mishmash of false signals up and down—and even beyond—the segment being received. Dynamic range is closely related to the third-order intercept point *(see)*, or IP3. Where possible, PASSPORT measures dynamic range and IP3 at the traditional 20 kHz and more challenging 5 kHz signal-separation points.
Earliest Heard (or Latest Heard). See key at the bottom of each Blue Page. If the PASSPORT monitoring team cannot establish the definite sign-on (or sign-off) time of a station, the earliest (or latest) time that the station could be traced is indicated by a left-facing or right-facing "arrowhead flag." This means that the station almost certainly operates beyond the time shown by that "flag." It also means that, unless you live relatively close to the station, you're unlikely to be able to hear it beyond that "flagged" time.
EBS. Economic Broadcasting Station, a type of station found in China.
ECSS (Exalted-Carrier Selectable Sideband). Manual tuning of a conventional AM-mode signal, using a receiver's single-sideband circuitry to zero-beat *(see)* the receiver's BFO with the transmitted signal's carrier. The better-sounding of the signal's sidebands is then selected by the listener. *See* Synchronous Detector.
Ed, Educ. Educational, Educação, Educadora.
Electrical Noise. *See* Noise.
Em. Emissora, Emisora, Emissor, Emetteur—in effect, "station" in various languages.
Enhanced Fidelity. Radios with good audio performance and certain types of high-tech circuitry can improve the fidelity of world band signals. Among the newer fidelity-enhancing techniques is synchronous detection (*see* Synchronous Detector), especially when coupled with selectable sideband. Another potential technological

advance to improve fidelity is digital world band transmission, which is actively being researched and tested *(see* Digital Radio Mondiale*)*.

EP. Emissor Provincial—Portuguese for "Provincial Station."

ER. Emissor Regional—Portuguese for "Regional Station."

Ergonomics. How handy and comfortable—intuitive—a set is to operate, especially hour after hour.

ES. External Service—Broadcasting intended primarily for audiences abroad. *Compare* DS.

External Service. *See* ES.

F. Friday.

Fax. *See* Radiofax.

Feeder, Shortwave. A utility transmission from the broadcaster's home country to a relay site or placement facility some distance away. Although these specialized transmissions carry world band programming, they are not intended to be received by the general public. Many world band radios can process these quasi-broadcasts anyway. Feeders operate in lower sideband (LSB), upper sideband (USB) or independent sideband (termed ISL if heard on the lower side, ISU if heard on the upper side) modes. Virtually all shortwave feeders have now been replaced by satellite and Internet audio feeders. *See* Single Sideband, Utility Stations.

First IF Rejection. A relatively uncommon source of false signals occurs when powerful transmitters operate on the same frequency as a receiver's first intermediate frequency (IF). The ability of receiving circuitry to avoid such transmitters' causing reception problems is called "IF rejection."

Frequency. The standard term to indicate where a station is located on the dial—regardless of whether it is "on-channel" or "off-channel" (*see* Channel). Measured in kilohertz (kHz) or Megahertz (MHz), which differ only in the placement of a decimal; e.g., 5970 kHz is the same as 5.97 MHz. Either measurement is equally valid, but to minimize confusion PASSPORT and most stations designate frequencies only in kHz.

Frequency Synthesizer. *See* Synthesizer, Frequency.

Front-End Selectivity. The ability of the initial stage of receiving circuitry to admit only limited frequency ranges into succeeding stages of circuitry. Good front-end selectivity keeps signals from other, powerful bands or segments from being superimposed upon the frequency range you're tuning. For example, a receiver with good front-end selectivity will receive only shortwave signals within the range 3200-3400 kHz. However, a receiver with mediocre front-end selectivity might allow powerful local mediumwave AM stations from 520-1700 kHz to be heard "ghosting in" between 3200 and 3400 kHz, along with the desired shortwave signals. Obviously, mediumwave AM signals don't belong on shortwave. Receivers with inadequate front-end selectivity can benefit from the addition of a preselector (*see*) or a high-pass filter.

GMT. Greenwich Mean Time—*See* World Time.

Hams. Government-licensed amateur radio hobbyists who *transmit* to each other by radio, often by single sideband (*see*), within special amateur bands. Many of these bands are within the shortwave spectrum (*see*). This is the same spectrum used by world band radio, but world band and ham radio, which laymen sometimes confuse with each other, are two very separate entities. The easiest way is to think of hams as making something like phone calls, whereas world band stations are like long-distance versions of ordinary FM or mediumwave AM stations.

Harmonic, Harmonic Radiation, Harmonic Signal. Usually, an unwanted weak spurious repeat of a signal in multiple(s) of the fundamental, or "real," frequency. Thus, the third harmonic of a mediumwave AM station on 1120 kHz might be heard faintly on 4480 kHz within the world band spectrum. Stations almost always try to minimize harmonic radiation, as it wastes energy and spectrum space. However, in rare cases stations have been known to amplify a harmonic signal so they can operate inexpensively on a second frequency. Also, *see* Subharmonic.

Hash. Electrical noise. *See* Noise.

High Fidelity. *See* Enhanced Fidelity.

HFCC (High Frequency Co-ordination Conference). Founded in 1990 and headquartered in Prague, the HFCC (www.hfcc.org) helps coordinate frequency usage by some 60 broadcasting organizations from more than 30 countries. These represent about 75 to 80 percent of the global output for international shortwave broadcasting. Coordination meetings take place twice yearly: once each for the "A" (summer) and "B" (winter) schedule seasons.

IBS. International Broadcasting Services, Ltd., publishers of *Passport to World Band Radio* and other publications.

Image. A common type of spurious signal found on low-cost radios where a strong signal appears at reduced strength, usually on a frequency 900 kHz or 910 kHz lower down. For example, the BBC on 5875 kHz might repeat on 4975 kHz, its "image frequency." *See* Spurious-Signal Rejection.

Independent Sideband. *See* Single Sideband.

Interference. Sounds from other signals, notably on the same ("co-channel") frequency or nearby channels, that are disturbing the one you are trying to hear. Worthy radios reduce interference by having good selectivity (*see*). Nearby television sets and cable television wiring may also generate a special type of radio interference called TVI, a "growl" heard every 15 kHz or so. Sometimes referred to as QRM, a term based on Morse-code shorthand.

International Reply Coupon (IRC). Sold by selected post offices in most parts of the world, IRCs amount to official international "scrip" that may be exchanged for postage in most countries of the world. Because they amount to an international form of postage repayment, they are handy for listeners trying to encourage foreign stations to write them back. However, IRCs are very costly for the amount in stamps that is provided in return. Too, an increasing number of countries are not forthcoming about "cashing in" IRCs. Specifics on this and related matters are provided in the Addresses PLUS section of this book.

International Telecommunication Union (ITU). The regulatory body, headquartered in Geneva, for all international telecommunications, including world band radio. Sometimes incorrectly referred to as the "International Telecommunications Union." In recent years, the ITU has become increasingly ineffective as a regulatory body for world band radio, with much of its former role having been taken up by the HFCC *(see)*.

Internet Radio. *See* Web radio.

Inverted-L Antenna. *See* Passive Antenna.

Ionosphere. *See* Propagation.

IP3. Third-order intercept point. *See* Dynamic Range.

IRC. *See* International Reply Coupon.

Irr. Irregular operation or hours of operation; i.e., schedule tends to be unpredictable.

ISB. Independent sideband. *See* Single Sideband.

ISL. Independent sideband, lower. *See* Feeder.

ISU. Independent sideband, upper. *See* Feeder.

ITU. *See* International Telecommunication Union.

Jamming. Deliberate interference to a transmission with the intent of discouraging listening. However, shortwave broadcasts are uniquely resistant to jamming. This ability to avoid "gatekeeping" is a major reason why shortwave continues to be the workhorse for international broadcasting. For now, jamming is practiced much less than it was during the Cold War.

Keypad. On a world band radio, like a computer, a keypad can be used to control many variables. However, unlike a computer, the keypad on most world band radios consists of only ten numeric or multifunction keys, usually supplemented by two more keys, as on a telephone keypad. Keypads are used primarily so you can enter a station's frequency for reception, and the best keypads have real keys (not a membrane) in the standard telephone format of 3x4 with "zero" under the "8" key. Many keypads are also used for presets, but this means you have to remember code numbers for stations (e.g., BBC 5975 kHz is "07"); handier radios have separate keys for presets, while some others use LCD-displayed "pages" to access presets.

kHz. Kilohertz, the most common unit for measuring where a station is on the world band dial. Formerly known as "kilocycles per second," or kc/s. 1,000 kilohertz equals one Megahertz. *See* Frequency.

Kilohertz. *See* kHz.

kW. Kilowatt(s), the most common unit of measurement for transmitter power (*see*).

LCD. Liquid-crystal display. LCDs, if properly designed, are fairly easily seen in bright light, but require illumination under darker conditions. LCDs, typically gray on gray, also tend to have mediocre contrast, and sometimes can be read from only a certain angle or angles, but they consume nearly no battery power.

LED. Light-emitting diode. LEDs are very easily read in the dark or in normal room light, but consume more battery power than LCDs and are hard to read in bright light.

Location. The physical location of a station's transmitter, which may be different from the studio location. Transmitter location is useful as a guide to reception quality. For example, if you're in eastern North America and wish to listen to the Voice of Russia, a transmitter located in St. Petersburg will almost certainly provide better reception than, say, one located in Siberia.

Longwave Band. The 148.5–283.5 kHz portion of the low-frequency (LF) radio spectrum used in Europe, the Near East, North Africa, Russia and Mongolia for domestic broadcasting. As a practical matter, these longwave signals, which have nothing to do with world band or other shortwave signals, are not usually audible in other parts of the world.

Longwire Antenna. *See* Passive Antenna.

LSB. Lower Sideband. *See* Feeder, Single Sideband.

LV. La Voix, La Voz—French and Spanish for "The Voice." In PASSPORT, this term is also used to represent "The Voice of."

M. Monday.

Mediumwave Band, Mediumwave AM Band. *See* AM Band.

Megahertz. *See* MHz.

Memory, Memories. *See* Preset.

Meters. An outdated unit of measurement used for individual world band segments of the shortwave spectrum. The frequency range covered by a given meters designation—also known as "wavelength"—can be gleaned from the following formula: *frequency (kHz) = 299,792 ÷ meters*. Thus, 49 meters comes out to a frequency of 6118 kHz—well within the range of frequencies included in that segment (*see* World Band Spectrum). Inversely, meters can be derived from the following: *meters = 299,792 ÷ frequency (kHz)*. The figure 299,792 is based on the speed of light as agreed upon internationally in 1983. However, in practice this is often rounded to 300,000 for computational purposes.

MHz. Megahertz, a common unit to measure where a station is on the dial. Formerly known as "Megacycles per second," or Mc/s. One Megahertz equals 1,000 kilohertz. *See* Frequency.

Mode. Method of transmission of radio signals. World band radio broadcasts are almost always in the analog AM mode, the same mode used in the mediumwave AM band (*see*). The AM mode consists of three components: two "sidebands," plus one "carrier" that resides between the two sidebands. Each sideband contains the same programming as the other, and the carrier carries no programming, so a few stations have experimented with the single-sideband (SSB) mode. SSB contains only one sideband, either the lower sideband (LSB) or upper sideband (USB), and a reduced carrier. It requires special radio circuitry to be demodulated, or made intelligible, which is the main reason SSB is unlikely to be widely adopted as a world band mode. However, major efforts are currently underway to implement digital-mode world band transmissions (*see* Digital Radio Mondiale). There are yet other modes used on shortwave, but not for world band. These include CW (Morse-type code), radiofax, RTTY (radioteletype) and narrow-band FM used by utility and ham stations. Narrow-band FM is not used for music, and is different from usual FM. *See* Single Sideband, ISB, ISL, ISU, LSB and USB.

N. New, Nueva, Nuevo, Nouvelle, Nacional, National, Nationale.

Nac. Nacional. Spanish and Portuguese for "National."

Nat, Natl, Nat'l. National, Nationale.

Noise. Static, buzzes, pops and the like caused by the earth's atmosphere (typically lightning), and to a lesser extent by galactic noise. Also, electrical noise emanates from such man-made sources as electric blankets, fish-tank heaters, heating pads, electrical and gasoline motors, light dimmers, flickering light bulbs, non-incandescent lights, computers and computer peripherals, office machines, electric fences, and faulty electric utility wiring and related components. Sometimes referred to as QRN, a term based on Morse-code shorthand.

Noise Floor. *See* Sensitivity.

Notch Filter, Tunable. A useful feature for reducing or rejecting annoying heterodyne interference—the whistles, howls and squeals for which shortwave has traditionally been notorious.

Other. Programs are in a language other than one of the world's primary languages.

Overall Distortion. Nothing makes listening quite so tiring as distortion. PASSPORT has devised techniques to measure overall cumulative distortion from signal input through audio output—not just distortion within the audio stage. This level of distortion is thus equal to what is heard by the ear.

Overloading. *See* Dynamic Range.

Passive Antenna. An antenna that is not electronically amplified. Typically, these are mounted outdoors, although the "tape-measure" type that comes as an accessory with some portables is usually strung indoors. For world band reception, virtually all outboard models for consumers are made from wire, rather than rods or tubular elements. The two most common designs are the inverted-L (so-called "longwire") and trapped dipole (mounted either horizontally or as a "sloper"). These antennas are preferable to active antennas (*see*), and are reviewed in detail in the Radio Database International White Paper, *PASSPORT Evaluation of Popular Outdoor Antennas (Unamplified)*.

PBS. People's Broadcasting Station.

Phase Noise. Synthesizers and other circuits can create a "rushing" noise that is usually noticed only when the receiver is tuned alongside the edge of a powerful broadcast or other carrier. In effect, the signal becomes "modulated" by the noise. Phase noise is a useful measurement if you tune weak signals alongside powerful signals. Measured in dBc (decibels below carrier).

PLL (Phase-Locked Loop). With world band receivers, a PLL circuit means that the radio can be tuned digitally, often using a number of handy tuning techniques, such as a keypad *(see)* and presets *(see)*.

Power. Transmitter power *before* amplification by the antenna, expressed in kilowatts (kW). The present range of world band powers is 0.01 to 1,000 kW.

Power Lock. *See* Travel Power Lock.

PR. People's Republic.

Preselector. A circuit—outboard as an accessory, or inboard as part of the receiver—that effectively limits the range of frequencies which can enter a receiver's circuitry or the circuitry of an active antenna (*see*); that is, which improves front-end selectivity (*see*). For example, a preselector may let in the range 15000-16000 kHz, thus helping ensure that your receiver or active antenna will not encounter problems within that range caused by signals from, say, 5730-6250 kHz or local mediumwave AM signals (520-1705 kHz). This range usually can be varied, manually or automatically, according to the frequency to which the receiver is being tuned. A preselector may be passive (unamplified) or active (amplified).

Preset. Allows you to select a station pre-stored in a radio's memory. The handiest presets require only one push of a button, as on a car radio.

Propagation. World band signals travel, like a basketball, up and down from the station to your radio. The "floor" below is the earth's surface, whereas the "player's hand" on high is the *ionosphere*, a gaseous layer that envelops the planet. While the earth's surface remains pretty much the same from day to day, the ionosphere—nature's own passive "satellite"—varies in how it propagates radio signals, depending on how much sunlight hits the "bounce points."

Thus, some world band segments do well mainly by day, whereas others are best by night. During winter there's less sunlight, so the "night bands" become unusually active, whereas the "day bands" become correspondingly less useful (*see* World Band Spectrum). Day-to-day changes in the sun's weather also cause short-term changes in world band radio reception; this explains why some days you can hear rare signals.

Additionally, the 11-year sunspot cycle has a long-term effect on propagation. Currently, the sunspot cycle is at a vigorous phase. This means that the upper world band segments will remain unusually lively over the coming years.

PS. Provincial Station, Pangsong.

Pto. Puerto, Porto.

QRM. *See* Interference.

QRN. *See* Noise.

QSL. *See* Verification.

R. Radio, Radiodiffusion, Radiodifusora, Radiodifusão, Radiophonikos, Radiostantsiya, Radyo, Radyosu, and so forth.

Radiofax, Radio Facsimile. Like ordinary telefax (facsimile by telephone lines), but by radio.

Radioteletype (RTTY). Characters, but not illustrations, transmitted by radio. *See* Baud.

RDI. Radio Database International®, a registered trademark of International Broadcasting Services, Ltd.

Receiver. Synonym for a radio, but sometimes—especially when called a "communications receiver"—implying a radio with superior tough-signal or utility-signal performance.

Reduced Carrier. *See* Single Sideband.

Reg. Regional.

Relay. A retransmission facility, often highlighted in "Worldwide Broadcasts in English" and "Voices from Home" in PASSPORT'S WorldScan® section. Relay facilities are generally considered to be located outside the broadcaster's country. Being closer to the target audience, they usually provide superior reception. *See* Feeder.

Rep. Republic, République, República.

RN. *See* R and N.

RS. Radio Station, Radiostantsiya, Radiostudiya, Radiophonikos Stathmos.

RT, RTV. Radiodiffusion Télévision, Radio Télévision, and so forth.

RTTY. *See* Radioteletype.

S. As an icon **S**: aired summer (midyear) only; *see* "HFCC." As an ordinary letter: San, Santa, Santo, São, Saint, Sainte. Also, South.

Sa. Saturday.

Scan, Scanning. Circuitry within a radio that allows it to bandscan or memory scan automatically.

Season, Schedule Season. *See* HFCC.

Segments. *See* Shortwave Spectrum.

Selectivity. The ability of a radio to reject interference (*see*) from signals on adjacent channels. Thus, also known as adjacent-channel rejection, a key variable in radio quality. *See* Bandwidth. *See* Shape Factor. *See* Ultimate Rejection. *See* Synchronous Detector.

Sensitivity. The ability of a radio to receive weak signals; thus, also known as weak-signal sensitivity. Of special importance if you are listening during the day or tuning domestic tropical band broadcasts—or if you are located in such parts of the world as Western North America, Hawaii or Australasia, where signals tend to be relatively weak. The best measurement of sensitivity is the noise floor.

Shape Factor. Skirt selectivity helps reduce interference and increase audio fidelity. It is important if you will be tuning stations that are weaker than adjacent-channel signals. Skirt selectivity is measured by the shape factor, the ratio between the bandwidth at -6 dB (adjacent signal at about the same strength as the received station) and -60 dB (adjacent signal relatively much stronger). A good shape factor provides the best defense against adjacent powerful signals' muscling their way in to disturb reception of the desired signal.

Shortwave Spectrum. The shortwave spectrum—also known as the High Frequency (HF) spectrum—is, strictly speaking, that portion of the radio spectrum from 3 MHz through 30 MHz (3,000-30,000 kHz). However, common usage places it at 2.3-30 MHz (2,300-30,000 kHz). World band operates on shortwave within 14 discrete segments ("bands") between 2.3 MHz and 26.1 MHz, with the rest of the shortwave spectrum being occupied by hams (*see*) and utility stations (*see*). Also, *see* the detailed "Best Times and Frequencies" chapter elsewhere in this edition.

Sideband. *See* Mode.

Single Sideband, Independent Sideband. Spectrum- and power-conserving modes of transmission commonly used mainly by utility stations and hams. These transmitted signals consist of one full sideband (lower sideband, LSB; or upper sideband, USB) and a vestigial carrier, but no second sideband. Very few broadcasters use, or are expected ever to use, these modes, although some quasi-broadcasts, such as the American AFRTS, operate in the single-sideband mode. Many world band radios are already capable of demodulating single-sideband transmissions, and some can even process independent-sideband signals. Certain single-sideband transmissions operate with a minimum of carrier reduction, which allows them to be listened to, albeit with some distortion, on ordinary radios not equipped to demodulate single sideband. Properly designed synchronous detectors (*see*) may prevent such distortion. *See* Feeder, Mode.

Site. *See* Location.

Skirt Selectivity. *See* Shape Factor.

Slew Controls. Elevator-button-type up and down controls to tune a radio. On many radios with synthesized tuning, slewing is used in lieu of tuning by knob. Better is when slew controls are complemented by a tuning knob, which is more versatile.

Sloper Antenna. *See* Passive Antenna.

SPR. Spurious (false) extra signal from a transmitter actually operating on another frequency. One such type is harmonic (*see*).

Spurious-Signal Rejection. The ability of a radio receiver to avoid producing false, or "ghost," signals that might otherwise interfere with the clarity of the station you're trying to hear. *See* Image.

St, Sta, Sto. Abbreviations for words that mean "Saint."

Stability. The ability of a receiver or transceiver to stay put on the tuned frequency without drifting.

Static. *See* Noise.

Su. Sunday.

Subharmonic. A harmonic heard at 1.5 or 0.5 times the operating frequency. This anomaly is caused by the way signals are generated within vintage-model transmitters, and thus cannot take place with modern transmitters. For example, the subharmonic of a station on 3360 kHz might be heard faintly on 5040 or 1680 kHz. Also, *see* Harmonic.

Sunspot Cycle. *See* Propagation.

Synchronous Detector. World band radios are increasingly coming equipped with this high-tech circuit that greatly reduces fading distortion. Better synchronous detectors also allow for synchronous selectable sideband; that is, the highly desirable ability to select the less-interfered of the two sidebands of a world band or other AM-mode signal. *See* Mode.

Synchronous Selectable Sideband. *See* Synchronous Detector.

Synthesizer, Frequency. Simple radios often use archaic needle-and-dial tuning that makes it difficult to find a desired channel or to tell which station you are hearing, except by ear. Other models utilize a digital frequency synthesizer to tune to signals without your having to hunt and peck. Among other things, such synthesizers allow for pushbutton tuning and presets, and display the exact frequency digitally—pluses that make tuning to the world considerably easier. Virtually a "must" feature.

Target. Where a transmission is beamed.

Th. Thursday.

Third Order Intercept Point. *See* Dynamic Range.

Travel Power Lock. Control to disable the on/off switch to prevent a radio from switching on accidentally.

Transmitter Power. *See* Power.

Trapped Dipole Antenna. *See* Passive Antenna.

Tu. Tuesday.

Ultimate Rejection, Ultimate Selectivity. The point at which a receiver is no longer able to reject adjacent-channel interference. Ultimate rejection is important if you listen to signals that are markedly weaker than are adjacent signals. *See* Selectivity.

Universal Day. *See* World Time.

Universal Time. *See* World Time.

URL. Universal Resource Locator; i.e., the Internet address for a given Webpage.

USB. Upper Sideband. *See* Feeder. *See* Single Sideband.

UTC. Coordinated Universal Time. *See* World Time.

Utility Stations. Most signals within the shortwave spectrum are not world band stations. Rather, they are utility stations—radio telephones, ships at sea, aircraft, ionospheric sounders, over-the-horizon radar and the like—that transmit strange sounds (growls, gurgles, dih-dah sounds, etc.). Although these can be picked up on many receivers, they are rarely intended to be utilized by the general public. *Compare* Broadcast, Hams and Feeders.

v. Variable frequency; i.e., one that is unstable or drifting because of a transmitter malfunction or, less often, to avoid jamming or other interference.

Verification. A "QSL" card or letter from a station verifying that a listener indeed heard that particular station. In order to stand a chance of qualifying for a verification card or letter, you should respond shortly after having heard the transmission. You need to provide the station heard with, at a minimum, the following information in a three-number "SIO" code, in which "SIO 555" is best and "SIO 111" is worst:

- **S**ignal strength, with 5 being of excellent quality, comparable to that of a local mediumwave AM station, and 1 being inaudible or at least so weak as to be virtually unintelligible. 2 (faint, but somewhat intelligible), 3 (moderate strength) and 4 (good strength) represent the signal-strength levels usually encountered with world band stations.
- **I**nterference from other stations, with 5 indicating no interference whatsoever, and 1 indicating such extreme interference that the desired signal is virtually drowned out. 2 (heavy interference), 3 (moderate interference) and 4 (slight interference) represent the differing degrees of interference more typically encountered with world band signals. If possible, indicate the names of the interfering station(s) and the channel(s) they are on. Otherwise, at least describe what the interference sounds like.
- **O**verall quality of the signal, with 5 being best, 1 worst.
- In addition to providing SIO findings, you should indicate which programs you've heard, as well as comments on how you liked or disliked those programs. Refer to the Addresses PLUS section of this edition for information on where and to whom your report should be sent, and whether return postage should be included.
- Because of the hassle involved, few stations wish to receive tape recordings of their transmissions.

Vo. Voice of.

W. As an icon **W**: aired winter only; *see* HFCC. As a regular letter: Wednesday.

Wavelength. *See* Meters.

Weak-Signal Sensitivity. *See* Sensitivity.

Webcasting. *See* Web Radio.

Web Radio, Webcasts. Broadcasts aired to the public over the Internet's World Wide Web. These thousands of stations worldwide include simulcast FM, mediumwave AM and world band stations, as well as Web-only "stations." Thus far listening to Webcasts in economically advanced countries for more than brief periods has been limited by phone line and related costs except within the United States. In developing countries, listening to Webcasts is almost invariably an uncommon exercise. Although Webcasting has been remarkably unfettered thus far, it is increasingly being subject to official gatekeeping, or censorship, and its future will be partly dependent on potentially onerous royalty fees being demanded by intellectual property owners.

World Band Radio. Similar to regular mediumwave AM band and FM band radio, except that world band stations can be heard over enormous distances, and thus often carry news, music and entertainment programs created especially for audiences abroad. Some world band stations have audiences of up to 120 million each day. Some 600 million people worldwide are believed to listen to world band radio.

World Band Spectrum. *See* "Best Times and Frequencies" elsewhere in this edition.

World Day. *See* World Time.

World Time. Also known as Coordinated Universal Time (UTC), Greenwich Mean Time (GMT) and Zulu time (Z). With nearly 170 countries on world band radio, if each announced its own local time you would need a calculator to figure it all out. To get around this, a single international time—World Time—is used. The differences between World Time and local time are detailed in the Addresses PLUS and Setting Your World Time Clock sections of this edition. World Time can also be determined simply by listening to World Time announcements given on the hour by world band stations—or minute by minute by WWV and WWVH in the United States on such frequencies as 5000, 10000 and 15000 kHz, or CHU in Canada on 3330, 7335 and 14670 kHz. A 24-hour clock format is used, so "1800 World Time" means 6:00 PM World Time. If you're in, say, North America, Eastern Time is five hours behind World Time winters and four hours behind World Time summers, so 1800 World Time would be 1:00 PM EST or 2:00 PM EDT. The easiest solution is to use a 24-hour digital clock set to World Time. Many radios already have these built in, and World Time clocks are also available as accessories. World Time also applies to the days of the week. So if it's 9:00 PM (21:00) Wednesday in New York during the winter, it's 0200 *Thursday* World Time.

WS. World Service.

Zero beat. When tuning a world band or other AM-mode signal in the single-sideband mode, there is a whistle, or "beat," whose pitch is the result of the difference in frequency between the receiver's internally generated carrier (BFO, or beat-frequency oscillator) and the station's transmitted carrier. By tuning carefully, the listener can reduce the difference between these two carriers to the point where the whistle is deeper and deeper, to the point where it no longer audible. This silent spot is known as "zero beat." *See* ECSS.

Printed in Canada

PASSPORT's Blue Pages—2002

Channel-by-Channel Guide to World Band Schedules

If you scan the world band airwaves, you'll discover lots more stations than those aimed your way. That's because shortwave signals are capriciously scattered by the heavens, so you can often hear stations not targeted to your area.

Blue Pages Help Identify Stations

But just dialing around can be frustrating if you don't have a "map"—PASSPORT's Blue Pages. Let's say that you've stumbled across something Asian-sounding on 7410 kHz at 2035 World Time. The Blue Pages show All India Radio beamed to Western Europe, with a hefty 500 kW of power from Bangalore. These clues suggest this is probably what you're hearing, even if you're not in Europe. You can also see that English from India will begin on that same channel in about ten minutes.

Schedules for Entire Year

Times and days of the week are in World Time; for local times in each country, see "Addresses PLUS." Some stations are shown as one hour earlier (◄) or later (►) midyear—typically April through October. Stations may also extend their hours for holidays, emergencies or sports events.

To be as useful as possible over the months to come, PASSPORT's schedules consist not just of observed activity, but also that which we have creatively opined will take place during the forthcoming year. This predictive material is based on decades of experience and is original from us. Although inherently not as exact as real-time data, over the years it's been of tangible value to PASSPORT readers.

Guide to Blue Pages Format

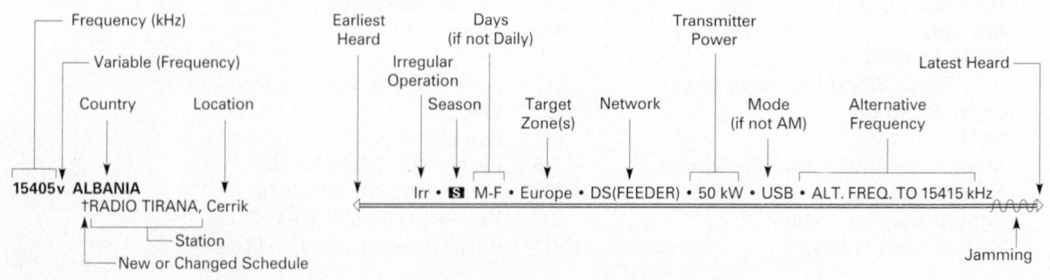

Frequency (kHz)
Variable (Frequency)
Country
Location
15405v ALBANIA
†RADIO TIRANA, Cerrik
Station
New or Changed Schedule
Earliest Heard
Days (if not Daily)
Irregular Operation
Season
Target Zone(s)
Network
Transmitter Power
Mode (if not AM)
Alternative Frequency
Latest Heard
Irr • S M-F • Europe • DS(FEEDER) • 50 kW • USB • ALT. FREQ. TO 15415 kHz
Jamming

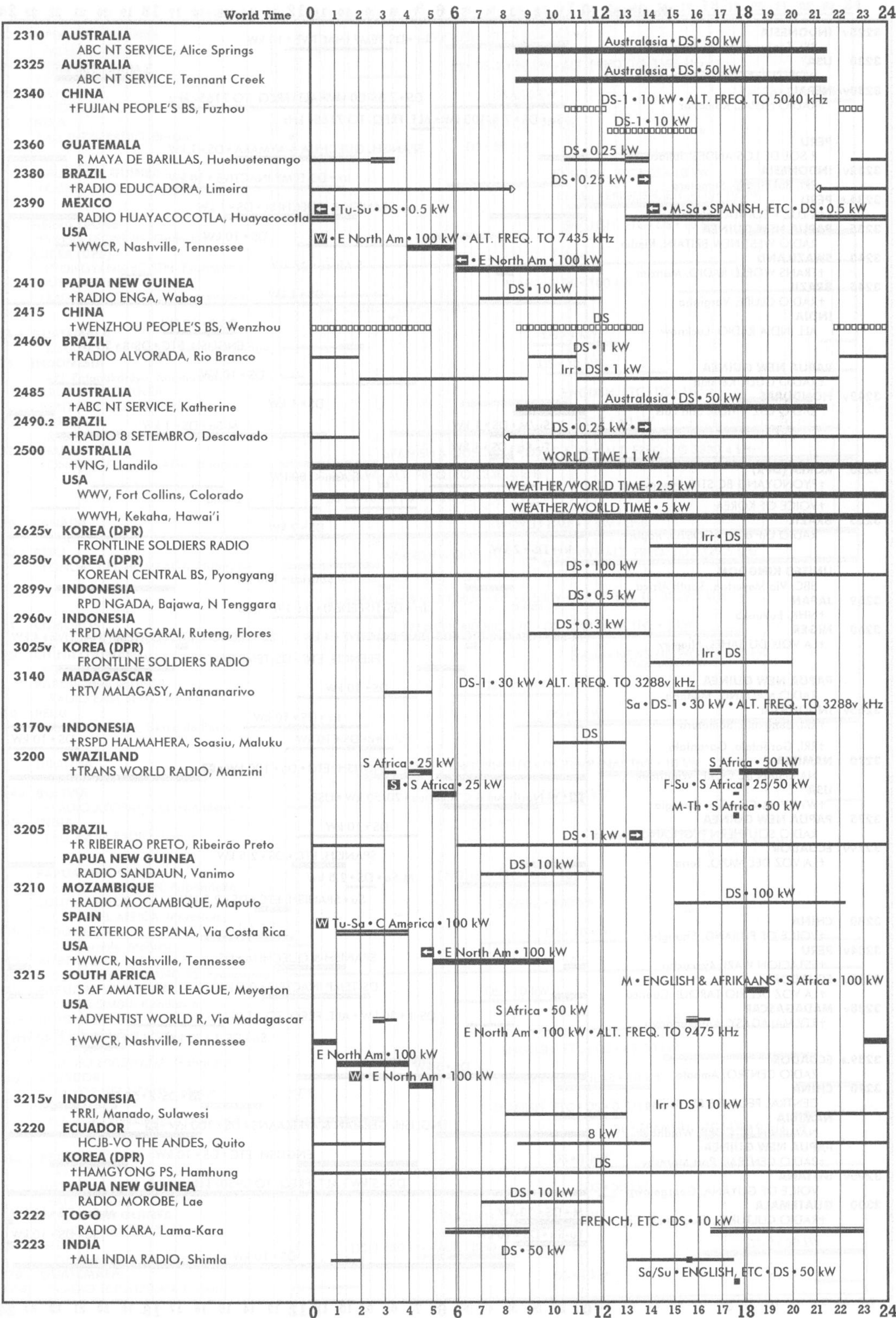
World Time
0 1 2 3 4 5 6 7 8 9 10 11 12 13 14 15 16 17 18 19 20 21 22 23 24
2310 AUSTRALIA
ABC NT SERVICE, Alice Springs
Australasia • DS • 50 kW
2325 AUSTRALIA
ABC NT SERVICE, Tennant Creek
Australasia • DS • 50 kW
2340 CHINA
†FUJIAN PEOPLE'S BS, Fuzhou
DS-1 • 10 kW • ALT. FREQ. TO 5040 kHz
DS-1 • 10 kW
2360 GUATEMALA
R MAYA DE BARILLAS, Huehuetenango
DS • 0.25 kW
2380 BRAZIL
†RADIO EDUCADORA, Limeira
DS • 0.25 kW
2390 MEXICO
RADIO HUAYACOCOTLA, Huayacocotla
Tu-Su • DS • 0.5 kW
M-Sa • SPANISH, ETC • DS • 0.5 kW
USA
†WWCR, Nashville, Tennessee
W • E North Am • 100 kW • ALT. FREQ. TO 7435 kHz
E North Am • 100 kW
2410 PAPUA NEW GUINEA
†RADIO ENGA, Wabag
DS • 10 kW
2415 CHINA
†WENZHOU PEOPLE'S BS, Wenzhou
DS
2460v BRAZIL
†RADIO ALVORADA, Rio Branco
DS • 1 kW
Irr • DS • 1 kW
2485 AUSTRALIA
†ABC NT SERVICE, Katherine
Australasia • DS • 50 kW
2490.2 BRAZIL
†RADIO 8 SETEMBRO, Descalvado
DS • 0.25 kW
2500 AUSTRALIA
†VNG, Llandilo
WORLD TIME • 1 kW
USA
WWV, Fort Collins, Colorado
WEATHER/WORLD TIME • 2.5 kW
WWVH, Kekaha, Hawai'i
WEATHER/WORLD TIME • 5 kW
2625v KOREA (DPR)
FRONTLINE SOLDIERS RADIO
Irr • DS
2850v KOREA (DPR)
KOREAN CENTRAL BS, Pyongyang
DS • 100 kW
2899v INDONESIA
RPD NGADA, Bajawa, N Tenggara
DS • 0.5 kW
2960v INDONESIA
†RPD MANGGARAI, Ruteng, Flores
DS • 0.3 kW
3025v KOREA (DPR)
FRONTLINE SOLDIERS RADIO
Irr • DS
3140 MADAGASCAR
†RTV MALAGASY, Antananarivo
DS-1 • 30 kW • ALT. FREQ. TO 3288v kHz
Sa • DS-1 • 30 kW • ALT. FREQ. TO 3288v kHz
3170v INDONESIA
†RSPD HALMAHERA, Soasiu, Maluku
DS
3200 SWAZILAND
†TRANS WORLD RADIO, Manzini
S Africa • 25 kW
S • S Africa • 25 kW
S Africa • 50 kW
F-Su • S Africa • 25/50 kW
M-Th • S Africa • 50 kW
3205 BRAZIL
†R RIBEIRAO PRETO, Ribeirão Preto
DS • 1 kW
PAPUA NEW GUINEA
RADIO SANDAUN, Vanimo
DS • 10 kW
3210 MOZAMBIQUE
†RADIO MOCAMBIQUE, Maputo
DS • 100 kW
SPAIN
†R EXTERIOR ESPANA, Via Costa Rica
W Tu-Sa • C America • 100 kW
USA
†WWCR, Nashville, Tennessee
E North Am • 100 kW
3215 SOUTH AFRICA
S AF AMATEUR R LEAGUE, Meyerton
M • ENGLISH & AFRIKAANS • S Africa • 100 kW
USA
†ADVENTIST WORLD R, Via Madagascar
S Africa • 50 kW
†WWCR, Nashville, Tennessee
E North Am • 100 kW • ALT. FREQ. TO 9475 kHz
E North Am • 100 kW
W • E North Am • 100 kW
3215v INDONESIA
†RRI, Manado, Sulawesi
Irr • DS • 10 kW
3220 ECUADOR
HCJB-VO THE ANDES, Quito
8 kW
KOREA (DPR)
†HAMGYONG PS, Hamhung
DS
PAPUA NEW GUINEA
RADIO MOROBE, Lae
DS • 10 kW
3222 TOGO
RADIO KARA, Lama-Kara
FRENCH, ETC • DS • 10 kW
3223 INDIA
†ALL INDIA RADIO, Shimla
DS • 50 kW
Sa/Su • ENGLISH, ETC • DS • 50 kW
0 1 2 3 4 5 6 7 8 9 10 11 12 13 14 15 16 17 18 19 20 21 22 23 24

SEASONAL S OR W 1-HR TIMESHIFT MIDYEAR ⇦ OR ⇨ JAMMING / OR ∧ EARLIEST HEARD ◁ LATEST HEARD ▷ NEW FOR 2002 †

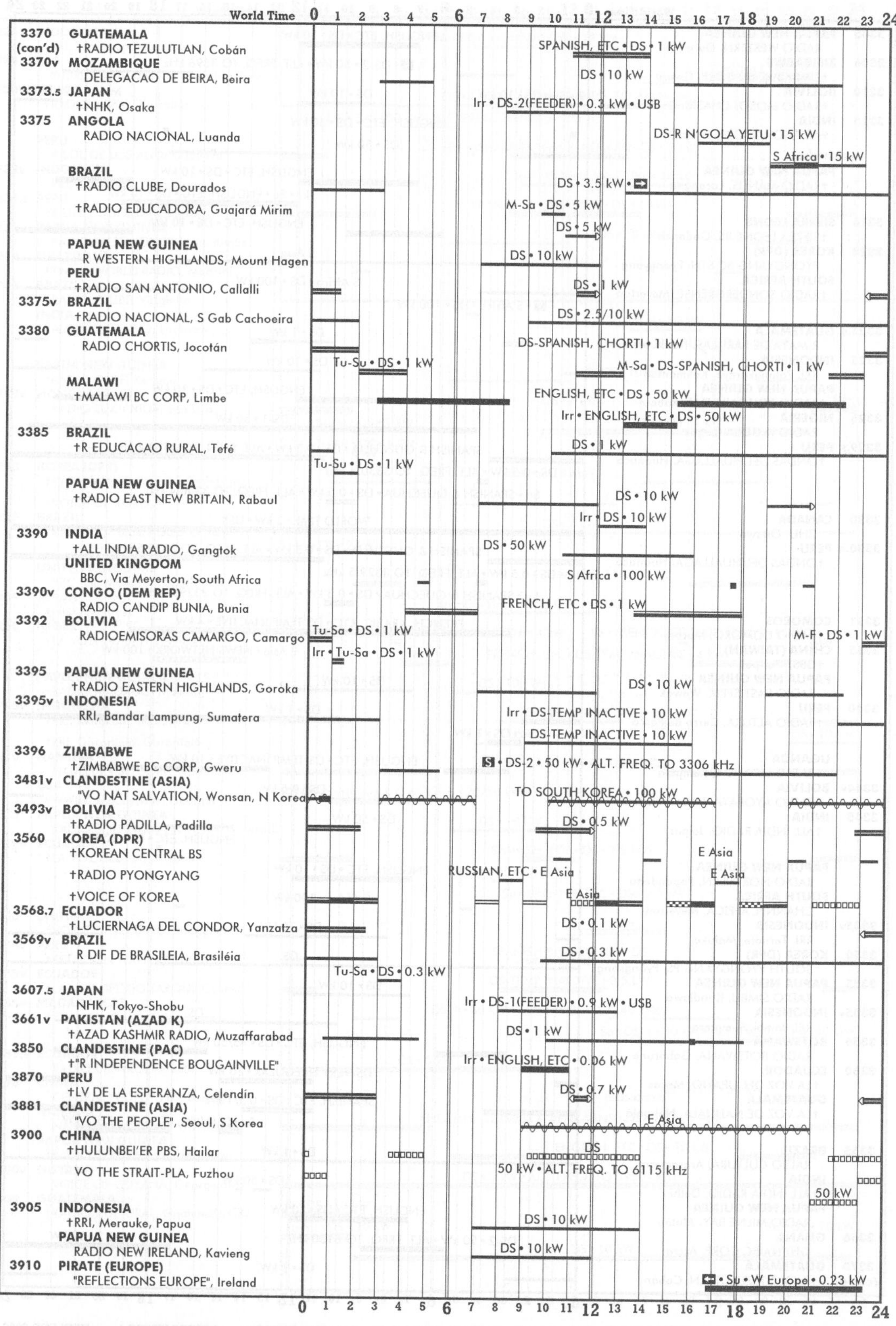
World Time 0 1 2 3 4 5 6 7 8 9 10 11 12 13 14 15 16 17 18 19 20 21 22 23 24
3370 (con'd) GUATEMALA
†RADIO TEZULUTLAN, Cobán
SPANISH, ETC • DS • 1 kW
3370v MOZAMBIQUE
DELEGACAO DE BEIRA, Beira
DS • 10 kW
3373.5 JAPAN
†NHK, Osaka
Irr • DS-2(FEEDER) • 0.3 kW • USB
3375 ANGOLA
RADIO NACIONAL, Luanda
DS-R N'GOLA YETU • 15 kW
S Africa • 15 kW
BRAZIL
†RADIO CLUBE, Dourados
DS • 3.5 kW
†RADIO EDUCADORA, Guajará Mirim
M-Sa • DS • 5 kW
DS • 5 kW
PAPUA NEW GUINEA
R WESTERN HIGHLANDS, Mount Hagen
DS • 10 kW
PERU
†RADIO SAN ANTONIO, Callalli
DS • 1 kW
3375v BRAZIL
†RADIO NACIONAL, S Gab Cachoeira
DS • 2.5/10 kW
3380 GUATEMALA
RADIO CHORTIS, Jocotán
DS-SPANISH, CHORTI • 1 kW
Tu-Su • DS • 1 kW
M-Sa • DS-SPANISH, CHORTI • 1 kW
MALAWI
†MALAWI BC CORP, Limbe
ENGLISH, ETC • DS • 50 kW
Irr • ENGLISH, ETC • DS • 50 kW
3385 BRAZIL
†R EDUCACAO RURAL, Tefé
DS • 1 kW
Tu-Su • DS • 1 kW
PAPUA NEW GUINEA
†RADIO EAST NEW BRITAIN, Rabaul
DS • 10 kW
Irr • DS • 10 kW
3390 INDIA
†ALL INDIA RADIO, Gangtok
DS • 50 kW
UNITED KINGDOM
BBC, Via Meyerton, South Africa
S Africa • 100 kW
3390v CONGO (DEM REP)
RADIO CANDIP BUNIA, Bunia
FRENCH, ETC • DS • 1 kW
3392 BOLIVIA
RADIOEMISORAS CAMARGO, Camargo
Tu-Sa • DS • 1 kW
Irr • Tu-Sa • DS • 1 kW
M-F • DS • 1 kW
3395 PAPUA NEW GUINEA
†RADIO EASTERN HIGHLANDS, Goroka
DS • 10 kW
3395v INDONESIA
RRI, Bandar Lampung, Sumatera
Irr • DS-TEMP INACTIVE • 10 kW
DS-TEMP INACTIVE • 10 kW
3396 ZIMBABWE
†ZIMBABWE BC CORP, Gweru
S • DS-2 • 50 kW • ALT. FREQ. TO 3306 kHz
3481v CLANDESTINE (ASIA)
"VO NAT SALVATION, Wonsan, N Korea
TO SOUTH KOREA • 100 kW
3493v BOLIVIA
†RADIO PADILLA, Padilla
DS • 0.5 kW
3560 KOREA (DPR)
†KOREAN CENTRAL BS
†RADIO PYONGYANG
RUSSIAN, ETC • E Asia
E Asia
E Asia
†VOICE OF KOREA
E Asia
3568.7 ECUADOR
†LUCIERNAGA DEL CONDOR, Yanzatza
DS • 0.1 kW
3569v BRAZIL
R DIF DE BRASILEIA, Brasiléia
DS • 0.3 kW
Tu-Sa • DS • 0.3 kW
3607.5 JAPAN
NHK, Tokyo-Shobu
Irr • DS-1(FEEDER) • 0.9 kW • USB
3661v PAKISTAN (AZAD K)
†AZAD KASHMIR RADIO, Muzaffarabad
DS • 1 kW
3850 CLANDESTINE (PAC)
†"R INDEPENDENCE BOUGAINVILLE"
Irr • ENGLISH, ETC • 0.06 kW
3870 PERU
†LV DE LA ESPERANZA, Celendín
DS • 0.7 kW
3881 CLANDESTINE (ASIA)
"VO THE PEOPLE", Seoul, S Korea
E Asia
3900 CHINA
†HULUNBEI'ER PBS, Hailar
DS
VO THE STRAIT-PLA, Fuzhou
50 kW • ALT. FREQ. TO 6115 kHz
50 kW
3905 INDONESIA
†RRI, Merauke, Papua
DS • 10 kW
PAPUA NEW GUINEA
RADIO NEW IRELAND, Kavieng
DS • 10 kW
3910 PIRATE (EUROPE)
"REFLECTIONS EUROPE", Ireland
Su • W Europe • 0.23 kW
0 1 2 3 4 5 6 7 8 9 10 11 12 13 14 15 16 17 18 19 20 21 22 23 24

ENGLISH ARABIC CHINESE FRENCH GERMAN RUSSIAN SPANISH OTHER

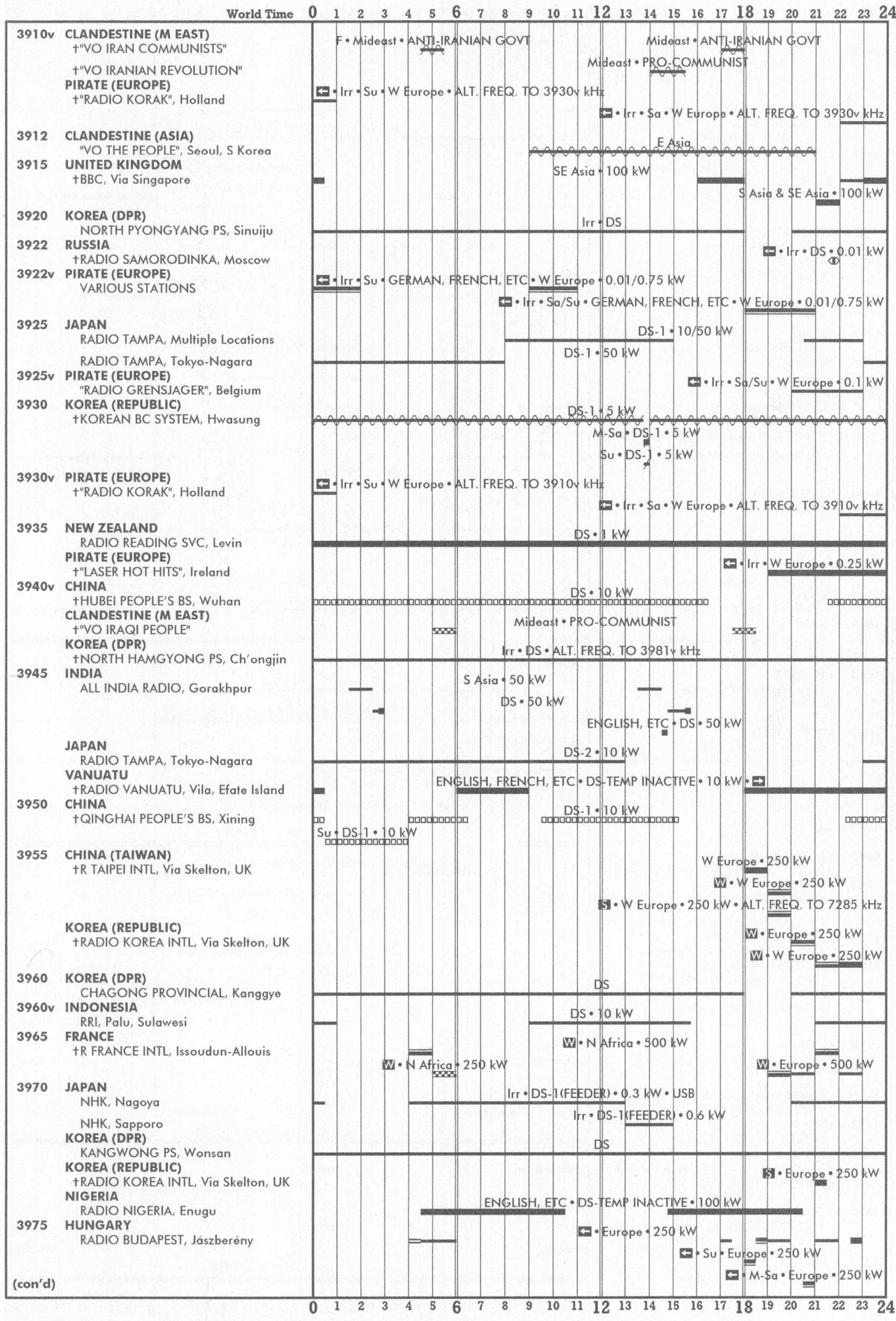
World Time 0 1 2 3 4 5 6 7 8 9 10 11 12 13 14 15 16 17 18 19 20 21 22 23 24
3910v CLANDESTINE (M EAST)
†"VO IRAN COMMUNISTS"
F • Mideast • ANTI-IRANIAN GOVT
Mideast • ANTI-IRANIAN GOVT
†"VO IRANIAN REVOLUTION"
Mideast • PRO-COMMUNIST
PIRATE (EUROPE)
†"RADIO KORAK", Holland
Irr • Su • W Europe • ALT. FREQ. TO 3930v kHz
Irr • Sa • W Europe • ALT. FREQ. TO 3930v kHz
3912 CLANDESTINE (ASIA)
"VO THE PEOPLE", Seoul, S Korea
E Asia
3915 UNITED KINGDOM
†BBC, Via Singapore
SE Asia • 100 kW
S Asia & SE Asia • 100 kW
3920 KOREA (DPR)
NORTH PYONGYANG PS, Sinuiju
Irr • DS
3922 RUSSIA
†RADIO SAMORODINKA, Moscow
Irr • DS • 0.01 kW
3922v PIRATE (EUROPE)
VARIOUS STATIONS
Irr • Su • GERMAN, FRENCH, ETC • W Europe • 0.01/0.75 kW
Irr • Sa/Su • GERMAN, FRENCH, ETC • W Europe • 0.01/0.75 kW
3925 JAPAN
RADIO TAMPA, Multiple Locations
DS-1 • 10/50 kW
RADIO TAMPA, Tokyo-Nagara
DS-1 • 50 kW
3925v PIRATE (EUROPE)
"RADIO GRENSJAGER", Belgium
Irr • Sa/Su • W Europe • 0.1 kW
3930 KOREA (REPUBLIC)
†KOREAN BC SYSTEM, Hwasung
DS-1 • 5 kW
M-Sa • DS-1 • 5 kW
Su • DS-1 • 5 kW
3930v PIRATE (EUROPE)
†"RADIO KORAK", Holland
Irr • Su • W Europe • ALT. FREQ. TO 3910v kHz
Irr • Sa • W Europe • ALT. FREQ. TO 3910v kHz
3935 NEW ZEALAND
RADIO READING SVC, Levin
DS • 1 kW
PIRATE (EUROPE)
†"LASER HOT HITS", Ireland
Irr • W Europe • 0.25 kW
3940v CHINA
†HUBEI PEOPLE'S BS, Wuhan
DS • 10 kW
CLANDESTINE (M EAST)
†"VO IRAQI PEOPLE"
Mideast • PRO-COMMUNIST
KOREA (DPR)
†NORTH HAMGYONG PS, Ch'ongjin
Irr • DS • ALT. FREQ. TO 3981v kHz
3945 INDIA
ALL INDIA RADIO, Gorakhpur
S Asia • 50 kW
DS • 50 kW
ENGLISH, ETC • DS • 50 kW
JAPAN
RADIO TAMPA, Tokyo-Nagara
DS-2 • 10 kW
VANUATU
†RADIO VANUATU, Vila, Efate Island
ENGLISH, FRENCH, ETC • DS-TEMP INACTIVE • 10 kW
3950 CHINA
†QINGHAI PEOPLE'S BS, Xining
DS-1 • 10 kW
Su • DS-1 • 10 kW
3955 CHINA (TAIWAN)
†R TAIPEI INTL, Via Skelton, UK
W Europe • 250 kW
W • W Europe • 250 kW
S • W Europe • 250 kW • ALT. FREQ. TO 7285 kHz
KOREA (REPUBLIC)
†RADIO KOREA INTL, Via Skelton, UK
W • Europe • 250 kW
W • W Europe • 250 kW
3960 KOREA (DPR)
CHAGONG PROVINCIAL, Kanggye
DS
3960v INDONESIA
RRI, Palu, Sulawesi
DS • 10 kW
3965 FRANCE
†R FRANCE INTL, Issoudun-Allouis
W • N Africa • 500 kW
W • N Africa • 250 kW
W • Europe • 500 kW
3970 JAPAN
NHK, Nagoya
Irr • DS-1(FEEDER) • 0.3 kW • USB
NHK, Sapporo
Irr • DS-1(FEEDER) • 0.6 kW
KOREA (DPR)
KANGWONG PS, Wonsan
DS
KOREA (REPUBLIC)
†RADIO KOREA INTL, Via Skelton, UK
S • Europe • 250 kW
NIGERIA
RADIO NIGERIA, Enugu
ENGLISH, ETC • DS-TEMP INACTIVE • 100 kW
3975 HUNGARY
RADIO BUDAPEST, Jászberény
Europe • 250 kW
Su • Europe • 250 kW
M-Sa • Europe • 250 kW
(con'd)
0 1 2 3 4 5 6 7 8 9 10 11 12 13 14 15 16 17 18 19 20 21 22 23 24

SEASONAL S OR W 1-HR TIMESHIFT MIDYEAR ◄ OR ► JAMMING / OR ∧ EARLIEST HEARD ◁ LATEST HEARD ▷ NEW FOR 2002 †

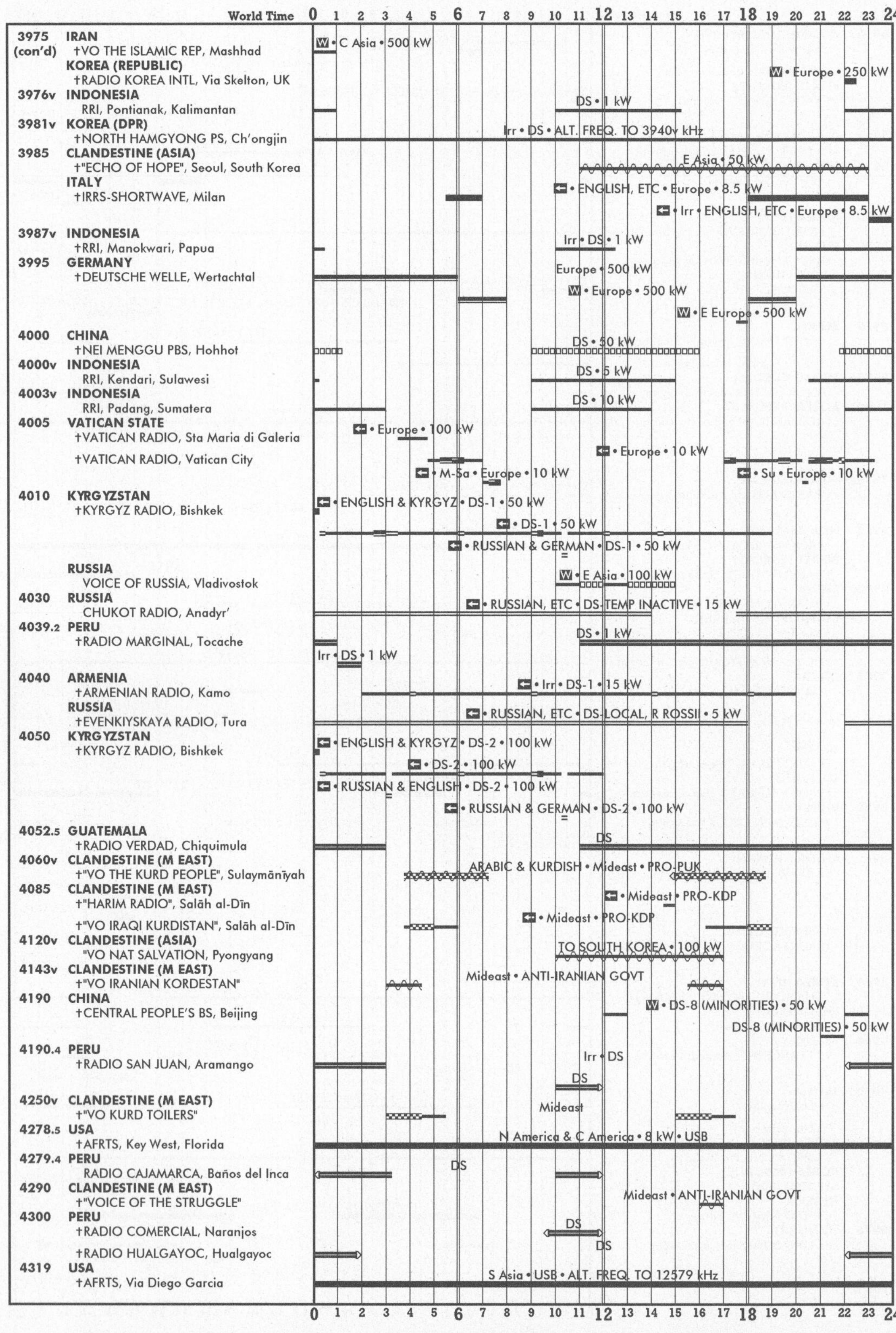
World Time 0 1 2 3 4 5 6 7 8 9 10 11 12 13 14 15 16 17 18 19 20 21 22 23 24
3975 (con'd) IRAN
†VO THE ISLAMIC REP, Mashhad
W • C Asia • 500 kW
KOREA (REPUBLIC)
†RADIO KOREA INTL, Via Skelton, UK
W • Europe • 250 kW
3976v INDONESIA
RRI, Pontianak, Kalimantan
DS • 1 kW
3981v KOREA (DPR)
†NORTH HAMGYONG PS, Ch'ongjin
Irr • DS • ALT. FREQ. TO 3940v kHz
3985 CLANDESTINE (ASIA)
†"ECHO OF HOPE", Seoul, South Korea
E Asia • 50 kW
ITALY
†IRRS-SHORTWAVE, Milan
• ENGLISH, ETC • Europe • 8.5 kW
• Irr • ENGLISH, ETC • Europe • 8.5 kW
3987v INDONESIA
†RRI, Manokwari, Papua
Irr • DS • 1 kW
3995 GERMANY
†DEUTSCHE WELLE, Wertachtal
Europe • 500 kW
W • Europe • 500 kW
W • E Europe • 500 kW
4000 CHINA
†NEI MENGGU PBS, Hohhot
DS • 50 kW
4000v INDONESIA
RRI, Kendari, Sulawesi
DS • 5 kW
4003v INDONESIA
RRI, Padang, Sumatera
DS • 10 kW
4005 VATICAN STATE
†VATICAN RADIO, Sta Maria di Galeria
• Europe • 100 kW
†VATICAN RADIO, Vatican City
• Europe • 10 kW
• M-Sa • Europe • 10 kW
• Su • Europe • 10 kW
4010 KYRGYZSTAN
†KYRGYZ RADIO, Bishkek
• ENGLISH & KYRGYZ • DS-1 • 50 kW
• DS-1 • 50 kW
• RUSSIAN & GERMAN • DS-1 • 50 kW
RUSSIA
VOICE OF RUSSIA, Vladivostok
W • E Asia • 100 kW
4030 RUSSIA
CHUKOT RADIO, Anadyr'
• RUSSIAN, ETC • DS-TEMP INACTIVE • 15 kW
4039.2 PERU
†RADIO MARGINAL, Tocache
DS • 1 kW
Irr • DS • 1 kW
4040 ARMENIA
†ARMENIAN RADIO, Kamo
• Irr • DS-1 • 15 kW
RUSSIA
†EVENKIYSKAYA RADIO, Tura
• RUSSIAN, ETC • DS-LOCAL, R ROSSII • 5 kW
4050 KYRGYZSTAN
†KYRGYZ RADIO, Bishkek
• ENGLISH & KYRGYZ • DS-2 • 100 kW
• DS-2 • 100 kW
• RUSSIAN & ENGLISH • DS-2 • 100 kW
• RUSSIAN & GERMAN • DS-2 • 100 kW
4052.5 GUATEMALA
†RADIO VERDAD, Chiquimula
DS
4060v CLANDESTINE (M EAST)
†"VO THE KURD PEOPLE", Sulaymānīyah
ARABIC & KURDISH • Mideast • PRO-PUK
4085 CLANDESTINE (M EAST)
†"HARIM RADIO", Salāh al-Dīn
• Mideast • PRO-KDP
†"VO IRAQI KURDISTAN", Salāh al-Dīn
• Mideast • PRO-KDP
4120v CLANDESTINE (ASIA)
"VO NAT SALVATION, Pyongyang
TO SOUTH KOREA • 100 kW
4143v CLANDESTINE (M EAST)
†"VO IRANIAN KORDESTAN"
Mideast • ANTI-IRANIAN GOVT
4190 CHINA
†CENTRAL PEOPLE'S BS, Beijing
W • DS-8 (MINORITIES) • 50 kW
DS-8 (MINORITIES) • 50 kW
4190.4 PERU
†RADIO SAN JUAN, Aramango
Irr • DS
DS
4250v CLANDESTINE (M EAST)
†"VO KURD TOILERS"
Mideast
4278.5 USA
†AFRTS, Key West, Florida
N America & C America • 8 kW • USB
4279.4 PERU
RADIO CAJAMARCA, Baños del Inca
DS
4290 CLANDESTINE (M EAST)
†"VOICE OF THE STRUGGLE"
Mideast • ANTI-IRANIAN GOVT
4300 PERU
†RADIO COMERCIAL, Naranjos
DS
†RADIO HUALGAYOC, Hualgayoc
DS
4319 USA
†AFRTS, Via Diego Garcia
S Asia • USB • ALT. FREQ. TO 12579 kHz
0 1 2 3 4 5 6 7 8 9 10 11 12 13 14 15 16 17 18 19 20 21 22 23 24
ENGLISH ARABIC CHINESE FRENCH GERMAN RUSSIAN SPANISH OTHER

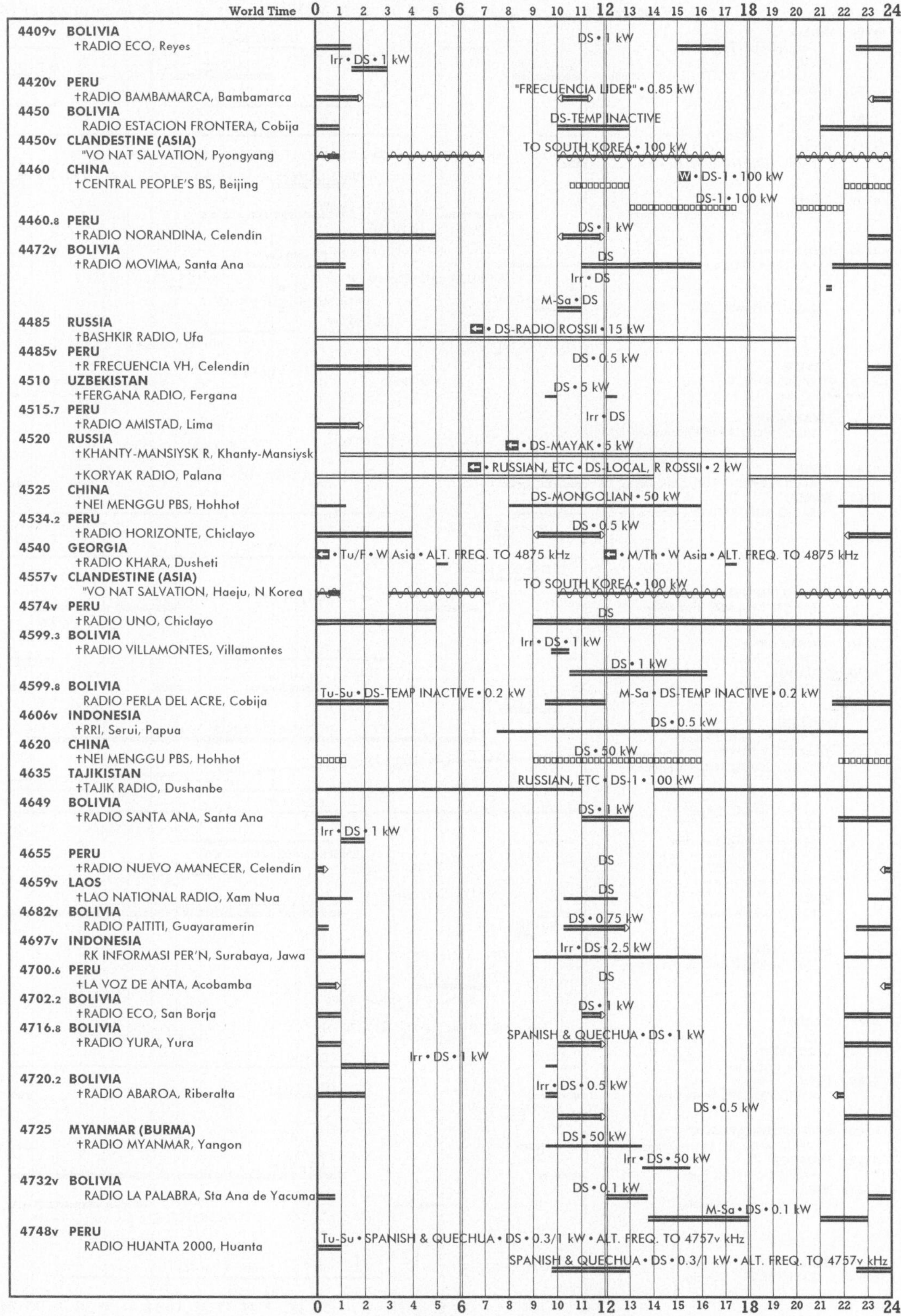

World Time 0 1 2 3 4 5 6 7 8 9 10 11 12 13 14 15 16 17 18 19 20 21 22 23 24
4409v BOLIVIA
†RADIO ECO, Reyes
DS • 1 kW
Irr • DS • 1 kW
4420v PERU
†RADIO BAMBAMARCA, Bambamarca
"FRECUENCIA LIDER" • 0.85 kW
4450 BOLIVIA
RADIO ESTACION FRONTERA, Cobija
DS-TEMP INACTIVE
4450v CLANDESTINE (ASIA)
"VO NAT SALVATION, Pyongyang
TO SOUTH KOREA • 100 kW
4460 CHINA
†CENTRAL PEOPLE'S BS, Beijing
W • DS-1 • 100 kW
DS-1 • 100 kW
4460.8 PERU
†RADIO NORANDINA, Celendín
DS • 1 kW
4472v BOLIVIA
†RADIO MOVIMA, Santa Ana
DS
Irr • DS
M-Sa • DS
4485 RUSSIA
†BASHKIR RADIO, Ufa
DS-RADIO ROSSII • 15 kW
4485v PERU
†R FRECUENCIA VH, Celendín
DS • 0.5 kW
4510 UZBEKISTAN
†FERGANA RADIO, Fergana
DS • 5 kW
4515.7 PERU
†RADIO AMISTAD, Lima
Irr • DS
4520 RUSSIA
†KHANTY-MANSIYSK R, Khanty-Mansiysk
DS-MAYAK • 5 kW
†KORYAK RADIO, Palana
RUSSIAN, ETC • DS-LOCAL, R ROSSII • 2 kW
4525 CHINA
†NEI MENGGU PBS, Hohhot
DS-MONGOLIAN • 50 kW
4534.2 PERU
†RADIO HORIZONTE, Chiclayo
DS • 0.5 kW
4540 GEORGIA
†RADIO KHARA, Dusheti
Tu/F • W Asia • ALT. FREQ. TO 4875 kHz
M/Th • W Asia • ALT. FREQ. TO 4875 kHz
4557v CLANDESTINE (ASIA)
"VO NAT SALVATION, Haeju, N Korea
TO SOUTH KOREA • 100 kW
4574v PERU
†RADIO UNO, Chiclayo
DS
4599.3 BOLIVIA
†RADIO VILLAMONTES, Villamontes
Irr • DS • 1 kW
DS • 1 kW
4599.8 BOLIVIA
RADIO PERLA DEL ACRE, Cobija
Tu-Su • DS-TEMP INACTIVE • 0.2 kW
M-Sa • DS-TEMP INACTIVE • 0.2 kW
4606v INDONESIA
†RRI, Serui, Papua
DS • 0.5 kW
4620 CHINA
†NEI MENGGU PBS, Hohhot
DS • 50 kW
4635 TAJIKISTAN
†TAJIK RADIO, Dushanbe
RUSSIAN, ETC • DS-1 • 100 kW
4649 BOLIVIA
†RADIO SANTA ANA, Santa Ana
DS • 1 kW
Irr • DS • 1 kW
4655 PERU
†RADIO NUEVO AMANECER, Celendín
DS
4659v LAOS
†LAO NATIONAL RADIO, Xam Nua
DS
4682v BOLIVIA
RADIO PAITITI, Guayaramerín
DS • 0.75 kW
4697v INDONESIA
RK INFORMASI PER'N, Surabaya, Jawa
Irr • DS • 2.5 kW
4700.6 PERU
†LA VOZ DE ANTA, Acobamba
DS
4702.2 BOLIVIA
†RADIO ECO, San Borja
DS • 1 kW
4716.8 BOLIVIA
†RADIO YURA, Yura
SPANISH & QUECHUA • DS • 1 kW
Irr • DS • 1 kW
4720.2 BOLIVIA
†RADIO ABAROA, Riberalta
Irr • DS • 0.5 kW
DS • 0.5 kW
4725 MYANMAR (BURMA)
†RADIO MYANMAR, Yangon
DS • 50 kW
Irr • DS • 50 kW
4732v BOLIVIA
RADIO LA PALABRA, Sta Ana de Yacuma
DS • 0.1 kW
M-Sa • DS • 0.1 kW
4748v PERU
RADIO HUANTA 2000, Huanta
Tu-Su • SPANISH & QUECHUA • DS • 0.3/1 kW • ALT. FREQ. TO 4757v kHz
SPANISH & QUECHUA • DS • 0.3/1 kW • ALT. FREQ. TO 4757v kHz
0 1 2 3 4 5 6 7 8 9 10 11 12 13 14 15 16 17 18 19 20 21 22 23 24

SEASONAL S OR W 1-HR TIMESHIFT MIDYEAR ⬅ OR ➡ JAMMING / OR ∧ EARLIEST HEARD ◁ LATEST HEARD ▷ NEW FOR 2002 †

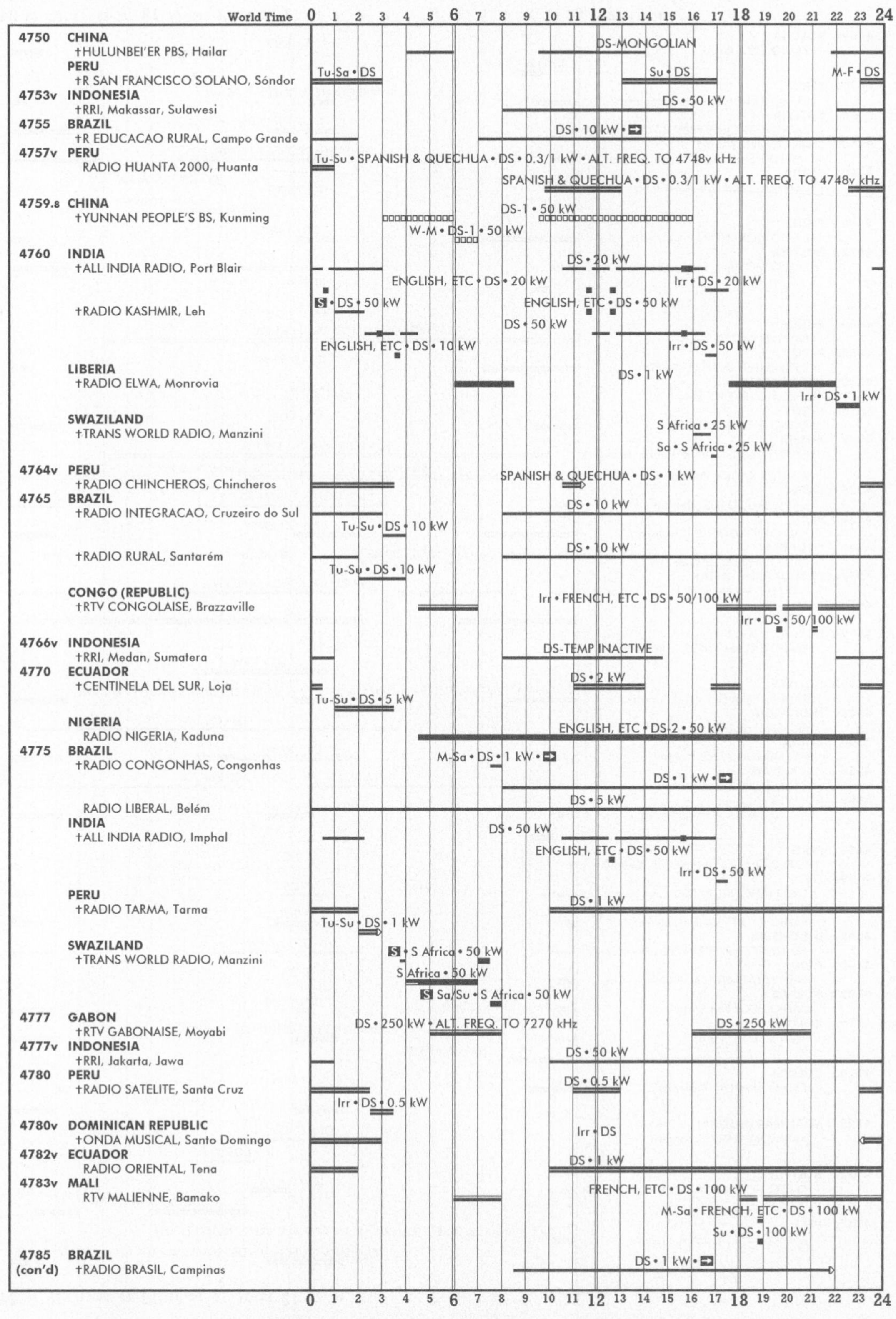
World Time 0 1 2 3 4 5 6 7 8 9 10 11 12 13 14 15 16 17 18 19 20 21 22 23 24
4750 CHINA
†HULUNBEI'ER PBS, Hailar
DS-MONGOLIAN
PERU
†R SAN FRANCISCO SOLANO, Sóndor
Tu-Sa • DS
Su • DS
M-F • DS
4753v INDONESIA
†RRI, Makassar, Sulawesi
DS • 50 kW
4755 BRAZIL
†R EDUCACAO RURAL, Campo Grande
DS • 10 kW •
4757v PERU
RADIO HUANTA 2000, Huanta
Tu-Su • SPANISH & QUECHUA • DS • 0.3/1 kW • ALT. FREQ. TO 4748v kHz
SPANISH & QUECHUA • DS • 0.3/1 kW • ALT. FREQ. TO 4748v kHz
4759.8 CHINA
†YUNNAN PEOPLE'S BS, Kunming
DS-1 • 50 kW
W-M • DS-1 • 50 kW
4760 INDIA
†ALL INDIA RADIO, Port Blair
DS • 20 kW
ENGLISH, ETC • DS • 20 kW
Irr • DS • 20 kW
†RADIO KASHMIR, Leh
S • DS • 50 kW
ENGLISH, ETC • DS • 50 kW
DS • 50 kW
ENGLISH, ETC • DS • 10 kW
Irr • DS • 50 kW
LIBERIA
†RADIO ELWA, Monrovia
DS • 1 kW
Irr • DS • 1 kW
SWAZILAND
†TRANS WORLD RADIO, Manzini
S Africa • 25 kW
Sa • S Africa • 25 kW
4764v PERU
†RADIO CHINCHEROS, Chincheros
SPANISH & QUECHUA • DS • 1 kW
4765 BRAZIL
†RADIO INTEGRACAO, Cruzeiro do Sul
DS • 10 kW
Tu-Su • DS • 10 kW
†RADIO RURAL, Santarém
DS • 10 kW
Tu-Su • DS • 10 kW
CONGO (REPUBLIC)
†RTV CONGOLAISE, Brazzaville
Irr • FRENCH, ETC • DS • 50/100 kW
Irr • DS • 50/100 kW
4766v INDONESIA
†RRI, Medan, Sumatera
DS-TEMP INACTIVE
4770 ECUADOR
†CENTINELA DEL SUR, Loja
DS • 2 kW
Tu-Su • DS • 5 kW
NIGERIA
RADIO NIGERIA, Kaduna
ENGLISH, ETC • DS-2 • 50 kW
4775 BRAZIL
†RADIO CONGONHAS, Congonhas
M-Sa • DS • 1 kW •
DS • 1 kW •
RADIO LIBERAL, Belém
DS • 5 kW
INDIA
†ALL INDIA RADIO, Imphal
DS • 50 kW
ENGLISH, ETC • DS • 50 kW
Irr • DS • 50 kW
PERU
†RADIO TARMA, Tarma
DS • 1 kW
Tu-Su • DS • 1 kW
SWAZILAND
†TRANS WORLD RADIO, Manzini
S • S Africa • 50 kW
S Africa • 50 kW
S Sa/Su • S Africa • 50 kW
4777 GABON
†RTV GABONAISE, Moyabi
DS • 250 kW • ALT. FREQ. TO 7270 kHz
DS • 250 kW
4777v INDONESIA
†RRI, Jakarta, Jawa
DS • 50 kW
4780 PERU
†RADIO SATELITE, Santa Cruz
DS • 0.5 kW
Irr • DS • 0.5 kW
4780v DOMINICAN REPUBLIC
†ONDA MUSICAL, Santo Domingo
Irr • DS
4782v ECUADOR
RADIO ORIENTAL, Tena
DS • 1 kW
4783v MALI
RTV MALIENNE, Bamako
FRENCH, ETC • DS • 100 kW
M-Sa • FRENCH, ETC • DS • 100 kW
Su • DS • 100 kW
4785 BRAZIL
(con'd) †RADIO BRASIL, Campinas
DS • 1 kW •
0 1 2 3 4 5 6 7 8 9 10 11 12 13 14 15 16 17 18 19 20 21 22 23 24

ENGLISH ▬ ARABIC ▭ CHINESE ▫▫▫ FRENCH ═ GERMAN ═ RUSSIAN ═ SPANISH ═ OTHER —

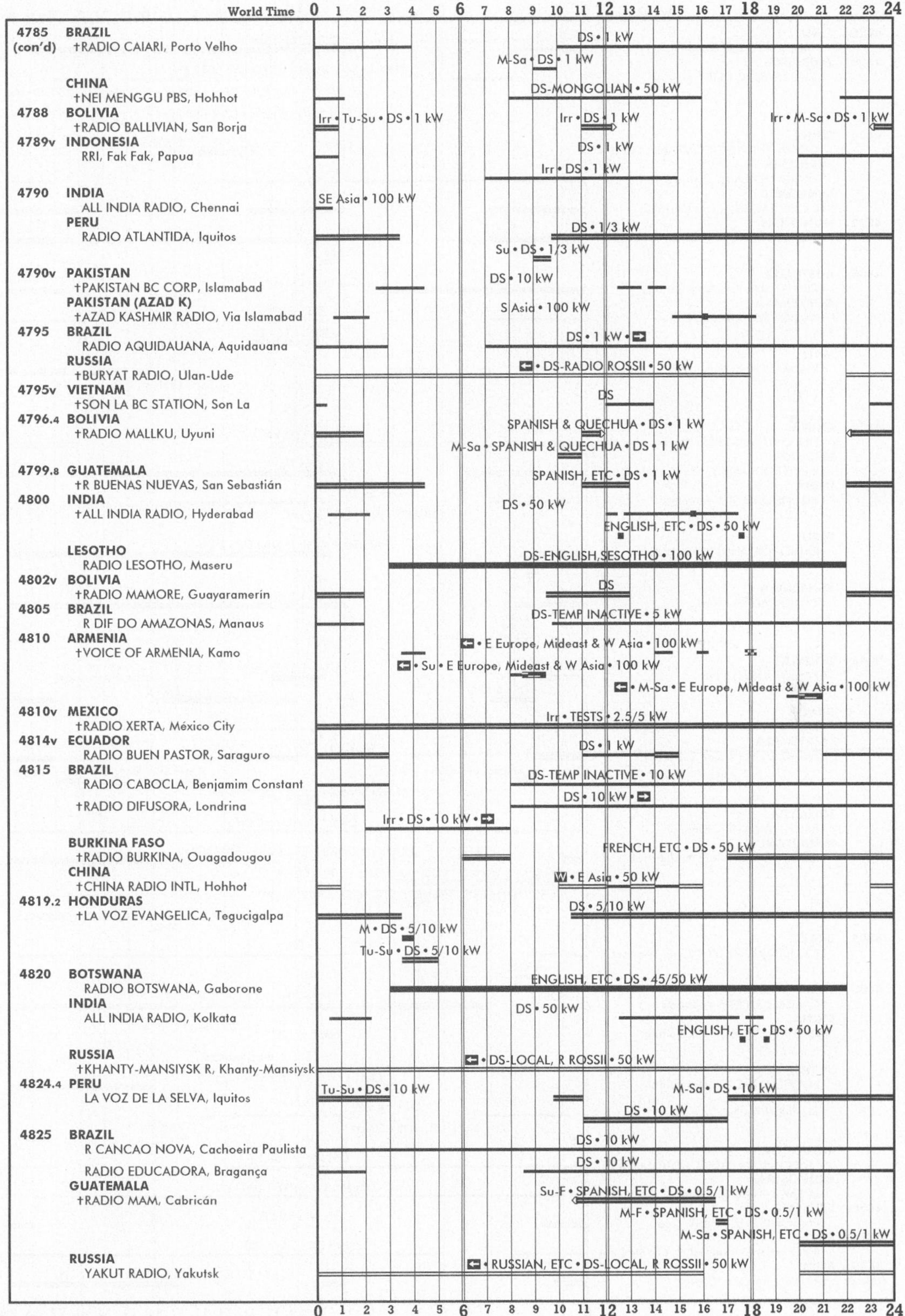
World Time 0 1 2 3 4 5 6 7 8 9 10 11 12 13 14 15 16 17 18 19 20 21 22 23 24
4785 (con'd) BRAZIL
†RADIO CAIARI, Porto Velho
DS • 1 kW
M-Sa • DS • 1 kW
CHINA
†NEI MENGGU PBS, Hohhot
DS-MONGOLIAN • 50 kW
4788 BOLIVIA
†RADIO BALLIVIAN, San Borja
Irr • Tu-Su • DS • 1 kW
Irr • DS • 1 kW
Irr • M-Sa • DS • 1 kW
4789v INDONESIA
RRI, Fak Fak, Papua
DS • 1 kW
Irr • DS • 1 kW
4790 INDIA
ALL INDIA RADIO, Chennai
SE Asia • 100 kW
PERU
RADIO ATLANTIDA, Iquitos
DS • 1/3 kW
Su • DS • 1/3 kW
4790v PAKISTAN
†PAKISTAN BC CORP, Islamabad
DS • 10 kW
PAKISTAN (AZAD K)
†AZAD KASHMIR RADIO, Via Islamabad
S Asia • 100 kW
4795 BRAZIL
RADIO AQUIDAUANA, Aquidauana
DS • 1 kW
RUSSIA
†BURYAT RADIO, Ulan-Ude
DS-RADIO ROSSII • 50 kW
4795v VIETNAM
†SON LA BC STATION, Son La
DS
4796.4 BOLIVIA
†RADIO MALLKU, Uyuni
SPANISH & QUECHUA • DS • 1 kW
M-Sa • SPANISH & QUECHUA • DS • 1 kW
4799.8 GUATEMALA
†R BUENAS NUEVAS, San Sebastián
SPANISH, ETC • DS • 1 kW
4800 INDIA
†ALL INDIA RADIO, Hyderabad
DS • 50 kW
ENGLISH, ETC • DS • 50 kW
LESOTHO
RADIO LESOTHO, Maseru
DS-ENGLISH,SESOTHO • 100 kW
4802v BOLIVIA
†RADIO MAMORE, Guayaramerín
DS
4805 BRAZIL
R DIF DO AMAZONAS, Manaus
DS-TEMP INACTIVE • 5 kW
4810 ARMENIA
†VOICE OF ARMENIA, Kamo
E Europe, Mideast & W Asia • 100 kW
Su • E Europe, Mideast & W Asia • 100 kW
M-Sa • E Europe, Mideast & W Asia • 100 kW
4810v MEXICO
†RADIO XERTA, México City
Irr • TESTS • 2.5/5 kW
4814v ECUADOR
RADIO BUEN PASTOR, Saraguro
DS • 1 kW
4815 BRAZIL
RADIO CABOCLA, Benjamim Constant
DS-TEMP INACTIVE • 10 kW
†RADIO DIFUSORA, Londrina
DS • 10 kW
Irr • DS • 10 kW
BURKINA FASO
†RADIO BURKINA, Ouagadougou
FRENCH, ETC • DS • 50 kW
CHINA
†CHINA RADIO INTL, Hohhot
W • E Asia • 50 kW
4819.2 HONDURAS
†LA VOZ EVANGELICA, Tegucigalpa
DS • 5/10 kW
M • DS • 5/10 kW
Tu-Su • DS • 5/10 kW
4820 BOTSWANA
RADIO BOTSWANA, Gaborone
ENGLISH, ETC • DS • 45/50 kW
INDIA
ALL INDIA RADIO, Kolkata
DS • 50 kW
ENGLISH, ETC • DS • 50 kW
RUSSIA
†KHANTY-MANSIYSK R, Khanty-Mansiysk
DS-LOCAL, R ROSSII • 50 kW
4824.4 PERU
LA VOZ DE LA SELVA, Iquitos
Tu-Su • DS • 10 kW
M-Sa • DS • 10 kW
DS • 10 kW
4825 BRAZIL
R CANCAO NOVA, Cachoeira Paulista
DS • 10 kW
RADIO EDUCADORA, Bragança
DS • 10 kW
GUATEMALA
†RADIO MAM, Cabricán
Su-F • SPANISH, ETC • DS • 0.5/1 kW
M-F • SPANISH, ETC • DS • 0.5/1 kW
M-Sa • SPANISH, ETC • DS • 0.5/1 kW
RUSSIA
YAKUT RADIO, Yakutsk
RUSSIAN, ETC • DS-LOCAL, R ROSSII • 50 kW
0 1 2 3 4 5 6 7 8 9 10 11 12 13 14 15 16 17 18 19 20 21 22 23 24

SEASONAL S OR W   1-HR TIMESHIFT MIDYEAR OR   JAMMING / OR ∧   EARLIEST HEARD ◁   LATEST HEARD ▷   NEW FOR 2002 †

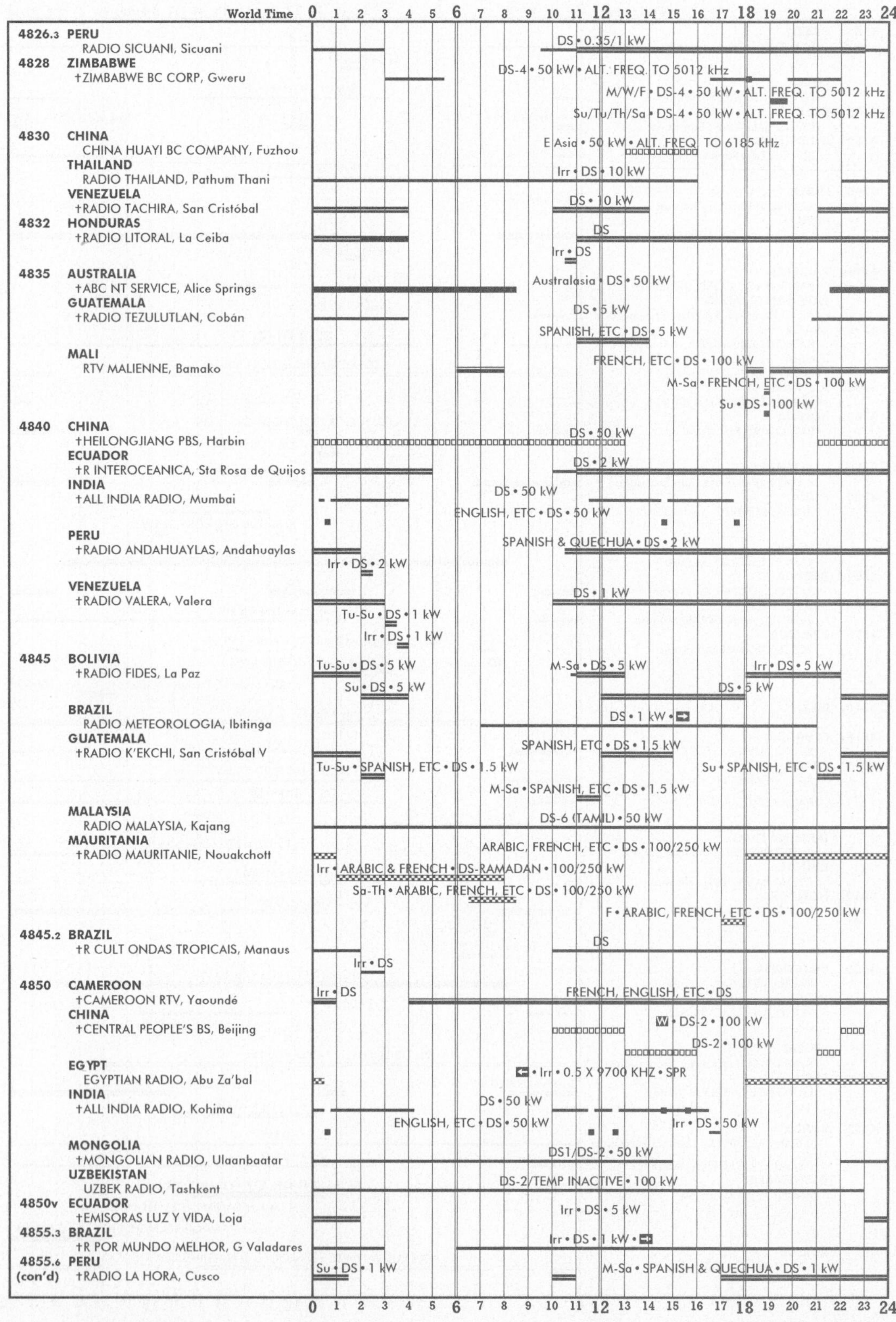
World Time 0 1 2 3 4 5 6 7 8 9 10 11 12 13 14 15 16 17 18 19 20 21 22 23 24
4826.3 PERU
RADIO SICUANI, Sicuani
DS • 0.35/1 kW
4828 ZIMBABWE
†ZIMBABWE BC CORP, Gweru
DS-4 • 50 kW • ALT. FREQ. TO 5012 kHz
M/W/F • DS-4 • 50 kW • ALT. FREQ. TO 5012 kHz
Su/Tu/Th/Sa • DS-4 • 50 kW • ALT. FREQ. TO 5012 kHz
4830 CHINA
CHINA HUAYI BC COMPANY, Fuzhou
E Asia • 50 kW • ALT. FREQ. TO 6185 kHz
THAILAND
RADIO THAILAND, Pathum Thani
Irr • DS • 10 kW
VENEZUELA
†RADIO TACHIRA, San Cristóbal
DS • 10 kW
4832 HONDURAS
†RADIO LITORAL, La Ceiba
DS
Irr • DS
4835 AUSTRALIA
†ABC NT SERVICE, Alice Springs
Australasia • DS • 50 kW
GUATEMALA
†RADIO TEZULUTLAN, Cobán
DS • 5 kW
SPANISH, ETC • DS • 5 kW
MALI
RTV MALIENNE, Bamako
FRENCH, ETC • DS • 100 kW
M-Sa • FRENCH, ETC • DS • 100 kW
Su • DS • 100 kW
4840 CHINA
†HEILONGJIANG PBS, Harbin
DS • 50 kW
ECUADOR
†R INTEROCEANICA, Sta Rosa de Quijos
DS • 2 kW
INDIA
†ALL INDIA RADIO, Mumbai
DS • 50 kW
ENGLISH, ETC • DS • 50 kW
PERU
†RADIO ANDAHUAYLAS, Andahuaylas
SPANISH & QUECHUA • DS • 2 kW
Irr • DS • 2 kW
VENEZUELA
†RADIO VALERA, Valera
DS • 1 kW
Tu-Su • DS • 1 kW
Irr • DS • 1 kW
4845 BOLIVIA
†RADIO FIDES, La Paz
Tu-Su • DS • 5 kW
M-Sa • DS • 5 kW
Irr • DS • 5 kW
Su • DS • 5 kW
DS • 5 kW
BRAZIL
RADIO METEOROLOGIA, Ibitinga
DS • 1 kW •
GUATEMALA
†RADIO K'EKCHI, San Cristóbal V
SPANISH, ETC • DS • 1.5 kW
Tu-Su • SPANISH, ETC • DS • 1.5 kW
Su • SPANISH, ETC • DS • 1.5 kW
M-Sa • SPANISH, ETC • DS • 1.5 kW
MALAYSIA
RADIO MALAYSIA, Kajang
DS-6 (TAMIL) • 50 kW
MAURITANIA
†RADIO MAURITANIE, Nouakchott
ARABIC, FRENCH, ETC • DS • 100/250 kW
Irr • ARABIC & FRENCH • DS-RAMADAN • 100/250 kW
Sa-Th • ARABIC, FRENCH, ETC • DS • 100/250 kW
F • ARABIC, FRENCH, ETC • DS • 100/250 kW
4845.2 BRAZIL
†R CULT ONDAS TROPICAIS, Manaus
DS
Irr • DS
4850 CAMEROON
†CAMEROON RTV, Yaoundé
Irr • DS
FRENCH, ENGLISH, ETC • DS
CHINA
†CENTRAL PEOPLE'S BS, Beijing
W • DS-2 • 100 kW
DS-2 • 100 kW
EGYPT
EGYPTIAN RADIO, Abu Za'bal
• Irr • 0.5 X 9700 KHZ • SPR
INDIA
†ALL INDIA RADIO, Kohima
DS • 50 kW
ENGLISH, ETC • DS • 50 kW
Irr • DS • 50 kW
MONGOLIA
†MONGOLIAN RADIO, Ulaanbaatar
DS1/DS-2 • 50 kW
UZBEKISTAN
UZBEK RADIO, Tashkent
DS-2/TEMP INACTIVE • 100 kW
4850v ECUADOR
†EMISORAS LUZ Y VIDA, Loja
Irr • DS • 5 kW
4855.3 BRAZIL
†R POR MUNDO MELHOR, G Valadares
Irr • DS • 1 kW •
4855.6 PERU
(con'd)
†RADIO LA HORA, Cusco
Su • DS • 1 kW
M-Sa • SPANISH & QUECHUA • DS • 1 kW
0 1 2 3 4 5 6 7 8 9 10 11 12 13 14 15 16 17 18 19 20 21 22 23 24
ENGLISH
ARABIC
CHINESE
FRENCH
GERMAN
RUSSIAN
SPANISH
OTHER

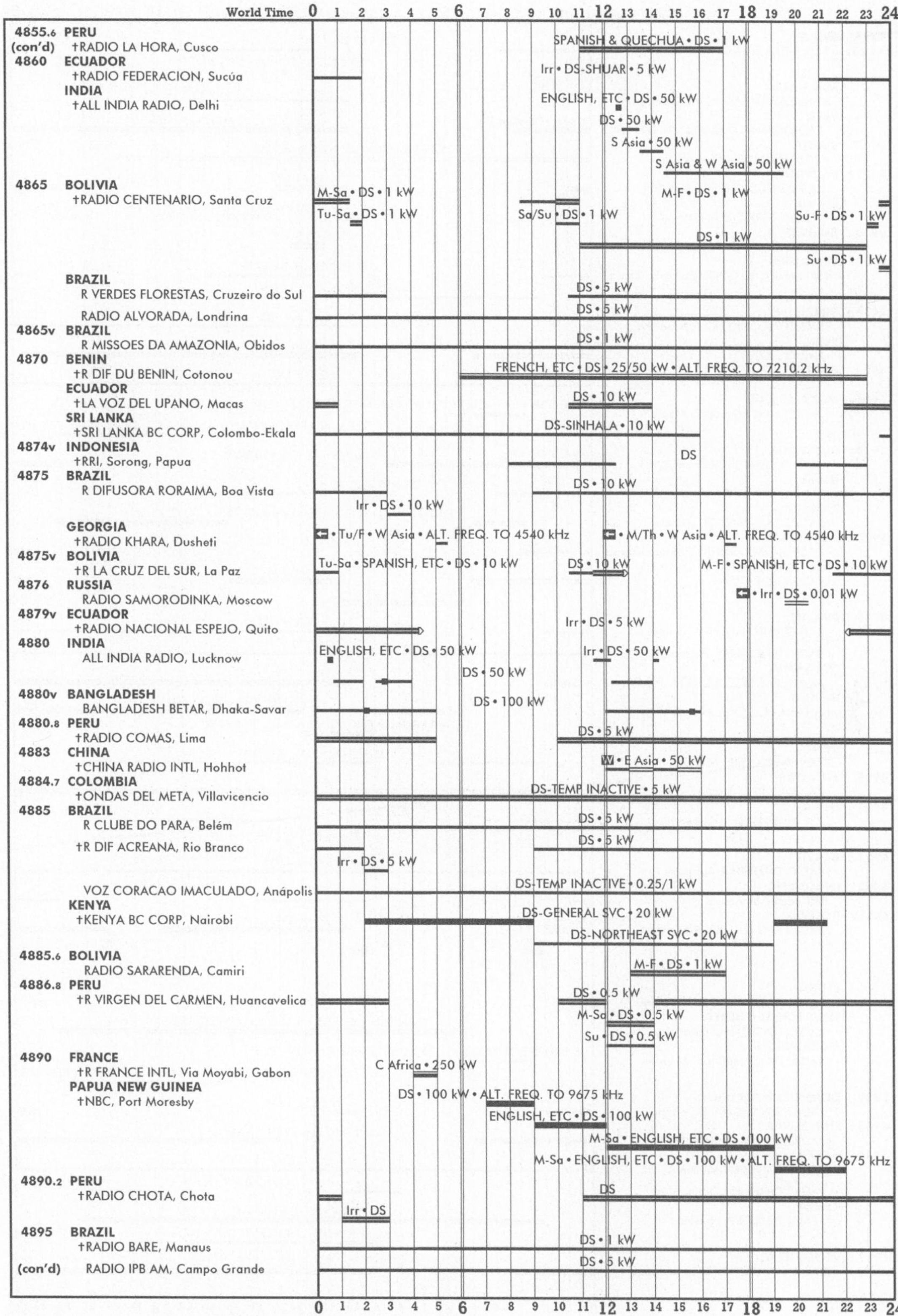
World Time 0 1 2 3 4 5 6 7 8 9 10 11 12 13 14 15 16 17 18 19 20 21 22 23 24
4855.6 PERU
(con'd) †RADIO LA HORA, Cusco
SPANISH & QUECHUA • DS • 1 kW
4860 ECUADOR
†RADIO FEDERACION, Sucúa
Irr • DS-SHUAR • 5 kW
INDIA
†ALL INDIA RADIO, Delhi
ENGLISH, ETC • DS • 50 kW
DS • 50 kW
S Asia • 50 kW
S Asia & W Asia • 50 kW
4865 BOLIVIA
†RADIO CENTENARIO, Santa Cruz
M-Sa • DS • 1 kW
M-F • DS • 1 kW
Tu-Sa • DS • 1 kW
Sa/Su • DS • 1 kW
Su-F • DS • 1 kW
DS • 1 kW
Su • DS • 1 kW
BRAZIL
R VERDES FLORESTAS, Cruzeiro do Sul
DS • 5 kW
RADIO ALVORADA, Londrina
DS • 5 kW
4865v BRAZIL
R MISSOES DA AMAZONIA, Obidos
DS • 1 kW
4870 BENIN
†R DIF DU BENIN, Cotonou
FRENCH, ETC • DS • 25/50 kW • ALT. FREQ. TO 7210.2 kHz
ECUADOR
†LA VOZ DEL UPANO, Macas
DS • 10 kW
SRI LANKA
†SRI LANKA BC CORP, Colombo-Ekala
DS-SINHALA • 10 kW
4874v INDONESIA
†RRI, Sorong, Papua
DS
4875 BRAZIL
R DIFUSORA RORAIMA, Boa Vista
DS • 10 kW
Irr • DS • 10 kW
GEORGIA
†RADIO KHARA, Dusheti
Tu/F • W Asia • ALT. FREQ. TO 4540 kHz
M/Th • W Asia • ALT. FREQ. TO 4540 kHz
4875v BOLIVIA
†R LA CRUZ DEL SUR, La Paz
Tu-Sa • SPANISH, ETC • DS • 10 kW
DS • 10 kW
M-F • SPANISH, ETC • DS • 10 kW
4876 RUSSIA
RADIO SAMORODINKA, Moscow
Irr • DS • 0.01 kW
4879v ECUADOR
†RADIO NACIONAL ESPEJO, Quito
Irr • DS • 5 kW
4880 INDIA
ALL INDIA RADIO, Lucknow
ENGLISH, ETC • DS • 50 kW
Irr • DS • 50 kW
DS • 50 kW
4880v BANGLADESH
BANGLADESH BETAR, Dhaka-Savar
DS • 100 kW
4880.8 PERU
†RADIO COMAS, Lima
DS • 5 kW
4883 CHINA
†CHINA RADIO INTL, Hohhot
W • E Asia • 50 kW
4884.7 COLOMBIA
†ONDAS DEL META, Villavicencio
DS-TEMP INACTIVE • 5 kW
4885 BRAZIL
R CLUBE DO PARA, Belém
DS • 5 kW
†R DIF ACREANA, Rio Branco
DS • 5 kW
Irr • DS • 5 kW
VOZ CORACAO IMACULADO, Anápolis
DS-TEMP INACTIVE • 0.25/1 kW
KENYA
†KENYA BC CORP, Nairobi
DS-GENERAL SVC • 20 kW
DS-NORTHEAST SVC • 20 kW
4885.6 BOLIVIA
RADIO SARARENDA, Camiri
M-F • DS • 1 kW
4886.8 PERU
†R VIRGEN DEL CARMEN, Huancavelica
DS • 0.5 kW
M-Sa • DS • 0.5 kW
Su • DS • 0.5 kW
4890 FRANCE
†R FRANCE INTL, Via Moyabi, Gabon
C Africa • 250 kW
PAPUA NEW GUINEA
†NBC, Port Moresby
DS • 100 kW • ALT. FREQ. TO 9675 kHz
ENGLISH, ETC • DS • 100 kW
M-Sa • ENGLISH, ETC • DS • 100 kW
M-Sa • ENGLISH, ETC • DS • 100 kW • ALT. FREQ. TO 9675 kHz
4890.2 PERU
†RADIO CHOTA, Chota
DS
Irr • DS
4895 BRAZIL
†RADIO BARE, Manaus
DS • 1 kW
(con'd) RADIO IPB AM, Campo Grande
DS • 5 kW
0 1 2 3 4 5 6 7 8 9 10 11 12 13 14 15 16 17 18 19 20 21 22 23 24

SEASONAL S OR W 1-HR TIMESHIFT MIDYEAR ⇦ OR ⇨ JAMMING / OR ∧ EARLIEST HEARD ◁ LATEST HEARD ▷ NEW FOR 2002 †

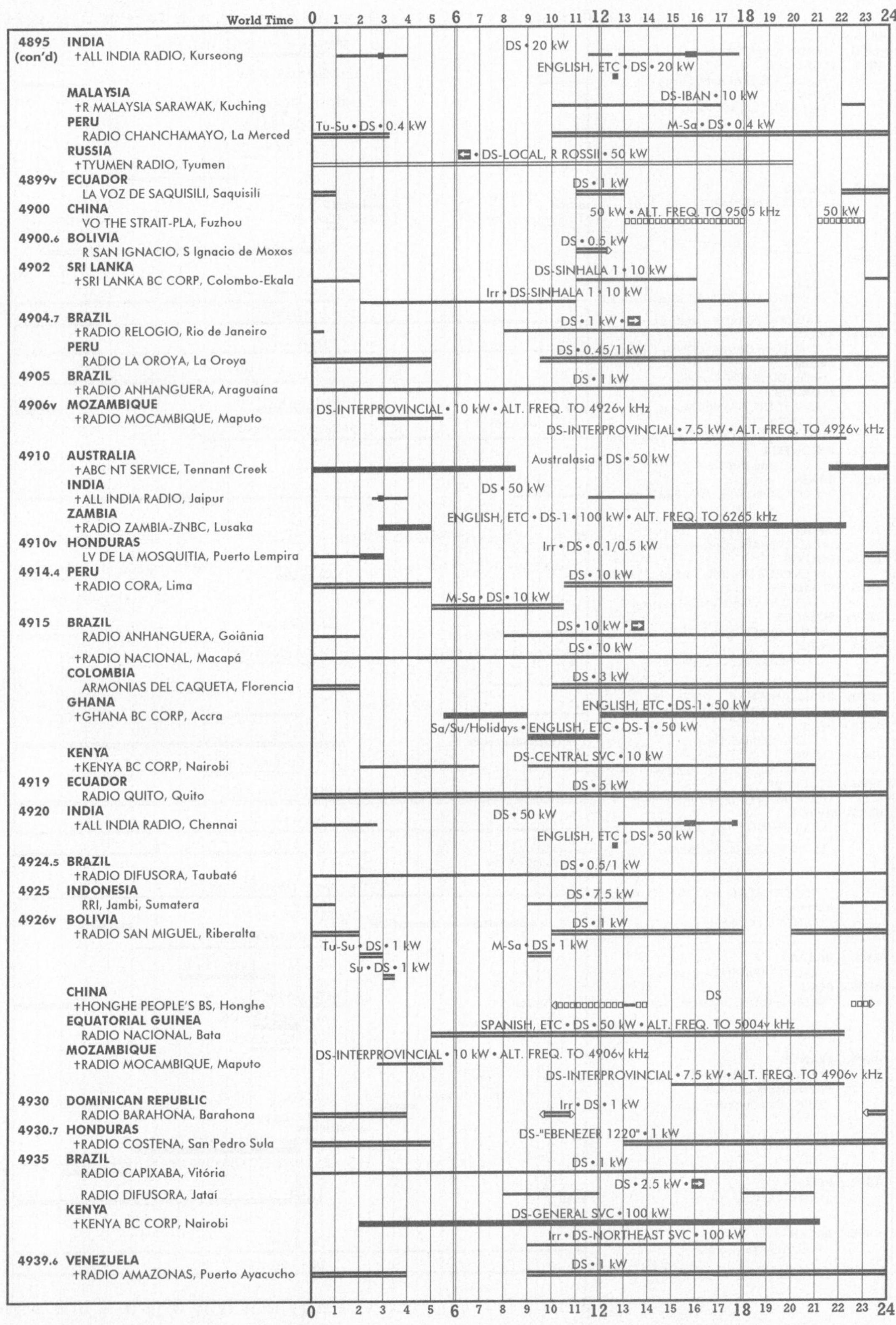
World Time 0 1 2 3 4 5 6 7 8 9 10 11 12 13 14 15 16 17 18 19 20 21 22 23 24
4895 (con'd) INDIA
†ALL INDIA RADIO, Kurseong
DS • 20 kW
ENGLISH, ETC • DS • 20 kW
MALAYSIA
†R MALAYSIA SARAWAK, Kuching
DS-IBAN • 10 kW
PERU
RADIO CHANCHAMAYO, La Merced
Tu-Su • DS • 0.4 kW
M-Sa • DS • 0.4 kW
RUSSIA
†TYUMEN RADIO, Tyumen
DS-LOCAL, R ROSSII • 50 kW
4899v ECUADOR
LA VOZ DE SAQUISILI, Saquisilí
DS • 1 kW
4900 CHINA
VO THE STRAIT-PLA, Fuzhou
50 kW • ALT. FREQ. TO 9505 kHz
50 kW
4900.6 BOLIVIA
R SAN IGNACIO, S Ignacio de Moxos
DS • 0.5 kW
4902 SRI LANKA
†SRI LANKA BC CORP, Colombo-Ekala
DS-SINHALA 1 • 10 kW
Irr • DS-SINHALA 1 • 10 kW
4904.7 BRAZIL
†RADIO RELOGIO, Rio de Janeiro
DS • 1 kW
PERU
RADIO LA OROYA, La Oroya
DS • 0.45/1 kW
4905 BRAZIL
†RADIO ANHANGUERA, Araguaína
DS • 1 kW
4906v MOZAMBIQUE
†RADIO MOCAMBIQUE, Maputo
DS-INTERPROVINCIAL • 10 kW • ALT. FREQ. TO 4926v kHz
DS-INTERPROVINCIAL • 7.5 kW • ALT. FREQ. TO 4926v kHz
4910 AUSTRALIA
†ABC NT SERVICE, Tennant Creek
Australasia • DS • 50 kW
INDIA
†ALL INDIA RADIO, Jaipur
DS • 50 kW
ZAMBIA
†RADIO ZAMBIA-ZNBC, Lusaka
ENGLISH, ETC • DS-1 • 100 kW • ALT. FREQ. TO 6265 kHz
4910v HONDURAS
LV DE LA MOSQUITIA, Puerto Lempira
Irr • DS • 0.1/0.5 kW
4914.4 PERU
†RADIO CORA, Lima
DS • 10 kW
M-Sa • DS • 10 kW
4915 BRAZIL
RADIO ANHANGUERA, Goiânia
DS • 10 kW
†RADIO NACIONAL, Macapá
DS • 10 kW
COLOMBIA
ARMONIAS DEL CAQUETA, Florencia
DS • 3 kW
GHANA
†GHANA BC CORP, Accra
ENGLISH, ETC • DS-1 • 50 kW
Sa/Su/Holidays • ENGLISH, ETC • DS-1 • 50 kW
KENYA
†KENYA BC CORP, Nairobi
DS-CENTRAL SVC • 10 kW
4919 ECUADOR
RADIO QUITO, Quito
DS • 5 kW
4920 INDIA
†ALL INDIA RADIO, Chennai
DS • 50 kW
ENGLISH, ETC • DS • 50 kW
4924.5 BRAZIL
†RADIO DIFUSORA, Taubaté
DS • 0.5/1 kW
4925 INDONESIA
RRI, Jambi, Sumatera
DS • 7.5 kW
4926v BOLIVIA
†RADIO SAN MIGUEL, Riberalta
DS • 1 kW
Tu-Su • DS • 1 kW
M-Sa • DS • 1 kW
Su • DS • 1 kW
CHINA
†HONGHE PEOPLE'S BS, Honghe
DS
EQUATORIAL GUINEA
RADIO NACIONAL, Bata
SPANISH, ETC • DS • 50 kW • ALT. FREQ. TO 5004v kHz
MOZAMBIQUE
†RADIO MOCAMBIQUE, Maputo
DS-INTERPROVINCIAL • 10 kW • ALT. FREQ. TO 4906v kHz
DS-INTERPROVINCIAL • 7.5 kW • ALT. FREQ. TO 4906v kHz
4930 DOMINICAN REPUBLIC
RADIO BARAHONA, Barahona
Irr • DS • 1 kW
4930.7 HONDURAS
†RADIO COSTENA, San Pedro Sula
DS-"EBENEZER 1220" • 1 kW
4935 BRAZIL
RADIO CAPIXABA, Vitória
DS • 1 kW
RADIO DIFUSORA, Jataí
DS • 2.5 kW
KENYA
†KENYA BC CORP, Nairobi
DS-GENERAL SVC • 100 kW
Irr • DS-NORTHEAST SVC • 100 kW
4939.6 VENEZUELA
†RADIO AMAZONAS, Puerto Ayacucho
DS • 1 kW
0 1 2 3 4 5 6 7 8 9 10 11 12 13 14 15 16 17 18 19 20 21 22 23 24
ENGLISH ARABIC CHINESE FRENCH GERMAN RUSSIAN SPANISH OTHER

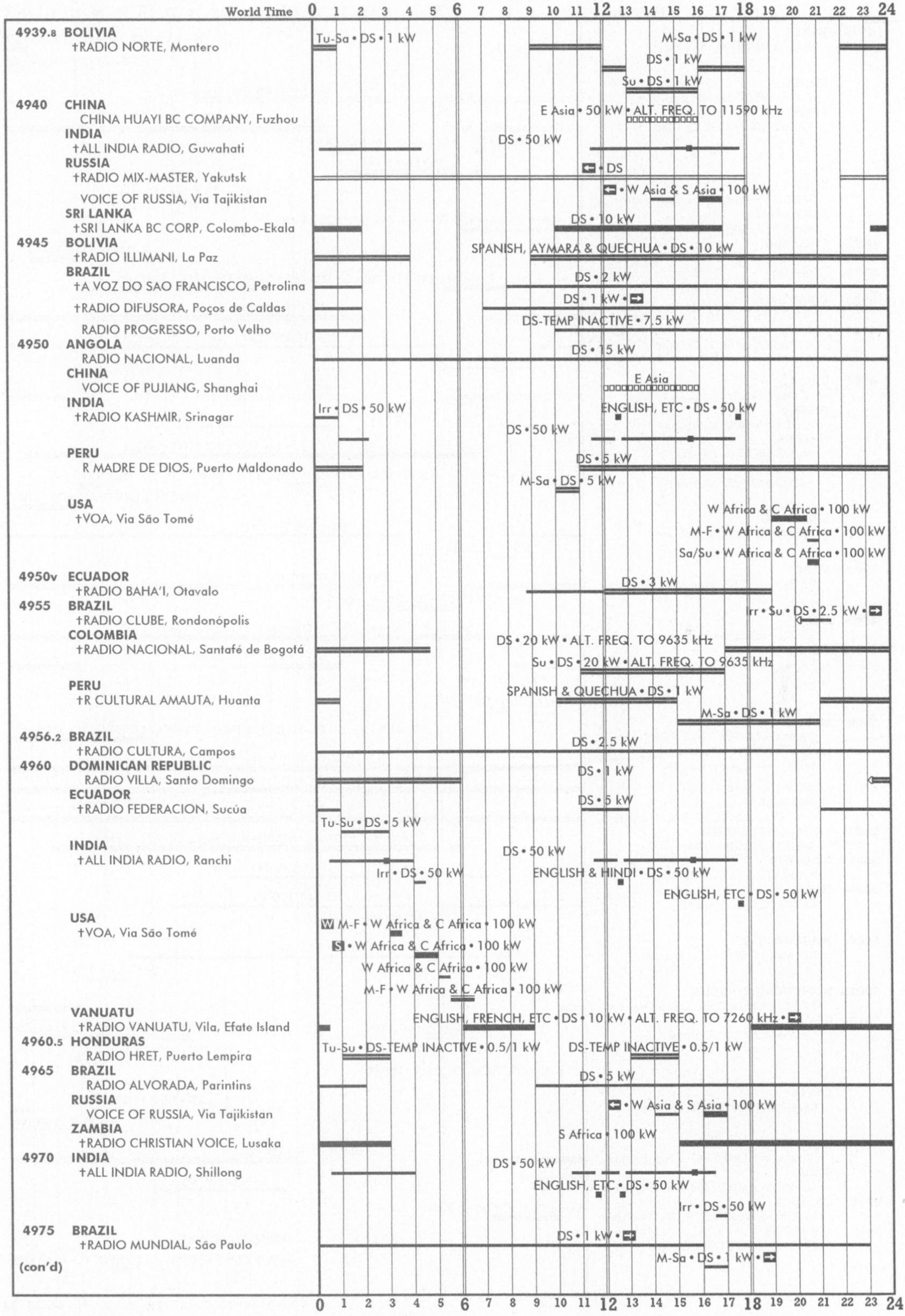
World Time 0 1 2 3 4 5 6 7 8 9 10 11 12 13 14 15 16 17 18 19 20 21 22 23 24
4939.8 BOLIVIA
†RADIO NORTE, Montero
Tu-Sa • DS • 1 kW
M-Sa • DS • 1 kW
DS • 1 kW
Su • DS • 1 kW
4940 CHINA
CHINA HUAYI BC COMPANY, Fuzhou
E Asia • 50 kW • ALT. FREQ. TO 11590 kHz
INDIA
†ALL INDIA RADIO, Guwahati
DS • 50 kW
RUSSIA
†RADIO MIX-MASTER, Yakutsk
DS
VOICE OF RUSSIA, Via Tajikistan
W Asia & S Asia • 100 kW
SRI LANKA
†SRI LANKA BC CORP, Colombo-Ekala
DS • 10 kW
4945 BOLIVIA
†RADIO ILLIMANI, La Paz
SPANISH, AYMARA & QUECHUA • DS • 10 kW
BRAZIL
†A VOZ DO SAO FRANCISCO, Petrolina
DS • 2 kW
†RADIO DIFUSORA, Poços de Caldas
DS • 1 kW
RADIO PROGRESSO, Porto Velho
DS-TEMP INACTIVE • 7.5 kW
4950 ANGOLA
RADIO NACIONAL, Luanda
DS • 15 kW
CHINA
VOICE OF PUJIANG, Shanghai
E Asia
INDIA
†RADIO KASHMIR, Srinagar
Irr • DS • 50 kW
ENGLISH, ETC • DS • 50 kW
DS • 50 kW
PERU
R MADRE DE DIOS, Puerto Maldonado
DS • 5 kW
M-Sa • DS • 5 kW
USA
†VOA, Via São Tomé
W Africa & C Africa • 100 kW
M-F • W Africa & C Africa • 100 kW
Sa/Su • W Africa & C Africa • 100 kW
4950v ECUADOR
†RADIO BAHA'I, Otavalo
DS • 3 kW
4955 BRAZIL
†RADIO CLUBE, Rondonópolis
Irr • Su • DS • 2.5 kW
COLOMBIA
†RADIO NACIONAL, Santafé de Bogotá
DS • 20 kW • ALT. FREQ. TO 9635 kHz
Su • DS • 20 kW • ALT. FREQ. TO 9635 kHz
PERU
†R CULTURAL AMAUTA, Huanta
SPANISH & QUECHUA • DS • 1 kW
M-Sa • DS • 1 kW
4956.2 BRAZIL
†RADIO CULTURA, Campos
DS • 2.5 kW
4960 DOMINICAN REPUBLIC
RADIO VILLA, Santo Domingo
DS • 1 kW
ECUADOR
†RADIO FEDERACION, Sucúa
DS • 5 kW
Tu-Su • DS • 5 kW
INDIA
†ALL INDIA RADIO, Ranchi
DS • 50 kW
Irr • DS • 50 kW
ENGLISH & HINDI • DS • 50 kW
ENGLISH, ETC • DS • 50 kW
USA
†VOA, Via São Tomé
W M-F • W Africa & C Africa • 100 kW
S • W Africa & C Africa • 100 kW
W Africa & C Africa • 100 kW
M-F • W Africa & C Africa • 100 kW
VANUATU
†RADIO VANUATU, Vila, Efate Island
ENGLISH, FRENCH, ETC • DS • 10 kW • ALT. FREQ. TO 7260 kHz
4960.5 HONDURAS
RADIO HRET, Puerto Lempira
Tu-Su • DS-TEMP INACTIVE • 0.5/1 kW
DS-TEMP INACTIVE • 0.5/1 kW
4965 BRAZIL
RADIO ALVORADA, Parintins
DS • 5 kW
RUSSIA
VOICE OF RUSSIA, Via Tajikistan
W Asia & S Asia • 100 kW
ZAMBIA
†RADIO CHRISTIAN VOICE, Lusaka
S Africa • 100 kW
4970 INDIA
†ALL INDIA RADIO, Shillong
DS • 50 kW
ENGLISH, ETC • DS • 50 kW
Irr • DS • 50 kW
4975 BRAZIL
†RADIO MUNDIAL, São Paulo
DS • 1 kW
M-Sa • DS • 1 kW
(con'd)
0 1 2 3 4 5 6 7 8 9 10 11 12 13 14 15 16 17 18 19 20 21 22 23 24

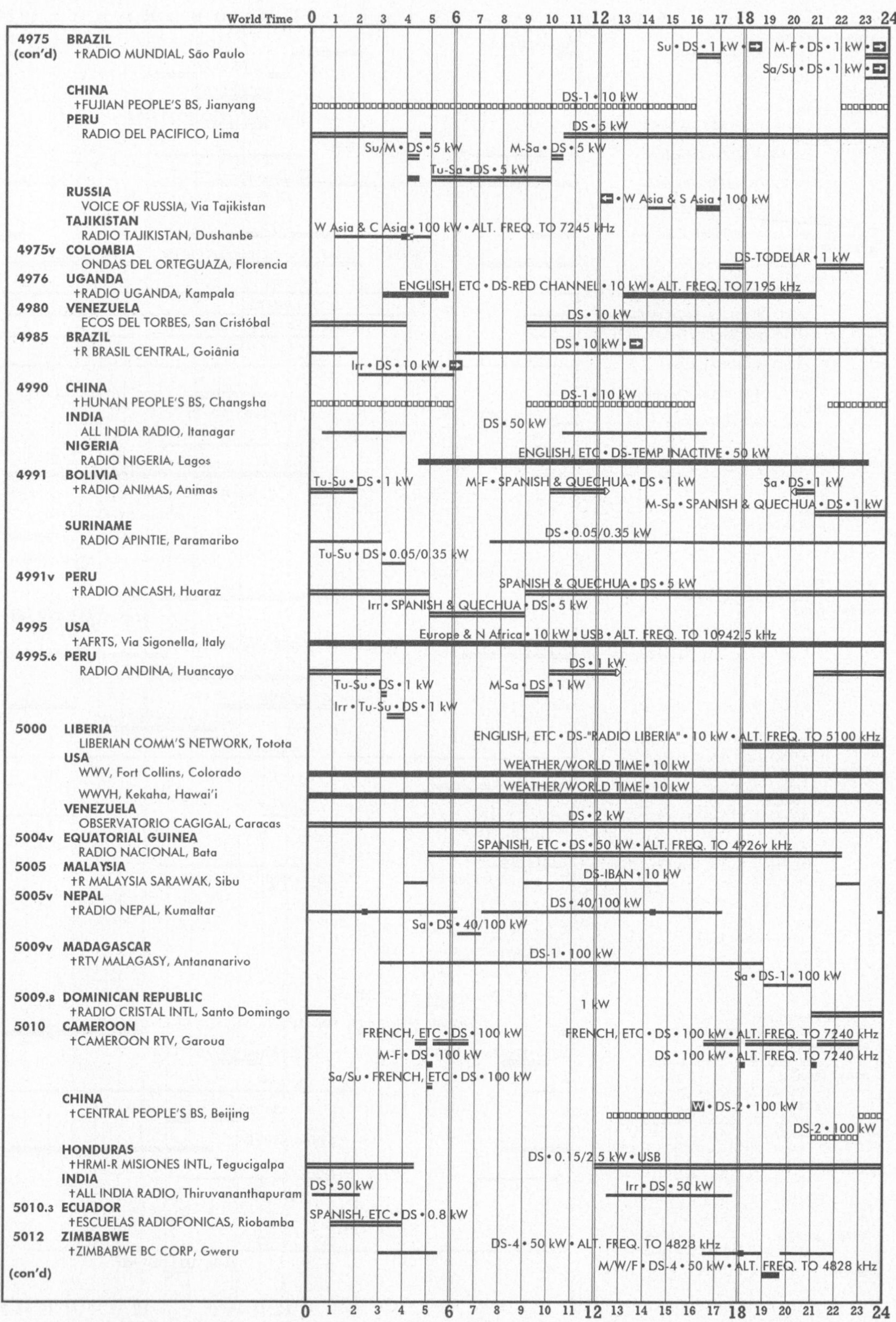
World Time 0 1 2 3 4 5 6 7 8 9 10 11 12 13 14 15 16 17 18 19 20 21 22 23 24
4975 (con'd) BRAZIL
†RADIO MUNDIAL, São Paulo
Su • DS • 1 kW
M-F • DS • 1 kW
Sa/Su • DS • 1 kW
CHINA
†FUJIAN PEOPLE'S BS, Jianyang
DS-1 • 10 kW
PERU
RADIO DEL PACIFICO, Lima
DS • 5 kW
Su/M • DS • 5 kW
M-Sa • DS • 5 kW
Tu-Sa • DS • 5 kW
RUSSIA
VOICE OF RUSSIA, Via Tajikistan
W Asia & S Asia • 100 kW
TAJIKISTAN
RADIO TAJIKISTAN, Dushanbe
W Asia & C Asia • 100 kW • ALT. FREQ. TO 7245 kHz
4975v COLOMBIA
ONDAS DEL ORTEGUAZA, Florencia
DS-TODELAR • 1 kW
4976 UGANDA
†RADIO UGANDA, Kampala
ENGLISH, ETC • DS-RED CHANNEL • 10 kW • ALT. FREQ. TO 7195 kHz
4980 VENEZUELA
ECOS DEL TORBES, San Cristóbal
DS • 10 kW
4985 BRAZIL
†R BRASIL CENTRAL, Goiânia
DS • 10 kW
Irr • DS • 10 kW
4990 CHINA
†HUNAN PEOPLE'S BS, Changsha
DS-1 • 10 kW
INDIA
ALL INDIA RADIO, Itanagar
DS • 50 kW
NIGERIA
RADIO NIGERIA, Lagos
ENGLISH, ETC • DS-TEMP INACTIVE • 50 kW
4991 BOLIVIA
†RADIO ANIMAS, Animas
Tu-Su • DS • 1 kW
M-F • SPANISH & QUECHUA • DS • 1 kW
Sa • DS • 1 kW
M-Sa • SPANISH & QUECHUA • DS • 1 kW
SURINAME
RADIO APINTIE, Paramaribo
DS • 0.05/0.35 kW
Tu-Su • DS • 0.05/0.35 kW
4991v PERU
†RADIO ANCASH, Huaraz
SPANISH & QUECHUA • DS • 5 kW
Irr • SPANISH & QUECHUA • DS • 5 kW
4995 USA
†AFRTS, Via Sigonella, Italy
Europe & N Africa • 10 kW • USB • ALT. FREQ. TO 10942.5 kHz
4995.6 PERU
RADIO ANDINA, Huancayo
DS • 1 kW
Tu-Su • DS • 1 kW
M-Sa • DS • 1 kW
Irr • Tu-Su • DS • 1 kW
5000 LIBERIA
LIBERIAN COMM'S NETWORK, Totota
ENGLISH, ETC • DS-"RADIO LIBERIA" • 10 kW • ALT. FREQ. TO 5100 kHz
USA
WWV, Fort Collins, Colorado
WEATHER/WORLD TIME • 10 kW
WWVH, Kekaha, Hawai'i
WEATHER/WORLD TIME • 10 kW
VENEZUELA
OBSERVATORIO CAGIGAL, Caracas
DS • 2 kW
5004v EQUATORIAL GUINEA
RADIO NACIONAL, Bata
SPANISH, ETC • DS • 50 kW • ALT. FREQ. TO 4926v kHz
5005 MALAYSIA
†R MALAYSIA SARAWAK, Sibu
DS-IBAN • 10 kW
5005v NEPAL
†RADIO NEPAL, Kumaltar
DS • 40/100 kW
Sa • DS • 40/100 kW
5009v MADAGASCAR
†RTV MALAGASY, Antananarivo
DS-1 • 100 kW
Sa • DS-1 • 100 kW
5009.8 DOMINICAN REPUBLIC
†RADIO CRISTAL INTL, Santo Domingo
1 kW
5010 CAMEROON
†CAMEROON RTV, Garoua
FRENCH, ETC • DS • 100 kW
FRENCH, ETC • DS • 100 kW • ALT. FREQ. TO 7240 kHz
M-F • DS • 100 kW
DS • 100 kW • ALT. FREQ. TO 7240 kHz
Sa/Su • FRENCH, ETC • DS • 100 kW
CHINA
†CENTRAL PEOPLE'S BS, Beijing
W • DS-2 • 100 kW
DS-2 • 100 kW
HONDURAS
†HRMI-R MISIONES INTL, Tegucigalpa
DS • 0.15/2.5 kW • USB
INDIA
†ALL INDIA RADIO, Thiruvananthapuram
DS • 50 kW
Irr • DS • 50 kW
5010.3 ECUADOR
†ESCUELAS RADIOFONICAS, Riobamba
SPANISH, ETC • DS • 0.8 kW
5012 ZIMBABWE
†ZIMBABWE BC CORP, Gweru
DS-4 • 50 kW • ALT. FREQ. TO 4828 kHz
M/W/F • DS-4 • 50 kW • ALT. FREQ. TO 4828 kHz
(con'd)
0 1 2 3 4 5 6 7 8 9 10 11 12 13 14 15 16 17 18 19 20 21 22 23 24
ENGLISH ARABIC CHINESE FRENCH GERMAN RUSSIAN SPANISH OTHER

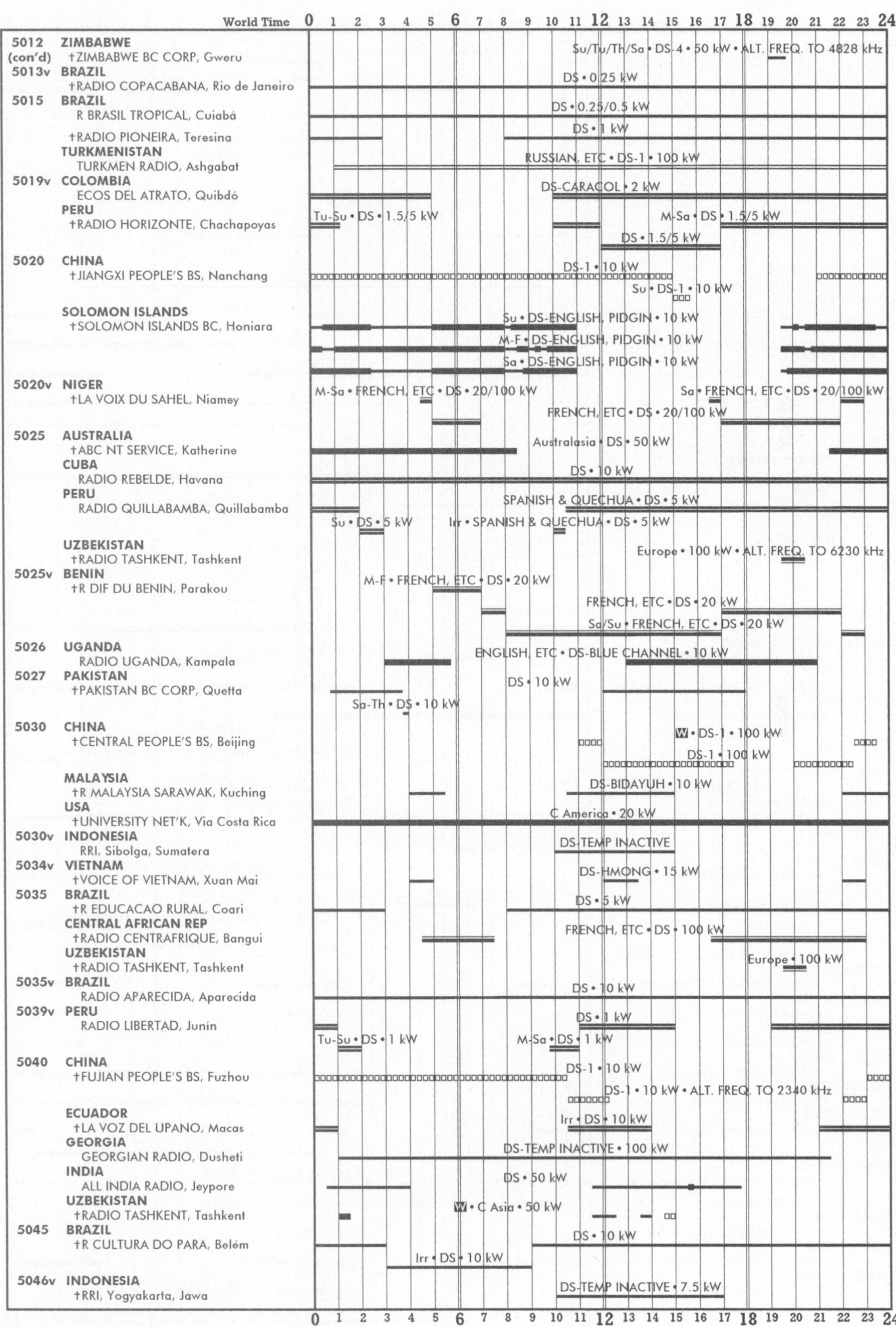
World Time 0 1 2 3 4 5 6 7 8 9 10 11 12 13 14 15 16 17 18 19 20 21 22 23 24
5012 (con'd) ZIMBABWE
†ZIMBABWE BC CORP, Gweru
Su/Tu/Th/Sa • DS-4 • 50 kW • ALT. FREQ. TO 4828 kHz
5013v BRAZIL
†RADIO COPACABANA, Rio de Janeiro
DS • 0.25 kW
5015 BRAZIL
R BRASIL TROPICAL, Cuiabá
DS • 0.25/0.5 kW
†RADIO PIONEIRA, Teresina
DS • 1 kW
TURKMENISTAN
TURKMEN RADIO, Ashgabat
RUSSIAN, ETC • DS-1 • 100 kW
5019v COLOMBIA
ECOS DEL ATRATO, Quibdó
DS-CARACOL • 2 kW
PERU
†RADIO HORIZONTE, Chachapoyas
Tu-Su • DS • 1.5/5 kW
M-Sa • DS • 1.5/5 kW
DS • 1.5/5 kW
5020 CHINA
†JIANGXI PEOPLE'S BS, Nanchang
DS-1 • 10 kW
Su • DS-1 • 10 kW
SOLOMON ISLANDS
†SOLOMON ISLANDS BC, Honiara
Su • DS-ENGLISH, PIDGIN • 10 kW
M-F • DS-ENGLISH, PIDGIN • 10 kW
Sa • DS-ENGLISH, PIDGIN • 10 kW
5020v NIGER
†LA VOIX DU SAHEL, Niamey
M-Sa • FRENCH, ETC • DS • 20/100 kW
Sa • FRENCH, ETC • DS • 20/100 kW
FRENCH, ETC • DS • 20/100 kW
5025 AUSTRALIA
†ABC NT SERVICE, Katherine
Australasia • DS • 50 kW
CUBA
RADIO REBELDE, Havana
DS • 10 kW
PERU
RADIO QUILLABAMBA, Quillabamba
SPANISH & QUECHUA • DS • 5 kW
Su • DS • 5 kW
Irr • SPANISH & QUECHUA • DS • 5 kW
UZBEKISTAN
†RADIO TASHKENT, Tashkent
Europe • 100 kW • ALT. FREQ. TO 6230 kHz
5025v BENIN
†R DIF DU BENIN, Parakou
M-F • FRENCH, ETC • DS • 20 kW
FRENCH, ETC • DS • 20 kW
Sa/Su • FRENCH, ETC • DS • 20 kW
5026 UGANDA
RADIO UGANDA, Kampala
ENGLISH, ETC • DS-BLUE CHANNEL • 10 kW
5027 PAKISTAN
†PAKISTAN BC CORP, Quetta
DS • 10 kW
Sa-Th • DS • 10 kW
5030 CHINA
†CENTRAL PEOPLE'S BS, Beijing
W • DS-1 • 100 kW
DS-1 • 100 kW
MALAYSIA
†R MALAYSIA SARAWAK, Kuching
DS-BIDAYUH • 10 kW
USA
†UNIVERSITY NET'K, Via Costa Rica
C America • 20 kW
5030v INDONESIA
RRI, Sibolga, Sumatera
DS-TEMP INACTIVE
5034v VIETNAM
†VOICE OF VIETNAM, Xuan Mai
DS-HMONG • 15 kW
5035 BRAZIL
†R EDUCACAO RURAL, Coari
DS • 5 kW
CENTRAL AFRICAN REP
†RADIO CENTRAFRIQUE, Bangui
FRENCH, ETC • DS • 100 kW
UZBEKISTAN
†RADIO TASHKENT, Tashkent
Europe • 100 kW
5035v BRAZIL
RADIO APARECIDA, Aparecida
DS • 10 kW
5039v PERU
RADIO LIBERTAD, Junín
DS • 1 kW
Tu-Su • DS • 1 kW
M-Sa • DS • 1 kW
5040 CHINA
†FUJIAN PEOPLE'S BS, Fuzhou
DS-1 • 10 kW
DS-1 • 10 kW • ALT. FREQ. TO 2340 kHz
ECUADOR
†LA VOZ DEL UPANO, Macas
Irr • DS • 10 kW
GEORGIA
GEORGIAN RADIO, Dusheti
DS-TEMP INACTIVE • 100 kW
INDIA
ALL INDIA RADIO, Jeypore
DS • 50 kW
UZBEKISTAN
†RADIO TASHKENT, Tashkent
W • C Asia • 50 kW
5045 BRAZIL
†R CULTURA DO PARA, Belém
DS • 10 kW
Irr • DS • 10 kW
5046v INDONESIA
†RRI, Yogyakarta, Jawa
DS-TEMP INACTIVE • 7.5 kW
0 1 2 3 4 5 6 7 8 9 10 11 12 13 14 15 16 17 18 19 20 21 22 23 24

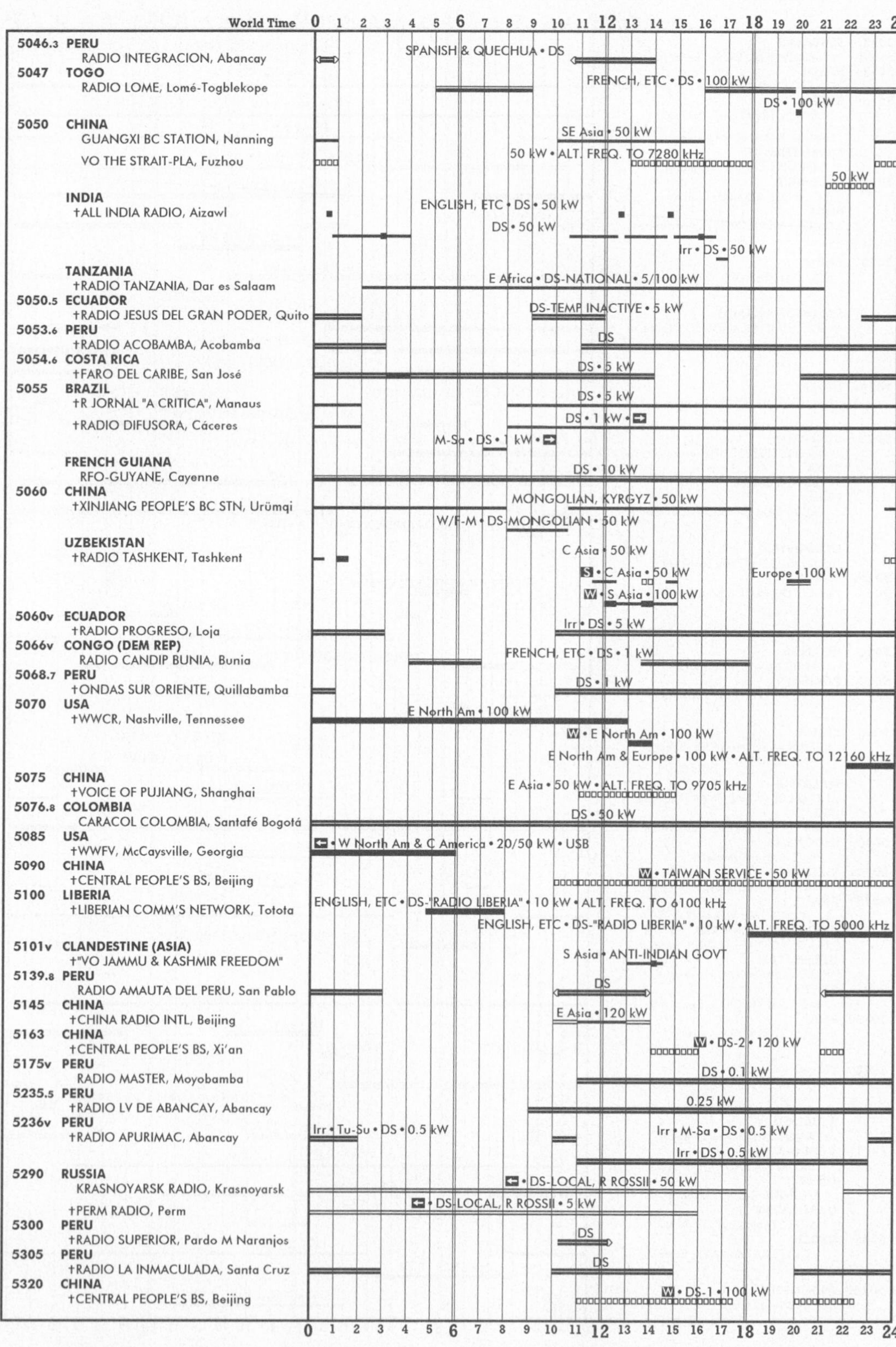
World Time 0 1 2 3 4 5 6 7 8 9 10 11 12 13 14 15 16 17 18 19 20 21 22 23 24
5046.3 PERU
RADIO INTEGRACION, Abancay
SPANISH & QUECHUA • DS
5047 TOGO
RADIO LOME, Lomé-Togblekope
FRENCH, ETC • DS • 100 kW
DS • 100 kW
5050 CHINA
GUANGXI BC STATION, Nanning
SE Asia • 50 kW
VO THE STRAIT-PLA, Fuzhou
50 kW • ALT. FREQ. TO 7280 kHz
50 kW
INDIA
†ALL INDIA RADIO, Aizawl
ENGLISH, ETC • DS • 50 kW
DS • 50 kW
Irr • DS • 50 kW
TANZANIA
†RADIO TANZANIA, Dar es Salaam
E Africa • DS-NATIONAL • 5/100 kW
5050.5 ECUADOR
†RADIO JESUS DEL GRAN PODER, Quito
DS-TEMP INACTIVE • 5 kW
5053.6 PERU
†RADIO ACOBAMBA, Acobamba
DS
5054.6 COSTA RICA
†FARO DEL CARIBE, San José
DS • 5 kW
5055 BRAZIL
†R JORNAL "A CRITICA", Manaus
DS • 5 kW
†RADIO DIFUSORA, Cáceres
DS • 1 kW
M-Sa • DS • 1 kW
FRENCH GUIANA
RFO-GUYANE, Cayenne
DS • 10 kW
5060 CHINA
†XINJIANG PEOPLE'S BC STN, Urümqi
MONGOLIAN, KYRGYZ • 50 kW
W/F-M • DS-MONGOLIAN • 50 kW
UZBEKISTAN
†RADIO TASHKENT, Tashkent
C Asia • 50 kW
S • C Asia • 50 kW
Europe • 100 kW
W • S Asia • 100 kW
5060v ECUADOR
†RADIO PROGRESO, Loja
Irr • DS • 5 kW
5066v CONGO (DEM REP)
RADIO CANDIP BUNIA, Bunia
FRENCH, ETC • DS • 1 kW
5068.7 PERU
†ONDAS SUR ORIENTE, Quillabamba
DS • 1 kW
5070 USA
†WWCR, Nashville, Tennessee
E North Am • 100 kW
W • E North Am • 100 kW
E North Am & Europe • 100 kW • ALT. FREQ. TO 12160 kHz
5075 CHINA
†VOICE OF PUJIANG, Shanghai
E Asia • 50 kW • ALT. FREQ. TO 9705 kHz
5076.8 COLOMBIA
CARACOL COLOMBIA, Santafé Bogotá
DS • 50 kW
5085 USA
†WWFV, McCaysville, Georgia
W North Am & C America • 20/50 kW • USB
5090 CHINA
†CENTRAL PEOPLE'S BS, Beijing
W • TAIWAN SERVICE • 50 kW
5100 LIBERIA
†LIBERIAN COMM'S NETWORK, Totota
ENGLISH, ETC • DS-"RADIO LIBERIA" • 10 kW • ALT. FREQ. TO 6100 kHz
ENGLISH, ETC • DS-"RADIO LIBERIA" • 10 kW • ALT. FREQ. TO 5000 kHz
5101v CLANDESTINE (ASIA)
†"VO JAMMU & KASHMIR FREEDOM"
S Asia • ANTI-INDIAN GOVT
5139.8 PERU
RADIO AMAUTA DEL PERU, San Pablo
DS
5145 CHINA
†CHINA RADIO INTL, Beijing
E Asia • 120 kW
5163 CHINA
†CENTRAL PEOPLE'S BS, Xi'an
W • DS-2 • 120 kW
5175v PERU
RADIO MASTER, Moyobamba
DS • 0.1 kW
5235.5 PERU
†RADIO LV DE ABANCAY, Abancay
0.25 kW
5236v PERU
†RADIO APURIMAC, Abancay
Irr • Tu-Su • DS • 0.5 kW
Irr • M-Sa • DS • 0.5 kW
Irr • DS • 0.5 kW
5290 RUSSIA
KRASNOYARSK RADIO, Krasnoyarsk
DS-LOCAL, R ROSSII • 50 kW
†PERM RADIO, Perm
DS-LOCAL, R ROSSII • 5 kW
5300 PERU
†RADIO SUPERIOR, Pardo M Naranjos
DS
5305 PERU
†RADIO LA INMACULADA, Santa Cruz
DS
5320 CHINA
†CENTRAL PEOPLE'S BS, Beijing
W • DS-1 • 100 kW
0 1 2 3 4 5 6 7 8 9 10 11 12 13 14 15 16 17 18 19 20 21 22 23 24
ENGLISH ARABIC CHINESE FRENCH GERMAN RUSSIAN SPANISH OTHER

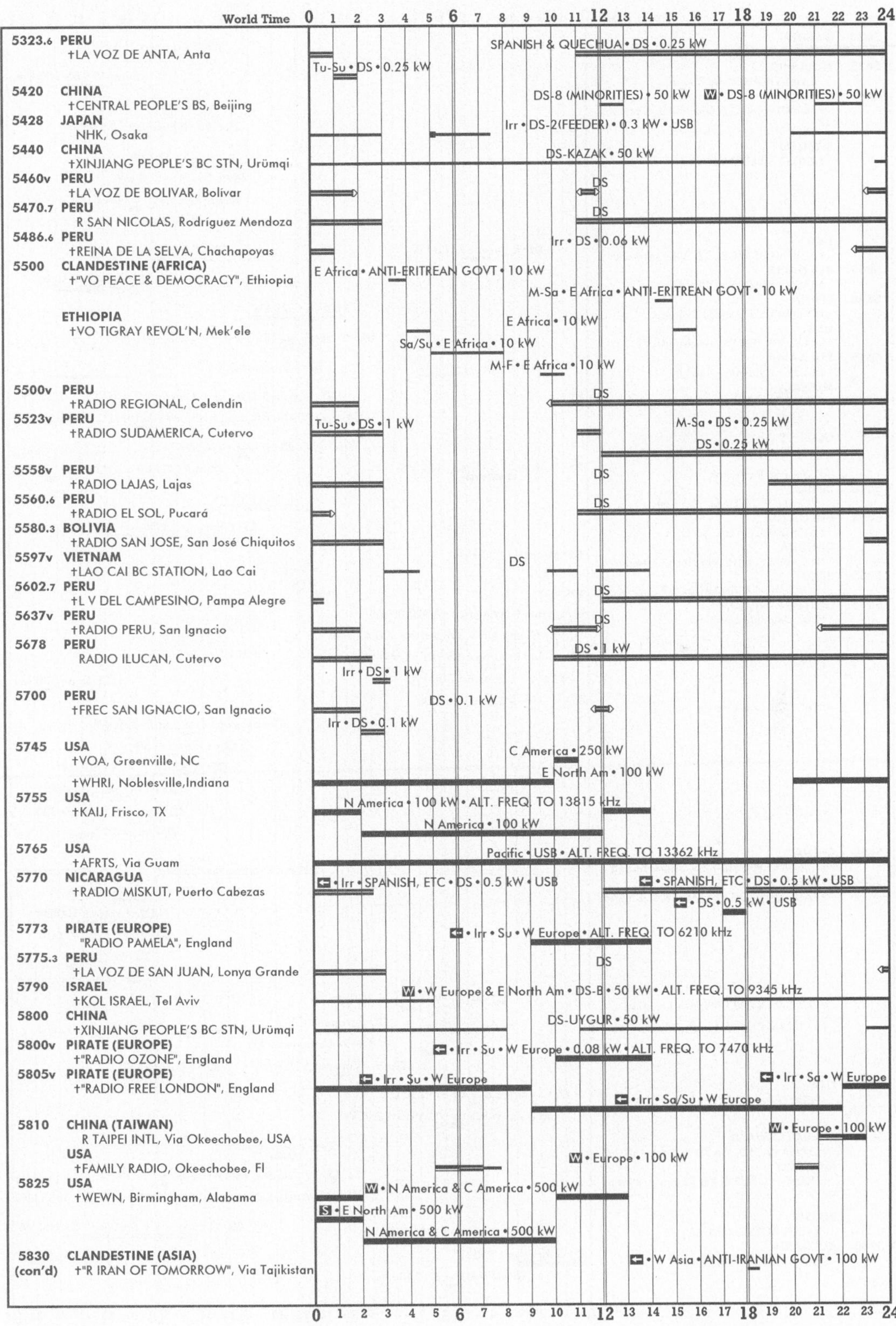
World Time 0 1 2 3 4 5 6 7 8 9 10 11 12 13 14 15 16 17 18 19 20 21 22 23 24
5323.6 PERU
†LA VOZ DE ANTA, Anta
SPANISH & QUECHUA • DS • 0.25 kW
Tu-Su • DS • 0.25 kW
5420 CHINA
†CENTRAL PEOPLE'S BS, Beijing
DS-8 (MINORITIES) • 50 kW
W • DS-8 (MINORITIES) • 50 kW
5428 JAPAN
NHK, Osaka
Irr • DS-2(FEEDER) • 0.3 kW • USB
5440 CHINA
†XINJIANG PEOPLE'S BC STN, Urümqi
DS-KAZAK • 50 kW
5460v PERU
†LA VOZ DE BOLIVAR, Bolívar
DS
5470.7 PERU
R SAN NICOLAS, Rodríguez Mendoza
DS
5486.6 PERU
†REINA DE LA SELVA, Chachapoyas
Irr • DS • 0.06 kW
5500 CLANDESTINE (AFRICA)
†"VO PEACE & DEMOCRACY", Ethiopia
E Africa • ANTI-ERITREAN GOVT • 10 kW
M-Sa • E Africa • ANTI-ERITREAN GOVT • 10 kW
ETHIOPIA
†VO TIGRAY REVOL'N, Mek'ele
E Africa • 10 kW
Sa/Su • E Africa • 10 kW
M-F • E Africa • 10 kW
5500v PERU
†RADIO REGIONAL, Celendín
DS
5523v PERU
†RADIO SUDAMERICA, Cutervo
Tu-Su • DS • 1 kW
M-Sa • DS • 0.25 kW
DS • 0.25 kW
5558v PERU
†RADIO LAJAS, Lajas
DS
5560.6 PERU
†RADIO EL SOL, Pucará
DS
5580.3 BOLIVIA
†RADIO SAN JOSE, San José Chiquitos
5597v VIETNAM
†LAO CAI BC STATION, Lao Cai
DS
5602.7 PERU
†L V DEL CAMPESINO, Pampa Alegre
DS
5637v PERU
†RADIO PERU, San Ignacio
DS
5678 PERU
RADIO ILUCAN, Cutervo
DS • 1 kW
Irr • DS • 1 kW
5700 PERU
†FREC SAN IGNACIO, San Ignacio
DS • 0.1 kW
Irr • DS • 0.1 kW
5745 USA
†VOA, Greenville, NC
C America • 250 kW
†WHRI, Noblesville,Indiana
E North Am • 100 kW
5755 USA
†KAIJ, Frisco, TX
N America • 100 kW • ALT. FREQ. TO 13815 kHz
N America • 100 kW
5765 USA
†AFRTS, Via Guam
Pacific • USB • ALT. FREQ. TO 13362 kHz
5770 NICARAGUA
†RADIO MISKUT, Puerto Cabezas
• Irr • SPANISH, ETC • DS • 0.5 kW • USB
• SPANISH, ETC • DS • 0.5 kW • USB
• DS • 0.5 kW • USB
5773 PIRATE (EUROPE)
"RADIO PAMELA", England
• Irr • Su • W Europe • ALT. FREQ. TO 6210 kHz
5775.3 PERU
†LA VOZ DE SAN JUAN, Lonya Grande
DS
5790 ISRAEL
†KOL ISRAEL, Tel Aviv
W • W Europe & E North Am • DS-B • 50 kW • ALT. FREQ. TO 9345 kHz
5800 CHINA
†XINJIANG PEOPLE'S BC STN, Urümqi
DS-UYGUR • 50 kW
5800v PIRATE (EUROPE)
†"RADIO OZONE", England
• Irr • Su • W Europe • 0.08 kW • ALT. FREQ. TO 7470 kHz
5805v PIRATE (EUROPE)
†"RADIO FREE LONDON", England
• Irr • Su • W Europe
• Irr • Sa • W Europe
• Irr • Sa/Su • W Europe
5810 CHINA (TAIWAN)
R TAIPEI INTL, Via Okeechobee, USA
W • Europe • 100 kW
USA
†FAMILY RADIO, Okeechobee, Fl
W • Europe • 100 kW
5825 USA
†WEWN, Birmingham, Alabama
W • N America & C America • 500 kW
S • E North Am • 500 kW
N America & C America • 500 kW
5830 CLANDESTINE (ASIA)
(con'd) †"R IRAN OF TOMORROW", Via Tajikistan
• W Asia • ANTI-IRANIAN GOVT • 100 kW
0 1 2 3 4 5 6 7 8 9 10 11 12 13 14 15 16 17 18 19 20 21 22 23 24

SEASONAL S OR W 1-HR TIMESHIFT MIDYEAR OR JAMMING / OR /\ EARLIEST HEARD ◁ LATEST HEARD ▷ NEW FOR 2002 †

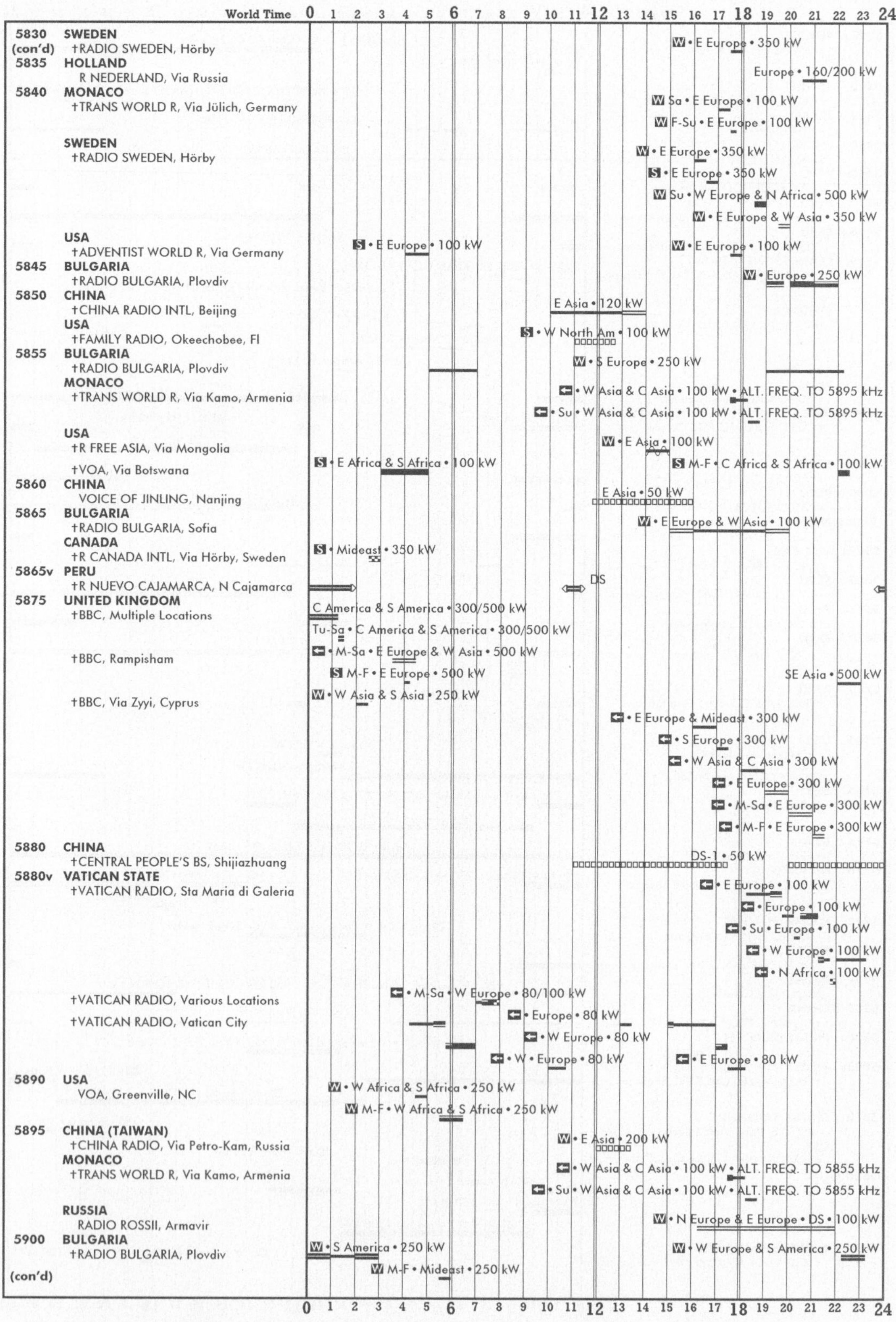
World Time 0 1 2 3 4 5 6 7 8 9 10 11 12 13 14 15 16 17 18 19 20 21 22 23 24
5830 SWEDEN
(con'd) †RADIO SWEDEN, Hörby
W • E Europe • 350 kW
5835 HOLLAND
R NEDERLAND, Via Russia
Europe • 160/200 kW
5840 MONACO
†TRANS WORLD R, Via Jülich, Germany
W Sa • E Europe • 100 kW
W F-Su • E Europe • 100 kW
SWEDEN
†RADIO SWEDEN, Hörby
W • E Europe • 350 kW
S • E Europe • 350 kW
W Su • W Europe & N Africa • 500 kW
W • E Europe & W Asia • 350 kW
USA
†ADVENTIST WORLD R, Via Germany
S • E Europe • 100 kW
W • E Europe • 100 kW
5845 BULGARIA
†RADIO BULGARIA, Plovdiv
W • Europe • 250 kW
5850 CHINA
†CHINA RADIO INTL, Beijing
E Asia • 120 kW
USA
†FAMILY RADIO, Okeechobee, Fl
S • W North Am • 100 kW
5855 BULGARIA
†RADIO BULGARIA, Plovdiv
W • S Europe • 250 kW
MONACO
†TRANS WORLD R, Via Kamo, Armenia
• W Asia & C Asia • 100 kW • ALT. FREQ. TO 5895 kHz
• Su • W Asia & C Asia • 100 kW • ALT. FREQ. TO 5895 kHz
USA
†R FREE ASIA, Via Mongolia
W • E Asia • 100 kW
†VOA, Via Botswana
S • E Africa & S Africa • 100 kW
S M-F • C Africa & S Africa • 100 kW
5860 CHINA
VOICE OF JINLING, Nanjing
E Asia • 50 kW
5865 BULGARIA
†RADIO BULGARIA, Sofia
W • E Europe & W Asia • 100 kW
CANADA
†R CANADA INTL, Via Hörby, Sweden
S • Mideast • 350 kW
5865v PERU
†R NUEVO CAJAMARCA, N Cajamarca
DS
5875 UNITED KINGDOM
†BBC, Multiple Locations
C America & S America • 300/500 kW
Tu-Sa • C America & S America • 300/500 kW
• M-Sa • E Europe & W Asia • 500 kW
†BBC, Rampisham
S M-F • E Europe • 500 kW
SE Asia • 500 kW
†BBC, Via Zyyi, Cyprus
W • W Asia & S Asia • 250 kW
• E Europe & Mideast • 300 kW
• S Europe • 300 kW
• W Asia & C Asia • 300 kW
• E Europe • 300 kW
• M-Sa • E Europe • 300 kW
• M-F • E Europe • 300 kW
5880 CHINA
†CENTRAL PEOPLE'S BS, Shijiazhuang
DS-1 • 50 kW
5880v VATICAN STATE
†VATICAN RADIO, Sta Maria di Galeria
• E Europe • 100 kW
• Europe • 100 kW
• Su • Europe • 100 kW
• W Europe • 100 kW
• N Africa • 100 kW
†VATICAN RADIO, Various Locations
• M-Sa • W Europe • 80/100 kW
†VATICAN RADIO, Vatican City
• Europe • 80 kW
• W Europe • 80 kW
• W • Europe • 80 kW
• E Europe • 80 kW
5890 USA
VOA, Greenville, NC
W • W Africa & S Africa • 250 kW
W M-F • W Africa & S Africa • 250 kW
5895 CHINA (TAIWAN)
†CHINA RADIO, Via Petro-Kam, Russia
W • E Asia • 200 kW
MONACO
†TRANS WORLD R, Via Kamo, Armenia
• W Asia & C Asia • 100 kW • ALT. FREQ. TO 5855 kHz
• Su • W Asia & C Asia • 100 kW • ALT. FREQ. TO 5855 kHz
RUSSIA
RADIO ROSSII, Armavir
W • N Europe & E Europe • DS • 100 kW
5900 BULGARIA
†RADIO BULGARIA, Plovdiv
W • S America • 250 kW
W • W Europe & S America • 250 kW
(con'd)
W M-F • Mideast • 250 kW
0 1 2 3 4 5 6 7 8 9 10 11 12 13 14 15 16 17 18 19 20 21 22 23 24

ENGLISH ARABIC CHINESE FRENCH GERMAN RUSSIAN SPANISH OTHER

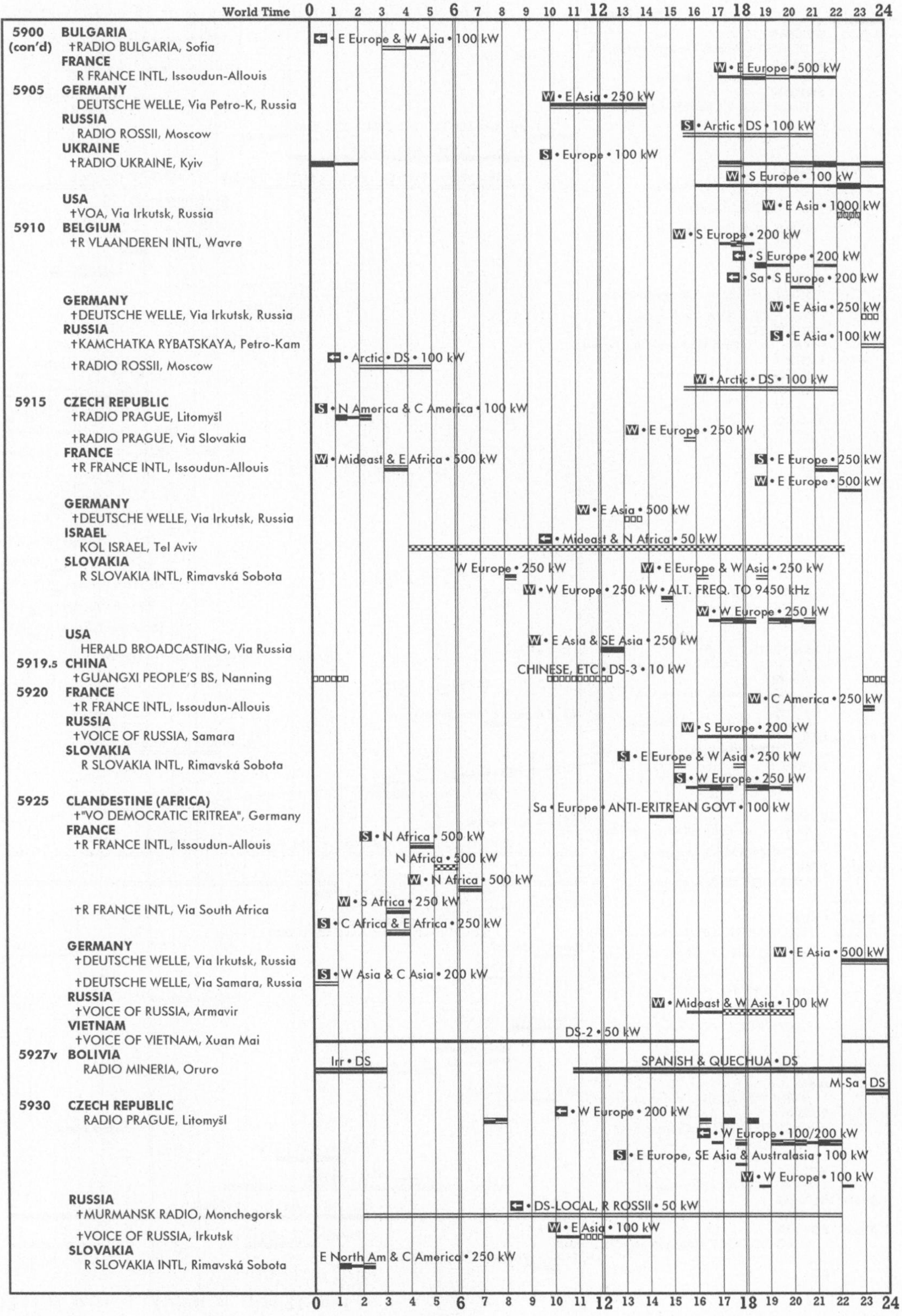
World Time 0 1 2 3 4 5 6 7 8 9 10 11 12 13 14 15 16 17 18 19 20 21 22 23 24
5900 (con'd) BULGARIA
†RADIO BULGARIA, Sofia
• E Europe & W Asia • 100 kW
FRANCE
R FRANCE INTL, Issoudun-Allouis
W • E Europe • 500 kW
5905 GERMANY
DEUTSCHE WELLE, Via Petro-K, Russia
W • E Asia • 250 kW
RUSSIA
RADIO ROSSII, Moscow
S • Arctic • DS • 100 kW
UKRAINE
†RADIO UKRAINE, Kyiv
S • Europe • 100 kW
W • S Europe • 100 kW
USA
†VOA, Via Irkutsk, Russia
W • E Asia • 1000 kW
5910 BELGIUM
†R VLAANDEREN INTL, Wavre
W • S Europe • 200 kW
• S Europe • 200 kW
• Sa • S Europe • 200 kW
GERMANY
†DEUTSCHE WELLE, Via Irkutsk, Russia
W • E Asia • 250 kW
RUSSIA
†KAMCHATKA RYBATSKAYA, Petro-Kam
S • E Asia • 100 kW
†RADIO ROSSII, Moscow
• Arctic • DS • 100 kW
W • Arctic • DS • 100 kW
5915 CZECH REPUBLIC
†RADIO PRAGUE, Litomyšl
S • N America & C America • 100 kW
†RADIO PRAGUE, Via Slovakia
W • E Europe • 250 kW
FRANCE
†R FRANCE INTL, Issoudun-Allouis
W • Mideast & E Africa • 500 kW
S • E Europe • 250 kW
W • E Europe • 500 kW
GERMANY
†DEUTSCHE WELLE, Via Irkutsk, Russia
W • E Asia • 500 kW
ISRAEL
KOL ISRAEL, Tel Aviv
• Mideast & N Africa • 50 kW
SLOVAKIA
R SLOVAKIA INTL, Rimavská Sobota
W Europe • 250 kW
W • E Europe & W Asia • 250 kW
W • W Europe • 250 kW • ALT. FREQ. TO 9450 kHz
W • W Europe • 250 kW
USA
HERALD BROADCASTING, Via Russia
W • E Asia & SE Asia • 250 kW
5919.5 CHINA
†GUANGXI PEOPLE'S BS, Nanning
CHINESE, ETC • DS-3 • 10 kW
5920 FRANCE
†R FRANCE INTL, Issoudun-Allouis
W • C America • 250 kW
RUSSIA
†VOICE OF RUSSIA, Samara
W • S Europe • 200 kW
SLOVAKIA
R SLOVAKIA INTL, Rimavská Sobota
S • E Europe & W Asia • 250 kW
S • W Europe • 250 kW
5925 CLANDESTINE (AFRICA)
†"VO DEMOCRATIC ERITREA", Germany
Sa • Europe • ANTI-ERITREAN GOVT • 100 kW
FRANCE
†R FRANCE INTL, Issoudun-Allouis
S • N Africa • 500 kW
N Africa • 500 kW
W • N Africa • 500 kW
†R FRANCE INTL, Via South Africa
W • S Africa • 250 kW
S • C Africa & E Africa • 250 kW
GERMANY
†DEUTSCHE WELLE, Via Irkutsk, Russia
W • E Asia • 500 kW
†DEUTSCHE WELLE, Via Samara, Russia
S • W Asia & C Asia • 200 kW
RUSSIA
†VOICE OF RUSSIA, Armavir
W • Mideast & W Asia • 100 kW
VIETNAM
†VOICE OF VIETNAM, Xuan Mai
DS-2 • 50 kW
5927v BOLIVIA
RADIO MINERIA, Oruro
Irr • DS
SPANISH & QUECHUA • DS
M-Sa • DS
5930 CZECH REPUBLIC
RADIO PRAGUE, Litomyšl
• W Europe • 200 kW
• W Europe • 100/200 kW
S • E Europe, SE Asia & Australasia • 100 kW
W • W Europe • 100 kW
RUSSIA
†MURMANSK RADIO, Monchegorsk
• DS-LOCAL, R ROSSII • 50 kW
†VOICE OF RUSSIA, Irkutsk
W • E Asia • 100 kW
SLOVAKIA
R SLOVAKIA INTL, Rimavská Sobota
E North Am & C America • 250 kW
0 1 2 3 4 5 6 7 8 9 10 11 12 13 14 15 16 17 18 19 20 21 22 23 24

SEASONAL S OR W 1-HR TIMESHIFT MIDYEAR ◀ OR ▶ JAMMING / OR ∧ EARLIEST HEARD ◁ LATEST HEARD ▷ NEW FOR 2002 †

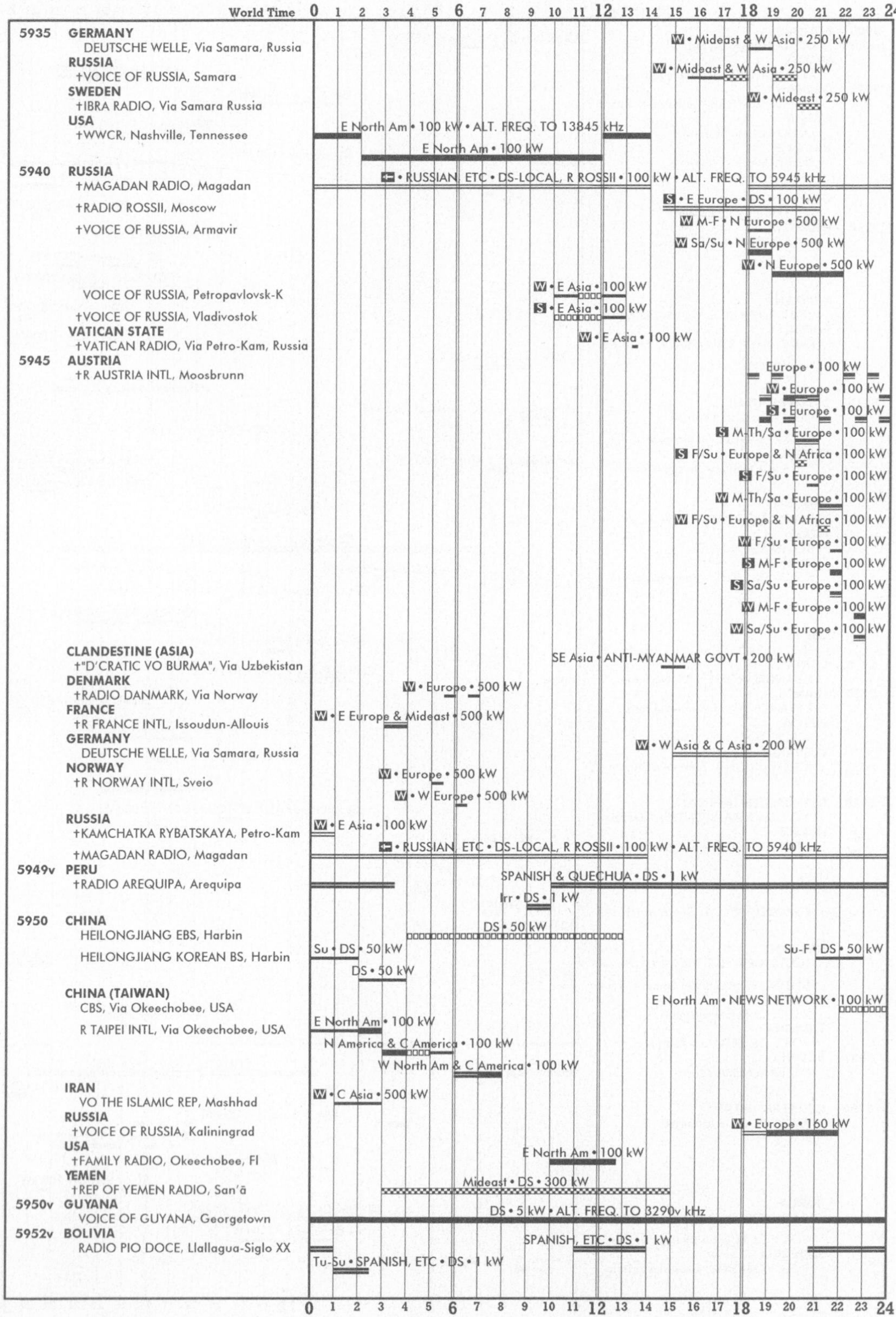
World Time 0 1 2 3 4 5 6 7 8 9 10 11 12 13 14 15 16 17 18 19 20 21 22 23 24
5935 GERMANY
DEUTSCHE WELLE, Via Samara, Russia
W • Mideast & W Asia • 250 kW
RUSSIA
†VOICE OF RUSSIA, Samara
W • Mideast & W Asia • 250 kW
SWEDEN
†IBRA RADIO, Via Samara Russia
W • Mideast • 250 kW
USA
†WWCR, Nashville, Tennessee
E North Am • 100 kW • ALT. FREQ. TO 13845 kHz
E North Am • 100 kW
5940 RUSSIA
†MAGADAN RADIO, Magadan
• RUSSIAN, ETC • DS-LOCAL, R ROSSII • 100 kW • ALT. FREQ. TO 5945 kHz
†RADIO ROSSII, Moscow
S • E Europe • DS • 100 kW
†VOICE OF RUSSIA, Armavir
W M-F • N Europe • 500 kW
W Sa/Su • N Europe • 500 kW
W • N Europe • 500 kW
VOICE OF RUSSIA, Petropavlovsk-K
W • E Asia • 100 kW
†VOICE OF RUSSIA, Vladivostok
S • E Asia • 100 kW
VATICAN STATE
†VATICAN RADIO, Via Petro-Kam, Russia
W • E Asia • 100 kW
5945 AUSTRIA
†R AUSTRIA INTL, Moosbrunn
Europe • 100 kW
W • Europe • 100 kW
S • Europe • 100 kW
S M-Th/Sa • Europe • 100 kW
S F/Su • Europe & N Africa • 100 kW
S F/Su • Europe • 100 kW
W M-Th/Sa • Europe • 100 kW
W F/Su • Europe & N Africa • 100 kW
W F/Su • Europe • 100 kW
S M-F • Europe • 100 kW
S Sa/Su • Europe • 100 kW
W M-F • Europe • 100 kW
W Sa/Su • Europe • 100 kW
CLANDESTINE (ASIA)
†"D'CRATIC VO BURMA", Via Uzbekistan
SE Asia • ANTI-MYANMAR GOVT • 200 kW
DENMARK
†RADIO DANMARK, Via Norway
W • Europe • 500 kW
FRANCE
†R FRANCE INTL, Issoudun-Allouis
W • E Europe & Mideast • 500 kW
GERMANY
DEUTSCHE WELLE, Via Samara, Russia
W • W Asia & C Asia • 200 kW
NORWAY
†R NORWAY INTL, Sveio
W • Europe • 500 kW
W • W Europe • 500 kW
RUSSIA
†KAMCHATKA RYBATSKAYA, Petro-Kam
W • E Asia • 100 kW
†MAGADAN RADIO, Magadan
• RUSSIAN, ETC • DS-LOCAL, R ROSSII • 100 kW • ALT. FREQ. TO 5940 kHz
5949v PERU
†RADIO AREQUIPA, Arequipa
SPANISH & QUECHUA • DS • 1 kW
Irr • DS • 1 kW
5950 CHINA
HEILONGJIANG EBS, Harbin
DS • 50 kW
HEILONGJIANG KOREAN BS, Harbin
Su • DS • 50 kW
Su-F • DS • 50 kW
DS • 50 kW
CHINA (TAIWAN)
CBS, Via Okeechobee, USA
E North Am • NEWS NETWORK • 100 kW
R TAIPEI INTL, Via Okeechobee, USA
E North Am • 100 kW
N America & C America • 100 kW
W North Am & C America • 100 kW
IRAN
VO THE ISLAMIC REP, Mashhad
W • C Asia • 500 kW
RUSSIA
†VOICE OF RUSSIA, Kaliningrad
W • Europe • 160 kW
USA
†FAMILY RADIO, Okeechobee, Fl
E North Am • 100 kW
YEMEN
†REP OF YEMEN RADIO, San'ā
Mideast • DS • 300 kW
5950v GUYANA
VOICE OF GUYANA, Georgetown
DS • 5 kW • ALT. FREQ. TO 3290v kHz
5952v BOLIVIA
RADIO PIO DOCE, Llallagua-Siglo XX
SPANISH, ETC • DS • 1 kW
Tu-Su • SPANISH, ETC • DS • 1 kW
0 1 2 3 4 5 6 7 8 9 10 11 12 13 14 15 16 17 18 19 20 21 22 23 24
ENGLISH ARABIC CHINESE FRENCH GERMAN RUSSIAN SPANISH OTHER

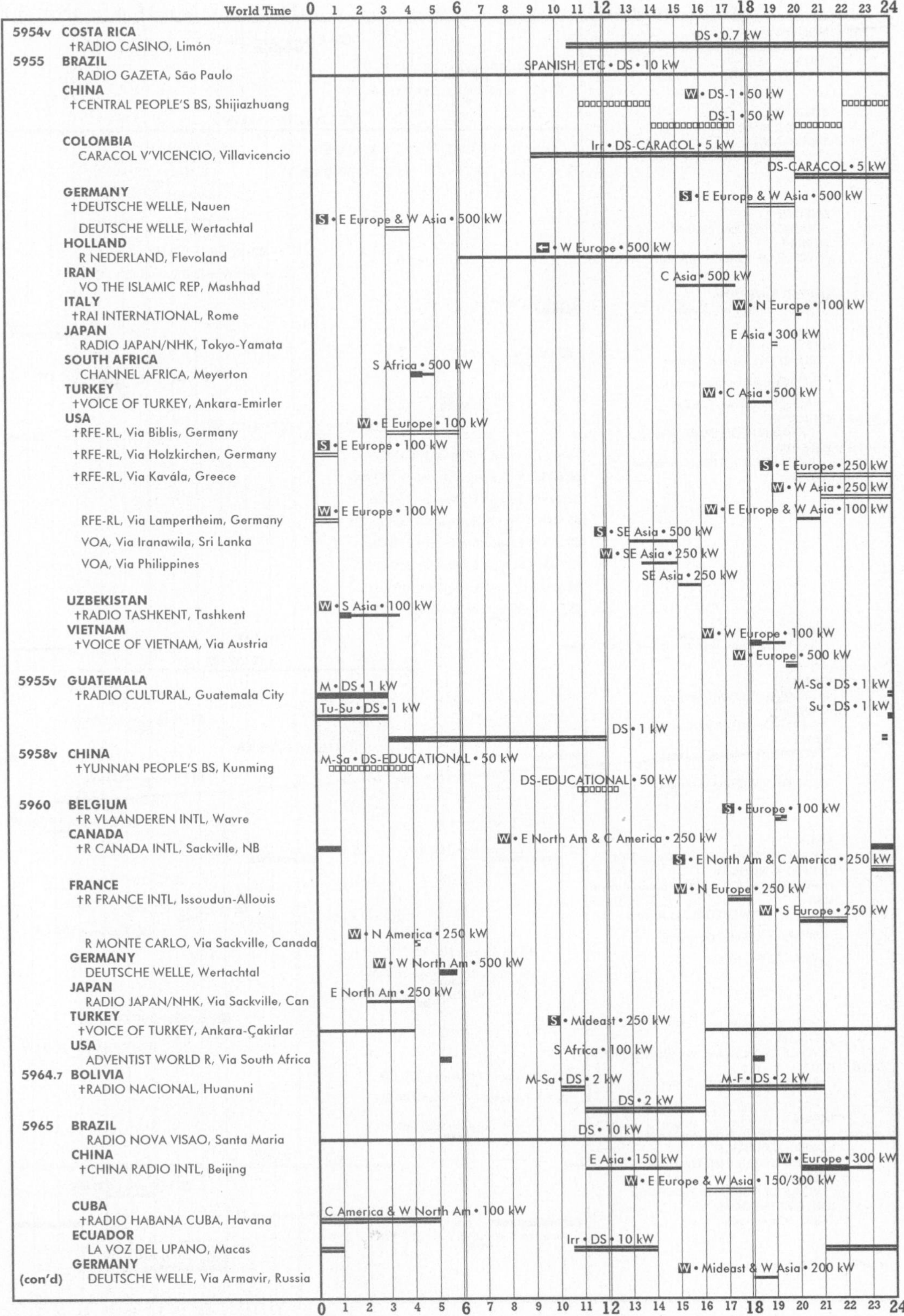
World Time 0 1 2 3 4 5 6 7 8 9 10 11 12 13 14 15 16 17 18 19 20 21 22 23 24
5954v COSTA RICA
†RADIO CASINO, Limón
DS • 0.7 kW
5955 BRAZIL
RADIO GAZETA, São Paulo
SPANISH, ETC • DS • 10 kW
CHINA
†CENTRAL PEOPLE'S BS, Shijiazhuang
W • DS-1 • 50 kW
DS-1 • 50 kW
COLOMBIA
CARACOL V'VICENCIO, Villavicencio
Irr • DS-CARACOL • 5 kW
DS-CARACOL • 5 kW
GERMANY
†DEUTSCHE WELLE, Nauen
S • E Europe & W Asia • 500 kW
DEUTSCHE WELLE, Wertachtal
S • E Europe & W Asia • 500 kW
HOLLAND
R NEDERLAND, Flevoland
W Europe • 500 kW
IRAN
VO THE ISLAMIC REP, Mashhad
C Asia • 500 kW
ITALY
†RAI INTERNATIONAL, Rome
W • N Europe • 100 kW
JAPAN
RADIO JAPAN/NHK, Tokyo-Yamata
E Asia • 300 kW
SOUTH AFRICA
CHANNEL AFRICA, Meyerton
S Africa • 500 kW
TURKEY
†VOICE OF TURKEY, Ankara-Emirler
W • C Asia • 500 kW
USA
†RFE-RL, Via Biblis, Germany
W • E Europe • 100 kW
†RFE-RL, Via Holzkirchen, Germany
S • E Europe • 100 kW
†RFE-RL, Via Kavála, Greece
S • E Europe • 250 kW
W • W Asia • 250 kW
RFE-RL, Via Lampertheim, Germany
W • E Europe • 100 kW
W • E Europe & W Asia • 100 kW
VOA, Via Iranawila, Sri Lanka
S • SE Asia • 500 kW
W • SE Asia • 250 kW
VOA, Via Philippines
SE Asia • 250 kW
UZBEKISTAN
†RADIO TASHKENT, Tashkent
W • S Asia • 100 kW
VIETNAM
†VOICE OF VIETNAM, Via Austria
W • W Europe • 100 kW
W • Europe • 500 kW
5955v GUATEMALA
†RADIO CULTURAL, Guatemala City
M • DS • 1 kW
M-Sa • DS • 1 kW
Tu-Su • DS • 1 kW
Su • DS • 1 kW
DS • 1 kW
5958v CHINA
†YUNNAN PEOPLE'S BS, Kunming
M-Sa • DS-EDUCATIONAL • 50 kW
DS-EDUCATIONAL • 50 kW
5960 BELGIUM
†R VLAANDEREN INTL, Wavre
S • Europe • 100 kW
CANADA
†R CANADA INTL, Sackville, NB
W • E North Am & C America • 250 kW
S • E North Am & C America • 250 kW
FRANCE
†R FRANCE INTL, Issoudun-Allouis
W • N Europe • 250 kW
W • S Europe • 250 kW
R MONTE CARLO, Via Sackville, Canada
W • N America • 250 kW
GERMANY
DEUTSCHE WELLE, Wertachtal
W • W North Am • 500 kW
JAPAN
RADIO JAPAN/NHK, Via Sackville, Can
E North Am • 250 kW
TURKEY
†VOICE OF TURKEY, Ankara-Çakirlar
S • Mideast • 250 kW
USA
ADVENTIST WORLD R, Via South Africa
S Africa • 100 kW
5964.7 BOLIVIA
†RADIO NACIONAL, Huanuni
M-Sa • DS • 2 kW
M-F • DS • 2 kW
DS • 2 kW
5965 BRAZIL
RADIO NOVA VISAO, Santa Maria
DS • 10 kW
CHINA
†CHINA RADIO INTL, Beijing
E Asia • 150 kW
W • Europe • 300 kW
W • E Europe & W Asia • 150/300 kW
CUBA
†RADIO HABANA CUBA, Havana
C America & W North Am • 100 kW
ECUADOR
LA VOZ DEL UPANO, Macas
Irr • DS • 10 kW
GERMANY
(con'd) DEUTSCHE WELLE, Via Armavir, Russia
W • Mideast & W Asia • 200 kW
0 1 2 3 4 5 6 7 8 9 10 11 12 13 14 15 16 17 18 19 20 21 22 23 24

SEASONAL S OR W 1-HR TIMESHIFT MIDYEAR ⇐ OR ⇒ JAMMING / OR ∧ EARLIEST HEARD ◁ LATEST HEARD ▷ NEW FOR 2002 †

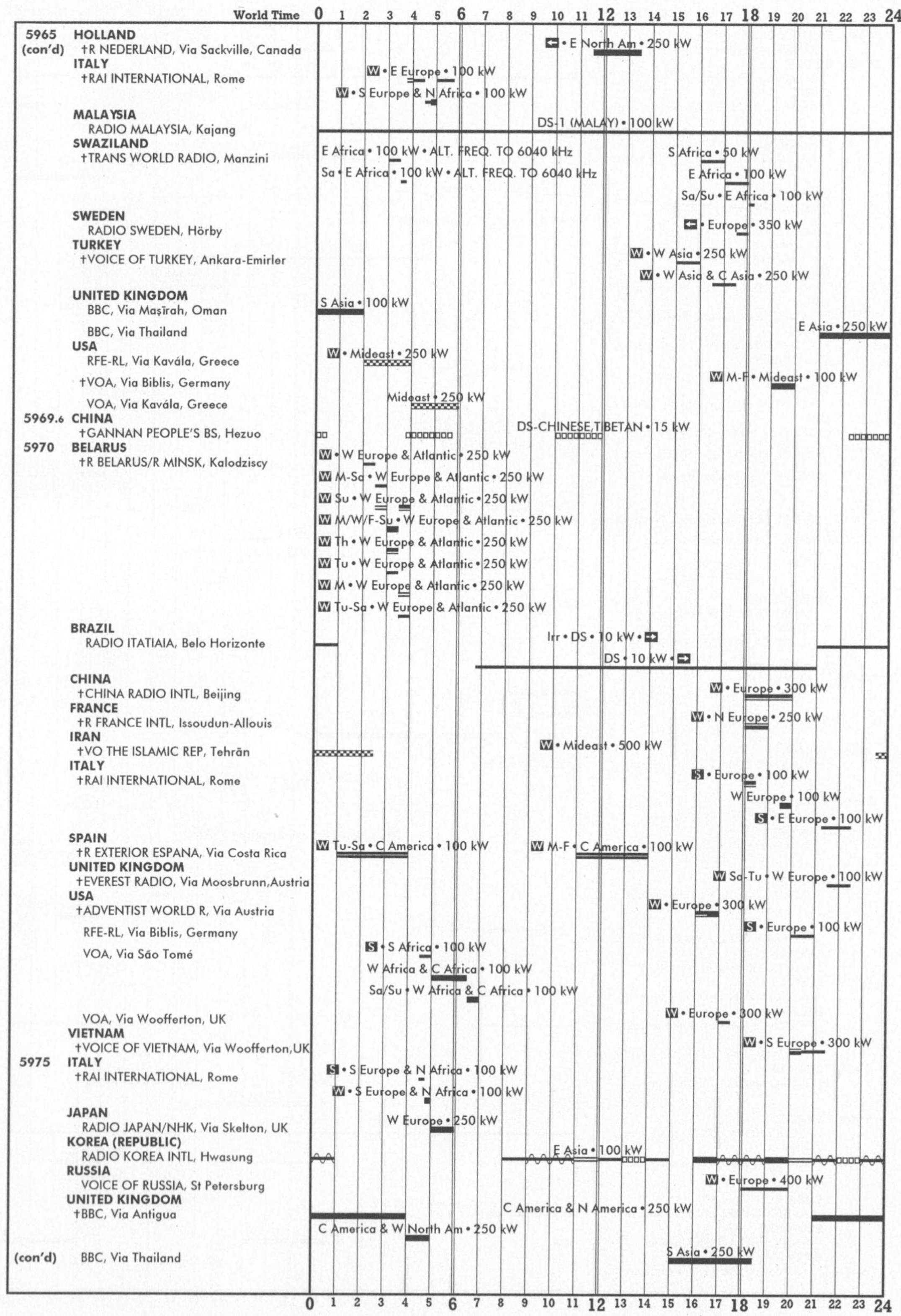
World Time 0 1 2 3 4 5 6 7 8 9 10 11 12 13 14 15 16 17 18 19 20 21 22 23 24
5965 (con'd) HOLLAND
†R NEDERLAND, Via Sackville, Canada
E North Am • 250 kW
ITALY
†RAI INTERNATIONAL, Rome
W • E Europe • 100 kW
W • S Europe & N Africa • 100 kW
MALAYSIA
RADIO MALAYSIA, Kajang
DS-1 (MALAY) • 100 kW
SWAZILAND
†TRANS WORLD RADIO, Manzini
E Africa • 100 kW • ALT. FREQ. TO 6040 kHz
Sa • E Africa • 100 kW • ALT. FREQ. TO 6040 kHz
S Africa • 50 kW
E Africa • 100 kW
Sa/Su • E Africa • 100 kW
SWEDEN
RADIO SWEDEN, Hörby
Europe • 350 kW
TURKEY
†VOICE OF TURKEY, Ankara-Emirler
W • W Asia • 250 kW
W • W Asia & C Asia • 250 kW
UNITED KINGDOM
BBC, Via Maşīrah, Oman
S Asia • 100 kW
BBC, Via Thailand
E Asia • 250 kW
USA
RFE-RL, Via Kavála, Greece
W • Mideast • 250 kW
†VOA, Via Biblis, Germany
W M-F • Mideast • 100 kW
VOA, Via Kavála, Greece
Mideast • 250 kW
5969.6 CHINA
†GANNAN PEOPLE'S BS, Hezuo
DS-CHINESE,TIBETAN • 15 kW
5970 BELARUS
†R BELARUS/R MINSK, Kalodziscy
W • W Europe & Atlantic • 250 kW
W M-Sa • W Europe & Atlantic • 250 kW
W Su • W Europe & Atlantic • 250 kW
W M/W/F-Su • W Europe & Atlantic • 250 kW
W Th • W Europe & Atlantic • 250 kW
W Tu • W Europe & Atlantic • 250 kW
W M • W Europe & Atlantic • 250 kW
W Tu-Sa • W Europe & Atlantic • 250 kW
BRAZIL
RADIO ITATIAIA, Belo Horizonte
Irr • DS • 10 kW
DS • 10 kW
CHINA
†CHINA RADIO INTL, Beijing
W • Europe • 300 kW
FRANCE
†R FRANCE INTL, Issoudun-Allouis
W • N Europe • 250 kW
IRAN
†VO THE ISLAMIC REP, Tehrān
W • Mideast • 500 kW
ITALY
†RAI INTERNATIONAL, Rome
S • Europe • 100 kW
W Europe • 100 kW
S • E Europe • 100 kW
SPAIN
†R EXTERIOR ESPANA, Via Costa Rica
W Tu-Sa • C America • 100 kW
W M-F • C America • 100 kW
UNITED KINGDOM
†EVEREST RADIO, Via Moosbrunn, Austria
W Sa-Tu • W Europe • 100 kW
USA
†ADVENTIST WORLD R, Via Austria
W • Europe • 300 kW
RFE-RL, Via Biblis, Germany
S • Europe • 100 kW
VOA, Via São Tomé
S • S Africa • 100 kW
W Africa & C Africa • 100 kW
Sa/Su • W Africa & C Africa • 100 kW
VOA, Via Woofferton, UK
W • Europe • 300 kW
VIETNAM
†VOICE OF VIETNAM, Via Woofferton, UK
W • S Europe • 300 kW
5975 ITALY
†RAI INTERNATIONAL, Rome
S • S Europe & N Africa • 100 kW
W • S Europe & N Africa • 100 kW
JAPAN
RADIO JAPAN/NHK, Via Skelton, UK
W Europe • 250 kW
KOREA (REPUBLIC)
RADIO KOREA INTL, Hwasung
E Asia • 100 kW
RUSSIA
VOICE OF RUSSIA, St Petersburg
W • Europe • 400 kW
UNITED KINGDOM
†BBC, Via Antigua
C America & N America • 250 kW
C America & W North Am • 250 kW
(con'd) BBC, Via Thailand
S Asia • 250 kW
0 1 2 3 4 5 6 7 8 9 10 11 12 13 14 15 16 17 18 19 20 21 22 23 24

ENGLISH ARABIC CHINESE FRENCH GERMAN RUSSIAN SPANISH OTHER

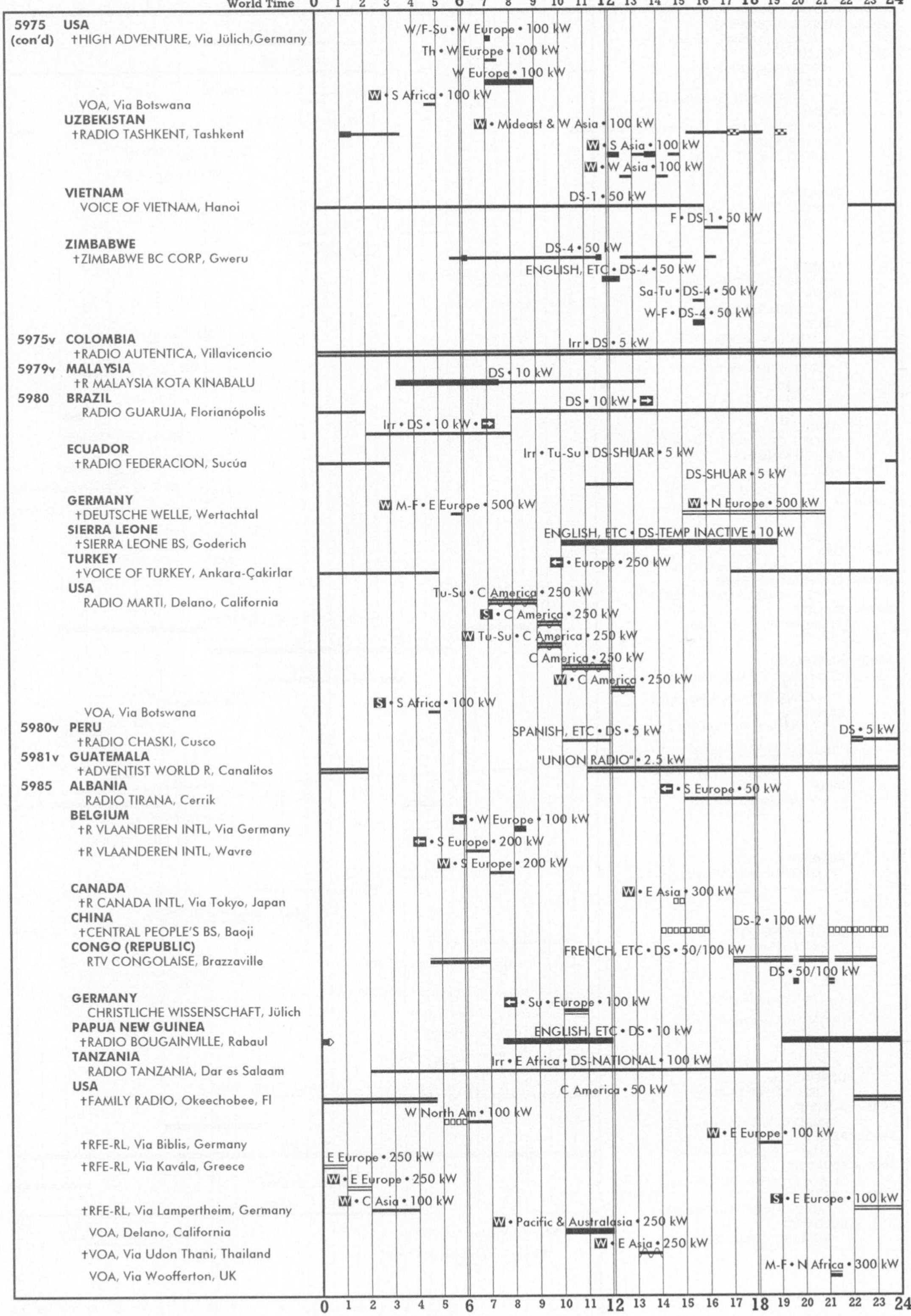
World Time 0 1 2 3 4 5 6 7 8 9 10 11 12 13 14 15 16 17 18 19 20 21 22 23 24
5975 (con'd) USA
†HIGH ADVENTURE, Via Jülich,Germany
W/F-Su • W Europe • 100 kW
Th • W Europe • 100 kW
W Europe • 100 kW
W • S Africa • 100 kW
VOA, Via Botswana
UZBEKISTAN
†RADIO TASHKENT, Tashkent
W • Mideast & W Asia • 100 kW
W • S Asia • 100 kW
W • W Asia • 100 kW
VIETNAM
VOICE OF VIETNAM, Hanoi
DS-1 • 50 kW
F • DS-1 • 50 kW
ZIMBABWE
†ZIMBABWE BC CORP, Gweru
DS-4 • 50 kW
ENGLISH, ETC • DS-4 • 50 kW
Sa-Tu • DS-4 • 50 kW
W-F • DS-4 • 50 kW
5975v COLOMBIA
†RADIO AUTENTICA, Villavicencio
Irr • DS • 5 kW
5979v MALAYSIA
†R MALAYSIA KOTA KINABALU
DS • 10 kW
5980 BRAZIL
RADIO GUARUJA, Florianópolis
DS • 10 kW
Irr • DS • 10 kW
ECUADOR
†RADIO FEDERACION, Sucúa
Irr • Tu-Su • DS-SHUAR • 5 kW
DS-SHUAR • 5 kW
GERMANY
†DEUTSCHE WELLE, Wertachtal
W M-F • E Europe • 500 kW
W • N Europe • 500 kW
SIERRA LEONE
†SIERRA LEONE BS, Goderich
ENGLISH, ETC • DS-TEMP INACTIVE • 10 kW
TURKEY
†VOICE OF TURKEY, Ankara-Çakirlar
• Europe • 250 kW
USA
RADIO MARTI, Delano, California
Tu-Su • C America • 250 kW
S • C America • 250 kW
W Tu-Su • C America • 250 kW
C America • 250 kW
W • C America • 250 kW
VOA, Via Botswana
S • S Africa • 100 kW
5980v PERU
†RADIO CHASKI, Cusco
SPANISH, ETC • DS • 5 kW
DS • 5 kW
5981v GUATEMALA
†ADVENTIST WORLD R, Canalitos
"UNION RADIO" • 2.5 kW
5985 ALBANIA
RADIO TIRANA, Cerrik
• S Europe • 50 kW
BELGIUM
†R VLAANDEREN INTL, Via Germany
• W Europe • 100 kW
†R VLAANDEREN INTL, Wavre
• S Europe • 200 kW
W • S Europe • 200 kW
CANADA
†R CANADA INTL, Via Tokyo, Japan
W • E Asia • 300 kW
CHINA
†CENTRAL PEOPLE'S BS, Baoji
DS-2 • 100 kW
CONGO (REPUBLIC)
RTV CONGOLAISE, Brazzaville
FRENCH, ETC • DS • 50/100 kW
DS • 50/100 kW
GERMANY
CHRISTLICHE WISSENSCHAFT, Jülich
• Su • Europe • 100 kW
PAPUA NEW GUINEA
†RADIO BOUGAINVILLE, Rabaul
ENGLISH, ETC • DS • 10 kW
TANZANIA
RADIO TANZANIA, Dar es Salaam
Irr • E Africa • DS-NATIONAL • 100 kW
USA
†FAMILY RADIO, Okeechobee, Fl
C America • 50 kW
W North Am • 100 kW
†RFE-RL, Via Biblis, Germany
W • E Europe • 100 kW
†RFE-RL, Via Kavála, Greece
E Europe • 250 kW
W • E Europe • 250 kW
W • C Asia • 100 kW
S • E Europe • 100 kW
†RFE-RL, Via Lampertheim, Germany
VOA, Delano, California
W • Pacific & Australasia • 250 kW
†VOA, Via Udon Thani, Thailand
W • E Asia • 250 kW
VOA, Via Woofferton, UK
M-F • N Africa • 300 kW
0 1 2 3 4 5 6 7 8 9 10 11 12 13 14 15 16 17 18 19 20 21 22 23 24

SEASONAL S OR W 1-HR TIMESHIFT MIDYEAR ← OR → JAMMING / OR ∧ EARLIEST HEARD ◁ LATEST HEARD ▷ NEW FOR 2002 †

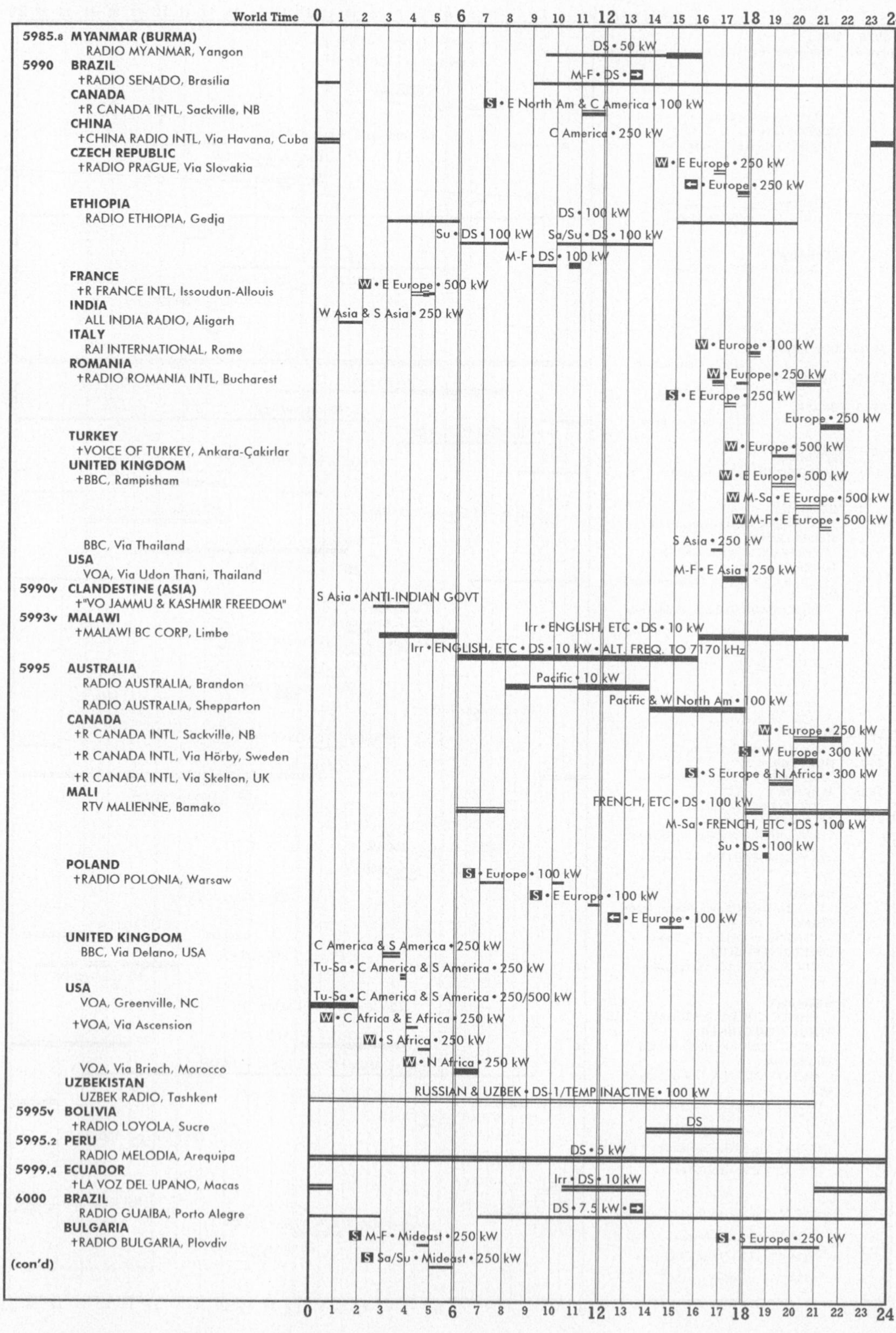
World Time 0 1 2 3 4 5 6 7 8 9 10 11 12 13 14 15 16 17 18 19 20 21 22 23 24
5985.8 MYANMAR (BURMA)
RADIO MYANMAR, Yangon
DS • 50 kW
5990 BRAZIL
†RADIO SENADO, Brasilia
M-F • DS •
CANADA
†R CANADA INTL, Sackville, NB
S • E North Am & C America • 100 kW
CHINA
†CHINA RADIO INTL, Via Havana, Cuba
C America • 250 kW
CZECH REPUBLIC
†RADIO PRAGUE, Via Slovakia
W • E Europe • 250 kW
Europe • 250 kW
ETHIOPIA
RADIO ETHIOPIA, Gedja
DS • 100 kW
Su • DS • 100 kW
Sa/Su • DS • 100 kW
M-F • DS • 100 kW
FRANCE
†R FRANCE INTL, Issoudun-Allouis
W • E Europe • 500 kW
INDIA
ALL INDIA RADIO, Aligarh
W Asia & S Asia • 250 kW
ITALY
RAI INTERNATIONAL, Rome
W • Europe • 100 kW
ROMANIA
†RADIO ROMANIA INTL, Bucharest
W • Europe • 250 kW
S • E Europe • 250 kW
Europe • 250 kW
TURKEY
†VOICE OF TURKEY, Ankara-Çakirlar
W • Europe • 500 kW
UNITED KINGDOM
†BBC, Rampisham
W • E Europe • 500 kW
W M-Sa • E Europe • 500 kW
W M-F • E Europe • 500 kW
BBC, Via Thailand
S Asia • 250 kW
USA
VOA, Via Udon Thani, Thailand
M-F • E Asia • 250 kW
5990v CLANDESTINE (ASIA)
†"VO JAMMU & KASHMIR FREEDOM"
S Asia • ANTI-INDIAN GOVT
5993v MALAWI
†MALAWI BC CORP, Limbe
Irr • ENGLISH, ETC • DS • 10 kW
Irr • ENGLISH, ETC • DS • 10 kW • ALT. FREQ. TO 7170 kHz
5995 AUSTRALIA
RADIO AUSTRALIA, Brandon
Pacific • 10 kW
RADIO AUSTRALIA, Shepparton
Pacific & W North Am • 100 kW
CANADA
†R CANADA INTL, Sackville, NB
W • Europe • 250 kW
†R CANADA INTL, Via Hörby, Sweden
S • W Europe • 300 kW
†R CANADA INTL, Via Skelton, UK
S • S Europe & N Africa • 300 kW
MALI
RTV MALIENNE, Bamako
FRENCH, ETC • DS • 100 kW
M-Sa • FRENCH, ETC • DS • 100 kW
Su • DS • 100 kW
POLAND
†RADIO POLONIA, Warsaw
S • Europe • 100 kW
S • E Europe • 100 kW
E Europe • 100 kW
UNITED KINGDOM
BBC, Via Delano, USA
C America & S America • 250 kW
Tu-Sa • C America & S America • 250 kW
USA
VOA, Greenville, NC
Tu-Sa • C America & S America • 250/500 kW
†VOA, Via Ascension
W • C Africa & E Africa • 250 kW
W • S Africa • 250 kW
VOA, Via Briech, Morocco
W • N Africa • 250 kW
UZBEKISTAN
UZBEK RADIO, Tashkent
RUSSIAN & UZBEK • DS-1/TEMP INACTIVE • 100 kW
5995v BOLIVIA
†RADIO LOYOLA, Sucre
DS
5995.2 PERU
RADIO MELODIA, Arequipa
DS • 5 kW
5999.4 ECUADOR
†LA VOZ DEL UPANO, Macas
Irr • DS • 10 kW
6000 BRAZIL
RADIO GUAIBA, Porto Alegre
DS • 7.5 kW •
BULGARIA
†RADIO BULGARIA, Plovdiv
S M-F • Mideast • 250 kW
S Sa/Su • Mideast • 250 kW
S • S Europe • 250 kW
(con'd)
0 1 2 3 4 5 6 7 8 9 10 11 12 13 14 15 16 17 18 19 20 21 22 23 24
ENGLISH ARABIC CHINESE FRENCH GERMAN RUSSIAN SPANISH OTHER

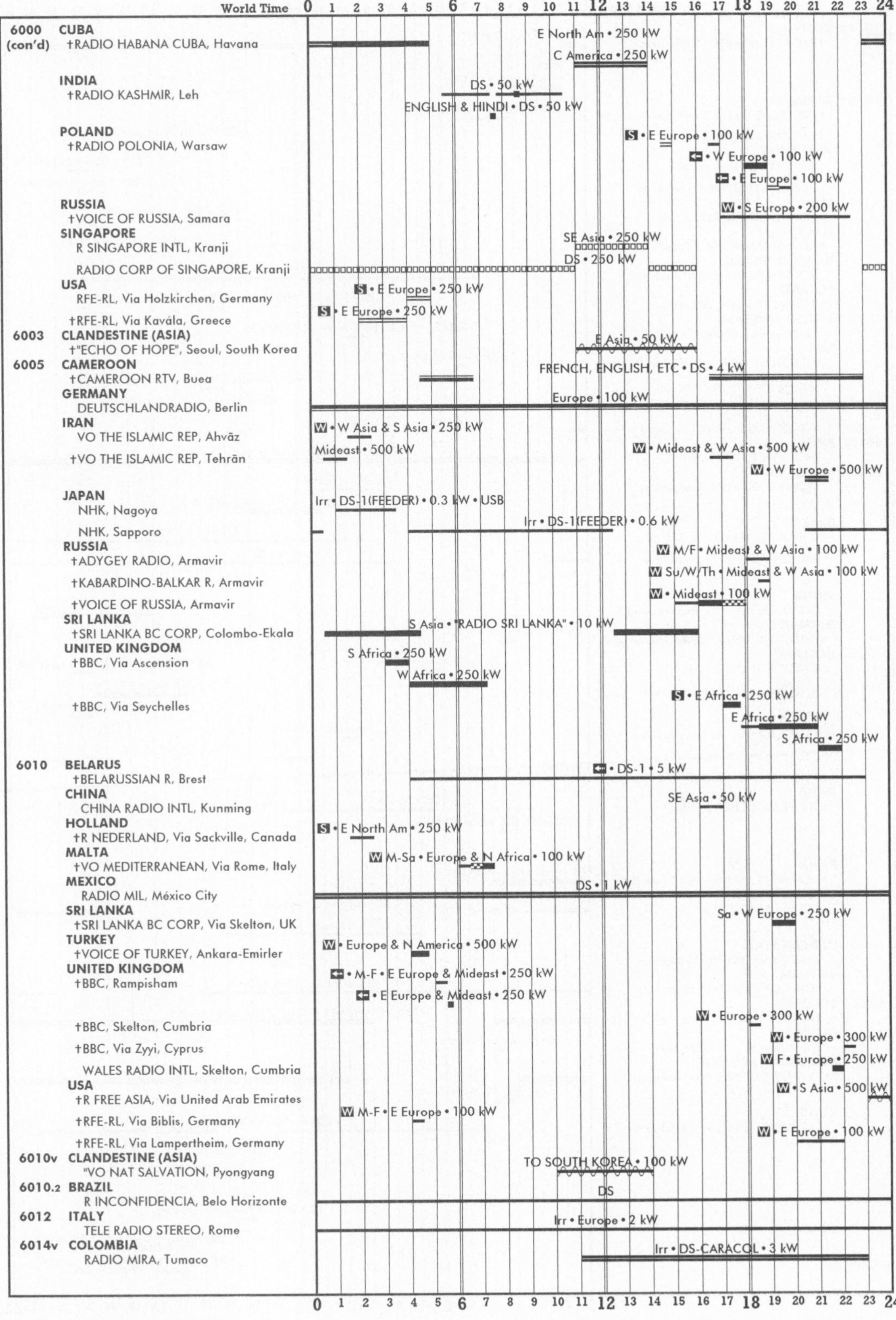
World Time 0 1 2 3 4 5 6 7 8 9 10 11 12 13 14 15 16 17 18 19 20 21 22 23 24
6000 (con'd) CUBA
†RADIO HABANA CUBA, Havana
E North Am • 250 kW
C America • 250 kW
INDIA
†RADIO KASHMIR, Leh
DS • 50 kW
ENGLISH & HINDI • DS • 50 kW
POLAND
†RADIO POLONIA, Warsaw
S • E Europe • 100 kW
• W Europe • 100 kW
• E Europe • 100 kW
RUSSIA
†VOICE OF RUSSIA, Samara
W • S Europe • 200 kW
SINGAPORE
R SINGAPORE INTL, Kranji
SE Asia • 250 kW
RADIO CORP OF SINGAPORE, Kranji
DS • 250 kW
USA
RFE-RL, Via Holzkirchen, Germany
S • E Europe • 250 kW
†RFE-RL, Via Kavála, Greece
S • E Europe • 250 kW
6003 CLANDESTINE (ASIA)
†"ECHO OF HOPE", Seoul, South Korea
E Asia • 50 kW
6005 CAMEROON
†CAMEROON RTV, Buea
FRENCH, ENGLISH, ETC • DS • 4 kW
GERMANY
DEUTSCHLANDRADIO, Berlin
Europe • 100 kW
IRAN
VO THE ISLAMIC REP, Ahvāz
W • W Asia & S Asia • 250 kW
†VO THE ISLAMIC REP, Tehrān
Mideast • 500 kW
W • Mideast & W Asia • 500 kW
W • W Europe • 500 kW
JAPAN
NHK, Nagoya
Irr • DS-1(FEEDER) • 0.3 kW • USB
NHK, Sapporo
Irr • DS-1(FEEDER) • 0.6 kW
RUSSIA
†ADYGEY RADIO, Armavir
W M/F • Mideast & W Asia • 100 kW
†KABARDINO-BALKAR R, Armavir
W Su/W/Th • Mideast & W Asia • 100 kW
†VOICE OF RUSSIA, Armavir
W • Mideast • 100 kW
SRI LANKA
†SRI LANKA BC CORP, Colombo-Ekala
S Asia • "RADIO SRI LANKA" • 10 kW
UNITED KINGDOM
†BBC, Via Ascension
S Africa • 250 kW
W Africa • 250 kW
†BBC, Via Seychelles
S • E Africa • 250 kW
E Africa • 250 kW
S Africa • 250 kW
6010 BELARUS
†BELARUSSIAN R, Brest
• DS-1 • 5 kW
CHINA
CHINA RADIO INTL, Kunming
SE Asia • 50 kW
HOLLAND
†R NEDERLAND, Via Sackville, Canada
S • E North Am • 250 kW
MALTA
†VO MEDITERRANEAN, Via Rome, Italy
W M-Sa • Europe & N Africa • 100 kW
MEXICO
RADIO MIL, México City
DS • 1 kW
SRI LANKA
†SRI LANKA BC CORP, Via Skelton, UK
Sa • W Europe • 250 kW
TURKEY
†VOICE OF TURKEY, Ankara-Emirler
W • Europe & N America • 500 kW
UNITED KINGDOM
†BBC, Rampisham
• M-F • E Europe & Mideast • 250 kW
• E Europe & Mideast • 250 kW
†BBC, Skelton, Cumbria
W • Europe • 300 kW
†BBC, Via Zyyi, Cyprus
W • Europe • 300 kW
WALES RADIO INTL, Skelton, Cumbria
W F • Europe • 250 kW
USA
†R FREE ASIA, Via United Arab Emirates
W • S Asia • 500 kW
†RFE-RL, Via Biblis, Germany
W M-F • E Europe • 100 kW
†RFE-RL, Via Lampertheim, Germany
W • E Europe • 100 kW
6010v CLANDESTINE (ASIA)
"VO NAT SALVATION, Pyongyang
TO SOUTH KOREA • 100 kW
6010.2 BRAZIL
R INCONFIDENCIA, Belo Horizonte
DS
6012 ITALY
TELE RADIO STEREO, Rome
Irr • Europe • 2 kW
6014v COLOMBIA
RADIO MIRA, Tumaco
Irr • DS-CARACOL • 3 kW
0 1 2 3 4 5 6 7 8 9 10 11 12 13 14 15 16 17 18 19 20 21 22 23 24

SEASONAL S OR W   1-HR TIMESHIFT MIDYEAR ⇐ OR ⇒   JAMMING / OR ⋀   EARLIEST HEARD ◁   LATEST HEARD ▷   NEW FOR 2002 †

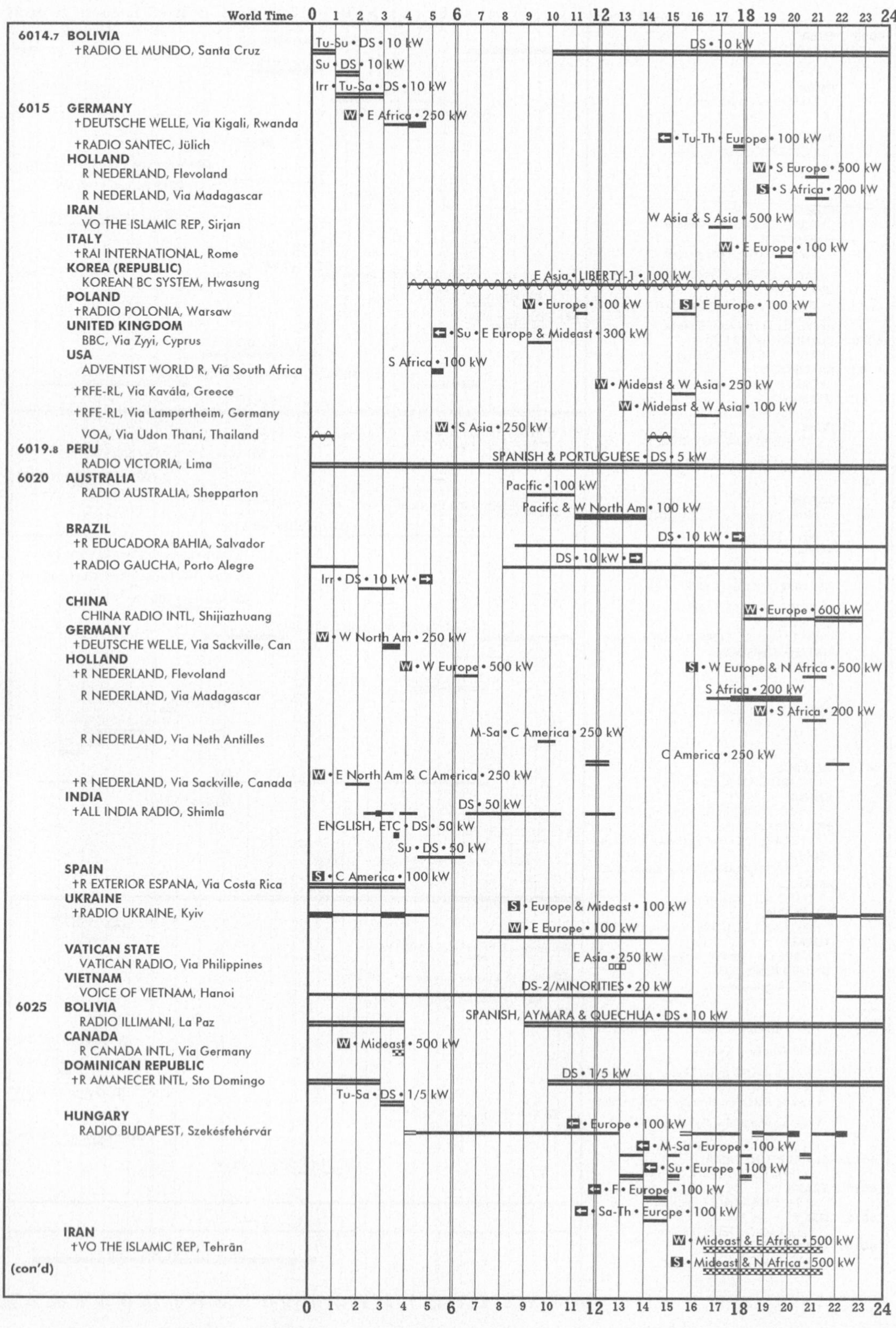
World Time 0 1 2 3 4 5 6 7 8 9 10 11 12 13 14 15 16 17 18 19 20 21 22 23 24
6014.7 BOLIVIA
†RADIO EL MUNDO, Santa Cruz
Tu-Su • DS • 10 kW
DS • 10 kW
Su • DS • 10 kW
Irr • Tu-Sa • DS • 10 kW
6015 GERMANY
†DEUTSCHE WELLE, Via Kigali, Rwanda
W • E Africa • 250 kW
†RADIO SANTEC, Jülich
• Tu-Th • Europe • 100 kW
HOLLAND
R NEDERLAND, Flevoland
W • S Europe • 500 kW
R NEDERLAND, Via Madagascar
S • S Africa • 200 kW
IRAN
VO THE ISLAMIC REP, Sirjan
W Asia & S Asia • 500 kW
ITALY
†RAI INTERNATIONAL, Rome
W • E Europe • 100 kW
KOREA (REPUBLIC)
KOREAN BC SYSTEM, Hwasung
E Asia • LIBERTY-1 • 100 kW
POLAND
†RADIO POLONIA, Warsaw
W • Europe • 100 kW
S • E Europe • 100 kW
UNITED KINGDOM
BBC, Via Zyyi, Cyprus
• Su • E Europe & Mideast • 300 kW
USA
ADVENTIST WORLD R, Via South Africa
S Africa • 100 kW
†RFE-RL, Via Kavála, Greece
W • Mideast & W Asia • 250 kW
†RFE-RL, Via Lampertheim, Germany
W • Mideast & W Asia • 100 kW
VOA, Via Udon Thani, Thailand
W • S Asia • 250 kW
6019.8 PERU
RADIO VICTORIA, Lima
SPANISH & PORTUGUESE • DS • 5 kW
6020 AUSTRALIA
RADIO AUSTRALIA, Shepparton
Pacific • 100 kW
Pacific & W North Am • 100 kW
BRAZIL
†R EDUCADORA BAHIA, Salvador
DS • 10 kW •
†RADIO GAUCHA, Porto Alegre
DS • 10 kW •
Irr • DS • 10 kW •
CHINA
CHINA RADIO INTL, Shijiazhuang
W • Europe • 600 kW
GERMANY
†DEUTSCHE WELLE, Via Sackville, Can
W • W North Am • 250 kW
HOLLAND
†R NEDERLAND, Flevoland
W • W Europe • 500 kW
S • W Europe & N Africa • 500 kW
R NEDERLAND, Via Madagascar
S Africa • 200 kW
W • S Africa • 200 kW
R NEDERLAND, Via Neth Antilles
M-Sa • C America • 250 kW
C America • 250 kW
†R NEDERLAND, Via Sackville, Canada
W • E North Am & C America • 250 kW
INDIA
†ALL INDIA RADIO, Shimla
DS • 50 kW
ENGLISH, ETC • DS • 50 kW
Su • DS • 50 kW
SPAIN
†R EXTERIOR ESPANA, Via Costa Rica
S • C America • 100 kW
UKRAINE
†RADIO UKRAINE, Kyiv
S • Europe & Mideast • 100 kW
W • E Europe • 100 kW
VATICAN STATE
VATICAN RADIO, Via Philippines
E Asia • 250 kW
VIETNAM
VOICE OF VIETNAM, Hanoi
DS-2/MINORITIES • 20 kW
6025 BOLIVIA
RADIO ILLIMANI, La Paz
SPANISH, AYMARA & QUECHUA • DS • 10 kW
CANADA
R CANADA INTL, Via Germany
W • Mideast • 500 kW
DOMINICAN REPUBLIC
†R AMANECER INTL, Sto Domingo
DS • 1/5 kW
Tu-Sa • DS • 1/5 kW
HUNGARY
RADIO BUDAPEST, Szekésfehérvár
• Europe • 100 kW
• M-Sa • Europe • 100 kW
• Su • Europe • 100 kW
• F • Europe • 100 kW
• Sa-Th • Europe • 100 kW
IRAN
†VO THE ISLAMIC REP, Tehrān
W • Mideast & E Africa • 500 kW
S • Mideast & N Africa • 500 kW
(con'd)
0 1 2 3 4 5 6 7 8 9 10 11 12 13 14 15 16 17 18 19 20 21 22 23 24
ENGLISH ARABIC CHINESE FRENCH GERMAN RUSSIAN SPANISH OTHER

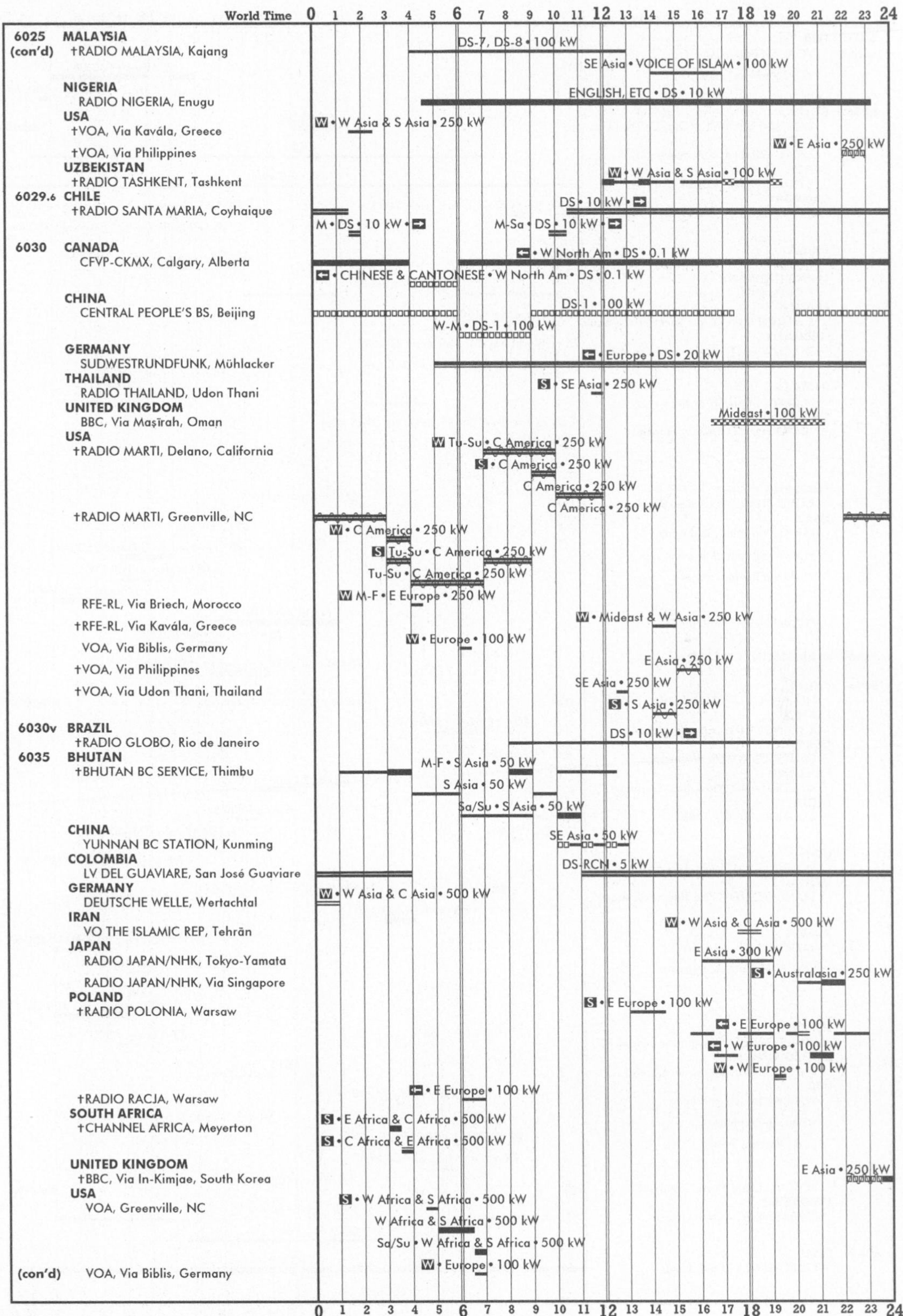
World Time 0 1 2 3 4 5 6 7 8 9 10 11 12 13 14 15 16 17 18 19 20 21 22 23 24
6025 (con'd) MALAYSIA
†RADIO MALAYSIA, Kajang
DS-7, DS-8 • 100 kW
SE Asia • VOICE OF ISLAM • 100 kW
NIGERIA
RADIO NIGERIA, Enugu
ENGLISH, ETC • DS • 10 kW
USA
†VOA, Via Kavála, Greece
W • W Asia & S Asia • 250 kW
†VOA, Via Philippines
W • E Asia • 250 kW
UZBEKISTAN
†RADIO TASHKENT, Tashkent
W • W Asia & S Asia • 100 kW
6029.6 CHILE
†RADIO SANTA MARIA, Coyhaique
DS • 10 kW
M • DS • 10 kW
M-Sa • DS • 10 kW
6030 CANADA
CFVP-CKMX, Calgary, Alberta
W North Am • DS • 0.1 kW
CHINESE & CANTONESE • W North Am • DS • 0.1 kW
CHINA
CENTRAL PEOPLE'S BS, Beijing
DS-1 • 100 kW
W-M • DS-1 • 100 kW
GERMANY
SUDWESTRUNDFUNK, Mühlacker
Europe • DS • 20 kW
THAILAND
RADIO THAILAND, Udon Thani
S • SE Asia • 250 kW
UNITED KINGDOM
BBC, Via Maşīrah, Oman
Mideast • 100 kW
USA
†RADIO MARTI, Delano, California
W Tu-Su • C America • 250 kW
S • C America • 250 kW
C America • 250 kW
C America • 250 kW
†RADIO MARTI, Greenville, NC
W • C America • 250 kW
S Tu-Su • C America • 250 kW
Tu-Su • C America • 250 kW
RFE-RL, Via Briech, Morocco
W M-F • E Europe • 250 kW
†RFE-RL, Via Kavála, Greece
W • Mideast & W Asia • 250 kW
VOA, Via Biblis, Germany
W • Europe • 100 kW
†VOA, Via Philippines
E Asia • 250 kW
†VOA, Via Udon Thani, Thailand
SE Asia • 250 kW
S • S Asia • 250 kW
6030v BRAZIL
†RADIO GLOBO, Rio de Janeiro
DS • 10 kW
6035 BHUTAN
†BHUTAN BC SERVICE, Thimbu
M-F • S Asia • 50 kW
S Asia • 50 kW
Sa/Su • S Asia • 50 kW
CHINA
YUNNAN BC STATION, Kunming
SE Asia • 50 kW
COLOMBIA
LV DEL GUAVIARE, San José Guaviare
DS-RCN • 5 kW
GERMANY
DEUTSCHE WELLE, Wertachtal
W • W Asia & C Asia • 500 kW
IRAN
VO THE ISLAMIC REP, Tehrān
W • W Asia & C Asia • 500 kW
JAPAN
RADIO JAPAN/NHK, Tokyo-Yamata
E Asia • 300 kW
RADIO JAPAN/NHK, Via Singapore
S • Australasia • 250 kW
POLAND
†RADIO POLONIA, Warsaw
S • E Europe • 100 kW
E Europe • 100 kW
W Europe • 100 kW
W • W Europe • 100 kW
†RADIO RACJA, Warsaw
E Europe • 100 kW
SOUTH AFRICA
†CHANNEL AFRICA, Meyerton
S • E Africa & C Africa • 500 kW
S • C Africa & E Africa • 500 kW
UNITED KINGDOM
†BBC, Via In-Kimjae, South Korea
E Asia • 250 kW
USA
VOA, Greenville, NC
S • W Africa & S Africa • 500 kW
W Africa & S Africa • 500 kW
Sa/Su • W Africa & S Africa • 500 kW
(con'd) VOA, Via Biblis, Germany
W • Europe • 100 kW
0 1 2 3 4 5 6 7 8 9 10 11 12 13 14 15 16 17 18 19 20 21 22 23 24

SEASONAL S OR W 1-HR TIMESHIFT MIDYEAR ⇐ OR ⇒ JAMMING / OR ∧ EARLIEST HEARD ◁ LATEST HEARD ▷ NEW FOR 2002 †

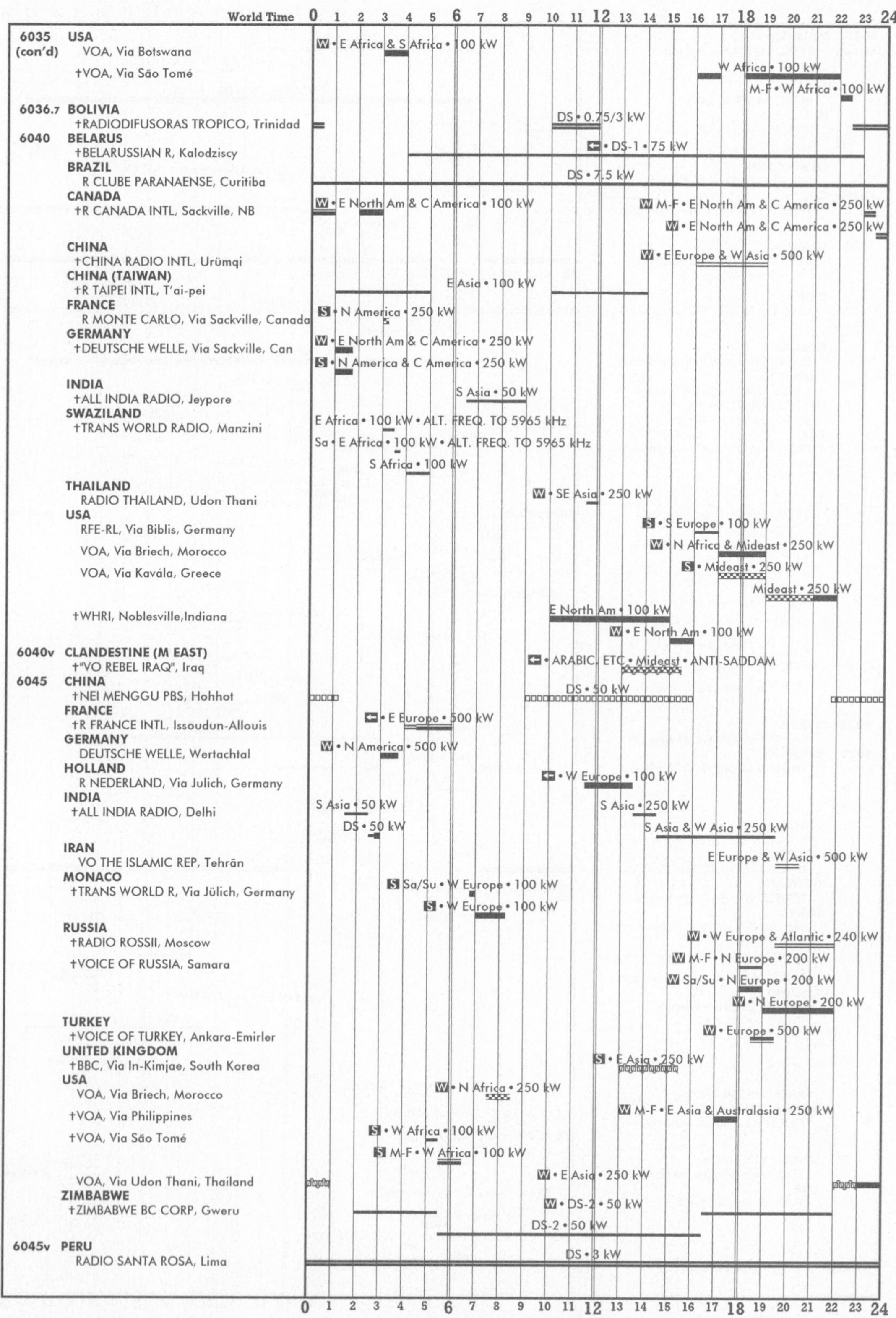
World Time
0 1 2 3 4 5 6 7 8 9 10 11 12 13 14 15 16 17 18 19 20 21 22 23 24
6035 (con'd) USA
VOA, Via Botswana
W • E Africa & S Africa • 100 kW
†VOA, Via São Tomé
W Africa • 100 kW
M-F • W Africa • 100 kW
6036.7 BOLIVIA
†RADIODIFUSORAS TROPICO, Trinidad
DS • 0.75/3 kW
6040 BELARUS
†BELARUSSIAN R, Kalodziscy
• DS-1 • 75 kW
BRAZIL
R CLUBE PARANAENSE, Curitiba
DS • 7.5 kW
CANADA
†R CANADA INTL, Sackville, NB
W • E North Am & C America • 100 kW
W M-F • E North Am & C America • 250 kW
W • E North Am & C America • 250 kW
CHINA
†CHINA RADIO INTL, Urümqi
W • E Europe & W Asia • 500 kW
CHINA (TAIWAN)
†R TAIPEI INTL, T'ai-pei
E Asia • 100 kW
FRANCE
R MONTE CARLO, Via Sackville, Canada
S • N America • 250 kW
GERMANY
†DEUTSCHE WELLE, Via Sackville, Can
W • E North Am & C America • 250 kW
S • N America & C America • 250 kW
INDIA
†ALL INDIA RADIO, Jeypore
S Asia • 50 kW
SWAZILAND
†TRANS WORLD RADIO, Manzini
E Africa • 100 kW • ALT. FREQ. TO 5965 kHz
Sa • E Africa • 100 kW • ALT. FREQ. TO 5965 kHz
S Africa • 100 kW
THAILAND
RADIO THAILAND, Udon Thani
W • SE Asia • 250 kW
USA
RFE-RL, Via Biblis, Germany
S • S Europe • 100 kW
VOA, Via Briech, Morocco
W • N Africa & Mideast • 250 kW
VOA, Via Kavála, Greece
S • Mideast • 250 kW
Mideast • 250 kW
†WHRI, Noblesville,Indiana
E North Am • 100 kW
W • E North Am • 100 kW
6040v CLANDESTINE (M EAST)
†"VO REBEL IRAQ", Iraq
• ARABIC, ETC • Mideast • ANTI-SADDAM
6045 CHINA
†NEI MENGGU PBS, Hohhot
DS • 50 kW
FRANCE
†R FRANCE INTL, Issoudun-Allouis
• E Europe • 500 kW
GERMANY
DEUTSCHE WELLE, Wertachtal
W • N America • 500 kW
HOLLAND
R NEDERLAND, Via Julich, Germany
• W Europe • 100 kW
INDIA
†ALL INDIA RADIO, Delhi
S Asia • 50 kW
S Asia • 250 kW
DS • 50 kW
S Asia & W Asia • 250 kW
IRAN
VO THE ISLAMIC REP, Tehrān
E Europe & W Asia • 500 kW
MONACO
†TRANS WORLD R, Via Jülich, Germany
S Sa/Su • W Europe • 100 kW
S • W Europe • 100 kW
RUSSIA
†RADIO ROSSII, Moscow
W • W Europe & Atlantic • 240 kW
†VOICE OF RUSSIA, Samara
W M-F • N Europe • 200 kW
W Sa/Su • N Europe • 200 kW
W • N Europe • 200 kW
TURKEY
†VOICE OF TURKEY, Ankara-Emirler
W • Europe • 500 kW
UNITED KINGDOM
†BBC, Via In-Kimjae, South Korea
S • E Asia • 250 kW
USA
VOA, Via Briech, Morocco
W • N Africa • 250 kW
†VOA, Via Philippines
W M-F • E Asia & Australasia • 250 kW
†VOA, Via São Tomé
S • W Africa • 100 kW
S M-F • W Africa • 100 kW
VOA, Via Udon Thani, Thailand
W • E Asia • 250 kW
ZIMBABWE
†ZIMBABWE BC CORP, Gweru
W • DS-2 • 50 kW
DS-2 • 50 kW
6045v PERU
RADIO SANTA ROSA, Lima
DS • 3 kW
0 1 2 3 4 5 6 7 8 9 10 11 12 13 14 15 16 17 18 19 20 21 22 23 24
ENGLISH ARABIC CHINESE FRENCH GERMAN RUSSIAN SPANISH OTHER

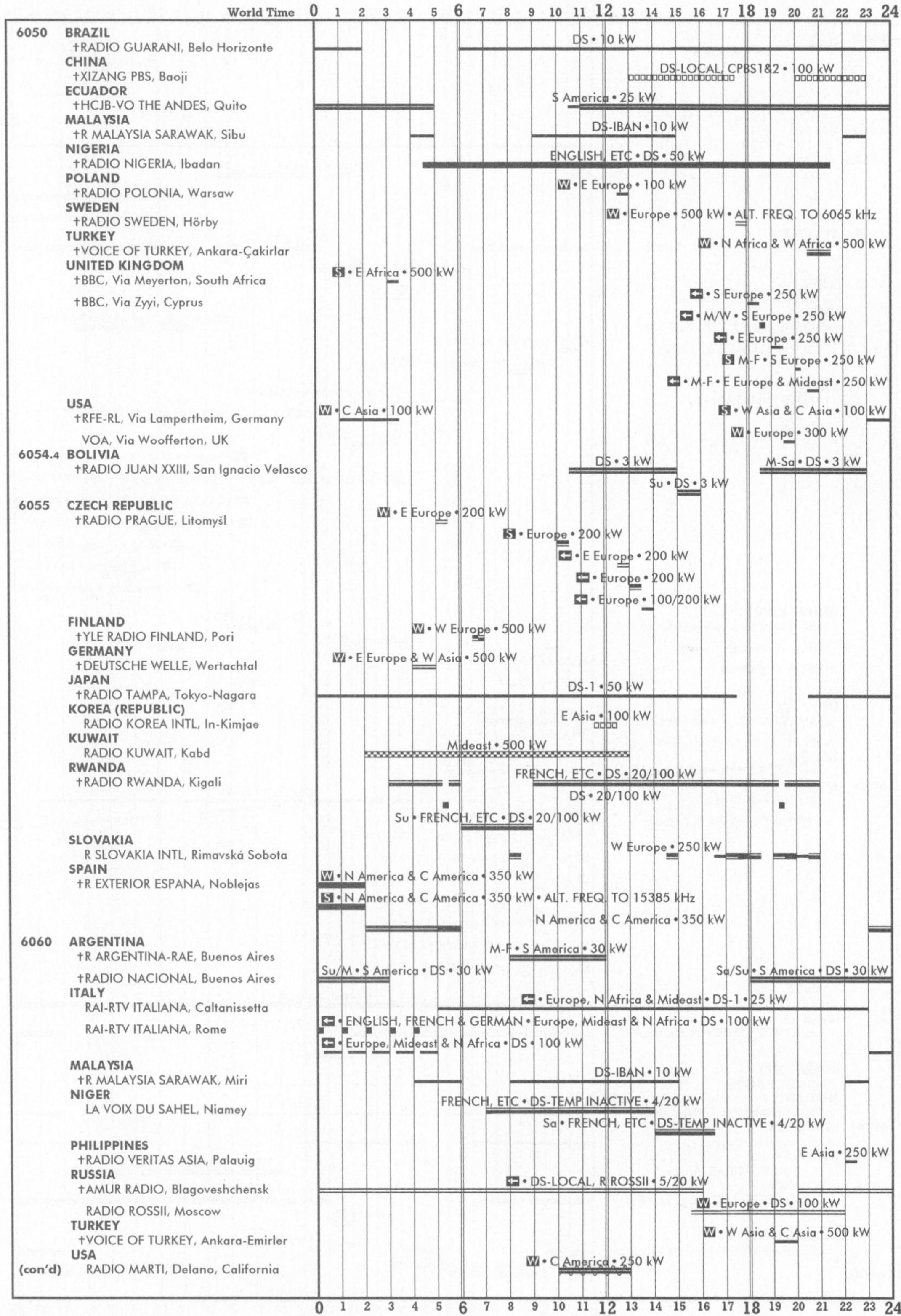
World Time 0 1 2 3 4 5 6 7 8 9 10 11 12 13 14 15 16 17 18 19 20 21 22 23 24
6050 BRAZIL
†RADIO GUARANI, Belo Horizonte
DS • 10 kW
CHINA
†XIZANG PBS, Baoji
DS-LOCAL, CPBS1&2 • 100 kW
ECUADOR
†HCJB-VO THE ANDES, Quito
S America • 25 kW
MALAYSIA
†R MALAYSIA SARAWAK, Sibu
DS-IBAN • 10 kW
NIGERIA
†RADIO NIGERIA, Ibadan
ENGLISH, ETC • DS • 50 kW
POLAND
†RADIO POLONIA, Warsaw
W • E Europe • 100 kW
SWEDEN
†RADIO SWEDEN, Hörby
W • Europe • 500 kW • ALT. FREQ. TO 6065 kHz
TURKEY
†VOICE OF TURKEY, Ankara-Çakirlar
W • N Africa & W Africa • 500 kW
UNITED KINGDOM
†BBC, Via Meyerton, South Africa
S • E Africa • 500 kW
†BBC, Via Zyyi, Cyprus
• S Europe • 250 kW
• M/W • S Europe • 250 kW
• E Europe • 250 kW
S M-F • S Europe • 250 kW
• M-F • E Europe & Mideast • 250 kW
USA
†RFE-RL, Via Lampertheim, Germany
W • C Asia • 100 kW
S • W Asia & C Asia • 100 kW
VOA, Via Woofferton, UK
W • Europe • 300 kW
6054.4 BOLIVIA
†RADIO JUAN XXIII, San Ignacio Velasco
DS • 3 kW
M-Sa • DS • 3 kW
Su • DS • 3 kW
6055 CZECH REPUBLIC
†RADIO PRAGUE, Litomyšl
W • E Europe • 200 kW
S • Europe • 200 kW
• E Europe • 200 kW
• Europe • 200 kW
• Europe • 100/200 kW
FINLAND
†YLE RADIO FINLAND, Pori
W • W Europe • 500 kW
GERMANY
†DEUTSCHE WELLE, Wertachtal
W • E Europe & W Asia • 500 kW
JAPAN
†RADIO TAMPA, Tokyo-Nagara
DS-1 • 50 kW
KOREA (REPUBLIC)
RADIO KOREA INTL, In-Kimjae
E Asia • 100 kW
KUWAIT
RADIO KUWAIT, Kabd
Mideast • 500 kW
RWANDA
†RADIO RWANDA, Kigali
FRENCH, ETC • DS • 20/100 kW
DS • 20/100 kW
Su • FRENCH, ETC • DS • 20/100 kW
SLOVAKIA
R SLOVAKIA INTL, Rimavská Sobota
W Europe • 250 kW
SPAIN
†R EXTERIOR ESPANA, Noblejas
W • N America & C America • 350 kW
S • N America & C America • 350 kW • ALT. FREQ. TO 15385 kHz
N America & C America • 350 kW
6060 ARGENTINA
†R ARGENTINA-RAE, Buenos Aires
M-F • S America • 30 kW
†RADIO NACIONAL, Buenos Aires
Su/M • S America • DS • 30 kW
Sa/Su • S America • DS • 30 kW
ITALY
RAI-RTV ITALIANA, Caltanissetta
• Europe, N Africa & Mideast • DS-1 • 25 kW
RAI-RTV ITALIANA, Rome
• ENGLISH, FRENCH & GERMAN • Europe, Mideast & N Africa • DS • 100 kW
• Europe, Mideast & N Africa • DS • 100 kW
MALAYSIA
†R MALAYSIA SARAWAK, Miri
DS-IBAN • 10 kW
NIGER
LA VOIX DU SAHEL, Niamey
FRENCH, ETC • DS-TEMP INACTIVE • 4/20 kW
Sa • FRENCH, ETC • DS-TEMP INACTIVE • 4/20 kW
PHILIPPINES
†RADIO VERITAS ASIA, Palauig
E Asia • 250 kW
RUSSIA
†AMUR RADIO, Blagoveshchensk
• DS-LOCAL, R ROSSII • 5/20 kW
RADIO ROSSII, Moscow
W • Europe • DS • 100 kW
TURKEY
†VOICE OF TURKEY, Ankara-Emirler
W • W Asia & C Asia • 500 kW
USA
(con'd) RADIO MARTI, Delano, California
W • C America • 250 kW
0 1 2 3 4 5 6 7 8 9 10 11 12 13 14 15 16 17 18 19 20 21 22 23 24

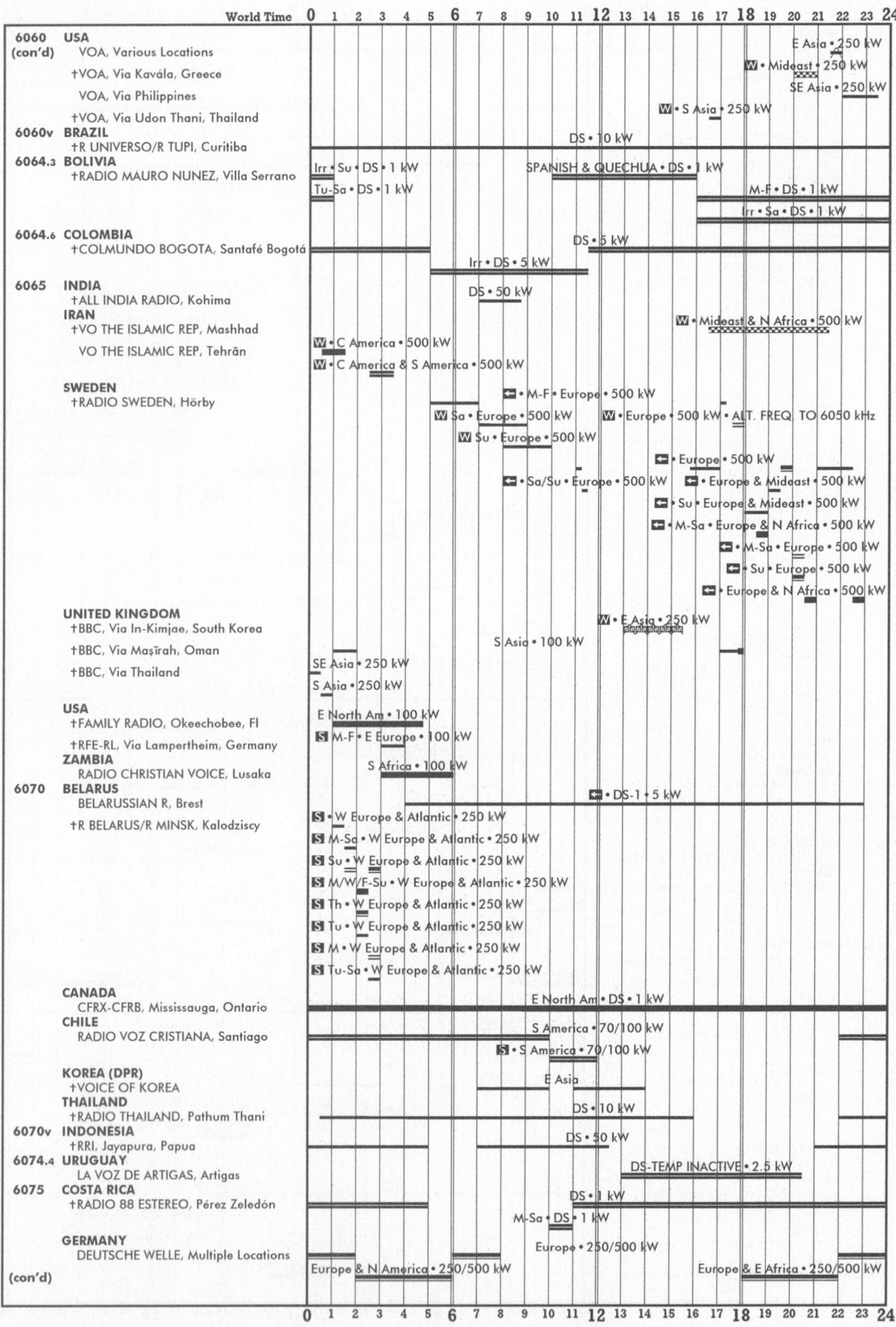
World Time 0 1 2 3 4 5 6 7 8 9 10 11 12 13 14 15 16 17 18 19 20 21 22 23 24
6060 (con'd) USA
VOA, Various Locations
E Asia • 250 kW
†VOA, Via Kavála, Greece
W • Mideast • 250 kW
VOA, Via Philippines
SE Asia • 250 kW
†VOA, Via Udon Thani, Thailand
W • S Asia • 250 kW
6060v BRAZIL
†R UNIVERSO/R TUPI, Curitiba
DS • 10 kW
6064.3 BOLIVIA
†RADIO MAURO NUNEZ, Villa Serrano
Irr • Su • DS • 1 kW
SPANISH & QUECHUA • DS • 1 kW
Tu-Sa • DS • 1 kW
M-F • DS • 1 kW
Irr • Sa • DS • 1 kW
6064.6 COLOMBIA
†COLMUNDO BOGOTA, Santafé Bogotá
DS • 5 kW
Irr • DS • 5 kW
6065 INDIA
†ALL INDIA RADIO, Kohima
DS • 50 kW
IRAN
†VO THE ISLAMIC REP, Mashhad
W • Mideast & N Africa • 500 kW
VO THE ISLAMIC REP, Tehrān
W • C America • 500 kW
W • C America & S America • 500 kW
SWEDEN
†RADIO SWEDEN, Hörby
M-F • Europe • 500 kW
W Sa • Europe • 500 kW
W • Europe • 500 kW • ALT. FREQ. TO 6050 kHz
W Su • Europe • 500 kW
• Europe • 500 kW
• Sa/Su • Europe • 500 kW
• Europe & Mideast • 500 kW
• Su • Europe & Mideast • 500 kW
• M-Sa • Europe & N Africa • 500 kW
• M-Sa • Europe • 500 kW
• Su • Europe • 500 kW
• Europe & N Africa • 500 kW
UNITED KINGDOM
†BBC, Via In-Kimjae, South Korea
W • E Asia • 250 kW
†BBC, Via Maṣīrah, Oman
S Asia • 100 kW
†BBC, Via Thailand
SE Asia • 250 kW
S Asia • 250 kW
USA
†FAMILY RADIO, Okeechobee, Fl
E North Am • 100 kW
†RFE-RL, Via Lampertheim, Germany
S M-F • E Europe • 100 kW
ZAMBIA
RADIO CHRISTIAN VOICE, Lusaka
S Africa • 100 kW
6070 BELARUS
BELARUSSIAN R, Brest
• DS-1 • 5 kW
†R BELARUS/R MINSK, Kalodziscy
S • W Europe & Atlantic • 250 kW
S M-Sa • W Europe & Atlantic • 250 kW
S Su • W Europe & Atlantic • 250 kW
S M/W/F-Su • W Europe & Atlantic • 250 kW
S Th • W Europe & Atlantic • 250 kW
S Tu • W Europe & Atlantic • 250 kW
S M • W Europe & Atlantic • 250 kW
S Tu-Sa • W Europe & Atlantic • 250 kW
CANADA
CFRX-CFRB, Mississauga, Ontario
E North Am • DS • 1 kW
CHILE
RADIO VOZ CRISTIANA, Santiago
S America • 70/100 kW
S • S America • 70/100 kW
KOREA (DPR)
†VOICE OF KOREA
E Asia
THAILAND
†RADIO THAILAND, Pathum Thani
DS • 10 kW
6070v INDONESIA
†RRI, Jayapura, Papua
DS • 50 kW
6074.4 URUGUAY
LA VOZ DE ARTIGAS, Artigas
DS-TEMP INACTIVE • 2.5 kW
6075 COSTA RICA
†RADIO 88 ESTEREO, Pérez Zeledón
DS • 1 kW
M-Sa • DS • 1 kW
GERMANY
DEUTSCHE WELLE, Multiple Locations
Europe • 250/500 kW
(con'd)
Europe & N America • 250/500 kW
Europe & E Africa • 250/500 kW
0 1 2 3 4 5 6 7 8 9 10 11 12 13 14 15 16 17 18 19 20 21 22 23 24
ENGLISH ARABIC CHINESE FRENCH GERMAN RUSSIAN SPANISH OTHER

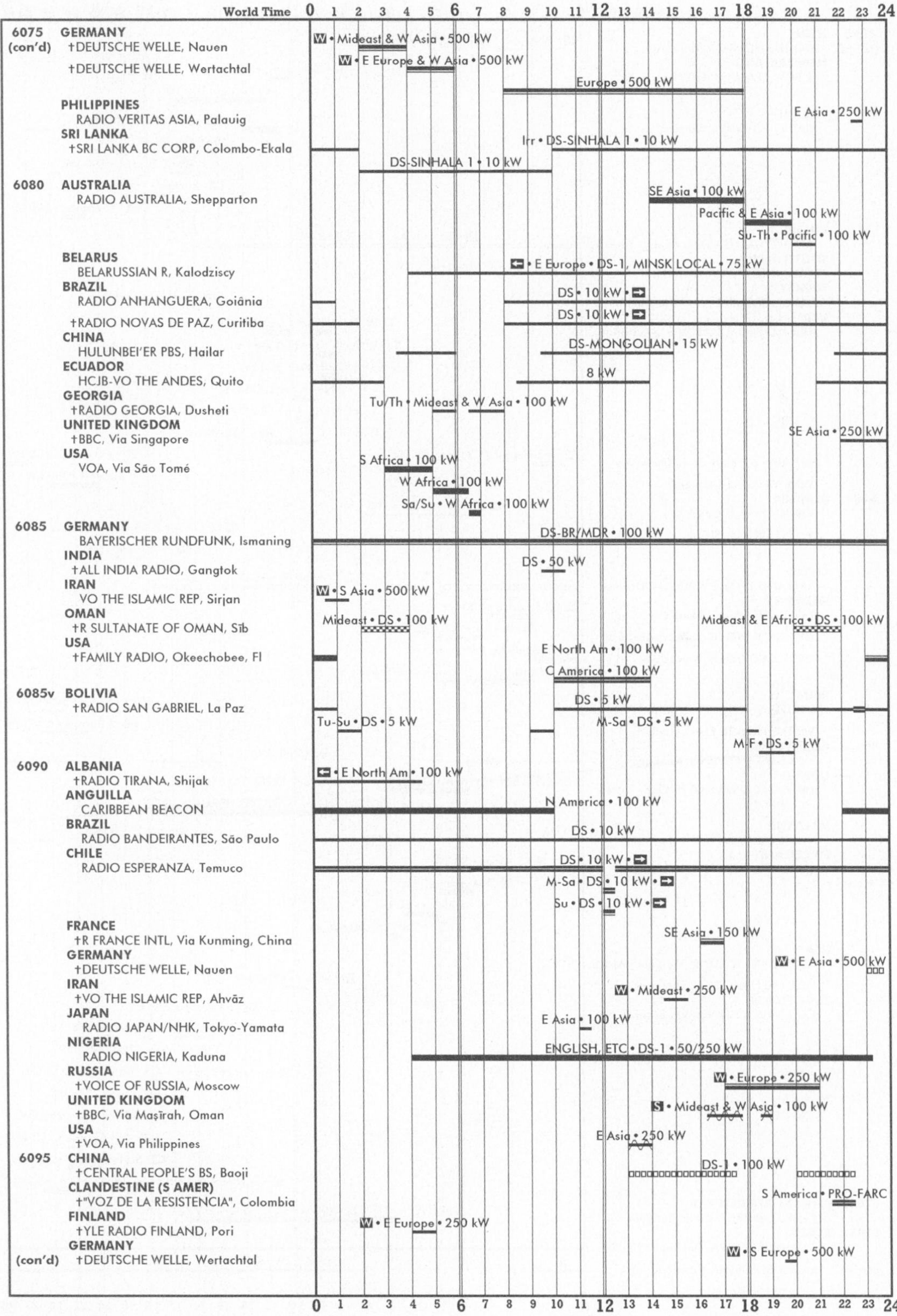
World Time 0 1 2 3 4 5 6 7 8 9 10 11 12 13 14 15 16 17 18 19 20 21 22 23 24
6075 (con'd) GERMANY
†DEUTSCHE WELLE, Nauen
W • Mideast & W Asia • 500 kW
W • E Europe & W Asia • 500 kW
†DEUTSCHE WELLE, Wertachtal
Europe • 500 kW
PHILIPPINES
RADIO VERITAS ASIA, Palauig
E Asia • 250 kW
SRI LANKA
†SRI LANKA BC CORP, Colombo-Ekala
Irr • DS-SINHALA 1 • 10 kW
DS-SINHALA 1 • 10 kW
6080 AUSTRALIA
RADIO AUSTRALIA, Shepparton
SE Asia • 100 kW
Pacific & E Asia • 100 kW
Su-Th • Pacific • 100 kW
BELARUS
BELARUSSIAN R, Kalodziscy
• E Europe • DS-1, MINSK LOCAL • 75 kW
BRAZIL
RADIO ANHANGUERA, Goiânia
DS • 10 kW •
†RADIO NOVAS DE PAZ, Curitiba
DS • 10 kW •
CHINA
HULUNBEI'ER PBS, Hailar
DS-MONGOLIAN • 15 kW
ECUADOR
HCJB-VO THE ANDES, Quito
8 kW
GEORGIA
†RADIO GEORGIA, Dusheti
Tu/Th • Mideast & W Asia • 100 kW
UNITED KINGDOM
†BBC, Via Singapore
SE Asia • 250 kW
USA
VOA, Via São Tomé
S Africa • 100 kW
W Africa • 100 kW
Sa/Su • W Africa • 100 kW
6085 GERMANY
BAYERISCHER RUNDFUNK, Ismaning
DS-BR/MDR • 100 kW
INDIA
†ALL INDIA RADIO, Gangtok
DS • 50 kW
IRAN
VO THE ISLAMIC REP, Sirjan
W • S Asia • 500 kW
OMAN
†R SULTANATE OF OMAN, Sīb
Mideast • DS • 100 kW
Mideast & E Africa • DS • 100 kW
USA
†FAMILY RADIO, Okeechobee, Fl
E North Am • 100 kW
C America • 100 kW
6085v BOLIVIA
†RADIO SAN GABRIEL, La Paz
DS • 5 kW
Tu-Su • DS • 5 kW
M-Sa • DS • 5 kW
M-F • DS • 5 kW
6090 ALBANIA
†RADIO TIRANA, Shijak
• E North Am • 100 kW
ANGUILLA
CARIBBEAN BEACON
N America • 100 kW
BRAZIL
RADIO BANDEIRANTES, São Paulo
DS • 10 kW
CHILE
RADIO ESPERANZA, Temuco
DS • 10 kW •
M-Sa • DS • 10 kW •
Su • DS • 10 kW •
FRANCE
†R FRANCE INTL, Via Kunming, China
SE Asia • 150 kW
GERMANY
†DEUTSCHE WELLE, Nauen
W • E Asia • 500 kW
IRAN
†VO THE ISLAMIC REP, Ahvāz
W • Mideast • 250 kW
JAPAN
RADIO JAPAN/NHK, Tokyo-Yamata
E Asia • 100 kW
NIGERIA
RADIO NIGERIA, Kaduna
ENGLISH, ETC • DS-1 • 50/250 kW
RUSSIA
†VOICE OF RUSSIA, Moscow
W • Europe • 250 kW
UNITED KINGDOM
†BBC, Via Maṣīrah, Oman
S • Mideast & W Asia • 100 kW
USA
†VOA, Via Philippines
E Asia • 250 kW
6095 CHINA
†CENTRAL PEOPLE'S BS, Baoji
DS-1 • 100 kW
CLANDESTINE (S AMER)
†"VOZ DE LA RESISTENCIA", Colombia
S America • PRO-FARC
FINLAND
†YLE RADIO FINLAND, Pori
W • E Europe • 250 kW
(con'd) GERMANY
†DEUTSCHE WELLE, Wertachtal
W • S Europe • 500 kW
0 1 2 3 4 5 6 7 8 9 10 11 12 13 14 15 16 17 18 19 20 21 22 23 24

SEASONAL S OR W 1-HR TIMESHIFT MIDYEAR OR JAMMING / OR /\ EARLIEST HEARD ◁ LATEST HEARD ▷ NEW FOR 2002 †

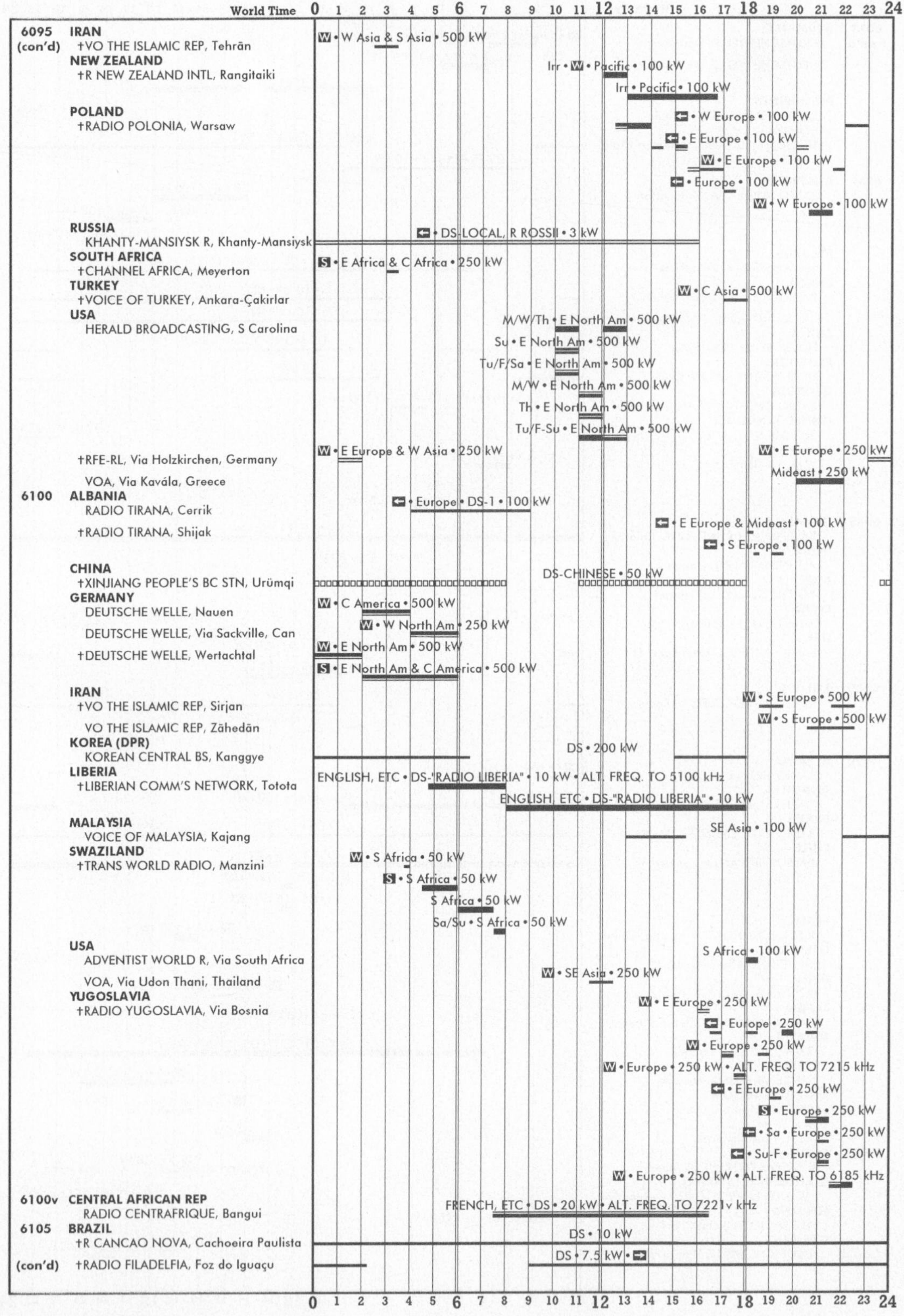
World Time 0 1 2 3 4 5 6 7 8 9 10 11 12 13 14 15 16 17 18 19 20 21 22 23 24
6095 (con'd) IRAN
†VO THE ISLAMIC REP, Tehrān
W • W Asia & S Asia • 500 kW
NEW ZEALAND
†R NEW ZEALAND INTL, Rangitaiki
Irr • W • Pacific • 100 kW
Irr • Pacific • 100 kW
POLAND
†RADIO POLONIA, Warsaw
• W Europe • 100 kW
• E Europe • 100 kW
W • E Europe • 100 kW
• Europe • 100 kW
W • W Europe • 100 kW
RUSSIA
KHANTY-MANSIYSK R, Khanty-Mansiysk
• DS-LOCAL, R ROSSII • 3 kW
SOUTH AFRICA
†CHANNEL AFRICA, Meyerton
S • E Africa & C Africa • 250 kW
TURKEY
†VOICE OF TURKEY, Ankara-Çakirlar
W • C Asia • 500 kW
USA
HERALD BROADCASTING, S Carolina
M/W/Th • E North Am • 500 kW
Su • E North Am • 500 kW
Tu/F/Sa • E North Am • 500 kW
M/W • E North Am • 500 kW
Th • E North Am • 500 kW
Tu/F-Su • E North Am • 500 kW
†RFE-RL, Via Holzkirchen, Germany
W • E Europe & W Asia • 250 kW
W • E Europe • 250 kW
VOA, Via Kavála, Greece
Mideast • 250 kW
6100 ALBANIA
RADIO TIRANA, Cerrik
• Europe • DS-1 • 100 kW
†RADIO TIRANA, Shijak
• E Europe & Mideast • 100 kW
• S Europe • 100 kW
CHINA
†XINJIANG PEOPLE'S BC STN, Urümqi
DS-CHINESE • 50 kW
GERMANY
DEUTSCHE WELLE, Nauen
W • C America • 500 kW
DEUTSCHE WELLE, Via Sackville, Can
W • W North Am • 250 kW
†DEUTSCHE WELLE, Wertachtal
W • E North Am • 500 kW
S • E North Am & C America • 500 kW
IRAN
†VO THE ISLAMIC REP, Sirjan
W • S Europe • 500 kW
VO THE ISLAMIC REP, Zāhedān
W • S Europe • 500 kW
KOREA (DPR)
KOREAN CENTRAL BS, Kanggye
DS • 200 kW
LIBERIA
†LIBERIAN COMM'S NETWORK, Totota
ENGLISH, ETC • DS-"RADIO LIBERIA" • 10 kW • ALT. FREQ. TO 5100 kHz
ENGLISH, ETC • DS-"RADIO LIBERIA" • 10 kW
MALAYSIA
VOICE OF MALAYSIA, Kajang
SE Asia • 100 kW
SWAZILAND
†TRANS WORLD RADIO, Manzini
W • S Africa • 50 kW
S • S Africa • 50 kW
S Africa • 50 kW
Sa/Su • S Africa • 50 kW
USA
ADVENTIST WORLD R, Via South Africa
S Africa • 100 kW
VOA, Via Udon Thani, Thailand
W • SE Asia • 250 kW
YUGOSLAVIA
†RADIO YUGOSLAVIA, Via Bosnia
W • E Europe • 250 kW
• Europe • 250 kW
W • Europe • 250 kW
W • Europe • 250 kW • ALT. FREQ. TO 7215 kHz
• E Europe • 250 kW
S • Europe • 250 kW
• Sa • Europe • 250 kW
• Su-F • Europe • 250 kW
W • Europe • 250 kW • ALT. FREQ. TO 6185 kHz
6100v CENTRAL AFRICAN REP
RADIO CENTRAFRIQUE, Bangui
FRENCH, ETC • DS • 20 kW • ALT. FREQ. TO 7221v kHz
6105 BRAZIL
†R CANCAO NOVA, Cachoeira Paulista
DS • 10 kW
(con'd) †RADIO FILADELFIA, Foz do Iguaçu
DS • 7.5 kW •
ENGLISH ARABIC CHINESE FRENCH GERMAN RUSSIAN SPANISH OTHER

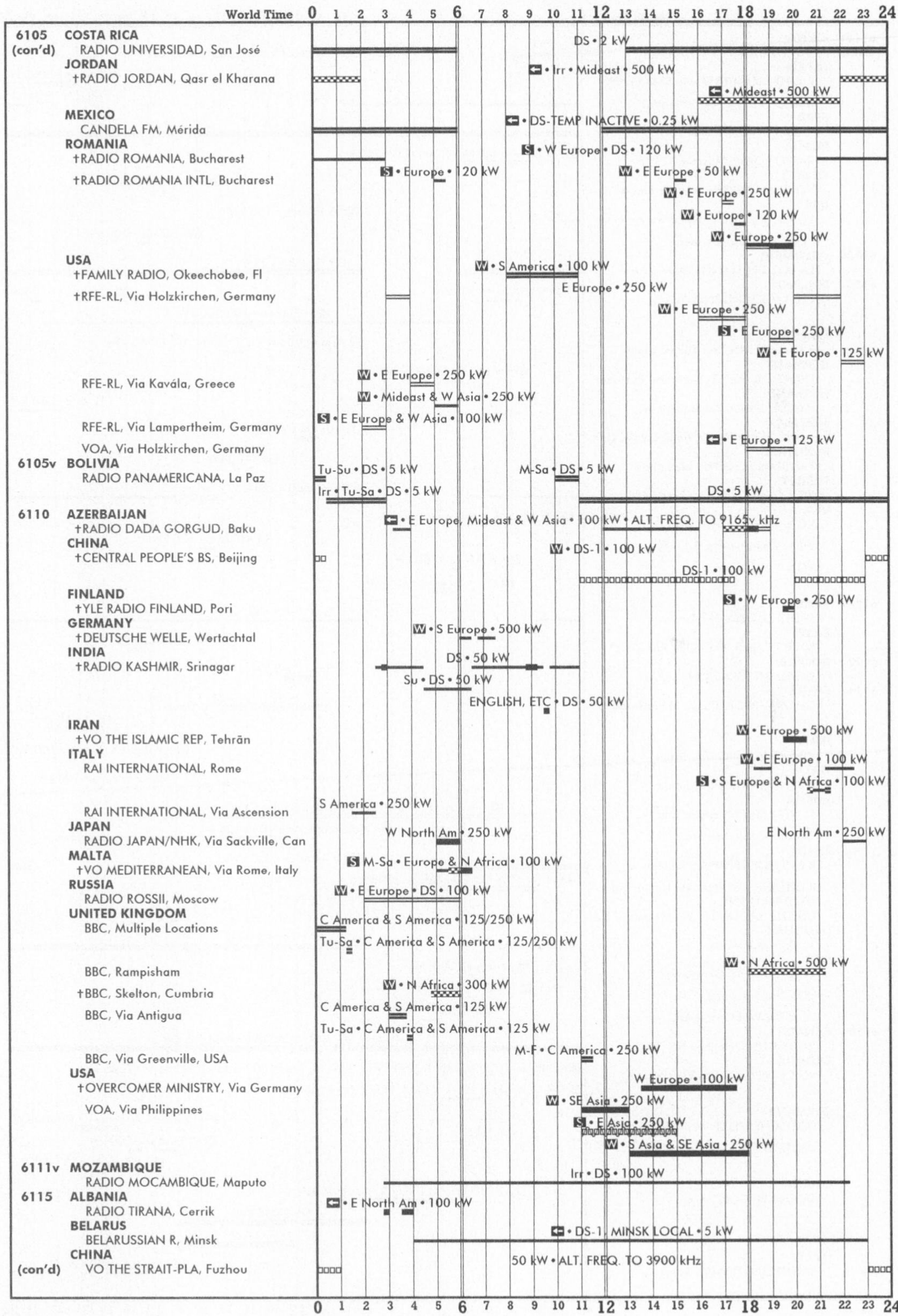
World Time 0 1 2 3 4 5 6 7 8 9 10 11 12 13 14 15 16 17 18 19 20 21 22 23 24
6105 (con'd) COSTA RICA
RADIO UNIVERSIDAD, San José
DS • 2 kW
JORDAN
†RADIO JORDAN, Qasr el Kharana
Irr • Mideast • 500 kW
Mideast • 500 kW
MEXICO
CANDELA FM, Mérida
DS-TEMP INACTIVE • 0.25 kW
ROMANIA
†RADIO ROMANIA, Bucharest
W Europe • DS • 120 kW
†RADIO ROMANIA INTL, Bucharest
Europe • 120 kW
E Europe • 50 kW
E Europe • 250 kW
Europe • 120 kW
Europe • 250 kW
USA
†FAMILY RADIO, Okeechobee, Fl
S America • 100 kW
†RFE-RL, Via Holzkirchen, Germany
E Europe • 250 kW
E Europe • 250 kW
E Europe • 250 kW
E Europe • 125 kW
RFE-RL, Via Kavála, Greece
E Europe • 250 kW
Mideast & W Asia • 250 kW
RFE-RL, Via Lampertheim, Germany
E Europe & W Asia • 100 kW
VOA, Via Holzkirchen, Germany
E Europe • 125 kW
6105v BOLIVIA
RADIO PANAMERICANA, La Paz
Tu-Su • DS • 5 kW
M-Sa • DS • 5 kW
Irr • Tu-Sa • DS • 5 kW
DS • 5 kW
6110 AZERBAIJAN
†RADIO DADA GORGUD, Baku
E Europe, Mideast & W Asia • 100 kW • ALT. FREQ. TO 9165v kHz
CHINA
†CENTRAL PEOPLE'S BS, Beijing
DS-1 • 100 kW
DS-1 • 100 kW
FINLAND
†YLE RADIO FINLAND, Pori
W Europe • 250 kW
GERMANY
†DEUTSCHE WELLE, Wertachtal
S Europe • 500 kW
INDIA
†RADIO KASHMIR, Srinagar
DS • 50 kW
Su • DS • 50 kW
ENGLISH, ETC • DS • 50 kW
IRAN
†VO THE ISLAMIC REP, Tehrān
Europe • 500 kW
ITALY
RAI INTERNATIONAL, Rome
E Europe • 100 kW
S Europe & N Africa • 100 kW
RAI INTERNATIONAL, Via Ascension
S America • 250 kW
JAPAN
RADIO JAPAN/NHK, Via Sackville, Can
W North Am • 250 kW
E North Am • 250 kW
MALTA
†VO MEDITERRANEAN, Via Rome, Italy
M-Sa • Europe & N Africa • 100 kW
RUSSIA
RADIO ROSSII, Moscow
E Europe • DS • 100 kW
UNITED KINGDOM
BBC, Multiple Locations
C America & S America • 125/250 kW
Tu-Sa • C America & S America • 125/250 kW
BBC, Rampisham
N Africa • 500 kW
†BBC, Skelton, Cumbria
N Africa • 300 kW
BBC, Via Antigua
C America & S America • 125 kW
Tu-Sa • C America & S America • 125 kW
BBC, Via Greenville, USA
M-F • C America • 250 kW
USA
†OVERCOMER MINISTRY, Via Germany
W Europe • 100 kW
VOA, Via Philippines
SE Asia • 250 kW
E Asia • 250 kW
S Asia & SE Asia • 250 kW
6111v MOZAMBIQUE
RADIO MOCAMBIQUE, Maputo
Irr • DS • 100 kW
6115 ALBANIA
RADIO TIRANA, Cerrik
E North Am • 100 kW
BELARUS
BELARUSSIAN R, Minsk
DS-1, MINSK LOCAL • 5 kW
CHINA (con'd)
VO THE STRAIT-PLA, Fuzhou
50 kW • ALT. FREQ. TO 3900 kHz
0 1 2 3 4 5 6 7 8 9 10 11 12 13 14 15 16 17 18 19 20 21 22 23 24

SEASONAL S OR W 1-HR TIMESHIFT MIDYEAR OR JAMMING / OR /\ EARLIEST HEARD ◁ LATEST HEARD ▷ NEW FOR 2002 †

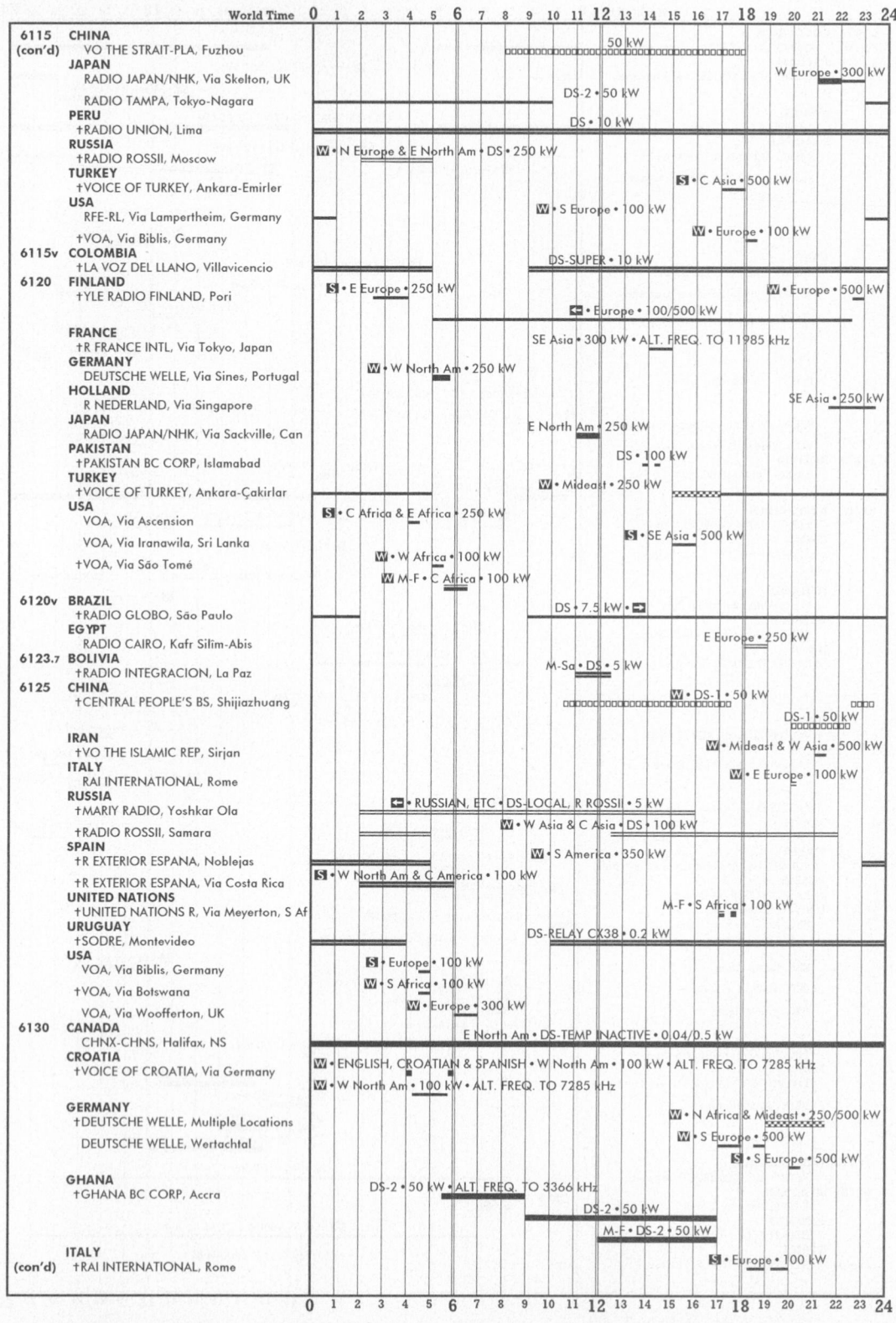

World Time 0 1 2 3 4 5 6 7 8 9 10 11 12 13 14 15 16 17 18 19 20 21 22 23 24

Frequency	Country / Station	Chart notes
6115 (con'd)	**CHINA**	
	VO THE STRAIT-PLA, Fuzhou	50 kW
	JAPAN	
	RADIO JAPAN/NHK, Via Skelton, UK	W Europe • 300 kW
	RADIO TAMPA, Tokyo-Nagara	DS-2 • 50 kW
	PERU	
	†RADIO UNION, Lima	DS • 10 kW
	RUSSIA	
	†RADIO ROSSII, Moscow	W • N Europe & E North Am • DS • 250 kW
	TURKEY	
	†VOICE OF TURKEY, Ankara-Emirler	S • C Asia • 500 kW
	USA	
	RFE-RL, Via Lampertheim, Germany	W • S Europe • 100 kW
	†VOA, Via Biblis, Germany	W • Europe • 100 kW
6115v	**COLOMBIA**	
	†LA VOZ DEL LLANO, Villavicencio	DS-SUPER • 10 kW
6120	**FINLAND**	
	†YLE RADIO FINLAND, Pori	S • E Europe • 250 kW; W • Europe • 500 kW; ← • Europe • 100/500 kW
	FRANCE	
	†R FRANCE INTL, Via Tokyo, Japan	SE Asia • 300 kW • ALT. FREQ. TO 11985 kHz
	GERMANY	
	DEUTSCHE WELLE, Via Sines, Portugal	W • W North Am • 250 kW
	HOLLAND	
	R NEDERLAND, Via Singapore	SE Asia • 250 kW
	JAPAN	
	RADIO JAPAN/NHK, Via Sackville, Can	E North Am • 250 kW
	PAKISTAN	
	†PAKISTAN BC CORP, Islamabad	DS • 100 kW
	TURKEY	
	†VOICE OF TURKEY, Ankara-Çakirlar	W • Mideast • 250 kW
	USA	
	VOA, Via Ascension	S • C Africa & E Africa • 250 kW
	VOA, Via Iranawila, Sri Lanka	S • SE Asia • 500 kW
	†VOA, Via São Tomé	W • W Africa • 100 kW; W M-F • C Africa • 100 kW
6120v	**BRAZIL**	
	†RADIO GLOBO, São Paulo	DS • 7.5 kW • →
	EGYPT	
	RADIO CAIRO, Kafr Silîm-Abis	E Europe • 250 kW
6123.7	**BOLIVIA**	
	†RADIO INTEGRACION, La Paz	M-Sa • DS • 5 kW
6125	**CHINA**	
	†CENTRAL PEOPLE'S BS, Shijiazhuang	W • DS-1 • 50 kW; DS-1 • 50 kW
	IRAN	
	†VO THE ISLAMIC REP, Sirjan	W • Mideast & W Asia • 500 kW
	ITALY	
	RAI INTERNATIONAL, Rome	W • E Europe • 100 kW
	RUSSIA	
	†MARIY RADIO, Yoshkar Ola	← • RUSSIAN, ETC • DS-LOCAL, R ROSSII • 5 kW
	†RADIO ROSSII, Samara	W • W Asia & C Asia • DS • 100 kW
	SPAIN	
	†R EXTERIOR ESPANA, Noblejas	W • S America • 350 kW
	†R EXTERIOR ESPANA, Via Costa Rica	S • W North Am & C America • 100 kW
	UNITED NATIONS	
	†UNITED NATIONS R, Via Meyerton, S Af	M-F • S Africa • 100 kW
	URUGUAY	
	†SODRE, Montevideo	DS-RELAY CX38 • 0.2 kW
	USA	
	VOA, Via Biblis, Germany	S • Europe • 100 kW
	†VOA, Via Botswana	W • S Africa • 100 kW
	VOA, Via Woofferton, UK	W • Europe • 300 kW
6130	**CANADA**	
	CHNX-CHNS, Halifax, NS	E North Am • DS-TEMP INACTIVE • 0.04/0.5 kW
	CROATIA	
	†VOICE OF CROATIA, Via Germany	W • ENGLISH, CROATIAN & SPANISH • W North Am • 100 kW • ALT. FREQ. TO 7285 kHz; W • W North Am • 100 kW • ALT. FREQ. TO 7285 kHz
	GERMANY	
	†DEUTSCHE WELLE, Multiple Locations	W • N Africa & Mideast • 250/500 kW
	DEUTSCHE WELLE, Wertachtal	W • S Europe • 500 kW; S • S Europe • 500 kW
	GHANA	
	†GHANA BC CORP, Accra	DS-2 • 50 kW • ALT. FREQ. TO 3366 kHz; DS-2 • 50 kW; M-F • DS-2 • 50 kW
(con'd)	**ITALY**	
	†RAI INTERNATIONAL, Rome	S • Europe • 100 kW

0 1 2 3 4 5 6 7 8 9 10 11 12 13 14 15 16 17 18 19 20 21 22 23 24

ENGLISH ▬ ARABIC ▦ CHINESE ▭ FRENCH ═ GERMAN ▬ RUSSIAN ═ SPANISH ═ OTHER —

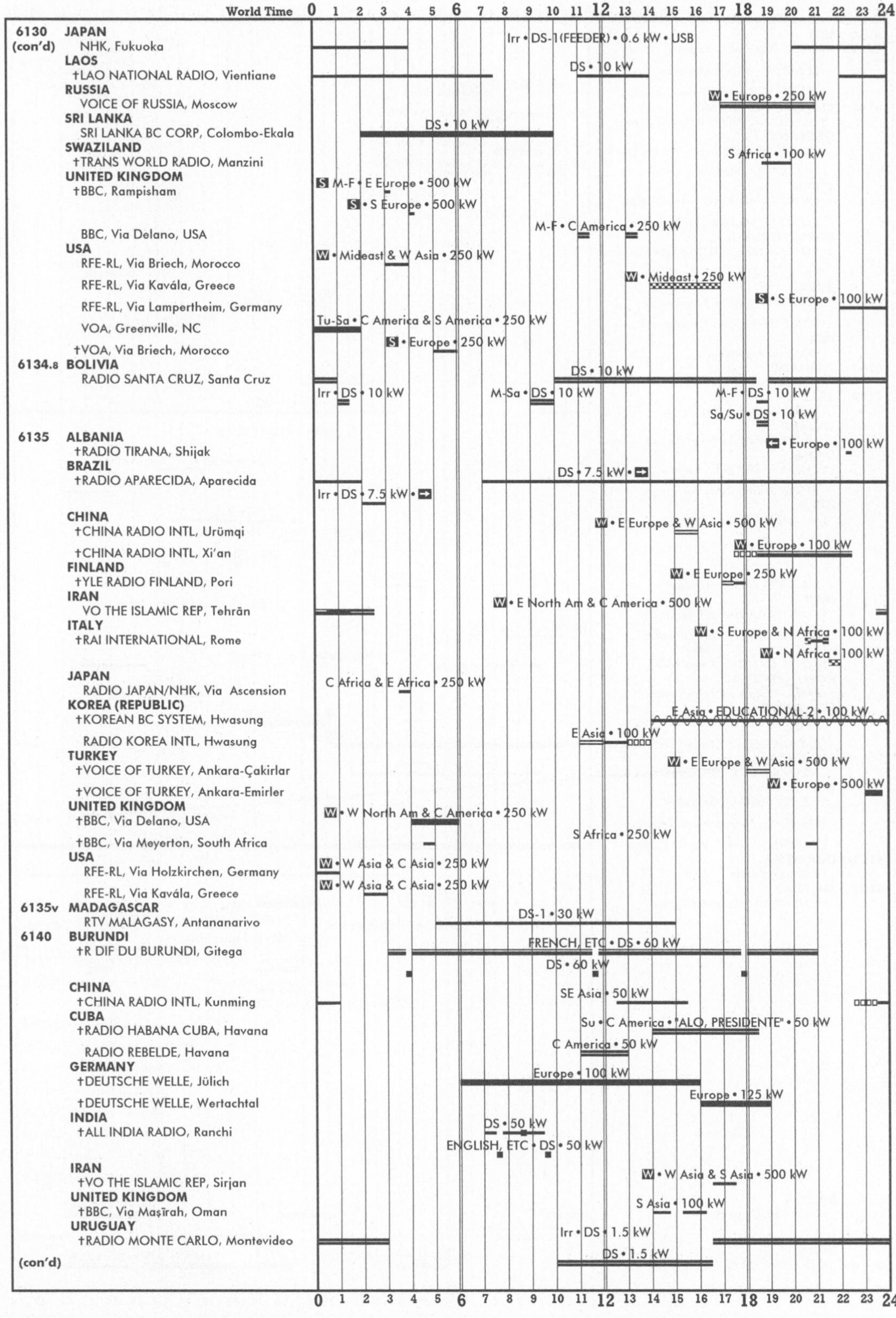

World Time 0 1 2 3 4 5 6 7 8 9 10 11 12 13 14 15 16 17 18 19 20 21 22 23 24
6130 (con'd) JAPAN
NHK, Fukuoka
Irr • DS-1(FEEDER) • 0.6 kW • USB
LAOS
†LAO NATIONAL RADIO, Vientiane
DS • 10 kW
RUSSIA
VOICE OF RUSSIA, Moscow
W • Europe • 250 kW
SRI LANKA
SRI LANKA BC CORP, Colombo-Ekala
DS • 10 kW
SWAZILAND
†TRANS WORLD RADIO, Manzini
S Africa • 100 kW
UNITED KINGDOM
†BBC, Rampisham
S M-F • E Europe • 500 kW
S • S Europe • 500 kW
BBC, Via Delano, USA
M-F • C America • 250 kW
USA
RFE-RL, Via Briech, Morocco
W • Mideast & W Asia • 250 kW
RFE-RL, Via Kavála, Greece
W • Mideast • 250 kW
RFE-RL, Via Lampertheim, Germany
S • S Europe • 100 kW
VOA, Greenville, NC
Tu-Sa • C America & S America • 250 kW
†VOA, Via Briech, Morocco
S • Europe • 250 kW
6134.8 BOLIVIA
RADIO SANTA CRUZ, Santa Cruz
DS • 10 kW
Irr • DS • 10 kW
M-Sa • DS • 10 kW
M-F • DS • 10 kW
Sa/Su • DS • 10 kW
6135 ALBANIA
†RADIO TIRANA, Shijak
• Europe • 100 kW
BRAZIL
†RADIO APARECIDA, Aparecida
DS • 7.5 kW •
Irr • DS • 7.5 kW •
CHINA
†CHINA RADIO INTL, Urümqi
W • E Europe & W Asia • 500 kW
†CHINA RADIO INTL, Xi'an
W • Europe • 100 kW
FINLAND
†YLE RADIO FINLAND, Pori
W • E Europe • 250 kW
IRAN
VO THE ISLAMIC REP, Tehrān
W • E North Am & C America • 500 kW
ITALY
†RAI INTERNATIONAL, Rome
W • S Europe & N Africa • 100 kW
W • N Africa • 100 kW
JAPAN
RADIO JAPAN/NHK, Via Ascension
C Africa & E Africa • 250 kW
KOREA (REPUBLIC)
†KOREAN BC SYSTEM, Hwasung
E Asia • EDUCATIONAL-2 • 100 kW
RADIO KOREA INTL, Hwasung
E Asia • 100 kW
TURKEY
†VOICE OF TURKEY, Ankara-Çakirlar
W • E Europe & W Asia • 500 kW
†VOICE OF TURKEY, Ankara-Emirler
W • Europe • 500 kW
UNITED KINGDOM
†BBC, Via Delano, USA
W • W North Am & C America • 250 kW
†BBC, Via Meyerton, South Africa
S Africa • 250 kW
USA
RFE-RL, Via Holzkirchen, Germany
W • W Asia & C Asia • 250 kW
RFE-RL, Via Kavála, Greece
W • W Asia & C Asia • 250 kW
6135v MADAGASCAR
RTV MALAGASY, Antananarivo
DS-1 • 30 kW
6140 BURUNDI
†R DIF DU BURUNDI, Gitega
FRENCH, ETC • DS • 60 kW
DS • 60 kW
CHINA
†CHINA RADIO INTL, Kunming
SE Asia • 50 kW
CUBA
†RADIO HABANA CUBA, Havana
Su • C America • "ALO, PRESIDENTE" • 50 kW
RADIO REBELDE, Havana
C America • 50 kW
GERMANY
†DEUTSCHE WELLE, Jülich
Europe • 100 kW
†DEUTSCHE WELLE, Wertachtal
Europe • 125 kW
INDIA
†ALL INDIA RADIO, Ranchi
DS • 50 kW
ENGLISH, ETC • DS • 50 kW
IRAN
†VO THE ISLAMIC REP, Sirjan
W • W Asia & S Asia • 500 kW
UNITED KINGDOM
†BBC, Via Maṣīrah, Oman
S Asia • 100 kW
URUGUAY
†RADIO MONTE CARLO, Montevideo
Irr • DS • 1.5 kW
DS • 1.5 kW
(con'd)
0 1 2 3 4 5 6 7 8 9 10 11 12 13 14 15 16 17 18 19 20 21 22 23 24

SEASONAL S OR W 1-HR TIMESHIFT MIDYEAR ⇐ OR ⇒ JAMMING / OR /\ EARLIEST HEARD ◁ LATEST HEARD ▷ NEW FOR 2002 †

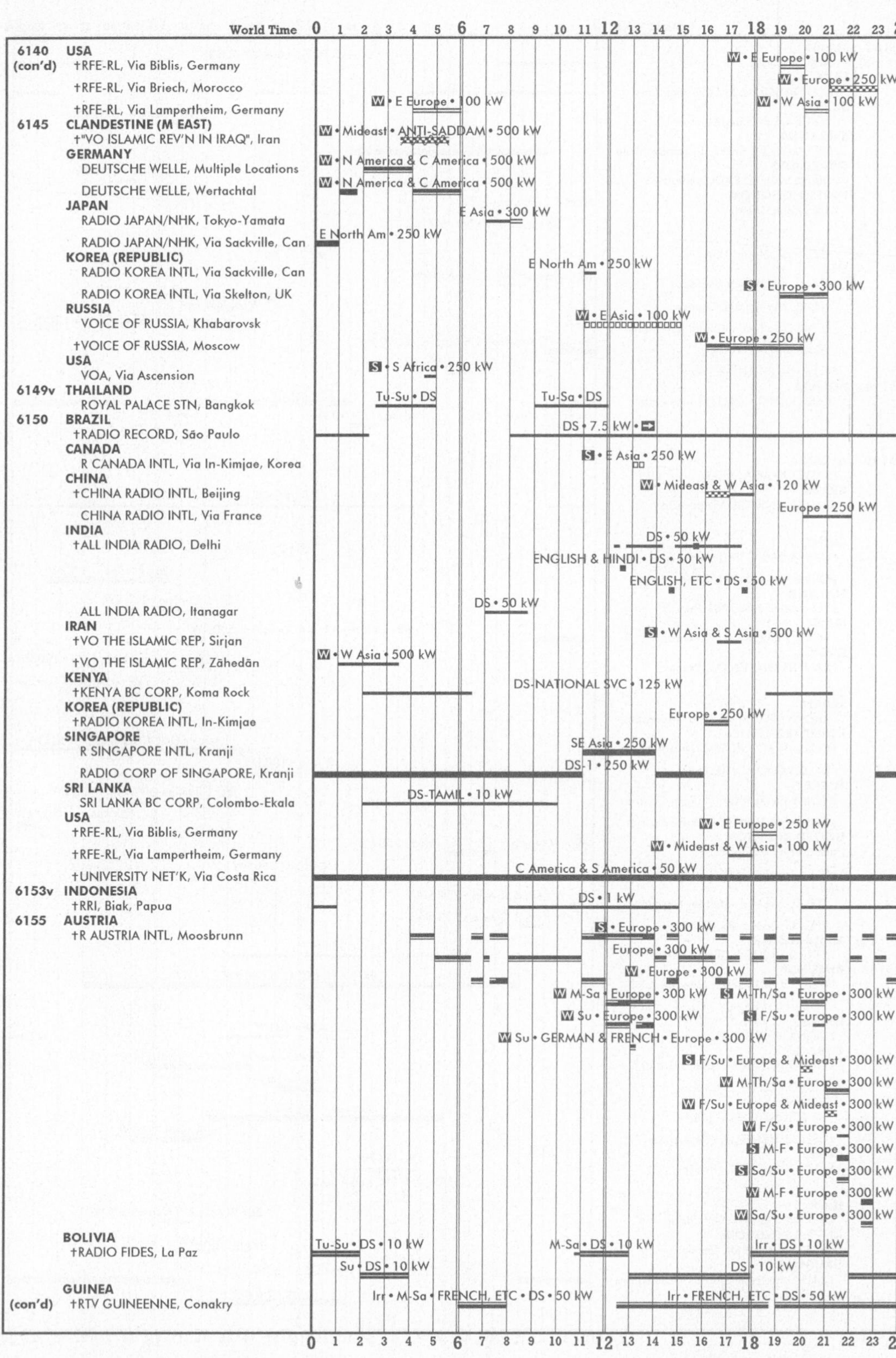
World Time 0 1 2 3 4 5 6 7 8 9 10 11 12 13 14 15 16 17 18 19 20 21 22 23 24
6140 USA (con'd)
†RFE-RL, Via Biblis, Germany
W • E Europe • 100 kW
†RFE-RL, Via Briech, Morocco
W • Europe • 250 kW
†RFE-RL, Via Lampertheim, Germany
W • E Europe • 100 kW
W • W Asia • 100 kW
6145 CLANDESTINE (M EAST)
†"VO ISLAMIC REV'N IN IRAQ", Iran
W • Mideast • ANTI-SADDAM • 500 kW
GERMANY
DEUTSCHE WELLE, Multiple Locations
W • N America & C America • 500 kW
DEUTSCHE WELLE, Wertachtal
W • N America & C America • 500 kW
JAPAN
RADIO JAPAN/NHK, Tokyo-Yamata
E Asia • 300 kW
RADIO JAPAN/NHK, Via Sackville, Can
E North Am • 250 kW
KOREA (REPUBLIC)
RADIO KOREA INTL, Via Sackville, Can
E North Am • 250 kW
RADIO KOREA INTL, Via Skelton, UK
S • Europe • 300 kW
RUSSIA
VOICE OF RUSSIA, Khabarovsk
W • E Asia • 100 kW
†VOICE OF RUSSIA, Moscow
W • Europe • 250 kW
USA
VOA, Via Ascension
S • S Africa • 250 kW
6149v THAILAND
ROYAL PALACE STN, Bangkok
Tu-Su • DS
Tu-Sa • DS
6150 BRAZIL
†RADIO RECORD, São Paulo
DS • 7.5 kW •
CANADA
R CANADA INTL, Via In-Kimjae, Korea
S • E Asia • 250 kW
CHINA
†CHINA RADIO INTL, Beijing
W • Mideast & W Asia • 120 kW
CHINA RADIO INTL, Via France
Europe • 250 kW
INDIA
†ALL INDIA RADIO, Delhi
DS • 50 kW
ENGLISH & HINDI • DS • 50 kW
ENGLISH, ETC • DS • 50 kW
ALL INDIA RADIO, Itanagar
DS • 50 kW
IRAN
†VO THE ISLAMIC REP, Sirjan
S • W Asia & S Asia • 500 kW
†VO THE ISLAMIC REP, Zāhedān
W • W Asia • 500 kW
KENYA
†KENYA BC CORP, Koma Rock
DS-NATIONAL SVC • 125 kW
KOREA (REPUBLIC)
†RADIO KOREA INTL, In-Kimjae
Europe • 250 kW
SINGAPORE
R SINGAPORE INTL, Kranji
SE Asia • 250 kW
RADIO CORP OF SINGAPORE, Kranji
DS-1 • 250 kW
SRI LANKA
SRI LANKA BC CORP, Colombo-Ekala
DS-TAMIL • 10 kW
USA
†RFE-RL, Via Biblis, Germany
W • E Europe • 250 kW
†RFE-RL, Via Lampertheim, Germany
W • Mideast & W Asia • 100 kW
†UNIVERSITY NET'K, Via Costa Rica
C America & S America • 50 kW
6153v INDONESIA
†RRI, Biak, Papua
DS • 1 kW
6155 AUSTRIA
†R AUSTRIA INTL, Moosbrunn
S • Europe • 300 kW
Europe • 300 kW
W • Europe • 300 kW
W M-Sa • Europe • 300 kW
S M-Th/Sa • Europe • 300 kW
W Su • Europe • 300 kW
S F/Su • Europe • 300 kW
W Su • GERMAN & FRENCH • Europe • 300 kW
S F/Su • Europe & Mideast • 300 kW
W M-Th/Sa • Europe • 300 kW
W F/Su • Europe & Mideast • 300 kW
W F/Su • Europe • 300 kW
S M-F • Europe • 300 kW
S Sa/Su • Europe • 300 kW
W M-F • Europe • 300 kW
W Sa/Su • Europe • 300 kW
BOLIVIA
†RADIO FIDES, La Paz
Tu-Su • DS • 10 kW
M-Sa • DS • 10 kW
Irr • DS • 10 kW
Su • DS • 10 kW
DS • 10 kW
GUINEA (con'd)
†RTV GUINEENNE, Conakry
Irr • M-Sa • FRENCH, ETC • DS • 50 kW
Irr • FRENCH, ETC • DS • 50 kW
0 1 2 3 4 5 6 7 8 9 10 11 12 13 14 15 16 17 18 19 20 21 22 23 24
ENGLISH ARABIC CHINESE FRENCH GERMAN RUSSIAN SPANISH OTHER

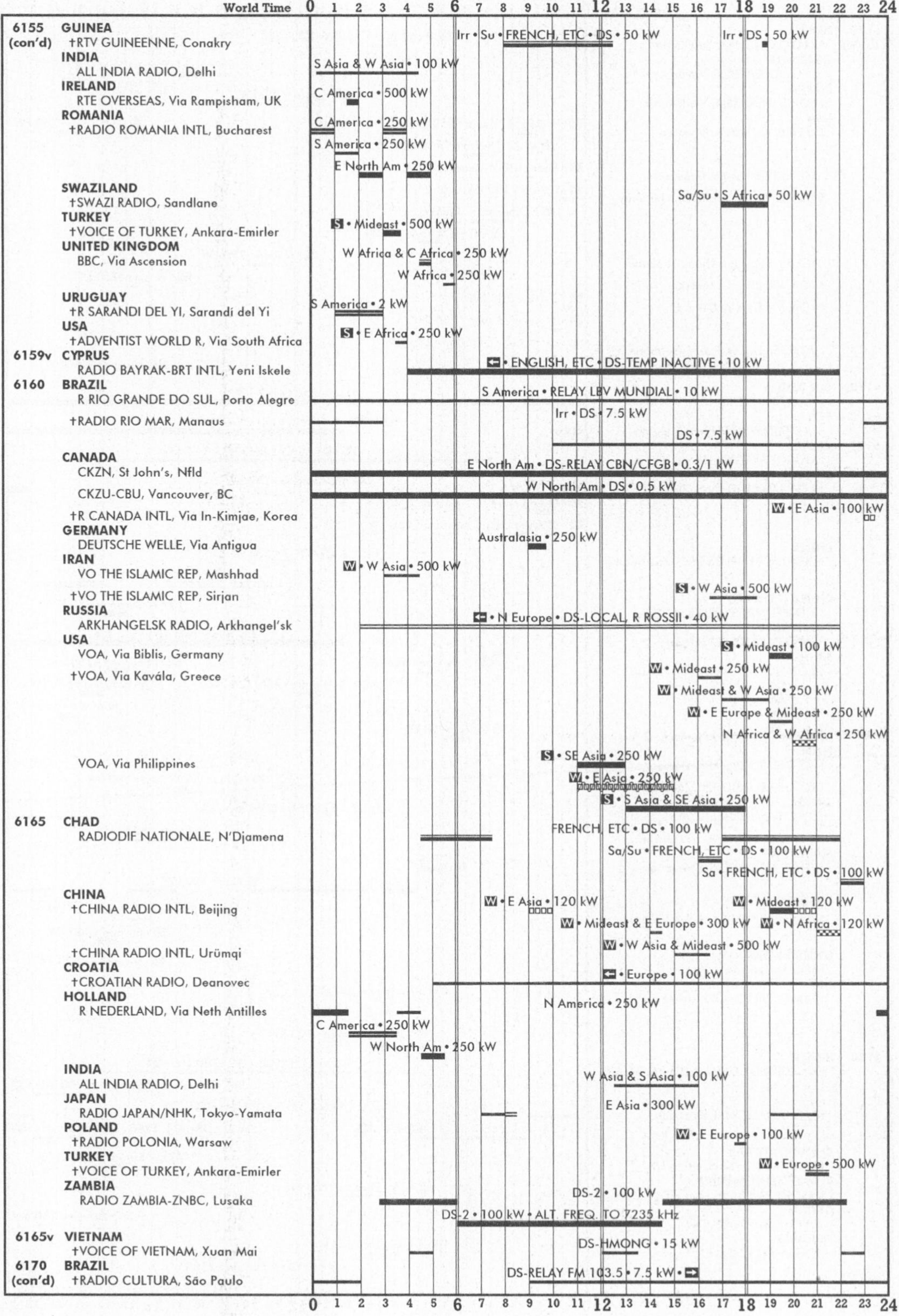
World Time 0 1 2 3 4 5 6 7 8 9 10 11 12 13 14 15 16 17 18 19 20 21 22 23 24
6155 (con'd) GUINEA
†RTV GUINEENNE, Conakry
Irr • Su • FRENCH, ETC • DS • 50 kW
Irr • DS • 50 kW
INDIA
ALL INDIA RADIO, Delhi
S Asia & W Asia • 100 kW
IRELAND
RTE OVERSEAS, Via Rampisham, UK
C America • 500 kW
ROMANIA
†RADIO ROMANIA INTL, Bucharest
C America • 250 kW
S America • 250 kW
E North Am • 250 kW
SWAZILAND
†SWAZI RADIO, Sandlane
Sa/Su • S Africa • 50 kW
TURKEY
†VOICE OF TURKEY, Ankara-Emirler
S • Mideast • 500 kW
UNITED KINGDOM
BBC, Via Ascension
W Africa & C Africa • 250 kW
W Africa • 250 kW
URUGUAY
†R SARANDI DEL YI, Sarandí del Yi
S America • 2 kW
USA
†ADVENTIST WORLD R, Via South Africa
S • E Africa • 250 kW
6159v CYPRUS
RADIO BAYRAK-BRT INTL, Yeni Iskele
ENGLISH, ETC • DS-TEMP INACTIVE • 10 kW
6160 BRAZIL
R RIO GRANDE DO SUL, Porto Alegre
S America • RELAY LBV MUNDIAL • 10 kW
†RADIO RIO MAR, Manaus
Irr • DS • 7.5 kW
DS • 7.5 kW
CANADA
CKZN, St John's, Nfld
E North Am • DS-RELAY CBN/CFGB • 0.3/1 kW
CKZU-CBU, Vancouver, BC
W North Am • DS • 0.5 kW
†R CANADA INTL, Via In-Kimjae, Korea
W • E Asia • 100 kW
GERMANY
DEUTSCHE WELLE, Via Antigua
Australasia • 250 kW
IRAN
VO THE ISLAMIC REP, Mashhad
W • W Asia • 500 kW
†VO THE ISLAMIC REP, Sirjan
S • W Asia • 500 kW
RUSSIA
ARKHANGELSK RADIO, Arkhangel'sk
N Europe • DS-LOCAL, R ROSSII • 40 kW
USA
VOA, Via Biblis, Germany
S • Mideast • 100 kW
†VOA, Via Kavála, Greece
W • Mideast • 250 kW
W • Mideast & W Asia • 250 kW
W • E Europe & Mideast • 250 kW
N Africa & W Africa • 250 kW
VOA, Via Philippines
S • SE Asia • 250 kW
W • E Asia • 250 kW
S • S Asia & SE Asia • 250 kW
6165 CHAD
RADIODIF NATIONALE, N'Djamena
FRENCH, ETC • DS • 100 kW
Sa/Su • FRENCH, ETC • DS • 100 kW
Sa • FRENCH, ETC • DS • 100 kW
CHINA
†CHINA RADIO INTL, Beijing
W • E Asia • 120 kW
W • Mideast • 120 kW
W • Mideast & E Europe • 300 kW
W • N Africa • 120 kW
†CHINA RADIO INTL, Urümqi
W • W Asia & Mideast • 500 kW
CROATIA
†CROATIAN RADIO, Deanovec
Europe • 100 kW
HOLLAND
R NEDERLAND, Via Neth Antilles
N America • 250 kW
C America • 250 kW
W North Am • 250 kW
INDIA
ALL INDIA RADIO, Delhi
W Asia & S Asia • 100 kW
JAPAN
RADIO JAPAN/NHK, Tokyo-Yamata
E Asia • 300 kW
POLAND
†RADIO POLONIA, Warsaw
W • E Europe • 100 kW
TURKEY
†VOICE OF TURKEY, Ankara-Emirler
W • Europe • 500 kW
ZAMBIA
RADIO ZAMBIA-ZNBC, Lusaka
DS-2 • 100 kW
DS-2 • 100 kW • ALT. FREQ. TO 7235 kHz
6165v VIETNAM
†VOICE OF VIETNAM, Xuan Mai
DS-HMONG • 15 kW
6170 (con'd) BRAZIL
†RADIO CULTURA, São Paulo
DS-RELAY FM 103.5 • 7.5 kW
0 1 2 3 4 5 6 7 8 9 10 11 12 13 14 15 16 17 18 19 20 21 22 23 24

SEASONAL S OR W 1-HR TIMESHIFT MIDYEAR ⇦ OR ⇨ JAMMING / OR ∧ EARLIEST HEARD ◁ LATEST HEARD ▷ NEW FOR 2002 †

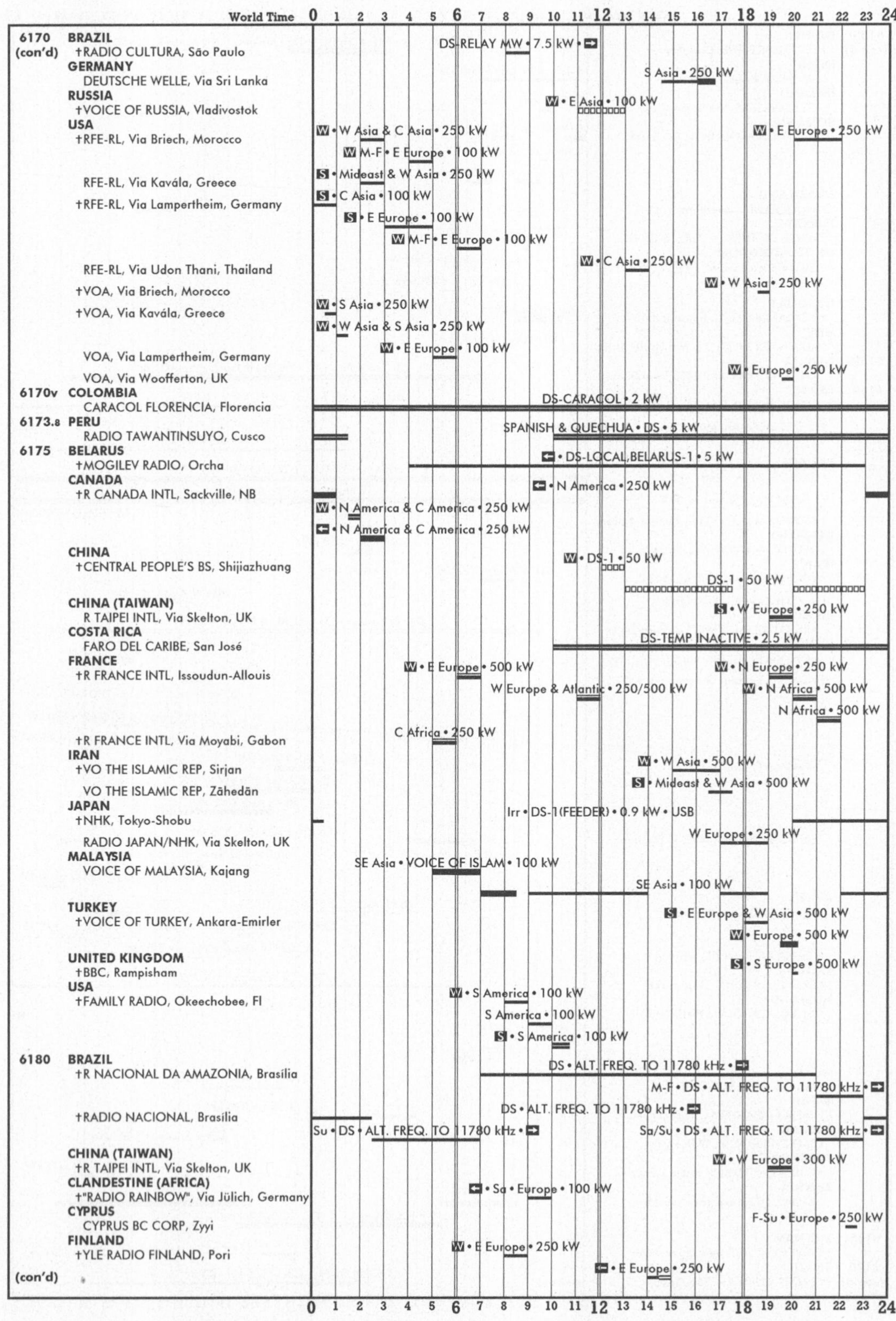
World Time 0 1 2 3 4 5 6 7 8 9 10 11 12 13 14 15 16 17 18 19 20 21 22 23 24
6170 (con'd) BRAZIL
†RADIO CULTURA, São Paulo
DS-RELAY MW • 7.5 kW •
GERMANY
DEUTSCHE WELLE, Via Sri Lanka
S Asia • 250 kW
RUSSIA
†VOICE OF RUSSIA, Vladivostok
W • E Asia • 100 kW
USA
†RFE-RL, Via Briech, Morocco
W • W Asia & C Asia • 250 kW
W • E Europe • 250 kW
W M-F • E Europe • 100 kW
RFE-RL, Via Kavála, Greece
S • Mideast & W Asia • 250 kW
†RFE-RL, Via Lampertheim, Germany
S • C Asia • 100 kW
S • E Europe • 100 kW
W M-F • E Europe • 100 kW
RFE-RL, Via Udon Thani, Thailand
W • C Asia • 250 kW
†VOA, Via Briech, Morocco
W • W Asia • 250 kW
†VOA, Via Kavála, Greece
W • S Asia • 250 kW
W • W Asia & S Asia • 250 kW
VOA, Via Lampertheim, Germany
W • E Europe • 100 kW
VOA, Via Woofferton, UK
W • Europe • 250 kW
6170v COLOMBIA
CARACOL FLORENCIA, Florencia
DS-CARACOL • 2 kW
6173.8 PERU
RADIO TAWANTINSUYO, Cusco
SPANISH & QUECHUA • DS • 5 kW
6175 BELARUS
†MOGILEV RADIO, Orcha
• DS-LOCAL,BELARUS-1 • 5 kW
CANADA
†R CANADA INTL, Sackville, NB
• N America • 250 kW
W • N America & C America • 250 kW
• N America & C America • 250 kW
CHINA
†CENTRAL PEOPLE'S BS, Shijiazhuang
W • DS-1 • 50 kW
DS-1 • 50 kW
CHINA (TAIWAN)
R TAIPEI INTL, Via Skelton, UK
S • W Europe • 250 kW
COSTA RICA
FARO DEL CARIBE, San José
DS-TEMP INACTIVE • 2.5 kW
FRANCE
†R FRANCE INTL, Issoudun-Allouis
W • E Europe • 500 kW
W • N Europe • 250 kW
W Europe & Atlantic • 250/500 kW
W • N Africa • 500 kW
N Africa • 500 kW
†R FRANCE INTL, Via Moyabi, Gabon
C Africa • 250 kW
IRAN
†VO THE ISLAMIC REP, Sirjan
W • W Asia • 500 kW
VO THE ISLAMIC REP, Zāhedān
S • Mideast & W Asia • 500 kW
JAPAN
†NHK, Tokyo-Shobu
Irr • DS-1(FEEDER) • 0.9 kW • USB
RADIO JAPAN/NHK, Via Skelton, UK
W Europe • 250 kW
MALAYSIA
VOICE OF MALAYSIA, Kajang
SE Asia • VOICE OF ISLAM • 100 kW
SE Asia • 100 kW
TURKEY
†VOICE OF TURKEY, Ankara-Emirler
S • E Europe & W Asia • 500 kW
W • Europe • 500 kW
UNITED KINGDOM
†BBC, Rampisham
S • S Europe • 500 kW
USA
†FAMILY RADIO, Okeechobee, Fl
W • S America • 100 kW
S America • 100 kW
S • S America • 100 kW
6180 BRAZIL
†R NACIONAL DA AMAZONIA, Brasília
DS • ALT. FREQ. TO 11780 kHz •
M-F • DS • ALT. FREQ. TO 11780 kHz •
†RADIO NACIONAL, Brasília
DS • ALT. FREQ. TO 11780 kHz •
Su • DS • ALT. FREQ. TO 11780 kHz •
Sa/Su • DS • ALT. FREQ. TO 11780 kHz •
CHINA (TAIWAN)
†R TAIPEI INTL, Via Skelton, UK
W • W Europe • 300 kW
CLANDESTINE (AFRICA)
†"RADIO RAINBOW", Via Jülich, Germany
• Sa • Europe • 100 kW
CYPRUS
CYPRUS BC CORP, Zyyi
F-Su • Europe • 250 kW
FINLAND
†YLE RADIO FINLAND, Pori
W • E Europe • 250 kW
• E Europe • 250 kW
(con'd)
0 1 2 3 4 5 6 7 8 9 10 11 12 13 14 15 16 17 18 19 20 21 22 23 24

ENGLISH ARABIC CHINESE FRENCH GERMAN RUSSIAN SPANISH OTHER

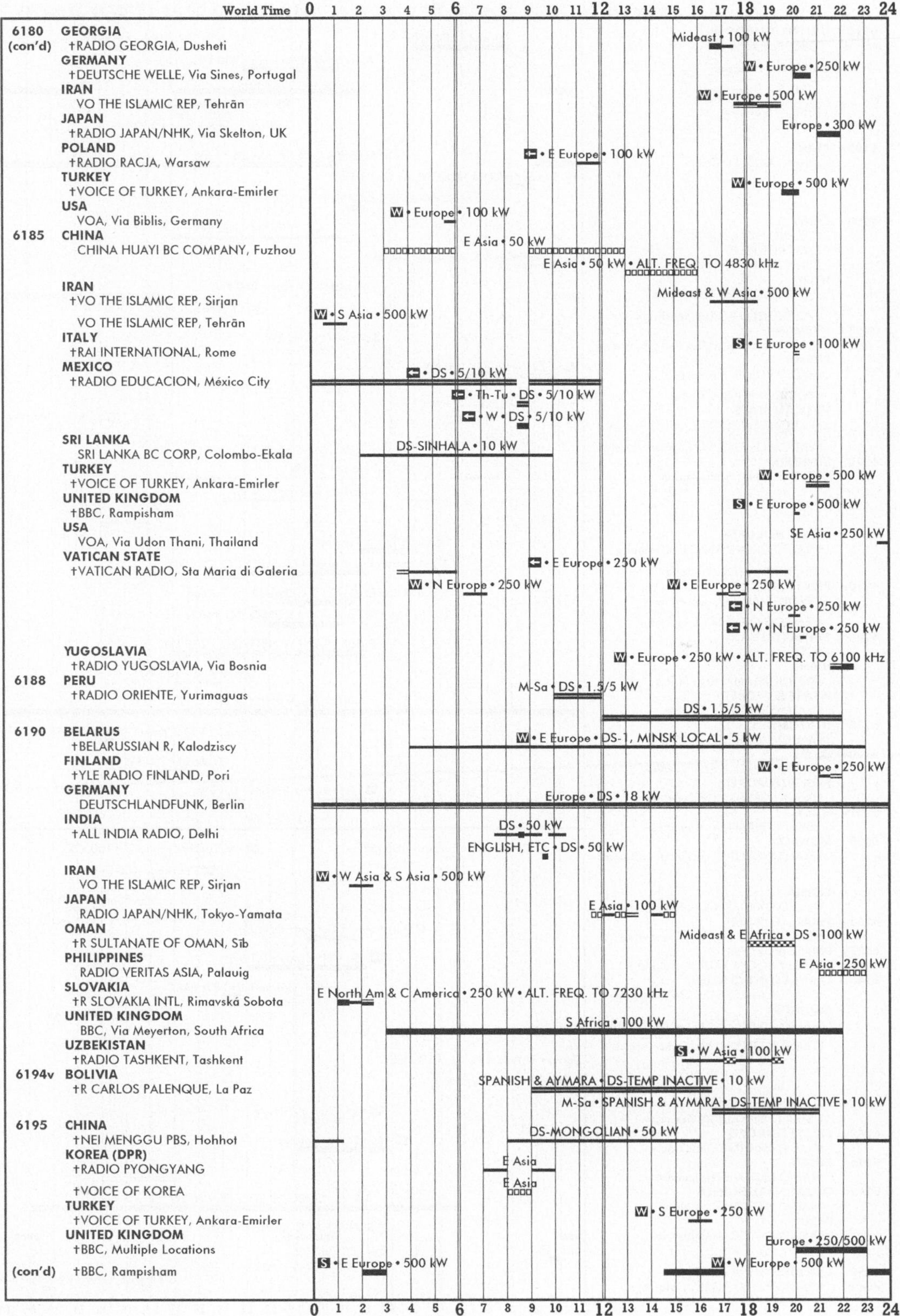
World Time 0 1 2 3 4 5 6 7 8 9 10 11 12 13 14 15 16 17 18 19 20 21 22 23 24
6180 (con'd) GEORGIA
†RADIO GEORGIA, Dusheti
Mideast • 100 kW
GERMANY
†DEUTSCHE WELLE, Via Sines, Portugal
W • Europe • 250 kW
IRAN
VO THE ISLAMIC REP, Tehrān
W • Europe • 500 kW
JAPAN
†RADIO JAPAN/NHK, Via Skelton, UK
Europe • 300 kW
POLAND
†RADIO RACJA, Warsaw
E Europe • 100 kW
TURKEY
†VOICE OF TURKEY, Ankara-Emirler
W • Europe • 500 kW
USA
VOA, Via Biblis, Germany
W • Europe • 100 kW
6185 CHINA
CHINA HUAYI BC COMPANY, Fuzhou
E Asia • 50 kW
E Asia • 50 kW • ALT. FREQ. TO 4830 kHz
IRAN
†VO THE ISLAMIC REP, Sirjan
Mideast & W Asia • 500 kW
VO THE ISLAMIC REP, Tehrān
W • S Asia • 500 kW
ITALY
†RAI INTERNATIONAL, Rome
S • E Europe • 100 kW
MEXICO
†RADIO EDUCACION, México City
DS • 5/10 kW
Th-Tu • DS • 5/10 kW
W • DS • 5/10 kW
SRI LANKA
SRI LANKA BC CORP, Colombo-Ekala
DS-SINHALA • 10 kW
TURKEY
†VOICE OF TURKEY, Ankara-Emirler
W • Europe • 500 kW
UNITED KINGDOM
†BBC, Rampisham
S • E Europe • 500 kW
USA
VOA, Via Udon Thani, Thailand
SE Asia • 250 kW
VATICAN STATE
†VATICAN RADIO, Sta Maria di Galeria
E Europe • 250 kW
W • N Europe • 250 kW
W • E Europe • 250 kW
N Europe • 250 kW
W • N Europe • 250 kW
YUGOSLAVIA
†RADIO YUGOSLAVIA, Via Bosnia
W • Europe • 250 kW • ALT. FREQ. TO 6100 kHz
6188 PERU
†RADIO ORIENTE, Yurimaguas
M-Sa • DS • 1.5/5 kW
DS • 1.5/5 kW
6190 BELARUS
†BELARUSSIAN R, Kalodziscy
W • E Europe • DS-1, MINSK LOCAL • 5 kW
FINLAND
†YLE RADIO FINLAND, Pori
W • E Europe • 250 kW
GERMANY
DEUTSCHLANDFUNK, Berlin
Europe • DS • 18 kW
INDIA
†ALL INDIA RADIO, Delhi
DS • 50 kW
ENGLISH, ETC • DS • 50 kW
IRAN
VO THE ISLAMIC REP, Sirjan
W • W Asia & S Asia • 500 kW
JAPAN
RADIO JAPAN/NHK, Tokyo-Yamata
E Asia • 100 kW
OMAN
†R SULTANATE OF OMAN, Sīb
Mideast & E Africa • DS • 100 kW
PHILIPPINES
RADIO VERITAS ASIA, Palauig
E Asia • 250 kW
SLOVAKIA
†R SLOVAKIA INTL, Rimavská Sobota
E North Am & C America • 250 kW • ALT. FREQ. TO 7230 kHz
UNITED KINGDOM
BBC, Via Meyerton, South Africa
S Africa • 100 kW
UZBEKISTAN
†RADIO TASHKENT, Tashkent
S • W Asia • 100 kW
6194v BOLIVIA
†R CARLOS PALENQUE, La Paz
SPANISH & AYMARA • DS-TEMP INACTIVE • 10 kW
M-Sa • SPANISH & AYMARA • DS-TEMP INACTIVE • 10 kW
6195 CHINA
†NEI MENGGU PBS, Hohhot
DS-MONGOLIAN • 50 kW
KOREA (DPR)
†RADIO PYONGYANG
E Asia
†VOICE OF KOREA
E Asia
TURKEY
†VOICE OF TURKEY, Ankara-Emirler
W • S Europe • 250 kW
UNITED KINGDOM
†BBC, Multiple Locations
Europe • 250/500 kW
(con'd) †BBC, Rampisham
S • E Europe • 500 kW
W • W Europe • 500 kW
0 1 2 3 4 5 6 7 8 9 10 11 12 13 14 15 16 17 18 19 20 21 22 23 24

SEASONAL S OR W 1-HR TIMESHIFT MIDYEAR ← OR → JAMMING / OR ⋀ EARLIEST HEARD ◁ LATEST HEARD ▷ NEW FOR 2002 †

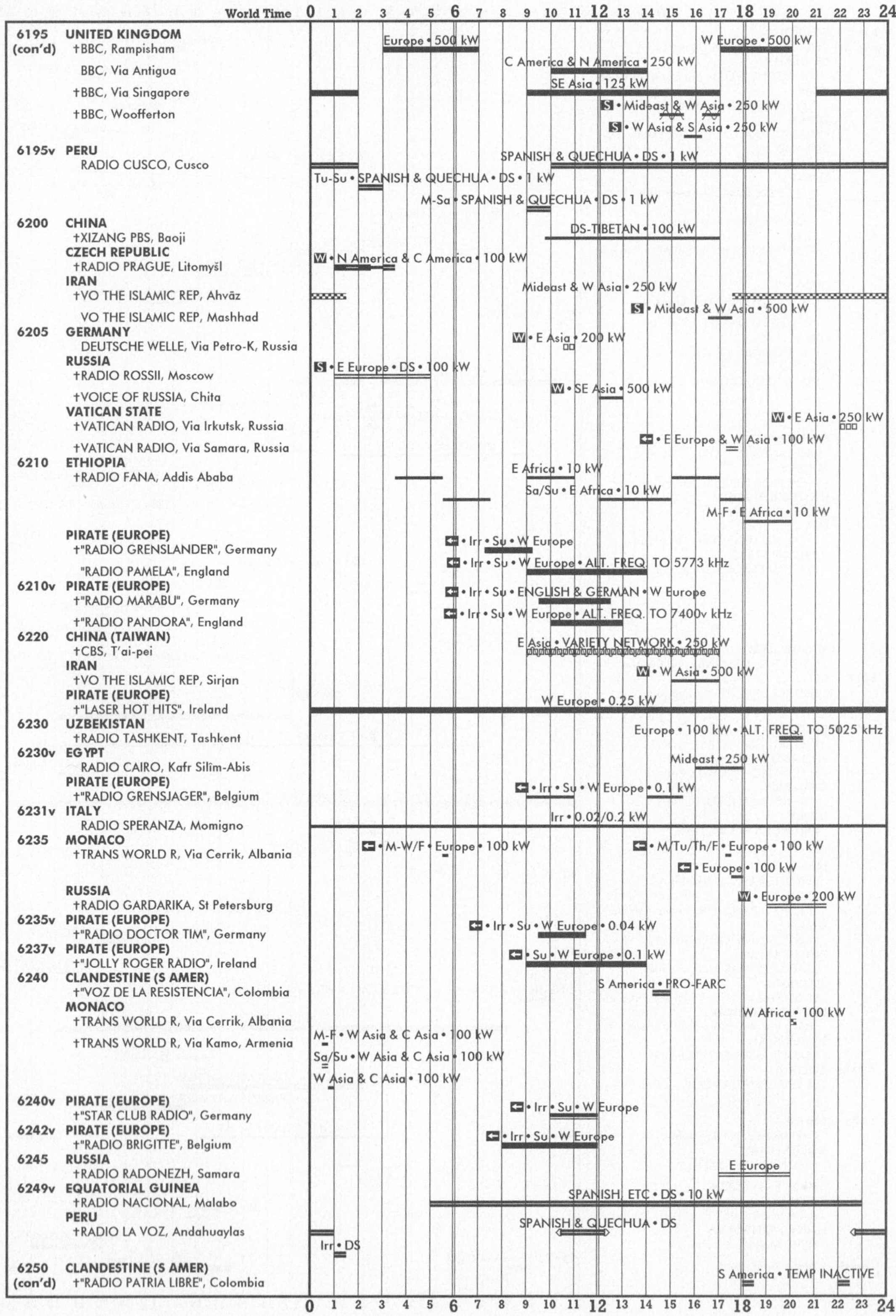
World Time 0 1 2 3 4 5 6 7 8 9 10 11 12 13 14 15 16 17 18 19 20 21 22 23 24
6195 (con'd) UNITED KINGDOM
†BBC, Rampisham — Europe • 500 kW; W Europe • 500 kW
BBC, Via Antigua — C America & N America • 250 kW
†BBC, Via Singapore — SE Asia • 125 kW
†BBC, Woofferton — S • Mideast & W Asia • 250 kW; S • W Asia & S Asia • 250 kW
6195v PERU
RADIO CUSCO, Cusco — SPANISH & QUECHUA • DS • 1 kW; Tu-Su • SPANISH & QUECHUA • DS • 1 kW; M-Sa • SPANISH & QUECHUA • DS • 1 kW
6200 CHINA
†XIZANG PBS, Baoji — DS-TIBETAN • 100 kW
CZECH REPUBLIC
†RADIO PRAGUE, Litomyšl — W • N America & C America • 100 kW
IRAN
†VO THE ISLAMIC REP, Ahvāz — Mideast & W Asia • 250 kW
VO THE ISLAMIC REP, Mashhad — S • Mideast & W Asia • 500 kW
6205 GERMANY
DEUTSCHE WELLE, Via Petro-K, Russia — W • E Asia • 200 kW
RUSSIA
†RADIO ROSSII, Moscow — S • E Europe • DS • 100 kW
†VOICE OF RUSSIA, Chita — W • SE Asia • 500 kW
VATICAN STATE
†VATICAN RADIO, Via Irkutsk, Russia — W • E Asia • 250 kW
†VATICAN RADIO, Via Samara, Russia — E Europe & W Asia • 100 kW
6210 ETHIOPIA
†RADIO FANA, Addis Ababa — E Africa • 10 kW; Sa/Su • E Africa • 10 kW; M-F • E Africa • 10 kW
PIRATE (EUROPE)
†"RADIO GRENSLANDER", Germany — Irr • Su • W Europe
"RADIO PAMELA", England — Irr • Su • W Europe • ALT. FREQ. TO 5773 kHz
6210v PIRATE (EUROPE)
†"RADIO MARABU", Germany — Irr • Su • ENGLISH & GERMAN • W Europe
†"RADIO PANDORA", England — Irr • Su • W Europe • ALT. FREQ. TO 7400v kHz
6220 CHINA (TAIWAN)
†CBS, T'ai-pei — E Asia • VARIETY NETWORK • 250 kW
IRAN
†VO THE ISLAMIC REP, Sirjan — W • W Asia • 500 kW
PIRATE (EUROPE)
†"LASER HOT HITS", Ireland — W Europe • 0.25 kW
6230 UZBEKISTAN
†RADIO TASHKENT, Tashkent — Europe • 100 kW • ALT. FREQ. TO 5025 kHz
6230v EGYPT
RADIO CAIRO, Kafr Silîm-Abis — Mideast • 250 kW
PIRATE (EUROPE)
†"RADIO GRENSJAGER", Belgium — Irr • Su • W Europe • 0.1 kW
6231v ITALY
RADIO SPERANZA, Momigno — Irr • 0.02/0.2 kW
6235 MONACO
†TRANS WORLD R, Via Cerrik, Albania — M-W/F • Europe • 100 kW; M/Tu/Th/F • Europe • 100 kW; Europe • 100 kW
RUSSIA
†RADIO GARDARIKA, St Petersburg — W • Europe • 200 kW
6235v PIRATE (EUROPE)
†"RADIO DOCTOR TIM", Germany — Irr • Su • W Europe • 0.04 kW
6237v PIRATE (EUROPE)
†"JOLLY ROGER RADIO", Ireland — Su • W Europe • 0.1 kW
6240 CLANDESTINE (S AMER)
†"VOZ DE LA RESISTENCIA", Colombia — S America • PRO-FARC
MONACO
†TRANS WORLD R, Via Cerrik, Albania — W Africa • 100 kW
†TRANS WORLD R, Via Kamo, Armenia — M-F • W Asia & C Asia • 100 kW; Sa/Su • W Asia & C Asia • 100 kW; W Asia & C Asia • 100 kW
6240v PIRATE (EUROPE)
†"STAR CLUB RADIO", Germany — Irr • Su • W Europe
6242v PIRATE (EUROPE)
†"RADIO BRIGITTE", Belgium — Irr • Su • W Europe
6245 RUSSIA
†RADIO RADONEZH, Samara — E Europe
6249v EQUATORIAL GUINEA
†RADIO NACIONAL, Malabo — SPANISH, ETC • DS • 10 kW
PERU
†RADIO LA VOZ, Andahuaylas — SPANISH & QUECHUA • DS; Irr • DS
6250 (con'd) CLANDESTINE (S AMER)
†"RADIO PATRIA LIBRE", Colombia — S America • TEMP INACTIVE
0 1 2 3 4 5 6 7 8 9 10 11 12 13 14 15 16 17 18 19 20 21 22 23 24
ENGLISH ARABIC CHINESE FRENCH GERMAN RUSSIAN SPANISH OTHER

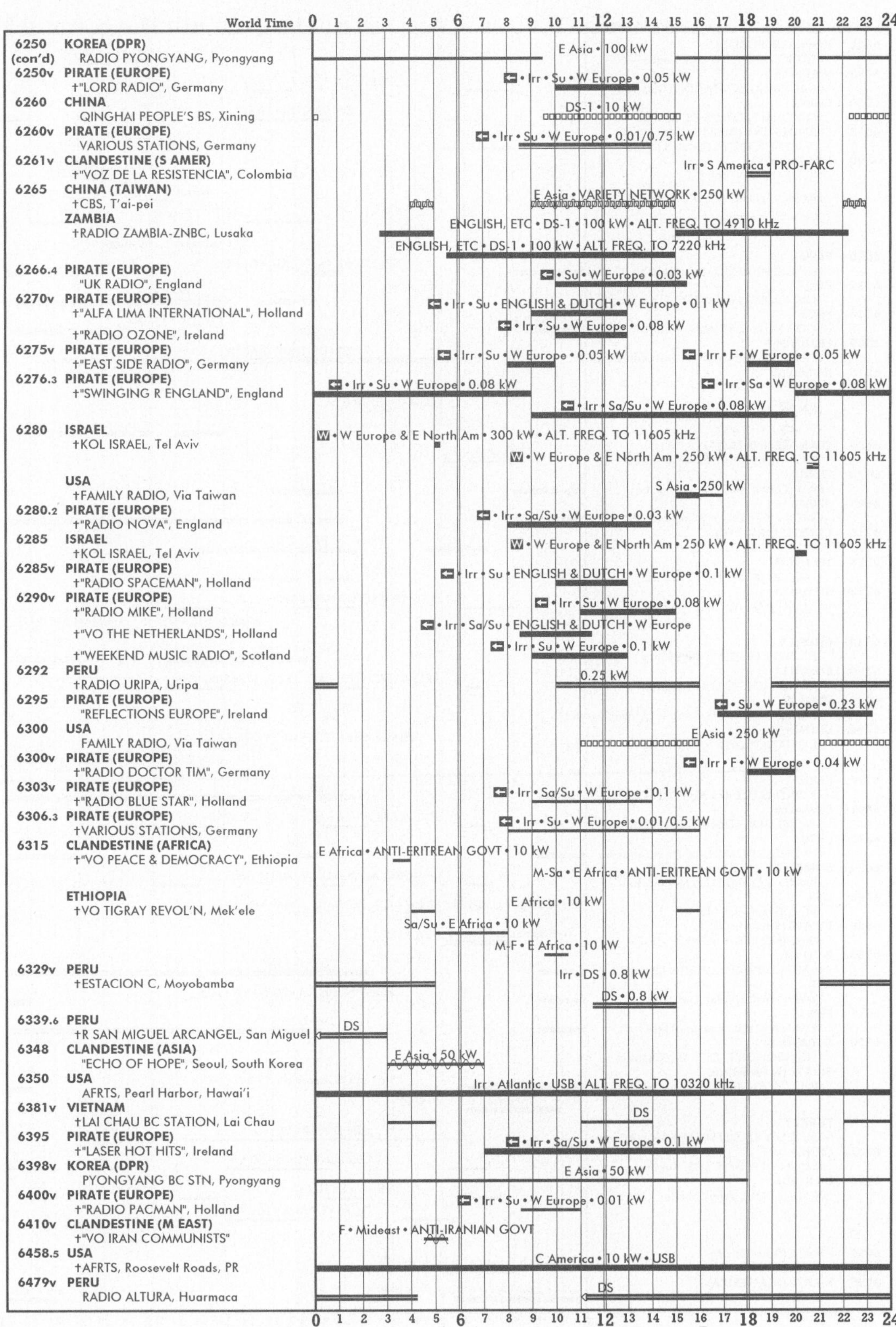
World Time 0 1 2 3 4 5 6 7 8 9 10 11 12 13 14 15 16 17 18 19 20 21 22 23 24
6250 (con'd) KOREA (DPR)
RADIO PYONGYANG, Pyongyang
E Asia • 100 kW
6250v PIRATE (EUROPE)
†"LORD RADIO", Germany
Irr • Su • W Europe • 0.05 kW
6260 CHINA
QINGHAI PEOPLE'S BS, Xining
DS-1 • 10 kW
6260v PIRATE (EUROPE)
VARIOUS STATIONS, Germany
Irr • Su • W Europe • 0.01/0.75 kW
6261v CLANDESTINE (S AMER)
†"VOZ DE LA RESISTENCIA", Colombia
Irr • S America • PRO-FARC
6265 CHINA (TAIWAN)
†CBS, T'ai-pei
E Asia • VARIETY NETWORK • 250 kW
ZAMBIA
†RADIO ZAMBIA-ZNBC, Lusaka
ENGLISH, ETC • DS-1 • 100 kW • ALT. FREQ. TO 4910 kHz
ENGLISH, ETC • DS-1 • 100 kW • ALT. FREQ. TO 7220 kHz
6266.4 PIRATE (EUROPE)
"UK RADIO", England
Su • W Europe • 0.03 kW
6270v PIRATE (EUROPE)
†"ALFA LIMA INTERNATIONAL", Holland
Irr • Su • ENGLISH & DUTCH • W Europe • 0.1 kW
†"RADIO OZONE", Ireland
Irr • Su • W Europe • 0.08 kW
6275v PIRATE (EUROPE)
†"EAST SIDE RADIO", Germany
Irr • Su • W Europe • 0.05 kW
Irr • F • W Europe • 0.05 kW
6276.3 PIRATE (EUROPE)
†"SWINGING R ENGLAND", England
Irr • Su • W Europe • 0.08 kW
Irr • Sa • W Europe • 0.08 kW
Irr • Sa/Su • W Europe • 0.08 kW
6280 ISRAEL
†KOL ISRAEL, Tel Aviv
W • W Europe & E North Am • 300 kW • ALT. FREQ. TO 11605 kHz
W • W Europe & E North Am • 250 kW • ALT. FREQ. TO 11605 kHz
USA
†FAMILY RADIO, Via Taiwan
S Asia • 250 kW
6280.2 PIRATE (EUROPE)
†"RADIO NOVA", England
Irr • Sa/Su • W Europe • 0.03 kW
6285 ISRAEL
†KOL ISRAEL, Tel Aviv
W • W Europe & E North Am • 250 kW • ALT. FREQ. TO 11605 kHz
6285v PIRATE (EUROPE)
†"RADIO SPACEMAN", Holland
Irr • Su • ENGLISH & DUTCH • W Europe • 0.1 kW
6290v PIRATE (EUROPE)
†"RADIO MIKE", Holland
Irr • Su • W Europe • 0.08 kW
†"VO THE NETHERLANDS", Holland
Irr • Sa/Su • ENGLISH & DUTCH • W Europe
†"WEEKEND MUSIC RADIO", Scotland
Irr • Su • W Europe • 0.1 kW
6292 PERU
†RADIO URIPA, Uripa
0.25 kW
6295 PIRATE (EUROPE)
"REFLECTIONS EUROPE", Ireland
Su • W Europe • 0.23 kW
6300 USA
FAMILY RADIO, Via Taiwan
E Asia • 250 kW
6300v PIRATE (EUROPE)
†"RADIO DOCTOR TIM", Germany
Irr • F • W Europe • 0.04 kW
6303v PIRATE (EUROPE)
†"RADIO BLUE STAR", Holland
Irr • Sa/Su • W Europe • 0.1 kW
6306.3 PIRATE (EUROPE)
†VARIOUS STATIONS, Germany
Irr • Su • W Europe • 0.01/0.5 kW
6315 CLANDESTINE (AFRICA)
†"VO PEACE & DEMOCRACY", Ethiopia
E Africa • ANTI-ERITREAN GOVT • 10 kW
M-Sa • E Africa • ANTI-ERITREAN GOVT • 10 kW
ETHIOPIA
†VO TIGRAY REVOL'N, Mek'ele
E Africa • 10 kW
Sa/Su • E Africa • 10 kW
M-F • E Africa • 10 kW
6329v PERU
†ESTACION C, Moyobamba
Irr • DS • 0.8 kW
DS • 0.8 kW
6339.6 PERU
†R SAN MIGUEL ARCANGEL, San Miguel
DS
6348 CLANDESTINE (ASIA)
"ECHO OF HOPE", Seoul, South Korea
E Asia • 50 kW
6350 USA
AFRTS, Pearl Harbor, Hawai'i
Irr • Atlantic • USB • ALT. FREQ. TO 10320 kHz
6381v VIETNAM
†LAI CHAU BC STATION, Lai Chau
DS
6395 PIRATE (EUROPE)
†"LASER HOT HITS", Ireland
Irr • Sa/Su • W Europe • 0.1 kW
6398v KOREA (DPR)
PYONGYANG BC STN, Pyongyang
E Asia • 50 kW
6400v PIRATE (EUROPE)
†"RADIO PACMAN", Holland
Irr • Su • W Europe • 0.01 kW
6410v CLANDESTINE (M EAST)
†"VO IRAN COMMUNISTS"
F • Mideast • ANTI-IRANIAN GOVT
6458.5 USA
†AFRTS, Roosevelt Roads, PR
C America • 10 kW • USB
6479v PERU
RADIO ALTURA, Huarmaca
DS
0 1 2 3 4 5 6 7 8 9 10 11 12 13 14 15 16 17 18 19 20 21 22 23 24

SEASONAL S OR W 1-HR TIMESHIFT MIDYEAR ⇦ OR ⇨ JAMMING / OR /\ EARLIEST HEARD ◁ LATEST HEARD ▷ NEW FOR 2002 †

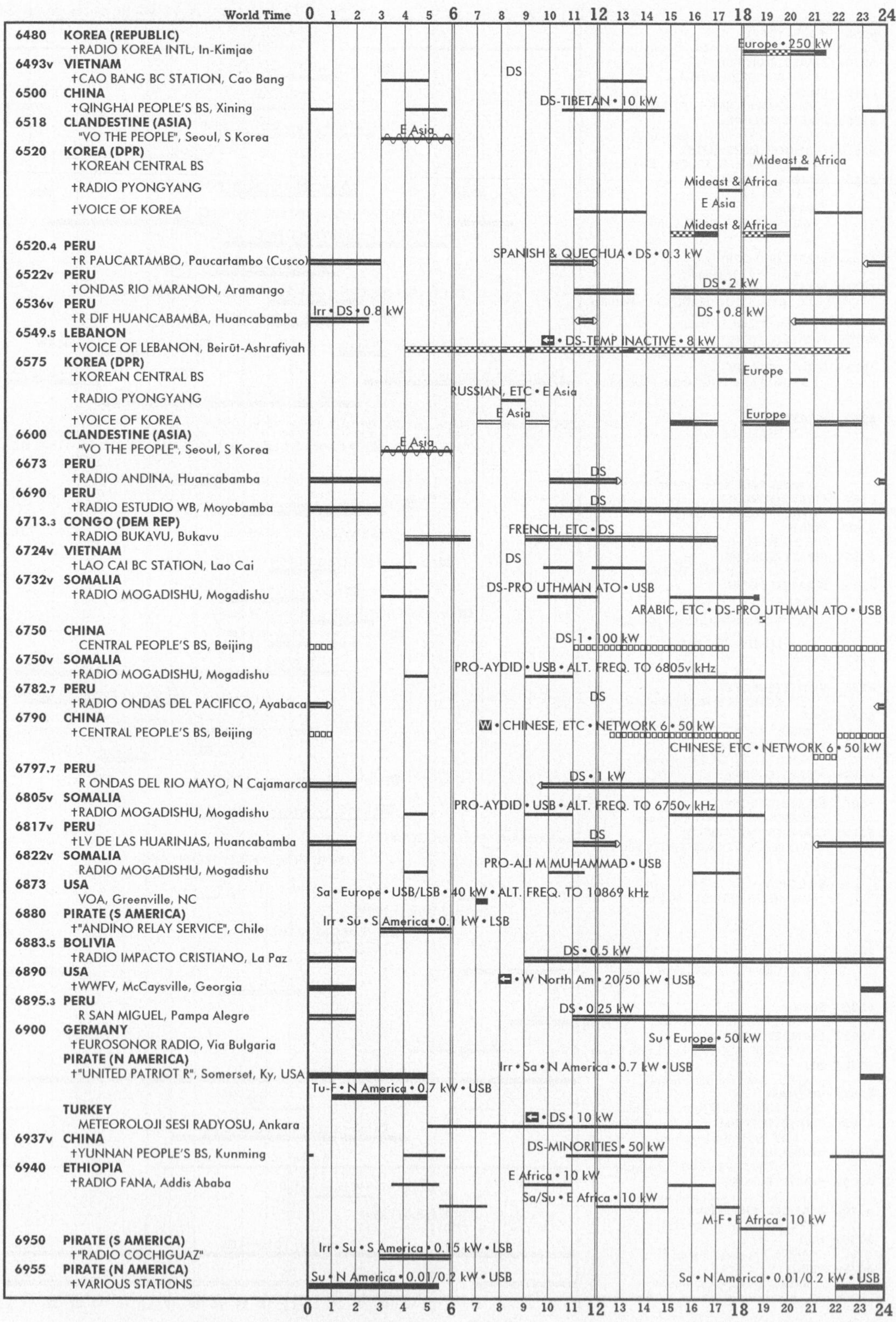
World Time 0 1 2 3 4 5 6 7 8 9 10 11 12 13 14 15 16 17 18 19 20 21 22 23 24
6480 KOREA (REPUBLIC)
†RADIO KOREA INTL, In-Kimjae
Europe • 250 kW
6493v VIETNAM
†CAO BANG BC STATION, Cao Bang
DS
6500 CHINA
†QINGHAI PEOPLE'S BS, Xining
DS-TIBETAN • 10 kW
6518 CLANDESTINE (ASIA)
"VO THE PEOPLE", Seoul, S Korea
E Asia
6520 KOREA (DPR)
†KOREAN CENTRAL BS
Mideast & Africa
†RADIO PYONGYANG
Mideast & Africa
†VOICE OF KOREA
E Asia
Mideast & Africa
6520.4 PERU
†R PAUCARTAMBO, Paucartambo (Cusco)
SPANISH & QUECHUA • DS • 0.3 kW
6522v PERU
†ONDAS RIO MARANON, Aramango
DS • 2 kW
6536v PERU
†R DIF HUANCABAMBA, Huancabamba
Irr • DS • 0.8 kW
DS • 0.8 kW
6549.5 LEBANON
†VOICE OF LEBANON, Beirūt-Ashrafiyah
• DS-TEMP INACTIVE • 8 kW
6575 KOREA (DPR)
†KOREAN CENTRAL BS
Europe
†RADIO PYONGYANG
RUSSIAN, ETC • E Asia
†VOICE OF KOREA
E Asia
Europe
6600 CLANDESTINE (ASIA)
"VO THE PEOPLE", Seoul, S Korea
E Asia
6673 PERU
†RADIO ANDINA, Huancabamba
DS
6690 PERU
†RADIO ESTUDIO WB, Moyobamba
DS
6713.3 CONGO (DEM REP)
†RADIO BUKAVU, Bukavu
FRENCH, ETC • DS
6724v VIETNAM
†LAO CAI BC STATION, Lao Cai
DS
6732v SOMALIA
†RADIO MOGADISHU, Mogadishu
DS-PRO UTHMAN ATO • USB
ARABIC, ETC • DS-PRO UTHMAN ATO • USB
6750 CHINA
CENTRAL PEOPLE'S BS, Beijing
DS-1 • 100 kW
6750v SOMALIA
†RADIO MOGADISHU, Mogadishu
PRO-AYDID • USB • ALT. FREQ. TO 6805v kHz
6782.7 PERU
†RADIO ONDAS DEL PACIFICO, Ayabaca
DS
6790 CHINA
†CENTRAL PEOPLE'S BS, Beijing
W • CHINESE, ETC • NETWORK 6 • 50 kW
CHINESE, ETC • NETWORK 6 • 50 kW
6797.7 PERU
R ONDAS DEL RIO MAYO, N Cajamarca
DS • 1 kW
6805v SOMALIA
†RADIO MOGADISHU, Mogadishu
PRO-AYDID • USB • ALT. FREQ. TO 6750v kHz
6817v PERU
†LV DE LAS HUARINJAS, Huancabamba
DS
6822v SOMALIA
RADIO MOGADISHU, Mogadishu
PRO-ALI M MUHAMMAD • USB
6873 USA
VOA, Greenville, NC
Sa • Europe • USB/LSB • 40 kW • ALT. FREQ. TO 10869 kHz
6880 PIRATE (S AMERICA)
†"ANDINO RELAY SERVICE", Chile
Irr • Su • S America • 0.1 kW • LSB
6883.5 BOLIVIA
†RADIO IMPACTO CRISTIANO, La Paz
DS • 0.5 kW
6890 USA
†WWFV, McCaysville, Georgia
• W North Am • 20/50 kW • USB
6895.3 PERU
R SAN MIGUEL, Pampa Alegre
DS • 0.25 kW
6900 GERMANY
†EUROSONOR RADIO, Via Bulgaria
Su • Europe • 50 kW
PIRATE (N AMERICA)
†"UNITED PATRIOT R", Somerset, Ky, USA
Irr • Sa • N America • 0.7 kW • USB
Tu-F • N America • 0.7 kW • USB
TURKEY
METEOROLOJI SESI RADYOSU, Ankara
• DS • 10 kW
6937v CHINA
†YUNNAN PEOPLE'S BS, Kunming
DS-MINORITIES • 50 kW
6940 ETHIOPIA
†RADIO FANA, Addis Ababa
E Africa • 10 kW
Sa/Su • E Africa • 10 kW
M-F • E Africa • 10 kW
6950 PIRATE (S AMERICA)
†"RADIO COCHIGUAZ"
Irr • Su • S America • 0.15 kW • LSB
6955 PIRATE (N AMERICA)
†VARIOUS STATIONS
Su • N America • 0.01/0.2 kW • USB
Sa • N America • 0.01/0.2 kW • USB
0 1 2 3 4 5 6 7 8 9 10 11 12 13 14 15 16 17 18 19 20 21 22 23 24
ENGLISH
ARABIC
CHINESE
FRENCH
GERMAN
RUSSIAN
SPANISH
OTHER

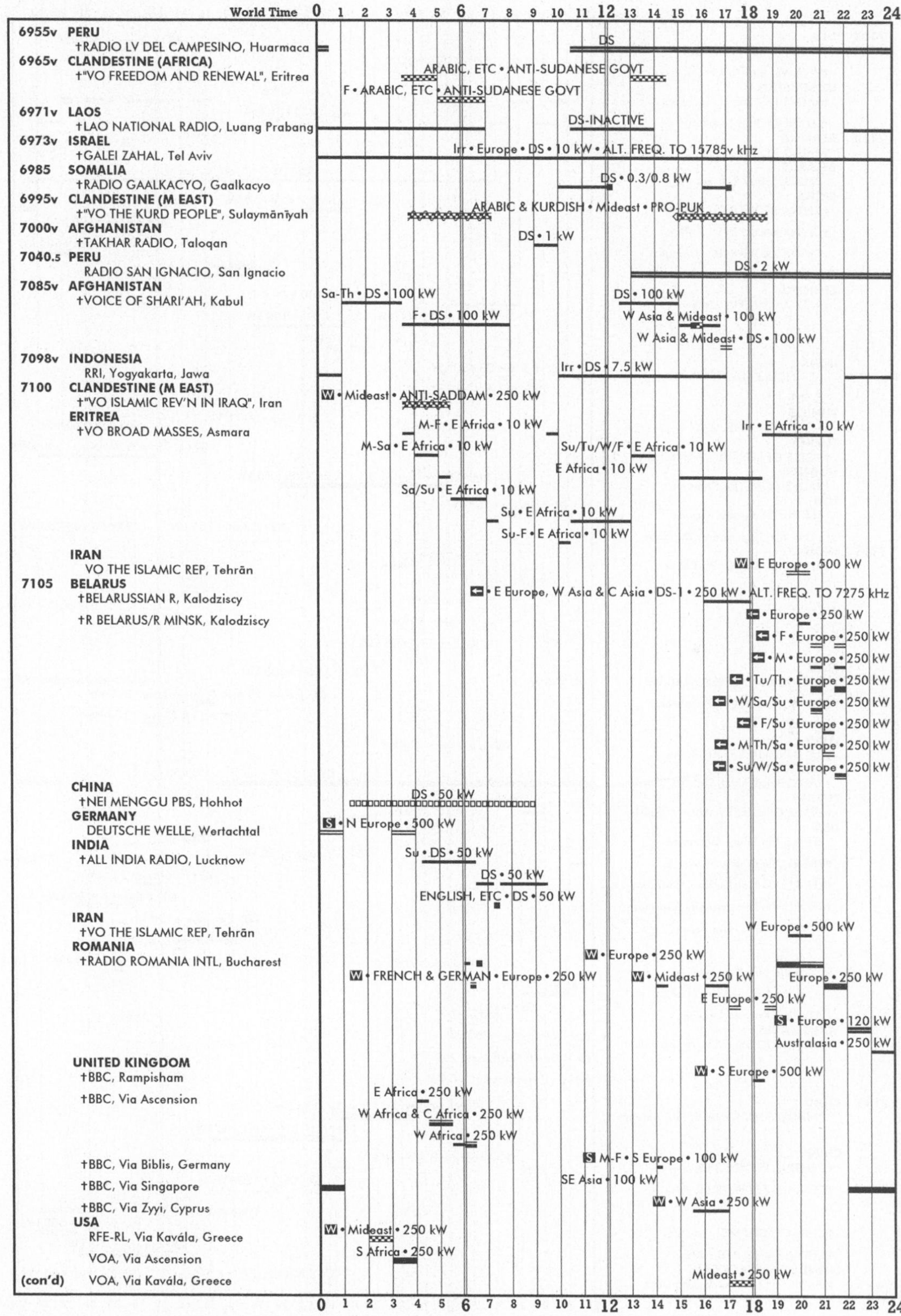
World Time 0 1 2 3 4 5 6 7 8 9 10 11 12 13 14 15 16 17 18 19 20 21 22 23 24
6955v PERU
†RADIO LV DEL CAMPESINO, Huarmaca
DS
6965v CLANDESTINE (AFRICA)
†"VO FREEDOM AND RENEWAL", Eritrea
ARABIC, ETC • ANTI-SUDANESE GOVT
F • ARABIC, ETC • ANTI-SUDANESE GOVT
6971v LAOS
†LAO NATIONAL RADIO, Luang Prabang
DS-INACTIVE
6973v ISRAEL
†GALEI ZAHAL, Tel Aviv
Irr • Europe • DS • 10 kW • ALT. FREQ. TO 15785v kHz
6985 SOMALIA
†RADIO GAALKACYO, Gaalkacyo
DS • 0.3/0.8 kW
6995v CLANDESTINE (M EAST)
†"VO THE KURD PEOPLE", Sulaymānīyah
ARABIC & KURDISH • Mideast • PRO-PUK
7000v AFGHANISTAN
†TAKHAR RADIO, Taloqan
DS • 1 kW
7040.5 PERU
RADIO SAN IGNACIO, San Ignacio
DS • 2 kW
7085v AFGHANISTAN
†VOICE OF SHARI'AH, Kabul
Sa-Th • DS • 100 kW
DS • 100 kW
F • DS • 100 kW
W Asia & Mideast • 100 kW
W Asia & Mideast • DS • 100 kW
7098v INDONESIA
RRI, Yogyakarta, Jawa
Irr • DS • 7.5 kW
7100 CLANDESTINE (M EAST)
†"VO ISLAMIC REV'N IN IRAQ", Iran
W • Mideast • ANTI-SADDAM • 250 kW
ERITREA
†VO BROAD MASSES, Asmara
M-F • E Africa • 10 kW
Irr • E Africa • 10 kW
M-Sa • E Africa • 10 kW
Su/Tu/W/F • E Africa • 10 kW
E Africa • 10 kW
Sa/Su • E Africa • 10 kW
Su • E Africa • 10 kW
Su-F • E Africa • 10 kW
IRAN
VO THE ISLAMIC REP, Tehrān
W • E Europe • 500 kW
7105 BELARUS
†BELARUSSIAN R, Kalodziscy
• E Europe, W Asia & C Asia • DS-1 • 250 kW • ALT. FREQ. TO 7275 kHz
†R BELARUS/R MINSK, Kalodziscy
• Europe • 250 kW
• F • Europe • 250 kW
• M • Europe • 250 kW
• Tu/Th • Europe • 250 kW
• W/Sa/Su • Europe • 250 kW
• F/Su • Europe • 250 kW
• M-Th/Sa • Europe • 250 kW
• Su/W/Sa • Europe • 250 kW
CHINA
†NEI MENGGU PBS, Hohhot
DS • 50 kW
GERMANY
DEUTSCHE WELLE, Wertachtal
S • N Europe • 500 kW
INDIA
†ALL INDIA RADIO, Lucknow
Su • DS • 50 kW
DS • 50 kW
ENGLISH, ETC • DS • 50 kW
IRAN
†VO THE ISLAMIC REP, Tehrān
W Europe • 500 kW
ROMANIA
†RADIO ROMANIA INTL, Bucharest
W • Europe • 250 kW
W • FRENCH & GERMAN • Europe • 250 kW
W • Mideast • 250 kW
Europe • 250 kW
E Europe • 250 kW
S • Europe • 120 kW
Australasia • 250 kW
UNITED KINGDOM
†BBC, Rampisham
W • S Europe • 500 kW
†BBC, Via Ascension
E Africa • 250 kW
W Africa & C Africa • 250 kW
W Africa • 250 kW
†BBC, Via Biblis, Germany
S M-F • S Europe • 100 kW
†BBC, Via Singapore
SE Asia • 100 kW
†BBC, Via Zyyi, Cyprus
W • W Asia • 250 kW
USA
RFE-RL, Via Kavála, Greece
W • Mideast • 250 kW
VOA, Via Ascension
S Africa • 250 kW
(con'd) VOA, Via Kavála, Greece
Mideast • 250 kW
0 1 2 3 4 5 6 7 8 9 10 11 12 13 14 15 16 17 18 19 20 21 22 23 24

SEASONAL S OR W 1-HR TIMESHIFT MIDYEAR OR JAMMING / OR /\ EARLIEST HEARD ◁ LATEST HEARD ▷ NEW FOR 2002 †

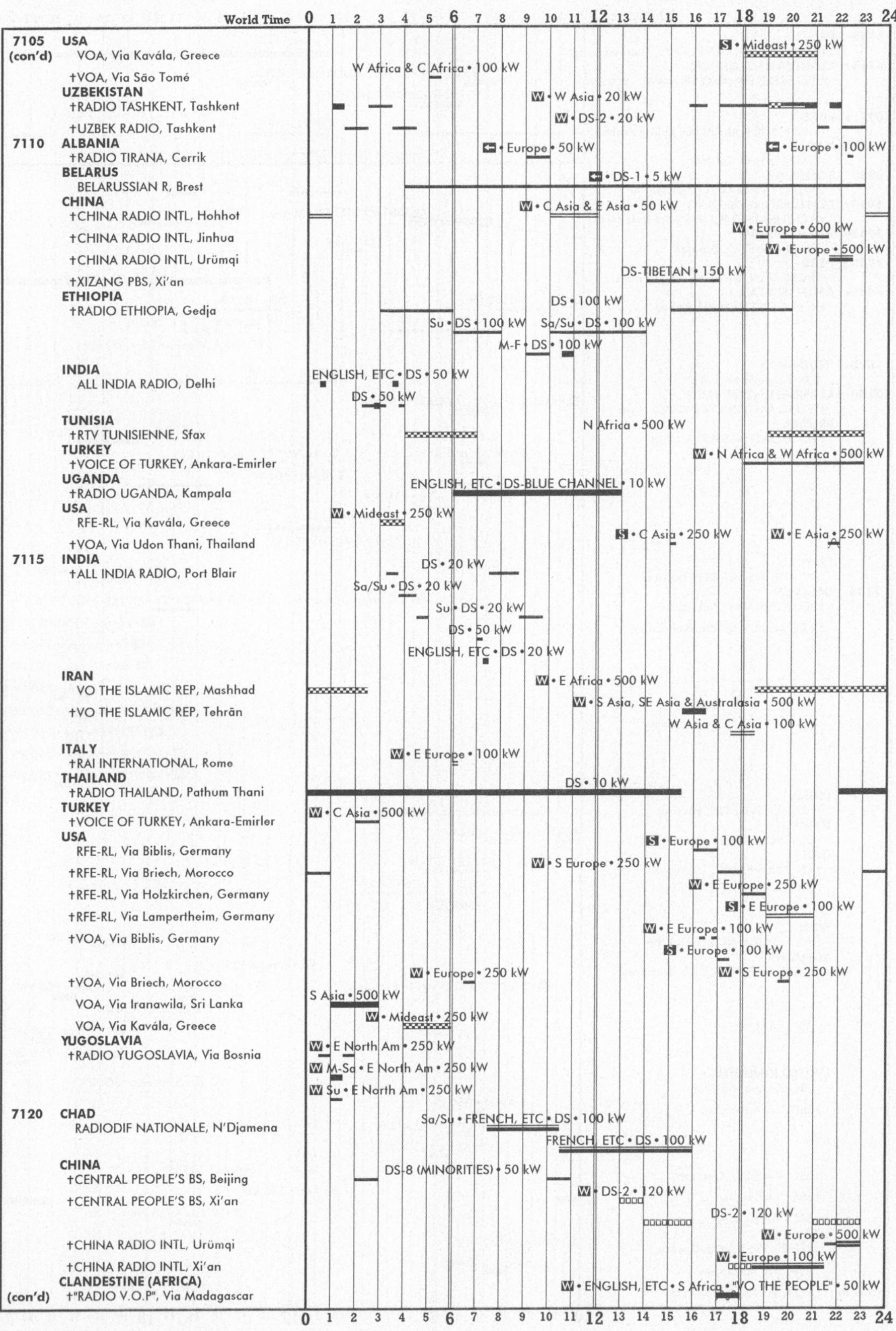
World Time 0 1 2 3 4 5 6 7 8 9 10 11 12 13 14 15 16 17 18 19 20 21 22 23 24
7105 (con'd) USA
VOA, Via Kavála, Greece
S • Mideast • 250 kW
†VOA, Via São Tomé
W Africa & C Africa • 100 kW
UZBEKISTAN
†RADIO TASHKENT, Tashkent
W • W Asia • 20 kW
†UZBEK RADIO, Tashkent
W • DS-2 • 20 kW
7110 ALBANIA
†RADIO TIRANA, Cerrik
• Europe • 50 kW
• Europe • 100 kW
BELARUS
BELARUSSIAN R, Brest
• DS-1 • 5 kW
CHINA
†CHINA RADIO INTL, Hohhot
W • C Asia & E Asia • 50 kW
†CHINA RADIO INTL, Jinhua
W • Europe • 600 kW
†CHINA RADIO INTL, Urümqi
W • Europe • 500 kW
†XIZANG PBS, Xi'an
DS-TIBETAN • 150 kW
ETHIOPIA
†RADIO ETHIOPIA, Gedja
DS • 100 kW
Su • DS • 100 kW
Sa/Su • DS • 100 kW
M-F • DS • 100 kW
INDIA
ALL INDIA RADIO, Delhi
ENGLISH, ETC • DS • 50 kW
DS • 50 kW
TUNISIA
†RTV TUNISIENNE, Sfax
N Africa • 500 kW
TURKEY
†VOICE OF TURKEY, Ankara-Emirler
W • N Africa & W Africa • 500 kW
UGANDA
†RADIO UGANDA, Kampala
ENGLISH, ETC • DS-BLUE CHANNEL • 10 kW
USA
RFE-RL, Via Kavála, Greece
W • Mideast • 250 kW
†VOA, Via Udon Thani, Thailand
S • C Asia • 250 kW
W • E Asia • 250 kW
7115 INDIA
†ALL INDIA RADIO, Port Blair
DS • 20 kW
Sa/Su • DS • 20 kW
Su • DS • 20 kW
DS • 50 kW
ENGLISH, ETC • DS • 20 kW
IRAN
VO THE ISLAMIC REP, Mashhad
W • E Africa • 500 kW
†VO THE ISLAMIC REP, Tehrān
W • S Asia, SE Asia & Australasia • 500 kW
W Asia & C Asia • 100 kW
ITALY
†RAI INTERNATIONAL, Rome
W • E Europe • 100 kW
THAILAND
†RADIO THAILAND, Pathum Thani
DS • 10 kW
TURKEY
†VOICE OF TURKEY, Ankara-Emirler
W • C Asia • 500 kW
USA
RFE-RL, Via Biblis, Germany
S • Europe • 100 kW
†RFE-RL, Via Briech, Morocco
W • S Europe • 250 kW
†RFE-RL, Via Holzkirchen, Germany
W • E Europe • 250 kW
†RFE-RL, Via Lampertheim, Germany
S • E Europe • 100 kW
†VOA, Via Biblis, Germany
W • E Europe • 100 kW
S • Europe • 100 kW
†VOA, Via Briech, Morocco
W • Europe • 250 kW
W • S Europe • 250 kW
VOA, Via Iranawila, Sri Lanka
S Asia • 500 kW
VOA, Via Kavála, Greece
W • Mideast • 250 kW
YUGOSLAVIA
†RADIO YUGOSLAVIA, Via Bosnia
W • E North Am • 250 kW
W M-Sa • E North Am • 250 kW
W Su • E North Am • 250 kW
7120 CHAD
RADIODIF NATIONALE, N'Djamena
Sa/Su • FRENCH, ETC • DS • 100 kW
FRENCH, ETC • DS • 100 kW
CHINA
†CENTRAL PEOPLE'S BS, Beijing
DS-8 (MINORITIES) • 50 kW
†CENTRAL PEOPLE'S BS, Xi'an
W • DS-2 • 120 kW
DS-2 • 120 kW
†CHINA RADIO INTL, Urümqi
W • Europe • 500 kW
†CHINA RADIO INTL, Xi'an
W • Europe • 100 kW
CLANDESTINE (AFRICA)
(con'd) †"RADIO V.O.P", Via Madagascar
W • ENGLISH, ETC • S Africa • "VO THE PEOPLE" • 50 kW
0 1 2 3 4 5 6 7 8 9 10 11 12 13 14 15 16 17 18 19 20 21 22 23 24
ENGLISH ARABIC CHINESE FRENCH GERMAN RUSSIAN SPANISH OTHER

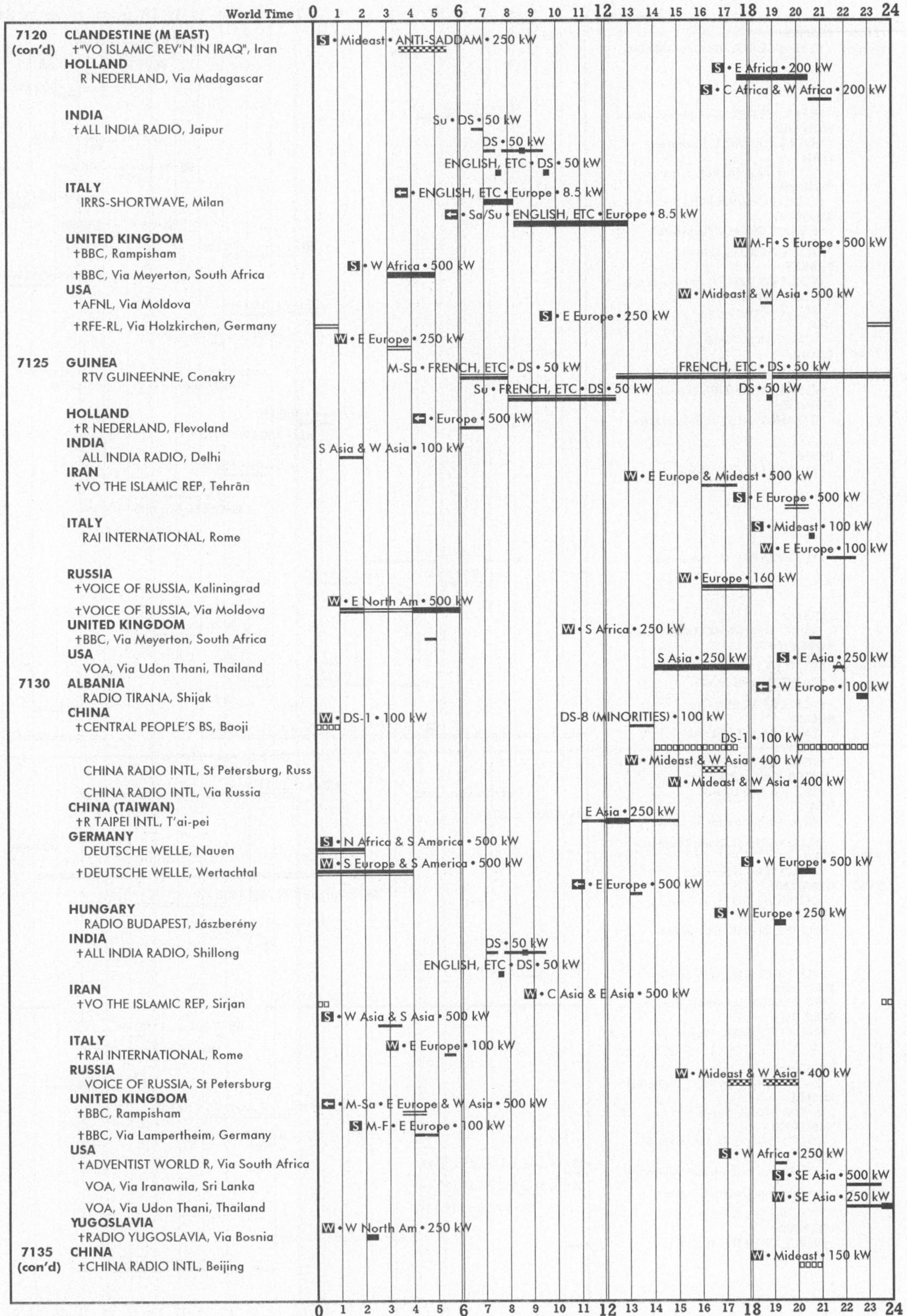
World Time 0 1 2 3 4 5 6 7 8 9 10 11 12 13 14 15 16 17 18 19 20 21 22 23 24
7120 (con'd) CLANDESTINE (M EAST)
†"VO ISLAMIC REV'N IN IRAQ", Iran
S • Mideast • ANTI-SADDAM • 250 kW
HOLLAND
R NEDERLAND, Via Madagascar
S • E Africa • 200 kW
S • C Africa & W Africa • 200 kW
INDIA
†ALL INDIA RADIO, Jaipur
Su • DS • 50 kW
DS • 50 kW
ENGLISH, ETC • DS • 50 kW
ITALY
IRRS-SHORTWAVE, Milan
ENGLISH, ETC • Europe • 8.5 kW
Sa/Su • ENGLISH, ETC • Europe • 8.5 kW
UNITED KINGDOM
†BBC, Rampisham
W M-F • S Europe • 500 kW
†BBC, Via Meyerton, South Africa
S • W Africa • 500 kW
USA
†AFNL, Via Moldova
W • Mideast & W Asia • 500 kW
†RFE-RL, Via Holzkirchen, Germany
S • E Europe • 250 kW
W • E Europe • 250 kW
7125 GUINEA
RTV GUINEENNE, Conakry
M-Sa • FRENCH, ETC • DS • 50 kW
FRENCH, ETC • DS • 50 kW
Su • FRENCH, ETC • DS • 50 kW
DS • 50 kW
HOLLAND
†R NEDERLAND, Flevoland
Europe • 500 kW
INDIA
ALL INDIA RADIO, Delhi
S Asia & W Asia • 100 kW
IRAN
†VO THE ISLAMIC REP, Tehrān
W • E Europe & Mideast • 500 kW
S • E Europe • 500 kW
ITALY
RAI INTERNATIONAL, Rome
S • Mideast • 100 kW
W • E Europe • 100 kW
RUSSIA
†VOICE OF RUSSIA, Kaliningrad
W • Europe • 160 kW
†VOICE OF RUSSIA, Via Moldova
W • E North Am • 500 kW
UNITED KINGDOM
†BBC, Via Meyerton, South Africa
W • S Africa • 250 kW
USA
VOA, Via Udon Thani, Thailand
S Asia • 250 kW
S • E Asia • 250 kW
7130 ALBANIA
RADIO TIRANA, Shijak
W Europe • 100 kW
CHINA
†CENTRAL PEOPLE'S BS, Baoji
W • DS-1 • 100 kW
DS-8 (MINORITIES) • 100 kW
DS-1 • 100 kW
CHINA RADIO INTL, St Petersburg, Russ
W • Mideast & W Asia • 400 kW
CHINA RADIO INTL, Via Russia
W • Mideast & W Asia • 400 kW
CHINA (TAIWAN)
†R TAIPEI INTL, T'ai-pei
E Asia • 250 kW
GERMANY
DEUTSCHE WELLE, Nauen
S • N Africa & S America • 500 kW
†DEUTSCHE WELLE, Wertachtal
W • S Europe & S America • 500 kW
S • W Europe • 500 kW
E Europe • 500 kW
HUNGARY
RADIO BUDAPEST, Jászberény
S • W Europe • 250 kW
INDIA
†ALL INDIA RADIO, Shillong
DS • 50 kW
ENGLISH, ETC • DS • 50 kW
IRAN
†VO THE ISLAMIC REP, Sirjan
W • C Asia & E Asia • 500 kW
S • W Asia & S Asia • 500 kW
ITALY
†RAI INTERNATIONAL, Rome
W • E Europe • 100 kW
RUSSIA
VOICE OF RUSSIA, St Petersburg
W • Mideast & W Asia • 400 kW
UNITED KINGDOM
†BBC, Rampisham
M-Sa • E Europe & W Asia • 500 kW
†BBC, Via Lampertheim, Germany
S M-F • E Europe • 100 kW
USA
†ADVENTIST WORLD R, Via South Africa
S • W Africa • 250 kW
VOA, Via Iranawila, Sri Lanka
S • SE Asia • 500 kW
VOA, Via Udon Thani, Thailand
W • SE Asia • 250 kW
YUGOSLAVIA
†RADIO YUGOSLAVIA, Via Bosnia
W • W North Am • 250 kW
7135 (con'd) CHINA
†CHINA RADIO INTL, Beijing
W • Mideast • 150 kW
0 1 2 3 4 5 6 7 8 9 10 11 12 13 14 15 16 17 18 19 20 21 22 23 24

SEASONAL S OR W   1-HR TIMESHIFT MIDYEAR ← OR →   JAMMING / OR ⋀   EARLIEST HEARD ◁   LATEST HEARD ▷   NEW FOR 2002 †

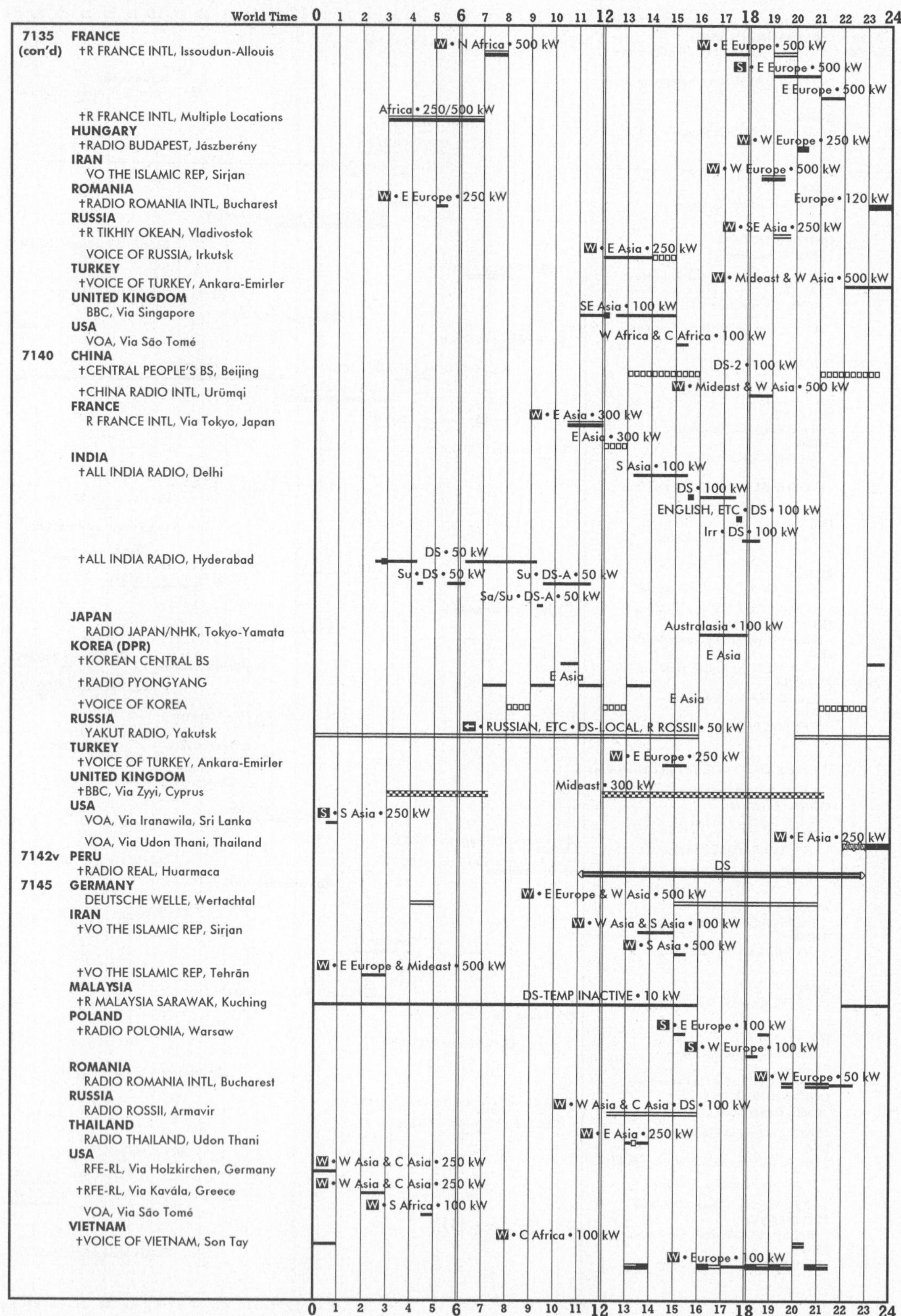
World Time 0 1 2 3 4 5 6 7 8 9 10 11 12 13 14 15 16 17 18 19 20 21 22 23 24
7135 (con'd) FRANCE
†R FRANCE INTL, Issoudun-Allouis
W • N Africa • 500 kW
W • E Europe • 500 kW
S • E Europe • 500 kW
E Europe • 500 kW
†R FRANCE INTL, Multiple Locations
Africa • 250/500 kW
HUNGARY
†RADIO BUDAPEST, Jászberény
W • W Europe • 250 kW
IRAN
VO THE ISLAMIC REP, Sirjan
W • W Europe • 500 kW
ROMANIA
†RADIO ROMANIA INTL, Bucharest
W • E Europe • 250 kW
Europe • 120 kW
RUSSIA
†R TIKHIY OKEAN, Vladivostok
W • SE Asia • 250 kW
VOICE OF RUSSIA, Irkutsk
W • E Asia • 250 kW
TURKEY
†VOICE OF TURKEY, Ankara-Emirler
W • Mideast & W Asia • 500 kW
UNITED KINGDOM
BBC, Via Singapore
SE Asia • 100 kW
USA
VOA, Via São Tomé
W Africa & C Africa • 100 kW
7140 CHINA
†CENTRAL PEOPLE'S BS, Beijing
DS-2 • 100 kW
†CHINA RADIO INTL, Urümqi
W • Mideast & W Asia • 500 kW
FRANCE
R FRANCE INTL, Via Tokyo, Japan
W • E Asia • 300 kW
E Asia • 300 kW
INDIA
†ALL INDIA RADIO, Delhi
S Asia • 100 kW
DS • 100 kW
ENGLISH, ETC • DS • 100 kW
Irr • DS • 100 kW
†ALL INDIA RADIO, Hyderabad
DS • 50 kW
Su • DS • 50 kW
Su • DS-A • 50 kW
Sa/Su • DS-A • 50 kW
JAPAN
RADIO JAPAN/NHK, Tokyo-Yamata
Australasia • 100 kW
KOREA (DPR)
†KOREAN CENTRAL BS
E Asia
†RADIO PYONGYANG
E Asia
†VOICE OF KOREA
E Asia
RUSSIA
YAKUT RADIO, Yakutsk
RUSSIAN, ETC • DS-LOCAL, R ROSSII • 50 kW
TURKEY
†VOICE OF TURKEY, Ankara-Emirler
W • E Europe • 250 kW
UNITED KINGDOM
†BBC, Via Zyyi, Cyprus
Mideast • 300 kW
USA
VOA, Via Iranawila, Sri Lanka
S • S Asia • 250 kW
VOA, Via Udon Thani, Thailand
W • E Asia • 250 kW
7142v PERU
†RADIO REAL, Huarmaca
DS
7145 GERMANY
DEUTSCHE WELLE, Wertachtal
W • E Europe & W Asia • 500 kW
IRAN
†VO THE ISLAMIC REP, Sirjan
W • W Asia & S Asia • 100 kW
W • S Asia • 500 kW
†VO THE ISLAMIC REP, Tehrān
W • E Europe & Mideast • 500 kW
MALAYSIA
†R MALAYSIA SARAWAK, Kuching
DS-TEMP INACTIVE • 10 kW
POLAND
†RADIO POLONIA, Warsaw
S • E Europe • 100 kW
S • W Europe • 100 kW
ROMANIA
RADIO ROMANIA INTL, Bucharest
W • W Europe • 50 kW
RUSSIA
RADIO ROSSII, Armavir
W • W Asia & C Asia • DS • 100 kW
THAILAND
RADIO THAILAND, Udon Thani
W • E Asia • 250 kW
USA
RFE-RL, Via Holzkirchen, Germany
W • W Asia & C Asia • 250 kW
†RFE-RL, Via Kavála, Greece
W • W Asia & C Asia • 250 kW
VOA, Via São Tomé
W • S Africa • 100 kW
VIETNAM
†VOICE OF VIETNAM, Son Tay
W • C Africa • 100 kW
W • Europe • 100 kW
0 1 2 3 4 5 6 7 8 9 10 11 12 13 14 15 16 17 18 19 20 21 22 23 24
ENGLISH ARABIC CHINESE FRENCH GERMAN RUSSIAN SPANISH OTHER

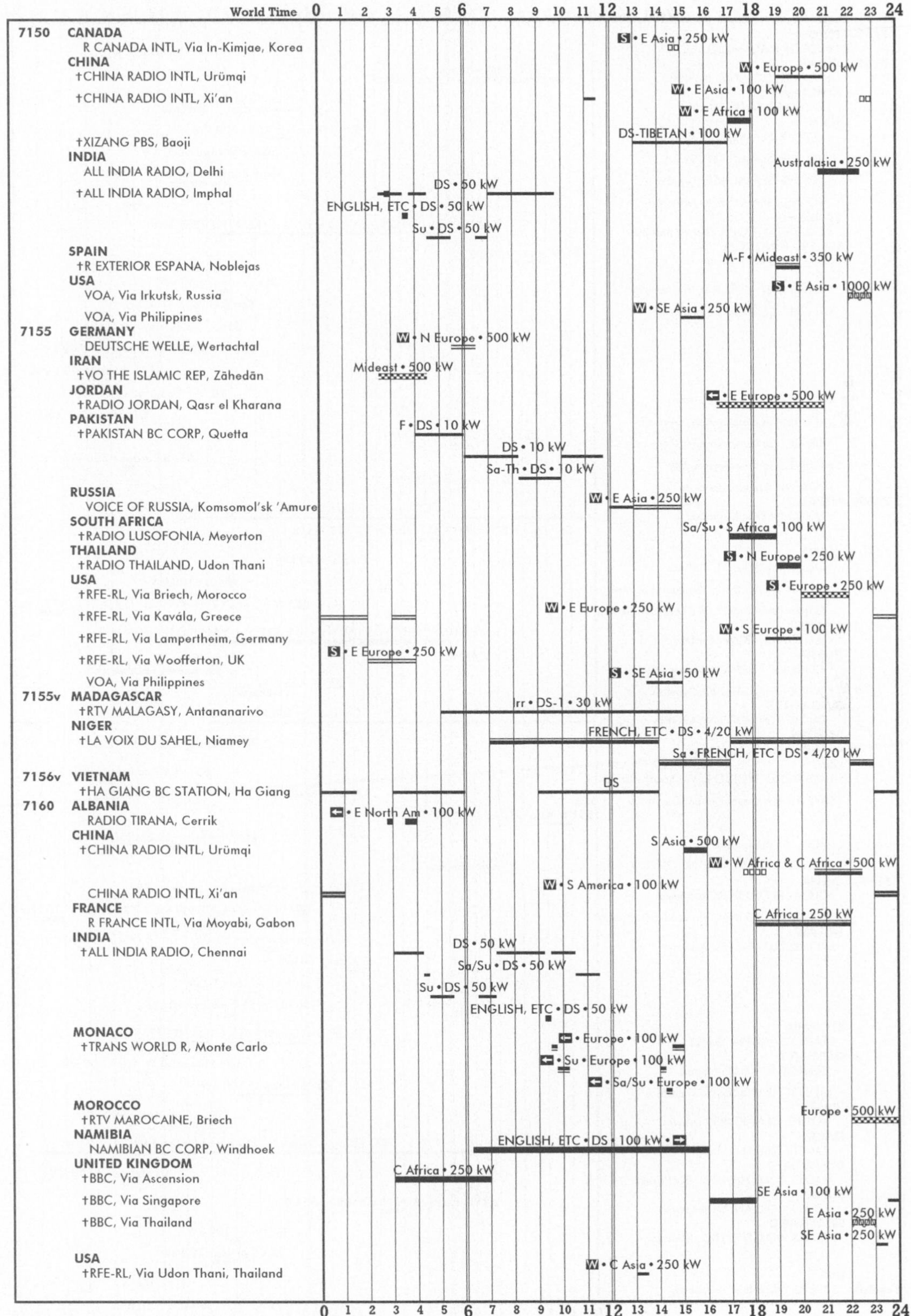
World Time 0 1 2 3 4 5 6 7 8 9 10 11 12 13 14 15 16 17 18 19 20 21 22 23 24
7150 CANADA
R CANADA INTL, Via In-Kimjae, Korea
S • E Asia • 250 kW
CHINA
†CHINA RADIO INTL, Urümqi
W • Europe • 500 kW
†CHINA RADIO INTL, Xi'an
W • E Asia • 100 kW
W • E Africa • 100 kW
†XIZANG PBS, Baoji
DS-TIBETAN • 100 kW
INDIA
ALL INDIA RADIO, Delhi
Australasia • 250 kW
†ALL INDIA RADIO, Imphal
DS • 50 kW
ENGLISH, ETC • DS • 50 kW
Su • DS • 50 kW
SPAIN
†R EXTERIOR ESPANA, Noblejas
M-F • Mideast • 350 kW
USA
VOA, Via Irkutsk, Russia
S • E Asia • 1000 kW
VOA, Via Philippines
W • SE Asia • 250 kW
7155 GERMANY
DEUTSCHE WELLE, Wertachtal
W • N Europe • 500 kW
IRAN
†VO THE ISLAMIC REP, Zāhedān
Mideast • 500 kW
JORDAN
†RADIO JORDAN, Qasr el Kharana
E Europe • 500 kW
PAKISTAN
†PAKISTAN BC CORP, Quetta
F • DS • 10 kW
DS • 10 kW
Sa-Th • DS • 10 kW
RUSSIA
VOICE OF RUSSIA, Komsomol'sk 'Amure
W • E Asia • 250 kW
SOUTH AFRICA
†RADIO LUSOFONIA, Meyerton
Sa/Su • S Africa • 100 kW
THAILAND
†RADIO THAILAND, Udon Thani
S • N Europe • 250 kW
USA
†RFE-RL, Via Briech, Morocco
S • Europe • 250 kW
†RFE-RL, Via Kavála, Greece
W • E Europe • 250 kW
†RFE-RL, Via Lampertheim, Germany
W • S Europe • 100 kW
†RFE-RL, Via Woofferton, UK
S • E Europe • 250 kW
VOA, Via Philippines
S • SE Asia • 50 kW
7155v MADAGASCAR
†RTV MALAGASY, Antananarivo
Irr • DS-1 • 30 kW
NIGER
†LA VOIX DU SAHEL, Niamey
FRENCH, ETC • DS • 4/20 kW
Sa • FRENCH, ETC • DS • 4/20 kW
7156v VIETNAM
†HA GIANG BC STATION, Ha Giang
DS
7160 ALBANIA
RADIO TIRANA, Cerrik
E North Am • 100 kW
CHINA
†CHINA RADIO INTL, Urümqi
S Asia • 500 kW
W • W Africa & C Africa • 500 kW
CHINA RADIO INTL, Xi'an
W • S America • 100 kW
FRANCE
R FRANCE INTL, Via Moyabi, Gabon
C Africa • 250 kW
INDIA
†ALL INDIA RADIO, Chennai
DS • 50 kW
Sa/Su • DS • 50 kW
Su • DS • 50 kW
ENGLISH, ETC • DS • 50 kW
MONACO
†TRANS WORLD R, Monte Carlo
Europe • 100 kW
Su • Europe • 100 kW
Sa/Su • Europe • 100 kW
MOROCCO
†RTV MAROCAINE, Briech
Europe • 500 kW
NAMIBIA
NAMIBIAN BC CORP, Windhoek
ENGLISH, ETC • DS • 100 kW
UNITED KINGDOM
†BBC, Via Ascension
C Africa • 250 kW
†BBC, Via Singapore
SE Asia • 100 kW
†BBC, Via Thailand
E Asia • 250 kW
SE Asia • 250 kW
USA
†RFE-RL, Via Udon Thani, Thailand
W • C Asia • 250 kW
0 1 2 3 4 5 6 7 8 9 10 11 12 13 14 15 16 17 18 19 20 21 22 23 24

SEASONAL S OR W 1-HR TIMESHIFT MIDYEAR ◄ OR ► JAMMING / OR ∧ EARLIEST HEARD ◁ LATEST HEARD ▷ NEW FOR 2002 †

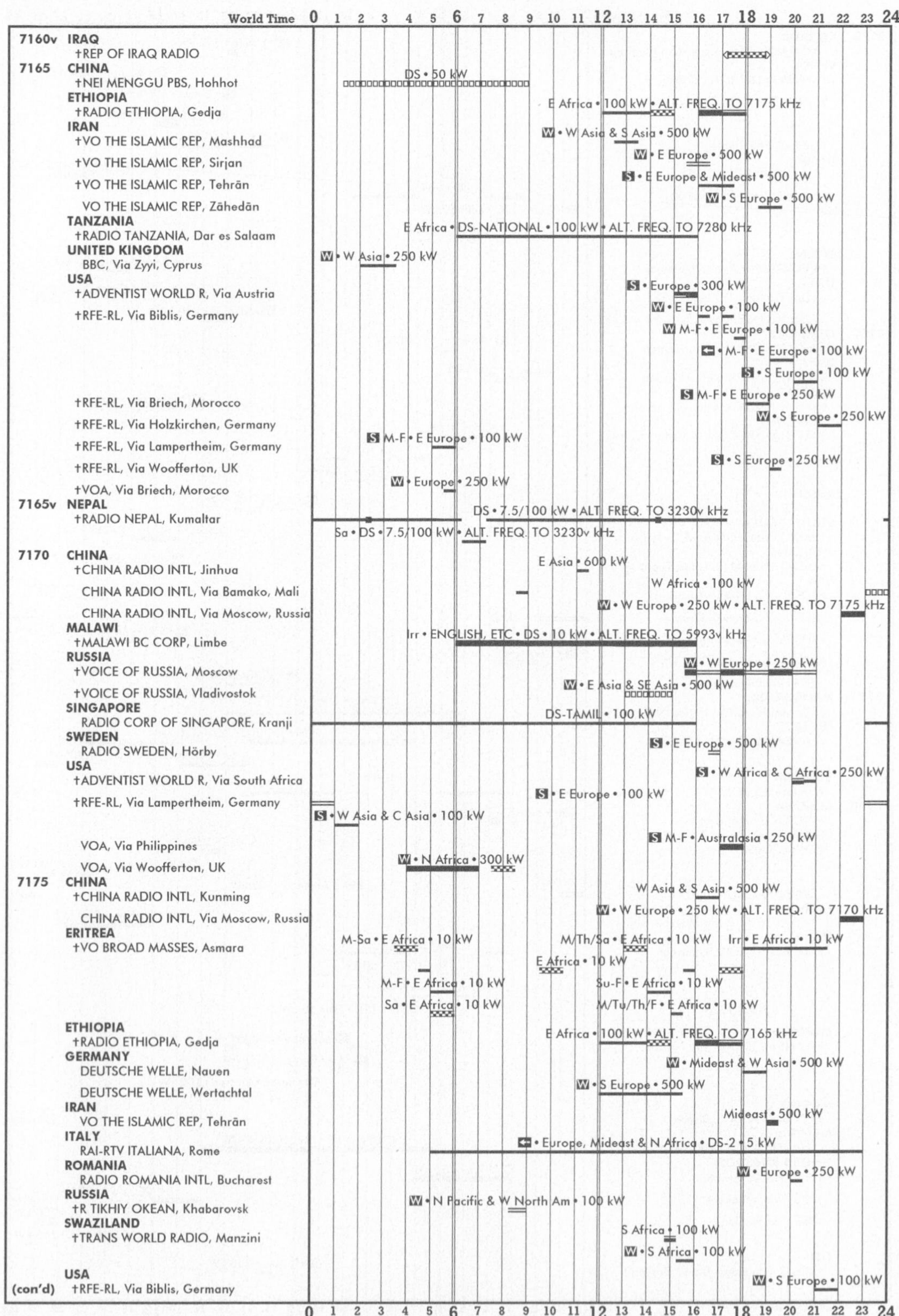
World Time 0 1 2 3 4 5 6 7 8 9 10 11 12 13 14 15 16 17 18 19 20 21 22 23 24
7160v IRAQ
†REP OF IRAQ RADIO
7165 CHINA
†NEI MENGGU PBS, Hohhot
DS • 50 kW
ETHIOPIA
†RADIO ETHIOPIA, Gedja
E Africa • 100 kW • ALT. FREQ. TO 7175 kHz
IRAN
†VO THE ISLAMIC REP, Mashhad
W • W Asia & S Asia • 500 kW
†VO THE ISLAMIC REP, Sirjan
W • E Europe • 500 kW
†VO THE ISLAMIC REP, Tehrān
S • E Europe & Mideast • 500 kW
VO THE ISLAMIC REP, Zāhedān
W • S Europe • 500 kW
TANZANIA
†RADIO TANZANIA, Dar es Salaam
E Africa • DS-NATIONAL • 100 kW • ALT. FREQ. TO 7280 kHz
UNITED KINGDOM
BBC, Via Zyyi, Cyprus
W • W Asia • 250 kW
USA
†ADVENTIST WORLD R, Via Austria
S • Europe • 300 kW
†RFE-RL, Via Biblis, Germany
W • E Europe • 100 kW
W M-F • E Europe • 100 kW
M-F • E Europe • 100 kW
S • S Europe • 100 kW
†RFE-RL, Via Briech, Morocco
S M-F • E Europe • 250 kW
†RFE-RL, Via Holzkirchen, Germany
W • S Europe • 250 kW
†RFE-RL, Via Lampertheim, Germany
S M-F • E Europe • 100 kW
†RFE-RL, Via Woofferton, UK
S • S Europe • 250 kW
†VOA, Via Briech, Morocco
W • Europe • 250 kW
7165v NEPAL
†RADIO NEPAL, Kumaltar
DS • 7.5/100 kW • ALT. FREQ. TO 3230v kHz
Sa • DS • 7.5/100 kW • ALT. FREQ. TO 3230v kHz
7170 CHINA
†CHINA RADIO INTL, Jinhua
E Asia • 600 kW
CHINA RADIO INTL, Via Bamako, Mali
W Africa • 100 kW
CHINA RADIO INTL, Via Moscow, Russia
W • W Europe • 250 kW • ALT. FREQ. TO 7175 kHz
MALAWI
†MALAWI BC CORP, Limbe
Irr • ENGLISH, ETC • DS • 10 kW • ALT. FREQ. TO 5993v kHz
RUSSIA
†VOICE OF RUSSIA, Moscow
W • W Europe • 250 kW
†VOICE OF RUSSIA, Vladivostok
W • E Asia & SE Asia • 500 kW
SINGAPORE
RADIO CORP OF SINGAPORE, Kranji
DS-TAMIL • 100 kW
SWEDEN
RADIO SWEDEN, Hörby
S • E Europe • 500 kW
USA
†ADVENTIST WORLD R, Via South Africa
S • W Africa & C Africa • 250 kW
†RFE-RL, Via Lampertheim, Germany
S • E Europe • 100 kW
S • W Asia & C Asia • 100 kW
VOA, Via Philippines
S M-F • Australasia • 250 kW
VOA, Via Woofferton, UK
W • N Africa • 300 kW
7175 CHINA
†CHINA RADIO INTL, Kunming
W Asia & S Asia • 500 kW
CHINA RADIO INTL, Via Moscow, Russia
W • W Europe • 250 kW • ALT. FREQ. TO 7170 kHz
ERITREA
†VO BROAD MASSES, Asmara
M-Sa • E Africa • 10 kW
M/Th/Sa • E Africa • 10 kW
Irr • E Africa • 10 kW
E Africa • 10 kW
M-F • E Africa • 10 kW
Su-F • E Africa • 10 kW
Sa • E Africa • 10 kW
M/Tu/Th/F • E Africa • 10 kW
ETHIOPIA
†RADIO ETHIOPIA, Gedja
E Africa • 100 kW • ALT. FREQ. TO 7165 kHz
GERMANY
DEUTSCHE WELLE, Nauen
W • Mideast & W Asia • 500 kW
DEUTSCHE WELLE, Wertachtal
W • S Europe • 500 kW
IRAN
VO THE ISLAMIC REP, Tehrān
Mideast • 500 kW
ITALY
RAI-RTV ITALIANA, Rome
Europe, Mideast & N Africa • DS-2 • 5 kW
ROMANIA
RADIO ROMANIA INTL, Bucharest
W • Europe • 250 kW
RUSSIA
†R TIKHIY OKEAN, Khabarovsk
W • N Pacific & W North Am • 100 kW
SWAZILAND
†TRANS WORLD RADIO, Manzini
S Africa • 100 kW
W • S Africa • 100 kW
USA
(con'd) †RFE-RL, Via Biblis, Germany
W • S Europe • 100 kW
0 1 2 3 4 5 6 7 8 9 10 11 12 13 14 15 16 17 18 19 20 21 22 23 24

ENGLISH ARABIC CHINESE FRENCH GERMAN RUSSIAN SPANISH OTHER

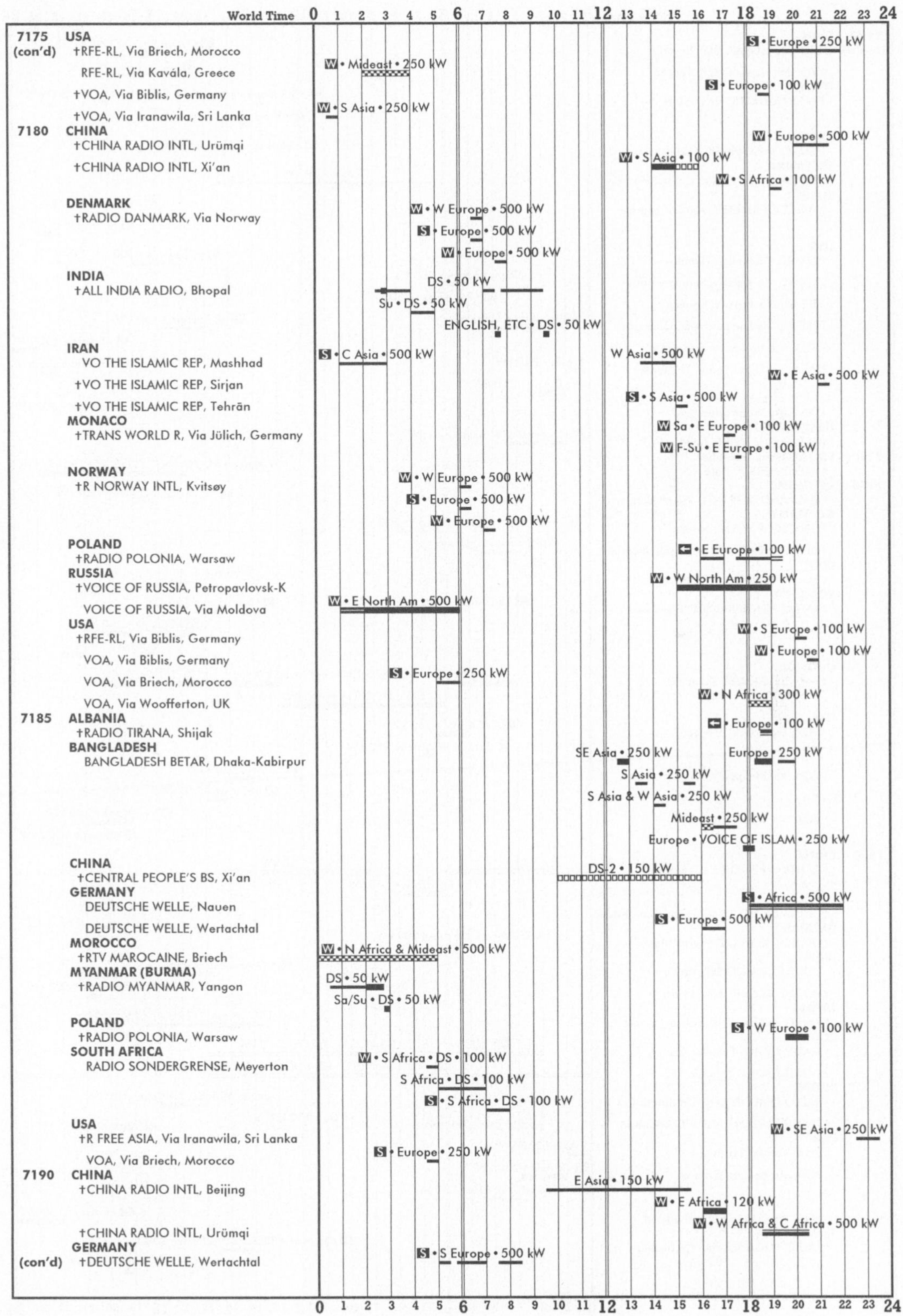
World Time 0 1 2 3 4 5 6 7 8 9 10 11 12 13 14 15 16 17 18 19 20 21 22 23 24
7175 USA
(con'd) †RFE-RL, Via Briech, Morocco
S • Europe • 250 kW
RFE-RL, Via Kavála, Greece
W • Mideast • 250 kW
†VOA, Via Biblis, Germany
S • Europe • 100 kW
†VOA, Via Iranawila, Sri Lanka
W • S Asia • 250 kW
7180 CHINA
†CHINA RADIO INTL, Urümqi
W • Europe • 500 kW
†CHINA RADIO INTL, Xi'an
W • S Asia • 100 kW
W • S Africa • 100 kW
DENMARK
†RADIO DANMARK, Via Norway
W • W Europe • 500 kW
S • Europe • 500 kW
W • Europe • 500 kW
INDIA
†ALL INDIA RADIO, Bhopal
DS • 50 kW
Su • DS • 50 kW
ENGLISH, ETC • DS • 50 kW
IRAN
VO THE ISLAMIC REP, Mashhad
S • C Asia • 500 kW
W Asia • 500 kW
†VO THE ISLAMIC REP, Sirjan
W • E Asia • 500 kW
†VO THE ISLAMIC REP, Tehrān
S • S Asia • 500 kW
MONACO
†TRANS WORLD R, Via Jülich, Germany
W Sa • E Europe • 100 kW
W F-Su • E Europe • 100 kW
NORWAY
†R NORWAY INTL, Kvitsøy
W • W Europe • 500 kW
S • Europe • 500 kW
W • Europe • 500 kW
POLAND
†RADIO POLONIA, Warsaw
E Europe • 100 kW
RUSSIA
†VOICE OF RUSSIA, Petropavlovsk-K
W • W North Am • 250 kW
VOICE OF RUSSIA, Via Moldova
W • E North Am • 500 kW
USA
†RFE-RL, Via Biblis, Germany
W • S Europe • 100 kW
VOA, Via Biblis, Germany
W • Europe • 100 kW
VOA, Via Briech, Morocco
S • Europe • 250 kW
VOA, Via Woofferton, UK
W • N Africa • 300 kW
7185 ALBANIA
†RADIO TIRANA, Shijak
Europe • 100 kW
BANGLADESH
BANGLADESH BETAR, Dhaka-Kabirpur
SE Asia • 250 kW
Europe • 250 kW
S Asia • 250 kW
S Asia & W Asia • 250 kW
Mideast • 250 kW
Europe • VOICE OF ISLAM • 250 kW
CHINA
†CENTRAL PEOPLE'S BS, Xi'an
DS-2 • 150 kW
GERMANY
DEUTSCHE WELLE, Nauen
S • Africa • 500 kW
DEUTSCHE WELLE, Wertachtal
S • Europe • 500 kW
MOROCCO
†RTV MAROCAINE, Briech
W • N Africa & Mideast • 500 kW
MYANMAR (BURMA)
†RADIO MYANMAR, Yangon
DS • 50 kW
Sa/Su • DS • 50 kW
POLAND
†RADIO POLONIA, Warsaw
S • W Europe • 100 kW
SOUTH AFRICA
RADIO SONDERGRENSE, Meyerton
W • S Africa • DS • 100 kW
S Africa • DS • 100 kW
S • S Africa • DS • 100 kW
USA
†R FREE ASIA, Via Iranawila, Sri Lanka
W • SE Asia • 250 kW
VOA, Via Briech, Morocco
S • Europe • 250 kW
7190 CHINA
†CHINA RADIO INTL, Beijing
E Asia • 150 kW
W • E Africa • 120 kW
†CHINA RADIO INTL, Urümqi
W • W Africa & C Africa • 500 kW
GERMANY
(con'd) †DEUTSCHE WELLE, Wertachtal
S • S Europe • 500 kW
0 1 2 3 4 5 6 7 8 9 10 11 12 13 14 15 16 17 18 19 20 21 22 23 24

SEASONAL S OR W 1-HR TIMESHIFT MIDYEAR ⬅ OR ➡ JAMMING / OR /\ EARLIEST HEARD ◁ LATEST HEARD ▷ NEW FOR 2002 †

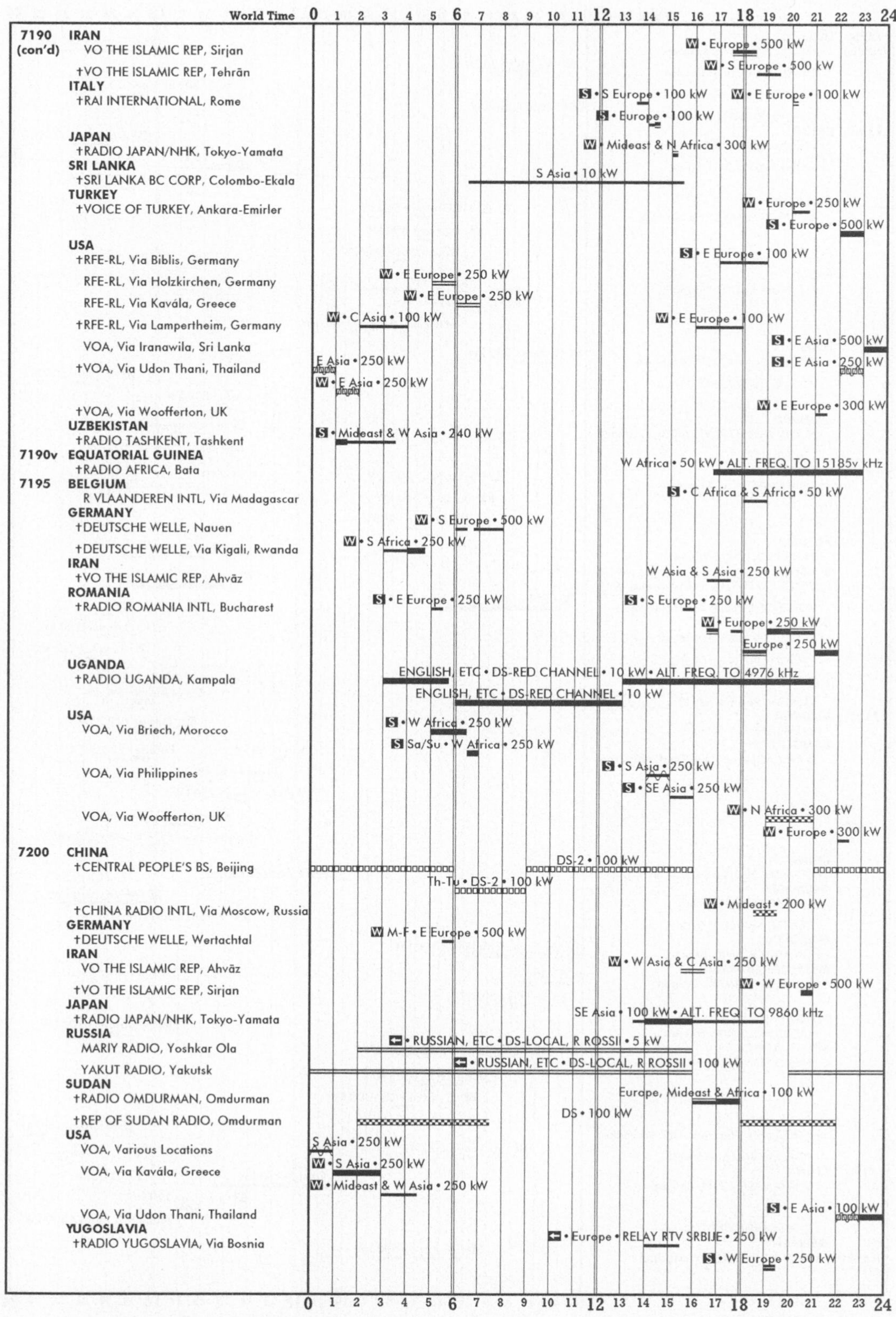
World Time 0 1 2 3 4 5 6 7 8 9 10 11 12 13 14 15 16 17 18 19 20 21 22 23 24
7190 (con'd) IRAN
VO THE ISLAMIC REP, Sirjan
W • Europe • 500 kW
†VO THE ISLAMIC REP, Tehrān
W • S Europe • 500 kW
ITALY
†RAI INTERNATIONAL, Rome
S • S Europe • 100 kW
W • E Europe • 100 kW
S • Europe • 100 kW
JAPAN
†RADIO JAPAN/NHK, Tokyo-Yamata
W • Mideast & N Africa • 300 kW
SRI LANKA
†SRI LANKA BC CORP, Colombo-Ekala
S Asia • 10 kW
TURKEY
†VOICE OF TURKEY, Ankara-Emirler
W • Europe • 250 kW
S • Europe • 500 kW
USA
†RFE-RL, Via Biblis, Germany
S • E Europe • 100 kW
RFE-RL, Via Holzkirchen, Germany
W • E Europe • 250 kW
RFE-RL, Via Kavála, Greece
W • E Europe • 250 kW
†RFE-RL, Via Lampertheim, Germany
W • C Asia • 100 kW
W • E Europe • 100 kW
VOA, Via Iranawila, Sri Lanka
S • E Asia • 500 kW
†VOA, Via Udon Thani, Thailand
E Asia • 250 kW
S • E Asia • 250 kW
W • E Asia • 250 kW
†VOA, Via Woofferton, UK
W • E Europe • 300 kW
UZBEKISTAN
†RADIO TASHKENT, Tashkent
S • Mideast & W Asia • 240 kW
7190v EQUATORIAL GUINEA
†RADIO AFRICA, Bata
W Africa • 50 kW • ALT. FREQ. TO 15185v kHz
7195 BELGIUM
R VLAANDEREN INTL, Via Madagascar
S • C Africa & S Africa • 50 kW
GERMANY
†DEUTSCHE WELLE, Nauen
W • S Europe • 500 kW
†DEUTSCHE WELLE, Via Kigali, Rwanda
W • S Africa • 250 kW
IRAN
†VO THE ISLAMIC REP, Ahvāz
W Asia & S Asia • 250 kW
ROMANIA
†RADIO ROMANIA INTL, Bucharest
S • E Europe • 250 kW
S • S Europe • 250 kW
W • Europe • 250 kW
Europe • 250 kW
UGANDA
†RADIO UGANDA, Kampala
ENGLISH, ETC • DS-RED CHANNEL • 10 kW • ALT. FREQ. TO 4976 kHz
ENGLISH, ETC • DS-RED CHANNEL • 10 kW
USA
VOA, Via Briech, Morocco
S • W Africa • 250 kW
S Sa/Su • W Africa • 250 kW
VOA, Via Philippines
S • S Asia • 250 kW
S • SE Asia • 250 kW
VOA, Via Woofferton, UK
W • N Africa • 300 kW
W • Europe • 300 kW
7200 CHINA
†CENTRAL PEOPLE'S BS, Beijing
DS-2 • 100 kW
Th-Tu • DS-2 • 100 kW
†CHINA RADIO INTL, Via Moscow, Russia
W • Mideast • 200 kW
GERMANY
†DEUTSCHE WELLE, Wertachtal
W M-F • E Europe • 500 kW
IRAN
VO THE ISLAMIC REP, Ahvāz
W • W Asia & C Asia • 250 kW
†VO THE ISLAMIC REP, Sirjan
W • W Europe • 500 kW
JAPAN
†RADIO JAPAN/NHK, Tokyo-Yamata
SE Asia • 100 kW • ALT. FREQ. TO 9860 kHz
RUSSIA
MARIY RADIO, Yoshkar Ola
RUSSIAN, ETC • DS-LOCAL, R ROSSII • 5 kW
YAKUT RADIO, Yakutsk
RUSSIAN, ETC • DS-LOCAL, R ROSSII • 100 kW
SUDAN
†RADIO OMDURMAN, Omdurman
Europe, Mideast & Africa • 100 kW
†REP OF SUDAN RADIO, Omdurman
DS • 100 kW
USA
VOA, Various Locations
S Asia • 250 kW
VOA, Via Kavála, Greece
W • S Asia • 250 kW
W • Mideast & W Asia • 250 kW
VOA, Via Udon Thani, Thailand
S • E Asia • 100 kW
YUGOSLAVIA
†RADIO YUGOSLAVIA, Via Bosnia
Europe • RELAY RTV SRBIJE • 250 kW
S • W Europe • 250 kW
0 1 2 3 4 5 6 7 8 9 10 11 12 13 14 15 16 17 18 19 20 21 22 23 24

ENGLISH ARABIC CHINESE FRENCH GERMAN RUSSIAN SPANISH OTHER

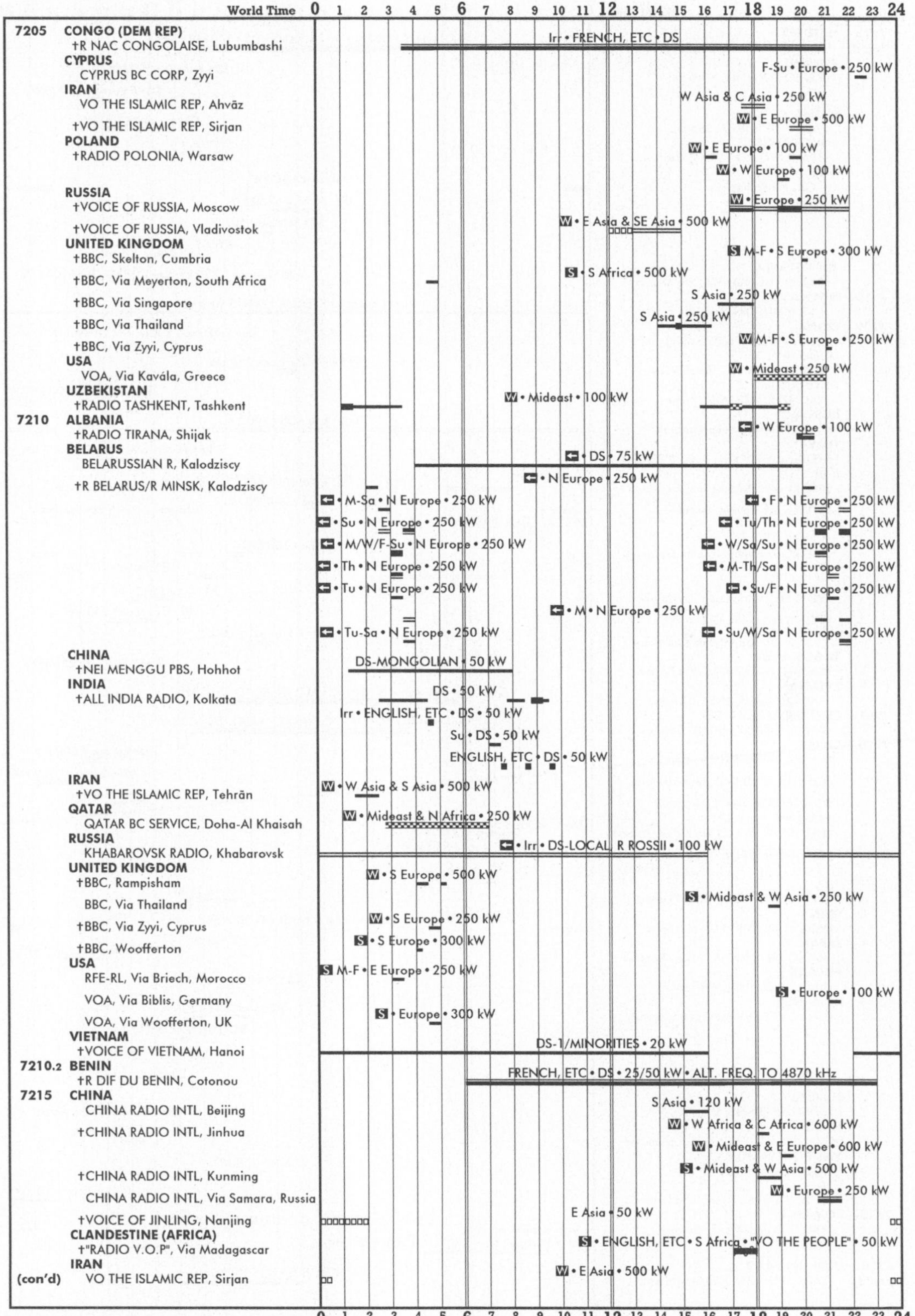
World Time 0 1 2 3 4 5 6 7 8 9 10 11 12 13 14 15 16 17 18 19 20 21 22 23 24
7205 CONGO (DEM REP)
†R NAC CONGOLAISE, Lubumbashi
Irr • FRENCH, ETC • DS
CYPRUS
CYPRUS BC CORP, Zyyi
F-Su • Europe • 250 kW
IRAN
VO THE ISLAMIC REP, Ahvāz
W Asia & C Asia • 250 kW
†VO THE ISLAMIC REP, Sirjan
W • E Europe • 500 kW
POLAND
†RADIO POLONIA, Warsaw
W • E Europe • 100 kW
W • W Europe • 100 kW
RUSSIA
†VOICE OF RUSSIA, Moscow
W • Europe • 250 kW
†VOICE OF RUSSIA, Vladivostok
W • E Asia & SE Asia • 500 kW
UNITED KINGDOM
†BBC, Skelton, Cumbria
S M-F • S Europe • 300 kW
†BBC, Via Meyerton, South Africa
S • S Africa • 500 kW
†BBC, Via Singapore
S Asia • 250 kW
†BBC, Via Thailand
S Asia • 250 kW
†BBC, Via Zyyi, Cyprus
W M-F • S Europe • 250 kW
USA
VOA, Via Kavála, Greece
W • Mideast • 250 kW
UZBEKISTAN
†RADIO TASHKENT, Tashkent
W • Mideast • 100 kW
7210 ALBANIA
†RADIO TIRANA, Shijak
• W Europe • 100 kW
BELARUS
BELARUSSIAN R, Kalodziscy
• DS • 75 kW
†R BELARUS/R MINSK, Kalodziscy
• N Europe • 250 kW
• M-Sa • N Europe • 250 kW
• F • N Europe • 250 kW
• Su • N Europe • 250 kW
• Tu/Th • N Europe • 250 kW
• M/W/F-Su • N Europe • 250 kW
• W/Sa/Su • N Europe • 250 kW
• Th • N Europe • 250 kW
• M-Th/Sa • N Europe • 250 kW
• Tu • N Europe • 250 kW
• Su/F • N Europe • 250 kW
• M • N Europe • 250 kW
• Tu-Sa • N Europe • 250 kW
• Su/W/Sa • N Europe • 250 kW
CHINA
†NEI MENGGU PBS, Hohhot
DS-MONGOLIAN • 50 kW
INDIA
†ALL INDIA RADIO, Kolkata
DS • 50 kW
Irr • ENGLISH, ETC • DS • 50 kW
Su • DS • 50 kW
ENGLISH, ETC • DS • 50 kW
IRAN
†VO THE ISLAMIC REP, Tehrān
W • W Asia & S Asia • 500 kW
QATAR
QATAR BC SERVICE, Doha-Al Khaisah
W • Mideast & N Africa • 250 kW
RUSSIA
KHABAROVSK RADIO, Khabarovsk
• Irr • DS-LOCAL, R ROSSII • 100 kW
UNITED KINGDOM
†BBC, Rampisham
W • S Europe • 500 kW
BBC, Via Thailand
S • Mideast & W Asia • 250 kW
†BBC, Via Zyyi, Cyprus
W • S Europe • 250 kW
†BBC, Woofferton
S • S Europe • 300 kW
USA
RFE-RL, Via Briech, Morocco
S M-F • E Europe • 250 kW
VOA, Via Biblis, Germany
S • Europe • 100 kW
VOA, Via Woofferton, UK
S • Europe • 300 kW
VIETNAM
†VOICE OF VIETNAM, Hanoi
DS-1/MINORITIES • 20 kW
7210.2 BENIN
†R DIF DU BENIN, Cotonou
FRENCH, ETC • DS • 25/50 kW • ALT. FREQ. TO 4870 kHz
7215 CHINA
CHINA RADIO INTL, Beijing
S Asia • 120 kW
†CHINA RADIO INTL, Jinhua
W • W Africa & C Africa • 600 kW
W • Mideast & E Europe • 600 kW
†CHINA RADIO INTL, Kunming
S • Mideast & W Asia • 500 kW
CHINA RADIO INTL, Via Samara, Russia
W • Europe • 250 kW
†VOICE OF JINLING, Nanjing
E Asia • 50 kW
CLANDESTINE (AFRICA)
†"RADIO V.O.P", Via Madagascar
S • ENGLISH, ETC • S Africa • "VO THE PEOPLE" • 50 kW
IRAN
(con'd) VO THE ISLAMIC REP, Sirjan
W • E Asia • 500 kW
0 1 2 3 4 5 6 7 8 9 10 11 12 13 14 15 16 17 18 19 20 21 22 23 24

SEASONAL S OR W 1-HR TIMESHIFT MIDYEAR ← OR → JAMMING / OR ∧ EARLIEST HEARD ◁ LATEST HEARD ▷ NEW FOR 2002 †

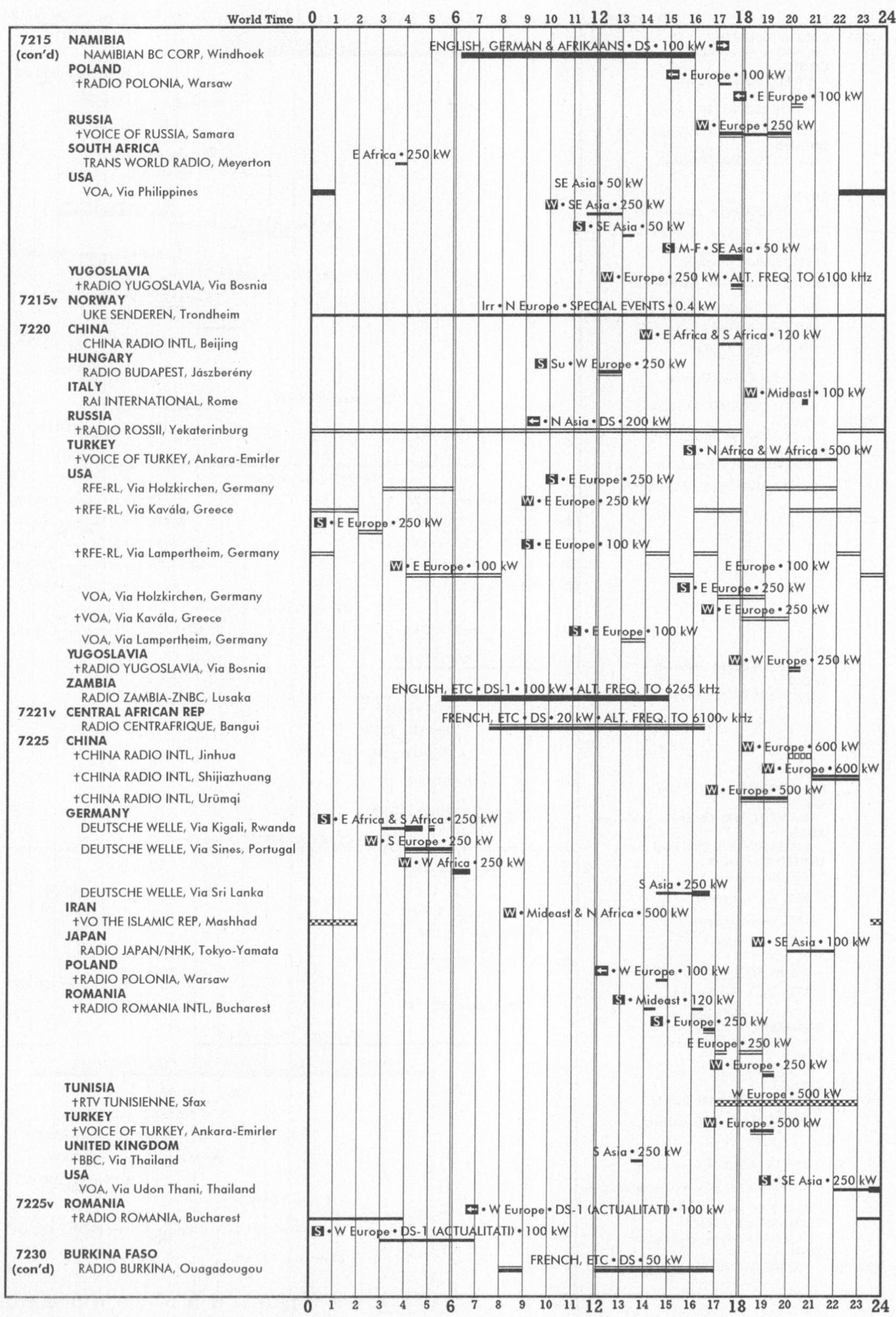
World Time 0 1 2 3 4 5 6 7 8 9 10 11 12 13 14 15 16 17 18 19 20 21 22 23 24
7215 (con'd) NAMIBIA
NAMIBIAN BC CORP, Windhoek
ENGLISH, GERMAN & AFRIKAANS • DS • 100 kW
POLAND
†RADIO POLONIA, Warsaw
Europe • 100 kW
E Europe • 100 kW
RUSSIA
†VOICE OF RUSSIA, Samara
W • Europe • 250 kW
SOUTH AFRICA
TRANS WORLD RADIO, Meyerton
E Africa • 250 kW
USA
VOA, Via Philippines
SE Asia • 50 kW
W • SE Asia • 250 kW
S • SE Asia • 50 kW
S M-F • SE Asia • 50 kW
YUGOSLAVIA
†RADIO YUGOSLAVIA, Via Bosnia
W • Europe • 250 kW • ALT. FREQ. TO 6100 kHz
7215v NORWAY
UKE SENDEREN, Trondheim
Irr • N Europe • SPECIAL EVENTS • 0.4 kW
7220 CHINA
CHINA RADIO INTL, Beijing
W • E Africa & S Africa • 120 kW
HUNGARY
RADIO BUDAPEST, Jászberény
S Su • W Europe • 250 kW
ITALY
RAI INTERNATIONAL, Rome
W • Mideast • 100 kW
RUSSIA
†RADIO ROSSII, Yekaterinburg
N Asia • DS • 200 kW
TURKEY
†VOICE OF TURKEY, Ankara-Emirler
S • N Africa & W Africa • 500 kW
USA
RFE-RL, Via Holzkirchen, Germany
S • E Europe • 250 kW
†RFE-RL, Via Kavála, Greece
W • E Europe • 250 kW
S • E Europe • 250 kW
†RFE-RL, Via Lampertheim, Germany
S • E Europe • 100 kW
W • E Europe • 100 kW
E Europe • 100 kW
VOA, Via Holzkirchen, Germany
S • E Europe • 250 kW
†VOA, Via Kavála, Greece
W • E Europe • 250 kW
VOA, Via Lampertheim, Germany
S • E Europe • 100 kW
YUGOSLAVIA
†RADIO YUGOSLAVIA, Via Bosnia
W • W Europe • 250 kW
ZAMBIA
RADIO ZAMBIA-ZNBC, Lusaka
ENGLISH, ETC • DS-1 • 100 kW • ALT. FREQ. TO 6265 kHz
7221v CENTRAL AFRICAN REP
RADIO CENTRAFRIQUE, Bangui
FRENCH, ETC • DS • 20 kW • ALT. FREQ. TO 6100v kHz
7225 CHINA
†CHINA RADIO INTL, Jinhua
W • Europe • 600 kW
†CHINA RADIO INTL, Shijiazhuang
W • Europe • 600 kW
†CHINA RADIO INTL, Urümqi
W • Europe • 500 kW
GERMANY
DEUTSCHE WELLE, Via Kigali, Rwanda
S • E Africa & S Africa • 250 kW
DEUTSCHE WELLE, Via Sines, Portugal
W • S Europe • 250 kW
W • W Africa • 250 kW
DEUTSCHE WELLE, Via Sri Lanka
S Asia • 250 kW
IRAN
†VO THE ISLAMIC REP, Mashhad
W • Mideast & N Africa • 500 kW
JAPAN
RADIO JAPAN/NHK, Tokyo-Yamata
W • SE Asia • 100 kW
POLAND
†RADIO POLONIA, Warsaw
W Europe • 100 kW
ROMANIA
†RADIO ROMANIA INTL, Bucharest
S • Mideast • 120 kW
S • Europe • 250 kW
E Europe • 250 kW
W • Europe • 250 kW
TUNISIA
†RTV TUNISIENNE, Sfax
W Europe • 500 kW
TURKEY
†VOICE OF TURKEY, Ankara-Emirler
W • Europe • 500 kW
UNITED KINGDOM
†BBC, Via Thailand
S Asia • 250 kW
USA
VOA, Via Udon Thani, Thailand
S • SE Asia • 250 kW
7225v ROMANIA
†RADIO ROMANIA, Bucharest
W Europe • DS-1 (ACTUALITATI) • 100 kW
S • W Europe • DS-1 (ACTUALITATI) • 100 kW
7230 (con'd) BURKINA FASO
RADIO BURKINA, Ouagadougou
FRENCH, ETC • DS • 50 kW
0 1 2 3 4 5 6 7 8 9 10 11 12 13 14 15 16 17 18 19 20 21 22 23 24
ENGLISH ARABIC CHINESE FRENCH GERMAN RUSSIAN SPANISH OTHER

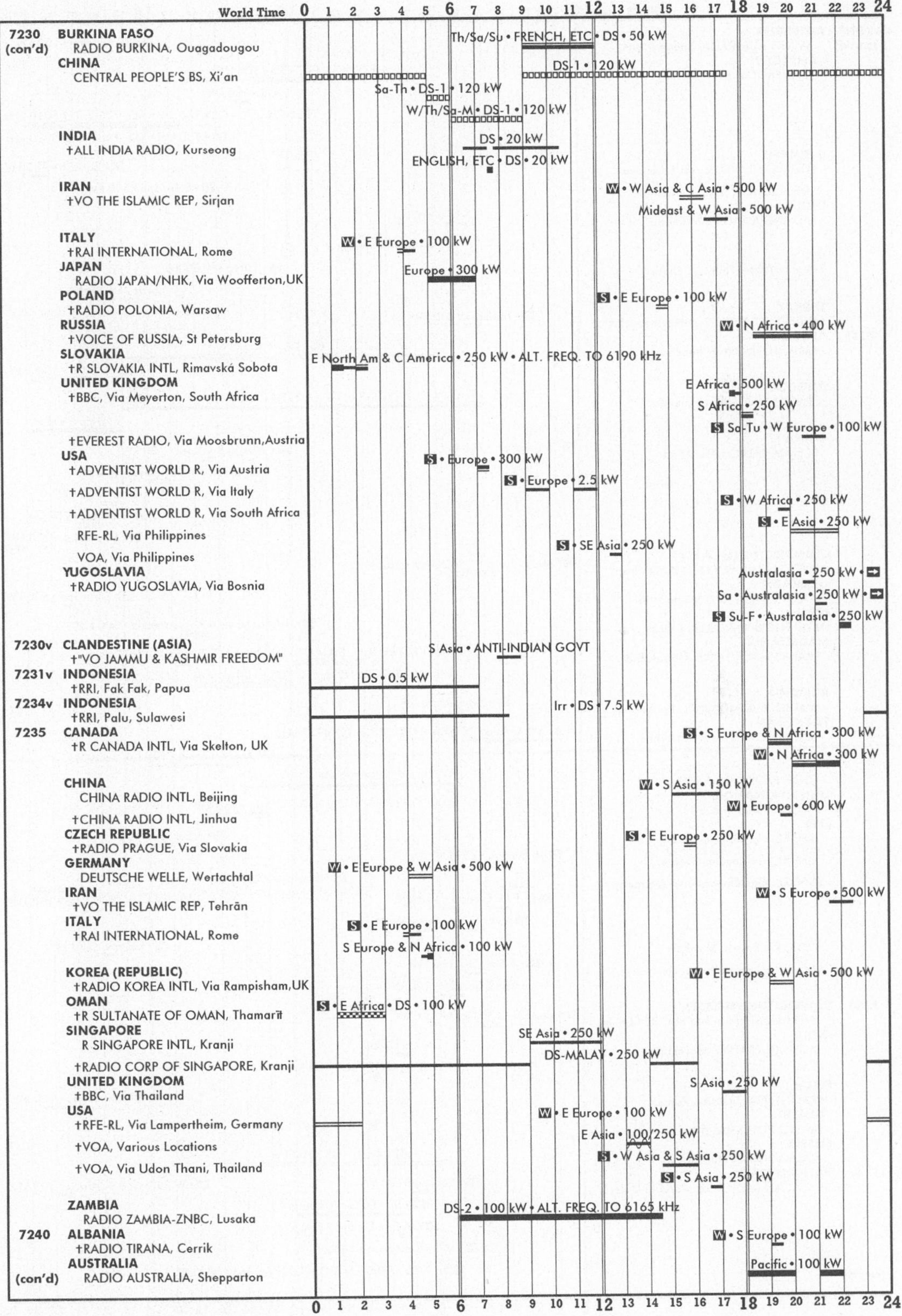
World Time 0 1 2 3 4 5 6 7 8 9 10 11 12 13 14 15 16 17 18 19 20 21 22 23 24
7230 (con'd) BURKINA FASO
RADIO BURKINA, Ouagadougou
Th/Sa/Su • FRENCH, ETC • DS • 50 kW
CHINA
CENTRAL PEOPLE'S BS, Xi'an
DS-1 • 120 kW
Sa-Th • DS-1 • 120 kW
W/Th/Sa-M • DS-1 • 120 kW
INDIA
†ALL INDIA RADIO, Kurseong
DS • 20 kW
ENGLISH, ETC • DS • 20 kW
IRAN
†VO THE ISLAMIC REP, Sirjan
W • W Asia & C Asia • 500 kW
Mideast & W Asia • 500 kW
ITALY
†RAI INTERNATIONAL, Rome
W • E Europe • 100 kW
JAPAN
RADIO JAPAN/NHK, Via Woofferton,UK
Europe • 300 kW
POLAND
†RADIO POLONIA, Warsaw
S • E Europe • 100 kW
RUSSIA
†VOICE OF RUSSIA, St Petersburg
W • N Africa • 400 kW
SLOVAKIA
†R SLOVAKIA INTL, Rimavská Sobota
E North Am & C America • 250 kW • ALT. FREQ. TO 6190 kHz
UNITED KINGDOM
†BBC, Via Meyerton, South Africa
E Africa • 500 kW
S Africa • 250 kW
†EVEREST RADIO, Via Moosbrunn,Austria
S Sa-Tu • W Europe • 100 kW
USA
†ADVENTIST WORLD R, Via Austria
S • Europe • 300 kW
†ADVENTIST WORLD R, Via Italy
S • Europe • 2.5 kW
†ADVENTIST WORLD R, Via South Africa
S • W Africa • 250 kW
RFE-RL, Via Philippines
S • E Asia • 250 kW
VOA, Via Philippines
S • SE Asia • 250 kW
YUGOSLAVIA
†RADIO YUGOSLAVIA, Via Bosnia
Australasia • 250 kW •
Sa • Australasia • 250 kW •
S Su-F • Australasia • 250 kW
7230v CLANDESTINE (ASIA)
†"VO JAMMU & KASHMIR FREEDOM"
S Asia • ANTI-INDIAN GOVT
7231v INDONESIA
†RRI, Fak Fak, Papua
DS • 0.5 kW
7234v INDONESIA
†RRI, Palu, Sulawesi
Irr • DS • 7.5 kW
7235 CANADA
†R CANADA INTL, Via Skelton, UK
S • S Europe & N Africa • 300 kW
W • N Africa • 300 kW
CHINA
CHINA RADIO INTL, Beijing
W • S Asia • 150 kW
†CHINA RADIO INTL, Jinhua
W • Europe • 600 kW
CZECH REPUBLIC
†RADIO PRAGUE, Via Slovakia
S • E Europe • 250 kW
GERMANY
DEUTSCHE WELLE, Wertachtal
W • E Europe & W Asia • 500 kW
IRAN
†VO THE ISLAMIC REP, Tehrān
W • S Europe • 500 kW
ITALY
†RAI INTERNATIONAL, Rome
S • E Europe • 100 kW
S Europe & N Africa • 100 kW
KOREA (REPUBLIC)
†RADIO KOREA INTL, Via Rampisham,UK
W • E Europe & W Asia • 500 kW
OMAN
†R SULTANATE OF OMAN, Thamarīt
S • E Africa • DS • 100 kW
SINGAPORE
R SINGAPORE INTL, Kranji
SE Asia • 250 kW
†RADIO CORP OF SINGAPORE, Kranji
DS-MALAY • 250 kW
UNITED KINGDOM
†BBC, Via Thailand
S Asia • 250 kW
USA
†RFE-RL, Via Lampertheim, Germany
W • E Europe • 100 kW
†VOA, Various Locations
E Asia • 100/250 kW
†VOA, Via Udon Thani, Thailand
S • W Asia & S Asia • 250 kW
S • S Asia • 250 kW
ZAMBIA
RADIO ZAMBIA-ZNBC, Lusaka
DS-2 • 100 kW • ALT. FREQ. TO 6165 kHz
7240 ALBANIA
†RADIO TIRANA, Cerrik
W • S Europe • 100 kW
AUSTRALIA (con'd)
RADIO AUSTRALIA, Shepparton
Pacific • 100 kW
0 1 2 3 4 5 6 7 8 9 10 11 12 13 14 15 16 17 18 19 20 21 22 23 24

SEASONAL S OR W 1-HR TIMESHIFT MIDYEAR ⬅ OR ➡ JAMMING / OR ∧ EARLIEST HEARD ◁ LATEST HEARD ▷ NEW FOR 2002 †

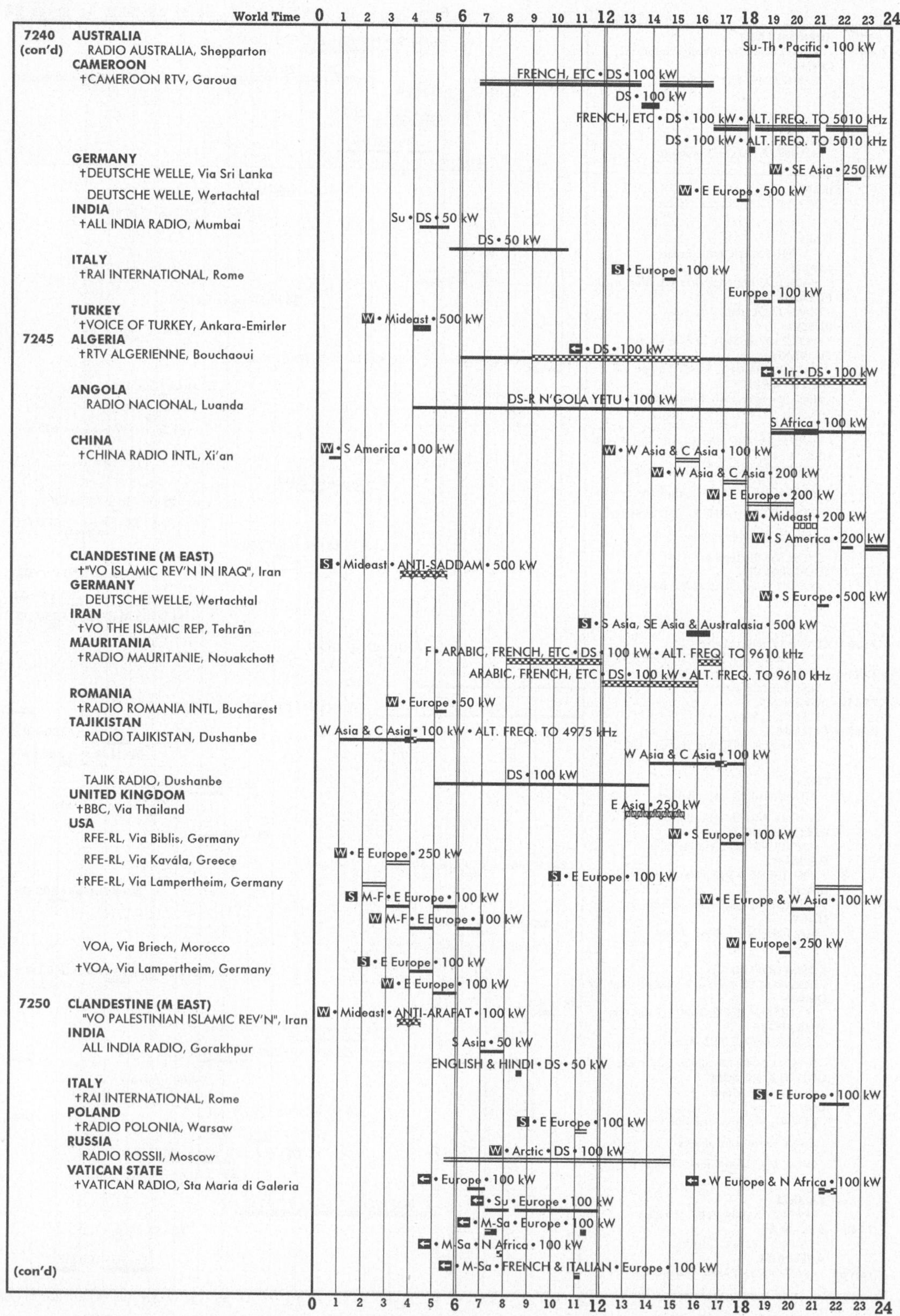
World Time 0 1 2 3 4 5 6 7 8 9 10 11 12 13 14 15 16 17 18 19 20 21 22 23 24
7240 (con'd) AUSTRALIA
RADIO AUSTRALIA, Shepparton
Su-Th • Pacific • 100 kW
CAMEROON
†CAMEROON RTV, Garoua
FRENCH, ETC • DS • 100 kW
DS • 100 kW
FRENCH, ETC • DS • 100 kW • ALT. FREQ. TO 5010 kHz
DS • 100 kW • ALT. FREQ. TO 5010 kHz
GERMANY
†DEUTSCHE WELLE, Via Sri Lanka
W • SE Asia • 250 kW
DEUTSCHE WELLE, Wertachtal
W • E Europe • 500 kW
INDIA
†ALL INDIA RADIO, Mumbai
Su • DS • 50 kW
DS • 50 kW
ITALY
†RAI INTERNATIONAL, Rome
S • Europe • 100 kW
Europe • 100 kW
TURKEY
†VOICE OF TURKEY, Ankara-Emirler
W • Mideast • 500 kW
7245 ALGERIA
†RTV ALGERIENNE, Bouchaoui
DS • 100 kW
Irr • DS • 100 kW
ANGOLA
RADIO NACIONAL, Luanda
DS-R N'GOLA YETU • 100 kW
S Africa • 100 kW
CHINA
†CHINA RADIO INTL, Xi'an
W • S America • 100 kW
W • W Asia & C Asia • 100 kW
W • W Asia & C Asia • 200 kW
W • E Europe • 200 kW
W • Mideast • 200 kW
W • S America • 200 kW
CLANDESTINE (M EAST)
†"VO ISLAMIC REV'N IN IRAQ", Iran
S • Mideast • ANTI-SADDAM • 500 kW
GERMANY
DEUTSCHE WELLE, Wertachtal
W • S Europe • 500 kW
IRAN
†VO THE ISLAMIC REP, Tehrān
S • S Asia, SE Asia & Australasia • 500 kW
MAURITANIA
†RADIO MAURITANIE, Nouakchott
F • ARABIC, FRENCH, ETC • DS • 100 kW • ALT. FREQ. TO 9610 kHz
ARABIC, FRENCH, ETC • DS • 100 kW • ALT. FREQ. TO 9610 kHz
ROMANIA
†RADIO ROMANIA INTL, Bucharest
W • Europe • 50 kW
TAJIKISTAN
RADIO TAJIKISTAN, Dushanbe
W Asia & C Asia • 100 kW • ALT. FREQ. TO 4975 kHz
W Asia & C Asia • 100 kW
TAJIK RADIO, Dushanbe
DS • 100 kW
UNITED KINGDOM
†BBC, Via Thailand
E Asia • 250 kW
USA
RFE-RL, Via Biblis, Germany
W • S Europe • 100 kW
RFE-RL, Via Kavála, Greece
W • E Europe • 250 kW
†RFE-RL, Via Lampertheim, Germany
S • E Europe • 100 kW
S M-F • E Europe • 100 kW
W • E Europe & W Asia • 100 kW
W M-F • E Europe • 100 kW
VOA, Via Briech, Morocco
W • Europe • 250 kW
†VOA, Via Lampertheim, Germany
S • E Europe • 100 kW
W • E Europe • 100 kW
7250 CLANDESTINE (M EAST)
"VO PALESTINIAN ISLAMIC REV'N", Iran
W • Mideast • ANTI-ARAFAT • 100 kW
INDIA
ALL INDIA RADIO, Gorakhpur
S Asia • 50 kW
ENGLISH & HINDI • DS • 50 kW
ITALY
†RAI INTERNATIONAL, Rome
S • E Europe • 100 kW
POLAND
†RADIO POLONIA, Warsaw
S • E Europe • 100 kW
RUSSIA
RADIO ROSSII, Moscow
W • Arctic • DS • 100 kW
VATICAN STATE
†VATICAN RADIO, Sta Maria di Galeria
Europe • 100 kW
W Europe & N Africa • 100 kW
Su • Europe • 100 kW
M-Sa • Europe • 100 kW
M-Sa • N Africa • 100 kW
M-Sa • FRENCH & ITALIAN • Europe • 100 kW
(con'd)
0 1 2 3 4 5 6 7 8 9 10 11 12 13 14 15 16 17 18 19 20 21 22 23 24
ENGLISH ARABIC CHINESE FRENCH GERMAN RUSSIAN SPANISH OTHER

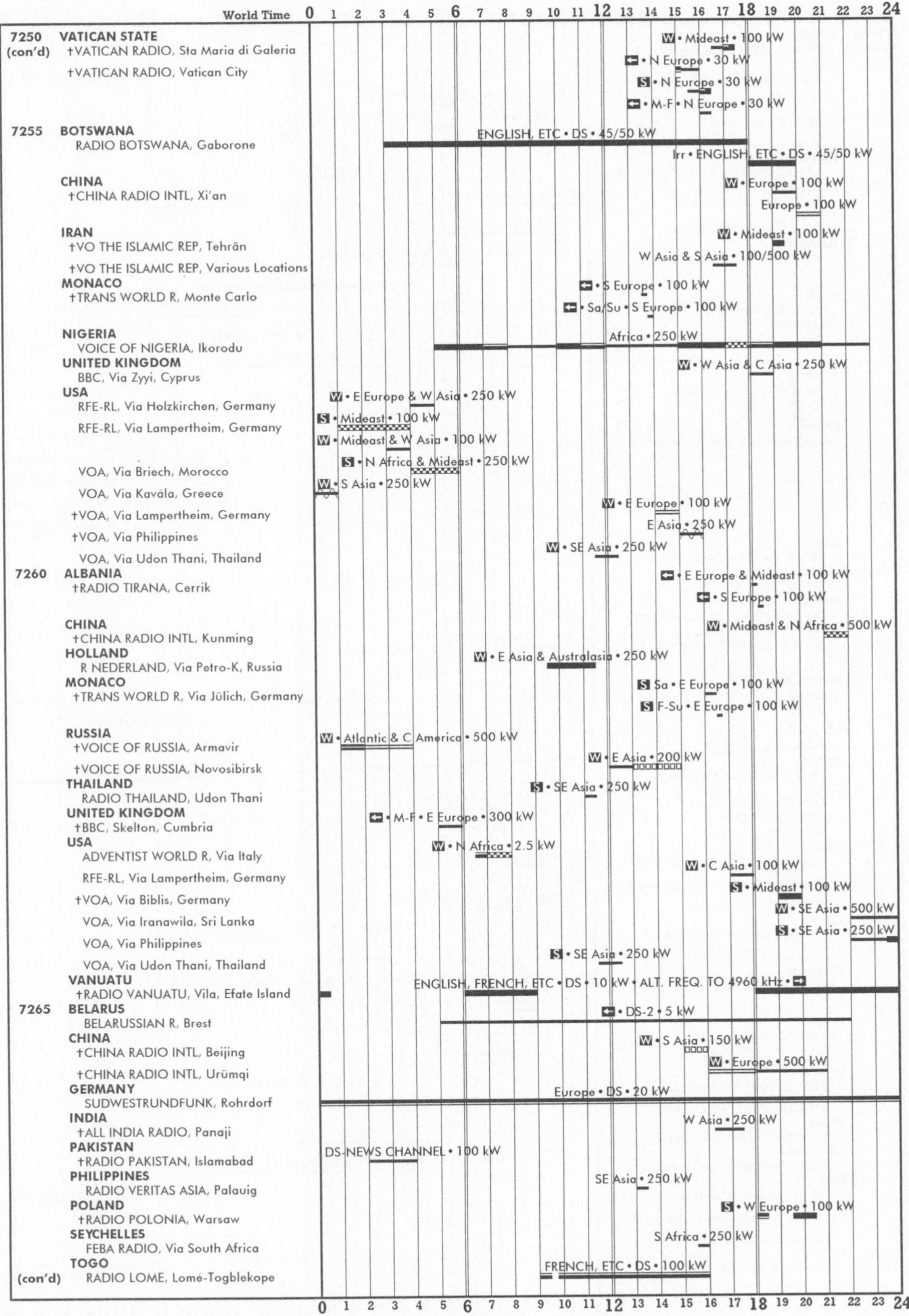
World Time 0 1 2 3 4 5 6 7 8 9 10 11 12 13 14 15 16 17 18 19 20 21 22 23 24
7250 VATICAN STATE (con'd)
†VATICAN RADIO, Sta Maria di Galeria
W • Mideast • 100 kW
†VATICAN RADIO, Vatican City
N Europe • 30 kW
S • N Europe • 30 kW
M-F • N Europe • 30 kW
7255 BOTSWANA
RADIO BOTSWANA, Gaborone
ENGLISH, ETC • DS • 45/50 kW
Irr • ENGLISH, ETC • DS • 45/50 kW
CHINA
†CHINA RADIO INTL, Xi'an
W • Europe • 100 kW
Europe • 100 kW
IRAN
†VO THE ISLAMIC REP, Tehrān
W • Mideast • 100 kW
†VO THE ISLAMIC REP, Various Locations
W Asia & S Asia • 100/500 kW
MONACO
†TRANS WORLD R, Monte Carlo
S Europe • 100 kW
Sa/Su • S Europe • 100 kW
NIGERIA
VOICE OF NIGERIA, Ikorodu
Africa • 250 kW
UNITED KINGDOM
BBC, Via Zyyi, Cyprus
W • W Asia & C Asia • 250 kW
USA
RFE-RL, Via Holzkirchen, Germany
W • E Europe & W Asia • 250 kW
RFE-RL, Via Lampertheim, Germany
S • Mideast • 100 kW
W • Mideast & W Asia • 100 kW
S • N Africa & Mideast • 250 kW
VOA, Via Briech, Morocco
W • S Asia • 250 kW
VOA, Via Kavála, Greece
W • E Europe • 100 kW
†VOA, Via Lampertheim, Germany
E Asia • 250 kW
†VOA, Via Philippines
W • SE Asia • 250 kW
VOA, Via Udon Thani, Thailand
7260 ALBANIA
†RADIO TIRANA, Cerrik
E Europe & Mideast • 100 kW
S Europe • 100 kW
CHINA
†CHINA RADIO INTL, Kunming
W • Mideast & N Africa • 500 kW
HOLLAND
R NEDERLAND, Via Petro-K, Russia
W • E Asia & Australasia • 250 kW
MONACO
†TRANS WORLD R, Via Jülich, Germany
S Sa • E Europe • 100 kW
S F-Su • E Europe • 100 kW
RUSSIA
†VOICE OF RUSSIA, Armavir
W • Atlantic & C America • 500 kW
†VOICE OF RUSSIA, Novosibirsk
W • E Asia • 200 kW
THAILAND
RADIO THAILAND, Udon Thani
S • SE Asia • 250 kW
UNITED KINGDOM
†BBC, Skelton, Cumbria
M-F • E Europe • 300 kW
USA
ADVENTIST WORLD R, Via Italy
W • N Africa • 2.5 kW
RFE-RL, Via Lampertheim, Germany
W • C Asia • 100 kW
†VOA, Via Biblis, Germany
S • Mideast • 100 kW
VOA, Via Iranawila, Sri Lanka
W • SE Asia • 500 kW
VOA, Via Philippines
S • SE Asia • 250 kW
VOA, Via Udon Thani, Thailand
S • SE Asia • 250 kW
VANUATU
†RADIO VANUATU, Vila, Efate Island
ENGLISH, FRENCH, ETC • DS • 10 kW • ALT. FREQ. TO 4960 kHz •
7265 BELARUS
BELARUSSIAN R, Brest
DS-2 • 5 kW
CHINA
†CHINA RADIO INTL, Beijing
W • S Asia • 150 kW
†CHINA RADIO INTL, Urümqi
W • Europe • 500 kW
GERMANY
SUDWESTRUNDFUNK, Rohrdorf
Europe • DS • 20 kW
INDIA
†ALL INDIA RADIO, Panaji
W Asia • 250 kW
PAKISTAN
†RADIO PAKISTAN, Islamabad
DS-NEWS CHANNEL • 100 kW
PHILIPPINES
RADIO VERITAS ASIA, Palauig
SE Asia • 250 kW
POLAND
†RADIO POLONIA, Warsaw
S • W Europe • 100 kW
SEYCHELLES
FEBA RADIO, Via South Africa
S Africa • 250 kW
TOGO (con'd)
RADIO LOME, Lomé-Togblekope
FRENCH, ETC • DS • 100 kW
0 1 2 3 4 5 6 7 8 9 10 11 12 13 14 15 16 17 18 19 20 21 22 23 24

SEASONAL S OR W 1-HR TIMESHIFT MIDYEAR OR JAMMING / OR /\ EARLIEST HEARD ◁ LATEST HEARD ▷ NEW FOR 2002 †

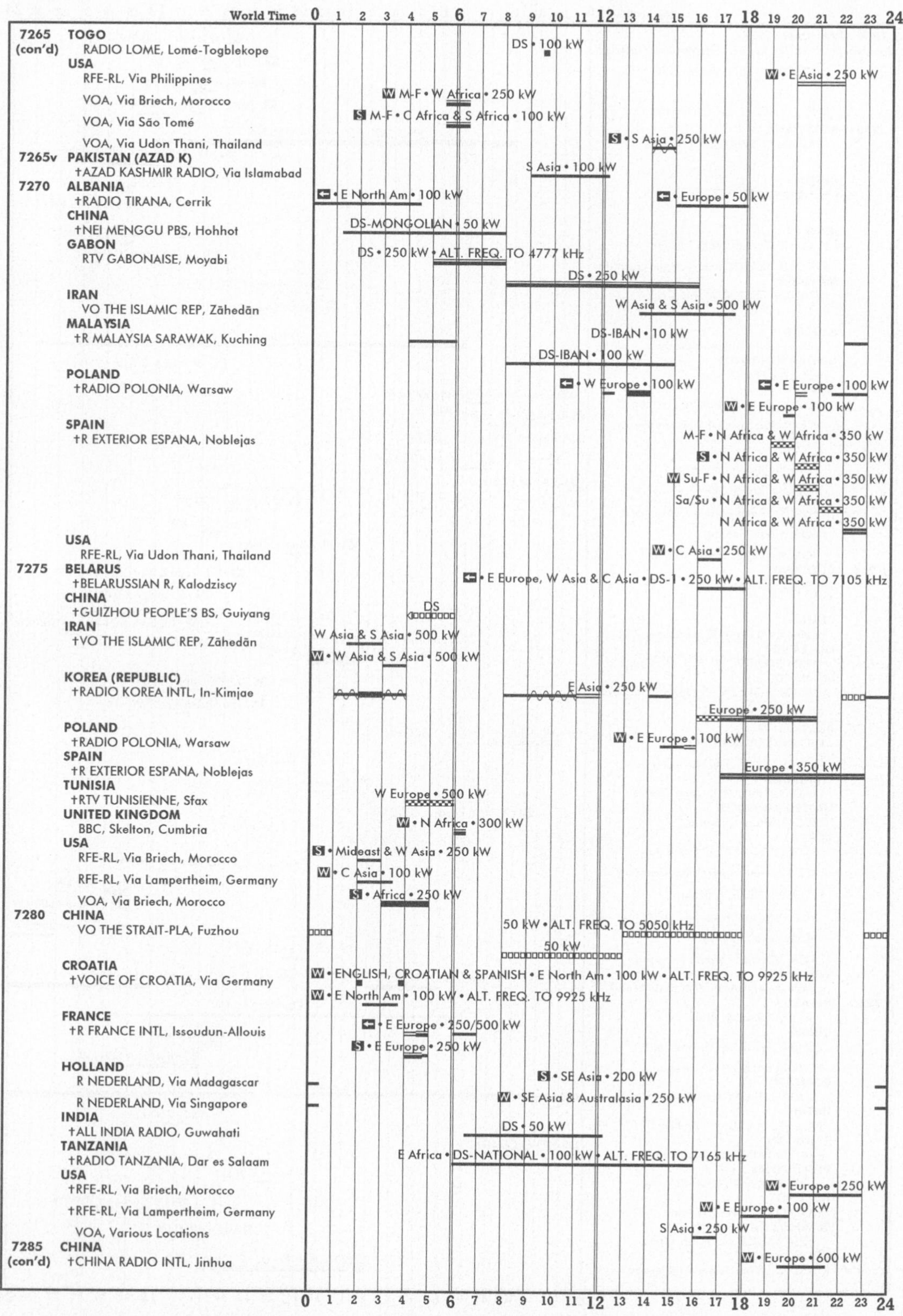
World Time 0 1 2 3 4 5 6 7 8 9 10 11 12 13 14 15 16 17 18 19 20 21 22 23 24
7265 (con'd) TOGO
RADIO LOME, Lomé-Togblekope
DS • 100 kW
USA
RFE-RL, Via Philippines
W • E Asia • 250 kW
VOA, Via Briech, Morocco
W M-F • W Africa • 250 kW
VOA, Via São Tomé
S M-F • C Africa & S Africa • 100 kW
VOA, Via Udon Thani, Thailand
S • S Asia • 250 kW
7265v PAKISTAN (AZAD K)
†AZAD KASHMIR RADIO, Via Islamabad
S Asia • 100 kW
7270 ALBANIA
†RADIO TIRANA, Cerrik
E North Am • 100 kW
Europe • 50 kW
CHINA
†NEI MENGGU PBS, Hohhot
DS-MONGOLIAN • 50 kW
GABON
RTV GABONAISE, Moyabi
DS • 250 kW • ALT. FREQ. TO 4777 kHz
DS • 250 kW
IRAN
VO THE ISLAMIC REP, Zāhedān
W Asia & S Asia • 500 kW
MALAYSIA
†R MALAYSIA SARAWAK, Kuching
DS-IBAN • 10 kW
DS-IBAN • 100 kW
POLAND
†RADIO POLONIA, Warsaw
• W Europe • 100 kW
• E Europe • 100 kW
W • E Europe • 100 kW
SPAIN
†R EXTERIOR ESPANA, Noblejas
M-F • N Africa & W Africa • 350 kW
S • N Africa & W Africa • 350 kW
W Su-F • N Africa & W Africa • 350 kW
Sa/Su • N Africa & W Africa • 350 kW
N Africa & W Africa • 350 kW
USA
RFE-RL, Via Udon Thani, Thailand
W • C Asia • 250 kW
7275 BELARUS
†BELARUSSIAN R, Kalodziscy
• E Europe, W Asia & C Asia • DS-1 • 250 kW • ALT. FREQ. TO 7105 kHz
CHINA
†GUIZHOU PEOPLE'S BS, Guiyang
DS
IRAN
†VO THE ISLAMIC REP, Zāhedān
W Asia & S Asia • 500 kW
W • W Asia & S Asia • 500 kW
KOREA (REPUBLIC)
†RADIO KOREA INTL, In-Kimjae
E Asia • 250 kW
Europe • 250 kW
POLAND
†RADIO POLONIA, Warsaw
W • E Europe • 100 kW
SPAIN
†R EXTERIOR ESPANA, Noblejas
Europe • 350 kW
TUNISIA
†RTV TUNISIENNE, Sfax
W Europe • 500 kW
UNITED KINGDOM
BBC, Skelton, Cumbria
W • N Africa • 300 kW
USA
RFE-RL, Via Briech, Morocco
S • Mideast & W Asia • 250 kW
RFE-RL, Via Lampertheim, Germany
W • C Asia • 100 kW
VOA, Via Briech, Morocco
S • Africa • 250 kW
7280 CHINA
VO THE STRAIT-PLA, Fuzhou
50 kW • ALT. FREQ. TO 5050 kHz
50 kW
CROATIA
†VOICE OF CROATIA, Via Germany
W • ENGLISH, CROATIAN & SPANISH • E North Am • 100 kW • ALT. FREQ. TO 9925 kHz
W • E North Am • 100 kW • ALT. FREQ. TO 9925 kHz
FRANCE
†R FRANCE INTL, Issoudun-Allouis
• E Europe • 250/500 kW
S • E Europe • 250 kW
HOLLAND
R NEDERLAND, Via Madagascar
S • SE Asia • 200 kW
R NEDERLAND, Via Singapore
W • SE Asia & Australasia • 250 kW
INDIA
†ALL INDIA RADIO, Guwahati
DS • 50 kW
TANZANIA
†RADIO TANZANIA, Dar es Salaam
E Africa • DS-NATIONAL • 100 kW • ALT. FREQ. TO 7165 kHz
USA
†RFE-RL, Via Briech, Morocco
W • Europe • 250 kW
†RFE-RL, Via Lampertheim, Germany
W • E Europe • 100 kW
VOA, Various Locations
S Asia • 250 kW
7285 (con'd) CHINA
†CHINA RADIO INTL, Jinhua
W • Europe • 600 kW
0 1 2 3 4 5 6 7 8 9 10 11 12 13 14 15 16 17 18 19 20 21 22 23 24
ENGLISH ARABIC CHINESE FRENCH GERMAN RUSSIAN SPANISH OTHER

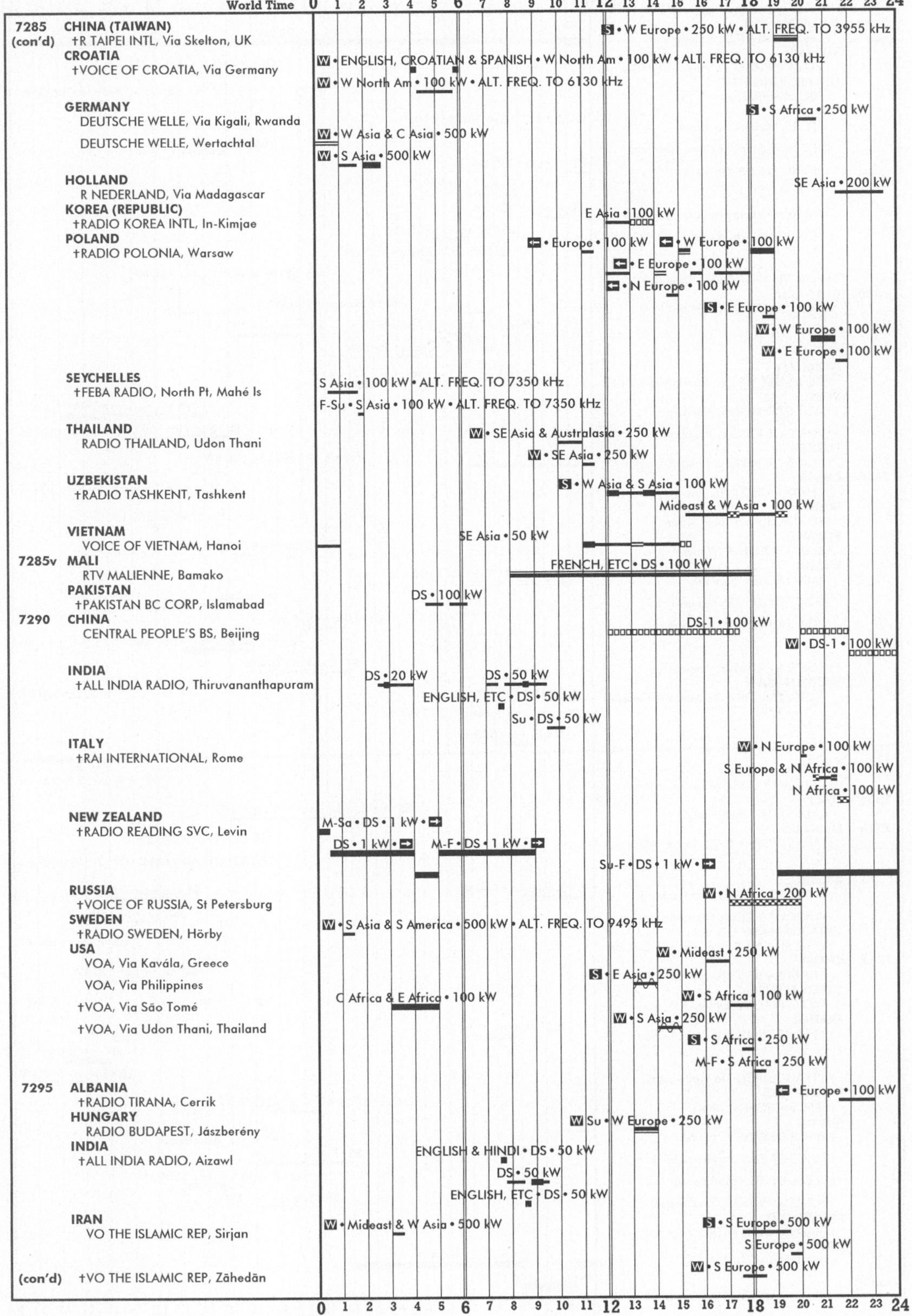
World Time 0 1 2 3 4 5 6 7 8 9 10 11 12 13 14 15 16 17 18 19 20 21 22 23 24
7285 (con'd) CHINA (TAIWAN)
†R TAIPEI INTL, Via Skelton, UK
S • W Europe • 250 kW • ALT. FREQ. TO 3955 kHz
CROATIA
†VOICE OF CROATIA, Via Germany
W • ENGLISH, CROATIAN & SPANISH • W North Am • 100 kW • ALT. FREQ. TO 6130 kHz
W • W North Am • 100 kW • ALT. FREQ. TO 6130 kHz
GERMANY
DEUTSCHE WELLE, Via Kigali, Rwanda
S • S Africa • 250 kW
DEUTSCHE WELLE, Wertachtal
W • W Asia & C Asia • 500 kW
W • S Asia • 500 kW
HOLLAND
R NEDERLAND, Via Madagascar
SE Asia • 200 kW
KOREA (REPUBLIC)
†RADIO KOREA INTL, In-Kimjae
E Asia • 100 kW
POLAND
†RADIO POLONIA, Warsaw
Europe • 100 kW
W Europe • 100 kW
E Europe • 100 kW
N Europe • 100 kW
S • E Europe • 100 kW
W • W Europe • 100 kW
W • E Europe • 100 kW
SEYCHELLES
†FEBA RADIO, North Pt, Mahé Is
S Asia • 100 kW • ALT. FREQ. TO 7350 kHz
F-Su • S Asia • 100 kW • ALT. FREQ. TO 7350 kHz
THAILAND
RADIO THAILAND, Udon Thani
W • SE Asia & Australasia • 250 kW
W • SE Asia • 250 kW
UZBEKISTAN
†RADIO TASHKENT, Tashkent
S • W Asia & S Asia • 100 kW
Mideast & W Asia • 100 kW
VIETNAM
VOICE OF VIETNAM, Hanoi
SE Asia • 50 kW
7285v MALI
RTV MALIENNE, Bamako
FRENCH, ETC • DS • 100 kW
PAKISTAN
†PAKISTAN BC CORP, Islamabad
DS • 100 kW
7290 CHINA
CENTRAL PEOPLE'S BS, Beijing
DS-1 • 100 kW
W • DS-1 • 100 kW
INDIA
†ALL INDIA RADIO, Thiruvananthapuram
DS • 20 kW
DS • 50 kW
ENGLISH, ETC • DS • 50 kW
Su • DS • 50 kW
ITALY
†RAI INTERNATIONAL, Rome
W • N Europe • 100 kW
S Europe & N Africa • 100 kW
N Africa • 100 kW
NEW ZEALAND
†RADIO READING SVC, Levin
M-Sa • DS • 1 kW
DS • 1 kW
M-F • DS • 1 kW
Su-F • DS • 1 kW
RUSSIA
†VOICE OF RUSSIA, St Petersburg
W • N Africa • 200 kW
SWEDEN
†RADIO SWEDEN, Hörby
W • S Asia & S America • 500 kW • ALT. FREQ. TO 9495 kHz
USA
VOA, Via Kavála, Greece
W • Mideast • 250 kW
VOA, Via Philippines
S • E Asia • 250 kW
†VOA, Via São Tomé
C Africa & E Africa • 100 kW
W • S Africa • 100 kW
†VOA, Via Udon Thani, Thailand
W • S Asia • 250 kW
S • S Africa • 250 kW
M-F • S Africa • 250 kW
7295 ALBANIA
†RADIO TIRANA, Cerrik
Europe • 100 kW
HUNGARY
RADIO BUDAPEST, Jászberény
W Su • W Europe • 250 kW
INDIA
†ALL INDIA RADIO, Aizawl
ENGLISH & HINDI • DS • 50 kW
DS • 50 kW
ENGLISH, ETC • DS • 50 kW
IRAN
VO THE ISLAMIC REP, Sirjan
W • Mideast & W Asia • 500 kW
S • S Europe • 500 kW
S Europe • 500 kW
(con'd) †VO THE ISLAMIC REP, Zāhedān
W • S Europe • 500 kW
0 1 2 3 4 5 6 7 8 9 10 11 12 13 14 15 16 17 18 19 20 21 22 23 24

SEASONAL S OR W 1-HR TIMESHIFT MIDYEAR ⇐ OR ⇒ JAMMING / OR ∧ EARLIEST HEARD ◁ LATEST HEARD ▷ NEW FOR 2002 †

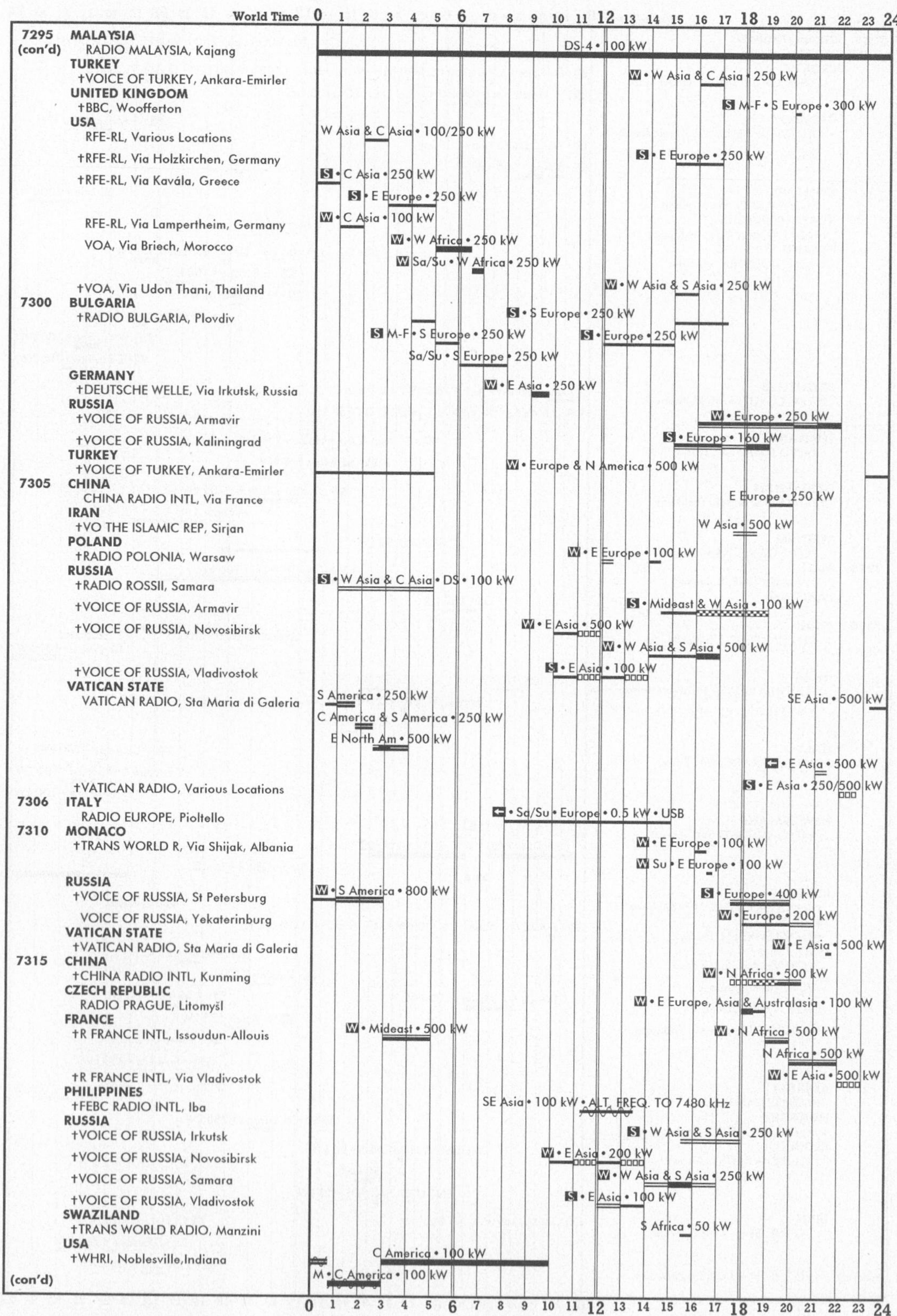

kHz	Country / Station	Schedule notes
7295 (con'd)	**MALAYSIA**	
	RADIO MALAYSIA, Kajang	DS-4 • 100 kW
	TURKEY	
	†VOICE OF TURKEY, Ankara-Emirler	W • W Asia & C Asia • 250 kW
	UNITED KINGDOM	
	†BBC, Woofferton	S M-F • S Europe • 300 kW
	USA	
	RFE-RL, Various Locations	W Asia & C Asia • 100/250 kW
	†RFE-RL, Via Holzkirchen, Germany	S • E Europe • 250 kW
	†RFE-RL, Via Kavála, Greece	S • C Asia • 250 kW
		S • E Europe • 250 kW
		W • C Asia • 100 kW
	RFE-RL, Via Lampertheim, Germany	
	VOA, Via Briech, Morocco	W • W Africa • 250 kW
		W Sa/Su • W Africa • 250 kW
	†VOA, Via Udon Thani, Thailand	W • W Asia & S Asia • 250 kW
7300	**BULGARIA**	
	†RADIO BULGARIA, Plovdiv	S • S Europe • 250 kW
		S M-F • S Europe • 250 kW
		S • Europe • 250 kW
		Sa/Su • S Europe • 250 kW
	GERMANY	
	†DEUTSCHE WELLE, Via Irkutsk, Russia	W • E Asia • 250 kW
	RUSSIA	
	†VOICE OF RUSSIA, Armavir	W • Europe • 250 kW
	†VOICE OF RUSSIA, Kaliningrad	S • Europe • 160 kW
	TURKEY	
	†VOICE OF TURKEY, Ankara-Emirler	W • Europe & N America • 500 kW
7305	**CHINA**	
	CHINA RADIO INTL, Via France	E Europe • 250 kW
	IRAN	
	†VO THE ISLAMIC REP, Sirjan	W Asia • 500 kW
	POLAND	
	†RADIO POLONIA, Warsaw	W • E Europe • 100 kW
	RUSSIA	
	†RADIO ROSSII, Samara	S • W Asia & C Asia • DS • 100 kW
	†VOICE OF RUSSIA, Armavir	S • Mideast & W Asia • 100 kW
	†VOICE OF RUSSIA, Novosibirsk	W • E Asia • 500 kW
		W • W Asia & S Asia • 500 kW
	†VOICE OF RUSSIA, Vladivostok	S • E Asia • 100 kW
	VATICAN STATE	
	VATICAN RADIO, Sta Maria di Galeria	S America • 250 kW
		SE Asia • 500 kW
		C America & S America • 250 kW
		E North Am • 500 kW
		← • E Asia • 500 kW
	†VATICAN RADIO, Various Locations	S • E Asia • 250/500 kW
7306	**ITALY**	
	RADIO EUROPE, Pioltello	← • Sa/Su • Europe • 0.5 kW • USB
7310	**MONACO**	
	†TRANS WORLD R, Via Shijak, Albania	W • E Europe • 100 kW
		W Su • E Europe • 100 kW
	RUSSIA	
	†VOICE OF RUSSIA, St Petersburg	W • S America • 800 kW
		S • Europe • 400 kW
	VOICE OF RUSSIA, Yekaterinburg	W • Europe • 200 kW
	VATICAN STATE	
	†VATICAN RADIO, Sta Maria di Galeria	W • E Asia • 500 kW
7315	**CHINA**	
	†CHINA RADIO INTL, Kunming	W • N Africa • 500 kW
	CZECH REPUBLIC	
	RADIO PRAGUE, Litomyšl	W • E Europe, Asia & Australasia • 100 kW
	FRANCE	
	†R FRANCE INTL, Issoudun-Allouis	W • Mideast • 500 kW
		W • N Africa • 500 kW
		N Africa • 500 kW
	†R FRANCE INTL, Via Vladivostok	W • E Asia • 500 kW
	PHILIPPINES	
	†FEBC RADIO INTL, Iba	SE Asia • 100 kW • ALT. FREQ. TO 7480 kHz
	RUSSIA	
	†VOICE OF RUSSIA, Irkutsk	S • W Asia & S Asia • 250 kW
	†VOICE OF RUSSIA, Novosibirsk	W • E Asia • 200 kW
	†VOICE OF RUSSIA, Samara	W • W Asia & S Asia • 250 kW
	†VOICE OF RUSSIA, Vladivostok	S • E Asia • 100 kW
	SWAZILAND	
	†TRANS WORLD RADIO, Manzini	S Africa • 50 kW
	USA	
	†WHRI, Noblesville, Indiana	C America • 100 kW
(con'd)		M • C America • 100 kW

World Time 0–24

ENGLISH ▬ ARABIC ▭▭ CHINESE ▫▫▫ FRENCH ═ GERMAN ═ RUSSIAN ═ SPANISH ═ OTHER —

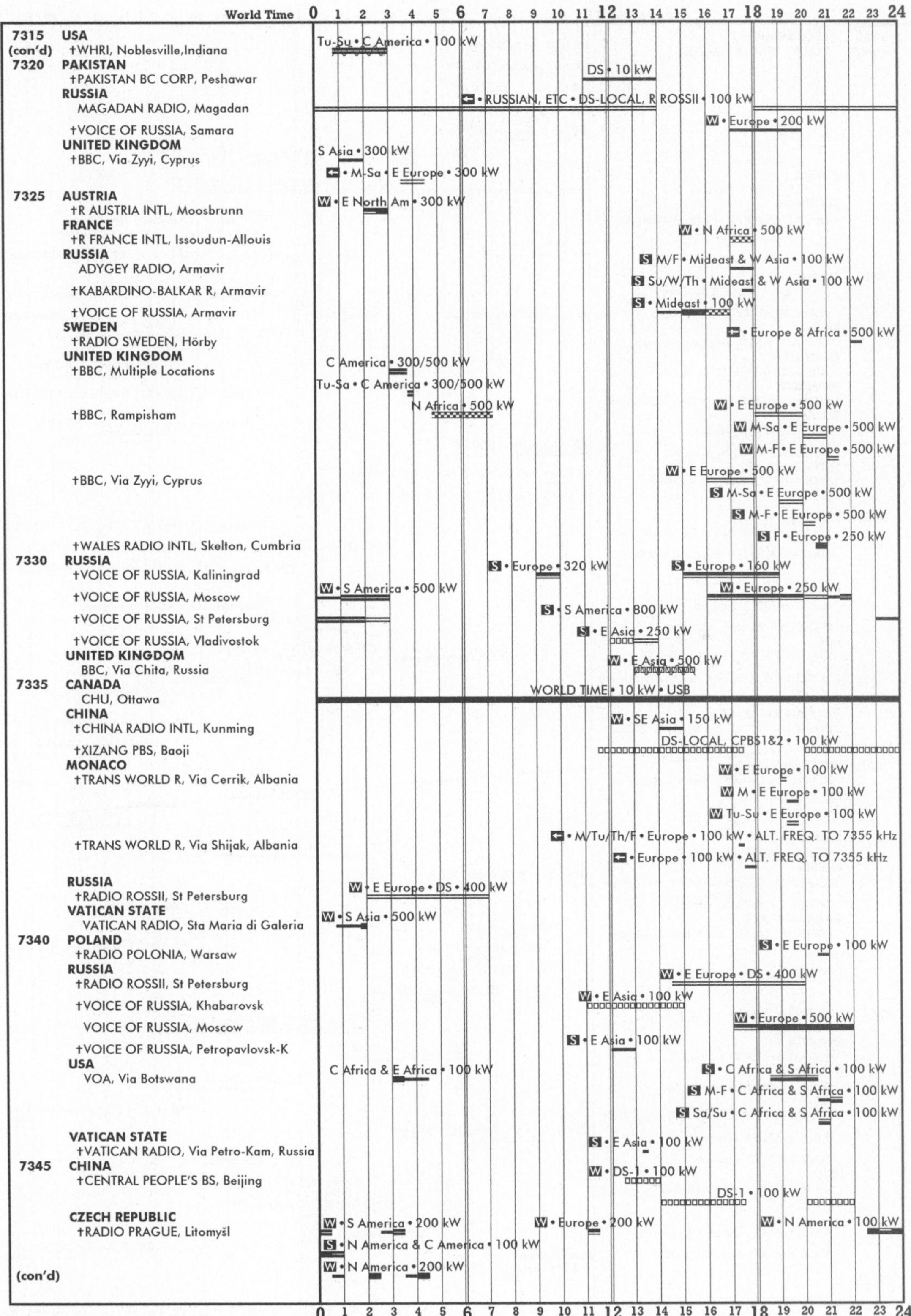
World Time 0 1 2 3 4 5 6 7 8 9 10 11 12 13 14 15 16 17 18 19 20 21 22 23 24
7315 (con'd) USA
†WHRI, Noblesville,Indiana
Tu-Su • C America • 100 kW
7320 PAKISTAN
†PAKISTAN BC CORP, Peshawar
DS • 10 kW
RUSSIA
MAGADAN RADIO, Magadan
RUSSIAN, ETC • DS-LOCAL, R ROSSII • 100 kW
†VOICE OF RUSSIA, Samara
Europe • 200 kW
UNITED KINGDOM
†BBC, Via Zyyi, Cyprus
S Asia • 300 kW
M-Sa • E Europe • 300 kW
7325 AUSTRIA
†R AUSTRIA INTL, Moosbrunn
E North Am • 300 kW
FRANCE
†R FRANCE INTL, Issoudun-Allouis
N Africa • 500 kW
RUSSIA
ADYGEY RADIO, Armavir
M/F • Mideast & W Asia • 100 kW
†KABARDINO-BALKAR R, Armavir
Su/W/Th • Mideast & W Asia • 100 kW
†VOICE OF RUSSIA, Armavir
Mideast • 100 kW
SWEDEN
†RADIO SWEDEN, Hörby
Europe & Africa • 500 kW
UNITED KINGDOM
†BBC, Multiple Locations
C America • 300/500 kW
Tu-Sa • C America • 300/500 kW
†BBC, Rampisham
N Africa • 500 kW
E Europe • 500 kW
M-Sa • E Europe • 500 kW
M-F • E Europe • 500 kW
†BBC, Via Zyyi, Cyprus
E Europe • 500 kW
M-Sa • E Europe • 500 kW
M-F • E Europe • 500 kW
F • Europe • 250 kW
†WALES RADIO INTL, Skelton, Cumbria
7330 RUSSIA
†VOICE OF RUSSIA, Kaliningrad
Europe • 320 kW
Europe • 160 kW
†VOICE OF RUSSIA, Moscow
S America • 500 kW
Europe • 250 kW
†VOICE OF RUSSIA, St Petersburg
S America • 800 kW
†VOICE OF RUSSIA, Vladivostok
E Asia • 250 kW
UNITED KINGDOM
BBC, Via Chita, Russia
E Asia • 500 kW
7335 CANADA
CHU, Ottawa
WORLD TIME • 10 kW • USB
CHINA
†CHINA RADIO INTL, Kunming
SE Asia • 150 kW
†XIZANG PBS, Baoji
DS-LOCAL, CPBS1&2 • 100 kW
MONACO
†TRANS WORLD R, Via Cerrik, Albania
E Europe • 100 kW
M • E Europe • 100 kW
Tu-Su • E Europe • 100 kW
†TRANS WORLD R, Via Shijak, Albania
M/Tu/Th/F • Europe • 100 kW • ALT. FREQ. TO 7355 kHz
Europe • 100 kW • ALT. FREQ. TO 7355 kHz
RUSSIA
†RADIO ROSSII, St Petersburg
E Europe • DS • 400 kW
VATICAN STATE
VATICAN RADIO, Sta Maria di Galeria
S Asia • 500 kW
7340 POLAND
†RADIO POLONIA, Warsaw
E Europe • 100 kW
RUSSIA
†RADIO ROSSII, St Petersburg
E Europe • DS • 400 kW
†VOICE OF RUSSIA, Khabarovsk
E Asia • 100 kW
VOICE OF RUSSIA, Moscow
Europe • 500 kW
†VOICE OF RUSSIA, Petropavlovsk-K
E Asia • 100 kW
USA
VOA, Via Botswana
C Africa & E Africa • 100 kW
C Africa & S Africa • 100 kW
M-F • C Africa & S Africa • 100 kW
Sa/Su • C Africa & S Africa • 100 kW
VATICAN STATE
†VATICAN RADIO, Via Petro-Kam, Russia
E Asia • 100 kW
7345 CHINA
†CENTRAL PEOPLE'S BS, Beijing
DS-1 • 100 kW
DS-1 • 100 kW
CZECH REPUBLIC
†RADIO PRAGUE, Litomyšl
S America • 200 kW
Europe • 200 kW
N America • 100 kW
N America & C America • 100 kW
N America • 200 kW
(con'd)
0 1 2 3 4 5 6 7 8 9 10 11 12 13 14 15 16 17 18 19 20 21 22 23 24

SEASONAL S OR W 1-HR TIMESHIFT MIDYEAR ◄ OR ► JAMMING / OR ∧ EARLIEST HEARD ◁ LATEST HEARD ▷ NEW FOR 2002 †

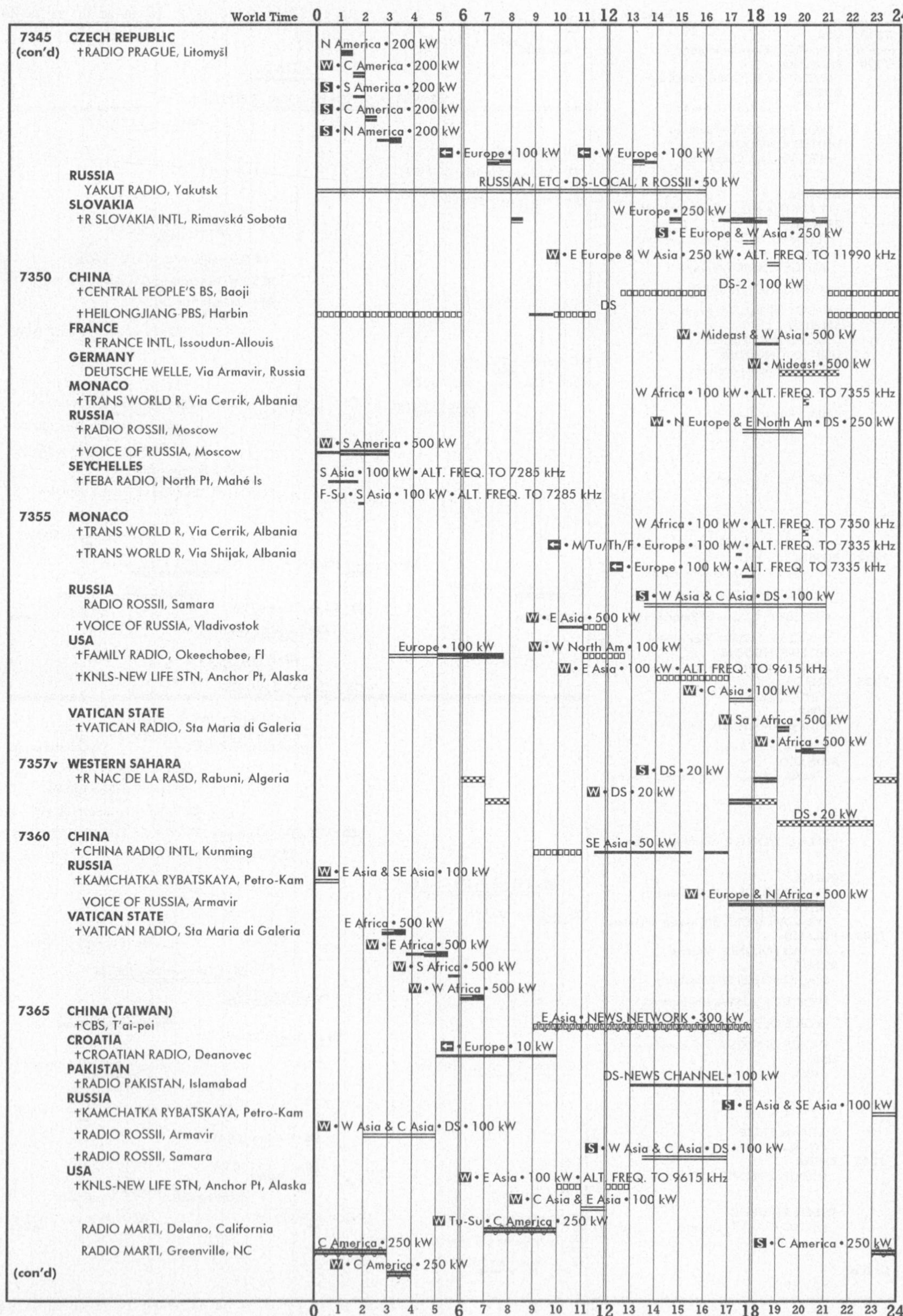
World Time 0 1 2 3 4 5 6 7 8 9 10 11 12 13 14 15 16 17 18 19 20 21 22 23 24
7345 (con'd) CZECH REPUBLIC
†RADIO PRAGUE, Litomyšl
N America • 200 kW
W • C America • 200 kW
S • S America • 200 kW
S • C America • 200 kW
S • N America • 200 kW
• Europe • 100 kW
• W Europe • 100 kW
RUSSIA
YAKUT RADIO, Yakutsk
RUSSIAN, ETC • DS-LOCAL, R ROSSII • 50 kW
SLOVAKIA
†R SLOVAKIA INTL, Rimavská Sobota
W Europe • 250 kW
S • E Europe & W Asia • 250 kW
W • E Europe & W Asia • 250 kW • ALT. FREQ. TO 11990 kHz
7350 CHINA
†CENTRAL PEOPLE'S BS, Baoji
DS-2 • 100 kW
†HEILONGJIANG PBS, Harbin
DS
FRANCE
R FRANCE INTL, Issoudun-Allouis
W • Mideast & W Asia • 500 kW
GERMANY
DEUTSCHE WELLE, Via Armavir, Russia
W • Mideast • 500 kW
MONACO
†TRANS WORLD R, Via Cerrik, Albania
W Africa • 100 kW • ALT. FREQ. TO 7355 kHz
RUSSIA
†RADIO ROSSII, Moscow
W • N Europe & E North Am • DS • 250 kW
†VOICE OF RUSSIA, Moscow
W • S America • 500 kW
SEYCHELLES
†FEBA RADIO, North Pt, Mahé Is
S Asia • 100 kW • ALT. FREQ. TO 7285 kHz
F-Su • S Asia • 100 kW • ALT. FREQ. TO 7285 kHz
7355 MONACO
†TRANS WORLD R, Via Cerrik, Albania
W Africa • 100 kW • ALT. FREQ. TO 7350 kHz
†TRANS WORLD R, Via Shijak, Albania
• M/Tu/Th/F • Europe • 100 kW • ALT. FREQ. TO 7335 kHz
• Europe • 100 kW • ALT. FREQ. TO 7335 kHz
RUSSIA
RADIO ROSSII, Samara
S • W Asia & C Asia • DS • 100 kW
†VOICE OF RUSSIA, Vladivostok
W • E Asia • 500 kW
USA
†FAMILY RADIO, Okeechobee, Fl
Europe • 100 kW
W • W North Am • 100 kW
†KNLS-NEW LIFE STN, Anchor Pt, Alaska
W • E Asia • 100 kW • ALT. FREQ. TO 9615 kHz
W • C Asia • 100 kW
VATICAN STATE
†VATICAN RADIO, Sta Maria di Galeria
W Sa • Africa • 500 kW
W • Africa • 500 kW
7357v WESTERN SAHARA
†R NAC DE LA RASD, Rabuni, Algeria
S • DS • 20 kW
W • DS • 20 kW
DS • 20 kW
7360 CHINA
†CHINA RADIO INTL, Kunming
SE Asia • 50 kW
RUSSIA
†KAMCHATKA RYBATSKAYA, Petro-Kam
W • E Asia & SE Asia • 100 kW
VOICE OF RUSSIA, Armavir
W • Europe & N Africa • 500 kW
VATICAN STATE
†VATICAN RADIO, Sta Maria di Galeria
E Africa • 500 kW
W • E Africa • 500 kW
W • S Africa • 500 kW
W • W Africa • 500 kW
7365 CHINA (TAIWAN)
†CBS, T'ai-pei
E Asia • NEWS NETWORK • 300 kW
CROATIA
†CROATIAN RADIO, Deanovec
• Europe • 10 kW
PAKISTAN
†RADIO PAKISTAN, Islamabad
DS-NEWS CHANNEL • 100 kW
RUSSIA
†KAMCHATKA RYBATSKAYA, Petro-Kam
S • E Asia & SE Asia • 100 kW
†RADIO ROSSII, Armavir
W • W Asia & C Asia • DS • 100 kW
†RADIO ROSSII, Samara
S • W Asia & C Asia • DS • 100 kW
USA
†KNLS-NEW LIFE STN, Anchor Pt, Alaska
W • E Asia • 100 kW • ALT. FREQ. TO 9615 kHz
W • C Asia & E Asia • 100 kW
RADIO MARTI, Delano, California
W Tu-Su • C America • 250 kW
RADIO MARTI, Greenville, NC
C America • 250 kW
S • C America • 250 kW
W • C America • 250 kW
(con'd)
0 1 2 3 4 5 6 7 8 9 10 11 12 13 14 15 16 17 18 19 20 21 22 23 24
ENGLISH ARABIC CHINESE FRENCH GERMAN RUSSIAN SPANISH OTHER

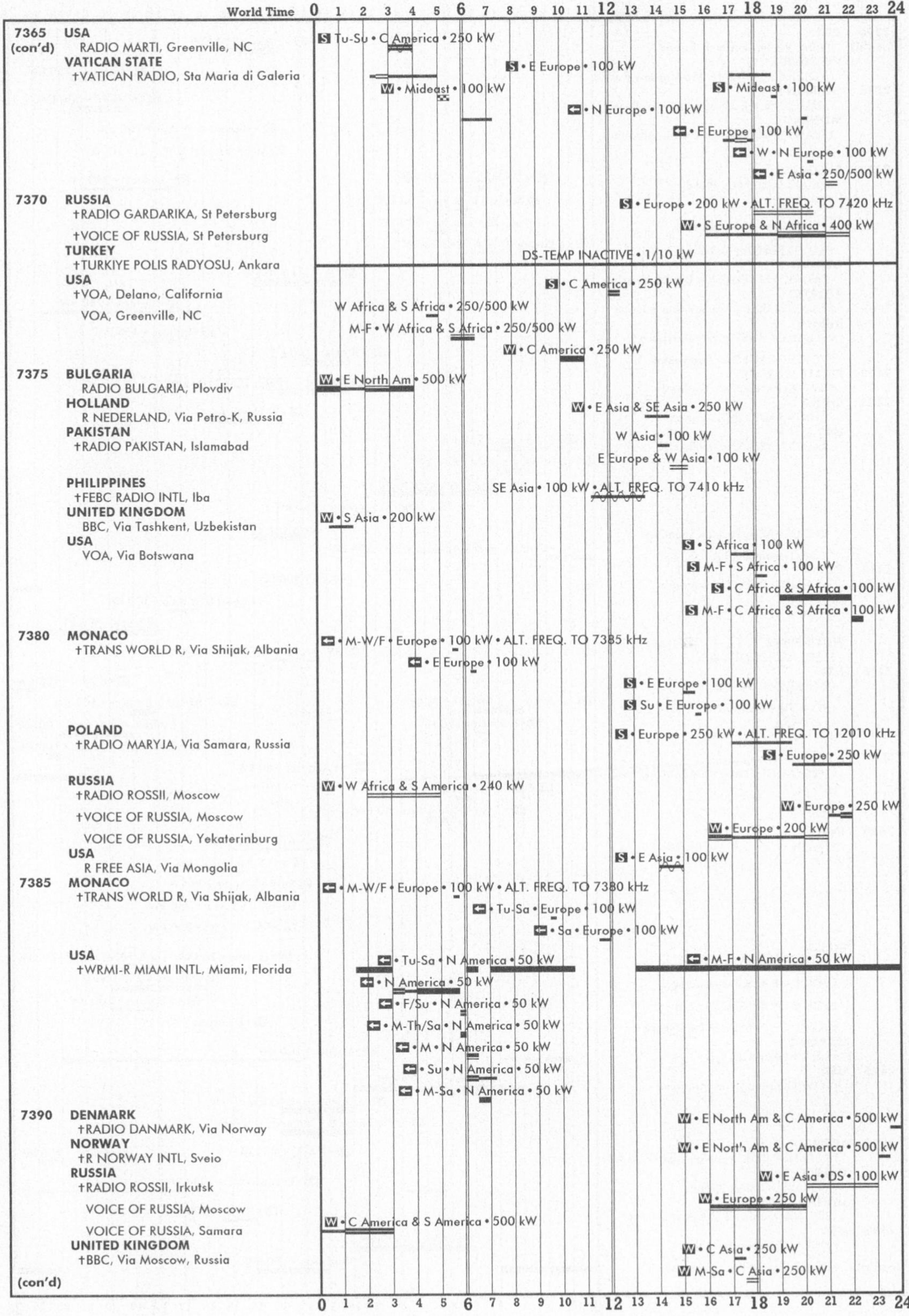

World Time 0 1 2 3 4 5 6 7 8 9 10 11 12 13 14 15 16 17 18 19 20 21 22 23 24
7365 (con'd) USA
RADIO MARTI, Greenville, NC
S Tu-Su • C America • 250 kW
VATICAN STATE
†VATICAN RADIO, Sta Maria di Galeria
S • E Europe • 100 kW
W • Mideast • 100 kW
S • Mideast • 100 kW
N Europe • 100 kW
E Europe • 100 kW
W • N Europe • 100 kW
E Asia • 250/500 kW
7370 RUSSIA
†RADIO GARDARIKA, St Petersburg
S • Europe • 200 kW • ALT. FREQ. TO 7420 kHz
†VOICE OF RUSSIA, St Petersburg
W • S Europe & N Africa • 400 kW
TURKEY
†TURKIYE POLIS RADYOSU, Ankara
DS-TEMP INACTIVE • 1/10 kW
USA
†VOA, Delano, California
S • C America • 250 kW
VOA, Greenville, NC
W Africa & S Africa • 250/500 kW
M-F • W Africa & S Africa • 250/500 kW
W • C America • 250 kW
7375 BULGARIA
RADIO BULGARIA, Plovdiv
W • E North Am • 500 kW
HOLLAND
R NEDERLAND, Via Petro-K, Russia
W • E Asia & SE Asia • 250 kW
PAKISTAN
†RADIO PAKISTAN, Islamabad
W Asia • 100 kW
E Europe & W Asia • 100 kW
PHILIPPINES
†FEBC RADIO INTL, Iba
SE Asia • 100 kW • ALT. FREQ. TO 7410 kHz
UNITED KINGDOM
BBC, Via Tashkent, Uzbekistan
W • S Asia • 200 kW
USA
VOA, Via Botswana
S • S Africa • 100 kW
S M-F • S Africa • 100 kW
S • C Africa & S Africa • 100 kW
S M-F • C Africa & S Africa • 100 kW
7380 MONACO
†TRANS WORLD R, Via Shijak, Albania
M-W/F • Europe • 100 kW • ALT. FREQ. TO 7385 kHz
E Europe • 100 kW
S • E Europe • 100 kW
S Su • E Europe • 100 kW
POLAND
†RADIO MARYJA, Via Samara, Russia
S • Europe • 250 kW • ALT. FREQ. TO 12010 kHz
S • Europe • 250 kW
RUSSIA
†RADIO ROSSII, Moscow
W • W Africa & S America • 240 kW
†VOICE OF RUSSIA, Moscow
W • Europe • 250 kW
VOICE OF RUSSIA, Yekaterinburg
W • Europe • 200 kW
USA
R FREE ASIA, Via Mongolia
S • E Asia • 100 kW
7385 MONACO
†TRANS WORLD R, Via Shijak, Albania
M-W/F • Europe • 100 kW • ALT. FREQ. TO 7380 kHz
Tu-Sa • Europe • 100 kW
Sa • Europe • 100 kW
USA
†WRMI-R MIAMI INTL, Miami, Florida
Tu-Sa • N America • 50 kW
M-F • N America • 50 kW
N America • 50 kW
F/Su • N America • 50 kW
M-Th/Sa • N America • 50 kW
M • N America • 50 kW
Su • N America • 50 kW
M-Sa • N America • 50 kW
7390 DENMARK
†RADIO DANMARK, Via Norway
W • E North Am & C America • 500 kW
NORWAY
†R NORWAY INTL, Sveio
W • E North Am & C America • 500 kW
RUSSIA
†RADIO ROSSII, Irkutsk
W • E Asia • DS • 100 kW
VOICE OF RUSSIA, Moscow
W • Europe • 250 kW
VOICE OF RUSSIA, Samara
W • C America & S America • 500 kW
UNITED KINGDOM
†BBC, Via Moscow, Russia
W • C Asia • 250 kW
W M-Sa • C Asia • 250 kW
(con'd)
0 1 2 3 4 5 6 7 8 9 10 11 12 13 14 15 16 17 18 19 20 21 22 23 24

SEASONAL S OR W 1-HR TIMESHIFT MIDYEAR OR JAMMING / OR /\ EARLIEST HEARD ◁ LATEST HEARD ▷ NEW FOR 2002 †

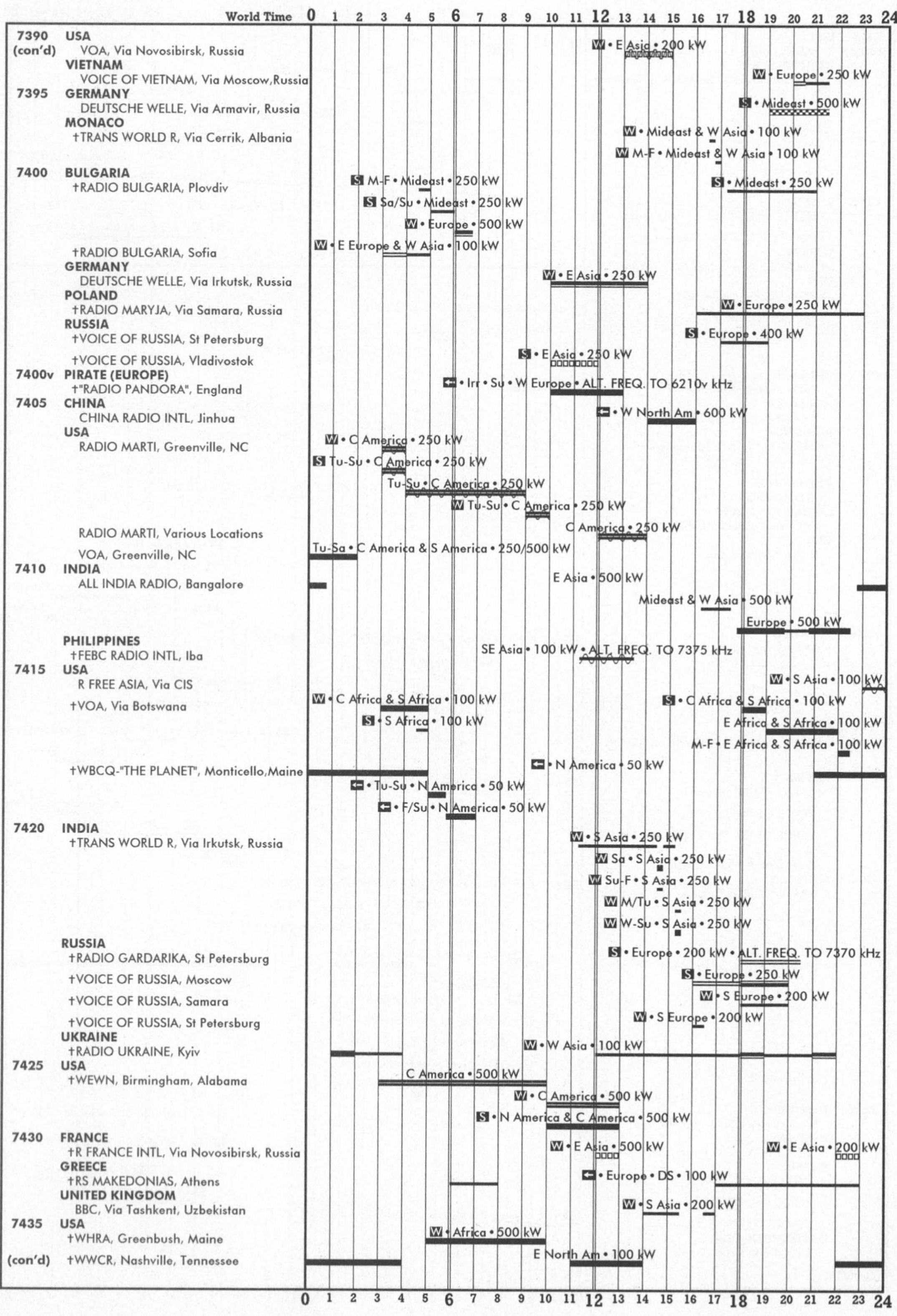
World Time 0 1 2 3 4 5 6 7 8 9 10 11 12 13 14 15 16 17 18 19 20 21 22 23 24
7390 (con'd) USA
VOA, Via Novosibirsk, Russia
W • E Asia • 200 kW
VIETNAM
VOICE OF VIETNAM, Via Moscow,Russia
W • Europe • 250 kW
7395 GERMANY
DEUTSCHE WELLE, Via Armavir, Russia
S • Mideast • 500 kW
MONACO
†TRANS WORLD R, Via Cerrik, Albania
W • Mideast & W Asia • 100 kW
W M-F • Mideast & W Asia • 100 kW
7400 BULGARIA
†RADIO BULGARIA, Plovdiv
S M-F • Mideast • 250 kW
S • Mideast • 250 kW
S Sa/Su • Mideast • 250 kW
W • Europe • 500 kW
W • E Europe & W Asia • 100 kW
†RADIO BULGARIA, Sofia
GERMANY
DEUTSCHE WELLE, Via Irkutsk, Russia
W • E Asia • 250 kW
POLAND
†RADIO MARYJA, Via Samara, Russia
W • Europe • 250 kW
RUSSIA
†VOICE OF RUSSIA, St Petersburg
S • Europe • 400 kW
†VOICE OF RUSSIA, Vladivostok
S • E Asia • 250 kW
7400v PIRATE (EUROPE)
†"RADIO PANDORA", England
• Irr • Su • W Europe • ALT. FREQ. TO 6210v kHz
7405 CHINA
CHINA RADIO INTL, Jinhua
• W North Am • 600 kW
USA
RADIO MARTI, Greenville, NC
W • C America • 250 kW
S Tu-Su • C America • 250 kW
Tu-Su • C America • 250 kW
W Tu-Su • C America • 250 kW
C America • 250 kW
RADIO MARTI, Various Locations
VOA, Greenville, NC
Tu-Sa • C America & S America • 250/500 kW
7410 INDIA
ALL INDIA RADIO, Bangalore
E Asia • 500 kW
Mideast & W Asia • 500 kW
Europe • 500 kW
PHILIPPINES
†FEBC RADIO INTL, Iba
SE Asia • 100 kW • ALT. FREQ. TO 7375 kHz
7415 USA
R FREE ASIA, Via CIS
W • S Asia • 100 kW
†VOA, Via Botswana
W • C Africa & S Africa • 100 kW
S • C Africa & S Africa • 100 kW
S • S Africa • 100 kW
E Africa & S Africa • 100 kW
M-F • E Africa & S Africa • 100 kW
• N America • 50 kW
†WBCQ-"THE PLANET", Monticello,Maine
• Tu-Su • N America • 50 kW
• F/Su • N America • 50 kW
7420 INDIA
†TRANS WORLD R, Via Irkutsk, Russia
W • S Asia • 250 kW
W Sa • S Asia • 250 kW
W Su-F • S Asia • 250 kW
W M/Tu • S Asia • 250 kW
W W-Su • S Asia • 250 kW
RUSSIA
†RADIO GARDARIKA, St Petersburg
S • Europe • 200 kW • ALT. FREQ. TO 7370 kHz
†VOICE OF RUSSIA, Moscow
S • Europe • 250 kW
†VOICE OF RUSSIA, Samara
W • S Europe • 200 kW
†VOICE OF RUSSIA, St Petersburg
W • S Europe • 200 kW
UKRAINE
†RADIO UKRAINE, Kyiv
W • W Asia • 100 kW
7425 USA
†WEWN, Birmingham, Alabama
C America • 500 kW
W • C America • 500 kW
S • N America & C America • 500 kW
7430 FRANCE
†R FRANCE INTL, Via Novosibirsk, Russia
W • E Asia • 500 kW
W • E Asia • 200 kW
GREECE
†RS MAKEDONIAS, Athens
• Europe • DS • 100 kW
UNITED KINGDOM
BBC, Via Tashkent, Uzbekistan
W • S Asia • 200 kW
7435 USA
†WHRA, Greenbush, Maine
W • Africa • 500 kW
(con'd) †WWCR, Nashville, Tennessee
E North Am • 100 kW
0 1 2 3 4 5 6 7 8 9 10 11 12 13 14 15 16 17 18 19 20 21 22 23 24
ENGLISH ARABIC CHINESE FRENCH GERMAN RUSSIAN SPANISH OTHER

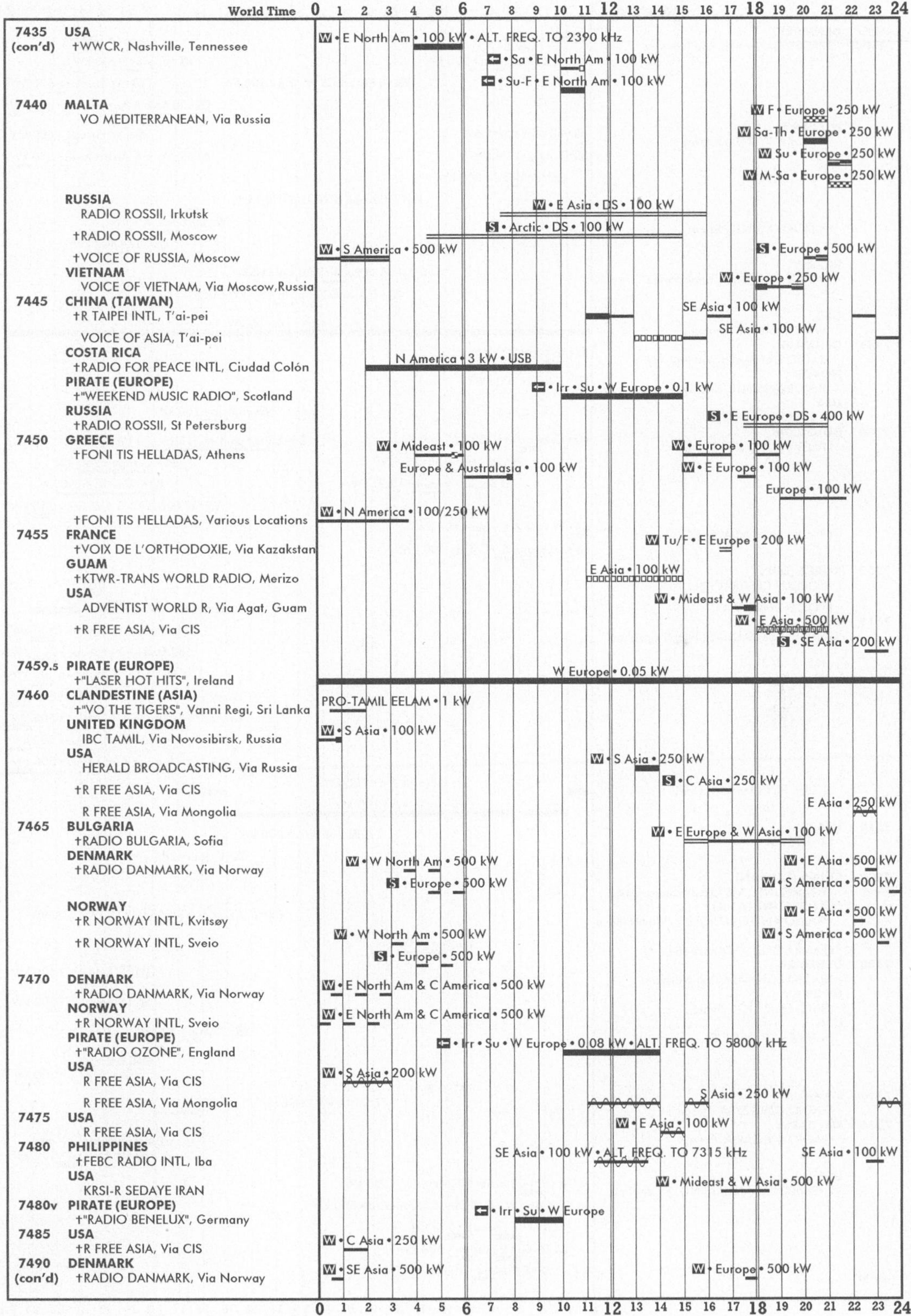
World Time 0 1 2 3 4 5 6 7 8 9 10 11 12 13 14 15 16 17 18 19 20 21 22 23 24
7435 (con'd) USA
†WWCR, Nashville, Tennessee
W • E North Am • 100 kW • ALT. FREQ. TO 2390 kHz
Sa • E North Am • 100 kW
Su-F • E North Am • 100 kW
7440 MALTA
VO MEDITERRANEAN, Via Russia
W F • Europe • 250 kW
W Sa-Th • Europe • 250 kW
W Su • Europe • 250 kW
W M-Sa • Europe • 250 kW
RUSSIA
RADIO ROSSII, Irkutsk
W • E Asia • DS • 100 kW
†RADIO ROSSII, Moscow
S • Arctic • DS • 100 kW
†VOICE OF RUSSIA, Moscow
W • S America • 500 kW
S • Europe • 500 kW
VIETNAM
VOICE OF VIETNAM, Via Moscow,Russia
W • Europe • 250 kW
7445 CHINA (TAIWAN)
†R TAIPEI INTL, T'ai-pei
SE Asia • 100 kW
VOICE OF ASIA, T'ai-pei
SE Asia • 100 kW
COSTA RICA
†RADIO FOR PEACE INTL, Ciudad Colón
N America • 3 kW • USB
PIRATE (EUROPE)
†"WEEKEND MUSIC RADIO", Scotland
Irr • Su • W Europe • 0.1 kW
RUSSIA
†RADIO ROSSII, St Petersburg
S • E Europe • DS • 400 kW
7450 GREECE
†FONI TIS HELLADAS, Athens
W • Mideast • 100 kW
W • Europe • 100 kW
Europe & Australasia • 100 kW
W • E Europe • 100 kW
Europe • 100 kW
†FONI TIS HELLADAS, Various Locations
W • N America • 100/250 kW
7455 FRANCE
†VOIX DE L'ORTHODOXIE, Via Kazakstan
W Tu/F • E Europe • 200 kW
GUAM
†KTWR-TRANS WORLD RADIO, Merizo
E Asia • 100 kW
USA
ADVENTIST WORLD R, Via Agat, Guam
W • Mideast & W Asia • 100 kW
†R FREE ASIA, Via CIS
W • E Asia • 500 kW
S • SE Asia • 200 kW
7459.5 PIRATE (EUROPE)
†"LASER HOT HITS", Ireland
W Europe • 0.05 kW
7460 CLANDESTINE (ASIA)
†"VO THE TIGERS", Vanni Regi, Sri Lanka
PRO-TAMIL EELAM • 1 kW
UNITED KINGDOM
IBC TAMIL, Via Novosibirsk, Russia
W • S Asia • 100 kW
USA
HERALD BROADCASTING, Via Russia
W • S Asia • 250 kW
†R FREE ASIA, Via CIS
S • C Asia • 250 kW
R FREE ASIA, Via Mongolia
E Asia • 250 kW
7465 BULGARIA
†RADIO BULGARIA, Sofia
W • E Europe & W Asia • 100 kW
DENMARK
†RADIO DANMARK, Via Norway
W • W North Am • 500 kW
W • E Asia • 500 kW
S • Europe • 500 kW
W • S America • 500 kW
NORWAY
†R NORWAY INTL, Kvitsøy
W • E Asia • 500 kW
†R NORWAY INTL, Sveio
W • W North Am • 500 kW
W • S America • 500 kW
S • Europe • 500 kW
7470 DENMARK
†RADIO DANMARK, Via Norway
W • E North Am & C America • 500 kW
NORWAY
†R NORWAY INTL, Sveio
W • E North Am & C America • 500 kW
PIRATE (EUROPE)
†"RADIO OZONE", England
Irr • Su • W Europe • 0.08 kW • ALT. FREQ. TO 5800v kHz
USA
R FREE ASIA, Via CIS
W • S Asia • 200 kW
R FREE ASIA, Via Mongolia
S Asia • 250 kW
7475 USA
R FREE ASIA, Via CIS
W • E Asia • 100 kW
7480 PHILIPPINES
†FEBC RADIO INTL, Iba
SE Asia • 100 kW • ALT. FREQ. TO 7315 kHz
SE Asia • 100 kW
USA
KRSI-R SEDAYE IRAN
W • Mideast & W Asia • 500 kW
7480v PIRATE (EUROPE)
†"RADIO BENELUX", Germany
Irr • Su • W Europe
7485 USA
†R FREE ASIA, Via CIS
W • C Asia • 250 kW
7490 (con'd) DENMARK
†RADIO DANMARK, Via Norway
W • SE Asia • 500 kW
W • Europe • 500 kW
0 1 2 3 4 5 6 7 8 9 10 11 12 13 14 15 16 17 18 19 20 21 22 23 24
SEASONAL S OR W
1-HR TIMESHIFT MIDYEAR OR
JAMMING / OR /\
EARLIEST HEARD ◁
LATEST HEARD ▷
NEW FOR 2002 †

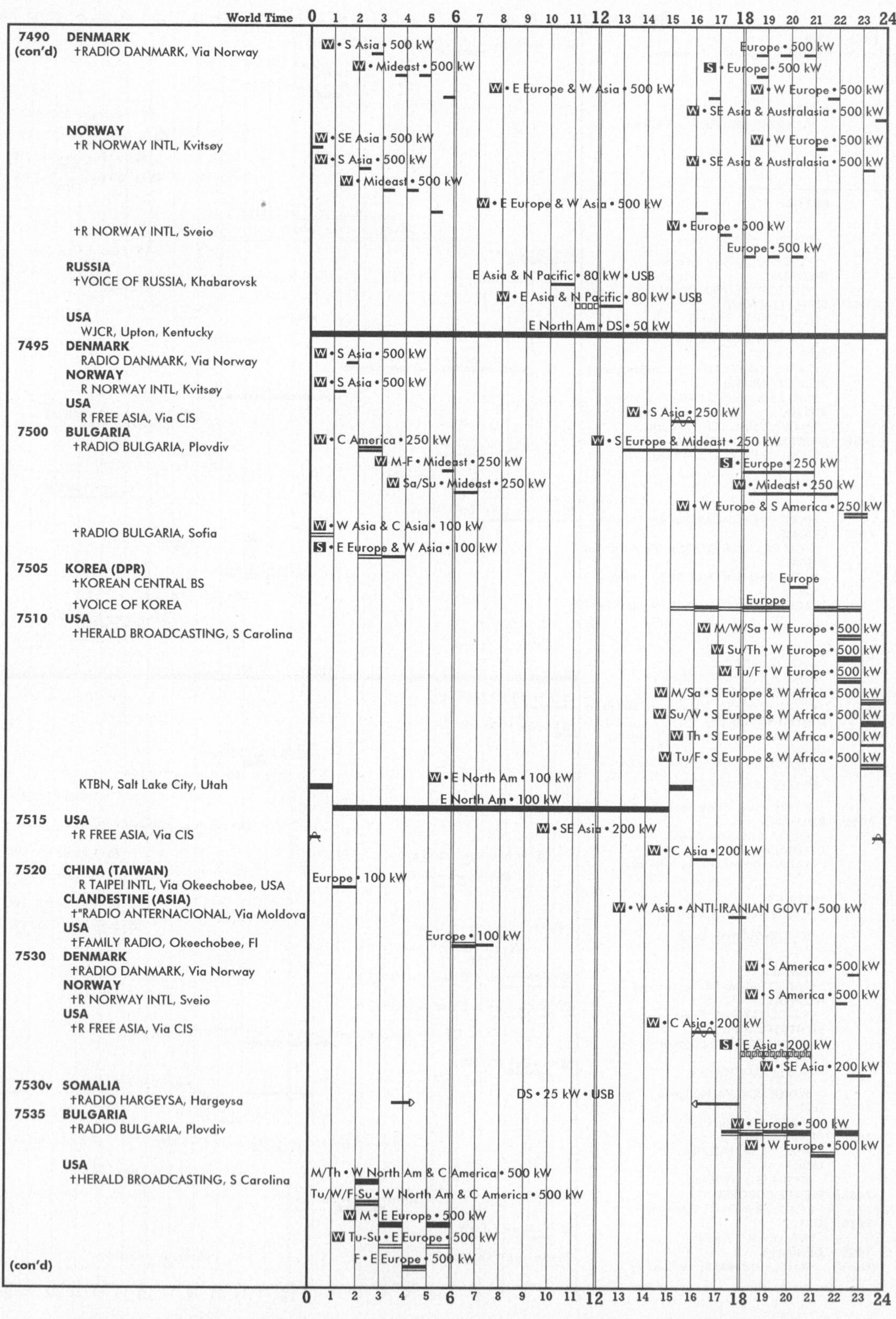
World Time 0 1 2 3 4 5 6 7 8 9 10 11 12 13 14 15 16 17 18 19 20 21 22 23 24
7490 DENMARK (con'd)
†RADIO DANMARK, Via Norway
W • S Asia • 500 kW
Europe • 500 kW
W • Mideast • 500 kW
S • Europe • 500 kW
W • E Europe & W Asia • 500 kW
W • W Europe • 500 kW
W • SE Asia & Australasia • 500 kW
NORWAY
†R NORWAY INTL, Kvitsøy
W • SE Asia • 500 kW
W • W Europe • 500 kW
W • S Asia • 500 kW
W • SE Asia & Australasia • 500 kW
W • Mideast • 500 kW
W • E Europe & W Asia • 500 kW
†R NORWAY INTL, Sveio
W • Europe • 500 kW
Europe • 500 kW
RUSSIA
†VOICE OF RUSSIA, Khabarovsk
E Asia & N Pacific • 80 kW • USB
W • E Asia & N Pacific • 80 kW • USB
USA
WJCR, Upton, Kentucky
E North Am • DS • 50 kW
7495 DENMARK
RADIO DANMARK, Via Norway
W • S Asia • 500 kW
NORWAY
R NORWAY INTL, Kvitsøy
W • S Asia • 500 kW
USA
R FREE ASIA, Via CIS
W • S Asia • 250 kW
7500 BULGARIA
†RADIO BULGARIA, Plovdiv
W • C America • 250 kW
W • S Europe & Mideast • 250 kW
W M-F • Mideast • 250 kW
S • Europe • 250 kW
W Sa/Su • Mideast • 250 kW
W • Mideast • 250 kW
W • W Europe & S America • 250 kW
†RADIO BULGARIA, Sofia
W • W Asia & C Asia • 100 kW
S • E Europe & W Asia • 100 kW
7505 KOREA (DPR)
†KOREAN CENTRAL BS
Europe
†VOICE OF KOREA
Europe
7510 USA
†HERALD BROADCASTING, S Carolina
W M/W/Sa • W Europe • 500 kW
W Su/Th • W Europe • 500 kW
W Tu/F • W Europe • 500 kW
W M/Sa • S Europe & W Africa • 500 kW
W Su/W • S Europe & W Africa • 500 kW
W Th • S Europe & W Africa • 500 kW
W Tu/F • S Europe & W Africa • 500 kW
KTBN, Salt Lake City, Utah
W • E North Am • 100 kW
E North Am • 100 kW
7515 USA
†R FREE ASIA, Via CIS
W • SE Asia • 200 kW
W • C Asia • 200 kW
7520 CHINA (TAIWAN)
R TAIPEI INTL, Via Okeechobee, USA
Europe • 100 kW
CLANDESTINE (ASIA)
†"RADIO ANTERNACIONAL, Via Moldova
W • W Asia • ANTI-IRANIAN GOVT • 500 kW
USA
†FAMILY RADIO, Okeechobee, Fl
Europe • 100 kW
7530 DENMARK
†RADIO DANMARK, Via Norway
W • S America • 500 kW
NORWAY
†R NORWAY INTL, Sveio
W • S America • 500 kW
USA
†R FREE ASIA, Via CIS
W • C Asia • 200 kW
S • E Asia • 200 kW
W • SE Asia • 200 kW
7530v SOMALIA
†RADIO HARGEYSA, Hargeysa
DS • 25 kW • USB
7535 BULGARIA
†RADIO BULGARIA, Plovdiv
W • Europe • 500 kW
W • W Europe • 500 kW
USA
†HERALD BROADCASTING, S Carolina
M/Th • W North Am & C America • 500 kW
Tu/W/F-Su • W North Am & C America • 500 kW
W M • E Europe • 500 kW
W Tu-Su • E Europe • 500 kW
F • E Europe • 500 kW
(con'd)
0 1 2 3 4 5 6 7 8 9 10 11 12 13 14 15 16 17 18 19 20 21 22 23 24
ENGLISH ARABIC CHINESE FRENCH GERMAN RUSSIAN SPANISH OTHER

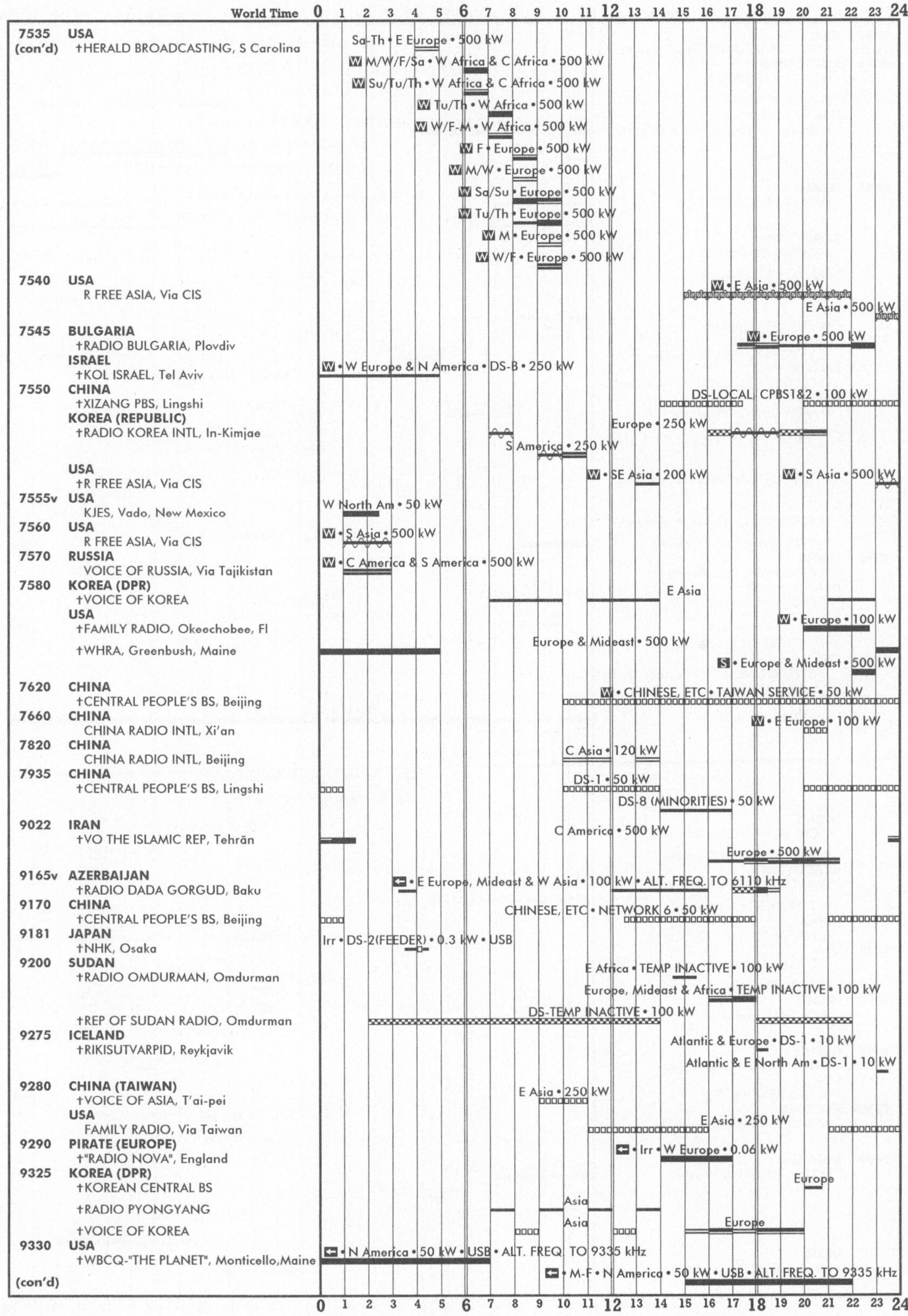
World Time 0 1 2 3 4 5 6 7 8 9 10 11 12 13 14 15 16 17 18 19 20 21 22 23 24
7535 (con'd) USA
†HERALD BROADCASTING, S Carolina
Sa-Th • E Europe • 500 kW
W M/W/F/Sa • W Africa & C Africa • 500 kW
W Su/Tu/Th • W Africa & C Africa • 500 kW
W Tu/Th • W Africa • 500 kW
W W/F-M • W Africa • 500 kW
W F • Europe • 500 kW
W M/W • Europe • 500 kW
W Sa/Su • Europe • 500 kW
W Tu/Th • Europe • 500 kW
W M • Europe • 500 kW
W W/F • Europe • 500 kW
7540 USA
R FREE ASIA, Via CIS
W • E Asia • 500 kW
E Asia • 500 kW
7545 BULGARIA
†RADIO BULGARIA, Plovdiv
W • Europe • 500 kW
ISRAEL
†KOL ISRAEL, Tel Aviv
W • W Europe & N America • DS-B • 250 kW
7550 CHINA
†XIZANG PBS, Lingshi
DS-LOCAL, CPBS1&2 • 100 kW
KOREA (REPUBLIC)
†RADIO KOREA INTL, In-Kimjae
Europe • 250 kW
S America • 250 kW
USA
†R FREE ASIA, Via CIS
W • SE Asia • 200 kW
W • S Asia • 500 kW
7555v USA
KJES, Vado, New Mexico
W North Am • 50 kW
7560 USA
R FREE ASIA, Via CIS
W • S Asia • 500 kW
7570 RUSSIA
VOICE OF RUSSIA, Via Tajikistan
W • C America & S America • 500 kW
7580 KOREA (DPR)
†VOICE OF KOREA
E Asia
USA
†FAMILY RADIO, Okeechobee, Fl
W • Europe • 100 kW
†WHRA, Greenbush, Maine
Europe & Mideast • 500 kW
S • Europe & Mideast • 500 kW
7620 CHINA
†CENTRAL PEOPLE'S BS, Beijing
W • CHINESE, ETC • TAIWAN SERVICE • 50 kW
7660 CHINA
CHINA RADIO INTL, Xi'an
W • E Europe • 100 kW
7820 CHINA
CHINA RADIO INTL, Beijing
C Asia • 120 kW
7935 CHINA
†CENTRAL PEOPLE'S BS, Lingshi
DS-1 • 50 kW
DS-8 (MINORITIES) • 50 kW
9022 IRAN
†VO THE ISLAMIC REP, Tehrān
C America • 500 kW
Europe • 500 kW
9165v AZERBAIJAN
†RADIO DADA GORGUD, Baku
• E Europe, Mideast & W Asia • 100 kW • ALT. FREQ. TO 6110 kHz
9170 CHINA
†CENTRAL PEOPLE'S BS, Beijing
CHINESE, ETC • NETWORK 6 • 50 kW
9181 JAPAN
†NHK, Osaka
Irr • DS-2(FEEDER) • 0.3 kW • USB
9200 SUDAN
†RADIO OMDURMAN, Omdurman
E Africa • TEMP INACTIVE • 100 kW
Europe, Mideast & Africa • TEMP INACTIVE • 100 kW
†REP OF SUDAN RADIO, Omdurman
DS-TEMP INACTIVE • 100 kW
9275 ICELAND
†RIKISUTVARPID, Reykjavik
Atlantic & Europe • DS-1 • 10 kW
Atlantic & E North Am • DS-1 • 10 kW
9280 CHINA (TAIWAN)
†VOICE OF ASIA, T'ai-pei
E Asia • 250 kW
USA
FAMILY RADIO, Via Taiwan
E Asia • 250 kW
9290 PIRATE (EUROPE)
†"RADIO NOVA", England
• Irr • W Europe • 0.06 kW
9325 KOREA (DPR)
†KOREAN CENTRAL BS
Europe
†RADIO PYONGYANG
Asia
†VOICE OF KOREA
Asia
Europe
9330 USA
†WBCQ-"THE PLANET", Monticello, Maine
• N America • 50 kW • USB • ALT. FREQ. TO 9335 kHz
• M-F • N America • 50 kW • USB • ALT. FREQ. TO 9335 kHz
(con'd)
0 1 2 3 4 5 6 7 8 9 10 11 12 13 14 15 16 17 18 19 20 21 22 23 24

SEASONAL S OR W 1-HR TIMESHIFT MIDYEAR OR JAMMING / OR /\ EARLIEST HEARD ◁ LATEST HEARD ▷ NEW FOR 2002 †

World Time 0 1 2 3 4 5 6 7 8 9 10 11 12 13 14 15 16 17 18 19 20 21 22 23 24

kHz	Country / Station	Schedule
9330 (con'd)	**USA**	
	†WBCQ-"THE PLANET", Monticello, Maine	← • M-Sa • N America • 50 kW • USB • ALT. FREQ. TO 9335 kHz
9335	**KOREA (DPR)**	
	†KOREAN CENTRAL BS	Europe
	†VOICE OF KOREA	Europe
	USA	
	†WBCQ-"THE PLANET", Monticello, Maine	← • N America • 50 kW • USB • ALT. FREQ. TO 9330 kHz
		← • M-F • N America • 50 kW • USB • ALT. FREQ. TO 9330 kHz
		← • M-Sa • N America • 50 kW • USB • ALT. FREQ. TO 9330 kHz
9345	**ISRAEL**	
	†KOL ISRAEL, Tel Aviv	S • W Europe & E North Am • DS-B • 50 kW
		W • W Europe & E North Am • DS-B • 50 kW • ALT. FREQ. TO 5790 kHz
	KOREA (DPR)	
	†KOREAN CENTRAL BS	Asia
	†RADIO PYONGYANG	Asia
	†VOICE OF KOREA	Asia
9350	**USA**	
	†R FREE ASIA, Via CIS	S • C Asia • 200 kW
9355	**CHINA (TAIWAN)**	
	R TAIPEI INTL, Via Okeechobee, USA	Europe • 100 kW; W • Europe • 100 kW
	FRANCE	
	†VOIX DE L'ORTHODOXIE, Via Kazakstan	S Tu/F • E Europe • 200 kW
	USA	
	†FAMILY RADIO, Okeechobee, Fl	Europe • 100 kW; S • S America • 100 kW
	†R FREE ASIA, Via CIS	W • SE Asia • 250 kW
		S • SE Asia • 250 kW
	†R FREE ASIA, Via Saipan, N Marianas	SE Asia • 100 kW; W • E Asia • 100 kW
		S • E Asia • 100 kW
	†R FREE ASIA, Via Tinian, N Marianas	S • E Asia • 500 kW
	†WEWN, Birmingham, Alabama	W • Europe • 500 kW
9365	**CHINA**	
	†CHINA RADIO INTL, Beijing	W • Europe • 150 kW
	USA	
	†R FREE ASIA, Via CIS	W • C Asia • 200 kW; W • S Asia • 500 kW
		S • S Asia • 500 kW
		W • SE Asia • 200 kW
9370	**USA**	
	ADVENTIST WORLD R, Via Agat, Guam	W • E Asia • 100 kW
	†R FREE ASIA, Via CIS	S • C Asia • 250 kW
	†WTJC, Newport, NC	← • N America • 50/61 kW
		← • M • N America • 50/61 kW
		← • Tu-Su • N America • 50/61 kW
		← • M-Sa • N America • 50/61 kW
		← • Su • N America • 50/61 kW
9375	**GREECE**	
	†FONI TIS HELLADAS, Athens	S • E Europe • 100 kW
	†FONI TIS HELLADAS, Kavála	← • E Europe • 250 kW
	UZBEKISTAN	
	†RADIO TASHKENT, Tashkent	S • W Asia • 20 kW
	†UZBEK RADIO, Tashkent	S • W Asia • DS-2 • 20 kW
9380	**CHINA**	
	†CENTRAL PEOPLE'S BS, Beijing	CHINESE, ETC • TAIWAN SERVICE • 50 kW
9385	**USA**	
	ADVENTIST WORLD R, Via Agat, Guam	Mideast • 100 kW
	†R FREE ASIA, Via CIS	S • SE Asia • 200 kW
9390	**ISRAEL**	
	†KOL ISRAEL, Tel Aviv	S • W Europe & E North Am • DS-B • 300 kW; W • W Europe & E North Am • DS-B • 250 kW
		W Europe & E North Am • DS-B • 250/300 kW
9395	**GREECE**	
	†FONI TIS HELLADAS, Athens	W • Europe • 100 kW
	USA	
	†R FREE ASIA, Via CIS	Irr • S • S Asia • 200 kW
9395v	**PAKISTAN**	
	†RADIO PAKISTAN, Islamabad	W Asia • 100 kW
		E Europe & W Asia • 100 kW
9400	**BULGARIA**	
	†RADIO BULGARIA, Plovdiv	← • E North Am • 500 kW
		← • Europe • 500 kW
		W • Mideast • 500 kW
		S • Europe • 500 kW
	INDIA	
(con'd)	†TRANS WORLD R, Via Irkutsk, Russia	S • S Asia • 250 kW

World Time 0 1 2 3 4 5 6 7 8 9 10 11 12 13 14 15 16 17 18 19 20 21 22 23 24

ENGLISH ▬ ARABIC ▭ CHINESE ▫▫▫ FRENCH ═ GERMAN ▬ RUSSIAN ═ SPANISH ═ OTHER —

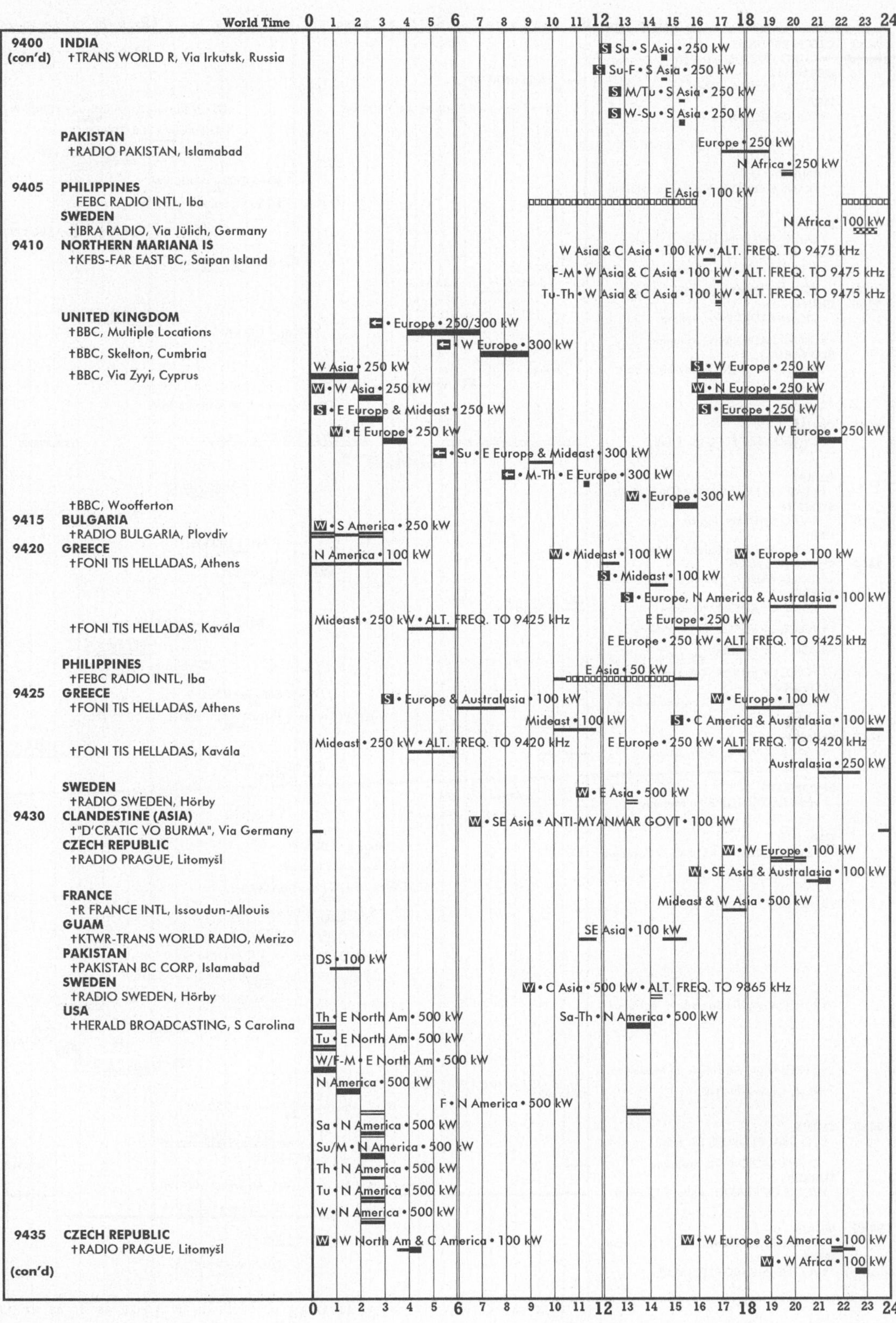
World Time 0 1 2 3 4 5 6 7 8 9 10 11 12 13 14 15 16 17 18 19 20 21 22 23 24
9400 INDIA
(con'd) †TRANS WORLD R, Via Irkutsk, Russia
S Sa • S Asia • 250 kW
S Su-F • S Asia • 250 kW
S M/Tu • S Asia • 250 kW
S W-Su • S Asia • 250 kW
PAKISTAN
†RADIO PAKISTAN, Islamabad
Europe • 250 kW
N Africa • 250 kW
9405 PHILIPPINES
FEBC RADIO INTL, Iba
E Asia • 100 kW
SWEDEN
†IBRA RADIO, Via Jülich, Germany
N Africa • 100 kW
9410 NORTHERN MARIANA IS
†KFBS-FAR EAST BC, Saipan Island
W Asia & C Asia • 100 kW • ALT. FREQ. TO 9475 kHz
F-M • W Asia & C Asia • 100 kW • ALT. FREQ. TO 9475 kHz
Tu-Th • W Asia & C Asia • 100 kW • ALT. FREQ. TO 9475 kHz
UNITED KINGDOM
†BBC, Multiple Locations
• Europe • 250/300 kW
†BBC, Skelton, Cumbria
• W Europe • 300 kW
†BBC, Via Zyyi, Cyprus
W Asia • 250 kW
S • W Europe • 250 kW
W • W Asia • 250 kW
W • N Europe • 250 kW
S • E Europe & Mideast • 250 kW
S • Europe • 250 kW
W • E Europe • 250 kW
W Europe • 250 kW
• Su • E Europe & Mideast • 300 kW
• M-Th • E Europe • 300 kW
W • Europe • 300 kW
†BBC, Woofferton
9415 BULGARIA
†RADIO BULGARIA, Plovdiv
W • S America • 250 kW
9420 GREECE
†FONI TIS HELLADAS, Athens
N America • 100 kW
W • Mideast • 100 kW
W • Europe • 100 kW
S • Mideast • 100 kW
S • Europe, N America & Australasia • 100 kW
Mideast • 250 kW • ALT. FREQ. TO 9425 kHz
†FONI TIS HELLADAS, Kavála
E Europe • 250 kW
E Europe • 250 kW • ALT. FREQ. TO 9425 kHz
PHILIPPINES
†FEBC RADIO INTL, Iba
E Asia • 50 kW
9425 GREECE
†FONI TIS HELLADAS, Athens
S • Europe & Australasia • 100 kW
W • Europe • 100 kW
Mideast • 100 kW
S • C America & Australasia • 100 kW
Mideast • 250 kW • ALT. FREQ. TO 9420 kHz
†FONI TIS HELLADAS, Kavála
E Europe • 250 kW • ALT. FREQ. TO 9420 kHz
Australasia • 250 kW
SWEDEN
†RADIO SWEDEN, Hörby
W • E Asia • 500 kW
9430 CLANDESTINE (ASIA)
†"D'CRATIC VO BURMA", Via Germany
W • SE Asia • ANTI-MYANMAR GOVT • 100 kW
CZECH REPUBLIC
†RADIO PRAGUE, Litomyšl
W • W Europe • 100 kW
W • SE Asia & Australasia • 100 kW
FRANCE
†R FRANCE INTL, Issoudun-Allouis
Mideast & W Asia • 500 kW
GUAM
†KTWR-TRANS WORLD RADIO, Merizo
SE Asia • 100 kW
PAKISTAN
†PAKISTAN BC CORP, Islamabad
DS • 100 kW
SWEDEN
†RADIO SWEDEN, Hörby
W • C Asia • 500 kW • ALT. FREQ. TO 9865 kHz
USA
†HERALD BROADCASTING, S Carolina
Th • E North Am • 500 kW
Sa-Th • N America • 500 kW
Tu • E North Am • 500 kW
W/F-M • E North Am • 500 kW
N America • 500 kW
F • N America • 500 kW
Sa • N America • 500 kW
Su/M • N America • 500 kW
Th • N America • 500 kW
Tu • N America • 500 kW
W • N America • 500 kW
9435 CZECH REPUBLIC
†RADIO PRAGUE, Litomyšl
W • W North Am & C America • 100 kW
W • W Europe & S America • 100 kW
W • W Africa • 100 kW
(con'd)
0 1 2 3 4 5 6 7 8 9 10 11 12 13 14 15 16 17 18 19 20 21 22 23 24

SEASONAL S OR W 1-HR TIMESHIFT MIDYEAR ⬅ OR ➡ JAMMING / OR ∧ EARLIEST HEARD ◃ LATEST HEARD ▹ NEW FOR 2002 †

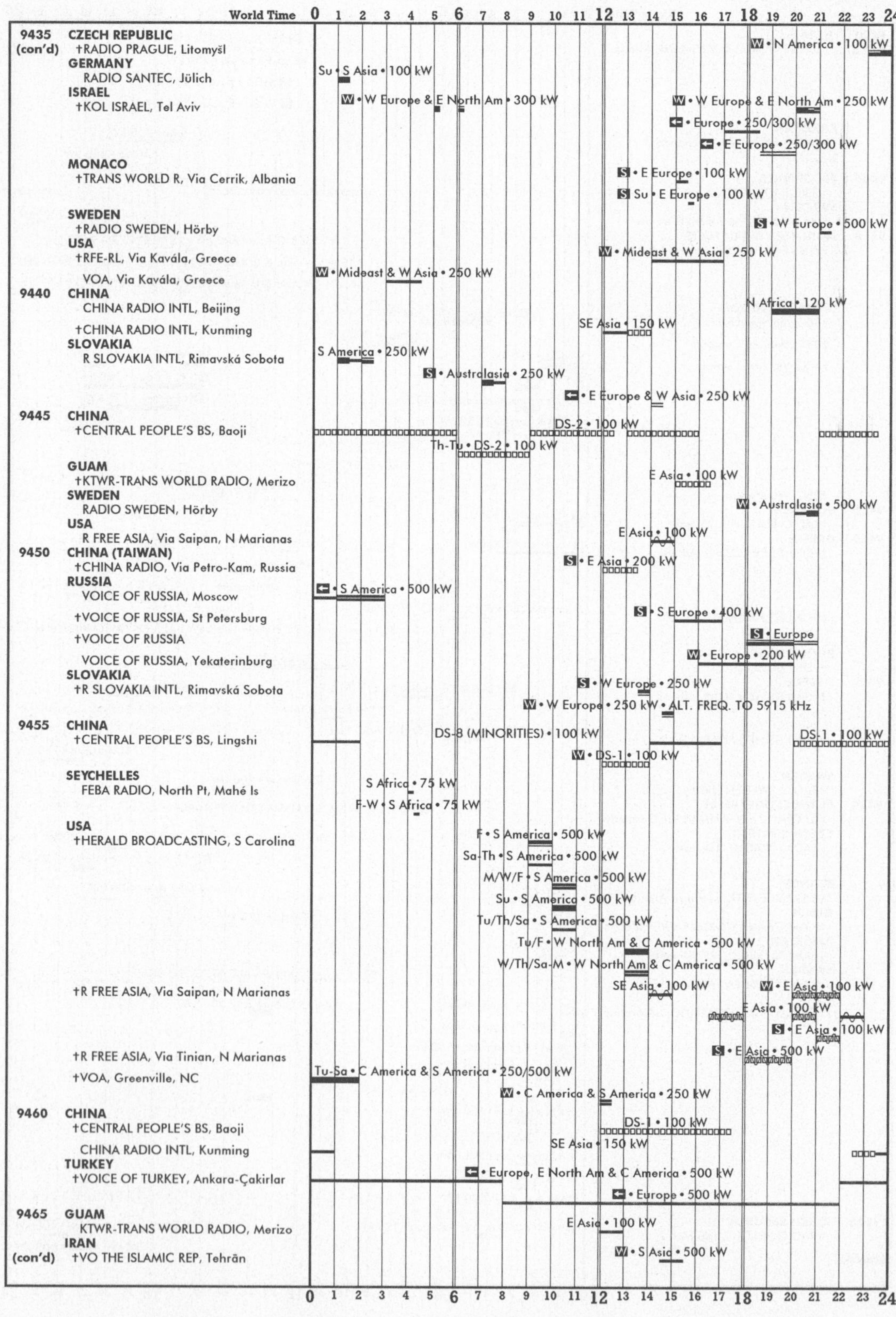
World Time 0 1 2 3 4 5 6 7 8 9 10 11 12 13 14 15 16 17 18 19 20 21 22 23 24
9435 CZECH REPUBLIC
(con'd) †RADIO PRAGUE, Litomyšl
W • N America • 100 kW
GERMANY
RADIO SANTEC, Jülich
Su • S Asia • 100 kW
ISRAEL
†KOL ISRAEL, Tel Aviv
W • W Europe & E North Am • 300 kW
W • W Europe & E North Am • 250 kW
• Europe • 250/300 kW
• E Europe • 250/300 kW
MONACO
†TRANS WORLD R, Via Cerrik, Albania
S • E Europe • 100 kW
S Su • E Europe • 100 kW
SWEDEN
†RADIO SWEDEN, Hörby
S • W Europe • 500 kW
USA
†RFE-RL, Via Kavála, Greece
W • Mideast & W Asia • 250 kW
VOA, Via Kavála, Greece
W • Mideast & W Asia • 250 kW
9440 CHINA
CHINA RADIO INTL, Beijing
N Africa • 120 kW
†CHINA RADIO INTL, Kunming
SE Asia • 150 kW
SLOVAKIA
R SLOVAKIA INTL, Rimavská Sobota
S America • 250 kW
S • Australasia • 250 kW
• E Europe & W Asia • 250 kW
9445 CHINA
†CENTRAL PEOPLE'S BS, Baoji
DS-2 • 100 kW
Th-Tu • DS-2 • 100 kW
GUAM
†KTWR-TRANS WORLD RADIO, Merizo
E Asia • 100 kW
SWEDEN
RADIO SWEDEN, Hörby
W • Australasia • 500 kW
USA
R FREE ASIA, Via Saipan, N Marianas
E Asia • 100 kW
9450 CHINA (TAIWAN)
†CHINA RADIO, Via Petro-Kam, Russia
S • E Asia • 200 kW
RUSSIA
VOICE OF RUSSIA, Moscow
• S America • 500 kW
†VOICE OF RUSSIA, St Petersburg
S • S Europe • 400 kW
†VOICE OF RUSSIA
S • Europe
VOICE OF RUSSIA, Yekaterinburg
W • Europe • 200 kW
SLOVAKIA
†R SLOVAKIA INTL, Rimavská Sobota
S • W Europe • 250 kW
W • W Europe • 250 kW • ALT. FREQ. TO 5915 kHz
9455 CHINA
†CENTRAL PEOPLE'S BS, Lingshi
DS-8 (MINORITIES) • 100 kW
DS-1 • 100 kW
W • DS-1 • 100 kW
SEYCHELLES
FEBA RADIO, North Pt, Mahé Is
S Africa • 75 kW
F-W • S Africa • 75 kW
USA
†HERALD BROADCASTING, S Carolina
F • S America • 500 kW
Sa-Th • S America • 500 kW
M/W/F • S America • 500 kW
Su • S America • 500 kW
Tu/Th/Sa • S America • 500 kW
Tu/F • W North Am & C America • 500 kW
W/Th/Sa-M • W North Am & C America • 500 kW
†R FREE ASIA, Via Saipan, N Marianas
SE Asia • 100 kW
W • E Asia • 100 kW
E Asia • 100 kW
S • E Asia • 100 kW
†R FREE ASIA, Via Tinian, N Marianas
S • E Asia • 500 kW
†VOA, Greenville, NC
Tu-Sa • C America & S America • 250/500 kW
W • C America & S America • 250 kW
9460 CHINA
†CENTRAL PEOPLE'S BS, Baoji
DS-1 • 100 kW
CHINA RADIO INTL, Kunming
SE Asia • 150 kW
TURKEY
†VOICE OF TURKEY, Ankara-Çakirlar
• Europe, E North Am & C America • 500 kW
• Europe • 500 kW
9465 GUAM
KTWR-TRANS WORLD RADIO, Merizo
E Asia • 100 kW
IRAN
(con'd) †VO THE ISLAMIC REP, Tehrān
W • S Asia • 500 kW
0 1 2 3 4 5 6 7 8 9 10 11 12 13 14 15 16 17 18 19 20 21 22 23 24

ENGLISH ARABIC CHINESE FRENCH GERMAN RUSSIAN SPANISH OTHER

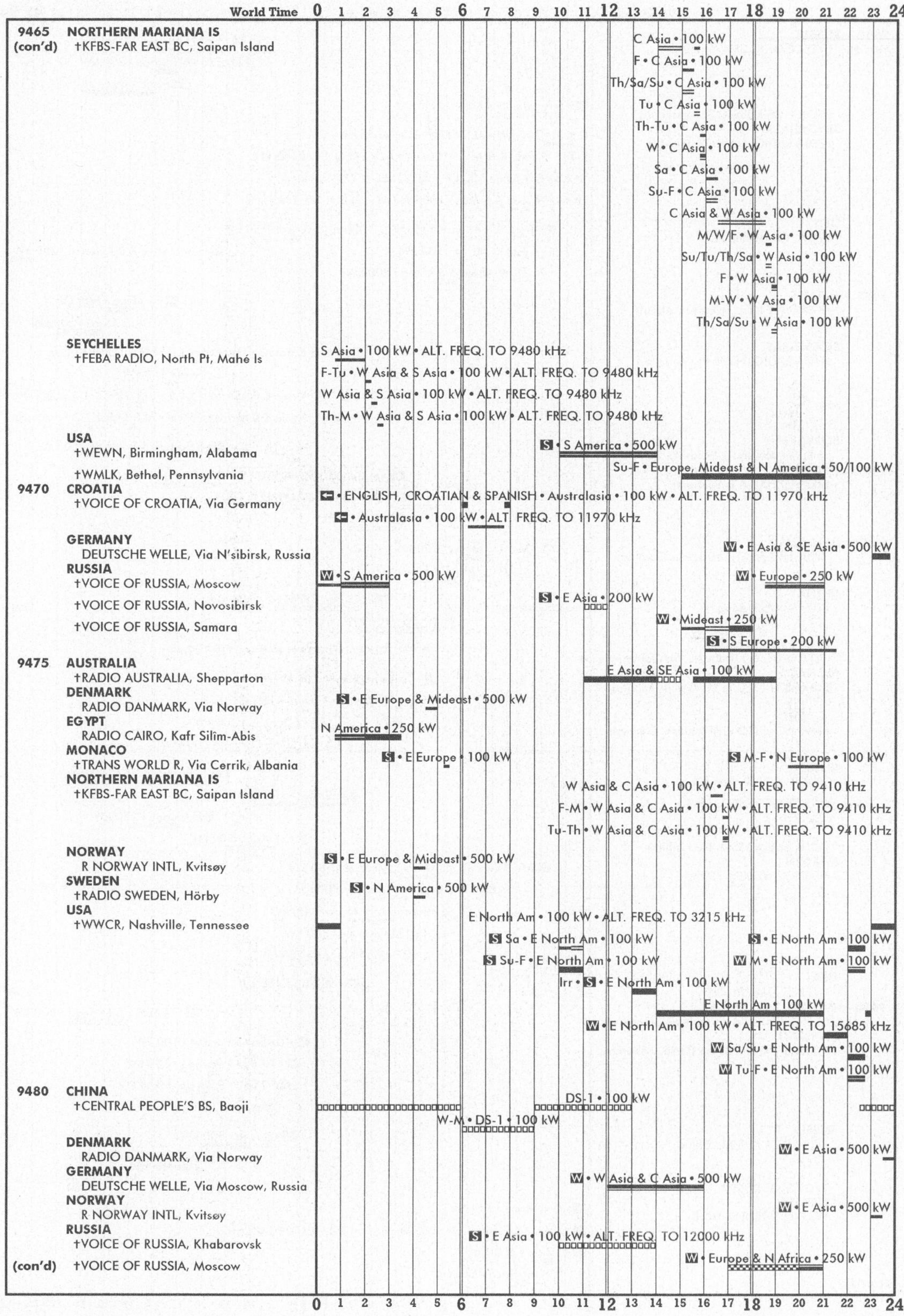
World Time 0 1 2 3 4 5 6 7 8 9 10 11 12 13 14 15 16 17 18 19 20 21 22 23 24
9465 (con'd) NORTHERN MARIANA IS
†KFBS-FAR EAST BC, Saipan Island
C Asia • 100 kW
F • C Asia • 100 kW
Th/Sa/Su • C Asia • 100 kW
Tu • C Asia • 100 kW
Th-Tu • C Asia • 100 kW
W • C Asia • 100 kW
Sa • C Asia • 100 kW
Su-F • C Asia • 100 kW
C Asia & W Asia • 100 kW
M/W/F • W Asia • 100 kW
Su/Tu/Th/Sa • W Asia • 100 kW
F • W Asia • 100 kW
M-W • W Asia • 100 kW
Th/Sa/Su • W Asia • 100 kW
SEYCHELLES
†FEBA RADIO, North Pt, Mahé Is
S Asia • 100 kW • ALT. FREQ. TO 9480 kHz
F-Tu • W Asia & S Asia • 100 kW • ALT. FREQ. TO 9480 kHz
W Asia & S Asia • 100 kW • ALT. FREQ. TO 9480 kHz
Th-M • W Asia & S Asia • 100 kW • ALT. FREQ. TO 9480 kHz
USA
†WEWN, Birmingham, Alabama
S • S America • 500 kW
†WMLK, Bethel, Pennsylvania
Su-F • Europe, Mideast & N America • 50/100 kW
9470 CROATIA
†VOICE OF CROATIA, Via Germany
• ENGLISH, CROATIAN & SPANISH • Australasia • 100 kW • ALT. FREQ. TO 11970 kHz
• Australasia • 100 kW • ALT. FREQ. TO 11970 kHz
GERMANY
DEUTSCHE WELLE, Via N'sibirsk, Russia
W • E Asia & SE Asia • 500 kW
RUSSIA
†VOICE OF RUSSIA, Moscow
W • S America • 500 kW
W • Europe • 250 kW
†VOICE OF RUSSIA, Novosibirsk
S • E Asia • 200 kW
†VOICE OF RUSSIA, Samara
W • Mideast • 250 kW
S • S Europe • 200 kW
9475 AUSTRALIA
†RADIO AUSTRALIA, Shepparton
E Asia & SE Asia • 100 kW
DENMARK
RADIO DANMARK, Via Norway
S • E Europe & Mideast • 500 kW
EGYPT
RADIO CAIRO, Kafr Silîm-Abis
N America • 250 kW
MONACO
†TRANS WORLD R, Via Cerrik, Albania
S • E Europe • 100 kW
S M-F • N Europe • 100 kW
NORTHERN MARIANA IS
†KFBS-FAR EAST BC, Saipan Island
W Asia & C Asia • 100 kW • ALT. FREQ. TO 9410 kHz
F-M • W Asia & C Asia • 100 kW • ALT. FREQ. TO 9410 kHz
Tu-Th • W Asia & C Asia • 100 kW • ALT. FREQ. TO 9410 kHz
NORWAY
R NORWAY INTL, Kvitsøy
S • E Europe & Mideast • 500 kW
SWEDEN
†RADIO SWEDEN, Hörby
S • N America • 500 kW
USA
†WWCR, Nashville, Tennessee
E North Am • 100 kW • ALT. FREQ. TO 3215 kHz
S Sa • E North Am • 100 kW
S • E North Am • 100 kW
S Su-F • E North Am • 100 kW
W M • E North Am • 100 kW
Irr • S • E North Am • 100 kW
E North Am • 100 kW
W • E North Am • 100 kW • ALT. FREQ. TO 15685 kHz
W Sa/Su • E North Am • 100 kW
W Tu-F • E North Am • 100 kW
9480 CHINA
†CENTRAL PEOPLE'S BS, Baoji
DS-1 • 100 kW
W-M • DS-1 • 100 kW
DENMARK
RADIO DANMARK, Via Norway
W • E Asia • 500 kW
GERMANY
DEUTSCHE WELLE, Via Moscow, Russia
W • W Asia & C Asia • 500 kW
NORWAY
R NORWAY INTL, Kvitsøy
W • E Asia • 500 kW
RUSSIA
†VOICE OF RUSSIA, Khabarovsk
S • E Asia • 100 kW • ALT. FREQ. TO 12000 kHz
(con'd) †VOICE OF RUSSIA, Moscow
W • Europe & N Africa • 250 kW
0 1 2 3 4 5 6 7 8 9 10 11 12 13 14 15 16 17 18 19 20 21 22 23 24

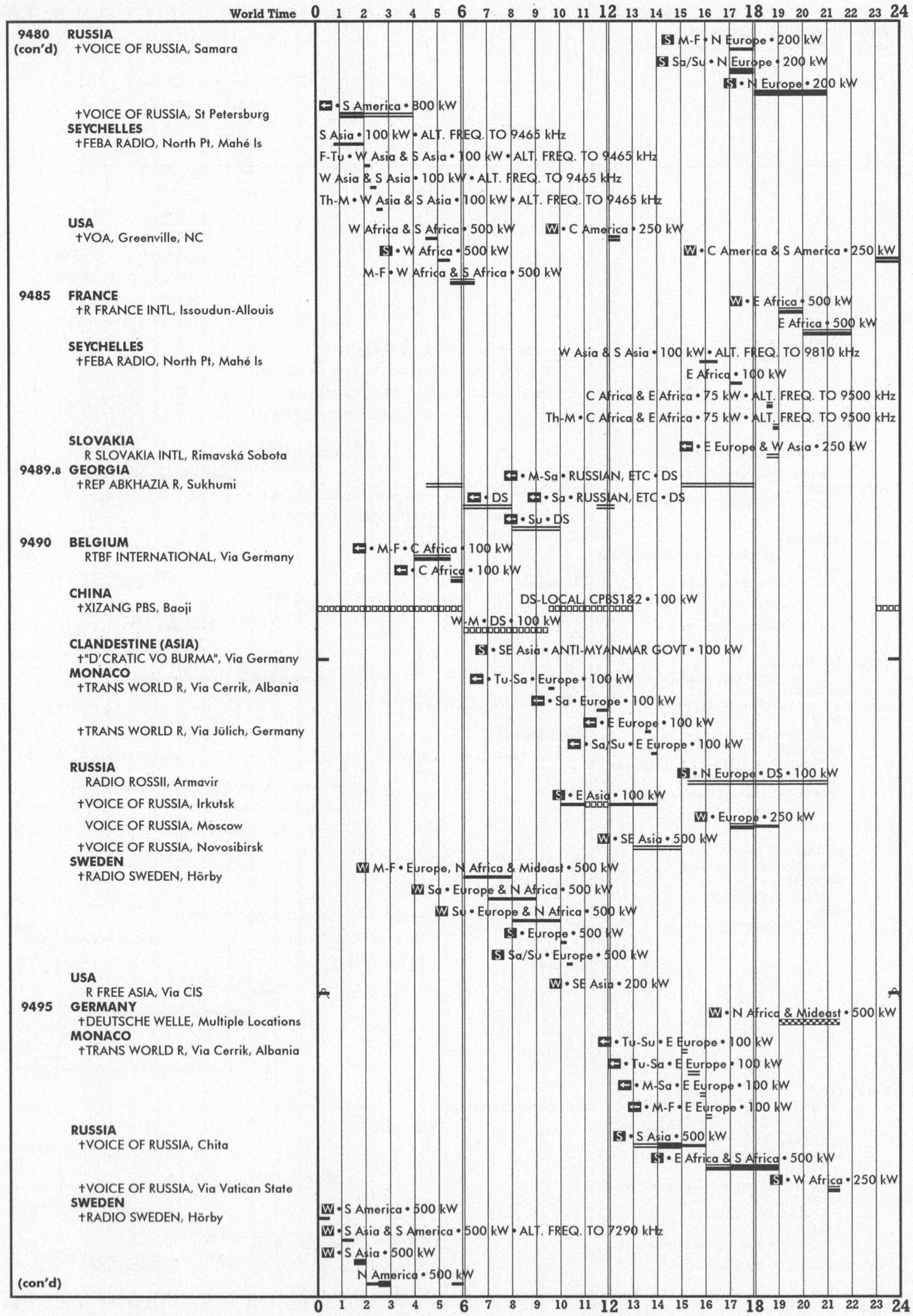
World Time 0 1 2 3 4 5 6 7 8 9 10 11 12 13 14 15 16 17 18 19 20 21 22 23 24
9480 (con'd) RUSSIA
†VOICE OF RUSSIA, Samara
S M-F • N Europe • 200 kW
S Sa/Su • N Europe • 200 kW
S • N Europe • 200 kW
†VOICE OF RUSSIA, St Petersburg
• S America • 800 kW
SEYCHELLES
†FEBA RADIO, North Pt, Mahé Is
S Asia • 100 kW • ALT. FREQ. TO 9465 kHz
F-Tu • W Asia & S Asia • 100 kW • ALT. FREQ. TO 9465 kHz
W Asia & S Asia • 100 kW • ALT. FREQ. TO 9465 kHz
Th-M • W Asia & S Asia • 100 kW • ALT. FREQ. TO 9465 kHz
USA
†VOA, Greenville, NC
W Africa & S Africa • 500 kW
W • C America • 250 kW
S • W Africa • 500 kW
W • C America & S America • 250 kW
M-F • W Africa & S Africa • 500 kW
9485 FRANCE
†R FRANCE INTL, Issoudun-Allouis
W • E Africa • 500 kW
E Africa • 500 kW
SEYCHELLES
†FEBA RADIO, North Pt, Mahé Is
W Asia & S Asia • 100 kW • ALT. FREQ. TO 9810 kHz
E Africa • 100 kW
C Africa & E Africa • 75 kW • ALT. FREQ. TO 9500 kHz
Th-M • C Africa & E Africa • 75 kW • ALT. FREQ. TO 9500 kHz
SLOVAKIA
R SLOVAKIA INTL, Rimavská Sobota
• E Europe & W Asia • 250 kW
9489.8 GEORGIA
†REP ABKHAZIA R, Sukhumi
• M-Sa • RUSSIAN, ETC • DS
• DS
• Sa • RUSSIAN, ETC • DS
• Su • DS
9490 BELGIUM
RTBF INTERNATIONAL, Via Germany
• M-F • C Africa • 100 kW
• C Africa • 100 kW
CHINA
†XIZANG PBS, Baoji
DS-LOCAL, CPBS1&2 • 100 kW
W-M • DS • 100 kW
CLANDESTINE (ASIA)
†"D'CRATIC VO BURMA", Via Germany
S • SE Asia • ANTI-MYANMAR GOVT • 100 kW
MONACO
†TRANS WORLD R, Via Cerrik, Albania
• Tu-Sa • Europe • 100 kW
• Sa • Europe • 100 kW
• E Europe • 100 kW
†TRANS WORLD R, Via Jülich, Germany
• Sa/Su • E Europe • 100 kW
RUSSIA
RADIO ROSSII, Armavir
S • N Europe • DS • 100 kW
†VOICE OF RUSSIA, Irkutsk
S • E Asia • 100 kW
VOICE OF RUSSIA, Moscow
W • Europe • 250 kW
†VOICE OF RUSSIA, Novosibirsk
W • SE Asia • 500 kW
SWEDEN
†RADIO SWEDEN, Hörby
W M-F • Europe, N Africa & Mideast • 500 kW
W Sa • Europe & N Africa • 500 kW
W Su • Europe & N Africa • 500 kW
S • Europe • 500 kW
S Sa/Su • Europe • 500 kW
USA
R FREE ASIA, Via CIS
W • SE Asia • 200 kW
9495 GERMANY
†DEUTSCHE WELLE, Multiple Locations
W • N Africa & Mideast • 500 kW
MONACO
†TRANS WORLD R, Via Cerrik, Albania
• Tu-Su • E Europe • 100 kW
• Tu-Sa • E Europe • 100 kW
• M-Sa • E Europe • 100 kW
• M-F • E Europe • 100 kW
RUSSIA
†VOICE OF RUSSIA, Chita
S • S Asia • 500 kW
S • E Africa & S Africa • 500 kW
†VOICE OF RUSSIA, Via Vatican State
S • W Africa • 250 kW
SWEDEN
†RADIO SWEDEN, Hörby
W • S America • 500 kW
W • S Asia & S America • 500 kW • ALT. FREQ. TO 7290 kHz
W • S Asia • 500 kW
N America • 500 kW
(con'd)
0 1 2 3 4 5 6 7 8 9 10 11 12 13 14 15 16 17 18 19 20 21 22 23 24

ENGLISH ▬ ARABIC ▭ CHINESE ▫▫▫ FRENCH ═ GERMAN ═ RUSSIAN ═ SPANISH ═ OTHER —

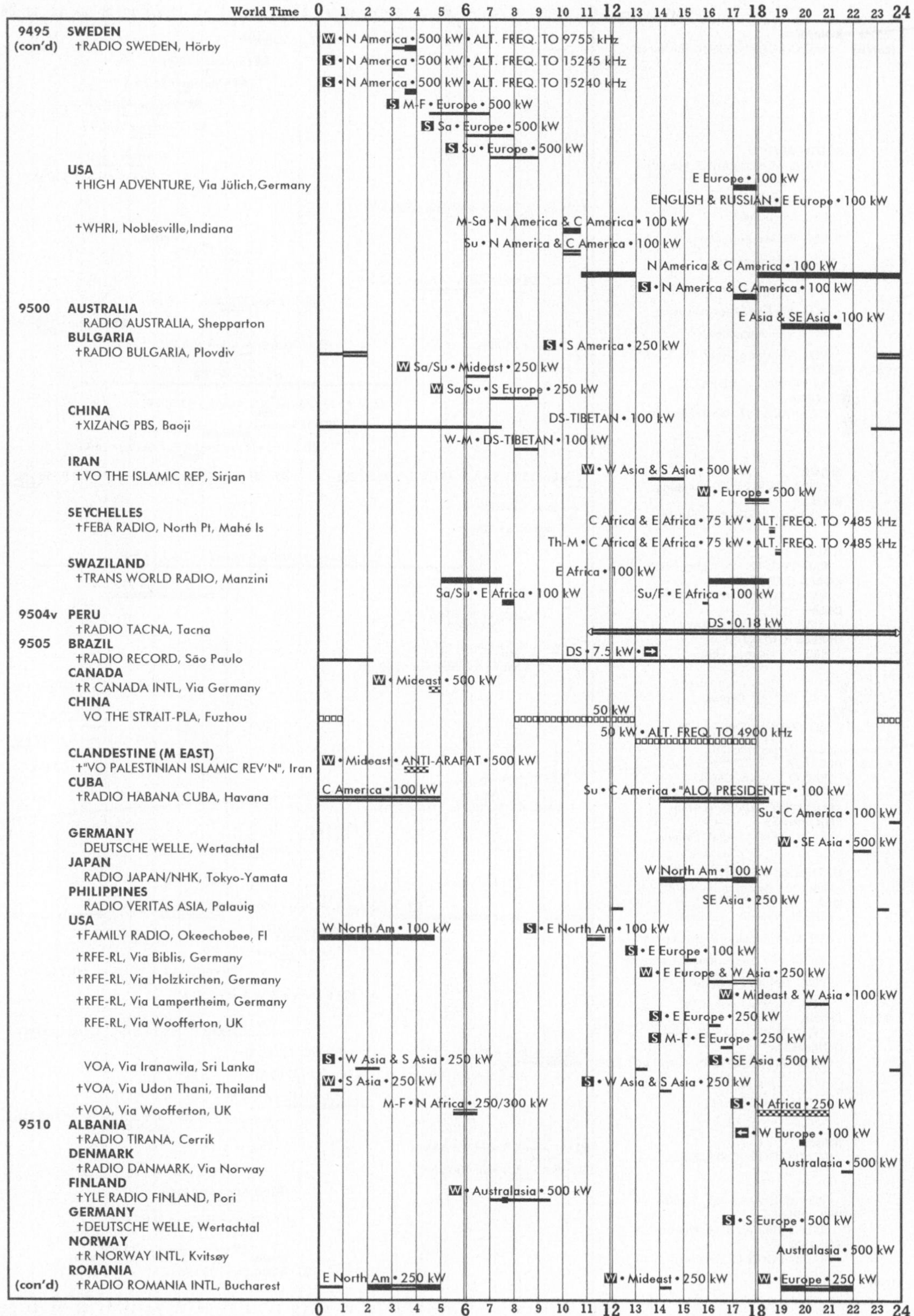
World Time 0 1 2 3 4 5 6 7 8 9 10 11 12 13 14 15 16 17 18 19 20 21 22 23 24
9495 (con'd) SWEDEN
†RADIO SWEDEN, Hörby
W • N America • 500 kW • ALT. FREQ. TO 9755 kHz
S • N America • 500 kW • ALT. FREQ. TO 15245 kHz
S • N America • 500 kW • ALT. FREQ. TO 15240 kHz
S M-F • Europe • 500 kW
S Sa • Europe • 500 kW
S Su • Europe • 500 kW
USA
†HIGH ADVENTURE, Via Jülich,Germany
E Europe • 100 kW
ENGLISH & RUSSIAN • E Europe • 100 kW
†WHRI, Noblesville,Indiana
M-Sa • N America & C America • 100 kW
Su • N America & C America • 100 kW
N America & C America • 100 kW
S • N America & C America • 100 kW
9500 AUSTRALIA
RADIO AUSTRALIA, Shepparton
E Asia & SE Asia • 100 kW
BULGARIA
†RADIO BULGARIA, Plovdiv
S • S America • 250 kW
W Sa/Su • Mideast • 250 kW
W Sa/Su • S Europe • 250 kW
CHINA
†XIZANG PBS, Baoji
DS-TIBETAN • 100 kW
W-M • DS-TIBETAN • 100 kW
IRAN
†VO THE ISLAMIC REP, Sirjan
W • W Asia & S Asia • 500 kW
W • Europe • 500 kW
SEYCHELLES
†FEBA RADIO, North Pt, Mahé Is
C Africa & E Africa • 75 kW • ALT. FREQ. TO 9485 kHz
Th-M • C Africa & E Africa • 75 kW • ALT. FREQ. TO 9485 kHz
SWAZILAND
†TRANS WORLD RADIO, Manzini
E Africa • 100 kW
Sa/Su • E Africa • 100 kW
Su/F • E Africa • 100 kW
9504v PERU
†RADIO TACNA, Tacna
DS • 0.18 kW
9505 BRAZIL
†RADIO RECORD, São Paulo
DS • 7.5 kW •
CANADA
†R CANADA INTL, Via Germany
W • Mideast • 500 kW
CHINA
VO THE STRAIT-PLA, Fuzhou
50 kW
50 kW • ALT. FREQ. TO 4900 kHz
CLANDESTINE (M EAST)
†"VO PALESTINIAN ISLAMIC REV'N", Iran
W • Mideast • ANTI-ARAFAT • 500 kW
CUBA
†RADIO HABANA CUBA, Havana
C America • 100 kW
Su • C America • "ALO, PRESIDENTE" • 100 kW
Su • C America • 100 kW
GERMANY
DEUTSCHE WELLE, Wertachtal
W • SE Asia • 500 kW
JAPAN
RADIO JAPAN/NHK, Tokyo-Yamata
W North Am • 100 kW
PHILIPPINES
RADIO VERITAS ASIA, Palauig
SE Asia • 250 kW
USA
†FAMILY RADIO, Okeechobee, Fl
W North Am • 100 kW
S • E North Am • 100 kW
†RFE-RL, Via Biblis, Germany
S • E Europe • 100 kW
†RFE-RL, Via Holzkirchen, Germany
W • E Europe & W Asia • 250 kW
†RFE-RL, Via Lampertheim, Germany
W • Mideast & W Asia • 100 kW
RFE-RL, Via Woofferton, UK
S • E Europe • 250 kW
S M-F • E Europe • 250 kW
VOA, Via Iranawila, Sri Lanka
S • W Asia & S Asia • 250 kW
S • SE Asia • 500 kW
†VOA, Via Udon Thani, Thailand
W • S Asia • 250 kW
S • W Asia & S Asia • 250 kW
†VOA, Via Woofferton, UK
M-F • N Africa • 250/300 kW
S • N Africa • 250 kW
9510 ALBANIA
†RADIO TIRANA, Cerrik
W Europe • 100 kW
DENMARK
†RADIO DANMARK, Via Norway
Australasia • 500 kW
FINLAND
†YLE RADIO FINLAND, Pori
W • Australasia • 500 kW
GERMANY
†DEUTSCHE WELLE, Wertachtal
S • S Europe • 500 kW
NORWAY
†R NORWAY INTL, Kvitsøy
Australasia • 500 kW
ROMANIA (con'd)
†RADIO ROMANIA INTL, Bucharest
E North Am • 250 kW
W • Mideast • 250 kW
W • Europe • 250 kW
0 1 2 3 4 5 6 7 8 9 10 11 12 13 14 15 16 17 18 19 20 21 22 23 24

SEASONAL S OR W 1-HR TIMESHIFT MIDYEAR ◄ OR ► JAMMING / OR ∧ EARLIEST HEARD ◁ LATEST HEARD ▷ NEW FOR 2002 †

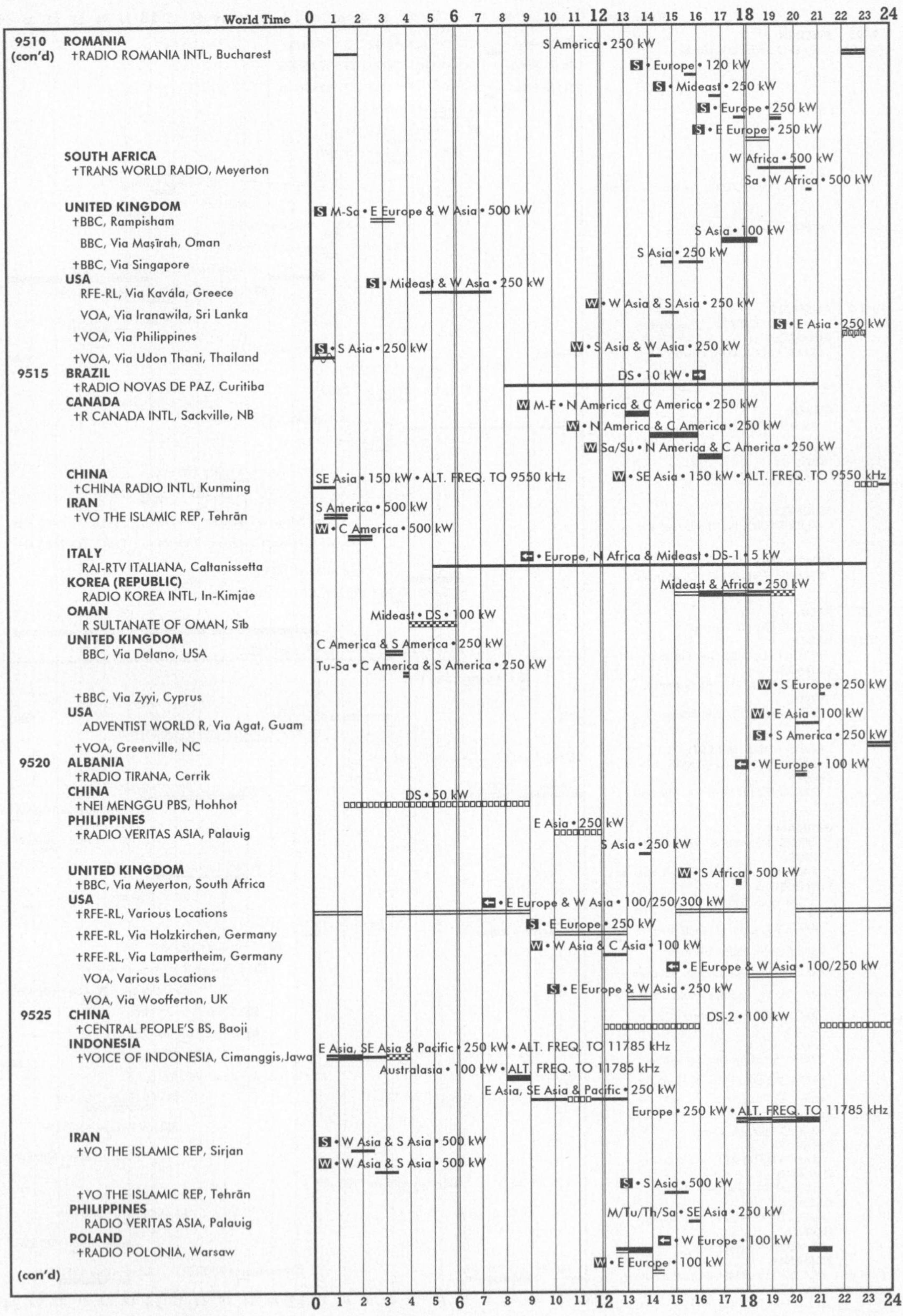
World Time 0 1 2 3 4 5 6 7 8 9 10 11 12 13 14 15 16 17 18 19 20 21 22 23 24
9510 (con'd) ROMANIA
†RADIO ROMANIA INTL, Bucharest
S America • 250 kW
S • Europe • 120 kW
S • Mideast • 250 kW
S • Europe • 250 kW
S • E Europe • 250 kW
SOUTH AFRICA
†TRANS WORLD RADIO, Meyerton
W Africa • 500 kW
Sa • W Africa • 500 kW
UNITED KINGDOM
†BBC, Rampisham
S M-Sa • E Europe & W Asia • 500 kW
BBC, Via Maṣīrah, Oman
S Asia • 100 kW
†BBC, Via Singapore
S Asia • 250 kW
USA
RFE-RL, Via Kavála, Greece
S • Mideast & W Asia • 250 kW
VOA, Via Iranawila, Sri Lanka
W • W Asia & S Asia • 250 kW
†VOA, Via Philippines
S • E Asia • 250 kW
†VOA, Via Udon Thani, Thailand
S • S Asia • 250 kW
W • S Asia & W Asia • 250 kW
9515 BRAZIL
†RADIO NOVAS DE PAZ, Curitiba
DS • 10 kW
CANADA
†R CANADA INTL, Sackville, NB
W M-F • N America & C America • 250 kW
W • N America & C America • 250 kW
W Sa/Su • N America & C America • 250 kW
CHINA
†CHINA RADIO INTL, Kunming
SE Asia • 150 kW • ALT. FREQ. TO 9550 kHz
W • SE Asia • 150 kW • ALT. FREQ. TO 9550 kHz
IRAN
†VO THE ISLAMIC REP, Tehrān
S America • 500 kW
W • C America • 500 kW
ITALY
RAI-RTV ITALIANA, Caltanissetta
Europe, N Africa & Mideast • DS-1 • 5 kW
KOREA (REPUBLIC)
RADIO KOREA INTL, In-Kimjae
Mideast & Africa • 250 kW
OMAN
R SULTANATE OF OMAN, Sīb
Mideast • DS • 100 kW
UNITED KINGDOM
BBC, Via Delano, USA
C America & S America • 250 kW
Tu-Sa • C America & S America • 250 kW
†BBC, Via Zyyi, Cyprus
W • S Europe • 250 kW
USA
ADVENTIST WORLD R, Via Agat, Guam
W • E Asia • 100 kW
†VOA, Greenville, NC
S • S America • 250 kW
9520 ALBANIA
†RADIO TIRANA, Cerrik
W Europe • 100 kW
CHINA
†NEI MENGGU PBS, Hohhot
DS • 50 kW
PHILIPPINES
†RADIO VERITAS ASIA, Palauig
E Asia • 250 kW
S Asia • 250 kW
UNITED KINGDOM
†BBC, Via Meyerton, South Africa
W • S Africa • 500 kW
USA
†RFE-RL, Various Locations
E Europe & W Asia • 100/250/300 kW
†RFE-RL, Via Holzkirchen, Germany
S • E Europe • 250 kW
†RFE-RL, Via Lampertheim, Germany
W • W Asia & C Asia • 100 kW
VOA, Various Locations
E Europe & W Asia • 100/250 kW
VOA, Via Woofferton, UK
S • E Europe & W Asia • 250 kW
9525 CHINA
†CENTRAL PEOPLE'S BS, Baoji
DS-2 • 100 kW
INDONESIA
†VOICE OF INDONESIA, Cimanggis, Jawa
E Asia, SE Asia & Pacific • 250 kW • ALT. FREQ. TO 11785 kHz
Australasia • 100 kW • ALT. FREQ. TO 11785 kHz
E Asia, SE Asia & Pacific • 250 kW
Europe • 250 kW • ALT. FREQ. TO 11785 kHz
IRAN
†VO THE ISLAMIC REP, Sirjan
S • W Asia & S Asia • 500 kW
W • W Asia & S Asia • 500 kW
†VO THE ISLAMIC REP, Tehrān
S • S Asia • 500 kW
PHILIPPINES
RADIO VERITAS ASIA, Palauig
M/Tu/Th/Sa • SE Asia • 250 kW
POLAND
†RADIO POLONIA, Warsaw
W Europe • 100 kW
W • E Europe • 100 kW
(con'd)
0 1 2 3 4 5 6 7 8 9 10 11 12 13 14 15 16 17 18 19 20 21 22 23 24
ENGLISH ARABIC CHINESE FRENCH GERMAN RUSSIAN SPANISH OTHER

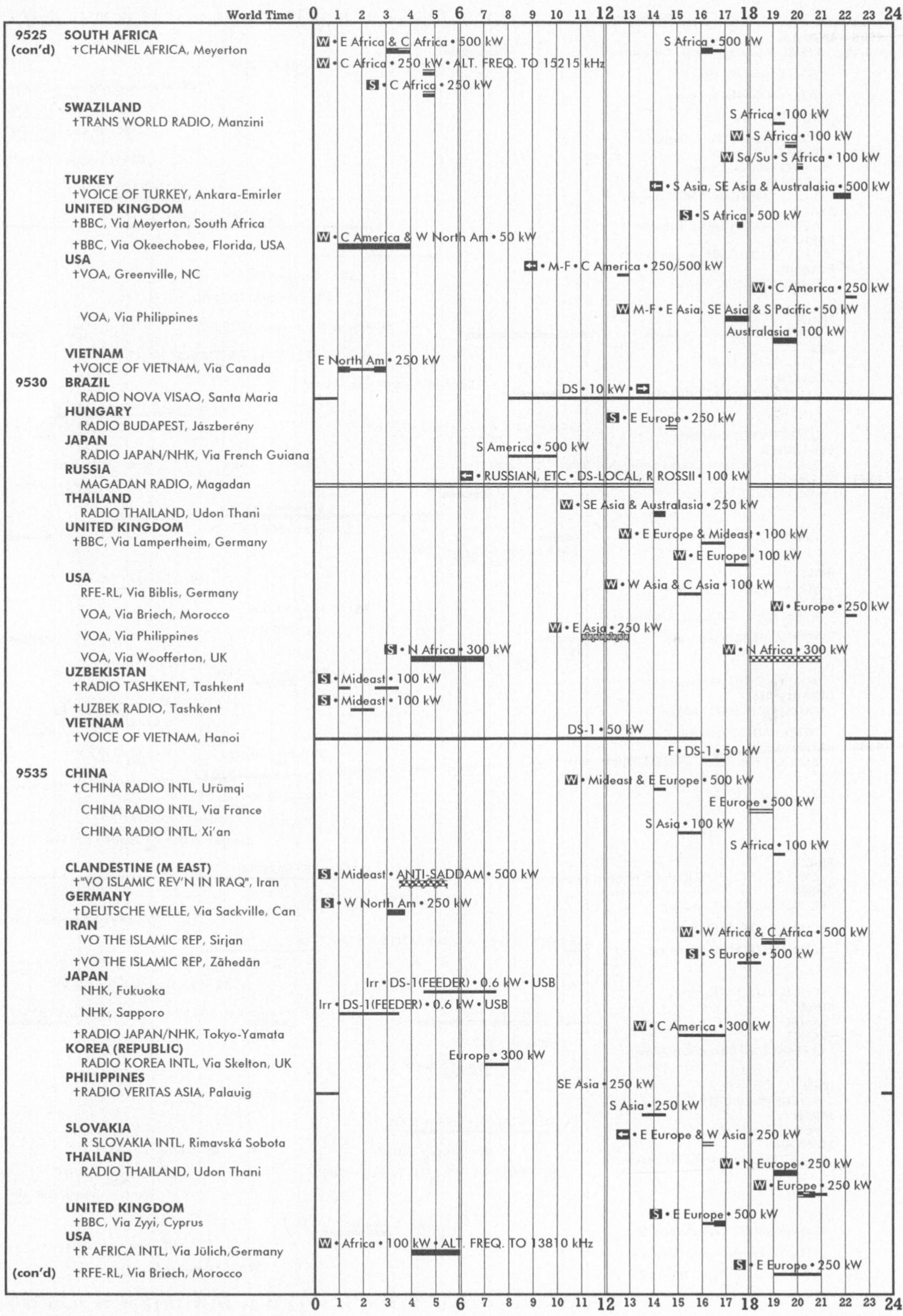
World Time 0 1 2 3 4 5 6 7 8 9 10 11 12 13 14 15 16 17 18 19 20 21 22 23 24
9525 (con'd) SOUTH AFRICA
†CHANNEL AFRICA, Meyerton
W • E Africa & C Africa • 500 kW
S Africa • 500 kW
W • C Africa • 250 kW • ALT. FREQ. TO 15215 kHz
S • C Africa • 250 kW
SWAZILAND
†TRANS WORLD RADIO, Manzini
S Africa • 100 kW
W • S Africa • 100 kW
W Sa/Su • S Africa • 100 kW
TURKEY
†VOICE OF TURKEY, Ankara-Emirler
• S Asia, SE Asia & Australasia • 500 kW
UNITED KINGDOM
†BBC, Via Meyerton, South Africa
S • S Africa • 500 kW
†BBC, Via Okeechobee, Florida, USA
W • C America & W North Am • 50 kW
USA
†VOA, Greenville, NC
• M-F • C America • 250/500 kW
W • C America • 250 kW
VOA, Via Philippines
W M-F • E Asia, SE Asia & S Pacific • 50 kW
Australasia • 100 kW
VIETNAM
†VOICE OF VIETNAM, Via Canada
E North Am • 250 kW
9530 BRAZIL
RADIO NOVA VISAO, Santa Maria
DS • 10 kW •
HUNGARY
RADIO BUDAPEST, Jászberény
S • E Europe • 250 kW
JAPAN
RADIO JAPAN/NHK, Via French Guiana
S America • 500 kW
RUSSIA
MAGADAN RADIO, Magadan
• RUSSIAN, ETC • DS-LOCAL, R ROSSII • 100 kW
THAILAND
RADIO THAILAND, Udon Thani
W • SE Asia & Australasia • 250 kW
UNITED KINGDOM
†BBC, Via Lampertheim, Germany
W • E Europe & Mideast • 100 kW
W • E Europe • 100 kW
USA
RFE-RL, Via Biblis, Germany
W • W Asia & C Asia • 100 kW
VOA, Via Briech, Morocco
W • Europe • 250 kW
VOA, Via Philippines
W • E Asia • 250 kW
VOA, Via Woofferton, UK
S • N Africa • 300 kW
W • N Africa • 300 kW
UZBEKISTAN
†RADIO TASHKENT, Tashkent
S • Mideast • 100 kW
†UZBEK RADIO, Tashkent
S • Mideast • 100 kW
VIETNAM
†VOICE OF VIETNAM, Hanoi
DS-1 • 50 kW
F • DS-1 • 50 kW
9535 CHINA
†CHINA RADIO INTL, Urümqi
W • Mideast & E Europe • 500 kW
CHINA RADIO INTL, Via France
E Europe • 500 kW
CHINA RADIO INTL, Xi'an
S Asia • 100 kW
S Africa • 100 kW
CLANDESTINE (M EAST)
†"VO ISLAMIC REV'N IN IRAQ", Iran
S • Mideast • ANTI-SADDAM • 500 kW
GERMANY
†DEUTSCHE WELLE, Via Sackville, Can
S • W North Am • 250 kW
IRAN
VO THE ISLAMIC REP, Sirjan
W • W Africa & C Africa • 500 kW
†VO THE ISLAMIC REP, Zāhedān
S • S Europe • 500 kW
JAPAN
NHK, Fukuoka
Irr • DS-1(FEEDER) • 0.6 kW • USB
NHK, Sapporo
Irr • DS-1(FEEDER) • 0.6 kW • USB
†RADIO JAPAN/NHK, Tokyo-Yamata
W • C America • 300 kW
KOREA (REPUBLIC)
RADIO KOREA INTL, Via Skelton, UK
Europe • 300 kW
PHILIPPINES
†RADIO VERITAS ASIA, Palauig
SE Asia • 250 kW
S Asia • 250 kW
SLOVAKIA
R SLOVAKIA INTL, Rimavská Sobota
• E Europe & W Asia • 250 kW
THAILAND
RADIO THAILAND, Udon Thani
W • N Europe • 250 kW
W • Europe • 250 kW
UNITED KINGDOM
†BBC, Via Zyyi, Cyprus
S • E Europe • 500 kW
USA
†R AFRICA INTL, Via Jülich, Germany
W • Africa • 100 kW • ALT. FREQ. TO 13810 kHz
(con'd) †RFE-RL, Via Briech, Morocco
S • E Europe • 250 kW
0 1 2 3 4 5 6 7 8 9 10 11 12 13 14 15 16 17 18 19 20 21 22 23 24

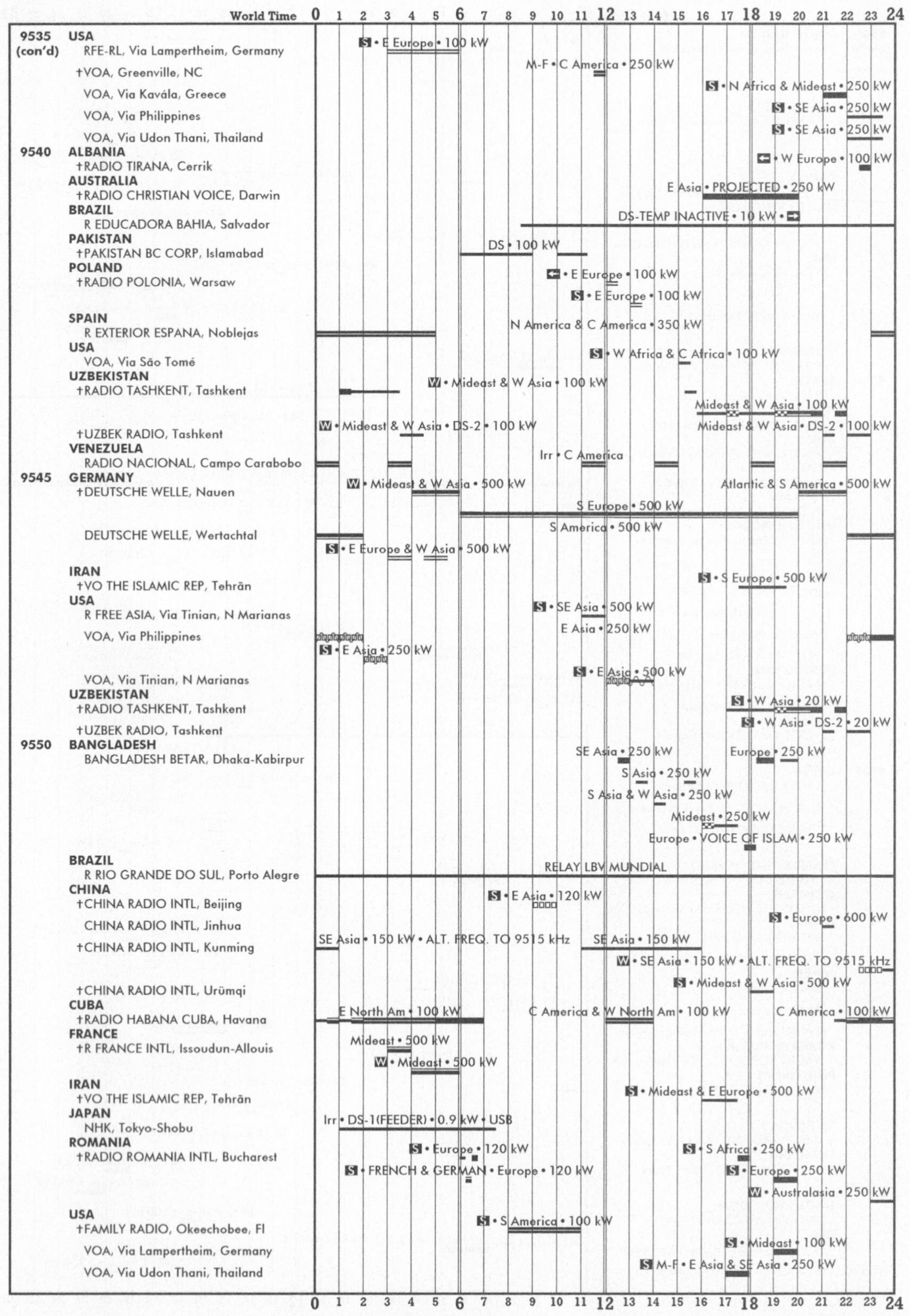
World Time 0 1 2 3 4 5 6 7 8 9 10 11 12 13 14 15 16 17 18 19 20 21 22 23 24
9535 (con'd) USA
RFE-RL, Via Lampertheim, Germany
S • E Europe • 100 kW
†VOA, Greenville, NC
M-F • C America • 250 kW
VOA, Via Kavála, Greece
S • N Africa & Mideast • 250 kW
VOA, Via Philippines
S • SE Asia • 250 kW
VOA, Via Udon Thani, Thailand
S • SE Asia • 250 kW
9540 ALBANIA
†RADIO TIRANA, Cerrik
W Europe • 100 kW
AUSTRALIA
†RADIO CHRISTIAN VOICE, Darwin
E Asia • PROJECTED • 250 kW
BRAZIL
R EDUCADORA BAHIA, Salvador
DS-TEMP INACTIVE • 10 kW
PAKISTAN
†PAKISTAN BC CORP, Islamabad
DS • 100 kW
POLAND
†RADIO POLONIA, Warsaw
E Europe • 100 kW
S • E Europe • 100 kW
SPAIN
R EXTERIOR ESPANA, Noblejas
N America & C America • 350 kW
USA
VOA, Via São Tomé
S • W Africa & C Africa • 100 kW
UZBEKISTAN
†RADIO TASHKENT, Tashkent
W • Mideast & W Asia • 100 kW
Mideast & W Asia • 100 kW
†UZBEK RADIO, Tashkent
W • Mideast & W Asia • DS-2 • 100 kW
Mideast & W Asia • DS-2 • 100 kW
VENEZUELA
RADIO NACIONAL, Campo Carabobo
Irr • C America
9545 GERMANY
†DEUTSCHE WELLE, Nauen
W • Mideast & W Asia • 500 kW
Atlantic & S America • 500 kW
S Europe • 500 kW
DEUTSCHE WELLE, Wertachtal
S America • 500 kW
S • E Europe & W Asia • 500 kW
IRAN
†VO THE ISLAMIC REP, Tehrān
S • S Europe • 500 kW
USA
R FREE ASIA, Via Tinian, N Marianas
S • SE Asia • 500 kW
VOA, Via Philippines
E Asia • 250 kW
S • E Asia • 250 kW
VOA, Via Tinian, N Marianas
S • E Asia • 500 kW
UZBEKISTAN
†RADIO TASHKENT, Tashkent
S • W Asia • 20 kW
†UZBEK RADIO, Tashkent
S • W Asia • DS-2 • 20 kW
9550 BANGLADESH
BANGLADESH BETAR, Dhaka-Kabirpur
SE Asia • 250 kW
Europe • 250 kW
S Asia • 250 kW
S Asia & W Asia • 250 kW
Mideast • 250 kW
Europe • VOICE OF ISLAM • 250 kW
BRAZIL
R RIO GRANDE DO SUL, Porto Alegre
RELAY LBV MUNDIAL
CHINA
†CHINA RADIO INTL, Beijing
S • E Asia • 120 kW
CHINA RADIO INTL, Jinhua
S • Europe • 600 kW
†CHINA RADIO INTL, Kunming
SE Asia • 150 kW • ALT. FREQ. TO 9515 kHz
SE Asia • 150 kW
W • SE Asia • 150 kW • ALT. FREQ. TO 9515 kHz
†CHINA RADIO INTL, Urümqi
S • Mideast & W Asia • 500 kW
CUBA
†RADIO HABANA CUBA, Havana
E North Am • 100 kW
C America & W North Am • 100 kW
C America • 100 kW
FRANCE
†R FRANCE INTL, Issoudun-Allouis
Mideast • 500 kW
W • Mideast • 500 kW
IRAN
†VO THE ISLAMIC REP, Tehrān
S • Mideast & E Europe • 500 kW
JAPAN
NHK, Tokyo-Shobu
Irr • DS-1(FEEDER) • 0.9 kW • USB
ROMANIA
†RADIO ROMANIA INTL, Bucharest
S • Europe • 120 kW
S • S Africa • 250 kW
S • FRENCH & GERMAN • Europe • 120 kW
S • Europe • 250 kW
W • Australasia • 250 kW
USA
†FAMILY RADIO, Okeechobee, Fl
S • S America • 100 kW
VOA, Via Lampertheim, Germany
S • Mideast • 100 kW
VOA, Via Udon Thani, Thailand
S M-F • E Asia & SE Asia • 250 kW
0 1 2 3 4 5 6 7 8 9 10 11 12 13 14 15 16 17 18 19 20 21 22 23 24

ENGLISH ▬ ARABIC ▭ CHINESE ▭ FRENCH ▬ GERMAN ▬ RUSSIAN ═ SPANISH ═ OTHER —

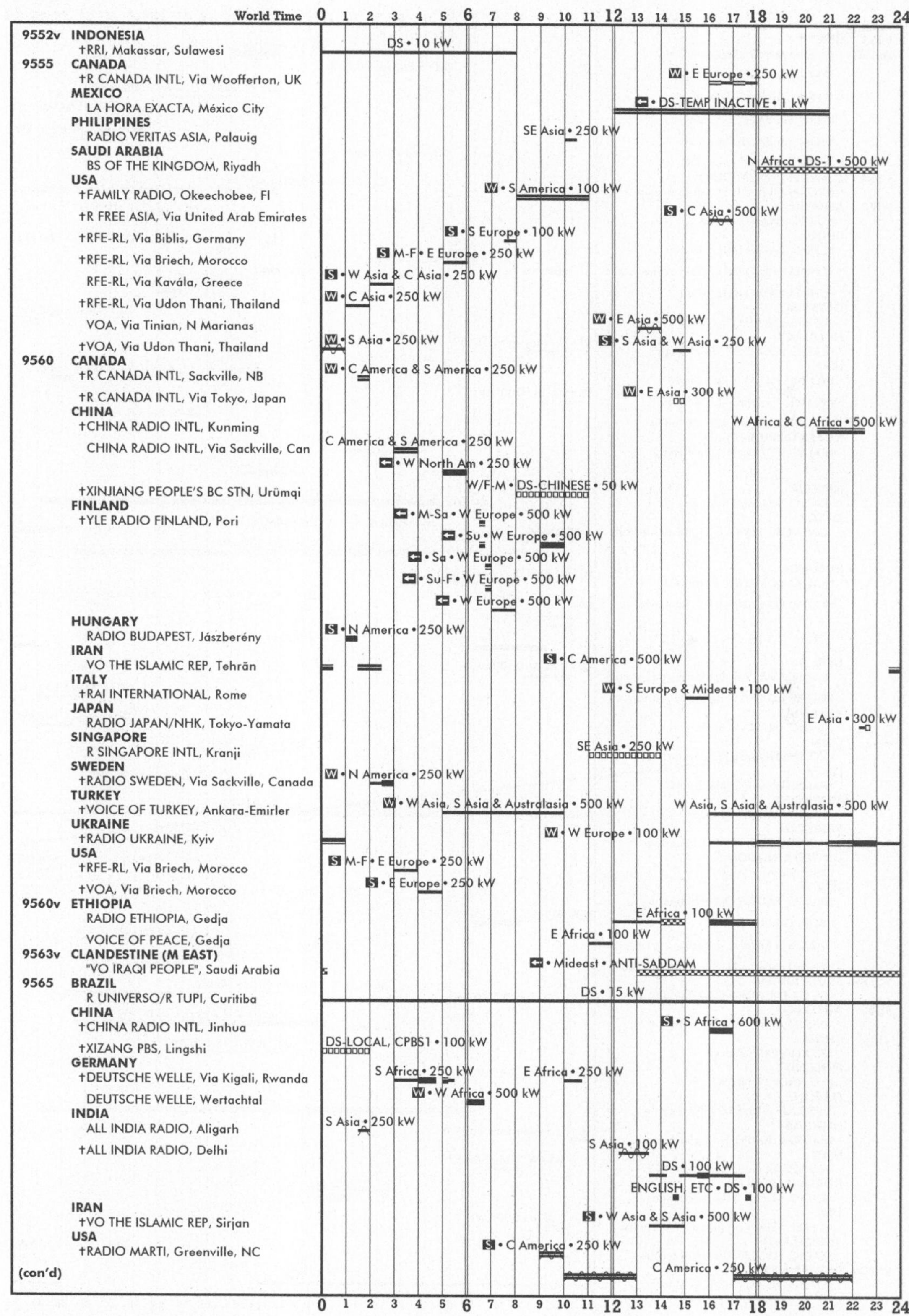
World Time 0 1 2 3 4 5 6 7 8 9 10 11 12 13 14 15 16 17 18 19 20 21 22 23 24
9552v INDONESIA
†RRI, Makassar, Sulawesi
DS • 10 kW
9555 CANADA
†R CANADA INTL, Via Woofferton, UK
W • E Europe • 250 kW
MEXICO
LA HORA EXACTA, México City
DS-TEMP INACTIVE • 1 kW
PHILIPPINES
RADIO VERITAS ASIA, Palauig
SE Asia • 250 kW
SAUDI ARABIA
BS OF THE KINGDOM, Riyadh
N Africa • DS-1 • 500 kW
USA
†FAMILY RADIO, Okeechobee, Fl
W • S America • 100 kW
†R FREE ASIA, Via United Arab Emirates
S • C Asia • 500 kW
†RFE-RL, Via Biblis, Germany
S • S Europe • 100 kW
†RFE-RL, Via Briech, Morocco
S M-F • E Europe • 250 kW
RFE-RL, Via Kavála, Greece
S • W Asia & C Asia • 250 kW
†RFE-RL, Via Udon Thani, Thailand
W • C Asia • 250 kW
VOA, Via Tinian, N Marianas
W • E Asia • 500 kW
†VOA, Via Udon Thani, Thailand
W • S Asia • 250 kW
S • S Asia & W Asia • 250 kW
9560 CANADA
†R CANADA INTL, Sackville, NB
W • C America & S America • 250 kW
†R CANADA INTL, Via Tokyo, Japan
W • E Asia • 300 kW
CHINA
†CHINA RADIO INTL, Kunming
W Africa & C Africa • 500 kW
CHINA RADIO INTL, Via Sackville, Can
C America & S America • 250 kW
• W North Am • 250 kW
†XINJIANG PEOPLE'S BC STN, Urümqi
W/F-M • DS-CHINESE • 50 kW
FINLAND
†YLE RADIO FINLAND, Pori
• M-Sa • W Europe • 500 kW
• Su • W Europe • 500 kW
• Sa • W Europe • 500 kW
• Su-F • W Europe • 500 kW
• W Europe • 500 kW
HUNGARY
RADIO BUDAPEST, Jászberény
S • N America • 250 kW
IRAN
VO THE ISLAMIC REP, Tehrãn
S • C America • 500 kW
ITALY
†RAI INTERNATIONAL, Rome
W • S Europe & Mideast • 100 kW
JAPAN
RADIO JAPAN/NHK, Tokyo-Yamata
E Asia • 300 kW
SINGAPORE
R SINGAPORE INTL, Kranji
SE Asia • 250 kW
SWEDEN
†RADIO SWEDEN, Via Sackville, Canada
W • N America • 250 kW
TURKEY
†VOICE OF TURKEY, Ankara-Emirler
W • W Asia, S Asia & Australasia • 500 kW
W Asia, S Asia & Australasia • 500 kW
UKRAINE
†RADIO UKRAINE, Kyiv
W • W Europe • 100 kW
USA
†RFE-RL, Via Briech, Morocco
S M-F • E Europe • 250 kW
†VOA, Via Briech, Morocco
S • E Europe • 250 kW
9560v ETHIOPIA
RADIO ETHIOPIA, Gedja
E Africa • 100 kW
VOICE OF PEACE, Gedja
E Africa • 100 kW
9563v CLANDESTINE (M EAST)
"VO IRAQI PEOPLE", Saudi Arabia
• Mideast • ANTI-SADDAM
9565 BRAZIL
R UNIVERSO/R TUPI, Curitiba
DS • 15 kW
CHINA
†CHINA RADIO INTL, Jinhua
S • S Africa • 600 kW
†XIZANG PBS, Lingshi
DS-LOCAL, CPBS1 • 100 kW
GERMANY
†DEUTSCHE WELLE, Via Kigali, Rwanda
S Africa • 250 kW
E Africa • 250 kW
DEUTSCHE WELLE, Wertachtal
W • W Africa • 500 kW
INDIA
ALL INDIA RADIO, Aligarh
S Asia • 250 kW
†ALL INDIA RADIO, Delhi
S Asia • 100 kW
DS • 100 kW
ENGLISH, ETC • DS • 100 kW
IRAN
†VO THE ISLAMIC REP, Sirjan
S • W Asia & S Asia • 500 kW
USA
†RADIO MARTI, Greenville, NC
S • C America • 250 kW
C America • 250 kW
(con'd)
0 1 2 3 4 5 6 7 8 9 10 11 12 13 14 15 16 17 18 19 20 21 22 23 24

SEASONAL S OR W 1-HR TIMESHIFT MIDYEAR ⬅ OR ➡ JAMMING / OR /\ EARLIEST HEARD ◁ LATEST HEARD ▷ NEW FOR 2002 †

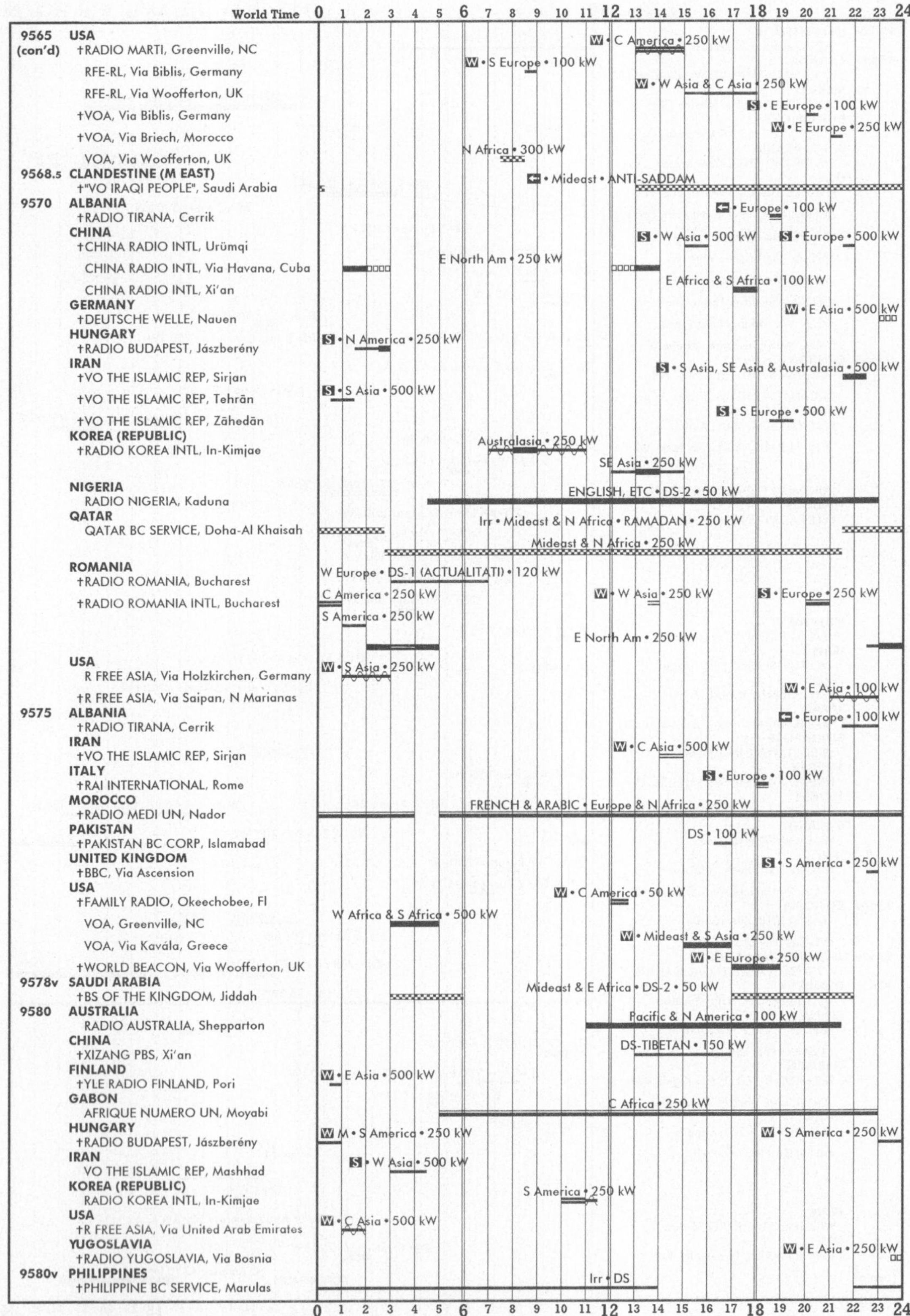
World Time 0 1 2 3 4 5 6 7 8 9 10 11 12 13 14 15 16 17 18 19 20 21 22 23 24
9565 (con'd) USA
†RADIO MARTI, Greenville, NC
W • C America • 250 kW
RFE-RL, Via Biblis, Germany
W • S Europe • 100 kW
RFE-RL, Via Woofferton, UK
W • W Asia & C Asia • 250 kW
†VOA, Via Biblis, Germany
S • E Europe • 100 kW
†VOA, Via Briech, Morocco
W • E Europe • 250 kW
VOA, Via Woofferton, UK
N Africa • 300 kW
9568.5 CLANDESTINE (M EAST)
†"VO IRAQI PEOPLE", Saudi Arabia
• Mideast • ANTI-SADDAM
9570 ALBANIA
†RADIO TIRANA, Cerrik
• Europe • 100 kW
CHINA
†CHINA RADIO INTL, Ürümqi
S • W Asia • 500 kW
S • Europe • 500 kW
CHINA RADIO INTL, Via Havana, Cuba
E North Am • 250 kW
CHINA RADIO INTL, Xi'an
E Africa & S Africa • 100 kW
GERMANY
†DEUTSCHE WELLE, Nauen
W • E Asia • 500 kW
HUNGARY
†RADIO BUDAPEST, Jászberény
S • N America • 250 kW
IRAN
†VO THE ISLAMIC REP, Sirjan
S • S Asia, SE Asia & Australasia • 500 kW
†VO THE ISLAMIC REP, Tehrān
S • S Asia • 500 kW
†VO THE ISLAMIC REP, Zāhedān
S • S Europe • 500 kW
KOREA (REPUBLIC)
†RADIO KOREA INTL, In-Kimjae
Australasia • 250 kW
SE Asia • 250 kW
NIGERIA
RADIO NIGERIA, Kaduna
ENGLISH, ETC • DS-2 • 50 kW
QATAR
QATAR BC SERVICE, Doha-Al Khaisah
Irr • Mideast & N Africa • RAMADAN • 250 kW
Mideast & N Africa • 250 kW
ROMANIA
†RADIO ROMANIA, Bucharest
W Europe • DS-1 (ACTUALITATI) • 120 kW
†RADIO ROMANIA INTL, Bucharest
C America • 250 kW
W • W Asia • 250 kW
S • Europe • 250 kW
S America • 250 kW
E North Am • 250 kW
USA
R FREE ASIA, Via Holzkirchen, Germany
W • S Asia • 250 kW
†R FREE ASIA, Via Saipan, N Marianas
W • E Asia • 100 kW
9575 ALBANIA
†RADIO TIRANA, Cerrik
• Europe • 100 kW
IRAN
†VO THE ISLAMIC REP, Sirjan
W • C Asia • 500 kW
ITALY
†RAI INTERNATIONAL, Rome
S • Europe • 100 kW
MOROCCO
†RADIO MEDI UN, Nador
FRENCH & ARABIC • Europe & N Africa • 250 kW
PAKISTAN
†PAKISTAN BC CORP, Islamabad
DS • 100 kW
UNITED KINGDOM
†BBC, Via Ascension
S • S America • 250 kW
USA
†FAMILY RADIO, Okeechobee, Fl
W • C America • 50 kW
VOA, Greenville, NC
W Africa & S Africa • 500 kW
VOA, Kavála, Greece
W • Mideast & S Asia • 250 kW
†WORLD BEACON, Via Woofferton, UK
W • E Europe • 250 kW
9578v SAUDI ARABIA
†BS OF THE KINGDOM, Jiddah
Mideast & E Africa • DS-2 • 50 kW
9580 AUSTRALIA
RADIO AUSTRALIA, Shepparton
Pacific & N America • 100 kW
CHINA
†XIZANG PBS, Xi'an
DS-TIBETAN • 150 kW
FINLAND
†YLE RADIO FINLAND, Pori
W • E Asia • 500 kW
GABON
AFRIQUE NUMERO UN, Moyabi
C Africa • 250 kW
HUNGARY
†RADIO BUDAPEST, Jászberény
W M • S America • 250 kW
W • S America • 250 kW
IRAN
VO THE ISLAMIC REP, Mashhad
S • W Asia • 500 kW
KOREA (REPUBLIC)
RADIO KOREA INTL, In-Kimjae
S America • 250 kW
USA
†R FREE ASIA, Via United Arab Emirates
W • C Asia • 500 kW
YUGOSLAVIA
†RADIO YUGOSLAVIA, Via Bosnia
W • E Asia • 250 kW
9580v PHILIPPINES
†PHILIPPINE BC SERVICE, Marulas
Irr • DS
0 1 2 3 4 5 6 7 8 9 10 11 12 13 14 15 16 17 18 19 20 21 22 23 24
ENGLISH ARABIC CHINESE FRENCH GERMAN RUSSIAN SPANISH OTHER

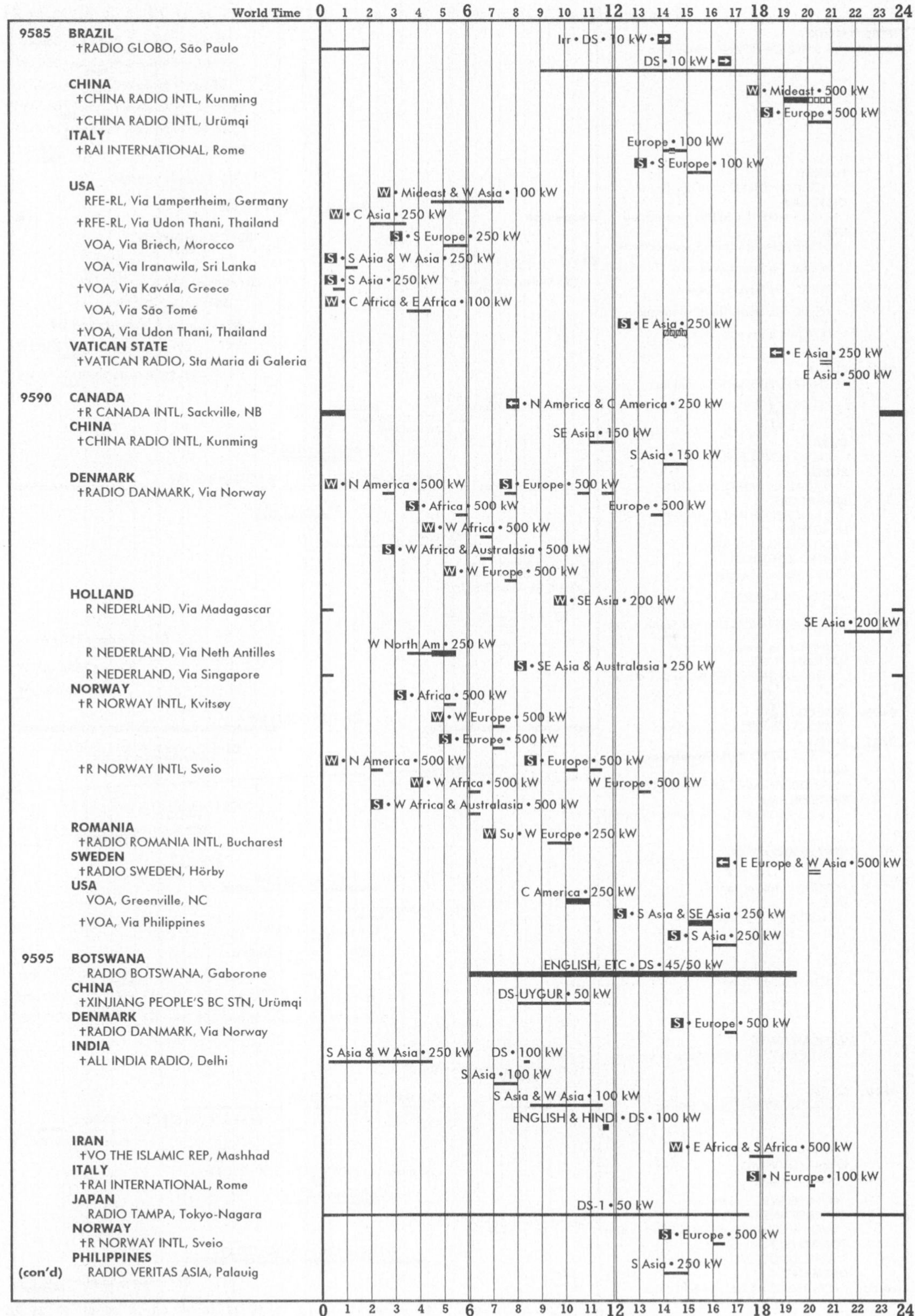
World Time 0 1 2 3 4 5 6 7 8 9 10 11 12 13 14 15 16 17 18 19 20 21 22 23 24
9585 BRAZIL
†RADIO GLOBO, São Paulo
Irr • DS • 10 kW •
DS • 10 kW •
CHINA
†CHINA RADIO INTL, Kunming
W • Mideast • 500 kW
†CHINA RADIO INTL, Urümqi
S • Europe • 500 kW
ITALY
†RAI INTERNATIONAL, Rome
Europe • 100 kW
S • S Europe • 100 kW
USA
RFE-RL, Via Lampertheim, Germany
W • Mideast & W Asia • 100 kW
†RFE-RL, Via Udon Thani, Thailand
W • C Asia • 250 kW
VOA, Via Briech, Morocco
S • S Europe • 250 kW
VOA, Via Iranawila, Sri Lanka
S • S Asia & W Asia • 250 kW
†VOA, Via Kavála, Greece
S • S Asia • 250 kW
VOA, Via São Tomé
W • C Africa & E Africa • 100 kW
†VOA, Via Udon Thani, Thailand
S • E Asia • 250 kW
VATICAN STATE
†VATICAN RADIO, Sta Maria di Galeria
• E Asia • 250 kW
E Asia • 500 kW
9590 CANADA
†R CANADA INTL, Sackville, NB
• N America & C America • 250 kW
CHINA
†CHINA RADIO INTL, Kunming
SE Asia • 150 kW
S Asia • 150 kW
DENMARK
†RADIO DANMARK, Via Norway
W • N America • 500 kW
S • Europe • 500 kW
S • Africa • 500 kW
Europe • 500 kW
W • W Africa • 500 kW
S • W Africa & Australasia • 500 kW
W • W Europe • 500 kW
HOLLAND
R NEDERLAND, Via Madagascar
W • SE Asia • 200 kW
SE Asia • 200 kW
R NEDERLAND, Via Neth Antilles
W North Am • 250 kW
R NEDERLAND, Via Singapore
S • SE Asia & Australasia • 250 kW
NORWAY
†R NORWAY INTL, Kvitsøy
S • Africa • 500 kW
W • W Europe • 500 kW
S • Europe • 500 kW
†R NORWAY INTL, Sveio
W • N America • 500 kW
S • Europe • 500 kW
W • W Africa • 500 kW
W Europe • 500 kW
S • W Africa & Australasia • 500 kW
ROMANIA
†RADIO ROMANIA INTL, Bucharest
W Su • W Europe • 250 kW
SWEDEN
†RADIO SWEDEN, Hörby
• E Europe & W Asia • 500 kW
USA
VOA, Greenville, NC
C America • 250 kW
†VOA, Via Philippines
S • S Asia & SE Asia • 250 kW
S • S Asia • 250 kW
9595 BOTSWANA
RADIO BOTSWANA, Gaborone
ENGLISH, ETC • DS • 45/50 kW
CHINA
†XINJIANG PEOPLE'S BC STN, Urümqi
DS-UYGUR • 50 kW
DENMARK
†RADIO DANMARK, Via Norway
S • Europe • 500 kW
INDIA
†ALL INDIA RADIO, Delhi
S Asia & W Asia • 250 kW
DS • 100 kW
S Asia • 100 kW
S Asia & W Asia • 100 kW
ENGLISH & HINDI • DS • 100 kW
IRAN
†VO THE ISLAMIC REP, Mashhad
W • E Africa & S Africa • 500 kW
ITALY
†RAI INTERNATIONAL, Rome
S • N Europe • 100 kW
JAPAN
RADIO TAMPA, Tokyo-Nagara
DS-1 • 50 kW
NORWAY
†R NORWAY INTL, Sveio
S • Europe • 500 kW
PHILIPPINES
(con'd) RADIO VERITAS ASIA, Palauig
S Asia • 250 kW
0 1 2 3 4 5 6 7 8 9 10 11 12 13 14 15 16 17 18 19 20 21 22 23 24

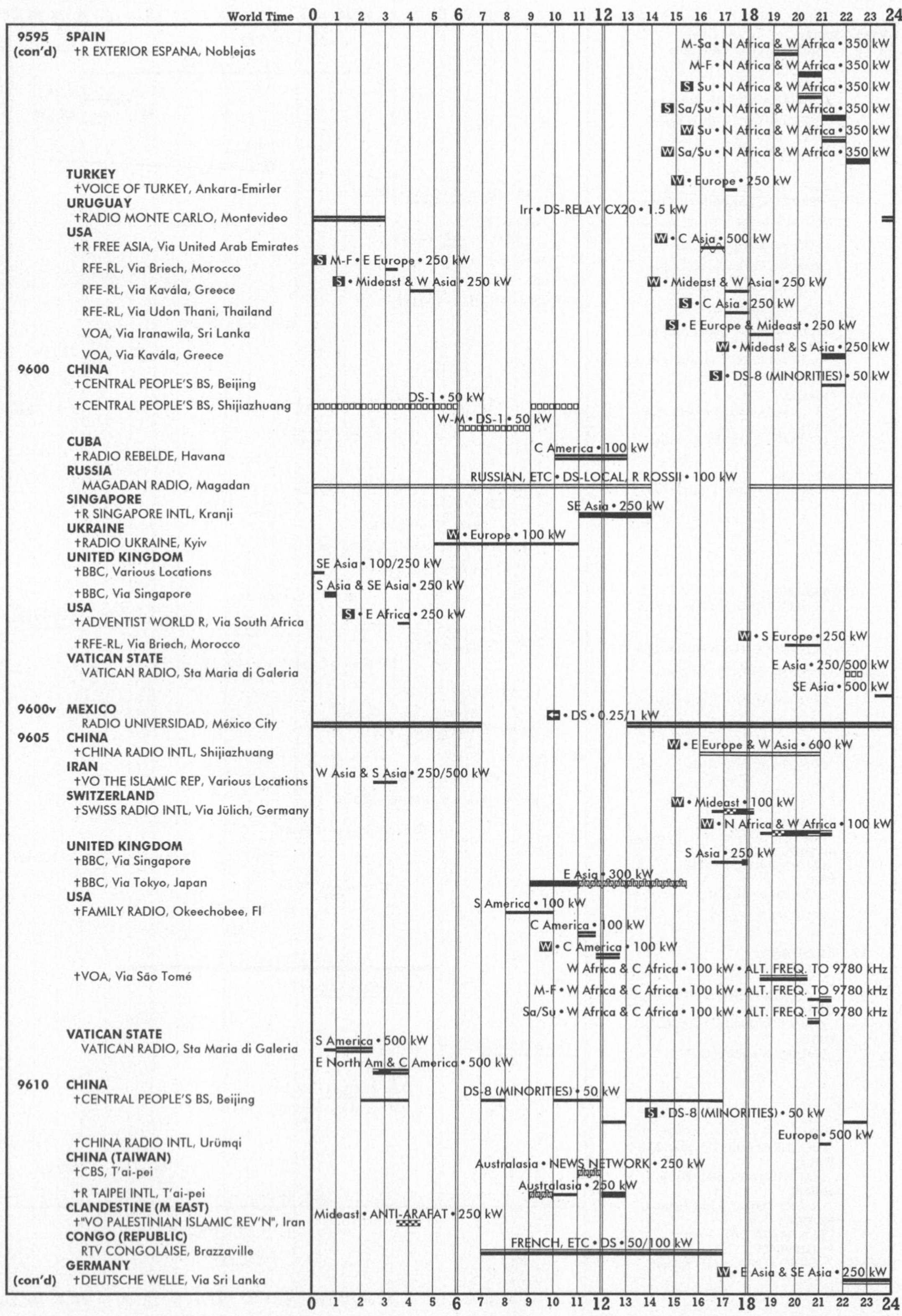
World Time 0 1 2 3 4 5 6 7 8 9 10 11 12 13 14 15 16 17 18 19 20 21 22 23 24
9595 (con'd) SPAIN
†R EXTERIOR ESPANA, Noblejas
M-Sa • N Africa & W Africa • 350 kW
M-F • N Africa & W Africa • 350 kW
S Su • N Africa & W Africa • 350 kW
S Sa/Su • N Africa & W Africa • 350 kW
W Su • N Africa & W Africa • 350 kW
W Sa/Su • N Africa & W Africa • 350 kW
TURKEY
†VOICE OF TURKEY, Ankara-Emirler
W • Europe • 250 kW
URUGUAY
†RADIO MONTE CARLO, Montevideo
Irr • DS-RELAY CX20 • 1.5 kW
USA
†R FREE ASIA, Via United Arab Emirates
W • C Asia • 500 kW
RFE-RL, Via Briech, Morocco
S M-F • E Europe • 250 kW
RFE-RL, Via Kavála, Greece
S • Mideast & W Asia • 250 kW
W • Mideast & W Asia • 250 kW
RFE-RL, Via Udon Thani, Thailand
S • C Asia • 250 kW
VOA, Via Iranawila, Sri Lanka
S • E Europe & Mideast • 250 kW
VOA, Via Kavála, Greece
W • Mideast & S Asia • 250 kW
9600 CHINA
†CENTRAL PEOPLE'S BS, Beijing
S • DS-8 (MINORITIES) • 50 kW
†CENTRAL PEOPLE'S BS, Shijiazhuang
DS-1 • 50 kW
W-M • DS-1 • 50 kW
CUBA
†RADIO REBELDE, Havana
C America • 100 kW
RUSSIA
MAGADAN RADIO, Magadan
RUSSIAN, ETC • DS-LOCAL, R ROSSII • 100 kW
SINGAPORE
†R SINGAPORE INTL, Kranji
SE Asia • 250 kW
UKRAINE
†RADIO UKRAINE, Kyiv
W • Europe • 100 kW
UNITED KINGDOM
†BBC, Various Locations
SE Asia • 100/250 kW
†BBC, Via Singapore
S Asia & SE Asia • 250 kW
USA
†ADVENTIST WORLD R, Via South Africa
S • E Africa • 250 kW
†RFE-RL, Via Briech, Morocco
W • S Europe • 250 kW
VATICAN STATE
VATICAN RADIO, Sta Maria di Galeria
E Asia • 250/500 kW
SE Asia • 500 kW
9600v MEXICO
RADIO UNIVERSIDAD, México City
• DS • 0.25/1 kW
9605 CHINA
†CHINA RADIO INTL, Shijiazhuang
W • E Europe & W Asia • 600 kW
IRAN
†VO THE ISLAMIC REP, Various Locations
W Asia & S Asia • 250/500 kW
SWITZERLAND
†SWISS RADIO INTL, Via Jülich, Germany
W • Mideast • 100 kW
W • N Africa & W Africa • 100 kW
UNITED KINGDOM
†BBC, Via Singapore
S Asia • 250 kW
†BBC, Via Tokyo, Japan
E Asia • 300 kW
USA
†FAMILY RADIO, Okeechobee, Fl
S America • 100 kW
C America • 100 kW
W • C America • 100 kW
†VOA, Via São Tomé
W Africa & C Africa • 100 kW • ALT. FREQ. TO 9780 kHz
M-F • W Africa & C Africa • 100 kW • ALT. FREQ. TO 9780 kHz
Sa/Su • W Africa & C Africa • 100 kW • ALT. FREQ. TO 9780 kHz
VATICAN STATE
VATICAN RADIO, Sta Maria di Galeria
S America • 500 kW
E North Am & C America • 500 kW
9610 CHINA
†CENTRAL PEOPLE'S BS, Beijing
DS-8 (MINORITIES) • 50 kW
S • DS-8 (MINORITIES) • 50 kW
†CHINA RADIO INTL, Urümqi
Europe • 500 kW
CHINA (TAIWAN)
†CBS, T'ai-pei
Australasia • NEWS NETWORK • 250 kW
†R TAIPEI INTL, T'ai-pei
Australasia • 250 kW
CLANDESTINE (M EAST)
†"VO PALESTINIAN ISLAMIC REV'N", Iran
Mideast • ANTI-ARAFAT • 250 kW
CONGO (REPUBLIC)
RTV CONGOLAISE, Brazzaville
FRENCH, ETC • DS • 50/100 kW
GERMANY
(con'd) †DEUTSCHE WELLE, Via Sri Lanka
W • E Asia & SE Asia • 250 kW
0 1 2 3 4 5 6 7 8 9 10 11 12 13 14 15 16 17 18 19 20 21 22 23 24

ENGLISH ARABIC CHINESE FRENCH GERMAN RUSSIAN SPANISH OTHER

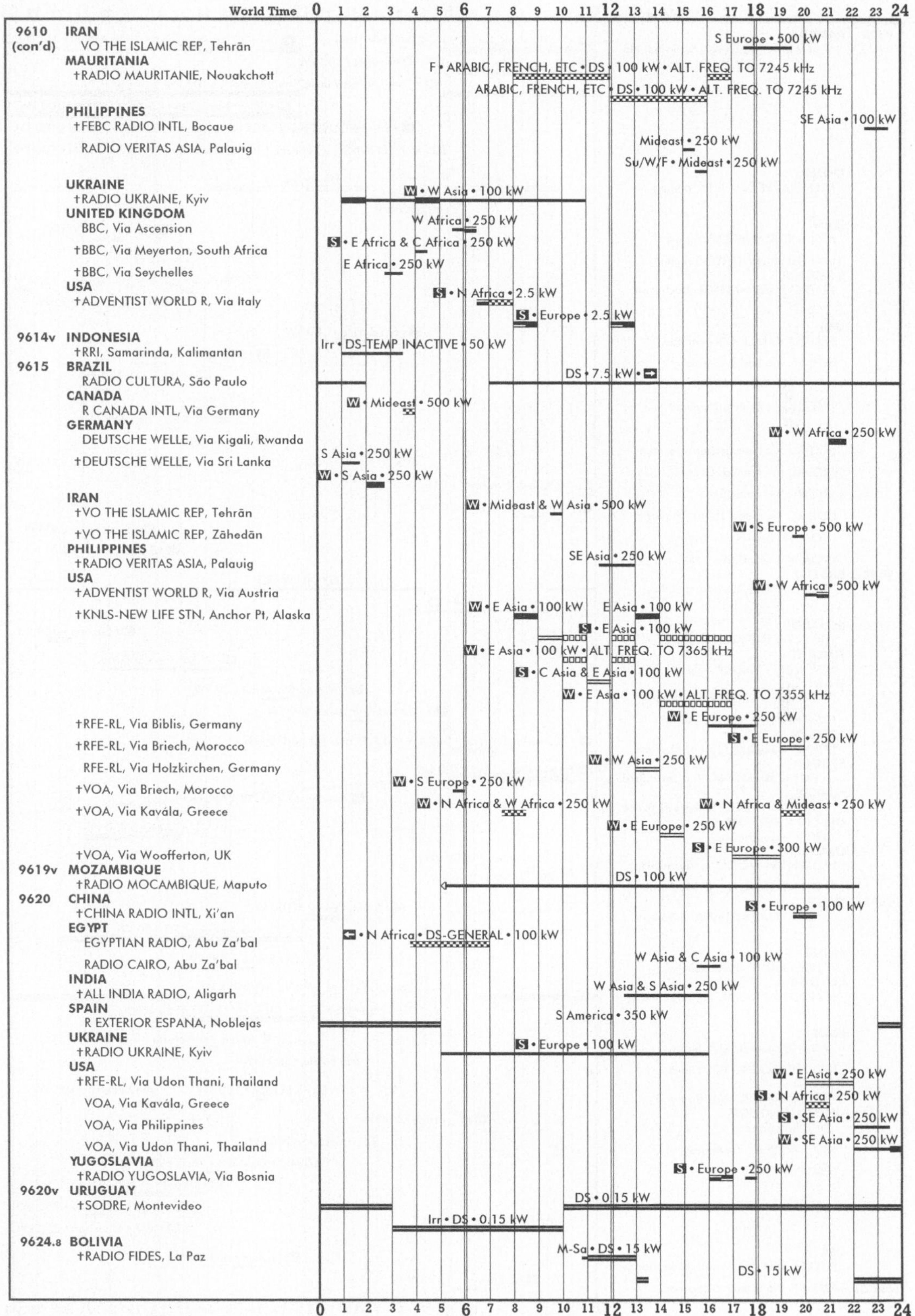
World Time 0 1 2 3 4 5 6 7 8 9 10 11 12 13 14 15 16 17 18 19 20 21 22 23 24
9610 (con'd) IRAN
VO THE ISLAMIC REP, Tehrān
S Europe • 500 kW
MAURITANIA
†RADIO MAURITANIE, Nouakchott
F • ARABIC, FRENCH, ETC • DS • 100 kW • ALT. FREQ. TO 7245 kHz
ARABIC, FRENCH, ETC • DS • 100 kW • ALT. FREQ. TO 7245 kHz
PHILIPPINES
†FEBC RADIO INTL, Bocaue
SE Asia • 100 kW
RADIO VERITAS ASIA, Palauig
Mideast • 250 kW
Su/W/F • Mideast • 250 kW
UKRAINE
†RADIO UKRAINE, Kyiv
W • W Asia • 100 kW
UNITED KINGDOM
BBC, Via Ascension
W Africa • 250 kW
†BBC, Via Meyerton, South Africa
S • E Africa & C Africa • 250 kW
†BBC, Via Seychelles
E Africa • 250 kW
USA
†ADVENTIST WORLD R, Via Italy
S • N Africa • 2.5 kW
S • Europe • 2.5 kW
9614v INDONESIA
†RRI, Samarinda, Kalimantan
Irr • DS-TEMP INACTIVE • 50 kW
9615 BRAZIL
RADIO CULTURA, São Paulo
DS • 7.5 kW • ➡
CANADA
R CANADA INTL, Via Germany
W • Mideast • 500 kW
GERMANY
DEUTSCHE WELLE, Via Kigali, Rwanda
W • W Africa • 250 kW
†DEUTSCHE WELLE, Via Sri Lanka
S Asia • 250 kW
W • S Asia • 250 kW
IRAN
†VO THE ISLAMIC REP, Tehrān
W • Mideast & W Asia • 500 kW
†VO THE ISLAMIC REP, Zāhedān
W • S Europe • 500 kW
PHILIPPINES
†RADIO VERITAS ASIA, Palauig
SE Asia • 250 kW
USA
†ADVENTIST WORLD R, Via Austria
W • W Africa • 500 kW
†KNLS-NEW LIFE STN, Anchor Pt, Alaska
W • E Asia • 100 kW
E Asia • 100 kW
S • E Asia • 100 kW
W • E Asia • 100 kW • ALT. FREQ. TO 7365 kHz
S • C Asia & E Asia • 100 kW
W • E Asia • 100 kW • ALT. FREQ. TO 7355 kHz
†RFE-RL, Via Biblis, Germany
W • E Europe • 250 kW
†RFE-RL, Via Briech, Morocco
S • E Europe • 250 kW
RFE-RL, Via Holzkirchen, Germany
W • W Asia • 250 kW
†VOA, Via Briech, Morocco
W • S Europe • 250 kW
†VOA, Via Kavála, Greece
W • N Africa & W Africa • 250 kW
W • N Africa & Mideast • 250 kW
W • E Europe • 250 kW
†VOA, Via Woofferton, UK
S • E Europe • 300 kW
9619v MOZAMBIQUE
†RADIO MOCAMBIQUE, Maputo
DS • 100 kW
9620 CHINA
†CHINA RADIO INTL, Xi'an
S • Europe • 100 kW
EGYPT
EGYPTIAN RADIO, Abu Za'bal
⬅ • N Africa • DS-GENERAL • 100 kW
RADIO CAIRO, Abu Za'bal
W Asia & C Asia • 100 kW
INDIA
†ALL INDIA RADIO, Aligarh
W Asia & S Asia • 250 kW
SPAIN
R EXTERIOR ESPANA, Noblejas
S America • 350 kW
UKRAINE
†RADIO UKRAINE, Kyiv
S • Europe • 100 kW
USA
†RFE-RL, Via Udon Thani, Thailand
W • E Asia • 250 kW
VOA, Via Kavála, Greece
S • N Africa • 250 kW
VOA, Via Philippines
S • SE Asia • 250 kW
VOA, Via Udon Thani, Thailand
W • SE Asia • 250 kW
YUGOSLAVIA
†RADIO YUGOSLAVIA, Via Bosnia
S • Europe • 250 kW
9620v URUGUAY
†SODRE, Montevideo
DS • 0.15 kW
Irr • DS • 0.15 kW
9624.8 BOLIVIA
†RADIO FIDES, La Paz
M-Sa • DS • 15 kW
DS • 15 kW
0 1 2 3 4 5 6 7 8 9 10 11 12 13 14 15 16 17 18 19 20 21 22 23 24

SEASONAL S OR W 1-HR TIMESHIFT MIDYEAR ⬅ OR ➡ JAMMING / OR ∧ EARLIEST HEARD ◁ LATEST HEARD ▷ NEW FOR 2002 †

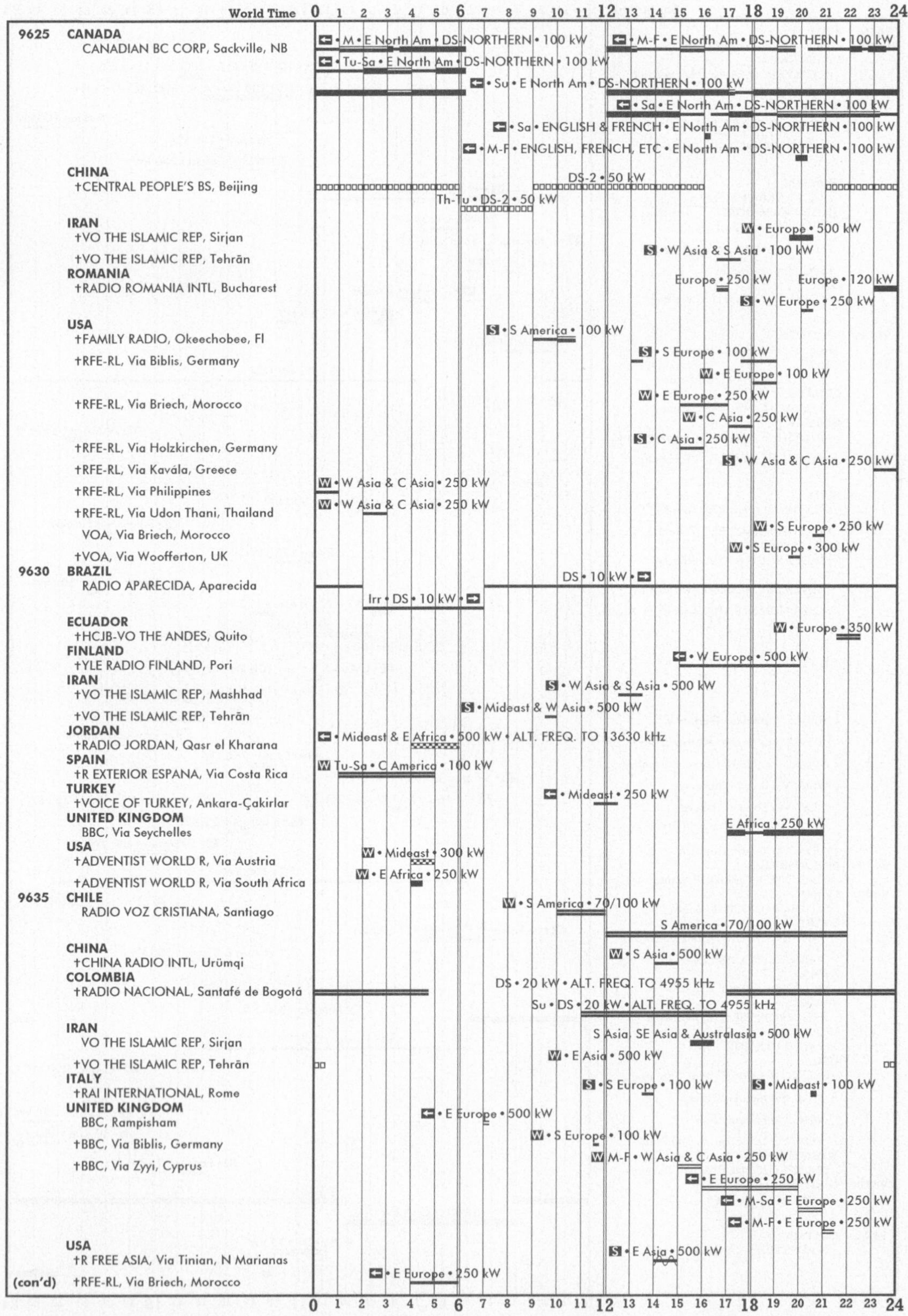
World Time
0 1 2 3 4 5 6 7 8 9 10 11 12 13 14 15 16 17 18 19 20 21 22 23 24
9625 CANADA
CANADIAN BC CORP, Sackville, NB
M • E North Am • DS-NORTHERN • 100 kW
M-F • E North Am • DS-NORTHERN • 100 kW
Tu-Sa • E North Am • DS-NORTHERN • 100 kW
Su • E North Am • DS-NORTHERN • 100 kW
Sa • E North Am • DS-NORTHERN • 100 kW
Sa • ENGLISH & FRENCH • E North Am • DS-NORTHERN • 100 kW
M-F • ENGLISH, FRENCH, ETC • E North Am • DS-NORTHERN • 100 kW
CHINA
†CENTRAL PEOPLE'S BS, Beijing
DS-2 • 50 kW
Th-Tu • DS-2 • 50 kW
IRAN
†VO THE ISLAMIC REP, Sirjan
W • Europe • 500 kW
†VO THE ISLAMIC REP, Tehrān
S • W Asia & S Asia • 100 kW
ROMANIA
†RADIO ROMANIA INTL, Bucharest
Europe • 250 kW
Europe • 120 kW
S • W Europe • 250 kW
USA
†FAMILY RADIO, Okeechobee, Fl
S • S America • 100 kW
†RFE-RL, Via Biblis, Germany
S • S Europe • 100 kW
W • E Europe • 100 kW
†RFE-RL, Via Briech, Morocco
W • E Europe • 250 kW
W • C Asia • 250 kW
S • C Asia • 250 kW
†RFE-RL, Via Holzkirchen, Germany
S • W Asia & C Asia • 250 kW
†RFE-RL, Via Kavála, Greece
†RFE-RL, Via Philippines
W • W Asia & C Asia • 250 kW
†RFE-RL, Via Udon Thani, Thailand
W • W Asia & C Asia • 250 kW
VOA, Via Briech, Morocco
W • S Europe • 250 kW
†VOA, Via Woofferton, UK
W • S Europe • 300 kW
9630 BRAZIL
RADIO APARECIDA, Aparecida
DS • 10 kW
Irr • DS • 10 kW
ECUADOR
†HCJB-VO THE ANDES, Quito
W • Europe • 350 kW
FINLAND
†YLE RADIO FINLAND, Pori
W Europe • 500 kW
IRAN
†VO THE ISLAMIC REP, Mashhad
S • W Asia & S Asia • 500 kW
†VO THE ISLAMIC REP, Tehrān
S • Mideast & W Asia • 500 kW
JORDAN
†RADIO JORDAN, Qasr el Kharana
Mideast & E Africa • 500 kW • ALT. FREQ. TO 13630 kHz
SPAIN
†R EXTERIOR ESPANA, Via Costa Rica
W Tu-Sa • C America • 100 kW
TURKEY
†VOICE OF TURKEY, Ankara-Çakirlar
Mideast • 250 kW
UNITED KINGDOM
BBC, Via Seychelles
E Africa • 250 kW
USA
†ADVENTIST WORLD R, Via Austria
W • Mideast • 300 kW
†ADVENTIST WORLD R, Via South Africa
W • E Africa • 250 kW
9635 CHILE
RADIO VOZ CRISTIANA, Santiago
W • S America • 70/100 kW
S America • 70/100 kW
CHINA
†CHINA RADIO INTL, Urümqi
W • S Asia • 500 kW
COLOMBIA
†RADIO NACIONAL, Santafé de Bogotá
DS • 20 kW • ALT. FREQ. TO 4955 kHz
Su • DS • 20 kW • ALT. FREQ. TO 4955 kHz
IRAN
VO THE ISLAMIC REP, Sirjan
S Asia, SE Asia & Australasia • 500 kW
†VO THE ISLAMIC REP, Tehrān
W • E Asia • 500 kW
ITALY
†RAI INTERNATIONAL, Rome
S • S Europe • 100 kW
S • Mideast • 100 kW
UNITED KINGDOM
BBC, Rampisham
E Europe • 500 kW
†BBC, Via Biblis, Germany
W • S Europe • 100 kW
†BBC, Via Zyyi, Cyprus
W M-F • W Asia & C Asia • 250 kW
E Europe • 250 kW
M-Sa • E Europe • 250 kW
M-F • E Europe • 250 kW
USA
†R FREE ASIA, Via Tinian, N Marianas
S • E Asia • 500 kW
(con'd)
†RFE-RL, Via Briech, Morocco
E Europe • 250 kW
0 1 2 3 4 5 6 7 8 9 10 11 12 13 14 15 16 17 18 19 20 21 22 23 24

ENGLISH ARABIC CHINESE FRENCH GERMAN RUSSIAN SPANISH OTHER

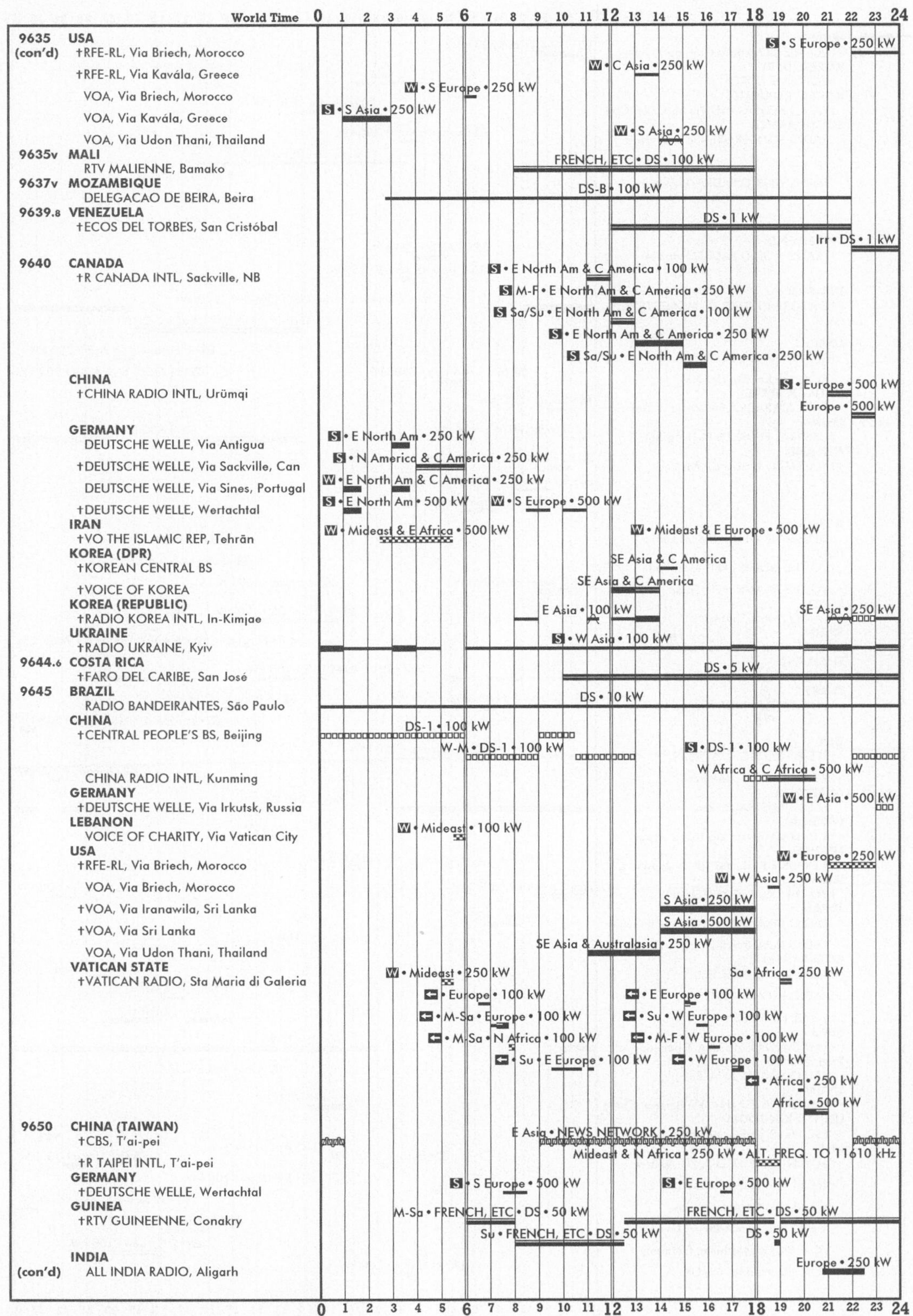
World Time 0 1 2 3 4 5 6 7 8 9 10 11 12 13 14 15 16 17 18 19 20 21 22 23 24
9635 (con'd) USA
†RFE-RL, Via Briech, Morocco
S • S Europe • 250 kW
†RFE-RL, Via Kavála, Greece
W • C Asia • 250 kW
VOA, Via Briech, Morocco
W • S Europe • 250 kW
VOA, Via Kavála, Greece
S • S Asia • 250 kW
VOA, Via Udon Thani, Thailand
W • S Asia • 250 kW
9635v MALI
RTV MALIENNE, Bamako
FRENCH, ETC • DS • 100 kW
9637v MOZAMBIQUE
DELEGACAO DE BEIRA, Beira
DS-B • 100 kW
9639.8 VENEZUELA
†ECOS DEL TORBES, San Cristóbal
DS • 1 kW
Irr • DS • 1 kW
9640 CANADA
†R CANADA INTL, Sackville, NB
S • E North Am & C America • 100 kW
S M-F • E North Am & C America • 250 kW
S Sa/Su • E North Am & C America • 100 kW
S • E North Am & C America • 250 kW
S Sa/Su • E North Am & C America • 250 kW
CHINA
†CHINA RADIO INTL, Urümqi
S • Europe • 500 kW
Europe • 500 kW
GERMANY
DEUTSCHE WELLE, Via Antigua
S • E North Am • 250 kW
†DEUTSCHE WELLE, Via Sackville, Can
S • N America & C America • 250 kW
DEUTSCHE WELLE, Via Sines, Portugal
W • E North Am & C America • 250 kW
†DEUTSCHE WELLE, Wertachtal
S • E North Am • 500 kW
W • S Europe • 500 kW
IRAN
†VO THE ISLAMIC REP, Tehrān
W • Mideast & E Africa • 500 kW
W • Mideast & E Europe • 500 kW
KOREA (DPR)
†KOREAN CENTRAL BS
SE Asia & C America
†VOICE OF KOREA
SE Asia & C America
KOREA (REPUBLIC)
†RADIO KOREA INTL, In-Kimjae
E Asia • 100 kW
SE Asia • 250 kW
UKRAINE
†RADIO UKRAINE, Kyiv
S • W Asia • 100 kW
9644.6 COSTA RICA
†FARO DEL CARIBE, San José
DS • 5 kW
9645 BRAZIL
RADIO BANDEIRANTES, São Paulo
DS • 10 kW
CHINA
†CENTRAL PEOPLE'S BS, Beijing
DS-1 • 100 kW
W-M • DS-1 • 100 kW
S • DS-1 • 100 kW
CHINA RADIO INTL, Kunming
W Africa & C Africa • 500 kW
GERMANY
†DEUTSCHE WELLE, Via Irkutsk, Russia
W • E Asia • 500 kW
LEBANON
VOICE OF CHARITY, Via Vatican City
W • Mideast • 100 kW
USA
†RFE-RL, Via Briech, Morocco
W • Europe • 250 kW
VOA, Via Briech, Morocco
W • W Asia • 250 kW
†VOA, Via Iranawila, Sri Lanka
S Asia • 250 kW
†VOA, Via Sri Lanka
S Asia • 500 kW
VOA, Via Udon Thani, Thailand
SE Asia & Australasia • 250 kW
VATICAN STATE
†VATICAN RADIO, Sta Maria di Galeria
W • Mideast • 250 kW
Sa • Africa • 250 kW
• Europe • 100 kW
• E Europe • 100 kW
• M-Sa • Europe • 100 kW
• Su • W Europe • 100 kW
• M-Sa • N Africa • 100 kW
• M-F • W Europe • 100 kW
• Su • E Europe • 100 kW
• W Europe • 100 kW
• Africa • 250 kW
Africa • 500 kW
9650 CHINA (TAIWAN)
†CBS, T'ai-pei
E Asia • NEWS NETWORK • 250 kW
†R TAIPEI INTL, T'ai-pei
Mideast & N Africa • 250 kW • ALT. FREQ. TO 11610 kHz
GERMANY
†DEUTSCHE WELLE, Wertachtal
S • S Europe • 500 kW
S • E Europe • 500 kW
GUINEA
†RTV GUINEENNE, Conakry
M-Sa • FRENCH, ETC • DS • 50 kW
FRENCH, ETC • DS • 50 kW
Su • FRENCH, ETC • DS • 50 kW
DS • 50 kW
INDIA (con'd)
ALL INDIA RADIO, Aligarh
Europe • 250 kW
0 1 2 3 4 5 6 7 8 9 10 11 12 13 14 15 16 17 18 19 20 21 22 23 24

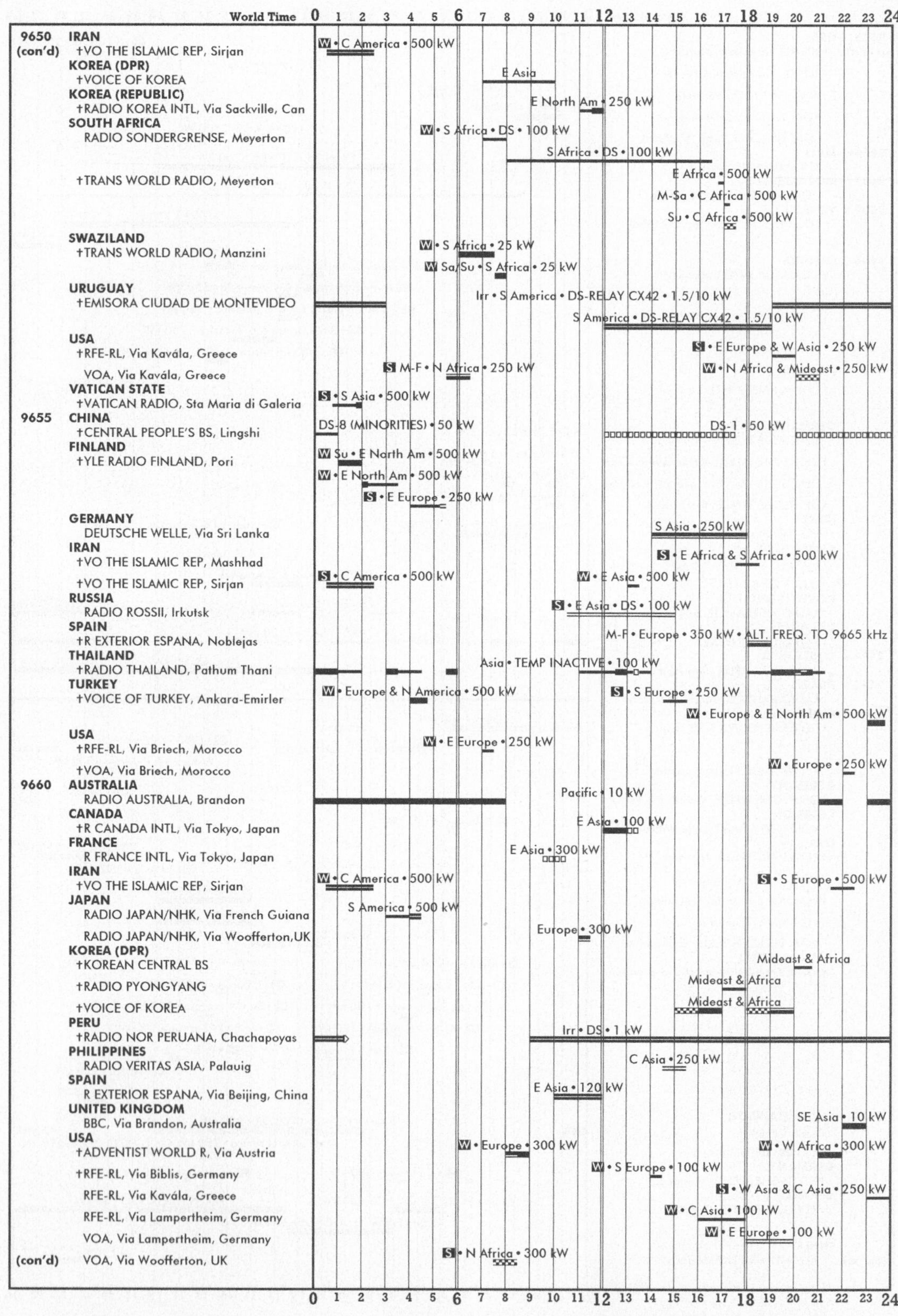
World Time 0 1 2 3 4 5 6 7 8 9 10 11 12 13 14 15 16 17 18 19 20 21 22 23 24
9650 (con'd) IRAN
†VO THE ISLAMIC REP, Sirjan
W • C America • 500 kW
KOREA (DPR)
†VOICE OF KOREA
E Asia
KOREA (REPUBLIC)
†RADIO KOREA INTL, Via Sackville, Can
E North Am • 250 kW
SOUTH AFRICA
RADIO SONDERGRENSE, Meyerton
W • S Africa • DS • 100 kW
S Africa • DS • 100 kW
†TRANS WORLD RADIO, Meyerton
E Africa • 500 kW
M-Sa • C Africa • 500 kW
Su • C Africa • 500 kW
SWAZILAND
†TRANS WORLD RADIO, Manzini
W • S Africa • 25 kW
W Sa/Su • S Africa • 25 kW
URUGUAY
†EMISORA CIUDAD DE MONTEVIDEO
Irr • S America • DS-RELAY CX42 • 1.5/10 kW
S America • DS-RELAY CX42 • 1.5/10 kW
USA
†RFE-RL, Via Kavála, Greece
S • E Europe & W Asia • 250 kW
VOA, Via Kavála, Greece
S M-F • N Africa • 250 kW
W • N Africa & Mideast • 250 kW
VATICAN STATE
†VATICAN RADIO, Sta Maria di Galeria
S • S Asia • 500 kW
9655 CHINA
†CENTRAL PEOPLE'S BS, Lingshi
DS-8 (MINORITIES) • 50 kW
DS-1 • 50 kW
FINLAND
†YLE RADIO FINLAND, Pori
W Su • E North Am • 500 kW
W • E North Am • 500 kW
S • E Europe • 250 kW
GERMANY
DEUTSCHE WELLE, Via Sri Lanka
S Asia • 250 kW
IRAN
†VO THE ISLAMIC REP, Mashhad
S • E Africa & S Africa • 500 kW
†VO THE ISLAMIC REP, Sirjan
S • C America • 500 kW
W • E Asia • 500 kW
RUSSIA
RADIO ROSSII, Irkutsk
S • E Asia • DS • 100 kW
SPAIN
†R EXTERIOR ESPANA, Noblejas
M-F • Europe • 350 kW • ALT. FREQ. TO 9665 kHz
THAILAND
†RADIO THAILAND, Pathum Thani
Asia • TEMP INACTIVE • 100 kW
TURKEY
†VOICE OF TURKEY, Ankara-Emirler
W • Europe & N America • 500 kW
S • S Europe • 250 kW
W • Europe & E North Am • 500 kW
USA
†RFE-RL, Via Briech, Morocco
W • E Europe • 250 kW
†VOA, Via Briech, Morocco
W • Europe • 250 kW
9660 AUSTRALIA
RADIO AUSTRALIA, Brandon
Pacific • 10 kW
CANADA
†R CANADA INTL, Via Tokyo, Japan
E Asia • 100 kW
FRANCE
R FRANCE INTL, Via Tokyo, Japan
E Asia • 300 kW
IRAN
†VO THE ISLAMIC REP, Sirjan
W • C America • 500 kW
S • S Europe • 500 kW
JAPAN
RADIO JAPAN/NHK, Via French Guiana
S America • 500 kW
RADIO JAPAN/NHK, Via Woofferton, UK
Europe • 300 kW
KOREA (DPR)
†KOREAN CENTRAL BS
Mideast & Africa
†RADIO PYONGYANG
Mideast & Africa
†VOICE OF KOREA
Mideast & Africa
PERU
†RADIO NOR PERUANA, Chachapoyas
Irr • DS • 1 kW
PHILIPPINES
RADIO VERITAS ASIA, Palauig
C Asia • 250 kW
SPAIN
R EXTERIOR ESPANA, Via Beijing, China
E Asia • 120 kW
UNITED KINGDOM
BBC, Via Brandon, Australia
SE Asia • 10 kW
USA
†ADVENTIST WORLD R, Via Austria
W • Europe • 300 kW
W • W Africa • 300 kW
†RFE-RL, Via Biblis, Germany
W • S Europe • 100 kW
RFE-RL, Via Kavála, Greece
S • W Asia & C Asia • 250 kW
RFE-RL, Via Lampertheim, Germany
W • C Asia • 100 kW
VOA, Via Lampertheim, Germany
W • E Europe • 100 kW
(con'd) VOA, Via Woofferton, UK
S • N Africa • 300 kW
0 1 2 3 4 5 6 7 8 9 10 11 12 13 14 15 16 17 18 19 20 21 22 23 24
ENGLISH ARABIC CHINESE FRENCH GERMAN RUSSIAN SPANISH OTHER

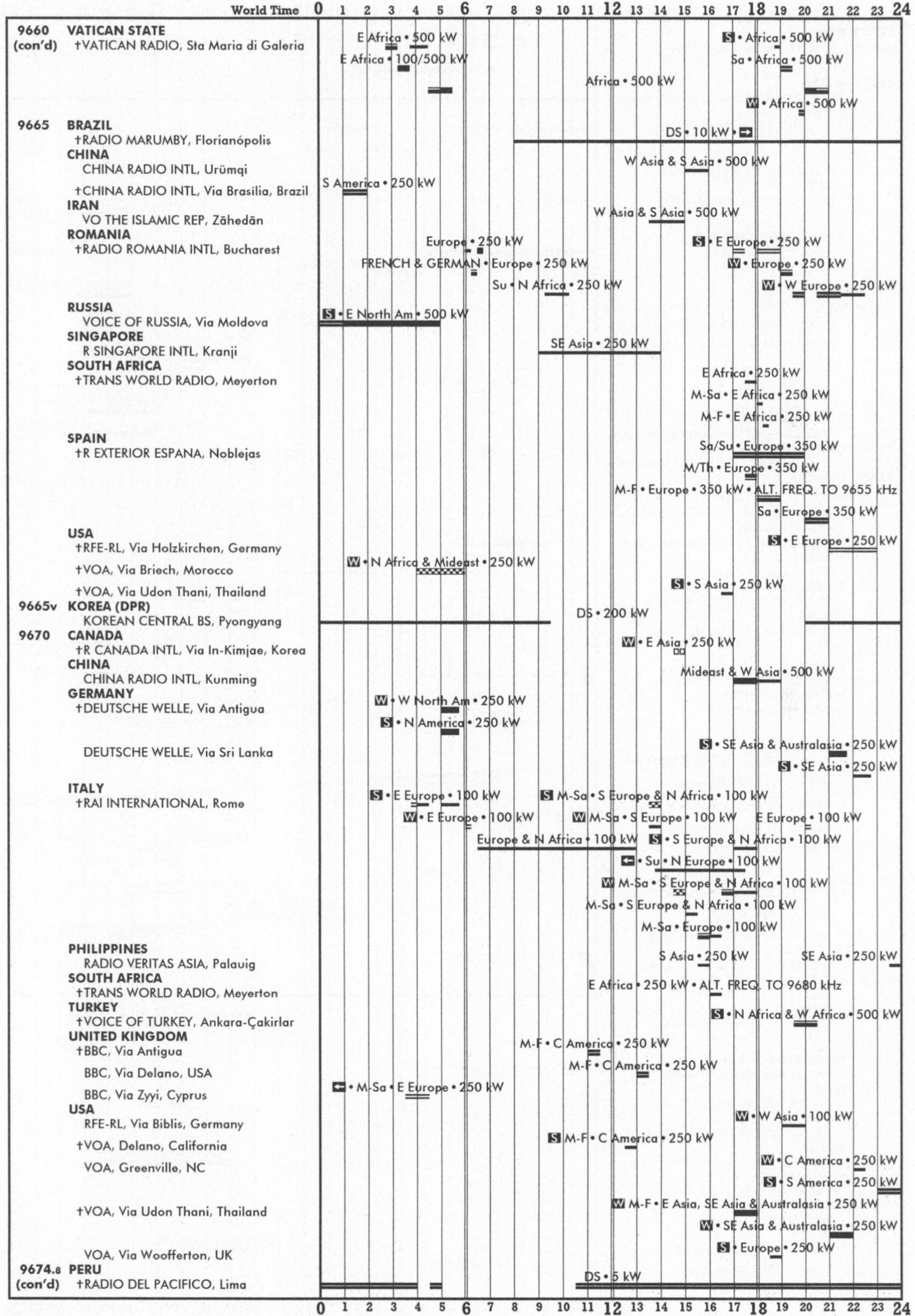
World Time 0 1 2 3 4 5 6 7 8 9 10 11 12 13 14 15 16 17 18 19 20 21 22 23 24
9660 (con'd) VATICAN STATE
†VATICAN RADIO, Sta Maria di Galeria
E Africa • 500 kW
E Africa • 100/500 kW
Africa • 500 kW
S • Africa • 500 kW
Sa • Africa • 500 kW
W • Africa • 500 kW
9665 BRAZIL
†RADIO MARUMBY, Florianópolis
DS • 10 kW
CHINA
CHINA RADIO INTL, Urümqi
W Asia & S Asia • 500 kW
†CHINA RADIO INTL, Via Brasília, Brazil
S America • 250 kW
IRAN
VO THE ISLAMIC REP, Zāhedān
W Asia & S Asia • 500 kW
ROMANIA
†RADIO ROMANIA INTL, Bucharest
Europe • 250 kW
FRENCH & GERMAN • Europe • 250 kW
Su • N Africa • 250 kW
S • E Europe • 250 kW
W • Europe • 250 kW
W • W Europe • 250 kW
RUSSIA
VOICE OF RUSSIA, Via Moldova
S • E North Am • 500 kW
SINGAPORE
R SINGAPORE INTL, Kranji
SE Asia • 250 kW
SOUTH AFRICA
†TRANS WORLD RADIO, Meyerton
E Africa • 250 kW
M-Sa • E Africa • 250 kW
M-F • E Africa • 250 kW
SPAIN
†R EXTERIOR ESPANA, Noblejas
Sa/Su • Europe • 350 kW
M/Th • Europe • 350 kW
M-F • Europe • 350 kW • ALT. FREQ. TO 9655 kHz
Sa • Europe • 350 kW
USA
†RFE-RL, Via Holzkirchen, Germany
S • E Europe • 250 kW
†VOA, Via Briech, Morocco
W • N Africa & Mideast • 250 kW
†VOA, Via Udon Thani, Thailand
S • S Asia • 250 kW
9665v KOREA (DPR)
KOREAN CENTRAL BS, Pyongyang
DS • 200 kW
9670 CANADA
†R CANADA INTL, Via In-Kimjae, Korea
W • E Asia • 250 kW
CHINA
CHINA RADIO INTL, Kunming
Mideast & W Asia • 500 kW
GERMANY
†DEUTSCHE WELLE, Via Antigua
W • W North Am • 250 kW
S • N America • 250 kW
DEUTSCHE WELLE, Via Sri Lanka
S • SE Asia & Australasia • 250 kW
S • SE Asia • 250 kW
ITALY
†RAI INTERNATIONAL, Rome
S • E Europe • 100 kW
W • E Europe • 100 kW
S M-Sa • S Europe & N Africa • 100 kW
W M-Sa • S Europe • 100 kW
E Europe • 100 kW
Europe & N Africa • 100 kW
S • S Europe & N Africa • 100 kW
Su • N Europe • 100 kW
W M-Sa • S Europe & N Africa • 100 kW
M-Sa • S Europe & N Africa • 100 kW
M-Sa • Europe • 100 kW
PHILIPPINES
RADIO VERITAS ASIA, Palauig
S Asia • 250 kW
SE Asia • 250 kW
SOUTH AFRICA
†TRANS WORLD RADIO, Meyerton
E Africa • 250 kW • ALT. FREQ. TO 9680 kHz
TURKEY
†VOICE OF TURKEY, Ankara-Çakirlar
S • N Africa & W Africa • 500 kW
UNITED KINGDOM
†BBC, Via Antigua
M-F • C America • 250 kW
BBC, Via Delano, USA
M-F • C America • 250 kW
BBC, Via Zyyi, Cyprus
M-Sa • E Europe • 250 kW
USA
RFE-RL, Via Biblis, Germany
W • W Asia • 100 kW
†VOA, Delano, California
S M-F • C America • 250 kW
VOA, Greenville, NC
W • C America • 250 kW
S • S America • 250 kW
†VOA, Via Udon Thani, Thailand
W M-F • E Asia, SE Asia & Australasia • 250 kW
W • SE Asia & Australasia • 250 kW
VOA, Via Woofferton, UK
S • Europe • 250 kW
9674.8 (con'd) PERU
†RADIO DEL PACIFICO, Lima
DS • 5 kW
0 1 2 3 4 5 6 7 8 9 10 11 12 13 14 15 16 17 18 19 20 21 22 23 24
SEASONAL S OR W
1-HR TIMESHIFT MIDYEAR OR
JAMMING / OR ⋀
EARLIEST HEARD ◁
LATEST HEARD ▷
NEW FOR 2002 †

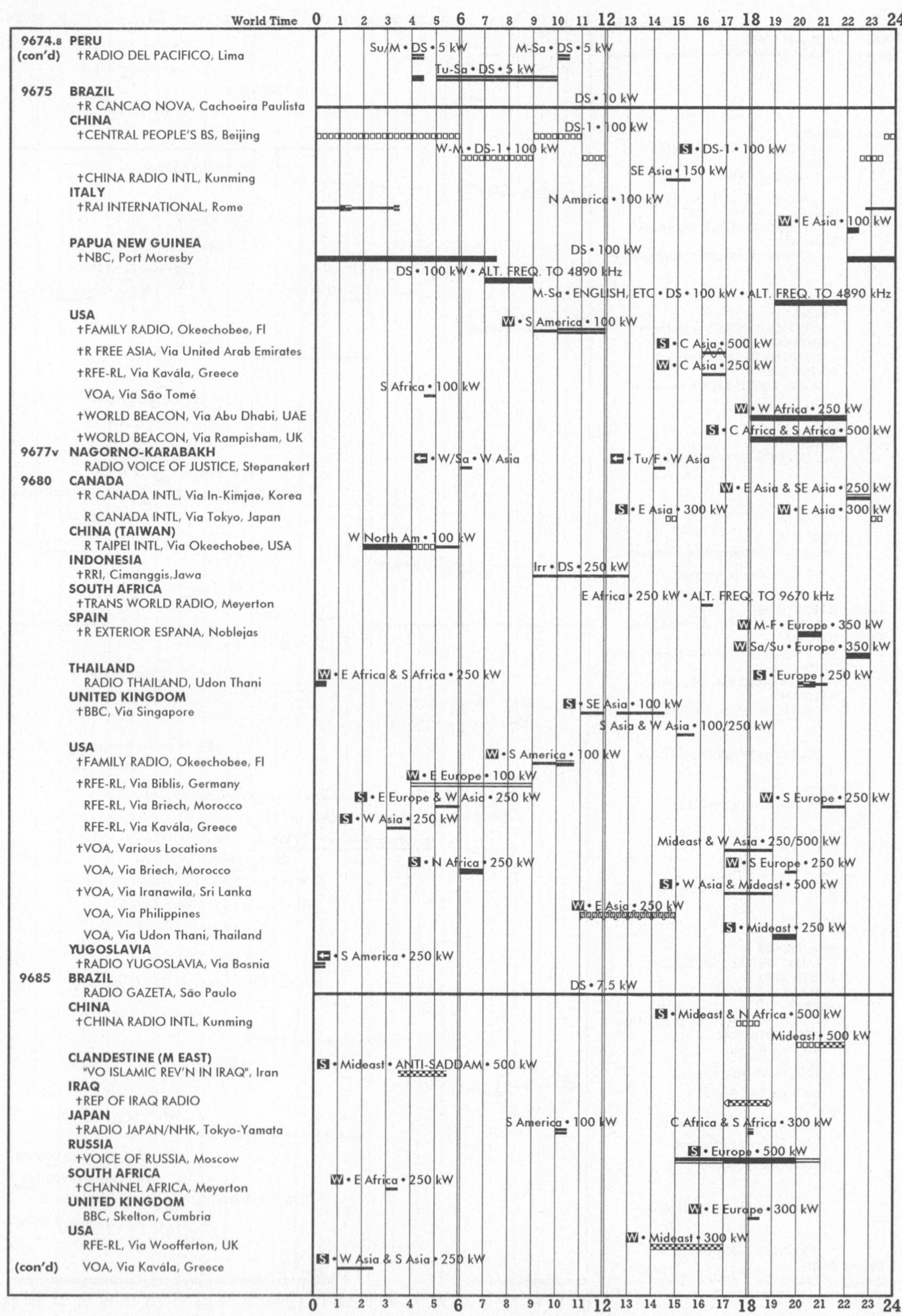
World Time 0 1 2 3 4 5 6 7 8 9 10 11 12 13 14 15 16 17 18 19 20 21 22 23 24
9674.8 PERU
(con'd) †RADIO DEL PACIFICO, Lima
Su/M • DS • 5 kW
M-Sa • DS • 5 kW
Tu-Sa • DS • 5 kW
9675 BRAZIL
†R CANCAO NOVA, Cachoeira Paulista
DS • 10 kW
CHINA
†CENTRAL PEOPLE'S BS, Beijing
DS-1 • 100 kW
W-M • DS-1 • 100 kW
S • DS-1 • 100 kW
†CHINA RADIO INTL, Kunming
SE Asia • 150 kW
ITALY
†RAI INTERNATIONAL, Rome
N America • 100 kW
W • E Asia • 100 kW
PAPUA NEW GUINEA
†NBC, Port Moresby
DS • 100 kW
DS • 100 kW • ALT. FREQ. TO 4890 kHz
M-Sa • ENGLISH, ETC • DS • 100 kW • ALT. FREQ. TO 4890 kHz
USA
†FAMILY RADIO, Okeechobee, Fl
W • S America • 100 kW
†R FREE ASIA, Via United Arab Emirates
S • C Asia • 500 kW
†RFE-RL, Via Kavála, Greece
W • C Asia • 250 kW
VOA, Via São Tomé
S Africa • 100 kW
†WORLD BEACON, Via Abu Dhabi, UAE
W • W Africa • 250 kW
†WORLD BEACON, Via Rampisham, UK
S • C Africa & S Africa • 500 kW
9677v NAGORNO-KARABAKH
RADIO VOICE OF JUSTICE, Stepanakert
W/Sa • W Asia
Tu/F • W Asia
9680 CANADA
†R CANADA INTL, Via In-Kimjae, Korea
W • E Asia & SE Asia • 250 kW
R CANADA INTL, Via Tokyo, Japan
S • E Asia • 300 kW
W • E Asia • 300 kW
CHINA (TAIWAN)
R TAIPEI INTL, Via Okeechobee, USA
W North Am • 100 kW
INDONESIA
†RRI, Cimanggis,Jawa
Irr • DS • 250 kW
SOUTH AFRICA
†TRANS WORLD RADIO, Meyerton
E Africa • 250 kW • ALT. FREQ. TO 9670 kHz
SPAIN
†R EXTERIOR ESPANA, Noblejas
W M-F • Europe • 350 kW
W Sa/Su • Europe • 350 kW
THAILAND
RADIO THAILAND, Udon Thani
W • E Africa & S Africa • 250 kW
S • Europe • 250 kW
UNITED KINGDOM
†BBC, Via Singapore
S • SE Asia • 100 kW
S Asia & W Asia • 100/250 kW
USA
†FAMILY RADIO, Okeechobee, Fl
W • S America • 100 kW
†RFE-RL, Via Biblis, Germany
W • E Europe • 100 kW
RFE-RL, Via Briech, Morocco
S • E Europe & W Asia • 250 kW
W • S Europe • 250 kW
RFE-RL, Via Kavála, Greece
S • W Asia • 250 kW
†VOA, Various Locations
Mideast & W Asia • 250/500 kW
VOA, Via Briech, Morocco
S • N Africa • 250 kW
W • S Europe • 250 kW
†VOA, Via Iranawila, Sri Lanka
S • W Asia & Mideast • 500 kW
VOA, Via Philippines
W • E Asia • 250 kW
VOA, Via Udon Thani, Thailand
S • Mideast • 250 kW
YUGOSLAVIA
†RADIO YUGOSLAVIA, Via Bosnia
S America • 250 kW
9685 BRAZIL
RADIO GAZETA, São Paulo
DS • 7.5 kW
CHINA
†CHINA RADIO INTL, Kunming
S • Mideast & N Africa • 500 kW
Mideast • 500 kW
CLANDESTINE (M EAST)
"VO ISLAMIC REV'N IN IRAQ", Iran
S • Mideast • ANTI-SADDAM • 500 kW
IRAQ
†REP OF IRAQ RADIO
JAPAN
†RADIO JAPAN/NHK, Tokyo-Yamata
S America • 100 kW
C Africa & S Africa • 300 kW
RUSSIA
†VOICE OF RUSSIA, Moscow
S • Europe • 500 kW
SOUTH AFRICA
†CHANNEL AFRICA, Meyerton
W • E Africa • 250 kW
UNITED KINGDOM
BBC, Skelton, Cumbria
W • E Europe • 300 kW
USA
RFE-RL, Via Wooﬀerton, UK
W • Mideast • 300 kW
(con'd) VOA, Via Kavála, Greece
S • W Asia & S Asia • 250 kW

ENGLISH ARABIC CHINESE FRENCH GERMAN RUSSIAN SPANISH OTHER

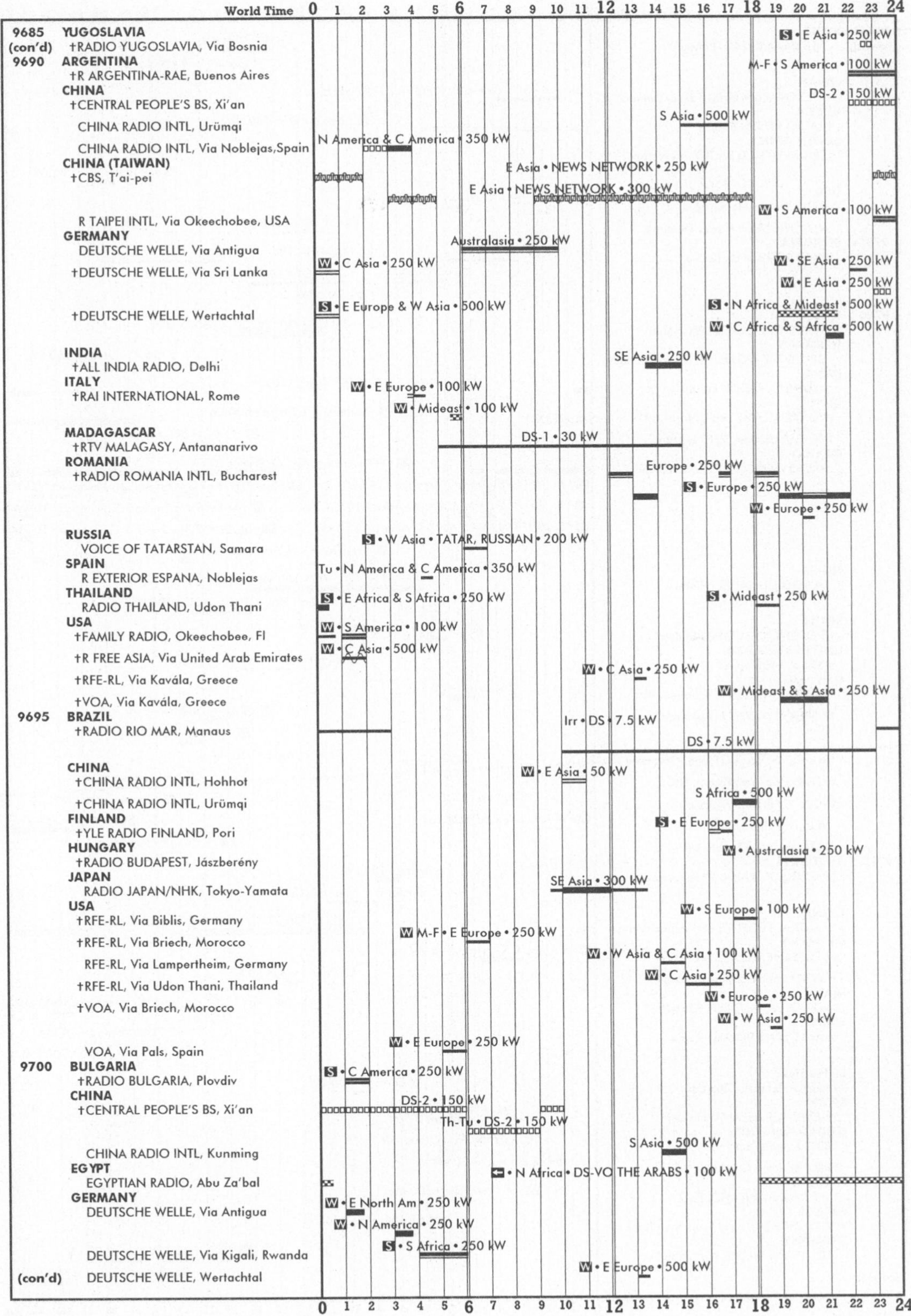
World Time 0 1 2 3 4 5 6 7 8 9 10 11 12 13 14 15 16 17 18 19 20 21 22 23 24
9685 (con'd) YUGOSLAVIA
†RADIO YUGOSLAVIA, Via Bosnia
S • E Asia • 250 kW
9690 ARGENTINA
†R ARGENTINA-RAE, Buenos Aires
M-F • S America • 100 kW
CHINA
†CENTRAL PEOPLE'S BS, Xi'an
DS-2 • 150 kW
CHINA RADIO INTL, Urümqi
S Asia • 500 kW
CHINA RADIO INTL, Via Noblejas,Spain
N America & C America • 350 kW
CHINA (TAIWAN)
†CBS, T'ai-pei
E Asia • NEWS NETWORK • 250 kW
E Asia • NEWS NETWORK • 300 kW
R TAIPEI INTL, Via Okeechobee, USA
W • S America • 100 kW
GERMANY
DEUTSCHE WELLE, Via Antigua
Australasia • 250 kW
†DEUTSCHE WELLE, Via Sri Lanka
W • C Asia • 250 kW
W • SE Asia • 250 kW
W • E Asia • 250 kW
†DEUTSCHE WELLE, Wertachtal
S • E Europe & W Asia • 500 kW
S • N Africa & Mideast • 500 kW
W • C Africa & S Africa • 500 kW
INDIA
†ALL INDIA RADIO, Delhi
SE Asia • 250 kW
ITALY
†RAI INTERNATIONAL, Rome
W • E Europe • 100 kW
W • Mideast • 100 kW
MADAGASCAR
†RTV MALAGASY, Antananarivo
DS-1 • 30 kW
ROMANIA
†RADIO ROMANIA INTL, Bucharest
Europe • 250 kW
S • Europe • 250 kW
W • Europe • 250 kW
RUSSIA
VOICE OF TATARSTAN, Samara
S • W Asia • TATAR, RUSSIAN • 200 kW
SPAIN
R EXTERIOR ESPANA, Noblejas
Tu • N America & C America • 350 kW
THAILAND
RADIO THAILAND, Udon Thani
S • E Africa & S Africa • 250 kW
S • Mideast • 250 kW
USA
†FAMILY RADIO, Okeechobee, Fl
W • S America • 100 kW
†R FREE ASIA, Via United Arab Emirates
W • C Asia • 500 kW
†RFE-RL, Via Kavála, Greece
W • C Asia • 250 kW
†VOA, Via Kavála, Greece
W • Mideast & S Asia • 250 kW
9695 BRAZIL
†RADIO RIO MAR, Manaus
Irr • DS • 7.5 kW
DS • 7.5 kW
CHINA
†CHINA RADIO INTL, Hohhot
W • E Asia • 50 kW
†CHINA RADIO INTL, Urümqi
S Africa • 500 kW
FINLAND
†YLE RADIO FINLAND, Pori
S • E Europe • 250 kW
HUNGARY
†RADIO BUDAPEST, Jászberény
W • Australasia • 250 kW
JAPAN
RADIO JAPAN/NHK, Tokyo-Yamata
SE Asia • 300 kW
USA
†RFE-RL, Via Biblis, Germany
W • S Europe • 100 kW
†RFE-RL, Via Briech, Morocco
W M-F • E Europe • 250 kW
RFE-RL, Via Lampertheim, Germany
W • W Asia & C Asia • 100 kW
†RFE-RL, Via Udon Thani, Thailand
W • C Asia • 250 kW
†VOA, Via Briech, Morocco
W • Europe • 250 kW
W • W Asia • 250 kW
VOA, Via Pals, Spain
W • E Europe • 250 kW
9700 BULGARIA
†RADIO BULGARIA, Plovdiv
S • C America • 250 kW
CHINA
†CENTRAL PEOPLE'S BS, Xi'an
DS-2 • 150 kW
Th-Tu • DS-2 • 150 kW
CHINA RADIO INTL, Kunming
S Asia • 500 kW
EGYPT
EGYPTIAN RADIO, Abu Za'bal
N Africa • DS-VO THE ARABS • 100 kW
GERMANY
DEUTSCHE WELLE, Via Antigua
W • E North Am • 250 kW
W • N America • 250 kW
DEUTSCHE WELLE, Via Kigali, Rwanda
S • S Africa • 250 kW
(con'd) DEUTSCHE WELLE, Wertachtal
W • E Europe • 500 kW
0 1 2 3 4 5 6 7 8 9 10 11 12 13 14 15 16 17 18 19 20 21 22 23 24

SEASONAL S OR W 1-HR TIMESHIFT MIDYEAR OR JAMMING / OR /\ EARLIEST HEARD ◁ LATEST HEARD ▷ NEW FOR 2002 †

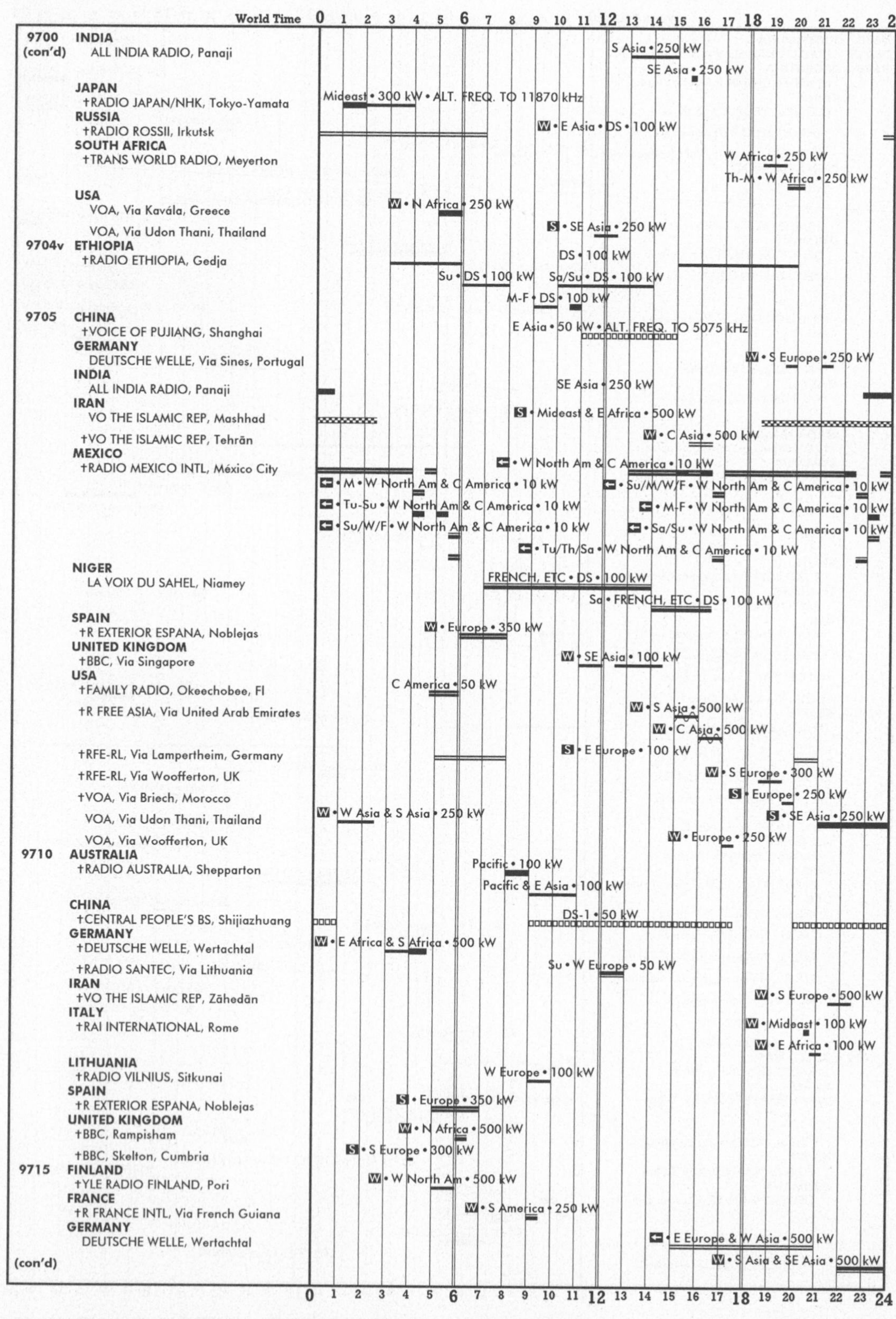
World Time 0 1 2 3 4 5 6 7 8 9 10 11 12 13 14 15 16 17 18 19 20 21 22 23 24
9700 (con'd) INDIA
ALL INDIA RADIO, Panaji
S Asia • 250 kW
SE Asia • 250 kW
JAPAN
†RADIO JAPAN/NHK, Tokyo-Yamata
Mideast • 300 kW • ALT. FREQ. TO 11870 kHz
RUSSIA
†RADIO ROSSII, Irkutsk
W • E Asia • DS • 100 kW
SOUTH AFRICA
†TRANS WORLD RADIO, Meyerton
W Africa • 250 kW
Th-M • W Africa • 250 kW
USA
VOA, Via Kavála, Greece
W • N Africa • 250 kW
VOA, Via Udon Thani, Thailand
S • SE Asia • 250 kW
9704v ETHIOPIA
†RADIO ETHIOPIA, Gedja
DS • 100 kW
Su • DS • 100 kW
Sa/Su • DS • 100 kW
M-F • DS • 100 kW
9705 CHINA
†VOICE OF PUJIANG, Shanghai
E Asia • 50 kW • ALT. FREQ. TO 5075 kHz
GERMANY
DEUTSCHE WELLE, Via Sines, Portugal
W • S Europe • 250 kW
INDIA
ALL INDIA RADIO, Panaji
SE Asia • 250 kW
IRAN
VO THE ISLAMIC REP, Mashhad
S • Mideast & E Africa • 500 kW
†VO THE ISLAMIC REP, Tehrān
W • C Asia • 500 kW
MEXICO
†RADIO MEXICO INTL, México City
• W North Am & C America • 10 kW
• M • W North Am & C America • 10 kW
• Su/M/W/F • W North Am & C America • 10 kW
• Tu-Su • W North Am & C America • 10 kW
• M-F • W North Am & C America • 10 kW
• Su/W/F • W North Am & C America • 10 kW
• Sa/Su • W North Am & C America • 10 kW
• Tu/Th/Sa • W North Am & C America • 10 kW
NIGER
LA VOIX DU SAHEL, Niamey
FRENCH, ETC • DS • 100 kW
Sa • FRENCH, ETC • DS • 100 kW
SPAIN
†R EXTERIOR ESPANA, Noblejas
W • Europe • 350 kW
UNITED KINGDOM
†BBC, Via Singapore
W • SE Asia • 100 kW
USA
†FAMILY RADIO, Okeechobee, Fl
C America • 50 kW
†R FREE ASIA, Via United Arab Emirates
W • S Asia • 500 kW
W • C Asia • 500 kW
†RFE-RL, Via Lampertheim, Germany
S • E Europe • 100 kW
†RFE-RL, Via Woofferton, UK
W • S Europe • 300 kW
†VOA, Via Briech, Morocco
S • Europe • 250 kW
VOA, Via Udon Thani, Thailand
W • W Asia & S Asia • 250 kW
S • SE Asia • 250 kW
VOA, Via Woofferton, UK
W • Europe • 250 kW
9710 AUSTRALIA
†RADIO AUSTRALIA, Shepparton
Pacific • 100 kW
Pacific & E Asia • 100 kW
CHINA
†CENTRAL PEOPLE'S BS, Shijiazhuang
DS-1 • 50 kW
GERMANY
†DEUTSCHE WELLE, Wertachtal
W • E Africa & S Africa • 500 kW
†RADIO SANTEC, Via Lithuania
Su • W Europe • 50 kW
IRAN
†VO THE ISLAMIC REP, Zāhedān
W • S Europe • 500 kW
ITALY
†RAI INTERNATIONAL, Rome
W • Mideast • 100 kW
W • E Africa • 100 kW
LITHUANIA
†RADIO VILNIUS, Sitkunai
W Europe • 100 kW
SPAIN
†R EXTERIOR ESPANA, Noblejas
S • Europe • 350 kW
UNITED KINGDOM
†BBC, Rampisham
W • N Africa • 500 kW
†BBC, Skelton, Cumbria
S • S Europe • 300 kW
9715 FINLAND
†YLE RADIO FINLAND, Pori
W • W North Am • 500 kW
FRANCE
†R FRANCE INTL, Via French Guiana
W • S America • 250 kW
GERMANY
DEUTSCHE WELLE, Wertachtal
• E Europe & W Asia • 500 kW
W • S Asia & SE Asia • 500 kW
(con'd)
0 1 2 3 4 5 6 7 8 9 10 11 12 13 14 15 16 17 18 19 20 21 22 23 24

ENGLISH ARABIC CHINESE FRENCH GERMAN RUSSIAN SPANISH OTHER

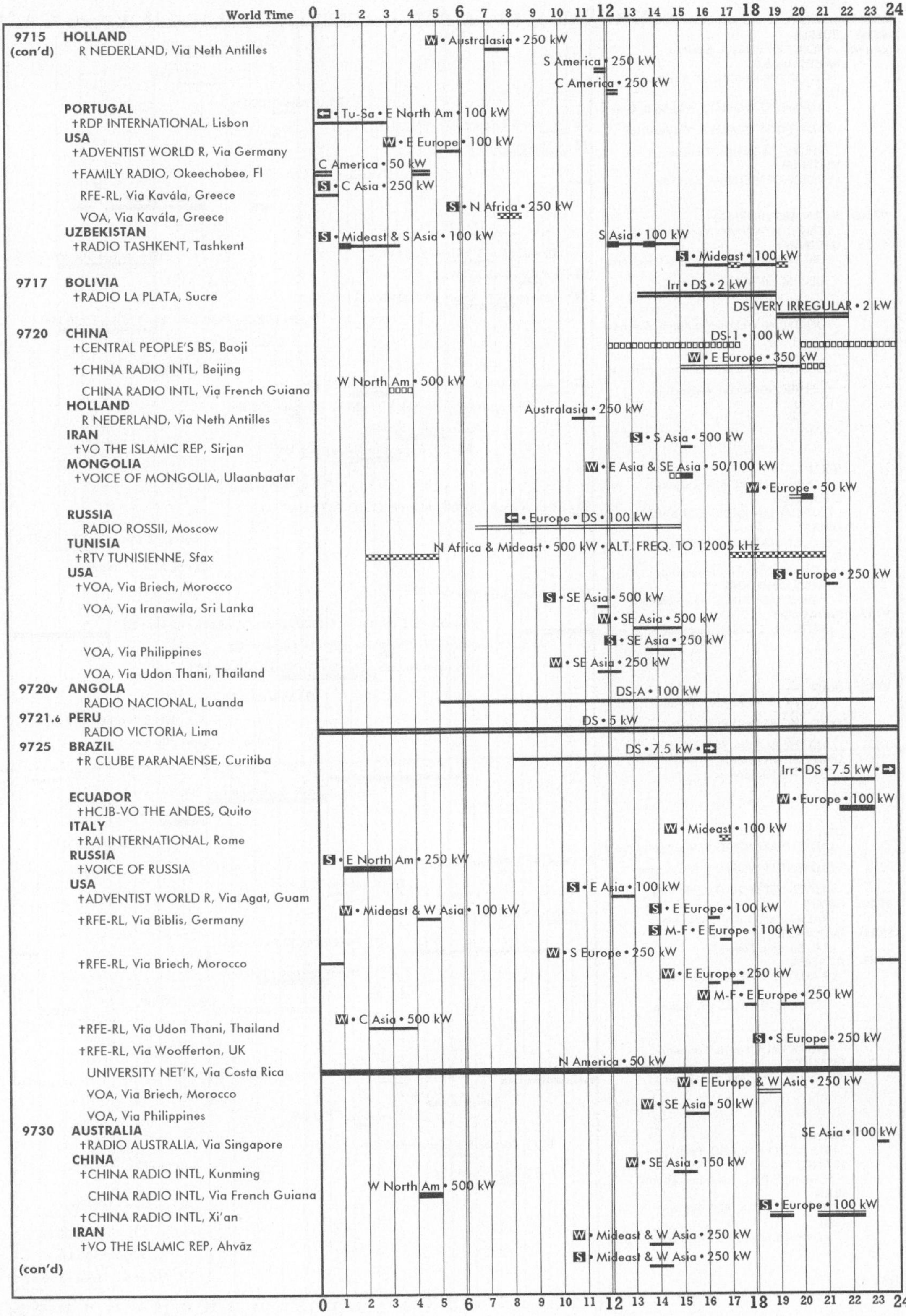
World Time 0 1 2 3 4 5 6 7 8 9 10 11 12 13 14 15 16 17 18 19 20 21 22 23 24
9715 (con'd) HOLLAND
R NEDERLAND, Via Neth Antilles
W • Australasia • 250 kW
S America • 250 kW
C America • 250 kW
PORTUGAL
†RDP INTERNATIONAL, Lisbon
Tu-Sa • E North Am • 100 kW
USA
†ADVENTIST WORLD R, Via Germany
W • E Europe • 100 kW
†FAMILY RADIO, Okeechobee, Fl
C America • 50 kW
RFE-RL, Via Kavála, Greece
S • C Asia • 250 kW
VOA, Via Kavála, Greece
S • N Africa • 250 kW
UZBEKISTAN
†RADIO TASHKENT, Tashkent
S • Mideast & S Asia • 100 kW
S Asia • 100 kW
S • Mideast • 100 kW
9717 BOLIVIA
†RADIO LA PLATA, Sucre
Irr • DS • 2 kW
DS-VERY IRREGULAR • 2 kW
9720 CHINA
†CENTRAL PEOPLE'S BS, Baoji
DS-1 • 100 kW
†CHINA RADIO INTL, Beijing
W • E Europe • 350 kW
CHINA RADIO INTL, Via French Guiana
W North Am • 500 kW
HOLLAND
R NEDERLAND, Via Neth Antilles
Australasia • 250 kW
IRAN
†VO THE ISLAMIC REP, Sirjan
S • S Asia • 500 kW
MONGOLIA
†VOICE OF MONGOLIA, Ulaanbaatar
W • E Asia & SE Asia • 50/100 kW
W • Europe • 50 kW
RUSSIA
RADIO ROSSII, Moscow
Europe • DS • 100 kW
TUNISIA
†RTV TUNISIENNE, Sfax
N Africa & Mideast • 500 kW • ALT. FREQ. TO 12005 kHz
USA
†VOA, Via Briech, Morocco
S • Europe • 250 kW
VOA, Via Iranawila, Sri Lanka
S • SE Asia • 500 kW
W • SE Asia • 500 kW
VOA, Via Philippines
S • SE Asia • 250 kW
VOA, Via Udon Thani, Thailand
W • SE Asia • 250 kW
9720v ANGOLA
RADIO NACIONAL, Luanda
DS-A • 100 kW
9721.6 PERU
RADIO VICTORIA, Lima
DS • 5 kW
9725 BRAZIL
†R CLUBE PARANAENSE, Curitiba
DS • 7.5 kW
Irr • DS • 7.5 kW
ECUADOR
†HCJB-VO THE ANDES, Quito
W • Europe • 100 kW
ITALY
†RAI INTERNATIONAL, Rome
W • Mideast • 100 kW
RUSSIA
†VOICE OF RUSSIA
S • E North Am • 250 kW
USA
†ADVENTIST WORLD R, Via Agat, Guam
S • E Asia • 100 kW
†RFE-RL, Via Biblis, Germany
W • Mideast & W Asia • 100 kW
S • E Europe • 100 kW
S M-F • E Europe • 100 kW
†RFE-RL, Via Briech, Morocco
W • S Europe • 250 kW
W • E Europe • 250 kW
W M-F • E Europe • 250 kW
W • C Asia • 500 kW
†RFE-RL, Via Udon Thani, Thailand
†RFE-RL, Via Woofferton, UK
S • S Europe • 250 kW
UNIVERSITY NET'K, Via Costa Rica
N America • 50 kW
VOA, Via Briech, Morocco
W • E Europe & W Asia • 250 kW
VOA, Via Philippines
W • SE Asia • 50 kW
9730 AUSTRALIA
†RADIO AUSTRALIA, Via Singapore
SE Asia • 100 kW
CHINA
†CHINA RADIO INTL, Kunming
W • SE Asia • 150 kW
CHINA RADIO INTL, Via French Guiana
W North Am • 500 kW
†CHINA RADIO INTL, Xi'an
S • Europe • 100 kW
IRAN
†VO THE ISLAMIC REP, Ahvāz
W • Mideast & W Asia • 250 kW
S • Mideast & W Asia • 250 kW
(con'd)
0 1 2 3 4 5 6 7 8 9 10 11 12 13 14 15 16 17 18 19 20 21 22 23 24

SEASONAL S OR W 1-HR TIMESHIFT MIDYEAR ⬅ OR ➡ JAMMING / OR /\ EARLIEST HEARD ◁ LATEST HEARD ▷ NEW FOR 2002 †

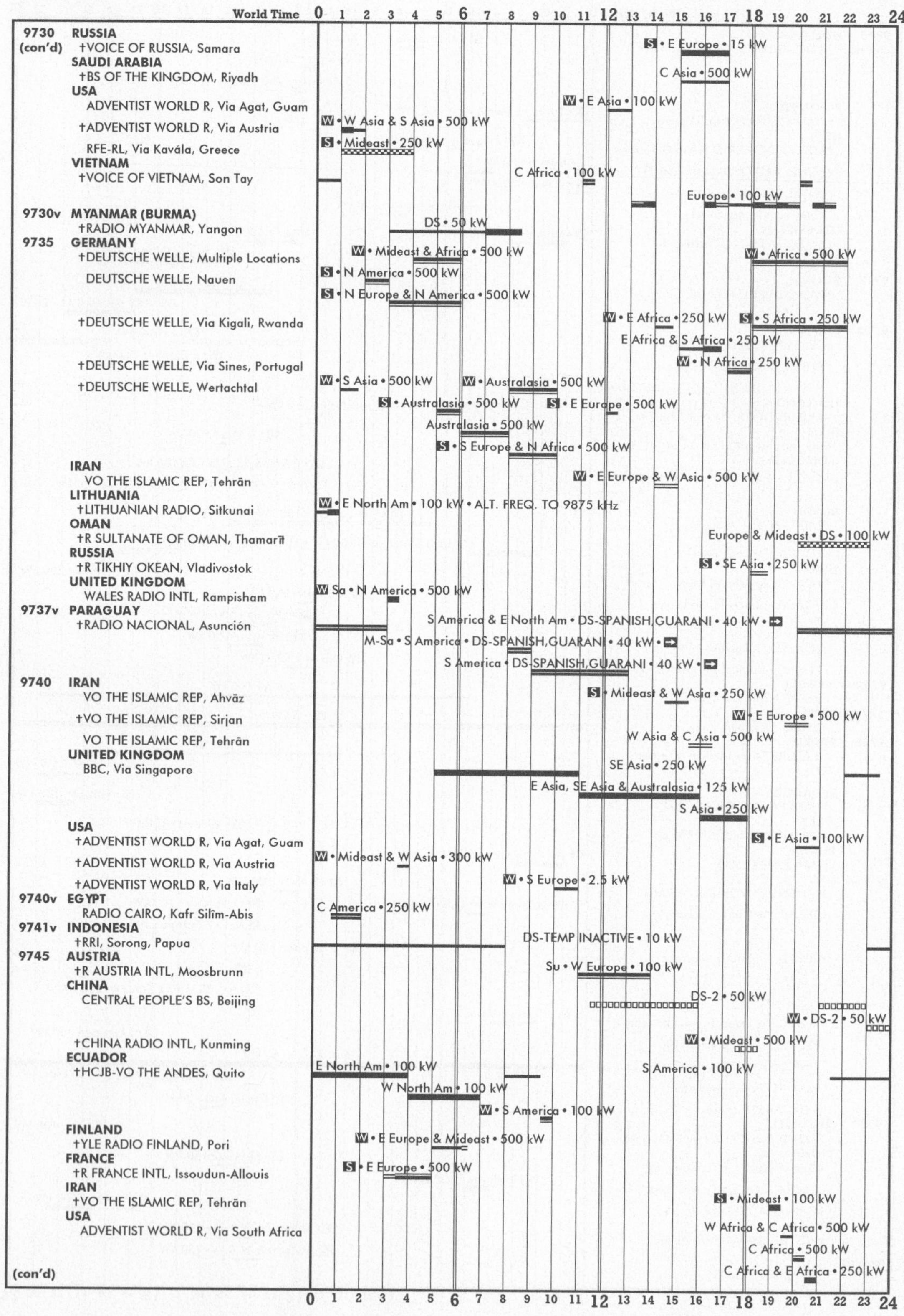
World Time 0 1 2 3 4 5 6 7 8 9 10 11 12 13 14 15 16 17 18 19 20 21 22 23 24
9730 (con'd) RUSSIA
†VOICE OF RUSSIA, Samara
S • E Europe • 15 kW
SAUDI ARABIA
†BS OF THE KINGDOM, Riyadh
C Asia • 500 kW
USA
ADVENTIST WORLD R, Via Agat, Guam
W • E Asia • 100 kW
†ADVENTIST WORLD R, Via Austria
W • W Asia & S Asia • 500 kW
RFE-RL, Via Kavála, Greece
S • Mideast • 250 kW
VIETNAM
†VOICE OF VIETNAM, Son Tay
C Africa • 100 kW
Europe • 100 kW
9730v MYANMAR (BURMA)
†RADIO MYANMAR, Yangon
DS • 50 kW
9735 GERMANY
†DEUTSCHE WELLE, Multiple Locations
W • Mideast & Africa • 500 kW
W • Africa • 500 kW
DEUTSCHE WELLE, Nauen
S • N America • 500 kW
S • N Europe & N America • 500 kW
†DEUTSCHE WELLE, Via Kigali, Rwanda
W • E Africa • 250 kW
S • S Africa • 250 kW
E Africa & S Africa • 250 kW
†DEUTSCHE WELLE, Via Sines, Portugal
W • N Africa • 250 kW
†DEUTSCHE WELLE, Wertachtal
W • S Asia • 500 kW
W • Australasia • 500 kW
S • Australasia • 500 kW
S • E Europe • 500 kW
Australasia • 500 kW
S • S Europe & N Africa • 500 kW
IRAN
VO THE ISLAMIC REP, Tehrān
W • E Europe & W Asia • 500 kW
LITHUANIA
†LITHUANIAN RADIO, Sitkunai
W • E North Am • 100 kW • ALT. FREQ. TO 9875 kHz
OMAN
†R SULTANATE OF OMAN, Thamarīt
Europe & Mideast • DS • 100 kW
RUSSIA
†R TIKHIY OKEAN, Vladivostok
S • SE Asia • 250 kW
UNITED KINGDOM
WALES RADIO INTL, Rampisham
W Sa • N America • 500 kW
9737v PARAGUAY
†RADIO NACIONAL, Asunción
S America & E North Am • DS-SPANISH,GUARANI • 40 kW
M-Sa • S America • DS-SPANISH,GUARANI • 40 kW
S America • DS-SPANISH,GUARANI • 40 kW
9740 IRAN
VO THE ISLAMIC REP, Ahvāz
S • Mideast & W Asia • 250 kW
†VO THE ISLAMIC REP, Sirjan
W • E Europe • 500 kW
VO THE ISLAMIC REP, Tehrān
W Asia & C Asia • 500 kW
UNITED KINGDOM
BBC, Via Singapore
SE Asia • 250 kW
E Asia, SE Asia & Australasia • 125 kW
S Asia • 250 kW
USA
†ADVENTIST WORLD R, Via Agat, Guam
S • E Asia • 100 kW
†ADVENTIST WORLD R, Via Austria
W • Mideast & W Asia • 300 kW
†ADVENTIST WORLD R, Via Italy
W • S Europe • 2.5 kW
9740v EGYPT
RADIO CAIRO, Kafr Silîm-Abis
C America • 250 kW
9741v INDONESIA
†RRI, Sorong, Papua
DS-TEMP INACTIVE • 10 kW
9745 AUSTRIA
†R AUSTRIA INTL, Moosbrunn
Su • W Europe • 100 kW
CHINA
CENTRAL PEOPLE'S BS, Beijing
DS-2 • 50 kW
W • DS-2 • 50 kW
†CHINA RADIO INTL, Kunming
W • Mideast • 500 kW
ECUADOR
†HCJB-VO THE ANDES, Quito
E North Am • 100 kW
S America • 100 kW
W North Am • 100 kW
W • S America • 100 kW
FINLAND
†YLE RADIO FINLAND, Pori
W • E Europe & Mideast • 500 kW
FRANCE
†R FRANCE INTL, Issoudun-Allouis
S • E Europe • 500 kW
IRAN
†VO THE ISLAMIC REP, Tehrān
S • Mideast • 100 kW
USA
ADVENTIST WORLD R, Via South Africa
W Africa & C Africa • 500 kW
C Africa • 500 kW
C Africa & E Africa • 250 kW
(con'd)

ENGLISH ARABIC CHINESE FRENCH GERMAN RUSSIAN SPANISH OTHER

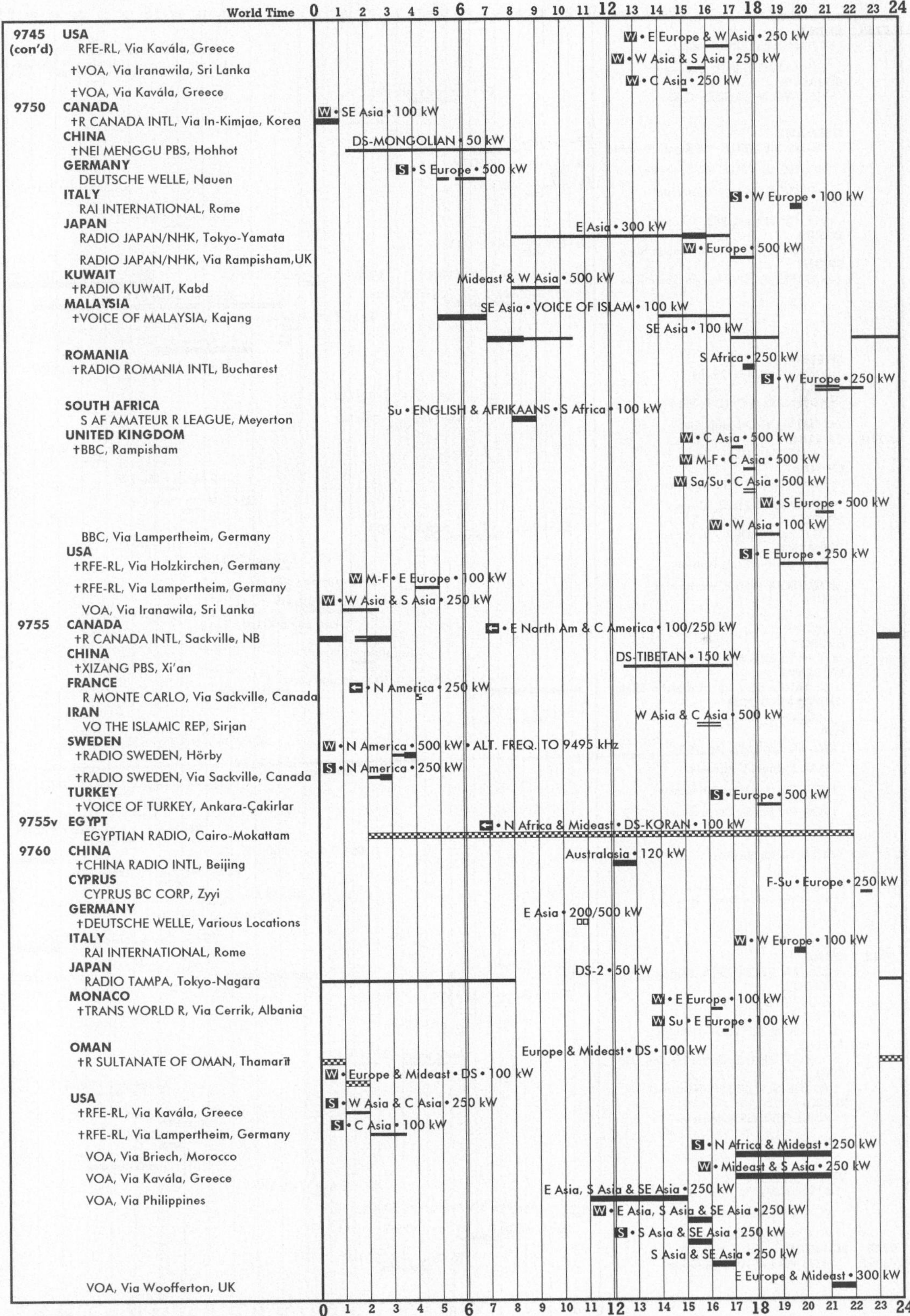
World Time 0 1 2 3 4 5 6 7 8 9 10 11 12 13 14 15 16 17 18 19 20 21 22 23 24
9745 (con'd) USA
RFE-RL, Via Kavála, Greece
W • E Europe & W Asia • 250 kW
†VOA, Via Iranawila, Sri Lanka
W • W Asia & S Asia • 250 kW
†VOA, Via Kavála, Greece
W • C Asia • 250 kW
9750 CANADA
†R CANADA INTL, Via In-Kimjae, Korea
W • SE Asia • 100 kW
CHINA
†NEI MENGGU PBS, Hohhot
DS-MONGOLIAN • 50 kW
GERMANY
DEUTSCHE WELLE, Nauen
S • S Europe • 500 kW
ITALY
RAI INTERNATIONAL, Rome
S • W Europe • 100 kW
JAPAN
RADIO JAPAN/NHK, Tokyo-Yamata
E Asia • 300 kW
RADIO JAPAN/NHK, Via Rampisham,UK
W • Europe • 500 kW
KUWAIT
†RADIO KUWAIT, Kabd
Mideast & W Asia • 500 kW
MALAYSIA
†VOICE OF MALAYSIA, Kajang
SE Asia • VOICE OF ISLAM • 100 kW
SE Asia • 100 kW
ROMANIA
†RADIO ROMANIA INTL, Bucharest
S Africa • 250 kW
S • W Europe • 250 kW
SOUTH AFRICA
S AF AMATEUR R LEAGUE, Meyerton
Su • ENGLISH & AFRIKAANS • S Africa • 100 kW
UNITED KINGDOM
†BBC, Rampisham
W • C Asia • 500 kW
W M-F • C Asia • 500 kW
W Sa/Su • C Asia • 500 kW
W • S Europe • 500 kW
W • W Asia • 100 kW
BBC, Via Lampertheim, Germany
S • E Europe • 250 kW
USA
†RFE-RL, Via Holzkirchen, Germany
W M-F • E Europe • 100 kW
†RFE-RL, Via Lampertheim, Germany
W • W Asia & S Asia • 250 kW
VOA, Via Iranawila, Sri Lanka
9755 CANADA
†R CANADA INTL, Sackville, NB
← • E North Am & C America • 100/250 kW
CHINA
†XIZANG PBS, Xi'an
DS-TIBETAN • 150 kW
FRANCE
R MONTE CARLO, Via Sackville, Canada
← • N America • 250 kW
IRAN
VO THE ISLAMIC REP, Sirjan
W Asia & C Asia • 500 kW
SWEDEN
†RADIO SWEDEN, Hörby
W • N America • 500 kW • ALT. FREQ. TO 9495 kHz
†RADIO SWEDEN, Via Sackville, Canada
S • N America • 250 kW
TURKEY
†VOICE OF TURKEY, Ankara-Çakirlar
S • Europe • 500 kW
9755v EGYPT
EGYPTIAN RADIO, Cairo-Mokattam
← • N Africa & Mideast • DS-KORAN • 100 kW
9760 CHINA
†CHINA RADIO INTL, Beijing
Australasia • 120 kW
CYPRUS
CYPRUS BC CORP, Zyyi
F-Su • Europe • 250 kW
GERMANY
†DEUTSCHE WELLE, Various Locations
E Asia • 200/500 kW
ITALY
RAI INTERNATIONAL, Rome
W • W Europe • 100 kW
JAPAN
RADIO TAMPA, Tokyo-Nagara
DS-2 • 50 kW
MONACO
†TRANS WORLD R, Via Cerrik, Albania
W • E Europe • 100 kW
W Su • E Europe • 100 kW
OMAN
†R SULTANATE OF OMAN, Thamarīt
Europe & Mideast • DS • 100 kW
W • Europe & Mideast • DS • 100 kW
USA
†RFE-RL, Via Kavála, Greece
S • W Asia & C Asia • 250 kW
†RFE-RL, Via Lampertheim, Germany
S • C Asia • 100 kW
VOA, Via Briech, Morocco
S • N Africa & Mideast • 250 kW
VOA, Via Kavála, Greece
W • Mideast & S Asia • 250 kW
VOA, Via Philippines
E Asia, S Asia & SE Asia • 250 kW
W • E Asia, S Asia & SE Asia • 250 kW
S • S Asia & SE Asia • 250 kW
S Asia & SE Asia • 250 kW
VOA, Via Woofferton, UK
E Europe & Mideast • 300 kW
0 1 2 3 4 5 6 7 8 9 10 11 12 13 14 15 16 17 18 19 20 21 22 23 24

SEASONAL S OR W 1-HR TIMESHIFT MIDYEAR ← OR → JAMMING / OR /\ EARLIEST HEARD ◁ LATEST HEARD ▷ NEW FOR 2002 †

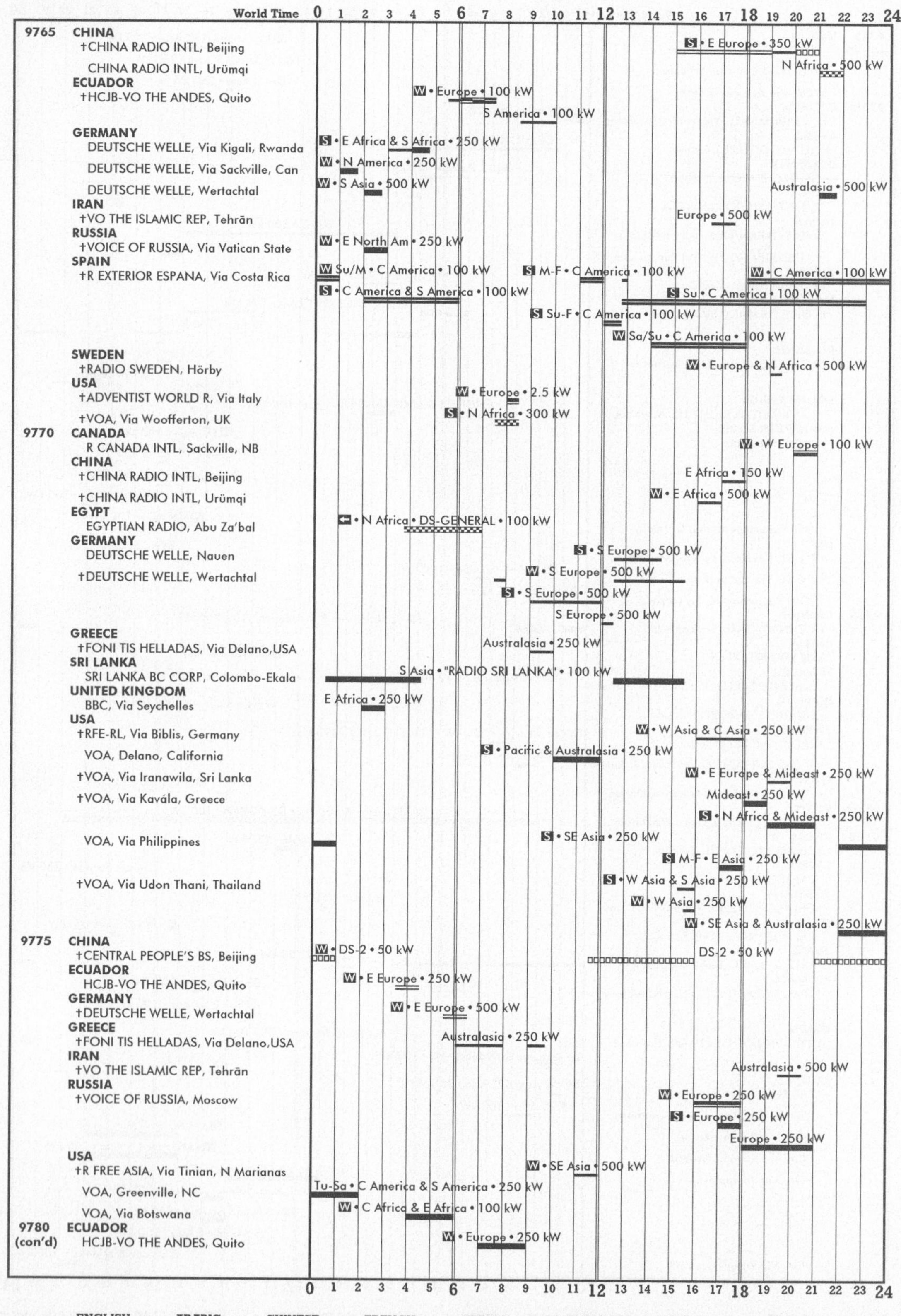
World Time 0 1 2 3 4 5 6 7 8 9 10 11 12 13 14 15 16 17 18 19 20 21 22 23 24
9765 CHINA
†CHINA RADIO INTL, Beijing
S • E Europe • 350 kW
CHINA RADIO INTL, Urümqi
N Africa • 500 kW
ECUADOR
†HCJB-VO THE ANDES, Quito
W • Europe • 100 kW
S America • 100 kW
GERMANY
DEUTSCHE WELLE, Via Kigali, Rwanda
S • E Africa & S Africa • 250 kW
DEUTSCHE WELLE, Via Sackville, Can
W • N America • 250 kW
DEUTSCHE WELLE, Wertachtal
W • S Asia • 500 kW
Australasia • 500 kW
IRAN
†VO THE ISLAMIC REP, Tehrān
Europe • 500 kW
RUSSIA
†VOICE OF RUSSIA, Via Vatican State
W • E North Am • 250 kW
SPAIN
†R EXTERIOR ESPANA, Via Costa Rica
W Su/M • C America • 100 kW
S M-F • C America • 100 kW
W • C America • 100 kW
S • C America & S America • 100 kW
S Su • C America • 100 kW
S Su-F • C America • 100 kW
W Sa/Su • C America • 100 kW
SWEDEN
†RADIO SWEDEN, Hörby
W • Europe & N Africa • 500 kW
USA
†ADVENTIST WORLD R, Via Italy
W • Europe • 2.5 kW
†VOA, Via Woofferton, UK
S • N Africa • 300 kW
9770 CANADA
R CANADA INTL, Sackville, NB
W • W Europe • 100 kW
CHINA
†CHINA RADIO INTL, Beijing
E Africa • 150 kW
†CHINA RADIO INTL, Urümqi
W • E Africa • 500 kW
EGYPT
EGYPTIAN RADIO, Abu Za'bal
• N Africa • DS-GENERAL • 100 kW
GERMANY
DEUTSCHE WELLE, Nauen
S • S Europe • 500 kW
†DEUTSCHE WELLE, Wertachtal
W • S Europe • 500 kW
S • S Europe • 500 kW
S Europe • 500 kW
GREECE
†FONI TIS HELLADAS, Via Delano,USA
Australasia • 250 kW
SRI LANKA
SRI LANKA BC CORP, Colombo-Ekala
S Asia • "RADIO SRI LANKA" • 100 kW
UNITED KINGDOM
BBC, Via Seychelles
E Africa • 250 kW
USA
†RFE-RL, Via Biblis, Germany
W • W Asia & C Asia • 250 kW
VOA, Delano, California
S • Pacific & Australasia • 250 kW
†VOA, Via Iranawila, Sri Lanka
W • E Europe & Mideast • 250 kW
†VOA, Via Kavála, Greece
Mideast • 250 kW
S • N Africa & Mideast • 250 kW
VOA, Via Philippines
S • SE Asia • 250 kW
S M-F • E Asia • 250 kW
†VOA, Via Udon Thani, Thailand
S • W Asia & S Asia • 250 kW
W • W Asia • 250 kW
W • SE Asia & Australasia • 250 kW
9775 CHINA
†CENTRAL PEOPLE'S BS, Beijing
W • DS-2 • 50 kW
DS-2 • 50 kW
ECUADOR
HCJB-VO THE ANDES, Quito
W • E Europe • 250 kW
GERMANY
†DEUTSCHE WELLE, Wertachtal
W • E Europe • 500 kW
GREECE
†FONI TIS HELLADAS, Via Delano,USA
Australasia • 250 kW
IRAN
†VO THE ISLAMIC REP, Tehrān
Australasia • 500 kW
RUSSIA
†VOICE OF RUSSIA, Moscow
W • Europe • 250 kW
S • Europe • 250 kW
Europe • 250 kW
USA
†R FREE ASIA, Via Tinian, N Marianas
W • SE Asia • 500 kW
VOA, Greenville, NC
Tu-Sa • C America & S America • 250 kW
VOA, Via Botswana
W • C Africa & E Africa • 100 kW
9780 (con'd) ECUADOR
HCJB-VO THE ANDES, Quito
W • Europe • 250 kW
0 1 2 3 4 5 6 7 8 9 10 11 12 13 14 15 16 17 18 19 20 21 22 23 24

ENGLISH ARABIC CHINESE FRENCH GERMAN RUSSIAN SPANISH OTHER

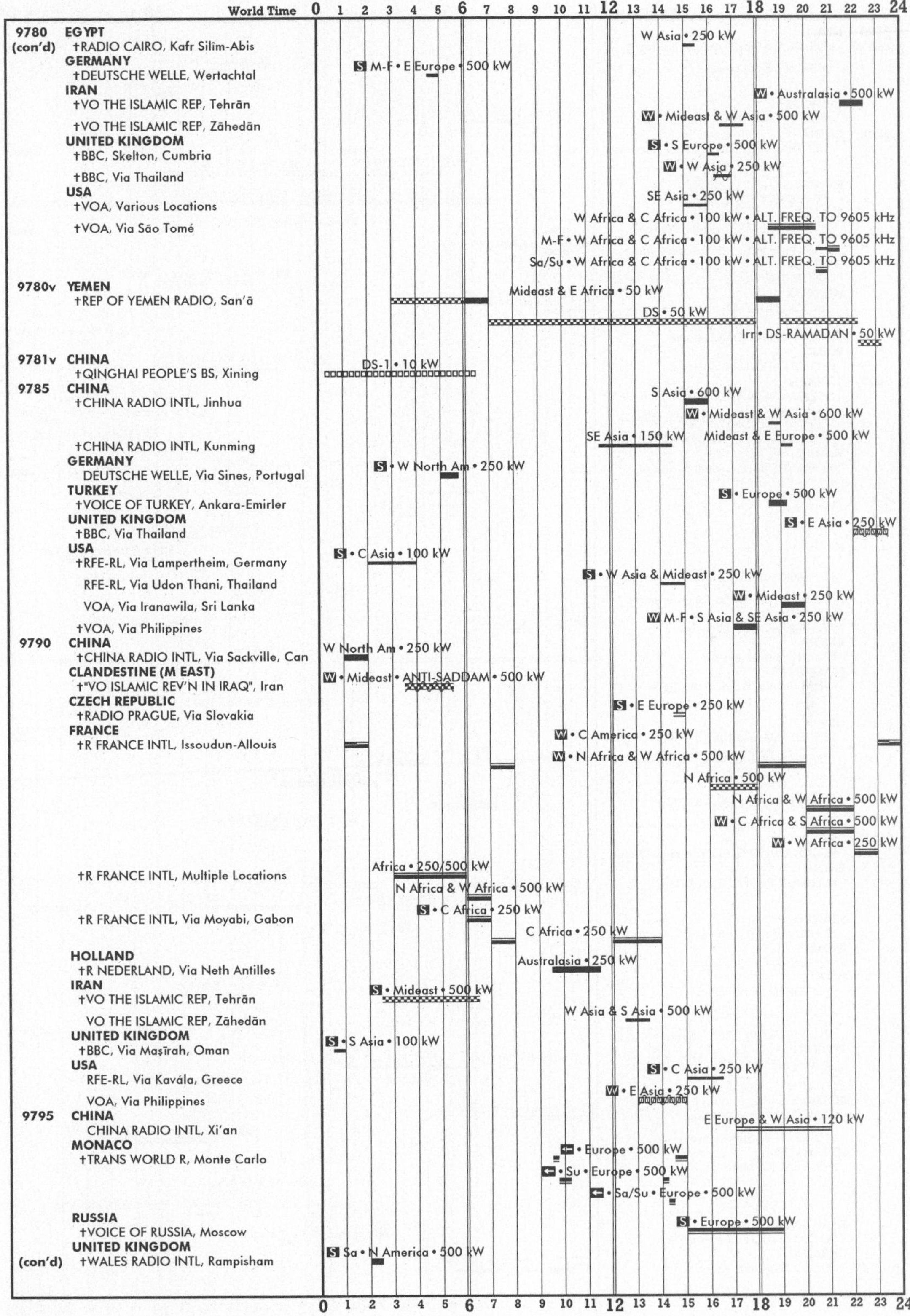
World Time 0 1 2 3 4 5 6 7 8 9 10 11 12 13 14 15 16 17 18 19 20 21 22 23 24
9780 (con'd) EGYPT
†RADIO CAIRO, Kafr Silīm-Abis
W Asia • 250 kW
GERMANY
†DEUTSCHE WELLE, Wertachtal
S M-F • E Europe • 500 kW
IRAN
†VO THE ISLAMIC REP, Tehrān
W • Australasia • 500 kW
†VO THE ISLAMIC REP, Zāhedān
W • Mideast & W Asia • 500 kW
UNITED KINGDOM
†BBC, Skelton, Cumbria
S • S Europe • 500 kW
†BBC, Via Thailand
W • W Asia • 250 kW
USA
†VOA, Various Locations
SE Asia • 250 kW
†VOA, Via São Tomé
W Africa & C Africa • 100 kW • ALT. FREQ. TO 9605 kHz
M-F • W Africa & C Africa • 100 kW • ALT. FREQ. TO 9605 kHz
Sa/Su • W Africa & C Africa • 100 kW • ALT. FREQ. TO 9605 kHz
9780v YEMEN
†REP OF YEMEN RADIO, San'ā
Mideast & E Africa • 50 kW
DS • 50 kW
Irr • DS-RAMADAN • 50 kW
9781v CHINA
†QINGHAI PEOPLE'S BS, Xining
DS-1 • 10 kW
9785 CHINA
†CHINA RADIO INTL, Jinhua
S Asia • 600 kW
W • Mideast & W Asia • 600 kW
†CHINA RADIO INTL, Kunming
SE Asia • 150 kW
Mideast & E Europe • 500 kW
GERMANY
DEUTSCHE WELLE, Via Sines, Portugal
S • W North Am • 250 kW
TURKEY
†VOICE OF TURKEY, Ankara-Emirler
S • Europe • 500 kW
UNITED KINGDOM
†BBC, Via Thailand
S • E Asia • 250 kW
USA
†RFE-RL, Via Lampertheim, Germany
S • C Asia • 100 kW
RFE-RL, Via Udon Thani, Thailand
S • W Asia & Mideast • 250 kW
VOA, Via Iranawila, Sri Lanka
W • Mideast • 250 kW
†VOA, Via Philippines
W M-F • S Asia & SE Asia • 250 kW
9790 CHINA
†CHINA RADIO INTL, Via Sackville, Can
W North Am • 250 kW
CLANDESTINE (M EAST)
†"VO ISLAMIC REV'N IN IRAQ", Iran
W • Mideast • ANTI-SADDAM • 500 kW
CZECH REPUBLIC
†RADIO PRAGUE, Via Slovakia
S • E Europe • 250 kW
FRANCE
†R FRANCE INTL, Issoudun-Allouis
W • C America • 250 kW
W • N Africa & W Africa • 500 kW
N Africa • 500 kW
N Africa & W Africa • 500 kW
W • C Africa & S Africa • 500 kW
W • W Africa • 250 kW
†R FRANCE INTL, Multiple Locations
Africa • 250/500 kW
N Africa & W Africa • 500 kW
†R FRANCE INTL, Via Moyabi, Gabon
S • C Africa • 250 kW
C Africa • 250 kW
HOLLAND
†R NEDERLAND, Via Neth Antilles
Australasia • 250 kW
IRAN
†VO THE ISLAMIC REP, Tehrān
S • Mideast • 500 kW
VO THE ISLAMIC REP, Zāhedān
W Asia & S Asia • 500 kW
UNITED KINGDOM
†BBC, Via Maşīrah, Oman
S • S Asia • 100 kW
USA
RFE-RL, Via Kavála, Greece
S • C Asia • 250 kW
VOA, Via Philippines
W • E Asia • 250 kW
9795 CHINA
CHINA RADIO INTL, Xi'an
E Europe & W Asia • 120 kW
MONACO
†TRANS WORLD R, Monte Carlo
• Europe • 500 kW
• Su • Europe • 500 kW
• Sa/Su • Europe • 500 kW
RUSSIA
†VOICE OF RUSSIA, Moscow
S • Europe • 500 kW
UNITED KINGDOM
(con'd) †WALES RADIO INTL, Rampisham
S Sa • N America • 500 kW
0 1 2 3 4 5 6 7 8 9 10 11 12 13 14 15 16 17 18 19 20 21 22 23 24

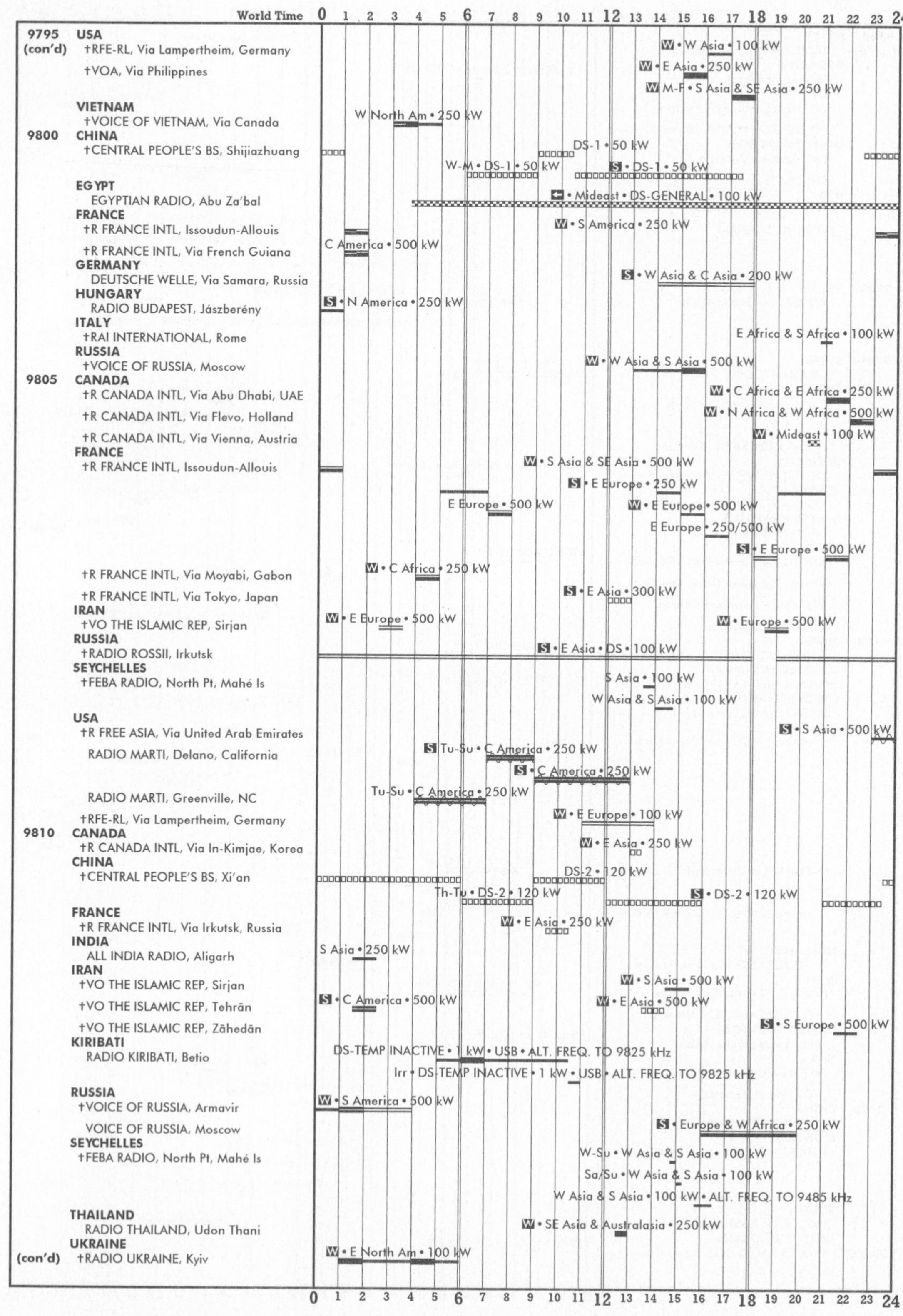
World Time
0 1 2 3 4 5 6 7 8 9 10 11 12 13 14 15 16 17 18 19 20 21 22 23 24
9795 USA
(con'd)
†RFE-RL, Via Lampertheim, Germany
W • W Asia • 100 kW
†VOA, Via Philippines
W • E Asia • 250 kW
W M-F • S Asia & SE Asia • 250 kW
VIETNAM
†VOICE OF VIETNAM, Via Canada
W North Am • 250 kW
9800 CHINA
†CENTRAL PEOPLE'S BS, Shijiazhuang
DS-1 • 50 kW
W-M • DS-1 • 50 kW
S • DS-1 • 50 kW
EGYPT
EGYPTIAN RADIO, Abu Za'bal
Mideast • DS-GENERAL • 100 kW
FRANCE
†R FRANCE INTL, Issoudun-Allouis
W • S America • 250 kW
†R FRANCE INTL, Via French Guiana
C America • 500 kW
GERMANY
DEUTSCHE WELLE, Via Samara, Russia
S • W Asia & C Asia • 200 kW
HUNGARY
RADIO BUDAPEST, Jászberény
S • N America • 250 kW
ITALY
†RAI INTERNATIONAL, Rome
E Africa & S Africa • 100 kW
RUSSIA
†VOICE OF RUSSIA, Moscow
W • W Asia & S Asia • 500 kW
9805 CANADA
†R CANADA INTL, Via Abu Dhabi, UAE
W • C Africa & E Africa • 250 kW
†R CANADA INTL, Via Flevo, Holland
W • N Africa & W Africa • 500 kW
†R CANADA INTL, Via Vienna, Austria
W • Mideast • 100 kW
FRANCE
†R FRANCE INTL, Issoudun-Allouis
W • S Asia & SE Asia • 500 kW
S • E Europe • 250 kW
E Europe • 500 kW
W • E Europe • 500 kW
E Europe • 250/500 kW
S • E Europe • 500 kW
†R FRANCE INTL, Via Moyabi, Gabon
W • C Africa • 250 kW
†R FRANCE INTL, Via Tokyo, Japan
S • E Asia • 300 kW
IRAN
†VO THE ISLAMIC REP, Sirjan
W • E Europe • 500 kW
W • Europe • 500 kW
RUSSIA
†RADIO ROSSII, Irkutsk
S • E Asia • DS • 100 kW
SEYCHELLES
†FEBA RADIO, North Pt, Mahé Is
S Asia • 100 kW
W Asia & S Asia • 100 kW
USA
†R FREE ASIA, Via United Arab Emirates
S • S Asia • 500 kW
RADIO MARTI, Delano, California
S Tu-Su • C America • 250 kW
S • C America • 250 kW
RADIO MARTI, Greenville, NC
Tu-Su • C America • 250 kW
†RFE-RL, Via Lampertheim, Germany
W • E Europe • 100 kW
9810 CANADA
†R CANADA INTL, Via In-Kimjae, Korea
W • E Asia • 250 kW
CHINA
†CENTRAL PEOPLE'S BS, Xi'an
DS-2 • 120 kW
Th-Tu • DS-2 • 120 kW
S • DS-2 • 120 kW
FRANCE
†R FRANCE INTL, Via Irkutsk, Russia
W • E Asia • 250 kW
INDIA
ALL INDIA RADIO, Aligarh
S Asia • 250 kW
IRAN
†VO THE ISLAMIC REP, Sirjan
W • S Asia • 500 kW
†VO THE ISLAMIC REP, Tehrān
S • C America • 500 kW
W • E Asia • 500 kW
†VO THE ISLAMIC REP, Zāhedān
S • S Europe • 500 kW
KIRIBATI
RADIO KIRIBATI, Betio
DS-TEMP INACTIVE • 1 kW • USB • ALT. FREQ. TO 9825 kHz
Irr • DS-TEMP INACTIVE • 1 kW • USB • ALT. FREQ. TO 9825 kHz
RUSSIA
†VOICE OF RUSSIA, Armavir
W • S America • 500 kW
VOICE OF RUSSIA, Moscow
S • Europe & W Africa • 250 kW
SEYCHELLES
†FEBA RADIO, North Pt, Mahé Is
W-Su • W Asia & S Asia • 100 kW
Sa/Su • W Asia & S Asia • 100 kW
W Asia & S Asia • 100 kW • ALT. FREQ. TO 9485 kHz
THAILAND
RADIO THAILAND, Udon Thani
W • SE Asia & Australasia • 250 kW
UKRAINE
(con'd)
†RADIO UKRAINE, Kyiv
W • E North Am • 100 kW
0 1 2 3 4 5 6 7 8 9 10 11 12 13 14 15 16 17 18 19 20 21 22 23 24

ENGLISH ARABIC CHINESE FRENCH GERMAN RUSSIAN SPANISH OTHER

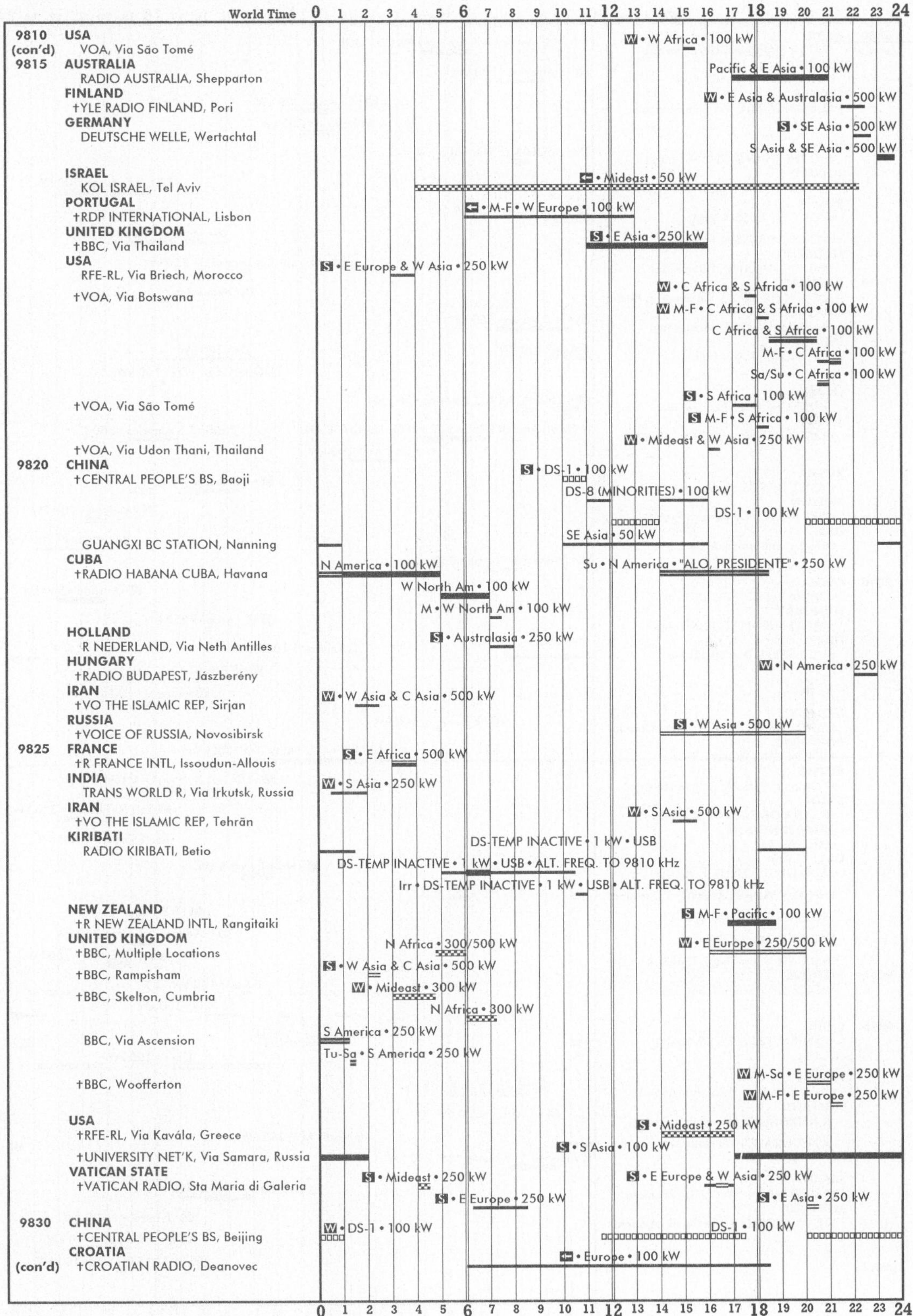
World Time 0 1 2 3 4 5 6 7 8 9 10 11 12 13 14 15 16 17 18 19 20 21 22 23 24
9810 (con'd) USA
VOA, Via São Tomé
W • W Africa • 100 kW
9815 AUSTRALIA
RADIO AUSTRALIA, Shepparton
Pacific & E Asia • 100 kW
FINLAND
†YLE RADIO FINLAND, Pori
W • E Asia & Australasia • 500 kW
GERMANY
DEUTSCHE WELLE, Wertachtal
S • SE Asia • 500 kW
S Asia & SE Asia • 500 kW
ISRAEL
KOL ISRAEL, Tel Aviv
• Mideast • 50 kW
PORTUGAL
†RDP INTERNATIONAL, Lisbon
• M-F • W Europe • 100 kW
UNITED KINGDOM
†BBC, Via Thailand
S • E Asia • 250 kW
USA
RFE-RL, Via Briech, Morocco
S • E Europe & W Asia • 250 kW
†VOA, Via Botswana
W • C Africa & S Africa • 100 kW
W M-F • C Africa & S Africa • 100 kW
C Africa & S Africa • 100 kW
M-F • C Africa • 100 kW
Sa/Su • C Africa • 100 kW
†VOA, Via São Tomé
S • S Africa • 100 kW
S M-F • S Africa • 100 kW
†VOA, Via Udon Thani, Thailand
W • Mideast & W Asia • 250 kW
9820 CHINA
†CENTRAL PEOPLE'S BS, Baoji
S • DS-1 • 100 kW
DS-8 (MINORITIES) • 100 kW
DS-1 • 100 kW
GUANGXI BC STATION, Nanning
SE Asia • 50 kW
CUBA
†RADIO HABANA CUBA, Havana
N America • 100 kW
Su • N America • "ALO, PRESIDENTE" • 250 kW
W North Am • 100 kW
M • W North Am • 100 kW
HOLLAND
R NEDERLAND, Via Neth Antilles
S • Australasia • 250 kW
HUNGARY
†RADIO BUDAPEST, Jászberény
W • N America • 250 kW
IRAN
†VO THE ISLAMIC REP, Sirjan
W • W Asia & C Asia • 500 kW
RUSSIA
†VOICE OF RUSSIA, Novosibirsk
S • W Asia • 500 kW
9825 FRANCE
†R FRANCE INTL, Issoudun-Allouis
S • E Africa • 500 kW
INDIA
TRANS WORLD R, Via Irkutsk, Russia
W • S Asia • 250 kW
IRAN
†VO THE ISLAMIC REP, Tehrān
W • S Asia • 500 kW
KIRIBATI
RADIO KIRIBATI, Betio
DS-TEMP INACTIVE • 1 kW • USB
DS-TEMP INACTIVE • 1 kW • USB • ALT. FREQ. TO 9810 kHz
Irr • DS-TEMP INACTIVE • 1 kW • USB • ALT. FREQ. TO 9810 kHz
NEW ZEALAND
†R NEW ZEALAND INTL, Rangitaiki
S M-F • Pacific • 100 kW
UNITED KINGDOM
†BBC, Multiple Locations
N Africa • 300/500 kW
W • E Europe • 250/500 kW
†BBC, Rampisham
S • W Asia & C Asia • 500 kW
†BBC, Skelton, Cumbria
W • Mideast • 300 kW
N Africa • 300 kW
BBC, Via Ascension
S America • 250 kW
Tu-Sa • S America • 250 kW
†BBC, Woofferton
W M-Sa • E Europe • 250 kW
W M-F • E Europe • 250 kW
USA
†RFE-RL, Via Kavála, Greece
S • Mideast • 250 kW
†UNIVERSITY NET'K, Via Samara, Russia
S • S Asia • 100 kW
VATICAN STATE
†VATICAN RADIO, Sta Maria di Galeria
S • Mideast • 250 kW
S • E Europe & W Asia • 250 kW
S • E Europe • 250 kW
S • E Asia • 250 kW
9830 CHINA
†CENTRAL PEOPLE'S BS, Beijing
W • DS-1 • 100 kW
DS-1 • 100 kW
(con'd) CROATIA
†CROATIAN RADIO, Deanovec
• Europe • 100 kW
0 1 2 3 4 5 6 7 8 9 10 11 12 13 14 15 16 17 18 19 20 21 22 23 24

SEASONAL S OR W   1-HR TIMESHIFT MIDYEAR ⬅ OR ➡   JAMMING / OR /\   EARLIEST HEARD ◁   LATEST HEARD ▷   NEW FOR 2002 †

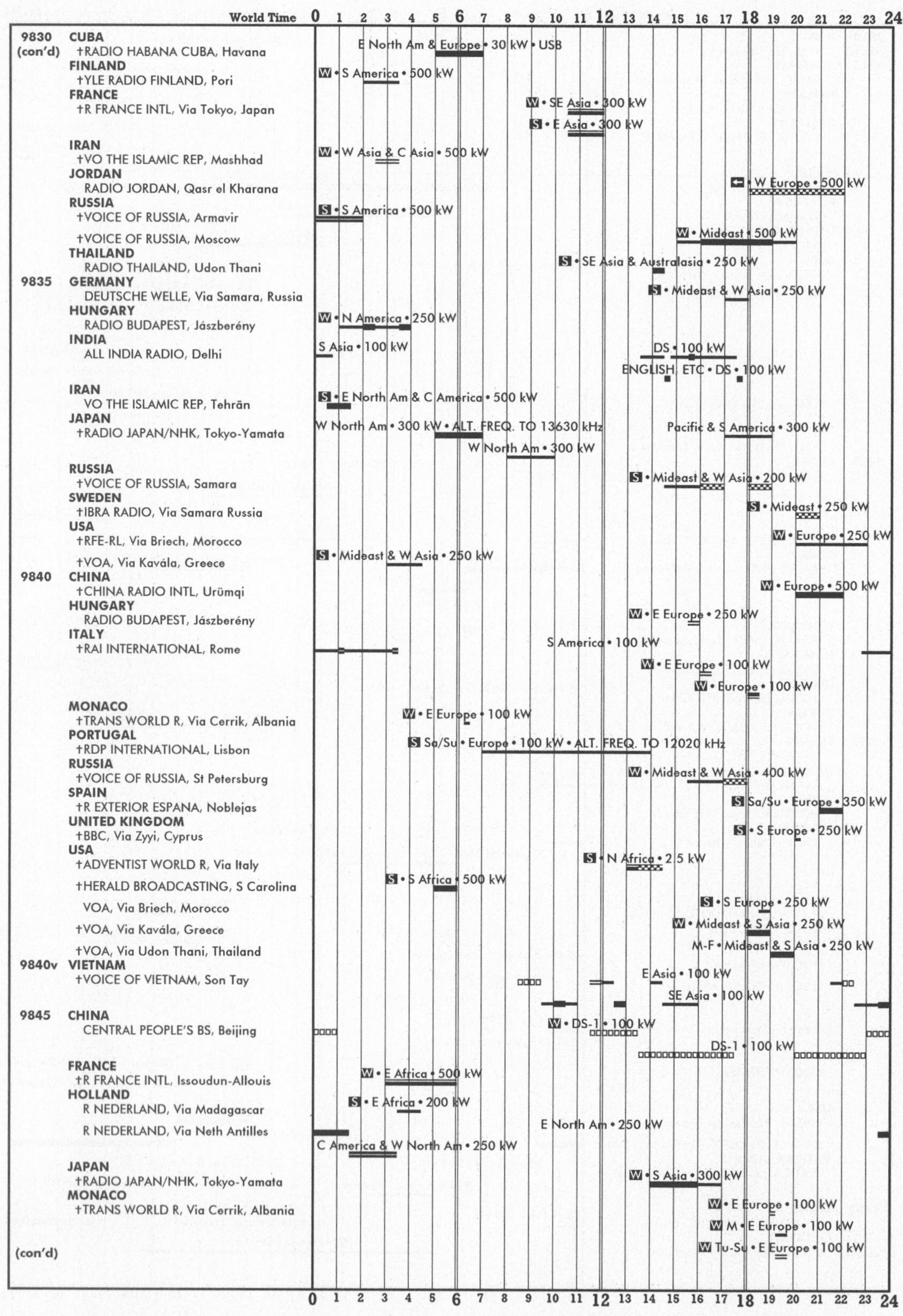
World Time 0 1 2 3 4 5 6 7 8 9 10 11 12 13 14 15 16 17 18 19 20 21 22 23 24
9830 (con'd) CUBA
†RADIO HABANA CUBA, Havana
E North Am & Europe • 30 kW • USB
FINLAND
†YLE RADIO FINLAND, Pori
W • S America • 500 kW
FRANCE
†R FRANCE INTL, Via Tokyo, Japan
W • SE Asia • 300 kW
S • E Asia • 300 kW
IRAN
†VO THE ISLAMIC REP, Mashhad
W • W Asia & C Asia • 500 kW
JORDAN
RADIO JORDAN, Qasr el Kharana
W Europe • 500 kW
RUSSIA
†VOICE OF RUSSIA, Armavir
S • S America • 500 kW
†VOICE OF RUSSIA, Moscow
W • Mideast • 500 kW
THAILAND
RADIO THAILAND, Udon Thani
S • SE Asia & Australasia • 250 kW
9835 GERMANY
DEUTSCHE WELLE, Via Samara, Russia
S • Mideast & W Asia • 250 kW
HUNGARY
RADIO BUDAPEST, Jászberény
W • N America • 250 kW
INDIA
ALL INDIA RADIO, Delhi
S Asia • 100 kW
DS • 100 kW
ENGLISH, ETC • DS • 100 kW
IRAN
VO THE ISLAMIC REP, Tehrān
S • E North Am & C America • 500 kW
JAPAN
†RADIO JAPAN/NHK, Tokyo-Yamata
W North Am • 300 kW • ALT. FREQ. TO 13630 kHz
Pacific & S America • 300 kW
W North Am • 300 kW
RUSSIA
†VOICE OF RUSSIA, Samara
S • Mideast & W Asia • 200 kW
SWEDEN
†IBRA RADIO, Via Samara Russia
S • Mideast • 250 kW
USA
†RFE-RL, Via Briech, Morocco
W • Europe • 250 kW
†VOA, Via Kavála, Greece
S • Mideast & W Asia • 250 kW
9840 CHINA
†CHINA RADIO INTL, Urümqi
W • Europe • 500 kW
HUNGARY
RADIO BUDAPEST, Jászberény
W • E Europe • 250 kW
ITALY
†RAI INTERNATIONAL, Rome
S America • 100 kW
W • E Europe • 100 kW
W • Europe • 100 kW
MONACO
†TRANS WORLD R, Via Cerrik, Albania
W • E Europe • 100 kW
PORTUGAL
†RDP INTERNATIONAL, Lisbon
S Sa/Su • Europe • 100 kW • ALT. FREQ. TO 12020 kHz
RUSSIA
†VOICE OF RUSSIA, St Petersburg
W • Mideast & W Asia • 400 kW
SPAIN
†R EXTERIOR ESPANA, Noblejas
S Sa/Su • Europe • 350 kW
UNITED KINGDOM
†BBC, Via Zyyi, Cyprus
S • S Europe • 250 kW
USA
†ADVENTIST WORLD R, Via Italy
S • N Africa • 2.5 kW
†HERALD BROADCASTING, S Carolina
S • S Africa • 500 kW
VOA, Via Briech, Morocco
S • S Europe • 250 kW
†VOA, Via Kavála, Greece
W • Mideast & S Asia • 250 kW
†VOA, Via Udon Thani, Thailand
M-F • Mideast & S Asia • 250 kW
9840v VIETNAM
†VOICE OF VIETNAM, Son Tay
E Asia • 100 kW
SE Asia • 100 kW
9845 CHINA
CENTRAL PEOPLE'S BS, Beijing
W • DS-1 • 100 kW
DS-1 • 100 kW
FRANCE
†R FRANCE INTL, Issoudun-Allouis
W • E Africa • 500 kW
HOLLAND
R NEDERLAND, Via Madagascar
S • E Africa • 200 kW
R NEDERLAND, Via Neth Antilles
E North Am • 250 kW
C America & W North Am • 250 kW
JAPAN
†RADIO JAPAN/NHK, Tokyo-Yamata
W • S Asia • 300 kW
MONACO
†TRANS WORLD R, Via Cerrik, Albania
W • E Europe • 100 kW
W M • E Europe • 100 kW
W Tu-Su • E Europe • 100 kW
(con'd)
0 1 2 3 4 5 6 7 8 9 10 11 12 13 14 15 16 17 18 19 20 21 22 23 24
ENGLISH ARABIC CHINESE FRENCH GERMAN RUSSIAN SPANISH OTHER

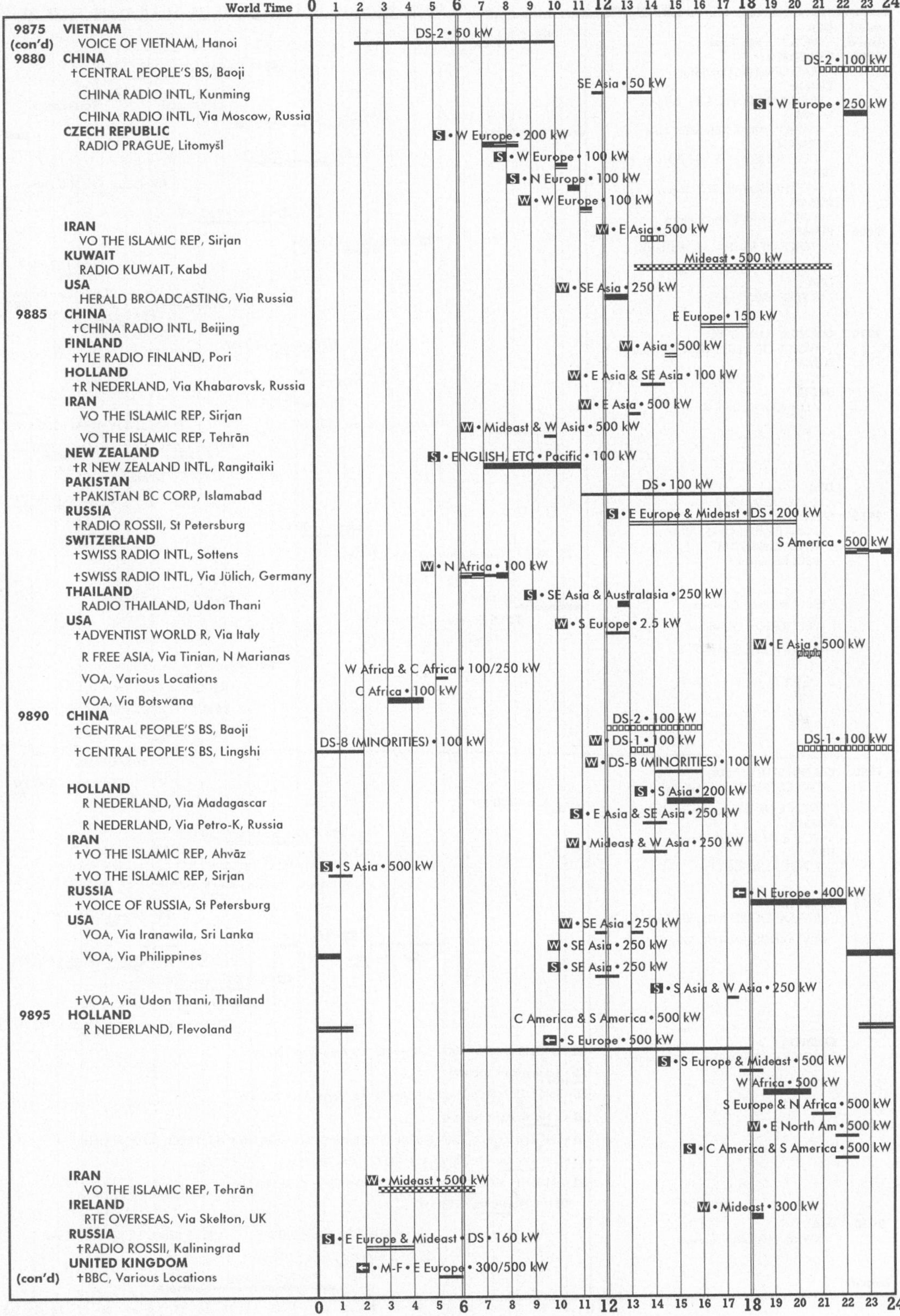
World Time 0 1 2 3 4 5 6 7 8 9 10 11 12 13 14 15 16 17 18 19 20 21 22 23 24
9875 (con'd) VIETNAM
VOICE OF VIETNAM, Hanoi
DS-2 • 50 kW
9880 CHINA
†CENTRAL PEOPLE'S BS, Baoji
DS-2 • 100 kW
CHINA RADIO INTL, Kunming
SE Asia • 50 kW
CHINA RADIO INTL, Via Moscow, Russia
S • W Europe • 250 kW
CZECH REPUBLIC
RADIO PRAGUE, Litomyšl
S • W Europe • 200 kW
S • W Europe • 100 kW
S • N Europe • 100 kW
W • W Europe • 100 kW
IRAN
VO THE ISLAMIC REP, Sirjan
W • E Asia • 500 kW
KUWAIT
RADIO KUWAIT, Kabd
Mideast • 500 kW
USA
HERALD BROADCASTING, Via Russia
W • SE Asia • 250 kW
9885 CHINA
†CHINA RADIO INTL, Beijing
E Europe • 150 kW
FINLAND
†YLE RADIO FINLAND, Pori
W • Asia • 500 kW
HOLLAND
†R NEDERLAND, Via Khabarovsk, Russia
W • E Asia & SE Asia • 100 kW
IRAN
VO THE ISLAMIC REP, Sirjan
W • E Asia • 500 kW
VO THE ISLAMIC REP, Tehrān
W • Mideast & W Asia • 500 kW
NEW ZEALAND
†R NEW ZEALAND INTL, Rangitaiki
S • ENGLISH, ETC • Pacific • 100 kW
PAKISTAN
†PAKISTAN BC CORP, Islamabad
DS • 100 kW
RUSSIA
†RADIO ROSSII, St Petersburg
S • E Europe & Mideast • DS • 200 kW
SWITZERLAND
†SWISS RADIO INTL, Sottens
S America • 500 kW
†SWISS RADIO INTL, Via Jülich, Germany
W • N Africa • 100 kW
THAILAND
RADIO THAILAND, Udon Thani
S • SE Asia & Australasia • 250 kW
USA
†ADVENTIST WORLD R, Via Italy
W • S Europe • 2.5 kW
R FREE ASIA, Via Tinian, N Marianas
W • E Asia • 500 kW
VOA, Various Locations
W Africa & C Africa • 100/250 kW
VOA, Via Botswana
C Africa • 100 kW
9890 CHINA
†CENTRAL PEOPLE'S BS, Baoji
DS-2 • 100 kW
†CENTRAL PEOPLE'S BS, Lingshi
DS-8 (MINORITIES) • 100 kW
W • DS-1 • 100 kW
DS-1 • 100 kW
W • DS-8 (MINORITIES) • 100 kW
HOLLAND
R NEDERLAND, Via Madagascar
S • S Asia • 200 kW
R NEDERLAND, Via Petro-K, Russia
S • E Asia & SE Asia • 250 kW
IRAN
†VO THE ISLAMIC REP, Ahvāz
W • Mideast & W Asia • 250 kW
†VO THE ISLAMIC REP, Sirjan
S • S Asia • 500 kW
RUSSIA
†VOICE OF RUSSIA, St Petersburg
N Europe • 400 kW
USA
VOA, Via Iranawila, Sri Lanka
W • SE Asia • 250 kW
VOA, Via Philippines
W • SE Asia • 250 kW
S • SE Asia • 250 kW
†VOA, Via Udon Thani, Thailand
S • S Asia & W Asia • 250 kW
9895 HOLLAND
R NEDERLAND, Flevoland
C America & S America • 500 kW
S Europe • 500 kW
S • S Europe & Mideast • 500 kW
W Africa • 500 kW
S Europe & N Africa • 500 kW
W • E North Am • 500 kW
S • C America & S America • 500 kW
IRAN
VO THE ISLAMIC REP, Tehrān
W • Mideast • 500 kW
IRELAND
RTE OVERSEAS, Via Skelton, UK
W • Mideast • 300 kW
RUSSIA
†RADIO ROSSII, Kaliningrad
S • E Europe & Mideast • DS • 160 kW
UNITED KINGDOM (con'd)
†BBC, Various Locations
M-F • E Europe • 300/500 kW
0 1 2 3 4 5 6 7 8 9 10 11 12 13 14 15 16 17 18 19 20 21 22 23 24

SEASONAL S OR W 1-HR TIMESHIFT MIDYEAR ⇐ OR ⇒ JAMMING / OR ∧ EARLIEST HEARD ◁ LATEST HEARD ▷ NEW FOR 2002 †

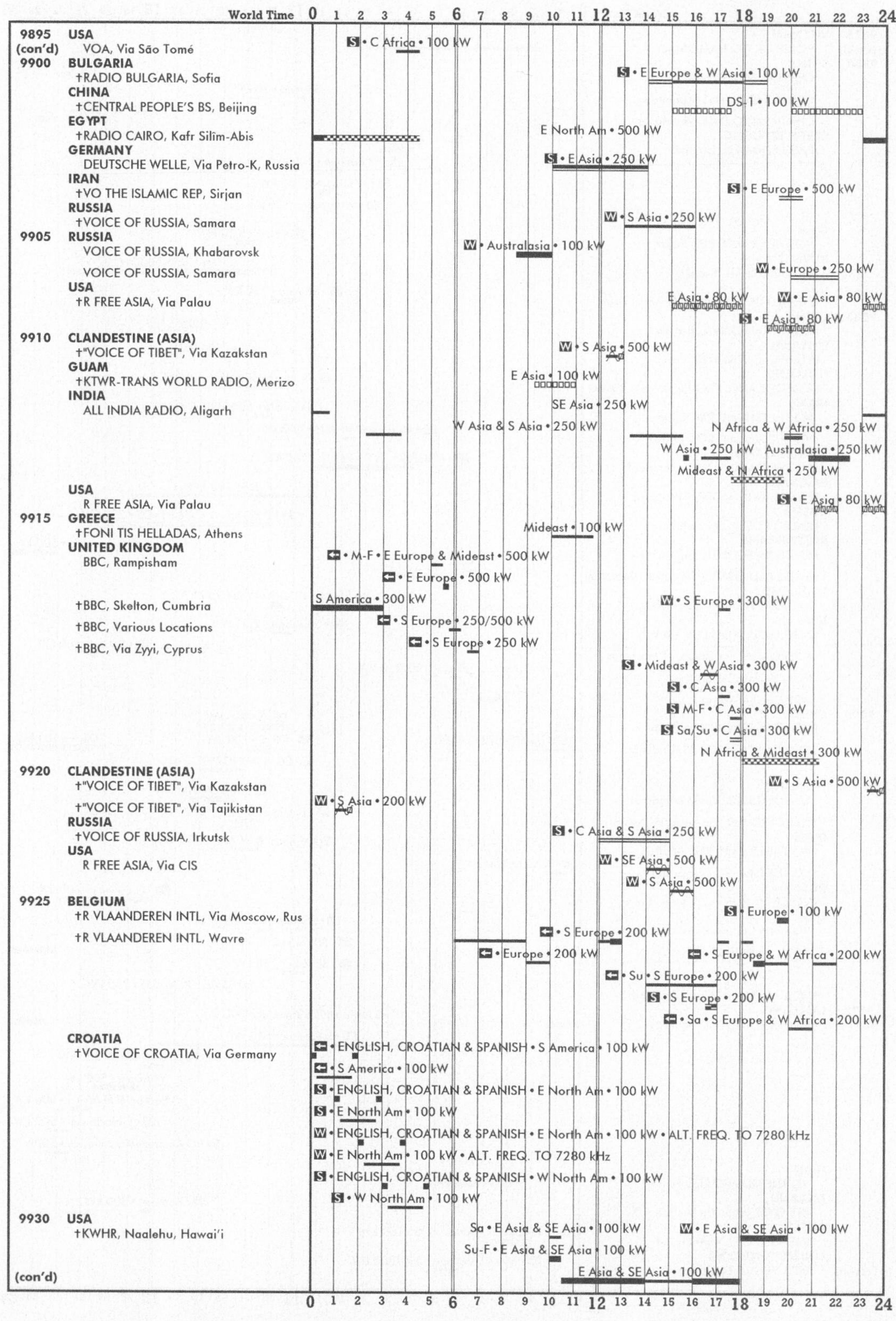
World Time 0 1 2 3 4 5 6 7 8 9 10 11 12 13 14 15 16 17 18 19 20 21 22 23 24
9895 USA
(con'd) VOA, Via São Tomé
S • C Africa • 100 kW
9900 BULGARIA
†RADIO BULGARIA, Sofia
S • E Europe & W Asia • 100 kW
CHINA
†CENTRAL PEOPLE'S BS, Beijing
DS-1 • 100 kW
EGYPT
†RADIO CAIRO, Kafr Silîm-Abis
E North Am • 500 kW
GERMANY
DEUTSCHE WELLE, Via Petro-K, Russia
S • E Asia • 250 kW
IRAN
†VO THE ISLAMIC REP, Sirjan
S • E Europe • 500 kW
RUSSIA
†VOICE OF RUSSIA, Samara
W • S Asia • 250 kW
9905 RUSSIA
VOICE OF RUSSIA, Khabarovsk
W • Australasia • 100 kW
VOICE OF RUSSIA, Samara
W • Europe • 250 kW
USA
†R FREE ASIA, Via Palau
E Asia • 80 kW
W • E Asia • 80 kW
S • E Asia • 80 kW
9910 CLANDESTINE (ASIA)
†"VOICE OF TIBET", Via Kazakstan
W • S Asia • 500 kW
GUAM
†KTWR-TRANS WORLD RADIO, Merizo
E Asia • 100 kW
INDIA
ALL INDIA RADIO, Aligarh
SE Asia • 250 kW
W Asia & S Asia • 250 kW
N Africa & W Africa • 250 kW
W Asia • 250 kW
Australasia • 250 kW
Mideast & N Africa • 250 kW
USA
R FREE ASIA, Via Palau
S • E Asia • 80 kW
9915 GREECE
†FONI TIS HELLADAS, Athens
Mideast • 100 kW
UNITED KINGDOM
BBC, Rampisham
M-F • E Europe & Mideast • 500 kW
E Europe • 500 kW
S America • 300 kW
†BBC, Skelton, Cumbria
W • S Europe • 300 kW
†BBC, Various Locations
S Europe • 250/500 kW
†BBC, Via Zyyi, Cyprus
S Europe • 250 kW
S • Mideast & W Asia • 300 kW
S • C Asia • 300 kW
S M-F • C Asia • 300 kW
S Sa/Su • C Asia • 300 kW
N Africa & Mideast • 300 kW
9920 CLANDESTINE (ASIA)
†"VOICE OF TIBET", Via Kazakstan
W • S Asia • 500 kW
†"VOICE OF TIBET", Via Tajikistan
W • S Asia • 200 kW
RUSSIA
†VOICE OF RUSSIA, Irkutsk
S • C Asia & S Asia • 250 kW
USA
R FREE ASIA, Via CIS
W • SE Asia • 500 kW
W • S Asia • 500 kW
9925 BELGIUM
†R VLAANDEREN INTL, Via Moscow, Rus
S • Europe • 100 kW
†R VLAANDEREN INTL, Wavre
S Europe • 200 kW
Europe • 200 kW
S Europe & W Africa • 200 kW
Su • S Europe • 200 kW
S • S Europe • 200 kW
Sa • S Europe & W Africa • 200 kW
CROATIA
†VOICE OF CROATIA, Via Germany
ENGLISH, CROATIAN & SPANISH • S America • 100 kW
S America • 100 kW
S • ENGLISH, CROATIAN & SPANISH • E North Am • 100 kW
S • E North Am • 100 kW
W • ENGLISH, CROATIAN & SPANISH • E North Am • 100 kW • ALT. FREQ. TO 7280 kHz
W • E North Am • 100 kW • ALT. FREQ. TO 7280 kHz
S • ENGLISH, CROATIAN & SPANISH • W North Am • 100 kW
S • W North Am • 100 kW
9930 USA
†KWHR, Naalehu, Hawai'i
Sa • E Asia & SE Asia • 100 kW
W • E Asia & SE Asia • 100 kW
Su-F • E Asia & SE Asia • 100 kW
(con'd)
E Asia & SE Asia • 100 kW
0 1 2 3 4 5 6 7 8 9 10 11 12 13 14 15 16 17 18 19 20 21 22 23 24
ENGLISH ARABIC CHINESE FRENCH GERMAN RUSSIAN SPANISH OTHER

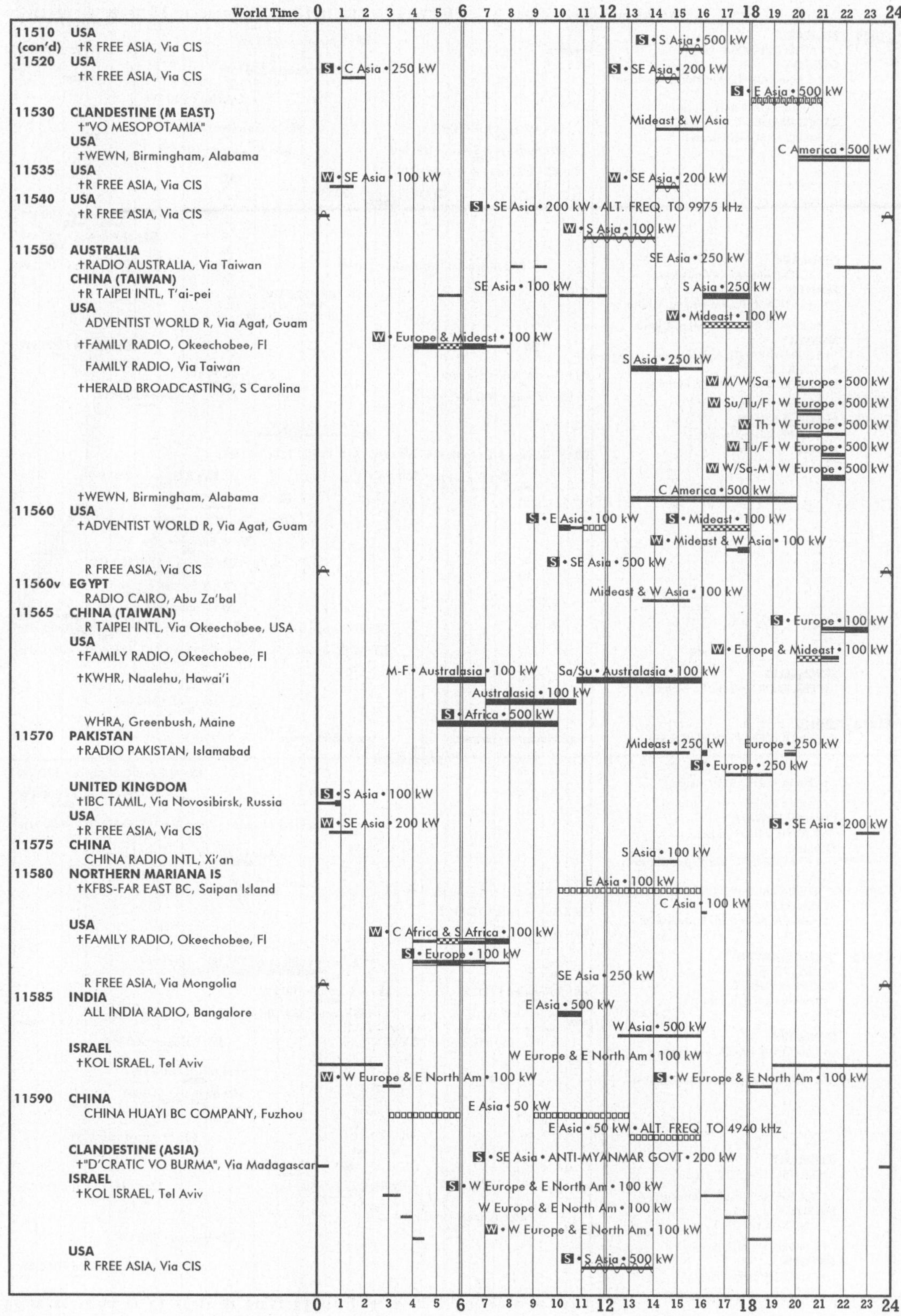
World Time 0 1 2 3 4 5 6 7 8 9 10 11 12 13 14 15 16 17 18 19 20 21 22 23 24
11510 (con'd) USA
†R FREE ASIA, Via CIS
S • S Asia • 500 kW
11520 USA
†R FREE ASIA, Via CIS
S • C Asia • 250 kW
S • SE Asia • 200 kW
S • E Asia • 500 kW
11530 CLANDESTINE (M EAST)
†"VO MESOPOTAMIA"
Mideast & W Asia
USA
†WEWN, Birmingham, Alabama
C America • 500 kW
11535 USA
†R FREE ASIA, Via CIS
W • SE Asia • 100 kW
W • SE Asia • 200 kW
11540 USA
†R FREE ASIA, Via CIS
S • SE Asia • 200 kW • ALT. FREQ. TO 9975 kHz
W • S Asia • 100 kW
11550 AUSTRALIA
†RADIO AUSTRALIA, Via Taiwan
SE Asia • 250 kW
CHINA (TAIWAN)
†R TAIPEI INTL, T'ai-pei
SE Asia • 100 kW
S Asia • 250 kW
USA
ADVENTIST WORLD R, Via Agat, Guam
W • Mideast • 100 kW
†FAMILY RADIO, Okeechobee, Fl
W • Europe & Mideast • 100 kW
FAMILY RADIO, Via Taiwan
S Asia • 250 kW
†HERALD BROADCASTING, S Carolina
W M/W/Sa • W Europe • 500 kW
W Su/Tu/F • W Europe • 500 kW
W Th • W Europe • 500 kW
W Tu/F • W Europe • 500 kW
W W/Sa-M • W Europe • 500 kW
†WEWN, Birmingham, Alabama
C America • 500 kW
11560 USA
†ADVENTIST WORLD R, Via Agat, Guam
S • E Asia • 100 kW
S • Mideast • 100 kW
W • Mideast & W Asia • 100 kW
R FREE ASIA, Via CIS
S • SE Asia • 500 kW
11560v EGYPT
RADIO CAIRO, Abu Za'bal
Mideast & W Asia • 100 kW
11565 CHINA (TAIWAN)
R TAIPEI INTL, Via Okeechobee, USA
S • Europe • 100 kW
USA
†FAMILY RADIO, Okeechobee, Fl
W • Europe & Mideast • 100 kW
†KWHR, Naalehu, Hawai'i
M-F • Australasia • 100 kW
Sa/Su • Australasia • 100 kW
Australasia • 100 kW
WHRA, Greenbush, Maine
S • Africa • 500 kW
11570 PAKISTAN
†RADIO PAKISTAN, Islamabad
Mideast • 250 kW
Europe • 250 kW
S • Europe • 250 kW
UNITED KINGDOM
†IBC TAMIL, Via Novosibirsk, Russia
S • S Asia • 100 kW
USA
†R FREE ASIA, Via CIS
W • SE Asia • 200 kW
S • SE Asia • 200 kW
11575 CHINA
CHINA RADIO INTL, Xi'an
S Asia • 100 kW
11580 NORTHERN MARIANA IS
†KFBS-FAR EAST BC, Saipan Island
E Asia • 100 kW
C Asia • 100 kW
USA
†FAMILY RADIO, Okeechobee, Fl
W • C Africa & S Africa • 100 kW
S • Europe • 100 kW
R FREE ASIA, Via Mongolia
SE Asia • 250 kW
11585 INDIA
ALL INDIA RADIO, Bangalore
E Asia • 500 kW
W Asia • 500 kW
ISRAEL
†KOL ISRAEL, Tel Aviv
W Europe & E North Am • 100 kW
W • W Europe & E North Am • 100 kW
S • W Europe & E North Am • 100 kW
11590 CHINA
CHINA HUAYI BC COMPANY, Fuzhou
E Asia • 50 kW
E Asia • 50 kW • ALT. FREQ. TO 4940 kHz
CLANDESTINE (ASIA)
†"D'CRATIC VO BURMA", Via Madagascar
S • SE Asia • ANTI-MYANMAR GOVT • 200 kW
ISRAEL
†KOL ISRAEL, Tel Aviv
S • W Europe & E North Am • 100 kW
W Europe & E North Am • 100 kW
W • W Europe & E North Am • 100 kW
USA
R FREE ASIA, Via CIS
S • S Asia • 500 kW
0 1 2 3 4 5 6 7 8 9 10 11 12 13 14 15 16 17 18 19 20 21 22 23 24

SEASONAL S OR W 1-HR TIMESHIFT MIDYEAR ⇦ OR ⇨ JAMMING / OR /\ EARLIEST HEARD ◁ LATEST HEARD ▷ NEW FOR 2002 †

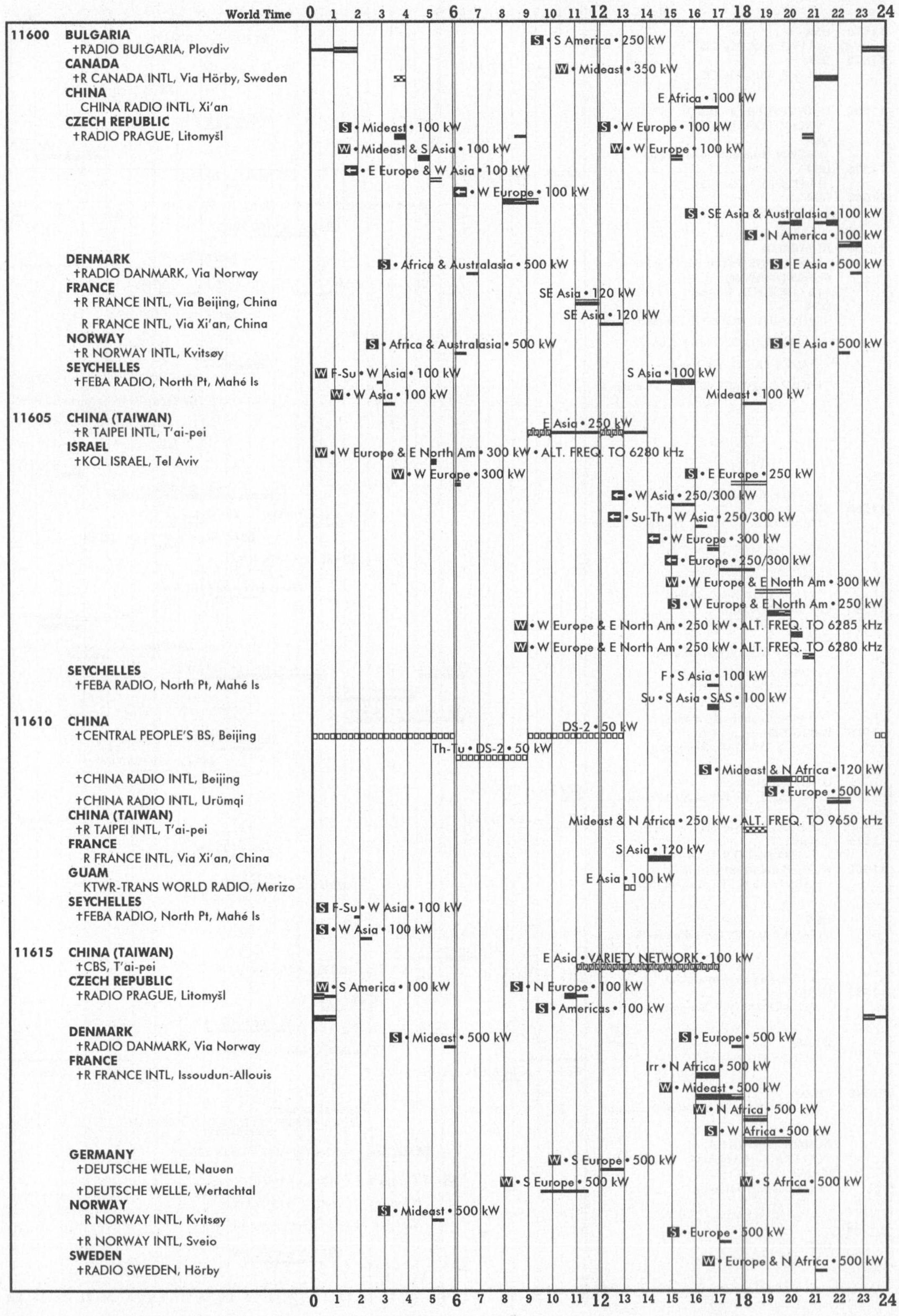
World Time 0 1 2 3 4 5 6 7 8 9 10 11 12 13 14 15 16 17 18 19 20 21 22 23 24
11600 BULGARIA
†RADIO BULGARIA, Plovdiv
S • S America • 250 kW
CANADA
†R CANADA INTL, Via Hörby, Sweden
W • Mideast • 350 kW
CHINA
CHINA RADIO INTL, Xi'an
E Africa • 100 kW
CZECH REPUBLIC
†RADIO PRAGUE, Litomyšl
S • Mideast • 100 kW
S • W Europe • 100 kW
W • Mideast & S Asia • 100 kW
W • W Europe • 100 kW
• E Europe & W Asia • 100 kW
• W Europe • 100 kW
S • SE Asia & Australasia • 100 kW
S • N America • 100 kW
DENMARK
†RADIO DANMARK, Via Norway
S • Africa & Australasia • 500 kW
S • E Asia • 500 kW
FRANCE
†R FRANCE INTL, Via Beijing, China
SE Asia • 120 kW
R FRANCE INTL, Via Xi'an, China
SE Asia • 120 kW
NORWAY
†R NORWAY INTL, Kvitsøy
S • Africa & Australasia • 500 kW
S • E Asia • 500 kW
SEYCHELLES
†FEBA RADIO, North Pt, Mahé Is
W F-Su • W Asia • 100 kW
S Asia • 100 kW
W • W Asia • 100 kW
Mideast • 100 kW
11605 CHINA (TAIWAN)
†R TAIPEI INTL, T'ai-pei
E Asia • 250 kW
ISRAEL
†KOL ISRAEL, Tel Aviv
W • W Europe & E North Am • 300 kW • ALT. FREQ. TO 6280 kHz
W • W Europe • 300 kW
S • E Europe • 250 kW
• W Asia • 250/300 kW
• Su-Th • W Asia • 250/300 kW
• W Europe • 300 kW
• Europe • 250/300 kW
W • W Europe & E North Am • 300 kW
S • W Europe & E North Am • 250 kW
W • W Europe & E North Am • 250 kW • ALT. FREQ. TO 6285 kHz
W • W Europe & E North Am • 250 kW • ALT. FREQ. TO 6280 kHz
SEYCHELLES
†FEBA RADIO, North Pt, Mahé Is
F • S Asia • 100 kW
Su • S Asia • SAS • 100 kW
11610 CHINA
†CENTRAL PEOPLE'S BS, Beijing
DS-2 • 50 kW
Th-Tu • DS-2 • 50 kW
†CHINA RADIO INTL, Beijing
S • Mideast & N Africa • 120 kW
†CHINA RADIO INTL, Urümqi
S • Europe • 500 kW
CHINA (TAIWAN)
†R TAIPEI INTL, T'ai-pei
Mideast & N Africa • 250 kW • ALT. FREQ. TO 9650 kHz
FRANCE
R FRANCE INTL, Via Xi'an, China
S Asia • 120 kW
GUAM
KTWR-TRANS WORLD RADIO, Merizo
E Asia • 100 kW
SEYCHELLES
†FEBA RADIO, North Pt, Mahé Is
S F-Su • W Asia • 100 kW
S • W Asia • 100 kW
11615 CHINA (TAIWAN)
†CBS, T'ai-pei
E Asia • VARIETY NETWORK • 100 kW
CZECH REPUBLIC
†RADIO PRAGUE, Litomyšl
W • S America • 100 kW
S • N Europe • 100 kW
S • Americas • 100 kW
DENMARK
†RADIO DANMARK, Via Norway
S • Mideast • 500 kW
S • Europe • 500 kW
FRANCE
†R FRANCE INTL, Issoudun-Allouis
Irr • N Africa • 500 kW
W • Mideast • 500 kW
W • N Africa • 500 kW
S • W Africa • 500 kW
GERMANY
†DEUTSCHE WELLE, Nauen
W • S Europe • 500 kW
†DEUTSCHE WELLE, Wertachtal
W • S Europe • 500 kW
W • S Africa • 500 kW
NORWAY
R NORWAY INTL, Kvitsøy
S • Mideast • 500 kW
†R NORWAY INTL, Sveio
S • Europe • 500 kW
SWEDEN
†RADIO SWEDEN, Hörby
W • Europe & N Africa • 500 kW
0 1 2 3 4 5 6 7 8 9 10 11 12 13 14 15 16 17 18 19 20 21 22 23 24

ENGLISH ▬ ARABIC ▭ CHINESE ▫▫▫ FRENCH ═ GERMAN ═ RUSSIAN ═ SPANISH ═ OTHER —

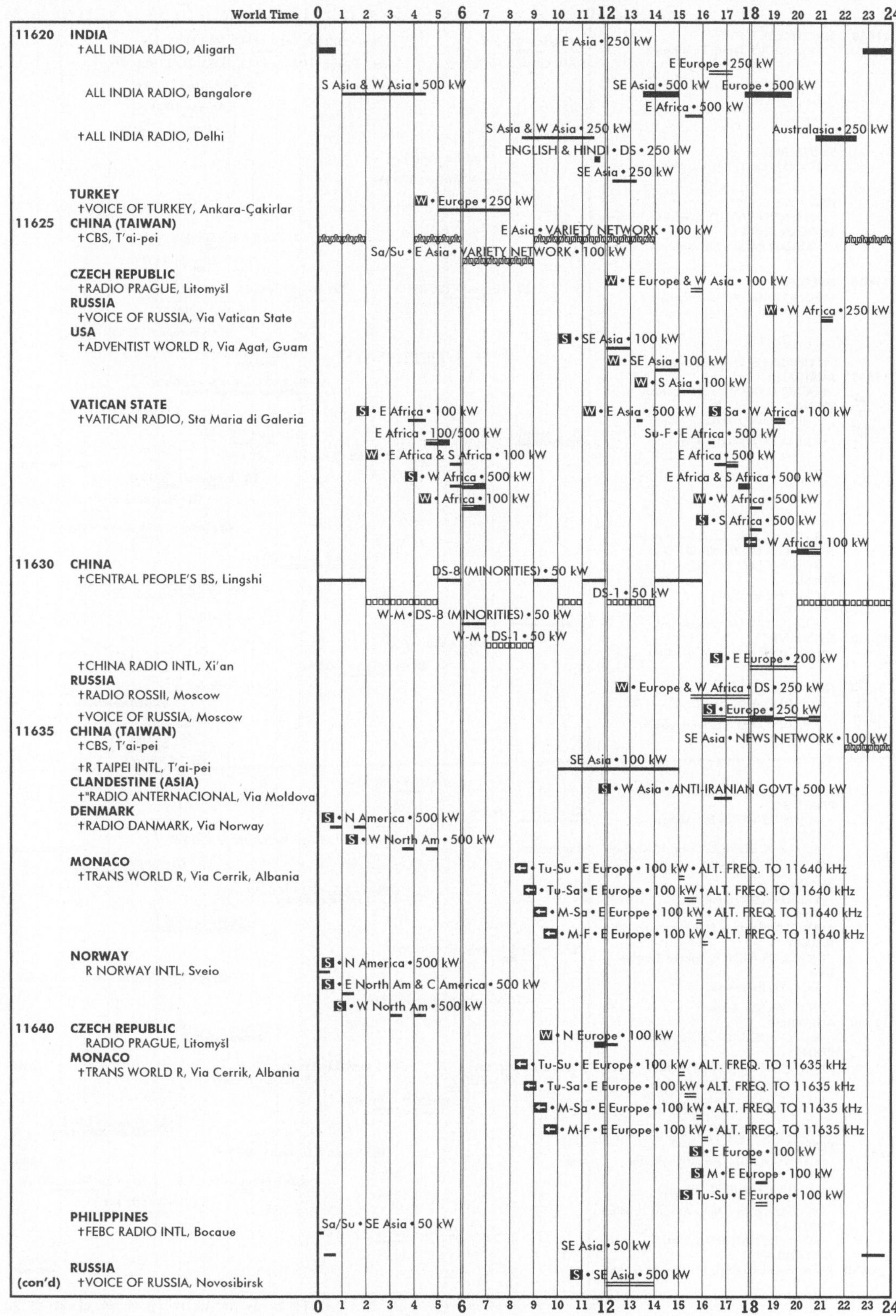
World Time 0 1 2 3 4 5 6 7 8 9 10 11 12 13 14 15 16 17 18 19 20 21 22 23 24
11620 INDIA
†ALL INDIA RADIO, Aligarh
E Asia • 250 kW
E Europe • 250 kW
ALL INDIA RADIO, Bangalore
S Asia & W Asia • 500 kW
SE Asia • 500 kW
Europe • 500 kW
E Africa • 500 kW
†ALL INDIA RADIO, Delhi
S Asia & W Asia • 250 kW
Australasia • 250 kW
ENGLISH & HINDI • DS • 250 kW
SE Asia • 250 kW
TURKEY
†VOICE OF TURKEY, Ankara-Çakirlar
W • Europe • 250 kW
11625 CHINA (TAIWAN)
†CBS, T'ai-pei
E Asia • VARIETY NETWORK • 100 kW
Sa/Su • E Asia • VARIETY NETWORK • 100 kW
CZECH REPUBLIC
†RADIO PRAGUE, Litomyšl
W • E Europe & W Asia • 100 kW
RUSSIA
†VOICE OF RUSSIA, Via Vatican State
W • W Africa • 250 kW
USA
†ADVENTIST WORLD R, Via Agat, Guam
S • SE Asia • 100 kW
W • SE Asia • 100 kW
W • S Asia • 100 kW
VATICAN STATE
†VATICAN RADIO, Sta Maria di Galeria
S • E Africa • 100 kW
W • E Asia • 500 kW
S Sa • W Africa • 100 kW
E Africa • 100/500 kW
Su-F • E Africa • 500 kW
W • E Africa & S Africa • 100 kW
E Africa • 500 kW
S • W Africa • 500 kW
E Africa & S Africa • 500 kW
W • Africa • 100 kW
W • W Africa • 500 kW
S • S Africa • 500 kW
W Africa • 100 kW
11630 CHINA
†CENTRAL PEOPLE'S BS, Lingshi
DS-8 (MINORITIES) • 50 kW
DS-1 • 50 kW
W-M • DS-8 (MINORITIES) • 50 kW
W-M • DS-1 • 50 kW
†CHINA RADIO INTL, Xi'an
S • E Europe • 200 kW
RUSSIA
†RADIO ROSSII, Moscow
W • Europe & W Africa • DS • 250 kW
†VOICE OF RUSSIA, Moscow
S • Europe • 250 kW
11635 CHINA (TAIWAN)
†CBS, T'ai-pei
SE Asia • NEWS NETWORK • 100 kW
†R TAIPEI INTL, T'ai-pei
SE Asia • 100 kW
CLANDESTINE (ASIA)
†"RADIO ANTERNACIONAL, Via Moldova
S • W Asia • ANTI-IRANIAN GOVT • 500 kW
DENMARK
†RADIO DANMARK, Via Norway
S • N America • 500 kW
S • W North Am • 500 kW
MONACO
†TRANS WORLD R, Via Cerrik, Albania
Tu-Su • E Europe • 100 kW • ALT. FREQ. TO 11640 kHz
Tu-Sa • E Europe • 100 kW • ALT. FREQ. TO 11640 kHz
M-Sa • E Europe • 100 kW • ALT. FREQ. TO 11640 kHz
M-F • E Europe • 100 kW • ALT. FREQ. TO 11640 kHz
NORWAY
R NORWAY INTL, Sveio
S • N America • 500 kW
S • E North Am & C America • 500 kW
S • W North Am • 500 kW
11640 CZECH REPUBLIC
RADIO PRAGUE, Litomyšl
W • N Europe • 100 kW
MONACO
†TRANS WORLD R, Via Cerrik, Albania
Tu-Su • E Europe • 100 kW • ALT. FREQ. TO 11635 kHz
Tu-Sa • E Europe • 100 kW • ALT. FREQ. TO 11635 kHz
M-Sa • E Europe • 100 kW • ALT. FREQ. TO 11635 kHz
M-F • E Europe • 100 kW • ALT. FREQ. TO 11635 kHz
S • E Europe • 100 kW
S M • E Europe • 100 kW
S Tu-Su • E Europe • 100 kW
PHILIPPINES
†FEBC RADIO INTL, Bocaue
Sa/Su • SE Asia • 50 kW
SE Asia • 50 kW
RUSSIA
(con'd) †VOICE OF RUSSIA, Novosibirsk
S • SE Asia • 500 kW
0 1 2 3 4 5 6 7 8 9 10 11 12 13 14 15 16 17 18 19 20 21 22 23 24

SEASONAL S OR W 1-HR TIMESHIFT MIDYEAR ⇐ OR ⇒ JAMMING / OR ∧ EARLIEST HEARD ◁ LATEST HEARD ▷ NEW FOR 2002 †

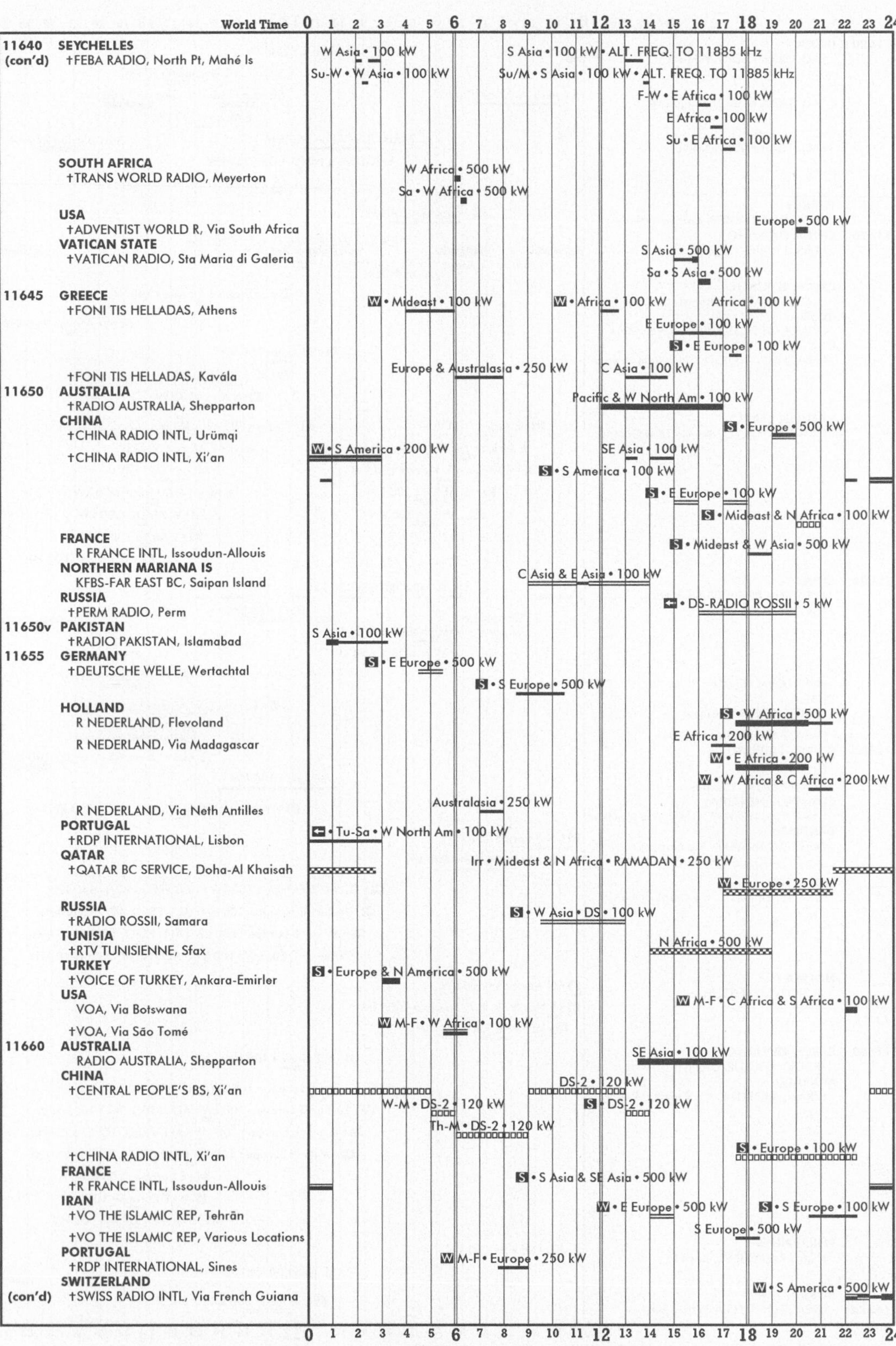
World Time 0 1 2 3 4 5 6 7 8 9 10 11 12 13 14 15 16 17 18 19 20 21 22 23 24
11640 (con'd) SEYCHELLES
†FEBA RADIO, North Pt, Mahé Is
W Asia • 100 kW
S Asia • 100 kW • ALT. FREQ. TO 11885 kHz
Su-W • W Asia • 100 kW
Su/M • S Asia • 100 kW • ALT. FREQ. TO 11885 kHz
F-W • E Africa • 100 kW
E Africa • 100 kW
Su • E Africa • 100 kW
SOUTH AFRICA
†TRANS WORLD RADIO, Meyerton
W Africa • 500 kW
Sa • W Africa • 500 kW
USA
†ADVENTIST WORLD R, Via South Africa
Europe • 500 kW
VATICAN STATE
†VATICAN RADIO, Sta Maria di Galeria
S Asia • 500 kW
Sa • S Asia • 500 kW
11645 GREECE
†FONI TIS HELLADAS, Athens
W • Mideast • 100 kW
W • Africa • 100 kW
Africa • 100 kW
E Europe • 100 kW
S • E Europe • 100 kW
†FONI TIS HELLADAS, Kavála
Europe & Australasia • 250 kW
C Asia • 100 kW
11650 AUSTRALIA
†RADIO AUSTRALIA, Shepparton
Pacific & W North Am • 100 kW
CHINA
†CHINA RADIO INTL, Urümqi
S • Europe • 500 kW
†CHINA RADIO INTL, Xi'an
W • S America • 200 kW
SE Asia • 100 kW
S • S America • 100 kW
S • E Europe • 100 kW
S • Mideast & N Africa • 100 kW
FRANCE
R FRANCE INTL, Issoudun-Allouis
S • Mideast & W Asia • 500 kW
NORTHERN MARIANA IS
KFBS-FAR EAST BC, Saipan Island
C Asia & E Asia • 100 kW
RUSSIA
†PERM RADIO, Perm
DS-RADIO ROSSII • 5 kW
11650v PAKISTAN
†RADIO PAKISTAN, Islamabad
S Asia • 100 kW
11655 GERMANY
†DEUTSCHE WELLE, Wertachtal
S • E Europe • 500 kW
S • S Europe • 500 kW
HOLLAND
R NEDERLAND, Flevoland
S • W Africa • 500 kW
R NEDERLAND, Via Madagascar
E Africa • 200 kW
W • E Africa • 200 kW
W • W Africa & C Africa • 200 kW
R NEDERLAND, Via Neth Antilles
Australasia • 250 kW
PORTUGAL
†RDP INTERNATIONAL, Lisbon
Tu-Sa • W North Am • 100 kW
QATAR
†QATAR BC SERVICE, Doha-Al Khaisah
Irr • Mideast & N Africa • RAMADAN • 250 kW
W • Europe • 250 kW
RUSSIA
†RADIO ROSSII, Samara
S • W Asia • DS • 100 kW
TUNISIA
†RTV TUNISIENNE, Sfax
N Africa • 500 kW
TURKEY
†VOICE OF TURKEY, Ankara-Emirler
S • Europe & N America • 500 kW
USA
VOA, Via Botswana
W M-F • C Africa & S Africa • 100 kW
†VOA, Via São Tomé
W M-F • W Africa • 100 kW
11660 AUSTRALIA
RADIO AUSTRALIA, Shepparton
SE Asia • 100 kW
CHINA
†CENTRAL PEOPLE'S BS, Xi'an
DS-2 • 120 kW
W-M • DS-2 • 120 kW
S • DS-2 • 120 kW
Th-M • DS-2 • 120 kW
†CHINA RADIO INTL, Xi'an
S • Europe • 100 kW
FRANCE
†R FRANCE INTL, Issoudun-Allouis
S • S Asia & SE Asia • 500 kW
IRAN
†VO THE ISLAMIC REP, Tehrān
W • E Europe • 500 kW
S • S Europe • 100 kW
†VO THE ISLAMIC REP, Various Locations
S Europe • 500 kW
PORTUGAL
†RDP INTERNATIONAL, Sines
W M-F • Europe • 250 kW
SWITZERLAND
(con'd) †SWISS RADIO INTL, Via French Guiana
W • S America • 500 kW
0 1 2 3 4 5 6 7 8 9 10 11 12 13 14 15 16 17 18 19 20 21 22 23 24
ENGLISH ARABIC CHINESE FRENCH GERMAN RUSSIAN SPANISH OTHER

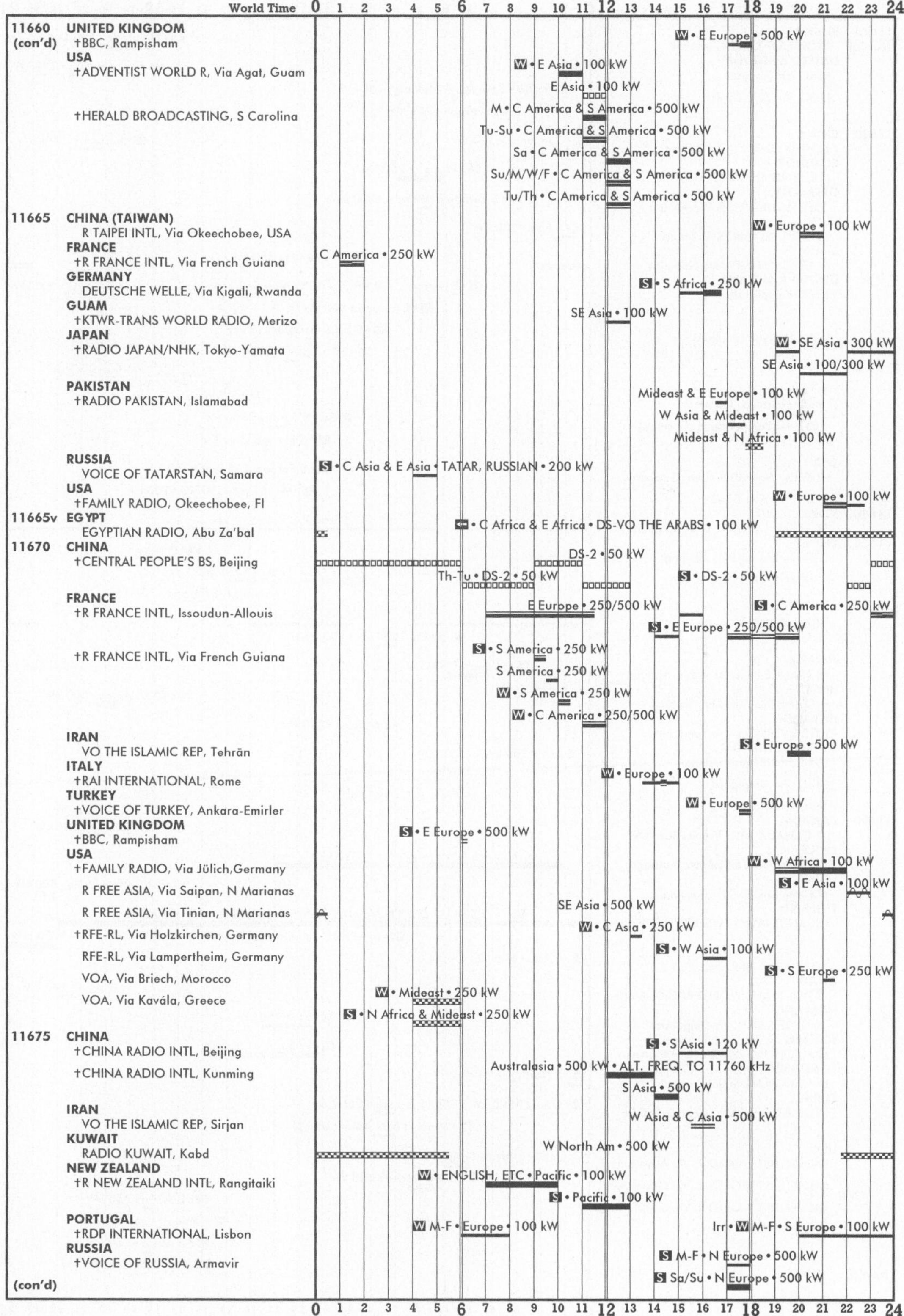
World Time 0 1 2 3 4 5 6 7 8 9 10 11 12 13 14 15 16 17 18 19 20 21 22 23 24
11660 (con'd) UNITED KINGDOM
†BBC, Rampisham
W • E Europe • 500 kW
USA
†ADVENTIST WORLD R, Via Agat, Guam
W • E Asia • 100 kW
E Asia • 100 kW
†HERALD BROADCASTING, S Carolina
M • C America & S America • 500 kW
Tu-Su • C America & S America • 500 kW
Sa • C America & S America • 500 kW
Su/M/W/F • C America & S America • 500 kW
Tu/Th • C America & S America • 500 kW
11665 CHINA (TAIWAN)
R TAIPEI INTL, Via Okeechobee, USA
W • Europe • 100 kW
FRANCE
†R FRANCE INTL, Via French Guiana
C America • 250 kW
GERMANY
DEUTSCHE WELLE, Via Kigali, Rwanda
S • S Africa • 250 kW
GUAM
†KTWR-TRANS WORLD RADIO, Merizo
SE Asia • 100 kW
JAPAN
†RADIO JAPAN/NHK, Tokyo-Yamata
W • SE Asia • 300 kW
SE Asia • 100/300 kW
PAKISTAN
†RADIO PAKISTAN, Islamabad
Mideast & E Europe • 100 kW
W Asia & Mideast • 100 kW
Mideast & N Africa • 100 kW
RUSSIA
VOICE OF TATARSTAN, Samara
S • C Asia & E Asia • TATAR, RUSSIAN • 200 kW
USA
†FAMILY RADIO, Okeechobee, Fl
W • Europe • 100 kW
11665v EGYPT
EGYPTIAN RADIO, Abu Za'bal
• C Africa & E Africa • DS-VO THE ARABS • 100 kW
11670 CHINA
†CENTRAL PEOPLE'S BS, Beijing
DS-2 • 50 kW
Th-Tu • DS-2 • 50 kW
S • DS-2 • 50 kW
FRANCE
†R FRANCE INTL, Issoudun-Allouis
E Europe • 250/500 kW
S • C America • 250 kW
S • E Europe • 250/500 kW
†R FRANCE INTL, Via French Guiana
S • S America • 250 kW
S America • 250 kW
W • S America • 250 kW
W • C America • 250/500 kW
IRAN
VO THE ISLAMIC REP, Tehrān
S • Europe • 500 kW
ITALY
†RAI INTERNATIONAL, Rome
W • Europe • 100 kW
TURKEY
†VOICE OF TURKEY, Ankara-Emirler
W • Europe • 500 kW
UNITED KINGDOM
†BBC, Rampisham
S • E Europe • 500 kW
USA
†FAMILY RADIO, Via Jülich,Germany
W • W Africa • 100 kW
R FREE ASIA, Via Saipan, N Marianas
S • E Asia • 100 kW
R FREE ASIA, Via Tinian, N Marianas
SE Asia • 500 kW
†RFE-RL, Via Holzkirchen, Germany
W • C Asia • 250 kW
RFE-RL, Via Lampertheim, Germany
S • W Asia • 100 kW
VOA, Via Briech, Morocco
S • S Europe • 250 kW
VOA, Via Kavála, Greece
W • Mideast • 250 kW
S • N Africa & Mideast • 250 kW
11675 CHINA
†CHINA RADIO INTL, Beijing
S • S Asia • 120 kW
†CHINA RADIO INTL, Kunming
Australasia • 500 kW • ALT. FREQ. TO 11760 kHz
S Asia • 500 kW
IRAN
VO THE ISLAMIC REP, Sirjan
W Asia & C Asia • 500 kW
KUWAIT
RADIO KUWAIT, Kabd
W North Am • 500 kW
NEW ZEALAND
†R NEW ZEALAND INTL, Rangitaiki
W • ENGLISH, ETC • Pacific • 100 kW
S • Pacific • 100 kW
PORTUGAL
†RDP INTERNATIONAL, Lisbon
W M-F • Europe • 100 kW
Irr • W M-F • S Europe • 100 kW
RUSSIA
†VOICE OF RUSSIA, Armavir
S M-F • N Europe • 500 kW
S Sa/Su • N Europe • 500 kW
(con'd)
0 1 2 3 4 5 6 7 8 9 10 11 12 13 14 15 16 17 18 19 20 21 22 23 24

SEASONAL S OR W   1-HR TIMESHIFT MIDYEAR ⇐ OR ⇒   JAMMING / OR /\   EARLIEST HEARD ◁   LATEST HEARD ▷   NEW FOR 2002 †

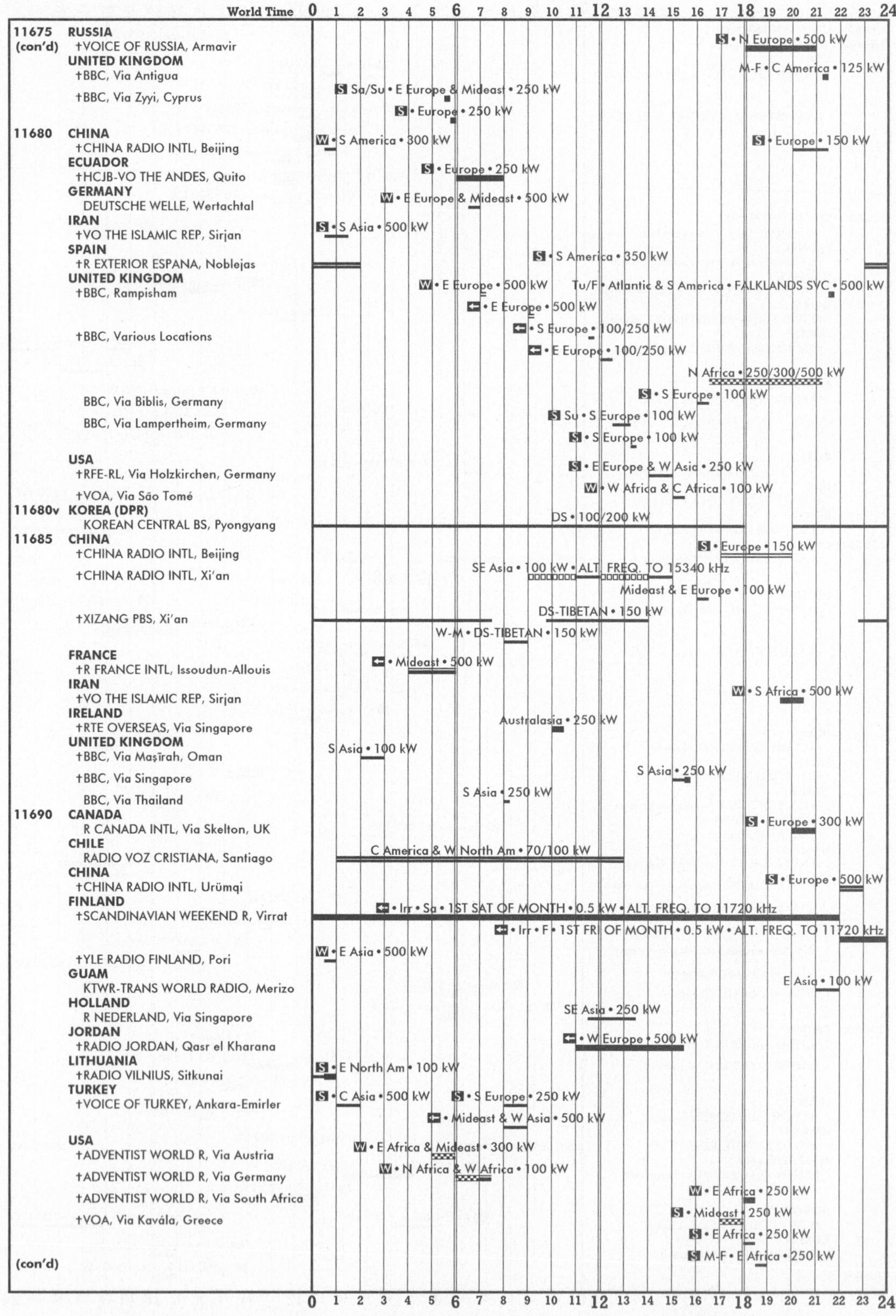
World Time 0 1 2 3 4 5 6 7 8 9 10 11 12 13 14 15 16 17 18 19 20 21 22 23 24
11675 (con'd) RUSSIA
†VOICE OF RUSSIA, Armavir
S • N Europe • 500 kW
UNITED KINGDOM
†BBC, Via Antigua
M-F • C America • 125 kW
†BBC, Via Zyyi, Cyprus
S Sa/Su • E Europe & Mideast • 250 kW
S • Europe • 250 kW
11680 CHINA
†CHINA RADIO INTL, Beijing
W • S America • 300 kW
S • Europe • 150 kW
ECUADOR
†HCJB-VO THE ANDES, Quito
S • Europe • 250 kW
GERMANY
DEUTSCHE WELLE, Wertachtal
W • E Europe & Mideast • 500 kW
IRAN
†VO THE ISLAMIC REP, Sirjan
S • S Asia • 500 kW
SPAIN
†R EXTERIOR ESPANA, Noblejas
S • S America • 350 kW
UNITED KINGDOM
†BBC, Rampisham
W • E Europe • 500 kW
Tu/F • Atlantic & S America • FALKLANDS SVC • 500 kW
• E Europe • 500 kW
†BBC, Various Locations
• S Europe • 100/250 kW
• E Europe • 100/250 kW
N Africa • 250/300/500 kW
S • S Europe • 100 kW
BBC, Via Biblis, Germany
S Su • S Europe • 100 kW
BBC, Via Lampertheim, Germany
S • S Europe • 100 kW
USA
†RFE-RL, Via Holzkirchen, Germany
S • E Europe & W Asia • 250 kW
†VOA, Via São Tomé
W • W Africa & C Africa • 100 kW
11680v KOREA (DPR)
KOREAN CENTRAL BS, Pyongyang
DS • 100/200 kW
11685 CHINA
†CHINA RADIO INTL, Beijing
S • Europe • 150 kW
†CHINA RADIO INTL, Xi'an
SE Asia • 100 kW • ALT. FREQ. TO 15340 kHz
Mideast & E Europe • 100 kW
†XIZANG PBS, Xi'an
DS-TIBETAN • 150 kW
W-M • DS-TIBETAN • 150 kW
FRANCE
†R FRANCE INTL, Issoudun-Allouis
• Mideast • 500 kW
IRAN
†VO THE ISLAMIC REP, Sirjan
W • S Africa • 500 kW
IRELAND
†RTE OVERSEAS, Via Singapore
Australasia • 250 kW
UNITED KINGDOM
†BBC, Via Maşīrah, Oman
S Asia • 100 kW
†BBC, Via Singapore
S Asia • 250 kW
BBC, Via Thailand
S Asia • 250 kW
11690 CANADA
R CANADA INTL, Via Skelton, UK
S • Europe • 300 kW
CHILE
RADIO VOZ CRISTIANA, Santiago
C America & W North Am • 70/100 kW
CHINA
†CHINA RADIO INTL, Urümqi
S • Europe • 500 kW
FINLAND
†SCANDINAVIAN WEEKEND R, Virrat
• Irr • Sa • 1ST SAT OF MONTH • 0.5 kW • ALT. FREQ. TO 11720 kHz
• Irr • F • 1ST FRI OF MONTH • 0.5 kW • ALT. FREQ. TO 11720 kHz
†YLE RADIO FINLAND, Pori
W • E Asia • 500 kW
GUAM
KTWR-TRANS WORLD RADIO, Merizo
E Asia • 100 kW
HOLLAND
R NEDERLAND, Via Singapore
SE Asia • 250 kW
JORDAN
†RADIO JORDAN, Qasr el Kharana
• W Europe • 500 kW
LITHUANIA
†RADIO VILNIUS, Sitkunai
S • E North Am • 100 kW
TURKEY
†VOICE OF TURKEY, Ankara-Emirler
S • C Asia • 500 kW
S • S Europe • 250 kW
• Mideast & W Asia • 500 kW
USA
†ADVENTIST WORLD R, Via Austria
W • E Africa & Mideast • 300 kW
†ADVENTIST WORLD R, Via Germany
W • N Africa & W Africa • 100 kW
†ADVENTIST WORLD R, Via South Africa
W • E Africa • 250 kW
†VOA, Via Kavála, Greece
S • Mideast • 250 kW
S • E Africa • 250 kW
S M-F • E Africa • 250 kW
(con'd)
0 1 2 3 4 5 6 7 8 9 10 11 12 13 14 15 16 17 18 19 20 21 22 23 24
ENGLISH ARABIC CHINESE FRENCH GERMAN RUSSIAN SPANISH OTHER

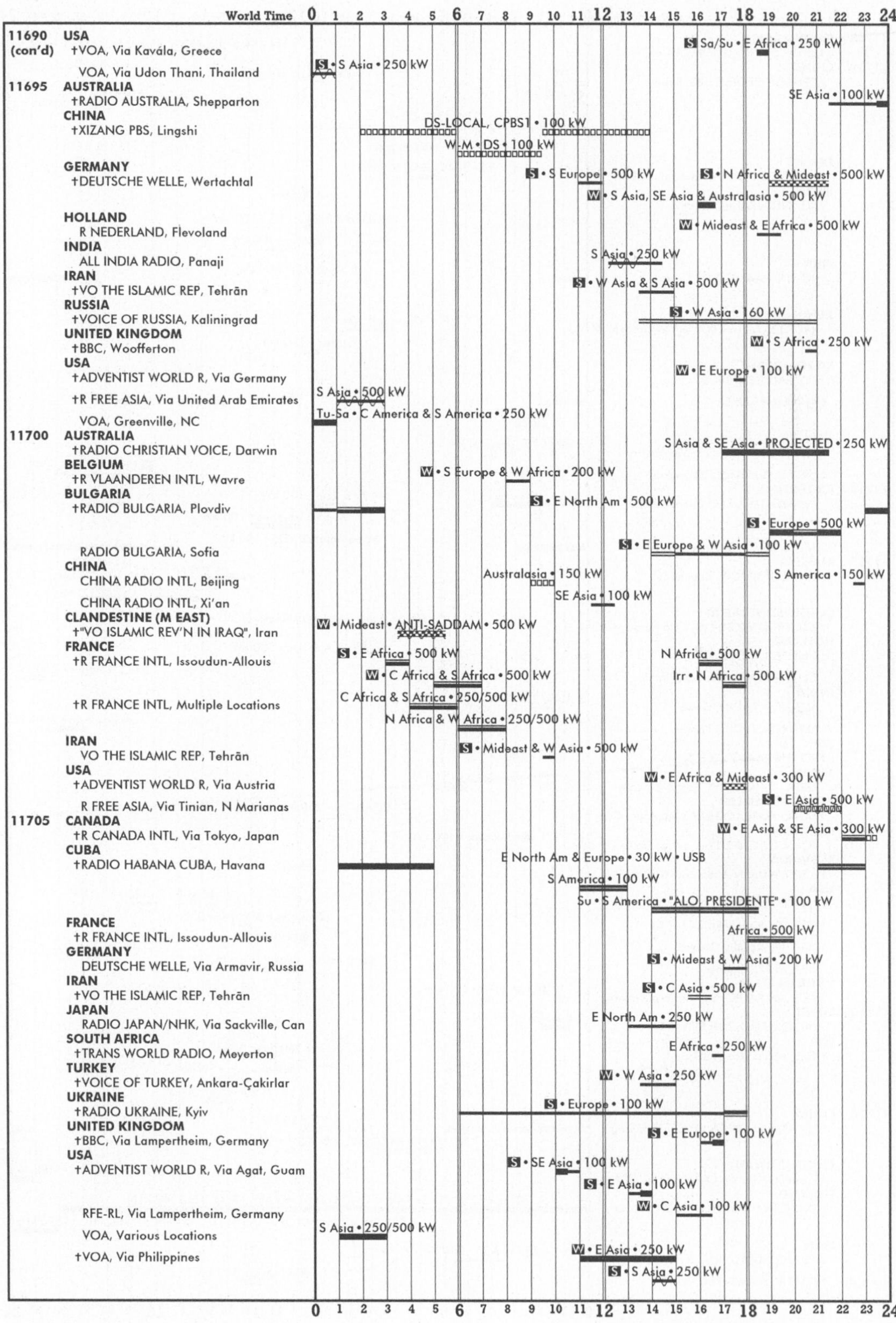
World Time 0 1 2 3 4 5 6 7 8 9 10 11 12 13 14 15 16 17 18 19 20 21 22 23 24
11690 (con'd) USA
†VOA, Via Kavála, Greece
S Sa/Su • E Africa • 250 kW
VOA, Via Udon Thani, Thailand
S • S Asia • 250 kW
11695 AUSTRALIA
†RADIO AUSTRALIA, Shepparton
SE Asia • 100 kW
CHINA
†XIZANG PBS, Lingshi
DS-LOCAL, CPBS1 • 100 kW
W-M • DS • 100 kW
GERMANY
†DEUTSCHE WELLE, Wertachtal
S • S Europe • 500 kW
S • N Africa & Mideast • 500 kW
W • S Asia, SE Asia & Australasia • 500 kW
HOLLAND
R NEDERLAND, Flevoland
W • Mideast & E Africa • 500 kW
INDIA
ALL INDIA RADIO, Panaji
S Asia • 250 kW
IRAN
†VO THE ISLAMIC REP, Tehrān
S • W Asia & S Asia • 500 kW
RUSSIA
†VOICE OF RUSSIA, Kaliningrad
S • W Asia • 160 kW
UNITED KINGDOM
†BBC, Woofferton
W • S Africa • 250 kW
USA
†ADVENTIST WORLD R, Via Germany
W • E Europe • 100 kW
†R FREE ASIA, Via United Arab Emirates
S Asia • 500 kW
VOA, Greenville, NC
Tu-Sa • C America & S America • 250 kW
11700 AUSTRALIA
†RADIO CHRISTIAN VOICE, Darwin
S Asia & SE Asia • PROJECTED • 250 kW
BELGIUM
†R VLAANDEREN INTL, Wavre
W • S Europe & W Africa • 200 kW
BULGARIA
†RADIO BULGARIA, Plovdiv
S • E North Am • 500 kW
S • Europe • 500 kW
S • E Europe & W Asia • 100 kW
RADIO BULGARIA, Sofia
CHINA
CHINA RADIO INTL, Beijing
Australasia • 150 kW
S America • 150 kW
CHINA RADIO INTL, Xi'an
SE Asia • 100 kW
CLANDESTINE (M EAST)
†"VO ISLAMIC REV'N IN IRAQ", Iran
W • Mideast • ANTI-SADDAM • 500 kW
FRANCE
†R FRANCE INTL, Issoudun-Allouis
S • E Africa • 500 kW
N Africa • 500 kW
W • C Africa & S Africa • 500 kW
Irr • N Africa • 500 kW
†R FRANCE INTL, Multiple Locations
C Africa & S Africa • 250/500 kW
N Africa & W Africa • 250/500 kW
IRAN
VO THE ISLAMIC REP, Tehrān
S • Mideast & W Asia • 500 kW
USA
†ADVENTIST WORLD R, Via Austria
W • E Africa & Mideast • 300 kW
R FREE ASIA, Via Tinian, N Marianas
S • E Asia • 500 kW
11705 CANADA
†R CANADA INTL, Via Tokyo, Japan
W • E Asia & SE Asia • 300 kW
CUBA
†RADIO HABANA CUBA, Havana
E North Am & Europe • 30 kW • USB
S America • 100 kW
Su • S America • "ALO, PRESIDENTE" • 100 kW
FRANCE
†R FRANCE INTL, Issoudun-Allouis
Africa • 500 kW
GERMANY
DEUTSCHE WELLE, Via Armavir, Russia
S • Mideast & W Asia • 200 kW
IRAN
†VO THE ISLAMIC REP, Tehrān
S • C Asia • 500 kW
JAPAN
RADIO JAPAN/NHK, Via Sackville, Can
E North Am • 250 kW
SOUTH AFRICA
†TRANS WORLD RADIO, Meyerton
E Africa • 250 kW
TURKEY
†VOICE OF TURKEY, Ankara-Çakirlar
W • W Asia • 250 kW
UKRAINE
†RADIO UKRAINE, Kyiv
S • Europe • 100 kW
UNITED KINGDOM
†BBC, Via Lampertheim, Germany
S • E Europe • 100 kW
USA
†ADVENTIST WORLD R, Via Agat, Guam
S • SE Asia • 100 kW
S • E Asia • 100 kW
W • C Asia • 100 kW
RFE-RL, Via Lampertheim, Germany
VOA, Various Locations
S Asia • 250/500 kW
†VOA, Via Philippines
W • E Asia • 250 kW
S • S Asia • 250 kW
0 1 2 3 4 5 6 7 8 9 10 11 12 13 14 15 16 17 18 19 20 21 22 23 24
SEASONAL S OR W
1-HR TIMESHIFT MIDYEAR OR
JAMMING / OR
EARLIEST HEARD
LATEST HEARD
NEW FOR 2002 †

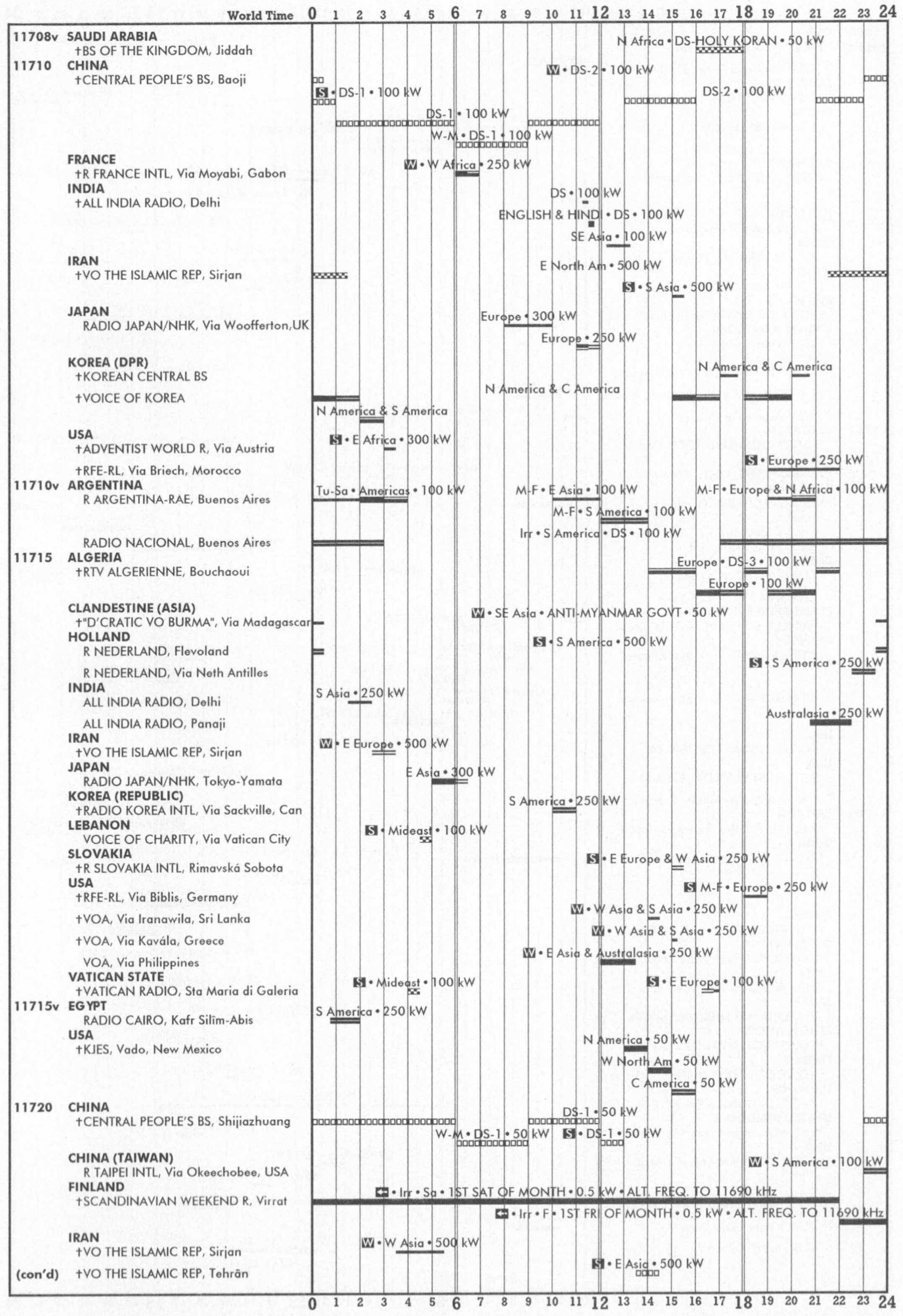
World Time 0 1 2 3 4 5 6 7 8 9 10 11 12 13 14 15 16 17 18 19 20 21 22 23 24
11708v SAUDI ARABIA
†BS OF THE KINGDOM, Jiddah
N Africa • DS-HOLY KORAN • 50 kW
11710 CHINA
†CENTRAL PEOPLE'S BS, Baoji
W • DS-2 • 100 kW
S • DS-1 • 100 kW
DS-2 • 100 kW
DS-1 • 100 kW
W-M • DS-1 • 100 kW
FRANCE
†R FRANCE INTL, Via Moyabi, Gabon
W • W Africa • 250 kW
INDIA
†ALL INDIA RADIO, Delhi
DS • 100 kW
ENGLISH & HINDI • DS • 100 kW
SE Asia • 100 kW
IRAN
†VO THE ISLAMIC REP, Sirjan
E North Am • 500 kW
S • S Asia • 500 kW
JAPAN
RADIO JAPAN/NHK, Via Woofferton,UK
Europe • 300 kW
Europe • 250 kW
KOREA (DPR)
†KOREAN CENTRAL BS
N America & C America
†VOICE OF KOREA
N America & C America
N America & S America
USA
†ADVENTIST WORLD R, Via Austria
S • E Africa • 300 kW
†RFE-RL, Via Briech, Morocco
S • Europe • 250 kW
11710v ARGENTINA
R ARGENTINA-RAE, Buenos Aires
Tu-Sa • Americas • 100 kW
M-F • E Asia • 100 kW
M-F • Europe & N Africa • 100 kW
M-F • S America • 100 kW
Irr • S America • DS • 100 kW
RADIO NACIONAL, Buenos Aires
11715 ALGERIA
†RTV ALGERIENNE, Bouchaoui
Europe • DS-3 • 100 kW
Europe • 100 kW
CLANDESTINE (ASIA)
†"D'CRATIC VO BURMA", Via Madagascar
W • SE Asia • ANTI-MYANMAR GOVT • 50 kW
HOLLAND
R NEDERLAND, Flevoland
S • S America • 500 kW
R NEDERLAND, Via Neth Antilles
S • S America • 250 kW
INDIA
ALL INDIA RADIO, Delhi
S Asia • 250 kW
ALL INDIA RADIO, Panaji
Australasia • 250 kW
IRAN
†VO THE ISLAMIC REP, Sirjan
W • E Europe • 500 kW
JAPAN
RADIO JAPAN/NHK, Tokyo-Yamata
E Asia • 300 kW
KOREA (REPUBLIC)
†RADIO KOREA INTL, Via Sackville, Can
S America • 250 kW
LEBANON
VOICE OF CHARITY, Via Vatican City
S • Mideast • 100 kW
SLOVAKIA
†R SLOVAKIA INTL, Rimavská Sobota
S • E Europe & W Asia • 250 kW
USA
†RFE-RL, Via Biblis, Germany
S M-F • Europe • 250 kW
†VOA, Via Iranawila, Sri Lanka
W • W Asia & S Asia • 250 kW
†VOA, Via Kavála, Greece
W • W Asia & S Asia • 250 kW
VOA, Via Philippines
W • E Asia & Australasia • 250 kW
VATICAN STATE
†VATICAN RADIO, Sta Maria di Galeria
S • Mideast • 100 kW
S • E Europe • 100 kW
11715v EGYPT
RADIO CAIRO, Kafr Silîm-Abis
S America • 250 kW
USA
†KJES, Vado, New Mexico
N America • 50 kW
W North Am • 50 kW
C America • 50 kW
11720 CHINA
†CENTRAL PEOPLE'S BS, Shijiazhuang
DS-1 • 50 kW
W-M • DS-1 • 50 kW
S • DS-1 • 50 kW
CHINA (TAIWAN)
R TAIPEI INTL, Via Okeechobee, USA
W • S America • 100 kW
FINLAND
†SCANDINAVIAN WEEKEND R, Virrat
Irr • Sa • 1ST SAT OF MONTH • 0.5 kW • ALT. FREQ. TO 11690 kHz
Irr • F • 1ST FRI OF MONTH • 0.5 kW • ALT. FREQ. TO 11690 kHz
IRAN
†VO THE ISLAMIC REP, Sirjan
W • W Asia • 500 kW
(con'd) †VO THE ISLAMIC REP, Tehrān
S • E Asia • 500 kW
0 1 2 3 4 5 6 7 8 9 10 11 12 13 14 15 16 17 18 19 20 21 22 23 24
ENGLISH ARABIC CHINESE FRENCH GERMAN RUSSIAN SPANISH OTHER

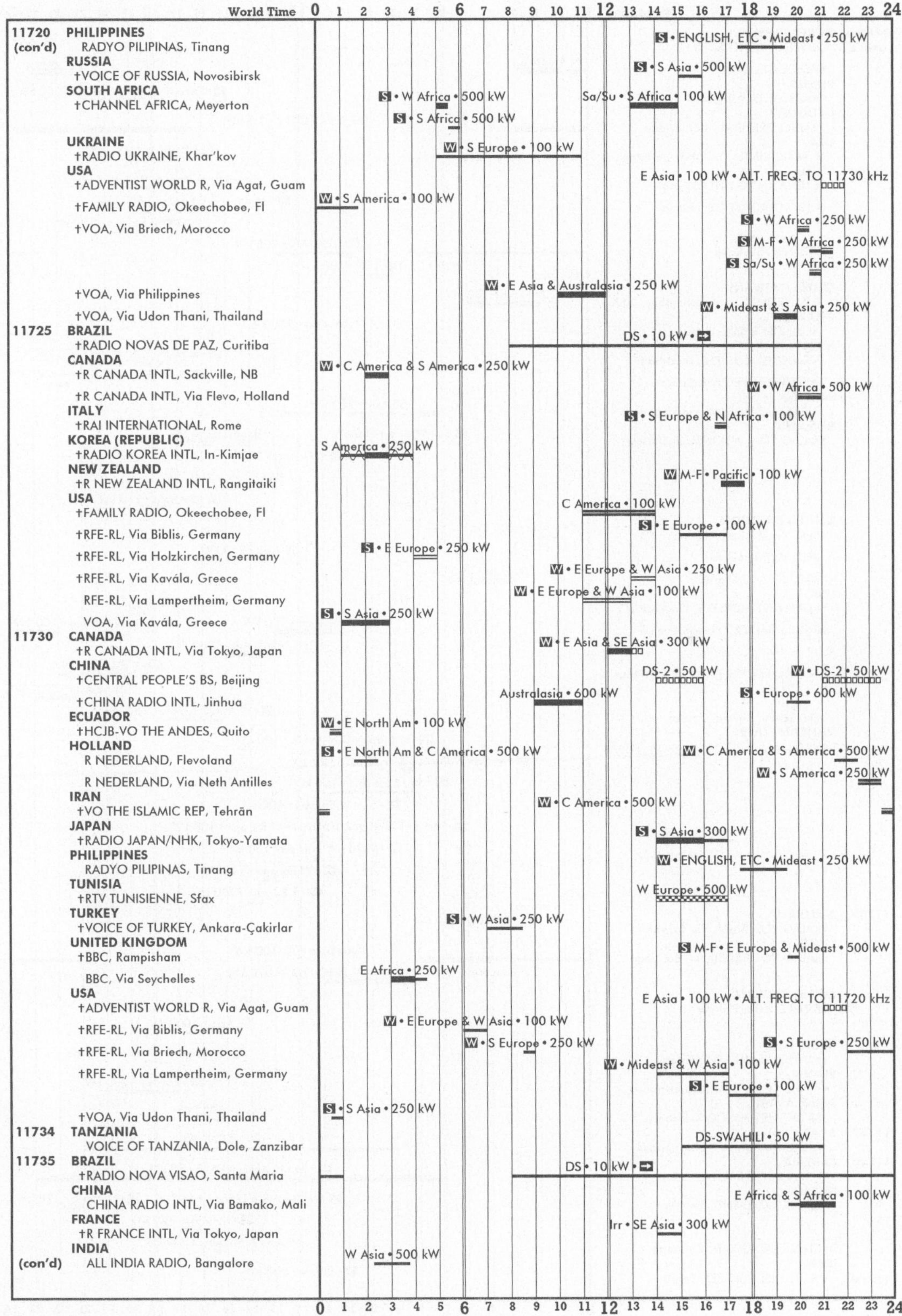
World Time 0 1 2 3 4 5 6 7 8 9 10 11 12 13 14 15 16 17 18 19 20 21 22 23 24
11720 (con'd) PHILIPPINES
RADYO PILIPINAS, Tinang
S • ENGLISH, ETC • Mideast • 250 kW
RUSSIA
†VOICE OF RUSSIA, Novosibirsk
S • S Asia • 500 kW
SOUTH AFRICA
†CHANNEL AFRICA, Meyerton
S • W Africa • 500 kW
Sa/Su • S Africa • 100 kW
S • S Africa • 500 kW
UKRAINE
†RADIO UKRAINE, Khar'kov
W • S Europe • 100 kW
USA
†ADVENTIST WORLD R, Via Agat, Guam
E Asia • 100 kW • ALT. FREQ. TO 11730 kHz
†FAMILY RADIO, Okeechobee, Fl
W • S America • 100 kW
†VOA, Via Briech, Morocco
S • W Africa • 250 kW
S M-F • W Africa • 250 kW
S Sa/Su • W Africa • 250 kW
†VOA, Via Philippines
W • E Asia & Australasia • 250 kW
†VOA, Via Udon Thani, Thailand
W • Mideast & S Asia • 250 kW
11725 BRAZIL
†RADIO NOVAS DE PAZ, Curitiba
DS • 10 kW •
CANADA
†R CANADA INTL, Sackville, NB
W • C America & S America • 250 kW
†R CANADA INTL, Via Flevo, Holland
W • W Africa • 500 kW
ITALY
†RAI INTERNATIONAL, Rome
S • S Europe & N Africa • 100 kW
KOREA (REPUBLIC)
†RADIO KOREA INTL, In-Kimjae
S America • 250 kW
NEW ZEALAND
†R NEW ZEALAND INTL, Rangitaiki
W M-F • Pacific • 100 kW
USA
†FAMILY RADIO, Okeechobee, Fl
C America • 100 kW
†RFE-RL, Via Biblis, Germany
S • E Europe • 100 kW
†RFE-RL, Via Holzkirchen, Germany
S • E Europe • 250 kW
†RFE-RL, Via Kavála, Greece
W • E Europe & W Asia • 250 kW
RFE-RL, Via Lampertheim, Germany
W • E Europe & W Asia • 100 kW
VOA, Via Kavála, Greece
S • S Asia • 250 kW
11730 CANADA
†R CANADA INTL, Via Tokyo, Japan
W • E Asia & SE Asia • 300 kW
CHINA
†CENTRAL PEOPLE'S BS, Beijing
DS-2 • 50 kW
W • DS-2 • 50 kW
†CHINA RADIO INTL, Jinhua
Australasia • 600 kW
S • Europe • 600 kW
ECUADOR
†HCJB-VO THE ANDES, Quito
W • E North Am • 100 kW
HOLLAND
R NEDERLAND, Flevoland
S • E North Am & C America • 500 kW
W • C America & S America • 500 kW
R NEDERLAND, Via Neth Antilles
W • S America • 250 kW
IRAN
†VO THE ISLAMIC REP, Tehrān
W • C America • 500 kW
JAPAN
†RADIO JAPAN/NHK, Tokyo-Yamata
S • S Asia • 300 kW
PHILIPPINES
RADYO PILIPINAS, Tinang
W • ENGLISH, ETC • Mideast • 250 kW
TUNISIA
†RTV TUNISIENNE, Sfax
W Europe • 500 kW
TURKEY
†VOICE OF TURKEY, Ankara-Çakirlar
S • W Asia • 250 kW
UNITED KINGDOM
†BBC, Rampisham
S M-F • E Europe & Mideast • 500 kW
BBC, Via Seychelles
E Africa • 250 kW
USA
†ADVENTIST WORLD R, Via Agat, Guam
E Asia • 100 kW • ALT. FREQ. TO 11720 kHz
†RFE-RL, Via Biblis, Germany
W • E Europe & W Asia • 100 kW
†RFE-RL, Via Briech, Morocco
W • S Europe • 250 kW
S • S Europe • 250 kW
†RFE-RL, Via Lampertheim, Germany
W • Mideast & W Asia • 100 kW
S • E Europe • 100 kW
†VOA, Via Udon Thani, Thailand
S • S Asia • 250 kW
11734 TANZANIA
VOICE OF TANZANIA, Dole, Zanzibar
DS-SWAHILI • 50 kW
11735 BRAZIL
†RADIO NOVA VISAO, Santa Maria
DS • 10 kW •
CHINA
CHINA RADIO INTL, Via Bamako, Mali
E Africa & S Africa • 100 kW
FRANCE
†R FRANCE INTL, Via Tokyo, Japan
Irr • SE Asia • 300 kW
INDIA (con'd)
ALL INDIA RADIO, Bangalore
W Asia • 500 kW
0 1 2 3 4 5 6 7 8 9 10 11 12 13 14 15 16 17 18 19 20 21 22 23 24

SEASONAL S OR W 1-HR TIMESHIFT MIDYEAR OR JAMMING / OR /\ EARLIEST HEARD LATEST HEARD NEW FOR 2002 †

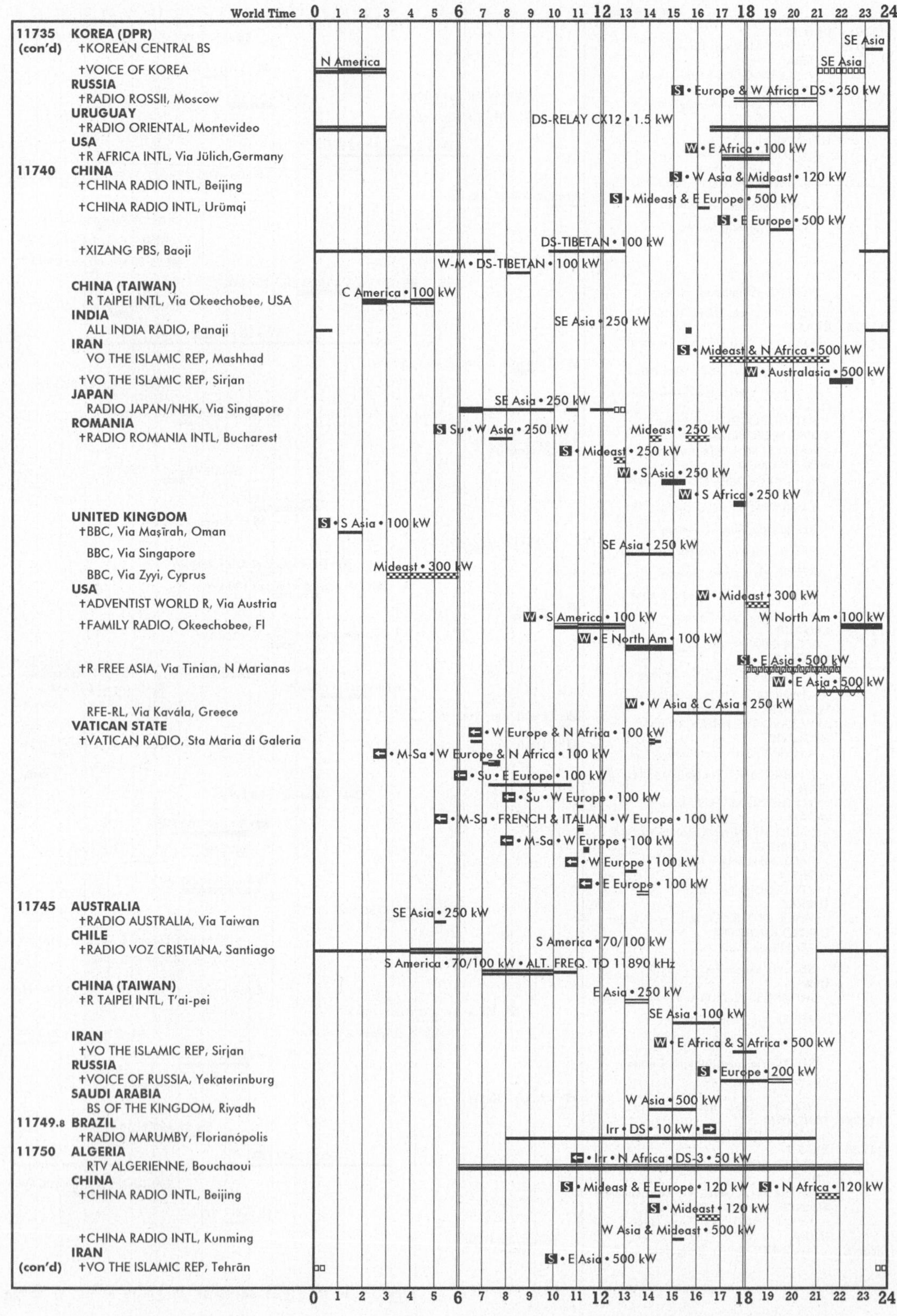
World Time 0 1 2 3 4 5 6 7 8 9 10 11 12 13 14 15 16 17 18 19 20 21 22 23 24
11735 (con'd) KOREA (DPR)
†KOREAN CENTRAL BS
SE Asia
†VOICE OF KOREA
N America
SE Asia
RUSSIA
†RADIO ROSSII, Moscow
S • Europe & W Africa • DS • 250 kW
URUGUAY
†RADIO ORIENTAL, Montevideo
DS-RELAY CX12 • 1.5 kW
USA
†R AFRICA INTL, Via Jülich,Germany
W • E Africa • 100 kW
11740 CHINA
†CHINA RADIO INTL, Beijing
S • W Asia & Mideast • 120 kW
†CHINA RADIO INTL, Urümqi
S • Mideast & E Europe • 500 kW
S • E Europe • 500 kW
†XIZANG PBS, Baoji
DS-TIBETAN • 100 kW
W-M • DS-TIBETAN • 100 kW
CHINA (TAIWAN)
R TAIPEI INTL, Via Okeechobee, USA
C America • 100 kW
INDIA
ALL INDIA RADIO, Panaji
SE Asia • 250 kW
IRAN
VO THE ISLAMIC REP, Mashhad
S • Mideast & N Africa • 500 kW
†VO THE ISLAMIC REP, Sirjan
W • Australasia • 500 kW
JAPAN
RADIO JAPAN/NHK, Via Singapore
SE Asia • 250 kW
ROMANIA
†RADIO ROMANIA INTL, Bucharest
S Su • W Asia • 250 kW
Mideast • 250 kW
S • Mideast • 250 kW
W • S Asia • 250 kW
W • S Africa • 250 kW
UNITED KINGDOM
†BBC, Via Maşīrah, Oman
S • S Asia • 100 kW
BBC, Via Singapore
SE Asia • 250 kW
BBC, Via Zyyi, Cyprus
Mideast • 300 kW
USA
†ADVENTIST WORLD R, Via Austria
W • Mideast • 300 kW
†FAMILY RADIO, Okeechobee, Fl
W • S America • 100 kW
W North Am • 100 kW
W • E North Am • 100 kW
†R FREE ASIA, Via Tinian, N Marianas
S • E Asia • 500 kW
W • E Asia • 500 kW
RFE-RL, Via Kavála, Greece
W • W Asia & C Asia • 250 kW
VATICAN STATE
†VATICAN RADIO, Sta Maria di Galeria
• W Europe & N Africa • 100 kW
• M-Sa • W Europe & N Africa • 100 kW
• Su • E Europe • 100 kW
• Su • W Europe • 100 kW
• M-Sa • FRENCH & ITALIAN • W Europe • 100 kW
• M-Sa • W Europe • 100 kW
• W Europe • 100 kW
• E Europe • 100 kW
11745 AUSTRALIA
†RADIO AUSTRALIA, Via Taiwan
SE Asia • 250 kW
CHILE
†RADIO VOZ CRISTIANA, Santiago
S America • 70/100 kW
S America • 70/100 kW • ALT. FREQ. TO 11890 kHz
CHINA (TAIWAN)
†R TAIPEI INTL, T'ai-pei
E Asia • 250 kW
SE Asia • 100 kW
IRAN
†VO THE ISLAMIC REP, Sirjan
W • E Africa & S Africa • 500 kW
RUSSIA
†VOICE OF RUSSIA, Yekaterinburg
S • Europe • 200 kW
SAUDI ARABIA
BS OF THE KINGDOM, Riyadh
W Asia • 500 kW
11749.8 BRAZIL
†RADIO MARUMBY, Florianópolis
Irr • DS • 10 kW •
11750 ALGERIA
RTV ALGERIENNE, Bouchaoui
• Irr • N Africa • DS-3 • 50 kW
CHINA
†CHINA RADIO INTL, Beijing
S • Mideast & E Europe • 120 kW
S • N Africa • 120 kW
S • Mideast • 120 kW
†CHINA RADIO INTL, Kunming
W Asia & Mideast • 500 kW
IRAN
(con'd) †VO THE ISLAMIC REP, Tehrān
S • E Asia • 500 kW
0 1 2 3 4 5 6 7 8 9 10 11 12 13 14 15 16 17 18 19 20 21 22 23 24
ENGLISH ARABIC CHINESE FRENCH GERMAN RUSSIAN SPANISH OTHER

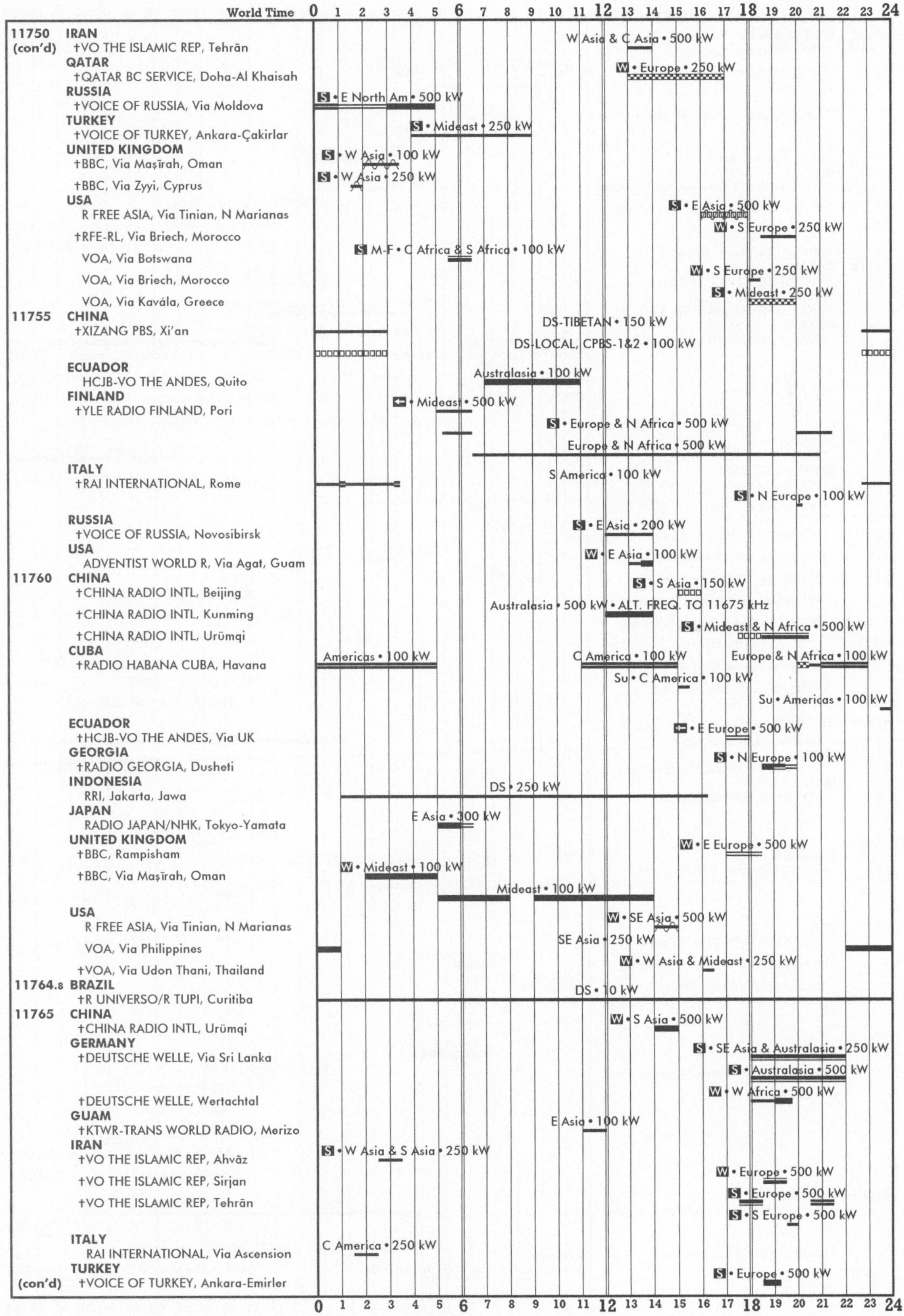
World Time 0 1 2 3 4 5 6 7 8 9 10 11 12 13 14 15 16 17 18 19 20 21 22 23 24
11750 (con'd) IRAN
†VO THE ISLAMIC REP, Tehrān
W Asia & C Asia • 500 kW
QATAR
†QATAR BC SERVICE, Doha-Al Khaisah
W • Europe • 250 kW
RUSSIA
†VOICE OF RUSSIA, Via Moldova
S • E North Am • 500 kW
TURKEY
†VOICE OF TURKEY, Ankara-Çakirlar
S • Mideast • 250 kW
UNITED KINGDOM
†BBC, Via Maşīrah, Oman
S • W Asia • 100 kW
†BBC, Via Zyyi, Cyprus
S • W Asia • 250 kW
USA
R FREE ASIA, Via Tinian, N Marianas
S • E Asia • 500 kW
†RFE-RL, Via Briech, Morocco
W • S Europe • 250 kW
VOA, Via Botswana
S M-F • C Africa & S Africa • 100 kW
VOA, Via Briech, Morocco
W • S Europe • 250 kW
VOA, Via Kavála, Greece
S • Mideast • 250 kW
11755 CHINA
†XIZANG PBS, Xi'an
DS-TIBETAN • 150 kW
DS-LOCAL, CPBS-1&2 • 100 kW
ECUADOR
HCJB-VO THE ANDES, Quito
Australasia • 100 kW
FINLAND
†YLE RADIO FINLAND, Pori
Mideast • 500 kW
S • Europe & N Africa • 500 kW
Europe & N Africa • 500 kW
ITALY
†RAI INTERNATIONAL, Rome
S America • 100 kW
S • N Europe • 100 kW
RUSSIA
†VOICE OF RUSSIA, Novosibirsk
S • E Asia • 200 kW
USA
ADVENTIST WORLD R, Via Agat, Guam
W • E Asia • 100 kW
11760 CHINA
†CHINA RADIO INTL, Beijing
S • S Asia • 150 kW
†CHINA RADIO INTL, Kunming
Australasia • 500 kW • ALT. FREQ. TO 11675 kHz
†CHINA RADIO INTL, Urümqi
S • Mideast & N Africa • 500 kW
CUBA
†RADIO HABANA CUBA, Havana
Americas • 100 kW
C America • 100 kW
Europe & N Africa • 100 kW
Su • C America • 100 kW
Su • Americas • 100 kW
ECUADOR
†HCJB-VO THE ANDES, Via UK
E Europe • 500 kW
GEORGIA
†RADIO GEORGIA, Dusheti
S • N Europe • 100 kW
INDONESIA
RRI, Jakarta, Jawa
DS • 250 kW
JAPAN
RADIO JAPAN/NHK, Tokyo-Yamata
E Asia • 300 kW
UNITED KINGDOM
†BBC, Rampisham
W • E Europe • 500 kW
†BBC, Via Maşīrah, Oman
W • Mideast • 100 kW
Mideast • 100 kW
USA
R FREE ASIA, Via Tinian, N Marianas
W • SE Asia • 500 kW
VOA, Via Philippines
SE Asia • 250 kW
†VOA, Via Udon Thani, Thailand
W • W Asia & Mideast • 250 kW
11764.8 BRAZIL
†R UNIVERSO/R TUPI, Curitiba
DS • 10 kW
11765 CHINA
†CHINA RADIO INTL, Urümqi
W • S Asia • 500 kW
GERMANY
†DEUTSCHE WELLE, Via Sri Lanka
S • SE Asia & Australasia • 250 kW
S • Australasia • 500 kW
†DEUTSCHE WELLE, Wertachtal
W • W Africa • 500 kW
GUAM
†KTWR-TRANS WORLD RADIO, Merizo
E Asia • 100 kW
IRAN
†VO THE ISLAMIC REP, Ahvāz
S • W Asia & S Asia • 250 kW
†VO THE ISLAMIC REP, Sirjan
W • Europe • 500 kW
†VO THE ISLAMIC REP, Tehrān
S • Europe • 500 kW
S • S Europe • 500 kW
ITALY
RAI INTERNATIONAL, Via Ascension
C America • 250 kW
TURKEY (con'd)
†VOICE OF TURKEY, Ankara-Emirler
S • Europe • 500 kW
0 1 2 3 4 5 6 7 8 9 10 11 12 13 14 15 16 17 18 19 20 21 22 23 24

SEASONAL S OR W 1-HR TIMESHIFT MIDYEAR ◄ OR ► JAMMING / OR /\ EARLIEST HEARD ◁ LATEST HEARD ▷ NEW FOR 2002 †

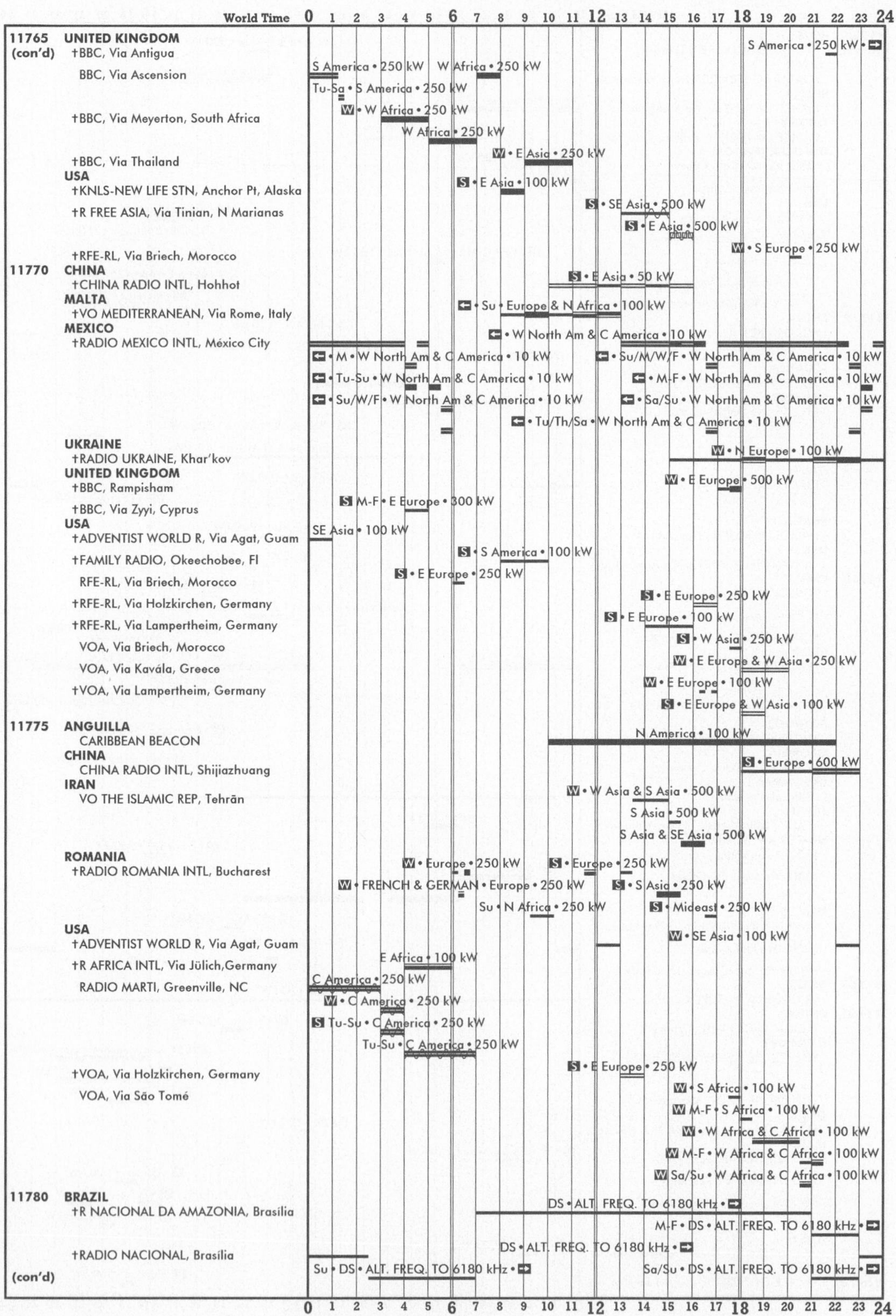
World Time 0 1 2 3 4 5 6 7 8 9 10 11 12 13 14 15 16 17 18 19 20 21 22 23 24
11765 (con'd) UNITED KINGDOM
†BBC, Via Antigua
S America • 250 kW •
BBC, Via Ascension
S America • 250 kW
W Africa • 250 kW
Tu-Sa • S America • 250 kW
W • W Africa • 250 kW
†BBC, Via Meyerton, South Africa
W Africa • 250 kW
W • E Asia • 250 kW
†BBC, Via Thailand
USA
†KNLS-NEW LIFE STN, Anchor Pt, Alaska
S • E Asia • 100 kW
†R FREE ASIA, Via Tinian, N Marianas
S • SE Asia • 500 kW
S • E Asia • 500 kW
†RFE-RL, Via Briech, Morocco
W • S Europe • 250 kW
11770 CHINA
†CHINA RADIO INTL, Hohhot
S • E Asia • 50 kW
MALTA
†VO MEDITERRANEAN, Via Rome, Italy
Su • Europe & N Africa • 100 kW
MEXICO
†RADIO MEXICO INTL, México City
• W North Am & C America • 10 kW
• M • W North Am & C America • 10 kW
• Su/M/W/F • W North Am & C America • 10 kW
• Tu-Su • W North Am & C America • 10 kW
• M-F • W North Am & C America • 10 kW
• Su/W/F • W North Am & C America • 10 kW
• Sa/Su • W North Am & C America • 10 kW
• Tu/Th/Sa • W North Am & C America • 10 kW
UKRAINE
†RADIO UKRAINE, Khar'kov
W • N Europe • 100 kW
UNITED KINGDOM
†BBC, Rampisham
W • E Europe • 500 kW
†BBC, Via Zyyi, Cyprus
S M-F • E Europe • 300 kW
USA
†ADVENTIST WORLD R, Via Agat, Guam
SE Asia • 100 kW
†FAMILY RADIO, Okeechobee, Fl
S • S America • 100 kW
RFE-RL, Via Briech, Morocco
S • E Europe • 250 kW
†RFE-RL, Via Holzkirchen, Germany
S • E Europe • 250 kW
†RFE-RL, Via Lampertheim, Germany
S • E Europe • 100 kW
VOA, Via Briech, Morocco
S • W Asia • 250 kW
VOA, Via Kavála, Greece
W • E Europe & W Asia • 250 kW
†VOA, Via Lampertheim, Germany
W • E Europe • 100 kW
S • E Europe & W Asia • 100 kW
11775 ANGUILLA
CARIBBEAN BEACON
N America • 100 kW
CHINA
CHINA RADIO INTL, Shijiazhuang
S • Europe • 600 kW
IRAN
VO THE ISLAMIC REP, Tehrān
W • W Asia & S Asia • 500 kW
S Asia • 500 kW
S Asia & SE Asia • 500 kW
ROMANIA
†RADIO ROMANIA INTL, Bucharest
W • Europe • 250 kW
S • Europe • 250 kW
W • FRENCH & GERMAN • Europe • 250 kW
S • S Asia • 250 kW
Su • N Africa • 250 kW
S • Mideast • 250 kW
USA
†ADVENTIST WORLD R, Via Agat, Guam
W • SE Asia • 100 kW
†R AFRICA INTL, Via Jülich,Germany
E Africa • 100 kW
RADIO MARTI, Greenville, NC
C America • 250 kW
W • C America • 250 kW
S Tu-Su • C America • 250 kW
Tu-Su • C America • 250 kW
†VOA, Via Holzkirchen, Germany
S • E Europe • 250 kW
VOA, Via São Tomé
W • S Africa • 100 kW
W M-F • S Africa • 100 kW
W • W Africa & C Africa • 100 kW
W M-F • W Africa & C Africa • 100 kW
W Sa/Su • W Africa & C Africa • 100 kW
11780 BRAZIL
†R NACIONAL DA AMAZONIA, Brasília
DS • ALT. FREQ. TO 6180 kHz •
M-F • DS • ALT. FREQ. TO 6180 kHz •
DS • ALT. FREQ. TO 6180 kHz •
†RADIO NACIONAL, Brasília
Su • DS • ALT. FREQ. TO 6180 kHz •
Sa/Su • DS • ALT. FREQ. TO 6180 kHz •
(con'd)
0 1 2 3 4 5 6 7 8 9 10 11 12 13 14 15 16 17 18 19 20 21 22 23 24

ENGLISH ARABIC CHINESE FRENCH GERMAN RUSSIAN SPANISH OTHER

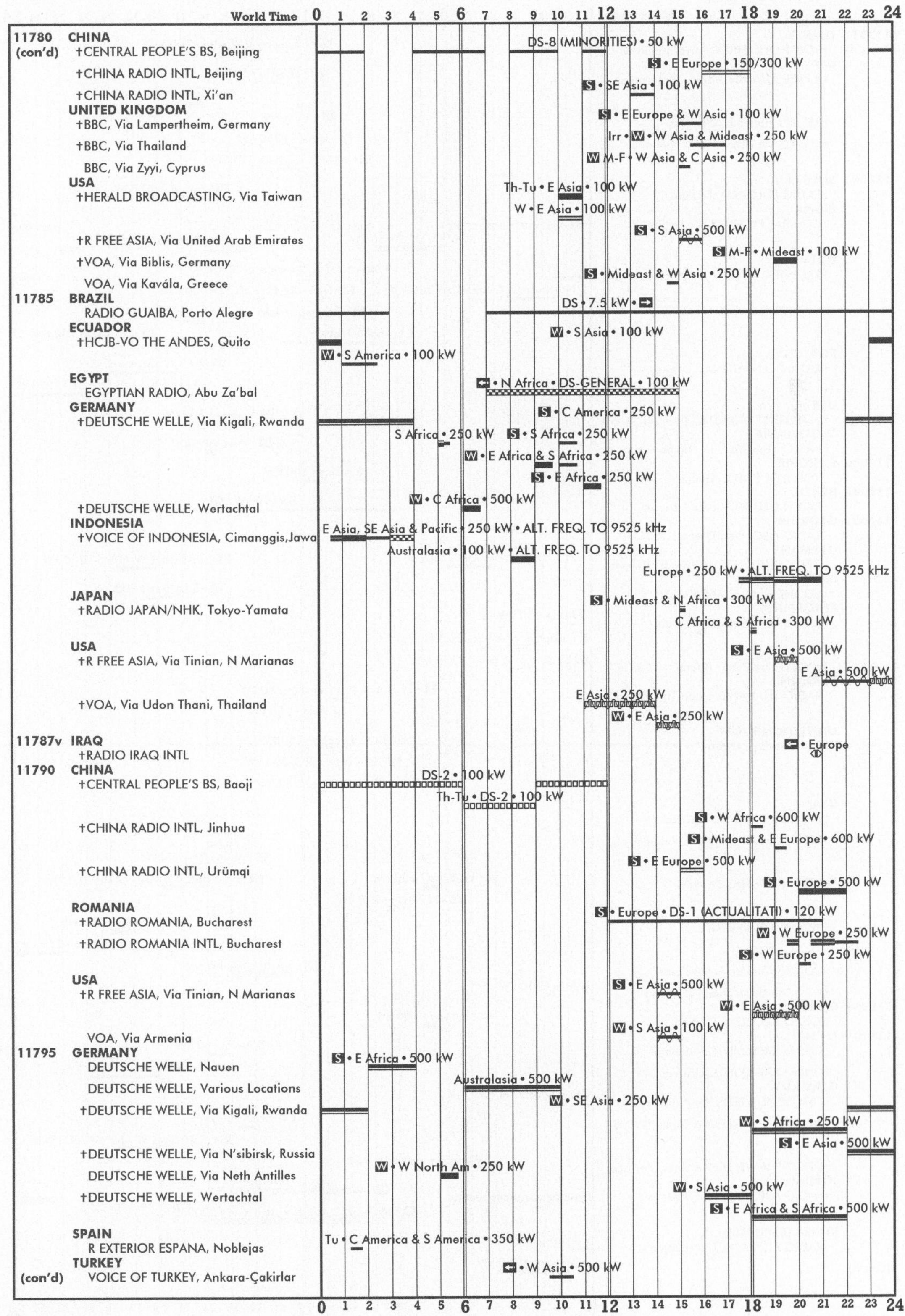
World Time 0 1 2 3 4 5 6 7 8 9 10 11 12 13 14 15 16 17 18 19 20 21 22 23 24
11780 CHINA
(con'd) †CENTRAL PEOPLE'S BS, Beijing
DS-8 (MINORITIES) • 50 kW
†CHINA RADIO INTL, Beijing
S • E Europe • 150/300 kW
†CHINA RADIO INTL, Xi'an
S • SE Asia • 100 kW
UNITED KINGDOM
†BBC, Via Lampertheim, Germany
S • E Europe & W Asia • 100 kW
†BBC, Via Thailand
Irr • W • W Asia & Mideast • 250 kW
BBC, Via Zyyi, Cyprus
W M-F • W Asia & C Asia • 250 kW
USA
†HERALD BROADCASTING, Via Taiwan
Th-Tu • E Asia • 100 kW
W • E Asia • 100 kW
†R FREE ASIA, Via United Arab Emirates
S • S Asia • 500 kW
†VOA, Via Biblis, Germany
S M-F • Mideast • 100 kW
VOA, Via Kavála, Greece
S • Mideast & W Asia • 250 kW
11785 BRAZIL
RADIO GUAIBA, Porto Alegre
DS • 7.5 kW •
ECUADOR
†HCJB-VO THE ANDES, Quito
W • S Asia • 100 kW
W • S America • 100 kW
EGYPT
EGYPTIAN RADIO, Abu Za'bal
N Africa • DS-GENERAL • 100 kW
GERMANY
†DEUTSCHE WELLE, Via Kigali, Rwanda
S • C America • 250 kW
S Africa • 250 kW
S • S Africa • 250 kW
W • E Africa & S Africa • 250 kW
S • E Africa • 250 kW
†DEUTSCHE WELLE, Wertachtal
W • C Africa • 500 kW
INDONESIA
†VOICE OF INDONESIA, Cimanggis,Jawa
E Asia, SE Asia & Pacific • 250 kW • ALT. FREQ. TO 9525 kHz
Australasia • 100 kW • ALT. FREQ. TO 9525 kHz
Europe • 250 kW • ALT. FREQ. TO 9525 kHz
JAPAN
†RADIO JAPAN/NHK, Tokyo-Yamata
S • Mideast & N Africa • 300 kW
C Africa & S Africa • 300 kW
USA
†R FREE ASIA, Via Tinian, N Marianas
S • E Asia • 500 kW
E Asia • 500 kW
†VOA, Via Udon Thani, Thailand
E Asia • 250 kW
W • E Asia • 250 kW
11787v IRAQ
†RADIO IRAQ INTL
• Europe
11790 CHINA
†CENTRAL PEOPLE'S BS, Baoji
DS-2 • 100 kW
Th-Tu • DS-2 • 100 kW
†CHINA RADIO INTL, Jinhua
S • W Africa • 600 kW
S • Mideast & E Europe • 600 kW
†CHINA RADIO INTL, Urümqi
S • E Europe • 500 kW
S • Europe • 500 kW
ROMANIA
†RADIO ROMANIA, Bucharest
S • Europe • DS-1 (ACTUALITATI) • 120 kW
†RADIO ROMANIA INTL, Bucharest
W • W Europe • 250 kW
S • W Europe • 250 kW
USA
†R FREE ASIA, Via Tinian, N Marianas
S • E Asia • 500 kW
W • E Asia • 500 kW
W • S Asia • 100 kW
VOA, Via Armenia
11795 GERMANY
S • E Africa • 500 kW
DEUTSCHE WELLE, Nauen
DEUTSCHE WELLE, Various Locations
Australasia • 500 kW
W • SE Asia • 250 kW
†DEUTSCHE WELLE, Via Kigali, Rwanda
W • S Africa • 250 kW
S • E Asia • 500 kW
†DEUTSCHE WELLE, Via N'sibirsk, Russia
DEUTSCHE WELLE, Via Neth Antilles
W • W North Am • 250 kW
†DEUTSCHE WELLE, Wertachtal
W • S Asia • 500 kW
S • E Africa & S Africa • 500 kW
SPAIN
R EXTERIOR ESPANA, Noblejas
Tu • C America & S America • 350 kW
TURKEY
(con'd) VOICE OF TURKEY, Ankara-Çakirlar
• W Asia • 500 kW
0 1 2 3 4 5 6 7 8 9 10 11 12 13 14 15 16 17 18 19 20 21 22 23 24

SEASONAL S OR W 1-HR TIMESHIFT MIDYEAR ⇐ OR ⇒ JAMMING / OR ∧ EARLIEST HEARD ◁ LATEST HEARD ▷ NEW FOR 2002 †

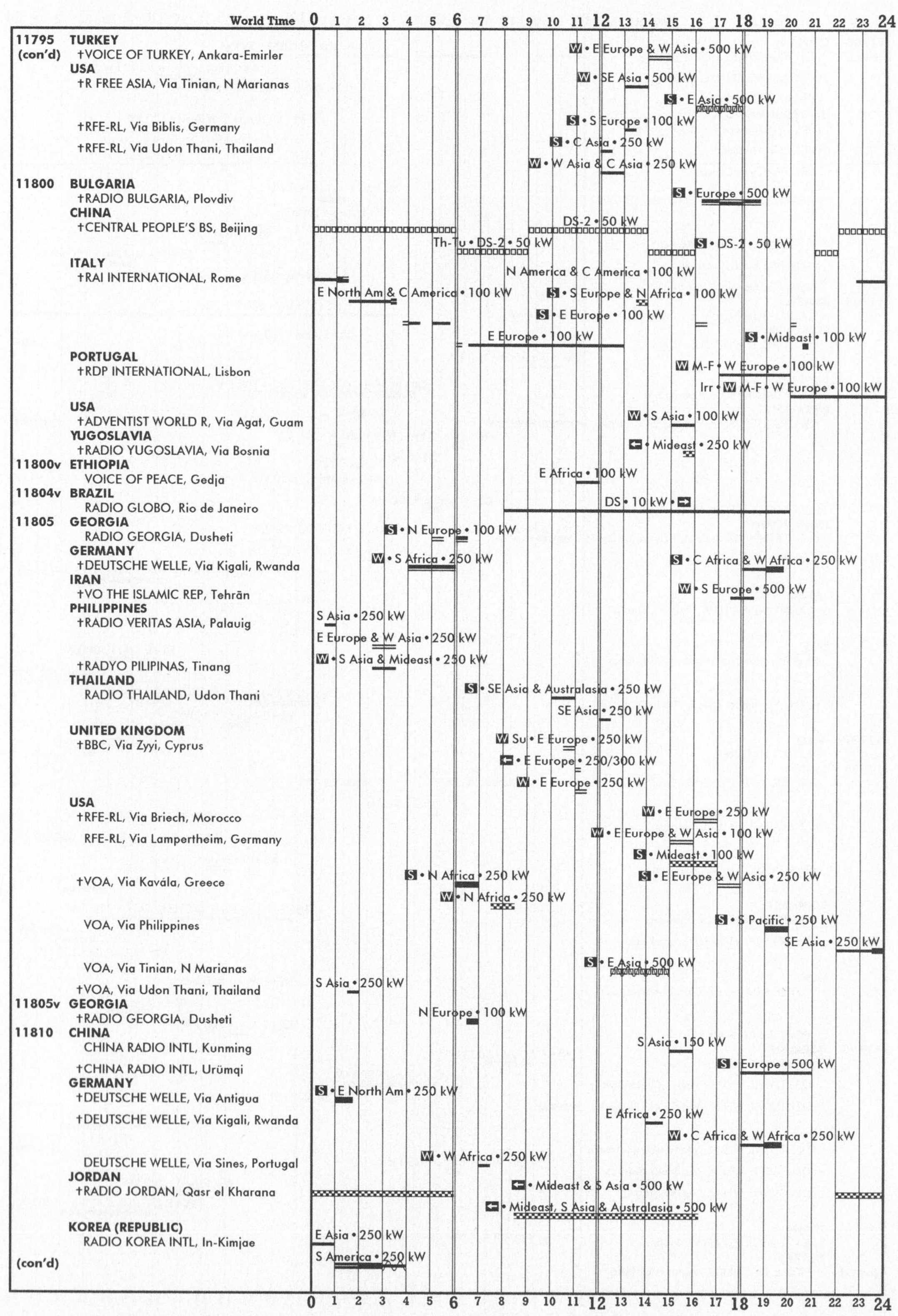
World Time 0 1 2 3 4 5 6 7 8 9 10 11 12 13 14 15 16 17 18 19 20 21 22 23 24
11795 (con'd) TURKEY
†VOICE OF TURKEY, Ankara-Emirler
W • E Europe & W Asia • 500 kW
USA
†R FREE ASIA, Via Tinian, N Marianas
W • SE Asia • 500 kW
S • E Asia • 500 kW
†RFE-RL, Via Biblis, Germany
S • S Europe • 100 kW
†RFE-RL, Via Udon Thani, Thailand
S • C Asia • 250 kW
W • W Asia & C Asia • 250 kW
11800 BULGARIA
†RADIO BULGARIA, Plovdiv
S • Europe • 500 kW
CHINA
†CENTRAL PEOPLE'S BS, Beijing
DS-2 • 50 kW
Th-Tu • DS-2 • 50 kW
S • DS-2 • 50 kW
ITALY
†RAI INTERNATIONAL, Rome
N America & C America • 100 kW
E North Am & C America • 100 kW
S • S Europe & N Africa • 100 kW
S • E Europe • 100 kW
E Europe • 100 kW
S • Mideast • 100 kW
PORTUGAL
†RDP INTERNATIONAL, Lisbon
W M-F • W Europe • 100 kW
Irr • W M-F • W Europe • 100 kW
USA
†ADVENTIST WORLD R, Via Agat, Guam
W • S Asia • 100 kW
YUGOSLAVIA
†RADIO YUGOSLAVIA, Via Bosnia
• Mideast • 250 kW
11800v ETHIOPIA
VOICE OF PEACE, Gedja
E Africa • 100 kW
11804v BRAZIL
RADIO GLOBO, Rio de Janeiro
DS • 10 kW •
11805 GEORGIA
RADIO GEORGIA, Dusheti
S • N Europe • 100 kW
GERMANY
†DEUTSCHE WELLE, Via Kigali, Rwanda
W • S Africa • 250 kW
S • C Africa & W Africa • 250 kW
IRAN
†VO THE ISLAMIC REP, Tehrān
W • S Europe • 500 kW
PHILIPPINES
†RADIO VERITAS ASIA, Palauig
S Asia • 250 kW
E Europe & W Asia • 250 kW
W • S Asia & Mideast • 250 kW
†RADYO PILIPINAS, Tinang
THAILAND
RADIO THAILAND, Udon Thani
S • SE Asia & Australasia • 250 kW
SE Asia • 250 kW
UNITED KINGDOM
†BBC, Via Zyyi, Cyprus
W Su • E Europe • 250 kW
• E Europe • 250/300 kW
W • E Europe • 250 kW
USA
†RFE-RL, Via Briech, Morocco
W • E Europe • 250 kW
RFE-RL, Via Lampertheim, Germany
W • E Europe & W Asia • 100 kW
S • Mideast • 100 kW
†VOA, Via Kavála, Greece
S • N Africa • 250 kW
S • E Europe & W Asia • 250 kW
W • N Africa • 250 kW
VOA, Via Philippines
S • S Pacific • 250 kW
SE Asia • 250 kW
VOA, Via Tinian, N Marianas
S • E Asia • 500 kW
†VOA, Via Udon Thani, Thailand
S Asia • 250 kW
11805v GEORGIA
†RADIO GEORGIA, Dusheti
N Europe • 100 kW
11810 CHINA
CHINA RADIO INTL, Kunming
S Asia • 150 kW
†CHINA RADIO INTL, Urümqi
S • Europe • 500 kW
GERMANY
†DEUTSCHE WELLE, Via Antigua
S • E North Am • 250 kW
†DEUTSCHE WELLE, Via Kigali, Rwanda
E Africa • 250 kW
W • C Africa & W Africa • 250 kW
DEUTSCHE WELLE, Via Sines, Portugal
W • W Africa • 250 kW
JORDAN
†RADIO JORDAN, Qasr el Kharana
• Mideast & S Asia • 500 kW
• Mideast, S Asia & Australasia • 500 kW
KOREA (REPUBLIC)
RADIO KOREA INTL, In-Kimjae
E Asia • 250 kW
S America • 250 kW
(con'd)
0 1 2 3 4 5 6 7 8 9 10 11 12 13 14 15 16 17 18 19 20 21 22 23 24

ENGLISH ARABIC CHINESE FRENCH GERMAN RUSSIAN SPANISH OTHER

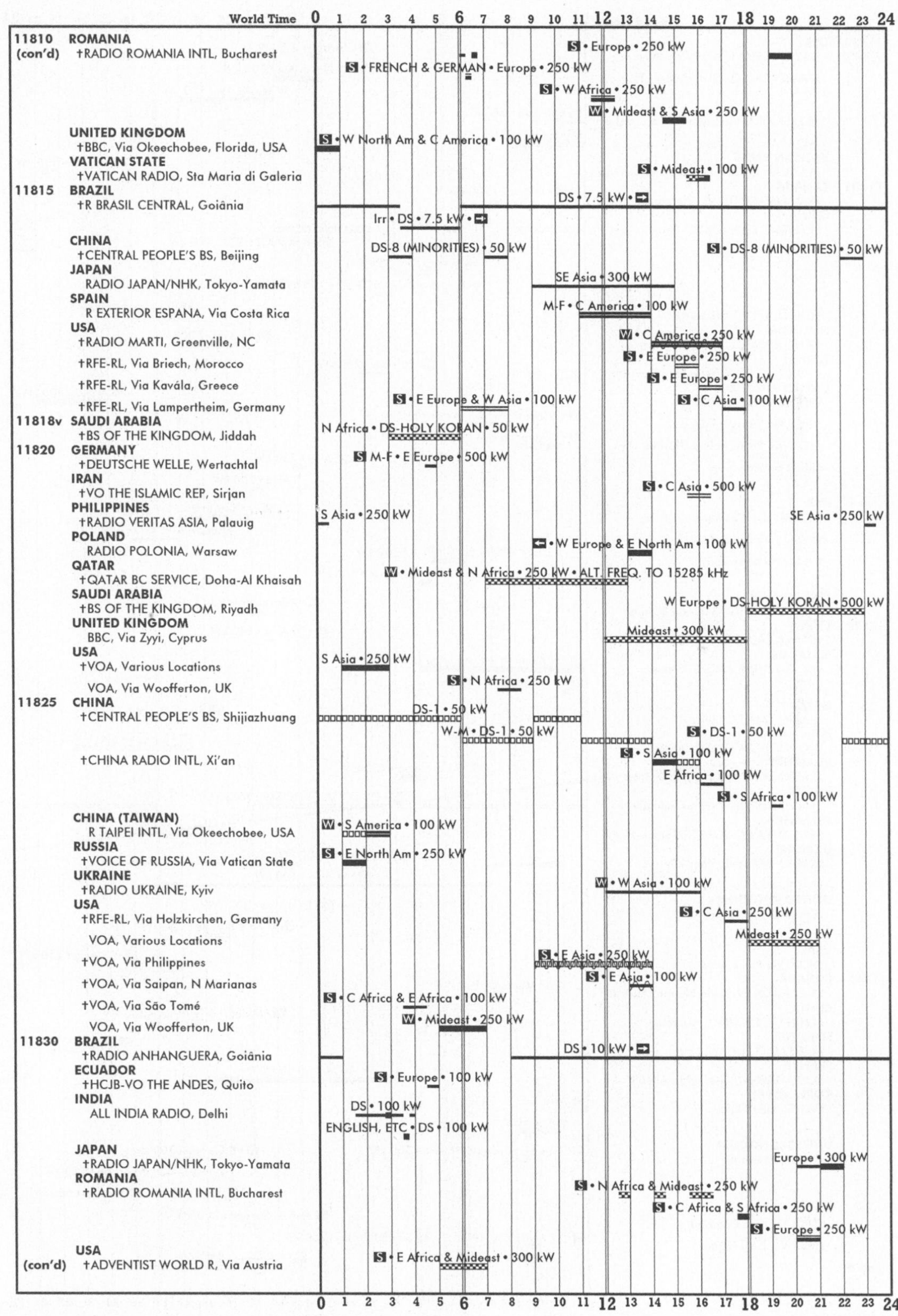
World Time 0 1 2 3 4 5 6 7 8 9 10 11 12 13 14 15 16 17 18 19 20 21 22 23 24
11810 (con'd) ROMANIA
†RADIO ROMANIA INTL, Bucharest
S • Europe • 250 kW
S • FRENCH & GERMAN • Europe • 250 kW
S • W Africa • 250 kW
W • Mideast & S Asia • 250 kW
UNITED KINGDOM
†BBC, Via Okeechobee, Florida, USA
S • W North Am & C America • 100 kW
VATICAN STATE
†VATICAN RADIO, Sta Maria di Galeria
S • Mideast • 100 kW
11815 BRAZIL
†R BRASIL CENTRAL, Goiânia
DS • 7.5 kW
Irr • DS • 7.5 kW
CHINA
†CENTRAL PEOPLE'S BS, Beijing
DS-8 (MINORITIES) • 50 kW
S • DS-8 (MINORITIES) • 50 kW
JAPAN
RADIO JAPAN/NHK, Tokyo-Yamata
SE Asia • 300 kW
SPAIN
R EXTERIOR ESPANA, Via Costa Rica
M-F • C America • 100 kW
USA
†RADIO MARTI, Greenville, NC
W • C America • 250 kW
†RFE-RL, Via Briech, Morocco
S • E Europe • 250 kW
†RFE-RL, Via Kavála, Greece
S • E Europe • 250 kW
†RFE-RL, Via Lampertheim, Germany
S • E Europe & W Asia • 100 kW
S • C Asia • 100 kW
11818v SAUDI ARABIA
†BS OF THE KINGDOM, Jiddah
N Africa • DS-HOLY KORAN • 50 kW
11820 GERMANY
†DEUTSCHE WELLE, Wertachtal
S M-F • E Europe • 500 kW
IRAN
†VO THE ISLAMIC REP, Sirjan
S • C Asia • 500 kW
PHILIPPINES
†RADIO VERITAS ASIA, Palauig
S Asia • 250 kW
SE Asia • 250 kW
POLAND
RADIO POLONIA, Warsaw
W Europe & E North Am • 100 kW
QATAR
†QATAR BC SERVICE, Doha-Al Khaisah
W • Mideast & N Africa • 250 kW • ALT. FREQ. TO 15285 kHz
SAUDI ARABIA
†BS OF THE KINGDOM, Riyadh
W Europe • DS-HOLY KORAN • 500 kW
UNITED KINGDOM
BBC, Via Zyyi, Cyprus
Mideast • 300 kW
USA
†VOA, Various Locations
S Asia • 250 kW
VOA, Via Woofferton, UK
S • N Africa • 250 kW
11825 CHINA
†CENTRAL PEOPLE'S BS, Shijiazhuang
DS-1 • 50 kW
W-M • DS-1 • 50 kW
S • DS-1 • 50 kW
†CHINA RADIO INTL, Xi'an
S • S Asia • 100 kW
E Africa • 100 kW
S • S Africa • 100 kW
CHINA (TAIWAN)
R TAIPEI INTL, Via Okeechobee, USA
W • S America • 100 kW
RUSSIA
†VOICE OF RUSSIA, Via Vatican State
S • E North Am • 250 kW
UKRAINE
†RADIO UKRAINE, Kyiv
W • W Asia • 100 kW
USA
†RFE-RL, Via Holzkirchen, Germany
S • C Asia • 250 kW
VOA, Various Locations
Mideast • 250 kW
†VOA, Via Philippines
S • E Asia • 250 kW
†VOA, Via Saipan, N Marianas
S • E Asia • 100 kW
†VOA, Via São Tomé
S • C Africa & E Africa • 100 kW
VOA, Via Woofferton, UK
W • Mideast • 250 kW
11830 BRAZIL
†RADIO ANHANGUERA, Goiânia
DS • 10 kW
ECUADOR
†HCJB-VO THE ANDES, Quito
S • Europe • 100 kW
INDIA
ALL INDIA RADIO, Delhi
DS • 100 kW
ENGLISH, ETC • DS • 100 kW
JAPAN
†RADIO JAPAN/NHK, Tokyo-Yamata
Europe • 300 kW
ROMANIA
†RADIO ROMANIA INTL, Bucharest
S • N Africa & Mideast • 250 kW
S • C Africa & S Africa • 250 kW
S • Europe • 250 kW
USA (con'd)
†ADVENTIST WORLD R, Via Austria
S • E Africa & Mideast • 300 kW
0 1 2 3 4 5 6 7 8 9 10 11 12 13 14 15 16 17 18 19 20 21 22 23 24

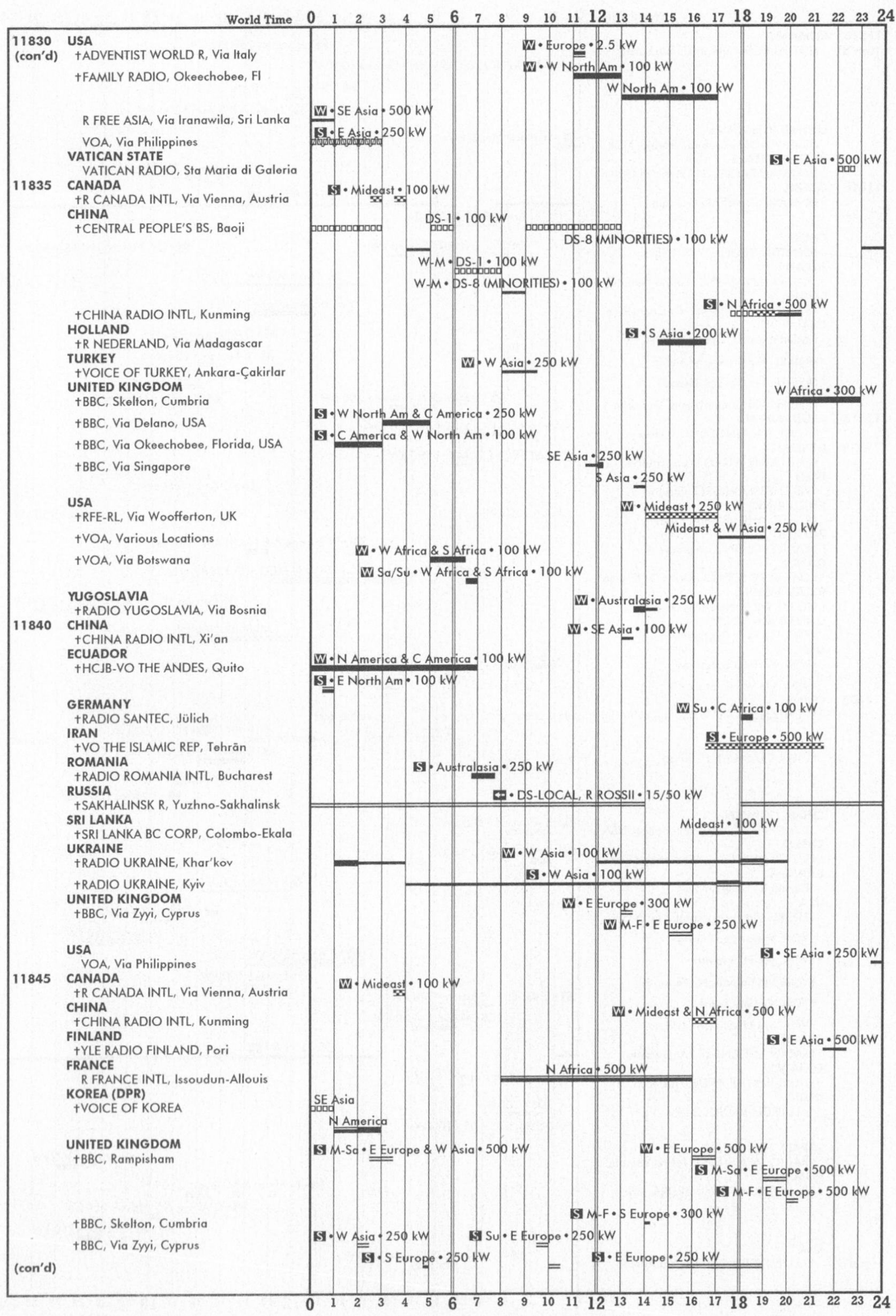
World Time 0 1 2 3 4 5 6 7 8 9 10 11 12 13 14 15 16 17 18 19 20 21 22 23 24
11830 (con'd) USA
†ADVENTIST WORLD R, Via Italy
W • Europe • 2.5 kW
†FAMILY RADIO, Okeechobee, Fl
W • W North Am • 100 kW
W North Am • 100 kW
R FREE ASIA, Via Iranawila, Sri Lanka
W • SE Asia • 500 kW
VOA, Via Philippines
S • E Asia • 250 kW
VATICAN STATE
VATICAN RADIO, Sta Maria di Galeria
S • E Asia • 500 kW
11835 CANADA
†R CANADA INTL, Via Vienna, Austria
S • Mideast • 100 kW
CHINA
†CENTRAL PEOPLE'S BS, Baoji
DS-1 • 100 kW
DS-8 (MINORITIES) • 100 kW
W-M • DS-1 • 100 kW
W-M • DS-8 (MINORITIES) • 100 kW
†CHINA RADIO INTL, Kunming
S • N Africa • 500 kW
HOLLAND
†R NEDERLAND, Via Madagascar
S • S Asia • 200 kW
TURKEY
†VOICE OF TURKEY, Ankara-Çakirlar
W • W Asia • 250 kW
UNITED KINGDOM
†BBC, Skelton, Cumbria
W Africa • 300 kW
†BBC, Via Delano, USA
S • W North Am & C America • 250 kW
†BBC, Via Okeechobee, Florida, USA
S • C America & W North Am • 100 kW
†BBC, Via Singapore
SE Asia • 250 kW
S Asia • 250 kW
USA
†RFE-RL, Via Woofferton, UK
W • Mideast • 250 kW
†VOA, Various Locations
Mideast & W Asia • 250 kW
†VOA, Via Botswana
W • W Africa & S Africa • 100 kW
W Sa/Su • W Africa & S Africa • 100 kW
YUGOSLAVIA
†RADIO YUGOSLAVIA, Via Bosnia
W • Australasia • 250 kW
11840 CHINA
†CHINA RADIO INTL, Xi'an
W • SE Asia • 100 kW
ECUADOR
†HCJB-VO THE ANDES, Quito
W • N America & C America • 100 kW
S • E North Am • 100 kW
GERMANY
†RADIO SANTEC, Jülich
W Su • C Africa • 100 kW
IRAN
†VO THE ISLAMIC REP, Tehrān
S • Europe • 500 kW
ROMANIA
†RADIO ROMANIA INTL, Bucharest
S • Australasia • 250 kW
RUSSIA
†SAKHALINSK R, Yuzhno-Sakhalinsk
DS-LOCAL, R ROSSII • 15/50 kW
SRI LANKA
†SRI LANKA BC CORP, Colombo-Ekala
Mideast • 100 kW
UKRAINE
†RADIO UKRAINE, Khar'kov
W • W Asia • 100 kW
†RADIO UKRAINE, Kyiv
S • W Asia • 100 kW
UNITED KINGDOM
†BBC, Via Zyyi, Cyprus
W • E Europe • 300 kW
W M-F • E Europe • 250 kW
USA
VOA, Via Philippines
S • SE Asia • 250 kW
11845 CANADA
†R CANADA INTL, Via Vienna, Austria
W • Mideast • 100 kW
CHINA
†CHINA RADIO INTL, Kunming
W • Mideast & N Africa • 500 kW
FINLAND
†YLE RADIO FINLAND, Pori
S • E Asia • 500 kW
FRANCE
R FRANCE INTL, Issoudun-Allouis
N Africa • 500 kW
KOREA (DPR)
†VOICE OF KOREA
SE Asia
N America
UNITED KINGDOM
†BBC, Rampisham
S M-Sa • E Europe & W Asia • 500 kW
W • E Europe • 500 kW
S M-Sa • E Europe • 500 kW
S M-F • E Europe • 500 kW
S M-F • S Europe • 300 kW
†BBC, Skelton, Cumbria
S • W Asia • 250 kW
S Su • E Europe • 250 kW
†BBC, Via Zyyi, Cyprus
S • S Europe • 250 kW
S • E Europe • 250 kW
(con'd)
0 1 2 3 4 5 6 7 8 9 10 11 12 13 14 15 16 17 18 19 20 21 22 23 24
ENGLISH ARABIC CHINESE FRENCH GERMAN RUSSIAN SPANISH OTHER

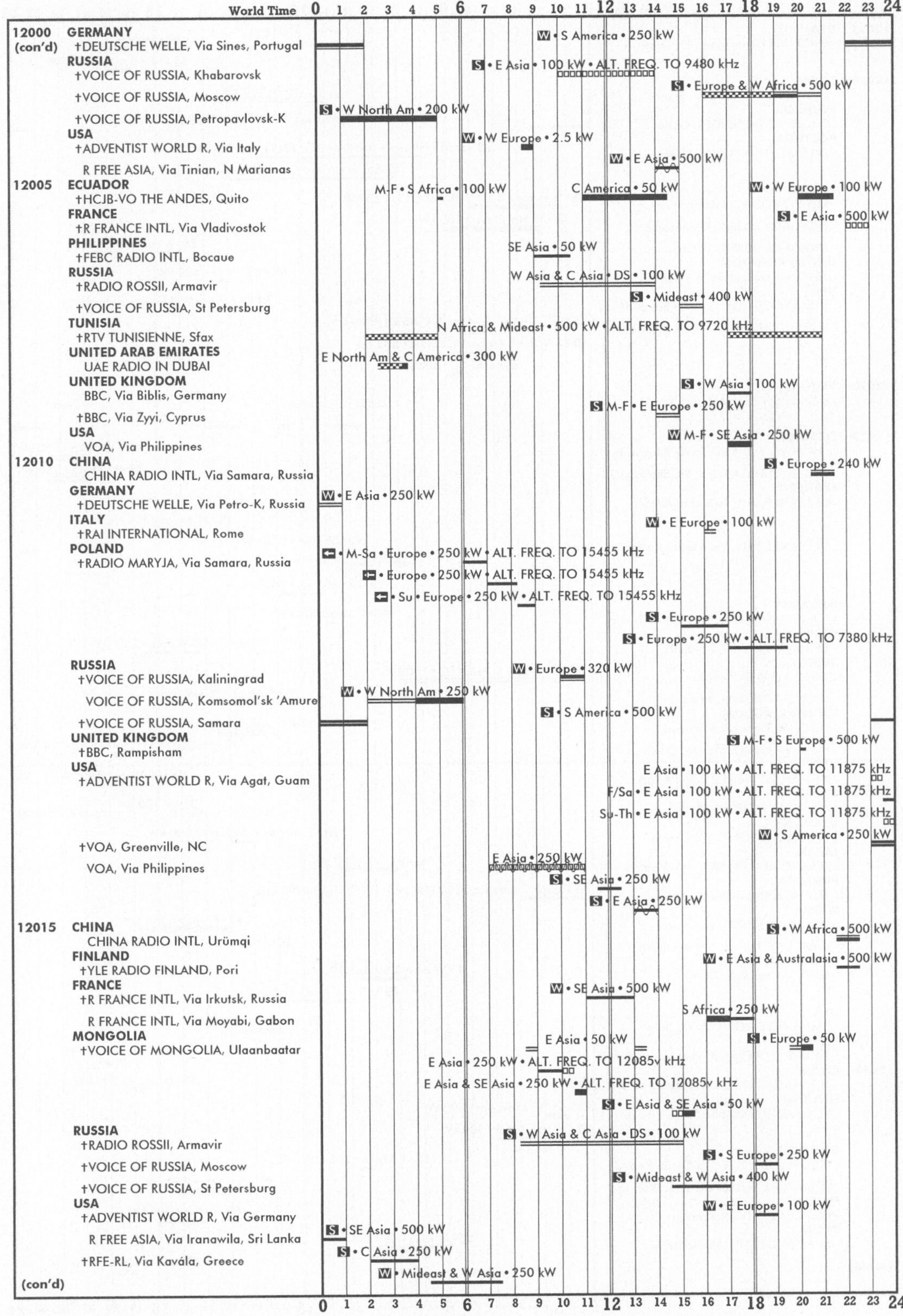
World Time 0 1 2 3 4 5 6 7 8 9 10 11 12 13 14 15 16 17 18 19 20 21 22 23 24
12000 (con'd) GERMANY
†DEUTSCHE WELLE, Via Sines, Portugal
W • S America • 250 kW
RUSSIA
†VOICE OF RUSSIA, Khabarovsk
S • E Asia • 100 kW • ALT. FREQ. TO 9480 kHz
†VOICE OF RUSSIA, Moscow
S • Europe & W Africa • 500 kW
†VOICE OF RUSSIA, Petropavlovsk-K
S • W North Am • 200 kW
USA
†ADVENTIST WORLD R, Via Italy
W • W Europe • 2.5 kW
R FREE ASIA, Via Tinian, N Marianas
W • E Asia • 500 kW
12005 ECUADOR
†HCJB-VO THE ANDES, Quito
M-F • S Africa • 100 kW
C America • 50 kW
W • W Europe • 100 kW
FRANCE
†R FRANCE INTL, Via Vladivostok
S • E Asia • 500 kW
PHILIPPINES
†FEBC RADIO INTL, Bocaue
SE Asia • 50 kW
RUSSIA
†RADIO ROSSII, Armavir
W Asia & C Asia • DS • 100 kW
†VOICE OF RUSSIA, St Petersburg
S • Mideast • 400 kW
TUNISIA
†RTV TUNISIENNE, Sfax
N Africa & Mideast • 500 kW • ALT. FREQ. TO 9720 kHz
UNITED ARAB EMIRATES
UAE RADIO IN DUBAI
E North Am & C America • 300 kW
UNITED KINGDOM
BBC, Via Biblis, Germany
S • W Asia • 100 kW
†BBC, Via Zyyi, Cyprus
S M-F • E Europe • 250 kW
USA
VOA, Via Philippines
W M-F • SE Asia • 250 kW
12010 CHINA
CHINA RADIO INTL, Via Samara, Russia
S • Europe • 240 kW
GERMANY
†DEUTSCHE WELLE, Via Petro-K, Russia
W • E Asia • 250 kW
ITALY
†RAI INTERNATIONAL, Rome
W • E Europe • 100 kW
POLAND
†RADIO MARYJA, Via Samara, Russia
M-Sa • Europe • 250 kW • ALT. FREQ. TO 15455 kHz
• Europe • 250 kW • ALT. FREQ. TO 15455 kHz
• Su • Europe • 250 kW • ALT. FREQ. TO 15455 kHz
S • Europe • 250 kW
S • Europe • 250 kW • ALT. FREQ. TO 7380 kHz
RUSSIA
†VOICE OF RUSSIA, Kaliningrad
W • Europe • 320 kW
VOICE OF RUSSIA, Komsomol'sk 'Amure
W • W North Am • 250 kW
†VOICE OF RUSSIA, Samara
S • S America • 500 kW
UNITED KINGDOM
†BBC, Rampisham
S M-F • S Europe • 500 kW
USA
†ADVENTIST WORLD R, Via Agat, Guam
E Asia • 100 kW • ALT. FREQ. TO 11875 kHz
F/Sa • E Asia • 100 kW • ALT. FREQ. TO 11875 kHz
Su-Th • E Asia • 100 kW • ALT. FREQ. TO 11875 kHz
W • S America • 250 kW
†VOA, Greenville, NC
E Asia • 250 kW
VOA, Via Philippines
S • SE Asia • 250 kW
S • E Asia • 250 kW
12015 CHINA
CHINA RADIO INTL, Urümqi
S • W Africa • 500 kW
FINLAND
†YLE RADIO FINLAND, Pori
W • E Asia & Australasia • 500 kW
FRANCE
†R FRANCE INTL, Via Irkutsk, Russia
W • SE Asia • 500 kW
R FRANCE INTL, Via Moyabi, Gabon
S Africa • 250 kW
MONGOLIA
†VOICE OF MONGOLIA, Ulaanbaatar
E Asia • 50 kW
S • Europe • 50 kW
E Asia • 250 kW • ALT. FREQ. TO 12085v kHz
E Asia & SE Asia • 250 kW • ALT. FREQ. TO 12085v kHz
S • E Asia & SE Asia • 50 kW
RUSSIA
†RADIO ROSSII, Armavir
S • W Asia & C Asia • DS • 100 kW
†VOICE OF RUSSIA, Moscow
S • S Europe • 250 kW
†VOICE OF RUSSIA, St Petersburg
S • Mideast & W Asia • 400 kW
USA
†ADVENTIST WORLD R, Via Germany
W • E Europe • 100 kW
R FREE ASIA, Via Iranawila, Sri Lanka
S • SE Asia • 500 kW
†RFE-RL, Via Kavála, Greece
S • C Asia • 250 kW
W • Mideast & W Asia • 250 kW
(con'd)
0 1 2 3 4 5 6 7 8 9 10 11 12 13 14 15 16 17 18 19 20 21 22 23 24

SEASONAL S OR W 1-HR TIMESHIFT MIDYEAR ⇐ OR ⇒ JAMMING / OR /\ EARLIEST HEARD ◁ LATEST HEARD ▷ NEW FOR 2002 †

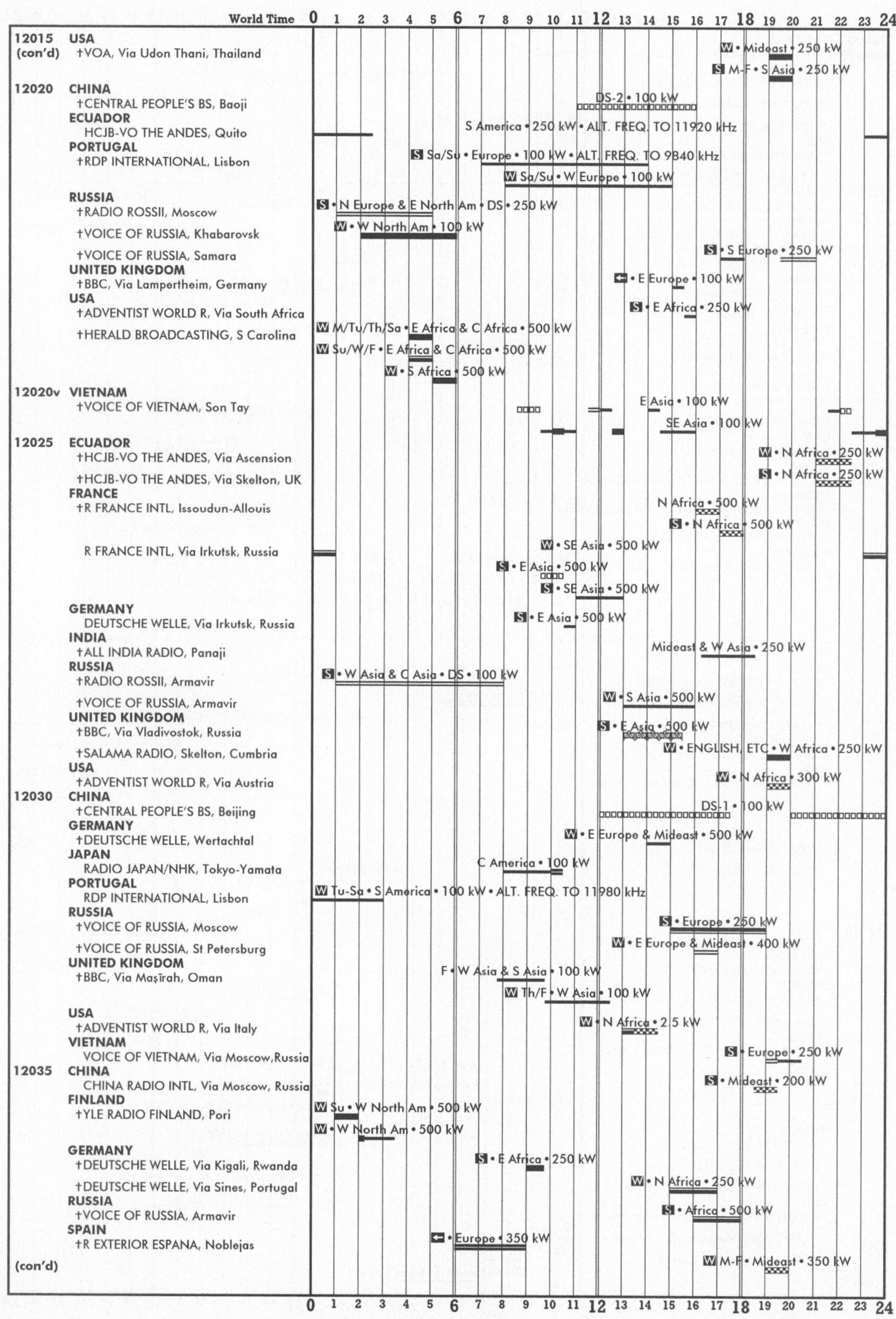
World Time 0 1 2 3 4 5 6 7 8 9 10 11 12 13 14 15 16 17 18 19 20 21 22 23 24
12015 (con'd) USA
†VOA, Via Udon Thani, Thailand
W • Mideast • 250 kW
S M-F • S Asia • 250 kW
12020 CHINA
†CENTRAL PEOPLE'S BS, Baoji
DS-2 • 100 kW
ECUADOR
HCJB-VO THE ANDES, Quito
S America • 250 kW • ALT. FREQ. TO 11920 kHz
PORTUGAL
†RDP INTERNATIONAL, Lisbon
S Sa/Su • Europe • 100 kW • ALT. FREQ. TO 9840 kHz
W Sa/Su • W Europe • 100 kW
RUSSIA
†RADIO ROSSII, Moscow
S • N Europe & E North Am • DS • 250 kW
†VOICE OF RUSSIA, Khabarovsk
W • W North Am • 100 kW
†VOICE OF RUSSIA, Samara
S • S Europe • 250 kW
UNITED KINGDOM
†BBC, Via Lampertheim, Germany
• E Europe • 100 kW
USA
†ADVENTIST WORLD R, Via South Africa
S • E Africa • 250 kW
†HERALD BROADCASTING, S Carolina
W M/Tu/Th/Sa • E Africa & C Africa • 500 kW
W Su/W/F • E Africa & C Africa • 500 kW
W • S Africa • 500 kW
12020v VIETNAM
†VOICE OF VIETNAM, Son Tay
E Asia • 100 kW
SE Asia • 100 kW
12025 ECUADOR
†HCJB-VO THE ANDES, Via Ascension
W • N Africa • 250 kW
†HCJB-VO THE ANDES, Via Skelton, UK
S • N Africa • 250 kW
FRANCE
†R FRANCE INTL, Issoudun-Allouis
N Africa • 500 kW
S • N Africa • 500 kW
R FRANCE INTL, Via Irkutsk, Russia
W • SE Asia • 500 kW
S • E Asia • 500 kW
S • SE Asia • 500 kW
GERMANY
DEUTSCHE WELLE, Via Irkutsk, Russia
S • E Asia • 500 kW
INDIA
†ALL INDIA RADIO, Panaji
Mideast & W Asia • 250 kW
RUSSIA
†RADIO ROSSII, Armavir
S • W Asia & C Asia • DS • 100 kW
†VOICE OF RUSSIA, Armavir
W • S Asia • 500 kW
UNITED KINGDOM
†BBC, Via Vladivostok, Russia
S • E Asia • 500 kW
†SALAMA RADIO, Skelton, Cumbria
W • ENGLISH, ETC • W Africa • 250 kW
USA
†ADVENTIST WORLD R, Via Austria
W • N Africa • 300 kW
12030 CHINA
†CENTRAL PEOPLE'S BS, Beijing
DS-1 • 100 kW
GERMANY
†DEUTSCHE WELLE, Wertachtal
W • E Europe & Mideast • 500 kW
JAPAN
RADIO JAPAN/NHK, Tokyo-Yamata
C America • 100 kW
PORTUGAL
RDP INTERNATIONAL, Lisbon
W Tu-Sa • S America • 100 kW • ALT. FREQ. TO 11980 kHz
RUSSIA
†VOICE OF RUSSIA, Moscow
S • Europe • 250 kW
†VOICE OF RUSSIA, St Petersburg
W • E Europe & Mideast • 400 kW
UNITED KINGDOM
†BBC, Via Maṣīrah, Oman
F • W Asia & S Asia • 100 kW
W Th/F • W Asia • 100 kW
USA
†ADVENTIST WORLD R, Via Italy
W • N Africa • 2.5 kW
VIETNAM
VOICE OF VIETNAM, Via Moscow, Russia
S • Europe • 250 kW
12035 CHINA
CHINA RADIO INTL, Via Moscow, Russia
S • Mideast • 200 kW
FINLAND
†YLE RADIO FINLAND, Pori
W Su • W North Am • 500 kW
W • W North Am • 500 kW
GERMANY
†DEUTSCHE WELLE, Via Kigali, Rwanda
S • E Africa • 250 kW
†DEUTSCHE WELLE, Via Sines, Portugal
W • N Africa • 250 kW
RUSSIA
†VOICE OF RUSSIA, Armavir
S • Africa • 500 kW
SPAIN
†R EXTERIOR ESPANA, Noblejas
• Europe • 350 kW
(con'd)
W M-F • Mideast • 350 kW
0 1 2 3 4 5 6 7 8 9 10 11 12 13 14 15 16 17 18 19 20 21 22 23 24
ENGLISH ARABIC CHINESE FRENCH GERMAN RUSSIAN SPANISH OTHER

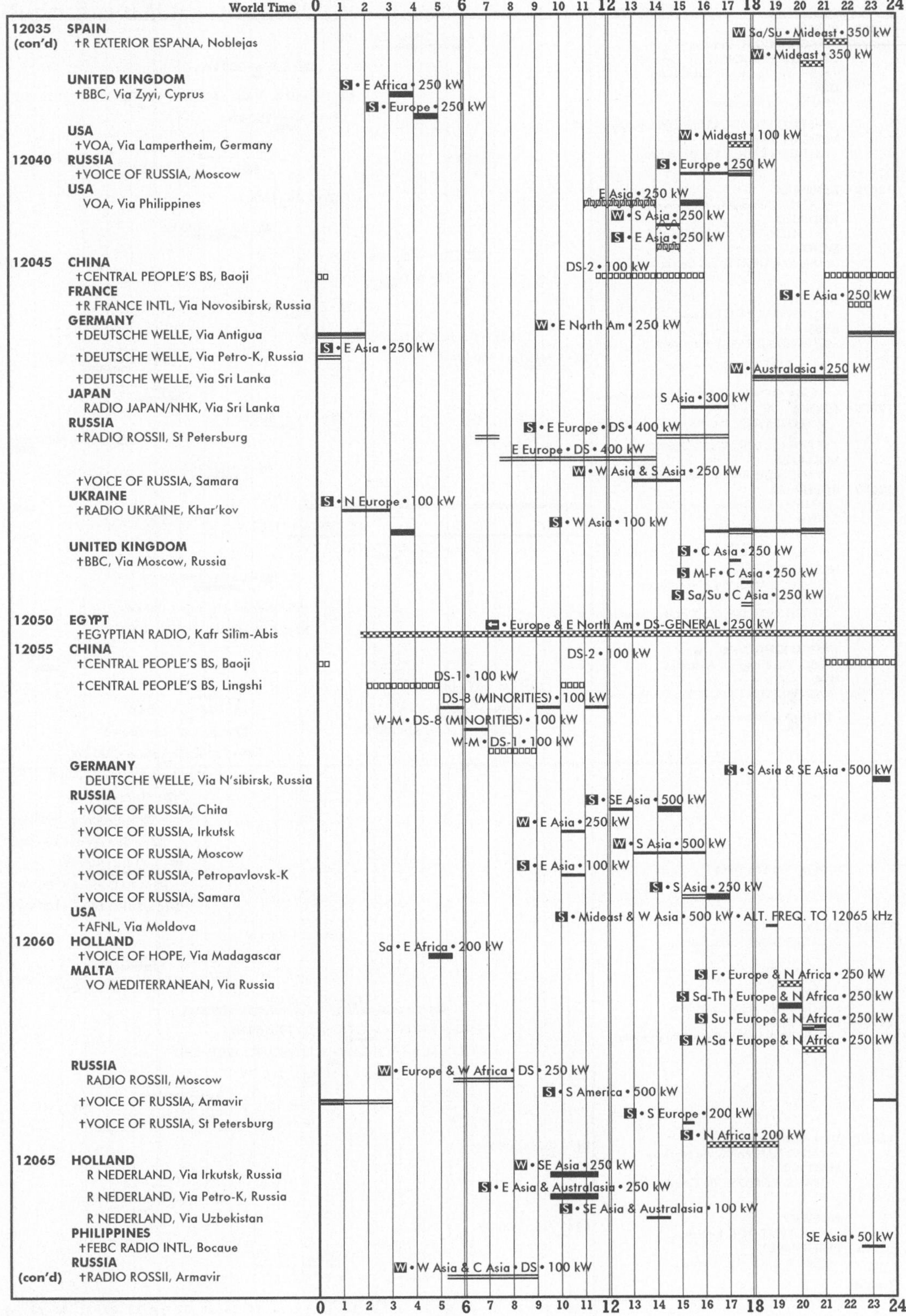
World Time 0 1 2 3 4 5 6 7 8 9 10 11 12 13 14 15 16 17 18 19 20 21 22 23 24
12035 SPAIN (con'd)
†R EXTERIOR ESPANA, Noblejas
W Sa/Su • Mideast • 350 kW
W • Mideast • 350 kW
UNITED KINGDOM
†BBC, Via Zyyi, Cyprus
S • E Africa • 250 kW
S • Europe • 250 kW
USA
†VOA, Via Lampertheim, Germany
W • Mideast • 100 kW
12040 RUSSIA
†VOICE OF RUSSIA, Moscow
S • Europe • 250 kW
USA
VOA, Via Philippines
E Asia • 250 kW
W • S Asia • 250 kW
S • E Asia • 250 kW
12045 CHINA
†CENTRAL PEOPLE'S BS, Baoji
DS-2 • 100 kW
FRANCE
†R FRANCE INTL, Via Novosibirsk, Russia
S • E Asia • 250 kW
GERMANY
†DEUTSCHE WELLE, Via Antigua
W • E North Am • 250 kW
†DEUTSCHE WELLE, Via Petro-K, Russia
S • E Asia • 250 kW
†DEUTSCHE WELLE, Via Sri Lanka
W • Australasia • 250 kW
JAPAN
RADIO JAPAN/NHK, Via Sri Lanka
S Asia • 300 kW
RUSSIA
†RADIO ROSSII, St Petersburg
S • E Europe • DS • 400 kW
E Europe • DS • 400 kW
†VOICE OF RUSSIA, Samara
W • W Asia & S Asia • 250 kW
UKRAINE
†RADIO UKRAINE, Khar'kov
S • N Europe • 100 kW
S • W Asia • 100 kW
UNITED KINGDOM
†BBC, Via Moscow, Russia
S • C Asia • 250 kW
S M-F • C Asia • 250 kW
S Sa/Su • C Asia • 250 kW
12050 EGYPT
†EGYPTIAN RADIO, Kafr Silîm-Abis
• Europe & E North Am • DS-GENERAL • 250 kW
12055 CHINA
†CENTRAL PEOPLE'S BS, Baoji
DS-2 • 100 kW
†CENTRAL PEOPLE'S BS, Lingshi
DS-1 • 100 kW
DS-8 (MINORITIES) • 100 kW
W-M • DS-8 (MINORITIES) • 100 kW
W-M • DS-1 • 100 kW
GERMANY
DEUTSCHE WELLE, Via N'sibirsk, Russia
S • S Asia & SE Asia • 500 kW
RUSSIA
†VOICE OF RUSSIA, Chita
S • SE Asia • 500 kW
†VOICE OF RUSSIA, Irkutsk
W • E Asia • 250 kW
†VOICE OF RUSSIA, Moscow
W • S Asia • 500 kW
†VOICE OF RUSSIA, Petropavlovsk-K
S • E Asia • 100 kW
†VOICE OF RUSSIA, Samara
S • S Asia • 250 kW
USA
†AFNL, Via Moldova
S • Mideast & W Asia • 500 kW • ALT. FREQ. TO 12065 kHz
12060 HOLLAND
†VOICE OF HOPE, Via Madagascar
Sa • E Africa • 200 kW
MALTA
VO MEDITERRANEAN, Via Russia
S F • Europe & N Africa • 250 kW
S Sa-Th • Europe & N Africa • 250 kW
S Su • Europe & N Africa • 250 kW
S M-Sa • Europe & N Africa • 250 kW
RUSSIA
RADIO ROSSII, Moscow
W • Europe & W Africa • DS • 250 kW
†VOICE OF RUSSIA, Armavir
S • S America • 500 kW
†VOICE OF RUSSIA, St Petersburg
S • S Europe • 200 kW
S • N Africa • 200 kW
12065 HOLLAND
R NEDERLAND, Via Irkutsk, Russia
W • SE Asia • 250 kW
R NEDERLAND, Via Petro-K, Russia
S • E Asia & Australasia • 250 kW
R NEDERLAND, Via Uzbekistan
S • SE Asia & Australasia • 100 kW
PHILIPPINES
†FEBC RADIO INTL, Bocaue
SE Asia • 50 kW
RUSSIA (con'd)
†RADIO ROSSII, Armavir
W • W Asia & C Asia • DS • 100 kW
0 1 2 3 4 5 6 7 8 9 10 11 12 13 14 15 16 17 18 19 20 21 22 23 24

SEASONAL S OR W 1-HR TIMESHIFT MIDYEAR ⇐ OR ⇒ JAMMING / OR /\ EARLIEST HEARD ◁ LATEST HEARD ▷ NEW FOR 2002 †

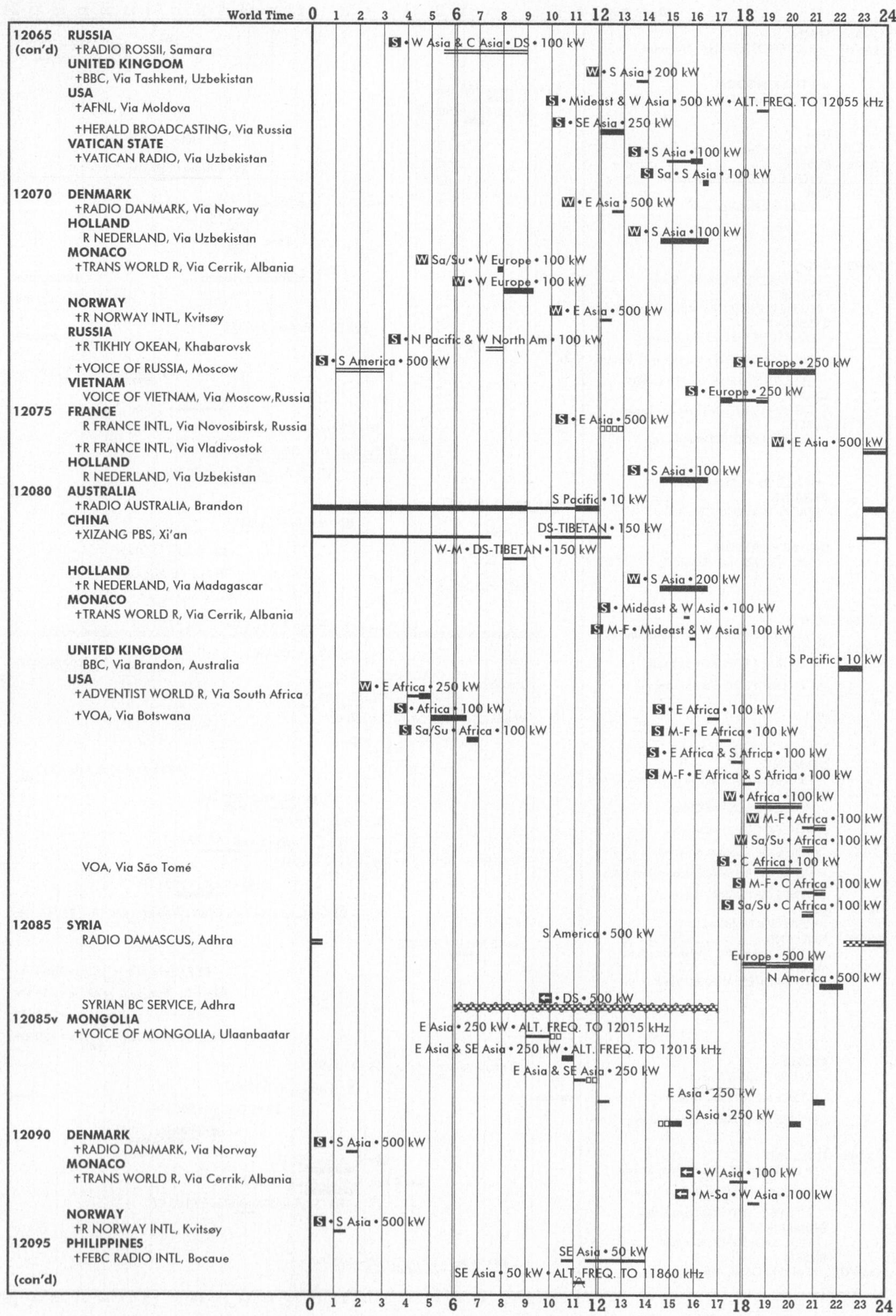

World Time 0 1 2 3 4 5 6 7 8 9 10 11 12 13 14 15 16 17 18 19 20 21 22 23 24

kHz	Country / Station	Schedule
12065 (con'd)	RUSSIA	
	†RADIO ROSSII, Samara	S • W Asia & C Asia • DS • 100 kW
	UNITED KINGDOM	
	†BBC, Via Tashkent, Uzbekistan	W • S Asia • 200 kW
	USA	
	†AFNL, Via Moldova	S • Mideast & W Asia • 500 kW • ALT. FREQ. TO 12055 kHz
	†HERALD BROADCASTING, Via Russia	S • SE Asia • 250 kW
	VATICAN STATE	
	†VATICAN RADIO, Via Uzbekistan	S • S Asia • 100 kW
		S Sa • S Asia • 100 kW
12070	DENMARK	
	†RADIO DANMARK, Via Norway	W • E Asia • 500 kW
	HOLLAND	
	R NEDERLAND, Via Uzbekistan	W • S Asia • 100 kW
	MONACO	
	†TRANS WORLD R, Via Cerrik, Albania	W Sa/Su • W Europe • 100 kW
		W • W Europe • 100 kW
	NORWAY	
	†R NORWAY INTL, Kvitsøy	W • E Asia • 500 kW
	RUSSIA	
	†R TIKHIY OKEAN, Khabarovsk	S • N Pacific & W North Am • 100 kW
	†VOICE OF RUSSIA, Moscow	S • S America • 500 kW
		S • Europe • 250 kW
	VIETNAM	
	VOICE OF VIETNAM, Via Moscow,Russia	S • Europe • 250 kW
12075	FRANCE	
	R FRANCE INTL, Via Novosibirsk, Russia	S • E Asia • 500 kW
	†R FRANCE INTL, Via Vladivostok	W • E Asia • 500 kW
	HOLLAND	
	R NEDERLAND, Via Uzbekistan	S • S Asia • 100 kW
12080	AUSTRALIA	
	†RADIO AUSTRALIA, Brandon	S Pacific • 10 kW
	CHINA	
	†XIZANG PBS, Xi'an	DS-TIBETAN • 150 kW
		W-M • DS-TIBETAN • 150 kW
	HOLLAND	
	†R NEDERLAND, Via Madagascar	W • S Asia • 200 kW
	MONACO	
	†TRANS WORLD R, Via Cerrik, Albania	S • Mideast & W Asia • 100 kW
		S M-F • Mideast & W Asia • 100 kW
	UNITED KINGDOM	
	BBC, Via Brandon, Australia	S Pacific • 10 kW
	USA	
	†ADVENTIST WORLD R, Via South Africa	W • E Africa • 250 kW
	†VOA, Via Botswana	S • Africa • 100 kW
		S Sa/Su • Africa • 100 kW
		S • E Africa • 100 kW
		S M-F • E Africa • 100 kW
		S • E Africa & S Africa • 100 kW
		S M-F • E Africa & S Africa • 100 kW
		W • Africa • 100 kW
		W M-F • Africa • 100 kW
		W Sa/Su • Africa • 100 kW
	VOA, Via São Tomé	S • C Africa • 100 kW
		S M-F • C Africa • 100 kW
		S Sa/Su • C Africa • 100 kW
12085	SYRIA	
	RADIO DAMASCUS, Adhra	S America • 500 kW
		Europe • 500 kW
		N America • 500 kW
	SYRIAN BC SERVICE, Adhra	← • DS • 500 kW
12085v	MONGOLIA	
	†VOICE OF MONGOLIA, Ulaanbaatar	E Asia • 250 kW • ALT. FREQ. TO 12015 kHz
		E Asia & SE Asia • 250 kW • ALT. FREQ. TO 12015 kHz
		E Asia & SE Asia • 250 kW
		E Asia • 250 kW
		S Asia • 250 kW
12090	DENMARK	
	†RADIO DANMARK, Via Norway	S • S Asia • 500 kW
	MONACO	
	†TRANS WORLD R, Via Cerrik, Albania	← • W Asia • 100 kW
		← • M-Sa • W Asia • 100 kW
	NORWAY	
	†R NORWAY INTL, Kvitsøy	S • S Asia • 500 kW
12095	PHILIPPINES	
	†FEBC RADIO INTL, Bocaue	SE Asia • 50 kW
(con'd)		SE Asia • 50 kW • ALT. FREQ. TO 11860 kHz

0 1 2 3 4 5 6 7 8 9 10 11 12 13 14 15 16 17 18 19 20 21 22 23 24

ENGLISH ▬ ARABIC ⩨ CHINESE ▫▫▫ FRENCH ═ GERMAN ═ RUSSIAN ═ SPANISH ═ OTHER —

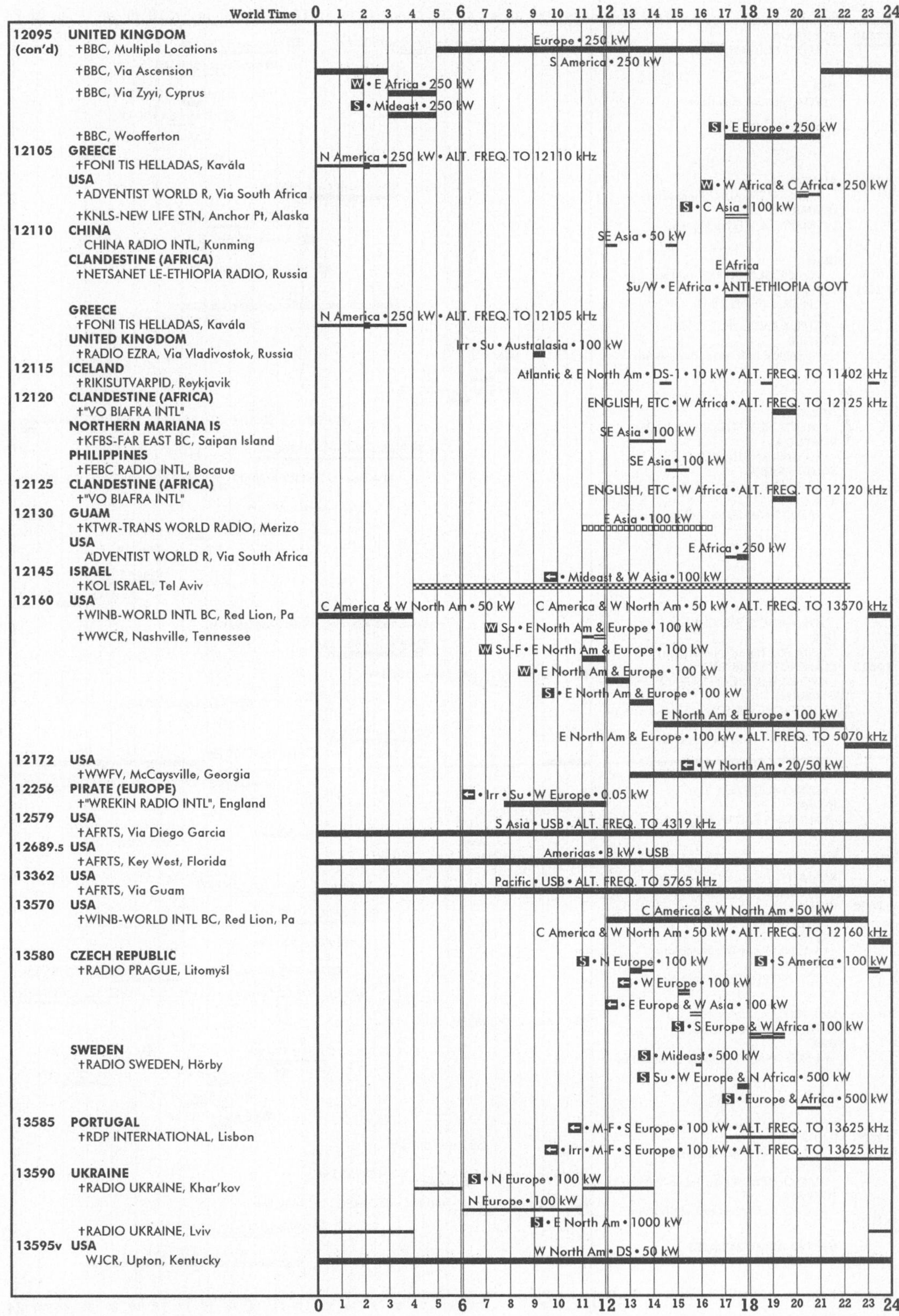
World Time 0 1 2 3 4 5 6 7 8 9 10 11 12 13 14 15 16 17 18 19 20 21 22 23 24
12095 (con'd) UNITED KINGDOM
†BBC, Multiple Locations
Europe • 250 kW
S America • 250 kW
†BBC, Via Ascension
†BBC, Via Zyyi, Cyprus
W • E Africa • 250 kW
S • Mideast • 250 kW
S • E Europe • 250 kW
†BBC, Woofferton
12105 GREECE
†FONI TIS HELLADAS, Kavála
N America • 250 kW • ALT. FREQ. TO 12110 kHz
USA
†ADVENTIST WORLD R, Via South Africa
W • W Africa & C Africa • 250 kW
†KNLS-NEW LIFE STN, Anchor Pt, Alaska
S • C Asia • 100 kW
12110 CHINA
CHINA RADIO INTL, Kunming
SE Asia • 50 kW
CLANDESTINE (AFRICA)
†NETSANET LE-ETHIOPIA RADIO, Russia
E Africa
Su/W • E Africa • ANTI-ETHIOPIA GOVT
GREECE
†FONI TIS HELLADAS, Kavála
N America • 250 kW • ALT. FREQ. TO 12105 kHz
UNITED KINGDOM
†RADIO EZRA, Via Vladivostok, Russia
Irr • Su • Australasia • 100 kW
12115 ICELAND
†RIKISUTVARPID, Reykjavik
Atlantic & E North Am • DS-1 • 10 kW • ALT. FREQ. TO 11402 kHz
12120 CLANDESTINE (AFRICA)
†"VO BIAFRA INTL"
ENGLISH, ETC • W Africa • ALT. FREQ. TO 12125 kHz
NORTHERN MARIANA IS
†KFBS-FAR EAST BC, Saipan Island
SE Asia • 100 kW
PHILIPPINES
†FEBC RADIO INTL, Bocaue
SE Asia • 100 kW
12125 CLANDESTINE (AFRICA)
†"VO BIAFRA INTL"
ENGLISH, ETC • W Africa • ALT. FREQ. TO 12120 kHz
12130 GUAM
†KTWR-TRANS WORLD RADIO, Merizo
E Asia • 100 kW
USA
ADVENTIST WORLD R, Via South Africa
E Africa • 250 kW
12145 ISRAEL
†KOL ISRAEL, Tel Aviv
Mideast & W Asia • 100 kW
12160 USA
†WINB-WORLD INTL BC, Red Lion, Pa
C America & W North Am • 50 kW
C America & W North Am • 50 kW • ALT. FREQ. TO 13570 kHz
†WWCR, Nashville, Tennessee
W Sa • E North Am & Europe • 100 kW
W Su-F • E North Am & Europe • 100 kW
W • E North Am & Europe • 100 kW
S • E North Am & Europe • 100 kW
E North Am & Europe • 100 kW
E North Am & Europe • 100 kW • ALT. FREQ. TO 5070 kHz
12172 USA
†WWFV, McCaysville, Georgia
W North Am • 20/50 kW
12256 PIRATE (EUROPE)
†"WREKIN RADIO INTL", England
Irr • Su • W Europe • 0.05 kW
12579 USA
†AFRTS, Via Diego Garcia
S Asia • USB • ALT. FREQ. TO 4319 kHz
12689.5 USA
†AFRTS, Key West, Florida
Americas • 8 kW • USB
13362 USA
†AFRTS, Via Guam
Pacific • USB • ALT. FREQ. TO 5765 kHz
13570 USA
†WINB-WORLD INTL BC, Red Lion, Pa
C America & W North Am • 50 kW
C America & W North Am • 50 kW • ALT. FREQ. TO 12160 kHz
13580 CZECH REPUBLIC
†RADIO PRAGUE, Litomyšl
S • N Europe • 100 kW
S • S America • 100 kW
W Europe • 100 kW
E Europe & W Asia • 100 kW
S • S Europe & W Africa • 100 kW
SWEDEN
†RADIO SWEDEN, Hörby
S • Mideast • 500 kW
S Su • W Europe & N Africa • 500 kW
S • Europe & Africa • 500 kW
13585 PORTUGAL
†RDP INTERNATIONAL, Lisbon
M-F • S Europe • 100 kW • ALT. FREQ. TO 13625 kHz
Irr • M-F • S Europe • 100 kW • ALT. FREQ. TO 13625 kHz
13590 UKRAINE
†RADIO UKRAINE, Khar'kov
S • N Europe • 100 kW
N Europe • 100 kW
†RADIO UKRAINE, Lviv
S • E North Am • 1000 kW
13595v USA
WJCR, Upton, Kentucky
W North Am • DS • 50 kW
0 1 2 3 4 5 6 7 8 9 10 11 12 13 14 15 16 17 18 19 20 21 22 23 24

SEASONAL S OR W 1-HR TIMESHIFT MIDYEAR ⇐ OR ⇒ JAMMING / OR ∧ EARLIEST HEARD ◁ LATEST HEARD ▷ NEW FOR 2002 †

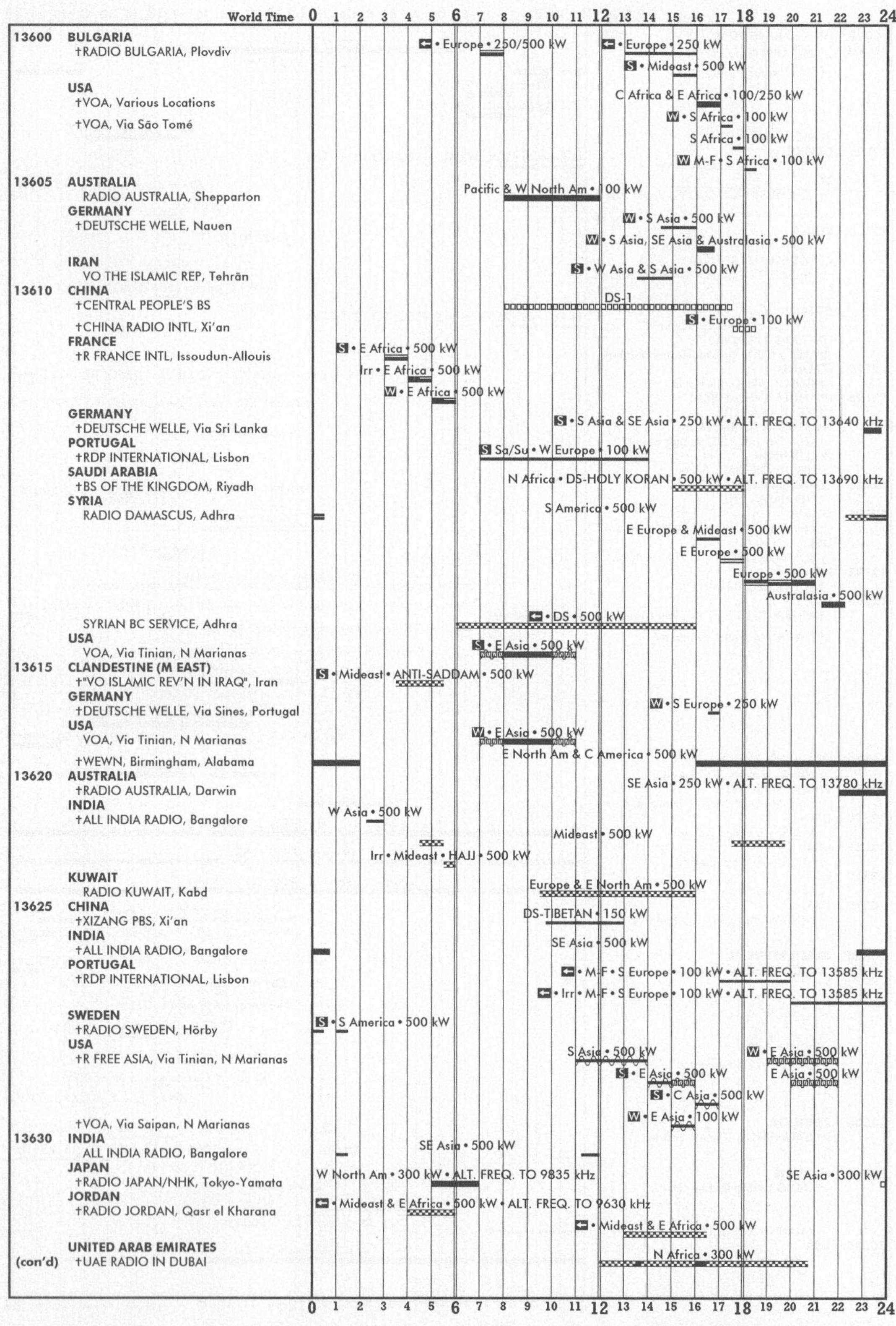
World Time 0 1 2 3 4 5 6 7 8 9 10 11 12 13 14 15 16 17 18 19 20 21 22 23 24
13600 BULGARIA
†RADIO BULGARIA, Plovdiv
• Europe • 250/500 kW
• Europe • 250 kW
S • Mideast • 500 kW
USA
†VOA, Various Locations
C Africa & E Africa • 100/250 kW
†VOA, Via São Tomé
W • S Africa • 100 kW
S Africa • 100 kW
W M-F • S Africa • 100 kW
13605 AUSTRALIA
RADIO AUSTRALIA, Shepparton
Pacific & W North Am • 100 kW
GERMANY
†DEUTSCHE WELLE, Nauen
W • S Asia • 500 kW
W • S Asia, SE Asia & Australasia • 500 kW
IRAN
VO THE ISLAMIC REP, Tehrān
S • W Asia & S Asia • 500 kW
13610 CHINA
†CENTRAL PEOPLE'S BS
DS-1
†CHINA RADIO INTL, Xi'an
S • Europe • 100 kW
FRANCE
†R FRANCE INTL, Issoudun-Allouis
S • E Africa • 500 kW
Irr • E Africa • 500 kW
W • E Africa • 500 kW
GERMANY
†DEUTSCHE WELLE, Via Sri Lanka
S • S Asia & SE Asia • 250 kW • ALT. FREQ. TO 13640 kHz
PORTUGAL
†RDP INTERNATIONAL, Lisbon
S Sa/Su • W Europe • 100 kW
SAUDI ARABIA
†BS OF THE KINGDOM, Riyadh
N Africa • DS-HOLY KORAN • 500 kW • ALT. FREQ. TO 13690 kHz
SYRIA
RADIO DAMASCUS, Adhra
S America • 500 kW
E Europe & Mideast • 500 kW
E Europe • 500 kW
Europe • 500 kW
Australasia • 500 kW
SYRIAN BC SERVICE, Adhra
• DS • 500 kW
USA
VOA, Via Tinian, N Marianas
S • E Asia • 500 kW
13615 CLANDESTINE (M EAST)
†"VO ISLAMIC REV'N IN IRAQ", Iran
S • Mideast • ANTI-SADDAM • 500 kW
GERMANY
†DEUTSCHE WELLE, Via Sines, Portugal
W • S Europe • 250 kW
USA
VOA, Via Tinian, N Marianas
W • E Asia • 500 kW
†WEWN, Birmingham, Alabama
E North Am & C America • 500 kW
13620 AUSTRALIA
†RADIO AUSTRALIA, Darwin
SE Asia • 250 kW • ALT. FREQ. TO 13780 kHz
INDIA
†ALL INDIA RADIO, Bangalore
W Asia • 500 kW
Mideast • 500 kW
Irr • Mideast • HAJJ • 500 kW
KUWAIT
RADIO KUWAIT, Kabd
Europe & E North Am • 500 kW
13625 CHINA
†XIZANG PBS, Xi'an
DS-TIBETAN • 150 kW
INDIA
†ALL INDIA RADIO, Bangalore
SE Asia • 500 kW
PORTUGAL
†RDP INTERNATIONAL, Lisbon
• M-F • S Europe • 100 kW • ALT. FREQ. TO 13585 kHz
• Irr • M-F • S Europe • 100 kW • ALT. FREQ. TO 13585 kHz
SWEDEN
†RADIO SWEDEN, Hörby
S • S America • 500 kW
USA
†R FREE ASIA, Via Tinian, N Marianas
S Asia • 500 kW
W • E Asia • 500 kW
S • E Asia • 500 kW
E Asia • 500 kW
S • C Asia • 500 kW
W • E Asia • 100 kW
†VOA, Via Saipan, N Marianas
13630 INDIA
ALL INDIA RADIO, Bangalore
SE Asia • 500 kW
JAPAN
†RADIO JAPAN/NHK, Tokyo-Yamata
W North Am • 300 kW • ALT. FREQ. TO 9835 kHz
SE Asia • 300 kW
JORDAN
†RADIO JORDAN, Qasr el Kharana
• Mideast & E Africa • 500 kW • ALT. FREQ. TO 9630 kHz
• Mideast & E Africa • 500 kW
UNITED ARAB EMIRATES
(con'd) †UAE RADIO IN DUBAI
N Africa • 300 kW
0 1 2 3 4 5 6 7 8 9 10 11 12 13 14 15 16 17 18 19 20 21 22 23 24
ENGLISH ARABIC CHINESE FRENCH GERMAN RUSSIAN SPANISH OTHER

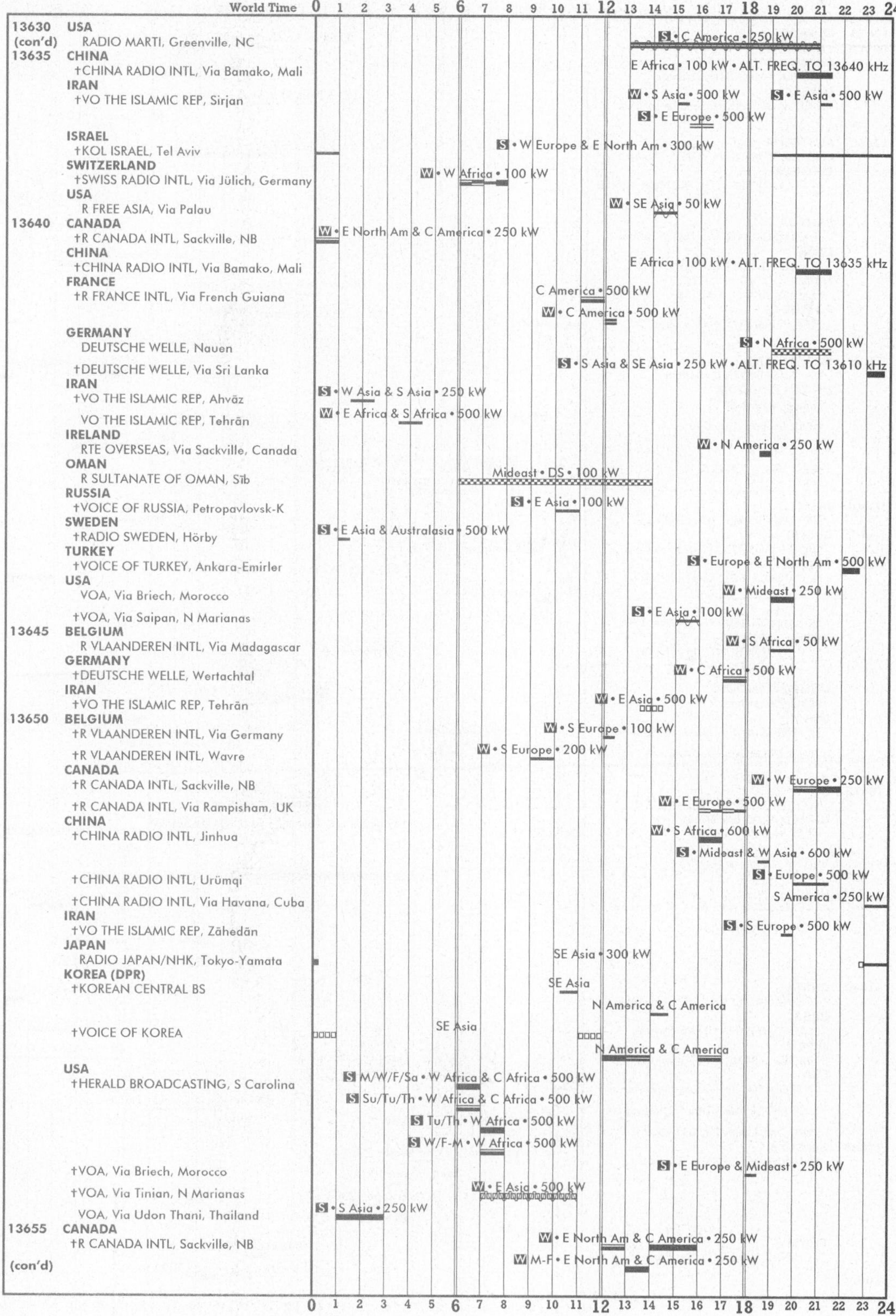
World Time 0 1 2 3 4 5 6 7 8 9 10 11 12 13 14 15 16 17 18 19 20 21 22 23 24
13630 (con'd) USA
RADIO MARTI, Greenville, NC
S • C America • 250 kW
13635 CHINA
†CHINA RADIO INTL, Via Bamako, Mali
E Africa • 100 kW • ALT. FREQ. TO 13640 kHz
IRAN
†VO THE ISLAMIC REP, Sirjan
W • S Asia • 500 kW
S • E Asia • 500 kW
S • E Europe • 500 kW
ISRAEL
†KOL ISRAEL, Tel Aviv
S • W Europe & E North Am • 300 kW
SWITZERLAND
†SWISS RADIO INTL, Via Jülich, Germany
W • W Africa • 100 kW
USA
R FREE ASIA, Via Palau
W • SE Asia • 50 kW
13640 CANADA
†R CANADA INTL, Sackville, NB
W • E North Am & C America • 250 kW
CHINA
†CHINA RADIO INTL, Via Bamako, Mali
E Africa • 100 kW • ALT. FREQ. TO 13635 kHz
FRANCE
†R FRANCE INTL, Via French Guiana
C America • 500 kW
W • C America • 500 kW
GERMANY
DEUTSCHE WELLE, Nauen
S • N Africa • 500 kW
†DEUTSCHE WELLE, Via Sri Lanka
S • S Asia & SE Asia • 250 kW • ALT. FREQ. TO 13610 kHz
IRAN
†VO THE ISLAMIC REP, Ahvāz
S • W Asia & S Asia • 250 kW
VO THE ISLAMIC REP, Tehrān
W • E Africa & S Africa • 500 kW
IRELAND
RTE OVERSEAS, Via Sackville, Canada
W • N America • 250 kW
OMAN
R SULTANATE OF OMAN, Sīb
Mideast • DS • 100 kW
RUSSIA
†VOICE OF RUSSIA, Petropavlovsk-K
S • E Asia • 100 kW
SWEDEN
†RADIO SWEDEN, Hörby
S • E Asia & Australasia • 500 kW
TURKEY
†VOICE OF TURKEY, Ankara-Emirler
S • Europe & E North Am • 500 kW
USA
VOA, Via Briech, Morocco
W • Mideast • 250 kW
†VOA, Via Saipan, N Marianas
S • E Asia • 100 kW
13645 BELGIUM
R VLAANDEREN INTL, Via Madagascar
W • S Africa • 50 kW
GERMANY
†DEUTSCHE WELLE, Wertachtal
W • C Africa • 500 kW
IRAN
†VO THE ISLAMIC REP, Tehrān
W • E Asia • 500 kW
13650 BELGIUM
†R VLAANDEREN INTL, Via Germany
W • S Europe • 100 kW
†R VLAANDEREN INTL, Wavre
W • S Europe • 200 kW
CANADA
†R CANADA INTL, Sackville, NB
W • W Europe • 250 kW
†R CANADA INTL, Via Rampisham, UK
W • E Europe • 500 kW
CHINA
†CHINA RADIO INTL, Jinhua
W • S Africa • 600 kW
S • Mideast & W Asia • 600 kW
†CHINA RADIO INTL, Urümqi
S • Europe • 500 kW
†CHINA RADIO INTL, Via Havana, Cuba
S America • 250 kW
IRAN
†VO THE ISLAMIC REP, Zāhedān
S • S Europe • 500 kW
JAPAN
RADIO JAPAN/NHK, Tokyo-Yamata
SE Asia • 300 kW
KOREA (DPR)
†KOREAN CENTRAL BS
SE Asia
N America & C America
†VOICE OF KOREA
SE Asia
N America & C America
USA
†HERALD BROADCASTING, S Carolina
S M/W/F/Sa • W Africa & C Africa • 500 kW
S Su/Tu/Th • W Africa & C Africa • 500 kW
S Tu/Th • W Africa • 500 kW
S W/F-M • W Africa • 500 kW
†VOA, Via Briech, Morocco
S • E Europe & Mideast • 250 kW
†VOA, Via Tinian, N Marianas
W • E Asia • 500 kW
VOA, Via Udon Thani, Thailand
S • S Asia • 250 kW
13655 CANADA
†R CANADA INTL, Sackville, NB
W • E North Am & C America • 250 kW
W M-F • E North Am & C America • 250 kW
(con'd)
0 1 2 3 4 5 6 7 8 9 10 11 12 13 14 15 16 17 18 19 20 21 22 23 24

SEASONAL S OR W 1-HR TIMESHIFT MIDYEAR ⇐ OR ⇒ JAMMING / OR ∧ EARLIEST HEARD ◁ LATEST HEARD ▷ NEW FOR 2002 †

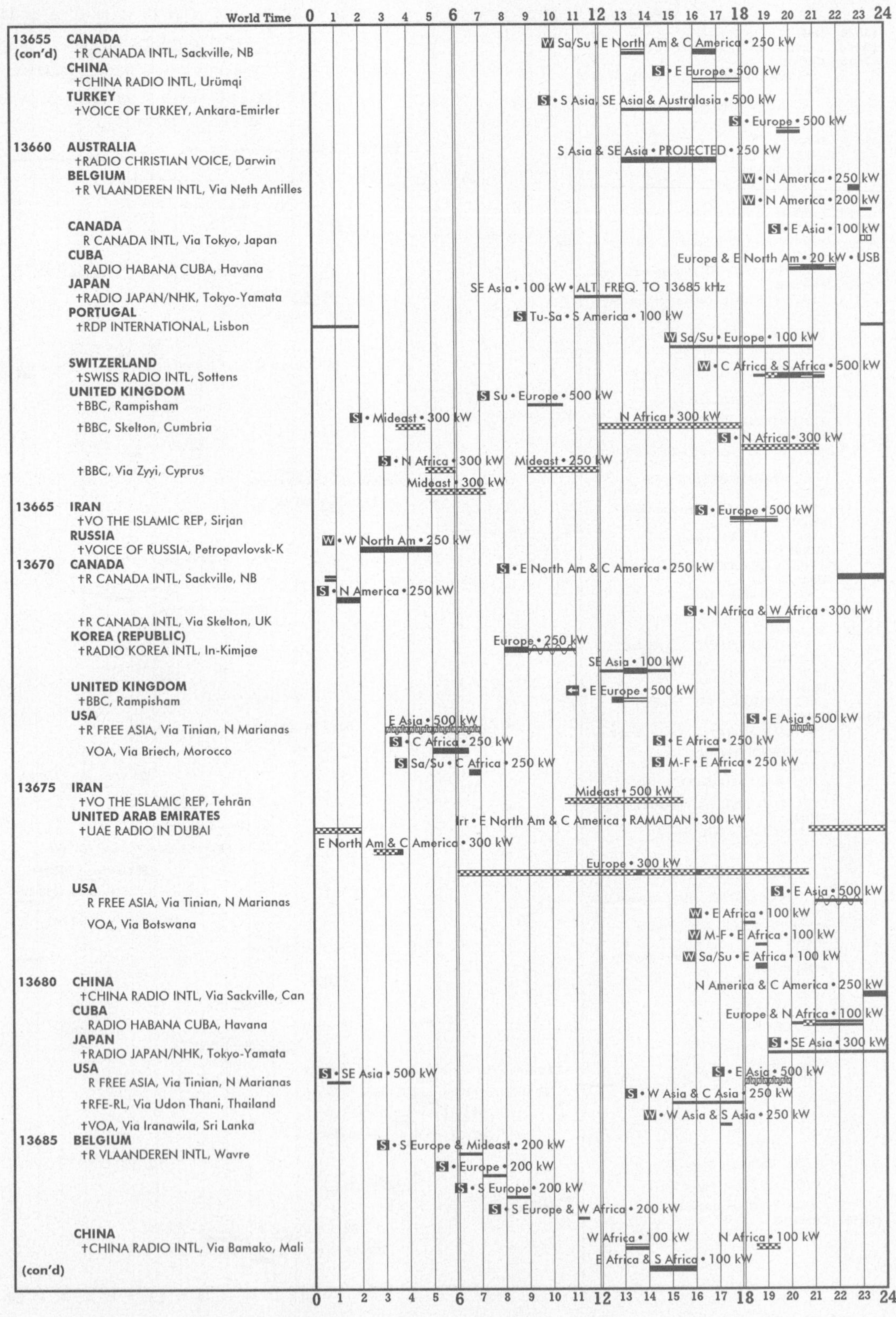
World Time 0 1 2 3 4 5 6 7 8 9 10 11 12 13 14 15 16 17 18 19 20 21 22 23 24
13655 (con'd) CANADA
†R CANADA INTL, Sackville, NB
W Sa/Su • E North Am & C America • 250 kW
CHINA
†CHINA RADIO INTL, Urümqi
S • E Europe • 500 kW
TURKEY
†VOICE OF TURKEY, Ankara-Emirler
S • S Asia, SE Asia & Australasia • 500 kW
S • Europe • 500 kW
13660 AUSTRALIA
†RADIO CHRISTIAN VOICE, Darwin
S Asia & SE Asia • PROJECTED • 250 kW
BELGIUM
†R VLAANDEREN INTL, Via Neth Antilles
W • N America • 250 kW
W • N America • 200 kW
CANADA
R CANADA INTL, Via Tokyo, Japan
S • E Asia • 100 kW
CUBA
RADIO HABANA CUBA, Havana
Europe & E North Am • 20 kW • USB
JAPAN
†RADIO JAPAN/NHK, Tokyo-Yamata
SE Asia • 100 kW • ALT. FREQ. TO 13685 kHz
PORTUGAL
†RDP INTERNATIONAL, Lisbon
S Tu-Sa • S America • 100 kW
W Sa/Su • Europe • 100 kW
SWITZERLAND
†SWISS RADIO INTL, Sottens
W • C Africa & S Africa • 500 kW
UNITED KINGDOM
†BBC, Rampisham
S Su • Europe • 500 kW
†BBC, Skelton, Cumbria
S • Mideast • 300 kW
N Africa • 300 kW
S • N Africa • 300 kW
†BBC, Via Zyyi, Cyprus
S • N Africa • 300 kW
Mideast • 250 kW
Mideast • 300 kW
13665 IRAN
†VO THE ISLAMIC REP, Sirjan
S • Europe • 500 kW
RUSSIA
†VOICE OF RUSSIA, Petropavlovsk-K
W • W North Am • 250 kW
13670 CANADA
†R CANADA INTL, Sackville, NB
S • E North Am & C America • 250 kW
S • N America • 250 kW
†R CANADA INTL, Via Skelton, UK
S • N Africa & W Africa • 300 kW
KOREA (REPUBLIC)
†RADIO KOREA INTL, In-Kimjae
Europe • 250 kW
SE Asia • 100 kW
UNITED KINGDOM
†BBC, Rampisham
• E Europe • 500 kW
USA
†R FREE ASIA, Via Tinian, N Marianas
E Asia • 500 kW
S • E Asia • 500 kW
VOA, Via Briech, Morocco
S • C Africa • 250 kW
S • E Africa • 250 kW
S Sa/Su • C Africa • 250 kW
S M-F • E Africa • 250 kW
13675 IRAN
†VO THE ISLAMIC REP, Tehrān
Mideast • 500 kW
UNITED ARAB EMIRATES
†UAE RADIO IN DUBAI
Irr • E North Am & C America • RAMADAN • 300 kW
E North Am & C America • 300 kW
Europe • 300 kW
USA
R FREE ASIA, Via Tinian, N Marianas
S • E Asia • 500 kW
VOA, Via Botswana
W • E Africa • 100 kW
W M-F • E Africa • 100 kW
W Sa/Su • E Africa • 100 kW
13680 CHINA
†CHINA RADIO INTL, Via Sackville, Can
N America & C America • 250 kW
CUBA
RADIO HABANA CUBA, Havana
Europe & N Africa • 100 kW
JAPAN
†RADIO JAPAN/NHK, Tokyo-Yamata
S • SE Asia • 300 kW
USA
R FREE ASIA, Via Tinian, N Marianas
S • SE Asia • 500 kW
S • E Asia • 500 kW
†RFE-RL, Via Udon Thani, Thailand
S • W Asia & C Asia • 250 kW
†VOA, Via Iranawila, Sri Lanka
W • W Asia & S Asia • 250 kW
13685 BELGIUM
†R VLAANDEREN INTL, Wavre
S • S Europe & Mideast • 200 kW
S • Europe • 200 kW
S • S Europe • 200 kW
S • S Europe & W Africa • 200 kW
CHINA
†CHINA RADIO INTL, Via Bamako, Mali
W Africa • 100 kW
N Africa • 100 kW
E Africa & S Africa • 100 kW
(con'd)
0 1 2 3 4 5 6 7 8 9 10 11 12 13 14 15 16 17 18 19 20 21 22 23 24

ENGLISH ▬ ARABIC ▬ CHINESE ▭ FRENCH ▬ GERMAN ▬ RUSSIAN ═ SPANISH ▬ OTHER —

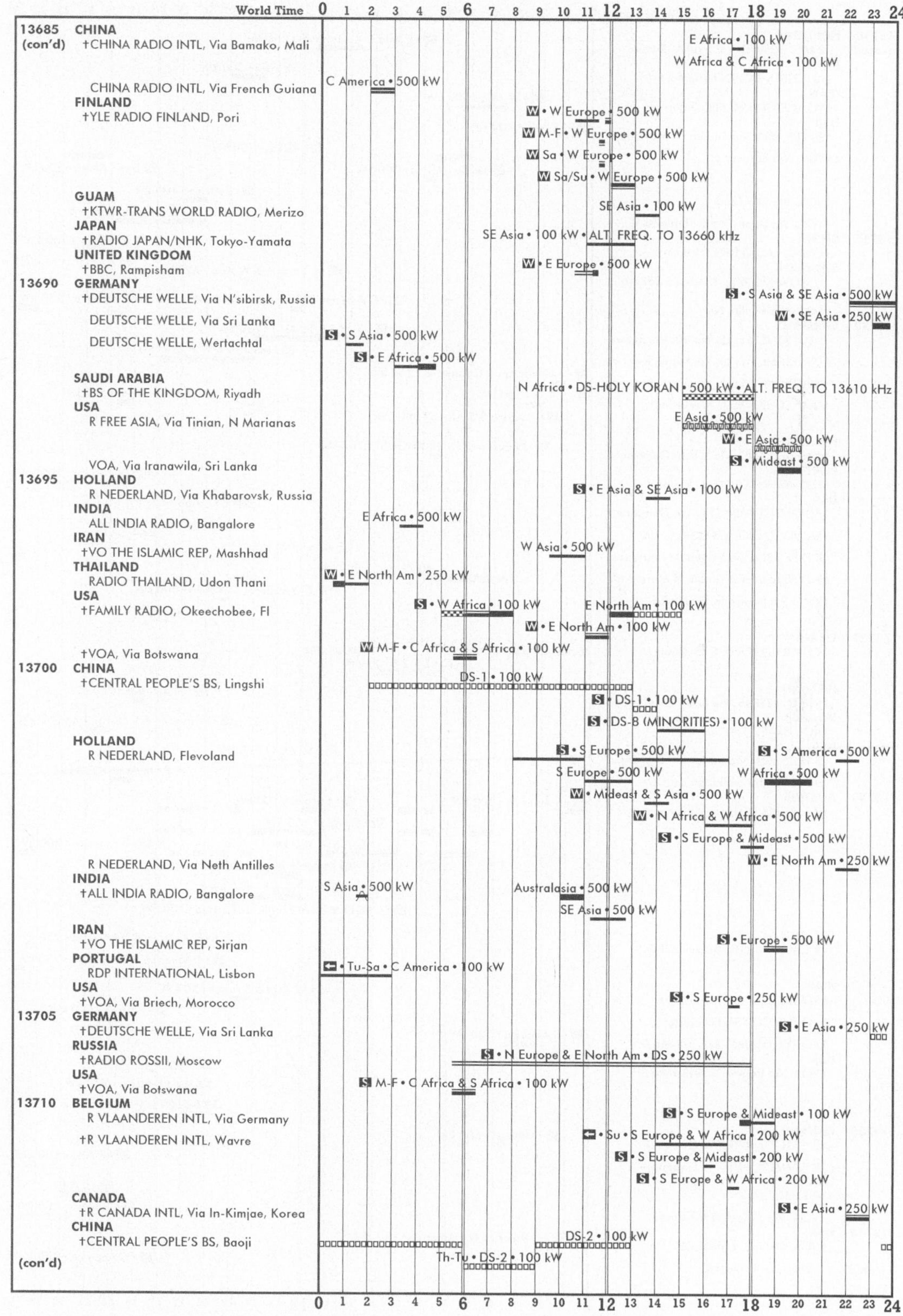
World Time 0 1 2 3 4 5 6 7 8 9 10 11 12 13 14 15 16 17 18 19 20 21 22 23 24
13685 (con'd) CHINA
†CHINA RADIO INTL, Via Bamako, Mali
E Africa • 100 kW
W Africa & C Africa • 100 kW
CHINA RADIO INTL, Via French Guiana
C America • 500 kW
FINLAND
†YLE RADIO FINLAND, Pori
W • W Europe • 500 kW
W M-F • W Europe • 500 kW
W Sa • W Europe • 500 kW
W Sa/Su • W Europe • 500 kW
GUAM
†KTWR-TRANS WORLD RADIO, Merizo
SE Asia • 100 kW
JAPAN
†RADIO JAPAN/NHK, Tokyo-Yamata
SE Asia • 100 kW • ALT. FREQ. TO 13660 kHz
UNITED KINGDOM
†BBC, Rampisham
W • E Europe • 500 kW
13690 GERMANY
†DEUTSCHE WELLE, Via N'sibirsk, Russia
S • S Asia & SE Asia • 500 kW
DEUTSCHE WELLE, Via Sri Lanka
W • SE Asia • 250 kW
DEUTSCHE WELLE, Wertachtal
S • S Asia • 500 kW
S • E Africa • 500 kW
SAUDI ARABIA
†BS OF THE KINGDOM, Riyadh
N Africa • DS-HOLY KORAN • 500 kW • ALT. FREQ. TO 13610 kHz
USA
R FREE ASIA, Via Tinian, N Marianas
E Asia • 500 kW
W • E Asia • 500 kW
VOA, Via Iranawila, Sri Lanka
S • Mideast • 500 kW
13695 HOLLAND
R NEDERLAND, Via Khabarovsk, Russia
S • E Asia & SE Asia • 100 kW
INDIA
ALL INDIA RADIO, Bangalore
E Africa • 500 kW
IRAN
†VO THE ISLAMIC REP, Mashhad
W Asia • 500 kW
THAILAND
RADIO THAILAND, Udon Thani
W • E North Am • 250 kW
USA
†FAMILY RADIO, Okeechobee, Fl
S • W Africa • 100 kW
E North Am • 100 kW
W • E North Am • 100 kW
†VOA, Via Botswana
W M-F • C Africa & S Africa • 100 kW
13700 CHINA
†CENTRAL PEOPLE'S BS, Lingshi
DS-1 • 100 kW
S • DS-1 • 100 kW
S • DS-B (MINORITIES) • 100 kW
HOLLAND
R NEDERLAND, Flevoland
S • S Europe • 500 kW
S • S America • 500 kW
S Europe • 500 kW
W Africa • 500 kW
W • Mideast & S Asia • 500 kW
W • N Africa & W Africa • 500 kW
S • S Europe & Mideast • 500 kW
R NEDERLAND, Via Neth Antilles
W • E North Am • 250 kW
INDIA
†ALL INDIA RADIO, Bangalore
S Asia • 500 kW
Australasia • 500 kW
SE Asia • 500 kW
IRAN
†VO THE ISLAMIC REP, Sirjan
S • Europe • 500 kW
PORTUGAL
RDP INTERNATIONAL, Lisbon
• Tu-Sa • C America • 100 kW
USA
†VOA, Via Briech, Morocco
S • S Europe • 250 kW
13705 GERMANY
†DEUTSCHE WELLE, Via Sri Lanka
S • E Asia • 250 kW
RUSSIA
†RADIO ROSSII, Moscow
S • N Europe & E North Am • DS • 250 kW
USA
†VOA, Via Botswana
S M-F • C Africa & S Africa • 100 kW
13710 BELGIUM
R VLAANDEREN INTL, Via Germany
S • S Europe & Mideast • 100 kW
†R VLAANDEREN INTL, Wavre
• Su • S Europe & W Africa • 200 kW
S • S Europe & Mideast • 200 kW
S • S Europe & W Africa • 200 kW
CANADA
†R CANADA INTL, Via In-Kimjae, Korea
S • E Asia • 250 kW
CHINA
†CENTRAL PEOPLE'S BS, Baoji
DS-2 • 100 kW
Th-Tu • DS-2 • 100 kW
(con'd)
0 1 2 3 4 5 6 7 8 9 10 11 12 13 14 15 16 17 18 19 20 21 22 23 24

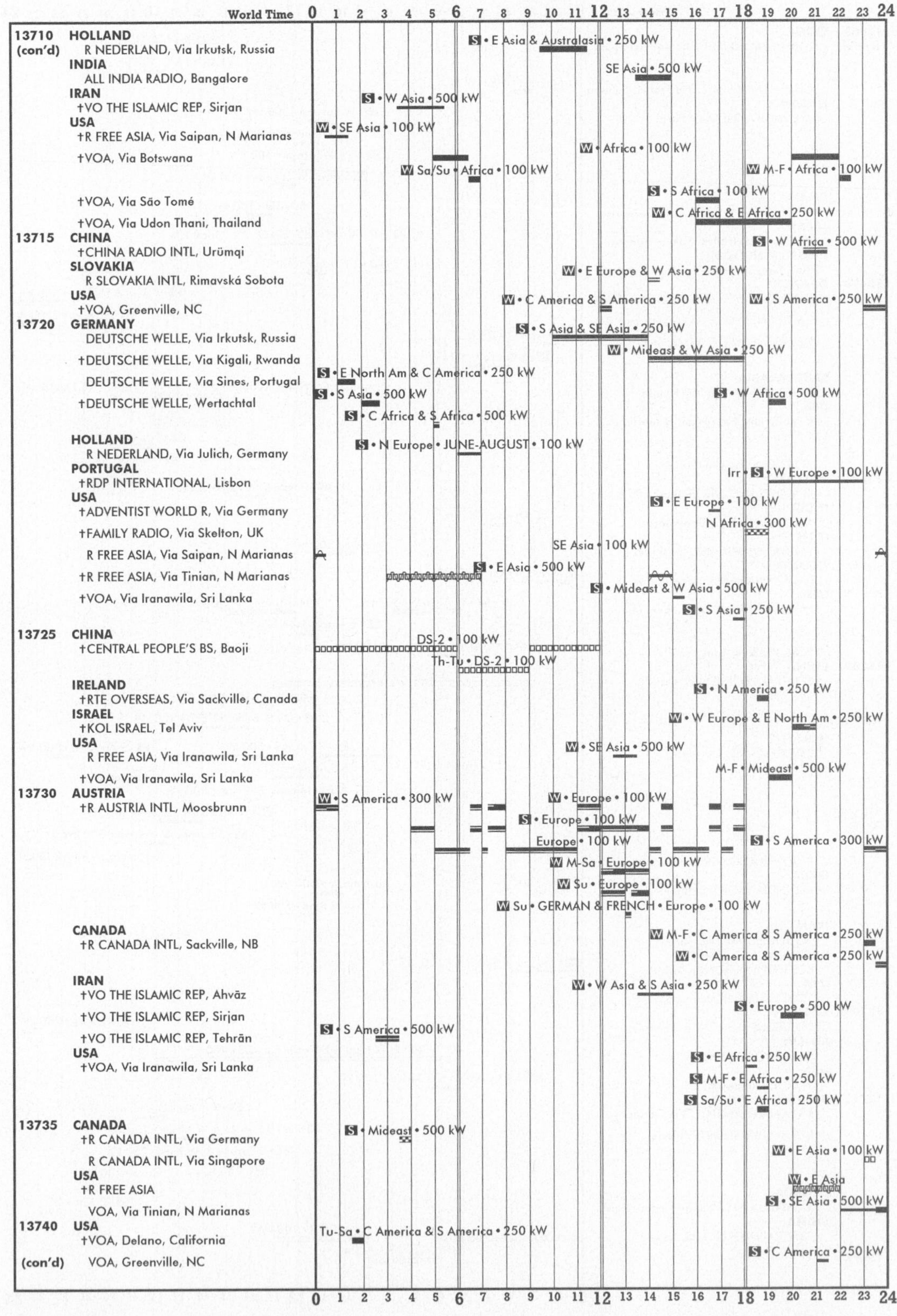
World Time 0 1 2 3 4 5 6 7 8 9 10 11 12 13 14 15 16 17 18 19 20 21 22 23 24
13710 (con'd) HOLLAND
R NEDERLAND, Via Irkutsk, Russia
S • E Asia & Australasia • 250 kW
INDIA
ALL INDIA RADIO, Bangalore
SE Asia • 500 kW
IRAN
†VO THE ISLAMIC REP, Sirjan
S • W Asia • 500 kW
USA
†R FREE ASIA, Via Saipan, N Marianas
W • SE Asia • 100 kW
†VOA, Via Botswana
W • Africa • 100 kW
W Sa/Su • Africa • 100 kW
W M-F • Africa • 100 kW
†VOA, Via São Tomé
S • S Africa • 100 kW
†VOA, Via Udon Thani, Thailand
W • C Africa & E Africa • 250 kW
13715 CHINA
†CHINA RADIO INTL, Urümqi
S • W Africa • 500 kW
SLOVAKIA
R SLOVAKIA INTL, Rimavská Sobota
W • E Europe & W Asia • 250 kW
USA
†VOA, Greenville, NC
W • C America & S America • 250 kW
W • S America • 250 kW
13720 GERMANY
DEUTSCHE WELLE, Via Irkutsk, Russia
S • S Asia & SE Asia • 250 kW
†DEUTSCHE WELLE, Via Kigali, Rwanda
W • Mideast & W Asia • 250 kW
DEUTSCHE WELLE, Via Sines, Portugal
S • E North Am & C America • 250 kW
†DEUTSCHE WELLE, Wertachtal
S • S Asia • 500 kW
S • W Africa • 500 kW
S • C Africa & S Africa • 500 kW
HOLLAND
R NEDERLAND, Via Julich, Germany
S • N Europe • JUNE-AUGUST • 100 kW
PORTUGAL
†RDP INTERNATIONAL, Lisbon
Irr • S • W Europe • 100 kW
USA
†ADVENTIST WORLD R, Via Germany
S • E Europe • 100 kW
†FAMILY RADIO, Via Skelton, UK
N Africa • 300 kW
R FREE ASIA, Via Saipan, N Marianas
SE Asia • 100 kW
†R FREE ASIA, Via Tinian, N Marianas
S • E Asia • 500 kW
†VOA, Via Iranawila, Sri Lanka
S • Mideast & W Asia • 500 kW
S • S Asia • 250 kW
13725 CHINA
†CENTRAL PEOPLE'S BS, Baoji
DS-2 • 100 kW
Th-Tu • DS-2 • 100 kW
IRELAND
†RTE OVERSEAS, Via Sackville, Canada
S • N America • 250 kW
ISRAEL
†KOL ISRAEL, Tel Aviv
W • W Europe & E North Am • 250 kW
USA
R FREE ASIA, Via Iranawila, Sri Lanka
W • SE Asia • 500 kW
†VOA, Via Iranawila, Sri Lanka
M-F • Mideast • 500 kW
13730 AUSTRIA
†R AUSTRIA INTL, Moosbrunn
W • S America • 300 kW
W • Europe • 100 kW
S • Europe • 100 kW
Europe • 100 kW
S • S America • 300 kW
W M-Sa • Europe • 100 kW
W Su • Europe • 100 kW
W Su • GERMAN & FRENCH • Europe • 100 kW
CANADA
†R CANADA INTL, Sackville, NB
W M-F • C America & S America • 250 kW
W • C America & S America • 250 kW
IRAN
†VO THE ISLAMIC REP, Ahvāz
W • W Asia & S Asia • 250 kW
†VO THE ISLAMIC REP, Sirjan
S • Europe • 500 kW
†VO THE ISLAMIC REP, Tehrān
S • S America • 500 kW
USA
†VOA, Via Iranawila, Sri Lanka
S • E Africa • 250 kW
S M-F • E Africa • 250 kW
S Sa/Su • E Africa • 250 kW
13735 CANADA
†R CANADA INTL, Via Germany
S • Mideast • 500 kW
R CANADA INTL, Via Singapore
W • E Asia • 100 kW
USA
†R FREE ASIA
W • E Asia
VOA, Via Tinian, N Marianas
S • SE Asia • 500 kW
13740 USA
†VOA, Delano, California
Tu-Sa • C America & S America • 250 kW
(con'd) VOA, Greenville, NC
S • C America • 250 kW
ENGLISH ARABIC CHINESE FRENCH GERMAN RUSSIAN SPANISH OTHER

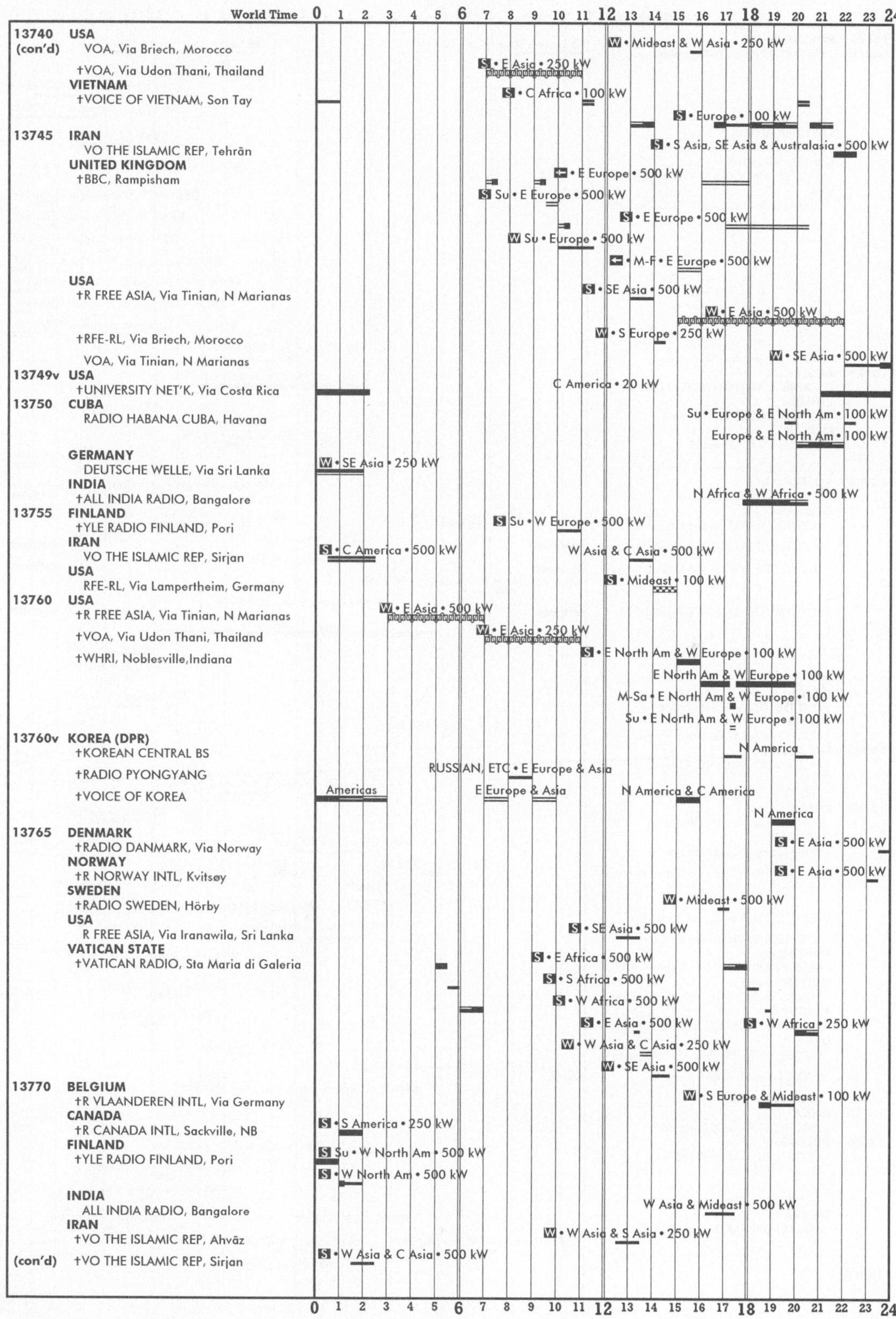
World Time 0 1 2 3 4 5 6 7 8 9 10 11 12 13 14 15 16 17 18 19 20 21 22 23 24
13740 (con'd) USA
VOA, Via Briech, Morocco
W • Mideast & W Asia • 250 kW
†VOA, Via Udon Thani, Thailand
S • E Asia • 250 kW
VIETNAM
†VOICE OF VIETNAM, Son Tay
S • C Africa • 100 kW
S • Europe • 100 kW
13745 IRAN
VO THE ISLAMIC REP, Tehrān
S • S Asia, SE Asia & Australasia • 500 kW
UNITED KINGDOM
†BBC, Rampisham
• E Europe • 500 kW
S Su • E Europe • 500 kW
S • E Europe • 500 kW
W Su • Europe • 500 kW
• M-F • E Europe • 500 kW
USA
†R FREE ASIA, Via Tinian, N Marianas
S • SE Asia • 500 kW
W • E Asia • 500 kW
†RFE-RL, Via Briech, Morocco
W • S Europe • 250 kW
VOA, Via Tinian, N Marianas
W • SE Asia • 500 kW
13749v USA
†UNIVERSITY NET'K, Via Costa Rica
C America • 20 kW
13750 CUBA
RADIO HABANA CUBA, Havana
Su • Europe & E North Am • 100 kW
Europe & E North Am • 100 kW
GERMANY
DEUTSCHE WELLE, Via Sri Lanka
W • SE Asia • 250 kW
INDIA
†ALL INDIA RADIO, Bangalore
N Africa & W Africa • 500 kW
13755 FINLAND
†YLE RADIO FINLAND, Pori
S Su • W Europe • 500 kW
IRAN
VO THE ISLAMIC REP, Sirjan
S • C America • 500 kW
W Asia & C Asia • 500 kW
USA
RFE-RL, Via Lampertheim, Germany
S • Mideast • 100 kW
13760 USA
†R FREE ASIA, Via Tinian, N Marianas
W • E Asia • 500 kW
†VOA, Via Udon Thani, Thailand
W • E Asia • 250 kW
†WHRI, Noblesville, Indiana
S • E North Am & W Europe • 100 kW
E North Am & W Europe • 100 kW
M-Sa • E North Am & W Europe • 100 kW
Su • E North Am & W Europe • 100 kW
13760v KOREA (DPR)
†KOREAN CENTRAL BS
N America
†RADIO PYONGYANG
RUSSIAN, ETC • E Europe & Asia
†VOICE OF KOREA
Americas
E Europe & Asia
N America & C America
N America
13765 DENMARK
†RADIO DANMARK, Via Norway
S • E Asia • 500 kW
NORWAY
†R NORWAY INTL, Kvitsøy
S • E Asia • 500 kW
SWEDEN
†RADIO SWEDEN, Hörby
W • Mideast • 500 kW
USA
R FREE ASIA, Via Iranawila, Sri Lanka
S • SE Asia • 500 kW
VATICAN STATE
†VATICAN RADIO, Sta Maria di Galeria
S • E Africa • 500 kW
S • S Africa • 500 kW
S • W Africa • 500 kW
S • E Asia • 500 kW
S • W Africa • 250 kW
W • W Asia & C Asia • 250 kW
W • SE Asia • 500 kW
13770 BELGIUM
†R VLAANDEREN INTL, Via Germany
W • S Europe & Mideast • 100 kW
CANADA
†R CANADA INTL, Sackville, NB
S • S America • 250 kW
FINLAND
†YLE RADIO FINLAND, Pori
S Su • W North Am • 500 kW
S • W North Am • 500 kW
INDIA
ALL INDIA RADIO, Bangalore
W Asia & Mideast • 500 kW
IRAN
†VO THE ISLAMIC REP, Ahvāz
W • W Asia & S Asia • 250 kW
(con'd) †VO THE ISLAMIC REP, Sirjan
S • W Asia & C Asia • 500 kW
0 1 2 3 4 5 6 7 8 9 10 11 12 13 14 15 16 17 18 19 20 21 22 23 24

SEASONAL S OR W 1-HR TIMESHIFT MIDYEAR ⇐ OR ⇒ JAMMING / OR /\ EARLIEST HEARD ◁ LATEST HEARD ▷ NEW FOR 2002 †

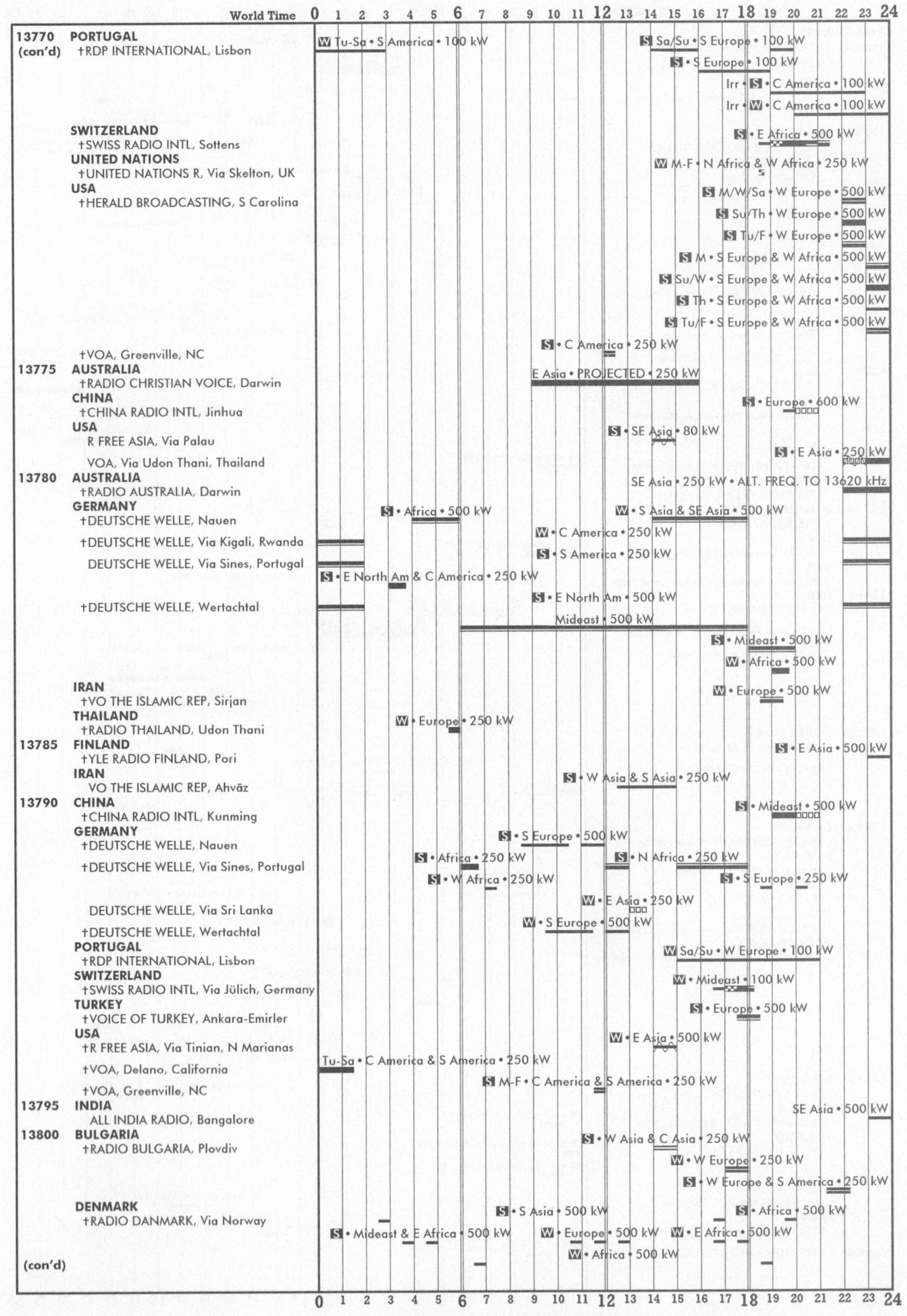
World Time 0 1 2 3 4 5 6 7 8 9 10 11 12 13 14 15 16 17 18 19 20 21 22 23 24
13770 (con'd) PORTUGAL
†RDP INTERNATIONAL, Lisbon
W Tu-Sa • S America • 100 kW
S Sa/Su • S Europe • 100 kW
S • S Europe • 100 kW
Irr • S • C America • 100 kW
Irr • W • C America • 100 kW
SWITZERLAND
†SWISS RADIO INTL, Sottens
S • E Africa • 500 kW
UNITED NATIONS
†UNITED NATIONS R, Via Skelton, UK
W M-F • N Africa & W Africa • 250 kW
USA
†HERALD BROADCASTING, S Carolina
S M/W/Sa • W Europe • 500 kW
S Su/Th • W Europe • 500 kW
S Tu/F • W Europe • 500 kW
S M • S Europe & W Africa • 500 kW
S Su/W • S Europe & W Africa • 500 kW
S Th • S Europe & W Africa • 500 kW
S Tu/F • S Europe & W Africa • 500 kW
†VOA, Greenville, NC
S • C America • 250 kW
13775 AUSTRALIA
†RADIO CHRISTIAN VOICE, Darwin
E Asia • PROJECTED • 250 kW
CHINA
†CHINA RADIO INTL, Jinhua
S • Europe • 600 kW
USA
R FREE ASIA, Via Palau
S • SE Asia • 80 kW
VOA, Via Udon Thani, Thailand
S • E Asia • 250 kW
13780 AUSTRALIA
†RADIO AUSTRALIA, Darwin
SE Asia • 250 kW • ALT. FREQ. TO 13620 kHz
GERMANY
†DEUTSCHE WELLE, Nauen
S • Africa • 500 kW
W • S Asia & SE Asia • 500 kW
†DEUTSCHE WELLE, Via Kigali, Rwanda
W • C America • 250 kW
DEUTSCHE WELLE, Via Sines, Portugal
S • S America • 250 kW
S • E North Am & C America • 250 kW
†DEUTSCHE WELLE, Wertachtal
S • E North Am • 500 kW
Mideast • 500 kW
S • Mideast • 500 kW
W • Africa • 500 kW
W • Europe • 500 kW
IRAN
†VO THE ISLAMIC REP, Sirjan
THAILAND
†RADIO THAILAND, Udon Thani
W • Europe • 250 kW
13785 FINLAND
†YLE RADIO FINLAND, Pori
S • E Asia • 500 kW
IRAN
VO THE ISLAMIC REP, Ahvāz
S • W Asia & S Asia • 250 kW
13790 CHINA
†CHINA RADIO INTL, Kunming
S • Mideast • 500 kW
GERMANY
†DEUTSCHE WELLE, Nauen
S • S Europe • 500 kW
†DEUTSCHE WELLE, Via Sines, Portugal
S • Africa • 250 kW
S • N Africa • 250 kW
S • W Africa • 250 kW
S • S Europe • 250 kW
DEUTSCHE WELLE, Via Sri Lanka
W • E Asia • 250 kW
†DEUTSCHE WELLE, Wertachtal
W • S Europe • 500 kW
PORTUGAL
†RDP INTERNATIONAL, Lisbon
W Sa/Su • W Europe • 100 kW
SWITZERLAND
†SWISS RADIO INTL, Via Jülich, Germany
W • Mideast • 100 kW
TURKEY
†VOICE OF TURKEY, Ankara-Emirler
S • Europe • 500 kW
USA
†R FREE ASIA, Via Tinian, N Marianas
W • E Asia • 500 kW
†VOA, Delano, California
Tu-Sa • C America & S America • 250 kW
†VOA, Greenville, NC
S M-F • C America & S America • 250 kW
13795 INDIA
ALL INDIA RADIO, Bangalore
SE Asia • 500 kW
13800 BULGARIA
†RADIO BULGARIA, Plovdiv
S • W Asia & C Asia • 250 kW
W • W Europe • 250 kW
S • W Europe & S America • 250 kW
DENMARK
†RADIO DANMARK, Via Norway
S • S Asia • 500 kW
S • Africa • 500 kW
S • Mideast & E Africa • 500 kW
W • Europe • 500 kW
W • E Africa • 500 kW
W • Africa • 500 kW
(con'd)
0 1 2 3 4 5 6 7 8 9 10 11 12 13 14 15 16 17 18 19 20 21 22 23 24
ENGLISH ARABIC CHINESE FRENCH GERMAN RUSSIAN SPANISH OTHER

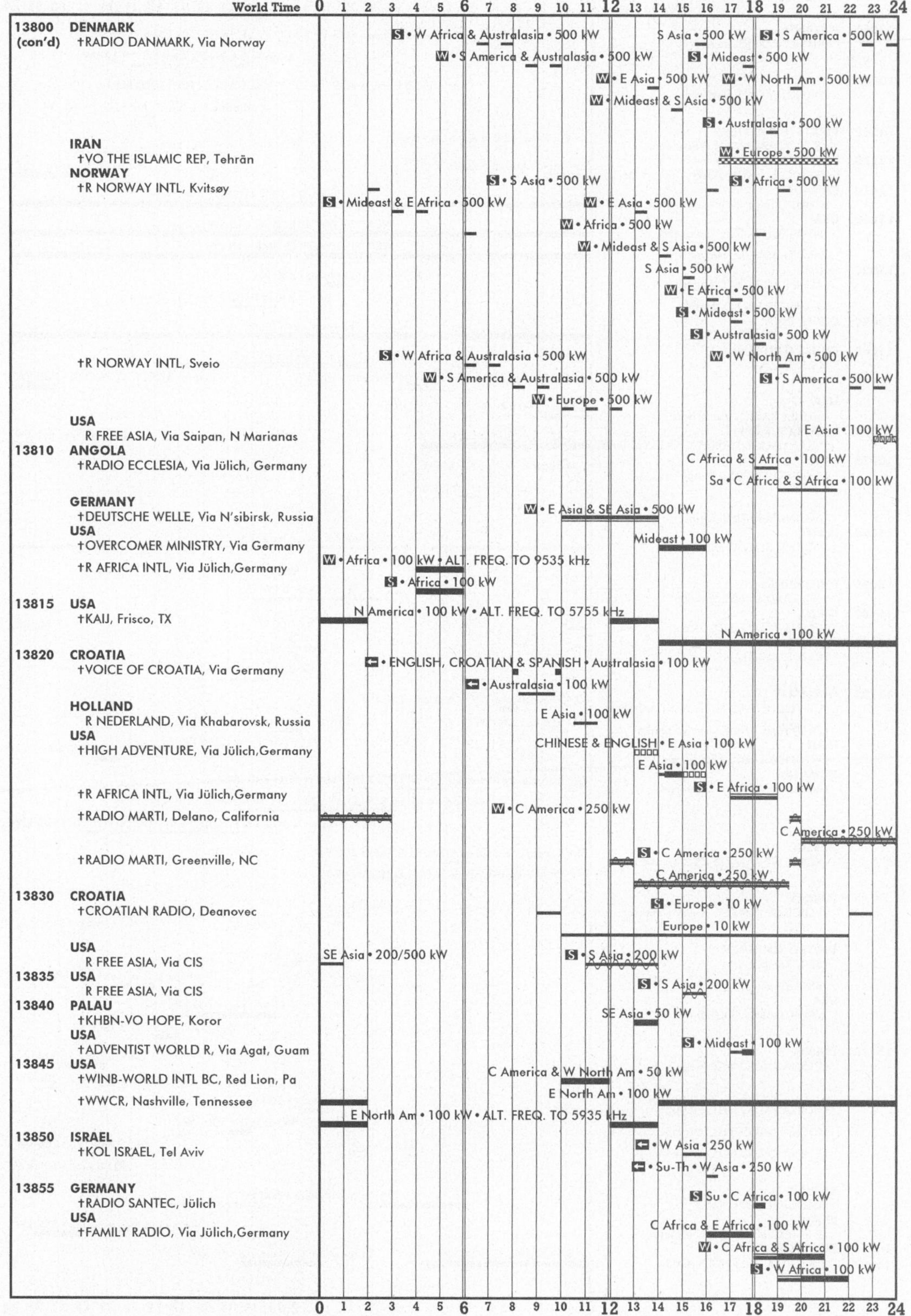
World Time 0 1 2 3 4 5 6 7 8 9 10 11 12 13 14 15 16 17 18 19 20 21 22 23 24
13800 DENMARK
(con'd) †RADIO DANMARK, Via Norway
S • W Africa & Australasia • 500 kW
S Asia • 500 kW
S • S America • 500 kW
W • S America & Australasia • 500 kW
S • Mideast • 500 kW
W • E Asia • 500 kW
W • W North Am • 500 kW
W • Mideast & S Asia • 500 kW
S • Australasia • 500 kW
IRAN
†VO THE ISLAMIC REP, Tehrān
W • Europe • 500 kW
NORWAY
†R NORWAY INTL, Kvitsøy
S • S Asia • 500 kW
S • Africa • 500 kW
S • Mideast & E Africa • 500 kW
W • E Asia • 500 kW
W • Africa • 500 kW
W • Mideast & S Asia • 500 kW
S Asia • 500 kW
W • E Africa • 500 kW
S • Mideast • 500 kW
S • Australasia • 500 kW
†R NORWAY INTL, Sveio
S • W Africa & Australasia • 500 kW
W • W North Am • 500 kW
W • S America & Australasia • 500 kW
S • S America • 500 kW
W • Europe • 500 kW
USA
R FREE ASIA, Via Saipan, N Marianas
E Asia • 100 kW
13810 ANGOLA
†RADIO ECCLESIA, Via Jülich, Germany
C Africa & S Africa • 100 kW
Sa • C Africa & S Africa • 100 kW
GERMANY
†DEUTSCHE WELLE, Via N'sibirsk, Russia
W • E Asia & SE Asia • 500 kW
USA
†OVERCOMER MINISTRY, Via Germany
Mideast • 100 kW
†R AFRICA INTL, Via Jülich,Germany
W • Africa • 100 kW • ALT. FREQ. TO 9535 kHz
S • Africa • 100 kW
13815 USA
†KAIJ, Frisco, TX
N America • 100 kW • ALT. FREQ. TO 5755 kHz
N America • 100 kW
13820 CROATIA
†VOICE OF CROATIA, Via Germany
• ENGLISH, CROATIAN & SPANISH • Australasia • 100 kW
• Australasia • 100 kW
HOLLAND
R NEDERLAND, Via Khabarovsk, Russia
E Asia • 100 kW
USA
†HIGH ADVENTURE, Via Jülich,Germany
CHINESE & ENGLISH • E Asia • 100 kW
E Asia • 100 kW
†R AFRICA INTL, Via Jülich,Germany
S • E Africa • 100 kW
†RADIO MARTI, Delano, California
W • C America • 250 kW
C America • 250 kW
†RADIO MARTI, Greenville, NC
S • C America • 250 kW
C America • 250 kW
13830 CROATIA
†CROATIAN RADIO, Deanovec
S • Europe • 10 kW
Europe • 10 kW
USA
R FREE ASIA, Via CIS
SE Asia • 200/500 kW
S • S Asia • 200 kW
13835 USA
R FREE ASIA, Via CIS
S • S Asia • 200 kW
13840 PALAU
†KHBN-VO HOPE, Koror
SE Asia • 50 kW
USA
†ADVENTIST WORLD R, Via Agat, Guam
S • Mideast • 100 kW
13845 USA
†WINB-WORLD INTL BC, Red Lion, Pa
C America & W North Am • 50 kW
†WWCR, Nashville, Tennessee
E North Am • 100 kW
E North Am • 100 kW • ALT. FREQ. TO 5935 kHz
13850 ISRAEL
†KOL ISRAEL, Tel Aviv
• W Asia • 250 kW
• Su-Th • W Asia • 250 kW
13855 GERMANY
†RADIO SANTEC, Jülich
S Su • C Africa • 100 kW
USA
†FAMILY RADIO, Via Jülich,Germany
C Africa & E Africa • 100 kW
W • C Africa & S Africa • 100 kW
S • W Africa • 100 kW
0 1 2 3 4 5 6 7 8 9 10 11 12 13 14 15 16 17 18 19 20 21 22 23 24

SEASONAL S OR W 1-HR TIMESHIFT MIDYEAR ⇐ OR ⇒ JAMMING / OR /\ EARLIEST HEARD ◁ LATEST HEARD ▷ NEW FOR 2002 †

kHz	Country / Station	Schedule notes
13860	**ICELAND** †RIKISUTVARPID, Reykjavik	Atlantic & Europe • DS-1 • 10 kW • ALT. FREQ. TO 13865 kHz; Atlantic & E North Am • DS-1 • 10 kW
13865	**ICELAND** †RIKISUTVARPID, Reykjavik	Atlantic & Europe • DS-1 • 10 kW • ALT. FREQ. TO 13860 kHz; Atlantic & E North Am • DS-1 • 10 kW
14540	**PIRATE (S AMERICA)** †"R CORSARIO INTL", Venezuela	Irr • C America & S America • LSB
14570	**PIRATE (S AMERICA)** †"RADIO BLANDENGUE"	Irr • Su • S America • LSB; Irr • Sa • S America • LSB
14670	**CANADA** †CHU, Ottawa	WORLD TIME • 3 kW • USB
15000	**USA** WWV, Fort Collins, Colorado	WEATHER/WORLD TIME • 10 kW
	WWVH, Kekaha, Hawai'i	WEATHER/WORLD TIME • 10 kW
15020	**INDIA** †ALL INDIA RADIO, Aligarh	E Asia & Australasia • 250 kW
	†ALL INDIA RADIO, Delhi	S Asia • 250 kW
15049v	**COSTA RICA** †RADIO FOR PEACE INTL, Ciudad Colón	N America • 10 kW
15060	**CHINA (TAIWAN)** †CBS, T'ai-pei	E Asia • VARIETY NETWORK • 100 kW; Sa/Su • E Asia • VARIETY NETWORK • 100 kW; E Asia • VARIETY NETWORK • 300 kW
	USA FAMILY RADIO, Via Taiwan	S Asia • 250 kW
15070	**PIRATE (EUROPE)** †"ALFA LIMA INTERNATIONAL", Holland	Irr • Su • 0.1 kW; Irr • Sa • 0.1 kW
15075	**INDIA** †ALL INDIA RADIO, Bangalore	Mideast & W Asia • 500 kW; E Africa • 500 kW
	ALL INDIA RADIO, Delhi	S Asia • 100 kW
15084v	**IRAN** VO THE ISLAMIC REP, Tehrān	Europe & C America • 500 kW; Europe • 500 kW
15095	**PHILIPPINES** †FEBC RADIO INTL, Bocaue	SE Asia • 100 kW
15100	**CHINA** CHINA RADIO INTL, Xi'an	SE Asia • 100 kW
15100v	**PAKISTAN** †RADIO PAKISTAN, Islamabad	E Asia • 250 kW; Mideast & N Africa • 250 kW
15105	**GERMANY** DEUTSCHE WELLE, Via Neth Antilles	S • W North Am & C America • 250 kW
	†DEUTSCHE WELLE, Via Sri Lanka	S • S Asia • 250 kW; S • SE Asia • 250 kW
	IRAN †VO THE ISLAMIC REP, Sirjan	W • S Africa • 500 kW
	ROMANIA †RADIO ROMANIA, Bucharest	W • Europe, N Africa & Mideast • DS-1 (ACTUALITATI) • 100 kW; Europe, N Africa & Mideast • DS-1 (ACTUALITATI) • 100 kW; S • Europe, N Africa & Mideast • DS-1 (ACTUALITATI) • 100 kW
	RUSSIA VOICE OF TATARSTAN, Samara	W • C Asia & E Asia • TATAR, RUSSIAN • 200 kW; W • W Asia • TATAR, RUSSIAN • 200 kW
	TURKEY †VOICE OF TURKEY, Ankara-Emirler	W • Mideast • 500 kW; W • E Asia • 500 kW
	UNITED KINGDOM †BBC, Rampisham	N Africa • 250 kW
	†BBC, Via Ascension	W Africa • 250 kW; W Africa & C Africa • 250 kW
	USA WHRI, Noblesville, Indiana	C America • 100 kW; W • C America • 100 kW
15110	**CHINA** †CHINA RADIO INTL, Beijing	S • Europe • 300 kW; S • S America • 300 kW
	†CHINA RADIO INTL, Hohhot	S • E Asia • 50 kW
	†CHINA RADIO INTL, Urümqi	S • S Asia • 500 kW
	†CHINA RADIO INTL, Xi'an	W • E Asia • 100 kW; S • S America • 200 kW; S • E Asia • 100 kW
	KUWAIT RADIO KUWAIT, Kabd	S Asia & SE Asia • 500 kW
	SPAIN †R EXTERIOR ESPANA, Noblejas	N America & C America • 350 kW
15115 (con'd)	**ECUADOR** †HCJB-VO THE ANDES, Quito	S • N America • 50 kW; N America & S America • 50 kW

World Time 0 1 2 3 4 5 6 7 8 9 10 11 12 13 14 15 16 17 18 19 20 21 22 23 24

ENGLISH ARABIC CHINESE FRENCH GERMAN RUSSIAN SPANISH OTHER

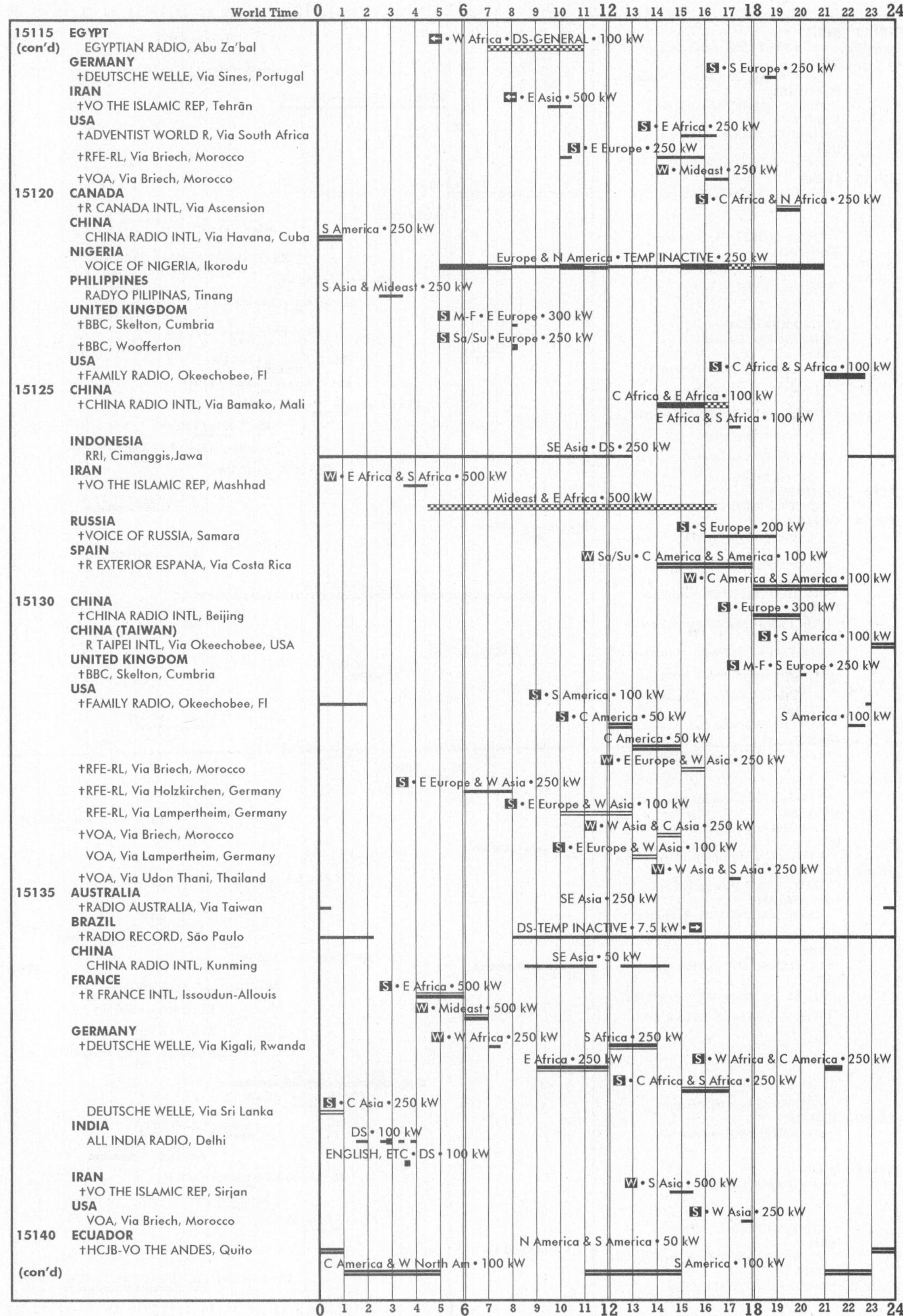

kHz	Country / Station	World Time 0–24
15115 (con'd)	**EGYPT**	
	EGYPTIAN RADIO, Abu Za'bal	⬅ • W Africa • DS-GENERAL • 100 kW
	GERMANY	
	†DEUTSCHE WELLE, Via Sines, Portugal	S • S Europe • 250 kW
	IRAN	
	†VO THE ISLAMIC REP, Tehrān	⬅ • E Asia • 500 kW
	USA	
	†ADVENTIST WORLD R, Via South Africa	S • E Africa • 250 kW
	†RFE-RL, Via Briech, Morocco	S • E Europe • 250 kW
	†VOA, Via Briech, Morocco	W • Mideast • 250 kW
15120	**CANADA**	
	†R CANADA INTL, Via Ascension	S • C Africa & N Africa • 250 kW
	CHINA	
	CHINA RADIO INTL, Via Havana, Cuba	S America • 250 kW
	NIGERIA	
	VOICE OF NIGERIA, Ikorodu	Europe & N America • TEMP INACTIVE • 250 kW
	PHILIPPINES	
	RADYO PILIPINAS, Tinang	S Asia & Mideast • 250 kW
	UNITED KINGDOM	
	†BBC, Skelton, Cumbria	S M-F • E Europe • 300 kW
	†BBC, Woofferton	S Sa/Su • Europe • 250 kW
	USA	
	†FAMILY RADIO, Okeechobee, Fl	S • C Africa & S Africa • 100 kW
15125	**CHINA**	
	†CHINA RADIO INTL, Via Bamako, Mali	C Africa & E Africa • 100 kW; E Africa & S Africa • 100 kW
	INDONESIA	
	RRI, Cimanggis,Jawa	SE Asia • DS • 250 kW
	IRAN	
	†VO THE ISLAMIC REP, Mashhad	W • E Africa & S Africa • 500 kW; Mideast & E Africa • 500 kW
	RUSSIA	
	†VOICE OF RUSSIA, Samara	S • S Europe • 200 kW
	SPAIN	
	†R EXTERIOR ESPANA, Via Costa Rica	W Sa/Su • C America & S America • 100 kW; W • C America & S America • 100 kW
15130	**CHINA**	
	†CHINA RADIO INTL, Beijing	S • Europe • 300 kW
	CHINA (TAIWAN)	
	R TAIPEI INTL, Via Okeechobee, USA	S • S America • 100 kW
	UNITED KINGDOM	
	†BBC, Skelton, Cumbria	S M-F • S Europe • 250 kW
	USA	
	†FAMILY RADIO, Okeechobee, Fl	S • S America • 100 kW; S • C America • 50 kW; S America • 100 kW; C America • 50 kW
	†RFE-RL, Via Briech, Morocco	W • E Europe & W Asia • 250 kW
	†RFE-RL, Via Holzkirchen, Germany	S • E Europe & W Asia • 250 kW
	RFE-RL, Via Lampertheim, Germany	S • E Europe & W Asia • 100 kW
	†VOA, Via Briech, Morocco	W • W Asia & C Asia • 250 kW
	VOA, Via Lampertheim, Germany	S • E Europe & W Asia • 100 kW
	†VOA, Via Udon Thani, Thailand	W • W Asia & S Asia • 250 kW
15135	**AUSTRALIA**	
	†RADIO AUSTRALIA, Via Taiwan	SE Asia • 250 kW
	BRAZIL	
	†RADIO RECORD, São Paulo	DS-TEMP INACTIVE • 7.5 kW • ➡
	CHINA	
	CHINA RADIO INTL, Kunming	SE Asia • 50 kW
	FRANCE	
	†R FRANCE INTL, Issoudun-Allouis	S • E Africa • 500 kW; W • Mideast • 500 kW
	GERMANY	
	†DEUTSCHE WELLE, Via Kigali, Rwanda	W • W Africa • 250 kW; S Africa • 250 kW; E Africa • 250 kW; S • W Africa & C America • 250 kW; S • C Africa & S Africa • 250 kW
	DEUTSCHE WELLE, Via Sri Lanka	S • C Asia • 250 kW
	INDIA	
	ALL INDIA RADIO, Delhi	DS • 100 kW; ENGLISH, ETC • DS • 100 kW
	IRAN	
	†VO THE ISLAMIC REP, Sirjan	W • S Asia • 500 kW
	USA	
	VOA, Via Briech, Morocco	S • W Asia • 250 kW
15140	**ECUADOR**	
	†HCJB-VO THE ANDES, Quito	N America & S America • 50 kW; C America & W North Am • 100 kW; S America • 100 kW
(con'd)		

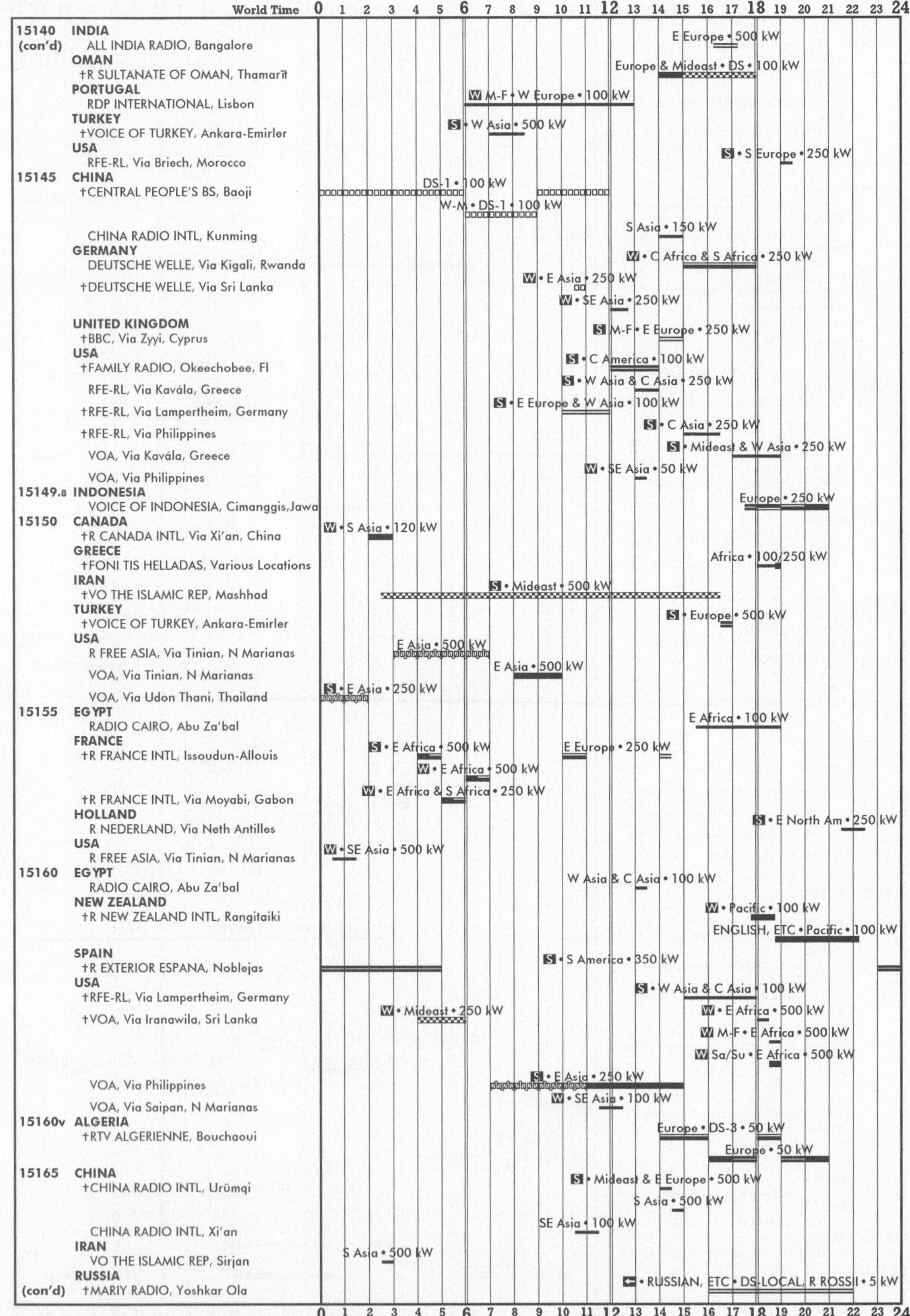
World Time 0 1 2 3 4 5 6 7 8 9 10 11 12 13 14 15 16 17 18 19 20 21 22 23 24
15140 (con'd) INDIA
ALL INDIA RADIO, Bangalore
E Europe • 500 kW
OMAN
†R SULTANATE OF OMAN, Thamarīt
Europe & Mideast • DS • 100 kW
PORTUGAL
RDP INTERNATIONAL, Lisbon
W M-F • W Europe • 100 kW
TURKEY
†VOICE OF TURKEY, Ankara-Emirler
S • W Asia • 500 kW
USA
RFE-RL, Via Briech, Morocco
S • S Europe • 250 kW
15145 CHINA
†CENTRAL PEOPLE'S BS, Baoji
DS-1 • 100 kW
W-M • DS-1 • 100 kW
CHINA RADIO INTL, Kunming
S Asia • 150 kW
GERMANY
DEUTSCHE WELLE, Via Kigali, Rwanda
W • C Africa & S Africa • 250 kW
†DEUTSCHE WELLE, Via Sri Lanka
W • E Asia • 250 kW
W • SE Asia • 250 kW
UNITED KINGDOM
†BBC, Via Zyyi, Cyprus
S M-F • E Europe • 250 kW
USA
†FAMILY RADIO, Okeechobee, Fl
S • C America • 100 kW
RFE-RL, Via Kavála, Greece
S • W Asia & C Asia • 250 kW
†RFE-RL, Via Lampertheim, Germany
S • E Europe & W Asia • 100 kW
†RFE-RL, Via Philippines
S • C Asia • 250 kW
VOA, Via Kavála, Greece
S • Mideast & W Asia • 250 kW
VOA, Via Philippines
W • SE Asia • 50 kW
15149.8 INDONESIA
VOICE OF INDONESIA, Cimanggis,Jawa
Europe • 250 kW
15150 CANADA
†R CANADA INTL, Via Xi'an, China
W • S Asia • 120 kW
GREECE
†FONI TIS HELLADAS, Various Locations
Africa • 100/250 kW
IRAN
†VO THE ISLAMIC REP, Mashhad
S • Mideast • 500 kW
TURKEY
†VOICE OF TURKEY, Ankara-Emirler
S • Europe • 500 kW
USA
R FREE ASIA, Via Tinian, N Marianas
E Asia • 500 kW
VOA, Via Tinian, N Marianas
E Asia • 500 kW
VOA, Via Udon Thani, Thailand
S • E Asia • 250 kW
15155 EGYPT
RADIO CAIRO, Abu Za'bal
E Africa • 100 kW
FRANCE
†R FRANCE INTL, Issoudun-Allouis
S • E Africa • 500 kW
E Europe • 250 kW
W • E Africa • 500 kW
W • E Africa & S Africa • 250 kW
†R FRANCE INTL, Via Moyabi, Gabon
HOLLAND
R NEDERLAND, Via Neth Antilles
S • E North Am • 250 kW
USA
R FREE ASIA, Via Tinian, N Marianas
W • SE Asia • 500 kW
15160 EGYPT
RADIO CAIRO, Abu Za'bal
W Asia & C Asia • 100 kW
NEW ZEALAND
†R NEW ZEALAND INTL, Rangitaiki
W • Pacific • 100 kW
ENGLISH, ETC • Pacific • 100 kW
SPAIN
†R EXTERIOR ESPANA, Noblejas
S • S America • 350 kW
USA
†RFE-RL, Via Lampertheim, Germany
S • W Asia & C Asia • 100 kW
†VOA, Via Iranawila, Sri Lanka
W • Mideast • 250 kW
W • E Africa • 500 kW
W M-F • E Africa • 500 kW
W Sa/Su • E Africa • 500 kW
VOA, Via Philippines
S • E Asia • 250 kW
VOA, Via Saipan, N Marianas
W • SE Asia • 100 kW
15160v ALGERIA
†RTV ALGERIENNE, Bouchaoui
Europe • DS-3 • 50 kW
Europe • 50 kW
15165 CHINA
†CHINA RADIO INTL, Urümqi
S • Mideast & E Europe • 500 kW
S Asia • 500 kW
CHINA RADIO INTL, Xi'an
SE Asia • 100 kW
IRAN
VO THE ISLAMIC REP, Sirjan
S Asia • 500 kW
RUSSIA
(con'd) †MARIY RADIO, Yoshkar Ola
• RUSSIAN, ETC • DS-LOCAL, R ROSSII • 5 kW
0 1 2 3 4 5 6 7 8 9 10 11 12 13 14 15 16 17 18 19 20 21 22 23 24

ENGLISH ARABIC CHINESE FRENCH GERMAN RUSSIAN SPANISH OTHER

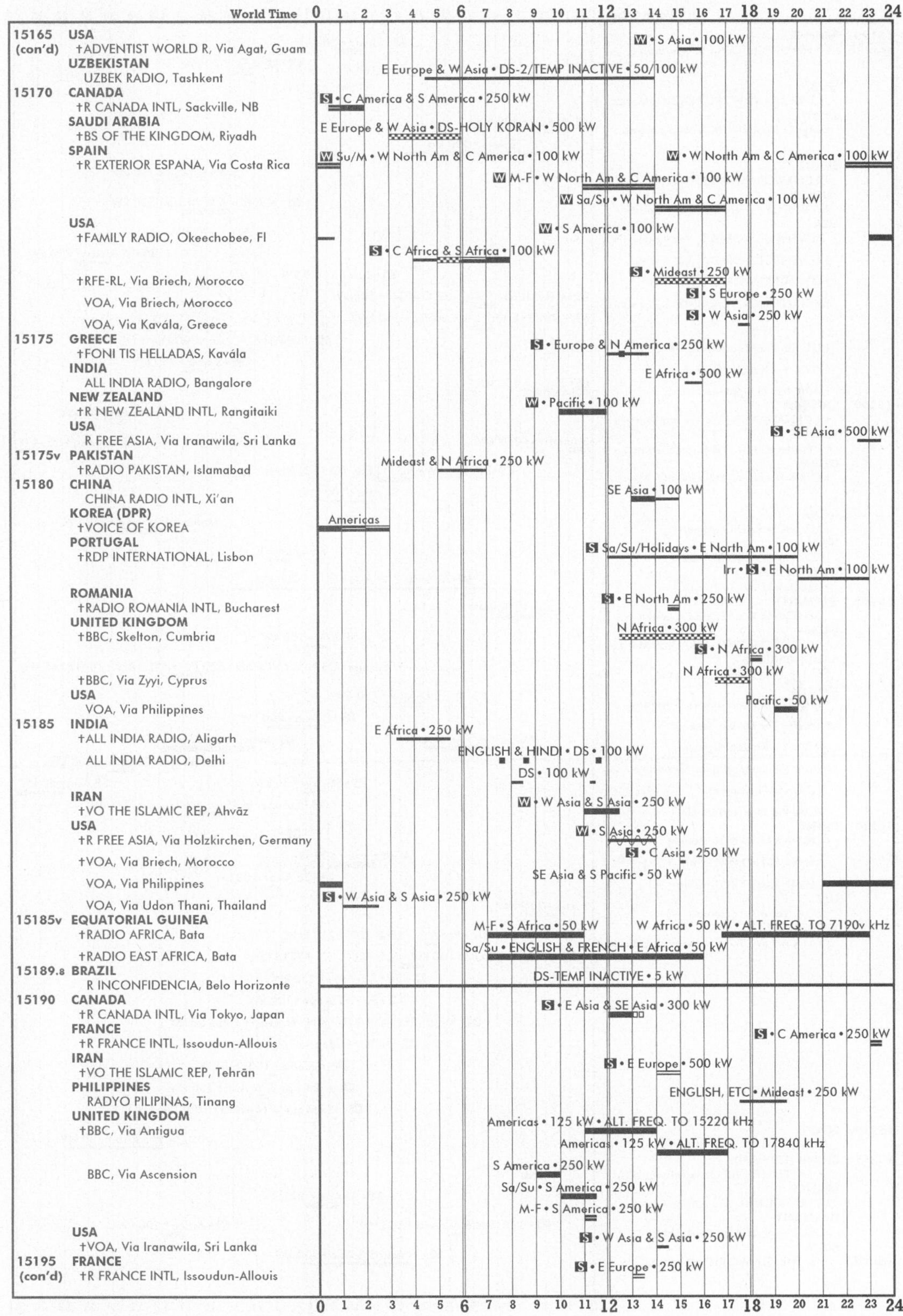
World Time 0 1 2 3 4 5 6 7 8 9 10 11 12 13 14 15 16 17 18 19 20 21 22 23 24
15165 (con'd) USA
†ADVENTIST WORLD R, Via Agat, Guam
W • S Asia • 100 kW
UZBEKISTAN
UZBEK RADIO, Tashkent
E Europe & W Asia • DS-2/TEMP INACTIVE • 50/100 kW
15170 CANADA
†R CANADA INTL, Sackville, NB
S • C America & S America • 250 kW
SAUDI ARABIA
†BS OF THE KINGDOM, Riyadh
E Europe & W Asia • DS-HOLY KORAN • 500 kW
SPAIN
†R EXTERIOR ESPANA, Via Costa Rica
W Su/M • W North Am & C America • 100 kW
W • W North Am & C America • 100 kW
W M-F • W North Am & C America • 100 kW
W Sa/Su • W North Am & C America • 100 kW
USA
†FAMILY RADIO, Okeechobee, Fl
W • S America • 100 kW
S • C Africa & S Africa • 100 kW
†RFE-RL, Via Briech, Morocco
S • Mideast • 250 kW
VOA, Via Briech, Morocco
S • S Europe • 250 kW
VOA, Via Kavála, Greece
S • W Asia • 250 kW
15175 GREECE
†FONI TIS HELLADAS, Kavála
S • Europe & N America • 250 kW
INDIA
ALL INDIA RADIO, Bangalore
E Africa • 500 kW
NEW ZEALAND
†R NEW ZEALAND INTL, Rangitaiki
W • Pacific • 100 kW
USA
R FREE ASIA, Via Iranawila, Sri Lanka
S • SE Asia • 500 kW
15175v PAKISTAN
†RADIO PAKISTAN, Islamabad
Mideast & N Africa • 250 kW
15180 CHINA
CHINA RADIO INTL, Xi'an
SE Asia • 100 kW
KOREA (DPR)
†VOICE OF KOREA
Americas
PORTUGAL
†RDP INTERNATIONAL, Lisbon
S Sa/Su/Holidays • E North Am • 100 kW
Irr • S • E North Am • 100 kW
ROMANIA
†RADIO ROMANIA INTL, Bucharest
S • E North Am • 250 kW
UNITED KINGDOM
†BBC, Skelton, Cumbria
N Africa • 300 kW
S • N Africa • 300 kW
†BBC, Via Zyyi, Cyprus
N Africa • 300 kW
USA
VOA, Via Philippines
Pacific • 50 kW
15185 INDIA
†ALL INDIA RADIO, Aligarh
E Africa • 250 kW
ALL INDIA RADIO, Delhi
ENGLISH & HINDI • DS • 100 kW
DS • 100 kW
IRAN
†VO THE ISLAMIC REP, Ahvāz
W • W Asia & S Asia • 250 kW
USA
†R FREE ASIA, Via Holzkirchen, Germany
W • S Asia • 250 kW
†VOA, Via Briech, Morocco
S • C Asia • 250 kW
VOA, Via Philippines
SE Asia & S Pacific • 50 kW
VOA, Via Udon Thani, Thailand
S • W Asia & S Asia • 250 kW
15185v EQUATORIAL GUINEA
†RADIO AFRICA, Bata
M-F • S Africa • 50 kW
W Africa • 50 kW • ALT. FREQ. TO 7190v kHz
†RADIO EAST AFRICA, Bata
Sa/Su • ENGLISH & FRENCH • E Africa • 50 kW
15189.8 BRAZIL
R INCONFIDENCIA, Belo Horizonte
DS-TEMP INACTIVE • 5 kW
15190 CANADA
†R CANADA INTL, Via Tokyo, Japan
S • E Asia & SE Asia • 300 kW
FRANCE
†R FRANCE INTL, Issoudun-Allouis
S • C America • 250 kW
IRAN
†VO THE ISLAMIC REP, Tehrān
S • E Europe • 500 kW
PHILIPPINES
RADYO PILIPINAS, Tinang
ENGLISH, ETC • Mideast • 250 kW
UNITED KINGDOM
†BBC, Via Antigua
Americas • 125 kW • ALT. FREQ. TO 15220 kHz
Americas • 125 kW • ALT. FREQ. TO 17840 kHz
BBC, Via Ascension
S America • 250 kW
Sa/Su • S America • 250 kW
M-F • S America • 250 kW
USA
†VOA, Via Iranawila, Sri Lanka
S • W Asia & S Asia • 250 kW
15195 (con'd) FRANCE
†R FRANCE INTL, Issoudun-Allouis
S • E Europe • 250 kW
0 1 2 3 4 5 6 7 8 9 10 11 12 13 14 15 16 17 18 19 20 21 22 23 24

SEASONAL S OR W 1-HR TIMESHIFT MIDYEAR ⇦ OR ⇨ JAMMING / OR ∧ EARLIEST HEARD ◁ LATEST HEARD ▷ NEW FOR 2002 †

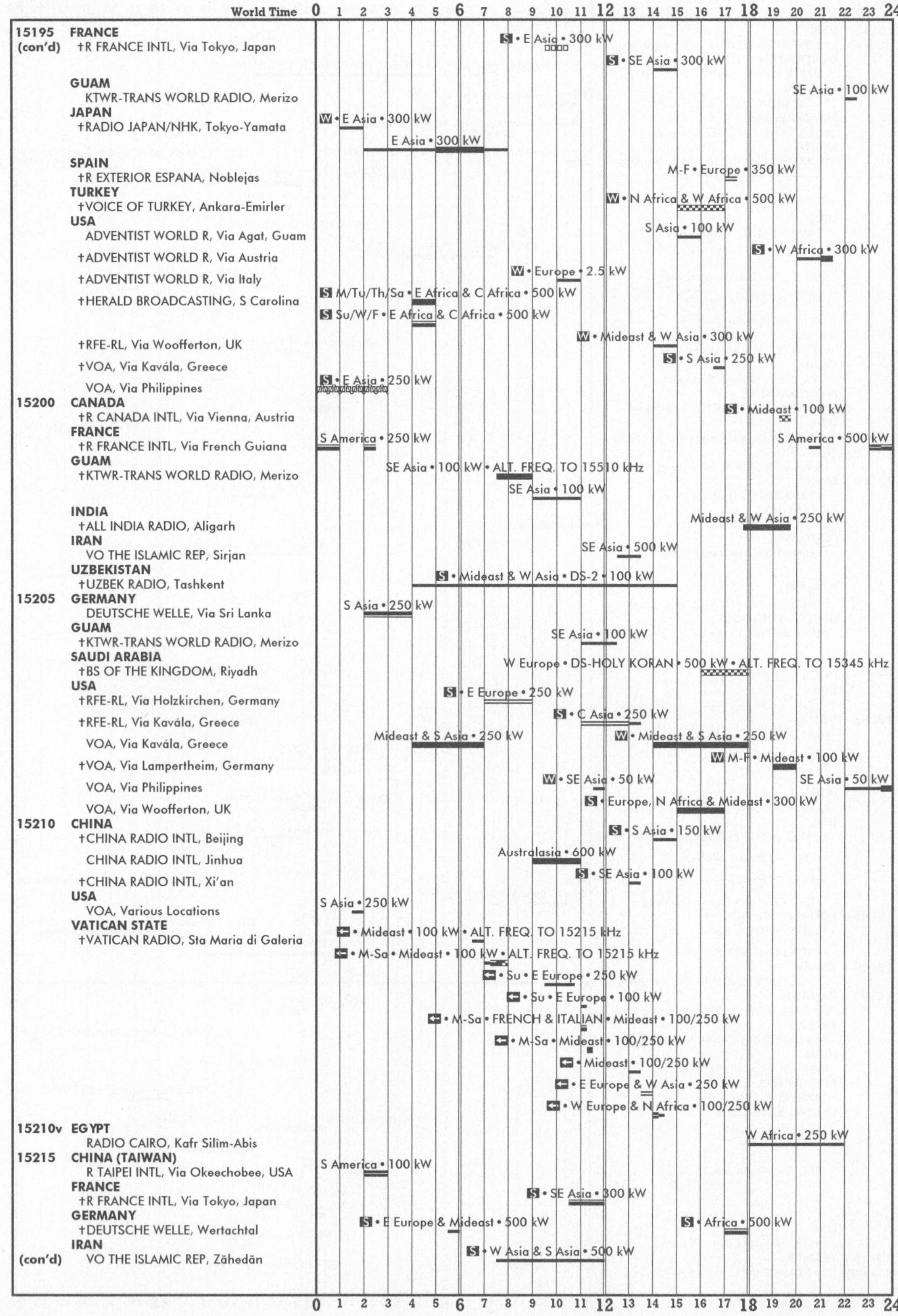
World Time 0 1 2 3 4 5 6 7 8 9 10 11 12 13 14 15 16 17 18 19 20 21 22 23 24
15195 (con'd) FRANCE
†R FRANCE INTL, Via Tokyo, Japan
S • E Asia • 300 kW
S • SE Asia • 300 kW
GUAM
KTWR-TRANS WORLD RADIO, Merizo
SE Asia • 100 kW
JAPAN
†RADIO JAPAN/NHK, Tokyo-Yamata
W • E Asia • 300 kW
E Asia • 300 kW
SPAIN
†R EXTERIOR ESPANA, Noblejas
M-F • Europe • 350 kW
TURKEY
†VOICE OF TURKEY, Ankara-Emirler
W • N Africa & W Africa • 500 kW
USA
ADVENTIST WORLD R, Via Agat, Guam
S Asia • 100 kW
†ADVENTIST WORLD R, Via Austria
S • W Africa • 300 kW
†ADVENTIST WORLD R, Via Italy
W • Europe • 2.5 kW
†HERALD BROADCASTING, S Carolina
S M/Tu/Th/Sa • E Africa & C Africa • 500 kW
S Su/W/F • E Africa & C Africa • 500 kW
†RFE-RL, Via Woofferton, UK
W • Mideast & W Asia • 300 kW
†VOA, Via Kavála, Greece
S • S Asia • 250 kW
VOA, Via Philippines
S • E Asia • 250 kW
15200 CANADA
†R CANADA INTL, Via Vienna, Austria
S • Mideast • 100 kW
FRANCE
†R FRANCE INTL, Via French Guiana
S America • 250 kW
S America • 500 kW
GUAM
†KTWR-TRANS WORLD RADIO, Merizo
SE Asia • 100 kW • ALT. FREQ. TO 15510 kHz
SE Asia • 100 kW
INDIA
†ALL INDIA RADIO, Aligarh
Mideast & W Asia • 250 kW
IRAN
VO THE ISLAMIC REP, Sirjan
SE Asia • 500 kW
UZBEKISTAN
†UZBEK RADIO, Tashkent
S • Mideast & W Asia • DS-2 • 100 kW
15205 GERMANY
DEUTSCHE WELLE, Via Sri Lanka
S Asia • 250 kW
GUAM
†KTWR-TRANS WORLD RADIO, Merizo
SE Asia • 100 kW
SAUDI ARABIA
†BS OF THE KINGDOM, Riyadh
W Europe • DS-HOLY KORAN • 500 kW • ALT. FREQ. TO 15345 kHz
USA
†RFE-RL, Via Holzkirchen, Germany
S • E Europe • 250 kW
†RFE-RL, Via Kavála, Greece
S • C Asia • 250 kW
VOA, Via Kavála, Greece
Mideast & S Asia • 250 kW
W • Mideast & S Asia • 250 kW
†VOA, Via Lampertheim, Germany
W M-F • Mideast • 100 kW
VOA, Via Philippines
W • SE Asia • 50 kW
SE Asia • 50 kW
VOA, Via Woofferton, UK
S • Europe, N Africa & Mideast • 300 kW
15210 CHINA
†CHINA RADIO INTL, Beijing
S • S Asia • 150 kW
CHINA RADIO INTL, Jinhua
Australasia • 600 kW
†CHINA RADIO INTL, Xi'an
S • SE Asia • 100 kW
USA
VOA, Various Locations
S Asia • 250 kW
VATICAN STATE
†VATICAN RADIO, Sta Maria di Galeria
• Mideast • 100 kW • ALT. FREQ. TO 15215 kHz
• M-Sa • Mideast • 100 kW • ALT. FREQ. TO 15215 kHz
• Su • E Europe • 250 kW
• Su • E Europe • 100 kW
• M-Sa • FRENCH & ITALIAN • Mideast • 100/250 kW
• M-Sa • Mideast • 100/250 kW
• Mideast • 100/250 kW
• E Europe & W Asia • 250 kW
• W Europe & N Africa • 100/250 kW
15210v EGYPT
RADIO CAIRO, Kafr Silîm-Abis
W Africa • 250 kW
15215 CHINA (TAIWAN)
R TAIPEI INTL, Via Okeechobee, USA
S America • 100 kW
FRANCE
†R FRANCE INTL, Via Tokyo, Japan
S • SE Asia • 300 kW
GERMANY
†DEUTSCHE WELLE, Wertachtal
S • E Europe & Mideast • 500 kW
S • Africa • 500 kW
IRAN
(con'd) VO THE ISLAMIC REP, Zāhedān
S • W Asia & S Asia • 500 kW
0 1 2 3 4 5 6 7 8 9 10 11 12 13 14 15 16 17 18 19 20 21 22 23 24
ENGLISH ARABIC CHINESE FRENCH GERMAN RUSSIAN SPANISH OTHER

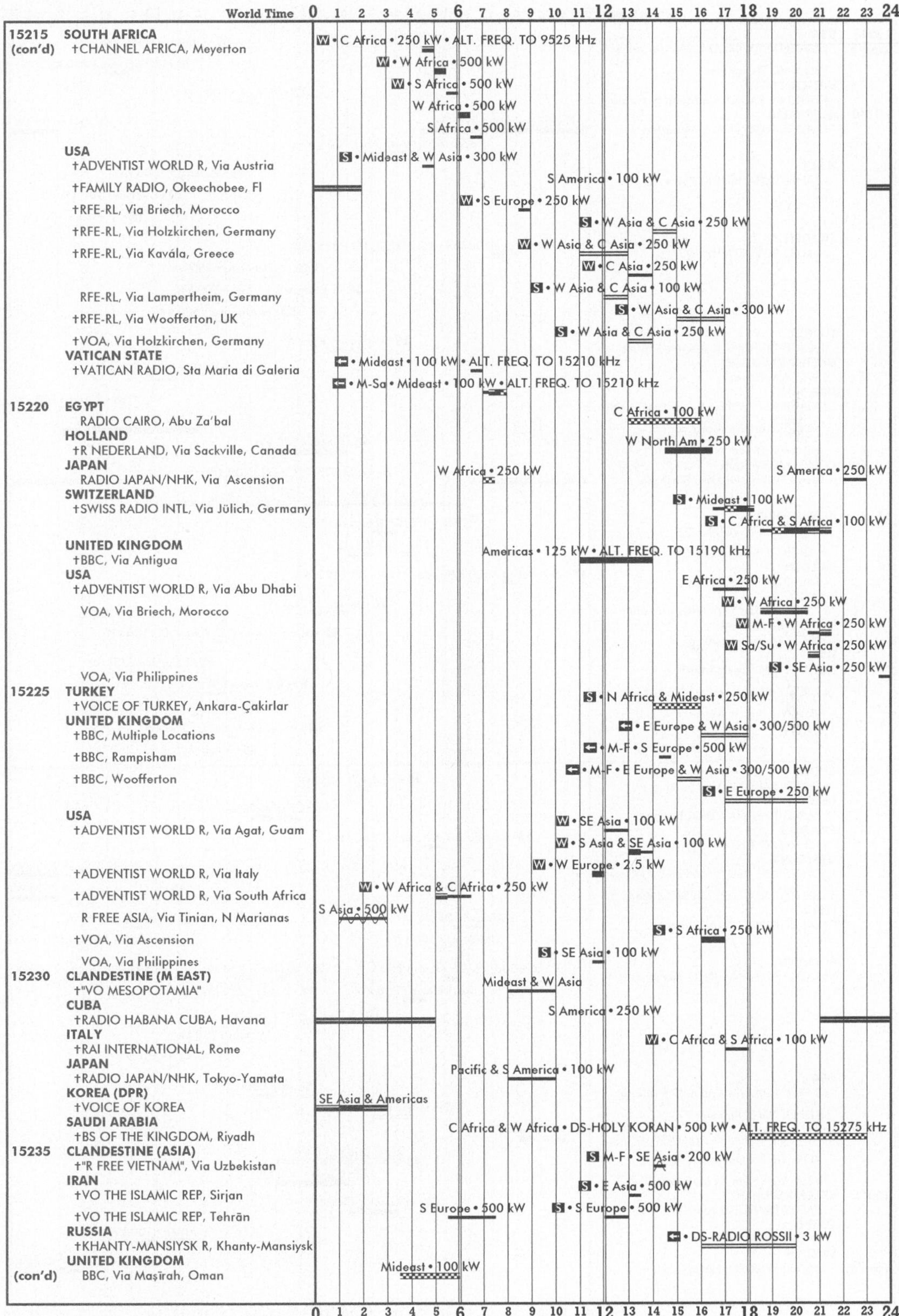

World Time 0 1 2 3 4 5 6 7 8 9 10 11 12 13 14 15 16 17 18 19 20 21 22 23 24
15215 (con'd) SOUTH AFRICA
†CHANNEL AFRICA, Meyerton
W • C Africa • 250 kW • ALT. FREQ. TO 9525 kHz
W • W Africa • 500 kW
W • S Africa • 500 kW
W Africa • 500 kW
S Africa • 500 kW
USA
†ADVENTIST WORLD R, Via Austria
S • Mideast & W Asia • 300 kW
†FAMILY RADIO, Okeechobee, Fl
S America • 100 kW
†RFE-RL, Via Briech, Morocco
W • S Europe • 250 kW
†RFE-RL, Via Holzkirchen, Germany
S • W Asia & C Asia • 250 kW
†RFE-RL, Via Kavála, Greece
W • W Asia & C Asia • 250 kW
W • C Asia • 250 kW
S • W Asia & C Asia • 100 kW
RFE-RL, Via Lampertheim, Germany
S • W Asia & C Asia • 300 kW
†RFE-RL, Via Woofferton, UK
S • W Asia & C Asia • 250 kW
†VOA, Via Holzkirchen, Germany
VATICAN STATE
†VATICAN RADIO, Sta Maria di Galeria
• Mideast • 100 kW • ALT. FREQ. TO 15210 kHz
• M-Sa • Mideast • 100 kW • ALT. FREQ. TO 15210 kHz
15220 EGYPT
RADIO CAIRO, Abu Za'bal
C Africa • 100 kW
HOLLAND
†R NEDERLAND, Via Sackville, Canada
W North Am • 250 kW
JAPAN
RADIO JAPAN/NHK, Via Ascension
W Africa • 250 kW
S America • 250 kW
SWITZERLAND
†SWISS RADIO INTL, Via Jülich, Germany
S • Mideast • 100 kW
S • C Africa & S Africa • 100 kW
UNITED KINGDOM
†BBC, Via Antigua
Americas • 125 kW • ALT. FREQ. TO 15190 kHz
USA
†ADVENTIST WORLD R, Via Abu Dhabi
E Africa • 250 kW
VOA, Via Briech, Morocco
W • W Africa • 250 kW
W M-F • W Africa • 250 kW
W Sa/Su • W Africa • 250 kW
VOA, Via Philippines
S • SE Asia • 250 kW
15225 TURKEY
†VOICE OF TURKEY, Ankara-Çakirlar
S • N Africa & Mideast • 250 kW
UNITED KINGDOM
†BBC, Multiple Locations
• E Europe & W Asia • 300/500 kW
†BBC, Rampisham
• M-F • S Europe • 500 kW
†BBC, Woofferton
• M-F • E Europe & W Asia • 300/500 kW
S • E Europe • 250 kW
USA
†ADVENTIST WORLD R, Via Agat, Guam
W • SE Asia • 100 kW
W • S Asia & SE Asia • 100 kW
†ADVENTIST WORLD R, Via Italy
W • W Europe • 2.5 kW
†ADVENTIST WORLD R, Via South Africa
W • W Africa & C Africa • 250 kW
R FREE ASIA, Via Tinian, N Marianas
S Asia • 500 kW
†VOA, Via Ascension
S • S Africa • 250 kW
VOA, Via Philippines
S • SE Asia • 100 kW
15230 CLANDESTINE (M EAST)
†"VO MESOPOTAMIA"
Mideast & W Asia
CUBA
†RADIO HABANA CUBA, Havana
S America • 250 kW
ITALY
†RAI INTERNATIONAL, Rome
W • C Africa & S Africa • 100 kW
JAPAN
†RADIO JAPAN/NHK, Tokyo-Yamata
Pacific & S America • 100 kW
KOREA (DPR)
†VOICE OF KOREA
SE Asia & Americas
SAUDI ARABIA
†BS OF THE KINGDOM, Riyadh
C Africa & W Africa • DS-HOLY KORAN • 500 kW • ALT. FREQ. TO 15275 kHz
15235 CLANDESTINE (ASIA)
†"R FREE VIETNAM", Via Uzbekistan
S M-F • SE Asia • 200 kW
IRAN
†VO THE ISLAMIC REP, Sirjan
S • E Asia • 500 kW
†VO THE ISLAMIC REP, Tehrān
S Europe • 500 kW
S • S Europe • 500 kW
RUSSIA
†KHANTY-MANSIYSK R, Khanty-Mansiysk
• DS-RADIO ROSSII • 3 kW
(con'd) UNITED KINGDOM
BBC, Via Maşīrah, Oman
Mideast • 100 kW
0 1 2 3 4 5 6 7 8 9 10 11 12 13 14 15 16 17 18 19 20 21 22 23 24

SEASONAL S OR W 1-HR TIMESHIFT MIDYEAR OR JAMMING / OR /\ EARLIEST HEARD ◁ LATEST HEARD ▷ NEW FOR 2002 †

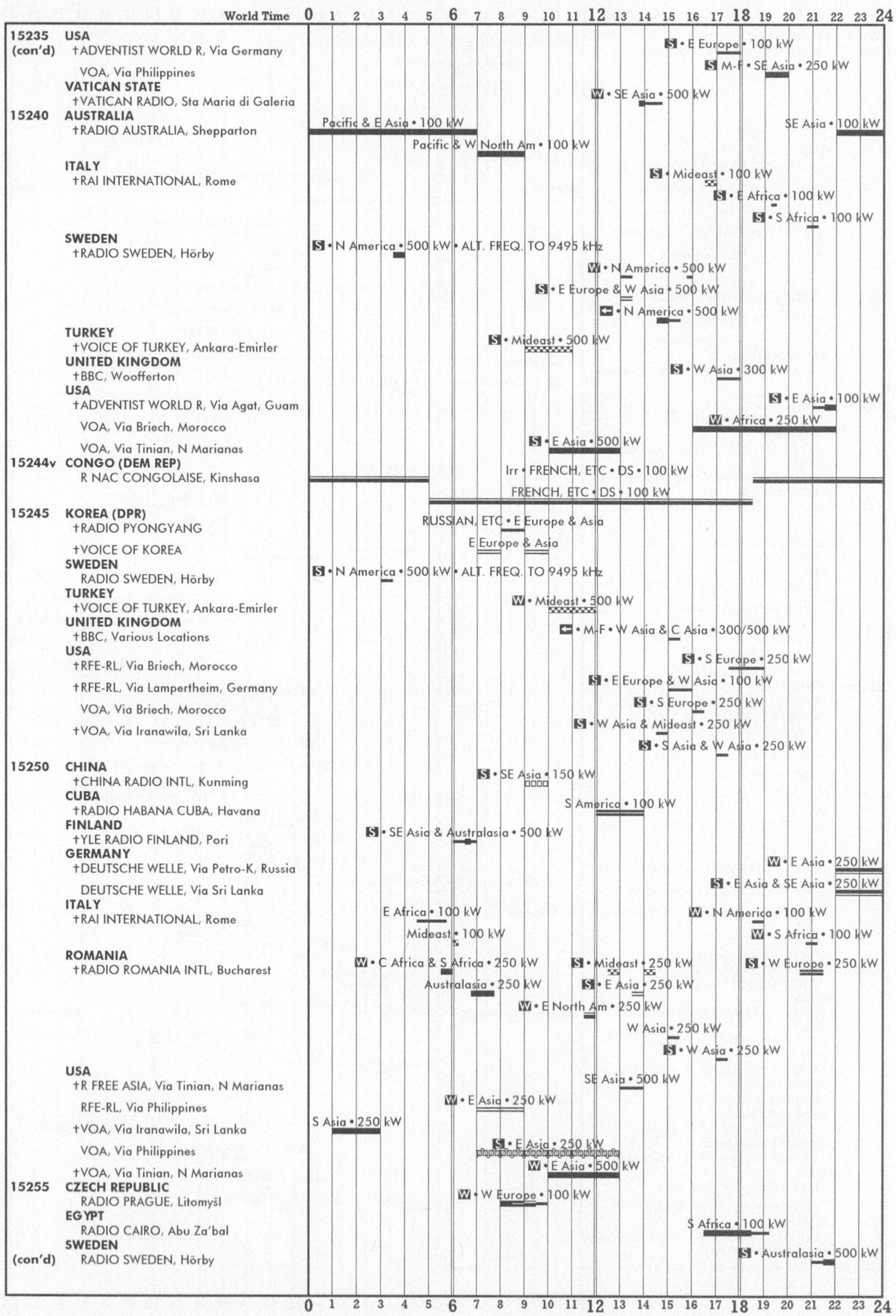
World Time 0 1 2 3 4 5 6 7 8 9 10 11 12 13 14 15 16 17 18 19 20 21 22 23 24
15235 (con'd) USA
†ADVENTIST WORLD R, Via Germany
S • E Europe • 100 kW
VOA, Via Philippines
S M-F • SE Asia • 250 kW
VATICAN STATE
†VATICAN RADIO, Sta Maria di Galeria
W • SE Asia • 500 kW
15240 AUSTRALIA
†RADIO AUSTRALIA, Shepparton
Pacific & E Asia • 100 kW
SE Asia • 100 kW
Pacific & W North Am • 100 kW
ITALY
†RAI INTERNATIONAL, Rome
S • Mideast • 100 kW
S • E Africa • 100 kW
S • S Africa • 100 kW
SWEDEN
†RADIO SWEDEN, Hörby
S • N America • 500 kW • ALT. FREQ. TO 9495 kHz
W • N America • 500 kW
S • E Europe & W Asia • 500 kW
N America • 500 kW
TURKEY
†VOICE OF TURKEY, Ankara-Emirler
S • Mideast • 500 kW
UNITED KINGDOM
†BBC, Woofferton
S • W Asia • 300 kW
USA
†ADVENTIST WORLD R, Via Agat, Guam
S • E Asia • 100 kW
VOA, Via Briech, Morocco
W • Africa • 250 kW
VOA, Via Tinian, N Marianas
S • E Asia • 500 kW
15244v CONGO (DEM REP)
R NAC CONGOLAISE, Kinshasa
Irr • FRENCH, ETC • DS • 100 kW
FRENCH, ETC • DS • 100 kW
15245 KOREA (DPR)
†RADIO PYONGYANG
RUSSIAN, ETC • E Europe & Asia
†VOICE OF KOREA
E Europe & Asia
SWEDEN
RADIO SWEDEN, Hörby
S • N America • 500 kW • ALT. FREQ. TO 9495 kHz
TURKEY
†VOICE OF TURKEY, Ankara-Emirler
W • Mideast • 500 kW
UNITED KINGDOM
†BBC, Various Locations
M-F • W Asia & C Asia • 300/500 kW
USA
†RFE-RL, Via Briech, Morocco
S • S Europe • 250 kW
†RFE-RL, Via Lampertheim, Germany
S • E Europe & W Asia • 100 kW
VOA, Via Briech, Morocco
S • S Europe • 250 kW
†VOA, Via Iranawila, Sri Lanka
S • W Asia & Mideast • 250 kW
S • S Asia & W Asia • 250 kW
15250 CHINA
†CHINA RADIO INTL, Kunming
S • SE Asia • 150 kW
CUBA
†RADIO HABANA CUBA, Havana
S America • 100 kW
FINLAND
†YLE RADIO FINLAND, Pori
S • SE Asia & Australasia • 500 kW
GERMANY
†DEUTSCHE WELLE, Via Petro-K, Russia
W • E Asia • 250 kW
DEUTSCHE WELLE, Via Sri Lanka
S • E Asia & SE Asia • 250 kW
ITALY
†RAI INTERNATIONAL, Rome
E Africa • 100 kW
W • N America • 100 kW
Mideast • 100 kW
W • S Africa • 100 kW
ROMANIA
†RADIO ROMANIA INTL, Bucharest
W • C Africa & S Africa • 250 kW
S • Mideast • 250 kW
S • W Europe • 250 kW
Australasia • 250 kW
S • E Asia • 250 kW
W • E North Am • 250 kW
W Asia • 250 kW
S • W Asia • 250 kW
USA
†R FREE ASIA, Via Tinian, N Marianas
SE Asia • 500 kW
RFE-RL, Via Philippines
W • E Asia • 250 kW
†VOA, Via Iranawila, Sri Lanka
S Asia • 250 kW
VOA, Via Philippines
S • E Asia • 250 kW
†VOA, Via Tinian, N Marianas
W • E Asia • 500 kW
15255 CZECH REPUBLIC
RADIO PRAGUE, Litomyšl
W • W Europe • 100 kW
EGYPT
RADIO CAIRO, Abu Za'bal
S Africa • 100 kW
SWEDEN (con'd)
RADIO SWEDEN, Hörby
S • Australasia • 500 kW
ENGLISH ARABIC CHINESE FRENCH GERMAN RUSSIAN SPANISH OTHER

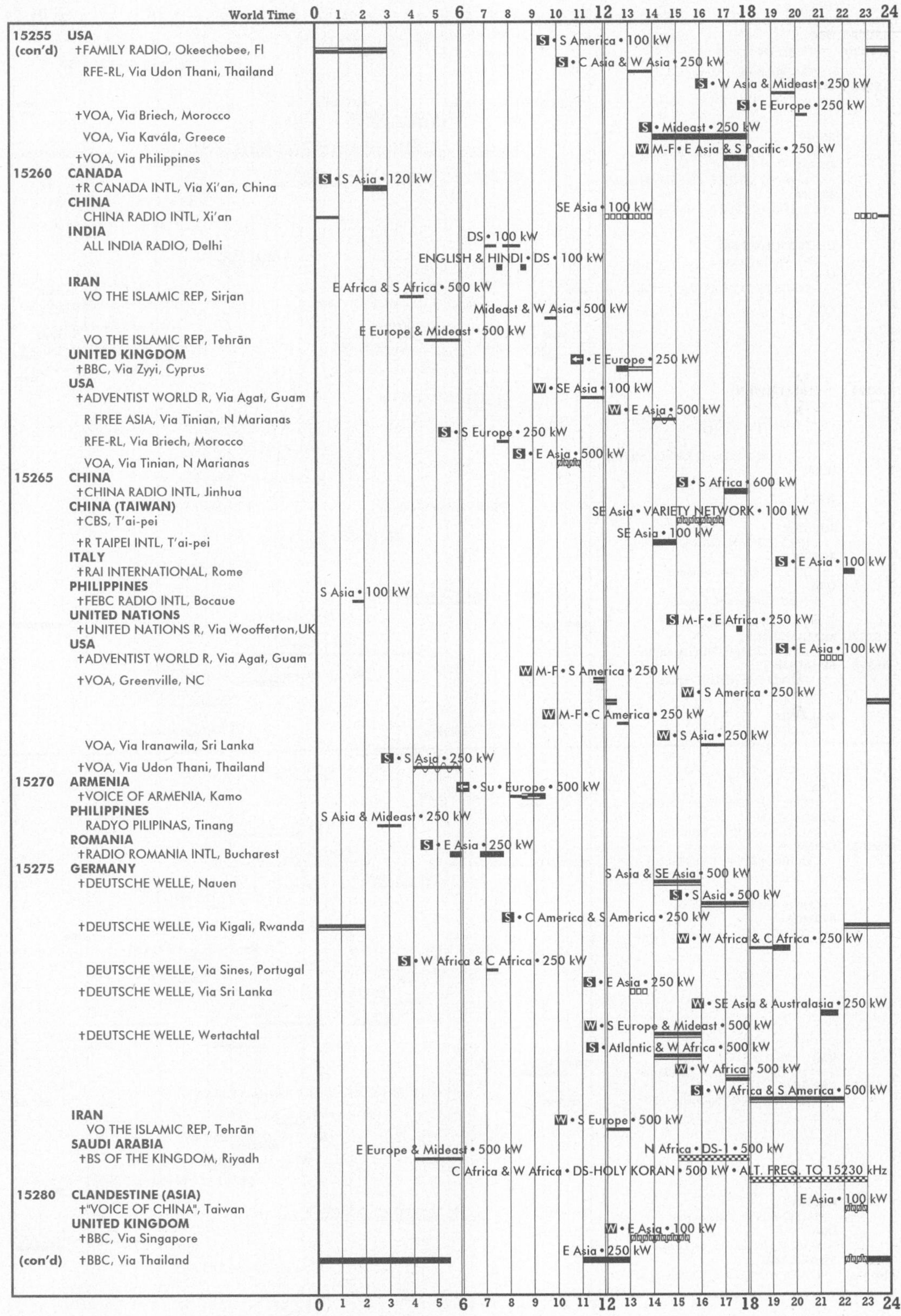
World Time 0 1 2 3 4 5 6 7 8 9 10 11 12 13 14 15 16 17 18 19 20 21 22 23 24
15255 USA
(con'd) †FAMILY RADIO, Okeechobee, Fl
S • S America • 100 kW
RFE-RL, Via Udon Thani, Thailand
S • C Asia & W Asia • 250 kW
S • W Asia & Mideast • 250 kW
†VOA, Via Briech, Morocco
S • E Europe • 250 kW
VOA, Via Kavála, Greece
S • Mideast • 250 kW
†VOA, Via Philippines
W M-F • E Asia & S Pacific • 250 kW
15260 CANADA
†R CANADA INTL, Via Xi'an, China
S • S Asia • 120 kW
CHINA
CHINA RADIO INTL, Xi'an
SE Asia • 100 kW
INDIA
ALL INDIA RADIO, Delhi
DS • 100 kW
ENGLISH & HINDI • DS • 100 kW
IRAN
VO THE ISLAMIC REP, Sirjan
E Africa & S Africa • 500 kW
Mideast & W Asia • 500 kW
VO THE ISLAMIC REP, Tehrān
E Europe & Mideast • 500 kW
UNITED KINGDOM
†BBC, Via Zyyi, Cyprus
• E Europe • 250 kW
USA
†ADVENTIST WORLD R, Via Agat, Guam
W • SE Asia • 100 kW
R FREE ASIA, Via Tinian, N Marianas
W • E Asia • 500 kW
RFE-RL, Via Briech, Morocco
S • S Europe • 250 kW
VOA, Via Tinian, N Marianas
S • E Asia • 500 kW
15265 CHINA
†CHINA RADIO INTL, Jinhua
S • S Africa • 600 kW
CHINA (TAIWAN)
†CBS, T'ai-pei
SE Asia • VARIETY NETWORK • 100 kW
†R TAIPEI INTL, T'ai-pei
SE Asia • 100 kW
ITALY
†RAI INTERNATIONAL, Rome
S • E Asia • 100 kW
PHILIPPINES
†FEBC RADIO INTL, Bocaue
S Asia • 100 kW
UNITED NATIONS
†UNITED NATIONS R, Via Woofferton,UK
S M-F • E Africa • 250 kW
USA
†ADVENTIST WORLD R, Via Agat, Guam
S • E Asia • 100 kW
†VOA, Greenville, NC
W M-F • S America • 250 kW
W • S America • 250 kW
W M-F • C America • 250 kW
W • S Asia • 250 kW
VOA, Via Iranawila, Sri Lanka
†VOA, Via Udon Thani, Thailand
S • S Asia • 250 kW
15270 ARMENIA
†VOICE OF ARMENIA, Kamo
• Su • Europe • 500 kW
PHILIPPINES
RADYO PILIPINAS, Tinang
S Asia & Mideast • 250 kW
ROMANIA
†RADIO ROMANIA INTL, Bucharest
S • E Asia • 250 kW
15275 GERMANY
†DEUTSCHE WELLE, Nauen
S Asia & SE Asia • 500 kW
S • S Asia • 500 kW
†DEUTSCHE WELLE, Via Kigali, Rwanda
S • C America & S America • 250 kW
W • W Africa & C Africa • 250 kW
DEUTSCHE WELLE, Via Sines, Portugal
S • W Africa & C Africa • 250 kW
†DEUTSCHE WELLE, Via Sri Lanka
S • E Asia • 250 kW
W • SE Asia & Australasia • 250 kW
†DEUTSCHE WELLE, Wertachtal
W • S Europe & Mideast • 500 kW
S • Atlantic & W Africa • 500 kW
W • W Africa • 500 kW
S • W Africa & S America • 500 kW
IRAN
VO THE ISLAMIC REP, Tehrān
W • S Europe • 500 kW
SAUDI ARABIA
†BS OF THE KINGDOM, Riyadh
E Europe & Mideast • 500 kW
N Africa • DS-1 • 500 kW
C Africa & W Africa • DS-HOLY KORAN • 500 kW • ALT. FREQ. TO 15230 kHz
15280 CLANDESTINE (ASIA)
†"VOICE OF CHINA", Taiwan
E Asia • 100 kW
UNITED KINGDOM
†BBC, Via Singapore
W • E Asia • 100 kW
(con'd) †BBC, Via Thailand
E Asia • 250 kW
0 1 2 3 4 5 6 7 8 9 10 11 12 13 14 15 16 17 18 19 20 21 22 23 24

SEASONAL S OR W 1-HR TIMESHIFT MIDYEAR ⇐ OR ⇒ JAMMING / OR ∧ EARLIEST HEARD ◁ LATEST HEARD ▷ NEW FOR 2002 †

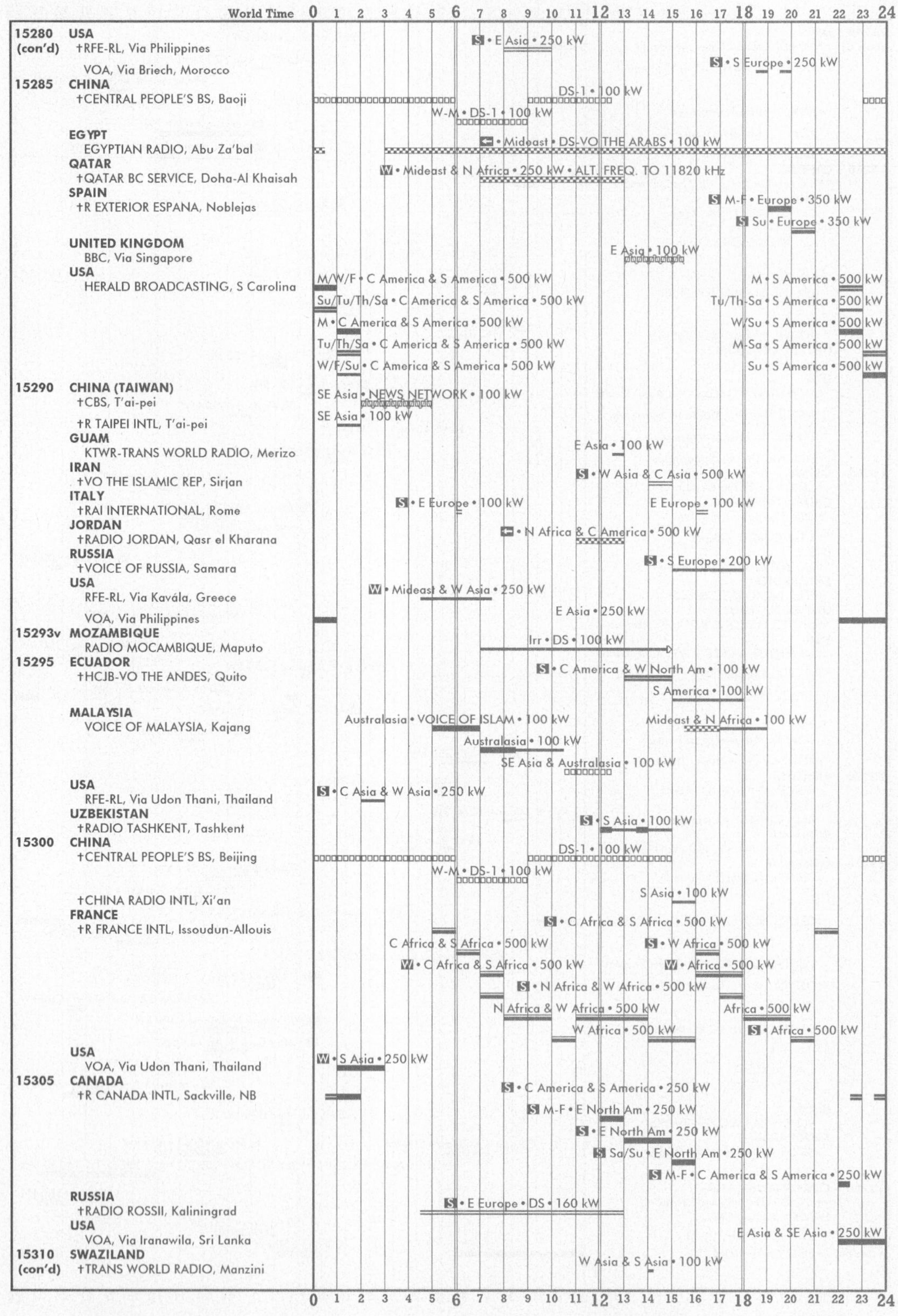
World Time 0 1 2 3 4 5 6 7 8 9 10 11 12 13 14 15 16 17 18 19 20 21 22 23 24
15280 (con'd) USA
†RFE-RL, Via Philippines
S • E Asia • 250 kW
VOA, Via Briech, Morocco
S • S Europe • 250 kW
15285 CHINA
†CENTRAL PEOPLE'S BS, Baoji
DS-1 • 100 kW
W-M • DS-1 • 100 kW
EGYPT
EGYPTIAN RADIO, Abu Za'bal
Mideast • DS-VO THE ARABS • 100 kW
QATAR
†QATAR BC SERVICE, Doha-Al Khaisah
W • Mideast & N Africa • 250 kW • ALT. FREQ. TO 11820 kHz
SPAIN
†R EXTERIOR ESPANA, Noblejas
S M-F • Europe • 350 kW
S Su • Europe • 350 kW
UNITED KINGDOM
BBC, Via Singapore
E Asia • 100 kW
USA
HERALD BROADCASTING, S Carolina
M/W/F • C America & S America • 500 kW
M • S America • 500 kW
Su/Tu/Th/Sa • C America & S America • 500 kW
Tu/Th-Sa • S America • 500 kW
M • C America & S America • 500 kW
W/Su • S America • 500 kW
Tu/Th/Sa • C America & S America • 500 kW
M-Sa • S America • 500 kW
W/F/Su • C America & S America • 500 kW
Su • S America • 500 kW
15290 CHINA (TAIWAN)
†CBS, T'ai-pei
SE Asia • NEWS NETWORK • 100 kW
†R TAIPEI INTL, T'ai-pei
SE Asia • 100 kW
GUAM
KTWR-TRANS WORLD RADIO, Merizo
E Asia • 100 kW
IRAN
†VO THE ISLAMIC REP, Sirjan
S • W Asia & C Asia • 500 kW
ITALY
†RAI INTERNATIONAL, Rome
S • E Europe • 100 kW
E Europe • 100 kW
JORDAN
†RADIO JORDAN, Qasr el Kharana
N Africa & C America • 500 kW
RUSSIA
†VOICE OF RUSSIA, Samara
S • S Europe • 200 kW
USA
RFE-RL, Via Kavála, Greece
W • Mideast & W Asia • 250 kW
VOA, Via Philippines
E Asia • 250 kW
15293v MOZAMBIQUE
RADIO MOCAMBIQUE, Maputo
Irr • DS • 100 kW
15295 ECUADOR
†HCJB-VO THE ANDES, Quito
S • C America & W North Am • 100 kW
S America • 100 kW
MALAYSIA
VOICE OF MALAYSIA, Kajang
Australasia • VOICE OF ISLAM • 100 kW
Mideast & N Africa • 100 kW
Australasia • 100 kW
SE Asia & Australasia • 100 kW
USA
RFE-RL, Via Udon Thani, Thailand
S • C Asia & W Asia • 250 kW
UZBEKISTAN
†RADIO TASHKENT, Tashkent
S • S Asia • 100 kW
15300 CHINA
†CENTRAL PEOPLE'S BS, Beijing
DS-1 • 100 kW
W-M • DS-1 • 100 kW
†CHINA RADIO INTL, Xi'an
S Asia • 100 kW
FRANCE
†R FRANCE INTL, Issoudun-Allouis
S • C Africa & S Africa • 500 kW
C Africa & S Africa • 500 kW
S • W Africa • 500 kW
W • C Africa & S Africa • 500 kW
W • Africa • 500 kW
S • N Africa & W Africa • 500 kW
N Africa & W Africa • 500 kW
Africa • 500 kW
W Africa • 500 kW
S • Africa • 500 kW
USA
VOA, Via Udon Thani, Thailand
W • S Asia • 250 kW
15305 CANADA
†R CANADA INTL, Sackville, NB
S • C America & S America • 250 kW
S M-F • E North Am • 250 kW
S • E North Am • 250 kW
S Sa/Su • E North Am • 250 kW
S M-F • C America & S America • 250 kW
RUSSIA
†RADIO ROSSII, Kaliningrad
S • E Europe • DS • 160 kW
USA
VOA, Via Iranawila, Sri Lanka
E Asia & SE Asia • 250 kW
15310 (con'd) SWAZILAND
†TRANS WORLD RADIO, Manzini
W Asia & S Asia • 100 kW
0 1 2 3 4 5 6 7 8 9 10 11 12 13 14 15 16 17 18 19 20 21 22 23 24

ENGLISH ARABIC CHINESE FRENCH GERMAN RUSSIAN SPANISH OTHER

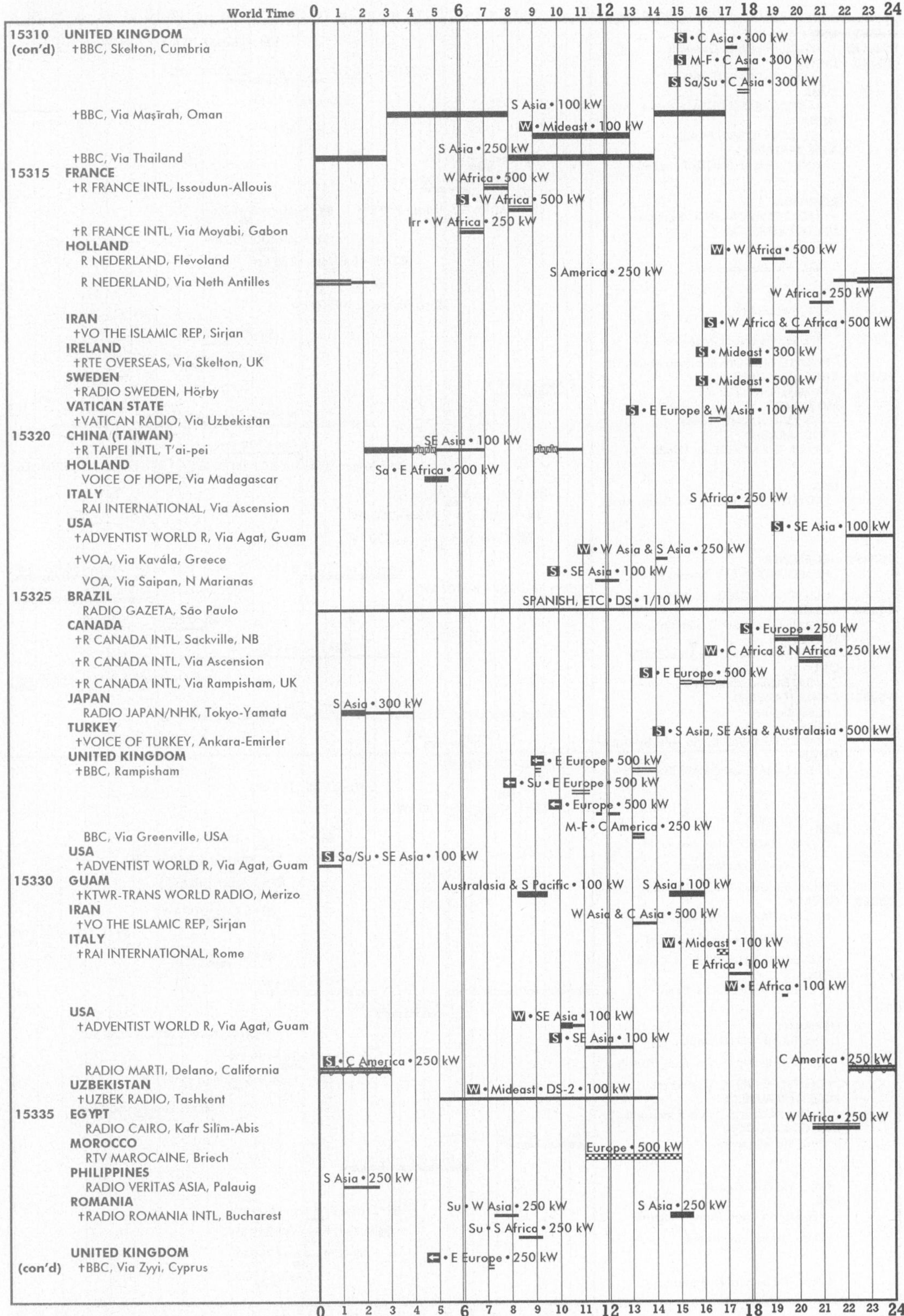
World Time 0 1 2 3 4 5 6 7 8 9 10 11 12 13 14 15 16 17 18 19 20 21 22 23 24
15310 UNITED KINGDOM
(con'd) †BBC, Skelton, Cumbria
S • C Asia • 300 kW
S M-F • C Asia • 300 kW
S Sa/Su • C Asia • 300 kW
†BBC, Via Maşīrah, Oman
S Asia • 100 kW
W • Mideast • 100 kW
†BBC, Via Thailand
S Asia • 250 kW
15315 FRANCE
†R FRANCE INTL, Issoudun-Allouis
W Africa • 500 kW
S • W Africa • 500 kW
†R FRANCE INTL, Via Moyabi, Gabon
Irr • W Africa • 250 kW
HOLLAND
R NEDERLAND, Flevoland
W • W Africa • 500 kW
R NEDERLAND, Via Neth Antilles
S America • 250 kW
W Africa • 250 kW
IRAN
†VO THE ISLAMIC REP, Sirjan
S • W Africa & C Africa • 500 kW
IRELAND
†RTE OVERSEAS, Via Skelton, UK
S • Mideast • 300 kW
SWEDEN
†RADIO SWEDEN, Hörby
S • Mideast • 500 kW
VATICAN STATE
†VATICAN RADIO, Via Uzbekistan
S • E Europe & W Asia • 100 kW
15320 CHINA (TAIWAN)
†R TAIPEI INTL, T'ai-pei
SE Asia • 100 kW
HOLLAND
VOICE OF HOPE, Via Madagascar
Sa • E Africa • 200 kW
ITALY
RAI INTERNATIONAL, Via Ascension
S Africa • 250 kW
USA
†ADVENTIST WORLD R, Via Agat, Guam
S • SE Asia • 100 kW
†VOA, Via Kavála, Greece
W • W Asia & S Asia • 250 kW
VOA, Via Saipan, N Marianas
S • SE Asia • 100 kW
15325 BRAZIL
RADIO GAZETA, São Paulo
SPANISH, ETC • DS • 1/10 kW
CANADA
†R CANADA INTL, Sackville, NB
S • Europe • 250 kW
†R CANADA INTL, Via Ascension
W • C Africa & N Africa • 250 kW
†R CANADA INTL, Via Rampisham, UK
S • E Europe • 500 kW
JAPAN
RADIO JAPAN/NHK, Tokyo-Yamata
S Asia • 300 kW
TURKEY
†VOICE OF TURKEY, Ankara-Emirler
S • S Asia, SE Asia & Australasia • 500 kW
UNITED KINGDOM
†BBC, Rampisham
• E Europe • 500 kW
• Su • E Europe • 500 kW
• Europe • 500 kW
BBC, Via Greenville, USA
M-F • C America • 250 kW
USA
†ADVENTIST WORLD R, Via Agat, Guam
S Sa/Su • SE Asia • 100 kW
15330 GUAM
†KTWR-TRANS WORLD RADIO, Merizo
Australasia & S Pacific • 100 kW
S Asia • 100 kW
IRAN
†VO THE ISLAMIC REP, Sirjan
W Asia & C Asia • 500 kW
ITALY
†RAI INTERNATIONAL, Rome
W • Mideast • 100 kW
E Africa • 100 kW
W • E Africa • 100 kW
USA
†ADVENTIST WORLD R, Via Agat, Guam
W • SE Asia • 100 kW
S • SE Asia • 100 kW
RADIO MARTI, Delano, California
S • C America • 250 kW
C America • 250 kW
UZBEKISTAN
†UZBEK RADIO, Tashkent
W • Mideast • DS-2 • 100 kW
15335 EGYPT
RADIO CAIRO, Kafr Silîm-Abis
W Africa • 250 kW
MOROCCO
RTV MAROCAINE, Briech
Europe • 500 kW
PHILIPPINES
RADIO VERITAS ASIA, Palauig
S Asia • 250 kW
ROMANIA
†RADIO ROMANIA INTL, Bucharest
Su • W Asia • 250 kW
S Asia • 250 kW
Su • S Africa • 250 kW
UNITED KINGDOM
(con'd) †BBC, Via Zyyi, Cyprus
• E Europe • 250 kW
0 1 2 3 4 5 6 7 8 9 10 11 12 13 14 15 16 17 18 19 20 21 22 23 24

SEASONAL S OR W 1-HR TIMESHIFT MIDYEAR OR JAMMING / OR /\ EARLIEST HEARD ◁ LATEST HEARD ▷ NEW FOR 2002 †

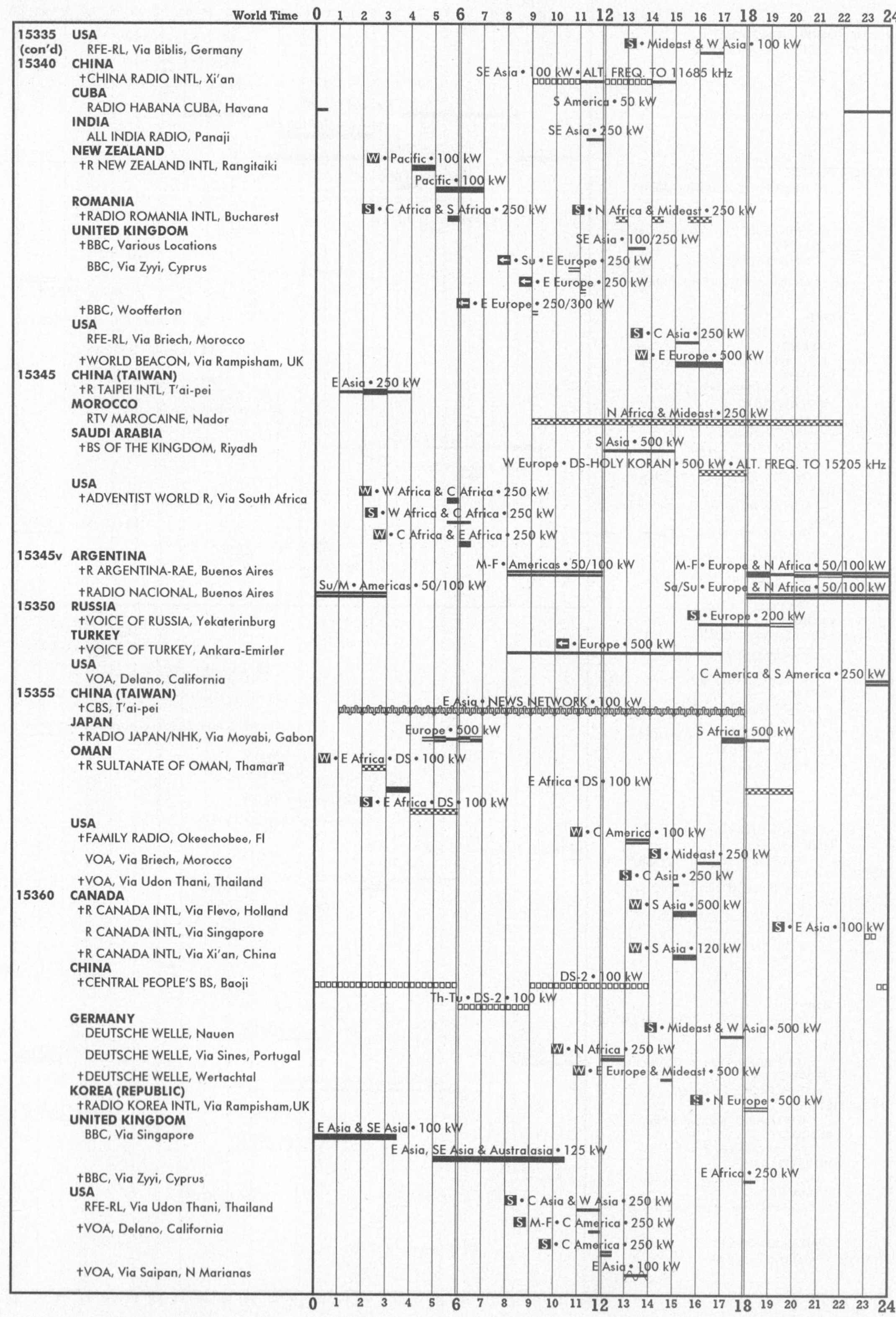
World Time 0 1 2 3 4 5 6 7 8 9 10 11 12 13 14 15 16 17 18 19 20 21 22 23 24
15335 (con'd) USA
RFE-RL, Via Biblis, Germany
S • Mideast & W Asia • 100 kW
15340 CHINA
†CHINA RADIO INTL, Xi'an
SE Asia • 100 kW • ALT. FREQ. TO 11685 kHz
CUBA
RADIO HABANA CUBA, Havana
S America • 50 kW
INDIA
ALL INDIA RADIO, Panaji
SE Asia • 250 kW
NEW ZEALAND
†R NEW ZEALAND INTL, Rangitaiki
W • Pacific • 100 kW
Pacific • 100 kW
ROMANIA
†RADIO ROMANIA INTL, Bucharest
S • C Africa & S Africa • 250 kW
S • N Africa & Mideast • 250 kW
UNITED KINGDOM
†BBC, Various Locations
SE Asia • 100/250 kW
BBC, Via Zyyi, Cyprus
Su • E Europe • 250 kW
E Europe • 250 kW
†BBC, Woofferton
E Europe • 250/300 kW
USA
RFE-RL, Via Briech, Morocco
S • C Asia • 250 kW
†WORLD BEACON, Via Rampisham, UK
W • E Europe • 500 kW
15345 CHINA (TAIWAN)
†R TAIPEI INTL, T'ai-pei
E Asia • 250 kW
MOROCCO
RTV MAROCAINE, Nador
N Africa & Mideast • 250 kW
SAUDI ARABIA
†BS OF THE KINGDOM, Riyadh
S Asia • 500 kW
W Europe • DS-HOLY KORAN • 500 kW • ALT. FREQ. TO 15205 kHz
USA
†ADVENTIST WORLD R, Via South Africa
W • W Africa & C Africa • 250 kW
S • W Africa & C Africa • 250 kW
W • C Africa & E Africa • 250 kW
15345v ARGENTINA
†R ARGENTINA-RAE, Buenos Aires
M-F • Americas • 50/100 kW
M-F • Europe & N Africa • 50/100 kW
†RADIO NACIONAL, Buenos Aires
Su/M • Americas • 50/100 kW
Sa/Su • Europe & N Africa • 50/100 kW
15350 RUSSIA
†VOICE OF RUSSIA, Yekaterinburg
S • Europe • 200 kW
TURKEY
†VOICE OF TURKEY, Ankara-Emirler
Europe • 500 kW
USA
VOA, Delano, California
C America & S America • 250 kW
15355 CHINA (TAIWAN)
†CBS, T'ai-pei
E Asia • NEWS NETWORK • 100 kW
JAPAN
†RADIO JAPAN/NHK, Via Moyabi, Gabon
Europe • 500 kW
S Africa • 500 kW
OMAN
†R SULTANATE OF OMAN, Thamarīt
W • E Africa • DS • 100 kW
E Africa • DS • 100 kW
S • E Africa • DS • 100 kW
USA
†FAMILY RADIO, Okeechobee, Fl
W • C America • 100 kW
VOA, Via Briech, Morocco
S • Mideast • 250 kW
†VOA, Via Udon Thani, Thailand
S • C Asia • 250 kW
15360 CANADA
†R CANADA INTL, Via Flevo, Holland
W • S Asia • 500 kW
R CANADA INTL, Via Singapore
S • E Asia • 100 kW
†R CANADA INTL, Via Xi'an, China
W • S Asia • 120 kW
CHINA
†CENTRAL PEOPLE'S BS, Baoji
DS-2 • 100 kW
Th-Tu • DS-2 • 100 kW
GERMANY
DEUTSCHE WELLE, Nauen
S • Mideast & W Asia • 500 kW
DEUTSCHE WELLE, Via Sines, Portugal
W • N Africa • 250 kW
†DEUTSCHE WELLE, Wertachtal
W • E Europe & Mideast • 500 kW
KOREA (REPUBLIC)
†RADIO KOREA INTL, Via Rampisham,UK
S • N Europe • 500 kW
UNITED KINGDOM
BBC, Via Singapore
E Asia & SE Asia • 100 kW
E Asia, SE Asia & Australasia • 125 kW
†BBC, Via Zyyi, Cyprus
E Africa • 250 kW
USA
RFE-RL, Via Udon Thani, Thailand
S • C Asia & W Asia • 250 kW
†VOA, Delano, California
S M-F • C America • 250 kW
S • C America • 250 kW
†VOA, Via Saipan, N Marianas
E Asia • 100 kW
0 1 2 3 4 5 6 7 8 9 10 11 12 13 14 15 16 17 18 19 20 21 22 23 24

ENGLISH ARABIC CHINESE FRENCH GERMAN RUSSIAN SPANISH OTHER

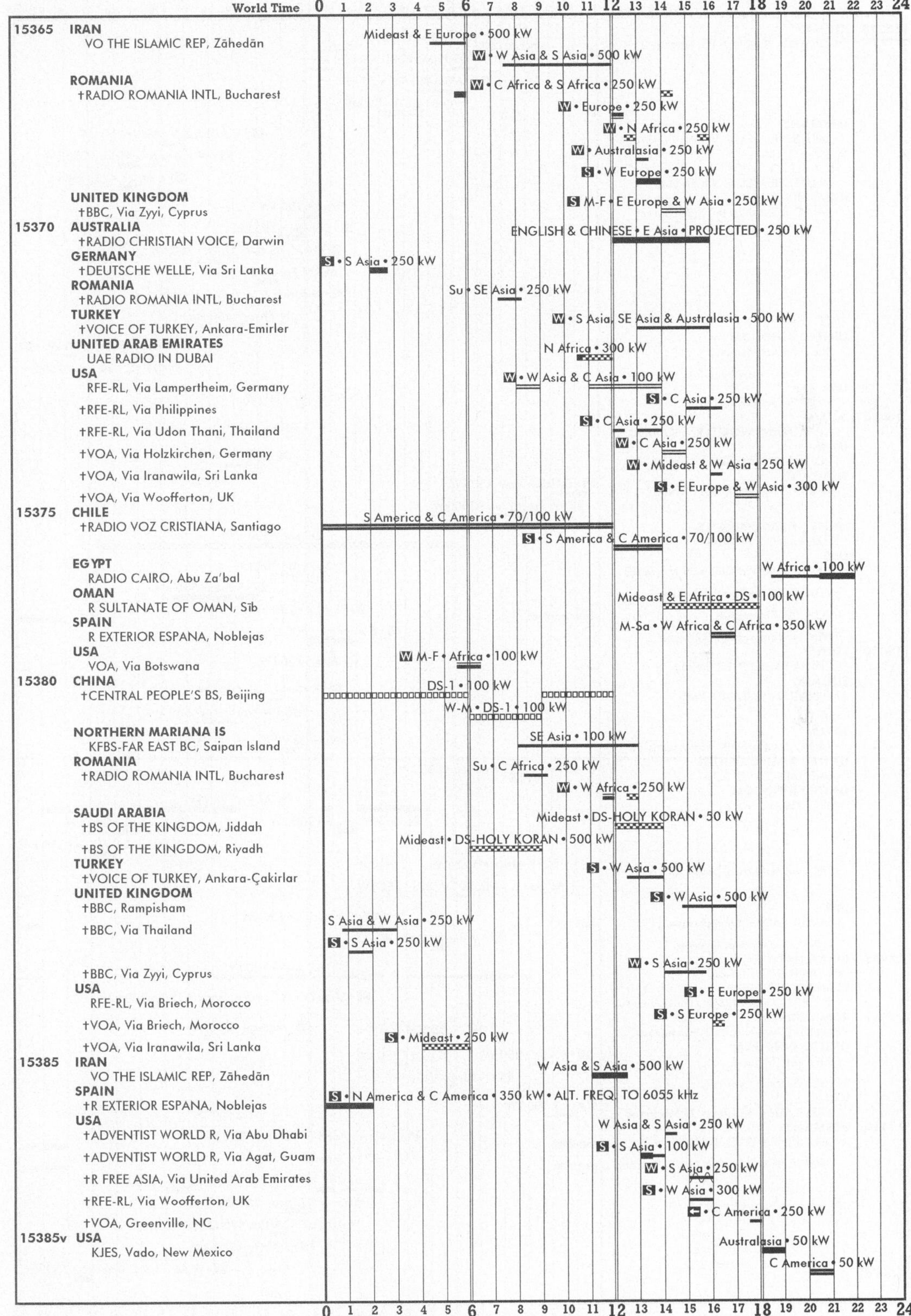
World Time 0 1 2 3 4 5 6 7 8 9 10 11 12 13 14 15 16 17 18 19 20 21 22 23 24
15365 IRAN
VO THE ISLAMIC REP, Zāhedān
Mideast & E Europe • 500 kW
W • W Asia & S Asia • 500 kW
ROMANIA
†RADIO ROMANIA INTL, Bucharest
W • C Africa & S Africa • 250 kW
W • Europe • 250 kW
W • N Africa • 250 kW
W • Australasia • 250 kW
S • W Europe • 250 kW
UNITED KINGDOM
†BBC, Via Zyyi, Cyprus
S M-F • E Europe & W Asia • 250 kW
15370 AUSTRALIA
†RADIO CHRISTIAN VOICE, Darwin
ENGLISH & CHINESE • E Asia • PROJECTED • 250 kW
GERMANY
†DEUTSCHE WELLE, Via Sri Lanka
S • S Asia • 250 kW
ROMANIA
†RADIO ROMANIA INTL, Bucharest
Su • SE Asia • 250 kW
TURKEY
†VOICE OF TURKEY, Ankara-Emirler
W • S Asia, SE Asia & Australasia • 500 kW
UNITED ARAB EMIRATES
UAE RADIO IN DUBAI
N Africa • 300 kW
USA
RFE-RL, Via Lampertheim, Germany
W • W Asia & C Asia • 100 kW
†RFE-RL, Via Philippines
S • C Asia • 250 kW
†RFE-RL, Via Udon Thani, Thailand
S • C Asia • 250 kW
†VOA, Via Holzkirchen, Germany
W • C Asia • 250 kW
†VOA, Via Iranawila, Sri Lanka
W • Mideast & W Asia • 250 kW
†VOA, Via Woofferton, UK
S • E Europe & W Asia • 300 kW
15375 CHILE
†RADIO VOZ CRISTIANA, Santiago
S America & C America • 70/100 kW
S • S America & C America • 70/100 kW
EGYPT
RADIO CAIRO, Abu Za'bal
W Africa • 100 kW
OMAN
R SULTANATE OF OMAN, Sīb
Mideast & E Africa • DS • 100 kW
SPAIN
R EXTERIOR ESPANA, Noblejas
M-Sa • W Africa & C Africa • 350 kW
USA
VOA, Via Botswana
W M-F • Africa • 100 kW
15380 CHINA
†CENTRAL PEOPLE'S BS, Beijing
DS-1 • 100 kW
W-M • DS-1 • 100 kW
NORTHERN MARIANA IS
KFBS-FAR EAST BC, Saipan Island
SE Asia • 100 kW
ROMANIA
†RADIO ROMANIA INTL, Bucharest
Su • C Africa • 250 kW
W • W Africa • 250 kW
SAUDI ARABIA
†BS OF THE KINGDOM, Jiddah
Mideast • DS-HOLY KORAN • 50 kW
†BS OF THE KINGDOM, Riyadh
Mideast • DS-HOLY KORAN • 500 kW
TURKEY
†VOICE OF TURKEY, Ankara-Çakirlar
S • W Asia • 500 kW
UNITED KINGDOM
†BBC, Rampisham
S • W Asia • 500 kW
†BBC, Via Thailand
S Asia & W Asia • 250 kW
S • S Asia • 250 kW
†BBC, Via Zyyi, Cyprus
W • S Asia • 250 kW
USA
RFE-RL, Via Briech, Morocco
S • E Europe • 250 kW
†VOA, Via Briech, Morocco
S • S Europe • 250 kW
†VOA, Via Iranawila, Sri Lanka
S • Mideast • 250 kW
15385 IRAN
VO THE ISLAMIC REP, Zāhedān
W Asia & S Asia • 500 kW
SPAIN
†R EXTERIOR ESPANA, Noblejas
S • N America & C America • 350 kW • ALT. FREQ. TO 6055 kHz
USA
†ADVENTIST WORLD R, Via Abu Dhabi
W Asia & S Asia • 250 kW
†ADVENTIST WORLD R, Via Agat, Guam
S • S Asia • 100 kW
†R FREE ASIA, Via United Arab Emirates
W • S Asia • 250 kW
†RFE-RL, Via Woofferton, UK
S • W Asia • 300 kW
†VOA, Greenville, NC
C America • 250 kW
15385v USA
KJES, Vado, New Mexico
Australasia • 50 kW
C America • 50 kW
0 1 2 3 4 5 6 7 8 9 10 11 12 13 14 15 16 17 18 19 20 21 22 23 24

SEASONAL S OR W 1-HR TIMESHIFT MIDYEAR ⇐ OR ⇒ JAMMING / OR ⋀ EARLIEST HEARD ◁ LATEST HEARD ▷ NEW FOR 2002 †

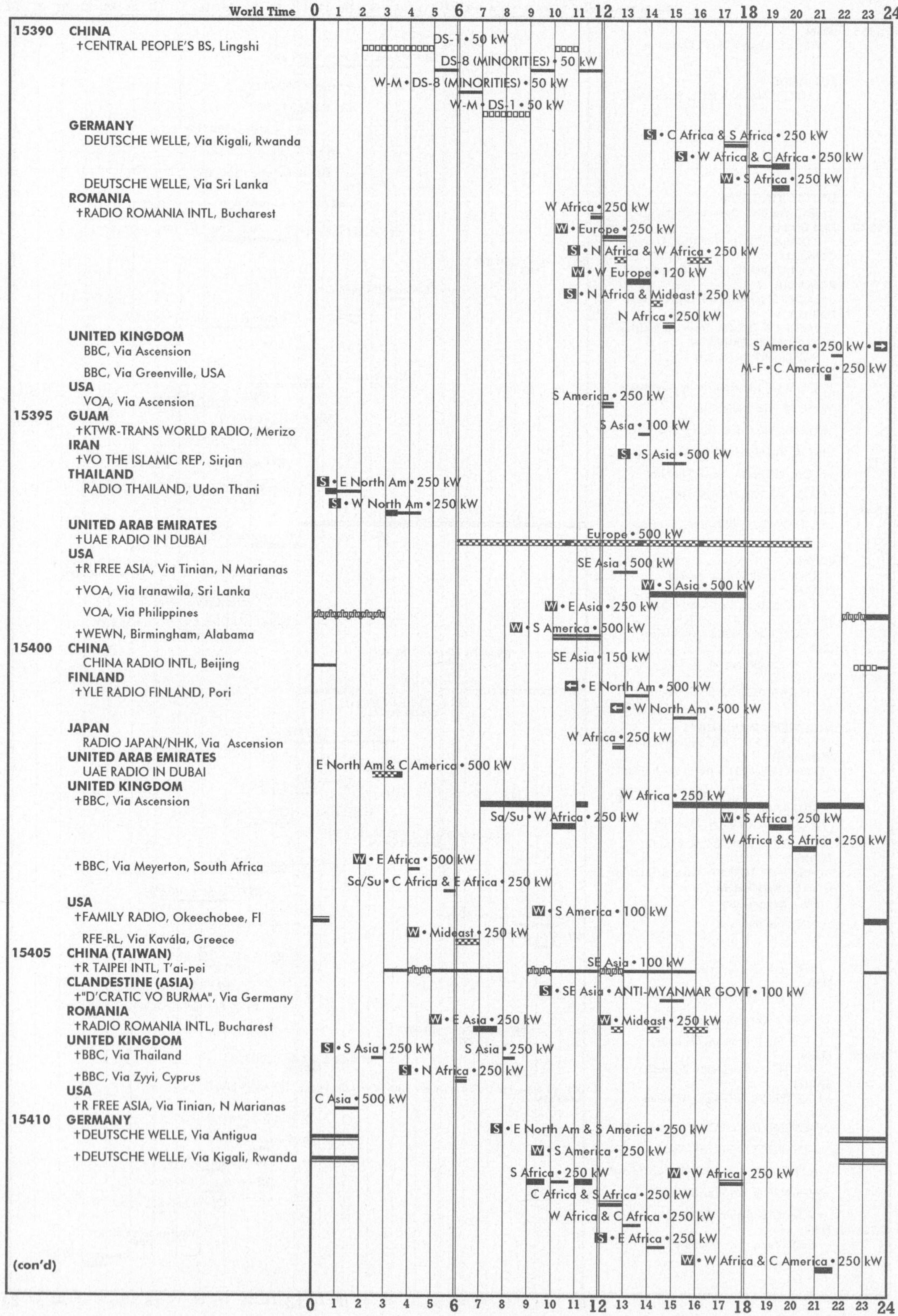
World Time 0 1 2 3 4 5 6 7 8 9 10 11 12 13 14 15 16 17 18 19 20 21 22 23 24
15390 CHINA
†CENTRAL PEOPLE'S BS, Lingshi
DS-1 • 50 kW
DS-8 (MINORITIES) • 50 kW
W-M • DS-8 (MINORITIES) • 50 kW
W-M • DS-1 • 50 kW
GERMANY
DEUTSCHE WELLE, Via Kigali, Rwanda
S • C Africa & S Africa • 250 kW
S • W Africa & C Africa • 250 kW
DEUTSCHE WELLE, Via Sri Lanka
W • S Africa • 250 kW
ROMANIA
†RADIO ROMANIA INTL, Bucharest
W Africa • 250 kW
W • Europe • 250 kW
S • N Africa & W Africa • 250 kW
W • W Europe • 120 kW
S • N Africa & Mideast • 250 kW
N Africa • 250 kW
UNITED KINGDOM
BBC, Via Ascension
S America • 250 kW •
BBC, Via Greenville, USA
M-F • C America • 250 kW
USA
VOA, Via Ascension
S America • 250 kW
15395 GUAM
†KTWR-TRANS WORLD RADIO, Merizo
S Asia • 100 kW
IRAN
†VO THE ISLAMIC REP, Sirjan
S • S Asia • 500 kW
THAILAND
RADIO THAILAND, Udon Thani
S • E North Am • 250 kW
S • W North Am • 250 kW
UNITED ARAB EMIRATES
†UAE RADIO IN DUBAI
Europe • 500 kW
USA
†R FREE ASIA, Via Tinian, N Marianas
SE Asia • 500 kW
†VOA, Via Iranawila, Sri Lanka
W • S Asia • 500 kW
VOA, Via Philippines
W • E Asia • 250 kW
†WEWN, Birmingham, Alabama
W • S America • 500 kW
15400 CHINA
CHINA RADIO INTL, Beijing
SE Asia • 150 kW
FINLAND
†YLE RADIO FINLAND, Pori
• E North Am • 500 kW
• W North Am • 500 kW
JAPAN
RADIO JAPAN/NHK, Via Ascension
W Africa • 250 kW
UNITED ARAB EMIRATES
UAE RADIO IN DUBAI
E North Am & C America • 500 kW
UNITED KINGDOM
†BBC, Via Ascension
W Africa • 250 kW
Sa/Su • W Africa • 250 kW
W • S Africa • 250 kW
W Africa & S Africa • 250 kW
†BBC, Via Meyerton, South Africa
W • E Africa • 500 kW
Sa/Su • C Africa & E Africa • 250 kW
USA
†FAMILY RADIO, Okeechobee, Fl
W • S America • 100 kW
RFE-RL, Via Kavála, Greece
W • Mideast • 250 kW
15405 CHINA (TAIWAN)
†R TAIPEI INTL, T'ai-pei
SE Asia • 100 kW
CLANDESTINE (ASIA)
†"D'CRATIC VO BURMA", Via Germany
S • SE Asia • ANTI-MYANMAR GOVT • 100 kW
ROMANIA
†RADIO ROMANIA INTL, Bucharest
W • E Asia • 250 kW
W • Mideast • 250 kW
UNITED KINGDOM
†BBC, Via Thailand
S • S Asia • 250 kW
S Asia • 250 kW
†BBC, Via Zyyi, Cyprus
S • N Africa • 250 kW
USA
†R FREE ASIA, Via Tinian, N Marianas
C Asia • 500 kW
15410 GERMANY
†DEUTSCHE WELLE, Via Antigua
S • E North Am & S America • 250 kW
W • S America • 250 kW
†DEUTSCHE WELLE, Via Kigali, Rwanda
S Africa • 250 kW
W • W Africa • 250 kW
C Africa & S Africa • 250 kW
W Africa & C Africa • 250 kW
S • E Africa • 250 kW
W • W Africa & C America • 250 kW
(con'd)
0 1 2 3 4 5 6 7 8 9 10 11 12 13 14 15 16 17 18 19 20 21 22 23 24
ENGLISH ARABIC CHINESE FRENCH GERMAN RUSSIAN SPANISH OTHER

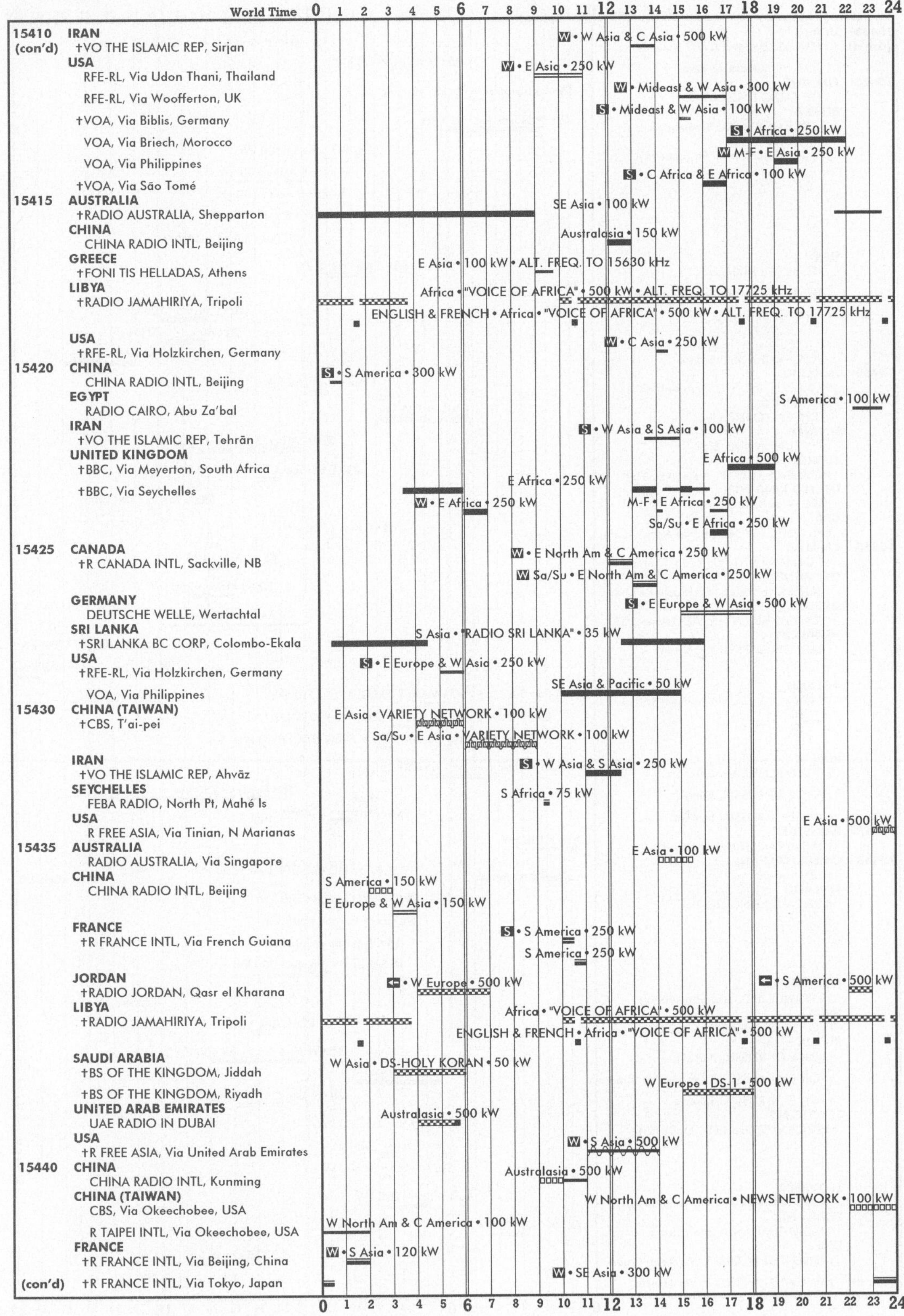
World Time 0 1 2 3 4 5 6 7 8 9 10 11 12 13 14 15 16 17 18 19 20 21 22 23 24
15410 (con'd) IRAN
†VO THE ISLAMIC REP, Sirjan
W • W Asia & C Asia • 500 kW
USA
RFE-RL, Via Udon Thani, Thailand
W • E Asia • 250 kW
RFE-RL, Via Woofferton, UK
W • Mideast & W Asia • 300 kW
†VOA, Via Biblis, Germany
S • Mideast & W Asia • 100 kW
VOA, Via Briech, Morocco
S • Africa • 250 kW
VOA, Via Philippines
W M-F • E Asia • 250 kW
†VOA, Via São Tomé
S • C Africa & E Africa • 100 kW
15415 AUSTRALIA
†RADIO AUSTRALIA, Shepparton
SE Asia • 100 kW
CHINA
CHINA RADIO INTL, Beijing
Australasia • 150 kW
GREECE
†FONI TIS HELLADAS, Athens
E Asia • 100 kW • ALT. FREQ. TO 15630 kHz
LIBYA
†RADIO JAMAHIRIYA, Tripoli
Africa • "VOICE OF AFRICA" • 500 kW • ALT. FREQ. TO 17725 kHz
ENGLISH & FRENCH • Africa • "VOICE OF AFRICA" • 500 kW • ALT. FREQ. TO 17725 kHz
USA
†RFE-RL, Via Holzkirchen, Germany
W • C Asia • 250 kW
15420 CHINA
CHINA RADIO INTL, Beijing
S • S America • 300 kW
EGYPT
RADIO CAIRO, Abu Za'bal
S America • 100 kW
IRAN
†VO THE ISLAMIC REP, Tehrān
S • W Asia & S Asia • 100 kW
UNITED KINGDOM
†BBC, Via Meyerton, South Africa
E Africa • 500 kW
†BBC, Via Seychelles
E Africa • 250 kW
W • E Africa • 250 kW
M-F • E Africa • 250 kW
Sa/Su • E Africa • 250 kW
15425 CANADA
†R CANADA INTL, Sackville, NB
W • E North Am & C America • 250 kW
W Sa/Su • E North Am & C America • 250 kW
GERMANY
DEUTSCHE WELLE, Wertachtal
S • E Europe & W Asia • 500 kW
SRI LANKA
†SRI LANKA BC CORP, Colombo-Ekala
S Asia • "RADIO SRI LANKA" • 35 kW
USA
†RFE-RL, Via Holzkirchen, Germany
S • E Europe & W Asia • 250 kW
VOA, Via Philippines
SE Asia & Pacific • 50 kW
15430 CHINA (TAIWAN)
†CBS, T'ai-pei
E Asia • VARIETY NETWORK • 100 kW
Sa/Su • E Asia • VARIETY NETWORK • 100 kW
IRAN
†VO THE ISLAMIC REP, Ahvāz
S • W Asia & S Asia • 250 kW
SEYCHELLES
FEBA RADIO, North Pt, Mahé Is
S Africa • 75 kW
USA
R FREE ASIA, Via Tinian, N Marianas
E Asia • 500 kW
15435 AUSTRALIA
RADIO AUSTRALIA, Via Singapore
E Asia • 100 kW
CHINA
CHINA RADIO INTL, Beijing
S America • 150 kW
E Europe & W Asia • 150 kW
FRANCE
†R FRANCE INTL, Via French Guiana
S • S America • 250 kW
S America • 250 kW
JORDAN
†RADIO JORDAN, Qasr el Kharana
W Europe • 500 kW
S America • 500 kW
LIBYA
†RADIO JAMAHIRIYA, Tripoli
Africa • "VOICE OF AFRICA" • 500 kW
ENGLISH & FRENCH • Africa • "VOICE OF AFRICA" • 500 kW
SAUDI ARABIA
†BS OF THE KINGDOM, Jiddah
W Asia • DS-HOLY KORAN • 50 kW
†BS OF THE KINGDOM, Riyadh
W Europe • DS-1 • 500 kW
UNITED ARAB EMIRATES
UAE RADIO IN DUBAI
Australasia • 500 kW
USA
†R FREE ASIA, Via United Arab Emirates
W • S Asia • 500 kW
15440 CHINA
CHINA RADIO INTL, Kunming
Australasia • 500 kW
CHINA (TAIWAN)
CBS, Via Okeechobee, USA
W North Am & C America • NEWS NETWORK • 100 kW
R TAIPEI INTL, Via Okeechobee, USA
W North Am & C America • 100 kW
FRANCE
†R FRANCE INTL, Via Beijing, China
W • S Asia • 120 kW
(con'd) †R FRANCE INTL, Via Tokyo, Japan
W • SE Asia • 300 kW
0 1 2 3 4 5 6 7 8 9 10 11 12 13 14 15 16 17 18 19 20 21 22 23 24

SEASONAL S OR W 1-HR TIMESHIFT MIDYEAR ◄ OR ► JAMMING / OR ∧ EARLIEST HEARD ◃ LATEST HEARD ▹ NEW FOR 2002 †

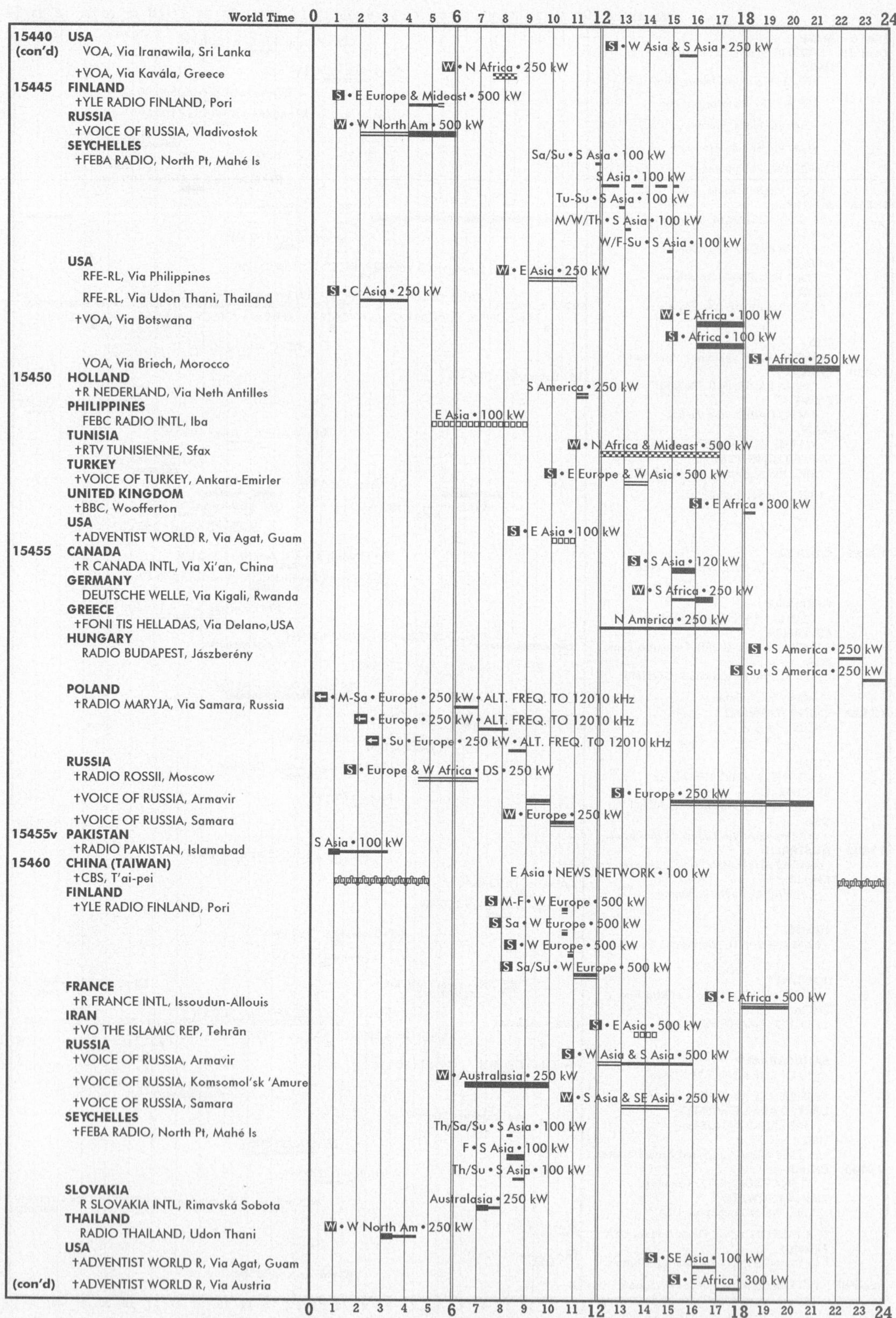
World Time 0 1 2 3 4 5 6 7 8 9 10 11 12 13 14 15 16 17 18 19 20 21 22 23 24
15440 (con'd) USA
VOA, Via Iranawila, Sri Lanka
S • W Asia & S Asia • 250 kW
†VOA, Via Kavála, Greece
W • N Africa • 250 kW
15445 FINLAND
†YLE RADIO FINLAND, Pori
S • E Europe & Mideast • 500 kW
RUSSIA
†VOICE OF RUSSIA, Vladivostok
W • W North Am • 500 kW
SEYCHELLES
†FEBA RADIO, North Pt, Mahé Is
Sa/Su • S Asia • 100 kW
S Asia • 100 kW
Tu-Su • S Asia • 100 kW
M/W/Th • S Asia • 100 kW
W/F-Su • S Asia • 100 kW
USA
RFE-RL, Via Philippines
W • E Asia • 250 kW
RFE-RL, Via Udon Thani, Thailand
S • C Asia • 250 kW
†VOA, Via Botswana
W • E Africa • 100 kW
S • Africa • 100 kW
VOA, Via Briech, Morocco
S • Africa • 250 kW
15450 HOLLAND
†R NEDERLAND, Via Neth Antilles
S America • 250 kW
PHILIPPINES
FEBC RADIO INTL, Iba
E Asia • 100 kW
TUNISIA
†RTV TUNISIENNE, Sfax
W • N Africa & Mideast • 500 kW
TURKEY
†VOICE OF TURKEY, Ankara-Emirler
S • E Europe & W Asia • 500 kW
UNITED KINGDOM
†BBC, Woofferton
S • E Africa • 300 kW
USA
†ADVENTIST WORLD R, Via Agat, Guam
S • E Asia • 100 kW
15455 CANADA
†R CANADA INTL, Via Xi'an, China
S • S Asia • 120 kW
GERMANY
DEUTSCHE WELLE, Via Kigali, Rwanda
W • S Africa • 250 kW
GREECE
†FONI TIS HELLADAS, Via Delano,USA
N America • 250 kW
HUNGARY
RADIO BUDAPEST, Jászberény
S • S America • 250 kW
S Su • S America • 250 kW
POLAND
†RADIO MARYJA, Via Samara, Russia
M-Sa • Europe • 250 kW • ALT. FREQ. TO 12010 kHz
Europe • 250 kW • ALT. FREQ. TO 12010 kHz
Su • Europe • 250 kW • ALT. FREQ. TO 12010 kHz
RUSSIA
†RADIO ROSSII, Moscow
S • Europe & W Africa • DS • 250 kW
†VOICE OF RUSSIA, Armavir
S • Europe • 250 kW
†VOICE OF RUSSIA, Samara
W • Europe • 250 kW
15455v PAKISTAN
†RADIO PAKISTAN, Islamabad
S Asia • 100 kW
15460 CHINA (TAIWAN)
†CBS, T'ai-pei
E Asia • NEWS NETWORK • 100 kW
FINLAND
†YLE RADIO FINLAND, Pori
S M-F • W Europe • 500 kW
S Sa • W Europe • 500 kW
S • W Europe • 500 kW
S Sa/Su • W Europe • 500 kW
FRANCE
†R FRANCE INTL, Issoudun-Allouis
S • E Africa • 500 kW
IRAN
†VO THE ISLAMIC REP, Tehrān
S • E Asia • 500 kW
RUSSIA
†VOICE OF RUSSIA, Armavir
S • W Asia & S Asia • 500 kW
†VOICE OF RUSSIA, Komsomol'sk 'Amure
W • Australasia • 250 kW
†VOICE OF RUSSIA, Samara
W • S Asia & SE Asia • 250 kW
SEYCHELLES
†FEBA RADIO, North Pt, Mahé Is
Th/Sa/Su • S Asia • 100 kW
F • S Asia • 100 kW
Th/Su • S Asia • 100 kW
SLOVAKIA
R SLOVAKIA INTL, Rimavská Sobota
Australasia • 250 kW
THAILAND
RADIO THAILAND, Udon Thani
W • W North Am • 250 kW
USA
†ADVENTIST WORLD R, Via Agat, Guam
S • SE Asia • 100 kW
(con'd) †ADVENTIST WORLD R, Via Austria
S • E Africa • 300 kW
0 1 2 3 4 5 6 7 8 9 10 11 12 13 14 15 16 17 18 19 20 21 22 23 24
ENGLISH ARABIC CHINESE FRENCH GERMAN RUSSIAN SPANISH OTHER

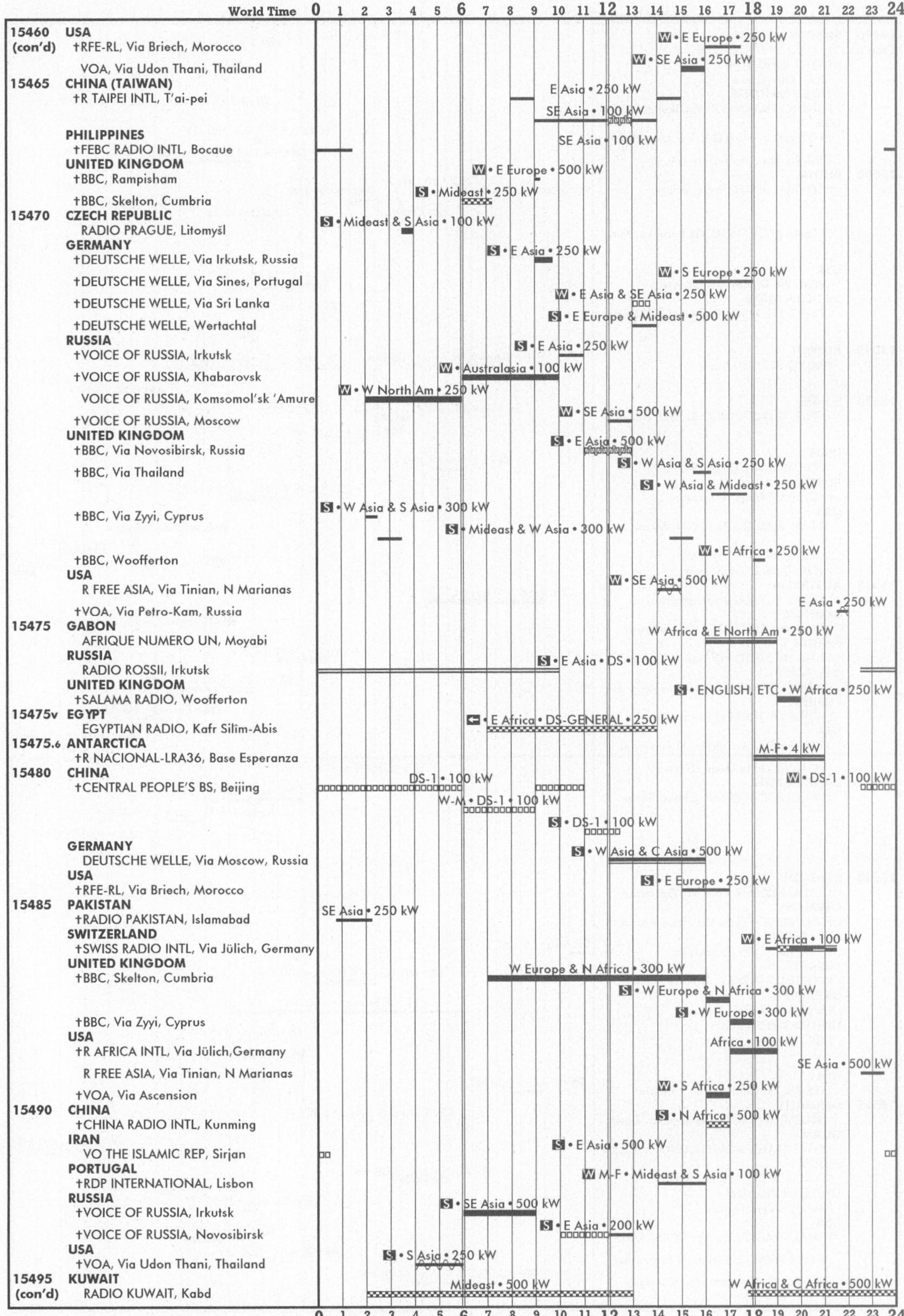
World Time 0 1 2 3 4 5 6 7 8 9 10 11 12 13 14 15 16 17 18 19 20 21 22 23 24
15460 (con'd) USA
†RFE-RL, Via Briech, Morocco
W • E Europe • 250 kW
VOA, Via Udon Thani, Thailand
W • SE Asia • 250 kW
15465 CHINA (TAIWAN)
†R TAIPEI INTL, T'ai-pei
E Asia • 250 kW
SE Asia • 100 kW
PHILIPPINES
†FEBC RADIO INTL, Bocaue
SE Asia • 100 kW
UNITED KINGDOM
†BBC, Rampisham
W • E Europe • 500 kW
†BBC, Skelton, Cumbria
S • Mideast • 250 kW
15470 CZECH REPUBLIC
RADIO PRAGUE, Litomyšl
S • Mideast & S Asia • 100 kW
GERMANY
†DEUTSCHE WELLE, Via Irkutsk, Russia
S • E Asia • 250 kW
†DEUTSCHE WELLE, Via Sines, Portugal
W • S Europe • 250 kW
†DEUTSCHE WELLE, Via Sri Lanka
W • E Asia & SE Asia • 250 kW
†DEUTSCHE WELLE, Wertachtal
S • E Europe & Mideast • 500 kW
RUSSIA
†VOICE OF RUSSIA, Irkutsk
S • E Asia • 250 kW
†VOICE OF RUSSIA, Khabarovsk
W • Australasia • 100 kW
VOICE OF RUSSIA, Komsomol'sk 'Amure
W • W North Am • 250 kW
†VOICE OF RUSSIA, Moscow
W • SE Asia • 500 kW
UNITED KINGDOM
†BBC, Via Novosibirsk, Russia
S • E Asia • 500 kW
†BBC, Via Thailand
S • W Asia & S Asia • 250 kW
S • W Asia & Mideast • 250 kW
†BBC, Via Zyyi, Cyprus
S • W Asia & S Asia • 300 kW
S • Mideast & W Asia • 300 kW
†BBC, Woofferton
W • E Africa • 250 kW
USA
R FREE ASIA, Via Tinian, N Marianas
W • SE Asia • 500 kW
†VOA, Via Petro-Kam, Russia
E Asia • 250 kW
15475 GABON
AFRIQUE NUMERO UN, Moyabi
W Africa & E North Am • 250 kW
RUSSIA
RADIO ROSSII, Irkutsk
S • E Asia • DS • 100 kW
UNITED KINGDOM
†SALAMA RADIO, Woofferton
S • ENGLISH, ETC • W Africa • 250 kW
15475v EGYPT
EGYPTIAN RADIO, Kafr Silîm-Abis
E Africa • DS-GENERAL • 250 kW
15475.6 ANTARCTICA
†R NACIONAL-LRA36, Base Esperanza
M-F • 4 kW
15480 CHINA
†CENTRAL PEOPLE'S BS, Beijing
DS-1 • 100 kW
W • DS-1 • 100 kW
W-M • DS-1 • 100 kW
S • DS-1 • 100 kW
GERMANY
DEUTSCHE WELLE, Via Moscow, Russia
S • W Asia & C Asia • 500 kW
USA
†RFE-RL, Via Briech, Morocco
S • E Europe • 250 kW
15485 PAKISTAN
†RADIO PAKISTAN, Islamabad
SE Asia • 250 kW
SWITZERLAND
†SWISS RADIO INTL, Via Jülich, Germany
W • E Africa • 100 kW
UNITED KINGDOM
†BBC, Skelton, Cumbria
W Europe & N Africa • 300 kW
S • W Europe & N Africa • 300 kW
S • W Europe • 300 kW
†BBC, Via Zyyi, Cyprus
USA
†R AFRICA INTL, Via Jülich,Germany
Africa • 100 kW
R FREE ASIA, Via Tinian, N Marianas
SE Asia • 500 kW
†VOA, Via Ascension
W • S Africa • 250 kW
15490 CHINA
†CHINA RADIO INTL, Kunming
S • N Africa • 500 kW
IRAN
VO THE ISLAMIC REP, Sirjan
S • E Asia • 500 kW
PORTUGAL
†RDP INTERNATIONAL, Lisbon
W M-F • Mideast & S Asia • 100 kW
RUSSIA
†VOICE OF RUSSIA, Irkutsk
S • SE Asia • 500 kW
†VOICE OF RUSSIA, Novosibirsk
S • E Asia • 200 kW
USA
†VOA, Via Udon Thani, Thailand
S • S Asia • 250 kW
15495 (con'd) KUWAIT
RADIO KUWAIT, Kabd
Mideast • 500 kW
W Africa & C Africa • 500 kW
0 1 2 3 4 5 6 7 8 9 10 11 12 13 14 15 16 17 18 19 20 21 22 23 24

SEASONAL S OR W 1-HR TIMESHIFT MIDYEAR ◄ OR ► JAMMING / OR ⋀ EARLIEST HEARD ◁ LATEST HEARD ▷ NEW FOR 2002 †

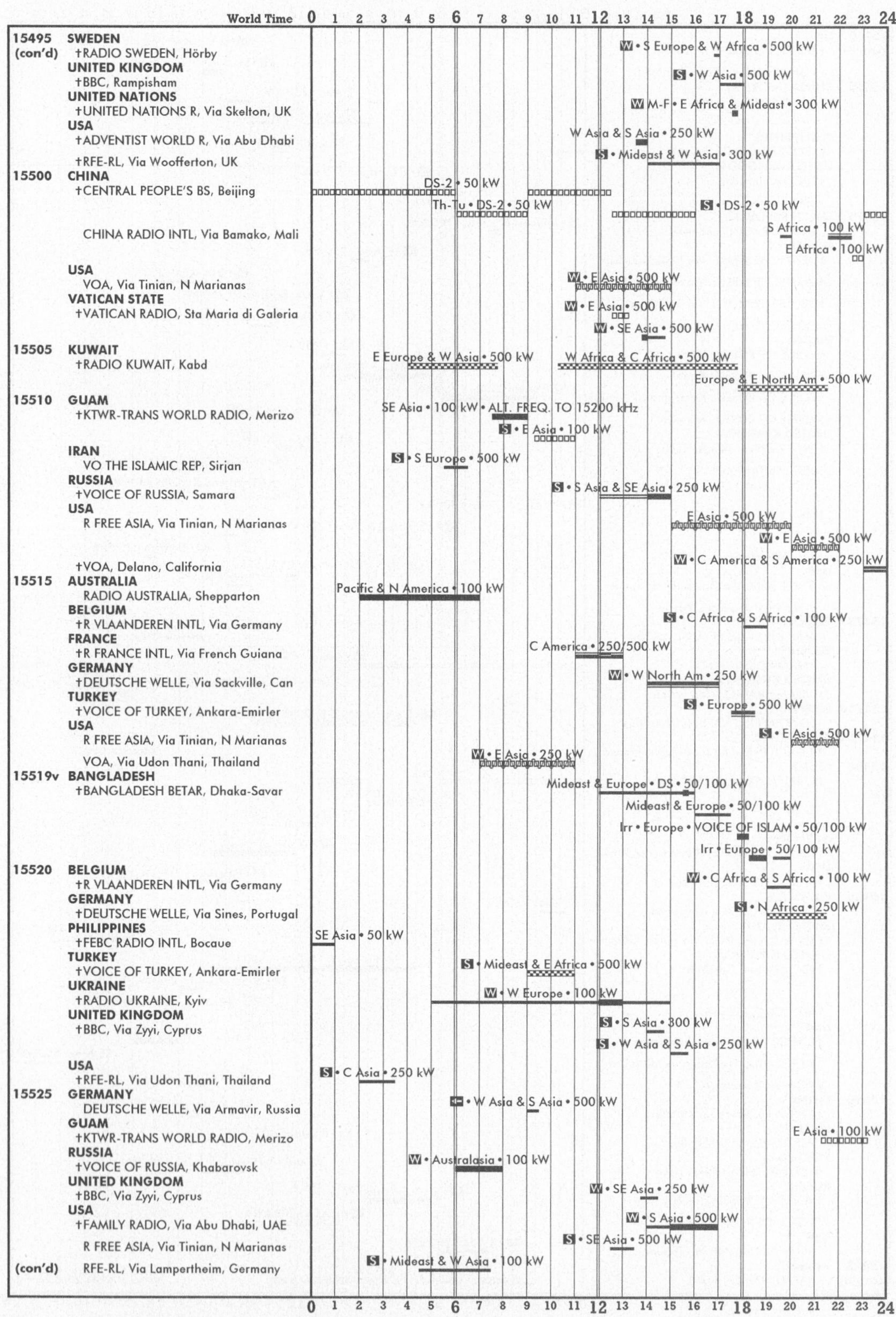
World Time 0 1 2 3 4 5 6 7 8 9 10 11 12 13 14 15 16 17 18 19 20 21 22 23 24
15495 (con'd) SWEDEN
†RADIO SWEDEN, Hörby
W • S Europe & W Africa • 500 kW
UNITED KINGDOM
†BBC, Rampisham
S • W Asia • 500 kW
UNITED NATIONS
†UNITED NATIONS R, Via Skelton, UK
W M-F • E Africa & Mideast • 300 kW
USA
†ADVENTIST WORLD R, Via Abu Dhabi
W Asia & S Asia • 250 kW
†RFE-RL, Via Woofferton, UK
S • Mideast & W Asia • 300 kW
15500 CHINA
†CENTRAL PEOPLE'S BS, Beijing
DS-2 • 50 kW
Th-Tu • DS-2 • 50 kW
S • DS-2 • 50 kW
CHINA RADIO INTL, Via Bamako, Mali
S Africa • 100 kW
E Africa • 100 kW
USA
VOA, Via Tinian, N Marianas
W • E Asia • 500 kW
VATICAN STATE
†VATICAN RADIO, Sta Maria di Galeria
W • E Asia • 500 kW
W • SE Asia • 500 kW
15505 KUWAIT
†RADIO KUWAIT, Kabd
E Europe & W Asia • 500 kW
W Africa & C Africa • 500 kW
Europe & E North Am • 500 kW
15510 GUAM
†KTWR-TRANS WORLD RADIO, Merizo
SE Asia • 100 kW • ALT. FREQ. TO 15200 kHz
S • E Asia • 100 kW
IRAN
VO THE ISLAMIC REP, Sirjan
S • S Europe • 500 kW
RUSSIA
†VOICE OF RUSSIA, Samara
S • S Asia & SE Asia • 250 kW
USA
R FREE ASIA, Via Tinian, N Marianas
E Asia • 500 kW
W • E Asia • 500 kW
†VOA, Delano, California
W • C America & S America • 250 kW
15515 AUSTRALIA
RADIO AUSTRALIA, Shepparton
Pacific & N America • 100 kW
BELGIUM
†R VLAANDEREN INTL, Via Germany
S • C Africa & S Africa • 100 kW
FRANCE
†R FRANCE INTL, Via French Guiana
C America • 250/500 kW
GERMANY
†DEUTSCHE WELLE, Via Sackville, Can
W • W North Am • 250 kW
TURKEY
†VOICE OF TURKEY, Ankara-Emirler
S • Europe • 500 kW
USA
R FREE ASIA, Via Tinian, N Marianas
S • E Asia • 500 kW
VOA, Via Udon Thani, Thailand
W • E Asia • 250 kW
15519v BANGLADESH
†BANGLADESH BETAR, Dhaka-Savar
Mideast & Europe • DS • 50/100 kW
Mideast & Europe • 50/100 kW
Irr • Europe • VOICE OF ISLAM • 50/100 kW
Irr • Europe • 50/100 kW
15520 BELGIUM
†R VLAANDEREN INTL, Via Germany
W • C Africa & S Africa • 100 kW
GERMANY
†DEUTSCHE WELLE, Via Sines, Portugal
S • N Africa • 250 kW
PHILIPPINES
†FEBC RADIO INTL, Bocaue
SE Asia • 50 kW
TURKEY
†VOICE OF TURKEY, Ankara-Emirler
S • Mideast & E Africa • 500 kW
UKRAINE
†RADIO UKRAINE, Kyiv
W • W Europe • 100 kW
UNITED KINGDOM
†BBC, Via Zyyi, Cyprus
S • S Asia • 300 kW
S • W Asia & S Asia • 250 kW
USA
†RFE-RL, Via Udon Thani, Thailand
S • C Asia • 250 kW
15525 GERMANY
DEUTSCHE WELLE, Via Armavir, Russia
• W Asia & S Asia • 500 kW
GUAM
†KTWR-TRANS WORLD RADIO, Merizo
E Asia • 100 kW
RUSSIA
†VOICE OF RUSSIA, Khabarovsk
W • Australasia • 100 kW
UNITED KINGDOM
†BBC, Via Zyyi, Cyprus
W • SE Asia • 250 kW
USA
†FAMILY RADIO, Via Abu Dhabi, UAE
W • S Asia • 500 kW
R FREE ASIA, Via Tinian, N Marianas
S • SE Asia • 500 kW
(con'd) RFE-RL, Via Lampertheim, Germany
S • Mideast & W Asia • 100 kW
0 1 2 3 4 5 6 7 8 9 10 11 12 13 14 15 16 17 18 19 20 21 22 23 24

ENGLISH ARABIC CHINESE FRENCH GERMAN RUSSIAN SPANISH OTHER

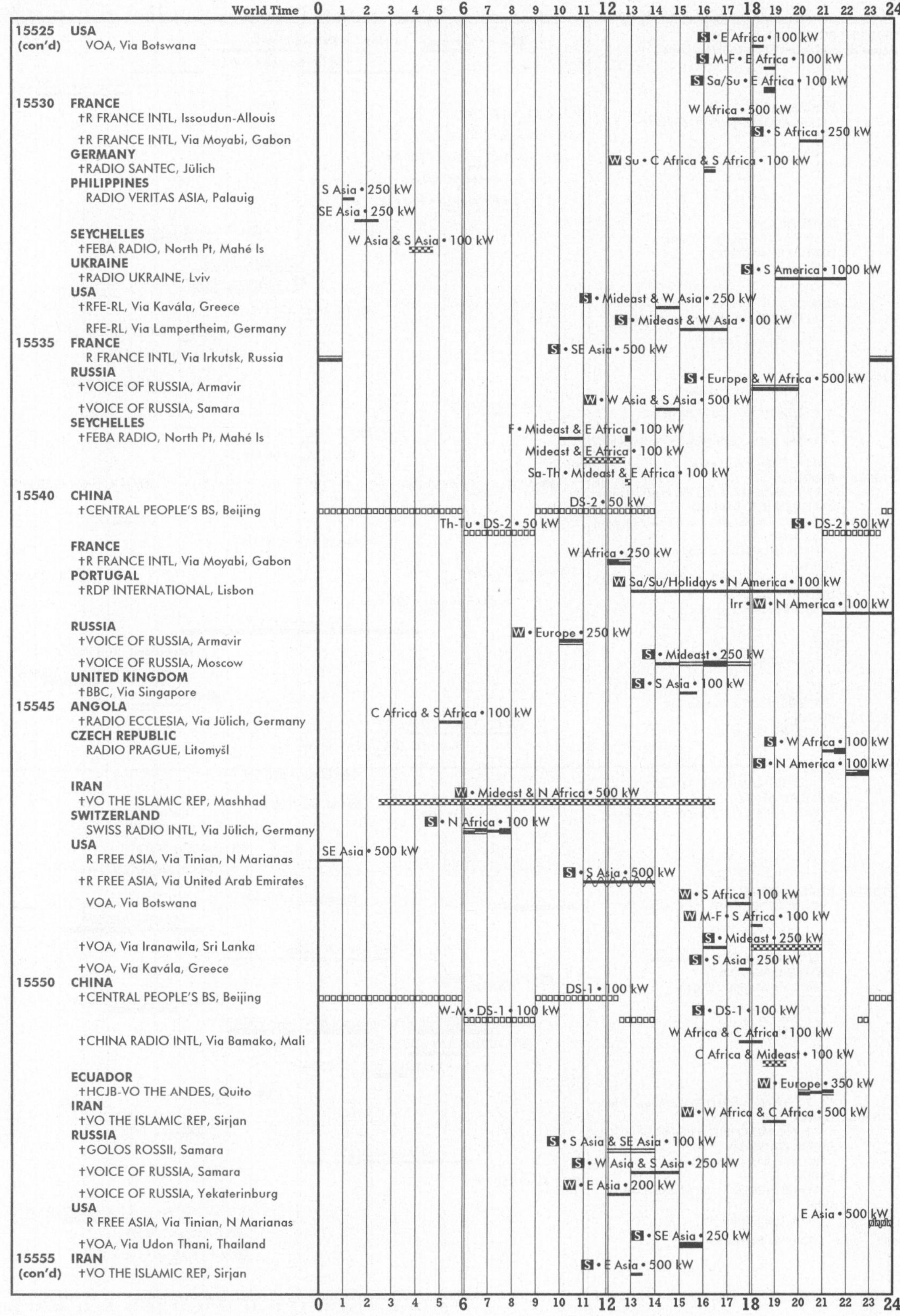
World Time 0 1 2 3 4 5 6 7 8 9 10 11 12 13 14 15 16 17 18 19 20 21 22 23 24
15525 (con'd) USA
VOA, Via Botswana
S • E Africa • 100 kW
S M-F • E Africa • 100 kW
S Sa/Su • E Africa • 100 kW
15530 FRANCE
†R FRANCE INTL, Issoudun-Allouis
W Africa • 500 kW
†R FRANCE INTL, Via Moyabi, Gabon
S • S Africa • 250 kW
GERMANY
†RADIO SANTEC, Jülich
W Su • C Africa & S Africa • 100 kW
PHILIPPINES
RADIO VERITAS ASIA, Palauig
S Asia • 250 kW
SE Asia • 250 kW
SEYCHELLES
†FEBA RADIO, North Pt, Mahé Is
W Asia & S Asia • 100 kW
UKRAINE
†RADIO UKRAINE, Lviv
S • S America • 1000 kW
USA
†RFE-RL, Via Kavála, Greece
S • Mideast & W Asia • 250 kW
RFE-RL, Via Lampertheim, Germany
S • Mideast & W Asia • 100 kW
15535 FRANCE
R FRANCE INTL, Via Irkutsk, Russia
S • SE Asia • 500 kW
RUSSIA
†VOICE OF RUSSIA, Armavir
S • Europe & W Africa • 500 kW
†VOICE OF RUSSIA, Samara
W • W Asia & S Asia • 500 kW
SEYCHELLES
†FEBA RADIO, North Pt, Mahé Is
F • Mideast & E Africa • 100 kW
Mideast & E Africa • 100 kW
Sa-Th • Mideast & E Africa • 100 kW
15540 CHINA
†CENTRAL PEOPLE'S BS, Beijing
DS-2 • 50 kW
Th-Tu • DS-2 • 50 kW
S • DS-2 • 50 kW
FRANCE
†R FRANCE INTL, Via Moyabi, Gabon
W Africa • 250 kW
PORTUGAL
†RDP INTERNATIONAL, Lisbon
W Sa/Su/Holidays • N America • 100 kW
Irr • W • N America • 100 kW
RUSSIA
†VOICE OF RUSSIA, Armavir
W • Europe • 250 kW
†VOICE OF RUSSIA, Moscow
S • Mideast • 250 kW
UNITED KINGDOM
†BBC, Via Singapore
S • S Asia • 100 kW
15545 ANGOLA
†RADIO ECCLESIA, Via Jülich, Germany
C Africa & S Africa • 100 kW
CZECH REPUBLIC
RADIO PRAGUE, Litomyšl
S • W Africa • 100 kW
S • N America • 100 kW
IRAN
†VO THE ISLAMIC REP, Mashhad
W • Mideast & N Africa • 500 kW
SWITZERLAND
SWISS RADIO INTL, Via Jülich, Germany
S • N Africa • 100 kW
USA
R FREE ASIA, Via Tinian, N Marianas
SE Asia • 500 kW
†R FREE ASIA, Via United Arab Emirates
S • S Asia • 500 kW
VOA, Via Botswana
W • S Africa • 100 kW
W M-F • S Africa • 100 kW
†VOA, Via Iranawila, Sri Lanka
S • Mideast • 250 kW
†VOA, Via Kavála, Greece
S • S Asia • 250 kW
15550 CHINA
†CENTRAL PEOPLE'S BS, Beijing
DS-1 • 100 kW
W-M • DS-1 • 100 kW
S • DS-1 • 100 kW
†CHINA RADIO INTL, Via Bamako, Mali
W Africa & C Africa • 100 kW
C Africa & Mideast • 100 kW
ECUADOR
†HCJB-VO THE ANDES, Quito
W • Europe • 350 kW
IRAN
†VO THE ISLAMIC REP, Sirjan
W • W Africa & C Africa • 500 kW
RUSSIA
†GOLOS ROSSII, Samara
S • S Asia & SE Asia • 100 kW
†VOICE OF RUSSIA, Samara
S • W Asia & S Asia • 250 kW
†VOICE OF RUSSIA, Yekaterinburg
W • E Asia • 200 kW
USA
R FREE ASIA, Via Tinian, N Marianas
E Asia • 500 kW
†VOA, Via Udon Thani, Thailand
S • SE Asia • 250 kW
15555 (con'd) IRAN
†VO THE ISLAMIC REP, Sirjan
S • E Asia • 500 kW
0 1 2 3 4 5 6 7 8 9 10 11 12 13 14 15 16 17 18 19 20 21 22 23 24

SEASONAL S OR W 1-HR TIMESHIFT MIDYEAR OR JAMMING / OR /\ EARLIEST HEARD LATEST HEARD NEW FOR 2002 †

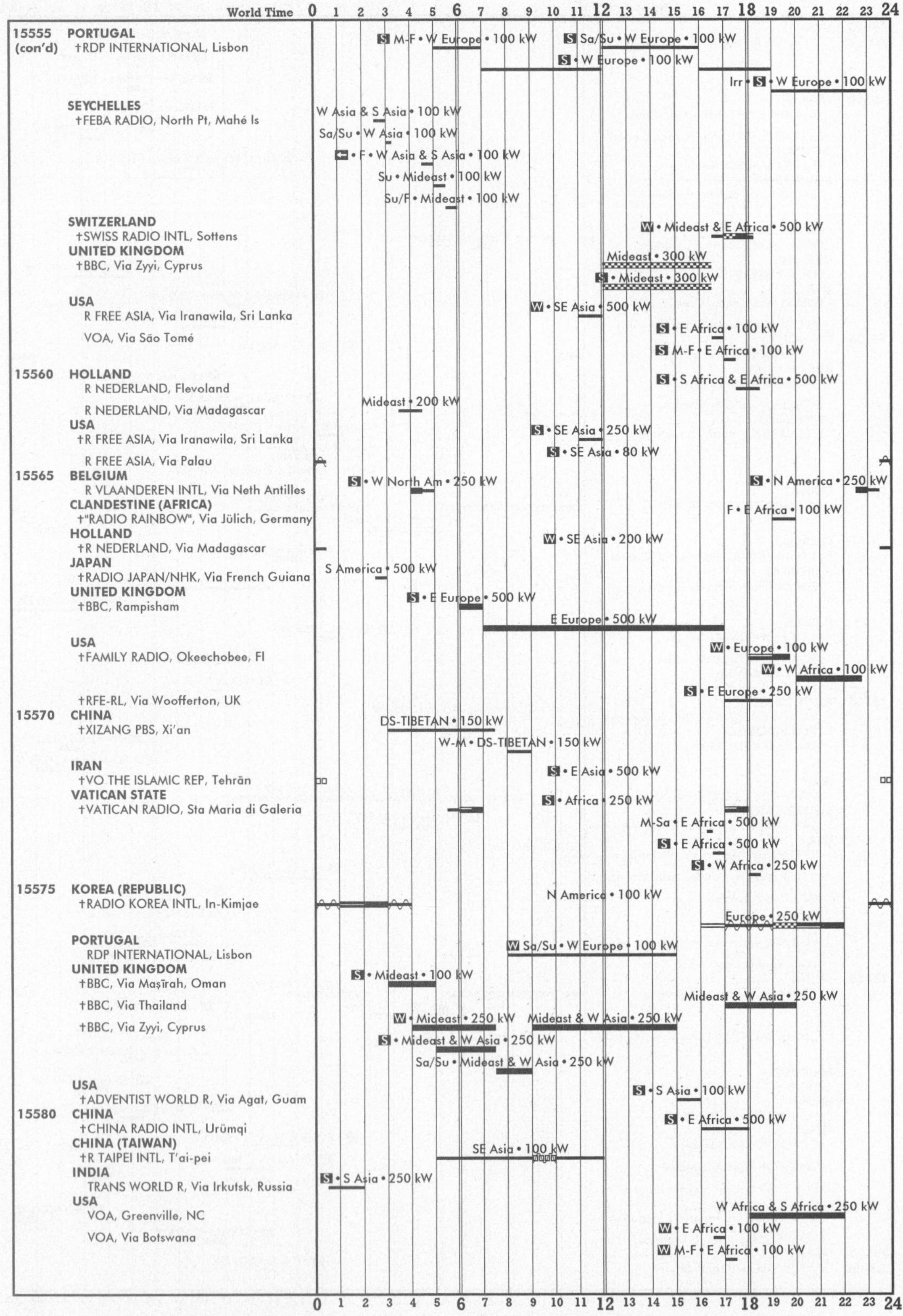
World Time 0 1 2 3 4 5 6 7 8 9 10 11 12 13 14 15 16 17 18 19 20 21 22 23 24
15555 (con'd) PORTUGAL
†RDP INTERNATIONAL, Lisbon
S M-F • W Europe • 100 kW
S Sa/Su • W Europe • 100 kW
S • W Europe • 100 kW
Irr • S • W Europe • 100 kW
SEYCHELLES
†FEBA RADIO, North Pt, Mahé Is
W Asia & S Asia • 100 kW
Sa/Su • W Asia • 100 kW
F • W Asia & S Asia • 100 kW
Su • Mideast • 100 kW
Su/F • Mideast • 100 kW
SWITZERLAND
†SWISS RADIO INTL, Sottens
W • Mideast & E Africa • 500 kW
UNITED KINGDOM
†BBC, Via Zyyi, Cyprus
Mideast • 300 kW
S • Mideast • 300 kW
USA
R FREE ASIA, Via Iranawila, Sri Lanka
W • SE Asia • 500 kW
VOA, Via São Tomé
S • E Africa • 100 kW
S M-F • E Africa • 100 kW
15560 HOLLAND
R NEDERLAND, Flevoland
S • S Africa & E Africa • 500 kW
R NEDERLAND, Via Madagascar
Mideast • 200 kW
USA
†R FREE ASIA, Via Iranawila, Sri Lanka
S • SE Asia • 250 kW
R FREE ASIA, Via Palau
S • SE Asia • 80 kW
15565 BELGIUM
R VLAANDEREN INTL, Via Neth Antilles
S • W North Am • 250 kW
S • N America • 250 kW
CLANDESTINE (AFRICA)
†"RADIO RAINBOW", Via Jülich, Germany
F • E Africa • 100 kW
HOLLAND
†R NEDERLAND, Via Madagascar
W • SE Asia • 200 kW
JAPAN
†RADIO JAPAN/NHK, Via French Guiana
S America • 500 kW
UNITED KINGDOM
†BBC, Rampisham
S • E Europe • 500 kW
E Europe • 500 kW
USA
†FAMILY RADIO, Okeechobee, Fl
W • Europe • 100 kW
W • W Africa • 100 kW
†RFE-RL, Via Woofferton, UK
S • E Europe • 250 kW
15570 CHINA
†XIZANG PBS, Xi'an
DS-TIBETAN • 150 kW
W-M • DS-TIBETAN • 150 kW
IRAN
†VO THE ISLAMIC REP, Tehrān
S • E Asia • 500 kW
VATICAN STATE
†VATICAN RADIO, Sta Maria di Galeria
S • Africa • 250 kW
M-Sa • E Africa • 500 kW
S • E Africa • 500 kW
S • W Africa • 250 kW
15575 KOREA (REPUBLIC)
†RADIO KOREA INTL, In-Kimjae
N America • 100 kW
Europe • 250 kW
PORTUGAL
RDP INTERNATIONAL, Lisbon
W Sa/Su • W Europe • 100 kW
UNITED KINGDOM
†BBC, Via Maşīrah, Oman
S • Mideast • 100 kW
†BBC, Via Thailand
Mideast & W Asia • 250 kW
†BBC, Via Zyyi, Cyprus
W • Mideast • 250 kW
Mideast & W Asia • 250 kW
S • Mideast & W Asia • 250 kW
Sa/Su • Mideast & W Asia • 250 kW
USA
†ADVENTIST WORLD R, Via Agat, Guam
S • S Asia • 100 kW
15580 CHINA
†CHINA RADIO INTL, Urümqi
S • E Africa • 500 kW
CHINA (TAIWAN)
†R TAIPEI INTL, T'ai-pei
SE Asia • 100 kW
INDIA
TRANS WORLD R, Via Irkutsk, Russia
S • S Asia • 250 kW
USA
VOA, Greenville, NC
W Africa & S Africa • 250 kW
VOA, Via Botswana
W • E Africa • 100 kW
W M-F • E Africa • 100 kW
0 1 2 3 4 5 6 7 8 9 10 11 12 13 14 15 16 17 18 19 20 21 22 23 24
ENGLISH ARABIC CHINESE FRENCH GERMAN RUSSIAN SPANISH OTHER

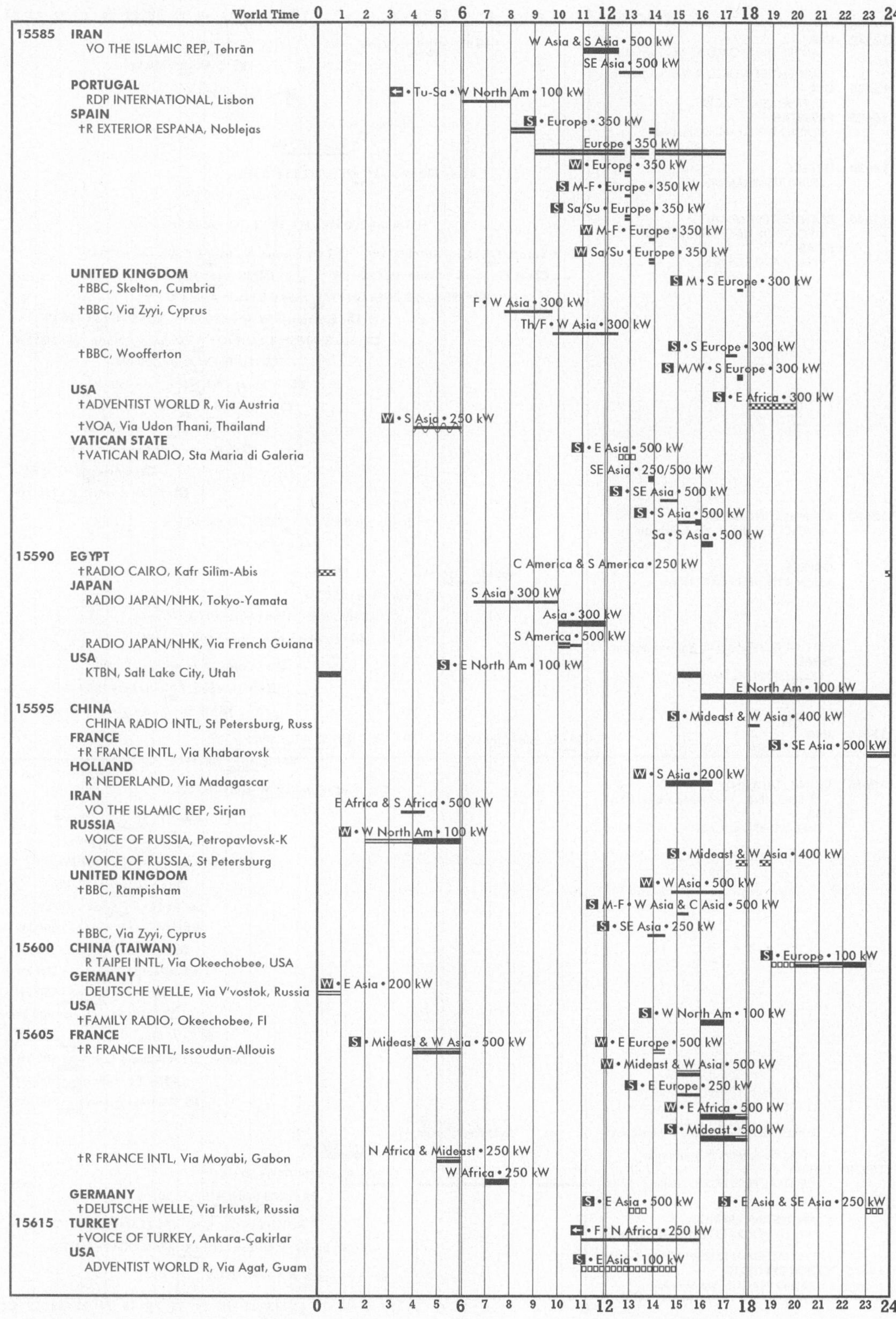
World Time 0 1 2 3 4 5 6 7 8 9 10 11 12 13 14 15 16 17 18 19 20 21 22 23 24
15585 IRAN
VO THE ISLAMIC REP, Tehrān
W Asia & S Asia • 500 kW
SE Asia • 500 kW
PORTUGAL
RDP INTERNATIONAL, Lisbon
• Tu-Sa • W North Am • 100 kW
SPAIN
†R EXTERIOR ESPANA, Noblejas
S • Europe • 350 kW
Europe • 350 kW
W • Europe • 350 kW
S M-F • Europe • 350 kW
S Sa/Su • Europe • 350 kW
W M-F • Europe • 350 kW
W Sa/Su • Europe • 350 kW
UNITED KINGDOM
†BBC, Skelton, Cumbria
S M • S Europe • 300 kW
†BBC, Via Zyyi, Cyprus
F • W Asia • 300 kW
Th/F • W Asia • 300 kW
†BBC, Woofferton
S • S Europe • 300 kW
S M/W • S Europe • 300 kW
USA
†ADVENTIST WORLD R, Via Austria
S • E Africa • 300 kW
†VOA, Via Udon Thani, Thailand
W • S Asia • 250 kW
VATICAN STATE
†VATICAN RADIO, Sta Maria di Galeria
S • E Asia • 500 kW
SE Asia • 250/500 kW
S • SE Asia • 500 kW
S • S Asia • 500 kW
Sa • S Asia • 500 kW
15590 EGYPT
†RADIO CAIRO, Kafr Silîm-Abis
C America & S America • 250 kW
JAPAN
RADIO JAPAN/NHK, Tokyo-Yamata
S Asia • 300 kW
Asia • 300 kW
RADIO JAPAN/NHK, Via French Guiana
S America • 500 kW
USA
KTBN, Salt Lake City, Utah
S • E North Am • 100 kW
E North Am • 100 kW
15595 CHINA
CHINA RADIO INTL, St Petersburg, Russ
S • Mideast & W Asia • 400 kW
FRANCE
†R FRANCE INTL, Via Khabarovsk
S • SE Asia • 500 kW
HOLLAND
R NEDERLAND, Via Madagascar
W • S Asia • 200 kW
IRAN
VO THE ISLAMIC REP, Sirjan
E Africa & S Africa • 500 kW
RUSSIA
VOICE OF RUSSIA, Petropavlovsk-K
W • W North Am • 100 kW
VOICE OF RUSSIA, St Petersburg
S • Mideast & W Asia • 400 kW
UNITED KINGDOM
†BBC, Rampisham
W • W Asia • 500 kW
S M-F • W Asia & C Asia • 500 kW
†BBC, Via Zyyi, Cyprus
S • SE Asia • 250 kW
15600 CHINA (TAIWAN)
R TAIPEI INTL, Via Okeechobee, USA
S • Europe • 100 kW
GERMANY
DEUTSCHE WELLE, Via V'vostok, Russia
W • E Asia • 200 kW
USA
†FAMILY RADIO, Okeechobee, Fl
S • W North Am • 100 kW
15605 FRANCE
†R FRANCE INTL, Issoudun-Allouis
S • Mideast & W Asia • 500 kW
W • E Europe • 500 kW
W • Mideast & W Asia • 500 kW
S • E Europe • 250 kW
W • E Africa • 500 kW
S • Mideast • 500 kW
†R FRANCE INTL, Via Moyabi, Gabon
N Africa & Mideast • 250 kW
W Africa • 250 kW
GERMANY
†DEUTSCHE WELLE, Via Irkutsk, Russia
S • E Asia • 500 kW
S • E Asia & SE Asia • 250 kW
15615 TURKEY
†VOICE OF TURKEY, Ankara-Çakirlar
• F • N Africa • 250 kW
USA
ADVENTIST WORLD R, Via Agat, Guam
S • E Asia • 100 kW
0 1 2 3 4 5 6 7 8 9 10 11 12 13 14 15 16 17 18 19 20 21 22 23 24

SEASONAL S OR W 1-HR TIMESHIFT MIDYEAR OR JAMMING / OR /\ EARLIEST HEARD ◁ LATEST HEARD ▷ NEW FOR 2002 †

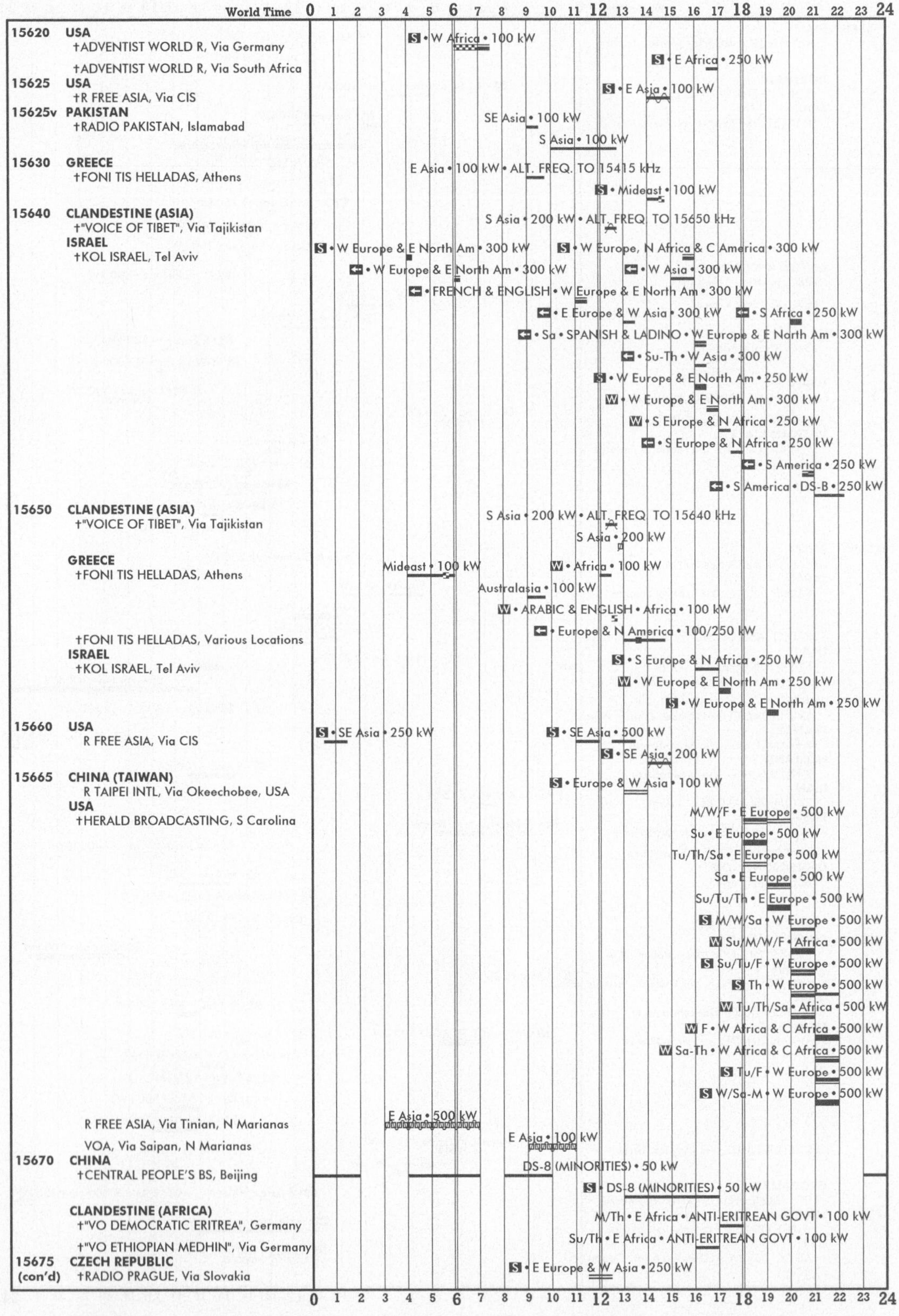
World Time 0 1 2 3 4 5 6 7 8 9 10 11 12 13 14 15 16 17 18 19 20 21 22 23 24
15620 USA
†ADVENTIST WORLD R, Via Germany
S • W Africa • 100 kW
†ADVENTIST WORLD R, Via South Africa
S • E Africa • 250 kW
15625 USA
†R FREE ASIA, Via CIS
S • E Asia • 100 kW
15625v PAKISTAN
†RADIO PAKISTAN, Islamabad
SE Asia • 100 kW
S Asia • 100 kW
15630 GREECE
†FONI TIS HELLADAS, Athens
E Asia • 100 kW • ALT. FREQ. TO 15415 kHz
S • Mideast • 100 kW
15640 CLANDESTINE (ASIA)
†"VOICE OF TIBET", Via Tajikistan
S Asia • 200 kW • ALT. FREQ. TO 15650 kHz
ISRAEL
†KOL ISRAEL, Tel Aviv
S • W Europe & E North Am • 300 kW
S • W Europe, N Africa & C America • 300 kW
• W Europe & E North Am • 300 kW
• W Asia • 300 kW
• FRENCH & ENGLISH • W Europe & E North Am • 300 kW
• E Europe & W Asia • 300 kW
• S Africa • 250 kW
• Sa • SPANISH & LADINO • W Europe & E North Am • 300 kW
• Su-Th • W Asia • 300 kW
S • W Europe & E North Am • 250 kW
W • W Europe & E North Am • 300 kW
W • S Europe & N Africa • 250 kW
• S Europe & N Africa • 250 kW
• S America • 250 kW
• S America • DS-B • 250 kW
15650 CLANDESTINE (ASIA)
†"VOICE OF TIBET", Via Tajikistan
S Asia • 200 kW • ALT. FREQ. TO 15640 kHz
S Asia • 200 kW
GREECE
†FONI TIS HELLADAS, Athens
Mideast • 100 kW
W • Africa • 100 kW
Australasia • 100 kW
W • ARABIC & ENGLISH • Africa • 100 kW
†FONI TIS HELLADAS, Various Locations
• Europe & N America • 100/250 kW
ISRAEL
†KOL ISRAEL, Tel Aviv
S • S Europe & N Africa • 250 kW
W • W Europe & E North Am • 250 kW
S • W Europe & E North Am • 250 kW
15660 USA
R FREE ASIA, Via CIS
S • SE Asia • 250 kW
S • SE Asia • 500 kW
S • SE Asia • 200 kW
15665 CHINA (TAIWAN)
R TAIPEI INTL, Via Okeechobee, USA
S • Europe & W Asia • 100 kW
USA
†HERALD BROADCASTING, S Carolina
M/W/F • E Europe • 500 kW
Su • E Europe • 500 kW
Tu/Th/Sa • E Europe • 500 kW
Sa • E Europe • 500 kW
Su/Tu/Th • E Europe • 500 kW
S M/W/Sa • W Europe • 500 kW
W Su/M/W/F • Africa • 500 kW
S Su/Tu/F • W Europe • 500 kW
S Th • W Europe • 500 kW
W Tu/Th/Sa • Africa • 500 kW
W F • W Africa & C Africa • 500 kW
W Sa-Th • W Africa & C Africa • 500 kW
S Tu/F • W Europe • 500 kW
S W/Sa-M • W Europe • 500 kW
R FREE ASIA, Via Tinian, N Marianas
E Asia • 500 kW
VOA, Via Saipan, N Marianas
E Asia • 100 kW
15670 CHINA
†CENTRAL PEOPLE'S BS, Beijing
DS-8 (MINORITIES) • 50 kW
S • DS-8 (MINORITIES) • 50 kW
CLANDESTINE (AFRICA)
†"VO DEMOCRATIC ERITREA", Germany
M/Th • E Africa • ANTI-ERITREAN GOVT • 100 kW
†"VO ETHIOPIAN MEDHIN", Via Germany
Su/Th • E Africa • ANTI-ERITREAN GOVT • 100 kW
15675 CZECH REPUBLIC
(con'd) †RADIO PRAGUE, Via Slovakia
S • E Europe & W Asia • 250 kW
0 1 2 3 4 5 6 7 8 9 10 11 12 13 14 15 16 17 18 19 20 21 22 23 24

ENGLISH ARABIC CHINESE FRENCH GERMAN RUSSIAN SPANISH OTHER

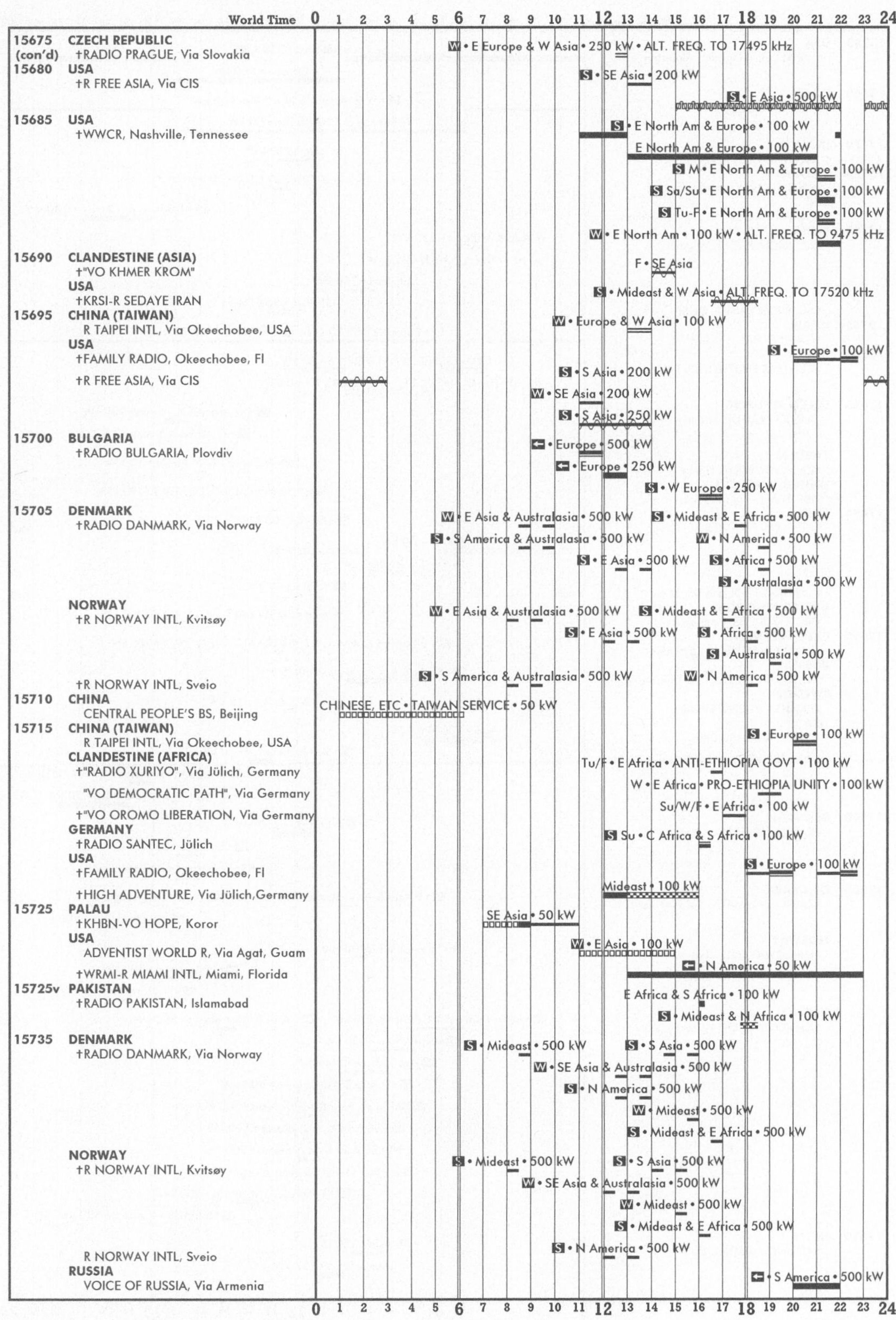
World Time 0 1 2 3 4 5 6 7 8 9 10 11 12 13 14 15 16 17 18 19 20 21 22 23 24
15675 (con'd) CZECH REPUBLIC
†RADIO PRAGUE, Via Slovakia
W • E Europe & W Asia • 250 kW • ALT. FREQ. TO 17495 kHz
15680 USA
†R FREE ASIA, Via CIS
S • SE Asia • 200 kW
S • E Asia • 500 kW
15685 USA
†WWCR, Nashville, Tennessee
S • E North Am & Europe • 100 kW
E North Am & Europe • 100 kW
S M • E North Am & Europe • 100 kW
S Sa/Su • E North Am & Europe • 100 kW
S Tu-F • E North Am & Europe • 100 kW
W • E North Am • 100 kW • ALT. FREQ. TO 9475 kHz
15690 CLANDESTINE (ASIA)
†"VO KHMER KROM"
F • SE Asia
USA
†KRSI-R SEDAYE IRAN
S • Mideast & W Asia • ALT. FREQ. TO 17520 kHz
15695 CHINA (TAIWAN)
R TAIPEI INTL, Via Okeechobee, USA
W • Europe & W Asia • 100 kW
USA
†FAMILY RADIO, Okeechobee, Fl
S • Europe • 100 kW
†R FREE ASIA, Via CIS
S • S Asia • 200 kW
W • SE Asia • 200 kW
S • S Asia • 250 kW
15700 BULGARIA
†RADIO BULGARIA, Plovdiv
• Europe • 500 kW
• Europe • 250 kW
S • W Europe • 250 kW
15705 DENMARK
†RADIO DANMARK, Via Norway
W • E Asia & Australasia • 500 kW
S • Mideast & E Africa • 500 kW
S • S America & Australasia • 500 kW
W • N America • 500 kW
S • E Asia • 500 kW
S • Africa • 500 kW
S • Australasia • 500 kW
NORWAY
†R NORWAY INTL, Kvitsøy
W • E Asia & Australasia • 500 kW
S • Mideast & E Africa • 500 kW
S • E Asia • 500 kW
S • Africa • 500 kW
S • Australasia • 500 kW
S • S America & Australasia • 500 kW
W • N America • 500 kW
†R NORWAY INTL, Sveio
15710 CHINA
CENTRAL PEOPLE'S BS, Beijing
CHINESE, ETC • TAIWAN SERVICE • 50 kW
15715 CHINA (TAIWAN)
R TAIPEI INTL, Via Okeechobee, USA
S • Europe • 100 kW
CLANDESTINE (AFRICA)
†"RADIO XURIYO", Via Jülich, Germany
Tu/F • E Africa • ANTI-ETHIOPIA GOVT • 100 kW
"VO DEMOCRATIC PATH", Via Germany
W • E Africa • PRO-ETHIOPIA UNITY • 100 kW
†"VO OROMO LIBERATION, Via Germany
Su/W/F • E Africa • 100 kW
GERMANY
†RADIO SANTEC, Jülich
S Su • C Africa & S Africa • 100 kW
USA
†FAMILY RADIO, Okeechobee, Fl
S • Europe • 100 kW
†HIGH ADVENTURE, Via Jülich,Germany
Mideast • 100 kW
15725 PALAU
†KHBN-VO HOPE, Koror
SE Asia • 50 kW
USA
ADVENTIST WORLD R, Via Agat, Guam
W • E Asia • 100 kW
†WRMI-R MIAMI INTL, Miami, Florida
• N America • 50 kW
15725v PAKISTAN
†RADIO PAKISTAN, Islamabad
E Africa & S Africa • 100 kW
S • Mideast & N Africa • 100 kW
15735 DENMARK
†RADIO DANMARK, Via Norway
S • Mideast • 500 kW
S • S Asia • 500 kW
W • SE Asia & Australasia • 500 kW
S • N America • 500 kW
W • Mideast • 500 kW
S • Mideast & E Africa • 500 kW
NORWAY
†R NORWAY INTL, Kvitsøy
S • Mideast • 500 kW
S • S Asia • 500 kW
W • SE Asia & Australasia • 500 kW
W • Mideast • 500 kW
S • Mideast & E Africa • 500 kW
R NORWAY INTL, Sveio
S • N America • 500 kW
RUSSIA
VOICE OF RUSSIA, Via Armenia
• S America • 500 kW
0 1 2 3 4 5 6 7 8 9 10 11 12 13 14 15 16 17 18 19 20 21 22 23 24
SEASONAL S OR W   1-HR TIMESHIFT MIDYEAR OR   JAMMING / OR ∧   EARLIEST HEARD ◁   LATEST HEARD ▷   NEW FOR 2002 †

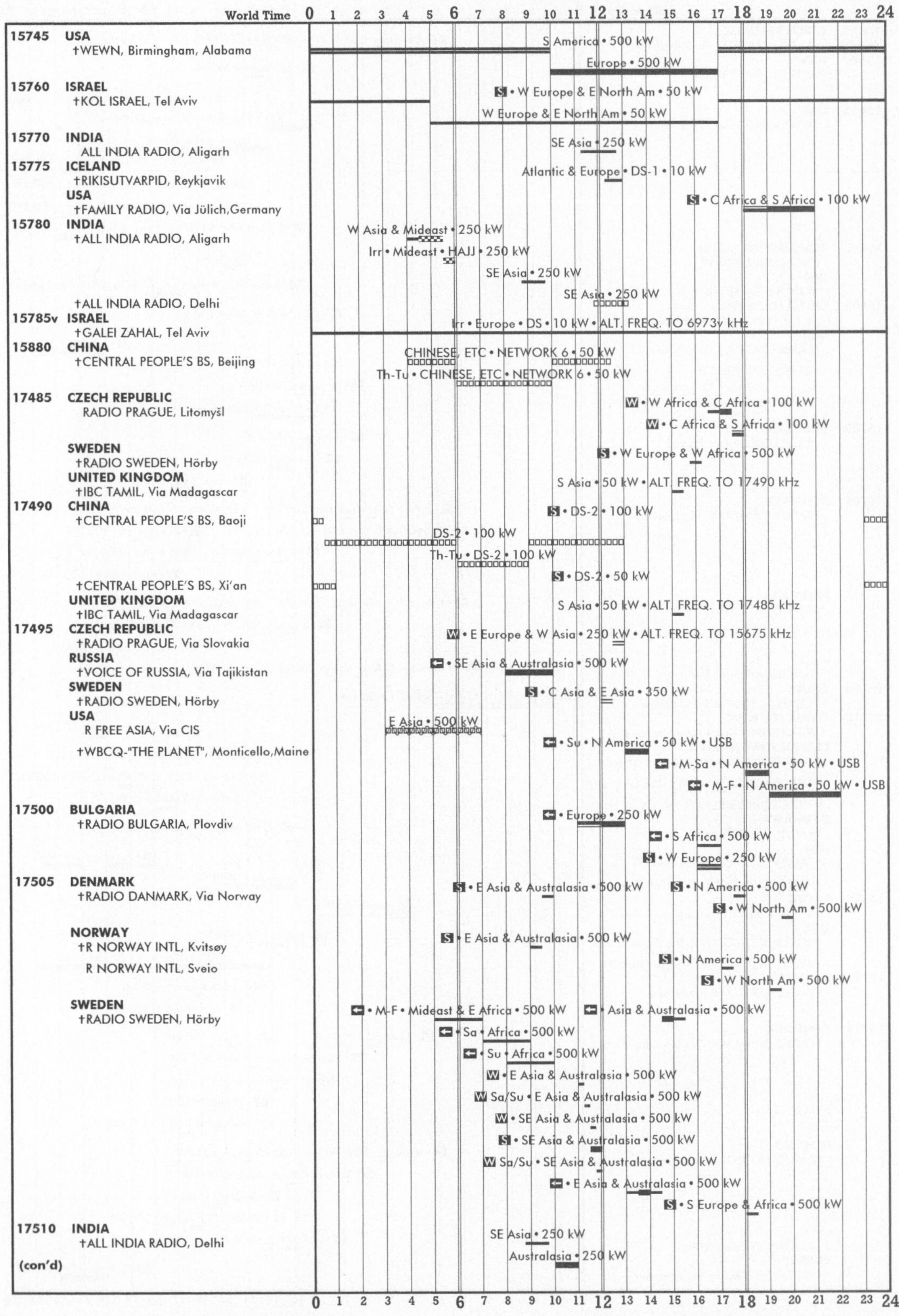
World Time 0 1 2 3 4 5 6 7 8 9 10 11 12 13 14 15 16 17 18 19 20 21 22 23 24
15745 USA
†WEWN, Birmingham, Alabama
S America • 500 kW
Europe • 500 kW
15760 ISRAEL
†KOL ISRAEL, Tel Aviv
S • W Europe & E North Am • 50 kW
W Europe & E North Am • 50 kW
15770 INDIA
ALL INDIA RADIO, Aligarh
SE Asia • 250 kW
15775 ICELAND
†RIKISUTVARPID, Reykjavik
Atlantic & Europe • DS-1 • 10 kW
USA
†FAMILY RADIO, Via Jülich,Germany
S • C Africa & S Africa • 100 kW
15780 INDIA
†ALL INDIA RADIO, Aligarh
W Asia & Mideast • 250 kW
Irr • Mideast • HAJJ • 250 kW
SE Asia • 250 kW
†ALL INDIA RADIO, Delhi
SE Asia • 250 kW
15785v ISRAEL
†GALEI ZAHAL, Tel Aviv
Irr • Europe • DS • 10 kW • ALT. FREQ. TO 6973v kHz
15880 CHINA
†CENTRAL PEOPLE'S BS, Beijing
CHINESE, ETC • NETWORK 6 • 50 kW
Th-Tu • CHINESE, ETC • NETWORK 6 • 50 kW
17485 CZECH REPUBLIC
RADIO PRAGUE, Litomyšl
W • W Africa & C Africa • 100 kW
W • C Africa & S Africa • 100 kW
SWEDEN
†RADIO SWEDEN, Hörby
S • W Europe & W Africa • 500 kW
UNITED KINGDOM
†IBC TAMIL, Via Madagascar
S Asia • 50 kW • ALT. FREQ. TO 17490 kHz
17490 CHINA
†CENTRAL PEOPLE'S BS, Baoji
S • DS-2 • 100 kW
DS-2 • 100 kW
Th-Tu • DS-2 • 100 kW
S • DS-2 • 50 kW
†CENTRAL PEOPLE'S BS, Xi'an
UNITED KINGDOM
†IBC TAMIL, Via Madagascar
S Asia • 50 kW • ALT. FREQ. TO 17485 kHz
17495 CZECH REPUBLIC
†RADIO PRAGUE, Via Slovakia
W • E Europe & W Asia • 250 kW • ALT. FREQ. TO 15675 kHz
RUSSIA
†VOICE OF RUSSIA, Via Tajikistan
SE Asia & Australasia • 500 kW
SWEDEN
†RADIO SWEDEN, Hörby
S • C Asia & E Asia • 350 kW
USA
R FREE ASIA, Via CIS
E Asia • 500 kW
†WBCQ-"THE PLANET", Monticello,Maine
Su • N America • 50 kW • USB
M-Sa • N America • 50 kW • USB
M-F • N America • 50 kW • USB
17500 BULGARIA
†RADIO BULGARIA, Plovdiv
Europe • 250 kW
S Africa • 500 kW
S • W Europe • 250 kW
17505 DENMARK
†RADIO DANMARK, Via Norway
S • E Asia & Australasia • 500 kW
S • N America • 500 kW
S • W North Am • 500 kW
NORWAY
†R NORWAY INTL, Kvitsøy
S • E Asia & Australasia • 500 kW
S • N America • 500 kW
R NORWAY INTL, Sveio
S • W North Am • 500 kW
SWEDEN
†RADIO SWEDEN, Hörby
M-F • Mideast & E Africa • 500 kW
Asia & Australasia • 500 kW
Sa • Africa • 500 kW
Su • Africa • 500 kW
W • E Asia & Australasia • 500 kW
W Sa/Su • E Asia & Australasia • 500 kW
W • SE Asia & Australasia • 500 kW
S • SE Asia & Australasia • 500 kW
W Sa/Su • SE Asia & Australasia • 500 kW
E Asia & Australasia • 500 kW
S • S Europe & Africa • 500 kW
17510 INDIA
†ALL INDIA RADIO, Delhi
SE Asia • 250 kW
Australasia • 250 kW
(con'd)
0 1 2 3 4 5 6 7 8 9 10 11 12 13 14 15 16 17 18 19 20 21 22 23 24
ENGLISH ARABIC CHINESE FRENCH GERMAN RUSSIAN SPANISH OTHER

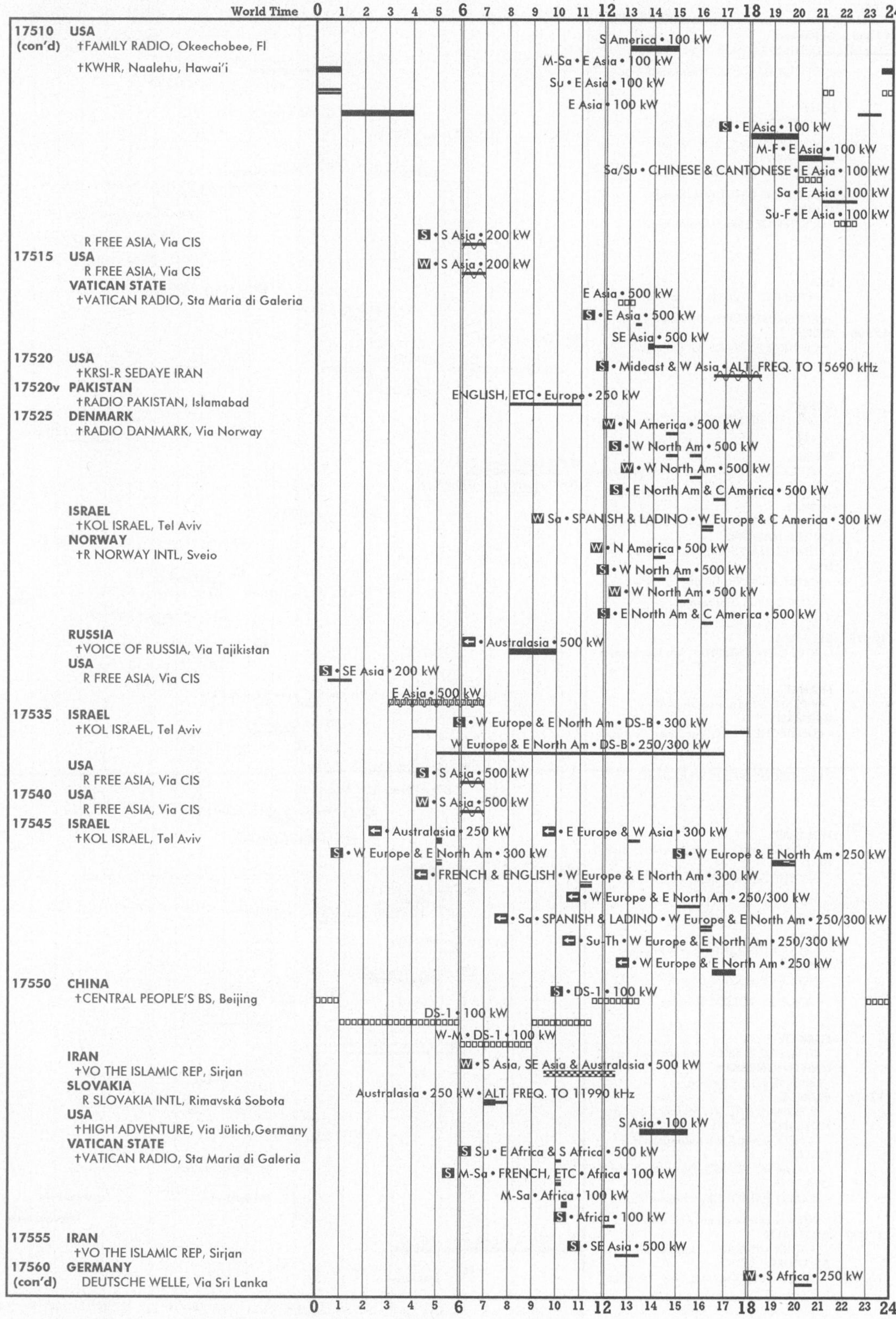
World Time 0 1 2 3 4 5 6 7 8 9 10 11 12 13 14 15 16 17 18 19 20 21 22 23 24
17510 (con'd) USA
†FAMILY RADIO, Okeechobee, Fl
S America • 100 kW
†KWHR, Naalehu, Hawai'i
M-Sa • E Asia • 100 kW
Su • E Asia • 100 kW
E Asia • 100 kW
S • E Asia • 100 kW
M-F • E Asia • 100 kW
Sa/Su • CHINESE & CANTONESE • E Asia • 100 kW
Sa • E Asia • 100 kW
Su-F • E Asia • 100 kW
R FREE ASIA, Via CIS
S • S Asia • 200 kW
17515 USA
R FREE ASIA, Via CIS
W • S Asia • 200 kW
VATICAN STATE
†VATICAN RADIO, Sta Maria di Galeria
E Asia • 500 kW
S • E Asia • 500 kW
SE Asia • 500 kW
17520 USA
†KRSI-R SEDAYE IRAN
S • Mideast & W Asia • ALT. FREQ. TO 15690 kHz
17520v PAKISTAN
†RADIO PAKISTAN, Islamabad
ENGLISH, ETC • Europe • 250 kW
17525 DENMARK
†RADIO DANMARK, Via Norway
W • N America • 500 kW
S • W North Am • 500 kW
W • W North Am • 500 kW
S • E North Am & C America • 500 kW
ISRAEL
†KOL ISRAEL, Tel Aviv
W Sa • SPANISH & LADINO • W Europe & C America • 300 kW
NORWAY
†R NORWAY INTL, Sveio
W • N America • 500 kW
S • W North Am • 500 kW
W • W North Am • 500 kW
S • E North Am & C America • 500 kW
RUSSIA
†VOICE OF RUSSIA, Via Tajikistan
• Australasia • 500 kW
USA
R FREE ASIA, Via CIS
S • SE Asia • 200 kW
E Asia • 500 kW
17535 ISRAEL
†KOL ISRAEL, Tel Aviv
S • W Europe & E North Am • DS-B • 300 kW
W Europe & E North Am • DS-B • 250/300 kW
USA
R FREE ASIA, Via CIS
S • S Asia • 500 kW
17540 USA
R FREE ASIA, Via CIS
W • S Asia • 500 kW
17545 ISRAEL
†KOL ISRAEL, Tel Aviv
• Australasia • 250 kW
• E Europe & W Asia • 300 kW
S • W Europe & E North Am • 300 kW
S • W Europe & E North Am • 250 kW
• FRENCH & ENGLISH • W Europe & E North Am • 300 kW
• W Europe & E North Am • 250/300 kW
• Sa • SPANISH & LADINO • W Europe & E North Am • 250/300 kW
• Su-Th • W Europe & E North Am • 250/300 kW
• W Europe & E North Am • 250 kW
17550 CHINA
†CENTRAL PEOPLE'S BS, Beijing
S • DS-1 • 100 kW
DS-1 • 100 kW
W-M • DS-1 • 100 kW
IRAN
†VO THE ISLAMIC REP, Sirjan
W • S Asia, SE Asia & Australasia • 500 kW
SLOVAKIA
R SLOVAKIA INTL, Rimavská Sobota
Australasia • 250 kW • ALT. FREQ. TO 11990 kHz
USA
†HIGH ADVENTURE, Via Jülich, Germany
S Asia • 100 kW
VATICAN STATE
†VATICAN RADIO, Sta Maria di Galeria
S Su • E Africa & S Africa • 500 kW
S M-Sa • FRENCH, ETC • Africa • 100 kW
M-Sa • Africa • 100 kW
S • Africa • 100 kW
17555 IRAN
†VO THE ISLAMIC REP, Sirjan
S • SE Asia • 500 kW
17560 (con'd) GERMANY
DEUTSCHE WELLE, Via Sri Lanka
W • S Africa • 250 kW
0 1 2 3 4 5 6 7 8 9 10 11 12 13 14 15 16 17 18 19 20 21 22 23 24

SEASONAL S OR W 1-HR TIMESHIFT MIDYEAR ← OR → JAMMING / OR /\ EARLIEST HEARD ◁ LATEST HEARD ▷ NEW FOR 2002 †

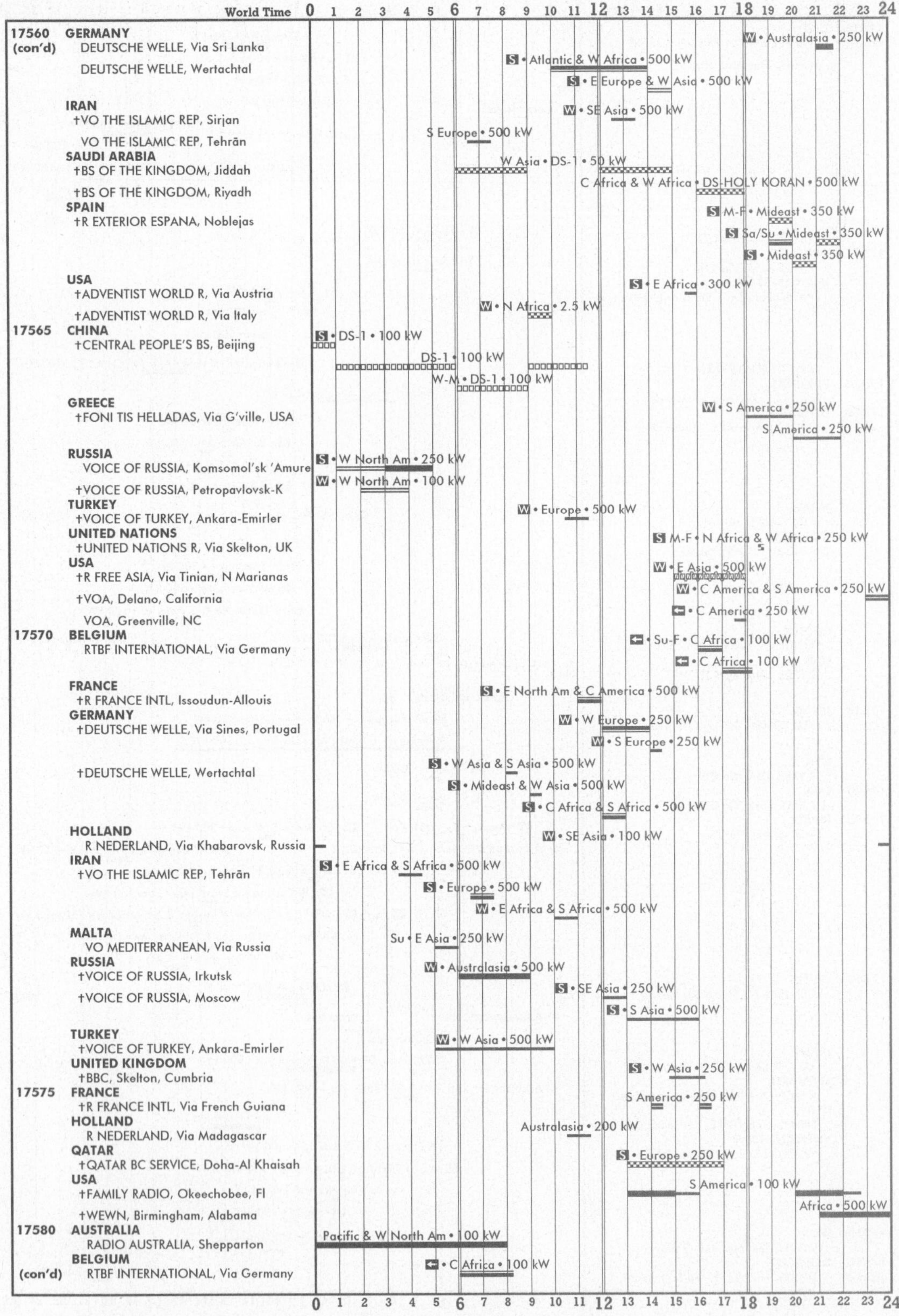
World Time 0 1 2 3 4 5 6 7 8 9 10 11 12 13 14 15 16 17 18 19 20 21 22 23 24
17560 (con'd) GERMANY
DEUTSCHE WELLE, Via Sri Lanka
W • Australasia • 250 kW
DEUTSCHE WELLE, Wertachtal
S • Atlantic & W Africa • 500 kW
S • E Europe & W Asia • 500 kW
IRAN
†VO THE ISLAMIC REP, Sirjan
W • SE Asia • 500 kW
VO THE ISLAMIC REP, Tehrān
S Europe • 500 kW
SAUDI ARABIA
†BS OF THE KINGDOM, Jiddah
W Asia • DS-1 • 50 kW
†BS OF THE KINGDOM, Riyadh
C Africa & W Africa • DS-HOLY KORAN • 500 kW
SPAIN
†R EXTERIOR ESPANA, Noblejas
S M-F • Mideast • 350 kW
S Sa/Su • Mideast • 350 kW
S • Mideast • 350 kW
USA
†ADVENTIST WORLD R, Via Austria
S • E Africa • 300 kW
†ADVENTIST WORLD R, Via Italy
W • N Africa • 2.5 kW
17565 CHINA
†CENTRAL PEOPLE'S BS, Beijing
S • DS-1 • 100 kW
DS-1 • 100 kW
W-M • DS-1 • 100 kW
GREECE
†FONI TIS HELLADAS, Via G'ville, USA
W • S America • 250 kW
S America • 250 kW
RUSSIA
VOICE OF RUSSIA, Komsomol'sk 'Amure
S • W North Am • 250 kW
†VOICE OF RUSSIA, Petropavlovsk-K
W • W North Am • 100 kW
TURKEY
†VOICE OF TURKEY, Ankara-Emirler
W • Europe • 500 kW
UNITED NATIONS
†UNITED NATIONS R, Via Skelton, UK
S M-F • N Africa & W Africa • 250 kW
USA
†R FREE ASIA, Via Tinian, N Marianas
W • E Asia • 500 kW
†VOA, Delano, California
W • C America & S America • 250 kW
VOA, Greenville, NC
• C America • 250 kW
17570 BELGIUM
RTBF INTERNATIONAL, Via Germany
Su-F • C Africa • 100 kW
• C Africa • 100 kW
FRANCE
†R FRANCE INTL, Issoudun-Allouis
S • E North Am & C America • 500 kW
GERMANY
†DEUTSCHE WELLE, Via Sines, Portugal
W • W Europe • 250 kW
W • S Europe • 250 kW
†DEUTSCHE WELLE, Wertachtal
S • W Asia & S Asia • 500 kW
S • Mideast & W Asia • 500 kW
S • C Africa & S Africa • 500 kW
HOLLAND
R NEDERLAND, Via Khabarovsk, Russia
W • SE Asia • 100 kW
IRAN
†VO THE ISLAMIC REP, Tehrān
S • E Africa & S Africa • 500 kW
S • Europe • 500 kW
W • E Africa & S Africa • 500 kW
MALTA
VO MEDITERRANEAN, Via Russia
Su • E Asia • 250 kW
RUSSIA
†VOICE OF RUSSIA, Irkutsk
W • Australasia • 500 kW
†VOICE OF RUSSIA, Moscow
S • SE Asia • 250 kW
S • S Asia • 500 kW
TURKEY
†VOICE OF TURKEY, Ankara-Emirler
W • W Asia • 500 kW
UNITED KINGDOM
†BBC, Skelton, Cumbria
S • W Asia • 250 kW
17575 FRANCE
†R FRANCE INTL, Via French Guiana
S America • 250 kW
HOLLAND
R NEDERLAND, Via Madagascar
Australasia • 200 kW
QATAR
†QATAR BC SERVICE, Doha-Al Khaisah
S • Europe • 250 kW
USA
†FAMILY RADIO, Okeechobee, Fl
S America • 100 kW
†WEWN, Birmingham, Alabama
Africa • 500 kW
17580 AUSTRALIA
RADIO AUSTRALIA, Shepparton
Pacific & W North Am • 100 kW
BELGIUM
(con'd) RTBF INTERNATIONAL, Via Germany
• C Africa • 100 kW
0 1 2 3 4 5 6 7 8 9 10 11 12 13 14 15 16 17 18 19 20 21 22 23 24

ENGLISH ARABIC CHINESE FRENCH GERMAN RUSSIAN SPANISH OTHER

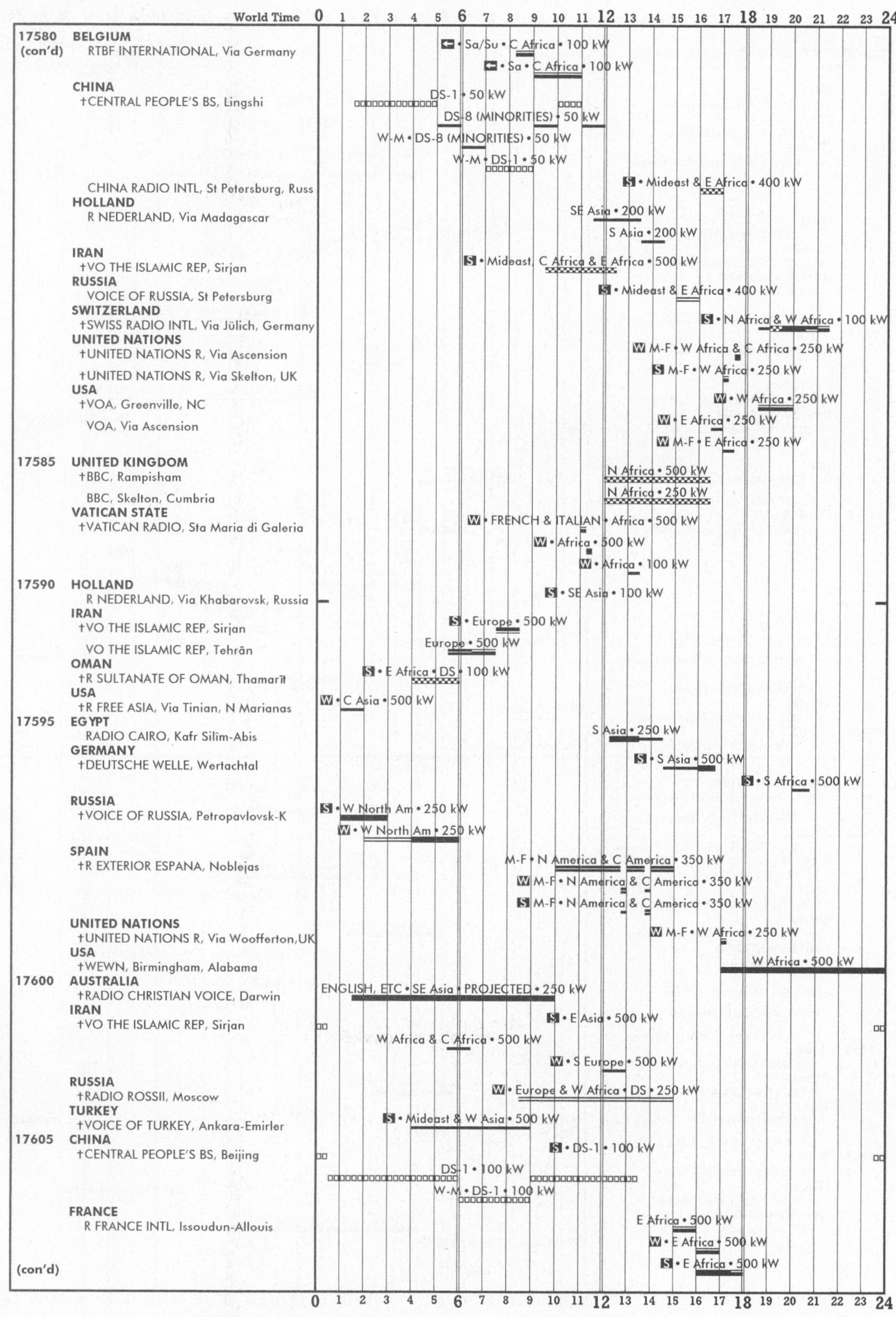
World Time 0 1 2 3 4 5 6 7 8 9 10 11 12 13 14 15 16 17 18 19 20 21 22 23 24
17580 (con'd) BELGIUM
RTBF INTERNATIONAL, Via Germany
Sa/Su • C Africa • 100 kW
Sa • C Africa • 100 kW
CHINA
†CENTRAL PEOPLE'S BS, Lingshi
DS-1 • 50 kW
DS-8 (MINORITIES) • 50 kW
W-M • DS-8 (MINORITIES) • 50 kW
W-M • DS-1 • 50 kW
CHINA RADIO INTL, St Petersburg, Russ
Mideast & E Africa • 400 kW
HOLLAND
R NEDERLAND, Via Madagascar
SE Asia • 200 kW
S Asia • 200 kW
IRAN
†VO THE ISLAMIC REP, Sirjan
Mideast, C Africa & E Africa • 500 kW
RUSSIA
VOICE OF RUSSIA, St Petersburg
Mideast & E Africa • 400 kW
SWITZERLAND
†SWISS RADIO INTL, Via Jülich, Germany
N Africa & W Africa • 100 kW
UNITED NATIONS
†UNITED NATIONS R, Via Ascension
M-F • W Africa & C Africa • 250 kW
†UNITED NATIONS R, Via Skelton, UK
M-F • W Africa • 250 kW
USA
†VOA, Greenville, NC
W Africa • 250 kW
VOA, Via Ascension
E Africa • 250 kW
M-F • E Africa • 250 kW
17585 UNITED KINGDOM
†BBC, Rampisham
N Africa • 500 kW
BBC, Skelton, Cumbria
N Africa • 250 kW
VATICAN STATE
†VATICAN RADIO, Sta Maria di Galeria
FRENCH & ITALIAN • Africa • 500 kW
Africa • 500 kW
Africa • 100 kW
17590 HOLLAND
R NEDERLAND, Via Khabarovsk, Russia
SE Asia • 100 kW
IRAN
†VO THE ISLAMIC REP, Sirjan
Europe • 500 kW
VO THE ISLAMIC REP, Tehrān
Europe • 500 kW
OMAN
†R SULTANATE OF OMAN, Thamarīt
E Africa • DS • 100 kW
USA
†R FREE ASIA, Via Tinian, N Marianas
C Asia • 500 kW
17595 EGYPT
RADIO CAIRO, Kafr Silîm-Abis
S Asia • 250 kW
GERMANY
†DEUTSCHE WELLE, Wertachtal
S Asia • 500 kW
S Africa • 500 kW
RUSSIA
†VOICE OF RUSSIA, Petropavlovsk-K
W North Am • 250 kW
W North Am • 250 kW
SPAIN
†R EXTERIOR ESPANA, Noblejas
M-F • N America & C America • 350 kW
M-F • N America & C America • 350 kW
M-F • N America & C America • 350 kW
UNITED NATIONS
†UNITED NATIONS R, Via Woofferton,UK
M-F • W Africa • 250 kW
USA
†WEWN, Birmingham, Alabama
W Africa • 500 kW
17600 AUSTRALIA
†RADIO CHRISTIAN VOICE, Darwin
ENGLISH, ETC • SE Asia • PROJECTED • 250 kW
IRAN
†VO THE ISLAMIC REP, Sirjan
E Asia • 500 kW
W Africa & C Africa • 500 kW
S Europe • 500 kW
RUSSIA
†RADIO ROSSII, Moscow
Europe & W Africa • DS • 250 kW
TURKEY
†VOICE OF TURKEY, Ankara-Emirler
Mideast & W Asia • 500 kW
17605 CHINA
†CENTRAL PEOPLE'S BS, Beijing
DS-1 • 100 kW
DS-1 • 100 kW
W-M • DS-1 • 100 kW
FRANCE
R FRANCE INTL, Issoudun-Allouis
E Africa • 500 kW
E Africa • 500 kW
E Africa • 500 kW
(con'd)
0 1 2 3 4 5 6 7 8 9 10 11 12 13 14 15 16 17 18 19 20 21 22 23 24

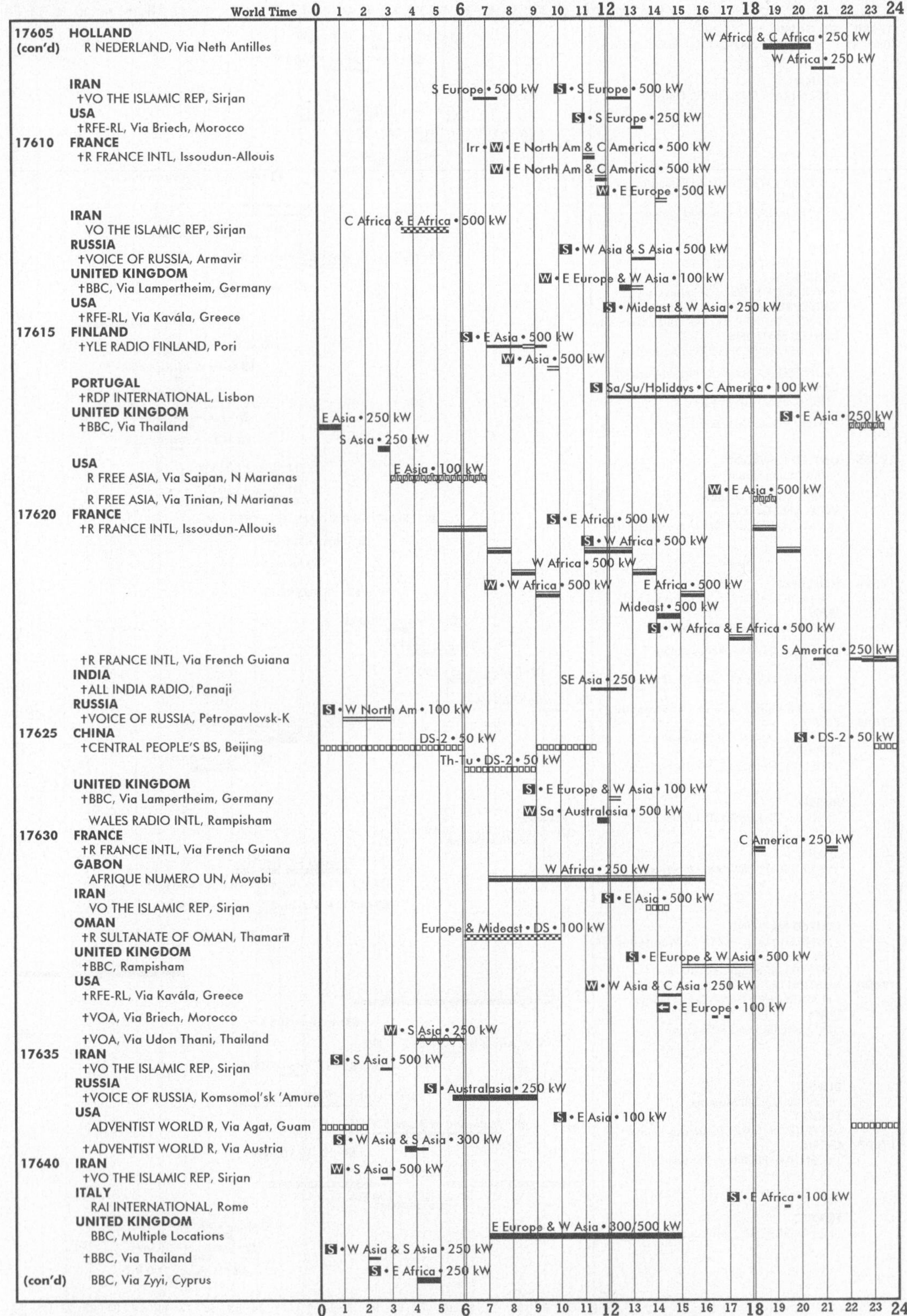
World Time 0 1 2 3 4 5 6 7 8 9 10 11 12 13 14 15 16 17 18 19 20 21 22 23 24
17605 (con'd) HOLLAND
R NEDERLAND, Via Neth Antilles
W Africa & C Africa • 250 kW
W Africa • 250 kW
IRAN
†VO THE ISLAMIC REP, Sirjan
S Europe • 500 kW
S • S Europe • 500 kW
USA
†RFE-RL, Via Briech, Morocco
S • S Europe • 250 kW
17610 FRANCE
†R FRANCE INTL, Issoudun-Allouis
Irr • W • E North Am & C America • 500 kW
W • E North Am & C America • 500 kW
W • E Europe • 500 kW
IRAN
VO THE ISLAMIC REP, Sirjan
C Africa & E Africa • 500 kW
RUSSIA
†VOICE OF RUSSIA, Armavir
S • W Asia & S Asia • 500 kW
UNITED KINGDOM
†BBC, Via Lampertheim, Germany
W • E Europe & W Asia • 100 kW
USA
†RFE-RL, Via Kavála, Greece
S • Mideast & W Asia • 250 kW
17615 FINLAND
†YLE RADIO FINLAND, Pori
S • E Asia • 500 kW
W • Asia • 500 kW
PORTUGAL
†RDP INTERNATIONAL, Lisbon
S Sa/Su/Holidays • C America • 100 kW
UNITED KINGDOM
†BBC, Via Thailand
E Asia • 250 kW
S Asia • 250 kW
S • E Asia • 250 kW
USA
R FREE ASIA, Via Saipan, N Marianas
E Asia • 100 kW
R FREE ASIA, Via Tinian, N Marianas
W • E Asia • 500 kW
17620 FRANCE
†R FRANCE INTL, Issoudun-Allouis
S • E Africa • 500 kW
S • W Africa • 500 kW
W Africa • 500 kW
W • W Africa • 500 kW
E Africa • 500 kW
Mideast • 500 kW
S • W Africa & E Africa • 500 kW
†R FRANCE INTL, Via French Guiana
S America • 250 kW
INDIA
†ALL INDIA RADIO, Panaji
SE Asia • 250 kW
RUSSIA
†VOICE OF RUSSIA, Petropavlovsk-K
S • W North Am • 100 kW
17625 CHINA
†CENTRAL PEOPLE'S BS, Beijing
DS-2 • 50 kW
Th-Tu • DS-2 • 50 kW
S • DS-2 • 50 kW
UNITED KINGDOM
†BBC, Via Lampertheim, Germany
S • E Europe & W Asia • 100 kW
WALES RADIO INTL, Rampisham
W Sa • Australasia • 500 kW
17630 FRANCE
†R FRANCE INTL, Via French Guiana
C America • 250 kW
GABON
AFRIQUE NUMERO UN, Moyabi
W Africa • 250 kW
IRAN
VO THE ISLAMIC REP, Sirjan
S • E Asia • 500 kW
OMAN
†R SULTANATE OF OMAN, Thamarīt
Europe & Mideast • DS • 100 kW
UNITED KINGDOM
†BBC, Rampisham
S • E Europe & W Asia • 500 kW
USA
†RFE-RL, Via Kavála, Greece
W • W Asia & C Asia • 250 kW
†VOA, Via Briech, Morocco
• E Europe • 100 kW
†VOA, Via Udon Thani, Thailand
W • S Asia • 250 kW
17635 IRAN
†VO THE ISLAMIC REP, Sirjan
S • S Asia • 500 kW
RUSSIA
†VOICE OF RUSSIA, Komsomol'sk 'Amure
S • Australasia • 250 kW
USA
ADVENTIST WORLD R, Via Agat, Guam
S • E Asia • 100 kW
†ADVENTIST WORLD R, Via Austria
S • W Asia & S Asia • 300 kW
17640 IRAN
†VO THE ISLAMIC REP, Sirjan
W • S Asia • 500 kW
ITALY
RAI INTERNATIONAL, Rome
S • E Africa • 100 kW
UNITED KINGDOM
BBC, Multiple Locations
E Europe & W Asia • 300/500 kW
†BBC, Via Thailand
S • W Asia & S Asia • 250 kW
(con'd) BBC, Via Zyyi, Cyprus
S • E Africa • 250 kW
0 1 2 3 4 5 6 7 8 9 10 11 12 13 14 15 16 17 18 19 20 21 22 23 24
ENGLISH ARABIC CHINESE FRENCH GERMAN RUSSIAN SPANISH OTHER

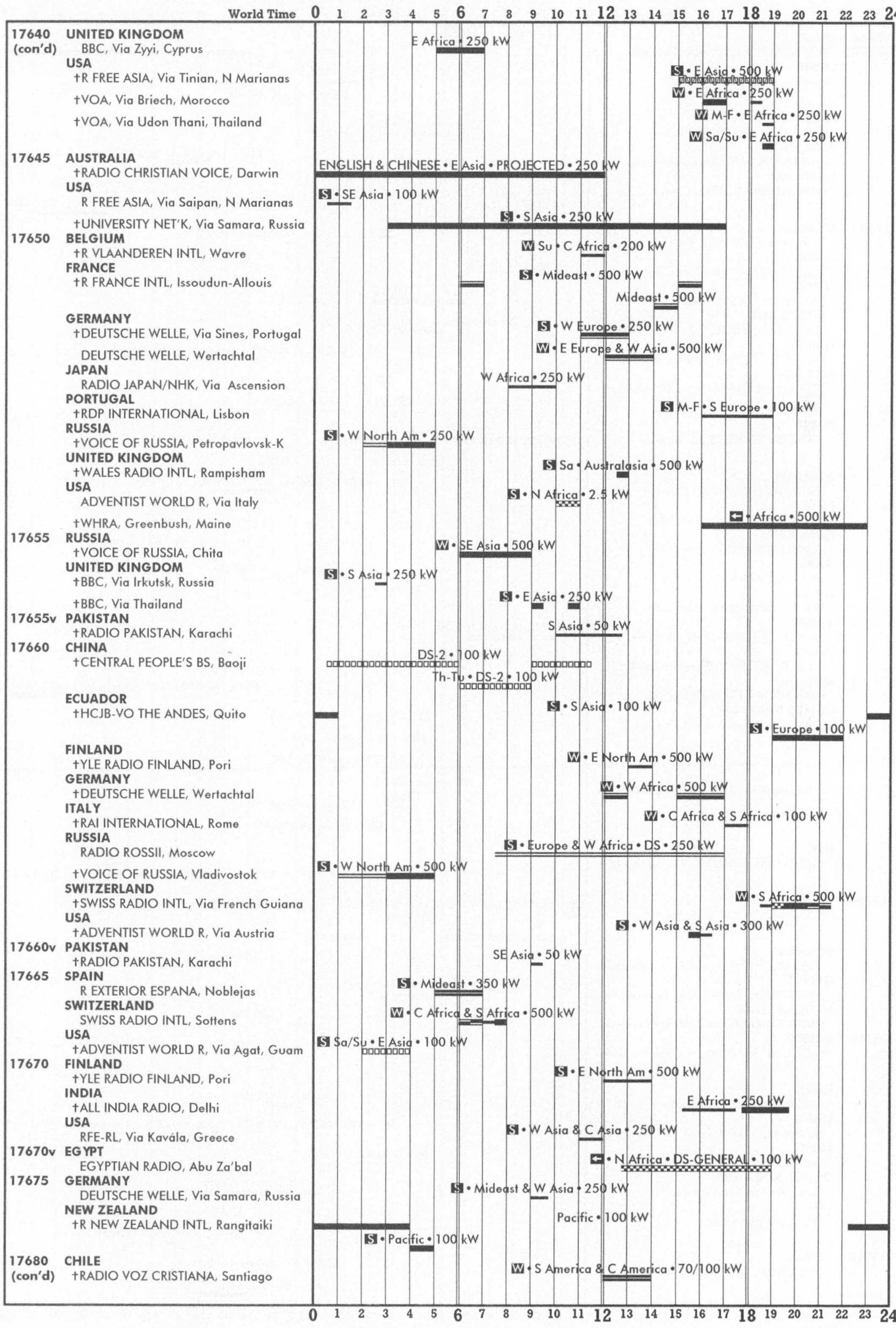
World Time 0 1 2 3 4 5 6 7 8 9 10 11 12 13 14 15 16 17 18 19 20 21 22 23 24
17640 (con'd) UNITED KINGDOM
BBC, Via Zyyi, Cyprus
E Africa • 250 kW
USA
†R FREE ASIA, Via Tinian, N Marianas
S • E Asia • 500 kW
†VOA, Via Briech, Morocco
W • E Africa • 250 kW
†VOA, Via Udon Thani, Thailand
W M-F • E Africa • 250 kW
W Sa/Su • E Africa • 250 kW
17645 AUSTRALIA
†RADIO CHRISTIAN VOICE, Darwin
ENGLISH & CHINESE • E Asia • PROJECTED • 250 kW
USA
R FREE ASIA, Via Saipan, N Marianas
S • SE Asia • 100 kW
†UNIVERSITY NET'K, Via Samara, Russia
S • S Asia • 250 kW
17650 BELGIUM
†R VLAANDEREN INTL, Wavre
W Su • C Africa • 200 kW
FRANCE
†R FRANCE INTL, Issoudun-Allouis
S • Mideast • 500 kW
Mideast • 500 kW
GERMANY
†DEUTSCHE WELLE, Via Sines, Portugal
S • W Europe • 250 kW
DEUTSCHE WELLE, Wertachtal
W • E Europe & W Asia • 500 kW
JAPAN
RADIO JAPAN/NHK, Via Ascension
W Africa • 250 kW
PORTUGAL
†RDP INTERNATIONAL, Lisbon
S M-F • S Europe • 100 kW
RUSSIA
†VOICE OF RUSSIA, Petropavlovsk-K
S • W North Am • 250 kW
UNITED KINGDOM
†WALES RADIO INTL, Rampisham
S Sa • Australasia • 500 kW
USA
ADVENTIST WORLD R, Via Italy
S • N Africa • 2.5 kW
†WHRA, Greenbush, Maine
Africa • 500 kW
17655 RUSSIA
†VOICE OF RUSSIA, Chita
W • SE Asia • 500 kW
UNITED KINGDOM
†BBC, Via Irkutsk, Russia
S • S Asia • 250 kW
†BBC, Via Thailand
S • E Asia • 250 kW
17655v PAKISTAN
†RADIO PAKISTAN, Karachi
S Asia • 50 kW
17660 CHINA
†CENTRAL PEOPLE'S BS, Baoji
DS-2 • 100 kW
Th-Tu • DS-2 • 100 kW
ECUADOR
†HCJB-VO THE ANDES, Quito
S • S Asia • 100 kW
S • Europe • 100 kW
FINLAND
†YLE RADIO FINLAND, Pori
W • E North Am • 500 kW
GERMANY
†DEUTSCHE WELLE, Wertachtal
W • W Africa • 500 kW
ITALY
†RAI INTERNATIONAL, Rome
W • C Africa & S Africa • 100 kW
RUSSIA
RADIO ROSSII, Moscow
S • Europe & W Africa • DS • 250 kW
†VOICE OF RUSSIA, Vladivostok
S • W North Am • 500 kW
SWITZERLAND
†SWISS RADIO INTL, Via French Guiana
W • S Africa • 500 kW
USA
†ADVENTIST WORLD R, Via Austria
S • W Asia & S Asia • 300 kW
17660v PAKISTAN
†RADIO PAKISTAN, Karachi
SE Asia • 50 kW
17665 SPAIN
R EXTERIOR ESPANA, Noblejas
S • Mideast • 350 kW
SWITZERLAND
SWISS RADIO INTL, Sottens
W • C Africa & S Africa • 500 kW
USA
†ADVENTIST WORLD R, Via Agat, Guam
S Sa/Su • E Asia • 100 kW
17670 FINLAND
†YLE RADIO FINLAND, Pori
S • E North Am • 500 kW
INDIA
†ALL INDIA RADIO, Delhi
E Africa • 250 kW
USA
RFE-RL, Via Kavála, Greece
S • W Asia & C Asia • 250 kW
17670v EGYPT
EGYPTIAN RADIO, Abu Za'bal
N Africa • DS-GENERAL • 100 kW
17675 GERMANY
DEUTSCHE WELLE, Via Samara, Russia
S • Mideast & W Asia • 250 kW
NEW ZEALAND
†R NEW ZEALAND INTL, Rangitaiki
Pacific • 100 kW
S • Pacific • 100 kW
17680 (con'd) CHILE
†RADIO VOZ CRISTIANA, Santiago
W • S America & C America • 70/100 kW
0 1 2 3 4 5 6 7 8 9 10 11 12 13 14 15 16 17 18 19 20 21 22 23 24

SEASONAL S OR W 1-HR TIMESHIFT MIDYEAR ◄ OR ► JAMMING / OR /\ EARLIEST HEARD ◁ LATEST HEARD ▷ NEW FOR 2002 †

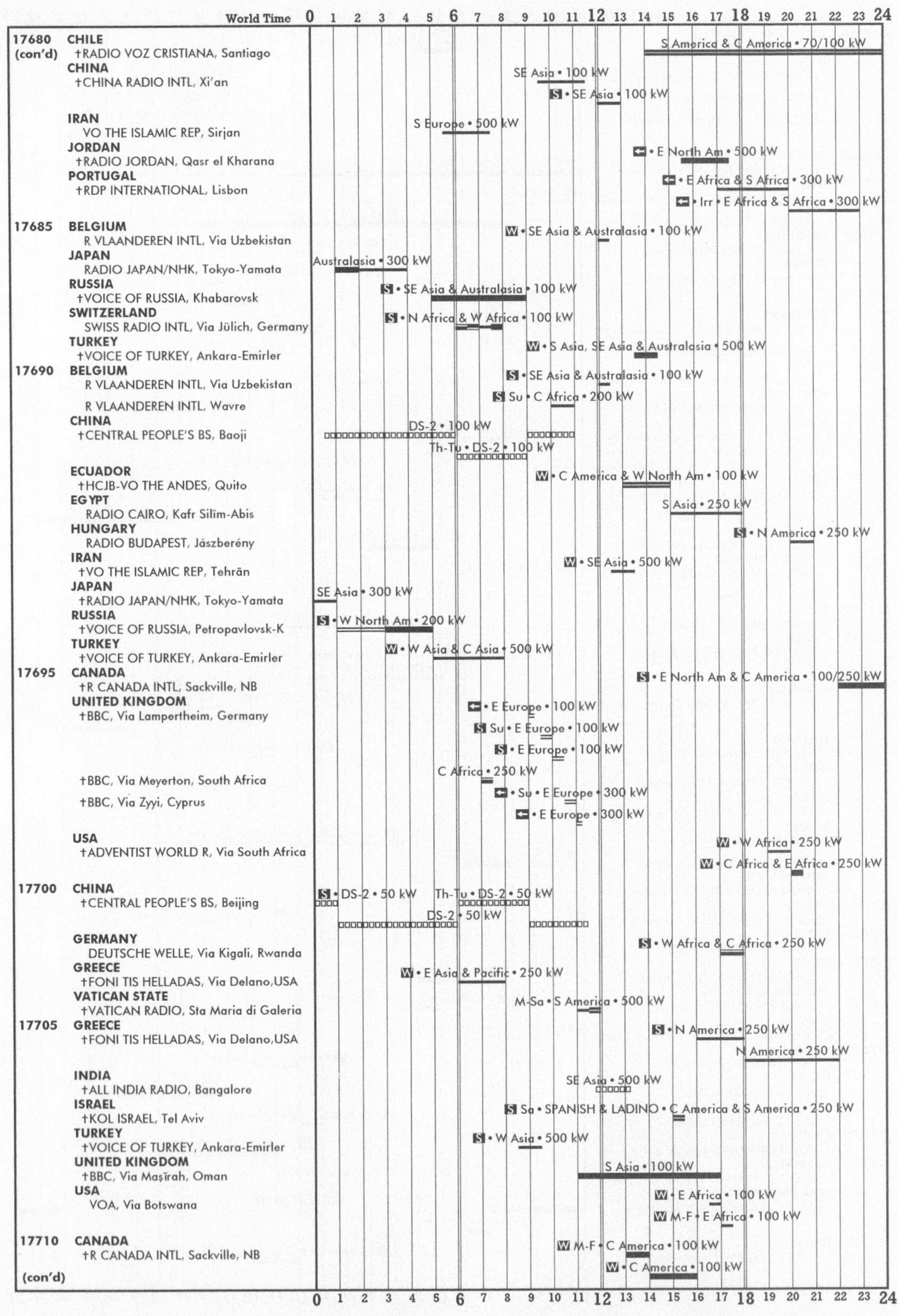
World Time 0 1 2 3 4 5 6 7 8 9 10 11 12 13 14 15 16 17 18 19 20 21 22 23 24
17680 (con'd) CHILE
†RADIO VOZ CRISTIANA, Santiago
S America & C America • 70/100 kW
CHINA
†CHINA RADIO INTL, Xi'an
SE Asia • 100 kW
S • SE Asia • 100 kW
IRAN
VO THE ISLAMIC REP, Sirjan
S Europe • 500 kW
JORDAN
†RADIO JORDAN, Qasr el Kharana
• E North Am • 500 kW
PORTUGAL
†RDP INTERNATIONAL, Lisbon
• E Africa & S Africa • 300 kW
• Irr • E Africa & S Africa • 300 kW
17685 BELGIUM
R VLAANDEREN INTL, Via Uzbekistan
W • SE Asia & Australasia • 100 kW
JAPAN
RADIO JAPAN/NHK, Tokyo-Yamata
Australasia • 300 kW
RUSSIA
†VOICE OF RUSSIA, Khabarovsk
S • SE Asia & Australasia • 100 kW
SWITZERLAND
SWISS RADIO INTL, Via Jülich, Germany
S • N Africa & W Africa • 100 kW
TURKEY
†VOICE OF TURKEY, Ankara-Emirler
W • S Asia, SE Asia & Australasia • 500 kW
17690 BELGIUM
R VLAANDEREN INTL, Via Uzbekistan
S • SE Asia & Australasia • 100 kW
R VLAANDEREN INTL, Wavre
S Su • C Africa • 200 kW
CHINA
†CENTRAL PEOPLE'S BS, Baoji
DS-2 • 100 kW
Th-Tu • DS-2 • 100 kW
ECUADOR
†HCJB-VO THE ANDES, Quito
W • C America & W North Am • 100 kW
EGYPT
RADIO CAIRO, Kafr Silîm-Abis
S Asia • 250 kW
HUNGARY
RADIO BUDAPEST, Jászberény
S • N America • 250 kW
IRAN
†VO THE ISLAMIC REP, Tehrān
W • SE Asia • 500 kW
JAPAN
†RADIO JAPAN/NHK, Tokyo-Yamata
SE Asia • 300 kW
RUSSIA
†VOICE OF RUSSIA, Petropavlovsk-K
S • W North Am • 200 kW
TURKEY
†VOICE OF TURKEY, Ankara-Emirler
W • W Asia & C Asia • 500 kW
17695 CANADA
†R CANADA INTL, Sackville, NB
S • E North Am & C America • 100/250 kW
UNITED KINGDOM
†BBC, Via Lampertheim, Germany
• E Europe • 100 kW
S Su • E Europe • 100 kW
S • E Europe • 100 kW
†BBC, Via Meyerton, South Africa
C Africa • 250 kW
†BBC, Via Zyyi, Cyprus
• Su • E Europe • 300 kW
• E Europe • 300 kW
USA
†ADVENTIST WORLD R, Via South Africa
W • W Africa • 250 kW
W • C Africa & E Africa • 250 kW
17700 CHINA
†CENTRAL PEOPLE'S BS, Beijing
S • DS-2 • 50 kW
Th-Tu • DS-2 • 50 kW
DS-2 • 50 kW
GERMANY
DEUTSCHE WELLE, Via Kigali, Rwanda
S • W Africa & C Africa • 250 kW
GREECE
†FONI TIS HELLADAS, Via Delano,USA
W • E Asia & Pacific • 250 kW
VATICAN STATE
†VATICAN RADIO, Sta Maria di Galeria
M-Sa • S America • 500 kW
17705 GREECE
†FONI TIS HELLADAS, Via Delano,USA
S • N America • 250 kW
N America • 250 kW
INDIA
†ALL INDIA RADIO, Bangalore
SE Asia • 500 kW
ISRAEL
†KOL ISRAEL, Tel Aviv
S Sa • SPANISH & LADINO • C America & S America • 250 kW
TURKEY
†VOICE OF TURKEY, Ankara-Emirler
S • W Asia • 500 kW
UNITED KINGDOM
†BBC, Via Maṣīrah, Oman
S Asia • 100 kW
USA
VOA, Via Botswana
W • E Africa • 100 kW
W M-F • E Africa • 100 kW
17710 CANADA
†R CANADA INTL, Sackville, NB
W M-F • C America • 100 kW
W • C America • 100 kW
(con'd)
0 1 2 3 4 5 6 7 8 9 10 11 12 13 14 15 16 17 18 19 20 21 22 23 24
ENGLISH ARABIC CHINESE FRENCH GERMAN RUSSIAN SPANISH OTHER

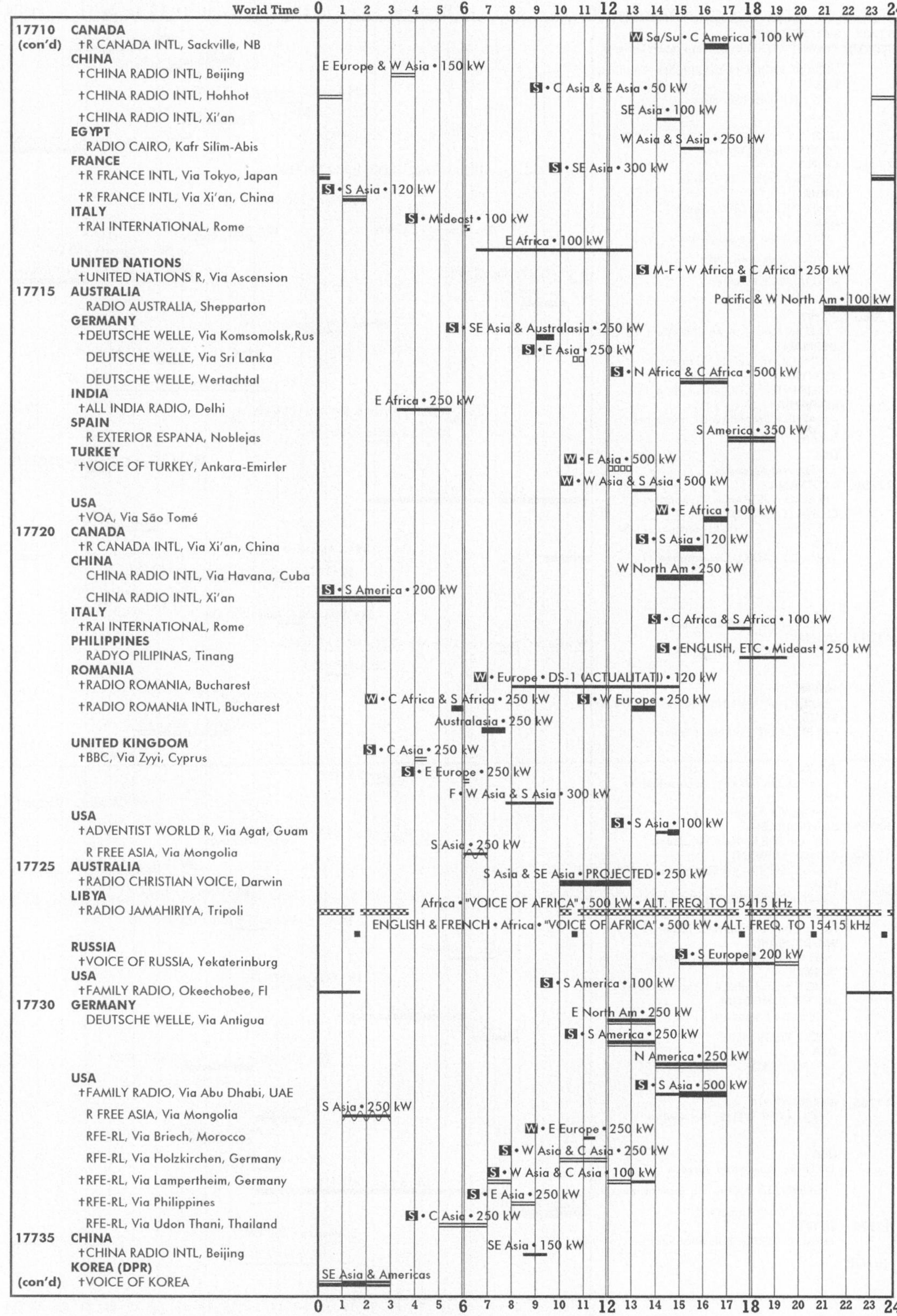
World Time 0 1 2 3 4 5 6 7 8 9 10 11 12 13 14 15 16 17 18 19 20 21 22 23 24
17710 CANADA
(con'd) †R CANADA INTL, Sackville, NB
W Sa/Su • C America • 100 kW
CHINA
†CHINA RADIO INTL, Beijing
E Europe & W Asia • 150 kW
†CHINA RADIO INTL, Hohhot
S • C Asia & E Asia • 50 kW
†CHINA RADIO INTL, Xi'an
SE Asia • 100 kW
EGYPT
RADIO CAIRO, Kafr Silîm-Abis
W Asia & S Asia • 250 kW
FRANCE
†R FRANCE INTL, Via Tokyo, Japan
S • SE Asia • 300 kW
†R FRANCE INTL, Via Xi'an, China
S • S Asia • 120 kW
ITALY
†RAI INTERNATIONAL, Rome
S • Mideast • 100 kW
E Africa • 100 kW
UNITED NATIONS
†UNITED NATIONS R, Via Ascension
S M-F • W Africa & C Africa • 250 kW
17715 AUSTRALIA
RADIO AUSTRALIA, Shepparton
Pacific & W North Am • 100 kW
GERMANY
†DEUTSCHE WELLE, Via Komsomolsk, Rus
S • SE Asia & Australasia • 250 kW
DEUTSCHE WELLE, Via Sri Lanka
S • E Asia • 250 kW
DEUTSCHE WELLE, Wertachtal
S • N Africa & C Africa • 500 kW
INDIA
†ALL INDIA RADIO, Delhi
E Africa • 250 kW
SPAIN
R EXTERIOR ESPANA, Noblejas
S America • 350 kW
TURKEY
†VOICE OF TURKEY, Ankara-Emirler
W • E Asia • 500 kW
W • W Asia & S Asia • 500 kW
USA
†VOA, Via São Tomé
W • E Africa • 100 kW
17720 CANADA
†R CANADA INTL, Via Xi'an, China
S • S Asia • 120 kW
CHINA
CHINA RADIO INTL, Via Havana, Cuba
W North Am • 250 kW
CHINA RADIO INTL, Xi'an
S • S America • 200 kW
ITALY
†RAI INTERNATIONAL, Rome
S • C Africa & S Africa • 100 kW
PHILIPPINES
RADYO PILIPINAS, Tinang
S • ENGLISH, ETC • Mideast • 250 kW
ROMANIA
†RADIO ROMANIA, Bucharest
W • Europe • DS-1 (ACTUALITATI) • 120 kW
†RADIO ROMANIA INTL, Bucharest
W • C Africa & S Africa • 250 kW
S • W Europe • 250 kW
Australasia • 250 kW
UNITED KINGDOM
†BBC, Via Zyyi, Cyprus
S • C Asia • 250 kW
S • E Europe • 250 kW
F • W Asia & S Asia • 300 kW
USA
†ADVENTIST WORLD R, Via Agat, Guam
S • S Asia • 100 kW
R FREE ASIA, Via Mongolia
S Asia • 250 kW
17725 AUSTRALIA
†RADIO CHRISTIAN VOICE, Darwin
S Asia & SE Asia • PROJECTED • 250 kW
LIBYA
†RADIO JAMAHIRIYA, Tripoli
Africa • "VOICE OF AFRICA" • 500 kW • ALT. FREQ. TO 15415 kHz
ENGLISH & FRENCH • Africa • "VOICE OF AFRICA" • 500 kW • ALT. FREQ. TO 15415 kHz
RUSSIA
†VOICE OF RUSSIA, Yekaterinburg
S • S Europe • 200 kW
USA
†FAMILY RADIO, Okeechobee, Fl
S • S America • 100 kW
17730 GERMANY
DEUTSCHE WELLE, Via Antigua
E North Am • 250 kW
S • S America • 250 kW
N America • 250 kW
USA
†FAMILY RADIO, Via Abu Dhabi, UAE
S • S Asia • 500 kW
R FREE ASIA, Via Mongolia
S Asia • 250 kW
RFE-RL, Via Briech, Morocco
W • E Europe • 250 kW
RFE-RL, Via Holzkirchen, Germany
S • W Asia & C Asia • 250 kW
†RFE-RL, Via Lampertheim, Germany
S • W Asia & C Asia • 100 kW
†RFE-RL, Via Philippines
S • E Asia • 250 kW
RFE-RL, Via Udon Thani, Thailand
S • C Asia • 250 kW
17735 CHINA
†CHINA RADIO INTL, Beijing
SE Asia • 150 kW
KOREA (DPR)
(con'd) †VOICE OF KOREA
SE Asia & Americas
0 1 2 3 4 5 6 7 8 9 10 11 12 13 14 15 16 17 18 19 20 21 22 23 24

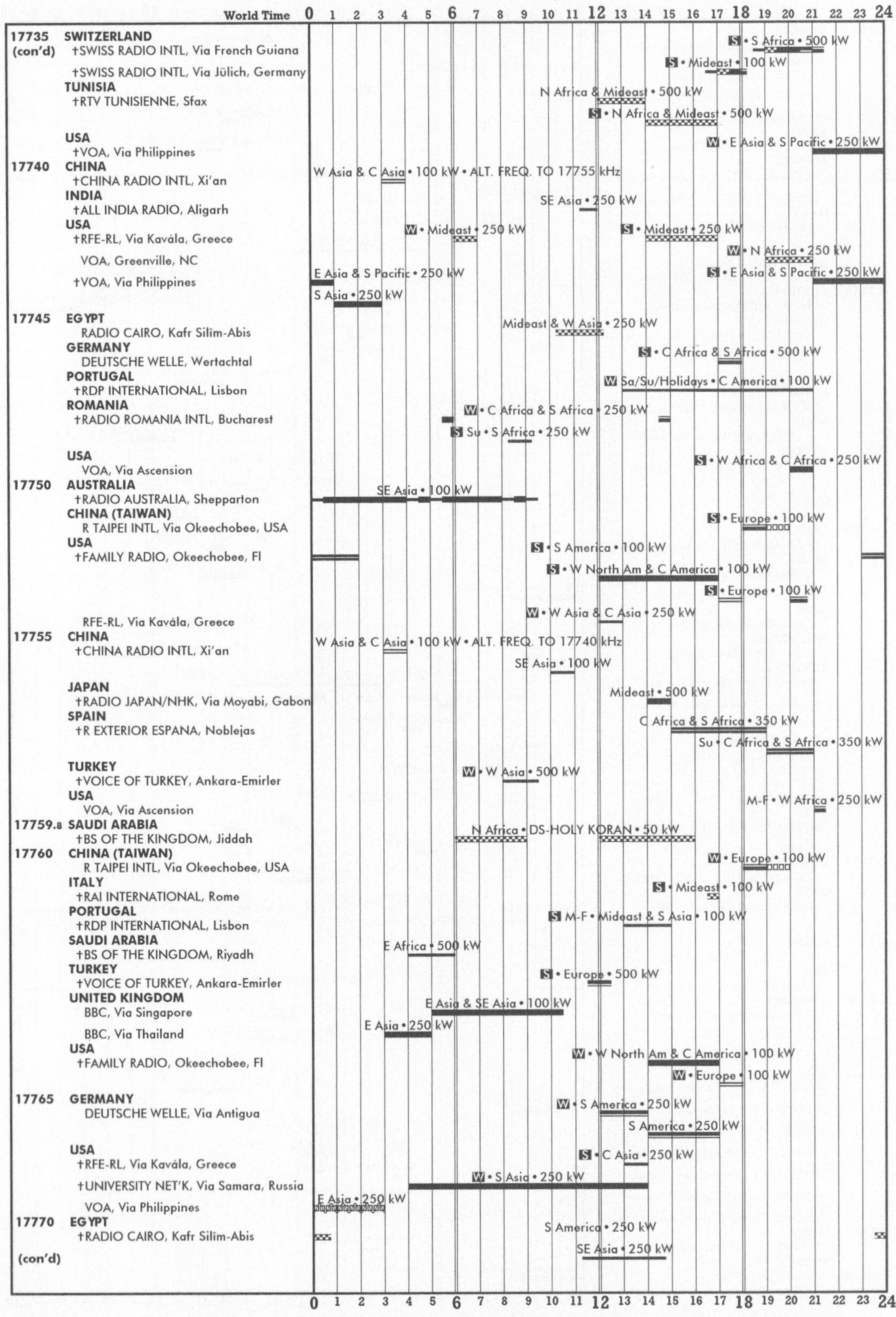
World Time 0 1 2 3 4 5 6 7 8 9 10 11 12 13 14 15 16 17 18 19 20 21 22 23 24
17735 (con'd) SWITZERLAND
†SWISS RADIO INTL, Via French Guiana
S • S Africa • 500 kW
†SWISS RADIO INTL, Via Jülich, Germany
S • Mideast • 100 kW
TUNISIA
†RTV TUNISIENNE, Sfax
N Africa & Mideast • 500 kW
S • N Africa & Mideast • 500 kW
USA
†VOA, Via Philippines
W • E Asia & S Pacific • 250 kW
17740 CHINA
†CHINA RADIO INTL, Xi'an
W Asia & C Asia • 100 kW • ALT. FREQ. TO 17755 kHz
INDIA
†ALL INDIA RADIO, Aligarh
SE Asia • 250 kW
USA
†RFE-RL, Via Kavála, Greece
W • Mideast • 250 kW
S • Mideast • 250 kW
VOA, Greenville, NC
W • N Africa • 250 kW
†VOA, Via Philippines
E Asia & S Pacific • 250 kW
S • E Asia & S Pacific • 250 kW
S Asia • 250 kW
17745 EGYPT
RADIO CAIRO, Kafr Silîm-Abis
Mideast & W Asia • 250 kW
GERMANY
DEUTSCHE WELLE, Wertachtal
S • C Africa & S Africa • 500 kW
PORTUGAL
†RDP INTERNATIONAL, Lisbon
W Sa/Su/Holidays • C America • 100 kW
ROMANIA
†RADIO ROMANIA INTL, Bucharest
W • C Africa & S Africa • 250 kW
S Su • S Africa • 250 kW
USA
VOA, Via Ascension
S • W Africa & C Africa • 250 kW
17750 AUSTRALIA
†RADIO AUSTRALIA, Shepparton
SE Asia • 100 kW
CHINA (TAIWAN)
R TAIPEI INTL, Via Okeechobee, USA
S • Europe • 100 kW
USA
†FAMILY RADIO, Okeechobee, Fl
S • S America • 100 kW
S • W North Am & C America • 100 kW
S • Europe • 100 kW
RFE-RL, Via Kavála, Greece
W • W Asia & C Asia • 250 kW
17755 CHINA
†CHINA RADIO INTL, Xi'an
W Asia & C Asia • 100 kW • ALT. FREQ. TO 17740 kHz
SE Asia • 100 kW
JAPAN
†RADIO JAPAN/NHK, Via Moyabi, Gabon
Mideast • 500 kW
SPAIN
†R EXTERIOR ESPANA, Noblejas
C Africa & S Africa • 350 kW
Su • C Africa & S Africa • 350 kW
TURKEY
†VOICE OF TURKEY, Ankara-Emirler
W • W Asia • 500 kW
USA
VOA, Via Ascension
M-F • W Africa • 250 kW
17759.8 SAUDI ARABIA
†BS OF THE KINGDOM, Jiddah
N Africa • DS-HOLY KORAN • 50 kW
17760 CHINA (TAIWAN)
R TAIPEI INTL, Via Okeechobee, USA
W • Europe • 100 kW
ITALY
†RAI INTERNATIONAL, Rome
S • Mideast • 100 kW
PORTUGAL
†RDP INTERNATIONAL, Lisbon
S M-F • Mideast & S Asia • 100 kW
SAUDI ARABIA
†BS OF THE KINGDOM, Riyadh
E Africa • 500 kW
TURKEY
†VOICE OF TURKEY, Ankara-Emirler
S • Europe • 500 kW
UNITED KINGDOM
BBC, Via Singapore
E Asia & SE Asia • 100 kW
BBC, Via Thailand
E Asia • 250 kW
USA
†FAMILY RADIO, Okeechobee, Fl
W • W North Am & C America • 100 kW
W • Europe • 100 kW
17765 GERMANY
DEUTSCHE WELLE, Via Antigua
W • S America • 250 kW
S America • 250 kW
USA
†RFE-RL, Via Kavála, Greece
S • C Asia • 250 kW
†UNIVERSITY NET'K, Via Samara, Russia
W • S Asia • 250 kW
VOA, Via Philippines
E Asia • 250 kW
17770 EGYPT
†RADIO CAIRO, Kafr Silîm-Abis
S America • 250 kW
SE Asia • 250 kW
(con'd)
0 1 2 3 4 5 6 7 8 9 10 11 12 13 14 15 16 17 18 19 20 21 22 23 24
ENGLISH ARABIC CHINESE FRENCH GERMAN RUSSIAN SPANISH OTHER

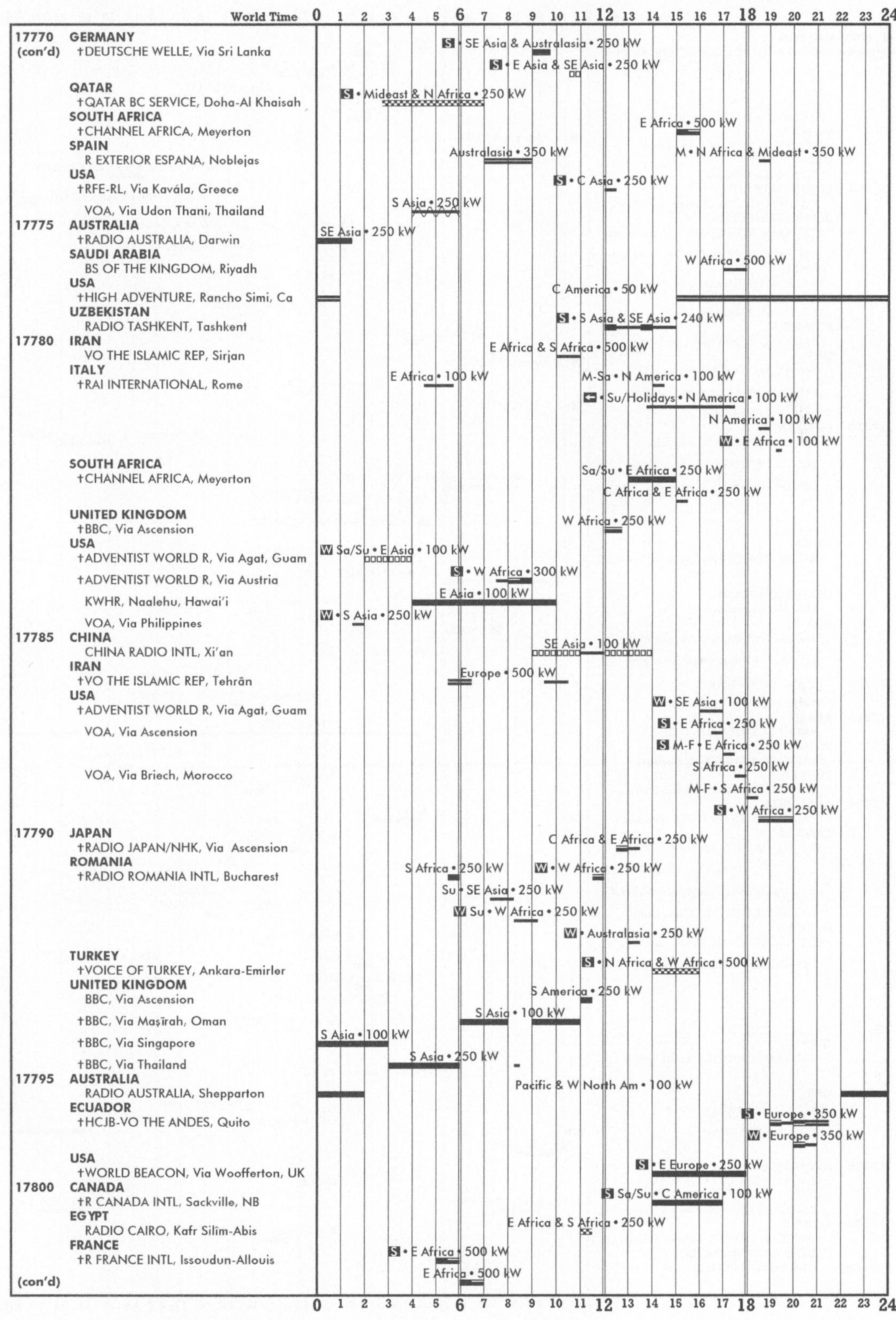
World Time 0 1 2 3 4 5 6 7 8 9 10 11 12 13 14 15 16 17 18 19 20 21 22 23 24
17770 (con'd) GERMANY
†DEUTSCHE WELLE, Via Sri Lanka
S • SE Asia & Australasia • 250 kW
S • E Asia & SE Asia • 250 kW
QATAR
†QATAR BC SERVICE, Doha-Al Khaisah
S • Mideast & N Africa • 250 kW
SOUTH AFRICA
†CHANNEL AFRICA, Meyerton
E Africa • 500 kW
SPAIN
R EXTERIOR ESPANA, Noblejas
Australasia • 350 kW
M • N Africa & Mideast • 350 kW
USA
†RFE-RL, Via Kavála, Greece
S • C Asia • 250 kW
VOA, Via Udon Thani, Thailand
S Asia • 250 kW
17775 AUSTRALIA
†RADIO AUSTRALIA, Darwin
SE Asia • 250 kW
SAUDI ARABIA
BS OF THE KINGDOM, Riyadh
W Africa • 500 kW
USA
†HIGH ADVENTURE, Rancho Simi, Ca
C America • 50 kW
UZBEKISTAN
RADIO TASHKENT, Tashkent
S • S Asia & SE Asia • 240 kW
17780 IRAN
VO THE ISLAMIC REP, Sirjan
E Africa & S Africa • 500 kW
ITALY
†RAI INTERNATIONAL, Rome
E Africa • 100 kW
M-Sa • N America • 100 kW
Su/Holidays • N America • 100 kW
N America • 100 kW
W • E Africa • 100 kW
SOUTH AFRICA
†CHANNEL AFRICA, Meyerton
Sa/Su • E Africa • 250 kW
C Africa & E Africa • 250 kW
UNITED KINGDOM
†BBC, Via Ascension
W Africa • 250 kW
USA
†ADVENTIST WORLD R, Via Agat, Guam
W Sa/Su • E Asia • 100 kW
†ADVENTIST WORLD R, Via Austria
S • W Africa • 300 kW
KWHR, Naalehu, Hawai'i
E Asia • 100 kW
VOA, Via Philippines
W • S Asia • 250 kW
17785 CHINA
CHINA RADIO INTL, Xi'an
SE Asia • 100 kW
IRAN
†VO THE ISLAMIC REP, Tehrān
Europe • 500 kW
USA
†ADVENTIST WORLD R, Via Agat, Guam
W • SE Asia • 100 kW
VOA, Via Ascension
S • E Africa • 250 kW
S M-F • E Africa • 250 kW
VOA, Via Briech, Morocco
S Africa • 250 kW
M-F • S Africa • 250 kW
S • W Africa • 250 kW
17790 JAPAN
†RADIO JAPAN/NHK, Via Ascension
C Africa & E Africa • 250 kW
ROMANIA
†RADIO ROMANIA INTL, Bucharest
S Africa • 250 kW
W • W Africa • 250 kW
Su • SE Asia • 250 kW
W Su • W Africa • 250 kW
W • Australasia • 250 kW
TURKEY
†VOICE OF TURKEY, Ankara-Emirler
S • N Africa & W Africa • 500 kW
UNITED KINGDOM
BBC, Via Ascension
S America • 250 kW
†BBC, Via Maṣīrah, Oman
S Asia • 100 kW
†BBC, Via Singapore
S Asia • 100 kW
†BBC, Via Thailand
S Asia • 250 kW
17795 AUSTRALIA
RADIO AUSTRALIA, Shepparton
Pacific & W North Am • 100 kW
ECUADOR
†HCJB-VO THE ANDES, Quito
S • Europe • 350 kW
W • Europe • 350 kW
USA
†WORLD BEACON, Via Woofferton, UK
S • E Europe • 250 kW
17800 CANADA
†R CANADA INTL, Sackville, NB
S Sa/Su • C America • 100 kW
EGYPT
RADIO CAIRO, Kafr Silîm-Abis
E Africa & S Africa • 250 kW
FRANCE
†R FRANCE INTL, Issoudun-Allouis
S • E Africa • 500 kW
E Africa • 500 kW
(con'd)
0 1 2 3 4 5 6 7 8 9 10 11 12 13 14 15 16 17 18 19 20 21 22 23 24

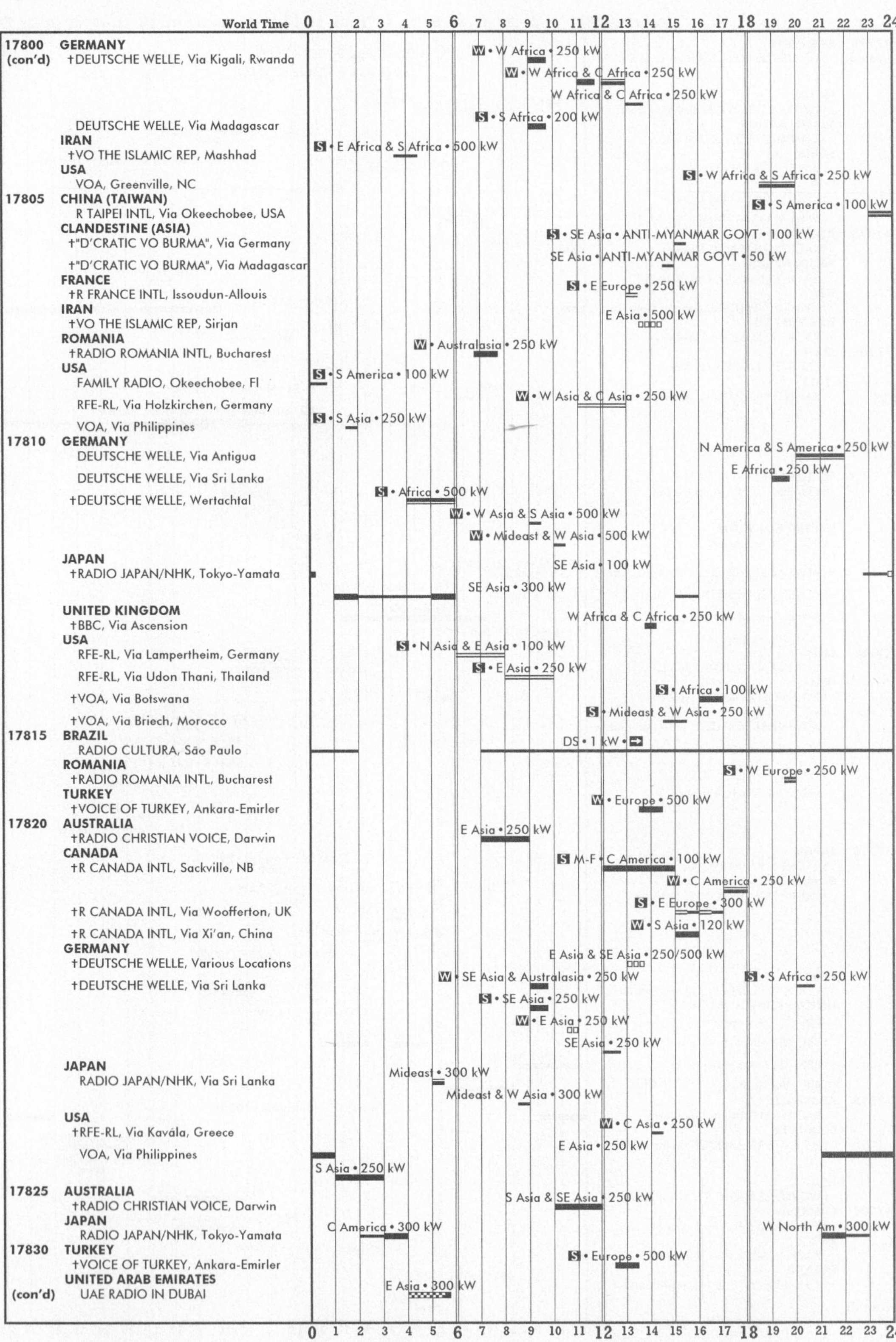
World Time 0 1 2 3 4 5 6 7 8 9 10 11 12 13 14 15 16 17 18 19 20 21 22 23 24
17800 (con'd) GERMANY
†DEUTSCHE WELLE, Via Kigali, Rwanda
W • W Africa • 250 kW
W • W Africa & C Africa • 250 kW
W Africa & C Africa • 250 kW
DEUTSCHE WELLE, Via Madagascar
S • S Africa • 200 kW
IRAN
†VO THE ISLAMIC REP, Mashhad
S • E Africa & S Africa • 500 kW
USA
VOA, Greenville, NC
S • W Africa & S Africa • 250 kW
17805 CHINA (TAIWAN)
R TAIPEI INTL, Via Okeechobee, USA
S • S America • 100 kW
CLANDESTINE (ASIA)
†"D'CRATIC VO BURMA", Via Germany
S • SE Asia • ANTI-MYANMAR GOVT • 100 kW
†"D'CRATIC VO BURMA", Via Madagascar
SE Asia • ANTI-MYANMAR GOVT • 50 kW
FRANCE
†R FRANCE INTL, Issoudun-Allouis
S • E Europe • 250 kW
IRAN
†VO THE ISLAMIC REP, Sirjan
E Asia • 500 kW
ROMANIA
†RADIO ROMANIA INTL, Bucharest
W • Australasia • 250 kW
USA
FAMILY RADIO, Okeechobee, Fl
S • S America • 100 kW
RFE-RL, Via Holzkirchen, Germany
W • W Asia & C Asia • 250 kW
VOA, Via Philippines
S • S Asia • 250 kW
17810 GERMANY
DEUTSCHE WELLE, Via Antigua
N America & S America • 250 kW
DEUTSCHE WELLE, Via Sri Lanka
E Africa • 250 kW
†DEUTSCHE WELLE, Wertachtal
S • Africa • 500 kW
W • W Asia & S Asia • 500 kW
W • Mideast & W Asia • 500 kW
JAPAN
†RADIO JAPAN/NHK, Tokyo-Yamata
SE Asia • 100 kW
SE Asia • 300 kW
UNITED KINGDOM
†BBC, Via Ascension
W Africa & C Africa • 250 kW
USA
RFE-RL, Via Lampertheim, Germany
S • N Asia & E Asia • 100 kW
RFE-RL, Via Udon Thani, Thailand
S • E Asia • 250 kW
†VOA, Via Botswana
S • Africa • 100 kW
†VOA, Via Briech, Morocco
S • Mideast & W Asia • 250 kW
17815 BRAZIL
RADIO CULTURA, São Paulo
DS • 1 kW •
ROMANIA
†RADIO ROMANIA INTL, Bucharest
S • W Europe • 250 kW
TURKEY
†VOICE OF TURKEY, Ankara-Emirler
W • Europe • 500 kW
17820 AUSTRALIA
†RADIO CHRISTIAN VOICE, Darwin
E Asia • 250 kW
CANADA
†R CANADA INTL, Sackville, NB
S M-F • C America • 100 kW
W • C America • 250 kW
†R CANADA INTL, Via Woofferton, UK
S • E Europe • 300 kW
†R CANADA INTL, Via Xi'an, China
W • S Asia • 120 kW
GERMANY
†DEUTSCHE WELLE, Various Locations
E Asia & SE Asia • 250/500 kW
†DEUTSCHE WELLE, Via Sri Lanka
W • SE Asia & Australasia • 250 kW
S • S Africa • 250 kW
S • SE Asia • 250 kW
W • E Asia • 250 kW
SE Asia • 250 kW
JAPAN
RADIO JAPAN/NHK, Via Sri Lanka
Mideast • 300 kW
Mideast & W Asia • 300 kW
USA
†RFE-RL, Via Kavála, Greece
W • C Asia • 250 kW
VOA, Via Philippines
E Asia • 250 kW
S Asia • 250 kW
17825 AUSTRALIA
†RADIO CHRISTIAN VOICE, Darwin
S Asia & SE Asia • 250 kW
JAPAN
RADIO JAPAN/NHK, Tokyo-Yamata
C America • 300 kW
W North Am • 300 kW
17830 TURKEY
†VOICE OF TURKEY, Ankara-Emirler
S • Europe • 500 kW
UNITED ARAB EMIRATES (con'd)
UAE RADIO IN DUBAI
E Asia • 300 kW
0 1 2 3 4 5 6 7 8 9 10 11 12 13 14 15 16 17 18 19 20 21 22 23 24
ENGLISH ARABIC CHINESE FRENCH GERMAN RUSSIAN SPANISH OTHER

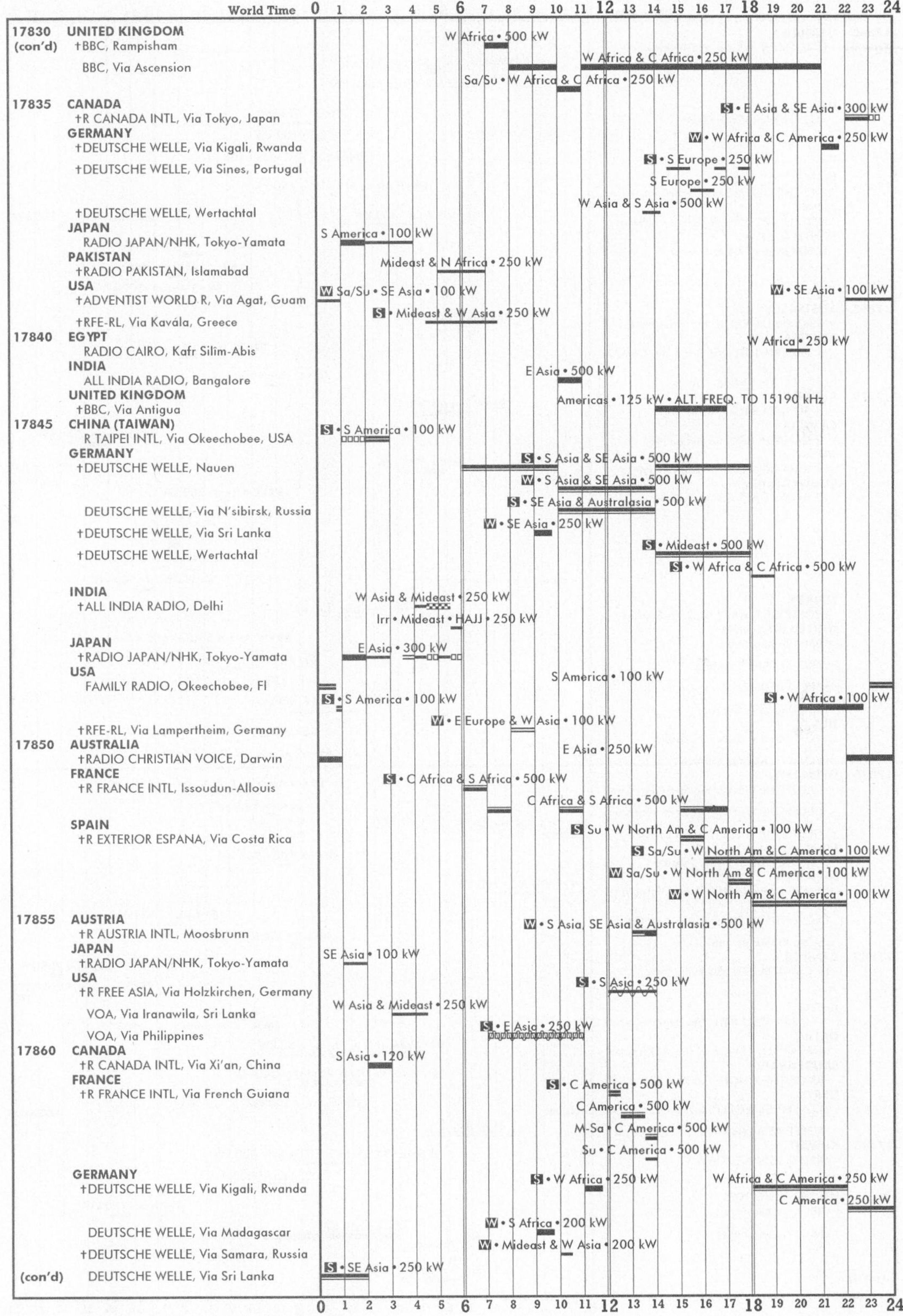
World Time 0 1 2 3 4 5 6 7 8 9 10 11 12 13 14 15 16 17 18 19 20 21 22 23 24
17830 (con'd) UNITED KINGDOM
†BBC, Rampisham
W Africa • 500 kW
BBC, Via Ascension
W Africa & C Africa • 250 kW
Sa/Su • W Africa & C Africa • 250 kW
17835 CANADA
†R CANADA INTL, Via Tokyo, Japan
S • E Asia & SE Asia • 300 kW
GERMANY
†DEUTSCHE WELLE, Via Kigali, Rwanda
W • W Africa & C America • 250 kW
†DEUTSCHE WELLE, Via Sines, Portugal
S • S Europe • 250 kW
S Europe • 250 kW
W Asia & S Asia • 500 kW
†DEUTSCHE WELLE, Wertachtal
JAPAN
RADIO JAPAN/NHK, Tokyo-Yamata
S America • 100 kW
PAKISTAN
†RADIO PAKISTAN, Islamabad
Mideast & N Africa • 250 kW
USA
†ADVENTIST WORLD R, Via Agat, Guam
W Sa/Su • SE Asia • 100 kW
W • SE Asia • 100 kW
†RFE-RL, Via Kavála, Greece
S • Mideast & W Asia • 250 kW
17840 EGYPT
RADIO CAIRO, Kafr Silîm-Abis
W Africa • 250 kW
INDIA
ALL INDIA RADIO, Bangalore
E Asia • 500 kW
UNITED KINGDOM
†BBC, Via Antigua
Americas • 125 kW • ALT. FREQ. TO 15190 kHz
17845 CHINA (TAIWAN)
R TAIPEI INTL, Via Okeechobee, USA
S • S America • 100 kW
GERMANY
†DEUTSCHE WELLE, Nauen
S • S Asia & SE Asia • 500 kW
W • S Asia & SE Asia • 500 kW
DEUTSCHE WELLE, Via N'sibirsk, Russia
S • SE Asia & Australasia • 500 kW
†DEUTSCHE WELLE, Via Sri Lanka
W • SE Asia • 250 kW
†DEUTSCHE WELLE, Wertachtal
S • Mideast • 500 kW
S • W Africa & C Africa • 500 kW
INDIA
†ALL INDIA RADIO, Delhi
W Asia & Mideast • 250 kW
Irr • Mideast • HAJJ • 250 kW
JAPAN
†RADIO JAPAN/NHK, Tokyo-Yamata
E Asia • 300 kW
USA
FAMILY RADIO, Okeechobee, Fl
S America • 100 kW
S • S America • 100 kW
S • W Africa • 100 kW
†RFE-RL, Via Lampertheim, Germany
W • E Europe & W Asia • 100 kW
17850 AUSTRALIA
†RADIO CHRISTIAN VOICE, Darwin
E Asia • 250 kW
FRANCE
†R FRANCE INTL, Issoudun-Allouis
S • C Africa & S Africa • 500 kW
C Africa & S Africa • 500 kW
SPAIN
†R EXTERIOR ESPANA, Via Costa Rica
S Su • W North Am & C America • 100 kW
S Sa/Su • W North Am & C America • 100 kW
W Sa/Su • W North Am & C America • 100 kW
W • W North Am & C America • 100 kW
17855 AUSTRIA
†R AUSTRIA INTL, Moosbrunn
W • S Asia, SE Asia & Australasia • 500 kW
JAPAN
†RADIO JAPAN/NHK, Tokyo-Yamata
SE Asia • 100 kW
USA
†R FREE ASIA, Via Holzkirchen, Germany
S • S Asia • 250 kW
VOA, Via Iranawila, Sri Lanka
W Asia & Mideast • 250 kW
VOA, Via Philippines
S • E Asia • 250 kW
17860 CANADA
†R CANADA INTL, Via Xi'an, China
S Asia • 120 kW
FRANCE
†R FRANCE INTL, Via French Guiana
S • C America • 500 kW
C America • 500 kW
M-Sa • C America • 500 kW
Su • C America • 500 kW
GERMANY
†DEUTSCHE WELLE, Via Kigali, Rwanda
S • W Africa • 250 kW
W Africa & C America • 250 kW
C America • 250 kW
DEUTSCHE WELLE, Via Madagascar
W • S Africa • 200 kW
†DEUTSCHE WELLE, Via Samara, Russia
W • Mideast & W Asia • 200 kW
(con'd) DEUTSCHE WELLE, Via Sri Lanka
S • SE Asia • 250 kW
0 1 2 3 4 5 6 7 8 9 10 11 12 13 14 15 16 17 18 19 20 21 22 23 24

SEASONAL S OR W 1-HR TIMESHIFT MIDYEAR ⇐ OR ⇒ JAMMING / OR /\ EARLIEST HEARD ◁ LATEST HEARD ▷ NEW FOR 2002 †

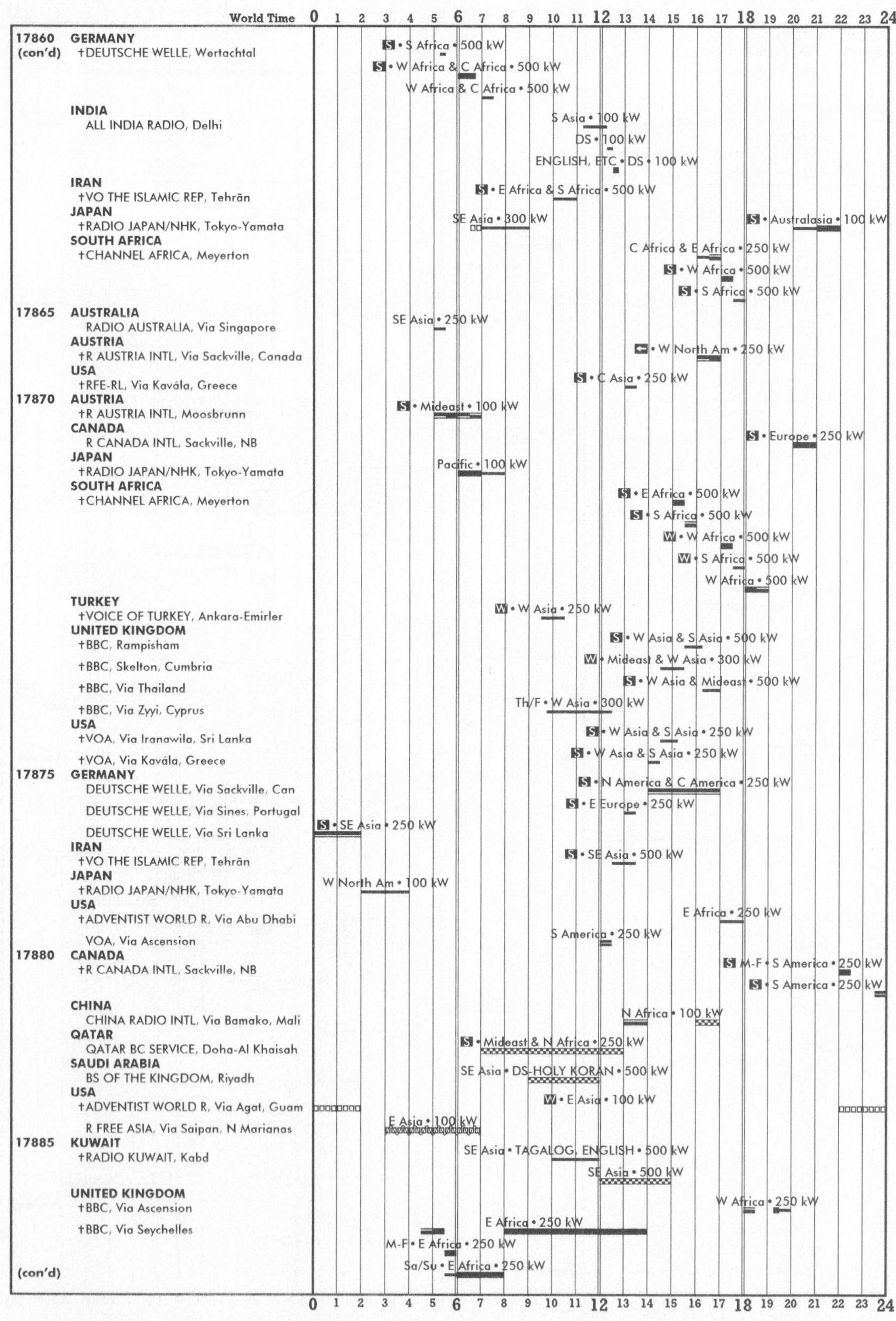
World Time 0 1 2 3 4 5 6 7 8 9 10 11 12 13 14 15 16 17 18 19 20 21 22 23 24
17860 (con'd) GERMANY
†DEUTSCHE WELLE, Wertachtal
S • S Africa • 500 kW
S • W Africa & C Africa • 500 kW
W Africa & C Africa • 500 kW
INDIA
ALL INDIA RADIO, Delhi
S Asia • 100 kW
DS • 100 kW
ENGLISH, ETC • DS • 100 kW
IRAN
†VO THE ISLAMIC REP, Tehrān
S • E Africa & S Africa • 500 kW
JAPAN
†RADIO JAPAN/NHK, Tokyo-Yamata
SE Asia • 300 kW
S • Australasia • 100 kW
SOUTH AFRICA
†CHANNEL AFRICA, Meyerton
C Africa & E Africa • 250 kW
S • W Africa • 500 kW
S • S Africa • 500 kW
17865 AUSTRALIA
RADIO AUSTRALIA, Via Singapore
SE Asia • 250 kW
AUSTRIA
†R AUSTRIA INTL, Via Sackville, Canada
• W North Am • 250 kW
USA
†RFE-RL, Via Kavála, Greece
S • C Asia • 250 kW
17870 AUSTRIA
†R AUSTRIA INTL, Moosbrunn
S • Mideast • 100 kW
CANADA
R CANADA INTL, Sackville, NB
S • Europe • 250 kW
JAPAN
†RADIO JAPAN/NHK, Tokyo-Yamata
Pacific • 100 kW
SOUTH AFRICA
†CHANNEL AFRICA, Meyerton
S • E Africa • 500 kW
S • S Africa • 500 kW
W • W Africa • 500 kW
W • S Africa • 500 kW
W Africa • 500 kW
TURKEY
†VOICE OF TURKEY, Ankara-Emirler
W • W Asia • 250 kW
UNITED KINGDOM
†BBC, Rampisham
S • W Asia & S Asia • 500 kW
†BBC, Skelton, Cumbria
W • Mideast & W Asia • 300 kW
†BBC, Via Thailand
S • W Asia & Mideast • 500 kW
†BBC, Via Zyyi, Cyprus
Th/F • W Asia • 300 kW
USA
†VOA, Via Iranawila, Sri Lanka
S • W Asia & S Asia • 250 kW
†VOA, Via Kavála, Greece
S • W Asia & S Asia • 250 kW
17875 GERMANY
DEUTSCHE WELLE, Via Sackville, Can
S • N America & C America • 250 kW
DEUTSCHE WELLE, Via Sines, Portugal
S • E Europe • 250 kW
DEUTSCHE WELLE, Via Sri Lanka
S • SE Asia • 250 kW
IRAN
†VO THE ISLAMIC REP, Tehrān
S • SE Asia • 500 kW
JAPAN
†RADIO JAPAN/NHK, Tokyo-Yamata
W North Am • 100 kW
USA
†ADVENTIST WORLD R, Via Abu Dhabi
E Africa • 250 kW
VOA, Via Ascension
S America • 250 kW
17880 CANADA
†R CANADA INTL, Sackville, NB
S M-F • S America • 250 kW
S • S America • 250 kW
CHINA
CHINA RADIO INTL, Via Bamako, Mali
N Africa • 100 kW
QATAR
QATAR BC SERVICE, Doha-Al Khaisah
S • Mideast & N Africa • 250 kW
SAUDI ARABIA
BS OF THE KINGDOM, Riyadh
SE Asia • DS-HOLY KORAN • 500 kW
USA
†ADVENTIST WORLD R, Via Agat, Guam
W • E Asia • 100 kW
R FREE ASIA, Via Saipan, N Marianas
E Asia • 100 kW
17885 KUWAIT
†RADIO KUWAIT, Kabd
SE Asia • TAGALOG, ENGLISH • 500 kW
SE Asia • 500 kW
UNITED KINGDOM
†BBC, Via Ascension
W Africa • 250 kW
†BBC, Via Seychelles
E Africa • 250 kW
M-F • E Africa • 250 kW
Sa/Su • E Africa • 250 kW
(con'd)
0 1 2 3 4 5 6 7 8 9 10 11 12 13 14 15 16 17 18 19 20 21 22 23 24
ENGLISH ARABIC CHINESE FRENCH GERMAN RUSSIAN SPANISH OTHER

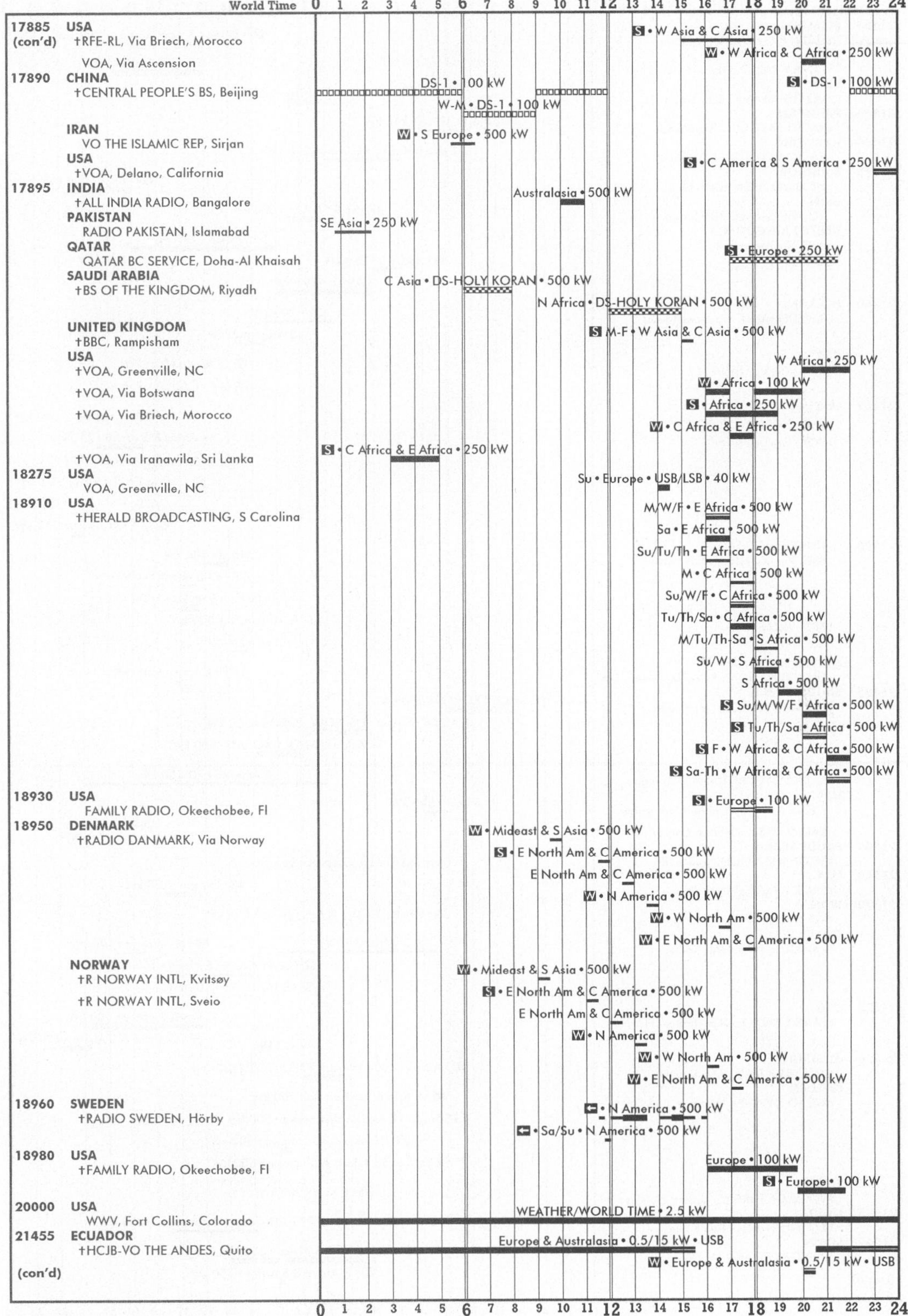
World Time 0 1 2 3 4 5 6 7 8 9 10 11 12 13 14 15 16 17 18 19 20 21 22 23 24
17885 USA
(con'd)
†RFE-RL, Via Briech, Morocco
S • W Asia & C Asia • 250 kW
VOA, Via Ascension
W • W Africa & C Africa • 250 kW
17890 CHINA
†CENTRAL PEOPLE'S BS, Beijing
DS-1 • 100 kW
S • DS-1 • 100 kW
W-M • DS-1 • 100 kW
IRAN
VO THE ISLAMIC REP, Sirjan
W • S Europe • 500 kW
USA
†VOA, Delano, California
S • C America & S America • 250 kW
17895 INDIA
†ALL INDIA RADIO, Bangalore
Australasia • 500 kW
PAKISTAN
RADIO PAKISTAN, Islamabad
SE Asia • 250 kW
QATAR
QATAR BC SERVICE, Doha-Al Khaisah
S • Europe • 250 kW
SAUDI ARABIA
†BS OF THE KINGDOM, Riyadh
C Asia • DS-HOLY KORAN • 500 kW
N Africa • DS-HOLY KORAN • 500 kW
UNITED KINGDOM
†BBC, Rampisham
S M-F • W Asia & C Asia • 500 kW
USA
†VOA, Greenville, NC
W Africa • 250 kW
†VOA, Via Botswana
W • Africa • 100 kW
†VOA, Via Briech, Morocco
S • Africa • 250 kW
W • C Africa & E Africa • 250 kW
†VOA, Via Iranawila, Sri Lanka
S • C Africa & E Africa • 250 kW
18275 USA
VOA, Greenville, NC
Su • Europe • USB/LSB • 40 kW
18910 USA
†HERALD BROADCASTING, S Carolina
M/W/F • E Africa • 500 kW
Sa • E Africa • 500 kW
Su/Tu/Th • E Africa • 500 kW
M • C Africa • 500 kW
Su/W/F • C Africa • 500 kW
Tu/Th/Sa • C Africa • 500 kW
M/Tu/Th-Sa • S Africa • 500 kW
Su/W • S Africa • 500 kW
S Africa • 500 kW
S Su/M/W/F • Africa • 500 kW
S Tu/Th/Sa • Africa • 500 kW
S F • W Africa & C Africa • 500 kW
S Sa-Th • W Africa & C Africa • 500 kW
18930 USA
FAMILY RADIO, Okeechobee, Fl
S • Europe • 100 kW
18950 DENMARK
†RADIO DANMARK, Via Norway
W • Mideast & S Asia • 500 kW
S • E North Am & C America • 500 kW
E North Am & C America • 500 kW
W • N America • 500 kW
W • W North Am • 500 kW
W • E North Am & C America • 500 kW
NORWAY
†R NORWAY INTL, Kvitsøy
W • Mideast & S Asia • 500 kW
†R NORWAY INTL, Sveio
S • E North Am & C America • 500 kW
E North Am & C America • 500 kW
W • N America • 500 kW
W • W North Am • 500 kW
W • E North Am & C America • 500 kW
18960 SWEDEN
†RADIO SWEDEN, Hörby
N America • 500 kW
Sa/Su • N America • 500 kW
18980 USA
†FAMILY RADIO, Okeechobee, Fl
Europe • 100 kW
S • Europe • 100 kW
20000 USA
WWV, Fort Collins, Colorado
WEATHER/WORLD TIME • 2.5 kW
21455 ECUADOR
†HCJB-VO THE ANDES, Quito
Europe & Australasia • 0.5/15 kW • USB
W • Europe & Australasia • 0.5/15 kW • USB
(con'd)
0 1 2 3 4 5 6 7 8 9 10 11 12 13 14 15 16 17 18 19 20 21 22 23 24

SEASONAL S OR W 1-HR TIMESHIFT MIDYEAR ⇐ OR ⇒ JAMMING / OR ∧ EARLIEST HEARD ◁ LATEST HEARD ▷ NEW FOR 2002 †

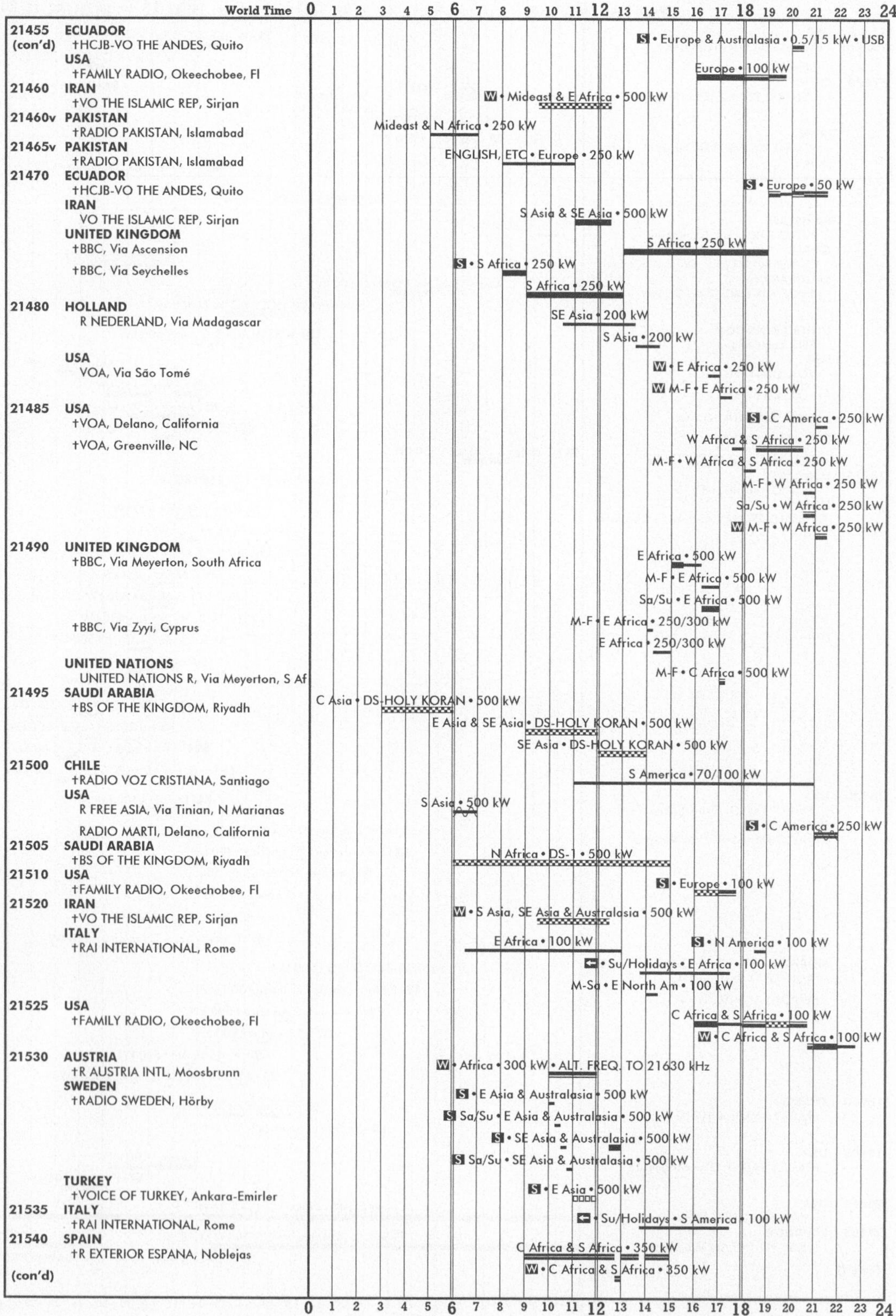
World Time 0 1 2 3 4 5 6 7 8 9 10 11 12 13 14 15 16 17 18 19 20 21 22 23 24
21455 ECUADOR
(con'd) †HCJB-VO THE ANDES, Quito
S • Europe & Australasia • 0.5/15 kW • USB
USA
†FAMILY RADIO, Okeechobee, Fl
Europe • 100 kW
21460 IRAN
†VO THE ISLAMIC REP, Sirjan
W • Mideast & E Africa • 500 kW
21460v PAKISTAN
†RADIO PAKISTAN, Islamabad
Mideast & N Africa • 250 kW
21465v PAKISTAN
†RADIO PAKISTAN, Islamabad
ENGLISH, ETC • Europe • 250 kW
21470 ECUADOR
†HCJB-VO THE ANDES, Quito
S • Europe • 50 kW
IRAN
VO THE ISLAMIC REP, Sirjan
S Asia & SE Asia • 500 kW
UNITED KINGDOM
†BBC, Via Ascension
S Africa • 250 kW
†BBC, Via Seychelles
S • S Africa • 250 kW
S Africa • 250 kW
21480 HOLLAND
R NEDERLAND, Via Madagascar
SE Asia • 200 kW
S Asia • 200 kW
USA
VOA, Via São Tomé
W • E Africa • 250 kW
W M-F • E Africa • 250 kW
21485 USA
†VOA, Delano, California
S • C America • 250 kW
†VOA, Greenville, NC
W Africa & S Africa • 250 kW
M-F • W Africa & S Africa • 250 kW
M-F • W Africa • 250 kW
Sa/Su • W Africa • 250 kW
W M-F • W Africa • 250 kW
21490 UNITED KINGDOM
†BBC, Via Meyerton, South Africa
E Africa • 500 kW
M-F • E Africa • 500 kW
Sa/Su • E Africa • 500 kW
†BBC, Via Zyyi, Cyprus
M-F • E Africa • 250/300 kW
E Africa • 250/300 kW
UNITED NATIONS
UNITED NATIONS R, Via Meyerton, S Af
M-F • C Africa • 500 kW
21495 SAUDI ARABIA
†BS OF THE KINGDOM, Riyadh
C Asia • DS-HOLY KORAN • 500 kW
E Asia & SE Asia • DS-HOLY KORAN • 500 kW
SE Asia • DS-HOLY KORAN • 500 kW
21500 CHILE
†RADIO VOZ CRISTIANA, Santiago
S America • 70/100 kW
USA
R FREE ASIA, Via Tinian, N Marianas
S Asia • 500 kW
RADIO MARTI, Delano, California
S • C America • 250 kW
21505 SAUDI ARABIA
†BS OF THE KINGDOM, Riyadh
N Africa • DS-1 • 500 kW
21510 USA
†FAMILY RADIO, Okeechobee, Fl
S • Europe • 100 kW
21520 IRAN
†VO THE ISLAMIC REP, Sirjan
W • S Asia, SE Asia & Australasia • 500 kW
ITALY
†RAI INTERNATIONAL, Rome
E Africa • 100 kW
S • N America • 100 kW
Su/Holidays • E Africa • 100 kW
M-Sa • E North Am • 100 kW
21525 USA
†FAMILY RADIO, Okeechobee, Fl
C Africa & S Africa • 100 kW
W • C Africa & S Africa • 100 kW
21530 AUSTRIA
†R AUSTRIA INTL, Moosbrunn
W • Africa • 300 kW • ALT. FREQ. TO 21630 kHz
SWEDEN
†RADIO SWEDEN, Hörby
S • E Asia & Australasia • 500 kW
S Sa/Su • E Asia & Australasia • 500 kW
S • SE Asia & Australasia • 500 kW
S Sa/Su • SE Asia & Australasia • 500 kW
TURKEY
†VOICE OF TURKEY, Ankara-Emirler
S • E Asia • 500 kW
21535 ITALY
†RAI INTERNATIONAL, Rome
Su/Holidays • S America • 100 kW
21540 SPAIN
†R EXTERIOR ESPANA, Noblejas
C Africa & S Africa • 350 kW
W • C Africa & S Africa • 350 kW
(con'd)
0 1 2 3 4 5 6 7 8 9 10 11 12 13 14 15 16 17 18 19 20 21 22 23 24

ENGLISH ARABIC CHINESE FRENCH GERMAN RUSSIAN SPANISH OTHER

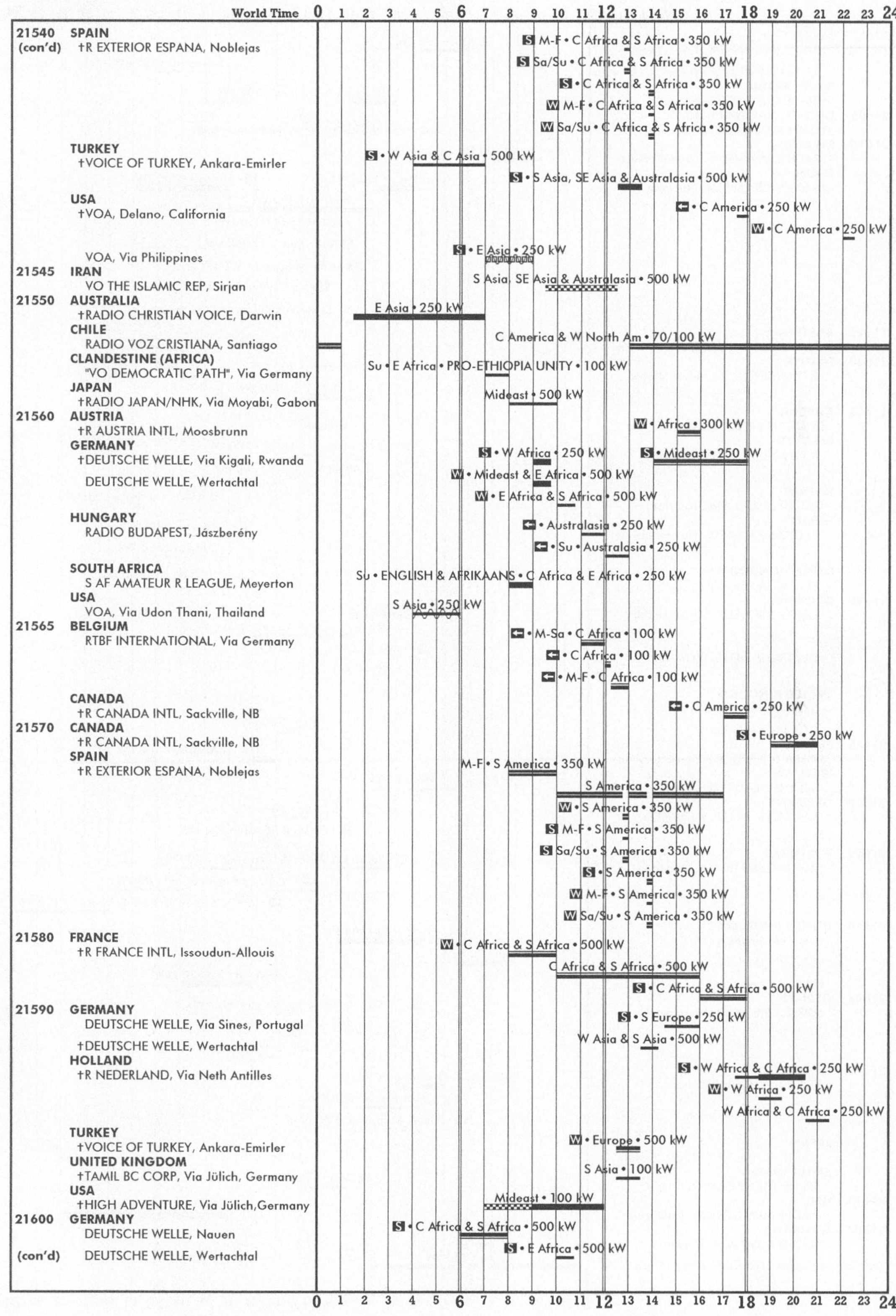
World Time 0 1 2 3 4 5 6 7 8 9 10 11 12 13 14 15 16 17 18 19 20 21 22 23 24
21540 SPAIN
(con'd) †R EXTERIOR ESPANA, Noblejas
S M-F • C Africa & S Africa • 350 kW
S Sa/Su • C Africa & S Africa • 350 kW
S • C Africa & S Africa • 350 kW
W M-F • C Africa & S Africa • 350 kW
W Sa/Su • C Africa & S Africa • 350 kW
TURKEY
†VOICE OF TURKEY, Ankara-Emirler
S • W Asia & C Asia • 500 kW
S • S Asia, SE Asia & Australasia • 500 kW
USA
†VOA, Delano, California
• C America • 250 kW
W • C America • 250 kW
VOA, Via Philippines
S • E Asia • 250 kW
21545 IRAN
VO THE ISLAMIC REP, Sirjan
S Asia, SE Asia & Australasia • 500 kW
21550 AUSTRALIA
†RADIO CHRISTIAN VOICE, Darwin
E Asia • 250 kW
CHILE
RADIO VOZ CRISTIANA, Santiago
C America & W North Am • 70/100 kW
CLANDESTINE (AFRICA)
"VO DEMOCRATIC PATH", Via Germany
Su • E Africa • PRO-ETHIOPIA UNITY • 100 kW
JAPAN
†RADIO JAPAN/NHK, Via Moyabi, Gabon
Mideast • 500 kW
21560 AUSTRIA
†R AUSTRIA INTL, Moosbrunn
W • Africa • 300 kW
GERMANY
†DEUTSCHE WELLE, Via Kigali, Rwanda
S • W Africa • 250 kW
S • Mideast • 250 kW
DEUTSCHE WELLE, Wertachtal
W • Mideast & E Africa • 500 kW
W • E Africa & S Africa • 500 kW
HUNGARY
RADIO BUDAPEST, Jászberény
• Australasia • 250 kW
• Su • Australasia • 250 kW
SOUTH AFRICA
S AF AMATEUR R LEAGUE, Meyerton
Su • ENGLISH & AFRIKAANS • C Africa & E Africa • 250 kW
USA
VOA, Via Udon Thani, Thailand
S Asia • 250 kW
21565 BELGIUM
RTBF INTERNATIONAL, Via Germany
• M-Sa • C Africa • 100 kW
• C Africa • 100 kW
• M-F • C Africa • 100 kW
CANADA
†R CANADA INTL, Sackville, NB
• C America • 250 kW
21570 CANADA
†R CANADA INTL, Sackville, NB
S • Europe • 250 kW
SPAIN
†R EXTERIOR ESPANA, Noblejas
M-F • S America • 350 kW
S America • 350 kW
W • S America • 350 kW
S M-F • S America • 350 kW
S Sa/Su • S America • 350 kW
S • S America • 350 kW
W M-F • S America • 350 kW
W Sa/Su • S America • 350 kW
21580 FRANCE
†R FRANCE INTL, Issoudun-Allouis
W • C Africa & S Africa • 500 kW
C Africa & S Africa • 500 kW
S • C Africa & S Africa • 500 kW
21590 GERMANY
DEUTSCHE WELLE, Via Sines, Portugal
S • S Europe • 250 kW
†DEUTSCHE WELLE, Wertachtal
W Asia & S Asia • 500 kW
HOLLAND
†R NEDERLAND, Via Neth Antilles
S • W Africa & C Africa • 250 kW
W • W Africa • 250 kW
W Africa & C Africa • 250 kW
TURKEY
†VOICE OF TURKEY, Ankara-Emirler
W • Europe • 500 kW
UNITED KINGDOM
†TAMIL BC CORP, Via Jülich, Germany
S Asia • 100 kW
USA
†HIGH ADVENTURE, Via Jülich,Germany
Mideast • 100 kW
21600 GERMANY
DEUTSCHE WELLE, Nauen
S • C Africa & S Africa • 500 kW
(con'd) DEUTSCHE WELLE, Wertachtal
S • E Africa • 500 kW
0 1 2 3 4 5 6 7 8 9 10 11 12 13 14 15 16 17 18 19 20 21 22 23 24

SEASONAL S OR W 1-HR TIMESHIFT MIDYEAR ← OR → JAMMING / OR ∧ EARLIEST HEARD ◁ LATEST HEARD ▷ NEW FOR 2002 †

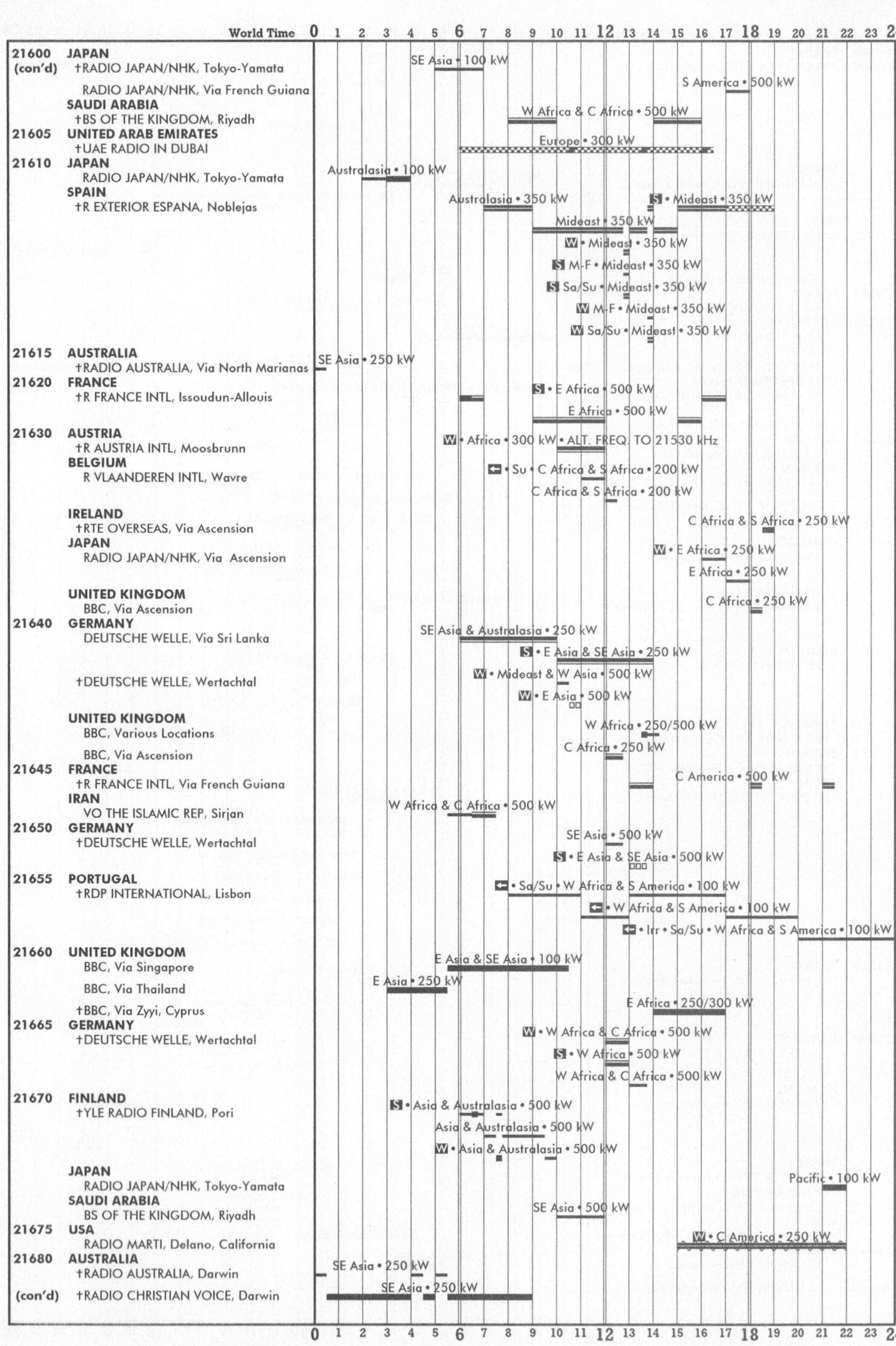
World Time 0 1 2 3 4 5 6 7 8 9 10 11 12 13 14 15 16 17 18 19 20 21 22 23 24
21600 JAPAN
(con'd) †RADIO JAPAN/NHK, Tokyo-Yamata
SE Asia • 100 kW
RADIO JAPAN/NHK, Via French Guiana
S America • 500 kW
SAUDI ARABIA
†BS OF THE KINGDOM, Riyadh
W Africa & C Africa • 500 kW
21605 UNITED ARAB EMIRATES
†UAE RADIO IN DUBAI
Europe • 300 kW
21610 JAPAN
RADIO JAPAN/NHK, Tokyo-Yamata
Australasia • 100 kW
SPAIN
†R EXTERIOR ESPANA, Noblejas
Australasia • 350 kW
S • Mideast • 350 kW
Mideast • 350 kW
W • Mideast • 350 kW
S M-F • Mideast • 350 kW
S Sa/Su • Mideast • 350 kW
W M-F • Mideast • 350 kW
W Sa/Su • Mideast • 350 kW
21615 AUSTRALIA
†RADIO AUSTRALIA, Via North Marianas
SE Asia • 250 kW
21620 FRANCE
†R FRANCE INTL, Issoudun-Allouis
S • E Africa • 500 kW
E Africa • 500 kW
21630 AUSTRIA
†R AUSTRIA INTL, Moosbrunn
W • Africa • 300 kW • ALT. FREQ. TO 21530 kHz
BELGIUM
R VLAANDEREN INTL, Wavre
Su • C Africa & S Africa • 200 kW
C Africa & S Africa • 200 kW
IRELAND
†RTE OVERSEAS, Via Ascension
C Africa & S Africa • 250 kW
JAPAN
RADIO JAPAN/NHK, Via Ascension
W • E Africa • 250 kW
E Africa • 250 kW
UNITED KINGDOM
BBC, Via Ascension
C Africa • 250 kW
21640 GERMANY
DEUTSCHE WELLE, Via Sri Lanka
SE Asia & Australasia • 250 kW
S • E Asia & SE Asia • 250 kW
†DEUTSCHE WELLE, Wertachtal
W • Mideast & W Asia • 500 kW
W • E Asia • 500 kW
UNITED KINGDOM
BBC, Various Locations
W Africa • 250/500 kW
BBC, Via Ascension
C Africa • 250 kW
21645 FRANCE
†R FRANCE INTL, Via French Guiana
C America • 500 kW
IRAN
VO THE ISLAMIC REP, Sirjan
W Africa & C Africa • 500 kW
21650 GERMANY
†DEUTSCHE WELLE, Wertachtal
SE Asia • 500 kW
S • E Asia & SE Asia • 500 kW
21655 PORTUGAL
†RDP INTERNATIONAL, Lisbon
Sa/Su • W Africa & S America • 100 kW
W Africa & S America • 100 kW
Irr • Sa/Su • W Africa & S America • 100 kW
21660 UNITED KINGDOM
BBC, Via Singapore
E Asia & SE Asia • 100 kW
BBC, Via Thailand
E Asia • 250 kW
†BBC, Via Zyyi, Cyprus
E Africa • 250/300 kW
21665 GERMANY
†DEUTSCHE WELLE, Wertachtal
W • W Africa & C Africa • 500 kW
S • W Africa • 500 kW
W Africa & C Africa • 500 kW
21670 FINLAND
†YLE RADIO FINLAND, Pori
S • Asia & Australasia • 500 kW
Asia & Australasia • 500 kW
W • Asia & Australasia • 500 kW
JAPAN
RADIO JAPAN/NHK, Tokyo-Yamata
Pacific • 100 kW
SAUDI ARABIA
BS OF THE KINGDOM, Riyadh
SE Asia • 500 kW
21675 USA
RADIO MARTI, Delano, California
W • C America • 250 kW
21680 AUSTRALIA
†RADIO AUSTRALIA, Darwin
SE Asia • 250 kW
(con'd) †RADIO CHRISTIAN VOICE, Darwin
SE Asia • 250 kW
0 1 2 3 4 5 6 7 8 9 10 11 12 13 14 15 16 17 18 19 20 21 22 23 24
ENGLISH ARABIC CHINESE FRENCH GERMAN RUSSIAN SPANISH OTHER

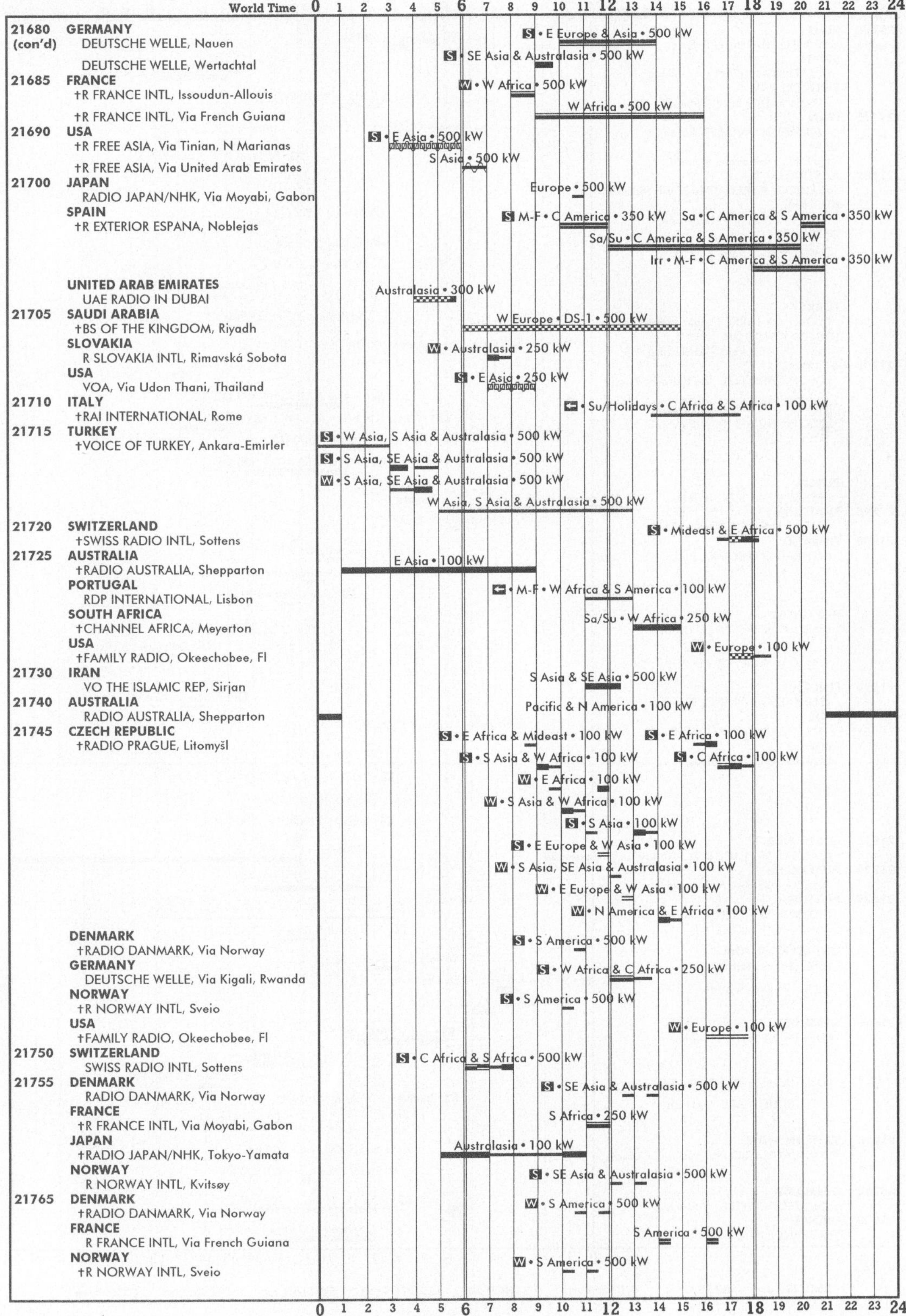
World Time 0 1 2 3 4 5 6 7 8 9 10 11 12 13 14 15 16 17 18 19 20 21 22 23 24
21680 (con'd) GERMANY
DEUTSCHE WELLE, Nauen
S • E Europe & Asia • 500 kW
DEUTSCHE WELLE, Wertachtal
S • SE Asia & Australasia • 500 kW
21685 FRANCE
†R FRANCE INTL, Issoudun-Allouis
W • W Africa • 500 kW
†R FRANCE INTL, Via French Guiana
W Africa • 500 kW
21690 USA
†R FREE ASIA, Via Tinian, N Marianas
S • E Asia • 500 kW
†R FREE ASIA, Via United Arab Emirates
S Asia • 500 kW
21700 JAPAN
RADIO JAPAN/NHK, Via Moyabi, Gabon
Europe • 500 kW
SPAIN
†R EXTERIOR ESPANA, Noblejas
S M-F • C America • 350 kW
Sa • C America & S America • 350 kW
Sa/Su • C America & S America • 350 kW
Irr • M-F • C America & S America • 350 kW
UNITED ARAB EMIRATES
UAE RADIO IN DUBAI
Australasia • 300 kW
21705 SAUDI ARABIA
†BS OF THE KINGDOM, Riyadh
W Europe • DS-1 • 500 kW
SLOVAKIA
R SLOVAKIA INTL, Rimavská Sobota
W • Australasia • 250 kW
USA
VOA, Via Udon Thani, Thailand
S • E Asia • 250 kW
21710 ITALY
†RAI INTERNATIONAL, Rome
• Su/Holidays • C Africa & S Africa • 100 kW
21715 TURKEY
†VOICE OF TURKEY, Ankara-Emirler
S • W Asia, S Asia & Australasia • 500 kW
S • S Asia, SE Asia & Australasia • 500 kW
W • S Asia, SE Asia & Australasia • 500 kW
W Asia, S Asia & Australasia • 500 kW
21720 SWITZERLAND
†SWISS RADIO INTL, Sottens
S • Mideast & E Africa • 500 kW
21725 AUSTRALIA
†RADIO AUSTRALIA, Shepparton
E Asia • 100 kW
PORTUGAL
RDP INTERNATIONAL, Lisbon
• M-F • W Africa & S America • 100 kW
SOUTH AFRICA
†CHANNEL AFRICA, Meyerton
Sa/Su • W Africa • 250 kW
USA
†FAMILY RADIO, Okeechobee, Fl
W • Europe • 100 kW
21730 IRAN
VO THE ISLAMIC REP, Sirjan
S Asia & SE Asia • 500 kW
21740 AUSTRALIA
RADIO AUSTRALIA, Shepparton
Pacific & N America • 100 kW
21745 CZECH REPUBLIC
†RADIO PRAGUE, Litomyšl
S • E Africa & Mideast • 100 kW
S • E Africa • 100 kW
S • S Asia & W Africa • 100 kW
S • C Africa • 100 kW
W • E Africa • 100 kW
W • S Asia & W Africa • 100 kW
S • S Asia • 100 kW
S • E Europe & W Asia • 100 kW
W • S Asia, SE Asia & Australasia • 100 kW
W • E Europe & W Asia • 100 kW
W • N America & E Africa • 100 kW
DENMARK
†RADIO DANMARK, Via Norway
S • S America • 500 kW
GERMANY
DEUTSCHE WELLE, Via Kigali, Rwanda
S • W Africa & C Africa • 250 kW
NORWAY
†R NORWAY INTL, Sveio
S • S America • 500 kW
USA
†FAMILY RADIO, Okeechobee, Fl
W • Europe • 100 kW
21750 SWITZERLAND
SWISS RADIO INTL, Sottens
S • C Africa & S Africa • 500 kW
21755 DENMARK
RADIO DANMARK, Via Norway
S • SE Asia & Australasia • 500 kW
FRANCE
†R FRANCE INTL, Via Moyabi, Gabon
S Africa • 250 kW
JAPAN
†RADIO JAPAN/NHK, Tokyo-Yamata
Australasia • 100 kW
NORWAY
R NORWAY INTL, Kvitsøy
S • SE Asia & Australasia • 500 kW
21765 DENMARK
†RADIO DANMARK, Via Norway
W • S America • 500 kW
FRANCE
R FRANCE INTL, Via French Guiana
S America • 500 kW
NORWAY
†R NORWAY INTL, Sveio
W • S America • 500 kW
0 1 2 3 4 5 6 7 8 9 10 11 12 13 14 15 16 17 18 19 20 21 22 23 24

SEASONAL S OR W 1-HR TIMESHIFT MIDYEAR ⬅ OR ➡ JAMMING / OR /\ EARLIEST HEARD ◁ LATEST HEARD ▷ NEW FOR 2002 †

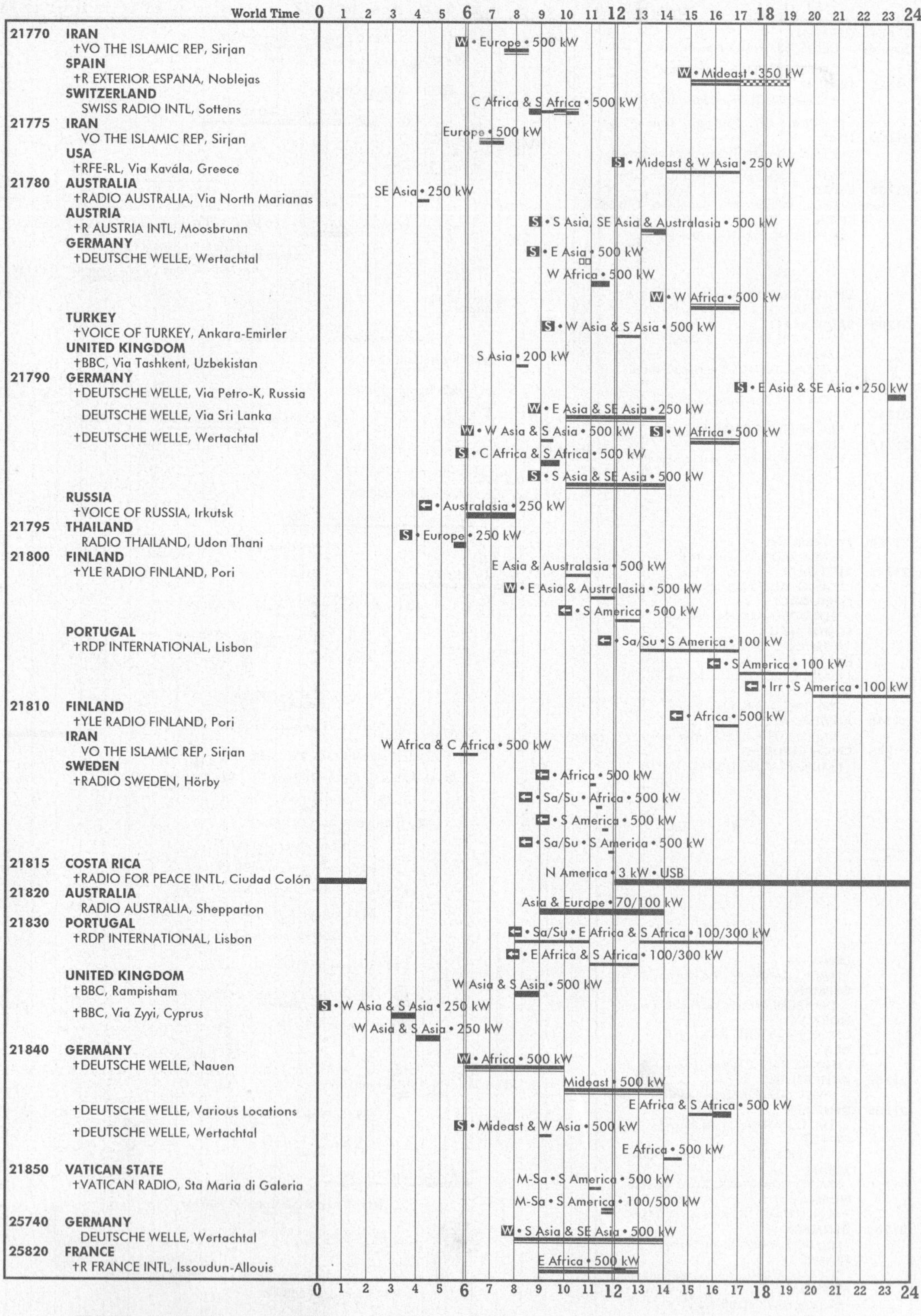
World Time 0 1 2 3 4 5 6 7 8 9 10 11 12 13 14 15 16 17 18 19 20 21 22 23 24
21770 IRAN
†VO THE ISLAMIC REP, Sirjan
W • Europe • 500 kW
SPAIN
†R EXTERIOR ESPANA, Noblejas
W • Mideast • 350 kW
SWITZERLAND
SWISS RADIO INTL, Sottens
C Africa & S Africa • 500 kW
21775 IRAN
VO THE ISLAMIC REP, Sirjan
Europe • 500 kW
USA
†RFE-RL, Via Kavála, Greece
S • Mideast & W Asia • 250 kW
21780 AUSTRALIA
†RADIO AUSTRALIA, Via North Marianas
SE Asia • 250 kW
AUSTRIA
†R AUSTRIA INTL, Moosbrunn
S • S Asia, SE Asia & Australasia • 500 kW
GERMANY
†DEUTSCHE WELLE, Wertachtal
S • E Asia • 500 kW
W Africa • 500 kW
W • W Africa • 500 kW
TURKEY
†VOICE OF TURKEY, Ankara-Emirler
S • W Asia & S Asia • 500 kW
UNITED KINGDOM
†BBC, Via Tashkent, Uzbekistan
S Asia • 200 kW
21790 GERMANY
†DEUTSCHE WELLE, Via Petro-K, Russia
S • E Asia & SE Asia • 250 kW
DEUTSCHE WELLE, Via Sri Lanka
W • E Asia & SE Asia • 250 kW
†DEUTSCHE WELLE, Wertachtal
W • W Asia & S Asia • 500 kW
S • W Africa • 500 kW
S • C Africa & S Africa • 500 kW
S • S Asia & SE Asia • 500 kW
RUSSIA
†VOICE OF RUSSIA, Irkutsk
• Australasia • 250 kW
21795 THAILAND
RADIO THAILAND, Udon Thani
S • Europe • 250 kW
21800 FINLAND
†YLE RADIO FINLAND, Pori
E Asia & Australasia • 500 kW
W • E Asia & Australasia • 500 kW
• S America • 500 kW
PORTUGAL
†RDP INTERNATIONAL, Lisbon
• Sa/Su • S America • 100 kW
• S America • 100 kW
• Irr • S America • 100 kW
21810 FINLAND
†YLE RADIO FINLAND, Pori
• Africa • 500 kW
IRAN
VO THE ISLAMIC REP, Sirjan
W Africa & C Africa • 500 kW
SWEDEN
†RADIO SWEDEN, Hörby
• Africa • 500 kW
• Sa/Su • Africa • 500 kW
• S America • 500 kW
• Sa/Su • S America • 500 kW
21815 COSTA RICA
†RADIO FOR PEACE INTL, Ciudad Colón
N America • 3 kW • USB
21820 AUSTRALIA
RADIO AUSTRALIA, Shepparton
Asia & Europe • 70/100 kW
21830 PORTUGAL
†RDP INTERNATIONAL, Lisbon
• Sa/Su • E Africa & S Africa • 100/300 kW
• E Africa & S Africa • 100/300 kW
UNITED KINGDOM
†BBC, Rampisham
W Asia & S Asia • 500 kW
†BBC, Via Zyyi, Cyprus
S • W Asia & S Asia • 250 kW
W Asia & S Asia • 250 kW
21840 GERMANY
†DEUTSCHE WELLE, Nauen
W • Africa • 500 kW
Mideast • 500 kW
†DEUTSCHE WELLE, Various Locations
E Africa & S Africa • 500 kW
†DEUTSCHE WELLE, Wertachtal
S • Mideast & W Asia • 500 kW
E Africa • 500 kW
21850 VATICAN STATE
†VATICAN RADIO, Sta Maria di Galeria
M-Sa • S America • 500 kW
M-Sa • S America • 100/500 kW
25740 GERMANY
DEUTSCHE WELLE, Wertachtal
W • S Asia & SE Asia • 500 kW
25820 FRANCE
†R FRANCE INTL, Issoudun-Allouis
E Africa • 500 kW
0 1 2 3 4 5 6 7 8 9 10 11 12 13 14 15 16 17 18 19 20 21 22 23 24
ENGLISH ARABIC CHINESE FRENCH GERMAN RUSSIAN SPANISH OTHER